The 21st Century Motherhood Movement

Mothers Speak Out on Why We Need to Change the World and How to Do It

The 21st Century Motherhood Movement

Mothers Speak Out on Why We Need to Change the World and How to Do It

Edited by

ANDREA O'REILLY

DEMETER

DEMETER PRESS
BRADFORD, ONTARIO

Demeter Press
c/o Motherhood Initiative for Research and
Community Involvement (MIRCI)
140 Holland St. West, P.O. 13022
Bradford, ON, L3Z 2Y5
Telephone: 905.775.5215
Email: info@demeterpress.org
Website: www.demeterpress.org

Demeter Press logo based on the sculpture *Demeter* by Maria-Luise Bodirsky <www.keramik-atelier.bodirsky.de>

Cover /Interior Design: Luciana Ricciutelli
Front Cover Photos: Courtesy contributors to this book.
Photo of Andrea O'Reilly and her daughters, Erin and Casey, courtesy Ivy Cuervo, CBC Toronto News Reporter
Back Cover Photo: Courtesy Linn Baran

Printed and Bound in Canada

Library and Archives Canada Cataloguing in Publication

The 21st century motherhood movement : mothers speak out on why we need to change the world and how to do it / edited by Andrea O'Reilly.

Includes bibliographical references.
ISBN 978-0-9866671-1-4

1. Motherhood—History—21st century.
2. Feminism—History—21st century. 3. Social change—History—21st century. I. O'Reilly, Andrea, 1961-

HQ759.T94 2011 306.874'3 C2011-903046-2

For Jessica Nathanson (1968-2011) and Sara Ruddick (1935-2011)

Table of Contents

SECTION VI: SOCIAL CHANGE AND SOCIAL JUSTICE

Acknowledgements

Writers, particularly those of us writing in the field of Motherhood Studies, frequently use, if not overuse, the language of birth to depict the writing process. The formation and development of ideas are likened to conception and pregnancy and the writing, as an arduous, lengthy, and indeed painful process, is compared to birth and those that sustain and support us in our writing are described as midwives. Though arguably an overused trope or metaphor, I find myself, as I struggle to put into words my thoughts and feelings as I complete this anthology, as I must do in an acknowledgement, that I am drawn to this language of birth as only it can convey both the pain and joy of this book's creation. This collection of 976 pages, with 80 plus contributors, is certainly the longest book I have edited in my many years of writing. Much time and needless to say effort was put into this book as it was conceived, gestated, and born over these many years. But more importantly, this collection, more so than any of my other books, was made possible only in and through the reproductive labour of so many individuals that I am blessed to have in my life. This book would not have been born without the love of my other mothers who sustained me as I created this book or the care of the midwives who attended its birth.

Particular thanks are due to Judith Stadtman Tucker who truly is the other mother of this book as the idea for it was born from our early conversations on motherhood activism. And to Sarah Malik, my research assistant, who I will never be able to thank adequately enough for the hundreds of hours she spent on this book corresponding with contributors, arranging and compiling chapters, and organizing the manuscript often under impossible deadlines and done with the utmost skill, diligence, grace and dedication. Thank you Sarah for never once complaining when my many emails marked "URGENT URGENT!" flooded your inbox, and for following through on every email request when most people are not able to understand my cryptic emails, and responding to them with prompt and efficient attention. My deepest appreciation to Melissa Nurse, who came to the rescue as the book was going into final production and copy-edited my chapters and proofed sections of the book in her final weeks of pregnancy. Only at Demeter Press, would copy-editing and proofing work be completed within hours of childbirth! And to Randy Chase: what could I possibly say to thank you for yet another superb job of proofing. That you were able to proof 976 pages of manuscript in a matter of weeks with such skill and dedication while working full time astounds me. This book would not have been born without the care and work of this man who is the best midwife any mother or writer could wish for. Thank you also to Luciana Ricciutelli; yet again you delivered another child under the most challenging of births. More so than anyone, this child came into being through your labour and love. And thank you for holding my hand, soothing my anguish, and forbearing my cries as I pushed this book into the world. Thanks to Kim Breland and Renée Knapp who worked throughout the weekend and pulled an all-nighter on last-minute proofing so we could meet our printing deadline. Finally, a HUGE thank you to the 80 plus contributors of the book: all editors should be so fortunate to work with such dedicated, smart, and passionate writers. And thank you for never once complaining for working under such impossible deadlines and amidst frequent chaos. I would also like to thank the Social Science and Humanities Research Council of Canada for its continued support of my research.

Most of the work on this book was done during a particularly difficult time in my life: in 2010 my beloved Association for Research on Mothering (ARM), very much my fourth child, which I had raised for 13 years, died and was reborn as the Motherhood Initiative for Research and Community Involvement (MIRCI). Those closest to me know how truly awful this time was for me as I mourned the loss of ARM, labored tirelessly to create MIRCI, and dealt with a serious health issue brought on by stress and exhaustion. During all of this I labored to complete this book because for me it signified and validated the need and importance of motherhood activism and scholarship that the closing of ARM had denied. I would not have survived that year nor would this book have been completed without the care and love of so many. Words can never convey how the hundreds of emails and letters I received in support of ARM and MIRCI sustained me through this most difficult year. I owe particular thanks to Angela Bosco, Linn Baran, Deborah Byrd, Christina Cudahy, Tracey Carlyle, Regina Edmonds, May Friedman, Fiona Green, Liz Podnieks, Jennifer O'Reilly, Sara Ruddick, and, of course, my partner Terry Conlin and my children Jesse, Casey, and Erin. Thank you for keeping the light on in the darkness.

And of course thank you to the hundreds of women who have worked so very hard and with so much passion to create the 21st century motherhood movement described in this collection. You have shown us why we need to change the world and how to do it so thank you!

Introduction

Maternal Activism as Matricentric Feminism: The History, Ideological Frameworks, Political Strategies and Activist Practices of the 21st Century Motherhood Movement

ANDREA O'REILLY

WRITING THE INTRODUCTION TO AN edited collection has always been a daunting undertaking for me. Never quite sure where or how to start, I return again and again to the chapters, revisit the books stacked beside my computer, and usually end up in the kitchen to make a second or third cup of tea. But such introductions are more than a beginning; they outline the middle and end of the anthology's "story." In essence, they are there to provide the thematic, theoretical, historical, cultural, social, and literary context for the reading of the chapters that follow. With the 81 chapters of this collection on the 21st century motherhood movement scattered across my desk and on my computer screen, I seek to find the organizing theme, as any good scholar should, or as I would instruct my students, the thesis statement: what is it about and what does it seek to prove or argue? However, I soon realize, such questions first require a definition of the term "the motherhood movement" and, more specifically, its twenty-first century manifestation. So I find myself back at the beginning; before I can describe the "when, where, who, how" of the 21st century motherhood movement, I must first define and explain "what" it is.

Defining the 21st Century Motherhood Movement: What Is In a Name?

If recent scholarship on the 21st century motherhood movement agrees on anything, it is that the term or concept "the 21st century motherhood movement" eludes a precise definition. While discussing the "Call for a Motherhood Movement" presented at the 2002 conference held at Barnard College and hosted by the Motherhood Project (see chapter 67) Stephanie Wilkinson, co-editor of *Brain, Child* magazine writes:

> Over the last six months, I've tried to track the progress of this thing—this shape-shifting, squishy, now-you-see-it, now-you-don't movement—and I've come to think that maybe the Call was more prophetic than prescriptive. All the seeds of schism are outlined there—all the issues that divide mothers working toward a movement. Would a movement be

> mother-focused or child-focused? Would it be a branch of feminism? What kind of feminism? Would it ask for legal rights for mothers? Would it be aligned with the political left or the right? (5)

"I'd envisioned my quest to find out what was going on in motherhood circles," Wilkinson continues, "as a journey. At the end, I hoped to find a nice place with a bunch of good people gathered together—kind of like a big family reunion. But as I went along, it came to seem more like a road trip between the houses of a bunch of relatives, some of whom don't exactly see eye to eye" (5). Likewise, Judith Stadtman Tucker, editor of the "Mothers Movement Online" and interviewed in the above article comments: "There are lots of seeds out there. But I don't believe there is a unifying politics of motherhood. Mothers don't think alike just because they are mothers" (qtd. in Wilkinson 10). Writing in the entry on "The Motherhood Movement" for the *Encyclopedia of Motherhood,* Caroline Gatrell explains that "the motherhood movement is difficult to define in part because of its lack of a political identity, and no officially elected leadership. Furthermore, no single group within the movement claims exclusive knowledge of the needs, beliefs and priorities among mothers within society" (823). "Unlike movements such as women's suffrage or campaigns for more woman-centred birth," she continues, "the motherhood movement today is not focused on any single aspect of women's needs" (823).

Indeed, it would seem that the motherhood movement lacks the criteria—political identity, leadership, common purpose, shared values and so forth—to qualify as a social movement, particularly when compared to other social movements such as the civil rights movement and the feminist movement. Wilkinson conducted a simple word association experiment for her article that seems to support such an argument. Friends and colleagues of Wilkinson were found to associate the civil rights movement with "Rosa Parks, integration, Martin Luther King, equality for African Americans; women's rights with Gloria Steinman, bra burning, and feminism" (3). However, when asked what mothers' rights were associated with, their responses were less certain: "(pause) … maternity leave? … childcare? I don't know I'd have to think about it…" (3). "Overall, the results were pretty clear" (3). Wilkinson concludes, "If there is a mothers' movement going on, it hasn't reached my neighborhood yet" (3). Judging by the above, it seems that the concept or term "the motherhood movement" appears to be "the problem with no name," to use Betty Friedan's famous quote, or in academic parlance, a sign without a referent.

However, as I will argue in this introduction, if situated in relation to its historical development and in ways specific to its twenty-first century context and the politics, principles, and practices of maternal activism, the 21st century motherhood movement may be understood to be, in both form and function, a social movement. Likewise, I believe this contention is further supported by the 80-plus motherhood organizations included in this collection. It should be noted that Wilkinson's article, entitled "You Say You Want a Revolution? Why the Mothers'

Revolution Hasn't Happened ... Yet," was written in 2005. In 2005, the concept and term "21st century motherhood movement" was difficult to define or describe with any precision because six years ago, this social movement was in its infancy. The majority of the organizations described in this collection were formed and established only in the first years of the twenty-first century. Similarly, the feminist movement would have been difficult to define and describe in the early to mid-1960s. Movements, traditions, and the like are definable only in retrospect when they have become established as such. I would argue that in 2011, with a decade plus of maternal activism and the creation of numerous motherhood organizations, the 21st century motherhood movement has become a social movement with its own specific mandate and objectives, one that is distinct from the larger feminist movement. However, the shape or character of the 21st century motherhood movement differs from early social movements because of its formation in the twenty-first century. The aforementioned absence of recognizable leaders in the motherhood movement, and the apparent lack of a shared agenda, were given as reasons why the motherhood movement does not function as a social movement. However, this more diffuse style of organizing is a chosen strategy for many in the motherhood movement; it is reflective of the eclectic and democratic nature of maternal activism. As Linda Lisi Jeurgens of the *National Association of Mother Centres* explains, "having a leader for each different area—one working on Social Security, and tax issues, another on universal pre-school bills— might be a more effective idea. You have a number of different champions, each working on their goals" (qtd. in Wilkinson 16). And as Enola Aird notes, most in the motherhood movement agree "that the male-power model of leadership needs to be looked at skeptically" (qtd. in Wilkinson 16).

Finally, this movement developed in the context of rapid technological change resulting in maternal activism being expressed in ways radically different than that of previous social movements. As rallies, marches, meetings, protests, and the like, characterized the activism of second-wave feminism and the civil rights movement, maternal activism, as with other forms of twenty-first century activism, is often expressed via technology—emails, blogs, websites, Facebook, Twitter, online communities, and so forth, and by way of more informal, grassroots, ad hoc, micro, spontaneous acts of "everyday activism." Indeed, many of the organizations described in this collection would not exist without the Internet. In this, twenty-first century maternal activism is closer to third-wave feminism than second-wave feminism in its philosophies and practices of social change. Moreover, as will be discussed at length below, maternal activism is often not recognized as such or dismissed as not "real" activism because of its specific and deliberate maternal stance. In my view, there is no doubt that a 21st century motherhood movement exists, but because it has developed and expresses itself in ways that do not conform to accepted and traditional, or more specifically masculine, norms and practices of activism, it remains for many difficult to define and classify.

The intent of this introduction is not to describe the chapters that follow but to provide a historical, thematic, and theoretical context for the reading of them.

More specifically, the introduction will provide an overview of the history and ideological frameworks of the 21st century motherhood movement, discuss the challenges and possibilities of maternalism—a philosophy central to much of twenty-first century motherhood activism—detail the specific practices and strategies of twenty-first century motherhood activism (including strategic essentialism, embodied activism, emotionality, maternal nurturance as resistance, matrifocality, maternal practice, and empowered maternal subjectivity) and consider motherhood activism in relation to feminism as both theory and practice. Overall, the introduction will argue that the 21st century motherhood movement is not only an autonomous social movement distinct from the larger feminist one, but that this movement, in being specifically mother-centred and concerned with the empowerment of mothers and social change for mothers, is urgently needed and long overdue. The 21st century motherhood movement, I contend, makes possible and gives rise to a specific and much-needed theory and politic of feminism for mothers that I have termed "matricentric feminism."

History

Writing the history of a movement that is only just beginning is a near impossible undertaking. Needless to say, a decade or so from now the significance of the events that are currently unfolding will be better understood as they are placed in the larger thematic and historical trajectory of twenty-first century maternal activism and, more specifically, the motherhood movement. To decide upon a starting date appears to be a challenging, if not problematic task. Although this collection considers twenty-first century motherhood organizations, several organizations that are important to contemporary maternal activism, such as Mothers Against Drunk Driving, National Association of Mother Centres, and La Leche League, began several years or decades earlier. Likewise, some others such as Another Mother for Peace, Mothers are Women, The Mothers of the Plaza de Mayo, while not currently active as organizations, are included in this collection and in discussions on the twenty-first century motherhood movement because of the pivotal role they play in contemporary theories and practices of maternal activism. Most agree that 1848, the date of the Seneca Falls convention, marks the beginning of the suffrage movement and the first wave of feminism. While a date or event to mark the inception of the second wave has not been agreed on, the year 1968 is usually given as the official date of the beginning of the contemporary, second-wave feminist movement (while recognizing the activism that preceded and gave rise to it). As well, with each wave, there is a text that is credited for the rise of the movement and becomes a symbol for it: Betty Friedan's *The Feminine Mystique* in the second wave, and Rebecca Walker's article "Becoming the Third Wave" for the third wave.

As I read the scholarship on twenty-first century maternal activism and the 80 plus chapters included in this collection, I looked to find a starting date for this movement or, at the very least, to determine key dates, events or texts in its development. While I will suggest some important moments in the movement's history thus far, I have no doubt that in a few years time such a trajectory will become clearer, for hindsight is 20/20 as they say. Being called the 21st century motherhood movement, I suspect the year 2000 will be the date given to mark the beginning of this movement. However, in my view, the diverse and disparate maternal activist groups and actions coalesce to create a cohesive whole, something that begins to be called the 21st century motherhood movement, around 2005. Significant dates and events in the history of the 21st century motherhood movement include 1998/99, when the Association for Research on Mothering and its journal (now the Motherhood Initiative for Research and Community Involvement and the *Journal of the Motherhood Initiative*), the first association and journal on motherhood, were formed (discussed in chapter 69), and the year 2000, when the Motherhood Project and Mothers Ought to Have Equal Rights (discussed in chapters 67 and 36) and the Million Mom March took place (discussed in chapter 45). Two years later in 2002, the Bernard College conference "Maternal Feminism: Lessons for a 21st Century Motherhood Movement" took place (discussed in chapter 67), and the following year saw the launch of the widely read e-newsletter, *Mothers Movement Online* in 2003 (discussed in chapter 44). Other significant dates and events include the 2005 article on the mothers' movement discussed above, published in *Brain, Child* magazine, as well as the launching of Demeter Press, the first press on motherhood, and the founding of MomsRising, both in 2006 (discussed in chapters 69 and 39). In addition, the international conference "You Say You Want a Revolution? The 21st Century Motherhood Movement" was held in 2008, then, in 2009, the International Mothers Network, now the International Mothers and Mothering Network was established (discussed in chapter 42). Lastly, the importance of the proposed date for the opening of the Museum of Motherhood in Seneca Falls, 2012, should not be overlooked (discussed in chapter 75).

As with the feminist movement of the 1960s, both lay and academic publications have played a pivotal role in the development of the 21st century motherhood movement. However, I would argue that motherhood scholarship largely predates and laid the foundation for contemporary maternal activism, particularly as it coalesced to form a unified movement. Such is a departure from the contemporary feminist movement wherein the academic discipline of Women's Studies was largely born from feminist activism. A cursory review of feminist publications reveals that most were published after 1968, the start of the second-wave feminist movement. In contrast, motherhood scholarship was published before the rise of the motherhood movement in this century. This is not to say that maternal activism did not exist prior to the twenty-first century, but rather suggests that the hundreds of books and articles on motherhood that were published in the 1990s and early 2000s, both lay and scholarly, provided the knowledge for understanding and responding to the discrimination, devaluation, and dissatisfaction mothers often experience, making possible an organized movement to challenge and change the status quo. In the *Brain, Child* article, Wilkinson argues that, "If the *Feminine Mystique* was the book that laid the seeds for the women's movement of the 1960s, Ann Crittenden's *Price of Motherhood* may someday be regarded as the one that did the same for the mothers' movement" (8). In other words, by documenting what Adrienne Rich described years earlier as the patriarchal institution of motherhood, scholarly and literary publications of the mid-1990s to the early 2000s provided the consciousness and language necessary for maternal activism to coalesce into a social movement. Among the notable publications of these formative years are *The Cultural Contradictions of Motherhood* (Hays); *Killing the Black Body: Race, Reproduction and the Meaning of Liberty* (Roberts); *The Impossibility of Motherhood* (DiQuinzio); *The Mask of Motherhood* (Maushart); *Unbending Gender: Why Family and Work Conflict and What to Do About It* (Williams); and *I Don't Know How She Does It* (Pearson), to name but a few.

As the motherhood movement gained momentum from approximately 2005 onwards, it made possible and gave rise to increased writing on motherhood, particularly in lay and literary genres (most notably the motherhood memoir). Significant publications include: *The Mommy Myth: The Idealization of Motherhood and How it Has Undermined Women* (Douglas and Michaels); *The Truth Behind the Mommy Wars* (Peskowitz); *Perfect Madness: Motherhood in the Age of Anxiety* (Warner); *The Motherhood Manifesto: What America's Moms Want and What to Do About It* (Blades and Rowe-Finkbeiner.); *Mother Shock* (Buchanan); *Dispatches from a Not-So-Perfect Life (Fox); Misconceptions (Wolf).* Throughout this time, the motherhood movement continued to be sustained by numerous scholarly works on motherhood: *Maternal Theory: Essential Readings* (O'Reilly 2007); *Opting Out? Why Women Really Quit Careers and Head Home* (Stone); *Mothering in the Third Wave* (Kinser); *Women's Studies Quarterly* special issue "Motherhood"; *Encyclopedia of Motherhood* (O'Reilly 2010a); *21st Century Motherhood: Experience, Identity, Policy, Agency* (O'Reilly 2010b), to name but a few. In turn, such motherhood scholarship coalesced to form a specific academic and scholarly discipline that I termed "Motherhood Studies" in 2006. The term is used to acknowledge and demarcate this new scholarship on motherhood as a legitimate and distinctive discipline grounded in the theoretical tradition of maternal theory developed by such scholars as Patricia Hill Collins, Adrienne Rich, and Sara Ruddick. As with the development of Women's Studies as an academic field in the 1970s, Motherhood Studies, while explicitly interdisciplinary and multidisciplinary, has developed as an autonomous and independent scholarly discipline over the last decade. In so doing, Motherhood Studies both sustains and is sustained by the 21st century motherhood movement and the maternal activism described in the chapters that follow.

Philosophies and Practices of Maternal Activism: Liberal Feminism, Maternalism, Ethic of Care Theory

Judith Stadtman Tucker, editor of *Mothers Movement Online*, has written extensively on the twenty-first century mothers' movement. Stadtman Tucker advances the concept of "political and ideological grounding" to understand and analyze a motherhood group's identity and its activism (Stadtman Tucker 2004, 2005, 2008, 2010). According to Stadtman Tucker, all motherhood organizations position themselves politically and ideologically in relation to what Patrice DiQuinzio (2006) has termed the trope or discourse of "essential motherhood:" the view that mothering is essential to women and all women are, or should be, mothers. Elsewhere I have argued that contemporary Western constructions of essential motherhood, though nuanced in their manifestations, are ideologically homogeneous and unambiguous, and are defined by a rigid and uniform philosophy of gender essentialism and the resulting binary opposition of the public and private sphere (O'Reilly 2010b). A central, if not defining, event in the rise of Western modernity was the emergence of the public/private dichotomy in which the work of production was assigned to the public sphere and the work of reproduction to the private sphere. This dichotomy was, of course, gender-coded: a man belonged in the public realm and was to embody the valued masculine traits of the emergent capitalist and industrial society, while a woman was to remain in the domain of the home and serve as the ornamental wife or, in the lexicon of the day, "The Angel in the House" (Woolf). Significantly, this gender polarity resulted in the emergence, or more accurately, the invention of full-time motherhood. While this notion of full-time motherhood was largely symbolic and restricted to middle class mothers, these mothers acquired moral superiority and cultural prestige (though of course not real societal power or respect) in and through their identity as Mother. This gendered schism converged to construct mothering as *essentially* and naturally the identity and purpose of women, and the family as fundamentally a private unit separate and distinct from the larger public, political, and social world. Susan Douglas and Meredith Michaels have termed the twenty-first century manifestation of this ideology the "New Momism" which, as they explain, begins with:

> [T]he insistence that no woman is truly complete or fulfilled unless she has kids, that women remain the best primary caretakers of children, and that to be a remotely decent mother, a woman has to devote her entire physical, psychological, emotional, intellectual being, 24/7, to her children. The new momism is a highly romanticized view of motherhood in which the standards for success are impossible to meet. (4)

However, as Douglas and Michaels go on to explain, "The new momism involves more than just impossible ideals about childrearing; it redefines all women, first and foremost, through their relationships to children. Thus, being a citizen, a worker, a governor [and so forth] are supposed to take a backseat to motherhood" (22). "The new momism," Douglas and Michaels continue, "insists that if you want to do anything else, you'd better first prove that you're a doting, totally involved mother before proceeding. The only recourse for women who want careers, or to do anything else besides stay at home with the kids all day, is to prove they can 'do it all'" (22). This type of gender essentialism, whether its conveyed as the "Angel in the House" (Woolf) ideology of the nineteenth century or this century's "New Momism," necessarily naturalizes mothering as "a woman's calling;" it is to be performed by the biological mother who must be a wife and nurturer in a heterosexual family wherein the father is the provider, and thus is not expected to engage in 'mothering.'

Stadtman Tucker argues that "several strands of political philosophy float through the logic and rhetoric of the emerging Mothers' Movement. The key variables are whether these different frameworks support or contest the dominant ideology of motherhood [described above] and whether they serve as a useful basis for developing advocacy positions that will advance rather that obstruct gender equality" (2004: 1-2). Stadtman Tucker explains further:

> Frameworks that challenge the dominant ideology of motherhood are attractive because of a growing awareness in popular culture that the idealization of "intensive" selfless mothering detracts from the lived experience of motherhood, isolates fathers from the core of family life, and limits mothers' personal freedom and occupational mobility. Frameworks that align with the dominant ideology of motherhood are politically appealing because they support a plea for better treatment of mothers without posing a serious threat to the status quo. (2004: 2).

"Activists and authors currently involved in the articulation of 'mothers' issues,'" Stadtman Tucker continues, "tend to sample from both conforming and non-conforming frameworks to legitimize their demands for social reforms" (2004: 2). She argues further that while there "are any number of philosophies and political theories that feed into the new thinking on motherhood as a social problem, the three predominant influences are liberal feminism, maternalism and feminist care theory" (2004: 2).

"Liberal feminism," she explains, "challenges the dominant ideology of motherhood and offers a vocabulary of rights, responsibilities, justice, equity, empowerment and identity" (2004: 2). "This framework," she continues, "is essential to their interpretation of mothers as persons with individual and social rights and responsibilities and is fundamental to the articulation of mothers' entitlement to self expression within and beyond the bounds of the maternal role—including self-expression through paid employment or civic engagement...; as well it qualifies mothers as equal citizens in an ideally egalitarian society ... and provides a context for the strategic separation of the needs and interests of women who mother from the needs and interests of the child they mother" (2004: 2). Motherhood organizations that work from a liberal feminist or equal rights paradigm include: MomsRising, Mothers and More, and Mothers Ought To Have Equal Rights. In contrast to Liberal Feminism, Maternalism, Stadtman Tucker explains, "conforms to the dominant ideology of motherhood and emphasizes the importance of maternal well-being to the health and safety of children" (2004: 2). "Maternalism," she continues, "overlaps with what has been called 'difference feminism'—particularly the idea that women are 'naturally' or intuitively more empathic, less exploitive, and more closely attuned to relational ambience then men" (2004: 2). In the *Encyclopedia of Motherhood*, Rachel V. Kutz-Flamenbaum writes that "maternalism, like paternalism, is an ideology and philosophy" (712). She continues:

> It asserts that "mother knows best" and that women, as a group, maintain a set of ideas, beliefs or experiences that reflect their motherly knowledge and motherly strengths. Maternalism suggests that women are (and should be) the moral conscience of humanity and asserts women's legitimate investment in political affairs through this emphasis. (712)

"Maternalist politics refers to," as Patrice DiQuinzio elaborates, "political activism and political movements that invoke motherhood as the basis of women's agency" (2006: 58). More numerous than equal rights based maternal activism (for reasons to be discussed below), groups that work from a maternalist politics include: Million Mom March, the Mothers of the Plaza de Mayo, The Mothers of Acari, The Mothers of Laleh Park, Mothers Against Drunk Driving, The Motherhood Project, Mainstreet Moms and Mothers In Charge.

In place of liberal feminism and maternalism, and what she views as their problematic emphasis on individualism and essentialism respectively, Stadtman Tucker develops and advocates a feminist ethic of care framework: "As with maternalism, a feminist ethic of care designates caring for others as an essential social function. But rather than valorizing maternal sensitivity and altruism as an innate vital resource, a feminist ethic of care aims to liberate caregiving from its peripheral status and reposition it as a primary human activity" (2006: 212). She goes on to explain that "for proponents of the contemporary mothers' movement, grounding the agenda in an ethic of care opens up the possibilities of developing a gender neutral approach to social policy and an opportunity to expand the language of care as a public good beyond the maternalist paradigm" (2006: 201). In positioning caregiving as a social responsibility rather than an exclusive maternal duty, a feminist ethic of care framework serves to reinvent normative motherhood both in terms of its individualism and essentialism. While currently few motherhood organizations work specifically from a feminist ethic of care framework, ones that model and practice some of its principals include Playground Revolution, Warriors Against Violence Society, The LGBTQ Parenting Network, Welfare Warriors, Feminist.com, and International Feminists for a Gift Economy. Other organizations, though they may be titled mothers groups, signify an ethic of care politics in the way that they position their organizations, the language they use to describe their mandates, and in the types of activism they undertake. As Heather Hewett notes, "The signature tag line of Stadtman Tucker's *Mothers Movement Online* website reads resources for and reporting for mothers and others who think about social change" (39). As well, Mothers

Acting Up, while seemingly a maternalist organization, includes an asterisk after the word mothers to include "mothers and others, on stilts and off, who exercise protective care over someone smaller;" and Mothers Ought To Have Equal Rights, though working from an equal rights perspective, frequently uses caregivers as well as mothers in its literature (Hewett 39). Other organizations that advance an ethic of care philosophy and practice in their challenge to the essentialism and individualism of normative motherhood include Mother Outlaws, The Latina Mami Collective, Jennifer Schumaker's 500 Mile Walk, and the Australian and Toronto Feminist Mothers Discussion Groups. While working from and advocating a feminist ethic of care politic, these organizations continue to use the word "mothers" because, as Hewett notes, "[such] reflects reality—women continue to perform most of the worlds' motherwork and carework" and affords, in Hewett's words "a *realpolitik* strategy of identity politics" (39).

Stadtman Tucker maintains that these competing frameworks have hindered the 21st century motherhood movement's progress and its attempts to develop a cohesive agenda and unified platform to achieve the social change it desires for mothers and motherhood. "The mothers' movement," she argues, "hasn't taken off yet because there's a divide that exists between whether this is a maternalist movement or if this is about the politics of motherhood aimed at resolving the social disadvantages of motherhood" (qtd. in Wilkinson 10). Contrary to Stadtman Tucker, I would suggest that most social movements are characterized by a wide range of differences in politics and ideologies, and that the aim of any movement should not be to determine what perspective or agenda is best, but how to best position such differences in terms of developing strategies for change. As DiQuinzio writes, "[T]hese tensions are exactly where the movement should begin in refining its ideological commitments, formulating its agenda, and developing strategies for change. Those of us engaged in this movement should not expect to resolve these tensions but rather should be prepared to negotiate and renegotiate them precisely as part of our strategies for change" (2006: 56). The contemporary women's movement has grown and flourished in spite of (and I would suggest as a result of) the many and diverse feminist ideologies that inform it: liberal, socialist, cultural, queer, womanist, and third wave, to name but a few. Moreover, as Stadtman Tucker herself argues (as noted above), most organizations draw from all three frameworks depending on the specific issue at hand and in order to develop the most effective strategy within a particular situation, context, or timeframe.

In her recent paper, "Harnessing the Radicalizing Experience of Motherhood to create Anti-Violence Activists," Susan Logsdon-Conradsen uses Mothers Acting Up as an example to argue that motherhood organizations tend to pick and choose, and mingle and blend the politics and strategies of the different frameworks. Logsdon-Conradsen argues that while the rhetoric of Mothers Acting Up is clearly maternalist, "it is their job, their honor," their mission is that of a feminist ethic of care: "advocating for the world's children" (16). She goes on to point out how "each of these frameworks provides a different pathway a mother may traverse on her path to becoming a mother-activist on any given issue" (4). In the context of mothers opposing violence the equal rights framework enables mothers to argue against violence on the grounds that all individuals have the right to live a life free of violence, while the maternalist perspective, in emphasizing women's role as caretaker and protector of children, empowers mothers to demand a safe world for their children. "A feminist care theory, with its emphasis on caring for all individuals as a social responsibility," as Logsdon-Conradsen explains, "clearly supports anti-violence activism and the need to protect and advocate for those with less power, including but not limited to children" (4). Moreover, these three frameworks are more complimentary than oppositional: they allow for a multitude of perspectives on any given motherhood issue, making possible the coalition building necessary for a successful social movement.

"Maternalism is Feminism for Hard Times": The Case Against Maternalist Politics for the 21st Century Motherhood Movement—Gender Essentialism, Emotionalism and Child-Centredness

If any debate has defined current discussions on maternal activism it is the role maternalist politics should or should not play in the 21st century motherhood movement. Most scholars, particularly those writing in the early years of the 21st century motherhood movement—Judith Stadtman Tucker, Heather Hewett, Patrice DiQuinzio—argue against maternalism as a politic or strategy for maternal activism. "The contemporary mothers' movement," DiQuinzio writes, "should strive to avoid the risk or pitfalls that maternalist politics present, even if that means sacrificing the advantages of maternalism; advantages that may be dubious anyway" (2006: 58).

Gender Essentialism: Co-opting Mothers/Normalizing Motherhoods

Critics of maternalism argue that this politic, as it is grounded in the discourse of essential motherhood, serves to reinforce and reify gender difference. Likewise, it renders sacrificial motherhood, which scholars agree causes mothering to be oppressive for women, as both normative and natural. Moreover, as DiQuinzio (2006) notes, maternalism may easily be manipulated or co-opted by others to oppose the interest of mothers; for example, the narrow definition of the "good" mother created from the discourse of essential motherhood may result in only "good" mothers' needs being addressed while the so defined "bad" mothers and their needs are ignored and demonized. In addition, DiQuinzio explains that mothers and maternal concerns "may be positioned on many sides of the same issue," and thus maternalism may be used to advance causes and organizations that most twenty-first century maternal activists would regard as antithetical to the objectives of the motherhood movement; mothers in support of war, and organizations such as *Security Moms for Bush* and *Armed Informed Mothers*, a pro-gun motherhood organization are examples of such" (2006: 61). Moreover,

DiQuinzio argues: "maternalist politics risks representing mothers and women as knowledgeable, interested, and entitled to political participation, only as mothers and only when they are acting on behalf of children or other dependent persons" (2006: 61). Finally, critics of maternalist politics worry that because maternalism is not inherently or necessarily feminist in its ideology or practice, it may serve to undermine women's demands for gender equity outside and beyond their role as mothers. As Hewett argues, "Feminism provides important theoretical underpinnings for current activism. Not to engage with feminist frameworks and history—not to understand its success as well as its failures is to run the risk of forgoing the opportunity to learn valuable knowledge and avoiding the same mistakes" (2006: 41).

Emotionalism: A Politics of Grief

Of equal concern to critics of maternalism is its strategy of what may be termed emotionalism. Michelle Moravec discusses the aforementioned in her recent article, "Another Mother for Peace: Reconsidering Maternalist Peace Rhetoric from a Historical Perspective, 1967-2007," arguing that "while motherhood may provide an emotionally resonate call for motivating peace activists it undercuts the political efficacy of women working to end war" (9). According to Moravec, the reason for this is maternal peace activist's reliance on gendered constructs of agency and resistance:

> Historically, women's exclusion from politics rested on a belief in women's innate characteristics, such as emotionality which rendered them too irrational. When women invoke the bonds of womanhood, when they speak from their personal grief, even when they read protest letters in public, they do not become politically efficacious acts. These forms of extra-political activism and emotive arguments run the risk of reinforcing a limited conception of women's participation in the public sphere and reifying the notion that women's true influence lies in persuading men. They reinscribe women's position as firmly on the margins. (24)

"The personal voice" she continues, "risks being misheard as an individualized expression of emotion. It threatens to push the debate about foreign policy deep into the realm of the emotional, which is not acceptable in American political discourse. The combination of emotion plus femininity yields even more disastrous political results because women are seen as protesting, not from a position of realpolitik, but out of fear and anxiety" (Moravec 23). Similarly, DiQuinzio argues that "Maternalist politics also tends to become a politics of grief, predicating women's political agency on either the pain or suffering of others or on the pain, suffering, and loss they experience as a result of harm or threats to their children or others for whom they care" (2006: 61). "But this representation of women's political agency in terms of emotion" she continues, "risks the delegitimation of maternal politics as irrational" (2006: 61).

"It's For the Children": Child-Centredness as Justification and Rationalization in Maternalism

In one of my earlier publications I argued that current thinking on maternal activism, in its emphasis upon children and in its strategies of rationalization and justification, has failed to develop a revolutionary mother-centred model of activism that takes the empowerment of mothers as its aim and focus (O'Reilly 2006a). In *Mother Without Child: Contemporary Fiction and the Crisis of Motherhood,* Elaine Tuttle Hansen argues that "the story of feminists thinking about motherhood since the early 1960s is told as a drama in three acts: repudiation, recuperation, and, in the latest and most difficult stage to conceptualize, an emerging critique of recuperation that coexists with ongoing efforts to deploy recuperative strategies" (5). Using Hansen's metaphor, I argued that, as feminist theory moved from a repudiation of patriarchal motherhood to a recuperation of motherhood (i.e., the formation of feminist mothering) we lost sight of what must be the primary and central aim of our challenge to patriarchal motherhood: the empowerment of mothers. In other words, as repudiation and recuperation define the first two acts of the feminist resistance to motherhood, the final act must be expressed more specifically as a revolution of motherhood for mothers themselves. Lately we have lost this revolutionary focus; our tone has become tame and timid, and our manner has turned cautious and circuitous. Instead of demanding change for mothers, we are now requesting them on behalf of children.

Through maternal activism, women use their position as mothers to lobby for social and political change, usually for and on behalf of children. However, maternal activism on behalf of children does not directly, or meaningfully, address the needs of mothers themselves. By defining activism in this manner I suggest we have, consciously or otherwise, discounted and disregarded what should be the first and primary aim of such activism: the empowerment of mothers. How and why patriarchal motherhood is oppressive to mothers has been well documented by feminist scholarship; however, when this same scholarship moves to a discussion on activism, the focus inexplicably shifts from the mother to children and/or to a world apart from the mother. In its first stage, a repudiation of patriarchal motherhood, the mother and her discontent was our foremost concern. However, in the second stage, recuperation, as we seek to re-conceive and reclaim mothering, the mother, while still crucial, frequently becomes instrumental to larger and seemingly more important objectives of social change. In other words, mothers are accorded agency to affect social change through activism, but little attention is paid to what this agency does or means for the mother herself in the context of *her own life*.

Equally troubling is how much of this literature justifies and rationalizes the reasons for empowering mothers. Too often, the demand to empower mothers is recast as a strategy for more effective parenting. For example, in her article "Resistance as a Site of Empowerment: The Journey Away from Maternal Sacrifice," Erika Horwitz argues that empowered mothering is characterized by women insisting on "the importance of mothers meeting their own needs," and the realization that "being a mother does not fulfill all of women's needs" (48). However, in spite of this realization, mothers' demands for agency and autonomy tend to be repositioned as requirements of their children in most instances, as a comment made by a woman in Horwitz's study illustrates: "If I was going to love that baby, have any quality of time with that baby, I had to get away from that baby. I had to meet my own needs" (48). Likewise, another woman in this study explained that she resisted patriarchal motherhood "to make me a better mother for my children" (52). In *A Potent Spell: Mother Love and the Power of Fea*r, Janna Malamud Smith makes reference to the myth of Demeter and Persephone in order to argue that children are best served by empowered mothers; she points out that Demeter "is able to save her daughter because she is a powerful goddess who can make winter permanent and destroy humankind" (59). "Demeter," she continues, "possesses the very qualities that Mothers so often have lacked—adequate resources and strength to protect their children, particularly daughters" (59). Therefore, what a child needs most in the world, Smith argues, "is a *free and happy* mother," an assertion that stands to contradict patriarchal wisdom (167, emphasis added). Smith elaborates further by citing Ann Crittenden: "Studies conducted on five continents have found that children are distinctly better off when the mother possesses enough income and authority in the family to make investing in children a priority" (qtd. in Smith 120). "The emergence of women as independent economic actors," Crittenden continues, "is not depriving children of vital support; it is giving them more powerful defenders. Depriving mothers of an income and influence of their own is harmful to children and a recipe for economic backwardness" (qtd. in Smith 130). To return to the story of Demeter: "It is only because Demeter has autonomy and independent resources," as Smith explains, "that she can protect Persephone" (241). Conversely, "when a culture devalues and enslaves the mother, she can [not] be like Demeter and protect her daughter" (Smith 244).

Re-reading my own work, I recognize that I too have been complicit in this questionable tactic of rationalization and justification. In both theory and practice, my demands for empowered mothering or maternal activism are defined and defended as necessary and essential *for children.* Like much of feminist scholarship on motherhood, my campaign for empowered mothering centred upon how this would benefit children. In *Mother Outlaws* (O'Reilly 2004c) I argue that empowered mothers are more effective mothers, using the metaphor of an airplane safety procedure to illustrate my argument. Anyone who has been on a plane knows the routine if oxygen masks are required: put on your mask and then assist children with theirs, which appears to defy common sense. But what these instructions recognize is that a parent must be masked first, because only then are they able to provide real and continued assistance to their child: unmasked they run they risk of becoming disoriented, ill or unconscious due to lack of oxygen which would render them of no use to their child. I argued that these instructions serve as a suitable metaphor for empowered mothering; that is, empowered mothers are better able to care for and protect their children.

While I do believe that empowered mothers are more effective mothers and that maternal activism on behalf of children is a worthwhile aim, I still wonder why the rhetoric of rationalization has become the strategy of choice among feminist activists and scholars today, and why our campaigns for social change center on children and not ourselves as mothers. Why can we not simply demand that motherhood be made better for mothers themselves? Why are our demands for maternity leaves, flex-time, greater involvement of partners in the home etc. always couched and explained as being for and about the children? Why are mothers' demands for more time, money, support, and validation only responded to when they are seen as benefiting children? I realize that this rhetoric is often employed strategically by feminists to make gains for mothers that would otherwise not be possible in a patriarchal culture. "In a social and political climate like the United States in which feminism is demonized or rejected as no longer necessary, feminists," as DiQuinzio observes, "can't argue explicitly for women's equality, rights or empowerment. So we have to sneak these issues in through the backdoor with rhetoric that 'it's all about the children' or 'it's good for families'" (2006: 63). She goes on to emphasize "that a mothers' movement that relies on images and rhetoric that might undermine or deligitimate women's claims on their own behalf, can't be a feminist movement" (DiQuinzio 2006: 63). While I appreciate the utility of this tactic—patriarchal culture will accord mothers resources if they use them on behalf children—I remain troubled by it and fear that it will ultimately backfire as real change for mothers cannot be achieved if such is always defined as being for and about children. I believe that we must also lobby for and on behalf of mothers: only then is a truly transformative and transgressive theory and mode of maternal activism made possible. Indeed, we must secure and guard a place for mothers between the proverbial baby and the bathwater.

Critics of maternalism maintain that such a politic, grounded as it is in gender essentialisiam and in its emotive and child-centred strategies, serves only to reinforce and reify gender difference and render normative and natural sacrificial motherhood that scholars agree causes mothering to be oppressive to women. As DiQuinzio concludes, "maternalist politics based on traditional sentimental representations of motherhood present significant risks and pitfalls for the merging mothers' movement" (2006: 66). "Sociologist Lisa Brush," she continues "puts it succinctly when she writes 'maternalism is feminism for hard times.' I take her to mean that maternalism is the feminism we resort to when we can't do any better on behalf of women" (DiQuinzio 2006: 66).

A Transgressive Maternalism: Strategic Essentialism, Experiential Maternalism, Experiential Essentialism and a Politics of the Heart

Strategic Essentialism, Experiential Maternalism and Experiential Essentialism

I would argue that maternalism, as both politic and practice, is more nuanced and multifaceted than the above authors suggest, which I believe is illustrated by the chapters that follow. In her recent article, "From Gestation to Delivery:

The Embodied Activist Mothering of Cindy Sheehan and Jennifer Shumaker" and in her chapters 40 and 58 in this collection, Natalie Wilson maintains that "motherhood need not be delivered as a static trope that ties women to outdated essential notions of motherhood" (232). Rather than being monolithic, the "trope of motherhood," as Wilson shows, "is varied, heterogeneous and contextual: utilized in various ways by activist movements" (201, 232). Wilson goes on to argue that maternal activism may be characterized by traditional maternalism and what she defines as 'activist mothering,' a politically aware and engaged type of mothering (such as feminist mothering, other mothering, maternal thinking, and outlaw mothering). She distinguishes between these two frameworks:

> While maternalism draws on essentialist notions of women as "natural" caretakers of children, and thus is problematic from a contemporary feminist perspective, it nevertheless gave many women an activist voice in society. It allowed mothers to move beyond the "private sphere" and gave them a public voice, albeit a voice that limited the ways in which they could speak.... As an extension of maternalism, activist mothering is aimed at social injustices at all levels and in all places but does not necessarily focus on or emphasize women *as mothers.* While maternalist-based movements chained women to their status as mothers by reifying "motherhood" ... activist mothering moves beyond this limiting frame by using motherhood as a launch rather than a base. (233)

"The maternalist framework employed by earlier activists," she continues, "can be read as a gestation period in which mothers nourished various budding forms of female activism in order to eventually deliver a full-fledged activist agenda" (234). "Hence, maternalism and activist mothering," Wilson emphasizes, "should not be read as two disparate modes but rather as a continuum of activism" (234). I concur that maternalism functions on a historical continuum of motherhood activism; likewise, I would argue that maternalism itself is enacted as and on a continuum. Maternalism, as shown in the chapters that follow, functions more often as a position rather than an identity; in other words, it is performed rather than essentially determined and derived.

Drawing upon Judith Butler's theory of the performativity of gender I argue that motherhood is similarly performed by maternalist activists. Gender, according to Butler, is performed rather than biologically inhabited and, as she explains, such "performativity is not a singular act but always a reiteration of a norm or set of norms, and to the extent that it acquires an act-like status in the present, it conceals or dissimulates the conventions of which it is a repetition" (12). "Essentialist," or good motherhood, is likewise performed by maternalist activists and is used/misused as circumstances dictate and as strategies require. In this, they engage in what Gayatri Spivak calls "strategic essentialism": "the strategic use of positivist essentialism in a scrupulously visible political interest" (qtd. in Kilburn). Spivak's strategy, as Michael Kilburn explains, "is deconstructive, like that of a good lawyer: when on defense, prod the prosecution's narrative until the cracks begin to appear and when prosecuting, piece together the case by understanding the criminal's motivation. [It] is like role-playing, briefly inhabiting the criminal mind in order to understand what makes it tick."

In contemporary maternalist politics, we see a similar deployment of strategic essentialism in Cynthia Edmonds-Cady's concept of "experiential maternalism" and Meghan Gibbon's notion of "experiential essentialism." In her recent article, "Mobilizing Motherhood: Race, Class and the Uses of Maternalism in the Welfare Rights Movement," Edmonds-Cady distinguishes between the sentimental maternalism of the middle-class white women, "Friends" in the welfare rights movement in Detroit, and the experiential maternalism of the "Recipients," the poor black women directly involved in this movement (2009). According to Edmonds-Cady, the middle-class white women held traditional (or in the context of this discussion, essentialist) assumptions about women, motherhood and work and "overemphasized a shared gender and motherhood status with the Recipients" (213). In contrast, the "Recipients took a more everyday practical approach to motherhood and their participation in the Welfare Rights Movement" (213). For these women, as Edmonds-Cady explains further:

> Recipients' use of experiential maternalism represented a pragmatic approach to motherhood as well as a way of emphasizing a desire to help poor women and children. Recipients did not perceive of motherhood as being a separate, romanticized vocation, as did many of the Friends. Instead their experience of poverty and the agency they employed through fighting the racist, classist welfare system allowed them to develop a more politicized activists' view of motherhood. Experiential maternalism was a way of viewing their social movement through the lens of their experiences of discrimination and stigmatization as poor black women, while they were simultaneously driven by the critical needs of their children. (214)

In other words, black women developed experiential maternalism from their specific and lived experiences of poverty and racism and deployed it, in Edmonds-Cady's words, "as a way to reach out to other poor mothers" (219). For these women, maternalism emerged from real and shared experiences of motherwork and not from a romanticized and essential concept of universal motherhood as with the white women. To paraphrase Spivak, these women used essentialism strategically to form, and lobby on behalf of, a community of mothers for a specific political cause: welfare rights.

Meghan Gibbon's concept of experiential essentialism developed in her recent chapter "Political Motherhood in the United States and Argentina" and in chapter 51 of this collection draws more from the deconstructive role-playing and decoding dimension of Spivak's strategic essentialism and Butler's concept of subjectivity as performance. In her examination of the *Madres de la Plaza de Mayo* (Mothers of the Plazo de Mayo) during the military dictatorship in Argentina, and of the organization Another Mother for Peace in the United States during the Vietnam War, Gibbons argues that these maternal activists used and misused the trope of maternal essentialism: performed "good" motherhood in order to achieve outlaw or activist mothering. Gibbons explains:

> These women were driven by something that was the product of their experiences (based in the biological and the social) and their treatment as mothers by the state (as citizens whose subject positions in the nation were manipulated to serve nationalist ends). Both groups of mothers showed great sophistication in dealing with the powerful force of essentialized motherhood. At times they rejected essentialism, but at other times they played on the power that it conferred upon them as mothers. In the end, the mothers rejected this binary and constructed a paradigm that reflected their social and political identities as well as their lived experience. (254-255)

Both groups, Gibbons emphasizes, "used their identities as mothers to authorize themselves to speak publicly about unpopular state policies" (254). But they did so strategically by "manipulating the maternal paradigm that was supposed to control them" (256). As women concerned with the wellbeing of their children, these mothers adhered to the script of normative motherhood, but by doing so in the public sphere and in the context of political protest, they violated the codes and frame (behaving in a non feminine manner and in the masculine realm) of this same script. With regard to the Madres, "they played on the cultural paradigm of *marianismo*, a Catholic model of ideal womanhood based on the Latin American cult of the Virgin Mary, in order to argue that they were only fulfilling the maternal obligations assigned to them by the state and the Church" (255-256). Moreover in presenting themselves "as pious, self-sacrificing, obedient and devoted to their families" (255) the mothers eventually gained national and international support and respect for their cause. In other words, the Madres performed good motherhood in order to enact and achieve outlaw maternal activism. In the context of strategic essentialism discussed above, they decoded and deconstructed what was expected of them as good mothers in order to role-play normative maternity to make possible their successful maternal activism. Through this, they redefined their identities as mothers as well as the larger meaning and practice of political engagement and protest.

A Politics of the Heart: Maternal Nurturance as Resistance and Embodied Activism

Central to maternalist politics is the practice of emotionalism which has been criticized by earlier scholars on motherhood activism. As evidenced in the chapters that follow, many motherhood organizations, MADD, UMOVE, Million Mom

March, and M.A.T.H., to name but a few, employ emotionalism and work from what DiQuinzio (2006) calls a "politics of grief." Such emotionalism, the above authors argue, "undercuts the political efficacy of women;" "risks being misheard as an individualized expression of emotion;" "predicates women's political agency on pain and suffering," and "risks the delegitimation of maternal politics as irrational." But is such a characterization of emotionalism just or accurate? As Logsdon-Conradsen argues, "Aren't many types of activism motivated by personal experience?" (21). "Why are mothers questioned for being emotionally motivated, while other activists are not? Does such an elitist perspective, in demanding that activism be based on rationality, not run the risk of devaluing both the feminine and the power of emotion? And is this just another way that society devalues motherhood and holds up the stereotypically masculine trait of unemotional as more legitimate?" (Logsdon-Conradsen 21). I would argue that emotionalism, similar to strategic essentialism, is an effective practice of resistance and protest if such is employed strategically and situated as a politic rather than a sentiment. Writing on the Madres of Argentina and Another Mother for Peace, Wilson notes that "emotion transformed the mothers, some of whom were timid housewives before their tragedies, into bold, public actors" (260). In so doing, as Wilson continues "[they] demonstrated that emotion could be a powerful motive for political struggle and significantly, by basing their campaigns on emotion, they challenged the privileging of reason in patriarchal culture and politics" (260). In this, mothers work from what I have termed a "politics of the heart:" a theory and practice that positions motherlove, or more specifically, maternal nurturance, as an act of resistance (O'Reilly 2004b).

In my previous writings on African American mothering and the fiction of Toni Morrison I argued that black mothers view and practice motherlove as a political act of resistance against a racist culture that seeks to harm their children (O'Reilly 2004b). Black mothers recognize that in fiercely loving their children—children who were regarded as unlovable within the institution of slavery and under the discourse of white supremacy—they were able to instill in them a loved sense of self to protect them from the hurts and harm of a racist culture. By way of maternal nurturance, black mothers sought to immunize their children from racist ideologies by loving them so that they could love themselves in a culture that defined them as not deserving or worthy of love. Through loving their children these mothers instilled them with a loved sense of self and self-esteem, enabling them to defy and subvert racist discourses that naturalize racial inferiority and commodify blacks as object and other. This practice of maternal nurturance builds upon the African American view of homeplace as a site of resistance. bell hooks explains:

> Historically, African-American people believed that the construction of a homeplace, however fragile and tenuous (the slave hut, the wooden shack), had a radical political dimension. Despite the brutal reality of racial apartheid, of domination, one's homeplace was one site where

> one could freely confront the issue of humanization, where one could resist. Black women resisted by making homes where all black people could strive to be subjects, not objects, where one could be affirmed in our minds and hearts despite poverty, hardship, and deprivation, where we could restore to ourselves the dignity denied to us on the outside in the public world. (42)

When she talks about homeplace, hooks emphasizes that she is not speaking merely of black women providing services for their families; rather, she refers to "the creation of a safe place" where, in her words, "black people could affirm one another and by so doing heal many of the wounds inflicted by racist domination … [a place where] [they] had the opportunity to grow and develop, to nurture [their] spirits" (42). For these mothers, motherlove was not innately derived or determined as in the trope of essential motherhood, but a consciously chosen act of resistance. However, as hooks continues: "[This] libratory struggle has been seriously undermined by contemporary efforts to change that subversive homeplace into a site of patriarchal domination" (42). "This shift in perspective, where homeplace is not viewed as a political site," she continues, "has had a negative impact on the construction of black female identity and political consciousness. Masses of black women, many of whom were not formally educated, had in the past been able to play a vital role in black liberation struggle" (42). I would argue that the rhetoric and strategy of maternal nurturance in maternalist politics functions in a similar manner: it is a consciously constituted strategy, motivated by mother love and, as theorized by Sara Ruddick, developed from the central demand of maternal practice, the preservation of children. However, as evidenced by the comments above, as it is enacted from the heart and not the mind, and as it is developed from the private realm of motherwork and not the public one of formal social action, it is often not considered as a real or legitimate form of resistance or protest.

As well, as Wilson has shown, emotionalism informs the highly successful strategy of "embodied activism" that characterizes much of modern motherhood activism. Embodied activism, Wilson explains, emphasizes "the embodied nature of existence" and refers to "a corporeally based political engagement" (235, 236). Activist mothers use their bodies and bodily actions to signify the inherent embodied nature of humanity and to enact their protests. Wilson explains: "Whether using the body as a sort of weapon to blockade factory entrances or as a manifestation of powerlessness and injustice (as when the body is purposefully rendered weak during a hunger strike so as to literally *materialize* various political injustices in ways that are visibly embodied) mothering activists have consistently refused to disembody their activism" (235, emphasis in original). Embodied activism, as Wilson continues, "delivers the message that injustices are not abstract wrongs that hurt a particular nation but literal wounds that injure living, breathing bodies" (236). Such activism marks the actions of the Argentine Madres who embodied their grief by wearing posters of their missing children and marching with life sized silhouettes, giving a physical presence to the bodies of their disappeared children. Similarly, as explored in chapter 40, Jennifer Schumaker embodies activist mothering in her 500-Mile Walk for Togetherness, as do CODEPINK (chapter 56) and Mothers Acting Up (chapter 63) in their flamboyant bodily displays (bright pink clothing, walking on stilts etc). Thus, both embodied activism and maternal nurturance are socially motivated and enacted forms of emotionalism through which they serve to transgress the essentially derived gender identity of traditional maternalism to become a consciously chosen political strategy.

A Transformative Maternalism, Matrifocality, Maternal Practice and Empowered Maternal Subjectivity

Matrifocality

The final concern with maternalism is its alleged child-centred focus and its attendant "It's for the child" justification and rationalization. However, a cursory review of the 81 chapters that follow demonstrate that the majority of contemporary motherhood organizations are mother-centred in both perspective and purpose. The organizations described in section one are concerned with empowering women in pregnancy, childbirth, and breastfeeding, while those in section two, three, and four focus upon providing support and community for mothers and delivering advocacy and activism on their behalf. The organizations described in the final section are also firmly mother-centred in their commitment to researching, narrating and performing women's lived experiences as mothers. In this, most contemporary motherhood organizations work from what I have termed elsewhere in reference to maternal discourses: a matrifocal narrative (O'Reilly and Caporale Bizzini). A matrifocal narrative is one in which a mother plays a role of cultural and social significance, one in which motherhood is thematically elaborated, valued, and structurally central to the plot. I would suggest that the majority of contemporary motherhood organizations may be understood to be political or social modes of maternal narratives; borrowing from literary theorists Brenda Daly and Maureen Reddy, they "begin with the mother in her own right, from her own perspective," and "hold fast to a maternal perspective" (2-3). And while children are certainly integral to the agenda or plots of these social matrifocal narratives, the mother remains a central character and her life an organizing theme therein.

Maternal Practice

I would further suggest that even explicitly child-focused organizations, such as those described in the sections on "Violence, Militarism, War and Peace" and "Social Change and Social Justice," may be considered mother-centred in so far as their concern is to better the lives of children. As Sara Ruddick theorized, maternal practice is characterized by three demands: preservation, growth, and social acceptance. "To be a mother," Ruddick explains, "is to be committed to meeting these demands by works of preservative love, nurturance, and training"

(17). The first duty of mothers is to protect and preserve their children: "to keep safe whatever is vulnerable and valuable in a child" (Ruddick 80). "Preserving the lives of children," Ruddick writes, "is the central constitutive, invariant aim of maternal practice: the commitment to achieving that aim is the constitutive maternal act" (19). "To be committed to meeting children's demand for preservation," Ruddick continues, "does not require enthusiasm or even love; it simply means to see vulnerability and to respond to it with care rather than abuse, indifference, or flight" (19). If we locate so-called child-focused organizations in the context of Ruddick's theory, they function as matrifocal organizations; they are able to aid mothers in their maternal practice, particularly its demand of preservation. An organization that seeks to protect children, or support their survival and development in general, likewise supports mothers by virtue of making motherwork easier. For example, organizations that address issues such as war and militarism, poverty, police/state brutality, drunken driving, environmental degradation, gun violence, etc. empower mothers by enabling them to fully and successfully perform the work they must do as mothers. I say this not to romanticize or "essentialize" motherhood, but to remind and emphasize that it is mothers who are responsible for children and childrearing in patriarchal culture. Since it is mothers who do the work of raising children under patriarchy, an organization that seeks to better the lives of children also betters the lives of mothers by improving, if you will, the working conditions under which mothers perform their reproductive labour.

Demeter and the Mamazon: Empowered Maternal Subjectivity

Earlier I argued that the Demeter-Persephone myth is frequently cited to make the argument that empowered mothers are more effective mothers; that is, mothers may ask for and be afforded power only if such is used for and on behalf of children. As discussed above, such a strategy of rationalization and justification is problematic because mothers are accorded agency only to affect social change on behalf of children, with little attention being paid to what this agency does or means for the mother herself in the context of *her own life*. However, I would argue that if we situate this strategy specifically in the context of maternal subjectivity, it opens up other possibilities and readings. In her book, *Of Woman Born*, Adrienne Rich interprets the Demeter/Persephone Myth, particularly as it was enacted in the Eleusinian mysteries as representing every daughter's "longing for a mother whose love for her and whose power were so great as to undo rape and bring her back from death" (240). The myth, Rich continues, bespeaks "*every mother's [longing] for the power of Demeter [and] the efficacy of her anger...*" (240, emphasis added). In patriarchal culture where there are so few examples, in either life or literature, of empowered mothering, Demeter's triumphant resistance serves as a powerful model of such. More significantly, in the context of this discussion on maternal subjectivity, this anger rendered Demeter powerful and in turn this power made her rage empowering. This enraged power and empowering rage transformed Demeter from being a passive witness to her daughter's abduction to an active opponent against it. As evidenced in many of the chapters that follow, particularly those in section five and six, the rage or grief that a mother feels as her child is threatened or killed radicalizes and mobilizes the mother, moving her to social action and political resistance. As these chapters demonstrate, mothers develop critical awareness, acquire confidence, build community, and achieve agency in and through their resistance on behalf of their children. In other words, while motherhood activism may originate from a child-centred perspective or purpose, it becomes matrifocal and arguably feminist in the way that it results in and gives rise to an empowered and powerful maternal subjectivity. The Demeter myth, though ostensibly about the rescue of a daughter and her rebirth as she returns from Hades (the place of the dead), simultaneously narrates a mother's rebirth in the transformation of her consciousness.

The archetype of the Mamazon similarly suggests the possibility of an empowered maternal subjectivity through motherhood activism on behalf of children. The term mamazon, as Sheri Lucas explains, "was created by merging the meanings of Amazon (the mythical tribe of warrior women who are represented as autonomous and competent, as physically, emotionally and intellectually strong) and 'mama'" (2010: 682). When the two are connected, Lucas goes on to explain, "it connotes primal and fierce 'mother bear' instincts; mothering practices that are nontraditional ... and the decision to mother outside of a committed monogamous relationship; and mother-driven political actions, particularly when it is loud, angry and assertive" (683). A "mamazon" identity and practice, Lucas continues, "[is] often considered threatening to conventional definitions of motherhood" (683). The mamazon trope, as with the Demeter archetype, reveals that child motivated and centred forms of motherhood activism do empower mothers and accord them a power not available to women in traditional motherhood. In so doing, this practice of maternalism, though purportedly child-centred, transforms both mothers and motherhood and give rises to what I and others have termed a 'mother outlaw' identity and a practice of 'outlaw mothering.' In the first instance, outlaw mothering functions as an oppositional discourse of motherhood; more specifically, it signifies a theory and practice of mothering that seeks to challenge the dominant discourse of motherhood, and change the various ways that the lived experience of patriarchal motherhood is limiting or oppressive to women. More pointedly, as I have argued elsewhere, the overarching aim of outlaw mothering is to confer to mothers the agency, authority, authenticity, autonomy, advocacy/activism denied to them in patriarchal motherhood (O'Reilly 2004c, 2004d, 2006a 2006b, 2007, 2008, 2009, 2010b; O'Reilly and Caporale-Bizzini). If we understand child motivated and centred activism from the perspective of the Mamazon and the Demeter archetype, it becomes evident that such forms of maternal activism do empower mothers and make possible a powerful matrifocal stance and practice. In so doing, such a perspective reveals that, contrary to traditional readings of maternalism, motherhood power is integral and central to maternalist politics and practice.

Matricentric Feminism: "Motherhood is the Unfinished Business of Feminism"

Motherhood activism, whether such is expressed as maternalism, equal rights for mothers, or as an ethic of care, works to empower mothers; I would argue that this makes it feminist. In a recent article Janice Nathanson contends that maternal activism promotes a feminist agenda in three specific ways:

> First, it exemplifies the very core of feminist ideology—that the personal is political. Second, it helps to negate essential notions of motherhood by transforming views of it from an "isolated or individualized experience ... [to] the inspiration for a foundation of visions of large-scale social change" (Orlect 3). And third, whether intentional or not, it upsets traditional gender and power relations. (244)

As discussed at length above and demonstrated in the chapters that follow, mothers come to political activism as a result of, and in response to, a personal situation or incident in their own lives or that of their children. Activist mothers recognize that their "personal troubles are politically constituted," and that only by political action can such personal troubles be remedied (Nathanson). In this, as Nathanson emphasizes, "they invoke one of feminism's most cherished ideologies—the personal is political" (245). As well, maternal activism, as detailed above and evidenced in the following chapters, defies and deconstructs essentialist notions of womanhood and motherhood by "reframing motherhood: expanding its boundaries (from private to public), and by endowing it with qualities normally attributed to the public realm" (Nathanson, 250). For activist mothers motherwork is neither private nor mundane, as is assumed and dictated by the normative ideology of patriarchal motherhood. Echoing the above sentiment and that of chapters that follow, Nathanson writes that, "mothers, in the process of their activism take on nontraditional roles in which their action and agency provide a new sense of empowerment that often upsets traditional gender roles" (251). Moreover, "women's activism," as Beth Roy emphasizes, "always challenges domestic as well as public power relations, because by the very act of taking a position in the public domain, women violate their patriarchal assignment to domesticity" (qtd. in Nathanson 251). In each instance, activist mothers redefine motherwork as a socially engaged enterprise and a site of power wherein mothers can effect social change, both in the home through feminist childrearing, and outside the home through maternal activism. Such maternal activism, in rendering the personal political, blurring the boundaries between the private and the public, and in inverting traditional gender roles, both disrupts and dislodges the gender essentialism (the naturalized opposition between the masculine/feminine, the private/public) that grounds and structures modern patriarchy. In this, motherhood activism emerges as a specific mode of feminist theory and practice, what I have termed "matricentric feminism."

I use the term matricentric feminism to distinguish it from maternal feminism and to mark it as a distinct motherhood politic and theory specific to its twenty-first century context. While matricentric feminism does borrow from maternalism in many of its strategies, it does so, as discussed above, strategically and in ways specific to its twenty-first century context. Moreover matricentric feminism also comprises the perspectives and philosophies of equal rights feminism and an ethic of care framework. Similar to Elaine Showalter who coined the term gynocentric to signify a woman-centred perspective, I use the term matricentric to denote a mother-centred standpoint and to emphasisize and designate it as a particular, long overdue and urgently needed mode of feminism.

It has been said that motherhood is the unfinished business of feminism. For example, a cursory review of recent scholarship on mothers and paid employment reveals that while women have made significant gains over the last three decades, mothers have not. Mothers in the paid labour force find themselves "mommy tracked," making sixty cents for every dollar earned by full-time fathers (Williams 2). Indeed, today the pay gap between mothers and non-mothers under thirty-five years is now larger than the wage gap between young men and women (Crittenden 94). And while the "glass ceiling" and the "sticky floor" are still to be found in the workplace, most scholars would argue that it is the maternal wall that impedes and hinders most women's progress in the workplace today. "Many childless women under the age of thirty five," Ann Crittenden writes, "believe that all the feminist battles have been won" (88) But, as Crittenden continues, "once a woman has a baby, the egalitarian office party is over" (88).

A discussion of the reasons for such "stalled feminism for mothers" is beyond the scope of this paper; however, what must be emphasized here in this introduction, is that with the 21st century motherhood movement we have, for the first time in the herstory of feminism, positioned mothers' needs and concerns as the starting point in theory and activism on and for women's empowerment. This is not to suggest that a matricentric feminism should replace traditional feminist thought; rather, it is to remind and emphasize that the category of mother is distinct from the category of woman, and that many of the problems mothers face—socially, economically, politically, culturally, psychologically and so forth—are specific to women's role and identity as mothers. Indeed, mothers are oppressed under patriarchy as women *and as mothers*. Consequently, mothers need a mother-centred or matricentric mode of feminism organized from and for their particular identity and work as mothers. If the eighty plus organizations described in this collection agree on anything, it is that a mother-centred feminism is urgently needed and long overdue because mothers, arguably more so than women in general, remain disempowered despite 40 years of feminism. Thus, the three models of motherhood activism—maternalism, equal rights, and an ethic of care—must be understood as complimentary. Rather than being seen as competing strategies for maternal empowerment, they must coalesce to form a specific feminist theory and practice, that of matricentric feminism. In this, motherhood activism is similar to feminism, which is likewise characterized by opposing theories and strategies for women's empowerment. Interestingly, the models of motherhood activism match those of feminism: maternalism resembles cultural feminism, equals rights resembles liberal feminism, and an ethic of care resembles socialist feminism. Such convergences suggest that motherhood activism is informed by feminist thought and is thus feminist in its agenda. Likewise, the divergences in motherhood theory signify a robust social movement and theory, not a fractured one as is often assumed in traditional interpretations of twenty-first century motherhood activism.

The motherhood organizations described in the chapters that follow, while widely diverse in their perspectives and aims, all embrace and advance matricentric feminism. Albeit with varying degrees of emphasis, they recognize that motherhood is disempowering if not oppressive as it is currently perceived and practiced in patriarchal societies for a multitude of reasons; namely, the societal devaluation of motherwork, the endless tasks of privatized mothering, and the impossible standards of idealized motherhood. For example, organizations concerned with maternal health argue that motherwork and female reproduction have a particularly deleterious impact on women's physical and mental agency; more specifically, mothers tend to prioritize the needs of other family members to the detriment of their own health, a significant number of mothers experience post partum depression, and thousands of women die every year globally and millions more suffer debilitating life-long injuries or infections relating to pregnancy and childbirth complications. Similarly, motherhood organizations concerned with mothers and paid work argue that the "second shift," the maternal wage gap, and ongoing employment discrimination prevent mothers from effectively combining family care responsibilities and paid employment, which consequently inhibits them from achieving agency and autonomy in their lives. Finally, as discussed above, each organization begins with the understanding that the category of mother is distinct from the category of woman, and that many of the problems mothers face—socially, economically, politically, culturally, psychologically and so forth—are specific to women's role and identity as mothers. Indeed, mothers are oppressed under patriarchy as women *and as mothers*. As a result, mothers need a mother-centred feminism organized from and for their particular identity and work as mothers.

The organizations described in the chapters that follow likewise recognize that mothers are (and have always been) leaders in various social justice movements for children, for families, and for peace and the environment. As well, each organization, even those that are child-centred in perspective, position maternal empowerment as a defining goal of their activism and seek to strengthen the social, personal, and political power of mothers. Each organization, albeit in different ways, seeks to grant women greater authority, resources, and status so that they can adequately care for their children while living full and purposeful lives. Likewise, each is concerned with exploring and addressing both the obstacles to and possibilities for maternal agency in order to bring about the necessary changes in law, public policy, education, family, health, the workplace, and motherwork in order to afford full and lasting authority, agency, respect, and empowerment for mothers in the twenty-first century. One point they all agree on is that maternal empowerment is needed for healthier mothers, families and society.

Overview of Collection

This book has been many years in the making. In 2004, Judith Stadtman Tucker and I began to work on a collection of essays on twenty-first century motherhood activism, but other projects and commitments intervened. In 2007, while writing on empowered mothering and maternal empowerment, I recognized the need and urgency to bring together motherhood organizations so that we could better understand motherhood activism, particularly as it was developing and coalescing to form a 21st century motherhood movement. To this end, the Association for Research on Mothering (now the Motherhood Initiative for Research and Community Involvement) hosted a two day conference in Toronto, Canada, in October 2008, "You Say You Want a Revolution? The 21st Century Motherhood Movement," bringing together 28 motherhood organizations. The objectives of this embedded conference, the first ever on the motherhood movement of the twenty-first century, were threefold. Firstly, we hoped to raise the public profile of the motherhood movement as a potential force for social change; secondly, we sought to provide a collective narrative of the history, core concerns, and objectives of the movement in its formative period; and thirdly, we wished to capture the diverse organizational backgrounds, personal perspectives and visions of those involved in the movement's inception, including independent activists and leaders/founders of groups involved in advocacy, support, education and consciousness raising for mothers. Our overall aim was to highlight the scope and diversity of this movement as it moved to create a more equitable world for mothers and their children. At this conference The International Mothers Network, now the The International Mothers and Mothering Network, the first ever global consortium of motherhood organizations (described in chapter 42), was formed and officially launched on March 8, 2009, International Women's Day. Though originally this anthology on the 21st century motherhood movement was to be the published papers of the organizations that participated in the 2008 conference, as I researched motherhood activism and as one motherhood group suggested another, the collection grew to include more than eighty organizations.

My criterion for the inclusion of chapters in this collection was that they were informed by the values of matricentric feminism described above, as well as being committed to improving the lives of mothers and working towards social change for mothers, children and society more generally. In this, each organization had to view and position itself as an activist and/or advocacy group that sought broad-based change and membership. In defining an organization this way, I looked for groups that not only provided services for mothers but also sought to change the larger meaning and experience of mothering/motherhood and/or address a particular social issue that had relevance to mothers' lives in their responsibility and practice of motherwork. Equally important in the selection of organization was that they covered diverse maternal identities and allowed for an international perspective on motherhood activism. While the volume includes various maternal perspectives—Aboriginal, Latina, African-American/Canadian, Queer/Lesbian, young and older, single, immigrant, poor, working class, incarcerated, disabled, and rural mothers—it remains largely North American in perspective like most contemporary scholarship on motherhood. This North American bias is corrected somewhat by the inclusion of motherhood organizations from Australia, Argentina, Brazil, England, Germany, Ireland, Iran and Russia, and from the inclusion of organizations that have an international perspective and membership. Some such organizations include the White Ribbon Alliance for Safe Motherhood and Save the Mothers Programs which work with and on behalf of mothers from the global south, and groups that have worldwide membership such as Mothers Acting Up, International Feminists for a Gift Economy, La Leche League International, The International MotherBaby Childbirth Organization, and the Mother Centers International Network. Each chapter discusses the context, history and mandate of the organization, and examines the organization's activities, challenges, future goals and its relationship to the larger movement. The contributors for this volume are either activists from the organization described or scholars who are knowledgeable about the organization, and are often both.

The volume is organized by way of seven sections. The first section is concerned with organizations that focus on women's experiences as they become mothers and includes chapters on pregnancy, childbirth, and breastfeeding. The second section, "Maternal Identities," considers groups that represent a particular demographic of mothers including young, Latina, incarcerated, and lesbian mothers, among many others. The third section focuses on organizations that provide support and advocacy for and on behalf of mothers, while section four describes groups that engage in activism on behalf of mothers. Organizations described in section five address issues of violence, militarism, war and peace while those in the sixth section are concerned with larger concerns of social justice and social change. The final section includes organizations that research and/or publish on motherhood such as research centres and mothering magazines. That being said, there is much overlap in any one organization's mandate, for example, those that support mothers may also engage in activism; likewise, some organizations included in the advocacy section provide such for a particular group of women. My overall aim was to arrange the groups by an organizing structure, however provisional, and to provide diversity across race/class/sexuality/ability/age in each section.

Conclusion

While reading the chapters for this collection on the 21st century motherhood movement, I am reminded of Adrienne Rich's groundbreaking distinction between two meanings of motherhood, "one superimposed on the other: the *potential relationship* of any women to her powers of reproduction and to children; and the *institution*, which aims at ensuring that that potential—and all women—shall remain under male control" (11, emphasis in original). Like Rich, the organizations described in this collection begin with the realization that motherhood, as it is currently perceived and practiced in patriarchal societies, is disempowering if not oppressive for a multitude of reasons; namely, the societal devaluation of motherwork, the endless tasks of privatized mothering, the current incompatibility of waged work and motherwork, and the impossible standards of idealized motherhood. However, like Rich they also recognize that mothering holds much potential for the empowerment of mothers, particularly the power of mothers to effect real and lasting change in their lives, in the lives of their children, and in the larger society. Both Rich and the organizations in this collection maintain that empowered mothers are more effective mothers for children, and that such mothers are healthier women and more productive workers, and that empowered mothering is beneficial for families and society at large. To realize and maximize the power of mothers, the organizations develop a plethora of theories and strategies that accord to mothers what is denied to them in patriarchal societies: agency, authority, authenticity, autonomy, advocacy and activism. Maternal agency, as Lynn O'Brien-Hallstein explains in her encyclopedia entry on the topic, "draws on the idea of agency—the ability to influence one's life, to a have power to control one's life—and explores how women have agency via mothering" (697). A theory of and programming for maternal agency focuses on, she continues, "mothering practices that facilitate women's authority and power and is revealed in mothers' efforts to challenge and act against aspects of institutionalized motherhood that constrain and limit women's lives and power as mothers" (O'Brien-Hallstein 697-698). Authenticity, as explained in Elizabeth Butterfield's encyclopedia entry, "is an ethical term that denotes being true to oneself, as in making decisions that are consistent with one's own beliefs and values" (700). In contrast, inauthenticity is generally understood to be an abdication of one's own authority and a loss of integrity. In the context of empowered mothering, maternal authenticity draws upon Ruddick's concept of the "conscientious mother" and O'Reilly's model of the "authentic feminist mother" (2009) and refers to "independence of mind and the courage to stand up to dominant values" and also to "being truthful about motherhood and remaining true to oneself in motherhood" (Butterfield; O'Reilly 2009). Similarly, maternal authority and autonomy refer to confidence and conviction in oneself, to holding power in the household, and to the ability to define and determine one's life and practices of mothering. Borrowing from Ruddick, authority and autonomy also reflect one's refusal to "relinquish or repudiate one's own perceptions and values" (Ruddick 112; O'Reilly 2009: 22). Finally, maternal advocacy/activism recognizes the potential political/social dimension of motherwork regardless of whether such is expressed in anti-sexist childrearing or maternal activism.

Overall, each organization seeks empowerment of and for mothers that, in varied and diverse ways, "names, analyzes and challenges oppression by way of the development of critical consciousness [and through] gaining control, exercising choices, and in engaging in collective social action" (Bernard Thomas and

Bernard 46). From this stance of maternal power, mothers are empowered to not only challenge and change patriarchal motherhood, as Rich advocated, but to transform the society in which they live in order to improve their own lives as women, as mothers, and in the context of the motherwork they undertake on behalf of children. From the perspective of Rich's theoretical model, the 21st century motherhood movement emerges as a viable and necessary social movement through realizing the potential of mothering and by empowering mothers to better their lives, those of their children, and the larger society. This movement, as noted in the title of this collection and demonstrated in the chapters that follow, shows us why we need to change the world and how to do it.

Works Cited

Bernard Thomas, Wanda and Candace Bernard. "Passing the Torch: A Mother and Daughter Reflect on their Experiences Across Generations." *Canadian Woman Studies/les cahiers de la femme* 18.2,3 (Summer/Fall 1998): 46-50.

Blades, Joan and Kristin Rowe-Finkbeiner. *The Motherhood Manifesto: What America's Moms Want and What to Do About It.* New York: Nation Books, 2006.

Buchanan, Andrea J. *Mother Shock: Loving Every (Other) Minute of It.* Emeryville, CA: Seal Press, 2003.

Butler, Judith. *Bodies That Matter: On the Discursive Limits of "Sex."* New York: Routledge, 1993.

Butterfield, Elizabeth. "Maternal Authenticity." *Encyclopedia of Motherhood.* Ed. Andrea O'Reilly. Los Angeles: Sage Press, 2010. 700-701.

Collins, Patricia Hill. *Black Feminist Thought: Knowledge, Consciousness, and the Politics of Empowerment.* New York: Routledge, 1999.

Crittenden, Ann. *The Price of Motherhood: Why the Most Important Job in the World Is Still the Least Valued.* New York: Henry Holt and Company, 2001.

Daly, Brenda O. and Maureen T. Reddy. "Narrating Mothers: Theorizing Maternal Subjectivities." *Narrating Mothers: Theorizing Maternal Subjectivities.* Eds. Brenda O. Daly and Maureen T. Reddy. Knoxville: University of Tennessee Press, 1991. 2-3.

DiQuinzio, Patrice. "The Politics of the Mothers Movement in the United States: Possibilities and Pitfalls." *Journal of the Association for Research on Mothering* 8.1,2 (Winter/Summer 2006): 55-71.

DiQuinzio, Patrice. *The Impossibility of Motherhood: Feminism, Individualism, and the Problem of Mothering.* New York: Routledge, 1999.

Douglas, Susan J. and Meredith W. Michaels. *The Mommy Myth: The Idealization of Motherhood and How It Has Undermined Women.* New York: Free Press, 2004.

Edmonds-Cady, Cynthia. "Mobilizing Motherhood: Race, Class and the Uses of Maternalism in the Welfare Rights Movement." *Women Studies Quarterly* 37.3,4. (Fall/Winter 2009): 206-222.

Fox, Faulkner. *Dispatches from a Not-So-Perfect Life or How I Learned to Love the House, the Man, the Child.* New York: Harmony Books, 2003.

Friedan, Betty. *The Feminine Mystique.* [1963]. New York: Norton, 2001.

Gatrell, Caroline. "Motherhood Movement." *Encyclopedia of Motherhood.* Ed. Andrea O'Reilly. Los Angeles: Sage Press, 2010. 821-823.

Gibbons, Meghan. "Political Motherhood in the United States and Argentina." *Mothers Who Deliver: Feminist Interventions in Public and Interpersonal Discourse.* Eds. Joceyln Fenton-Stitt and Pageen Reichert Powell. Albany, NY: SUNY Press, 2010. 253-278.

Hansen, Elaine Tuttle. *Mother Without Child: Contemporary Fiction and the Crisis of Motherhood.* Berkeley: University of California Press, 1997.

Hays, Sharon. *The Cultural Contradictions of Motherhood.* New Haven: Yale University Press, 1996.

Hewett, Heather. "'Talkin' Bout a Revolution: Building a Mothers' Movement in the Third Wave." *Journal of the Association for Research on Mothering* 8.1,2 (Winter/Summer 2006): 34-54.

hooks, bell. *Yearning: Race, Gender, and Cultural Politics.* Boston: South End Books, 1990.

Horwitz, Erika. "Resistance as a Site of Empowerment: The Journey Away from Maternal Sacrifice." *Mother Outlaws: Theories and Practices of Empowered Mothering.* Ed. Andrea O'Reilly. Toronto: Women's Press, 2004. 43-58.

Kilburn, Michael. "Glossary of Key Terms in the Work of Gayatri Chakravorty Spivak." *Emory University.* Spring 2006. Web. <http://www.english.emory.edu/Bahri/Glossary.html>.

Kinser, Amber, ed. *Mothering in the Third Wave.* Toronto: Demeter Press, 2008.

Kutz-Flamebaum, Rachel V. "Maternalism." *Encyclopedia of Motherhood.* Ed. Andrea O'Reilly. Los Angeles: Sage Press, 2010. 712-716

Logsdon-Conradsen, Susan. "Harnessing the Radicalizing Experience of Motherhood to Create Anti-Violence Activists." NWSA conference paper, Nov. 2010.

Lucas, Sheri. "Mamazons." *Encyclopedia of Motherhood.* Ed. Andrea O'Reilly. Los Angeles: Sage Press, 2010. 682-683.

Maushart, Susan. *The Mask of Motherhood: How Becoming a Mother Changes Everything and Why We Pretend It Doesn't.* New York: Penguin Books, 2000.

Moravec, Michelle. "Another Mother for Peace: Reconsidering Maternalist Peace Rhetoric from a Historical Perspecrive 1967-2007." *Journal of the Motherhood Initiative* 1.1 (Spring 2010): 9-29.

Nathanson, Janice. "Maternal Activism: How Feminist Is It?" *Feminist Mothering.* Ed. Andrea O'Reilly. Albany, NY: SUNY Press, 2008. 243- 256.

O'Brien-Hallstein, Lynn. "Maternal Agency." *Encyclopedia of Motherhood.* Ed. Andrea O'Reilly. Los Angeles: Sage Press, 2010. 697-699.

O'Reilly, Andrea. *Mother Matters: Motherhood as Discourse and Practice.* Toronto: Association for Research on Mothering, 2004a.

O'Reilly, Andrea. *Toni Morrison and Motherhood: A Politics of the Heart.* Albany, NY: SUNY Press, 2004b.

O'Reilly, Andrea, ed. *Mother Outlaws: Theories and Practices of Empowered Mothering.* Toronto: Women's Press, 2004c.

O'Reilly, Andrea, ed. *From Motherhood to Mothering: The Legacy of Adrienne Rich's Of Woman Born.* Albany, NY: SUNY Press, 2004d.

O'Reilly, Andrea. "Between the Baby and the Bathwater: Some Thoughts on a Mother Centred Theory and Practice of Feminist Mothering." *Journal of the Association for Research on Mothering* 8.1,2 (Winter/Summer 2006a): 323-330.

O'Reilly, Andrea. *Rocking the Cradle: Thoughts on Motherhood, Feminism, and the Possibility of Empowered Mothering.* Toronto: Demeter Press, 2006b.

O'Reilly, Andrea, ed. *Maternal Theory: Essential Readings.* Toronto: Demeter Press, 2007.

O'Reilly, Andrea. *Feminist Mothering.* Albany, NY: SUNY Press, 2008.

O'Reilly, Andrea. *Maternal Thinking: Philosophy, Politics, Practice.* Toronto: Demeter Press, 2009.

O'Reilly, Andrea. *Encyclopedia of Mothering.* Los Angeles: Sage Press, 2010a.

O'Reilly, Andrea. *21st Century Motherhood: Experience, Identity, Policy, Agency.* New York: Columbia University Press, 2010b.

O'Reilly, Andrea and Silvia Caporale-Bizzini. *From Personal to Political: Towards a New Theory of Maternal Narrative.* Selinsgrove, PA: Susquehanna University Press, 2009.

Pearson, Allison. *I Don't Know How She Does It: The Life of Kate Reddy, Working Mother.* New York: Knopf, 2002.

Peskowitz, Miriam. *The Truth Behind the Mommy Wars: Who Decides What Makes a Good Mother.* Emeryville, CA: Seal, 2005.

Rich, Adrienne. *Of Woman Born: Motherhood as Experience and Institution.* 1976. New York: W.W. Norton, 1986.

Roberts, Dorothy. *Killing the Black Body: Race, Reproduction, and the Meaning of Liberty.* New York: Pantheon Books, 1997.

Ruddick, Sara. *Maternal Thinking: Toward a Politics of Peace.* New York: Beacon Press, 1989.

Showalter, Elaine. "Towards a Feminist Poetics." *Women Writing About Women.* Ed. Mary Jacobus. London: Croom Helm, 1979. 25- 36.

Smith, Janna Malamud. *A Potent Spell: Mother Love and the Power of Fear.* Boston: Houghton Mifflin Company, 2003.

Stadtman Tucker, Judith. "The Motherhood Papers: Morality or equality? Maternal thinking and the social agenda." *The Mothers Movement Online.* June 2003. Web. <http://www.mothersmovement.org/features/mhoodpapers/maternalism/morality_equality.htm>,

Stadtman Tucker, Judith. "Motherhood and its Discontents: The Political and Ideological Grounding of the 21st Century Mothers' Movement." Paper presented at the Association for Research on Mothering Conference "Motherhood and Feminism," Toronto, 2004.

Stadtman Tucker, Judith. "The Motherhood Papers: The New Future of Motherhood: Mothers don't 'choose' their way into the motherhood problem, and we can't choose our way out of it. So where do we go from here." *The Mothers Movement Online*. May 2005. Web. <http://www.mothersmovement.org/features/mhoodpapers/new_future/0505_1.htm>.

Stadtman Tucker, Judith. "Rocking the Boat: Feminism and the Ideological Grounding to the Twenty-First Mothers' Movement." *Feminist Mothering*. Ed. Andrea O'Reilly. Albany, NY: SUNY Press, 2008. 205-218.

Stadtman Tucker, Judith. "From Choice to Change: Rewriting the Script of the Motherhood as Maternal Activism." *21st Century Motherhood: Experience, Identity, Policy, Agency*. Ed. Andrea O'Reilly. New York: Columbia University Press, 2010. 293-309.

Stone, Pamela. *Opting Out? Why Women Really Quit Careers and Head Home*. Berkeley: University of California Press, 2007.

Walker, Rebecca. "Becoming the Third Wave." *Ms* (New York: Liberty Media for Women) (January/February 1992): 39-41.

Warner, Judith. *Perfect Madness: Motherhood in the Age of Anxiety*. New York: Riverhead Books, 2005.

Wilkinson, Stephanie. "Say You Want A Revolution? Why the Mothers' Revolution Hasn't Happened ... Yet." *Brain, Child* 2005. Web. <http://www.brainchildmag.com/essays/fall2005_wilkinson.html>.

Williams, Joan. *Unbending Gender: Why Family and Work Conflict and What to Do About It*. New York: Oxford University Press, 2000.

Wilson, Natalie. "From Gestation to Delivery: The Embodied Activist Mothering of Cindy Sheehan and Jennifer Schumaker." *Mothers Who Deliver: Feminist Interventions in Public and Interpersonal Discourse*. Eds. Joceyln Fenton-Stitt and Pageen Reichert Powell. Albany, NY: SUNY Press, 2010. 231-252.

Wolf, Naomi. *Misconceptions: Truth, Lies and the Unexpected on the Journey to Motherhood*. New York: Doubleday, 2001.

Woolf, Virginia. *A Room of One's Own*. [1929]. New York: A Harvest Book, 1981.

Women's Studies Quarterly. Special Issue on Motherhood. Fall/Winter 2009.

I.
Becoming a Mother: Pregnancy, Childbirth, Breastfeeding

1. Empowering Women to Become Mothers

Midwifery in Ontario, 1990-2010

JUDITH MINTZ

> ...April 1981, one month before our daughter Norah was born, a home birth naturally; a midwife; you could almost hear the guitars plinking in the background, except we did not feast on the placenta as some of our friends were doing at the time. (Shields 3)

AS SOON AS I DISCOVERED that I was pregnant with my first child in early 2004, I called my local midwifery collective. At that time, I was living in an isolated A-frame house thirty minutes' drive from the nearest hospital. I was told at my first meeting that I could have a home birth, complete with birthing pool, provided that I was in good health and my pregnancy progressed "normally." I read up on "natural" childbirth methods, nutrition and herbs. I was also working full-time as a shiatsu therapist and yoga instructor and was well acquainted with holistic bodywork practices. My midwives supported each aspect of my journey as a mother-to-be, honouring my needs and choices, but Canadian pregnant and birthing women in previous generations have not always been able to get the support and respect they need. In this chapter, I will explore how midwifery empowers mothers as both a public project and a private experience.

Midwifery and its legal regulatory processes have been a feminist project in Canada for only two generations. Feminist historians such as Wendy Mitchinson; Cheryl Krasnick Warsh; C. Lesley Biggs; and Kathryn McPherson and Veronica Strong-Boag have documented the history of women's engagement with the Canadian medical system and giving birth since the mid-1980s, exposing how the medicalization of childbirth has been to women's disadvantage. Anthropologist Margaret MacDonald (2006) has examined the contemporary significance of "natural bodies and natural births" and how midwives and their clients together have moved away from essentializing constructions of "natural childbirth" to reflect appropriate use of biomedical technology and appropriate medical intervention (236).

Ontario midwives have been advocating for women and their families with a feminist framework since the mid 1990s. In this chapter, I will explore how midwifery is a vital part of the motherhood movement. Midwifery, I argue, puts mothers at the centre of the family and birthing process. By way of introduction, I will identify the issues that indicate a rationale for midwifery through a brief literature review and historiography. Through a review of current documents from the Association of Ontario Midwives (AOM) and the College of Midwives of Ontario (CMO), I will show how the midwives' ethics of care mandate exemplifies matrifocality, and discuss challenges and the significance of midwifery within the larger motherhood movement. I have embedded into this chapter my own personal narrative of how I was empowered as a mother through my contact with midwives.

Drawing on maternal theory by Andrea O'Reilly and Silvia Caporale Bizzini, I argue that midwives create a matrifocal narrative (10) in their advocacy for mothers. O'Reilly and Caporale Bizzini articulate that matrifocal narratives "begin with the mother in her own right, from her own perspective" (10). Citing Miriam Johnson's 1989 discussion in *Strong Mothers Weak Wives,* they explain,

> ...matrifocal societies tend to have greater gender equality because of the power of a maternal paradigm. In these societies, regardless of the particular type of kinship system, women play roles of cultural and social significance and define themselves less as wives than as mothers. (226)

It could be suggested, then, that contemporary midwifery collectives exemplify part of the continuum of matrifocal societies in how women receive non-hierarchical care in the prenatal period, through parturition and six-week post-partum phase. Indeed, many women remain emotionally if not physically connected to their midwifery practices, since many have annual picnics where families gather to reunite with their midwives and meet other families who share similar relationships to birthing and early motherhood practices.

Introduction

There has been much cross-disciplinary writing on the medicalization of childbirth and the renaissance of midwifery in Canada. Before launching into a discussion of midwifery in Ontario since its 1994 legislation, it is important here to briefly review some of this literature in order to contextualize how and why contemporary midwifery practices have evolved. The eighteenth century development of the forceps by William Smellie (Campbell 184) accelerated the movement of childbirth into the hands of physicians who sought the territory of obstetrics as a way of augmenting their medical practices. In the eighteenth and nineteenth century, doctors were proliferating as authoritative holders of scientific knowledge while simultaneously displacing midwives as careless and antiquated. In her brief review of the history of midwifery in Canada, MacDonald pointed out that obstetricians were intent on saving women from the risks of childbirth, which they purported to be able to decrease (2006: 237).

C. Lesley Biggs (1990) pointed out that in mid-nineteenth-century Ontario, midwives' practices declined because doctors projected an aura of the infallibility of science. Biggs states that the Victorian-era Ontario government legislated midwifery so that only women who had accredited medical training, of which there were very few, could legally assist women in childbirth (20). Midwives at that time, it should be noted, charged $3 less than most physicians' $5 for childbirth services, so it was fiduciary prudence for doctors to bully midwives out of practice. Biggs points out that many doctors resented the incursion that midwives made onto their territory, citing that their costly and time-consuming medical training was far superior to midwives' knowledge and experience (27). Biggs therefore argues that the medicalization of childbirth and the perinatal period was largely political, rather than generating from a genuine concern for mothers and their babies. Further, Biggs contends that doctors' increasing professionalization and the concomitant vilification of midwives in order to achieve this goal led to a decline in the quality of perinatal care.

Interestingly, physicians were not the only group who were intent on medicalizing childbirth. As Judith Walzer Leavitt points out, early twentieth century feminists such as Francis Carmody lobbied passionately for wider distribution and access to the pain-relieving drug, scopolamine, also known as Twilight Sleep. Walzer Leavitt demonstrates that Twilight Sleep was touted as a drug that would prevent "nervous exhaustion" endemic to the "modern woman" and her delicate constitution. The early suffragists, she adds, felt that the dread and pain of childbirth was a universal experience for all (upper class, white) women, who could avoid such pain through the use of the drug. The notion that working class (and racialized) women's bodies were more suited to hard labour and thus had a higher pain threshold, however, disputes this essentializing notion about sisterhood (150). Despite the fact that women who received the drug were afforded no memory of the birth of their babies, Twilight Sleep had a brief period of popularity, in part because of the mystique of the powers of what many considred "modern" science but also importantly, because the women who lobbied for it believed that they were fighting for their right to a pain-free childbirth. As Adrienne Rich put it in her classic text, *Of Woman Born*, "...this 'freedom from pain', like 'sexual liberation,' places a woman physically at men's disposal..." (171).

Research by Marlene Epp shows that by the mid twentieth century, physician-attended hospital births were normalized and midwifery care had become all but obsolete except in some Mennonite and isolated First Nations communities (336-338). Wendy Mitchinson advised that we not dichotomize our thinking about the differences between midwives and doctors, and this is indeed a challenge that the Ontario Midwives Association has risen to meet (10-11). Midwives provide appropriate support and respect for their clients' needs and demands for their pregnancy and birth through an equitable, thoughtful approach to using biotechnology in conjunction with unaugmented births. Mitchinson has pointed out that there is a risk that birth reformers have romanticized childbirth, and Margaret MacDonald (2006) has articulated that contemporary midwifery now seeks to rejoin "natural" with appropriate use of technology (238). Representations of medicalized childbirth in fiction writing suggest that consumer demand can actually spark change.

Canadian fiction writers such as Margaret Atwood, Carol Shields, and most recently, Ami McKay have taken up the issue of women's birthing rights since the mid-1970s. Atwood's 1977 painful play-by-play description in "Giving Birth," the last short story in *Dancing Girls and Other Stories*, exemplifies how doctors and by extension, nurses, have been trumping women's agency in childbirth for as long as our grandmothers can remember. Thirty-three years later, Atwood's character, Jeanine's feet-in-stirrups, medicalized birthing experience seems utterly archaic to contemporary readers who sympathize with midwifery and holistic health. Through writing "Giving Birth," Atwood asserts that although it seems impossible to envision any other way to have a baby, women desire pregnancy and childbirth to be woman-centered rather than focused on doctors' convenience. This desire, expressed through fiction writing, evolved into the consumer movement that spurred the rebirth of midwifery.

In addition to the inspiration from literature, midwifery began its slow rebirth as an outgrowth of the activism of the 1970s "second wave of feminism." With publications such as *Our Bodies, Ourselves,* which was first published in 1970, women in the United States and Canada began to question the pathologization and medicalization of childbirth and reclaim their bodies by resisting interventions at the hospitals (2). Ivy Lynn Bourgeault, Cecilia Benoit and Robbie Davis-Floyd point out that lay-midwifery arose in response to women's (and men's) shifts in consciousness about birthing (7). Ina May Gaskin's now cult-status *Spiritual Midwifery*, first published in 1977 by the small commune (known as "The Farm") in Summertown, Tennessee, from where she based her midwifery practice. It is representative of the back-to-the-land movement that engendered renewed interest in holistic health in North America. This movement also called for women's reclamation of their maternal bodies from pathologizing obstetric practices that had normalized biotechnological intervention. Indeed, Gaskin reports an unprecedented number of home births and vaginal breech births. Of 1,917 births between 1970 and 2004, Gaskin confirms that 96 percent of the babies born under The Farm midwifery care were born at home, with medical intervention rates hovering at around .05 percent (473).

Bourgeault, Benoit, and Davis-Floyd (2004) referred to midwifery today as being in a state of "ferment and change" and therefore, "new" (3). They pointed out that in Canada in the late 1980s, lobby groups who were pushing for "family-centered" (8) maternity brought routine obstetric care into question by arguing that women should be offered more agency and choice in their pregnancy and childbirth experiences. This reclamation of the maternal body, however, was not seized without rebellion. With midwives regulated only since 1994, the renaissance of midwifery is fairly recent but there is a growing and hard-won respect and understanding from many doctors toward midwifery practices in hospital settings.

By the latter part of the twentieth century, concurrent with feminism's second wave and the environmental movement, women began demanding alternative care paradigms and midwifery began to experience what Farah M. Shroff called a "rebirth" (17). Shroff, writing three years after Ontario regulation had been passed in 1994, points out that midwifery's "ancient herstory" is at "at least recognized if not respected" thoughout the world (15), but that despite its legalized regulation, midwives still are at odds with doctors and nurses. Midwifery, MacDonald (2006) concurs, remains on the "interstices of mainstream and alternative health care…" (238) This challenge will be addressed later in the chapter.

A Brief History of the Renaissance of Midwifery in Ontario

I situate myself as not only an interested feminist researcher, but also as a former midwifery client who is grateful for the empowerment that midwives facilitated for me in difficult birthing situations. Thus, my position is admittedly that of biased supporter of midwifery. I am also keenly aware of the hard-won respect that midwives have fought for from the medical community in the name of women's autonomy over their bodies and childbirth experience. In this section, I will provide a very brief overview of the renaissance of midwifery in Ontario. Drawing on Wendy Mitchinson's 1991 monograph, *The Nature of Their Bodies*, Lesley Biggs (2004) articulates that midwifery's demise was not attributable to a single cause (27). One of the causes Biggs points out that she failed to identify in her earlier writings is that midwives were a diverse group that failed to "…organize and lobby for professional status as a result of class, linguistic and geographic barriers…" (30). Midwives' and women's failure to organize shifted by the 1980s. As the College of Midwives of Ontario website states,

> In 1983, a small group of consumers, health care providers and other supporters of midwifery met with midwives from the Ontario Association of Midwives (OAM) to discuss the status of midwifery in Ontario. Subsequently, these consumers established the Midwifery Task Force of Ontario (MTF-O) to promote legislation and recognition of midwifery.[1]

It was a decade longer before The College of Midwives of Ontario was formed on December 31, 1993 in conjunction with the establishment of midwives into the Regulated Health Practitioners Act (RHPA). The College of Midwives of Ontario states that June, 1991, saw the passing of the *Midwifery Act*, which recognized, funded and regulated midwifery in Ontario. The Interim Regulatory Council on Midwifery (IRCM) then set about developing standards for the profession. What I am interested in here is how midwives, in my personal experience, have sought to maintain professional standards while providing the demanding care and personal support that birthing mothers need. Now that midwives are generally accepted within the seemingly oxymoronic professional holistic childbirthing paradigm, how do women remain at the centre of their birthing experience?

Mandate

I argue that midwives endeavour to make women at the centre of the childbirth experience. According to the Association of Ontario Midwives, midwifery is based on three principles, and I quote their webpage here so that readers may observe the official statement:

> *Continuity of Care:*
> Midwives provide care throughout pregnancy, labour, birth, and the first six weeks following birth. Midwives develop relationships with women and are available to clients 24 hours a day, seven days a week by pager.
>
> *Informed Choice:*
> Women are active decision-makers in the care they receive; midwives give information to help women make informed decisions.
>
> *Choice of Birthplace:*
> Women may choose to give birth safely at home or in hospital. Midwives have hospital privileges in Ontario hospitals. This means that they can admit and discharge clients at hospitals and access hospital resources needed by clients, including a consultation from a doctor if there is a concern or complication. Midwives are the only health care professional specifically trained in home birth. (Association of Ontario Midwives webpage)[2]

These three aspects, Continuity of Care, Informed Choice and Choice of Birthplace, are interconnected and place the mother at the centre. For example, my second pregnancy threatened to end eight weeks prematurely, and my midwives were by my side or accessible by pager from the moment my water broke in the middle of the night, through my extended hospital stay, post-natal iatrogenic illness and subsequent quarantine and to the eventual discharge from their care at six weeks post partum. They worked as a team so that there was always a midwife on call for me if and when I needed their support. The midwives negotiated with the obstetricians into whose care my pregnancy was transferred, and helped me to navigate the different turns of events as they unfolded. Very importantly, my midwives recognized from a holistic perspective how my body was manifesting my emotional stressors into my pregnancy, and supported me throughout the dreaded but increasing medicalization of my childbirth experience.

For both of my pregnancies, I did not wish to have my babies in hospital, and my midwives helped me to understand and accept why it was necessary for me to do so. The CMO mandate states that, "Midwives promote decision-making as a shared responsibility, between the woman, her family (as defined by the woman) and her caregivers. The mother is recognized as the primary decision maker" (College of Midwives of Ontario website).[3] Thus, midwifery is both officially, and as I demonstrate, experientially woman-centered. At the beginning of the third trimester of my first pregnancy, my so-called "normal" pregnancy took a serious and dramatic turn. A scare over lack of foetal movement turned into a diagnosis of oligohydramnios (low amniotic fluid). Although my midwives assured me that both my baby and I were completely healthy, the midwives advised me against home birth and I had to have regular ultrasounds to monitor fluid levels. They gently and diplomatically explained exactly what the risks of not following their recommendations were (cord compression and stillbirth were worst outcomes), and why the risks of a homebirth to the baby and me were high in comparison to a hospital birth. As the Association of Ontario Midwives website states,

> A home birth is not appropriate for all women. Your health during pregnancy and labour and your personal circumstances are considerations to discuss with your midwife when making this decision.[4]

Before making this recommendation, my primary midwife consulted with other midwives (a protocol considered "level 1" in the College of Midwives regulations). Then, they decided that my situation was serious enough to warrant consulting with an obstetrician (consulting protocol level 2) who recommended the bi-weekly and then weekly ultrasounds. The midwives were very supportive emotionally, and remained my primary care givers throughout the rest of my pregnancy. The obstetrician recommended that my labour be induced medically a few days prior to my due date. My midwives also supported my holistic background and often provided me with suggestions of their own. Indeed, the Association of Ontario Midwives (2008) explicitly points out how interprofessional care is mandated to allow midwives to work as a team with hospital employees such as nurses and doctors (IPC Position Paper 2).

True to the CMO mandate of informed choice, the midwives did due diligence in helping me to understand all of the potential outcomes of my decisions. My midwives non-judgmentally provided me with all of the options for all of the potential situations, from tests to procedures. I agreed to the hospital birth and induction, but I was determined to avoid further medical intervention. Although they ultimately failed to produce the desired effect, my midwives supported my efforts at trying to self-induce through acupuncture, chiropractic and homeopathy. When those methods failed, I agreed to have my labour induced. The midwives took turns caring for me once my labour started. My primary midwife was there in the first part of my labour until late morning when the second midwife arrived to relieve her. The midwife showed my husband how to help me feel more comfortable with shiatsu massage and she gave me visualization and sounding techniques that helped my body relax. The primary midwife returned late afternoon to relieve the secondary one, and eventually administered nitrous oxide, which helped me relax from the incessant contractions just enough to allow my cervix to complete its painful journey to full dilation. I gave three quick pushes and the midwife caught my daughter as she emerged, eyes open, into the world at 6:30 p.m.

As per professional protocol, my midwifery care did not stop when I was discharged from hospital the next afternoon. The midwives visited me and the baby at home at least twice in the immediate post-partum period and then we followed up with office visits until the six-week post-partum mark. The reassurance and support that I received from my midwives encouraged me to continue breastfeeding even when I felt like giving up. One night, around two weeks' post-partum, I was desperate enough to call my primary midwife for breastfeeding support. Initially, the baby and I had a lot of trouble breastfeeding. The baby seemed incessantly hungry and cried whenever I put her down. My midwife came over, weighed the baby and gave me tips on getting the best latch.

As the CMO website testifies, midwives maintain up-to-date knowledge on breastfeeding counseling.[5] Although I was a new mother who was highly committed to breastfeeding my baby, it should be noted that midwives also link new mothers with different support services, such as La Leche League (LLL) and the local Family Resource Centre (Ontario Early Years Centre has more links to parenting programs). They also provided me with a care package that included a book, a Parent Child Mother Goose cassette tape, OEYC program listings and schedules, and women's health information. Because I lived in an isolated area distant from my family and other supports, my midwife facilitated my being put at the top of a wait list for the Parent Child Mother Goose program, a weekly song and story group for caregivers with babies under age one.

A regular prenatal appointment with a midwife is usually about forty-five minutes, and includes counseling and education as an integral aspect in providing women with confidence and support. Shroff points out that these longer appointments are a point of difference from the prenatal care offered by an obstetrician or family physician, who usually only spend about ten minutes with their patients (21). I always felt that seeing my midwife for my regular prenatal appointment afforded me the opportunity to explore all of my issues from every angle; medical, physical, through nutrition, holistic modalities and very importantly, emotionally. The midwives' support was unequivocally non-judgmental. This non-judgmental care is also represented in the midwives' commitment to diversity.

The AOM diversity statement stipulates that in addition to adhering to the Ontario Human Rights Code, it recognizes that

> inequality is maintained by discrimination against and systemic marginalization of people based on, but not exclusive to, ability, age, class, socioeconomic status, educational background, ethnicity, gender, geographic location, language, race, religion, reproductive and parenting decisions and sexual orientation.[6]

This statement covers a wide range of diversity issues that would each warrant major study. For the purposes of brevity then, I would argue that midwifery is committed to providing inclusive care for pregnant, parturient and post-partum women. In 2009, the southern-Ontario based Best Start Resource Centre created the Newcomer Guide for health care practitioners. Its goal is to

> help service providers find ways to provide "culturally competent care," which has been defined as "the ability to provide care with a client-centered orientation, recognizing the significant impact of cultural values and beliefs as well as power and hierarchy often inherent in clinical interactions, particularly between clients from marginalized groups and health care organizations." (5) [7]

This 60-page guide arguably fills in some of the gaps in women's reproductive health care pointed out by Carolyn Egan and Linda Gardner, who suggest that discriminatory racism is endemic in the health care system and that immigrant women suffer from insufficient and inattentive health care. Further, Pamela Pinto argued that women with disabilities are often assumed by doctors to be unable to carry a healthy baby to term. While midwifery can not necessarily solve all of these structural problems, its commitment to equality through the AODA and Human Rights Code, as well as its practical mandate of 45 minute appointment times and advocating for women in hospital settings even in the event of transfer of care, suggests that midwifery is the best option for any pregnant woman who wishes holistic care and delivery in either a hospital or home setting.

Pat Israel pointed out that disabled women could benefit immensely from midwifery (85), and at the time of her writing, midwives' offices were often more accessible than doctors and they were more willing to explore birthing position options (85). Recent studies such as those by Suzanne C. Smelzer (88-89) and Deborah Payne and Kathryn M. McPherson (630) identify many of the needs that disabled pregnant women may have. The *Accessibility for Ontarians with Disabilities Act* (also known as AODA), which was brought into effect in August 2007, indicates in Section 6 that all spaces serving the public must have an accessibility standard.[8] This will accommodate for members of the public with a range of disabilities, including provisions for visual impairment in elevators, ramps, bars and wide power assisted doors. With these legislated changes, midwives are well situated to provide equitable care to disabled women through advocating for their clients' needs, negotiating with other health care practitioners, and offering longer appointment times.

Challenges

During my labour and delivery, midwives and the obstetrician, as I was blithely unaware at the time, were working collaboratively to provide me with the best care. Midwives' hospital privileges (the ability to admit and discharge a person from hospital), are neither easily gained nor taken for granted. Interestingly, my personal experience in childbirth shows that midwives do not wish to acknowledge that tension may exist between themselves and doctors. This is, in my opinion, largely because to challenge the dynamic could jeopardize the relationship between doctors and midwives and ultimately be detrimental to women and their birth experiences. The AOM actively lobbies the Ministry of Health and Long Term Care in order to improve collaboration between health care practitioners, in an initiative called "interprofessional care."

Collaboration with doctors and nurses is a high priority of the AOM, as their 2008 position paper on Interprofessional Care (IPC) attests, and they make a point of stating explicitly how they will do this, stating, "AOM provides comprehensive steps for building a strong foundation upon which successful IPC initiatives can flourish."(3) It begs the question however, if doctors are doing as much work as the AOM to promote this high level of interprofessional care.

The biggest challenge that midwives face is the continuous need to maintain positive outreach and public relations to community members, doctors and nurses. In its 2008 position paper on interprofessional care, the AOM identifies the gaps that currently pose as a challenge for maternity care. It states to the Ministry of Health and Long Term Care that there is a shortage of midwives (the CMO website states that currently there are 500 midwives practicing in Ontario) and accessible birthing facilities. The AOM further stipulates that in order to improve maternity care, doctors must collaborate with midwives through interprofessional care models (5). As the AOM position paper points out, midwives must be able to work within their full capacities in a hospital setting in order to meet their mandate of complete woman-centered care (6). Unfortunately, this protocol is inconsistent from facility to facility. Case in point: I had my first baby in one hospital that allowed midwives more privileges than in another hospital within the midwives' jurisdiction. My second baby was born in this second hospital where the midwives were not afforded the same capacities of care. This exemplifies the gaps in interprofessional care that the AOM identify.

It should be noted here that The College of Midwives of Ontario and the Association of Ontario Midwives represent an official position, and it is not entirely synchronous with that of the personal stories of practicing midwives or birthing mothers. Margaret MacDonald demonstrates through her anthropological research with midwives and their clients that there is a gap between traditional midwifery and the newer midwifery that utilizes its recent professionalization (2004: 56) as a way to work interprofessionally with doctors and nurses. MacDonald suggests that professionalization created conflict for some of the "grandmothered" midwives who practiced before regulation. One of the midwives in MacDonald's study was quoted as saying, "I don't ever want to see my practice get to the point where I am just checking off boxes and examining test results … I see it becoming very professionalized…" (2004: 54). I have experienced this tension personally, and argue that the midwives I had the opportunity to work with provided me with care that moved gracefully between the professional demands of the hospital and the messier, more complicated demands of my difficult second pregnancy.

Despite how well midwifery is generally accepted in hospitals, public health documents and government legislation, some people remain uneducated about it. In my former professional shiatsu practice, I was disheartened to find out from some of my clients that they had no idea that midwifery appointments offered this level of care, time and respect. Many of my shiatsu clients over the years did not realize that OHIP covers midwifery care. Further, many women today still think that midwives only do homebirths or that it is not possible to have pain relief (with an epidural). Fortunately, some women's lack of knowledge about midwifery does not affect its popularity and waiting lists are the norm. While these wait lists are likely to be cumbersome for midwifery practices administratively, anecdotally the wait lists represent a bigger worry for many pregnant women who are unsure of whether they will be able to be cared for by a midwife.

Conclusion

The relationship of midwifery to the larger motherhood movement is implicit in its ethics of care. Through offering unequivocal respect to pregnant, parturient and post-natal women, midwives place mothers at the centre of the birthing continuum. Midwives in Ontario have faced a massive overhaul from traditional notions of practice, to virtual invisibility, and back to regulation and a new paradigm of care within the medical system. Despite the challenges of having to "earn" a place within the hegemonic framework of medicalized birthing, it is evident through the examination of official College of Midwives of Ontario (CMO) and Association of Ontario Midwives (AOM) documents that midwives and their supporters are well-organized activists for mothers. Midwives' constant activism through specific and directed outreach and communications ensures that low-risk women's care in pregnancy, childbirth and the post-partum period remains at the centre of the mandate. Further, the AOM proves that the Ministry of Health and Long Term Care requires more midwives and funding for birthing centres in order to meet the growing demands of Ontario's childbearing women who may not have access to family doctors or who live in remote communities.

Although I was unable to have the home birth I had hoped for, my personal experiences with midwives have proven that not only do midwives empower mothers to have a healthy pregnancy and birth, but also that midwives inspire women to look deep within themselves to find their highest potential. I birthed my babies, yes, but my midwives also encouraged my work in academia and supported my enthusiasm about writing and women's health advocacy. I write this chapter for my midwives in gratitude.

[1]Please see <http://www.cmo.on.ca/about_college.php> and <http://www.cmo.on.ca/history.php> for further details.

[2]See<http://www.aom.on.ca/Midwifery_Care/What_is_a_Midwife.aspx>.

[3]See<http://www.cmo.on.ca/midwife_philosophy.php>.

[4]See the Association of Ontario Midwives website <http://www.aom.on.ca/Midwifery_Care/Choice_of_Birthplace/>.

[5]See<http://www.cmo.on.ca/midwife_care.php>.
[6]See<http://www.aom.on.ca/Communications/Position_Statements/DiversityStatement.aspx>.
[7]For a full document on perinatal care for newcomers to Canada, see <http://www.aom.on.ca/files/Communications/Reports_and_Studies/Newcomer__Guide_Final_Best_Start_09.pdf>.
[8]See the full AODA at <http://www.aoda.ca/?page_id=8>.

Works Cited

Atwood, Margaret. *Dancing Girls and Other Stories.* Toronto: McClelland and Stewart, 1977.

Association of Ontario Midwives. *Midwives and Interprofessional Care.* Toronto: Association of Ontario Midwives, 2008. Online. <http://www.aom.on.ca/files/Communications/Position_Statements/IPC_Position_Paper_Final.pdf>.

Best Start Resource Centre. *Giving Birth in a New Land: Strategies for Service Providers Working with Newcomers.* Toronto: Best Start Resource Centre, 2009. Online. <http://www.aom.on.ca/files/Communications/Reports_and_Studies/Newcomer__Guide_Final_Best_Start_09.pdf>.

Biggs, C. Lesley. "'The Case of the Missing Midwives': A History of Midwifery in Ontario From 1795-1900." *Delivering Motherhood: Maternal Ideologies and Practices in the 19th and 20th Centuries.* Eds. Katherine Arnup, Andrée Lévesque, Ruth Roach Pierson and Margaret Brennan. London: Routledge, 1990. 20-35.

Biggs, C. Lesley. "Rethinking the History of Midwifery in Canada." *Reconceiving Midwifery.* Eds. Ivy Bourgeault, Cecilia Benoit and Robbie Davis-Floyd. Montreal: McGill-Queen's University Press, 2004. 17-45.

Boston Women's Collective. *Our Bodies, Our Selves.* New York: Simon and Schuster, 1984.

Bourgeault, Ivy, Cecilia Benoit and Robbie Davis-Floyd. "Introduction." *Reconceiving Midwifery.* Eds. Ivy Bourgeault, Cecilia Benoit and Robbie Davis-Floyd. Montreal: McGill-Queen's University Press, 2004. 3-14.

Campbell, Melissa. "William Smellie's Obstetrical Forceps." *Australia and New Zealand Journal of Obstetrics and Gynaecology* 44 (1994): 184-185. Online. January 10, 2011.

Davis, Kathy. *Making of Our Bodies, Ourselves: How Feminism Travels Across Borders.* Durham, NC: Duke University Press, 2007. Online. January 27, 2011.

Egan, Carolyn, and Gardner, Linda. "Racism, Women's Health and Reproductive Freedom." *Scratching the Surface: Canadian, Anti-Racist, Feminist Thought.* Eds. Enakshi Dua, Angela Robertson. Toronto: Women's Press, 1999. 295-308.

Epp, Marlene. "Midwife-Healers in Canadian Mennonite Immigrant Communities: Women who 'made things right'." *Histoire sociale/Social History* 40/80 (November 2007): 324-342.

Gaskin, Ina May. *Spiritual Midwifery.* 3rd Edition. Summertown, TN: The Book

Publishing Company, 1990.

Israel, Pat. "Experiences of Mothers with Disabilities and Implications for the Practice of Midwifery." *The New Midwifery: Reflections on Renaissance and Regulation*. Ed. Farah M. Shroff. Toronto: Women's Press, 1997. 83-92.

Leavitt, Judith Walzer. "Birthing and Anesthesia: The Debate over Twilight Sleep." *Signs* 6.1 (Autumn 1980): 148.

MacDonald, Margaret. "Tradition as a Political Symbol in the New Midwifery in Canada." *Reconceiving Midwifery*. Eds. Ivy Bourgeault; Cecilia Benoit, Robbie Davis-Floyd. Montreal: McGill-Queen's University Press, 2004. 46-66.

MacDonald, Margaret. "Gender Expectations: Natural Bodies and Natural Births in the New Midwifery in Canada." *Medical Anthropology Quarterly* 20.2 (2006): 235-256.

McKay, Ami. *The Birth House*. Toronto: Vintage Canada, 2007.

Mitchinson, Wendy. *Giving Birth in Canada: 1900-1950*. Toronto: University of Toronto Press, 2002.

O'Reilly, Andrea and Silvia Caporale Bizzini, eds. *From the Personal to the Political: Toward a New Theory of Maternal Narrative*. Selinsgrove, New Jersey: Susquehanna University Press, 2009.

Payne, Deborah and Kathryn M. McPherson. "Becoming Mothers, Multiple Sclerosis and Motherhood: A Qualitative Study." *Disability and Rehabilitation* 32.8 (2010): 629-638. Online. January 12, 2011.

Pinto, Pamela. "Women, Disability and the Right to Health." *Women's Health: Intersections of Policy, Research and Practice*. Eds. Pat Armstrong and Jennifer Deadman. Toronto: Women's Press, 2008. 119-133.

Rich, Adrienne. *Of Woman Born: Motherhood as Experience and Institution*. 1976. New York, London: W.W. Norton & Company, 1986.

Shields, Carol. *Unless*. Toronto: Vintage Canada. 2002.

Shroff, Farah M. "Introduction." *The New Midwifery: Reflections on Renaissance and Regulation*. Ed. Farah M. Shroff. Toronto: Women's Press, 1997. 15-37.

Smeltzer, Suzanne C. "Pregnancy in Women with Physicial Disabilities." *Journal of Obstetric Gynecology and Neo Natal Nursing* 36.1 (January-February 2007): 88-96. Online. January 12, 2011.

Website Links:

Accessibility for Ontarians with Disabilities Act (AODA) <http://www.aoda.ca>

College of Midwives of Ontario <http://www.cmo.on.ca/about_college.php>

La Leche League (LLL) <http://www.lllc.ca>

Ontario Midwives Association (OMA) <http://www.aom.on.ca>

Ontario Early Years Centres (OEYC) <http://www.children.gov.on.ca/htdocs/English/topics/earlychildhood/oeyc/index.aspx>

Parent Child Mother Goose Program <http://www.nald.ca/mothergooseprogram/start.htm>

2. Public Education and the Midwives Alliance of North America

Giving Birth to "Mothers Naturally"

MELISSA CHEYNEY, ELIZABETH MOORE AND GERADINE SIMKINS

IN 2012, THE MIDWIVES ALLIANCE of North America (MANA) will celebrate her 30th anniversary. The Midwives Alliance was conceived of and born nearly three decades ago as a network of birth professionals and activists advocating for women's ascendancy in their own reproductive lives, to promote midwifery as a high-quality maternity care option, and to shelter a place for the burgeoning normal birth movement.[1] Since the early 1980s, the Midwives Alliance has conceived of itself as the Mothership—a vessel that has helped smaller crafts to set sail. Throughout the years, our organization had a hand in launching a fleet of organizations designed to promote midwifery and the gentle birth movement. These include the North American Registry of Midwives (NARM), Midwifery Education Accreditation Council (MEAC), Foundation for the Advancement of Midwifery (FAM), Citizens for Midwifery (CfM), National Association of Certified Professional Midwives (NACPM) and Association of Midwifery Educators (AME). The Midwives Alliance has also been a co-partner in the conception, birth and nurturing of the Certified Professional Midwife (CPM) credential, an innovative and autonomous midwifery credential created and sustained by and for midwives who specialize in home and free-standing birth center maternity care.

In 2006, the leadership of the Midwives Alliance gathered to examine our goals as an organization and to reflect on the fact that even with all of the publicity surrounding rising caesarean section rates (Martin et al.) and poor maternal and infant health outcomes (Althabe and Belizan; Declercq et al.)[2] in the U.S., the rate of women choosing home and birth center deliveries with midwives has remained relatively constant and low over the last 50 years. Today, only about one to two percent of women choose to deliver outside of the hospital (Boucher et al.; MacDorman et al.).[3] The obstacles we identified included: public perception that it is necessary to deliver in a hospital, fear surrounding childbirth, perceived lack of safety, misconceptions about midwives and their competencies and knowledge, and women's fear and lack of confidence about natural birth and their own bodies' innate wisdom. Multiple generations of high-tech, low-touch, medicalized childbirth, a general ignorance of maternal-child health outcomes in the United States, and wide spread "emergency birth" programming and media exploitation of birth-as-dangerous-medical-event, combine to produce and reproduce cultural norms that can function to curtail choice in birth setting and provider type, despite the burgeoning body of research that demonstrates the safety of midwife-attended home and birth center deliveries (de Jonge et al.; Fullerton et al.; Janssen et al.; Johnson and Daviss).

Mandate

As the Midwives Alliance leadership thinks about how to best advocate for women's choices in childbearing, a few themes and questions continually emerge. How do we grow the profession of midwifery so that in every state and in every region in North America, women have access to a diversity of providers, including Certified Professional Midwives, Certified Nurse-Midwives, family practice physicians, obstetricians, and perinatologist when needed? How can we work together to make standards of care for mothers and babies align more closely with evidence-based medicine instead of with the "medicine-based evidence" that currently plays such a powerful role in constructing normative behaviors around childbirth? And perhaps most importantly, how can we raise awareness about midwives and their approaches to woman-centered care with the ultimate goal of increasing the number of births attended by midwives in home and birth center settings? In this chapter, we describe the birth of "*Mothers Naturally: for what you care about most*"—a public education campaign created by the Midwives Alliance to increase access to safe and positive birth experiences through expanding education about natural birth options and by empowering women to make pregnancy and birth choices that fit with their own lives and values.

Activities

The primary tool in the *Mothers Naturally* campaign is a public website that invites women and their families to explore the concepts of natural pregnancy and care with a midwife.[4] The website is designed to encourage women to celebrate the journey of natural pregnancy, to trust their innate abilities to nourish a healthy pregnancy, to create their own ideal birth environments by seeking out both physical and emotional support, and to discover the safe and personalized care of a midwife. In the pages that follow, we describe the content in three major areas of the campaign: 1) promoting natural pregnancy; 2) benefits of natural pregnancy and birth; and 3) tips for achieving a natural birth. Throughout, we problematize the use of the term "natural" and critically examine the explicit and implicit content—the text and the subtext—as a way of illuminating how the personal and the political intertwine in the *Mothers Naturally* campaign.

Promoting Natural Pregnancy

Because the vast majority of women in the United States today begin their pregnancies with a call to their obstetrician/gynecologist, without ever considering other options, we wanted to design a campaign that would begin with a basic commonality that many reproductive-aged women share—the interest in, and desire for, a healthy lifestyle, especially as it pertains to pregnancy. Constructs of "natural pregnancy" in this section of the *Mothers Naturally* campaign were designed to capture women's attention around a healthy/natural lifestyle as a point of entry—a place to start the conversation. By functionally equating natural and healthy, the website introduces women to a model of birthing care that builds on a desire for a more "natural" way of life that may already exist. The Midwives Alliance believes that every mother and baby deserve a healthy start regardless of race, education level, marital status or ability to pay, and so *Mothers Naturally* starts the discussion there: What does it mean to have a natural pregnancy?

Natural pregnancy is founded on the belief that being pregnant and giving birth are normal life experiences that the vast majority of women's bodies are well-equipped to accommodate. Natural pregnancy includes creating an internal and external environment of health-promoting and birth-positive elements that incorporates balanced, mindful eating, regular exercise, listening to positive birth stories, gathering knowledge, planning for a model of care that fits with a woman's own beliefs and values, and partnering with a caregiver that will guide a woman and her family through each step of pregnancy and delivery safely and confidently. In a culture where few women have seen deliveries before they themselves give birth, birth knowledge is second hand and often gained through books and Internet resources. Knowledge acquired from these sources can build or undermine confidence, diminish fear or enhance it. The *Mothers Naturally* campaign aims to overturn fear and doubt by providing women with practical tools for defining and working toward a natural pregnancy and birth. Through the website, the Midwives Alliance seeks to promote natural pregnancy by opening a dialogue in several key arenas, including: eating mindfully and appreciatively, moving and playing, and surrounding mothers-to-be with goodness. These discussions are designed to help guide women through their journeys into motherhood.

Eat Mindfully and Appreciatively

By moving beyond the banal "make sure to eat a healthy diet" recommendation or the ubiquitous "eating for two" pamphlets that pass for prenatal dietary counseling in mainstream prenatal care (Cheyney and Moreno-Black), the *Mothers Naturally* campaign aims to provide targeted, clear and evidence-based guidelines for nourishing a healthy pregnancy: "A natural pregnancy starts with a natural diet. You are nourishing yourself and your baby. Be sure to eat nutrient rich, whole foods and to avoid highly processed foods and empty calories. This includes eating a variety of fresh vegetables, fruits, beans and lean meats (organic when possible). If you are craving sugar, eat protein. It will alleviate your craving. Be sure to drink two to three liters of water per day. Avoid artificially sweetened drinks and carbonated sodas. Natural juices may be enjoyed in moderation."

Here the term natural is operationalized to refer to less processed, whole foods that are closer to their natural (i.e., unprocessed) condition, and thus, healthier. Natural foods become a metaphor for nourishing a healthy pregnancy; as women consume these foods, they begin to embody the *Mothers Naturally* philosophy of a natural pregnancy. This approach acknowledges that food is more than calories and micronutrients; preparing and eating natural foods during pregnancy does more than simply provide the building blocks for growing and nurturing a baby. Eating mindfully and appreciatively allows women to engage holistic meanings of food and food choice as a "warm-up" or practice for making decisions around more natural (i.e., less technologically processed, and therefore, healthier) birth experienccs.

Move and Play

Mothers Naturally messages about exercise aim to move women out of the gym, into the fresh air as a way of connecting them to constructions of nature and what is natural. The goal is to return joy to exercise and to undermine mother-blaming constructs of women who are not "fit enough" or "strong enough" to deliver without medical or pharmacological intervention. The *Mothers Naturally* campaign encourages women to:

> Love your growing body and know that you are blessed with the ability to nourish your child with everything he or she needs—including physical activity balanced with indulgent rest. Be sure to make your activities fun and full of joy. Skip the drudgery of a workout if you are dreading it. Instead, dance, hike in nature or walk to a flower store—anything that keeps you moving and makes you smile. If your job requires that you sit for long periods of time, sit on a yoga ball to increase circulation, improve posture and help your baby's position.

Again, by providing women with tools that connect them with concepts of nature and the natural, the goal is to increase faith in the processes of pregnancy, birth and breastfeeding and to promote a healthy pregnancy.

In this section, perhaps more than anywhere else in the *Mothers Naturally* campaign, the Midwives Alliance is conscious of the White, middle-class overtones of the "move and play" message. Women living in the inner city may not feel safe getting out for a walk, and fresh air and flower shops are hard to come by in many marginalized communities. While this message is designed to appeal to the average U.S. woman who is likely to consider a midwife-attended birth, and especially a birth enter or home delivery, when read through the lens of current health disparities in access to prenatal care, we are made acutely aware of the White privilege that undergirds so much of the alternative and natural birth movements. We are self critical of the role the Midwives Alliance and other organizations have played in producing and reproducing class- and race-based inequality in access to maternity care.[5] The leadership and women of color section of the Midwives Alliance are working diligently to open the dialogue around institutionalized racism and birth choice in North America. We are asking ourselves: How can we work to make our messages more inclusive? And perhaps more importantly, what kinds of social change need to occur if we are to see the gaps between the experiences of rich and poor mothers in our countries decreased? What roles should midwives play in social justice movements aimed at improving maternal and infant health outcomes and reducing health disparities?

Surround Yourself with Goodness

A third concept used by *Mothers Naturally* to promote natural pregnancy involves the recommendation to: "Surround yourself with people and stories that will fuel your confidence and prepare you for a positive journey. Avoid watching TV stories about birth and say 'no thanks' to the negative birth stories people love to tell." Natural birth is confident and positive birth, not birth undermined by messages of fear, suffering and looming danger, death or impairment. *Mothers Naturally* content is constructed in opposition to more medicalized notions of birth and pregnancy that have been argued to be excessively focused on surveillance, prenatal testing and being prepared "in case something goes wrong" (Cheyney; Davis-Floyd). Midwives believe that women who go through pregnancy worried about all of the "what if's" will emerge as mothers with very different experiences and perspectives than those who are nurtured through the same processes with an attitude of hopeful anticipation, where a healthy pregnancy and infant are expected. While complications are closely monitored and appropriately treated under midwifery models of care, the primary focus is on practice strategies that promote the likelihood of a healthy and empowering, i.e., a natural birth.

Benefits of Natural Birth

In addition to communicating ways of defining and promoting natural pregnancy, the *Mothers Naturally* campaign attempts to delineate the benefits of natural birth. The Midwives Alliance aspires to create a culture of birthing where pregnancy and childbirth are viewed as normal and natural life events. As a small percentage of women in our culture reject notions of the pregnant body as inherently faulty and in need of massive medical surveillance, questions about place of birth inevitably follow. The *Mothers Naturally* website states:

> If you are enjoying a natural pregnancy consider natural childbirth! You want to give your child a safe and healthy start. A woman's body is innately prepared with the strength, stamina, and ability to nourish a safe and natural pregnancy and childbirth. By supporting the body's own instinctive knowledge, unnecessary medical intervention can often be avoided. With a midwife, you will have a wealth of resources to call upon to support each step of your pregnancy and birth, rather than being limited to medical intervention alone. With the best options, knowledge, holistic care, and positive support you will be better suited to enable your

> body to do its work, and to avoid unnecessary medical intervention. What more could you want for what you care about most?

Visitors to the site are then asked to explore a few questions regarding place of delivery:

> Natural home childbirth is a safe and reasonable alternative to giving birth in a hospital. Take a few minutes to breathe deeply and envision the most perfect childbirth.... Who is with you? What kind of beautiful or familiar environment are you in? What surrounds you to give you strength and comfort? Ahhhh.... It feels good to be in control and have things your way, doesn't it? It's comforting, freeing and empowering. This is natural homebirth.

It goes on to encourage:

> Without the stresses generally associated with physician-attended births (unfamiliar people and environment, hospital schedules and policies, bright unnatural lighting, unknown tests, etc.), you are able to relax into your labor. In a warm, familiar environment, you are able to give yourself the gift of space: for your body's rhythm to take its natural course, to discover strength within yourself, and most importantly, to love your baby. Just as each woman's dream childbirth is different, each natural, home childbirth story is different. It is the role of a midwife to help each dream come true, within the parameters set by the baby's unique journey into the world. The midwife is a guide, mentor, educator, and professional dedicated to the most modern techniques to guard the safety of mother and baby. For women with low-risk pregnancies, natural homebirth with a qualified midwife is as safe as hospital births.. In fact, reducing stress and elevating comfort and joy has been shown to reduce pain and the need for unnecessary procedures, which can lead to other complications.

The *Mothers Naturally* campaign attempts to move women through processes of envisioning their ideal birth by painting a picture of natural birth that many women may lack the imagery for. The focus on comfort, control and trust are designed to bring women to the place where they can at least begin to think about giving birth another way.

Choice

The Midwives Alliance believes that in the United States today, biomedical hegemony and institutionalized racism heavily structure access to maternity care and the extent to which women have the right to choose where and with whom to give birth (Davis-Floyd and Johnson; Kitzinger; Wagner). Cultural and political-economic factors, far more than scientific research, determine what constitutes "safe birthing options" and "appropriate" care providers. A unique set of historical and political-economic factors have produced a virtual monopoly by U.S. physicians over the process of childbirth (De Vries et al.; Wagner), even though a large body of literature now exists that supports midwifery care both in and out-of-hospital as a safe and viable option. The overt dominance of high-tech obstetrics is both unusual from a global maternal and infant health perspective, and extremely powerful because unquestioned biomedical authority structures reality, making a limited number of birthing "choices" seem reasonable. *Mothers Naturally* attempts to overturn the medical model stronghold on birthing options by making a woman's role in birth choice explicit and by highlighting the advantages of the homebirth-with-a-midwife alternative.

The *Mothers Naturally* website states: "Motherhood is all about choices. Where your child is born is one of the first and most transformative choices you will make for yourself and your child. When you choose to birth at home you are empowering yourself, the mother—not the doctors—to create a safe, nurturing and loving entrance *for what you care about most*—your baby." The site goes on to describe:

> Homebirth with a midwife provides:
> •Personal attention and respectful treatment in safe, familiar and private surroundings.
> •Woman-centered care.
> •Family-oriented birth with no strangers present.
> •An opportunity for immediate bonding and breastfeeding.
> •Less disruption and stress for the whole family.
> •Emotional support and affirmation that birth is normal.
> •Guidance and education at each step of the process.

To many, this emotionally supported, holistic care seems desirable, but the Midwives Alliance acknowledges that most mothers still question the safety of birth outside of the hospital. A majority of U.S. women have internalized the notion of doctor-as-expert, and by extension, the idea that the hospital is the only safe place to deliver a baby. The *Mothers Naturally* campaign aims to call this cultural assumption into question and to provide women with the tools and references to begin to think in a more nuanced and critical way about what the safety evidence says. At the end of this section of the website, we arrive at the crux—the perceived safety of midwife-attended home or birth center delivery. How can mothers today hear past, or think outside of, the years of socialization into normative constructs of medicalized childbirth?

Safety

The *Mothers Naturally* campaign addresses the safety question this way: "The safety and benefits of midwifery care have been proven again and again in countries across the world. World Health Organization statistics show that births attended by midwives have lower infection rates, lower C-section rates, fewer complications, and healthier outcomes—and thus, lower overall medical costs—than physician-attended, hospital births. In addition, there is no difference in infant mortality between midwife-attended and physician-attended births for low-risk women. Countries such as the Netherlands, Sweden, and New Zealand, which have some of the best birth outcome statistics in the world, use midwives as their primary maternity care providers. Midwife-attended home births are as safe as hospital births, with the benefits of fewer interventions and infections, more support, and greater client satisfaction."

The website goes on to encourage readers to consider the following research findings:

- Families receive more personalized attention and care for all aspects (physical, emotional and clinical) of the pregnancy and birth, which greatly improves both mother's and baby's experience.
- Midwives act as confidence boosters. They promote self-care and help women feel capable and comfortable throughout pregnancy and labor.
- When appropriate, midwives collaborate with medical care providers to ensure the safety of mother and baby.
- Midwife-attended home births are more cost effective than hospital births because unnecessary interventions are avoided.
- Homebirths reduce maternal morbidity rates from complications due to interventions and infections, risks from hospital errors or insufficient staffing levels.
- Homebirths increase the prospects for successful bonding and breast-feeding.

And to consider the following facts:

- Studies have proven that a warm and familiar setting enables the body's physiology to naturally curb pain and labor more effectively.
- Each intervention in the natural process can beget another intervention. This cascade effect, or action/reaction, can lead to unnecessary complications or infections.
- Without drug intervention, babies are less likely to experience complications.
- The rate of C-sections in the U.S. has risen to over 30 percent. However, at home your risk of transferring for a C-section is 3.8 percent.

The intended "take-home" messages in this section of the campaign are that pregnancy and childbirth are natural experiences that should be supported by holistic providers like midwives, whose approaches take into consideration the complete woman—physical, mental, emotional, spiritual and cultural. In so doing, *Mothers Naturally* and the Midwives Alliance are asserting that to address only the clinical aspects of birthing care as more medicalized approaches are designed to do, results in incomplete and insufficient care. Midwives embrace the whole woman in her familial and social environment. Natural birth then, as it is constructed through the campaign, is healthy, positive, socially supported, empowering, safe and holistic. However, the birth itself is seen as only one piece of the puzzle for a woman as she embraces the vast and culturally under-supported role of mother. *Mothers Naturally* attempts to connect the experiences of pregnancy, birth and the postpartum periods, rejecting artificial separations between ante-, intra- and postpartum care. The *Mothers Naturally* campaign claims that what is particularly unique to the care of midwives is that they support the bridge to motherhood by nurturing the family, and by providing breastfeeding support and extensive aftercare. Natural birth is integrated into what comes before, and what comes after, the actual delivery.

Bonding and Breastfeeding

In relation to the potent, yet vulnerable, time immediately following the birth experience, the *Mothers Naturally* campaign stresses that: "Birthing at home with a midwife gives you and your family the space to focus on what matters most: getting to know each other, bonding, nesting and restoring. A midwife's care will continue for six to eight weeks after your baby arrives. During postnatal visits, initially at your home, a midwife will check and weigh your baby, provide encouragement and suggestions for mother's rest and restoration. She also helps your family welcome and adjust to a new baby. Most importantly, she will help with breastfeeding."

Because research clearly demonstrates that the best predictor of a successful breastfeeding relationship is social support (Entwistle et al.; Meedya et al.; Mushtaq et al; Vaaler et al.; Whalen and Cramton), the *Mothers Naturally* website emphasizes that natural birth is also about breastfeeding:

> Breastfeeding plays a key role in bonding and physical health of both mother and baby. Breast milk is especially designed to meet the physiological needs of the human infant. It can help protect children from cancer, diabetes, diarrhea, ear infections, emotional neglect, low I.Q., sudden infant death syndrome, urinary tract infections, and other illnesses. Breastfeeding may also offer some protection to the mother from breast and ovarian cancers and obesity.

Public heath campaigns send some of the same messages,[6] and many women in the U.S. today are familiar with research that demonstrates "breast is best." At the Midwives Alliance, we are concerned, however, that to educate women about the benefits of breastfeeding, without providing the social support or the removal of institutional barriers (like the lack of paid maternity leave relative to other high-income nations, or baby unfriendly work environments) is a disservice to women. To know that breastfeeding carries enormous benefits, but then to feel like you have "failed" at its delivery, effectively applies additional blame to women who already carry the burden of social judgments when they do not meet cultural standards for what constitutes a "good mother." Choosing a midwife means that a woman will have the necessary support as she transitions through the postpartum period and establishes breastfeeding.

Family Support

A final category *Mothers Naturally* integrates into the definition of natural birth involves the central role of the family. Natural birth is supportive birth and it takes into consideration not just the birth of the baby, but also the birth of the larger social unit. The website describes it this way: "Through your pregnancy, your midwife will get to know you and your family personally. She will offer help and suggestions during this time of transition. She will include family and friends in the birth process, as you wish. This bonding process may include having a sibling listen to your baby's heartbeat and feel the baby. Your midwife also knows how important it is for you to feel connected and supported during pregnancy and motherhood. To help, she may refer you to prenatal yoga classes, La Leche League meetings and prenatal groups to help you connect with others who share the physical, emotional, and social changes you are experiencing. She can also help guide you through changes in your relationship and family. Your midwife offers information for sibling preparation and guidance about mommy's need for space during her birth."

With reference to the actual delivery, messages are aimed at inclusiveness as a way of emphasizing that birth is not just a clinical process, but also a rite of passage that has the ability to transform all participants as they transition to their new status as members of a family with a new addition. *Mothers Naturally* emphasizes the emotional needs of family members, as well as the pragmatics of mobilizing community to help with the needs of a new baby: "During labor, if extended family or friends are present, the midwife will stay connected with them, providing reassurance as to length and progress of labor. She will also offer postpartum support for day-to-day work, such as encouraging women to arrange for trusted friends and family to help with meals, siblings, pet care, watering plants, and laundry." Collectively, these messages communicate that natural birth is not something a woman does alone. Natural birth is healthy, positive, socially supported, holistic, empowering, safe and transformative. It is designed to meet a wide range of needs for birthing mothers, as well as for their extended families and communities.

Tips for Natural Birth

A third area of *Mothers Naturally* content—tips for natural birth—is designed to walk women through the final stages of thinking about natural birth with a midwife at home or in a birth center, moving them toward the actual implementation: "Once you've chosen to have a natural childbirth at home, you have already made a statement about yourself and your dedication to your baby: 'Birth is beautiful, and I am empowered with strength and grace to bring my baby into the world safely and gently.'" The Midwives Alliance sees support as one of women's greatest needs once they come to the place of planning a natural birth. Many women experience judgment from their families, friends and other care providers as they choose to birth outside the dominant paradigm of more medicalized, hospital delivery (Cheyney). To counter these pressures, *Mothers Naturally* offers a few ideas to help support a woman's confidence in her choice to give birth naturally:

•Think positively about your changing body.
•Learn as much as you can about normal, natural, unmedicated birth.
•Read positive natural birth stories, but stay away from TV birth stories.
•Surround yourself with support that celebrates and trusts natural birth.
•Eat and drink in a way that supports your healthy body and nourishes your baby.
•Stay active and get out to play as much as is appropriate for you.
•Practice relaxation, visualizations, and breathing with your partner before the birth.
•Make a music play list with both calm, relaxing music, and active dance rhythms.
•Sprinkle positive affirmations and happy drawings around the house.
•When in labor, practice the art of meeting each surge with relaxed breath.
•During labor, use touch. Massage, nipple stimulation and being close to your partner all help labor progress.
•Use water therapy: like a shower, bath, or water birth tub.
•Use aromatherapy.
•Let your body take over and trust your instincts. Don't let your busy mind interfere with your body's ancient wisdom.
•Trust that this is the most powerful experience of your life and worth every bit of effort.
•Choose your caregiver wisely because he or she will have an enormous impact on your experience.

Challenges

The public education campaign of the Midwives Alliance—"*Mothers Naturally —for what you care about most*"—operationalizes a very specific notion of "natural birth" designed to appeal to mothers' desires for a healthy pregnancy, social support, safety, family integration and empowerment. The aim is to enable women to choose a midwife-attended birth if that is what feels right to them. The Midwives Alliance, however, acknowledges that this choice is not for everyone, and that the *Mothers Naturally* campaign has an explicit agenda—to encourage women to consider a natural birth with a midwife. It makes no claim to objectivity, but instead seeks to provide practical tools women can use as they claim ascendancy in their reproductive choices. As such, campaign content may be seen as exclusive and even alienating to women who choose a hospital delivery with a physician. We reconcile this by acknowledging the support that already exists in the form of powerful cultural norms for those mothers who choose to deliver in the hospital. The *Mothers Naturally* campaign explicitly seeks to educate and facilitate mothers on the margins who are exploring other options. We are simultaneously hopeful that some parts of the website will resonate with families who may, in reading about *Mothers Naturally's* constructions of natural pregnancy and birth, seek out a doula or intensive breastfeeding help in the form of a support group or lactation consultation.

We at the Midwives Alliance acknowledge and have discussed at length the culturally constructed nature of the term "natural." We have reflected on Pamela Klassen's (2001) work on homebirth as spiritual practice and the ways she and others (MacDonald; Westfall and Benoit) have critiqued the use of the term "natural" in connection with childbirth rhetoric. As it is used in popular discussions, "natural birth" can mean one with no pain medications even when IV's and continuous, electronic fetal monitoring and artificial hormones like pitocin are used for augmentation or induction of labor. Other women use "natural" to mean any birth that is vaginal, and not by cesarean section, regardless of other interventions. "Natural birth" then, is itself, a cultural construct. Even so, we would argue that "natural birth" as a concept has meaning among women in our culture. Although, academics and researchers have moved away from its usage, due largely to some of the complexities of meaning identified above, and have engaged newer terminologies like "normal," "physiologic" or "humanistic" labor and birth, it is our sense that the latter terms may be less meaningful or even alienating to many of the women *Mothers Naturally* is designed to engage. While, we acknowledge the complexities of the term, we strive through the website content to create meaning around natural birth that resonates with the experiences of women and what we hear being shared in the stories of mothers who are looking for alternatives to medicalized hospital birth.

Future Goals

In October of 2010, the Midwives Alliance membership responded to a survey question that queried: "What is the one thing that must be done to sustain the midwifery profession?" The number one response was: "Increase public awareness and educate the public about the midwifery model of care." As a result, our board affirmed its intention to continue focusing on raising awareness through public education and to broaden its reach by designing three new interrelated media campaigns. These campaigns will focus on: 1) highlighting midwives as maternity care providers and recruiting new midwives into the profession; 2) beneficial, low-tech strategies for avoiding unnecessary and costly, high-tech childbirth interventions, especially cesarean sections; and 3) using midwifery care to decrease health disparities among marginalized populations and communities of color, highlighting strategies to ensure that all babies are born full-term, of normal weight, and healthy. Because public education is slow, while technology is moves rapidly, the Midwives Alliance has designed these education campaigns to appeal to "digital natives" who are used to receiving information quickly and in multiple formats. The key features of each of these campaigns will be short video interviews with midwifery researchers, activists and consumers across the United States. It is our hope that together, they will create a rapid, viral, social media effect that will transform the way childbirth happens in our country.

Mothers Naturally in Relationship to the Larger Motherhood Movement

In response to increasing levels of intervention in childbirth, high cesarean section rates and dissatisfaction with the practices of biomedical models of maternity care, grassroots supporters in the Motherhood Movement are fighting for the right to give birth where and with whom they choose, and specifically, in out-of-hospital settings. As activist groups organize for change, the Midwives Alliance is one of the few U.S. groups that can provide a truly alternative model for giving birth that maintains a woman's ascendancy in her own reproductive processes. We seek to change cultural narratives and to shape the ways childbirth is performed. The conversations about "natural pregnancy," "natural birth" and "natural parenting" that permeate our public education campaign, *Mothers Naturally,* play key roles in shaping women's attitudes, while simultaneously influencing the institutions where birth takes place.

Conclusion

In conclusion, feminist theories of the body have helped to expose scientific facts about the pregnant and birthing body as power-laden, cultural constructs that emerge from our society's patriarchal and technocratic foundations (Davis-Floyd; Kaufman and Morgan). As Margaret MacDonald (95) describes: "Women's bodies have been scientifically constructed as essentially faulty; their reproductive bodies as potentially dangerous to babies; childbirth as so fraught with danger as to be unthinkable without biomedical surveillance and intervention." Just as feminist scholarship has worked to expose these unfounded assumptions, the Midwives Alliance, via the *Mothers Naturally* public education campaign, desires to peel away the fictions of medicalized prenatal care to expose strong and capable women who grow and birth babies outside of the regulatory and self-regulatory processes naturalized by modern, technocratic obstetrics. As families and midwives embrace the vision of natural birth defined by *Mothers Naturally*, they challenge the authority of more medicalized approaches, create new meanings around birth as a rite of passage, and make the personal political. Helping to birth mothers and families that are healthy, socially supported, safe, transformed and empowered is what we at the Midwives Alliance care about most.

[1]When MANA initially formed, its members represented a diversity of locales and issues across North America. However, over the last thirty years, our organization has become more U.S. focused due to the increasing number of professional and activist groups that have formed in Canada and in Mexico. While many of the issues raised in this article are relevant to our sister midwives and mothers in North America and beyond, women in the United States are the predominant focus of the *Mothers Naturally* Campaign.

[2]See "Birth by the Numbers" at: <http://www.theunnecesarean.com/blog/2009/9/3/birth-by-the-numbers-on-updated-lamaze-video-library.html>.

[3]According to MacDorman and colleagues, in 2006, there were 38,568 out-of-hospital births in the United States, including 24,970 homebirths and 10,781 births occurring in freestanding birthing centers. The total number of out-of-hospital births rose 3% from .87% in 2004 to .9% in 2006, and 65% of these births occurred at home.

[4]<http://www.mothersnaturally.org/index.html>.

[5]See Craven and Fraser (1995; 1998) for critical assessments of race- and class-based power dynamics in alternative birth and midwifery movements.

[6]See: 1) The National Breastfeeding Campaign at: <http://www.womenshealth.gov/breastfeeding/government-programs/national-breastfeeding-campaign>; 2) Healthy People 2020: Breastfeeding Objectives at: <http://www.healthypeople.gov/hp2020/objectives/ViewObjective.aspx?Id=203&TopicArea=Maternal%2C+Infant+and+Child+Health&Objective=MICH+HP2020%E2%80%9328&TopicAreaId=32>; 3) Breastfeeding Report Card—United States 2010 at: <http://www.cdc.gov/breastfeeding/data/reportcard.htm>; 4) Breastfeeding Promotion and Support in WIC at: <http://www.fns.usda.gov/wic/breastfeeding/mainpage.htm>; and 5) U.S. Department of Health and Human Services. Executive Summary: The Surgeon General's Call to Action to Support Breastfeeding. Washington, DC: U.S. Department of Health and Human Services, Office of the Surgeon General; January 20, 2011, for examples.

Works Cited

Althabe, F. and J. F. Belizan. "Caesarean Section: The Paradox." *The Lancet* 368 (2006): 1472-1473.

Boucher, D., C. Bennett, B. McFarlin, and R. Freeze. "Staying Home to Give Birth: Why Women in the United State Choose Home Birth." *Journal of Midwifery and Women's Health* 54 (2009): 119-126.

Cheyney, Melissa. "Homebirth as Systems-Challenging Praxis: Knowledge, Power and Intimacy in the Birthplace." *Qualitative Health Research* 18.2 (2008): 254-267.

Cheyney, M. and G. Moreno-Black. "Nutritional Counseling in Midwifery and Obstetric Practice." *Ecology of Food and Nutrition* 49.1 (2009): 1-29.

Craven, C. "'Consumer's Right' to Choose a Midwife: Shifting Meanings for Reproductive Rights under Neoliberalism." *American Anthropologist* 109.4 (2007): 701-712.

Davis, Floyd, R. *Birth as an American Rite of Passage.* [1992]. Berkeley: University of California Press, 2004.

Davis-Floyd, R. and C. B. Johnson. *Mainstreaming Midwives: The Politics of Change.* New York: Routledge, 2006.

de Jonge, A., B. van der Goes, A. Ravelli, M. Amelink-Verburg, B. Mol, J. Nijhuis, J. Bennebroek Gravenhorst, and S. Buitendijk. "Perinatal Mortality and Morbidity in a Nationwide Cohort of 529,688 Low-risk Planned Home and Hospital Births." *International Journal of Obstetrics and Gynecology* 116.9 (2009): 1177-1184.

Declercq, E., M. Barger, H. Cabral, S. Evans, M. Kotelchuck, C. Simon, J. Weiss, and L. Heffner. "Maternal Outcomes Associated with Planned Primary Cesareans Compared to Planned Vaginal Births." *Obstetrics and Gynecology* 109 (2007): 669-677.

DeVries, R., C. Benoit, E. van Teijlingen, and S. Wrede, eds. 2001. *Birth by Design: Pregnancy, Maternity Care and Midwifery in North America and Europe.* New York: Routledge.

Entwistle F., S. Kendall and M. Mead. "Breastfeeding Support—The Importance of Self-Efficacy for Low-Income Women." *Maternal & Child Nutrition* 6 (3) (2010): 228-42.

Fraser, G. "Modern Bodies, Modern Minds: Midwifery and Reproductive Change in an African American Community." *Conceiving the New World Order: The Global Politics of Reproduction.* Eds. F. Ginsburg and R. Rapp. Berkeley: University of California Press, 1995. 42-58.

Fraser, G. *African American Midwifery in the South: Dialogues of Birth, Race, and Memory.* Cambridge: Harvard University Press, 1998.

Fullerton, J., A. Navarro, and S. Young. "Outcomes of Planned Home Births: An Integrative Review." *Journal of Midwifery and Women's Health* 52.4 (2007): 323-333.

Janssen, Patricia, Lee Saxell, Lesley Page, Michael Klein, Robert Liston, and Shoo Lee. "Outcomes of Planned Home Birth with Registered Midwife versus Planned Hospital Birth with Midwife or Physician." *Canadian Medical Association Journal* 181.6-7 (2009): 377-383.

Johnson, Kenneth, and Betty-Anne Daviss. "Outcomes of Planned Home Births with Certified Professional Midwives: Large Prospective Study in North America." *British Medical Journal* 330.7505 (2005): 1416-1422.

Kaufman, S. R., and L. M. Morgan. "The Anthropology of the Beginnings and Ends of Life." *Annual Review of Anthropology* 34 (2005): 317-341.

Kitzinger, S. *The Politics of Birth*. Edinburgh: Elsevier Butterworth Heinemann, 2005.

Klassen Pamela. *Blessed Events: Religion and Home Birth in America*. Princeton, NJ: Princeton University Press, 2001.

MacDonald, Margaret. *At Work in the Field of Birth: Midwifery Narratives of Nature, Tradition, and Home*. Nashville, TN: Vanderbilt University Press, 2007.

MacDorman, M., F. Menacker and E. Declercq. "Trends and Characteristics of Home and Other Out-of-Hospital Births in the United States, 1990-2006." *National Vital Statistics Report* 58 (11) (2010): 1-15.

Martin, Joyce, Brady Hamilton, Paul Sutton, Stephanie Ventura, T.J. Matthews, Sharon Kirmeyer, and Michelle Osterman. "Births: Final Data for 2007." *National Vital Statistics Reports* 58.24 (2010):1-85.

Meedya S., K. Fahy and A. Kable. "Factors that Positively influence Breastfeeding Duration To 6 Months: A Literature Review." *Women and Birth: Journal of the Australian College of Midwives* 23.4 (2010): 135-45.

Mothers Naturally. Online: <http://www.mothersnaturally.org>.

Mushtaq N., V. J. Skaggs, and D. M. Thompson. "Effect of Breastfeeding Education and Support on Promoting Breastfeeding: A Literature Review." *The Journal of the Oklahoma State Medical Association* 101.10 (2008): 231-6.

Vaaler M. L., B. C. Castrucci, S. E. Parks, J. Clark, J. Stagg, and T. Erickson. "Men's attitudes Toward Breastfeeding: Findings from the 2007 Texas Behavioral Risk Factor Surveillance System." *Maternal and Child Health Journal* 15.2 (2011): 148-57.

Wagner, M. *Born in the USA: How a Broken Maternity System Must Be Fixed to Put Mothers and Babies First.* Berkeley: University of California Press, 2006.

Westfall, Rachel, and Cecilia Benoit. "The Rhetoric of 'Natural' in Natural Childbirth: Childbearing Women's Perspectives on Prolonged Pregnancy and Induction of Labour." *Social Science and Medicine* 59.7 (2004): 1397-1408.

Whalen, B. and R. Cramtom. "Overcoming Barriers to Breastfeeding Continuation and Exclusivity." *Current Opinion in Pediatrics* 22.5 (2010): 655-663.

3
Articulating a Rhetoric of Agency for Pregnancy Through Intersectionality

The National Advocates for Pregnant Women

MICHELLE TRIM

NATIONAL ADVOCATES FOR PREGNANT WOMEN (NAPW) is a non-profit organization dedicated to advocating on behalf of women on issues primarily related to pregnancy and parenting. Their mission statement reads: "National Advocates for Pregnant Women (NAPW) works to secure the human and civil rights, health and welfare of all women, focusing particularly on pregnant and parenting women, and those who are most vulnerable—low income women, women of color, and drug-using women." NAPW (not to be confused with the National Association for Professional Women) is different from other women's advocacy organizations in that it focuses on one particular life- stage—reproduction—but does not limit its scope to identity or lifestyle. In other words, NAPW operates at the intersection of pregnancy, drug policy, and reproductive rights, representing a broad and diverse population of women and their families.

NAPW makes visible pregnancy-related issues that are often obscured or ignored by the abortion debate. As a result, both feminists and non-feminists alike can benefit by NAPW's consciousness-raising about the lack of agency afforded to pregnant women under the law. Examples of issues of concern to NAPW include discrimination against pregnant or fertile women by employers; labor policies that are incompatible with pregnancy and childbirth; punitive laws targeting drug-using pregnant women; and agency in healthcare decisions related to alternative birth methods and/or invasive procedures. Their small staff of eight people includes program associates, highly credentialed litigators, and healthcare professionals, including Executive Director, Lynn M. Paltrow, JD. While their offices are located in New York, their litigation and advocacy support is provided nationwide.

History

Litigation

Founded in 2001, NAPW's primary goal has been to achieve recognition of of pregnant women as autonomous people, endowed with both legal and human rights (Paltrow). In their first year of activity, the organization provided significant legal advocacy and legal support by joining amicus briefs in cases involving preg-

NAPW activists at 2004 March for Women's Lives

nant defendants and drug use/ drug testing (NAPW 2002: 4). An amicus brief is a document that is submitted for consideration by the judge; it becomes part of the official record for that case. Amicus briefs usually contain information related to the case, such as scientific data or professional opinions, but are not submitted by people directly involved in the case. Although these efforts were unsuccessful in getting some of the cases involved overturned (or even reconsidered), other cases initiated prior to the organization's formation, such as *Ferguson v. City of Charleston* heard by the U.S. Supreme Court in 2001, were ultimately victories for pregnant women's rights (NAPW 2002: 7). Cases heard by the U.S. Supreme Court spend many years in lower courts; thus, it can take a substantially long time for a final decision to be rendered. Litigation support, research, and amicus brief activities continued in states such as South Carolina, Hawaii, Texas, Arizona, and Missouri through 2003 (NAPW 2003: 2-8). One case in particular involved the interpretation of a new Texas fetal rights law by the 47th judicial district attorney, Rebecca King. She had instructed healthcare providers to report drug use of pregnant women to the police for prosecution NAPW 2003: 10). NAPW helped by providing local agencies opposed to this new policy with research supporting the lack of legal foundation in the D.A.'s request while also offering organizing support for local activists interested in raising awareness about the problem. Efforts related to this practice are ongoing and include the participation of the American Civil Liberties Union (ACLU) (NAPW 2003: 10-11).

By 2004, other legal victories had been realized. A case of abuse filed in New York against a mother who used alcohol while pregnant was dismissed in 2004 (NAPW 2005: 4). Other noteworthy litigation activities included a case in which a drug using couple was prohibited from procreating until they could prove their parent-worthiness (NAPW 2005: 4). The original order from Judge Marilyn L. O'Connor of Monroe County, New York, Family Court cited drug use by the parents as cause for "neglect" of their fourth child (NAPW 2005: 4). Partnering with "public health, children's rights and social justice organizations including the Child Welfare Organizing Project, Doctors of the World-USA and the Family Defense Clinic ... both Feminists for Life of New York and Planned Parenthood of the Rochester/Syracuse Region," NAPW organized an amicus brief in support of vacating (dismissing) the judge's order (NAPW 2005: 5). NAPW provided litigation support for defendants in cases in Kentucky and Missouri which were also dismissed, both long fought victories. In the 2002 case, *State of Kentucky v. Harris*, a mother was charged with child abuse for allegedly injecting herself with oxycontin during her pregnancy. NAPW provided legal, public health and local organizational support. The case was dismissed in 2002, and the state's appeal in 2004 was also dismissed (NAPW 2005: 5). In the 2003 case, State *of Missouri v. Keila Lewis,* a mother was charged with felony child endangerment because her child tested positive for marijuana at birth. Lewis admitted to using the drug once during pregnancy, but as the amicus brief organized by NAPW pointed out, there was no scientific evidence that one exposure to the drug could have negative consequences for the unborn child. The case was dismissed in 2004 (NAPW 2005: 5) In Pennsylvania in 2004, NAPW lent advocacy support to a family who narrowly escaped a court order forcing a caesarian surgery. The resulting public education campaign was surprisingly large and involved other women coming forward who had been compelled to have an un-consented caesarian delivery (NAPW 2005: 7-8). In 2006 NAPW continued advocacy efforts by providing research to support defendants in cases in South Carolina, New Mexico, Arizona, Alabama, Colorado, Georgia, Missouri, North Dakota, and New Hampshire who were being arrested for child abuse based on substance use during pregnancy (Paltrow 2006). Such efforts continued, focusing on an increase of arrests in Alabama in 2008 (Paltrow 2008).

Public Education

Although the litigation efforts of the organization have been noteworthy, some of their most impressive work has involved public education around the intersection of issues such as addiction, drug use and pregnancy. In 2003, Lynn Paltrow drafted a letter to the *New York Times* arguing that they discontinue their use of the term "Crack baby" as it has no concrete medical justification (NAPW 2004: 12). A part of the letter was published by the newspaper, and NAPW reports that further use of the term by the *New York Times* has been stopped (12). Additional public education efforts seeking to undermine the pervasive "crack baby" myth have continued. NAPW regularly speaks to university associations, foundations, policy groups, and organizes workshops at national conferences, such as the National Conference on Harm Reduction. The goal of these talks can vary, but usually involves educating attendees as to the ways that fetal rights laws result in punishment of pregnant women rather than offering the support and treatment they need, drug using or not. The intersectionality within which NAPW operates also results in their tackling related issues such as child welfare, drug policy, and birth decisions. In 2006 the organization was a co-sponsor of the "National Harm Reduction Conference." The Harm Reduction Coalition (HRC) sponsors the only National Conference of its kind. It convenes biannually and, "... provide[s] a critical and unique forum for the exploration and development of harm reduction practice, theory, and policy, and serve[s] as crucial networking mechanisms for individuals working in harm reduction." In 2006, 2007, and 2008 NAPW hosted the "National Summit to Ensure the Health and Humanity of Pregnant Women." In 2009, NAPW co-sponsored a symposium, "Drugs, Pregnancy and Parenting: What the Experts in Social Work Medicine and Law Have to Say," at the New York University School of Law. A sequel symposium of the same title was also co-sponsored in 2010. A similar event was held in at the University of Alabama at Birmingham in October of that same year.

Press coverage of the organization's activities has ranged from television talk shows to popular magazines to local newspapers to national newspapers to publications such as the *Ford Foundation Report* (NAPW 2002; 2003, 2004). NAPW organized its first national conference in 2002 in New York City; it was entitled, "Maternal-State Conflicts: Claims of Fetal Rights and the Well-Being of Women and Families." In 2004, NAPW participated in the March for Women's Lives in Washington, DC. Lynn Paltrow was among those who spoke to the assembled mass of marchers that day (NAPW 2005: 1). The event was covered by national media outlets including C-SPAN and CNN. Following the event, Paltrow was interviewed for the television and radio program *Democracy Now*, joining Susan Sarandon and Margaret Cho on that broadcast (NAPW 2005: 19). Since 2004, Paltrow and other representatives of NAPW have joined panels, provided content for columns in the *New York Times* and the *Washington Post,* and contributed articles to the *Huffington Post* (an online newspaper) as well as publications in law and academic journals.

Context

Perhaps what distinguishes the mission of NAPW the most is their emphasis on advocating for the rights of drug-using women. This is not a hushed or sidelined issue; it is clearly announced and interwoven into the rhetoric of the organization's website. As part of their coverage of court cases in which pregnant mothers have been arrested for child endangerment as a result of drug use, the locations of prisons and drug treatment centers in Alabama are graphically charted on a large map on the organization's home page. Prisons are shown to significantly outnumber treatment centers. Likewise, NAPW maintains a blog covering court decisions related to fetal rights. This coverage helps educate viewers about fetal separatist movements and their connection to efforts undermining the rights of the mother. The home page also includes a link to a recent book, *Our Bodies, Our*

Crimes: The Policing of Women's Reproduction in America, written by the board president, Jeanne Flavin. Other newsworthy events such as a conference presentation at the American Anthropological Association, a roundtable discussion at Princeton University, and a presentation at the recent National Conference for the Harm Reduction Coalition showcase the intellectual nature of the activism promoted by the organization.

It is no surprise that non-native speakers, poor women, and women of color tend to have less agency in their reproductive choices and pregnancy processes. In several states, for example, pregnant women are required by law to be screened for STDs and/ or AIDS at multiple points during their pregnancies (Peters 2007). Lifestyle, sexual behavior, the patient's wishes are not always considered, and it is not uncommon (in my personal experience) for practitioners to throw in drug screening without informing the patient. While the intention behind such testing may not be nefarious, the resulting lack of agency available to the pregnant mother is problematic, especially for those women whose economic, immigrant, or cultural status would prevent them from resisting such a directive and/or make them targets for punitive enforcements.

Objectives

There seem to be three main ways that NAPW works to achieve its objectives. The organization engages in public education on issues related to the mother's agency in pregnancy; it offers litigation support for those pregnant women who fail drug screenings and/or give birth to newborns who test positive for drugs and whose mothers are charged with neglect; it provides local and national grass roots organizing support. NAPW has been recognized by the expert reviewers of Philanthropedia as "a very small organization with big, bold cutting-edge ideas and advocacy" and "a strong legal capacity."

Activities—Public Education

The organization provides access to important information in ways that expand the means for pregnant women to make informed choices. For example, a recent report, "A Woman's Guide to VBAC: Navigating the NIH Consensus Recommendations," is linked to the homepage. This important site contains incredibly empowering and useful information for women seeking to make informed and agentive decisions about their birth choices after having previously had a cesarean delivery. As one such woman, I found this information following the disturbing discovery that not all health care providers will perform VBAC (vaginal birth after cesarean). Because of this report, and the information provided about the low rates of complications due to VBAC, I felt able to confidently ask my midwife to plan for a VBAC rather than a repeat cesarean. Without this information, I would have felt less able to advocate for my own preferences. By linking to this site, NAPW communicates clearly their desire for all women to be able to be participants in the decision-making part of the birth process.

Publications such as academic journal articles and legal briefs are also items of information posted to the NAPW site. These documents, dating back to 1991, provide readers with a variety of resources ranging from legal decisions to arguments against punitive responses to drug using women. The range of documents also communicates the established nature of the organization. In fact, NAPW has been named "one of the top 2010 top non-profit organizations working in the women's reproductive health, rights, and justice field at the national level" according to Sonya Shields, NAPW Director of Development. They are also known for their persuasive op-ed pieces and ability to reframe the issue of drug-using pregnant women in human rights terms through publications and public lectures. While some might criticize NAPW's lack of close collaboration with other Choice-based organizations, I disagree. Part of what makes this organization's efforts so important is its ability to advocate for the autonomy of women in pregnancy and parenting while also joining in larger social movements dealing with drug use and poverty. This seems to be part of their success in that they are able to side-step the larger abortion debate in order to focus on the smaller, less visible, less publicized and thus more insidious legal actions that are slowly chipping away at the freedoms protected by the right to choose.

Litigation

In addition to public education efforts, NAPW provides substantial litigation support. One of the most famous cases the organization worked on involved a South Carolina woman, Regina McKnight who was charged with homicide following the stillbirth of her child. The charge was based on the allegation that the mother had used cocaine and thus caused the death of her unborn child. She was sentenced to 20 years in prison. Litigation related to this case and that which followed the initial conviction began in 2002 and continued until McKnight's release in 2008 (NAPW 2003; Wen). The lack of scientific or medical proof connecting cocaine use to stillbirth was one of the key pieces of information provided by NAPW in the case. A very recent case targeted for support by NAPW also involved a mother charged with homicide after a stillbirth. This time, the defendant is a teenager. The organization's website tracks developments in cases like this in the blog section.

Grassroots Organizing Support

NAPW offers both indirect and direct organizing support in localities across the U.S. The organization has a Facebook presence and delivers important action items, press releases, and links to activities to its network of Facebook "friends." Likewise, NAPW maintains an email subscription list of supporters, donors and friends of the organization. These individuals receive reports on ongoing activities, important accomplishments and fundraising efforts. A good example of a

Laura Pemberton, a woman taken into custody by a Florida Sheriff and forced to undergo unconsented cesarean surgery, presents at NAPW 2007 National Summit to Ensure the Health and Humanity of Pregnant and Birthing Women.

recent event that utilized social networking technology involved NAPW Executive director's open letter to Sarah Palin, "How Will You Lead? What Will You Say?" This letter was in response to the January 8, 2011, shooting of Congresswoman Giffords, Paltrow's cousin. The letter invited Governor Palin to reconsider her previous use of violent imagery and metaphors in her political rhetoric (Paltrow). After the letter was published in the *Huffington Post*, Paltrow was interviewed on Keith Olbermann's *Countdown*, a nationally known news commentary program. Both the publication of the letter and Paltrow's appearance on *Countdown* were announced on Facebook, Twitter, and via email to the organization's friends and supporters.

Most of NAPW's organizing efforts involve bringing together different organizations and groups in locations where litigation efforts and/or dubious prosecutions are happening. From the NAPW website:

> Examples of local organizing include providing advocacy and training to local healthcare providers and women in recovery in South Carolina; bringing together pro-choice, drug policy, mental health and social justice activists in Utah to collaborate in challenges to the Rowland case; co-sponsoring a coalition of grassroots women's health activists in South Carolina; and sending our National Educator to Utah, Kansas

> and other states to help build and support locally-based reproductive justice collaborations.

At the national level, the organization conducts letter-writing campaigns and organizes experts and health-care providers to join amicus briefs. Some of their most effective organizing often results in press coverage that then enables the organization to reach an even broader audience, as in the example of the open letter to Governor Palin.

Relationship to Larger Motherhood Movement

In their 2002 annual report, the organization clarifies their relationship to the larger Choice movements:

> By focusing on the rights of pregnant women, including those who are continuing their pregnancies to term, we are simultaneously expanding the reproductive rights movement and promoting drug policy and criminal justice reform. (NAPW 2003: 1)

One of the strengths of both NAPW's litigation and grassroots organizing support is its ability to form partnerships with a wide range of agencies and organizations. They regularly partner with pediatric, maternal health, social service, and drug policy organizations. Because NAPW tries to make the legal and social effects of pregnancy and intersectional issues such as poverty, drug use, and parenting the focus of their advocacy efforts, they do not exclusively target motherhood or feminist organizations for support. In other words, NAPW has recast the disenfranchisement of pregnant women as a human rights issue—not just a feminist or a motherhood issue.

Since NAPW is seeking change in federal and state policies and laws, allying themselves with other organizations representing intersectional issues makes them harder to dismiss. Although NAPW supports Choice, they are able to organize around other important issues related to pregnant women's agency, particularly those issues directly affecting non-white, working-class, drug-using, and poor women. Not unlike feminist mainstream movements, motherhood movements have largely been regarded as white, middle-class activities representing a small portion of motherhood concerns. In addition, tensions regarding the role of a mother and her validation in society are constantly contested by feminist and post-feminist critics. Are mothers to be valued as nurturers? Where do pregnant women fit in the theoretical framework that argues for recognition of the "other? Is pregnancy a mark of privilege? Or, are pregnant women simply people whose multiple identities include a feminine gender and a pregnant body? In all of the grassroots organizing by groups such as MomsRising for paid maternity leave, affordable childcare, fair pay and other legislation favorable to working women, how much effort is being put towards policies or support systems for women working minimum-wage jobs or who cannot afford to work?

One of the largest tensions in my view is between the vision of mother as divinity—nurturing and sacrificing—and that of the drug-using, impoverished, abused mother who is not living up to societal expectations. NAPW's role in the larger motherhood movement is crucial for this reason. Because their advocacy efforts explicitly capitalize on the intersection of identities and concerns facing their clients, NAPW makes visible a deeper social problem that has the potential to affect every woman. If legislative efforts fail, for example, and drug-using pregnant women can be convicted and sentenced to jail for child abuse/ neglect/ endangerment in every state, the rights of all pregnant women become open to question. Currently, a problematic U.S. drug policy mixed with racial and economic bias is facilitating enforcement, instead of treatment, efforts against pregnant women who test positive for illegal drugs, but one wonders if such enforcement were to become the norm, what would be the next worst offence? Would pregnant women be prosecuted for drinking alcohol, playing sports, exercising, drinking coffee, refusing to take prenatal vitamins, working long shifts, eating bad food or caring for too many other children? This is part of the problem that NAPW is trying to address; once the right to choose, whether that is the right to choose an abortion or the right to carry a pregnancy to term, is nullified, all women lose.

Conclusion

In pregnancy, women can threaten established social norms by not performing the culturally prescribed image of motherhood, but, they are simultaneously vulnerable. The state, partners, religions and even families often assert control over the pregnant woman's body, rendering her wishes subordinate. While birth plans may seem to provide the rhetorical agency pregnant women need, "seeking to avoid technological intervention into a 'natural' process," they lack the legal power of other health care documents, such as living wills or DNRs (Owens 248). Other women caught in the web of poverty and addiction often find themselves fighting for autonomy on multiple fronts. They risk losing their children, their liberty, even their lives. In fact, when confronted with the policies and practices of particular health care providers and state laws, some women find themselves in need of more than rhetorical agency—they need autonomy over their own bodies.

Literacy expert, Mary P. Sheridan-Rabideau argues that "myth building can facilitate social change" by providing new meanings rather than simply critiquing old ways of thinking (464). In other words, Judith Tucker's "change narratives" are myth-building examples of ways feminists can work to re-inscribe activities, such as caregiving, as "human activity" rather than "women's work" (Tucker). I would argue that it is the myth of the pregnant woman as dependent, as incapable of negotiating the birthing and parenting process without state and medical control that NAPW is working to change. In reading their website, a new narrative of the pregnant woman as agent, as autonomous actor in control over her own body is formed and given meaning. This new rhetoric offers something unique to women—including the most vulnerable among us—empowering all women, pregnant, parenting or just hoping to maintain the right of control over their own bodies.

Works Cited

Harm Reduction Coalition (HRC). 2010. Web. 30 December 2010. <http://www.harmreduction.org/section.php?id=57>.

MomsRising. Web. <http://www.momsrising.org>.

National Advocates for Pregnant Women (NAPW). Web. <http://advocatesforpregnantwomen.org>.

National Advocates for Pregnant Women (NAPW). *2002 Annual Report.* New York: NAPW, 2003.

National Advocates for Pregnant Women (NAPW). *2003 Annual Report.* New York: NAPW, 2004.

National Advocates for Pregnant Women (NAPW). 2004 *Annual Report.* New York: NAPW, 2005.

National Advocates for Pregnant Women (NAPW). 2010. Web. 15 Jan 2011. <http:// advocatesforpregnantwomen.org/>.

"National Advocates for Pregnant Women Ranked Nonprofits: National Reproductive Health, Rights and Justice." Philanthropedia 2010. Web. <http://www.myphilanthropedia.org>. 20 Nov 2010.

Owens, Kim Hensley. "Confronting Rhetorical Disability: A Critical Analysis of Women's Birth Plans." *Written Communication* 26 (3) (2009): 247-272.

Paltrow, Lynn. "Arrests Continue, But So Do The Challenges." NAPW Web. <http://advocatesforpregnantwomen.org/blog/> Blog entry, 2006.

Paltrow, Lynn. "Prosecutions in Alabama? Say No!" NAPW Web. <http://advocatesforpregnantwomen.org/blog/> Blog entry, 2008.

Paltrow, Lynn. Personal interview. 9 December 2010.

Peters, Jeremy W. "New Jersey Requires HIV Test in Pregnancy." *New York Times* 27 December 2007. Web. 15 November 2010. <http://www.nytimes.com/2007/12/27/nyregion/27hiv.html?_r=2&ref=nyregion>

Philanthropedia. Web. <http://www.myphilanthropedia.org/top-nonprofits/national/reproductive-health-rights-justice/national-advocates-for-pregnant-women>.

Sheridan-Rabideau, Mary P. "The Stuff that Myths Are Made Of: Myth Building as Social Action." *Communication* 18 (4) (2001): 440-469. Print.

Tucker, Judith Stadtman. "The Builders of New Myths: Friedan, Feminism, and the Future." *The Mothers Movement Online.* Web. <http://www.mothersmovement.org/features/06/03/newmyths_1.html> 2006. Jan 2011.

Wen. "Regina McKnight—Victory at Long Last." NAPW Web. <http://advocatesforpregnantwomen.org/blog/> Blog entry, 2008.

4.
Different Songs, Same Harmony
SisterSong's Women of Color Reproductive Justice Collective

JENNIFER MUSIAL

We are SisterSong because we are women of color from many cultures and orientations who may sing different songs yet we all sing the women's song in harmony, from the same score, on the same sheet of music.
—Juanita Williams, Management Circle Member, quilter and HIV/AIDS survivor, 1997

IN 1996-1997, FUNDING FROM the Ford Foundation facilitated the assemblage of 16 Indigenous women and women of color organizations into one umbrella organization, SisterSong: The Women of Color Reproductive Health Project. Laura Jimenez recalls the name SisterSong was chosen to honor the sentiments expressed at an early SisterSong gathering by HIV/AIDS survivor and founding member of the group Juanita Williams, who conveys that diverse groups of women can share a goal of reproductive justice (Jimenez). Initially interested in bringing together activists, advocates and community organizers to talk about reproductive health, particularly reproductive tract infections, and sexual rights in the late 1990s, SisterSong went on to host its first national conference in 2003, which was attended by over 600 individuals representing multiple communities, regions and perspectives and was instrumental in organizing the March for Women's Lives in Washington, DC, in 2004. SisterSong has addressed the gaps in "mainstream" feminist organizing that has become too focused on a pro-choice/abortion rights stance to the exclusion of other important concerns to women of color such as the right to parent and the right to retain children in the face of child removal through residential schools, deportation and foster care, according to SisterSong national co-ordinator Loretta Ross. Radical in its politics and organizational structure, SisterSong continues to exemplify a workable feminist collective model that recognizes racial, ethnic, spiritual, gender identity, sexuality and class differences amongst its member organizations and persons served while simultaneously sharing a commitment to freedom from reproductive oppression through a social justice framework. In this chapter, I will outline SisterSong's mandate, herstory, notable activities, challenges and strategies, plans for growth and connection to the motherhood movement at large. Through this chapter, I will demonstrate the importance of SisterSong in representing Indigenous women and women of color, often marginalized, excluded or simply unaccounted for within feminist reproductive health organizing, and highlight SisterSong's trailblazing collectivist model that borrows from international human rights scaffolding to argue that women's rights are human rights.

Philosophy and Purpose

SisterSong is organized around three core principles. First, SisterSong shares with the mainstream pro-choice/abortion rights movement a belief that women have the right to avoid or circumvent reproduction through birth control, emergency contraception, abortion and other family planning methods. Second, using a historical, anti-racist analysis, SisterSong points out that in a white supremacist society, racialized women have been coerced, persuaded and otherwise influenced in their reproductive decision-making. Noting forced breeding programs for African-Americans that took place in plantation slave economies (Roberts 27-29), non-consensual sterilization abuse of Indigenous women, African-American women and Latina women, testing of hormonal birth control on Puerto Rican women, continued disproportionate prescriptions of long-acting, arguably unsafe, hormonal birth control to women of color and welfare "reform" that limits social assistance to women who have "too many" children, SisterSong maintains that women have the right to have children. Since eugenic, classist, colonial and racist efforts have gone into preventing and dissuading Indigenous women and women of color from reproducing, the contention that all women have the right to parent is truly revolutionary. Following this, the third part of SisterSong's mandate is all women have the right to parent the children they currently have. In addition to efforts to prevent reproduction, Indigenous women and women of color disproportionately face removal of children by foster care, residential schooling, and separation from children through incarceration, deportation and other restrictive immigration laws. By supporting women's parenting of their born children, SisterSong prioritizes keep families together and rooted in their communities of support.

Through these core principles, SisterSong addresses reproductive oppression, which is the "control and exploitation of women, girls, and individuals through our bodies, sexuality, labor and reproduction" (Ross, "Reproductive Justice 101," Part 1). SisterSong employs the United Nations' Universal Declaration of Human Rights (1948) to counter reproductive oppression. The international human rights paradigm is different from a neo-liberal notion of human rights. Neo-liberalism emphasizes an individual's "civil and political rights" (such as equality, non-discrimination, voting, free speech, etc.); the international rights model adds "economic, social and cultural human rights" as well (Ross et. al. 85). Economic, social and cultural human rights encompass the right to a living wage, health care, education, social assistance, religion and language. Beyond these, international human rights acknowledges environmental rights (clean air, a non-toxic living and working environment, access to clean water), development rights (ability to control natural resources), and importantly to SisterSong, sexual rights (right to have or not have children, freely express sexuality and gender identity, access to birth control and abortion, and the ability to marry and self-define one's family) (Ross, "Interview with Loretta Ross of SisterSong Part 2"). Influenced by feminists and activists around the world, SisterSong argues that these are mutually constitutive such that one cannot achieve equality without access to clean drinking water and one cannot be free of discrimination if he/she/ze does not have access to family planning etc. To understand why women choose to mother or not to mother, one must consider poverty, security in intimate relationships, access to health care, protection from pregnancy discrimination at work, etc. as factors in women's reproductive lives. This is why SisterSong says the language of "reproductive *rights*" is reductive: they argue it reminds too much of neo-liberal, individualist application of rights. Ross, Brownlee, Diallo, Dixon and Rodriguez argue that racialized and Indigenous women cannot find peace, security and freedom in their lives if the rights of their communities are not recognized (85-86). Further, constitutional language of "reproductive rights" does not work for Indigenous women and women of color who do not have a great deal of choice or privacy (overpolicing, hyper-surveillance) and are otherwise rooted in their communities rather than solely individual human actors (Ross, "Interview with Loretta Ross of SisterSong Part 2"). Instead, "reproductive justice" is preferred because it is historically and collectively minded, and borrows from an international tradition used by women outside the United States. Ross maintains the United States has a long way to go to implement international human rights. Not only has the United States failed to ratify the Convention to End All Forms of Discrimination Against Women and the Equal Rights Amendment, the United States has actively *denied* human rights within its borders (for instance, the denial of Indigenous land claims or the refusal to recognize and honor transgendered identities in the prison system).

History/Herstory

During the 1970's and 1980's, many Indigenous women and women of color groups began organizing around reproductive justice. Whether the focus was pro-choice/abortion rights, HIV/AIDS, reproductive tract infections, unsafe medical procedures, anti-sterilization or simply "women's health," various groups met to discuss how to deliver services and address inadequacies in sexual and reproductive health care. In 1997-1998, through Ford Foundation funding, 16 organizations from around the country (four representing Black/African-American women, four representing Hispanic/Latina women, four representing Asian/Pacific Islander women and four representing Indigenous women) were brought together to dialogue, share resources, conduct research and address gaps in services and appropriate treatment for women. This initial group was called "SisterSong: Women of Color Reproductive Health Project."

In the second phase of development, SisterSong changed its name from a "project" to a "collective" and looked to solidify national and international infrastructure and visibility. In 2003, SisterSong took up a reproductive justice vis-à-vis human rights framework and organized its first national conference (over 600 folks attended). That same year, SisterSong welcomed BrotherBeat, a men of color-allied organization, into their collective structure. Next, SisterSong co-organized the March for Women's Lives in Washington, DC, in 2004, highlighting the presence of Indigenous women and women of color in the reproductive health movement. A national office was established in 2005 in Atlanta and moved into Mother House, a central office and organizing location in 2007. Also that year, SisterSong put on the "Let's Talk about Sex" conference that was attended by over 1000 people. Additionally, SisterSong began to see the limitations and exclusions of dividing racialization and ethnicity into four categories. And so they added organizations that serve Middle Eastern, Muslim, North African, African-Latina, African-Caribbean women because, as Loretta Ross says, SisterSong had a "radical progressive analysis that turned out to be attractive to people" (Ross, "Reproductive Justice 101," Part 1).

The latest phase of SisterSong, 2006 to today (2011), involves outreach, strengthening existing relationships and building new alliances. SisterSong continues to offer trainings such as "Reproductive Justice 101" to Indigenous and women of color organizations. These trainings introduce participants to the reproductive justice framework and explain the origins and potential applications of the term. Trainings are often provided for staff and/or volunteers in other reproductive health organizations, university classrooms, campus service units and other social justice groups (Jimenez). In addition to trainings, SisterSong researches needs and gaps in service for marginalized populations, builds solidarity with other allied social justice movements such as prison abolition and environmental justice groups and shares resources through their website. In 2006, SisterSong became a federally recognized non-profit so they were approved for 501(c)3 [tax exempt] status (Ross, "Reproductive Justice 101," Part 1). Humbly beginning with 16 member organizations, by 2011 SisterSong welcomed 40 member organizations and 56 affiliate organizations into their collective structure ("Member and Affiliate Organizations").

Activities

SisterSong builds bridges and fosters a larger reproductive health community through its national gatherings. The first national conference, "SisterSong Reproductive Health and Sexual Rights National Conference," was held in 2003. This gathering involved speakers, workshops, caucus break-out sessions, each one-teach one sharing, leadership seminars, visioning and planning activities, and ceremonies to honor activist pioneers. During the conference, there was talk of and planning for the 2004 March for Women's Lives in Washington, DC. Initially, the "big four" organizations (Planned Parenthood, Feminist Majority, National Association for

SisterSong, "March for Women's Lives."

the Repeal of Abortion Laws (NARAL) and National Organization for Women (NOW)) called the gathering as the "March for Freedom of Choice." When people within these organizations protested the limits of "choice" discourse, SisterSong was approached. SisterSong demanded to change the name to the March for Women's Lives so as to enact a more inclusive mandate focused on reproductive justice (Buttenwieser). There was concern that the pro-choice/abortion rights movement would co-opt the march thereby marginalizing the efforts and interests of women of color. SisterSong was adamant that Indigenous and racialized women needed to be on the speaker's list, there had to be pre- and post-march breakout and sharing sessions for Indigenous women and women of color and talk of reproductive justice had to move beyond talk of pro-choice/abortion rights. Further, the "big four" organizations invested money to reach out and mobilize grassroots Indigenous and women of color groups to encourage the presence of racialized women at the march (Lancz).

Building on the momentum established through these efforts, SisterSong hosted their second national conference called "Let's Talk about Sex" in Chicago in 2007. Celebrating their tenth anniversary as a collective, SisterSong's goal was to promote pro-sex politics in reproductive justice organizing. In their newsletter "Collective Voices," SisterSong explains, "Since the right to have sex is a topic rarely discussed when addressing reproductive health and rights issues, SisterSong believes that sexual prohibitions are not only promoted by moral conservatives in this country, but also by reproductive rights advocates who fail to promote a sex-positive culture. Sex is not for pro-creation and sexual pleasure – sex is a human right" (SisterSong, "Collective Voices," 20). This theme is so important to SisterSong that they are revisiting it for SisterSong's third national conference in 2011 in Miami called "Let's Talk about Sex: Love, Legislation and Leadership." According to the call on the website, SisterSong's looking for "workshop proposals that highlight cutting edge visions that address issues on sex, sexuality, and sexual pleasure" and hopes to include workshops and plenary sessions on topics such as birth control, senior sexuality, STDs, microbicides, gynecological health and wellness, erotica, militarism, youth sexuality, and more, all through a reproductive justice lens" with expected attendance of 1,300 people.

In addition to promoting healthy sexuality through a national gathering, SisterSong advocates for access to abortion and is critical of oppressive anti-abortion rhetoric. One example of this is the recent activity by groups like Priests for Life and Too Many Aborted who funded billboards and organized "Freedom Rides" in 2010 protesting abortion as a mechanism of genocide in communities of color. When billboards featuring a racialized child and slogans such as "black children are an endangered species" and "black and unwanted" began to appear on American roadsides, SisterSong vocally opposed targeting African American women's reproductive decision-making. Taking this rhetoric one step further, Priests for Life co-ordinated "Freedom Rides," which were initiatives to car-pool and organize buses to travel to the site of the 1963 church burning in Birmingham Alabama that killed four African American girls. Offended that predominantly African

American leaders would use the racially motivated hate crime as a touchtone for anti-abortion activism, SisterSong critiqued these actions as a "thinly-veiled attack on Black women's rights with a Black figurehead" and opposed the use of civil rights iconography and public sites for anti-abortion rhetoric.

To counter this action and demonstrate that spirituality and reproductive justice are not incompatible, SisterSong, SPARK Reproductive Justice NOW! and SisterLove, Inc. "invited faith-based leaders, civil rights leaders, and women's health supporters to the King Center on July 24, 2010, 2:30 pm in Atlanta" to address the inappropriate use of civil rights language and clarify the importance of a reproductive justice politic that "call[s] on the public to trust Black women to make their own decisions about what's best for them and their families" ("SisterSong, SPARK, and SisterLove Expose Hijacking of Civil Rights Movement"). In an interview with Laura Flanders at GritTV, Loretta Ross argues, "you will not re-enslave us to suit your political agenda" ("GritTV: Loretta Ross & Lynn Paltrow: Conspiracy Tactics"). By drawing on a historical analysis of slave breeding programs directed towards African-American women, Ross ties this latest campaign back to the racialized legacy of a capitalist slave economy wherein women's reproduction served as profit for white slave owners and plantation managers. Overall, Ross says, "You cannot save Black babies by discriminating against Black women" ("SisterSong, SPARK, and SisterLove Expose Hijacking of Civil Rights Movement").

SisterSong continues to lobby for Indigenous and racialized women's rights to reproductive and parental decision-making. Beyond opposing the "Freedom Rides" described above, SisterSong lobbied against HB1155, the Prenatal Nondiscrimination Bill (also known as the Sex and Race Selection Bill), which is a federal law that prohibits targeting racialized women for abortion services and bans sex-selective abortions. Though sensible "on paper," SisterSong predicted the practice would criminaliz[e] women of color "without any regard to the broader ubiquitous issues of gender discrimination that are deeply embedded in the fabrics of our lived experiences" (SisterSong "HB1155 Action Alert"). SisterSong feared that if passed, HB1155 would put the onus on abortion providers to verify that they were *not* soliciting women of color, a potentially difficult thing to prove, which may result in interrupted or delayed abortion services ("SisterSong Collective Opposes HB1155 The Sex and Race Selection Bill"). While HB1155 stalled in the House Judiciary Non-Civil Committee, SB 529 "*OB/GYN Criminalization and Racial Discrimination Act*" was taken up at the state level and passed in the Georgia Senate; SB 529 is a companion piece to HB1155 written in the same spirit that also holds abortion providers responsible (criminally and civilly) for "alleged" targeting and coercion of an abortion-seeker (ex. if a parent urges his/her daughter to have an abortion, the abortion doctor may face criminal or civil charges). As Loretta Ross points out, this bill demonstrates how state legislation acts in contrast to federal protections for abortion care ("GritTV: Loretta Ross & Lynn Paltrow: Conspiracy Tactics").

To encourage an intersectional approach and pro-woman mandate, SisterSong conducts on-going trainings, workshops and skills-sharing across the United

States and internationally. These sessions promote a reproductive justice analysis to service providers and feminist organizations (a sample of these talks by Loretta Ross can be found on YouTube). As a non-profit organization, SisterSong also accepts donations that may be used towards the $1.1 million "Supporting Our Community of Sisters" Expansion and Capital Campaign to maintain and grow their public site Mother House, scholarships to subsidize travel for activists and advocates to national SisterSong gatherings, and the Reproductive Justice Training Fund that allows SisterSong to travel around the United States to offer training to activists, educators, health care providers, policymakers and practitioners alike.

Challenges and Strategies

As a reproductive justice non-profit, SisterSong faces funding challenges, as all activist organizations do, to continue serving Indigenous women and women of color. Beyond establishing economic sustainability, SisterSong faces distinct challenges from feminism, communities of color, domestic U.S. politics and international politics. First, as I alluded to earlier, SisterSong plays a unique role within broader feminist movements. Starting as a collective run by Indigenous women and women of color organizations, Loretta Ross explains that SisterSong quickly found many racialized women doing similar work were *not* in women of color-specific organizations (ex. Planned Parenthood). Some of these women were isolated and marginalized as they struggled to bring an analysis of racism into these places. In an effort to reach out, build solidarity and offer support, SisterSong opened up the collective structure to individual racialized women and allied white women (Ross, "Reproductive Justice 101," Part 1). This allowed SisterSong to grow its base of support too. In her interviews, Ross states one of the biggest contentions within SisterSong is its relationship to the "big four" (Planned Parenthood, Feminist Majority, NARAL and NOW). SisterSong remains wary of these organizations appropriating the phrase "reproductive justice" as a cover to mean abortion rights without approaching this work from an intersectional and community-based framework or being self-reflexive about racism, classism, heterosexism and colonialism within current operations. While they will help out when asked and when they can, SisterSong was "not created to fix the mainstream" and therefore does not want to be distracted by requests from Planned Parenthood, Feminist Majority, NARAL and NOW at the expense of marginalized Indigenous women and women of color. Ross maintains SisterSong's focus is grassroots, community focused organizing primarily with women of color (Ross, "Community Women's Voices").

Second, SisterSong identifies the "Veil of Silence" as a challenge to dialogue within racialized communities. The "Veil of Silence" refers to the shame and secrecy that surrounds frank discussions about sexuality and reproduction in some communities. This "Veil of Silence" is observed worldwide (Ross, Brownlee, Diallo, Dixon and Rodriguez 85). SisterSong identifies the "Veil of Silence" an important issue because it often results in the perpetuation of dangerous myths and misinforma-

SisterSong, "March for Women's Lives."

tion that puts women's health at risk. With piecemeal advice, presumptions and rumours, and nowhere to access non-judgmental, factual and clear education or resources, some women are situated as reproductive decision-makers who cannot make informed choices about their bodies. SisterSong empowers women to break the "Veil of Silence" by offering training and workshop programs to educate women as knowledgeable leaders and educators in their communities.

Third, this organization faces difficult challenges in lobbying for change with (and sometimes against) conservative policymakers and public opinion. George

W. Bush administration era abstinence-only education contributed to a "Veil of Silence" and prevented open dialogue about and access to adequate sexual health services and education, which disproportionately affected marginalized racialized women. Clawing back reproductive justice legislation, such as the passing of the *"Partial Birth" Abortion Ban Act* in 2003, parental notification laws, fetal rights legislation that criminalizes pregnant women for behavior, drug use or anti-medicalized pregnancy/labor care (ex. refusing a caesarian section) present a major obstacle towards realizing reproductive justice for all. Added to this, one may consider neo-population control tactics such as initiatives aimed at getting poor Indigenous women and women of color to accept sterilization through financial incentives or long-acting contraception, judicial decisions that include limiting women's fertility as part of their incarceration, or new sterilization techniques and pharmaceuticals that are not approved by international health and safety boards put women at risk of incarceration, poverty, injury or death. Finally, public fear that President Obama's health care plan will provide federally-funded abortion services make SisterSong's work that much more difficult and that much more necessary.

Fourth, SisterSong faces international challenges to provide resources and support to women worldwide. As I discussed earlier, SisterSong is in dialogue with a global women's movement for reproductive justice. To negotiate economic instability, some international organizations and non-governmental organizations (NGOs) are turning to questionable sources of financial support. Ross et. al. call attention to this by stating, "Even more troubling, many international women's rights organizations are now dependent on the financial and political support of population control organizations" (Ross, Brownlee, Diallo, Dixon and Rodriquez 86). By taking money from the United States Agency for International Development (USAID), for example, some organizations become complicit in a history of eugenic, colonial reproductive oppression that sought to limit "undesirable" women's reproduction in the Global South. Moreover, since the United States has yet to ratify the Convention to End All Forms of Discrimination Against Women (CEDAW), they cannot be held internationally accountable for treatment of and service provision to women within a global human rights framework.

Plans for Growth and Future Goals

Since 2006, SisterSong has been in "Phase Three" called "Expanding Our Impact." This phase calls for: 1) reproductive justice advocacy through trainings, research and collaboration; 2) building and strengthening Indigenous women and women of color organizations through networking, skills sharing, needs assessment and scholarships; 3) working across movements to find allies and solidarity with other social justice organizations; and, 4) providing information and resources through the Collective Voices newsletter, Mapping Our Rights website and creating an archive of online material that can be accessed through the SisterSong website (SisterSong, "The SisterSong Matrix: Organizational Structure"). Planning the

March for Women's Lives in 2004 demonstrated the power of web-based activism as word spread through communities online. SisterSong is trying to capitalize on that by amassing an impressive collection of articles on their website under the "Publications and Articles" section and now has a presence on Facebook, a social networking site.

In response to the discourse that black women's abortion is genocide, SisterSong supports Trust Black Women, established in 2010, as a partnership of multiple organizations and individuals who conduct research, media campaigns to dispel myths about abortion, lobby for public policies that sustain reproductive decision-making, advocate for truthful and responsible health education, and network between allied organizations (SisterSong, "Trust Black Women"). Also, SisterSong's website promises Latina Encuentro to start soon. Lastly, SisterSong collaborated with Charles and Hunter Stuart of STV Productions to create a documentary called *Abortion Conspiracy: Splitting the Vote* (2010). The documentary is available in five parts online and SisterSong is working to produce a feature-length DVD that can be purchased and distributed.

Connection to Motherhood Movement

In an interview for MothersMovement.org, Marlene Fried was clear that a strong Motherhood Movement must take race and class into consideration. If the Motherhood Movement operated from an intersectional analysis, the issue of access to motherhood itself (i.e. the right to parent) would be key, according to Fried (Buttenwieser). Loretta Ross concurs that "Women of color are not only undervalued as mothers, they are at times ridiculed for being mothers, their motherhood seen as social detriment: teenage mothers, African American mothers to African American sons" (Buttenwieser). Hence, SisterSong questions the pathologizing and stereotyping of Indigenous mothers and mothers of color, and challenges the pro-choice/abortion rights movement to unlearn racist, classist and colonialist ways of thinking and take motherhood seriously by supporting the rights of all women to parent if they so choose.

Moreover, SisterSong centralizes the role of community for mothers. The reason why pro-choice/abortion rights is *perceived* to be a "white woman's issue" is because so often this politic is articulated as an individual's right to choose. SisterSong intervenes by saying that limiting, denying and controlling women's reproduction is a mechanism of domination over their communities (Buttenwieser).

Finally, SisterSong is unique because they borrow from the international human rights model. Here, they point out that when a woman becomes pregnant, her decision-making about mothering is linked to various categories within the Universal Declaration of Human Rights. For instance, a pregnant woman will consider whether her wage is enough to support a(nother) child and whether she can access adequate parental leave from work, which are basic economic human rights. She will consider if she can provide food, clothing, shelter and access social assistance if she needs it, which are basic social human rights. She will consider if she has access to prenatal care and maternity support in the language of her choosing, which is a basic cultural human right. These factors heavily influence a woman's maternal decision-making and must be accounted for within reproductive justice and motherhood movement organizing.

Conclusion

SisterSong's core intentions to support, mentor and advocate for Indigenous women and women of color's right to determine their reproductive lives are realized through their collective structure, national gatherings and lobbying efforts. Though at least three previous efforts failed to draw women of color organizations together nationally, SisterSong was successful in creating a reproductive justice coalition. Through a commitment to non-judgment and trust in women to make the most appropriate decision for their bodies, lives, and communities, SisterSong truly manages to look globally and act locally through borrowing an international human rights model and applying it to grassroots, community action. Thus, SisterSong is revolutionary in its demonstrated awareness of history, intersectionality, reproduction, and social justice.

Works Cited

Buttenwieser, Sarah Werthan. "Motherhood and Reproductive Justice: An Interview with Loretta Ross and Marlene Gerber Fried." *MothersMovement.* Feb. 2005. Web. 12 Dec. 2010. <http://www.mothersmovement.org/features/05/s_buttenwieser_0205/undivided_rights_1.htm>.

GritTV. *Abortion Conspiracy: Splitting the Vote.* 2010.

GritTV. "Loretta Ross & Lynn Paltrow: Conspiracy Tactics." 2010. Web. 10 Dec. 2010. <http://vodpod.com/watch/5090374-grittv-loretta-ross-lynn-paltrow-conspiracy-tactics>.

Lancz, Linda Thompson. "The March for Women's Lives – An Analysis." *LaborStandard.* 2004. Web. 10 Dec. 2010.

<http://www.laborstandard.org/New_Postings/March_for_Women%27s_Lives.htm>.

Jimenez, Laura. Personal Interview. 21 January 2011.

Roberts, Dorothy. *Killing the Black Body: Race, Reproduction, and the Meaning of Liberty.* New York: Pantheon Books, 1997.

Ross, Loretta. "Reproductive Justice 101 Part 1." YouTube.com. 21 Oct. 2008. Web. 1 Dec. 2010. <http://www.youtube.com/watch?v=JRcT_NMa6aI>.

Ross, Loretta. "Interview with Loretta Ross of SisterSong Part 1." YouTube.com. 2006. Community Women's Voices. Web. 1 Dec. 2010. <http://www.youtube.com/watch?v=84dIHnpz_g0>

Ross, Loretta. "Interview with Loretta Ross of SisterSong Part 2." YouTube.com. 2006. Community Women's Voices. Web. 1 Dec. 2010. <http://www.youtube.

com/watch?v=K0B6Fa8_Hq8&NR=1>

Ross, Loretta. "Interview with Loretta Ross of SisterSong Part 3." YouTube.com. 2006. Community Women's Voices. Web. 1 Dec. 2010. <http://www.youtube.com/watch?v=Y4o4H0JQwdA&NR=1>.

Ross, Loretta J., Brownlee, Sarah L., Diallo, Dázon Dixon and Luz Rodriguez. "The 'SisterSong Collective': Women of Color, Reproductive Health and Human Rights." *American Journal of Health Studies Special Issue: "The Health of Women of Color."* 17.2 (2001): 79-88.

SisterSong. "Collective Voices." 2.5 (2006-2007): 1-20.

SisterSong. "HB1155 Action Alert: The Sex and Race Selection Bill." *Sistersong.* February 2010. Web. 10 Dec. 2010. <http://www.SisterSong.net/latest_news.html>.

SisterSong. "Member Organizations." *SisterSong.* 2007. Web. 10 Dec. 2010. <http://www.SisterSong.net/member_affiliate_orgs_list.html>.

SisterSong. "SisterSong Collective Opposes HB1155: The Sex and Race Selection Bill." *Sistersong.* 12 Feb. 2010. Web. 10 Dec. 2010. <http://www.SisterSong.net/latest_news.html>.

SisterSong. "SisterSong, SPARK and Sisterlove Disappointed in the Passage of SB 529." Sistersong. 26 Mar. 2010. Web. 10 Dec. 2010. <http://www.SisterSong.net/latest_news.html>.

SisterSong. "SisterSong, SPARK, and SisterLove Expose Hijacking of Civil Rights Movement." *Sistersong.* 22 July 2010. Web. 10 Dec. 2010. <http://www.SisterSong.net/latest_news.html>.

SisterSong. "The SisterSong Matrix: Organizational Structure." *Sistersong.* 2008. Web. 29 Nov. 2010. <http://www.SisterSong.net/SisterSong_Matrix_2008.pdf>.

SisterSong. "Trust Black Women." *SisterSong.* 2010. Web. 10 Dec. 2010. <http://www.SisterSong.net/trust_black_women.html>.

5.
Birth Trauma Canada

Advocating for the Rights of Childbearing Women

PENNY CHRISTENSEN

BIRTH TRAUMA CANADA IS AN independent, volunteer run organization working collaboratively with similar organizations around the world to champion better maternity care that reflects the values and choices of all childbearing women. It began October 5, 1998 and we have had an on-line presence since April, 2007. The organization offers an anonymous and non-judgmental platform for women to talk openly about their obstetrical treatment. We believe ending the taboo of speaking about birth trauma and its causes is the first step to solving this serious problem. We also believe that violence to childbearing women and inhumanity in obstetrics will not end until women band together and force change.

Birth Trauma Canada has listened to horror stories from hundreds of women from Canada and around the world, primarily from the 'developed' world. We are mindful of how difficult it is for women to talk about negative childbirth experiences. We understand and support women who have had negative childbirth experiences, we recognize how common these experiences are, we campaign for reproductive choice and genuine informed consent for women and we fight for an end to systemic misogyny and inhumanity in obstetrics. We are frank and honest with women considering motherhood. We encourage women to demand better treatment and to report abuses. We encourage them to believe that obstetrical care should be about them and not about the people providing their care. We are strong advocates for better quality obstetrical research and genuine evidence based obstetrical policies that respect the human rights of women and their individual values and choices. We advocate for accountability, transparency and reporting in obstetrics, believing that if hospitals had to report their names and statistics often, honestly and consistently the inhumanity in obstetrics could be reduced. We work cooperatively with other similar organizations around the world to affect change, reduce world wide maternal mortality and morbidity and elevate the status and value placed on mothers in our society. We want a woman's right to choice about delivery options legally entrenched and we want the already legally entrenched right to informed consent respected for pregnant women.

The motherhood movement is about the ascendency of mothers to a place in society where their real value is recognized and appreciated. The obstacles to achieving that goal are numerous. Birth Trauma Canada believes the best role we can play in the motherhood movement is to start where motherhood starts—in the hearts and minds of those providing obstetrical services and, most importantly, in the hearts and minds of mothers and those women considering motherhood. Obstetrics has long been a field that has resisted feminist enlightenment and that needs to change.

Challenges

Misogyny is, and has always been, systemic in obstetrics. Women are denied informed consent or the agency to make their own decisions. They are not given honest information about all the risks they face that would allow them to make informed decisions. Obstetrical research still has a well deserved reputation for being the most biased and scientifically dishonest research in medicine. Scientifically dishonest research is used to deny effective pain relief and disparage maternal request cesarean birth. It has been used to justify routine episiotomies, "twilight sleep," routine shaving and enemas, routine vaginal deliveries with forceps, long hospital confinements, birthing in lithotomy position and a host of other inhumane practices. Obstetrics is the only medical specialty that refuses or limits pain relief when they have the safe means to do so. They have had this ability for decades, just as all medical specialties have. Pregnant and birthing women are ridiculed, gossiped about, ignored, blamed, threatened, scolded, shamed, judged, humiliated, coerced and manipulated. They are vulnerable targets of sexual violence in labour, delivery and postpartum wards. They are subjected to lewd language and sexual innuendos and a lack of privacy. They are made to feel like abnormal failures if they had an epidural or required a cesarean or assisted vaginal delivery. They are left with no memory of all or parts of the birthing experience—a clear indication of traumatic amnesia or receiving pharmaceuticals that erase their memory, very rarely with their prior knowledge or consent. Their bodies are used for training purposes, often with coerced consent, no consent or without medical necessity. They endure all manner of inhumane procedures. They deal with traumatic stress and depression just as combat soldiers and torture victims do. Their childbirth experiences leave them with permanent physical and psychological damage that often negatively affect them for the rest of their lives. They are considered mere vessels for something more precious. Their suffering is trivialized and dismissed. They are expected to sacrifice and suffer because they are women. Suffering by women is considered acceptable and normal, even necessary, by a significant percentage of those working in the field of women's health. There is even a significant number in the field of obstetrics and gynecology that find the sexual violence associated with vaginal deliveries exciting. Obstetrics is the only field of medicine delusional enough to believe that if something is natural it must be good. Nature, sadly, is also often cruel, unfair and tragic.

A patient education pamphlet titled *Postpartum Depression* published by the American College of Obstetricians and Gynecologists (ACOG) states that 70 to 80 percent of women are depressed, anxious, upset and have trouble sleeping after they have a baby. They go on to state "*Many new mothers feel sadness, fear, anger and anxiety after having a baby. This is normal.*" Other associations of midwives and physicians share this sentiment. It is not unique to the ACOG. How badly must one hate women to accept that any of these things are normal? Sadness, fear, anger, depression, anxiety and difficulty getting to sleep or staying asleep are indicative of post-traumatic stress. Obstetrics is the only medical specialty where a significant proportion of practitioners believe trauma symptoms are caused by hormones or personal weakness but let's be very clear and state what should be obvious. Symptoms of trauma and stress are caused by trauma and stress. Given these realities, is it any wonder mothers are the highest users of anti-depressants/ anti-anxiety pharmaceuticals?

Trauma symptoms occur in three board categories: re-experiencing the original trauma (nightmares, intrusive memories, flashbacks); an avoidance of situations or people likely to act as reminders of the original trauma (often includes emotional numbing and detachment) and the need to protect themselves and their children from further trauma (vigilance). The current diagnosis of Post Traumatic Stress Disorder (PTSD) requires symptoms from each category for a month or more. Current studies looking at the prevalence of PTSD after childbirth currently range from 6 to 15 percent. The number of postpartum women who experience some of the symptoms of PTSD is higher still. I expect if women could answer appropriate questionnaires independent of the medical community and anonymously to avoid the inevitable stigma associated with admitting psychological distress after childbirth, these numbers would be higher. Traumatized people, regardless of gender or age, often suffer from insomnia and sleep deprivation, an inability to focus or concentrate, emotional detachment, hopelessness, powerlessness, fear, sadness, crying, an inability to enjoy activities that were once enjoyable, low self-confidence, panic and anxiety attacks, obsessive compulsive behaviours, headaches, shortness of breath, chest tightness and constant fatigue. They are understandably unwilling to trust people, especially those who have betrayed them; they worry about ways they could be hurt again or that their child could be hurt; they understandably avoid medical personnel and hospitals or any other person or situation likely to serve as a trigger to nightmares or unpleasant memories. Many are unwilling to talk about the experience (denial) or have an overwhelming need to talk about and understand what happened and why. Many have a heightened awareness of social injustice, a lack of interest in or fear of sex, profound grief and a sense of loss and/or isolation. Some traumatized mothers will have an inability to bond with their baby. Other trauma symptoms include feelings of inadequacy or feeling overwhelmed or uncomfortable in social situations or constricted places. It is important to remember that childbirth is often a series of traumatic experiences. Extreme pain, loss of control and privacy, and feeling violated/ disrespected are three separate traumatizing experiences. We will continue as a society that grossly undervalues mothers until we have an obstetrical industry that recognizes that psychological and physical damage to childbearing women is never trivial, acceptable or normal.

A joint policy statement issued by the Society of Obstetricians and Gynaecologists of Canada (SOGC), the Association of Women's Health, Obstetric and Neonatal Nurses of Canada (AWHONN) Canada),[1] the Canadian Association of Midwives (CAM), the College of Family Physicians (CFPC) and the Society of Rural Physicians of Canada (SRPC) states that "normal" birth, playing by their rules, can include postpartum hemorrhage, pelvic floor damage, perineal trauma and repair, admission to the neonatal intensive care unit, augmentation and induction of labour, artificial rupture of membranes and electronic fetal monitoring. They consider cesareans abnormal and epidurals abnormal during labour and only very recently decided they considered epidurals normal for vaginal deliveries. What chance do childbearing women in Canada have when professionals tasked with protecting women's health consider these things normal?

Women don't consider these things normal and they have a number of ways to protect themselves from those who do.

1) Avoiding motherhood is the most common and effective form of protection. It is the simplest and only guaranteed way to avoid obstetrical "normal"; to protect themselves from the short and long term physical and psychological damage of pregnancy and childbirth; to ensure future generations of women are not subjected to the same attitudes and treatment and to ensure they don't occupy the same under-valued position in society their mothers do.

2) Women have one child and then avoid pregnancy again. They have been so traumatized and betrayed by the cruelty shown them they will not subject themselves to the same treatment again.

3) Some women who have one traumatizing childbirth experience control the circumstances surrounding their second pregnancy after several years building up their courage to try again. Some use elaborate birth plans and/or legal counsel prior to another planned vaginal birth, hoping for protection. Many insist on a planned cesarean delivery to avoid the previous trauma associated with their past planned vaginal childbirth experience. Some choose to birth at home. Some women free birth. This is unassisted childbirth, primarily by women experiencing a second or subsequent pregnancy. Anyone who has caused problems for them in the past, or could potentially cause problems for them, is banned from their planned vaginal delivery. This includes all medical personnel—midwives, physicians and nurses. The risks are high but, for these women, the risks associated with another planned vaginal birth at the hands of the obstetrical community are higher.

Maternal mortality has diminished considerably in the developed world from earlier highs at the beginning of this century thanks in large part to modern medicine (predominantly blood transfusions, higher standards of hygiene, antibiotics, surgical competence, regional anesthesia) but the path taken to reduce maternal mortality by obstetrical professionals has knowingly (and profitably) resulted in shameful levels of inhumanity and maternal morbidity. Until society decides to value childbearing women in developed countries we will continue to see birth rates decline.

A well-worn joke among obstetricians is that they spend the first part of their careers supporting the perineum and the second half of their careers being supported by it. By this they mean they spend the first part of their careers making money by attending vaginal births and the second half of their careers making money by repairing the damage from those vaginal births. I have no idea why this would be guffaw worthy but it is true. Surgical correction of pelvic organ prolapse, urinary incontinence and anal incontinence is a billion dollar industry in the U.S. alone. Only about ten percent of those who suffer these problems seek medical attention for them. Most suffer in isolation, silence and secrecy; feeling it is better to suffer this way than approach the medical community for help—an understandable claim by those who have already been damaged or violated by those working in obstetrics and gynecology. By 2050, in the United States alone, it is projected that 43.8-58.2 million mothers will have at least one pelvic floor disorder, including 28.1–41.0 million with urinary incontinence, 16.8 -25.3 million with fecal incontinence and 4.9–9.2 million with POP (Pelvic Floor Prolapse) if obstetrical policy does not change. In 2010, 28.1 million American mothers have at least one pelvic floor disorder; 18.3 million with urinary incontinence, 10.6 million with fecal incontinence and 3.3 million with POP (Wu). Women have the right to know this but only 15 percent, according to the same study, are told. This is not informed consent and it is inexcusable. This study is significant for several reasons. Firstly, it is a rare quality study. Many obstetrical studies are not. Secondly, it mirrors the information I get daily from women who have had planned vaginal deliveries—spontaneous, assisted and emergency cesareans done after initiation of second stage. Thirdly, it highlights the staggering amount of maternal morbidity mothers cope with, and that obstetrical caregivers know about, and have known about since there were such things as midwives, nurses and physicians.

Pelvic physiotherapy, pharmaceuticals for incontinence and the resulting anxiety and depression, medical devices for prolapse and absorbent products are costs born by women that far exceed the costs associated with gynecological repair surgeries and medical appointments. The financial hardship associated with women's inability to work or participate in their communities because of their childbirth related health problems are costs that women also bear. Yet women are encouraged to birth vaginally without being told these facts. The risks of planned cesareans are overstated and the risks associated with planned vaginal deliveries are consistently understated. Women are told it is best to avoid surgery (and surgery certainly does carry risks) but are not told they will require reconstructive surgery to their genital tracts and their external genitalia after a vaginal birth. This surgery takes as long, if not longer, than a cesarean. Nor are they told of the high number of subsequent gynecological surgeries required throughout their lives to repair botched jobs done immediately after vaginal birth or to repair those women who required reconstructive surgery after their vaginal birth but were denied it because their obstetrical care provider didn't want their record to look bad. This childish game of one-up-manship between midwives and physicians (and physicians and physicians) leaves many of these women with dire consequences associated with unreconstructed secondary healing. They are not told they have a far greater risk of pelvic organ prolapse, sexual dysfunction, urinary and anal incontinence with vaginal deliveries than with planned, unlaboured cesareans at term. Many are unaware of the significant risk they face of assisted vaginal deliveries using forceps or a vacuum extractor to force the baby from their bodies, nor are they aware of the significant risk of an emergency cesarean as a common end to planned vaginal deliveries. Less than half of all deliveries in Canada are uncomplicated vaginal deliveries (43 percent of them were in 2002-2003) (Minister of Public Works and Government Services Canada; Canadian Institute for Health Informaton) and it is worth noting that they do not consider most obstetrical lacerations or other genital tract trauma as a complication. (Women, however, understandably do. If the same destruction was levelled at men or children there would be justifiable outrage.) Thirty two percent of women who had vaginal deliveries had complications before or during delivery. This figure does not include VBACs (vaginal births after cesarean). Including VBACs would increase the figure of 32 percent. The rate of assisted vaginal deliveries (vacuum extractor and forceps) averages around 16-17 percent of all vaginal deliveries in Canada. In my home province of Alberta, the worst in the land, the rate is higher. Calgary's rate is 22.6 percent of all attempted vaginal deliveries (17.8 percent vacuum extractor, 3.3 percent forceps) and East Central Alberta is even worse with a rate of 23.3 percent (14.8 percent vacuum extractor, 6.5 percent forceps). Inductions account for 21.3 percent of all deliveries. The average episiotomy rate was 23.8 percent in 2000-2001 (Minister of Public Works and Government Services Canada; Canadian Institute for Health Informaton). The rate of assisted deliveries, episiotomies and cesareans vary widely across the country. There are certain trends. Where cesarean rates are higher the rate of assisted deliveries goes down. When the episiotomy rate goes down the rate of spontaneous lacerations goes up. One of the most common comments I hear from mothers who have had vaginal deliveries or emergency cesareans after reaching second stage is "*I did not know that would happen or that it happens so frequently. Why wasn't I told this would happen?*" In truth there is no good reason women aren't informed of these risks.

Emergency cesareans, done for complications arising from labour and/or delivery or when the mother is pushed to the point of exhaustion by sleep deprivation, the force of contractions and the hours or days spent in excruciating pain, have serious consequences for both mother and baby. Often obstetrical researchers and medical staff use terrifying (and true) statistics from these unplanned cesareans to denigrate maternal request cesareans when they know full well these two procedures are not comparable. Assisted vaginal deliveries carry more risk for mothers and their babies than those already associated with spontaneous vaginal births. Most young women are not made aware of the high level of sexual dysfunction women experience after a vaginal birth. Intercourse can become painful, their vaginas too large or the nerve damage to their genitalia and pelvic region renders them incapable of sensation or with chronic pain. The toll on intimate relationships and self-esteem among women who have sustained this damage is incalculable.

Anti-cesarean bias is abundant in obstetrics. Obstetrical caregivers in Canada claim that vaginal birth following a normal pregnancy is safer for mother and child than a cesarean section and that cesarean section is abnormal (SOGC and AWHONN). The independent U.S. National Institute of Health states that "available information comparing the risks and benefits of maternal request cesarean delivery versus planned vaginal birth do not provide the basis for a recommendation in either direction" (U.S. National Institute of Health). Who is lying? If planned vaginal deliveries are safer than planned cesarean births we would expect to see evidence of that in several ways. Anecdotal evidence and quality, scientifically honest research would support that bias. It does not.

If planned vaginal births were safer than planned cesarean births Birth Trauma Canada (and other similar organizations that non-judgmentally support and listen to women with traumatizing childbirth experiences) would hear horror stories from those with planned cesareans. Yet the overwhelming majority of these stories are about planned vaginal deliveries, not planned cesareans. The overwhelming majority of women who contact us have psychological and physical damage related to planned vaginal births—spontaneous, assisted and emergency laboured cesareans. This reality is confirmed by every organization similar to ours across the world.

Quality hospitals with competent medical staff routinely and consistently perform planned cesareans with fewer—often considerably fewer—adverse events and morbidity for both mothers and their babies than possible with planned vaginal deliveries. This has been true for years. Armed with knowledge of this reality the situation fails to be about how safe planned cesareans are. Clearly they *can* be done safer than planned vaginal deliveries. It becomes a far more sinister question about why substandard hospitals and incompetent medical personnel can't (or won't) do them safely.

Further, if planned cesarean births were inherently more dangerous than planned vaginal deliveries we would never expect to see a hospital or region with high cesarean rates and low (or no) maternal mortality, yet this is a reality at many quality hospitals in Canada and around the world. Again, we need to ask the uncomfortable question about why all hospitals won't do this.

There are limited suitable answers to this question. First, those maintaining the status quo and denigrating a woman's right to reproductive choice in obstetrics do so because they profit from the status quo. Systemic misogyny that persistently places women as second class citizens is the other reason.

I have yet to read one quality study supporting the safety of planned vaginal deliveries over planned cesareans. This isn't to say there are no studies claiming to prove planned vaginal births are safest for both mother and baby. There are hundreds of them but, in my position as Executive Director of Birth Trauma Canada, I've come to realize that not all information is valuable. In obstetrics most of it is not.

Women are told cesareans increase their risk of infection, postpartum hemorrhage, blood clots, pain, recovery time and length of hospital stay. What they are not told is that the first five are only true in substandard hospitals with incompetent medical personnel or with emergency cesareans (which are planned vaginal deliveries). The length of hospital stay is, and always has been, primarily a function of how long hospitals get paid to keep you in them. Quality hospitals routinely and consistently perform planned cesareans with fewer adverse events than possible with planned vaginal deliveries and that has been true for years. They do this by paying attention to hospital (and their own) cleanliness and aseptic technique during surgery and by using prophylactic antibiotics. A good anesthesiologist can manage surgical and post surgical pain so the mother experiences neither. A good surgeon has a number of techniques to minimize adhesions and minimize trauma to soft tissue during cesarean surgery. Compression stockings, early mobility and blood thinners are tools used to manage thromboembolitic risks. None of these things are new. They have existed for decades. There is no better proof of misogyny in obstetrics than the phrase "too posh to push" levelled at women who want to avoid the risks associated with planned vaginal deliveries by planning cesarean births. No one else undergoing surgery is subjected to this abuse.

Without access to quality reporting concerning individual hospital quality of care women don't have the information they need to make informed decisions about how they give birth or where. This lack of accountability and transparency is a serious problem with the health care system in Canada. I want to also point out that the variation among hospitals with respect to cesarean births also applies to vaginal births. There is also huge, risk adjusted variation in the rates of episiotomies, assisted vaginal deliveries, postpartum hemorrhage, third- and fourth-degree obstetrical lacerations, blood transfusions and infections among hospitals in Canada for those giving birth vaginally. Those women who desire a planned vaginal delivery have the right to know which hospitals are safer for them.

Poor quality obstetrical research and bias are used to deny women effective pain relief during vaginal childbirth. Obstetrics is the only medical specialty that denies effective pain relief to women when the technology and skills exist to provide that service. I once asked a midwife why she was so opposed to epidurals. She had a raft of "studies" denigrating them as unsafe that she used to back her claim. None of them passed scientific muster. One by one I deconstructed each study and showed her why these claims were bogus. I asked the same question again. Her answer this time was that "*Women needed to suffer terrible pain and sorrow to keep them from becoming too powerful. Women who weren't made submissive risk upsetting the natural order of the world.*" Internalized misogyny is still misogyny and it is a sad fact that some women can be very cruel to other women. Upsetting the 'natural order of the world' is a sentiment eerily echoed by the Canadian Association of Midwives in the 2007 version of their position paper against maternal request cesareans. They stated that "*Cesarean surgery on demand will have disastrous social and financial consequences for health internationally.*" They were subjected to justifiable criticism for their viciousness in blaming women who choose cesarean section for destroying the social and financial fabric of the world. Only after this criticism did they revise the wording to something less inflammatory but their initial honesty revealed a level of misogyny that pervades all levels of obstetrical care. This attitude is not exclusive to midwives.

Bias and poor quality research have been factors in several past abuses of women in obstetrics. Generations of women were subjected to routine episiotomies. Physicians knew the majority of women giving birth the first time would sustain second-degree obstetrical lacerations. The rest would sustain 3rd or 4th degree lacerations. They reasoned that deliberately cutting a second-degree laceration would prevent the more severe lacerations that involved the anal sphincters and that repairs to a straight incision would be easier to repair than the jagged ones that would inevitably result from spontaneous vaginal births. Routine episiotomies became the standard for decades. Studies supporting routine episiotomies were commonplace. All of them were flawed. None of them were scientifically literate or scientifically honest. Routine episiotomies increase the risk of third- and fourth-degree obstetrical lacerations, a realization that would require decades to admit. The evidence to support the reality that routine episiotomies did not protect the pelvic floor was always there but it was never subjected to quality review. Like all medical biases, it was made legitimate and entrenched through an absence of evidence based science and rational thought. As a consequence millions of women were subjected to an obstetrical policy that made their lives worse.

The same plethora of studies supported the "twilight sleep" chapter in obstetrical history; none were based on sound evidence. Women gave birth strapped to a table in the lithotomy position, often delivered with forceps, after being drugged with scopolamine and morphine. They would scream in agony because morphine is not very effective against the excruciating pain of childbirth, especially in the low doses necessary to avoid death or damage to their baby. Modern women know scopolamine better as a date rape drug. It erases memory. This was how women gave birth until the late 1960s (mid- 1970s in Canada) before it was considered too barbaric. That realization took three decades.

Relation to Larger Motherhood Movement

What does this all mean in relation to the larger motherhood movement? I believe we can all accept that a society that values mothers is also one that has entrenched policies recognizing maternal autonomy and diversity. Obstetrics is considered the last frontier of feminist influence and thought. Women have long struggled to achieve their basic human rights in all aspects of society from financial independence to reproductive rights. That forward trajectory has resulted in the first generation of childbearing women truly raised to believe they are equal and that they are not second-class citizens. Yet, we still have a society that treats mothers as undervalued members of society. Their real worth is not acknowledged and pregnancy is used as an excuse to ignore their universal human rights to agency, autonomy and security of person. That disconnect can't continue in any society that wants to be considered enlightened and progressive. The larger motherhood movement recognizes that and Birth Trauma Canada is one organization working to make that enlightenment a reality. We recognize the value of mothers (and their supporters) working cohesively together for positive change; indeed it is the only way progress in the area of human rights for women has ever been achieved. It is mothers who must wrestle control away from those wishing to maintain or increase their market share of a lucrative birthing industry by dictating to women what is "natural" or "normal" or best for them. Humans very rarely do the right thing when they profit from doing the wrong thing.

A genuine respect for maternal autonomy is critical to the motherhood movement and it is central to Birth Trauma Canada's mandate. Mothers need to fight for their own maternal autonomy while respecting every other woman's right to her own maternal autonomy whether they agree with their choices or not. Removing the right to individual autonomy has always been an effective means to control other humans and it is often done under the guise of beneficence and empowerment. It is not choice if the only choice they have is to agree with those controlling them. Birth Trauma Canada can act as an instrument for change but we need mothers to endorse the principles we hold dear. One organization has only a feeble chance of forcing transformational change. The whole motherhood movement, however, is a formidable force. I want to be very clear about the principles involved in establishing the supremacy of maternal autonomy and I believe all mothers will view them as self-evident. These are the principles we will continue to advocate for. We can't change the past but we can change the future.

- We need to stop being a mother-bashing society. Mothers are subjected to enormous pressure from the moment they become pregnant. Every generation of mothers contends with a new choir of the self-righteous singing a different song about what women do wrong as mothers. The problem is systemic. Each generation brings new 'experts' in public health, obstetrics and pediatrics, armed with bad science, self-righteous arrogance and their own prejudices, to clarify for women what good motherhood looks like. Years pass, old directives are laid to rest but the mothers subjected to shame and abuses because of them are never apologized to or given restitution. There are many ways to be a good mother that vary with each mother. Until we, as a society, understand and appreciate that we won't ever value mothers.
- No mother should be subjected to ridicule, insults, coercion, threats, manipulation and humiliation by their families, friends, other mothers or by any working in the field of women's health.
- Human suffering and morbidity are not normal. They do not become normal when they happen to women. Normalizing the abnormal has always been how the wicked justify cruelty.
- Women have the ethical and legal right to complete, unbiased, unvarnished, scientifically honest information about all the risks associated

with planned vaginal births and planned caesarean births and they have the right to use that information to make informed decisions about the birth option best for them based on the risks they are willing to accept. Anything less is a denial of their right to informed consent. This includes honest statistical information related to the competence of the individual obstetrical care provider(s) and the quality of care at the hospital they are considering as a birth place and it means they get to choose where they birth and who they birth with based on that information. I think we have to levy significant fines on journals that publish bad science or statistically dishonest research and hospitals and birth centres must be legally required to make an independent assessment of their quality of care publicly accessible.

•Women must be recognized as the diverse individuals they are. No two are alike, nor should we expect them to be. Some women are empowered by pain and adversity. Others see nothing noble in suffering. They are both right. There can be no cookie cutter obstetrics. There is no single correct way to give birth.

•Maternal request caesarean section is a legitimate and justifiable birth option for those women wishing to avoid the risks of a planned vaginal delivery. To denigrate or deny this birth option is a clear violation of a woman's right to benefit from scientific advancement.

•Home birthing is an option for those women desiring that option and the barriers placed to prevent them should be replaced with policies to make them possible and safer. Demonizing or criminalizing women who opt for home births or unassisted births is inexcusable. The overwhelming majority of women making these choices do so after experiencing hospital births and they have determined avoiding the inhumanity of another hospital birth is a better option. Given the stories I hear of, on a near daily basis, their position is understandable. They have no other options available to make sure they control their birth experience. The answer is to make hospital births less inhumane to them or give them the resources necessary to make birthing at home a safer option. For decades the medical establishment, with the full cooperation of the state, has deliberately placed legal and monetary barriers to home births by refusing to allow the most qualified obstetrical care providers to attend and by making scientific advancements available only in hospitals. Their behaviour speaks more about the need to control women than beneficence.

•The state and the medical profession should never have the legal right to force women to birth in a manner that is unacceptable to them.

•There is no place for fanaticism and ideology in obstetrics that cannot be backed with facts, nor is there any place in obstetrics for encouraging unrealistic expectations of childbirth. When we dismiss or trivialize the very real risks mothers face we also dismiss and under value them.

Obstetrics can't continue as a contest of beliefs fuelled by the fanaticism of some.

•A women's right to privacy and dignity must be respected.

•Obstetrics must be mother-centred. Mothers must occupy a position at the apex of the obstetrical hierarchy instead of left to flounder somewhere near the middle or the bottom. There can only be one ultimate authority on what is best for mothers and that is the woman herself.

•Sadists, those with sexual perversions and those thrilled by violence to women are screened before they can gravitate to careers in women's health. This applies equally to men and women.

•People who wish to force all women to birth naturally, who themselves live unnatural lives availing themselves of technology and human innovation, should be recognized as the hypocrites they are.

•Extreme pain, lack of control and lack of privacy and dignity cause post-traumatic stress and depression. Reducing this means women must have control over all three.

•Women have the right to birth experiences that don't leave them feeling raped and I say that fully aware of how loaded that word is. I have been unsuccessful in finding another term that adequately describes the experiences I have heard since 1998. Prior consent by the mother, gained without duress and with full disclosure, is required for anything that will be done to her or could be done to her.

•The needs of women are not the same as the needs of obstetrical caregivers. When women are armed with that knowledge they can better recognize obstetrical bias and lobbying and guard themselves against it. Obstetrical caregivers will act to increase/maintain their market share of a lucrative birthing industry. It is in their best interest to denigrate certain birth options (and oppose maternal autonomy) if they don't possess the skills or ability to profit from them, if their careers depend on that behaviour or if it makes their job easier. Often they cloak their aspirations with terms like empowerment or beneficence when that is patently untrue. They are not god-like. They have the same character flaws as any other human.

Birth Trauma Canada will continue, as we have since 1998, to advocate on behalf of mothers. We will continue to listen to mothers, offer validation and understanding and serve as a forum for their views and comments anonymously. We will continue to be a strong and passionate feminist voice for mothers.

Conclusion

No woman should be forced to give birth in a manner that is unacceptable to her. Making an informed decision about what is acceptable to her requires honest, unbiased, evidence-based information about all the risks associated with planned vaginal deliveries and planned cesarean deliveries. The woman, and only the woman, has to assess those risks and decide which, if any, of those risks she is personally willing to take. She has the right to do so without bullying, coercion, manipulation, threats or judgement. As an individual each woman will assess risks differently and obstetrical caregivers must be prepared to work for women competently within those expectations. If those expectations don't match their ideology they should respectfully suggest another obstetrical caregiver who does possess the required attitude. It means prospective mothers need clear and easy access to hospital quality of care statistics so they can decide where to birth *and* they have to be given the right to make that decision. New mothers must have the right to rate their childbirth experience and their caregivers anonymously and that information has to be gathered outside the medical community to ensure honesty and impartiality. Mothers are not mere vessels for something more precious. They are just as precious. They are the fundamental reason we exist as a species and have a society. The fact they will sacrifice so much for the benefit of their children should not be used as a license for cruelty.

[1]It is worth noting that the Obstetric and Neonatal Nurses of the United States (AWOHONN) did not endorse this position paper and it has been condemned by a number of medical and birthing support organizations around the world, including Birth Trauma Canada.

Works Cited

Canadian Institute for Health Information. *Giving Birth in Canada: Regional Trends from 2001-2002 to 2005-2006.* Ottawa: Author, 2007.

Minister of Public Works and Government Services Canada.*Canadian Perinatal Health Report.* Ottawa: Author, 2003.

Society of Obstetricians and Gynaecologists of Canada (SOGC) and the Association of Women's Health, Obstetric and Neonatal Nurses of Canada (AWHONN) Canada. "Joint Policy Statement." *Journal of Obstetrics and Gynaecoloy Canada* 30.12 (2008): 1163-1165

U.S. National Institute of Health. *Cesarean Delivery on Maternal Request.* March 29, 2006.

Wu, Jennifer M. et al. "Forecasting the Prevalence of Pelvic Floor Disorders in U.S. Women: 2010-2050." *Obstetrics and Gynecology* 114.6 (December 2009): 1278-1283.

6.
Maternity Coalition

Australia's National Maternity Consumer Advocacy Organization

LAREEN NEWMAN, KERREEN REIGER AND MONICA CAMPO

THIS CHAPTER TELLS THE STORY of the Maternity Coalition (MC), an Australian advocacy organization which represents an often "forgotten" strand of the women's movement—the maternalist feminist emphasis on reclaiming women's rights in birth and breastfeeding (Reiger, *Our Bodies*). Having originated in the late 1980s to lobby state government inquiries for improved maternity services in the Australian states of New South Wales (NSW) and Victoria, by 2008 the organization was established nationally and was acknowledged as a key stakeholder in the incoming federal government's agenda for improving maternity care. This chapter first examines how the Maternity Coalition developed, its rationale and mothering discourse, and then considers challenges that the organization faces in the early twenty-first century. Developing from a state-based to a national organization, MC faces internal sustainability difficulties in terms of communicating and managing a voluntary organization mostly comprised of busy young mothers. The external challenges are also considerable—MC aims to change the entrenched system of maternity services but in a cultural context which values technology and professional expertise and a political economic context in which the medical profession holds significant power. Nonetheless, Australia's Maternity Coalition has achieved a national profile and credibility, bringing women's rights to options and optimal care in birth to public attention at a level not achieved in many comparable countries.

History, Purpose and Philosophy

In the 1980s several developments laid the groundwork for what would emerge as the Maternity Coalition (MC). Childbirth groups supporting normal birth and decrying excessive medicalization in maternity care had been established in Australia from the late 1960s, rapidly expanding in the 1970s in the context of the women's movement. In Australia, and to a lesser extent elsewhere, childbirth education, homebirth and breastfeeding support groups, of mostly white and middle class women, formed a separate "movement" to the mainstream feminist women's health movement. The movement is best interpreted as maternalist;

that is, emphasizing women's embodied knowledge and mothering roles (Reiger, *Reconceiving Citizenship; Our Bodies)*. MC as an organization went further than support groups, developing a more political role primarily focused on advocacy for improved maternity care. How MC has interpreted that mission has varied locally but reflects its beginnings in political activities around the government reviews of birthing services in the states of NSW and Victoria in the late 1980s. In exploring key factors that have shaped the organization's philosophy and purpose, the following discussion also reveals wider social and organizational challenges facing the international movement to "reclaim" women's autonomy in childbirth (Goer).

MC began in mid-1988 as a Task Force of a Sydney-based consumer group, Maternity Alliance (MA). MA had commenced in June 1987 in response to the need for effective, rather than tokenistic, consumer input into the NSW review of obstetrics (the Shearman Review). MA's stress was on being a *consumer* organization, reflecting the influence of the recently developed Consumer Health Forum. The Alliance achieved two consumer representatives and a midwife on the NSW review. Responding to the initiative of MA representatives, a specific Victorian group formed to lobby the Birthing Services Review (BSR). The background to the Review already lay in local activism, especially through the direct precursor to what became MC—Mothers & Midwives Action (MAMA). MAMA had gained political support for maternity reform from key women politicians and from feminist health bureaucrats, and problems with perinatal care had been identified by the *Why Women's Health* report in 1985 (Reiger). The Victorian Taskforce of MA initially focused on forming a flexible umbrella group to prepare a major submission, and succeeded in getting the message out to women that the review team wanted to hear a broad range of voices. A variety of skills and backgrounds contributed to effective action: Gennie MacGregor from MAMA understood the background politics, and Irene Shaw was a member of the Review consultative group but also a childbirth educator and researcher of the birth centre movement. Along with homebirth groups, the involvement of those supporting technological birth, including multiple birth and neonatal death support groups, led to some lively debates over changing birth practices to better benefit women.

In the process of engaging with the Review, the Victorian Task Force moved away from Maternity Alliance (MA) primarily over philosophical differences of opinion about organizational processes. The MA general committee strongly held the position that professionals could not hold office in a "consumer" organization and also discouraged actual branches, preferring only informal flexible groups. In Victoria, while midwives were not strongly involved in the Task Force itself, they were essential participants in the precursor organization MAMA, which emphasized mothers' and midwives' shared interests in changing the system of maternity care. Maternity Coalition then also encouraged a *coalition* of women and midwives. While it formed as an umbrella group in which smaller organizations retained independence and freedom such as in local networking, MC sought a coherent organizational direction based on advocacy.

Top: Maternity Coalition Rally, c2004. Bottom: Pooling Resources at Birth Information Night.

In the early-mid 1990s MC's main focus was on promoting the outcome of the Victorian review. The review report, *Having a Baby in Victoria* (1990) gave strong policy support to implementing the concept of women-centered and family-friendly care, such as through family birth centers and an increased professional role for the (then nurse-trained) midwives staffing the hospital system, as well as the few working independently in community-based practice. Midwives had begun to develop new professional networks and heightened consciousness of the need for system change and to practice more autonomously than as obstetric nurses.

Nationally, maternity reform was also given formal legitimacy during the 1990s, first in NSW and Victoria, then later in Western Australia and South Australia and at federal level (Reiger, *Neoliberal Quickstep*). While Queensland came later to this process, it was home to important advocacy groups, especially the Home Midwifery Association that developed a complex network of homebirth groups. In sum then, the mandate of MC was to promote change within the maternity care system and to use community gatherings to bring attention to problems faced by women as new mothers. In its role of watchdog over the slow implementation of reform, MC in Victoria developed not only as a support group but also as a formal organization that was increasingly seen by health managers and bureaucrats as credible and representative in lobbying. MC remained small in terms of direct membership, but the largely Melbourne-based group developed a constitution in 1991, and incorporated as a charitable organization that provided the basis for later geographical expansion.

The working committee of MC was bound by commitment to the social value of mothering, as both physiological and social process. Close personal ties were forged over several years: as a community with a shared interest in women's lives as mothers, MC brought old and new members together, more babies arrived, toddlers grew into teenagers, marriages dissolved and families re-formed, and women's paid jobs had to be juggled. Informal monthly meetings were held over weekend lunches, often in a members' home or later in community locations, in a largely unsuccessful effort to become more socially inclusive. MC membership however, has unfortunately remained predominantly white middle class, albeit with the goal of working for improvements to benefit *all* women. Regular MC meetings were eventually arranged to overlap over lunch with meetings of Midwives in Private Practice, bringing some midwives and MC mothers together in a shared agenda. Compared with the emphasis on "intensive mothering" common in some homebirth and breastfeeding groups, a fairly pragmatic approach to styles of mothering and managing paid work became accepted in MC, possibly reflecting diverse interests of professional women, including midwives. Commitment to promoting normal physiological birth and to supporting breastfeeding has remained the taken-for-granted basis of MC's philosophy.

By the mid-1990s the goals and philosophy of MC were formally articulated, becoming refined over time as follows:

> Maternity Coalition is a national non-profit, non-political and non-sectarian consumer advocacy organization in Australia. The organization acts as an umbrella to bring together support groups and individuals for effective lobbying, information sharing, networking and support in maternity services across Australia. It works to unite women in their efforts and to share skills and resources to achieve beneficial changes in the health care system in the interests of improving birthing services. It was developed to support both consumer and midwife participation at all levels of health policy planning, decision-making and service delivery.

Executive Meeting South Australian birth groups.

The philosophy of the Maternity Coalition is to:

- •encourage a woman-centered approach to the birth process;
- •regard pregnancy and childbirth as normal physiological processes, not illnesses;
- •stress the social, cultural and psychological factors influencing childbirth;
- •support midwives as the primary caregivers for women in normal birth;
- •emphasize women's rights to make informed choices about their caregiver and place of birth;
- •promote continuous assessment and critical evaluation of technologies used in maternity care;
- •support the development of services sensitive to women's varied cultural and physical needs. (Source: www.maternitycoalition.org.au)

As the organization grew into the later 1990s, the MC journal *Birth Matters* was inaugurated in April 1997 by founding member Irene Shaw to offer a steady flow of information-sharing as a base for further advocacy action. Early issues, in a similar way to more recent ones, report frustration at the difficulty of changing hospital practices in spite of MC submissions and contributions to government consultations and committees. They have also regularly included birth stories and articles on what is often now termed "gentle" or "natural" mothering. New people coming onto the MC committee increased the passion and energy for political advocacy efforts, soon seeking to expand MC's work beyond Victoria as networking increased. In a cultural environment where health awareness was becoming more common, then president Robyn Payne established the "Choices for Childbirth" public birth information series in Melbourne in 1999, with similar programs emerging in other areas. Under Robyn's leadership the governance of MC continued to be reviewed to maintain a range of skills and interests in the organization, including balancing mothers and midwives in formal positions. For many years, MC successfully managed the possible conflicts between their interests, involving midwives on the committee such as Jenny Parratt as treasurer and Joy Johnston in editing *Birth Matters*. Although the MC Management Committee recognized that a more socially and culturally diverse community base of women was desirable, MC's mandate was an umbrella group to advocate at various levels for improved maternity services. To this end, bringing new members on board slowly was regarded as important, allowing them to become familiar with the enormous and increasing range of information about birth and maternity care, the local policy context, and the culture and principles of MC, which had gained it considerable legitimacy with health professionals and bureaucrats.

Maternity Coalition in the Twenty-first Century

By the 2000s members from other states were seeking expansion of MC in light of developments in their own states and at federal government level. The midwifery profession was also mobilizing for change through conferences and the nationally funded Australian Midwifery Action Research project. In several Australian states this was a period of major shake-up in the health sector, including closures of rural units, and community concern about the health implications of policies promoting early discharge after birth but with a decline in maternal and child health support. In a conscious effort to expand, the Victorian MC committee supported its relatively new Canberra members Barb Vernon and Justine Caines to attend the annual MC meeting in Melbourne in November 2001. They accepted an invitation to stand as, respectively, MC President and Media Officer, and a new era of development began. A period of major advance for MC as an increasingly national voluntary organization was made possible both by members' increased access to information technologies, and by a political climate in which midwifery was becoming more assertive as a profession and health departments somewhat more responsive to consumer advocacy.

Going National: The National Maternity Action Plan

The first real blueprint for overall reform of Australia's maternity services—the National Maternity Action Plan (NMAP)—was developed by a coalition of groups, notably by MC's revitalized leadership team along with the Australian Society of Independent Midwives, and Community Midwifery WA (http://www.maternitycoalition.org.au/nmap/nmap.html). The NMAP greatly extended MC's agenda and profile. It strongly emphasized women's right to choose a known midwife to care for them throughout pregnancy, birth and the first few weeks after birth as both the optimal model of evidence-based care (Sakala and Corry) and as a human right of women in reproduction.

Advancing the seemingly radical agenda of NMAP—that is seeking to challenge the obstetric-led maternity care system—attracted professional and political attention and gave MC increased visibility. By the mid- to late 2000s MC was firmly established with a local president and one or more branches in every state and territory, although patterns of local activity varied. In Queensland, local advocacy efforts placed maternity reform on the political agenda for the first time and established MC as an articulate voice. In some states many of the more active MC members were also active members of other groups with a similar purpose and philosophy, with MC acting as an effective umbrella organization, channeling information between state and national levels. This meant easier planning of joint events such as public birth information nights, and shared efforts in promoting normal birth and midwifery care (e.g., at regional Parents and Babies Expos), while state groups could still be involved in national reform campaigns. On the other hand, in other states MC was *the* main organization and benefited from having just one broad membership base. As MC's profile and credibility increased, MC members were also invited by many local health departments, hospitals and midwifery educators to sit on various committees as consumer representatives. MC also gained valuable support in some states from local politicians, particularly women politicians, who were sympathetic to its cause and who offered some opportunities to meet Ministers, or helped MC executive members build their understanding of how to effectively advocate to politicians.

Organizational Challenges and Future Directions

MC continues to face challenges in two main areas: first, the *internal* issues associated with sustaining a national organization run totally by volunteers and, second, *external* issues associated with advocating physiologically normal birth within a professional and political environment which continues to resist fundamental change to the mainstream system of medicalized birth. In view of both sets of challenges, it is hardly surprising that tensions and struggles regarding the focus, philosophy and strategies of the group continue to generate internal tension and test the strength of purpose and connectedness which motivates mostly mothers, but a few men also, to belong to MC.

Internal Organizational Challenges

As MC grew beyond the initial one or two states, it faced challenges because its internal organizational processes and structures no longer met the needs of what was becoming a national organization. By 2007 several unresolved issues started to stand in the way of further expansion. Accordingly a small Federal government grant was sought and obtained by then national MC President, Louise Hartley. This allowed MC to bring state/territory presidents and other delegates face-to-face in two workshops to discuss the mission and strategies to move the organization effectively into the twenty-first century. Several structural challenges had to be addressed, especially relationships between national, state and regional branches, with emerging local grassroots entities, and with midwifery organizations.

The "Choices for Childbirth" public education seminars and, more latterly, the "Birth & Babies" (BaBs) mothers' support groups were never officially included in the organizational accountability and reporting structures. Furthermore, in states where MC is not the sole maternity consumer advocacy organization, diverse groups often have different philosophical or strategic focus points, such as homebirth advocacy (including the practice of "free birth"), caesarean birth awareness, or community antenatal education. Their different views of mothering in turn affect their capacity to work together or to attract a broader range of mothers. Some groups, for example, have an additional focus on radical feminist activism, "attachment parenting" and extended breastfeeding, and on organic foods, natural clothing and natural living. As they vary in their self-identification, some therefore prefer to remain small and independent.

All local groups work to improve maternity services and experiences for women, especially valuing and promoting midwifery services. Although MC started as an explicit collaboration between birthing women and midwives, by the mid-2000s, as midwives established a heightened sense of professional identity, state authorities, and some members, encouraged the discursive positioning of MC more specifically as a health *consumer* organization. Whilst the "mothers-midwives coalition" remains important, it has therefore become less pivotal to MC organizational identity and the balance between focusing on midwifery interests and "consumer" issues has remained controversial. The diverse community-based birthing groups have nonetheless continued to work successfully with midwives on many occasions to run public events either under a local banner or under the MC banner. In several locations in 2007-8, shared events included for example screenings of the Ricki Lake documentary film, *The Business of Being Born*, and a protest outside the federal parliament in response to changes to insurance and registration requirements around home birth midwifery access in 2009.

In a country as large as Australia, and with only the limited funds from membership and local fundraising, MC's communication challenges have been considerable. It has been difficult for state presidents to come together or even to meet with regional representatives to build the relationships required for concerted advocacy efforts. The Internet has enabled a shared interactive national online list-serve, and some at local levels, and email and teleconferences also allow office bearers and members to work together more effectively, such as on the national newsletter, although such "distanciated" relationships cannot replace the interpersonal trust and local knowledge of "real time and space." Conflicts and misunderstandings, which can become especially acute in the emotionally-laden field of childbirth, can also become amplified in the absence of personal bonds and knowledge of each other.

Sustaining involvement is also a challenge in an organization run by volunteers who are at the same time mostly mothers with young children and families to care for, and often also women in part-time or full-time paid work. Not only are those most active in the organization at risk of finding themselves burnt-out from working a "triple shift" (mothering and caring work, paid work outside the home, unpaid advocacy work) but for many, activism around birth is part of a life cycle stage, soon replaced by joining kindergarten and school groups as their children grow up. Those with longest involvement have often been midwives, researchers, or activists who go on to doula, or midwifery training, finding their involvement to be a great opportunity to "bond in sisterhood" to work to improve women's lives. The shared commitment to widening women's birthing options, especially birth centers and homebirth, and to improving mainstream hospital-based services, has remained MC's central focus, but has also been challenged by the external political environment.

Confronting the Challenges of Political Advocacy

The *external* challenges faced by the Maternity Coalition include the continuing power of the medical lobby and of a biomedical paradigm which diminishes women's agency in reproduction (Rothman, *In Labour*; Martin) and contributes to the cultural dominance of medicalized birth. The Australian Federal Government's National Review of Maternity Services in 2008-9 generated a key period of mobilization and consumed an enormous amount of MC's time and energy, although with very disappointing and demoralizing results. Auspiced by a reformist Labor government elected in late 2007 as part of its larger health reform agenda, the MSR was responding to several pressures for reform of the maternity system, significantly those put on the agenda by MC via the NMAP in 2002. MC leaders played a key stakeholder role in the MSR process, notably Justine Caines (also representing Homebirth Australia) who contributed enormously to public media discussion. From the initial consulting period, there was genuine optimism that changes to the power dynamic of Australian maternity care were a real possibility.

MC advocates, and others in related organizations, worked tirelessly to encourage women to write submissions to the Review, providing templates and holding gatherings where women submitted letters "en masse," advocating for the right to be able to choose their own midwife and birthplace. Following its formal report in February 2009, the MSR resulted in legislation to facilitate new arrangements for midwives and nurse practitioners, designed to enable those of them registered as "eligible" professionals to access state health insurance (Medicare) rebates and pharmaceutical benefits, along with indemnity insurance. However, as such "eligible" midwives are now required to work in "collaborative arrangements" with obstetricians or hospitals, a new form of control has been instituted over both women's choices and midwives' practice. Despite vigorous campaigning by mothers and supporters—a 3000 strong rally to protest outside the national Parliament, letter writing, media work and meetings with politicians—the legislation was passed in 2010. Activism around the MSR has confirmed the power of the medical lobby and hence also revealed the limitations of women's role as consumers and their political effectiveness in changing a mainstream system.

Gaining and Maintaining Credibility as a Voice for Women

While Maternity Coalition gained a heightened public profile during the MSR process, members nevertheless had difficulty representing a coherent public voice. Internal differences emerged within MC itself, between MC and other groups, and within the midwifery community. These continue to reflect longstanding tensions which split the Australian homebirth movement in the early 1990s and which MC had since sought to overcome. Some saw the struggle over the MSR primarily as *ideological*, requiring a huge cultural paradigm shift to remove childbirth, an intrinsically "natural part of life," entirely away from government or medical control. They draw on counter cultural, and often essentialist, radical feminist imagery to emphasize women's embodied capacities and the importance of rejecting mainstream services. Others instead interpret maternity reform in more pragmatic and reformist terms as using state policy to slowly change a health system to ensure greater equity for socially disadvantaged women as well as offer increased choices and autonomy for all. In spite of some overlap of objectives and shared strategies, both strands within the birth movement are evident within MC, which also faces continued challenges associated with public image. Unlike in the 1970s, "alternative" birthing is not exactly fashionable in a contemporary technocratic, risk-oriented and celebrity-obsessed culture.

Medical dominance is so taken for granted in Australia that few women question it, or even see that the adverse health outcomes they often experience with birth are caused by the way the system is often set up to fail them (and not to provide, for example, the emotional care and time they need to give birth under their own steam), so that women have no option but instead to "trust" their doctors, and then blame themselves and their own bodies for negative experiences of birth and early motherhood (Campo). Reflecting the cultural dominance of biomedicine, the media also often derogatively present birth advocacy groups as "hippies" and "feminists" driven by ideology and irrational hatred of "modern" medicine (e.g. Devine). It is usually doctors and their organizations, rather than women and their midwifery advocates, who are then sought for opinion by journalists. As a volunteer-run organization supported by a relatively narrow membership base, MC struggles to compete with the united front presented by powerful medical interests supported by paid executive officers, paid professional media teams, etc. During the MSR for example, doctors lobbied vigorously in favor of supporting the status-quo of medically-led birth. While they claimed achieving low levels of infant and maternal mortality rates as their success, they ignored evidence presented concerning high levels of maternal morbidity—postnatal depression, post-traumatic stress disorder, relatively high levels of caesarean and perineal trauma, and low breastfeeding rates.

Ironically, the constraints of neo-liberal health care provision both open up new possibilities for health care reform, including stress on increased "choices" in childbirth, but also constrain the agendas (Reiger, *Neoliberal Quickstep*). Health professionals and policy advisors with a "health-risk" rather than "wellness" attitude to pregnancy and birth provide the main input to the service system design, planning and management, often marginalizing attempts by women as consumers seeking service redesign to be more woman-centered. A decade and more of conservative governments has seen the demise of many feminist-oriented agencies within federal and state bureaucracies, limiting MC's capacity to mobilize support outside of health policy decision-making. However, in advocating for women's needs, MC has benefited from the resources now associated with health consumer advocacy more generally, and from having well-educated members with skills to use the Internet to gather and analyze the same scientific research evidence to which doctors alone traditionally had access. MC has also been supported in this regard by some members whose professional lives in academia (feminist and women's studies, midwifery, sociology, and public health in particular) facilitates informed critique of the status quo, challenges medical views, and highlights research on models of care which give more benefit to women (see, e.g., Newman, *Why Planned Attended Homebirth; Health Care System*). MC has also had support from some professional groups whose mandate includes increasing the provision of woman-centered care, in particular the Australian College of Midwives, and from doctors—more often in the public than the private health system—who support less medicalized models of care because they acknowledge the rights of women to be autonomous decision-makers in reproductive health care and respect the professional role of midwives.

Conclusion

That the Maternity Coalition's advocacy work for Australian women in childbirth can sometimes feel like an uphill battle is hardly surprising in view of the internal and external challenges it involves. Organizations such as MC will have a reason to exist as long as obstetrics, despite increased women entering the profession, continues to act as an institutional bastion of male domination of women, over-riding women's agency in childbirth and maintaining masculine "medicine" versus feminine "illness." The medical, scientific focus remains on mechanistic and reductionist explanations and "controlling" approaches to childbirth care, while alternative "birth models that work," emphasizing interaction, holistic care and the integrity of organisms, struggle for legitimacy and support (Davis-Floyd et al). This means that activist mothers need coalitions within a renewed women's movement in order to achieve a paradigm shift to give women their rightful and respected central place in the reproductive process. The many roles that are required to run a national organization mostly of young mothers, let alone to recruit new members and also undertake advocacy, can be very demanding. It is testimony to women's amazing energy, abilities, creative force and passion that women-led organizations such as Maternity Coalition *are* able to exist and continue to remind us that, as Barbara Katz Rothman put it some time ago: "Birth is not only about making babies. It's about making mothers—strong, competent, capable mothers who trust themselves and believe in their inner strength" (Rothman 1996: 254).

The authors acknowledge all the women (and a few good men!) who have worked tirelessly over the years to develop MC into the national organization that it is today. They also thank the following for their helpful comments on an earlier draft of the chapter: Lisa Metcalfe, MC Immediate Past National President; Ann Catchlove, MC Acting National President; Bruce Teakle, Member of MC National Executive Committee and former MC Queensland State Branch President; and Leslie Arnott, Victorian consumer representative and former MC National President.

Works Cited

Campo, Monica. "Trust, Power and Agency in Childbirth: Women's Relationships with Obstetricians." *Outskirts: Feminisms Along the Edge* 22 (May 2010). <http://www.chloe.uwa.edu.au/outskirts/archive/volume22/campo>. Accessed: 28 August 2010.

Davis-Floyd, Robbie, Leslie Barclay and Jan Tritten, eds. *Birth Models That Work.* Berkeley: University of California Press, 2009.Devine, Miranda. "Caesarean scar mongers should zip it." *Sydney Morning Herald* 21 February 2009. <http://www.smh.com.au/opinion/caesarean-scar-mongers-should-zip-it-20090220-8dkm.html>. Accessed: 1 Sept. 2010:

Goer, Henci. "Humanizing Birth: A Global Grassroots Movement." *Birth: Issues in Perinatal Care* 31.4 (2004): 308-314.

Martin, Emily. *The Woman in the Body: A Cultural Analysis of Reproduction.* Milton Keynes: Open University Press, 1989.

Maternity Coalition. <www.maternitycoalition.org.au>.

Newman, Lareen. "Why Planned Attended Homebirth Should Be More Widely Supported in Australia." *Australian & New Zealand Journal of Obstetrics & Gynaecology* 48 (2008): 450-453.

Newman, Lareen. "The Health Care System as a Social Determinant of Health: Qualitative Insights from South Australian Maternity Consumers." *Australian Health Review* 33.1 (2008): 62-71.

Reiger, Kerreen M. "Reconceiving Citizenship: The Challenge of Mothers as Political Activists." *Feminist Theory* 1.3 (2000): 309-327.

Reiger, Kerreen M. *Our Bodies, Our Babies: The Forgotten Women's Movement.* Carlton: Melbourne University Press, 2001.

Reiger, Kerreen M. "The Neoliberal Quickstep: Contradictions in Australian Maternity Policy." *Health Sociology Review* 15.4 (2006): 330-340

Rothman, Barbara Katz. *In Labour: Women and Power in the Birthplace.* London: Junction, 1982.

Rothman, Barbara Katz. "Women Providers and Control." *Journal of Obstetric, Gynecologic, & Neonatal Nursing* 25.3 (1996): 224-256.

Sakala, Carol and M. Corry. *Evidence-Based Maternity Care: What it Is and What it Can Achieve.* 2008. Childbirth Connection, the Reforming States Group, and the Milbank Memorial Fund: <www.childbirthconnection.org/article.asp?ck=10575>. Accessed: 15 Sept. 2009.

7.

Caritas, donum vitae, pro familia, and *Sozialdienst katholischer Frauen*

Supporting Mothers and Sustaining the Next Generation of Germany

SONJA M. ALLEN

GERMANY IS CURRENTLY ENGAGED IN contentious debates, revolving around sustaining the natural birth rate. The topics of discussion include, on one hand, ways to encourage young families to grow and, on the other hand, utilizing medical procedures to determine the health of a future child through pre-implantation diagnostics and pre-natal testing.

This chapter will introduce four organizations who participate in this debate: *Caritas, donum vitae, pro familia,* and *Sozialdienst katholischer Frauen* (Social Services of Catholic Women; abbreviated as *SkF*). *Caritas* and *SkF* are closely associated with the Catholic Church and are mostly funded through them. *donum vitae* is inspired by Christian belief, but not affiliated with any religious institutions. Its offices across Germany receive financial support from respective state governments. *pro familia* is neither affiliated with a political party nor religious institutions, but receives some funding from the different levels of government for its services and programs. All four organizations are non-profit charitable organizations and rely on fundraising and volunteers for support.

The four organizations exist to support women, their families, and to promote their ideals, particularly regarding unwanted pregnancies, abortions, genetic testing, and helping women and mothers in need. Each of the four associations has its own philosophy and offers specialized services. They advocate the prevention of unwanted pregnancies; support pregnant women and mothers in crisis; offer anonymous counselling services (online, email, or in person) for infertility, family planning, adjusting to a new baby, prenatal diagnostic testing, miscarriage, stillbirth, and abortion; and give advice and provide support during pregnancy, child birth, and postpartum. Many services offered by *Caritas, donum vitae,* and *Sozialdienst katholischer Frauen (SkF)* are dedicated to helping mothers cope with motherhood and become better mothers. However, little support is offered to mothers who would like to fulfill their dreams and goals, and shape their identity outside the realm of motherhood.

This chapter will inform about the situation of mothers in Germany. I will explain the rules and regulations related to pregnancy, maternity, and motherhood, including abortion and maternity leave. Then, I will attempt to draw attention to the challenges and issues for women in Germany today. Finally, I will introduce *Caritas, donum vitae, pro familia,* and *SkF* and look at their organizational activities, challenges, future goals, as well as their contributions to the broader mothering movement.

Context

Over the past two centuries, the three waves of feminism and its associated women's movements have demanded more rights and equal opportunity for women. As such, motherhood in Germany has changed from the traditional role of home parenting, taking care of household and children, to a new model of working motherhood.

In 2008, Germany had 6.9 million mothers, who were of employable age. The percentage of women who were employed was directly related to the age of their children. Less than one third of mothers, whose children were under the age of three, pursued employment. Of those who had children in the age range three to five, six of ten mothers worked. When children attended elementary school (age six to nine), the statistics showed that 65 percent of mothers went to work. And for the age range 10-14, the proportion of mothers, who were working, increased by another five percent. These numbers alone, however, do not paint the full picture, as one also has to consider whether mothers hold full-time or part-time positions. Statistics from the same year conclude that of all employable mothers in Germany, 73 percent work on a part-time basis. Stefan Rübenach explains that part-time work allows mothers to balance their time between their career and family more efficiently, but at the same time reduces their income and contribution to a pension plan.[1]

Further differences exist between the geographical locations of the former German Democratic Republic (GDR; eastern Germany) and the former Federal Republic of Germany (FRG; western Germany), as the aforementioned geographical region benefits from a well established childcare infrastructure from pre-reunification times. Hence, almost twice as many mothers hold full-time employment in eastern Germany than in western Germany. Further reasons play a factor in this divide: mothers living in eastern Germany often need to work for economic reasons, while mothers in western Germany are encouraged and tend to choose a traditional role within their family.

Maternity Leave

Working mothers-to-be are protected by laws that outline their rights and the obligations of their employers. All employers offer to their employees government-mandated insurance, which is paid out during the mandatory maternity leave (*Mutterschutzfrist*), six weeks prior and eight weeks after the delivery or adoption. The amount of maternity benefit (*Mutterschaftsgeld*) is 67 percent of a woman's income (to a maximum of €1800 per month) and consists of a portion from the State Health Insurers, supplemented by the employer (*Arbeitgeberzuschuss*), for up to 12 months or 14 months in the case of a single parent. The following months of maternity leave, up to 36 in total, are unpaid. Maternity leave is also commonly referred to as parental leave, as a father may choose to stay home with his child for the 34 months, after the mother has finished two months of mandatory maternity leave. If another child is born during parental leave, the periods of parental leave can be served consecutively. Those mothers who were receiving unemployment benefits during pregnancy are paid fully by the State Health Insurer. The Maternity Allowance Department (*Mutterschaftsgeldstelle)* provides support for women insured through a private health insurance company, as well as women working part-time, and women insured through a family member. Self-employed persons without Sick Leave Insurance (*Krankengeldanspruch*) receive no assistance.

Fertility

According to the Statistics of the European Commission from 2007, 30 percent of women in Germany do not have children; the figure rises among female university graduates to 40 percent.[2] The average age of women in Germany bearing their first child is 30.2 years, with a trend to start a family later. This made them, in 2007, the oldest first-time mothers in Europe. Most women in Germany who have children opt to have one or two. Germany's birth rate has been for years one of the lowest in Europe with an average of 1.36 children per woman.[3]

Birth Control

Several factors contribute to this low fertility rate: the political taint and correlation of motherhood with fascism, lengthy education times, consumerism, and the fear of an uncertain future. Additionally, German women have had access to various birth control methods, which have allowed them to postpone or opt out of motherhood.

Abortion

Abortion has played a role in reducing the birth rate. In 2009, 110,694 abortions were performed in Germany.[4] However, abortion was not always legal in Germany and over the decades many battles have been fought in an effort to legalize this procedure. For example, the second women's movement in Germany demanded since the 1960s that terminating pregnancies should not be punishable. Advancements seemed to occur after 1971, when more than 350 women admitted in the German magazine *Stern* (Star) that they had aborted their fetuses. With the introduction of new oral contraceptives in the mid-twentieth century, this discussion was fueled with more controversies, since women had now the ability to prevent pregnancies with the birth control pill. The women's movement finally succeeded in Germany in the 1990s, when abortion was legally declared non-punishable, if conducted prior to the fourteenth week of pregnancy, counselling was received, and alternatives were considered.[5] By law, a woman may now terminate a pregnancy during the first twelve weeks after fertilization (fourteen weeks into the pregnancy), as long as she has received counselling from a state-recognized pregnancy counselling institution and has waited three more days before undergoing the medical procedure. Abortion beyond 14 weeks is only legal if the pregnancy poses a current or future physical or mental threat to the woman and the only available solution is to terminate the pregnancy. The diagnosis of fetal abnormalities would be one such circumstance.

An abortion costs approximately €410 and is to be paid by the patient herself. However, medical tests performed before and after the procedure and medical treatments due to complications are covered by health insurance. Abortions conducted for medical reasons or abortions of pregnancies resulting from rape are covered by the patient's insurance plan and the government respectively. Women with a low income may apply for financial aid to cover the cost of the abortion.[6]

Women in Germany, who were seeking an abortion in 1999, were confronted with two organizations stopping the issuance of counselling certification. Pope John Paul II had announced that Catholic pregnancy counselling centers (in Germany) would be disallowed to issue counselling certificates for the purpose of aborting unborn children. *Caritas* and *SkF* who have strong ties to and are (partially) funded by the Catholic Church were directly affected by this announcement and conformed to the Pope's demands.

Incentives to Have More Children

In recent years, the German government has attempted to encourage women (and parents) to have more children, by offering a lengthy maternity leave. (For more information on the details, please refer to the section entitled "Maternity Leave.") Parents (or guardians) of children under 18 years can apply for government child benefit (*Kindergeld*). To qualify, they must live and work in Germany and pay income tax there. The benefit amount is dependent on how many children the parent has and the children's ages. For the first, second, and third child, the parent receives monthly payments of €154 per child. For each additional child they get €179 more. This benefit can be extended to age 25, if a child pursues post-secondary education or an apprenticeship. Additionally, each child living with a parent or guardian is considered a dependant, for which parents can receive a child tax credit (*Kinderfreibetrag*) on their income tax.

Challenges

With respect to women and their role in the family and the work force, Germany still maintains fairly traditional attitudes. The government demonstrates its opinion that women should stay at home through mandatory maternity leaves, financial incentives, and a lack of childcare initiatives. Career-oriented women in Germany face ad campaigns and public opinion that endorse motherhood.[7] There are few support options for working women, especially working mothers. Many services are geared towards stay-at-home mothers and mothers working part-time. All of these factors act as obstacles for working mothers, but are in line with Germany's Christian politics and conservatism (Spiess and Dunkelberg). Until the attitudes of people in Germany change and mothers receive more childcare support and more family-friendly employment opportunities, the labour market will remain inequitable for women.

This chapter is going to look at these challenges and issues in the context of *Caritas, donum vitae, pro familia,* and *SkF,* and will explain how these institutions are making a difference to mothers of Germany.

Mandate

The following paragraphs will briefly introduce the mandate of each organization, focusing on its differences.

Caritas, a humanitarian agency with origins in the Catholic community of Germany, is guided by Christian charity and promotes together with its partners the spirit of social solidarity. Its intent is to offer an extensive spectrum of services to aid disadvantaged people, including mothers.

SkF, an organization funded by the Catholic Church, advocates for the interests of women at all political levels. It collaborates with other ecclesiastical, political, and social women's associations to fight for more rights and better work conditions for women. Its goal is for women to lead a variance of lifestyles that allows them to be equally active as an individual, in their family, as an employee/employer, and as a part of society. *SkF* focuses on supporting and strengthening women in general and working mothers in specific, regardless of their nationality or religious affiliation, so that they may lead a fulfilled life on all levels.

donum vitae focuses on reducing the termination of pregnancies. For this reason, this Catholic inspired organization assists women of unplanned or unwanted pregnancies to deal with their difficult situation, educates its client about their choices and considers this act as their attempt to save the life of an unborn child.

pro familia advocates for the right of the individual to freely decide, if, when, and how many children s/he would like to have and it campaigns to simplify the abortion process. This organization strives to promote responsible sexual freedom of humankind within the concept of social justice and believes that abortion should be an easily available method of birth control.

History

This historic overview will explain how each organization evolved from its infancy. It will begin with the oldest organization and conclude with the youngest.

Lorenz Werthmann, a young Catholic priest, founded *Caritas* in Cologne on November 9, 1897, to help people in crisis including pregnant women and mothers. It continued to operate during World War I and II as the number of people in dire need increased. When Nazi Germany collapsed in 1945, the members of *Caritas* coordinated aid from abroad and reunified families. The organization began to provide international emergency relief and disaster aid during the 1950s and continued to expand these services during the following three decades. Since

Germany's reunification (1990), they have been focused on rebuilding the association in eastern Germany and on establishing pregnancy counselling for mothers in crisis, as well as opening medical retreat centers, where mothers can regain strength and their health. Today, *Caritas* employs almost half a million people, making it the largest private employer of Germany.

Agnes Neuhaus (1854-1944) also recognized around the time when *Caritas* was established, that there are circumstances in which women require help from women. Other women joined her effort as a demonstration of religious belief. In 1900, this initiative of women founded *SkF*. Their work is guided by individuality, solidarity, and subsidiary.

The non-religious, social organization *pro familia*, founded in 1952 in Kassel, Germany, educates the public about the methods of regulating conception and planned parenthood. *pro familia* successfully lobbied for the reform of punishment for sexual misdemeanors (Paragraph 218). After this, the volunteers of this association established its federal network of counselling centers. Since Germany's reunification in 1990, *pro familia* has merged with its East German partner "EHE und FAMILIE" (marriage and family) and expanded its range of information and counselling services on the topic of sexuality and family planning.

donum vitae, the youngest of the four organizations, was founded in September 1999 in reaction to Pope John Paul II prohibiting Catholic pregnancy consultation services for women who wanted to abort. The founding members of *donum vitae* wanted to specifically target these women, so that they could save more lives (fetuses). They developed a Catholic-inspired counselling service for pregnant women that is state-recognized and able to fulfill the requirements for legal abortion. *donum vitae* has since its infancy created one hundred and ninety counselling centers across Germany to advise and help women, men, and couples of all nationalities and denominations.

Organizational Activities

As a group, combined with government initiatives, *Caritas*, *donum vitae*, *pro familia*, and *SkF* form a solid base of services to mothers and their families which deal with contraception, pregnancy, abortion, and genetic testing. They all dedicate resources towards pregnancy prevention, of which *pro familia* and *donum vitae* make it a priority, and provide sexual education to the public. *pro familia* offers at all locales prescription free emergency contraception and cost-free contraceptives. Five specialized centers offer integrated counselling services and perform medical procedures like fitting a diaphragm, sterilizing men and women, and terminating pregnancies. *donum vitae* integrates additional topics into their sexual education classes, which engage with the worthiness of an unborn child, assist participants in formulating their wishes and aspirations, and encourage reflection about their hopes, about love, relationships, partnerships, and faithfulness. *SkF* and *Caritas* also participate in pregnancy prevention by providing information, but do not offer additional services like *pro familia* or *donum vitae*. All four organizations offer (pregnancy) counselling and can assist mothers in crisis. The following sections will highlight the activities of each organization that are distinctive and most representative of what type of work it does with regard to the women's movement.

Caritas has a number of programs that are intended to assist mothers pre and post birth. One of these programs is the preventative care and rehabilitation program *Catholic Consortium for the Convalescence of Mothers* (*Katholische Arbeitsgemeinschaft für Müttergenesung e.V.*).[8] To attend this program, a person must exhibit: 1) psychological, social, and physical stress symptoms; 2) burn-out syndrome and psychosomatic symptoms; 3) co-existence of two or more long-term conditions; or 4) restrictions in activities around the household and/or at work and dysfunctional interactions (i.e. between mother and child).[9] After being referred to the program by a medical professional, patients undergo a therapy regime designed specifically for mothers, which typically consists of medical treatment, exercise, group and one-on-one discussions, psychological guidance, relaxation methods, nutrition classes, and creative and musical programs. Specialized medical professionals treat the attendees holistically.[10] Most of the costs of attending are covered by medical insurance, including travel, accommodations, meals, and the cost of a caregiver for the children left at home. The aim of mothers attending the program is to allow them to focus on themselves, their health and well-being, while knowing their families are taken care of. After finishing the program, they participate in follow-up care for one year. This program is designed to, and is very effective at, assisting mothers in coping with the stressors and obstacles of being a mother. For women who choose to be primarily mothers, this program can be very empowering, for those women with additional aspirations (i.e. developing a professional career), the program has a limited effect.

Caritas also offers services focused on supporting parents with mentally and/or physically disabled children. This service ranges from supporting the parents when they learn of their children's disability, during pregnancy and after birth, to providing assisted living. *Caritas* has specialized help centers that are able to discuss concerns a parent may have about this new life situation. *Caritas'* staff will educate the parents about social assistance and governmental services that they can avail of, such as respite care. They also refer mothers of disabled children to associations dedicated to particular disabilities and empower them to seek assistance from others, so that their vision of a future with a child of special needs is enhanced. These services offer mothers a way of coping with having a disabled child and help them grow and become stronger. Though these sessions are not intended to assist mothers with gaining employment, the coping mechanisms and the support services offered could make it more of a possibility.

donum vitae, through *Anonymous Birth* (*Anonyme Geburt*), empowers girls and women by giving them a safe and confidential way of dealing with an unplanned pregnancy. This is especially the case for women, who, for religious/moral reasons, choose not to terminate their pregnancy. In the states of Bavaria and Saarland, girls/women are able to secretly and without cost give birth in a medically-supervised setting. The attendees have the duty to treat all medical files confidentially and can refuse to testify in court. *donum vitae* further supports these mothers beyond the pregnancy and birthing process and assists them in finding a solution that is appropriate for them and their child(ren). Assisting women in this manner gives them choice and empowers them to make decisions that are right for themselves and their unique situation.

pro familia enables women through "Sextra" and "Sexundso." These programs are geared to youth and young adults and provide information and advice on love, friendship, and sexuality.[11]

Sextra helps inform women through individual online chat and its public website, which provides immediate answers to common questions about sexuality. Sexundso expands on this offering through more immediate email and telephone support for those, who may need time sensitive information about the morning after pill (*Pille danach*). Their website also contains information about topics like "the first time and after" and "totally crazy, totally in love." Through these two programs and through pedagogical sexuality events, *pro familia* plays an active role in educating Germany's youth and advocating planned motherhood.

For expecting/young mothers under the age of twenty-three, *pro familia* offers a program called "MamaMia."[12] It is a project that supports the balancing act between being a young adult and a parent. It teaches them coping mechanisms for a life with child. Group meetings allow them to share experiences, respect, and assistance from each other. Although this program intends to help attendees be better mothers, it doesn't seem to enable them to be self-sufficient (get an income, find meaningful employment). *pro familia* empowers women and mothers in their reproductive choices.

SkF's 2010 initiative, "Strengthening Women" (*Frauen stärken*), is a public campaign intended to build the confidence of women and mothers of all walks of lives and to give them hope. Many females responded and expressed their thoughts on what makes them strong. They asked women to finish the sentence: "I am strong because ..." One of the responses was: "I am *strong* because I can be and want to be strong."[13] *SkF* presented a selection of the replies at the second church congress in Munich (May 2010) and summarized the responses into two statements: 1) Having the courage to ask for and accept help strengthens women, gives them a sense of hope, and boosts their confidence level. 2) Strong women/mothers can help make other women/mothers stronger.[14]

SkF prepares expecting mothers for a lifestyle with a child and remains a source of support after birth, in an attempt to help them live a fulfilled life. Staff helps them find suitable accommodations and refers them, if the circumstances require it, to state or church-structured foundations for financial assistance. Depending on the location, it may be one of their own Girls' Residences (*Mädchenwohngruppen*) or Mother-Child-Houses (*Mutter-Kind-Häuser*).

Mosaik–Girls' Residences (*Mosaik–Mädchenwohngruppen*), through these services and career education, empower girls to become independent and self-sufficient. These residences accommodate girls in group homes, who have experienced personal problems with their parents/families or school/place of employment and

were referred by the youth welfare office. During their stay at a Mosaik Residence, girls focus on their education, employment training, and mental and physical well-being. Each group normally consists of six girls (13 years or older), of which one is a young mother. These girls live in single and double rooms and handle the household together, while they remain in close contact with a psychologist, homework supervisor, and education leader. Girls who intend to move out receive their own quarters, which helps them acquire skills for independent living.

Mother-Child-Houses (*Mutter-Kind-Häuser*) lodge pregnant women and mothers with less than two children, one under the age of six, who are dealing with life events/obstacles (i.e. unplanned pregnancy, abuse, divorce, unemployment). Living with other single-mothers allows them to talk about their situation and to relate to one another. With *SkF*'s help, each mother and her child(ren) build an individual plan that identifies realistic solutions and goals (education, employment, etc) and is actively working towards achieving them.

Through *Mosaik – Girls' Group Residences* and *Mother-Child Houses, SkF* empowers girls and young women, some of them being single mothers, by giving them a chance to attend educational institutions, become apprentices, and acquire the skills and support system for an independent life.

SkF assists women who want to live a variety of lifestyles and promotes women and mothers being equally active as individuals, family members, employees/employers, and as a part of society. They lead by example and create flexible employment opportunities that enable mothers to pursue a career while caring for their family. They also run 31 daycare centers throughout Germany (see "Kindergarten/Kinderhort.").

These organizations focus on supporting motherhood mostly independent of other aspirations. When it comes to empowering women and providing them choices, *pro familia* provides a substantial range of support prior to birth. The remaining organizations focus on motherhood, but do little to support women with multiple ambitions, i.e., mothers who wish to establish careers. For these women, *SkF* offers the broadest range of services, although some services are restricted to specific demographics. Though it has its limitations, including those imposed by the church, *SkF* is, of the four organizations, the one that offers a more comprehensive range of services and does the most to empower women and mothers regardless of their aspirations.

Limitations and Challenges

As all charities, these four organizations depend on finding permanent and continuous sources of funding, increasing its membership base, and attracting volunteers. Two of the organizations are limited by their ties with the Catholic Church. The following sections will outline the challenges and limitations of the individual groups.

One of the largest challenges for *Caritas* today is engaging with the topic of preimplantation diagnostics (PID). PID is a practice of screening a fetus for diseases, medical conditions, and other characteristics, such as gender. As an organization of Christian belief, *Caritas* has great concern for discriminating life and has asked the public to consider the implications. Peter Neher, the President of *Caritas*, acknowledged that couples wish for more security when it comes to the health of their future children. At the same time, he was alarmed that the ideal of perfectionism appears to be more important than ever (Neher 2010a).

donum vitae is currently faced with the challenge of standardizing its services. While some offices and their services are already well established, others are still in development. Their focus is often dispersed and sometimes in opposing directions. *donum vitae* initiated for this reason in 2008 a federal conference in hopes of starting the process and overcoming this challenge. While some of the concerns addressed during this first meeting have been resolved, others are still in progress or need to be dealt with in future.

pro familia is known for pushing the boundaries regarding reproductive rights and motherhood and as such often encounters confrontation on political, legal, and moral levels. When the organization was founded, it overcame resistance regarding the idea of planned parenthood. Later on, it held its ground when it came to terminating pregnancies and established medical clinics that would offer this service. In 2011, *pro familia* is dealing with institutions and other opponents who are against the legalization of PID. *pro familia* will be drawing on its previous experiences to anticipate and establish new services, in order to strengthen those women and couples, who wish to have their future children genetically tested prior to implantation.

SkF will be focused on expanding its *Early Help* (*Frühe Hilfe*) program, which assists mothers during the first few months after the arrival of a newborn. They believe, this challenge has arisen due to changes in the social environment that has left new mothers without the support from their extended family. With the success of *SkF's* pilot project, their major challenges are likely to be with funding,

donum vitae Federal Conference, 2008

training, and the national implementation. *SkF* also believes, the first obstacle to be overcome, when attempting to assist/empower women, is to encourage them to ask for help.

The Future of *Caritas, donum vitae, pro familia,* and *SkF*

In order to serve mothers better in future, *Caritas, donum vitae, pro familia,* and *SkF* are attempting to address challenges and make plans to assist, enable, and empower mothers in new ways. This means adjusting to the changing social demands while upholding their philosophy.

Caritas plans to evaluate and analyze all of its ongoing projects to improve its efficiency of services and address potential shortcomings. In addition to this, one of its primary goals is to ensure that there is no discrimination of fetuses via PID. *Caritas* will continue to lobby against genetic testing prior to implantation. Neher, the President of *Caritas*, has stated that German society should not be questioning parents with disabled children about why they did not prevent the disability, but be asking, how they can help.[14] In an effort to enable the accomplishment of *Caritas*' future goals, *Caritas* continues education and training of counselors and social workers at its academy in Freiburg.

donum vitae is focused on creating programs to cope with the negatively perceived changes to federal law regarding prenatal diagnostics. They are also enhancing their services for marginalized clients and preparing to lobby for changes in legislation around genetic testing, pre-implementation diagnostics, anonymous birth places and baby drop-offs.

pro familia intends to continue advocating for the individual's right to choice about their life and partnerships. These topics will include abortion, contraception, reproductive methods, genetic technologies, and prostitution. Additionally, they will focus efforts on sexual education, stopping the trafficking of women and sexual violence.

SkF plans to strengthen the protection of abused women and children through a new service *gewalt-los* ("non-violent") and advocating for new protective laws against violence.[15] They are also attempting to increase funding, to expand their permanent services.

Relationship to Larger Motherhood Movement

The formation of *Caritas* took place during the first wave of feminism in the late nineteenth century, when women in Germany were fighting for the equality of the sexes, were organizing congresses, and were articulating how they felt doubly burdened by work and the responsibilities at home. Members of *Caritas* helped mothers to deal with these conflicts and arranged its first services during its formative years. One such service was the creation of childcare centers, where children would be taken care of while their mothers pursued employment—a service that appears to be no longer offered. During the same time, the Catholic women's initiative *SkF* committed to helping other women in need, assisting them to cope with their role as a mother, but also empowering them with combined women power.

During the second wave of feminism, the women's movement began to advocate planned parenthood and demanded the freedom to terminate early pregnancies. *Caritas* established more preventive services and offered counselling to women who were contemplating abortions. As the women's movement made progress, *SkF* modified its already established repertoire to better suit these new developments and created new services to continue their support for women in crisis and need, while upholding their Christian mandate. *pro familia*'s foundation took place during this time frame. Women wanted to live sexually fulfilled lives and decide for themselves when it was time to have a family. The mandate of *pro familia* is based on these views. Some may even go as far as calling *pro familia* an anti-mother organization. But ultimately, *pro familia* has played a role in advancing the motherhood movement, giving women the right to decide when, where, with whom, and how many children they would like to have. This includes being supportive of alternative lifestyles. Additionally, *pro familia* supports genetic testing on embryos and fetuses.

When abortion was legalized in Germany during the 1990s, the federal government stipulated by law that expecting mothers opting for this procedure must seek counselling at one of their recognized institutions. *Caritas*, *SkF*, and *pro familia* belonged to the group of organizations who had been granted the right to issue abortion certificates by the federal government. This changed, however, in 1999, when the motherhood movement in Germany experienced a set-back. Pope John Paul II used his authority to prohibit Catholic pregnancy counselling centers from issuing certificates. Both *Caritas* and *SkF* conformed to this request while still counselling women considering abortion. This ruling, combined with the well-established pregnancy and birth counselling services, and the three waves of the German motherhood movement, led to the establishment of *donum vitae* and paved the way for its current array of services, including recognized abortion counselling.

Conclusion

Motherhood in Germany is more traditional. Most mothers exclusively raise their children while young and tend to work only in part-time jobs as their children get older. Only a change in public attitude, coupled with an increase in support services (i.e. childcare), will allow mothers to pursue a career.[16] The four German organizations introduced in this chapter, *Caritas, donum vitae, pro familia,* and *Sozialdienst katholischer Frauen,* each provide an array of basic services, including the prevention of unwanted pregnancies and counselling for mothers-to-be. They are complimented by specialized programs, projects and services that help women cope with motherhood. While their explicit focus is not the empowerment of women so that they may live a more fulfilled lives and form identities outside the realm of motherhood, the relentless and incessant work of these four organizations for (expecting) mothers in Germany helps sustain the next generation of Germany, and plays a role in shaping the future of Germany and the role that women can play in that future.

[1]See Rübenach for all statistics mentioned in this paragraph.
[2]All statistics of the sub-heading "Fertility" stem from the year 2007 and are referenced, unless otherwise indicated, in Allen.
[3]Statisics from *European Commision*, 2010. See: "Total Fertility Rates." <epp.eurostat.ec.europa.eu>. (Path: Eurostat; Population; Data; Main Tables; Population – Demography – Fertilità) Accessed: 4 January 2011
[4]Less than five percent of those are performed for medical or crime related reasons; the majority of abortions take place after the state required counselling.
[5]Women of the German Democratic Republic had since 1972 the legal ability to request the termination of a pregnancy before the twelfth week.
[6]In 2008, an income under €966 per month was classified as "low income." See "Eine Kampagne für mehr Kinderfreundlichkeit."
[7]Since this national program is of much demand, it has its own website <http://www.kag-muettergenesung.de>, where detailed information can be found. More information about this program can also be found at: <http://www.beratung-caritas.de/kurberatung_fuer_muetter.html>.
[8]See "Das Leitsyndrom mütterlicher Erkrankungen."
[9]A list of clinics focusing on the treatment of certain diseases, conditions, symptoms, is available through *KAG-Müttergenesung*. See: "Schwerpunkte in den Kliniken."

To see what kind of benefits women who attended the program experienced, see: "Qualitätssicherung."

[10]More information about "Sextra" and "Sexundso" can be found at <https://pro-familia.sextra.de> and <http://www.sexundso.de> respectively.

[11]For more information, please consult <http://www.profamilia.de/fileadmin/projekte/MamaMia.pdf>.

[12]This is my own translation of Sainjargal Schmidt-Häusler's "*Ich bin STARK weil ich stark sein kann und will.*"

[13]*SkF*'s first letter of 2010 contained a three-page article about "*Frauen stärken*" (Altweger and Jachmann-Willmer).

[14]See Neher 2010a, 2010b for more detailed information.

[15]In December 2010, *non-violent* (*gewalt-los*) won the third place *Deutsche Engagementpreis* (German Dedication Award). More information about *non-violent* can be found at <www.gewalt-los.de>.

[16]Relevant articles can be found on the website for the Ministry of Family, Seniors, Women and Youth, including these two: "Familie und Arbeitswelt," *Bundesministerium für Familie, Senioren, Frauen und Jugend* (December 2010); "Gute Kinderbetreuung," *Bundesministerium für Familie, Senioren, Frauen und Jugend* (November 2010).

Works Cited

Allen, Sonja. "Germany." *Encyclopedia of Motherhood.* Vol. I. Ed. Andrea O'Reilly. Thousand Oaks, CA: Sage Publications, 2010.

Altweger, Barbara and Renate Jachmann-Willmer. "Frauen Stärken: Der SkF auf dem Weg zum ÖKT." *Da sein: Leben helfen: Korrespondenzblatt* 10.1 (2010): 9-12. <http://www.skf-zentrale.de/2010_1_KorrBlatt.pdf>. Accessed: 10 December 2010.

Caritas. <www.caritas.de>.

"Das Leitsyndrom mütterlicher Erkrankungen." *kag-muettergenesung.de* [n.d.]. <http://www.kag-muettergenesung.de/11843.html>. Accessed: 15 January 2011.

donum vitae. <www.donumvitae.org>.

"Eine Kampagne für mehr Kinderfreundlichkeit." *Du-bist-Deutschland* [n.d.]. <http://www.du-bist-deutschland.de>. Accessed: 15 January 2011.

"Kindergarten/Kinderhort." *skf-zentrale.de* [n.d.] <http://www.skf-zentrale.de/html/buh_kindergartenhort.html>. Accessed: 15 January 2011.

Ministry of Family, Seniors, Women and Youth. "Familie und Arbeitswelt." *Bundesministerium für Familie, Senioren, Frauen und Jugend.* 2 December 2010. Web.: <http://www.bmfsfj.de/BMFSFJ/Familie/familie-und-arbeitswelt.html>. Accessed: 17 January 2011.

Ministry of Family, Seniors, Women and Youth. "Gute Kinderbetreuung." *Bundesministerium für Familie, Senioren, Frauen und Jugend. 17* November 2010. Web: <http://www.bmfsfj.de/BMFSFJ/Kinder-und-Jugend/kinderbetreuung.

html>. Accessed: 17 January 2011.

Neher, Peter. "Caritas spricht sich gegen Präimplentationsdiagnostik (PID) aus." Press Release. *Deutscher Caritasverband* 10 November 2010a.

Neher, Peter. "Werdende Eltern und Menschen mit Behinderung unterstützen, Präimplantationsdiagnostik verbieten." *Comment, Deutscher Caritasverband* 9 November 2010a. Web: <http://www.caritas.de/2338.asp?detail=true&id=27697>. Accessed: 29 November 2010b.

pro familia. <www.profamilia.de>.

Qualitätssicherung," *kag-muettergenesung.de* [n.d.]. <http://www.kag-muettergenesung.de/11842.html>. Accessed: 15 January 2011.

Rübenach, Stefan. "Alles beim Alten: Mütter stellen Erwerbstätigkeit hinten an." *Statistisches Bundesamt Deutschland* 4 March 2010. Web: <http://www.destatis.de>. Accessed: 13 January 2011.

"Schwerpunkte in den Kliniken." *kag-muettergenesung.de* [n.d.]. <http://www.kag-muettergenesung.de/11845.html>. Accessed: 15 January 2011.

Sozialdienst katholischer Frauen (SkF). <www.skf-zentrale.de>.

Spiess, C. Katharina and Annalena Dunkelberg. "The Impact of Child and Maternal Health Indicators on Female Labor Force Participation after Childbirth: Evidence for Germany." *Journal of Comparative Family Studies* 40.1 (2009): 119-138.

8. The White Ribbon Alliance for Safe Motherhood

Confronting Maternal Mortality as the Health Scandal of Our Time

LYNN COMERFORD

THE WHITE RIBBON ALLIANCE (WRA) is an international coalition advocating for safe motherhood as a basic human right and is a leader among those holding governments and institutions accountable for the tragedy of maternal mortality. The organization puts pressure on governments to enforce change and is dedicated solely to saving the lives of the world's poorest women who die because they do not have access to basic healthcare. The name of the organization derives from the fact that in some cultures white symbolizes life and hope, while in others it symbolizes mourning; the white ribbon is dedicated to women who have died needlessly in pregnancy and childbirth.

Mandate

The WRA mandate is to stop women and girls from dying needlessly in pregnancy and childbirth, and improve maternal, newborn and child health by demanding that donor and developing country governments invest the money required to create, strengthen, integrate, and make more efficient health systems which deliver tangible outcomes for women and children.

Maternal mortality has been described as the health scandal of our time (Fathalla). Easily treatable problems such as high blood pressure, infection, obstructed labor, or heavy bleeding needlessly kill mothers every day in developing nations. Women die while giving birth because there are no clamps to stop a mother's bleeding or no health worker to hold them. Even where a woman has access to a cesarean section, the sutures that are needed to sew her up may not be available. Women die because there is no one to dispense the three cents worth of magnesium sulphate required to stop death due to high blood pressure associated with pre-eclempsia. And, women die because they are vulnerable to infection when they give birth outside or from the use of nonsterilized equipment or when there is a lack of medicine to treat infection (see Kabakchieva). More than 90 percent of maternal deaths occur in developing countries and approximately 80 percent of maternal deaths can be avoided by effective intervention (WHO 2004; Campbell and Graham).

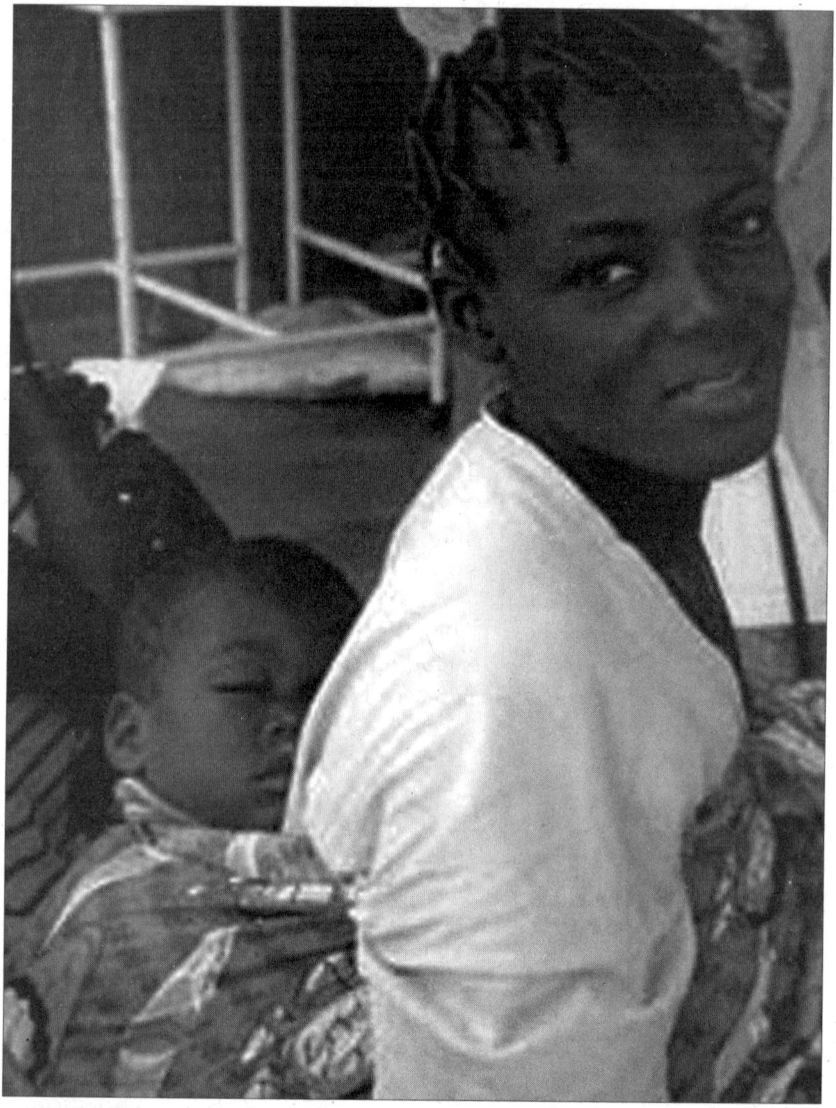

Annually, across the globe, over 200 million women will get pregnant, approximately 40 percent of these women will experience an abnormality during the course of delivery, 15 percent will suffer a serious complication, and 1.7 percent will die (see De Bernis et al.). During the time it takes to read this chapter, ten expectant mothers will have died and hundreds of others will be in labor after having walked for days to their nearest maternity unit. Due to a dearth of clinics in remote areas, poor transportation, and poverty, women often end up giving birth on the roadside in the dark with no trained assistant: many bleed to death. According to many studies, the number of mothers dying in childbirth remains exactly the same as it was in the mid-1980s. For every mother that dies, 30 other women are left suffering from injuries and disabilities that resulted from the complications of childbirth (see Igberase).

History

Since 1999, the White Ribbon Alliance (WRA) has expanded to include members in 148 countries and affiliated National Alliances in 15 – Bangladesh, Burkina Faso, India, Indonesia, Kenya, Malawi, Nepal, Pakistan, Rwanda, South Africa, Sweden, Tanzania, Uganda, Yemen and Zambia. The WRA is funded by the Bill & Melinda Gates Foundation, the United States Agency for International Development (USAID), the United Nations Population Fund (UNFPA), the United Kingdom Department for International Development (DFID), the John D. and Catherine T. MacArthur Foundation, and the Ministry of Foreign Affairs of Norway, as well as individual donations. In 2008, Sarah Brown, wife of Gordon Brown, a former Prime Minister of the United Kingdom, became the Patron of the White Ribbon Alliance for Safe Motherhood. Sarah Brown and Theresa Shaver, President and Executive Director of WRA, appointed supermodel Naomi Campbell Global Ambassador to the White Ribbon Alliance at the *Leadership for Health* summit for African first ladies in Los Angeles, California. Campbell brought international attention to the WRA and raised funds in September 2008 with her charity catwalk show called "Fashion for Relief."

Context

Half of the world's women today give birth with no pain relief, no drugs to speed delivery or thwart infections and no ambulance service. The lives of more than 500,000 women are claimed each year as a result of pregnancy-related complications: 10,000 every week; one every minute. According to the Global Health Observatory (GHO), every day in the year 2008, approximately 1,000 women died of severe bleeding after childbirth, infections, hypertensive disorders, and/or unsafe abortions. Of these 1,000 women, 570 lived in sub-Saharan Africa, 300 in South Asia, and five in high-income countries. Because the vast majority of maternal mortality is needless, this problem must be seen as a gross violation of human rights and the worst form of discrimination against women. It is also economically dysfunctional; for in addition to holding the fabric of the family and community together, women are often a country's economic engines as well. In many parts of Africa, for example, women do 80 percent of the farming and transport two-thirds of all goods in their arms, and on their heads and backs. Women in Southeast Asia do 90 percent of the labor for rice cultivation.

The contrast for pregnant women in developing versus developed countries is stark: the risk of a woman in a developing country dying from a pregnancy-related cause during her lifetime is about 36 times higher than a woman living in a developed country. Expectant mothers who die during childbirth leave behind a million orphans annually. When a newborn is left motherless, s/he is ten times more likely to die within the first week of birth. The orphans left behind are three to ten times more likely to die within two years than those with two living parents. The older girls left behind without a mother are frequently taken out of school to do a mother's work or are married off at an early age. The plight of the child-mother is particularly disturbing: young girls in many parts of the world cannot say no to sex or marriage. In some countries, girls as young as ten are married and then die in childbirth because their bodies are too undeveloped to handle a pregnancy.

Complicating maternal mortality is gender inequality. The women most at risk for dying while giving birth have no political power and when they die they are silenced forever. They are often buried in remote areas and not even counted. Because males typically rule household decision-making, women often give up control over their own health decisions. Frequently, poor expectant fathers do not have enough money to pay for a taxi-ride to the health center; for too many expectant fathers, the cost of travel and treatment is more expensive than letting his wife die and replacing her with a new wife. An expectant father may make this decision because of his desperate need to protect his surviving children from debt (see Lawoyin et. al).

In the *International Statistical Classification of Diseases and Related Health Problems, Tenth Revision*, 1992, the World Health Organization (WHO) defines maternal death as: "The death of a woman pregnant or within 42 days of termination of pregnancy, irrespective of the duration and site of the pregnancy, from any cause related to or aggravated by the pregnancy or its management but not from accidental or incidental causes." This definition allows the cause of maternal death to be identified as either direct or indirect. Direct obstetric deaths result from obstetric complications of the pregnant state (pregnancy, delivery, and postpartum). These complications include incorrect treatment, interventions, or omissions in treatment. An omission in treatment may include, for example, the lack of available blood from a blood bank. Direct obstetric deaths would include, for example, hemorrhage, pre-eclampsia/eclampsia or to complications of anesthesia or cesarean section. Indirect obstetric deaths, on the other hand, are those that result from a pre-existing disease or diseases that developed during pregnancy and which were not due to direct obstetric causes. Indirect obstetric deaths would include, for example, deaths due to the aggravation of an existing cardiac or renal disease.

In raw numbers, in 2008, by country, India had the largest number of maternal deaths (63,000), followed by Nigeria (50,000), the Democratic Republic of the Congo (19,000), Afghanistan (18,000), Ethiopia (14,000), Pakistan (14,000), the United Republic of Tanzania (14,000), Bangladesh (12,000), Indonesia (10,000), Sudan (9,700), and Kenya (7,900) (WHO, 2009). These 11 countries comprised an estimated 65 percent of the global maternal deaths reported in 2008. In contrast, 27 countries (all middle- or high-income countries) had five or fewer maternal deaths in 2008.[1] Between the years 2000 and 2008, less than half of all pregnant women globally received the WHO-recommended minimum of four antenatal visits. In Africa and South-East Asia fewer than 50 percent of all women giving birth had a skilled attendant present (see Chou et. al.). On most of the continent of Africa, the ratio is one doctor for every 60-80,000 people. In Nigeria, for example, in a recent study, the most common causes of maternal mortalities were puerperal sepsis, abortion complications, pre-eclampsia/eclampsia, prolonged obstructed labor, and hemorrhaging (Igberase and Ebeigbe). Not surprisingly, the researchers found that the percentage of mortality for those who do not go to a health center to give birth was ten times higher than those who do go to a health center to give birth.

In 2000, all 191 United Nations member states agreed to achieve eight Millennium Development Goals (MDGs) by 2015. The United Nations Millennium Declarations commits world leaders to: 1) eradicate extreme poverty and hunger; 2) achieve universal primary education; 3) promote gender equality and empower women; 4) reduce child mortality; 5) improve maternal health; 6) combat HIV/AIDS, malaria, and other diseases; 7) ensure environmental sustainability; and 8) develop a global partnership for development. One of the specific targets of Millennium Development Goal 5 (MDG-5), the goal the WRA is most focused on, should have been one of the more easily achievable: to reduce the number of mothers dying in childbirth by three quarters by 2015. Little progress has been made, even though "the right to the highest possible standard of physical and mental health, known as the Universal Right to Health, is enshrined in the International Covenant on Economic, Social and Cultural Rights, to which all states are legally bound" (ICESR Art.12). Saving the lives of mothers is one of the most crucial steps toward achieving some of the other MDGs such as reducing infant mortality and educating and vaccinating all children. Maternal deaths represent a gross violation of the universal right to health, to which all states are legally bound.

Objectives

During the 2010-2011 year the WRA focused on initiating and coordinating action by campaign supporters for: 1) finding more resources for maternal, newborn and child health, 2) making maternal mortality a key indicator of a functioning health system, 3) increasing the recruiting, training, and retaining of health workers in order to address the global gap in skill care for women and newborns during and after pregnancy and childbirth, and 4) removing barriers to quality healthcare for women and children.

The five-year plan for the objectives of the WRA as they work towards the 2015 deadline include: 1) making the public more aware of maternal and newborn mortality and increasing demands for political leadership and action to champion the issue, 2) holding donors and political leaders locally, nationally and internationally accountable for their promises to act, and 3) creating a "Framework for Action on Maternal, Newborn and Child Health" that includes a strategy, quantifiable targets, an accountability mechanism, and a work plan with time-bound commitments from all actors involved so progress can be monitored to the 2015 deadline.

In order for these short-term and long-term objectives to be met, the WRA must keep the political pressure up on all governments to deliver on their promises of more resources for maternal, newborn and child health. The WRA's effort to keep up the political pressure include: 1) building on the work being done by the G8 on an MDG accountability framework which includes tracking and reporting on whether donor financial commitments for health are being met, 2) joining forces with regional and national forces to track and report on the delivery of domestic resources for maternal, newborn and child health, 3) pressing for an increase of at least $10 billion during the year 2010-2011 in an effort to meet MDGs 4-6, 4) considering whether the time is right to create a Global Health Fund (GHF) that includes comprehensive maternal, newborn and child health within its' mandate.

Activities

In 2010 the activities of the WRA included: 1) working toward the creation of a UN Maternal and Newborn Health Envoy, 2) working with national governments, foundations, including the Gates Foundation, and advisers, to link MDGs 4, 5 and 6, and create a program that includes health checklists, kits, and well trained health workers to improve the quality of care, 3) working with government and NGO partners to create a marketing campaign for maternal and newborn health products that have been proven to reduce mortality, and 4) raising awareness and funds.

An example of the kind of work that the WRA initiates is what WRA India recently did in their 2008 *Deliver Now for Women and Children* campaign (see WRA 2010). The campaign mobilized stakeholders including policymakers, health service providers, and the media, to put the spotlight on India's maternal and child health programs. The WRA surveyed mother's health services in 12 districts of Orissa state using the state's own checklists based on services women were entitled to through the government's National Rural Health Mission. The WRA study concluded that women needlessly died during childbirth in health facilities in spite of government promises to prevent maternal mortality: annually, in the state of Orissa, 75,000 women give birth and 2,500 women die during the process. The WRA Orissa study highlighted major gaps in basic health instruments and drug availability such as the lack of blood transfusion supplies, weighing machines, blood pressure equipment, and stethoscopes. The WRA study also revealed that nearly half of First Referral Units were not active and that there were few gynecologists available to women giving birth.

The WRA used these research findings to hold the government accountable by holding public hearings (attended by 11,000 women) and inviting the media so that the problem of maternal mortality in India received national attention. As a result of the publicity, a national focus on the problem of maternal mortality was spurred and led to an investigation of 800 maternal deaths. It was discovered that nearly all of these deaths were preventable. A follow-up media tour highlighted the dysfunctional state of women's health facilities. As a result of the WRA campaign, the Ministers of Finance, Health, and Information of Orissa publicly pledged to improve the quality of maternal and child health services. The improvements promised included an adequate supply of post-delivery and neonatal medicines, increases in trained health workers, improved emergency transport, and economic reimbursement to women who deliver their babies in public-funded health centers.

Challenges

The efforts by WRA to help meet MDG 5 have been thwarted for many reasons. First, the WRA cannot be effective if the necessary funding (between $10-20 billion) is not available to implement what is already known is needed to save the lives of women and newborns. It is up to the G8 to come up with the funding. Unfortunately, due to the recent global downturn, many governments froze or cancelled international-aid budgets. African leaders have committed themselves to improving health services, and in 2001 pledged to put aside 15 per cent of their annual budgets to improve health access; however, by 2004, only Botswana and Gambia had met that target. African priorities appear to be elsewhere. Chad, for example, is using its money from oil to buy weapons.

Second, the WRA has not contributed as effectively as it would like to MDG–5 because basic healthcare is not currently understood internationally to be a legal right for expectant mothers. The current shortage of 350,000 midwives increases maternal mortality simply because women lack access to skilled birth attendants or basic medical care. The WRA wants governments to absorb midwives as part of their workforce. Governments must commit to paying for maternal healthcare and to the training and hiring of more doctors, nurses, and midwives (there is a gap of 800,000 health workers in Africa alone, worldwide there is a 4 million healthcare worker gap).

WRA members face uphill battles fighting, at the local, national and international levels, for increased coordination between transportation sources and local clinics and hospitals, increased data on maternal mortality at all levels, more professional behavior from health workers, increased education in tribal areas, increased blood banks or blood storage units, increased medical staff (particularly gynecologists and anesthesiologists), and increased permanent local clinics (many currently function in rented buildings).

Government-run hospitals lack sufficient resources, equipment, and staff. Patients are told to buy their own supplies such as gloves, syringes, needles, cotton, wool and maternity pads. To overcome the decline in government financing, many hospitals and clinics ask patients to pay for services as well. In Kenya, for example, the government introduced hospital and clinic "user fees" as part of a World Bank push for cost-sharing in public services. In India, many pregnant women die because they cannot afford private healthcare, or the bribes asked for by public health workers, and end up turning to untrained midwives and quacks that maim them and their babies. Hospitals regularly have poor electric service, no air conditioning, broken lights, and few (if any) medical supplies. Doctors often pay for sutures out of their own pockets because hospitals have none. Before a caesarean section can start, for example, a patient's family must provide all necessary intravenous fluids and bags, medications, catheters, blood for transfusions, and surgical gloves for the doctors and nurses.

Third, the effectiveness of the WRA is challenged by grinding gender inequality. It was not until 2008 that, for the first time in history, "Women in Childbirth" made the G8 agenda. Societies with high maternal mortality rates tend to be male-dominated societies where women are not allowed to participate in their own healthcare decisions unless they get consent from a male relative. Because one of the most dangerous things a woman can do in many parts of the developing world is to become pregnant, it is hard to believe that if men were dying at these rates the United Nations Security Council would not have appointed a global minister of paternal mortality long ago. Currently, laws on health delivery are not effective enough to compel husbands to act more responsibly when their wife is about to give birth. Women continue to die from complications related to pregnancy or childbirth without attracting much interest because the victims are typically among the most voiceless people in the world: impoverished, rural, uneducated and female.

Birth control and abortion on demand are excellent ways to reduce maternal deaths (fewer pregnancies mean fewer deaths). However, for women in countries with the highest maternal mortality rates, birth control and legal abortions are often difficult (if not impossible) to get. Women have few rights and receive poor care because their lives are not valued in their cultures and traditions as much as the lives of men. There is little dignity or respect shown for women giving birth in many developing nations. Doctors and nurses are often harsh and contemptuous toward uneducated women and frequently intimidate them into staying away until it is too late; if doctors and nurses had better bedside manners more women would go to hospitals and more lives would be saved. Medical personnel should have a higher stake in protecting a mother's survival because mothers increase the survival rates of family members as she is often the person responsible for preventing malaria infections, feeding her family, and ensuring that her children attend school and receive their immunizations. In order to rectify these health disparities, the WRA would like to see more women in developing countries involved in the allocation of healthcare money.

Fourth, it is difficult for the WRA to be effective at reducing maternal mortality if governments make no effort to educate women. The WRA argues that women and their communities must be provided information about pregnancy and reproductive health so that they will be able to better care for themselves and be more aware of the danger signs during pregnancy and delivery. For example, in order to reduce anemia, pregnant women should be instructed to take their prenatal vitamins even when they fast for three weeks in observance of the Muslim holy month of Ramadan. Improved communication between hospitals, clinics and families (particularly rural families) would provide WRA much needed communication networks so that important pregnancy information could be disseminated to all pregnant women.

A related problem is that governments and donor agencies tend to focus on specific themes, such as malaria, HIV infection, and tuberculosis *individually*, and fail to take a holistic approach to healthcare systems. Maternal mortality rarely gets attention from international donors because they are so focused on individual global health threats however, if the treatment of these health threats were combined with maternal healthcare, more lives would be saved.

Finally, the WRA cannot be effective in reducing maternal mortality if the world continues to look the other way. Political leaders from both rich and poor countries must keep their promises to dramatically reduce the needless deaths of mothers and their newborns. Advocacy must be made at the highest level of governance by all stakeholders, as well as at the grassroots levels. The UN Secretary-General must make reducing maternal mortality a top priority and have maternal mortality recognized as a key indicator of a functioning health system. This will only be achieved with increased networking and collaboration between governments, health workers and charitable organizations.

At the 2010 G8/G20 summits, UN secretary-general, Ban Ki-Moon, called for a substantial financial plan in order to try to meet the MDGs. The stakes for women around the world could not be higher. Ban is seeking commitments from donor and developing countries, business, philanthropists, and NGOs, of $26 billion by 2011 and $42 billion by 2015 in order to adopt an action plan on maternal health. Governments of both rich and poor countries have pledged their political and economic support many times. The WHO Commission on Macro-Economics and Health recommended that, in addition to developing countries' domestic allocations, donor countries allocate at least 0.1 percent of their Gross National Income (GNI) to health aid and meeting the health-related MDGs. The U.S. government has recently made a commitment to supporting international maternal health. In a reversal of the Bush Administration, which cut off all U.S. money for the U.N. Population Fund, President Obama has moved to restore the money by unveiling his Global Health Initiative which doubles U.S. funding for maternal and child health. And, a bill was introduced in the U.S. Congress titled, *The Newborn, Child, and Mother Survival Act*, in March, 2010, which would establish U.S. leadership in this area. Thus far, it has attracted little attention.

Future Goals

The WRA, representing its members in 148 countries, joined the International Confederation of Midwives, International Council of Nurses, International Federation of Gynecology and Obstetrics, and International Pediatricians Association to petition G8 leaders as a unified force of 15 million people to "deliver the extra

$10 billion per year to build the health systems needed to cut maternal mortality by 75 percent by 2015." At the G8 Summit, the *2009 G8 Leaders Declaration: Responsible Leadership for a Sustainable Future* reflected the recommendations of the Partnership for Maternal, Newborn & Child Health with the following statement: "We warmly support building a global consensus on maternal, newborn and child health as a way to accelerate progress on the Millennium Development Goals for both maternal and child health, through: 1) political and community leadership and engagement; 2) a quality package of evidence based interventions through effective health systems; 3) the removal of barriers to access for all women and children, and free healthcare at the point of use where countries chose to provide it; 4) skilled health workers; 5) accountability for results." (see *Millennium Development Goals Report*, 2010). The G8 Summit responded positively and committed $5 billion towards the $30 billion needed by 2015 to end the decades-long crisis of women dying in childbirth for lack of basic health care. G8 leaders agreed to produce an accountability report at the 2011 Summit in France that will document each country's assistance per pledges made. The WRA will be watching and pressuring governments to fulfill these commitments.

Relationship to Larger Motherhood Movement

The WRA works in concert with the Global Strategy for Women's and Children's Health (GSWCH). In 2010, the United Nations Secretary-General launched the GSWCH. The GSWCH is an effort to renew and enhance all financial and policy commitments made by all partners to improve women's and children's health. These include: 1) improving access to reproductive health services; 2) identifying a comprehensive package of essential interventions and services for women and children that include family planning, antenatal care, skilled care at birth, emergency obstetric and newborn care, safe abortion services (where abortion is not prohibited by law) and prevention of mother-to-child transmission of HIV services; 3) improving health systems and insuring that high-quality services are available in underserved communities; 4) addressing the critical shortage of health workers by implementing national plans to train, retain and deploy health workers; and, 5) developing, funding and implementing a prioritized, coordinated and innovative research agenda for women's and children's health.

Although the motherhood movement is largely a North American rights movement, it is imperative that it partner with international motherhood organizations, such as the White Ribbon Alliance, so that mothers in developing countries are not overlooked.

Conclusion

In sum, the WRA tackles the global problem of maternal mortality on many fronts and with many strategies in order to reduce obstacles to maternal healthcare. The WRA advocates for the availability of skilled birth attendants and obstetric care for all women and infants at well-supplied health centers that women can afford to access and works from the grassroots up for more efficient healthcare, better hospital equipment, and improved coordination between clinics and ambulance drivers. In short, the WRA understands that maternal mortality is no longer an issue of knowledge; it is an issue of advocacy and political will.

[1]According to the WHO 2010 report, *Trends in Maternal Mortality: 1990 to 2008*, based on estimates developed by WHO, UNICF, UNFPA, and the World Bank, developing countries continued to account for 99 percent (355,000) of maternal deaths. In 2008, Sub-Saharan Africa and South Asia accounted for 87 percent (313,000) of global maternal deaths, and eleven countries including Afghanistan, Bangladesh, the Democratic Republic of the Congo, Ethiopia, India, Indonesia, Kenya, Nigeria, Pakistan, Sudan, and the United Republic of Tanzania, comprised 65 percent of all maternal deaths. Sub-Saharan Africa had the highest maternal mortality ratio (MMR) at 640 maternal deaths per 100,000 live births in 2008, followed by South Asia (280), Oceania (230), South-Eastern Asia (160). Forty-five countries had high estimated MMR (MMR ≥300) with four countries (Afghanistan, Chad, Guinea-Bissau, and Somalia), having extremely high MMR (MMR ≥1000). Outside of sub-Saharan Africa, the seven countries with high MMR were: Afghanistan (1400), the Lao People's Democratic Republic (580), Nepal (380), Timor-Leste (370), Bangladesh (340), Haiti (300), and Cambodia (290). Among developing regions, the adult lifetime risk of maternal death (the probability that a 15-year-old female will die eventually from a maternal cause) as measured in 2008 is highest in sub-Saharan Africa (at 1 in 31), followed by Oceania (1 in 110) and South Asia (1 in 120), while the developed regions had the smallest lifetime risk (1 in 4300). Of all 172 countries and territories for which estimates were made, Afghanistan had the highest estimated lifetime risk of 1 in 11.

Works Cited

Campbell O. M. R. and W. J. Graham. "Strategies For Reducing Maternal Mortality: Getting On With What Works." *Lancet* 368 (2006): 1284-1299.

Chou, D., M. Inoue, C. Mathers, M. Oestergaard, L. Say, S. Mills, E. Suzuki and J. Wilmoth. *Trends in Maternal Mortality: 1990 to 2008. Estimates Developed by WHO, UNICEF, UNFPA, and The World Bank.* Geneva: World Health Organization, 2010.

De Bernis, L., D. R. Sherratt, C. AbouZahr and W. Van Lerberghe. "Skilled Attendants for Pregnancy, Childbirth and Postnatal Care." *British Medical Bulletin* 67 (2003): 39-57.

Fathalla, M. F. "Imagine a World Where Motherhood Is Safe for All Women: You Can Make It Happen." *International Journal of Gynecology and Obstetrics* 72 (2001): 207-213.

Global Health Observatory. *Primary Health Care: Now More Than Ever.* Geneva: World Health Organization, 2008.

Igberase, G. O. and P. N. Ebeigbe. "Maternal Mortality in a Rural Referral Hospital in the Niger Delta, Nigeria." *Journal of Obstetrics and Gynecology* 27.3 (2007): 275-278.

International Charter of Human Rights. *The International Covenant on Economic Social and Cultural Rights* (ICESR), (art. 12). The Office of the United Nations High Commissioner for Human Rights, 1966. Web. <http://www2.ohchr.org/english/law/cescr.htm>.

International Statistical Classification of Diseases and Related Health Problems. Tenth Revision., 1992. World Health Organization Publications, 1992. Web. <http://www.who.int/classifications/icd/en/index.htm>.

Kabakchieva, Velika. "Maternal Morbidity and Mortality in the United States." *Journal of Children and Poverty* 15.1 (2009): 63-69.

Lawoyin, Taio, Olusheyi Lawoyin and David Adewole. "Men's Perception of Maternal Mortality in Nigeria." *Journal of Public Health Policy* 28.3 (2007): 229-318.

Millennium Development Goals Report 2010. New York: United Nations, 2010.

UNICEF. Global Databases. 2010. <http://www. childinfo.org/delivery_care_country data.php>.

United Nations. *Secretary-General Ban Ki-Moon: Global Strategy for Women's and Children's Health* (GSWCH). Fact Sheet, 2010. Web. <http://www.un.org/sg/hf/Global_StategyEN.pdf>.

World Health Organization (WHO). *African Union Atlas of Birth: Investing inthe Future—Why the African Union Summit Must Increase Health Spending to Save the Lives of Africa's Women and Children.* Fact Sheet. Geneva: World Health Organization, 2010.

World Health Organization (WHO). *Maternal Mortality in 2000: Estimates Developed by WHO, UNICEF and UNFPA.* Fact Sheet. Geneva: World Health Organization, 2004.

World Health Organization (WHO). *Trends in Maternal Mortality: 1990 to 2008: Estimates Developed by WHO, UNICEF, UNFPA, and the World Bank.* Geneva: World Health Organization Press, 2010.

World Health Organization (WHO). *Women and Health: Today's Evidence, Tomorrow's Agenda.* Fact Sheet. Geneva: World Health Organization Press, 2009.

White Ribbon Alliance. <http://www.whiteribbonalliance.org>.

White Ribbon Alliance. "Report 2010." *The White Ribbon Alliance: Members Matter* 3.7 (August 2010). <www.whiteribbonalliance.org/globalmaternal-mortality.cfm>.

White Ribbon Alliance. *The White Ribbon Alliance for Safe Motherhood: Strategic Plan 2001-2013.* London: Author, 2009.

9.
Save the Mothers Programs

JACQUELINE CICCIO PARSONS

FEMALE REPRODUCTIVE HEALTH IS ONE of the most important factors contributing to the overall health of women and girls worldwide. According to the World Health Organization in 2010, the leading causes of death among women of childbearing age were HIV/AIDS and maternal conditions. These two causes clearly dominate the list, accounting for more than 33 per cent of all deaths, and more deaths than the next eight causes combined. The maternal conditions category includes post-delivery bleeding, maternal high blood pressure, unsafe abortion, post-delivery infections, and other related issues. Any efforts which are intended to improve the health of women worldwide must certainly address reproductive health as a top priority.

During the period from 1990 to 2008, deaths due to childbirth and pregnancy declined by an encouraging 36 per cent (WHO 2010). Unfortunately, these improvements have been unevenly distributed. Currently 99 per cent of deaths due to maternal factors occur in developing countries, led by sub-Saharan Africa, which alone accounts for 570 of the 1000 deaths which occur daily worldwide. A woman in a developing country is 36 times more likely than a woman from a developed country to die from conditions related to childbirth, and one woman per minute dies in developing countries from these conditions. This disparity suggests that poverty plays a direct role in these death rates. If this is the case, then fairly simple solutions may emerge.

Major NGOs such as the World Health Organization, the United Nations Children's Fund, and the World Bank all have programs to address these issues. The UN has eight Millennium Developmental Goals and Goal Five is improving maternal health. In September 2010, the UN established a commission on Women's Health, and pledged 40 billion dollars to the effort. Other major programs include the Peace Corps and Doctors Without Borders. Particularly notable is the annual Continuing Promise (CP) program, which combines military and NGO resources to provide care, education, public health and even infrastructure upgrades. The 2010 version of CP included healthcare professionals from the militaries of eight countries, along with those representing 40 NGOs. They spent four months in five countries and provided over 160,000 medical services.

FIGO and Save the Mothers (STM)

Many smaller NGOs are involved as well. The Duke University Library Guide to NGOs lists over 40 NGOs which pursue women's health. One NGO that has actively addressed these issues is the International Federation of Gynecology and Obstetrics (FIGO). Founded in 1954, FIGO's mission is to "promote the wellbeing of women and to raise the standards of practice in obstetrics and gynecology." Currently FIGO is engaged in six initiatives, one of which is called the "FIGO Saving the Mothers and Infants Initiative," which runs from 2006–2011. It was created by Dr. Mahmoud Fathalla, professor of obstetrics and gynecology at Assuit University, Egypt, and a past president of FIGO. Its budget of $2.6M is dwarfed by the budgets of United Nations and WHO projects, but it leverages this money very efficiently. The backbone of this project consists of the midwifery societies and Obstetrical/Gynecological professional societies of the involved countries. In the main pilot program, ten developing countries are each paired with a developed country, creating a partnership which leads to improved services and then to better health outcomes in the developing countries.

The developing countries that participate in the pilot projects are Haiti, Kenya, Kosovo, Moldova, Nigeria, Pakistan, Peru, Uganda, Ukraine, and Uruguay. Related projects operate in Ethiopia, Nicaragua, El Salvador, Guatemala, and Honduras. Each country has a separate project with a unique name and focus. Some of these have a very specific emphasis, like the venture in Haiti which works with a single facility, while others have extremely broad, nation-wide efforts, such as that seen in Kosovo. Other projects concentrate their resources on the poorest regions or states, like the Nigerian project, which is spread among six hospitals in three states, or the Pakistani project, which emphasizes two impoverished regions. The projects also emphasize different health issues. For example, the Uruguay project targets only abortion related health concerns, while the Ukraine project aims at the top five major childbirth health issues: obstructed labor, hemorrhage, sepsis, hypertensive disorders, and complications due to unsafe abortion. And finally, the projects propose different mechanisms for change. The Ukrainian project relies on process auditing, the Kosovo project attempts to strengthen professional organizations, and the Moldova undertaking is essentially a combination of these two: increased data analysis combined with strengthened professional associations.

Each venture is also unique in that each uses different partner-nations. The Haitian project is partnered with Canada, Pakistan is partnered with the UK, and Central American countries partner with the United States. The cultures and professional healthcare models of both the developed and developing countries naturally influence the form each program takes.

The Central American "Save the Mothers" Project has seen an interesting evolution. Central America was not an area originally targeted by FIGO for activity, but upon the urging of Dr. Edgar Kestler, a Guatemalan OB/GYN, a new service in Central America was added, serving women in Nicaragua, El Salvador, Guatemala, and Honduras. This project partners extensively with the Pan American Health

Alliance, which brings together healthcare resources from all the Americas. The South American project is essentially a training and collaboration vehicle, which brings members of the American College of Obstetrics and Gynecology (ACOG) in the US to work with their sister organizations in other participating countries. ACOG members travel to Central America and conduct training workshops to boost the skills of their Central American colleagues. Although it is not one of the pilot programs, this program has seen remarkable success; a 2002 study suggests that emergency obstetric care capacity has increased (Mekbib).

Ethiopia-Sweden Collaboration

Another non-pilot program of significance is the Ethiopia-Sweden collaboration. This project is a collaboration between the Ethiopia Society of Obstetricians and Gynecologists and the Swedish Society of Obstetricians and Gynecologists. The STM partnership between Ethiopia and Sweden is noteworthy for several reasons. First, it is one of the oldest of the STM initiatives, originating in 1998. Second, it has been well studied and documented, including a rigorous study performed by Mekbib et al. in 2003. The program includes training, supplies, materials, and equipment, all aimed at increasing the capacity of three emergency OB facilities in the impoverished and underserved West Showa Zone. The Mekbib study was able to document several significant improvements after a very short time. The rate of caesarian sections increased by more than a factor of five in less than three years, indicating a dramatic increase in surgical capacity. Much more importantly, Mekbib was able to demonstrate a measurable decrease in maternal death rate, with a reduction of almost 50 per cent. This provided the most concrete proof that the STM initiatives are producing positive results. All of this benefit was accrued with a three-year expenditure of less than $100,000. This showed that the STM model can be both effective and efficient, when given a nominally acceptable sociopolitical/economic climate.

Uganda-Canada Collaborative

Similar improvements have been shown in the Uganda–Canada collaboration, which has seen increased access to emergency care. One of the original ten pilot programs, this project began in 2008, with a $4M cash infusion from the Swedish International Development Cooperation Agency. Although the professional societies of the two countries had been partnering at least since 1998, this was the first time that resources were plentiful enough to generate tangible progress. The latest phase of the project ended in 2010, but further work will continue when funds become available.

Even though Uganda and Canada have similar populations, the death rates for childbearing women and infants is strikingly different. In Canada, approximately ten women per year die in childbirth; in Uganda the number hovers near 6000. More than a dozen factors work against Ugandan mothers, including poor infrastructure, cultural barriers, second-class citizen status, poverty, and political instability. The Ugandan STM project focused on six facilities in the poorest region of Uganda, seeking to increase capacity of emergency and delivery services, while increasing the impact of the midwife and OB/GYN professional societies. One unique element of this program is that it also seeks to improve transportation to help the mother get to the medical care. Most of the mothers who are dying live in remote and rural areas, so in some cases transportation can be the only barrier to access.

Ugandan mothers are also vulnerable to malaria, which strikes pregnant women in alarming numbers throughout the region. A 2005 study, not directly related to STM, tested the efficacy of a combination of increased antenatal care, malaria prevention drugs, and insecticide impregnated mosquito netting. The study found a huge unmet demand for all of these services (Kiwuwa and Mubenga). Fortunately, some of the largest and best-funded NGOs, such as the Gates Foundation, have anti-malarial programs which may prove very helpful. If the incidence of malaria in child-bearing women can be decreased, it should improve their overall resiliency, thus amplifying the effects of the STM initiatives.

The momentum of the Uganda STM initiative may have been an influencing factor in the rise of emphasis on surgical modalities as public health tools. OB/GYN is a surgical specialty, and the Uganda STM program placed a heavy emphasis on acute emergency care during and just prior to childbirth. It is not surprising, therefore, that in 2008, a multidisciplinary task force convened in Uganda expressly for the purpose of improving utilization of surgical services. As described by Luboga (2010), this was the beginning of a new prominence for surgical and emergency medical service in sub-Saharan Africa. It is hoped that this new attention on surgery will enhance the visibility of related programs, including STM.

The FIGO STM collaborative also dovetails with a professional education program, which is also called "Save the Mothers." The OB/GYN societies of Uganda and Canada had already been partnering together for several years when, in 2005, the Save the Mothers degree program began. This two-year diploma program leads to a Master's degree in Public Health Leadership from Uganda Christian University. The mission of this Master's degree is "To train a multi-disciplinary team of professionals who will understand the complex issues around safe motherhood and will be competent leaders to initiate substantial change through a multitude of specializations, professional skills and influence."

The "Save the Mothers" degree program is the brainchild of Dr. Jean Chamberlain Froese, M.D. Dr. Froese is an obstetrician and director of the International Women's Health Program at McMaster University, in Hamilton, Ontario. Dr. Froese lives in Uganda eight months of the year running a maternal/child health program. In 2008, the "FIGO Save the Mothers" program came to Uganda and capitalized on the existing Canada-Uganda relationship formed by Dr. Froese. Then in 2010, Dr. Froese published a book, "Where Have All The Mothers Gone?" on the challenges mothers experience with childbirth throughout the world.

The integration of this degree program with all the other aspects of STM shows intriguing promise. One of the advantages of education is that it is portable; after an adequate number of Ugandans earn this degree, the university can begin exporting its expertise by educating professionals from surrounding nations. This increased education level could have the long term effect of amplifying the benefits of other STM undertakings.

Conclusion

The diverse Save the Mothers programs around the world have all produced significant benefits with limited resources. After the original ten pilot projects began, new projects have sprung up in five different countries. This is encouraging because it suggests that the model is repeatable and flexible enough to apply to a wide range of settings. Some of the STM projects also work in concert with related programs which increase professional education, surgery awareness, and malaria control. If these relationships increase and spread to other countries, the synergistic effects could be significant. Because it has been applied in so many diverse environments, the model has proved itself to be exportable, flexible, and replicable. It will be interesting to see if funding is available after the program's end in 2011. The lives of many women and babies may hang in the balance.

Works Cited

Black, Harvey. "Pairing Up Saves Mothers in Central America." *Perspectives in Health Newsletter* 6.1 (2001) <http://www.paho.org/english/dpi/Number11_article5.htm>.

Curet, L. B. "FIGO Save the Mothers Initiative: the Central America and USA collaboration." *International Journal of Gynecology and Obstetrics* Feb 2003. <www.ncbi.nlm.nih.gov/pubmed/12566201>.

Duke University Libraries. 15 Jan 2008. Duke University. 5 Nov 2010 <http://library.duke.edu/research/subject/guides/ngo_guide/ngo_links/women.html>.

International Federation of Gynecology and Obstetrics. "Saving mothers and Newborns." 18 June 2010 <http://www.figo.org/projects/newborns>.

Kiwuwa, M. S. and P. Mufabenga. "Use of Antenatal Care, Maternity Services, Intermittent Presumptive Treatment and Insecticide Treated Bed Nets by Pregnant Women in Luwero District, Uganda." *Malaria Journal* 7.44 (March 1, 2008). Web. <http://www.ncbi.nlm.nih.gov/pubmed/18312682>.

Lalonde, A. B. "The FIGO Save the Mothers Initiative: The Uganda-Canada Collaboration." *International Journal of Gynecology and Obstetrics* Feb 2003. <http://www.ncbi.nlm.nih.gov/pubmed/12566200>.

Lobhi, S. K. "FIGO save the Mothers Initiative: The Pakistan–UK Collaboration." *International Journal of Gynecology and Obstetrics* Oct. 2004. Web. <http://www.ijgo.org/article/S0020-7292(04)00242-5/abstract>.

Luboga, S. "Key Aspects of Health Policy Development to Improve Surgical

Services in Uganda." *World Journal of Surgery* 34.11 (2010). Web. <http://www.ncbi.nlm.nih.gov/pmc/articles/PMC2949567>.

Mekbib, T. et al. "The FIGO Save the Mothers Initiative: the Ethiopia-Sweden collaboration." *International Journal of Gynecology and Obstetrics* 81.4 (April 2003). <http://www.ncbi.nlm.nih.gov/pubmed/12676407>. Accessed: 1 December 2010.

Save the Mothers Program. 2009-2010. <http://www.savethemothers.org>

Uganda Christian University. "Save the Mothers Program." 2011. <http://ucu.ac.ug/content/view/151/43/>.

United States Southern Command. "Continuing Promise 2010." 19 November 2010. <http://www.southcom.mil/appssc/factFiles.php?id=155>.

World Health Organization (WHO). "Maternal deaths worldwide drop by third." 15 September 2010. <http://www.who.int/mediacentre/news/releases/2010/maternal_mortality_20100915/en/index.html>. Accessed: 7 December 2010.

World Health Organization. (WHO). <http://gamapserver.who.int/gho/interactive_charts/women_and_health/causes_death/chart.html>.

10.
Association for Improvements in the Maternity Services (AIMS) Ireland

Supporting Women, Promoting Change

CHRISTINA BERMINGHAM

THE ASSOCIATION FOR IMPROVEMENTS IN the Maternity Services (AIMS) Ireland was formed in 2007 by mothers dissatisfied with the maternity services in Ireland. AIMS IRELAND was set up with the support of AIMS UK, an organization that has been at the forefront of improving maternity services over the past forty years. AIMS IRELAND is a consumer-led voluntary organization whose mission is to highlight normal birth and campaign for mother- and baby-friendly birth practices that are supported by evidence-based research and international best practice. In addition to its campaign work, the organization offers independent, confidential support and information on maternity choices and care to women and their families. The organization has undergone tremendous growth and change during the past few years and today plays a key role representing the voices and interests of maternity service users in the Republic of Ireland. Drawing on my personal involvement in the group and using information collected as part of my ongoing Ph.D. research exploring birth activism in the Republic of Ireland, this chapter provides details of the organization's formation, mission, and activities. It highlights some of the key achievements and obstacles identified by former and current organizational leaders while exploring the role organizations like AIMS IRELAND play in the larger motherhood movement.

Maternity Services in the Republic of Ireland

In order to understand how and why birth organizations like AIMS Ireland have developed it is important to first present some background on the maternity system in Ireland. In the Republic of Ireland, according to the latest annual figures (2008) an average of over 75,000 women experience birth (ESRI). Of the average 75,000 or more births a year, less than one percent of women give birth outside a hospital setting (ESRI; Kennedy, 2002, 2004, 2005). The development of maternity services in Ireland reflects the increasing control and management of childbirth by the medical profession (Begley; Devane, Murphy-Lawless and Begley; Grey; Kennedy 2002, 2004, 2005; Murphy-Lawless 1998; Devane and

Photo of AIMS IRELAND *members, including the author and her son, Oliver, at the official launch of an* AIMS IRELAND *branch in Galway, West of Ireland. March 2008. Photo: Reg Gordon.*

Murphey-Lawless; O'Connor). In the Republic of Ireland, being pregnant and giving birth occurs within a highly centralized maternity system consisting of mostly obstetric-led units managed by the Health Services Executive (HSE) where the medical model of birth is dominant. This medical model "views women as a problem to be solved and pregnancy as a pathological state" (Kennedy 2005: 18). It has been so successfully integrated into the maternity services in Ireland (and elsewhere) as a result of the stringent efforts of the obstetric profession to dominate the area of childbirth; a process in play for over two hundred years (Murphy-Lawless).

The successful medicalization of birth by obstetrics in Ireland is reflected in, as well as reinforced and sustained through legislation, state policy and institutional structures (Devane, Murphy-Lawless and Begley; Kennedy 2002, 2004, 2005; McAdam-O'Connell; O'Malley). Tracing the development of maternity care policies in Ireland, Patricia Kennedy (2002) states: "There has been a very serious lack of attention in Ireland to policies which relate specifically to the health of women as they experience pregnancy, childbirth and the postpartum period" (6).

The main legislation guiding maternity practice is the Mother and Infant Care Scheme (see Ireland) and in this policy, obstetricians are identified as the lead professional in maternity service provision. Since the seventies, Ireland's maternity system has been subject to widespread centralization as smaller units throughout the country have been closed in favor of larger, consultant-led units. There are no national guidelines governing maternity service provision and the type and quality of care varies considerably throughout the country. This inconsistent service provision is a feature of a maternity system that has been designed with limited involvement of anyone outside of the obstetric profession. According to Devane

Devane, Jo Murphy-Lawless, and Cecily M. Begley, "Women have had minimal, if any input to influence the direction of maternity-care decisions effectively at strategic policy levels" (93). The current Irish maternity system and the policy-making processes that have contributed to the design of this system severely lack accountability and transparency.

Among those who advocate for maternity care improvements, this lack of accountability, transparency, and consistency has many negative consequences for women who avail of Irish maternity services. "Active Management of Labour," a unique Irish contribution to the medicalization of childbirth worldwide, has drastically impacted the provision of maternity care and the ways in which women experience pregnancy and birth since the late 1960s (Kennedy 2002; Murphy-Lawless). Among those who oppose this medicalized system, there are strong efforts to draw attention to the lack of choice and control women have under the medical model. For many, the Irish maternity system does not place the needs and concerns of women at the centre. It has contributed to a system of care often referred to as an "assembly line" where women, as patients, undergo a variety of technology-based interventions designed to hurry them through labour under the constant management of the medical profession (Murphy-Lawless; Begley; Grey; Devane, Murphy-Lawless and Begley).

This system is referred to as the "Irish Childbirth Regime" by Jane Grey who uses the term *regime* "to emphasize the extent to which these practices and ideas appear to be uncontested within certain boundaries of time and space—that is, they have a character peculiar to modern Ireland ... the absence of any significant public challenge to the process is extraordinary" (247-248). That these ideas and practices remain so largely uncontested are a testament to the success of obstetrics in dominating birth. It also calls into question the ways in which the political, cultural and economic conditions of Irish society have contributed to the success of this regime and the lack of public contestation. Declan Devane and Jo Murphy-Lawless draw attention to the impact of social norms on the development of medicalized birth in Ireland: "The social norms stemming from a rigidly stratified, conservative and impoverished Catholic society helped to strengthen immeasurably the power of the obstetricians and what was their growing bias towards a medical model..." (13). In response to all these features of Irish maternity care, individuals, groups and organizations have emerged to contest the power, knowledge and authority of the obstetric profession and to seek alternative ways of birthing. Such efforts are not entirely unique to Ireland, and throughout the world there is evidence of similar collective action taking place within the larger motherhood movement.

And so, this is the maternity system that I quite suddenly found myself a part of when in June of 2007, while five months pregnant, I moved with my partner to a small city in the West of Ireland. In the course of trying to navigate this system and educate myself about childbirth and the maternity services I first learned of AIMS Ireland after coming across the group's website while researching online. After the birth of my son, I became involved in a local branch of AIMS IRELAND serving as branch secretary and later (when branches were abolished in favor of returning to a national structure) as a "regional liaison officer." My personal experiences within the Irish maternity services and my growing involvement in AIMSI and birth activism sparked a research interest. In February 2008, I was awarded a Ph.D. Studentship from the School of Nursing at Dublin City University to carry out research on the politics of childbirth and maternity care in Ireland and the development of birth activism in Ireland.

The information compiled in this chapter comes from both my personal involvement with the organization and from data collected as part of my Ph.D. research. The information included in this chapter has been gathered from (1) a brief survey conducted of birth organizations in Ireland; (2) in-depth interviews with both current and former organizational leaders and members of AIMS IRELAND; and (3) analysis of secondary sources and organizational documents such as press releases, website content, informational brochures, etc... Additionally, the current AIMSI committee members have given a great deal of their time and energy in assisting me with compiling and organizing this information and their feedback has been invaluable.

Philosophy/Purpose

AIMS IRELAND's mission is to highlight normal birth[1] and campaign for mother- and baby-friendly birth practices which are supported by evidence-based research and international best practices. AIMS Ireland provides independent, confidential support and information on maternity choices and care to women and their families. Through contact with service users, consumer interest groups and healthcare practitioners, the organization stays informed of key issues in maternity care and services which they are then able to feed back to service providers, media, the Health Services Executive (HSE) and government in an effort to improve maternity services on a local and national level.[2]

History

AIMS IRELAND was formed in 2007 by mothers dissatisfied with the maternity care system in Ireland. The four founding members, all mothers, met on a parenting website which discussed childbirth and birth choices in 2006. They originally established a group called "Maternity Care Matters" and focused on the issue of birth partners—the ban on doulas attending births in some Irish hospitals, and additional birth partners in Dublin. After contacting the Association for Improvements in the Maternity Services (AIMS) UK, they were invited by AIMS UK Chair, Beverly Beech, to become AIMS IRELAND. AIMS UK has been at the forefront of improving maternity services for over 40 years. They publish a well-respected and widely read quarterly journal that focuses on current issues in maternity care, provides news about ongoing campaigns and analysis of the latest research.[3] AIMS IRELAND strives to do the same in bringing information to women and families and bringing about improvements in the maternity system. An earlier IRISH AIMS was established in Ireland in 1979 by Dee Neeson who, along with other mothers, similarly dissatisfied with the maternity services, organized to campaign for changes. AIMS IRELAND played an instrumental role in the early stages of birth activism in Ireland but by the nineties no longer existed.

Activities

Providing Information and Support

AIMS IRELAND provides information and support to women and their families in a number of ways including via their website, local public meetings, and Birth Healing Workshops. The organization's appointed Support and Information Aide responds to hundreds of birth-related inquiries via e-mail and telephone each year. In 2010, the organization redesigned their website, online discussion forums and Facebook profile with feedback from the public and members to ensure greater clarity and ease in navigating the information and content made available through these Internet sources. The organization holds public meetings that are informal and open to the public where AIMS IRELAND representatives provide updates on initiatives and developments taking place locally and nationally and also offer parents and practitioners a forum to share experiences and discuss concerns and opportunities relating to maternity services in their area. From the start, the organization's founding members have been particularly concerned with raising awareness of birth-related trauma. Based on additional feedback from surveys and contact with both women and providers, AIMS IRELAND has organized a number of Birth Healing Workshops. These workshops are designed for women who have suffered a distressing or traumatic birth experience and wish to take steps toward healing. They are full-day workshops facilitated by qualified psychotherapists with experience in supporting and helping women in coming to terms with difficult birth experiences.[4] The latest workshop held in Dublin in late Spring 2010 was fully booked with a waiting list.

One of the group's key priorities lies in carrying out research via surveys to gather details of women's experiences with the maternity services. Given the lack of women's voices and interests in Irish maternity services these surveys remain the only opportunity for women to evaluate their maternity services. The surveys themselves help raise awareness among women, and then AIMSI's reports and presentations on the results and success in getting the media to report on them, comprise a huge accomplishment in terms of making women's voices heard. The latest survey report, *What Matters to You* (AIMSI 2010) has been recognized within the HSE and working groups as a key document, and as a model for satisfaction surveys in hospital settings.

As AIMS IRELAND's recognition as a consumer group has increased, it has been asked to serve on a number of hospital consumer groups and government-backed steering committees. In addition AIMS IRELAND organizes, participates in and attends local, national and international conferences, workshops and seminars.

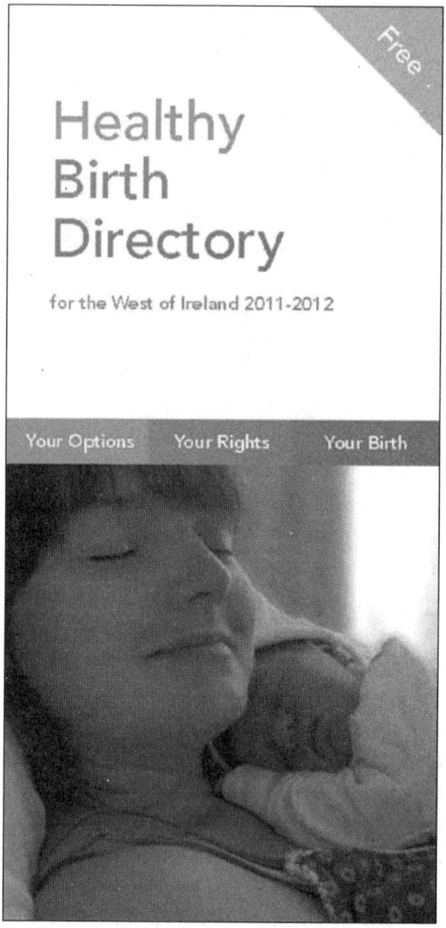

They host information booths exhibited at conferences and birth fairs throughout the country. The organization produces informational brochures/leaflets and flyers for upcoming events. They engage with media through press releases and interviews with reporters from newspapers, radio and television. Membership with the organization includes a copy of the AIMS IRELAND Bi-Annual Newsletter; access to additional research and information; up-to-date information via e-mail on the latest initiatives, articles, surveys, etc; free delivery of AIMS books; and the opportunity to serve as an AIMS IRELAND Representative. In September 2010, AIMS IRELAND hosted a Joint Committee Meeting and Seminar Day with AIMS UK in Dublin focused on the key issue of consent in maternity care. This public seminar included presentations, discussions and a workshop and followed with a public lecture on midwife-led care held a few days later in Galway.

A group of AIMS IRELAND members in the West of Ireland have been working on a Healthy Birth Directory modeled on a similar guide produced by U.S.-based Choices in Childbirth. The guide is organized into three sections: Your Options, Your Rights and Your Birth. It includes a directory of individual practitioners in the community who have signed up to a model of care called the International MotherBaby Childbirth Initiative (IMBCI). The IMBCI outlines what good maternity care is drawing on a women-centered standard of care that AIMS IRELAND hopes will grow to inform and influence all policies and practices throughout the Irish maternity services. The guide, recently launched in Galway on March 8, 2011 to celebrate International Women's Day, is freely available to download via the AIMS IRELAND website and by request in print form.

Campaigns

AIMS IRELAND is involved in campaigning and lobbying efforts and work with a variety of organizations, groups and individuals both nationally and internationally to raise awareness of maternity and birth issues and seek improvements in the maternity care system. As indicated in the organization's mandate a majority of the organization's campaigning results from the feedback gathered from those who contact the organization with a query or concern or from issues identified in surveys conducted by the organization. The focus of AIMS IRELAND campaigns are also reflective of the problems that exist within the current maternity system as identified at the start of this chapter. For instance, the organization has been campaigning for: (1) the creation of national guidelines for clinical practice which would be in agreement with international best practice as set by the World Health Organization; (2) publication of obstetric clinical reports for all hospitals in annual reports with adequate follow-up investigation for any major deviations from set national guidelines; and (3) provision of a national consultative body, which would include representatives from all stakeholders in maternity care, to monitor all hospital statistics and deal with complaints in a clear, structured and independent manner.

Another key campaign AIMS IRELAND has engaged in during the last few years that is closely linked to the ones mentioned above has centered on Informed Choice and Consent. AIMS IRELAND has called for an independent review of consent-related practices within the Irish maternity system to be implemented in concurrence with the creation and implementation of National Guidelines for Clinical Practice in Maternity Care. This recommendation stems from a report released by the group in March of 2008 publishing its findings of a national electronic survey, *The Availaibility of Information and Consent*. Of the 161 women surveyed (anonymously and self-selecting) 75.6 percent of respondents stated they feel that consent is an issue of concern in the Irish maternity system. More than half of respondents (57.6 percent) were not given the option to refuse a procedure, test or treatment. Invasive procedures such as ARM, Episiotomy, the use of Oxytocin, Membrane Sweeps, assisted delivery, internal fetal scalp monitoring and the management of the third stage of labour were all areas cited, feeding into AIMS IRELAND's recommendation for National Guidelines for Clinical Practice in Maternity Care. To date, the organization's efforts to engage with the HSE and government officials regarding these issues has resulted in several meetings with politicians and the HSE.

Additionally a great deal of the issues the organization has focused on recently have come from outside variables such as legislation or scandals emerging in the media. For instance in light of the recent Irish miscarriage misdiagnosis scandal, AIMS IRELAND emerged as a major birth consumer group receiving widespread recognition from the media, the HSE, midwives and those involved in training midwives. As of November 2010, the organization's campaigning efforts were largely centred on pending legislation for the 2010 Nurses and Midwives Bill. As highlighted in Martina Hynan's chapter on Keeping Mum, this legislation in its current form, denies women and midwives autonomy, choice and control in birth. AIMS IRELAND has led the joint campaign protesting the legislation including an online petition[5] that has received over 3,400 signatures to date, a protest

Protesting the 2010 Irish Nurses and Midwives Bill outside The Dáil in Dublin, Ireland, Nov. 3, 2010. Holding AIMS IRELAND Banner: (on left) Tracy Donegan (AIMSI member; Doula Ireland, founder) and (on right) Jene Kelly (co-founder, current Co-Chair of AIMSI). Photo: AIMS IRELAND.

picketing outside the Irish government, and drafting of suggested amendments to be made to the current bill. AIMS IRELAND's efforts to raise concerns about the bill drew national and international media coverage and involvement from individuals and groups with AIMS IRELAND acting as an "umbrella" organization leading these efforts to challenge the bill. The legislation is still pending and AIMSI is still actively campaigning against the proposed bill.

Achievements and Challenges

In the few short years since it has been established, AIMS IRELAND has experienced significant growth and undergone tremendous change. One of the key challenges the organization faces is a lack of personnel and high turn over rate of those involved. As a voluntary organization the demands of the work faced by a relatively few key officers is extremely demanding. Balancing family, work and their voluntary responsibilities creates a great deal of strain for the relatively few core organizers. Many of the organizers note the personal and professional sacrifices involved in carrying out their work in the organization. Adding to this is the emotional difficulty of processing the stories individuals share with them. This includes experiences of trauma, inequitable treatment and/or instances of inadequate care that fails to meet "best practice" standards. This is particularly difficult for those who are pregnant themselves and/or may still be dealing with traumatic birth experiences. Often those involved with AIMS IRELAND must detach themselves emotionally from these experiences and it can be challenging to make a clear distinction between personal experiences and the generalized situation.

The lack of resources on all levels is challenging particularly in regards to funding. The organization does not have any paid staff nor does it receive any additional funding outside of donations and membership dues. Volunteers are left to carry the financial burden of many activities including phone calls, printing, etc. It is often difficult to organize and pay for babysitting, parking, and petrol costs to attend meetings and events. The majority of the non-AIMS IRELAND meetings (i.e. various committees, meetings with government bodies and officials) that members must attend are held during weekdays between 9:00-5:00 and members are spread throughout the country, so coordinating meetings is very difficult. A great deal of organizing and organizational work is done online (via email) and by phone. The development of and access to technology in order to facilitate this is great but it also results in additional time away from family when one is on the computer or telephone so much. Some members of the current board identified the stress that their roles have placed on their partners, most of whom are required to increase their own family/house responsibilities in order for their partners to carry out AIMS IRELAND work.

In addition to the personal difficulties of fulfilling the responsibilities that come with the group's growing recognition and involvement in maternity care issues in Ireland is the constraints associated with serving as representatives on an increasing number of consumer groups and steering committees. While the group has paved the way in terms of being asked to join these committees it is still a struggle to have their recommendations heard and implemented. Also, serving on committees that like the current system lack transparency and accountability has presented many challenges for AIMS IRELAND representatives who struggle to ensure that true consumer representation in a democratic process of policymaking takes place. In the words of one AIMS IRELAND member, "There can be a feeling that consumer representation is a ticked box rather than a tool for understanding the concerns and issues for women accessing the Irish maternity system."[6]

Relationship to Larger Motherhood Movement

The challenges identified above by former and current AIMS IRELAND leaders and members are ones echoed throughout my interviews and surveys of those involved in birth activism in Ireland. As we struggle to increase choice and control in birth for women and their partners and fight for women's rights in birth within systems that deny women's rights and continue to stifle women's voices we undoubtedly come face-to-face with challenges such as these. To a large extent the issues AIMSI is campaigning for are the same ones earlier generations of mothers and midwives fought for. One of the biggest challenges for AIMS IRELAND and other Irish birth organizations included in my research has been working successfully with each other and other groups. However, the latest campaign led by AIMS IRELAND concerning the 2010 Nurses and Midwives Bill brought together groups both within and outside of Ireland in an unprecedented way resulting in a growing movement that is, I believe, becoming increasingly more effective and powerful. I believe that this coming together of individuals, groups and organizations both within Ireland and outside who support women's choice and control and seek to make heard women's voices and experiences is what will define the movement going forward paving the way for change. I also believe that this book undoubtedly contributes to this by bringing together groups from around the world who are part of the motherhood movement. We may all have our individual goals, differing activities and campaigns, but in the end we are united in our struggle for women's rights, equality and true representation.

Special thanks to AIMS IRELAND Co-Chairs, Jene Kelly and Krysia Lynch, and former Secretary, Tara Durkin, for all their support and feedback in compiling information for this chapter.

[1]AIMS IRELAND defines "normal birth" in accordance with the World Health Organization's (1997) definition: "…spontaneous in onset, low-risk at the start of labour and remaining so throughout labour and delivery. The infant is born spontaneously in the vertex position between 37 and 42 completed weeks of pregnancy. After birth mother and infant are in good condition…. In normal birth there should be a valid reason to interfere with the natural process."
[2]See: http://www.aimsireland.com/homepage/?topic=home
[3]AIMS UK website: <http://www.aims.org.uk>
[4]For more information about past Birth Healing Workshops organized by AIMS Ireland please see: <http://www.aimsireland.com/events/?topic=birthHealing>.
[5]AIMS IRELAND's petition: <www.gopetition.com/petition/39693.html>.
[6]AIMS IRELAND. Personal Communication. December 2010.

Works Cited

AIMS Ireland: Association for Improvements in the Maternity Services Ireland. 2010 <http://www.aimsireland.com>.

Begley, Cecily M. "'Giving Midwifery Care': Student Midwives' Views of Their Working Role." *Midwifery* 17 (2001): 24-34.

Devane, Declan and Jo Murphy-Lawless. "Maternity Care in Ireland." *Home Birth Association Ireland Information Booklet.* Oct. 2008: 12-14.

Devane, Declan, Jo Murphy-Lawless, and Cecily M. Begley. "Childbirth Policies and Practices in Ireland and the Journey Towards Midwifery-Led Care." *Midwifery* 23 (2007): 92-101.

Economic and Social Research Institute (ESRI).Health Research and Information Division. *Perinatal Statistics Report 2008.* Dublin. December 21, 2010. <http://www.esri.ie/publications/latest_publications/view/index.xml?id=3151>.

Grey, Jane. "The Drama of Childbirth." *Ireland Unbound: A Turn of the Century Chronicle.* Irish Sociological Chronicles, Vol. 3, 1999-2000. Ed. M. P. Corcoran and M. Peillon. Dublin: Institute of Public Administration, 2002. 247-259.

Ireland. Department of Health and Children. *Report of the Maternity and Infant Care Scheme.* Dublin: Department of Health and Children Ireland, 1994.

Kennedy, Patricia. *Maternity in Ireland: A Woman-Centred Perspective.* Dublin: The Liffey Press, 2002.

Kennedy, Patricia. *Motherhood in Ireland: Creation and Context.* Cork: Mercier Press, 2004.

Kennedy, Patricia. "Moving Towards Consumer Involvement in Maternity Services in the North-east of Ireland." *International Journal of Consumer Studies* 32 (2005): 27-33.

McAdam-O'Connell, Bridget. "Risk, Responsibility and Choice: The Medical Model of Birth and Alternatives." *Returning Birth to Women: Challenging Policies and Practices.* Ed. Patricia Kennedy and Jo Murphy-Lawless. Dublin: Centre for Women's Studies, Trinity College Dublin and WERRC, University College Dublin 1998. 21-29.

Murphy-Lawless, Jo. *Reading Birth and Death: A History of Obstetric Thinking.* Cork: Cork University Press, 1998.

O'Connor, Marie. Birthtides: Turning Towards Home Birth. London: Harper Collins, 1995.

O'Malley, Mary Pat. "Silence as a Means of Preserving the Status-Quo: The Case of Ante-Natal Care in Ireland." *Multilingua* 24 (2005): 39-54.

11.
Keeping Mum, Community Art Project

Joining the Dots ... Mapping Maternal Identity in Ireland

MARTINA HYNAN

KEEPING MUM, COMMUNITY ART PROJECT and Clare Birth Choice, Activist Group are based in County Clare Ireland. Keeping Mum ostensibly began as the creative arm of Clare Birth Choice, a voluntary organization lobbying for improved maternity services in Ireland. They are in effect the same organization, but the two names are assigned to different causes: Keeping Mum is identified with artistic expression, whereas Clare Birth Choice promotes social and political awareness of maternity issues in Ireland.

At the time of writing this chapter, Clare Birth Choice is immersed in a national campaign to challenge proposed new legislation that, if passed in its current form, will adversely affect mothers and midwives. The opening of this chapter will give an overview of this struggle to date. The remainder of the chapter will be devoted to a review of the work of Keeping Mum.

Clare Birth Choice and Political Activism

Clare Birth Choice was started in 2004 by a group of mothers, all non-Irish nationals, who began lobbying for maternity service in Co. Clare. There has been no maternity service here since 1987. Women have to travel up to eighty miles to maternity hospitals in Limerick or Galway. In 2004 all members of Clare Birth Choice had experienced giving birth in an Irish maternity hospital and all passionately believed that this system failed them and their families.

We are currently challenging proposed new legislation; however, right now the government is in crisis and we expect a general election in March 2011. The Minister for Health has just resigned and it is very difficult to know what will happen with the *Nurses and Midwives Bill 2010*.

This new bill could effectively criminalize independent midwives:[1] Section 40 weaves mandatory insurance into statute and effectively means that if a midwife without mandatory insurance attends a woman who falls outside the very strict guidelines for home birth, then, she will be fined and possibly imprisoned. This denies a midwife the right to provide her service and contravenes European Law (Directive 2005/36/EC) that guarantees a midwife the right to offer her services

Demonstration outside Government Buildings, Dublin.

independently. If Section 24 of the new *Nurses and Midwives Bill 2010* is passed midwives will be the only health professionals in Ireland without the ability to govern themselves.

We are working with other organizations and individuals including; Association for the Improvement of Maternity Services (AIMS) Ireland, the Community Midwives Association, Doula Ireland, Health Services Action Group and Home Birth Association, as well as many lecturers in nursing and midwifery courses in Ireland (including Trinity College Dublin, University College Cork and the National University of Ireland Galway) to change this legislation.

Krysia Lynch, co-chair, AIMS Ireland commented that the bill is: "an affront to women's rights and also basic human rights,"[2] and as such, must be challenged.

Those involved in the current campaign recognise the challenge that this new bill could create, and as I write, I can hear the words of Helene Cixous in her seminal essay "The Laugh of the Medusa," when she wrote: "Censor the body and you censor breath and speech at the same time. Write yourself. Your body must be heard" (880). Women in Ireland must write their bodies into this new bill or they could be silenced for a very long time.

We are actively lobbying members of parliament and are continuing our efforts to garner support as well as raise awareness in press and media. Letters of support have been published in the *Irish Times*[3] and other national and local papers. On a local level in Co. Clare, we met with local journalist, Jessica Quinn, who wrote a substantial article on the subject in *The Clare Champion* in January 2011.

Mandate of Keeping Mum, Community Art Project

Keeping Mum creates art activist programmes that challenge cultural and socio-political concepts, perceptions and representations of birth in Ireland. By raising awareness in this way we are seeking to create change and move towards a positive and holistic understanding of birth.

History

In May 2008 I approached members of Clare Birth Choice and suggested that they create a series of artworks from personal memories of giving birth. Thus Keeping Mum, Community Art Project was born.

When we began to meet, questions were raised about Irish culture, the history of obstetric care, the legacy of colonialism, the influence of the Catholic Church, the representation of women in Ireland, the inter-connections of the image and concepts of mother with that of Mother Ireland. This changing birthing landscape in Ireland reflects the social, political, psychological and cultural developments that have and are taking place here; our approach to our memories were drenched in this cultural morass.

When Ireland gained independence from Britain in 1922 it began its campaign to establish a separate and distinct post-colonial identity, and integral to this new identity was the control over women's sexuality. "The determination to be different in every way was … reinforced by projecting the Irish female as chaste, unsophisticated, even unworldly, whose sole role within the new state was that of mother and homemaker" (Breathnach-Lynch 85). Enshrining a woman's place within the home was confirmed in the 1937 Constitution, which states, "In particular by her life within the home, woman gives to the state a support without which the common good cannot be achieved" (Connor 511). Both the cultural and political lives of the new post-colonial Ireland have worked hard to promulgate an Irish female identity premised on anti-Britishness and focused on an evolving Catholic ethos that repressed all citizens but women in particular.[4]

So much of the cultural, social, physical and political landscape of Ireland has been dominated by the Catholic Church, and very often at the expense of women. As Mary Condren, theologian and feminist theorist puts it many of the battles have often: "been carved out, literally, over the bodies of women" (xvii).

Objectives and Practice

There is a very strong belief within the group that it is only by sharing, by being informed and by helping to inform each other that we will help other mothers and parents-to-be, both men and women, to understand and value the experience of becoming a mother. Our objective is to develop a creative arts and activist programme that will include the reflections of more mothers, father, midwives and others in our community.

Ballyportry Sheela-na-gig, Clare Museum, Ennis, Co. Clare.

When we started Keeping Mum, we decided to create a group logo and after much discussion we all felt that our logo should derive from the medieval Sheela-na-Gig[5] image. Sheela-na-gigs are often considered a continuation of earlier pagan customs associated with pagan spirit/ Mother Earth/ Earth Goddess/ fertility symbols. Sometimes she is referred to as a midwife. The most commonly agreed meaning is that of "the old hag of the breasts." We settled on the Sheela-na-gig as the most appropriate image for our logo.

We began our art project with eight women. One woman is from Austria, one from Cuba, one from Venezuela, three are from the UK and two from Ireland. All seven of us who have experienced birth have done so in Ireland. The eighth member is an independent midwife. English is not the first language for three members, so working in the visual language is helpful on various levels.

From the outset, the group's descriptions of their birthing experiences have been shrouded in feelings of fear, sadness, frustration, anger, disappointment and powerlessness, because prior to their engagement with the maternity services in Ireland they were unaware of the history of the "active management of birth"[6] in Ireland with the inevitable "the cascade of interventions" (Murphy-Lawless 204).

Context

> Suppose that we redefine our labours and the moment of birth, not as empty time to be got through, but as a sort of happiness, an intensity, a completeness, a memory that in its crystal clarity, lives as long as we do. The moment of birth as a point of revolution – this is a tool with which to re-take control, to energetically contest how our bodies in labour have been written and to write our experiences anew. (Murphy-Lawless)[7]

Jo Murphy-Lawless made this statement during the launch of her book *Reading Birth and Death: A History of Obstetric Thinking*. I wasn't able to attend the launch because I had given birth to our daughter five weeks earlier. I had a home birth, and it was undoubtedly the most empowering and enlightening experience I have ever had. Ironically, if I were pregnant today, I would not have the same choice of where to give birth that I had in 1998 because our maternity services have become increasingly medicalized with a growing emphasis on hospital births. Prior to 1994 the health care system stated that, "where a decision is made by a woman to give birth in her own home, health personnel would respect that decision" (O'Connor 117); however, after this time slowly and inexorably this decision has been eroded in part due to litigation against the state[8] and growing fears of further litigation.

Activities

When we created the artworks for Keeping Mum we met weekly over a period of approximately three months. We now meet monthly and discuss ways of developing both Clare Birth Choice and Keeping Mum.

We work on a voluntary basis and have no secure funding which means that we can only provide visual art workshops when we have the resources. For example, I ran a 'taster workshop'[9] in April 2010 with a group of women interested in joining Keeping Mum; however, we have not secured any further funding yet.

The existing core group membership is comprised of a dynamic and diverse group of women. One is a dance teacher with expertise in teaching belly dancing to pregnant women, and she is also training to be a Doula. Another has recently qualified as a yoga teacher. Both of these women are running classes and hope the women they work with will join Keeping Mum.

To increase the awareness of issues surrounding birth we hosted the showing of a new documentary, *Natural Traditions*[10] on 3rd December 2010. It documents the history of community midwifery in the West Cork area of Ireland. It was not only an opportunity to discuss the proposed new legislation but also a chance to show the artwork of Keeping Mum and encourage other women to reflect on their birthing experiences and invite women to join our group. It was also a fundraiser for Keeping Mum. Five more women have expressed their desire to join our group.

When we began Keeping Mum in 2008, I introduced the group to the work of women artists, particularly work created during the past thirty years. I wanted to introduce some of the critical debates about the politics of the gaze,[11] the medical gaze, the male gaze, the female gaze and the feminist gaze. Some of the women artist's work we looked at included: Louise Bourgeois, Judy Chicago, Pauline Cummins, Rita Duffy, Mona Hatoum, Mary Kelly, Ana Mendieta, Annette Messager, Kiki Smith and Nancy Spero, to name some.

Several of the women said that they had never seen art like this before, and Cecilia, who is from Cuba, commented that she had never felt a connection with the visual arts until she had seen the work of these women artists. Not only did this open up the world of the visual in a new way for the group, but I believe it engaged them with visual art from within a feminist cultural perspective, elicit-

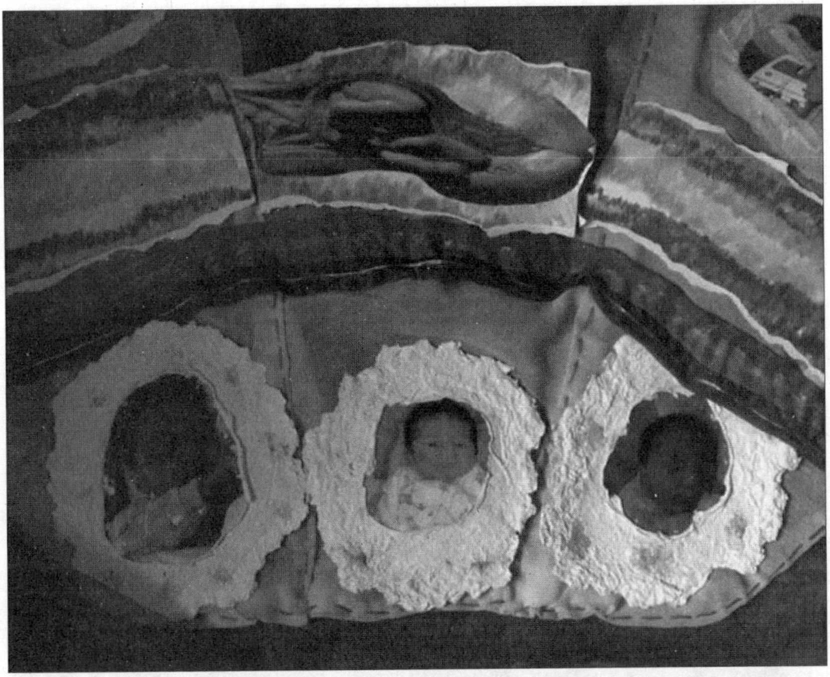

"Memory Flashes" by Silvia Cardona-Grijalva.

"Our Crowning Rose" by Cecilia Martinez-Conway.

"Like a Tree, I Am Alive" by Armella Karas-Doyle

ing powerful responses. This was a very deliberate strategy on my part. I choose images by women artists whose vision and aesthetic simultaneously challenged patriarchal representations of women's bodies and contributed to a more woman centred worldview, and I believe it was this worldview that so moved the women in Keeping Mum.

When we looked at an image by Judy Chicago called "Tear/Tear" from *The Birth Project*[12] the women expressed their interest and affinity with the ideas behind the work and the method employed.

To my dismay, I discovered that there were too few images of birth in

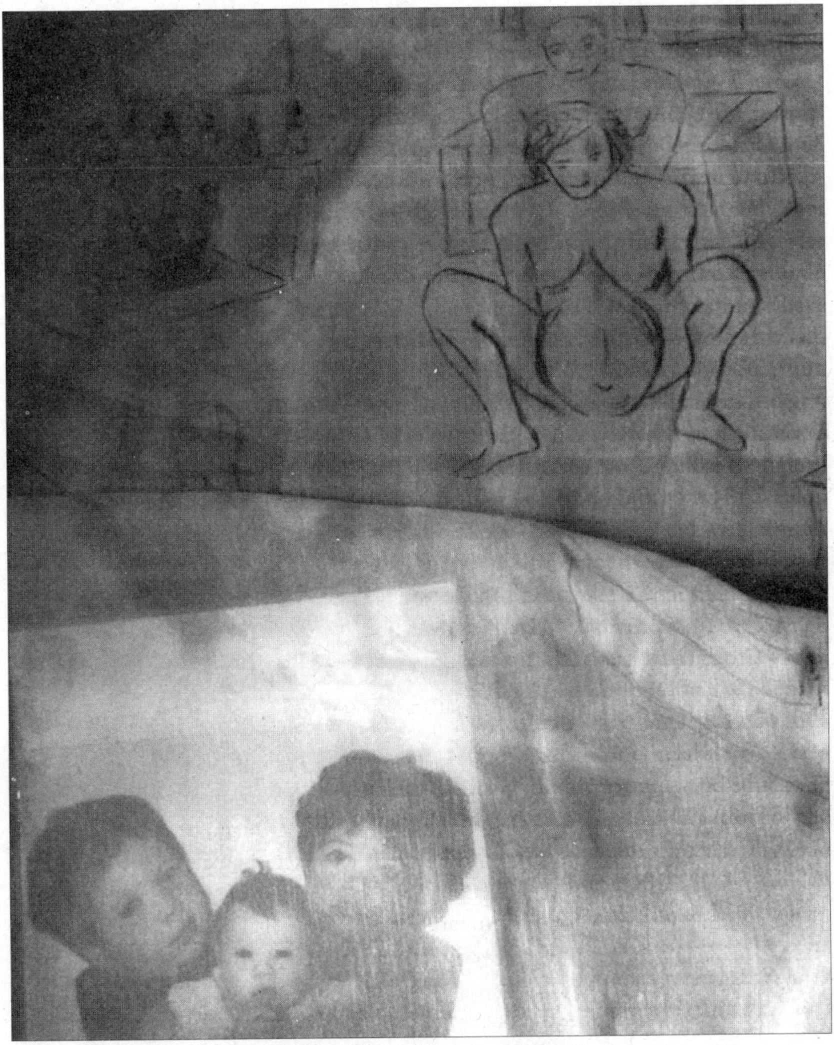

"Peace of Mind" by Cecilia Martinez-Conway

> Western art, an omission I set out to counter through an extended series of painted and needle-worked images of birth. To behold the vulva in labour as a woman is giving birth is to be confronted with sheer female power. I wanted to celebrate that power and to explore and express the range of birth experiences—the painful and the joyous—and the act of creation itself. (Chicago 68)

Suddenly there was a real sense of possibility, of hope and a growing desire to create artworks. The women expressed their keen desire to draw, paint, make paper and sew. They wanted the experience to be "hands on." We had limited time and

Keeping Mum — KEEPING MUM!

resources[13] so decided to focus on one aspect of our individual experiences. While most of the group had mixed birthing experiences they were determined to represent a positive aspect of their experience. We discussed just what a positive image was for each of us and why. The artworks created are mixed media and include fabric painting, sewing, photography and paper-making. We exhibit the work in a gazebo and attach the artworks onto muslin fabric panels. This makes it lightweight, easily transportable and freestanding, a veritable "room of one's own."

To date the work has been shown in eight venues nationally and internationally. When we exhibited it during our International Women's Day Celebrations in Ennis, County Clare, 2009, hosted by the Clare Women's Network, we invited Jo Murphy-Lawless to speak. Jo is currently lecturer at the School of Nursing and Midwifery, at Trinity College Dublin. Since then, it has travelled to Canada where it was shown at the 2009 Annual Conference of the Association for Research on Mothering (ARM), and recently, we showed at the International Day of the Midwife Celebrations at the University of Limerick at the invitation of the teaching staff on the nursing and midwifery course whom we had met at the Birth Project conference, Trinity College Dublin in April 2010.

Challenges

The challenge facing both Keeping Mum and Clare Birth Choice is to plot a course that will enable the group to continue their critical engagement with the social, cultural and political experiences of birth in Ireland from a creative and feminist perspective.

Future Goals

Our goal is to secure funding so that we can create the arts programme we are devising which will strengthen our connection between art and political activism. In the interim, we will continue working voluntarily to raise awareness of policy issues and invite women to share their birthing experiences with us in Keeping Mum. We are determined to further develop the connection between art activism and political activism.

Relationship to the Larger Motherhood Movement

It is also important to us that we learn from the experiences of other countries such as Canada and New Zealand to see if their models of care and the trajectories that their maternity services have taken can help to change perceptions and policy for women in Ireland. In collaboration with other organizations such as Motherhood Initiative for Research and Community Involvement (MIRCI) (formerly the Association for Research on Mothering), MaMSIE[14] and the other organizations named in this chapter, we will continue to question and challenge our maternity services.

Conclusion

We have helped to create national momentum on issues relating to birth and our role as an art and activist group will be to continue to build on this momentum.

[1]Further information on the *Nurses and Midwives Bill 2010* and other issues relating to maternity services in Ireland see <http://www.aimsireland.com>.
[2]More from this quotation: "They want the right to choose home birth. If this Bill is passed, these rights will be taken away from many women.... AIMS IRELAND see Section 40 of the proposed Bill as an affront to women's rights and also basic human rights" (Krysia Lynch, Co-Chair AIMS IRELAND, 2010).
[3]See *Irish Times,* Letters Page, "Defending Midwives Role."
[4]See Sandra L. MacAvoy's chapter, "The Regulation of Sexuality in the Irish Free State, 1929-1935" in *Medicine, Disease and the State in Ireland 1650-1940* for details of legislation relating to the banning of contraceptives and information about contraceptives, and also the extensive banning of literature that continued up to the late 1960s.
[5]Source for meaning of Sheela-na-gig are taken from Freitag and McMahon and Roberts.

[6]For a detailed description of the "active management of birth," devised by Kieran O'Driscoll in 1960s, see Murphy-Lawless (205).
[7]I would like to thank Jo Murphy-Lawless for allowing me to use this quotation from her speech at the book launch of *Reading Birth and Death: A History of Obstetrics,* 12 November, 1998.
[8]See Murphy-Lawless which details the case of the Dunne family against the National Maternity Hospital (214-220).
[9]Funding for this workshop was provided through County Clare Arts Office.
[10]*Natural Traditions* was screened at Glór, Ennis, County Clare, Ireland on Friday 3 December 2010. The event was a fundraiser for the Community Midwives Association and Clare Birth Choice. The screening was followed by a discussion. The film was produced by Frameworks Films in collaboration with the Community Midwives Association for Cork Community Television.
[11]The gaze I'm referring to here draws extensively on visual cultural and feminist theoretical readings of looking that rely on feminist readings such as Laura Mulvey, Lucy Lippard, Griselda Pollock, as well as psychoanalytic readings from Freud, Lacan and Bracha Ettinger. I am particularly interested in exploring the readings of the power of the gaze from Foucault through to contemporary feminist readings of the power relationships between medicine and women's bodies.
[12]We looked at this image in *When Women Rule the World* (see Mitchell). We also looked at image from "The Birth Project" online <www. http://throughtheflower.org/page.php?p=12&n=2>.
[13]We did receive a grant from CREATE, the national development agency for collaborative arts for the initial Research and Development Phase of the project. I would like to add that much of the work has been created in a voluntary capacity.
[14]Mapping Maternal Subjectivities, Identities and Ethics (MaMSIE) creates spaces for interdisciplinary conversations about the maternal across different knowledge and practice communities including feminism, psychoanalysis, the social sciences, philosophy, visual and performance art, literature, and creative writing." Taken from MaMSIE website. See: <http://mamsie.wikispaces.com/>.

Works Cited

Breathnach-Lynch, Sighle. *Ireland's Art Ireland's History Representing Ireland, 1845 to Present.* Creighton University Press, 2007.

Cixous, Helene. "The Laugh of the Medusa." *Signs* 1.4 (1976): 875-893.

Chicago, Judy. *The Birth Project.* Web. <http://throughtheflower.org/page.php?p=12&n=2>.

Chicago, Judy and Elizabeth A. Sackler. *Judy Chicago.* New York: Watson-Guptil Publications, 2002. 68. ed.

Condren, Mary. *The Serpent and the Goddess: Women, Religion and Power in Celtic Ireland.* Dublin: New Island Books, 2002.

Connor, Valerie. "Feminism, Democratic Politics and Citizenship." *Third Text* 19.5 (2005): 511-524.

Freitag, Barbara. *Sheela-na-gigs: Unravelling An Enigma.* New York: Routledge, 2004.

Irish Times. Letters Page: "Defending Midwives Role." 17 Jan 2011. Web. <http://www.irishtimes.com/newspaper/letters/2011/0117/1224287680198.html>.

Keeping Mum and Clare Birth Choice. Web. <www.martinahynan.com>.

Lynch, Krysia. Co-Chair, AIMS IRELAND, 2010. Web. <www.aimsireland.com/news/?topic=newsdropdown>.

MacAvoy, Sandra L. "The Regulation of Sexuality in the Irish Free State." *Medicine, Disease and the State in Ireland 1650-1940.* Eds. Greta Jones and Elizabeth Malcolm. Cork: Cork University Press, 1999. 1929-1935.

McMahon, Joanne and Jack Roberts. *The Sheela-na-Gigs of Ireland and Britain: The Divine Hag of the Christian Celts: An Illustrated Guide.* Cork: Mercier Press, 2000.

Mitchell, Allyson. (curator) *When Women Rule the World: Judy Chicago in Thread.* Textile Museum of Canada and The Art Gallery of Calgary, co-publishers, 2009.

Murphy-Lawless, Jo. *Reading Birth and Death: A History of Obstetric Thinking.* Bloomington: Indiana Press, 1998.

O'Connor, Marie. "Conjuring Choice While Subverting Autonmy: Medical Technocracy and Home Birth in Ireland." *Risk and Choice in Maternity Care.* Ed. Andrew Symon. Philadelphia: Elsevier Ltd. 2006. 109-122.

Quinn, Jessica. "Making the case for the 'baby catchers'." *The Clare Champion* January 2011. Web. <http://www.clarechampion.ie/index.php?option=com_content&view=article&id=4553:making-the-case-for-the-baby-catchers&catid=73:feature&Itemid=55>.

12.
A BOLD Theatre Action

The Birth on Labor Day Movement to Make Maternity Care Mother-Friendly

KRYN FREEHLING-BURTON

BOLD'S MISSION IS TO "MAKE maternity care mother-friendly." The organization began in 2003 with a play inspired by women's birth stories and developed into an annual "Birth on Labor Day" or BOLD event at the beginning of September. BOLD has three areas of focus: a play centering on birth called *Birth*, talk-backs following performances of the play, and Red Tent events designed for women to share their own birth stories. Karen Brody, the playwright and founder of BOLD, believes that the honest sharing of all kinds of birth experiences can challenge the medicalization of birth in the United States (and increasingly around the world) that leads to higher mortality and morbidity rates, as well as to increased dissatisfaction with the limited choices and information women face during childbirth. The goal of BOLD is to empower mothers as well as encourage dialogue with birth professionals in individual communities. Each of the following sections of the paper begins with an excerpt from the play. This chapter discusses the context for the creation of BOLD, the mandate for BOLD, the history of the organization, the main aspects of BOLD's actions, challenges and responses to the organization and its work, how it is organized and how BOLD connects with other mothering activism.

Context for the Creation of BOLD and Mandate for Action

You know, it always feels good to tell someone my story. It's like this big secret I live with. I know people frown upon women who tell pregnant women horror birth stories. I know this. But my story is different.

Though there are many organizations challenging the appalling state of childbirth in the United States (according to the United Nations, the U.S. ranks below the high-income nations and several low-income nations in birth outcomes), BOLD's artistic approach that adapts real stories for theatrical presentation allows people to enter into these discussions in unique ways not readily accessible in other situations and venues (e.g. childbirth classes in which an "expert" is the single provider of information generally focusing on a single model of birth). The vari-

Performing "Birth" in Fernie, British Columbia. Photo: Jennifer Gardiner

ous surges of the women's movements in the United States (and indeed, around the world) have intentionally used theater and performance as a subversive and women-centered model to present ideas and demand action. Feminist theatre practitioners recognize the power of telling women's stories to start discussions and agitate for social change.

On the BOLD website, playwright Karen Brody describes the process of writing about birth:

> Perhaps I am a pioneer ... I couldn't believe there wasn't a mainstream play depicting childbirth. Women got *The Vagina Monologues*. But somehow childbirth has been left out of the dialogue about women's bodies. Nobody wants to touch birth. Believe me, in the fall of 2003 I knocked on every door of every editor of every mainstream magazine. The response? Lots of shut doors.... A prenatal yoga article? Yes. A hypnobirthing piece? Absolutely. But the act of giving birth? The door was slammed tight. "Please don't tell me about the baby coming out," one editor told me. That made up my mind. I was going in.[1]

In this climate, how can women and their families possibly access the information needed to make informed decisions about our health care?

BOLD aligns its actions and foci for mother-friendly maternity care with the way it is defined by the Coalition for Improving Maternity Services (CIMS). These concepts include the normalcy of the birthing process, empowerment, autonomy, do no harm, and responsibility of the childbirth professional community to support mothers.

The three core beliefs of the BOLD organization are outlined on the website in this way: "Art is a powerful medium that can inspire individuals and communities to take action. Mothers are unstoppable change agents when they spot an injustice to themselves, their family or community. You cannot make maternity care mother-friendly without addressing issues of race, class, poverty, and environment. BOLD dreams of a day when every woman in the world can get superior, mother-friendly maternity care."

History of BOLD

> *I went to [Abby's] birth. Wow ... to watch a baby being born like that. I hadn't seen anything like it before. It was beautiful. Abby made these incredible howling noises. I wouldn't have thought the sound of a whale in distress would be too nice. You know:*
> *Waaa...hooo!!!!!!!!! Waaa...hooo!!!!!!!!*
> *Abby waahoo-ed for hours. After it was over I walked out thinking: I want what SHE got. I began to seek safe passage. I finally began to walk through all my birth baggage.*

Karen Brody's play, *Birth*, was conceived in 2003 and its prenatal care provided by the Coalition for Improving Maternity Services conference in Washington, D.C. The first performance was a staged reading at the Horizon Theatre under Georgetown theatre department chair, Leslie Jacob's direction in 2005. As the theatre filled to overflowing with standing-room only, a social movement centered on the politics and theatricality of childbirth was delivered.

Though she was not a playwright before writing *Birth*, Karen Brody placed the stories she was entrusted with into the medium that seemed to best suit the spirit in which they were told to her. She had no pre-conceived ideas as a researcher going into the initial phase of the project but after about twenty-five interviews, Brody realized that certain questions were critical. She did focus her interviews on low-risk women's stories and the women with whom she spoke tended to be college educated or professional individuals with likely access to books about childbirth, and the interviews were anonymous. From the more than 115 interviews conducted, Brody chose eight women's narratives that represented common themes that were repeated over and over by the participants. Brody believes "That was the hardest part—choosing only eight. An impossible task.... Some birth stories had to be dropped. I chose the most typical ones I heard; the most common themes. Namely: epidurals, cesareans and natural births." By concentrating on these through stories of our cultural experiences of birth, Brody taps into some essential issues for American childbirth.

During Labor Day weekend in 2006, this play grew to be more than merely a theatrical event. *Birth*, a play by Karen Brody, became The Birth on Labor Day activism movement, or BOLD. Communities throughout the U.S. produced the play with mothers, doulas, midwives, nurses, and actors portraying each of the characters that had been drawn from real-life interviews conducted by the playwright. According to the website, "Twenty-one communities [participated in 2006]—from Seattle, Washington to Delhi, India—and over $50,000 was raised for organizations and causes devoted to making maternity care mother-friendly. On Labor Day that weekend, Brody hosted a kick-off production of the play in New York City with well-known birth professionals—Debra Pascali-Bonaro, Barbara Harper and Henci Goer—as part of the cast. Dr. Christiane Northrup, former obstetrician and popular women's health author, spoke after the play on a panel."

All of these early performances included a talk-back following the show covering a range of issues related to women's experiences with birthing and initiated frank discussions with traditional medical practitioners, alternative birthing practitioners and mothers. In four years the BOLD movement raised over $350,000 and reached nearly 500,000 people worldwide.

Aspects of BOLD's Actions: The Play, The Talk-Backs, The Red Tent Events

The Play

> *The baby was fine when he came out. Totally healthy. Not me.... Fourth degree tear. They were sewing me up for a* LONG *time after the birth. I just wanted to close my legs for one freaking minute. I just wanted to be finished. To be alone with my baby. You know, my body ached to hold him. Oh, where was my family? They were all in the room with me. (Beat) Still watching soccer..*

By placing birth center stage, Brody encourages an interrogation of women's experiences with childbirth through the eight narratives presented. Audiences vicariously experience more than ten births through the storytelling. Scenes are filled with multiple characters and lots of birth sounds. The inclusion of the variety of birth sounds is important to Brody, especially when it became apparent that many actors had not experienced birth or even been to someone else's birth. "*Birth* was the first play to offer an intimate portrayal of birth sounds and the possibility that birth is for some women not a fearful scary moment, but a powerful life-changing opportunity to experience pleasure and normality." The popular culture depiction of birth as an emergency fraught with out-of-control mothers swearing and screaming at hapless fathers collapses the range of ways that birth is experienced. Brody laments that "having a baby is about the *baby* in entertainment" and mothers are often sidelined or presented as caricatures in these pop culture narratives. These depictions are rampant on TV and movie screens; *Birth* provides a counter-narrative; some births are quiet, some sound sensual, and some are loud with positive affirmations like one character's mantra, "my body rocks!" All present the birthing mother at the center of her story whether or not she is listened to, heard, or respected.

Mother-centered birthing at a performance in Paris, France.

> Storytelling is an ancient ritual—a gift—with tremendous power and value in society. The more we tell our stories … [the] greater [the] probability that we will be inspired to take action. Storytelling has the power to heal and transform our lives on a profound level. With maternity care systems ailing so deeply it is crucial to tell our birth stories, celebrate the happy ones, heal from the unhappy ones, and unite as a community to create the best births possible for mothers (BOLD website).

The Talk-Backs

> *I must have thanked the anesthesiologist a million times that morning. He was like my knight-in-shining-armor. That epidural took me out of a very dark, lonely place.*

A required component for organizations and communities producing the play is after-performance talk-backs. In the tradition of the feminist consciousness-raising groups of the sixties and seventies, talk-backs have been an integral part of activist theatre for decades. As one performer at a 2008 performance said, "I think [the audience] needed decompression time … a lot of questions and issues and emotions were raised by the play, and [the audience] definitely needed a time to talk about those feelings and ask questions." Talk-backs are often organized around a particular issue, such as the skyrocketing c-section rates in the U.S. or supporting midwives in areas where midwife-assisted delivery of babies at home is a felony. The talk-backs are facilitated by a panel of experts that can include obstetricians, midwives, doulas, mothers, and nurses. Since each community faces different challenges and issues related to childbirth, the talk-backs allow for the organizers and producers to provide space for these particular issues to be addressed.

The creation of a College Campaign encourages performances for audiences who often have not yet given much thought to how choices about childbirth could affect them. One director notes that the talk-back following a community performance had a more political feel with participants ready to take action on the issues, whereas a college performance was question-based and focused on audience members asking for information which is an expected response for audiences primarily comprised of students who are not parents. Both formats contribute to the literacy around childbirth rights, advocacy, and options in different situations with different needs represented.

The Red Tent

> *I've told my partner that if I am dying on my doorstep don't take me to the hospital where I gave birth to Rachel. Rachel's birth should have been the happiest day of my life. ...Beware of those beautiful birthing rooms! My room was gorgeous. Lots of mahogany wood; but that's just looks. A nice room isn't going to determine your birth experience.*

Brody believes that "theatre for social change starts with people having hope." In order to produce actions for change, we must first be educated about the issues and speak/hear truths about peoples' experiences. This belief is at the heart of the performances and talk-backs. It is also at the heart of the additional form of activism BOLD organizes, the Red Tent. "Mothers today are silenced by a culture that does not encourage women to tell their birth stories in detail.... Each BOLD Red Tent invites mothers to tell their birth stories in vivid detail and receive the transformative power of telling their story.... This silent, deep listening from compassionate women in the circle allows each mother to stand in her story and process it how she needs to."

BOLD Red Tents have been held all over the world and any money raised goes to support local projects that are working to make maternity care mother-friendly. "BOLD Red Tents have been held in living rooms, yoga studios, outdoors, as well as in prisons and teen mom programs." Red Tent events open space for women to share their own birth experiences, and like the excerpts from the play included throughout this article, allow us to laugh and cry together and above all, to be heard.

Additional Work of BOLD

The past two years have seen not only an increase in U.S. performances of *Birth,* but increasing numbers of performances around the world and the translation of the script into French, German and Spanish. Indeed, as the website describes, "BOLD is more than our performances and BOLD Red Tents. BOLD events support innovative gatherings and campaigns to educate and change

BOLD *Red Tent sharing in 2009*

attitudes towards childbirth and a woman's right to choose where and how to give birth. These include seed money and promotion of the Second Annual Breech Birth Conference in Ottawa, Canada; re-opening a birth center in Alliston, Ontario; the "Where's My Midwife?" campaign in Wilmington, North Carolina ... BOLD events money has been raised for homeless shelters for pregnant women and teens, prison-based doula programs, organizations educating mothers about VBAC (vaginal birth after cesarean), the International Cesarean Awareness Network, the Coalition for Improving Maternity Services, and many local birth networks and organizations working hard to provide mother-friendly services to pregnant mothers." The money raised by BOLD events translates into real programs and support that supplement the more intangible aspects of watching the play or sharing in discussions about birth.

Challenges and Responses to the Organization and its Work

Who said I wasn't a good mother? It was the most bizarre experience, people telling me how I was feeling. I didn't feel disappointed. I just didn't feel a c-section was called for. My instincts told me to wait, that the baby wasn't fully cooked, that I should let labor unfold. Maybe a week later I would have felt panicky and gone for a c-section. But my decision would have been based on whatever communication I was having with the baby. (pauses). I *was the mother.*

An overriding theme of the play is "I want what she got." The typical view of childbirth, mitigated by the media and communities that surround us, inspired Brody to craft a work that encourages women to "connect with our innate power. That we don't have to lose that power when we give birth." All women tell their stories differently. Each narrative has its own rhythm, so while Brody uses artistic license in cutting to the essential parts of each woman's story, she preserves the individual rhythm of each story. This preservation reminds audiences that these are real women's stories and allows actors to access the words in ways that help audiences distinguish between the characters.

An interesting phenomenon arises out of audience response to the stories presented. The stories presented show a range of childbirth professionals in a variety of lights—good and bad obstetricians and positive and negative midwives, mothers who choose c-sections and mothers who choose home births. Brody carefully crafts the structure of the story presentations to have a balance of "natural" birth and medical birth stories so that one does not dominate in time or substance. And yet the responses at talk-backs and on audience feedback forms from around the U.S. as well as interviews conducted by a research team in Oregon find that natural and home birth proponents feel that there are not enough of these stories or are frustrated that some midwives in the play are portrayed in a negative light. Proponents and supporters of a more medical or technocratic model of childbirth feel that hospitals and obstetricians are painted in a negative light. Many women feel quite defensive of their own stories and the stories of women close to them. This difference speaks to the larger divide in our culture about women and our choices, particularly those choices related to mothering—constrained as these choices might actually be. This divide is also what drives the work of BOLD activists, from Brody to the individual directors, organizers, and actors. Women can only make informed choices when we are aware of the range of options available and are supported by our families and our health care providers. Brody explains in her blog, "The play is not an advertisement for natural birth, although I do think it makes a strong statement that if you want natural birth today you're going to have to work hard to get it."

While there are no scientific studies about *Birth* and BOLD events that can be generalized, we do have ample anecdotal information about how individual event participants and audience members are changed. Missouri participated in the first two years of the Birth on Labor Day events before subsequent legislation was passed to legalize midwives. Brody and the event organizers believe that the play and accompanying discussions helped prepare the climate for the successful passing of this legislation. Another specific example occurred in Maui when Kaiser Permanente invited moms and organizers of a BOLD event to talk with hospital staff about the World Health Organization's mother-friendly hospital initiative.

The play, the talk-backs, and the Red Tent events are opening up space for women to share their own stories as well as to hear from others. "Telling birth stories can be a very powerful way to process an individual's birth as well as a way to get to know how mothers are giving birth." Those who have attended a performance of the play can attest to the birth sharings that occur during intermission, after the play, and even for weeks after attending a BOLD event. These continued conversations are testament to the ripples of change that BOLD is initiating around the world.

Organizing the Organization

Karen Brody is the artistic and executive director of BOLD and like most grassroots goups, works from her home, storing boxes of paperwork in her garage and conducting business by phone and email. Most of the staff members who work with Brody are mothers and their work is organized into 20-hour a week segments in the recognition that it is hard for moms to carve out time for any kind of work, particularly work that brings in little monetary compensation. Like activists in many areas of the women's and mothers' movements, we do this work because we believe in it passionately. As with many organizations, funding remains a challenge and volunteers conduct most of the work of BOLD. The Advisory Board collaborates with Brody on the vision of the organization and is working on raising money for an executive director position. In many ways, BOLD is still a baby and the infrastructure is still growing to support this important aspect of the mothering movement.

How BOLD Connects with Other Mothering Activism

> *Three hours later I was ten centimeters. They told me to push. Tish was on one side, Deb was on the other and the obstetrician and two labor and delivery nurses were at the end of the bed.... and I was in the middle.... A baby came out of me! I couldn't believe it...I also couldn't believe the whole scene. Everyone cheering for me ... telling me when to push. It was really fun. Yes, pushing was such a wonderful moment. Deb and Tish cheering me on, my obstetrician screaming like a soccer mom, and two groovy labor and delivery nurses hooting and hollering. They were all so into it. And into me. I was the star..*

Many participants compare the play to *The Vagina Monologues* even though Brody was inspired to format the stories in dramatic form by the play entitled *The Exonerated* by Jessica Blank and Erik Jensen. Like Ensler's V-Day organization, BOLD provides opportunity for a range of actions around the issues and a centralized way to communicate and connect with other producers of the play and Red Tent events. The focus and centering of individual mothers' experiences in challenging the androcentric technocratic views of women's bodies reminds one of La Leche League's work in trusting the mother and her knowledge of her body and her baby. BOLD is a natural partner for organizations like the Midwives Alliance of North America and the Big Push for Midwives that offer training and support for midwives and the women they serve as well as working with legislation to protect a mother's right to choose how, where, and with whom she gives birth.

Brody's play elucidates the central tenants and common threads of feminist activist theatre like the classic ovarian theatre productions of *For Colored Girls Who Have Considered Suicide When the Rainbow is Enuf* by Ntozake Shange, *Top Girls* by Carol Churchill, and *The Vagina Monologues* by Eve Ensler. In fact, Ensler's play about women's experiences with their vaginas originally did not even include a scene about birth. Shange's play includes an abortion story and Churchill uses menstruation in a pivotal scene indicating the importance of overt discussions of female body processes as women reclaim theatre stages. *Birth* focuses on real women's stories, told in their own words, with little interruption or alteration. This centrality of women's stories allows audiences to hear narratives in women's voices with the women as the central character. The characters act with agency or their lack of agency is problematized within the narrative. Since Brody bases the scenes and monologues on the interviews conducted with women around the country, we see the characters as they see themselves, in the ways that they define and wrestle with their identity during this critical time in their lives. *Birth* is also an example of feminist activist theatre in that it focuses explicitly on women's bodies, not shying away from depictions and discussions of the ways women's bodies work, don't work, or are pathologized by medical professionals. Finally, *Birth* employs storytelling techniques that defy expectations of the typical two-act narrative with freedom for the directors and producers to present the play with as much or as little set design as the production and performance space demands. Some productions use realistic set pieces like birthing beds with stirrups for the hospital scenes; others perform with little more than the actors' bodies. Still others incorporate technology and the visual arts like a Chicago production that projected slides behind the actors in lieu of a traditional set. These common themes that run through much of feminist theatre produced over the last century provide the BOLD mothers' movement with the example and the freedom to work within the contemporary health movement and women's movement in agitating for change as well as giving voice to the varied stories and experiences depicted in the play and by the mothers who share in Red Tents.[2]

Conclusion

> *My body rocks! ... This was a pretty important image for me to hold onto when I gave birth. Imagery worked like magic. When Jamie would tell me "My body rocks!" I imagined myself standing on the top of a mountain showing off my beefy muscles. That woman on top of the mountain could give birth. She* rocked*!*

BOLD rocks expectations about birth at the same time it gives voice to individual experiences of women during birthing. Through the dramatic performances, talk-backs with experts, and Red Tent sharing events, BOLD continues to revitalize activism around the experience of birthing. As founder and playwright Karen Brody believes, change is possible when we acknowledge the vastness of women's experiences, expand the choices to which pregnant individuals have access, and give voice to mothers.

Special thanks to Karen Brody for sharing the story of BOLD's birth with me on a lovely afternoon in a New York city park. Other colleagues who contributed in various ways to this narrative include Melissa Cheyney, Courtney Everson, Tasha Galardi, Kimberly Gifford, Elle Bublitz, Charlotte Headrick, Paige Polcene, and Melodie Narramore Yocum. My four children and my partner—in theatre and in life—continually inspire me to make the world better and safer for women in all stages of our lives.

[1]The information about BOLD and quotations in this piece are from BOLD Action's website and from an interview-conversation with Karen Brody on June 26, 2008. Additional comments from participants in events are drawn from interviews following Oregon State University's production in 2008. Quotes from the play are from the *Birth* performance script copyright 2011. Any errors are my own.
[2]Theatre Practitioners Elaine Aston and Delores Ringer's ideas about feminist theatre informed the development of my own concepts as they relate to theatre as activism.

13. The International MotherBaby Childbirth Organization

Working To Create Optimal Maternity Care Worldwide

ROBBIE DAVIS-FLOYD, DEBRA PASCALI-BONARO, MAYRI SAGADY LESLIE, RAE DAVIES, HÉLÈNE VADEBONCOEUR AND RODOLFO GÓMEZ PONCE DE LEÓN

FAR TOO MANY WOMEN (OVER 300,000) die every year for childbirth-related reasons; far more suffer from many types of morbidity, often the result of the massive overuse of unnecessary, non-evidence based medical procedures during labor, birth, and the postpartum period. These unnecessary interventions impede and often damage the physiological and emotional processes of both birth and breastfeeding. This chapter tells the story of the creation of an international initiative designed to improve childbirth care and childbirth and breastfeeding outcomes for all women and, most specifically, of the organization and the individuals behind it. This initiative arose from a dream and is well on its way to becoming a reality grounded in a strong evidence basis and in a clear human rights framework. The specifics of this initiative and the process of its creation form the subject matter of this chapter. In telling this story, we hope to offer a template for positive change—a template that builds on the prior work of many others, created by and for the birth-giving women of the world.

History of the International MotherBaby Childbirth Organization (IMBCO)

The Role of CIMS

The Coalition for Improving Maternity Services (CIMS) was founded in 1996 in the U.S. and today incorporates in its membership 50 childbirth-related organizations representing over 90,000 members. Its mission was then and continues to be to promote a wellness model of maternity care that will improve birth outcomes and substantially reduce costs. During its inceptional meeting at Mt. Madonna (an apt site) in California, the founders of CIMS (including two of us, Robbie and Mayri) began work on creating the *Mother-Friendly Childbirth Initiative (MFCI): 10 Steps to Mother-Friendly Hospitals, Birth Centers, and Home Birth Services* for the U.S. (For the history and full text of the MFCI, go to www.motherfriendly.org.) The MFCI was modeled, in part, after the Baby-Friendly Hospital Initiative (BFHI). Individuals who had participated in the development of the original WHO/UNICEF

BFHI initiative were invited to meetings during the creation of the BFHI. Much dialogue and discussion ensued about ways to integrate the MFCI and the BFHI, therefore ensuring that 'mother-friendly care' supported 'baby-friendly' care. As a result, the tenth step of the MFCI specifies that a mother-friendly service "strives to achieve the WHO/UNICEF 'Ten Steps of the Baby-Friendly Hospital Initiative' to promote successful breastfeeding,"—a strategy that was later replicated in the International MotherBaby Childbirth Initiative (IMBCI).

After the MFCI was released in 1996, it didn't take long before the initiative went global via the Internet. The MFCI was translated into multiple languages and put to work in many countries, most often by consumer organizations. In subsequent years, CIMS received many requests from organizations and advocacy groups both large and small in multiple countries to help them create their own initiatives. To these requests, CIMS consistently responded with the message that its U.S.-based initiative, the MFCI, was freely available and could be adapted by any country to meet its own needs. We did not want to seem in any way to be "American imperialists," so we kept repeating that message.

CIMS did hold an internationally-oriented meeting in 2002 in response to requests from international organizations to take the MFCI around the world, with midwives Mary Kroeger and Jan Tritten as co-chairs. Mary Kroeger's vision had long been to create an international document that addressed the mother and baby as one unit. This informal 2002 meeting and a series of others solidified the idea in the minds of those who attended, and over time, more and more international birth activists and practitioners, including a growing number of international obstetricians, including most prominently Dr. Jose Gorrin from Puerto Rico, kept showing up at CIMS conferences in the U.S., and repeating their requests for CIMS to create a global initiative that would work for all countries.

The year 2002 was pivotal for the international birth and breastfeeding communities. CIMS was represented at the special United Nations General Assembly on Children in New York City; CIMS representatives presented the MFCI at the International Congress of Midwives (ICM) Congress in Vienna, to the Ministry of Health in Brazil, and at many conferences around the world. Mary Kroeger was instrumental in the development of the World Alliance for Breastfeeding Action (WABA) Global Forum II with birthing practices as a core theme. In 2003, the World Health Organization embraced "Mother-Friendly" concepts in their publication *Global Strategy for Infant and Young Child Feeding: A Tool for Assessing National Practices, Policies, and Programs.*

The global stage was set as the demand for CIMS to develop an international version of the MFCI continued to grow. The rationale was that we had done it once, so we were better equipped to do it again! And, they repeated, we had the international advantage of creating such an initiative in English, which was increasingly becoming the global lingua franca, and that CIMS had more resources for creating this initiative than the nascent country organizations could have.

The CIMS International Committee

Finally, CIMS gave up protesting that each country should create its own initiative, and in 2005 formally created an International Committee with the idea that this Committee would create a global initiative based on the MFCI. It was midwife Mary Kroeger who held the vision for the creation of this committee. She had worked to invite delegates from around the world to the first official CIMS International meeting in Virginia in 2005 and had planned to chair this first meeting. Yet she fell ill, and convinced Debra Pascali Bonaro to chair "just this one meeting!" in her place. Together they had requested and received funding for scholarships to bring international representatives to this meeting from the New Hampshire Charitable Trust Foundation as well as support from the Johnson and Johnson Pediatric Institute. Representatives from Europe, Asia and the Americas attended this ground-breaking meeting February 25 and 26 in Arlington, Virginia. Their advocacy for the creation of an international initiative was, to say the least, enthusiastic and convincing, as was—to her astonishment—their advocacy for Debra to become the first Chair of the new CIMS International Committee. This one day meeting ended with a vision and a list of next steps:

1. Develop a global data base of every regional and country-level birth and breastfeeding organization—including NGOs, government, and grassroots organizations—in the world, with the assistance of four regional representatives, and develop country contacts around the world.
2. Create and administer a survey of these organizations on the 10 Steps of the MFCI.
3. Hold a meeting in Geneva with global representation of major organizations within one year.

With survey input, international organizations, and committee input, we envisioned that we would create a global document that would be culturally appropriate and effect change in all regions of the world.

Debra remembers waking the day after she returned home, looking at the list tucked into her pajamas, and feeling overwhelmed with the task of creating a global initiative. Then the phone rang. Jane Arnold, a nurse-midwifery faculty member, had communicated the results of our meeting to her colleagues at the Center for Women's Health Research at the University of North Carolina at Chapel Hill; its Director Katherine Hartmann was willing to lend a hand. Canadian midwife Bridget Lynch, who is now the Director of the International Confederation of Midwives, was instrumental in helping us outline the above tasks and helped us to organize a series of calls, create a steering committee and working groups, and guide us to key contacts.

The CIMS International Committee set out on a global search. Via a grant and the support of Childbirth Connection, a U.S. based leader in maternity care quality improvement, we created an international network of regional and country representatives from the four major regions of the world—Africa, Asia-Pacifica, Europe, and the Americas encompassing 163 countries. These regional representatives included Flavia Previtali from Uruguay, regional rep for the Americas; Lucie Rytova, MA, and Eliska Kodysova, MA, from the Czech Republic, regional reps for Europe; Mandisa Singata, MBA, RM, RN, from South Africa, regional rep for Africa; and Mun Tip Lew from Malaysia, regional rep for Asia. They went to work developing country contacts who could gather information for organizations of pregnancy, birth, and breastfeeding providers, consumers, grassroots consumer groups, advocacy groups, women's health groups, health care professionals, and both governmental and non-govermental organizations, generating the world's largest international database on maternity and breastfeeding organizations.

The Center for Women's Health Research at the University of North Carolina used this database to conduct a global survey of the "10 Steps of the Mother-Friendly Childbirth Initiative" (MFCI). This survey did not include Step 9 on circumcision, which is not an issue in most countries (as it is not routinely performed), yet did include an additional question on informed decision making—a point strongly emphasized by the international representatives. Using a Likert scale, the survey (conducted online), requested feedback on the other nine steps of the MFCI and included a few open-ended questions about barriers to best practices. The multidisciplinary team at the Cecil G. Sheps Center for Health Services Research evaluated the results, which showed an 80-95 percent agreement on each of the steps included in the survey and a huge consensus on the importance of respect for the mother and informed decision-making, which everyone recommended should become Step 1 of the IMBCI "10 Steps to Optimal MotherBaby Maternity Care."

This survey assured the CIMS International Committee that there was indeed strong international support for the principles and goals of the U.S. MFCI, and that support gave us a sound basis for creating what we eventually called the International MotherBaby Childbirth Initiative (IMBCI). We chose this name because we wanted to draw attention to the mother and baby as one integral unit, a dyad that should not be separated, and because our Initiative places a great deal of emphasis on the impact of birth practices on breastfeeding, which was fully documented in Mary Kroeger's book, *The Impact of Birthing Practices on Breastfeeding: Protecting the Mother and Baby Continuum.*

A second CIMS International Committee meeting followed in Boston in March 2006 at the CIMS annual meeting that was attended by 50 international birth advocates and professionals from 22 countries, most of whom represented organizations. The New Hampshire Charitable Trust and Johnson and Johnson Pediatric Institute again offered scholarships and support that enabled us to bring in representatives from Africa, Israel, the Philippines, South America, and Europe. J. Nikki McKoy, from The Center for Women's Health Research at the University of North Carolina at Chapel Hill, presented our first look at the international survey, which included over 160 countries. Maureen Corry, Executive Director of Childbirth Connection (formerly called the Maternity Center Association), was also present and was recruited to co-chair the newly formed Committee with Debra. Other members of the CIMS International Committee came quickly to include Rae Davies, Mayri Sagady Leslie, and Robbie Davis-Floyd. As in, we went to a meeting just to be supportive, and came out of it as a fully-formed group with a mandate to create a global initiative! Inspired by the level of international support, Debra and Maureen and the rest of us went to work immediately.

Creation of the IMBCI

In May 2006, the CIMS International Committee held a Steering Committee meeting in Chapel Hill at the University of North Carolina to hear the survey results again, in more detail, and to work on the wording for an initial draft of what at the time we were calling the Global Mother-Friendly Childbirth Initiative (because our grounding at the time, our solid basis as confirmed by the survey, was the CIMS Mother-Friendly Childbirth Initiative). Funded by the New Hampshire Charitable Trust Foundation, this meeting was attended by midwifery instructor Jane Arnold, Maureen Corry, Rae Davies, Rosha Forman (a budding midwifery student, friend and apprentice of Mary Kroeger, she has since attended and graduated from midwifery school), Katherine Hartmann, who was then professor and researcher at the Center for Women's Health Research at University of Carolina, Miriam Labbok, former director of the BFHI for UNICEF Nikki McKoy, then project manager at the Center for Women's Health Research (University of Carolina), Debra Pascali-Bonaro, and Robbie Davis-Floyd.

We had in our hands the MFCI, the Better Birth Initiative (which originated in South Africa), and various other related documents. We felt daunted by the task ahead, yet we were not working from scratch! We very much wanted to keep our new international initiative to 10 Steps, following the MFCI and the BFHI, as ten is a powerful round number that works to "keep it simple" and maintain a strong focus. We also had a very clear mandate from our international survey on what Step 1 should be: All of the international organizations surveyed noted that respect for the woman and her choices, along with full information provided to her, should be the foundation of any and all models of birth care. So, of course, Step 1 reads that "An optimal MotherBaby maternity service has written policies, implemented in education and practice, requiring that its health care providers":

> treat every woman with respect and dignity, fully informing and involving her in decision making about care for herself and her baby in language that she understands, and providing her the right to informed consent and refusal.

Our fearless Chairwomen Debra Pascali Bonaro and Maureen Corry had many international contacts, and helped us realize that any attempt at creating a global initiative would have to have the support of the already-existing global maternal health-related organizations. Yet how to proceed? Bridget Lynch again was instrumental in guiding us. She suggested that we develop a Technical Advisory Group consisting of representatives from all the major international agencies involved with maternity care. She opened many doors for us, one of which led to Maureen and Debra holding several meetings with Nancy Terrari from UNICEF. These and many other discussions led to the creation of the Technical Advisory Group.

As we had predicted earlier, it quickly became obvious that a face-to-face meeting of these representatives would have to be held for rapid progress to be made. Debra and Maureen obtained funding for such a meeting from the New Hampshire Charitable Trust Foundation, from a fund that later came to be known as the Transforming Birth Fund—we are forever grateful to its founders!

Thus the CIMS International Committee, with the direct participation of Childbirth Connection, held a Technical Advisory Group meeting in Geneva, Switzerland in June 2006, to present and refine the initial draft of the Initiative and to gauge the level of interest in supporting and promoting the Initiative. This meeting, for which we all came well-prepared with our ideas and our initial draft of the Initiative, was chaired by Monir Islam, the current director of Making Pregnancy Safer (WHO). The participants in this Geneva meeting included representatives from WHO, UNICEF, USAIDS, CIMS, Childbirth Connection, Lamaze International, DONA, La Leche League International, Wellstart International, the World Alliance of Breastfeeding Associations (WABA), the International Lactation Consultant Association (ILCA), the International Confederation of Midwives (ICM), the International Council of Nurses (ICN), the International Pediatric Association (IPA), and JPHIEGO. We recruited these organizations because of our profound respect for the international work they had already done, and because we knew that we could not create such an Initiative in isolation.

There was tremendous support for developing this initiative from all present, and we spent hours refining the wording of the document in a very rewarding group consensus process—well, it turned out to be very rewarding, yet it was very trying for one of us (Robbie)—as designated editor (she had been the lead editor for the MFCI, along with Roberta Scaer and Henci Goer, back in 1995, so it made sense for her to be lead editor this next time around), she had our preliminary draft from Chapel Hill up on PowerPoint, and for two afternoons straight she took verbal suggestions from the TAG reps, sometimes shouted out with much discussion around every word—a huge challenge to change the wording on computer, on the spot, yet lots of fun—a most creative and exciting process! Each night Robbie sat up late incorporating all the verbal suggestions, to present it all again the next day, while Debra, Maureen, Rae, and the rest of our Committee worked on strategy.

During this most amazing TAG meeting, after Dr. Katherine Hartmann presented the encouraging results of the international survey on the MFCI 10 Steps done by the Center for Women's Health Research (University of North Carolina), we not only worked on the wording of the IMBCI but also on making preliminary plans for pilot testing the IMBCI in various hospitals around the world and conceptualizing its future. We culminated the meeting with a huge round of applause for Debra and Maureen for all their work in bringing us all together to create this global initiative, for which everyone present agreed there was a huge need.

It was most serendipitous that right after this TAG meeting, Robbie, accompanied by Rae Davies (who later became our IMBCO Administrative Director) was headed to give some talks at the Hecvsante Nursing and Midwifery School in Lausanne, Switzerland. Although the IMBCI was not on the schedule, we convinced the entire faculty of the school to meet with us to review the PowerPoint of the IMBCI as it then stood in its initial stage. Many of its major steps regarding humane care had long been implemented in Switzerland, so the faculty went beyond those to encouraging us to include a whole step on collaborative care—a major issue for Swiss midwives, as obstetricians there often took a top-down approach and did not bother to collaborate in an egalitarian way with the professional midwives. Robbie and Rae realized that collaborative care was also a major issue in many other countries. The Swiss midwives' suggestion about collaborative care ultimately became Step 9: "Provide a continuum of collaborative care with all relevant health care providers, institutions, and organizations."

As Editor for the IMBCI, Robbie had the responsibility over the next year of gathering international input on the document. Wishing to be as inclusive as possible, Robbie sent it out far and wide. As a result, the IMBCI was ultimately reviewed by representatives of all of the organizations listed above and around 100 high-level childbirth experts, midlevel practitioners, and grassroots activists from many countries—the full range from bottom-up to top-down. At first, as previously mentioned, wanting to remain connected to the MFCI, we used the title "Global MotherBaby-Friendly Initiative" and then, wanting also to honor Mary Kroeger's insistence on the integrity of the motherbaby, "International MotherBaby-Friendly Initiative."

We were on draft #57 when we were asked by UNICEF and WHO—the creators of the international Baby-Friendly Hospital Initiative (BFHI)—and also by the World Alliance of Breastfeeding Organizations (WABA) not to use the phrase "motherbaby-friendly" because that made it sound as if we were the umbrella organization for Baby-Friendly worldwide. (The Baby-Friendly Hospital Initiative had already been in existence for over 20 years and had designated many thousands of hospitals in many countries, whereas we were in our incipient stage.) So after much debate, we chose the final name *International MotherBaby Childbirth Initiative (IMBCI: 10 Steps to Optimal MotherBaby Maternity Care.* (See below re the term "MotherBaby.")

At first, Robbie worked closely on the writing of the IMBCI with the members of the official editorial committee who had volunteered for the job at the TAG meeting, yet it in the end it turned out that the ones who had the most patience for the very stressful and lengthy wording process were our other Board members at that time—Debra Pascali Bonaro, Maureen Corry, Rae Davies, and Mayri Sagady Leslie. The crafting of the IMBCI narrowed down to the five of us—we struggled over and carefully considered every single word. This care was necessary because we were writing an initiative that we intended to be applicable to the entire world, and the needs and resources of developed and developing countries differ widely. Robbie's education as an anthropologist and her wide knowledge of these differences helped enormously, as did the international experiences of Debra, Maureen, and Rae, in particular Maureen's thorough knowledge of the scientific evidence and Mayri's long years in nurse-midwifery clinical experience, plus her strong research and epidemiological background.

Our cumulative awareness of those differences led to many difficult yet rewarding conversations—for example, should we say that an optimal MotherBaby facility should offer both drug- and drug-free pain relief options? Clearly, the epidural is experienced by many women as a humanistic pain-relieving option during labor. Yet it carries risks and complications, especially if given too early in labor. So that issue had to be debated at length. In the end, we came down to reality—to insist in our Initiative that pain-relieving drugs, including the epidural, be included in the IMBCI would be to ask developing countries that cannot afford such drugs to provide them; to include such drugs as a requirement would be most unrealistic and unfair. (Again, we were very aware that we were creating this initiative for all countries and all settings.) On the other hand, drug-free pain-relieving interventions cost almost nothing and can be provided in any setting in any country, and are evidence-based as helping to relieve pain while causing no harm. So Step 4 reads:

> Provide drug-free comfort and pain-relieving methods during labour [we used the British spelling as it has become the global standard], explaining their benefits for facilitating normal birth and avoiding unnecessary harm, and showing women (and their companions) how to use these methods, including touch, holding, massage, laboring in water, and coping/relaxation techniques. Respect women's preferences and choices.

After a full year of intensive work, we finalized the wording of the IMBCI in February of 2008, and launched the International MotherBaby Childbirth Initiative at the CIMS Annual Meeting in Florida on International Women's Day in March 2008. Of course we had to launch it at CIMS—its mother organization! It was a marvelous occasion. Debra and Robbie presented the IMBCI step-by-step on Powerpoint. The many international representatives present organized themselves into a line, and one-by-one stepped up to the microphone to read the Principles we included in the document to pinpoint the underlying philosophy of the IMBCI. Here are a few of the Basic Principles of the IMBCI:

- Women's and children's rights are human rights.
- Access to humane and effective health care is a basic human right.
- Consideration and respect for every woman should be the foundation

of all maternity care.

•Pregnancy, labour, birth, and breastfeeding are normal and healthy processes that in most cases need only attention and support from caregivers. Current evidence demonstrates the safety and superior outcomes of this approach.

•Midwives, who are the primary care providers for millions of birthing women in most countries, have developed a model of care based on the normal physiology, sociology, and psychology of pregnancy, labour, birth, and the postpartum period. The International MotherBaby Childbirth Initiative draws on the midwifery model of care and affirms that midwifery knowledge, skills, and behavior are essential for optimal MotherBaby care.

The MotherBaby

An important contribution of the IMBCI is the "MotherBaby" model of care. "MotherBaby" is a term first used by Audrey Naylor, MD, Ph.D. Dr. Naylor is CEO of Wellstart International, a pediatrician and a longtime champion of breastfeeding in the international arena. In referring to her use of the term, she said:

> I strongly believe that mothers and babies are an interdependent, biologic unit that must stay together for at least six months during the period of exclusive breastfeeding and continue for about nine months after birth during the introduction of nutritious complementary foods. Breastfeeding should continue for two or more years while the baby is introduced to nutritious complementary family foods. Words are powerful. If we use a single word for this motherbaby unit it may help. (Audrey Naylor, e-mail message to Mayri Sagady Leslie, August 8, 2010.)

The IMBCI promotes the idea that the MotherBaby is Naylor's "single unit," inseparable throughout the continuum of care:

> The mother and baby constitute an integral unit during pregnancy, birth, and infancy (referred to herein as the "MotherBaby") and should be treated as such, as the care of one significantly impacts the care of the other.... This MotherBaby Model of Care promotes the health and wellbeing of all women and babies during pregnancy, birth, and breastfeeding, setting the gold standard for excellence and superior outcomes in maternity care. All maternity service providers should be educated in, provide, and support this MotherBaby Model of Care. (www.imbci.org)

Our launching of the IMBCI in March 2008 turned into a powerful ceremony, complete with tears, whistles, and balloons!

"Launching at CIMS 047." The IMBCO Board and International Representatives

"Board meeting New York, 185." Left to right: Mayri Sagady Leslie, Debra Pascali Bonaro, Rae Davies, Rodolfo Gomez, Robbie Davis-Floyd, Maureen Corry.

Creation of the International MotherBaby Childbirth Organization (IMBCO)

Before this launching, in 2007, with the full support of CIMS, the CIMS International Committee became a separate organization, called the International MotherBaby

Childbirth Organization (IMBCO). The separation was clearly necessary—we could no longer be the CIMS International Committee, as CIMS is U.S.-based and U.S.-focused, whereas our agenda is international. The CIMS International Committee members at the time became the new Board members of the IMBCO; again, they included Co-Chairs Debra Pascali-Bonaro and Maureen Corry; Rae Davies, Secretary; Robbie Davis-Floyd, Editor; and Mayri Lesley Sagady, CIMS Liaison. This small group of middle-class white girls had worked well to create the wording of the IMBCI (remember, we took input from over 100 international experts and grass-roots participants), yet we knew that in order to implement this initiative, the Board would have to expand considerably.

We achieved a major breakthrough in that endeavor when we were finally able to hire, with support from the Transforming Birth Fund, an Argentinean obstetrician and epidemiologist, Rodolfo Gomez Ponce de Leon, MD, MPH, Ph.D., to be our Executive Director as a half-time position. "Rodo" had worked as an obstetrician-gynecologist for 15 years in a marvelous public hospital in Tucuman, Argentina—Hospital Avellaneda—that had maintained its cesarean rates at below 15 percent for years in favor of supporting the normal physiology of birth via midwifery care and upright positions for labor and birth. He had gone on to earn a doctorate in Public Health in the U.S. and to work for IPAS. Rae Davies, our Board secretary, went off the Board to accept a part-time position as Administrative Director, so that she could handle the logistics of our operation and leave Rodolfo freer to concentrate on promoting it—which he did at many international conferences—and to work with other members of the IMBCO Board on developing guides and evaluation tools for the hospitals and other birth facilities that we hoped would come on board to implement the IMBCI and evaluate the results.

We did not stop with that expansion. We put out an international call for new Board members, and subsequently added Petra ten-Hoope Bender, former Secretary General of the International Confederation of Midwives and former Executive Director of the Partnership for Maternal, Newborn and Child Health (PMNCH); Daphne Rattner, MD, a Brazilian epidemiologist, professor, and former Director of the Women's Health Program for the Brazilian Ministry of Health; Hélène Vadeboncoeur, a longtime researcher, birth activist and scholar who authored the first Canadian book on VBAC and helped the Quebec Ministry of Health develop the first birth centers in Quebec; and Debrah Lewis, the Director and a practicing midwife at Mamatoto Resource and Birth Centre in Trinidad who currently serves as the Americas Regional Board Member of the International Confederation of Midwives (ICM). We also created an Advisory Council of nine members representing various international organizations. (See <www.imbci.org> for full bios of all of the above.)

Now fully-fledged and formed as an organization, we needed a logo. We envisioned a mother and baby with the world around them, embodying our global outreach and the connection of MotherBaby to Mother Earth. Board member Mayri's daughter Crystal Sagady was a graphic artist—using our vision, she created a beautiful logo that now graces all our documents. And thanks to the tireless efforts of our Administrative Director Rae Davies, we have become a 501c3 in the U.S, so that we can officially accept tax-free donations for our ongoing work.

IMBCO's Ongoing Work

Once the IMBCI logo was completed and beautifully formatted by Crystal Sagady, we immediately incorporated it into the IMBCI and posted the final document on our newly created website www.imbci.org, informing all our international representatives. They went to work on translation—the IMBCI has now been translated into over 15 languages—and on putting it to work in their countries and regions. A number of NGOs have taken the IMBCI as their chartering document, and are working to implement it in their countries.

A common course for international initiatives is to seek to have them ratified in a formal process by all major and relevant organizations. CIMS did pass through that process, from 1995-1996, with all major U.S.-based childbirth reform organizations, all of which did eventually ratify the CIMS Mother-Friendly Childbirth Initiative (MFCI). IMBCO did not choose that course, recognizing that international formal ratification by all of our TAG participants could have held dissemination of the document up for years! We understood that the first step should instead be pilot/demonstration-site testing of the efficacy of the IMBCI 10 Steps. So we put out an international call, and have received applications from pilot/demonstration sites in six countries; to date we have accepted the following sites:

- Pavillon des Naissances, Hôpital Brome Missisquoi Perkins, Cowansville, Centre de Santé et Services Sociaux La Pommeraie, in Quebec, Canada;
- Hospital Sofia Feldman, Belo Horizonte, Brazil;
- Community Hospital Feldbach, Feldbach, Austria;
- Kwazakhele Unit, Port Elizabeth, South Africa;
- Banashankari Maternity Hospital, Bengaluru, Karnataka, India;
- Dr. Jose Fabella Memorial Hospital, Manila, the Philippines;
- Hospital Central de Maputo, Maputo, Provincia de Maputo, Mozambique;
- Beira Central Hospital, Beira, Sofala, Mozambique.[1]

These hospitals are paving the way for demonstrating how maternity care services can offer women optimal MotherBaby maternity care. We have by now visited all these sites and worked directly with their key staff members. They are beginning the process of implementing the IMBCI 10 Steps in their respective institutions, and we will be carefully documenting and evaluating the effects. IMBCO has developed guides and evaluation tools for these and future sites to utilize.

We are currently seeking funding for the research components of the implementation of the IMBCI. IMBCO would also welcome any researchers who care to study the process of implementation and document both the barriers these sites may face and the outcomes we hope they achieve. Each site will also determine its most pressing needs in terms of implementing this step or that step, and IMBCO will help in identifying local, regional or international resources to support them. In 2011, these sites will be organized in a communication network so that they can learn from each other around the IMBCI implementation process.

In addition, seeking to aid the many independent sites that want to implement the IMBCI on their own, we have created MotherBaby Networks (MBnets):

> MotherBaby Networks are a result of increased interest throughout the world in supporting the International MotherBaby Childbirth Initiative (IMBCI) and promoting the 10 Steps to Optimal MotherBaby Maternity Services. MBnets consist of individuals such as midwives and physicians; or a collaboration of individuals, community grassroots advocates and organizations, and careproviders; or a facility such as a birth center, clinic or hospital where women give birth.

MBnets are an unlimited number of sites throughout the world which, by their own initiative, are using the International MotherBaby Childbirth Initiative (IMBCI) to promote the 10 Steps to Optimal MotherBaby Maternity Services in their own contextual surroundings. These sites have contacted the International MotherBaby Childbirth Organization (IMBCO) to inform us of their work, completed our online questionnaire, and confirmed their support of the IMBCI. As such, they are recognized by IMBCO as being part of the MotherBaby Network of sites engaged in the promotion of the IMBCI. As a result, they have access to IMBCO resources and will have the opportunity to share their victories and/or challenges through the IMBCO website (quoted from <www.imbci.org>).

Relationship to the Larger Motherhood Movement

International initiatives that seek to remedy global problems in maternal and child health include the Safe Motherhood Initiative, Making Pregnancy Safer, the International Initiative for Maternal Mortality and Human Rights, and the Global Strategy for Infant and Young Child Feeding. They also include the Baby-friendly Hospital Initiative (BFHI) and the International Code of Marketing of Breast-milk Substitutes, both of which were reaffirmed by the 2005 Innocenti Declaration on the Protection, Promotion, and Support of Breastfeeding and endorsed by the 2006 World Health Assembly.

To these efforts, the International MotherBaby Childbirth Initiative (IMBCI) adds a vital emphasis on the quality of the mother's birth experience and its impact on the short- and long-term health of the mother, baby, and family. The IMBCI focuses on the scientific evidence showing the benefits of MotherBaby-centered care based on the normal physiology of pregnancy, birth, and breastfeeding and the risks of inappropriate medical interventions, and on the importance of attention to women's individual needs.

The IMBCI complements pre-existing maternal and infant survival and breastfeeding support efforts (including recent Mother-friendly additions to the BFHI), emphasizing the need for the continuum of humanistic care proven necessary for the best outcomes. The IMBCI originated from the work of the International Committee of the Coalition for Improving Maternity Services (CIMS) and continues at a global level the work begun in 1996 by the CIMS Mother-Friendly Childbirth Initiative in the United States, which focuses on facilitating normal birth, avoiding unnecessary interventions, and supporting breastfeeding.

The IMBCI also contributes to achieving at least five of the eight United Nations Millennium Development Goals targeted for 2015:

> *Goal 1:* Eradicate extreme poverty and hunger. The IMBCI promotes optimal maternal nutrition and infant feeding.
> *Goal 3:* Promote gender equality and empower women. The IMBCI calls for empowering women through education and respectful, caring treatment during pregnancy, birth, and the postpartum period.
> *Goal 4:* Reduce child mortality.
> *Goal 5:* Improve maternal health and reduce the maternal mortality ratio by ¾. The IMBCI calls for skilled birth attendance, effective emergency care, and reserving medical intervention for cases where potential benefits outweigh potential harms to reduce infant and maternal morbidity and mortality, and emphasizes wellness and prevention measures before, during, and after birth to increase maternal and infant survival and health.
> *Goal 6:* Combat HIV/AIDS malaria, and other diseases. The IMBCI calls for education and prevention measures, and for informed birth and feeding practices that reduce the transmission of HIV from mother to baby.

Conclusion

The purpose of the IMBCI 10 Steps is to improve care throughout the childbearing continuum, in order to save lives, prevent illness and harm from the overuse of obstetric technologies, and promote health for mothers and babies. Rising cesarean rates around the world, the increasing overuse of obstetric technologies, and failure to implement the scientific evidence in favor of normal, physiological birth have created the need for clear guidelines for providing optimal maternity care.

This Initiative addresses the needs of all nations and birthing women for evidence-based and humanistic improvements in the quality of maternity care. The IMBCI is both educational and instrumental in purpose. Its educational purpose is to call global attention to the importance of the quality of the mother's birth experience and its impact on the outcome, the risks to mother and baby from inappropriate medical interventions, and the scientific evidence showing the benefits of MotherBaby-centered care based on the normal physiology of pregnancy, birth, and breastfeeding and on attention to women's individual needs. The instrumental purpose of the IMBCI 10 Steps is to put into worldwide awareness and practice the MotherBaby Model of Care—a woman-centered, non-interventive approach that promotes the health and wellbeing of all women and babies during pregnancy, birth, and breastfeeding, setting the gold standard for excellence and superior outcomes in maternity care.

The mission of the International MotherBaby Childbirth Organization (IMBCO), in collaboration with other organizations, is to develop, regularly update, and promulgate the International MotherBaby Childbirth Initiative worldwide to improve care throughout the childbearing continuum, in order to save lives, prevent illness and harm, and promote health for mothers and babies around the world.

The full text of the IMBCI is available at <www.imbci.org> for anyone in any country to download and work with in their area. Individuals and organizations can sign on as supporters of the IMBCI, adopt it as a focal point for their work, use it as an educational instrument and guide to help birth facilities to improve their maternity care, and become either formal demonstration sites or informal MBnets. We believe that the IMBCI sets the global gold standard for optimal maternity care, and that those who truly wish to achieve that kind of care for mothers and babies will utilize the IMBCI in every way possible to meet that goal. Ultimately, our vision is that every birth facility will operate according to the IMBCI 10 Steps, resulting in vastly improved and evidence-based care that will dramatically reduce mortality and morbidity and enhance birth outcomes, including breastfeeding, for the mothers and babies of the world. We welcome your support!

[1]See <www.imbi.org> for full descriptions of all these facilities.

Works Cited

Kroeger, Mary, with Linda Smith. *The Impact of Birthing Practices on Breastfeeding: Protecting the Mother and Baby Continuum.* Sudbury, MA: Jones and Bartlett, 2004.

World Health Organization (WHO). *Global Strategy for Infant and Young Child Feeding: A Tool for Assessing National Practices, Policies and Programs.* Geneva: Author, 2003. Web. < http://www.who.int/nutrition/publications/infantfeeding/9241562544/en/index.html>.

14.
Surgery is a Natural Birth Plan for Many Women

The Organization electivecesarean.com

PAULINE MCDONAGH HULL

ELECTIVECESAREAN.COM BEGAN LIFE ONLINE in February 2006 as a resource offering support and information to women whose birth plan is a cesarean. Its aims are to encourage clarity in the reporting of cesarean risks and benefits, which can only be achieved by separating data on different types of cesareans (for example, planned versus emergency, primary versus repeat, and maternal request with no indication versus medical or obstetrical indications), and to campaign for recognition that a planned cesarean at 39+ gestational weeks is a legitimate birth plan, even in a healthy pregnancy, provided the woman has an individualized consultation and is planning a small family.

All too often, the idea that cesarean surgery might be a very much *wanted* and satisfactory birth outcome is strongly criticized, and even ridiculed by some, but in fact the arguments against it are grounded in a very basic yet common misunderstanding of the risks that are *specific* to this type of surgery. Fortunately, things are beginning to change, and with the advent of more accurate comparative studies looking at the outcomes of different birth *plans* (rather than outcomes alone, in isolation), researchers have demonstrated better health outcomes for mothers and babies (Larsson, Källen and Andolf; "Women choosing caesarean have low death rate"; Berger and Sachs; Dahlgren et al.; Hankins, Clark and Munn) and greater levels of satisfaction (Graham et al.; Ryding, Wijma and Wijma; Robson et al.; Wiklund, Edman and Andolf; Mould et al.; Torkan et al.; Weiss, Fawcett and Aber) with a planned cesarean compared with a *planned* vaginal birth (and all its possible outcomes, including forceps, vacuum and/or emergency cesarean delivery).

But importantly, electivecesarean.com does not advocate cesarean birth as a natural choice for *all* women; rather, it aims to ensure that women who *do* make this informed decision are not disrespected, disparaged or refused a priori. Also, like many grass roots organizations, it did not initially set out to be part of a larger *motherhood movement*; it simply saw a need to redress the balance in the perception of cesarean birth. However, it gratefully appreciates the opportunity to be included here in the context of this wider, ongoing endeavor, and this chapter will explain why the organization was founded, what it has achieved to date, the challenges it has faced, and what it hopes to achieve in the future.

Mandate/Context

Initially, electivecesarean.com set out to address the overwhelmingly negative public attitude towards cesarean birth, and in particular, a planned or *elective* cesarean. Its portrayal as a dangerous, *unwanted* and *unnatural* procedure, to be considered only when *absolutely necessary* in a life or death situation (and even then, only begrudgingly or mournfully so) was at odds with the organization's view that advances in the safety of cesarean surgery is also something to be celebrated. Both in terms of the millions of lives it has saved and the devastating injuries it has prevented, but also because it provides contemporary women with a new birth choice and (for some) a welcome alternative to the more unpredictable nature of labor. That said, electivecesarean.com is very clear that it does *not* provide medical advice for any individual, and that a cesarean *request* (as opposed to *demand*) should always be subject to consultation with a doctor. It also emphasizes the very real and serious risks associated with planned surgery (such as adhesions, future placental complications, re-hospitalization and infection etc.), so that there can be no mistake that this is a very serious and significant decision—and not one to be taken lightly.

Cesareans are Not Born Equal

First and foremost, electivecesarean.com wanted to emphasize the differences in risk between different types of surgery, as this is crucial to understand. For example, it is well established that *a planned cesarean birth has lower risks than an emergency cesarean birth*. Not all countries separate the two when collating their birth data, and although some do separate *primary versus repeat cesareans* data, it is not known whether the repeat cesarean followed a previous planned or emergency surgery. What *is* known is that *a repeat planned cesarean birth has greater risks than a primary planned cesarean birth*, and because there is strong evidence of increased risks with multiple cesarean surgeries, women choosing a cesarean are advised to keep their family size small (a proviso that is understandably more readily accepted by women who *choose* a cesarean than women who don't, and a trend reflected in the very low fertility rates of most of the developed world too).

It is also a recognized fact that *a planned cesarean birth at 39+ weeks' gestation has lower risks for babies than those carried out at fewer than 39 weeks' gestation*, and since maternal request surgery is *only* advised after 39 weeks (in order to reduce the risk of respiratory illness), it is completely irrelevant to criticize this birth choice by citing research that includes outcomes of babies born *prior* to 39 weeks (which have usually been scheduled early for medical or obstetrical reasons). Accuracy of gestational age is admittedly sometimes an issue, but this is why individualized consultation is so important—did the woman have an early ultrasound scan (which provides the best estimate of gestation) for example?

There is also a difference in the way in which a maternal request cesarean can be referred to, and the semantics here are very telling. It is called a "*cesarean with*

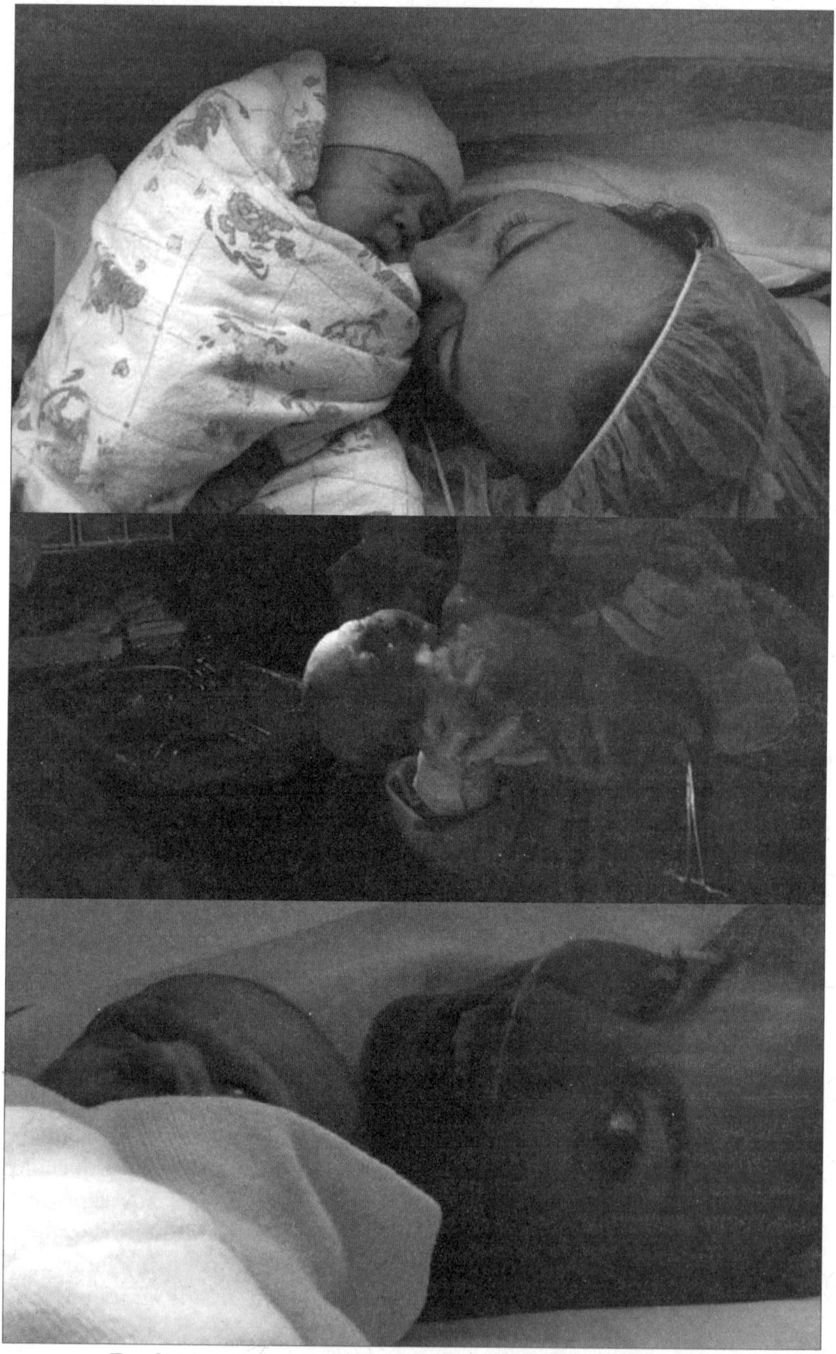

Top: Charlotte Hull, born on September 19, 2007. Middle and bottom: Jack Hull, born on May 27, 2009, and their mother, Pauline McDonagh Hull.

no indication" but by some, it is described as a "*prophylactic cesarean.*" In effect, while the first definition dismisses any notion of medical or obstetrical need whatsoever, the second infers that because the intention of the surgery is to *avoid* the established medical problems associated with planned vaginal birth (e.g. infant birth injuries, pelvic floor damage and psychological trauma), there *is* in fact an indication—it's just a *preventative* one.

Finally, a cesarean birth can be *wanted* or *unwanted* by mothers, and this self-assessed definition of surgical birth is far more helpful when looking at birth outcomes than any third party labeling of whether it was "*necessary or unnecessary*" (this appraisal has its place, but only after first establishing that the cesarean was unwanted, otherwise it is a waste of effort and resources). Unfortunately, this distinction is almost never acknowledged, and as a consequence, many of the strategies currently being employed by hospitals and governments to reduce cesarean rates across the board are analogous with the gardener who uses a lawnmower to remove the weeds from his blossoming flowerbed. All that matters is that the rate gets cut.

History

When the *National Institute for Clinical Excellence* (*NICE*) published its cesarean guideline in 2004, for Pauline McDonagh Hull, who was at the time working as a broadcast journalist with *BBC News* in London, it was the last straw. For years, she had been increasingly frustrated by media headlines warning women inclined to choose a cesarean that they were "*five to seven times more likely to die*" and "*putting their babies' lives at risk,*" when in fact the truth is that a large percentage of these more dangerous outcomes are related to emergency surgeries (the vast majority of which originate as planned vaginal births) or are surgeries planned due to pre-existing medical or obstetrical complications, and therefore inherently more likely to have greater risks attached. In contrast, a cesarean requested on the grounds of wanting to avoid the unpredictability of labor, to deliver the baby quickly and safely at 39+ weeks, and to reduce the risk of serious damage to the pelvic floor, is a completely different entity.

So when the newly published *NICE* guideline announced firmly that maternal request is "*not on its own an indication*" for surgery, and the derision of "*too posh to push*" mothers went into overdrive, Pauline was concerned about the women who would be *"too poor to pay"* private hospital fees when refused their preferred birth plan. And so she embarked upon an almost two year process (including three months' unpaid leave from the *BBC*) of researching, writing, designing and creating web pages, as well as conducting in-depth interviews with doctors and mothers—all with the purpose of setting the record straight. In February 2006, the organization electivecesarean.com was born.

All visitors are asked to answer a survey in order to become members of the site, and the thousands and thousands of answers (which remain anonymous) have provided an invaluable insight into the women who are requesting cesareans and their reasons for doing so. In fact in the past year, Pauline has worked with other researchers (who have statistical and analytical expertise) with a view to publishing some of the results of these surveys in a medical journal. In October 2008, electivecesarean.com co-founded the *Coalition for Childbirth Autonomy* (*CCA*) with three other organizations that share its values and beliefs (*Birth Trauma Canada*, *c-sections.org* and *The Birth Trauma Association*), and in a joint press release, the *CCA* called on the *World Health Organization* (*WHO*) to provide evidence for its "*dangerous and outdated*" 1985 recommendation of a 15 percent cesarean rate threshold ("Birth Group, CCA, Calls on WHO"). And while the two events are likely entirely coincidental, in 2009, the *WHO* admitted that it has no empirical evidence for its 15 percent figure and that there is actually *no known optimum rate* of cesarean births.

Activities

The organization spends a great deal of time defending the legitimacy of a planned cesarean at 39 weeks' gestation, even in a healthy pregnancy, through media interviews (radio, print, online and most recently, for a documentary on birth), writing comments on news stories, submitting letters to medical journals, blogging on electivecesarean.com's sister site *cesareandebate.blogspot.com*, and various other campaign work. It also spends time communicating with women who contact the site looking for help, and as far as it can, with very limited time and resources, the organization offers them support through emails and occasionally phone calls too. But while this activity can be very rewarding, it can also be very distressing too, hearing stories from women who are repeatedly refused the chance to even *consider* a cesarean birth plan and are either coerced into very traumatic vaginal birth experiences or are left feeling so desperate (often suffering from tokophobia—an acute fear of labor and birth) that some of them terminate their much wanted pregnancies.

So when the opportunity arose for electivecesarean.com to become actively involved in the development of an update to the 2004 *NICE* guideline (the original catalyst for establishing the organization), the organization immediately registered as a stakeholder and Pauline attended a meeting in London to discuss the proposed scope of the update. Incredibly, maternal request was not scheduled to be included in the partial review, and so electivecesarean.com, together with other Stakeholders, submitted evidence in support of its inclusion, and fortunately *NICE* agreed. The final publication of the update is scheduled for the end of 2011.

Similarly, the organization has been increasingly busy with activities at a governmental level too. In 2009, it applied to become a member of the *Maternity Care Working Party* (*MCWP*) in Britain (attending two meetings in London to date), and in 2010, Pauline spoke at an All-party parliamentary group meeting on Maternity in London, corresponded with her local Member of Parliament and the Department of Health by email, and in 2011 is arranging to meet with the new chair of the *MCWP*—all with the aim of presenting evidence in support of maternal request and urging caution in blanket policies to reduce national cesarean rates. Unfortunately, a necessary aspect of defending the benefits of planning a cesarean is highlighting the various *increased* risks associated with vaginal birth that many women want to avoid. This can lead to unintentional conflict with other birth groups who disagree with electivecesarean.com's perspective, and as a result, communication with these groups has evolved as an activity—trying to stress the importance of autonomy across the *whole* spectrum of birth choices and of working with (rather than against) each other.

Other activities that the organization is involved in are as diverse as attending two national birth conferences in the United States (Pauline was invited as a speaker at one), aligning itself with the group *MomsRising.org* in 2008, and spending time on the phone helping journalists with background information for their stories on cesarean birth. This latter activity is extremely important because the articles that journalists write have the power to influence the public perception of cesareans. With this in mind, electivecesarean.com has issued a number of press releases on the subject of planned cesareans, and it has also published an online petition titled "*Prophylactic planned cesarean birth at 39 weeks confirmed gestation for informed women planning a small family is a legitimate decision*" via the website *GoPetition.com*.

Challenges

The main challenge that electivecesarean.com faces (like so many other organizations) is a financial one. From its very inception, the site has been funded by its founder, and has been kept going through a sheer passion for and commitment to the work that the organization carries out. It has no sponsors or advertising revenue to date, and interestingly, one company with a cesarean-related product wrote to say that it was fearful of being seen as pro-surgery and anti-natural birth by advertising on electivecesarean.com, but that it might reconsider in the future (when this birth choice is more accepted). So in 2008, the organization reluctantly introduced a one-time $5 charge for membership to help with running costs, and while the vast majority of members have been perfectly happy to pay this fee (it is automatically waived for any pregnant woman who says she cannot afford it), there has been strong disapproval by some of its cesarean critics. The organization finds this criticism ironic given the income that is generated by many proponents of vaginal birth, but it would still like to find a solution to its funding challenge in the future so that essential works and new features can be carried out as planned.

Staying with the subject of money, another challenge for the organization is to refute the very commonly held belief that planned cesareans cost more than planned vaginal births, and especially in countries with socialized healthcare systems financed by tax-payers, where maternal request is often viewed as an unaffordable "lifestyle choice" (although as an interesting aside here, there are numerous other lifestyle choices, including alcohol, smoking, drugs and lack of exercise, for which treatment is afforded indiscriminately and without question).

Again, this involves questioning the value of traditional comparative models and making the prophylactic nature of a cesarean better understood. For example, simply comparing the cost of spontaneous vaginal birth outcomes alone with *all* (or even just planned) cesarean birth outcomes is misleading, since a planned vaginal birth has many different short- and long-term cost outcomes that must be attributed to it too.

Staff must be available 24 hours a day, seven days a week in case forceps, vacuum, an epidural and/or emergency surgery is required at any time during labor (ironically, the comparative *cost-effectiveness* of planned surgery has been cited as a criticism of its overuse in some countries), and there may be counseling needed after a traumatic birth, repair of damage to the pelvic floor (e.g. prolapse and incontinence surgeries) and/or the treatment of infant birth injuries (e.g. physiotherapy and surgery) too. But without doubt, the biggest (and most overlooked) birth cost is litigation settlements. The financial ramifications when a planned vaginal birth goes wrong are enormous, and hundreds of millions of dollars are paid out to families devastated by the loss or injury of mothers and (especially) babies every year. And yet this cost is routinely kept to one side and completely disassociated from the planned vaginal birth account, which is where the vast majority of it belongs. The challenge for electivecesarean.com is to make the public more aware of the evidence that exists on cesarean cost (Kazandjian et al.; Bost; Morrison and MacKenzie; NIH State-of-the-Science).

Finally, perhaps the organization's greatest challenge is to communicate that any attempt to reduce overall cesarean rates should *not* be allowed to impact on the growing sub-group of prophylactic maternal request cesareans by women with healthy pregnancies at 39+ weeks and plans for a small family (whatever impact that may have on overall rates), without being accused of advocating (or ignoring the potential risks associated with) ever increasing rates. But again, this is why clarity of data is so crucial, because without knowing *which* type of cesareans are increasing or reducing, and only concentrating on the overall "*total cesarean number*," there is a real danger that strategies and targets could be making the situation worse and not better. For example, by reducing the numbers of (planned) cesareans with the lowest risks and increasing the numbers of (emergency) cesareans with the highest risks, it's possible that the overall number may fall but the outcomes for mothers and babies are not improved.

Future Goals

Ultimately, electivecesarean.com sees its role in the future as trying to facilitate change, both in the way that birth plans are perceived and the way that birth outcomes are assessed. As such, the main goal of the organization is, and will continue to be, campaigning for the recognition of maternal request prophylactic cesarean as a legitimate birth plan, and greater transparency in the collation and presentation of birth data. Without this, we are in danger of forever more being in a situation where "*no one can say for sure*" whether a planned vaginal or cesarean birth has the lowest risk of death and serious morbidity in mothers and babies. And while many doctors and professional organizations have already suggested that advances in surgical technique (albeit often unappreciated and under-celebrated) may have already reached a level of parity with the benefits of natural birth, if uncertainty reigns, nothing will change.

Interestingly, in the same year (2003) that the American College of Obstetricians and Gynecologists said: "*the burden of proof should fall on those who advocate for a change in policy in support of elective cesarean delivery*" ("New ACOG Opinion Addresses Elective Cesarean Controversy"), two Australian doctors were discussing whether or not there should be a term cephalic trial to properly compare different birth *plans*, and wrote: "*What a disaster it would be if it was found elective cesarean was safer than vaginal birth*" (Robson and Ellwood). Indeed some doctors are already predicting that even more women will opt for a cesarean birth once they learn the truth about all the possible consequences of planning a vaginal birth, and this is even without the results of a landmark study. But while electivecesarean.com understands that this vision of the future of birth is completely unthinkable for some, it remains adamant that establishing the *facts* about different birth types and *informing* women about these facts must take precedence over any ideological concerns of what women might then decide to do with those facts.

The last thing to mention in terms of electivecesarean.com's future goals is the publication of a book that its founder has written with her co-author, Dr. Magnus Murphy, who is Chief of the Division of Urogynecology and Pelvic Floor Disorders at the *Calgary Regional Health Authority* and a Clinical Assistant Professor at the *University of Calgary*. The book, titled *Choosing Cesarean – A Natural Birth Plan*, is being published by Prometheus Books and takes an in-depth look at the whole controversy regarding maternal request cesareans. It has been written for pregnant women and medical professionals alike, with a strong emphasis on facts, figures and opinion that readers may not have seen anywhere else, as well as birth stories, birth preparation and recovery tips and a review of the politics and evolution of cesarean rates around the world.

Relationship to Larger Motherhood Movement

The work of electivecesarean.com is important in relation to the wider motherhood movement because it identifies a group of women and mothers who are often misrepresented and misunderstood in the context of birth plans and experiences. Furthermore, it shares the movement's aim of empowering mothers, by providing them with a platform for communication and education, and the information and support they might need when preparing for what can sometimes be very daunting, difficult and even confrontational antenatal consultations. So embedded in our social fabric is the idea of natural birth as an empowering, valuable and desirable rite of passage, which *all* pregnant women want to experience, it often seems as though the only mothers whose birth stories are heard and sympathized with are those who plan a spontaneous vaginal birth and do not have this outcome. And yet the stories relayed by mothers to electivecesarean.com are just as heartbreaking and infuriating.

For example, women who avoid getting pregnant because they cannot find a supportive doctor or hospital, women who terminate their pregnancies when their cesarean request is refused, women who are criticized or belittled by other mothers because of their birth choice, women who fight for their birth plan and win, only for their doctor to be unavailable on the day and other doctors either refuse to perform the surgery or make negative comments throughout the birth, and women who (after being coerced into having a trial of labor) end up with devastating injuries to their baby or themselves. These mothers, their experiences and their voices deserve our attention too.

electivecesarean.com believes that what's important in the context of the work being done by all well-meaning birth groups is the recognition and acceptance that when it comes to birth choices, mothers are no longer all moving together in the same direction—partly because they don't *want* to but also because they don't *have* to. And what this organization aims to offer these women, who very often don't recognize their desires, thoughts and choices on other birth websites, is a place where they can come to feel accepted, supported and *normal.*

Conclusion

In very simple terms, there are two ways that a baby can be born: vaginally or surgically. And whereas the latter method of delivery originated as a last resort means for mankind to intervene and save the lives of mothers and babies destined to die at the hands of Mother Nature, it has developed into an arguably evolutionary answer to the enduring challenge of getting a large head and wide shoulders out of a relatively narrow pelvic opening. Why engage with the vagaries of a trial of labor when you can bypass it completely? But of course cesarean surgery is *not* a risk-free procedure, and therefore the fact that perfectly healthy women are *choosing* a cesarean without ever attempting labor at all is understandably shocking and frustrating to people who still view the cesarean as a last resort measure. Why risk major surgery when there is a very strong likelihood that a natural physiological birth is achievable?

This is just the briefest summation of what has brought us to probably the greatest debate in today's obstetrical world: whether or not a planned cesarean birth on maternal request, with no medical or obstetrical indication, is indeed prophylactic in comparison with a trial of labor and should it be offered in principle (albeit subject to individualized consultation, as with any surgical procedure), or even made available, to pregnant women in an antenatal setting? It is a complex question, and one fraught with passion and opinion on both sides, but the inescapable truth is that while debate rages on around the world, increasing numbers of women and indeed medical professionals ("Gallup Survey Reveals"; Wax et al.; Gabbe and Holzman) are deciding to give birth surgically. It would appear that in the historical context of human birth, cesareans may have had a relatively short and limited presence thus far, but looking to the future, it is likely that their presence will most certainly not be short-lived.

Works Cited

Berger, M. and B. P. Sachs. "Maternal Mortality With Cesarean Delivery in Massachusetts (1995-2003) and a Review of the Literature." "NIH State-of-the-Science Conference Cesarean Abstracts" (March 27-29, 2006). Web. <http://consensus.nih.gov/2006/cesareanabstracts.pdf>.

"Birth Group, CCA, Calls on WHO to Re-examine 'Outdated and Unsafe' 10-15% Recommended Cesarean Rate." The Coalition for Childbirth Autonomy. News Release. October 29, 2008. Web. <http://www.mmdnewswire.com/birth-group-cca-calls-on-who-to-re-examine-outdated-and-unsafe-10-15-recommended-cesarean-rate-4073.html>.

Bost, Brent W. "Cesarean Delivery on Demand: What Will It Cost?" *American Journal of Obstetrics & Gynecology* 188.6 (2003): 1418-1423.

Dahlgren, Leanne S. et al. "Caesarean section on maternal request: risks and benefits in healthy nulliparous women and their infants." *Journal of Obstetrics and Gynaecology Canada* 31.9 (September 2009): 808-817. Web. <http://highwire.stanford.edu/cgi/medline/pmid;19941705>.

electivecesarean.com. Web. <http://www.electivecesarean.com>.

Gabbe, S. G. and G. B. Holzman. "Obstetricians' Choice of Delivery." *Lancet* 357.9257 (March 3, 2001): 722. Web. <http://www.thelancet.com/journals/lancet/article/PIISO140-6736(05)71484-7/fulltext>.

"Gallup Survey Reveals Women Ob-Gyns Benefit from 'Insider Knowledge'." [n.d.]. Web. <http://www.acog.org/from_home/publications/press_releases/nr12-09-03-2.cfm>.

Graham, W. J. et al. "An Investigation of Women's Involvement in the Decision to Deliver by Caesarean Section,." *British Journal of Obstetrics and Gynaecology* 106.3 (1999): 213-220, Web. <http://www.ncbi.nlm.nih.gov/pubmed/10426639>.

Hankins, Gary D. V., Shannon M. Clark, and Mary B. Munn. "Cesarean Section on Request at 39 Weeks: Impact on Shoulder Dystocia, Fetal Trauma, Neonatal Encephalopathy, and Intrauterine Fetal Demise." *Seminars in Perinatology* 30 (5) (2006): 276-287.

Kazandjian, Vahé A. et al. "Does a Cesarean Section Delivery Always Cost More Than A Vaginal Delivery?" *Journal of Evaluation in Clinical Practice* 13.1 (2007): 16-20.

Larsson C., K. Källen and E. Andolf. "Cesarean Section and Risk of Pelvic Organ Prolapse: A Nested Case-Control Study." *American Journal of Obstetrics and Gynaecology* 200.3 (2009): 243.e1-4. Web. < http://www.ncbi.nlm.nih.gov/pubmed/19254581>.

Morrison, Joanne and I. Z. MacKenzie. "Cesarean Section on Demand." *Seminars in Perinatology* 27.1 (2003): 20-33.

Mould T. A. et al. "Women's Involvement with the Decision Preceding Their Caesarean Section and Their Degree of Satisfaction." *British Journal of Obstetrics and Gynaecology* 103.11 (1996): 1074-1077. Web. <http://www.ncbi.nlm.nih.gov/pubmed/8916991>.

National Institute for Clinical Excellence (NICE). *Cesarean Section: Clinical Guide 13.* London: Author, April 2004. Web. <www.nice.org.uk/nicemedia/pdf/GC-013NICEguideline.pdf>.

"New ACOG Opinion Addresses Elective Cesarean Controversy." ACOG Office of Communications News Release. October 31, 2003. Web. <http://www.acog.org/from_home/publications/press_releases/nr10-31-03-1.cfm>.

"NIH State-of-the-Science Conference Statement on Cesarean Delivery on Maternal Request." *NIH Consensus and State-of-the-Science Statements* 23.1 (March 27, 2006): 1-29.

Robson, Stephen and David Ellwood, "Should Obstetricians Support a 'Term Cephalic Trial'?" *The Australian & New Zealand Journal of Obstetrics & Gynaecology* 43.5 (2003): 341-343. Web. <http://www.ncbi.nlm.nih.gov/pubmed/14717307>.

Robson, Stephen et al. "Elective Caesarean Delivery At Maternal Request: A Preliminary Study Of Motivations Influencing Women's Decision-Making." *The Australian & New Zealand Journal of Obstetrics & Gynaecology* 48.4 (2008): 415-420. Web. <http://www.ncbi.nlm.nih.gov/pubmed/18837848>.

Ryding, E. L., K. Wijma and B. Wijma. "Psychological Impact of Emergency Cesarean Section in Comparison with Elective Cesarean Section, Instrumental and Normal Vaginal Delivery." *Journal of Psychosomatic Obstetrics and Gynaecology* 19.3 (1998): 135-144. Web. <http://www.ncbi.nlm.nih.gov/pubmed/9844844>.

Torkan, Behnaz et al. "Postnatal Quality of Life in Women After Normal Vaginal Delivery and Caesarean Section." *BMC Pregnancy and Childbirth* 9.1 (2009): 4 Web. <http://www.biomedcentral.com/1471-2393/9/4>.

Wax, Joseph R. et al. "Patient Choice Cesarean: The Maine Experience." *Birth* 32.3 (2005): 203-206. Web. <http://www.ncbi.nlm.nih.gov/pubmed/16128974>.

Weiss, Marianne, Jacqueline Fawcett, and Cynthia Aber. "Adaptation, Postpartum Concerns, and Learning Needs in the First Two Weeks After Caesarean Birth." *Journal of Clinical Nursing* 18.21 (2009): 2938-2948. Web. <http://www.ncbi.nlm.nih.gov/pubmed/19821872>.

Wiklund, Ingela, Gunnar Edman, and Ellika Andolf. "Cesarean Section on Maternal Request: Reasons for the Request, Self-Estimated Health, Expectations, Experience of Birth and Signs of Depression Among First-Time Mothers." *Acta Obstetricia Et Gynecologica Scandinavica* 86.4 (2007): 451-456. Web. <http://www.ncbi.nlm.nih.gov/pubmed/17486467>.

"Women choosing caesarean have low death rate." *Telegraph* [n.d.]. Web. <http://www.telegraph.co.uk/news/uknews/1584671/Women-choosing-caesarean-have-low-death-rate.html>.

15. La Leche League International

CINDY COWAN

DURING THE MIDDLE OF THE twentieth century, breastfeeding rates in North America, and particularly the U.S., dropped as low as 30 percent. Women who wanted to breastfeed often had difficulty in finding help when they ran into challenges and were often given inaccurate information, based on bottle-feeding norms and a lack of understanding of the biology of breastfeeding.

In 1956, a group of seven mothers (Marian Tompson, Mary White, Edwina Froehlich, Mary Ann Cahill, Betty Wagner, Viola Lennon and Mary Ann Kerwin) who had breastfed their own babies decided to start an organization to help other women who wanted to breastfeed. The organization began by meeting in women's homes. Few other resources for breastfeeding mothers were available in North America at the time, and the organization grew rapidly at first. It is currently an active presence in 68 countries around the world.

The World Health Organization once named La Leche League (LLL) the world's foremost authority on breastfeeding, and the organization's information sheets on various breastfeeding topics as well as its book for mothers (*The Womanly Art of Breastfeeding*) are widely known and used.

At the time of LLL's birth, the word breastfeeding was considered risqué. The Founders took the name La Leche from an old statue in St. Augustine, Florida, showing Mary, the mother of Jesus, and bearing the title *Nuestra Senora de la Leche y Buen Parto* which meant "Our Lady of Happy Delivery and Plentiful Milk." *La Leche* is Spanish for "the milk." League was added for alliteration.

The trained volunteers who help mothers and lead group meetings are called Leaders. Research has shown that the peer support provided by LLL is the most effective way to increase the duration of exclusive breastfeeding and the overall duration of breastfeeding.

Mandate

La Leche League's mandate is expressed through the organization's current mission statement:

> Our Mission is to help mothers worldwide to breastfeed through mother-to-mother support, encouragement, information, and education, and to promote a better understanding of breastfeeding as an important element in the healthy development of the baby and mother.

This is further expanded upon in the Purpose statements: La Leche League was founded to give information and encouragement, mainly through personal help, to all mothers who want to breastfeed their babies. While complementing the care of the physician and other health care professionals, it recognizes the unique importance of one mother helping another to perceive the needs of her child and to learn the best means of fulfilling those needs.

LLL believes that breastfeeding, with its many important physical and psychological advantages, is best for baby and mother and is the ideal way to initiate good parent-child relationships. The loving help and support of the father enables the mother to focus on mothering so that together the parents develop close relationships which strengthen the family and thus the whole fabric of society.

LLL further believes that mothering through breastfeeding deepens a mother's understanding and acceptance of the responsibilities and rewards of her special role in the family. As a woman grows in mothering she grows as a human being, and every other role she may fill in her lifetime is enriched by the insights and humanity she brings to it from her experiences as a mother.

The League's purpose is distinct. This singleness of purpose does not prevent interaction with other organizations with compatible purposes, but La Leche League will carefully guard against allying itself with another cause, however worthwhile that cause may be.

Philosophy Statements

Early in their planning for the organization, the seven women who founded La Leche League decided to have a set of guidelines or principles to define their underlying beliefs. These are generally known as the "Philosophy Statements."

These have been edited and revised slightly over the years and currently read:

- Mothering through breastfeeding is the most natural and effective way of understanding and satisfying the needs of the baby.
- Mother and baby need to be together early and often to establish a satisfying relationship and an adequate milk supply.
- In the early years the baby has an intense need to be with his mother which is as basic as his need for food.
- Breast milk is the superior infant food.
- For the healthy, full-term baby, breast milk is the only food necessary until the baby shows signs of needing solids, about the middle of the first year after birth.

- •Ideally the breastfeeding relationship will continue until the baby outgrows the need.
- •Alert and active participation by the mother in childbirth is a help in getting breastfeeding off to a good start.
- •Breastfeeding is enhanced and the nursing couple sustained by the loving support, help, and companionship of the baby's father. A father's unique relationship with his baby is an important element in the child's development from early infancy.
- •Good nutrition means eating a well-balanced and varied diet of foods in as close to their natural state as possible.
- •From infancy on, children need loving guidance which reflects acceptance of their capabilities and sensitivity to their feelings.

The "taglines" used over the years to describe the organization have also changed with time. An early one was "Good Mothering Through Breastfeeding." Currently, it is "Happy Mothers, Breastfed Babies."

History

Founded in 1956 in Chicago, Illinois, the organization grew rapidly in the early years. Groups were formed in Canada in the early 1960s and eventually La Leche League Canada was established as an affiliate of La Leche League International (LLLI). Affiliates were also formed in New Zealand and the UK. LLLI has been largely U.S.-based, but in recent years has moved to establish a separate LLLUSA.

As the organization grew, it was organized into Groups, Chapters and Areas. Groups are local organizations headed by one or more accredited Leaders, Chapters are made up of several Groups in a community, and Areas are geographically-defined collections of Groups or Chapters. One or more Areas could make up a Division (in the U.S.), or an Affiliate. In recent years, the Executive Director and Board of Directors have initiated a re-organization in which 20 or more Leaders create agreements to form an Area; five or more Areas can again come together with written agreements to form an Area Network, which can then "connect" to La Leche League International. This process has been controversial and is still incomplete.

Context

Many of the challenges facing breastfeeding mothers are the same today as in the years when LLL was founded; others are new. These include:

- •Difficulty in getting accurate information about how to initiate, establish and sustain breastfeeding, or being given conflicting information on these topics.
- •Lack of information on how to resolve breastfeeding problems (such as sore nipples, mastitis, etc.).

- •Concerns about being harassed or embarrassed when breastfeeding in public.
- •Concerns about fitting breastfeeding into a busy life, including when returning to work.
- •Concerns about how breastfeeding will affect other relationships.
- •Overcoming special challenges such as breastfeeding after breast surgery, breastfeeding an adopted baby, breastfeeding a premature baby, etc.

Activities

1. Mother to Mother Support

La Leche League from the beginning has been based on the concept of mother-to-mother help: the idea that an experienced breastfeeding mother can provide sensitive and practical help to a new mother with questions and concerns about breastfeeding. This help is given during group meetings where the volunteer Leaders facilitate discussion, over the phone, and during visits to the mother's home or in the hospital. In recent years, help by email has been increasingly common. Mothers can also submit questions to be answered by Leaders through the LLLI website, or can participate in forums hosted there.

During meetings or one-to-one helping situations, Leaders provide the accurate and practical information the mother needs to make decisions and find solutions to her concerns.

2. Training and Educating Volunteers

Preparing mothers to become volunteers is another major activity of the organization. Women must meet specific requirements to become Leaders; these have changed over the years and are likely to continue to change in the future, but include having breastfed at least one baby for at least nine months at the time of the application, having read the current edition of *The Womanly Art of Breastfeeding* and demonstrating through a written personal history commitment to the LLL philosophy statements. Typically, a prospective Leader works with another, more experienced Leader and a representative of LLLI's Leader Applicant department to discuss her personal history, learn about how to access and share breastfeeding information, and learn how to counsel women who call for help with sensitivity and respect.

For a number of years, LLLI had a "peer counselling" program. The system of recruiting and training Leaders has led to a situation where most Leaders are white and financially fairly well-off, and women from other backgrounds may not see them as peers. The peer counselling program sought out women from other ethnic and socio-economic backgrounds who might not have met the criteria to qualify as Leaders—for example, they might have only breastfeed for six months—and provided them with training in order to enable them to work with women in their community. This program was discontinued recently as part of the re-organization.

3. Providing Written Materials

LLLI has also created a wealth of written material on breastfeeding, starting with *The Womanly Art of Breastfeeding* which was first published in 1958. The eighth edition of this book was published in 2010. Other books published by LLLI include a series of cookbooks focusing on healthy foods for families, books on tandem nursing, breastfeeding after breast surgery, weaning, and other related topics. The *Breastfeeding Answer Book* was long a primary resource both for Leaders and for health professionals who worked with breastfeeding mothers. LLLI has recently discontinued its publishing program but is now working with a mainstream publisher to continue to produce books under its name. Many of the information sheets and informative articles once sold at meetings or distributed by mail are now available through the website.

These written materials can provide information and support for mothers with less-common difficulties (such as breastfeeding after breast reduction).

A magazine for Leaders (called *Leaven)* is still produced. *New Beginnings,* which was an international magazine for LLL members, has been discontinued but may be taken on by LLLUSA (since the majority of the subscribers were located in the US). A new publication, *Breastfeeding Today,* is published online.

Affiliates such as La Leche League Canada maintain their own websites and produce newsletters, brochures and information sheets as needed in their countries.

4. Organizing Conferences, Workshops and Seminars

La Leche League International did, in the past, organize an International Conference every two years; all but one of these were located in the U.S. (The other one was held in Toronto.). The last of these was in 2007. LLLI also used to organize workshops and seminars aimed at physicians and other health care professionals; these were discontinued at about the same time. Some affiliates, countries and areas continue to organize conferences and seminars.

These events provide an opportunity for breastfeeding parents and volunteers to gather and learn more about overcoming challenges, and to build a sense of community.

5. Advocacy

The amount of advocacy done by the organization has varied over the years, but has not been a priority, since the primary focus is on providing practical help to mothers.

Challenges and Organizational Responses

The earliest challenge faced by the brand-new LLL was the high level of demand. Despite the low breastfeeding rates, many women wanted to breastfeed and the number of monthly meetings held expanded rapidly. Women in other communities wrote to the mothers and asked for information, and the Founders wrote personal letters back. In 1958, they began a newsletter, and published the first edition of *The Womanly Art of Breastfeeding* (this consisted of mimeographed pages in duo-tang binders). A 1963 article by Karen Pryor in *Reader's Digest* entitled "They Teach the Joys of Breastfeeding" brought the group national attention and more growth. The training process for volunteer Leaders was quite basic at first and based on the assumption that having breastfed a baby herself would go a long way to preparing a mother to help other mothers. As time went on, a more formal process was developed that helped potential Leaders learn counselling skills and obtain information to help mothers with various breastfeeding challenges (from breastfeeding a premature baby or an infant with Down syndrome to identifying and getting treatment for conditions such as mastitis and thrush).

Another challenge was the lack of acceptance from the medical community. Although LLL began in consultation with two medical doctors (Mary White's husband, Dr. Gregory White, and his friend, Dr. Herbert Ratner), and has maintained a Medical Advisory Board, many of the recommendations made by the organization, although evidence-based, did not coincide with the advice given by most physicians. For example, LLL recommended breastfeeding from birth and feeding on demand; usual practice in the 1950s was to give only a "trial bottle" of sugar water in the first 24 hours and then feed on a strict four-hour schedule. LLL also recommended that solid foods only be started around the middle of the first year, in response to indications from the baby that he was ready to eat other foods. The current practice in this area was to start solid foods as early as possible but certainly by six weeks of age. LLL also came under fire for recommending that babies continue to breastfeed until they outgrew the need, at a time when many doctors recommending weaning by six months at the latest.

It is interesting to see that current recommendations from all major medical organizations now support the recommendations that LLL was making more than 50 years ago about initiating breastfeeding, starting solids, breastfeeding duration, etc.

Another challenge the organization faced early on was finding a way to move on from its Catholic roots. The seven women who founded LLL were all members of the Catholic church. They decided from the beginning that they wanted LLL to be open to all women, but their strong faith led to some difficulties. In particular, there was some disagreement about whether or not the organization should take a stand on abortion. In the end, it did not. Another issue which may be related to these religious roots is the philosophy statement on the role of fathers, and its reflection in the earlier versions of the *The Womanly Art of Breastfeeding.* While single mothers and lesbian mothers were welcomed at meetings, the written materials emphasized "husbands" and made no reference to unmarried partners or same-sex partners. The most recent (2010) edition of *The Womanly Art of Breastfeeding* uses the term partner rather than husband, and refers to single mothers and same-sex partners as well.

From the beginning, LLL volunteers have been accused of "making mothers feel guilty about not breastfeeding" and called "nipple Nazis" and similar derogatory names. This is surprising, to a certain extent, since the LLL Founders were clear that their goal was to help women who *wanted* to breastfeed, and they were not interested in trying to coerce women who didn't want to. However, many of the volunteers and members feel quite passionately about the value and importance of breastfeeding and this may be the root of the perception that they "make mothers feel guilty." On the other hand, this may also be the result of mothers getting a rather mixed message from their health care professionals: "Breast is best, but formula is just as good" which is then contradicted by the factual information given out by LLL highlighting potential risks of not breastfeeding.

Another aspect which has drawn criticism is the organization's emphasis on mothering that extends beyond its link to breastfeeding. Some felt that the earlier tagline "Good mothering through breastfeeding" suggested that only breastfeeding mothers could be good mothers, for example. La Leche League differed from researchers and some health care professionals in emphasizing the breastfeeding relationship, rather than the milk, and seeing the way of caring for the baby that best fit with breastfeeding as a model for mothering and a way of learning to be a good mother. In other words, because breastfeeding is most easily established and milk production maintained when the mother and baby are together most if not all of the time, and the mother responds promptly to the baby's cues, this available and responsive type of mothering became the model for the good mother.

Discussion continues within the organization about whether it is strictly a "breastfeeding" support group or a "mothering through breastfeeding" support group, with strong opinions on either side. While many Leaders and members practise an "attachment parenting" approach, there is no official stand on parenting styles.

A current challenge faced by the organization is a change in how women volunteer. In the past, a significant number of women continued to work at home once their children were in school, and these women often valued becoming deeply involved in volunteer work. Today, with more women working from the time their children are small, it is difficult to find volunteers willing or able to commit the amount of time and energy that Leaders and, in particular, administrators within LLL, were able to do in the past. This has made it increasingly difficult to find volunteers to take on the responsibilities of managing the organization without pay, and attempts have been made to cut the work into smaller "chunks," encourage more team-work, and change the structure of the organization to rely less on volunteer management.

Contentious Issues

One of the philosophy statements says: *In the early years the baby has an intense need to be with his mother which is as basic as his need for food.* The meaning of this statement and how it should be interpreted has varied over the years and in different countries.

This statement identifies a need that the baby has for his mother's presence separately from the need for her milk, but doesn't define how a mother should respond to that need. LLL has always provided information, help and support to breastfeeding mothers who were working or who experienced extended separations from their babies for other reasons, and this has not changed. However, LLL requires that prospective Leaders demonstrate their understanding and commitment to these philosophy statements in their own lives and behaviours as mothers. For many years, this particular statement was interpreted fairly strictly. A prospective Leader (known as a Leader applicant) was expected to be with her baby or at least available to her baby continuously (except, perhaps, while the baby slept) for the first year, and having only brief, occasional separations until the child was three years old. The interpretation has changed over the years, although even a few years ago, a mother who was employed and away from her baby (under a year old) while at work was not eligible for Leadership. However, the guidelines have become increasingly flexible and mothers who have ongoing, regular separation from their babies are now sometimes accredited as Leaders. This change has caused some controversy and concern among Leaders who agreed with and supported the previous interpretation of the statement and feel that the current trend towards accrediting Leaders with substantial amounts of separation from their babies is a negative change.

Another philosophy statement that has been controversial is: *Breastfeeding is enhanced and the nursing couple sustained by the loving support, help, and companionship of the baby's father. A father's unique relationship with his baby is an important element in the child's development from early infancy.* Some Leaders and members have pointed out that many babies are raised by single mothers with the support of friends and family, or by same-sex couples, and this statement ignores and may even be read as criticizing those situations. They would like to see it changed to something that is more inclusive and that recognizes the roles that all kinds of loving relationships play in a baby's life and development. Others see it as an important statement about fathers and their role, and object to any attempts to change it.

In the early years of LLL, mothers were encouraged to be discreet about breastfeeding in public, and in meetings mothers might be helped to practise getting baby latched on without revealing too much skin. Some breastfeeding advocates felt this made things more difficult for mothers whose babies were uncooperative about nursing under a blanket or other cover-up, and that it ultimately was not helpful to the breastfeeding cause. Seeing breastfeeding in public situations helps to convey the message that breastfeeding is normal and not something to be hidden away. In recent years, the emphasis on discretion has diminished.

Another area of controversy stems from the philosophy statement that breastfeeding should (ideally) continue until the baby outgrows the need. LLLI supports the concept of "baby-led (or child-led) weaning, and many mothers involved in the organization will still be breastfeeding when their children are older—sometimes as old as six or seven years. While breastfeeding past the first couple of years is not unusual in many parts of the world, breastfeeding into early childhood is sometimes labelled sexual abuse in North America and LLLI has been criticized for supporting this. Others feel that the concept of child-led weaning can put unreasonable demands on the mother, who may feel that she is expected to continue breastfeeding even if she would prefer to stop, and recent publications (including the LLLI-published book *How Weaning Happens)* have put more emphasis on the mother's role in encouraging weaning while continuing to be sensitive to her child's needs. While medical organizations at one time recommended early weaning from the breast, current recommendations from the Canadian Pediatric Society and the American Association of Pediatricians encourage mothers to breastfeed for two years and beyond, and the AAP specifically notes that "there is no upper limit" to the duration of breastfeeding. As the 2010 edition of *The Womanly Art of Breastfeeding* points out, even if mothers do nothing at all to encourage it, all children do eventually wean.

LLL has been described as "the gateway drug to alternative lifestyles." Although LLL as an organization has been clear that it takes no stand on a number of potentially controversial issues, many women first learn about such things as babywearing, homeschooling, elimination communication, the anti-vaccination movement, etc., during LLL gatherings. (Elimination communication or "diaper-free baby" means that, rather than use diapers, mothers learn to recognize their babies' cues for urinating and defecating and take the baby to a toilet or potty when he signals this need. This can be done from birth, and is common in many other parts of the world, but is new to most North Americans.) This may be because mothers who become involved with LLL tend to be those who question the advice given by the medical community, and they then go on to question other "norms" of their society.

Since many members of LLL are involved in these other causes, which are often related to mothering, the organization puts considerable emphasis on "avoiding mixing causes." This causes some conflict among Leaders because many of these causes are an essential part of their daily lives. For example, if a Leader uses a sling to carry her baby around at a meeting, is she suggesting to the mothers who attend that belonging to LLL would require them to use baby slings as well? Or if she brings her obviously school-aged children to meetings during the day, is she suggesting that LLL supports homeschooling (when it in fact has no position on this issue)? The concern is that a mother may feel reluctant to contact the organization for breastfeeding help if she is put off by the connection to other issues unrelated to breastfeeding.

While medical associations have come to support most of La Leche League's positions over the years, some remain controversial. One is co-sleeping or bed-sharing. LLL publications recommend bed-sharing as one approach to night-time parenting for breastfeeding mothers and babies, provided certain safety guidelines are followed. They point to evidence that shows breastfeeding mothers orient themselves to the baby while sleeping differently than mothers who are not breastfeeding, and to studies that show bed-sharing can significantly increase breastfeeding duration. Current public health statements in North America are generally opposed to any bed-sharing, without differentiating between breastfed and non-breastfed babies.

Another area of controversy is the supplementation of exclusively breastfed babies with Vitamin D. As the concern about plummeting Vitamin D levels in the population as a whole has grown (thanks to increased use of sunscreen and more time spent indoors), health professionals and official organizations have recommended that all exclusively breastfed babies be supplemented with Vitamin D drops. While recognizing that Vitamin D is essential, LLL has suggested that parents take a more individualized approach: a fair-skinned parent with an equally fair-skinned infant, who is outside for a period of time most days, and is not completely covered up, is likely to have good Vitamin D status. A dark-skinned mother and baby, who is covered completely for religious or other reasons and/or rarely goes outdoors, may both need supplemental Vitamin D. Generally, if a baby has poor Vitamin D status, his or her mother does as well, and supplementing the baby does not help the mother.

Financial Challenges and Re-organization

In the past twenty years or so, as breastfeeding rates have climbed, other sources of breastfeeding support have emerged. Many public health programs, such as Women, Infants and Children (WIC) in the U.S. or Best Start in Canada, offer group meetings and other supports for breastfeeding mothers now. As the Internet has expanded, many websites now offer extensive information and opportunities for email support. LLL has expanded its website offerings as well and created mother-to-mother forums.

These changes, though, have contributed to ongoing financial challenges for the organization, which relied on mothers and Leaders paying membership fees for support. Despite increasing numbers of mothers breastfeeding and frequently turning to Leaders or the LLLI website for help and information, attendance at meetings dropped in many communities and fewer mothers paid for memberships. These financial problems, in part, led to a decision by the Board of Directors and Executive Director to restructure the organization. The process (involving the creation of agreements among volunteers and the various sub-groups of the organization) has been lengthy and continues to be controversial; one of the surviving Founders, Marian Tompson, recently resigned in protest.

Relation to Larger Motherhood Movement

It is difficult to clearly place LLL in relation to the larger motherhood movement. The organization has worked hard to keep its focus strictly on breastfeeding and helping mothers one-to-one; there has been little political lobbying or interest in connecting with other organizations. The breastfeeding cause is supported by women who may disagree strongly about other issues; while some members and volunteers describe themselves as feminists, others would adamantly resist that description. This singleness of purpose is one of the organization's strengths but can also be seen as a weakness, because it makes collaboration with others difficult even when that collaboration might enable the organization to reach more women or effect change.

La Leche League's contributions to the larger motherhood movement have largely been through example, and these may be significant. Most agree that LLL contributed to the rising breastfeeding rates in North America in the last half of the twentieth century, and this provided concrete evidence of the power of women to change their society and their circumstances. LLL insisted that women did not have to blindly follow the recommendations of their health care providers or others; women were capable of reading research, understanding evidence, and making their own decisions about how to give birth, how to feed their babies, how to manage breastfeeding and when to wean. Fifty years ago, these were revolutionary ideas, especially coming from women with no particular political power.

Future Goals

There continues to be a need for support for mothers who want to breastfeed: although breastfeeding rates are significantly higher than in the 1950s in North America, the percentage of mothers who breastfeed to six months or twelve months continues to be low, and even fewer breastfeed exclusively.

The challenge for LLL is figuring out how this support can best be provided in today's environment. Mothers today are less likely to attend meetings or read books about breastfeeding and often seek support and information online. While LLL does provide information through its websites, the kind of personalized support and assessment of breastfeeding problems traditionally provided at meetings or during home visits is not possible in an online approach. In addition, this does not provide LLL with the funding needed to sustain the organization.

Conclusion

La Leche League International has played an important role in reclaiming breastfeeding for mothers and babies after this "art" was almost lost in North America. The organization's biggest strength is the large number of deeply committed volunteers, who commit significant amounts of time to helping mothers with breastfeeding. The mother-to-mother peer helper approach used in LLLI has been demonstrated by research to be the single most effective way to increase the duration of breastfeeding. The organization has also faced a number of challenges over the past fifty years and has at times struggled to adapt to them; if LLLI does continue as an organization it is likely to look rather different in the future than it does now. The changes in organizational structure allow volunteers to work in more diverse ways: we may see greater reliance on online communications, more specialized helping (for example, groups for Muslim women), increased collaboration with health professionals, more sessions offered at workplaces, and more "drop-in" gatherings rather than formal meetings.

Works Cited

La Leche League International. *The Womanly Art of Breastfeeding.* 8th ed. New York: Ballantine Books, 2010.

Pryor, Karen. "They Teach the Joys of Breastfeeding." *Reader's Digest.* 1963.

16. Middle-Class Mothers as Activists for Change

The Australian Breastfeeding Association

VIRGINIA THORLEY

THE NURSING MOTHERS' ASSOCIATION, NOW the Australian Breastfeeding Association (ABA), was founded in Melbourne, Australia, in February 1964 by Mary Paton (the Founder) and five other mothers, each of whom had worked in a professional area before marriage. The association has been described both as an organization of conservative, middle-class women and an activist organization. This chapter will demonstrate the relevance of these images, simplistic on their own, in the context of the organization's history, philosophy, purpose and challenges, and the ABA's role as an agent for change.

The organization's philosophy is best described as providing mother-to-mother support within a structure that values motherhood and mothers, while engaging with society and governments to create change. The ABA's purpose is to assist mothers who plan to breastfeed to meet their goals, within the context of mothering generally; that is, breastfeeding is not placed in isolation from the woman's life. The association's statement of its vision incorporates this purpose along with the desire to be the foremost authority on breastfeeding in Australia and to have society regard breastfeeding as normal. In discussing the ABA's history, this chapter will examine why this organization was founded, the training of its volunteers, and efforts to outreach to minority groups and professionals. Some of the obstacles and challenges the association has faced were peculiar to the ABA, while others were influenced by economic and societal change. Looking to the future, the association has articulated its goals in the 2009-2012 strategic plan. This chapter will show that the ABA had a role in the motherhood movement, while generally its office-bearers did not perceive themselves as part of a wider movement.

Philosophy, Purpose and Mission

The association's philosophy is described on the ABA website as espousing the values of mother-to-mother support and "skilled and loving parenting" in the community, through an organizational ideology of excellence that emphasizes cooperation and teamwork, through communication that is "honest, open and respectful" with transparent processes (ABA, "Vision"). An underlying factor is the association's strong focus on its Code of Ethics, which spells out its status as a lay organization which does not give medical advice and whose office bearers do not criticize individual health care professionals or encroach into professional domains. Thus, sessions on the Code of Ethics form part of ongoing education for those holding volunteer positions. When over zealously interpreted, it occasionally is restrictive in a way that was never intended.

Since its inception, the purpose of the ABA has been to provide women who wish to breastfeed the accurate information and personal support that many mothers need in order to achieve this goal. From the earliest years, the ABA has viewed breastfeeding as a part of "skilled and loving mothering," with the word "mothering" now changed to "parenting" to include fathers. The association's latest statement of its mission is:

> As Australia's leading authority on breastfeeding, we educate and support mothers, using up-to-date research findings and the practical experiences of many women. We work to influence our society to acknowledge breastfeeding as the norm for infant nutrition and as an aid to skilled and loving parenting. (ABA, "Strategic Plan")

History

The ABA had its genesis as the Nursing Mothers' Association when suburban Melbourne mother, Mary Paton (the Founder) had difficulty finding accurate information to help her breastfeed her baby. Maternity hospital practices were not conducive to a good start with breastfeeding and the printed information available was inadequate (Reiger, *Disenchantment* 143; Thorley, "Printed Advice" 77-89). She read an article in a 1963 *Reader's Digest* about the formation of La Leche League as the world's first organization providing mother-to-mother support on breastfeeding. Realizing this sort of assistance was lacking in Australia, she drew together several other mothers and they devoured printed materials from La Leche League. After considerable reflection, they decided to found a separate organization that would be based in Australia. The first official meeting was held in February 1964. After consideration of possible names for their group, and advice that the word "breastfeeding" was unacceptable for the telephone directory, they decided on the "Nursing Mothers' Association." "Of Australia" was added to the name in 1969, when branches in other states were formed. A further name change came in August 2001, after an overwhelming vote of the membership to rename it the "Australian Breastfeeding Association."

There was a tradition of involvement in maternal and child health by middle-class women on a voluntary basis; indeed, in most Australian states middle-class women had been instrumental in fund-raising for well-baby clinics in the community and hiring trained staff for them (Gandevia 125; McCalman 50-51; Davis 161-73). Even in Queensland, where state government policy discouraged the participation of the volunteer sector in welfare, the Mothercraft Association of Queensland (MAQ), in the years 1931-1961, managed to find a role to play (Thorley, "Softly" 80-92). When the ABA was founded, most Australian mothers were primarily homemakers, either by choice or because employment was generally closed to women on marriage. Volunteerism provided an outlet for their energy. For the more active members volunteer work for the association involved similar amounts of time and effort as a paid job would have, though this was not perceived as "work." Indeed, in the mid-1980s, the appropriateness of the breastfeeding mother's return to paid employment was hotly debated in the association's newsletter for its counsellors, *Talkabout.* This debate reflected community attitudes and was not unique to the ABA.

Training of Lay Counsellors

When the first breastfeeding counsellors were trained, they qualified in particular roles, as Group Leaders, Assistant Group Leaders, Telephone Counsellors or Letter Counsellors. Trainees were encouraged to become Group Leaders as the basic unit of the NMAA was, and still is, the local group. Eventually, the term "breastfeeding counsellor" was used generically for all of these categories. In 1986 another category was established, that of the "community educator," who became increasing involved at group and local level.

Initially the training system was similar to that of La Leche League during the same period, with trainees being required to make written responses to a set of questions based on real situations. The training system has been updated a number of times to develop counselling skills as well as the capacity to provide accurate information to assist the mother in making decisions in her own situation. The current training system involves completion of a Certificate IV in Breastfeeding Education (Counselling), which provides ABA counsellors with a recognized qualification. ABA 's community educators now study for their own Certificate IV in Breastfeeding Education (Community).

Outreach Programs

While a high level of training and ongoing education has always been one of the ABA's strengths, the obverse of the coin is that the reading level necessary makes it difficult to recruit minority women and those from lower socio-economic backgrounds (Phillips, *Talkabout* 24). Yet these are the sections of the community least likely to breastfeed for long. The association has conducted outreach programs, usually on short-term funding from state governments, to train minority women to support other women to breastfeed and to develop culturally appropriate materials for some of Australia's marginalized groups. In 1983-1984 the Thallikool program in the Northern Rivers District of New South Wales used a state government grant to train two Aboriginal women from local communities in breastfeeding and counselling, and to develop educational materials (Mangleson 99-104). Related programs followed on both sides of the New South Wales/Queensland border, again with state government grants and employing ABA counsellors as project workers. Some in the association were initially uneasy about counsellors being paid for this work. While to some extent this may have reflected old middle-class attitudes that volunteering was laudable, but paid employment was not a role for mothers, the underlying concern appears to have been that this was unfair to others who volunteered their time. In another outreach program, ABA counsellors worked with Punjabi mothers in a farming community in northern New South Wales. One outcome of this program was that the Indian mothers produced a hand-written breastfeeding manual in Punjabi. Another outreach program, in Victoria, targeted adolescent mothers.

Structure

Once the NMAA had spread from Victoria into other states, state and territory branches were created. As the branches developed they have not necessarily used state or territory boundary, for logistical reasons. The branches occupy a level of structure between the local groups, which is how most members experience the organization, and the national level. In the larger states these branches divided into regions, answerable to the branch "representative" (later renamed the branch president). The Founder has always considered the association's structure as one of its strengths, with the national hierarchy supporting the grassroots groups Australia-wide. Kerreen Reiger has termed the NMAA structure a "maternalist bureaucracy," as evidenced by the concept of the organization as a family, which has impacted on the decision-making processes, with uneasiness about factions or personal power" (Reiger, *Our Bodies* 85-87).

In the early years members of the Executive Committee (later the Board of Directors, after the association was incorporated) stored their files under their beds and elsewhere in their homes. Tasks such as the collating of newsletters and the sewing of an early sale item, the *meh tai* baby sling, were initially done at kitchen tables. As the workload became greater, the need for a national office with paid staff became pressing. The first NMAA National Headquarters was established in a Melbourne suburb in 1970 and subsequent national offices have always been located in Melbourne. "Working groups," which are responsible for a number of national administrative and policy areas, consist of volunteer conveners and members across Australia.

Outreach to the Health Professions

In providing support and information to mothers who wished to breastfeed their babies, it became apparent very early that educating health care professionals would be an advantage to mothers, who depended on professional assistance in the maternity hospitals where most Australian women gave birth. The first issue of the association's peer-reviewed journal for health professionals, *Breastfeeding Review*, appeared in August 1982. The old Research Department, later the Information Service, was restructured in 1988 as the Lactation Resource Centre (LRC) to provide the association's counsellors and outside subscribers with the most accurate information available on breastfeeding and human lactation. LRC subscribers have always included individual health care professionals and hospitals. The LRC also sells a range of textbooks and other education material on breastfeeding.

A home study kit for health care professionals was planned from the mid-1980s and the first edition was published in 1990 as *Breastfeeding Management in Australia* (Brodribb). This first edition was printed in Mackay, Queensland, where the editor, ABA counsellor and medical practitioner, Dr. Wendy Brodribb, was then living, and collated by local members. The third edition in 2004, for an international readership, was retitled *Breastfeeding Management.*

In addition to larger educational events with visiting speakers, in recent years the LRC has conducted a "Research, Ethics and Knowledge" course in Melbourne and Brisbane for health care professionals and lay counsellors. The target group includes the increasing number of individuals preparing for the examination of the International Board of Lactation Consultant Examiners or seeking to upgrade their knowledge base.

Activism

Although claiming to be apolitical, as a young organization in the early-1970s the association campaigned to ban the French atomic tests in the Pacific, with an appeal in French addressed to the "mothers of France." The association has also, on a number of occasions, been involved in representations about pesticide use in relation to the safety of mothers and their babies. After media reports in 1970 about increased pesticide levels in mothers' milk, the association produced a Research Bulletin on the subject to provide non-sensationalist information to members and the public. Spokeswomen became involved in media interviews and liaised with other concerned groups. Ten years later the pesticides issue again appeared in the media and, once again, the ABA became involved in providing information and reassurance to mothers that there was no imperative to wean their babies. As concerned consumers, in 1980 ABA formed a special committee, based in Brisbane, to address the issue. The committee's submission to the Hazardous Chemicals Enquiry, a Federal Parliamentary Standing Committee, recommended more research, alternative methods of pest control and the monitoring of pesticide use ("Herbicide" 4).

The ABA was involved in campaigning for the implementation in Australia of the 1981 *International Code of Marketing of Breast Milk Substitutes* (World Health Organization), known in Australia as the WHO Code. This code and subsequent World Health Assembly resolutions to which Australia is a signatory were designed to protect vulnerable new mothers from unrestrained marketing of breastfeeding substitutes. From the 1980s, the association educated members about the issues the WHO Code covered, made representations to the national Trade Practices Commission about unethical marketing practices and continued to monitor local breaches of the international marketing code. Representatives of the association were invited to the signing of the "Marketing in Australia of Infant Formula" (MAIF) Agreement in 1992, an agreement which covers only parts of the WHO Code and, unlike national legislation restricting the advertising of medications, provides no penalties for breaches.

In the 1980s the association developed the innovative Mother Friendly Workplace Award to acknowledge workplaces that met certain criteria for enabling women to continue breastfeeding or providing their babies with their milk after the return to work. To encourage workplaces to maintain standards, this was reconceptualized in 2002 as an accreditation process, and renamed the Breastfeeding Friendly Workplace Accreditation.

The ABA at branch and national level has fostered relations with departments of health and governments, becoming influential in a number of ways. Examples are the specific addition to state anti-discrimination legislation to include the right to breastfeed anywhere a woman could legally be and the 2007 House of Representatives Inquiry into the Health Effects of Breastfeeding, the latter the result of representations to the federal government by ABA. The 479 submissions to the inquiry came from the public health sector, numerous individual ABA members and other individuals, as well as ABA at national and state level. An ABA representative sits on the International Board of Lactation Consultant Examiners, the body that certifies lactation consultants globally.

Challenges

Financial Sustainability

As with other voluntary organizations, money and sustainability have always been a concern. When the association began in Melbourne, members were encouraged to bring items that could be sold for recycling or an item to donate for sale at the meeting, to raise money. The bring-and-buy method of raising modest funds continued for some years. Other forms of fund-raising at local and branch level that have endured across the years include fashion parades, barbecues, cake stalls, and the hire of equipment, including—latterly—breast pumps.

The rapid expansion of membership during the 1970s put heavier financial demands on the organization. In May 1975 the 15,000th member joined and two months later, in July, the 16,000th member joined (*Talkabout* 25). To meet the needs of members and non-members who sought the support of the association for information and advice, more breastfeeding counsellors needed to be trained, and this cost money, more than could be covered by membership subscriptions. So the association's volunteers began to write grant applications, despite initial fears about government involvement.

Neither the old methods of raising money nor funding from grants could ensure sustainability of income. Grant money is, almost by definition, tied to a specific project or purpose, invariably for a fixed term, with no guarantee of a further grant at the end of the period. One of the strategies to provide an income stream was to separate the organizational arm from the trading arm, with a company established to sell NMAA products and other merchandise. Originally named "Merrily Merrily Enterprises" and later renamed "Mothers Direct," the trading arm had mixed success.

In 1986 the NMAA faced a challenge that threatened its financial stability.

Someone injured a finger while using an ice-crushing machine hired from a local NMAA group and she sued the NMAA for damages. When the High Court of Queensland found against the NMAA, the company that provided public liability insurance refused to pay the full claim. The eventual cost exceeded $AUD 75,000 (Paterson 11). A special appeal to members resulted in donations from over 4,500 individuals, who rallied to the call to "save" the association.

The association again faced a critical financial situation at the turn of the twenty-first century. Income had plunged and the ABA had an estimated budget loss of $160,000 in the first half of the financial year, to February 2002. Mothers Direct, established to provide profits for ABA, instead lost money and had to be supported from association funds. A management consultant was employed as desperate times meant new strategies to reduce costs and generate income. A "100-Day Challenge" was implemented at all levels of the association to halt the

Brisbane Mothers Direct shop and ABA office. Photo: Lesley McBurney.

losses and reverse the financial plight (Croker). The overall loss for the financial year ending at 30 June 2003 was $172,442, of which $147,735 was lost by the trading arm. In the next financial year, to June 2004, the loss had been reduced to $14,251 for the ABA and $15,979 for Mothers Direct (ABA 2004 Annual Report). Both the association and Mothers Direct were once again profitable by the 2004-2005 financial year (ABA 2005 Annual Report). Today the Mothers Direct brand has profitable shops in Melbourne and (since 2007) in Brisbane, as well as a mail-order business.

Grant money has come largely from the federal government and state governments, but other funding has been received from the gaming industry's mandatory community grants, from city or regional councils, and from commercial entities. Policies were eventually developed to preclude the acceptance of money from companies which manufacture products used for artificial feeding, to avoid a conflict of interest and adhere to the *International Code of Marketing of Breast-Milk Substitutes* (WHO).

National fund-raising initiatives have in recent years included an annual lottery and regular appeal letters to the membership, as well as conferences and lectures for the further education of both the association's counsellors and health care professionals. These educational offerings make a profit and also raise the association's profile.

Geographical Isolation

Australia is an island continent the size of the contiguous United States, with a relatively small population predominantly situated on the coast. Thus geographical distance has always been an issue impacting upon how the ABA operates. With the goal of providing consistent, up-to-date advice and support to mothers wherever they may live, it was important for the association to attempt to overcome as many of the disadvantages of geographical isolation as possible. In the late-1960s few members lived outside the main population areas in the southeast, but by the 1970s numbers, everywhere, were burgeoning. Residents of small towns then paid a high price for telephone calls outside their immediate area as long-distance telephone calls were billed in three-minute increments. This put pressure on both the caller and the counsellor to restrict the time. The alternative was letter counselling, at a time when mail services were slow, even in towns and cities with daily mail services. In the early-1970s letters from the association's national headquarters in Melbourne to the only Queensland counsellor in a small town southwest of Townsville could take up to two weeks. In remote areas and on farms, weekly mail services were common.

Several correspondence groups were set up to serve isolated mothers on cattle and sheep stations (ranches), in mining camps and in small towns. Initially, the correspondence group discussion took the form of a "round robin," that is, the group leader would write an introduction to the topic and send it, with a list of names and addresses, to the first member. Each member, in turn, would add her comments and send the package to the next member on the list, a process that could take many weeks. The process became fine-tuned over time (Thorley, *Mother to Mother*, 24-25).

The federal government later reformed telephone billing to reflect the reality of life in rural areas. The ABA established telephone counselling rosters in the major cities to improve access by mothers, though the technical telephony problems involved took up time at branch business meetings. One of the recommendations of the 2007 House of Representatives Inquiry into the Health Benefits of Breastfeeding was for the federal government to provide funding for a national telephone helpline for the ABA, which mothers anywhere in Australia could access for the cost of a local call. This was made possible by a federal government grant of $AUD 500,000 a year for five years in 2008.

As technology improved, new ways of communicating across the country became available. The Internet enabled communication by email to begin, at first in a small way, and in the late-1990s the association began an email counselling roster. This has grown exponentially, with an increasing number of counsellors joining the email roster to meet demand. Once Internet access in country areas improved, women anywhere in Australia could use this mode of counselling; rural counsellors could also increase their counselling experience. Access details for the email roster are listed on the ABA website. Because of insurance limitations, ABA cannot provide counselling to mothers in North America, though requests for help by email are accepted from other countries, as well as Australia.

Distance has also impacted upon counsellor training and ongoing education, and a large cost borne by distant groups has always been sending their counsellors to branch conferences, or even trainee meetings in their own large regions. Money for this necessary travel has been found through innovative fund-raising such as the group that undertook the contract to deliver telephone directories in their city, or through partial grants (Thorley, *Mother to Mother*, 56). Isolated counsellors and trainees were also given a special section of counsellor newsletters to discuss issues specific to them.

Conflicts

In any organization, conflicts will occur and maternalist organizations are not immune. Local or branch personality conflicts in ABA seem to have been handled quietly, sometimes with mediation. However, at a national level in the mid-1970s a conflict which in retrospect appears to be related to differing views on presidential style and accountability split the association into two factions, with both sides campaigning by letter and telephone, before it was resolved.

Shrinking Availability of Volunteers

Dependence on volunteers has always been both a strength and a weakness for the ABA. The whole concept of mother-to-mother support for breastfeeding necessitates experienced mothers to be recruited for training for counsellor roles, to provide a dimension of support and more time than professionals

ABA's magazine, Essence, *covers news, information and issues.*

can provide. Although few mothers had paid employment in the early years of the association, rapid growth in membership led to a shortage of counsellors and a heavy load for existing ones. Since the latter part of the twentieth century this demographic, mothers of young children, has had fewer hours to devote to the association because of employment commitments. The retention of long-serving volunteers and developments in technology, such as the Internet, have enabled the association to continue to provide services. Telephone and email counselling shifts for counsellors on roster gradually shrank to shorter blocks of time, to suit those with work commitments. Breastfeeding classes for pregnant women and their partners are now commonly scheduled for weekends or evenings to cater for women who are working, whether they are prospective members or ABA's counsellors and community educators themselves.

Future Goals

In the Strategic Plan for 2009-2012, the ABA has set out six "key result areas." These are: 1) breastfeeding support; 2) financial viability; 3) training, education and resources; 4) advocacy, policy and research; 5) public awareness, profile and marketing; and 6) governance and organizational development (ABA "Strategic Plan"). These six areas bring the goals that have driven the organization for most of its life into the future. They include some of the ABA 's strengths, as already discussed, and one of the association's continual challenges, financial sustainability.

The first key area is the underpinning reason for ABA's existence. Whether through the local mother-support group, the national 1-800 telephone helpline, email contact, breastfeeding classes for couples or the website, breastfeeding support is how most mothers experience ABA. The explanation supporting this key result area includes to "Educate the broader community that breastfeeding is normal" (ABA Strategic Plan) overlap with the third key result area, except that one concerns the community, while the other is about counsellor training.

The second key result area is an ongoing concern for most voluntary organizations, the ABA included. Memories of the organization's parlous financial state in the early 2000s, and the strategies used to pull it out of this pit, are still fresh in the collective mind of ABA volunteers in national and state administrative roles. So there is an emphasis on the wise use of existing financial assets to increase them, and on local responsibility. The training and ongoing education of counsellors, including building on resources they can use, is at the forefront of the third key result area and specifically linked to the provision of "skilled, knowledgeable and practical" support to breastfeeding mothers (ABA Strategic Plan).

The seemingly diverse areas of advocacy, policy and research are grouped together in the fourth key result area. The rationale for this is that these factors, together, are elements in improving breastfeeding outcomes. The "marketing" in the fifth key result area, means promoting the ABA "brand" to raise the association's profile and increase public awareness of breastfeeding. Earlier, the old *NMAA Newsletter* was given a new look as a magazine under a new title, *Essence*, all the better to reflect the ABA brand. Finally, the sixth key result area, governance and organizational development, pulls the other key areas together by making the association strong and effective.

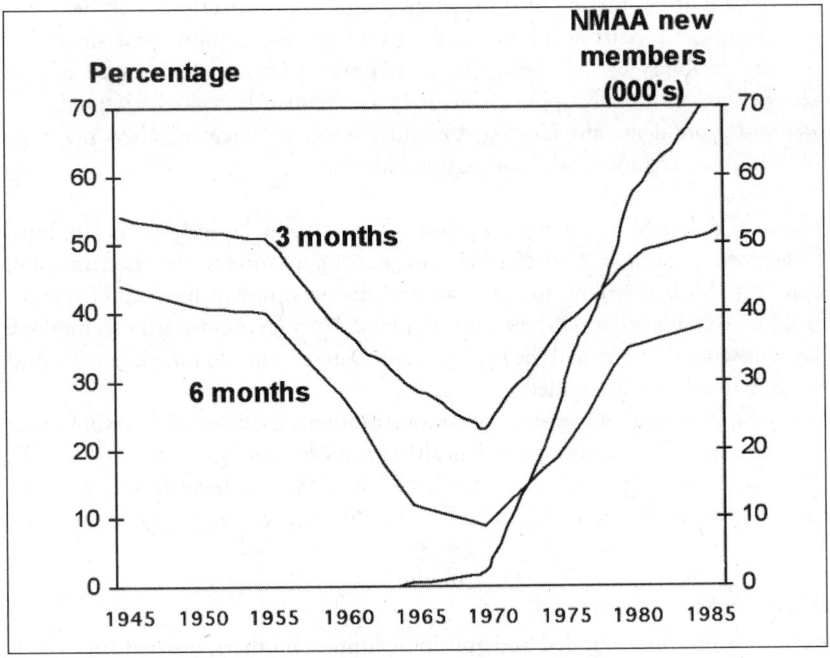

Percentage of mothers completely breastfeeding at three months and six months (adapted from Smibert 1989).

The Organization's Importance in the Motherhood Movement

The genesis of the ABA occurred at a time when maternalist organizations promoting and campaigning for women's rights in reproductive areas of life were being established in Australia. Some, such as childbirth groups and the ABA, focused on women as mothers, while other organizations, such as the Women's Electoral Lobby, concentrated on other aspects of women's fertility and on women's rights generally. ABA women viewed the organization in the context of other mother-to-mother breastfeeding support groups overseas. Other social influences at the time, which may have had a bearing on the increased interest in breastfeeding among mothers, included the growth of the consumer movement and nostalgia for an idealized, more natural past.

During the early period of rapid growth the position of the ABA as a self-help group appears not to have been recognized. Yet the organization fits the 1976 definition of Alfred H. Katz and Eugene I. Bender:

> Self-help groups are voluntary, small group structures for mutual aid and the accomplishment of a special purpose. They are usually formed by peers who have come together for mutual assistance in satisfying a common need ... and bringing about desired social and/or personal change. The initiators and members of such groups perceive that their needs are not, or cannot be, met by or through existing social institutions. Self-help groups emphasize social interactions and the assumption of personal responsibility by members. They often provide material assistance, as well as emotional support; thus they are frequently "cause"-oriented, and promulgate any ideology or values through which members may attain an enhanced sense of personal identity.

This is a remarkably close description of the ABA in its early years (Phillips, *Breastfeeding Review,* 37-39). Furthermore, the organization is non-governmental, though today it is willing to apply for and use government funding of specific projects. As with other self-help and mutual aid groups, advances in technology have subsequently widened the means of communication and interaction beyond the face-to-face group model.

The rapid growth of membership among mothers, the association's willingness from its earliest years to engage with health care professional groups, and the credit given to the organization for the reversal of the decline in breastfeeding rates by medical writers (Wilmot 15; Smibert 499-503), increased its respectability.

Conclusion

As an organization founded and run by volunteer mothers, assisted by a small paid staff, the ABA has often placed a heavy load on its volunteers. Nevertheless, held together by a consistent vision and a strong and evolving organizational structure, the ABA is still providing mother-to-mother support to women who wish to breastfeed and continuing its activism. Challenges such as rapid growth, geographical spread, financial difficulties and internal conflict have been turned into opportunities to strengthen the organizational structure and to involve members in holding the association together. The current strategic plan looks positively towards the future.

Works Cited

Australian Breastfeeding Association (ABA). *2004 Annual Report.* Web. <http://www.breastfeeding.asn.au/aboutaba/annual.html> Accessed: 10 July 2010.

Australian Breastfeeding Association (ABA). *2005 Annual Report.* Web. <http://www.breastfeeding.asn.au/aboutaba/annual.htm>. Accessed 10 July 2010.

Australian Breastfeeding Association (ABA). "ABA Vision, Mission, Values and Objectives." 2009. Web. <http://www.breastfeeding.asn.au/aboutaba/purpose.html>. Accessed 10 July 2010.

Australian Breastfeeding Association (ABA). "Strategic Plan." Web. <http://www.breastfeeding.asn.au>. Accessed 10 July 2010.

Brodribb, Wendy, ed. *Breastfeeding Management in Australia.* Nunawading, Victoria: Nursing Mothers' Association of Australia, 1990.

Croker, Anne. "100-day Challenge Final Update." ABA Listserv. 18 June 2002.

Davis, Annette. "Infant Mortality and Child Saving: The Campaign of Women's Organisations in Western Australia, 1900-1922." *Childhood and Society in Western Australia.* Ed. Penelope Hetherington. Nedlands: University of Western Australia Press, 1988. 161-173.

Gandevia, Bryan. *Tears Often Shed: Child Health and Welfare in Australia from 1788.* Rushcutters Bay, New South Wales: Pergamon Press, 1978.

"Herbicide and Pesticide Levels in Breastmilk." *Talkabout* 11.6 (1980): 4.

Katz, Alfred H. and Eugene I. Bender. *The Strength in Us: Self-Help Groups in the Modern World.* New York: New Viewpoints, 1976.

Mangleson, Jan. "Thallikool." *Breastfeeding Review* 1.13 (1988): 99-104.

McCalman, Janet. *Struggletown: Public and Private Life in Richmond 1900-1965.* Carlton, Melbourne University Press, 1985.

Paterson, Helen. "Special Appeal Closed – Affirmation of NMAA. An End to Court Case and Public Liability Insurance Saga." *NMAA Newsletter* 22.9 (Nov 1986): 11.

Phillips, Virginia [Thorley, Virginia]. "NMAA As a Self-Help Organisation." *Breastfeeding Review* 1.2 (1983): 37-39.

Phillips, Virginia [Thorley, Virginia]. *Talkabout* 8.4 (July 1977): 24.

Reiger, Kerreen M. *The Disenchantment of the Home: Modernizing the Australian Family 1880-1940.* Melbourne: Oxford University Press, 1985.

Reiger, Kerreen M. *Our Bodies Our Babies: The Forgotten Women's Movement.* Carlton South, Victoria: Melbourne University Press, 2001.

Smibert, James. "Postnatal Care in the 20th Century." *Australian Family Physician* 18.5: 499-503.

Talkabout 6.3 (August 1975): 25.

Thorley, Virginia. *Mother to Mother: The History of the Queensland Branch of the Australian Breastfeeding Association.* Coorparoo, Queensland: Queensland Branch of ABA, 2009.

Thorley, Virginia. "Printed Advice on Initiating and Maintaining Breastfeeding in Mid-Twentieth Century Queensland." *Journal of Human Lactation* 19.1 (2003): 77-89.

Thorley, Virginia. "Softly, Softly: How the Mothercraft Association of Queensland Co-existed with Government Policy, 1931-1961." *Health and History* 3.2 (2001): 80-93.

Wilmot, Elizabeth. "Annual Report for the Calendar Year 1972 of the Director of Maternal Infant and Pre-School Welfare." Melbourne: Government Printer, 1973.

World Health Organization (WHO). *International Code of Marketing of Breast-Milk Substitutes.* World Health Assembly, WHA 34.22, May 1981.

II.
Maternal Identities

17. Project GirlMom

An Affirmation of Positive Maternal Identity

SANDY M. MAY

Girls like me have raised presidents. We've raised messiahs and musicians, writers and settlers. Girls like me won't compromise and we won't fail.

—Allison Crews

IN 1999 BEE LAVENDER FOUNDED Girl-Mom.com, a feminist pro-choice advocacy website dedicated to empowering, educating and supporting young mothers. Rooted in her own experience of teenage pregnancy and mothering, Lavender envisaged a safe and supportive space where young mothers could gain encouragement, advice, and community from one another and their own writing; a positive space, which reflected the lives and experiences of young mothers and their children, rather than the dominant cultural messages of shame and blame. Eleven years later the community continues to provide the crucial online resource of mother-to-mother support, advice, encouragement, and advocacy for young mothers.

Girl-Mom.com is broadly structured around the needs and interests of its community members. If the content and direction of the organization are wide-ranging and fluid in accordance with this structure, its guiding principle remains unwavering in the belief that young mothers, like all mothers, need and are entitled to, support and respect.

Philosophy, Purpose, and Mission

A quick glance at any supermarket checkout magazine rack tells us pregnancy and motherhood are key milestones in a woman's life to be celebrated and embraced. If pregnancy and motherhood happen to occur within (culturally and historically specific) defined margins of "normative" fertility and motherhood they are generally accepted as "natural" social activities (Lessa). Teenage pregnancy and mothering fall decidedly outside contemporary Western boundaries.

Although teenage pregnancy is arguably less stigmatized (in some respects) than in previous decades (Lessa; Vinovskis), it continues to be viewed by many as the consequence of irresponsible behaviour, or punishment for "messing up." The underlying editorial philosophy of Girl-Mom.com challenges any notions that pregnancy and motherhood are consequences to be suffered, advocating instead, that young women are equally entitled to celebrate and embrace pregnancy and motherhood as key milestones in their lives.

GirlMom's philosophy of self-empowerment, mother-to-mother support, and skilled and loving parenting, parallels that of countless organizations and parenting support groups. This seemingly unobjectionable message of support and empowerment is at odds with cultural narratives of shame and blame however, and is thus often taken to mean that support for teenage mothers equals support for teenage pregnancy. GirlMom is unmistakably clear in stating that the project does not advocate that teenagers or anyone of any age get pregnant. GirlMom's mandate is to provide a supportive environment for young women who have already chosen to become mothers and are moving forward in their lives.

GirlMom.com has nevertheless found itself the frequent target of online harassment. Encroachments on Girl-Mom.com, an intended safe space for young mothers, have unfortunately resulted in GirlMom's going offline for extended periods. To be sure, a foremost frustration and impediment to carrying out research, and concluding this chapter, has been the lack of online accessibility to Girl-Mom.com. It was particularly fortuitous and surprising that Girl-Mom.com should resurface online at the eleventh-hour so to speak.

That GirlMom aims to facilitate a positive environment, and mother-to-mother support for teenage mothers stands in contrast to dominant ways of conceptualizing and speaking about teenage pregnancy and mothering (Kelly 1996). Inevitably this transforms Girl-Mom's mandate from one of direct dialogue between young mothers, to one of direct dialogue with larger questions of identity, agency, and advocacy.

Excerpts from Girl-Mom.com's main page illustrate the project's intertwining of the personal and the political: "GirlMom encourages mothers. We encourage all young women who have chosen to become mothers"; "We believe that teenagers have the ability to parent well, but are socially conditioned to believe they are irresponsible and reckless. We encourage all young mothers to stand up for themselves, to fight for their children, to empower themselves and to defy the notion that being young means that you are unworthy of parenthood."

In discussing the history of Girl-Mom.com, this chapter will further examine why GirlMom was founded, and by extension, the broader social contexts within which teenage pregnancy and mothering are framed as problematic and undesirable, the structure of GirlMom and the involvement of its community members, and the different challenges and obstacles unique to the organization. This chapter will also demonstrate GirlMom's role as an agent for change in the motherhood movement, while alternatively, illustrating the absence of young mothers' voices and experiences from the motherhood movement, and to that end, the broader feminist community.

History

When Bee Lavender informed her parents she was pregnant in the spring of 1991, she was 18 years old, an A+ student, and the first person in her working-class family to go to university. The origins of Girl-Mom.com are rooted in Lavender's experience of social exclusion, teenage pregnancy, and mothering from that point on.

In 2007, Lavender detailed many of her experiences for *The Guardian* newspaper in her essay, "Young, Gifted, and Pregnant." Lavender recounts approaching her university's student support centre shortly after learning she was pregnant. Looking to discuss a plan for staying in school, Lavender was told that having a baby was inconsistent with continuing her studies and she was advised to drop out. When Lavender turned to a professor for advice, she was not only told to go home, but also informed that it was anti-feminist to become a mother at her age.

Accepting she had squandered her academic prospects, Lavender took their counsel. She forfeited the merit scholarships that had enabled her to attend a post-secondary institution, withdrew from her program, and moved home. Any marginalization Lavender experienced at the university was only amplified upon returning home. Throughout "Young, Gifted, and Pregnant," Lavender gives countless examples of overbearing and condescending doctors, nurses, and interns. She recounts her post-labour hospital stay, an experience that saw her sharing a hospital room with two young women who intended to place their children for adoption, and another addicted to crack-cocaine, while other mothers were grouped together according to preferred parenting styles (i.e., mothers planning to breastfeed).

As a young mother Lavender encountered no shortage of high-handed professionals, unsolicited opinions, and overbearing strangers with advice on everything from the importance of staying in school to how to best discipline her child. Lavender returned to university full-time when her daughter was four weeks old, finishing her undergraduate degree in half the allotted time, and continuing on to graduate school. Ultimately Lavender found that it did not matter if she looked respectable, changed her hairstyle and wardrobe, drove the right kind of car, or owned her own home. Having a child placed Lavender outside the social norms of motherhood and adolescence and it was a phenomenon that did not diminish with time, education or career success.

If teenage mothers face considerable barriers in contemporary Western culture, the most significant challenge Lavender faced as a single teenage mother was not economic hardship, diminished educational, or professional opportunities, or even the day-to-day challenges that come with being a parent at any age. It was the dismissive and judgmental attitudes of other people. "When I became a parent it seemed like the whole world was determined to shame me, that I was destined to be an outcast, just for loving and keeping my baby."

It was not until Lavender finished her Master's degree and entered the professional work force, that she realized her experience of stigma and marginalization

Sandy May and her daughter, Allie.

was not unique. She also realized that the key element missing from her early life was a group of peers. "I had no role models, no mentors, no advice, no encouragement." She decided it was important and necessary to change the dialogue, to help other young mothers going through the same thing.

Membership and Structure

The scope of Girl-Mom.com is impressively diverse and expansive. Visitors to the website can find articles, essays, and stories on any number of topics. A narrative by Kathleen Asseni, for example, recounts the author's experience of pregnancy and parenting as a transsexual teenage mother, while Allison Crews' essay "When I Was Garbage," tells of her experience of pregnancy in grade 10, and her subsequent decision against allowing an older, wealthy couple to adopt her son.

Individual discussion threads on the website encompass everything from vegetarian recipes, maternity clothing, and different methods of birth control. A more service-oriented format is used for such topics as: advice on breastfeeding, dealing with custody conflicts, navigating student aid programs, and "How to Tell Your Parents You're Pregnant."

As an organization, Girl-Mom.com is structured around general community members, online moderators, a producer, and the publisher. As the publisher of *Girl-Mom.com*, Bee Lavender provides financial backing and technical support. Moderators of the website nominate the producer, and the moderators (who are always active members of the community) are chosen internally by members who have typically occupied the position themselves. The entire process, according to Lavender, is consensus based and privately conducted.

Unfortunately the conditions under which general members are admitted to the community remain unclear. GirlMom membership may be reserved for mothers with young children, as my own inquiries and attempts to join as a former/older "teenage mother" have gone unanswered. Admission appears to be at the discretion of the producer of Girl-Mom.com.

Challenges and Conflicts

The most obvious challenge GirlMom faces as an organization is its culture clash with dominant discourse about teenage pregnancy and mothering. As noted earlier, the website has responded to online harassment by periodically going offline. This lack of continuity may pose practical challenges in terms of the projects' cohesiveness and overall stability. Girl-Mom.com has also taken the additional precaution of screening members. While this is both understandable and reasonable it raises questions about exclusivity, accessibility, and possible challenges with respect to community outreach.

Additional challenges to outreach might also include the general social isolation, and income insecurity experienced by many teenage mothers. Older mothers are naturally entitled to social supports and networking via play dates and "mommy groups," where congregations of teenage mothers evoke public panic over trends and epidemics. And while the Internet opens up a wealth of possibilities for grassroots organizations, many young mothers simply do not have extra room in their budgets for computers and monthly Internet bills.

A final challenge to consider is whether Girl-Mom.com might not be paradoxical in and of itself as an organization and political project. If GirlMom stands as a testament to alternative models of mothering, it does so on account teenage mothers' experiences of exclusion. Teenage pregnancy and teenage mothers fall decidedly outside the social norms of normative fertility and motherhood, but such norms are decidedly rooted in white, middle-class assumptions about success, and the correct sequence of markers of success in a woman's life that should ideally be acquired before pregnancy and motherhood occurs (Kelly 1997; Geronimus and Korenman). It is unclear whether GirlMom challenges these markers and the basis of these markers, or simply the "natural" sequence within which these markers should follow. Does GirlMom mean to challenge white, middle-class standards of "legitimate" motherhood, or simply dispute their exclusion? Is such a paradox even reconcilable, and if so does GirlMom mean to?

Future Goals

The future goals of Girl-Mom.com continue to be those upon which the organization was originally founded. Girl-Mom.com aims to facilitate a supportive environment where young mothers can gain encouragement, advice, education, advocacy, and community from one another and through their own writing.

GirlMom's Importance in the Motherhood Movement

If the motherhood movement and contemporary feminist debate are engaged in ongoing questions over the meanings of such concepts as maternity, power, and success (Hirshman), it is generally established that 1) women choose pregnancy and motherhood for diverse, complex, and innumerable reasons (Pillow 101), and 2) that women's experiences of pregnancy and motherhood are wide-ranging and unique.

Young women's experiences of pregnancy and mothering remain largely excluded from this umbrella. While there are countless examples from which to draw, Allison Crews' *Girl-Mom.com* essay, "And So I Chose," is particularly relevant and pointed. "And So I Chose" is Crews' narrative of teenage pregnancy, her staunchly pro-life upbringing, and her search for support and acceptance from segments of the online pro-choice feminist community. Crews had supposed that she would find support from the feminists and pro-choice activists who had fought, in various ways, to secure and protect her reproductive rights. She supposed she would not be condemned for not having wanted an abortion, or even for being a pregnant teenager. She supposed her reproductive rights extended to her right to choose to become a mother.

Instead she found no less judgment and rhetoric from pro-choice activists than the pro-life activists she had grown up around. She was questioned/interrogated and openly made fun of for her decision to choose motherhood. She was called an irresponsible teenager, counseled to have an abortion and "save herself" before it was too late, and informed that "girls like her" were responsible for the backsliding of the feminist movement.

The attitudes Crews came up against are not uncommon in pro-choice, and feminist circles. Feminist blogger Rebecca Traister provides another example of such sentiments in her 2009 *salon.com* editorial "Bristol Palin stammers the truth," to say nothing of the countless vitriolic responses from "pro-choice" feminists. What Traister and many of those in agreement with her refuse to acknowledge however, is the simple fact that reproductive choice cannot apply only to the right to choose abortion.

Concepts of choice are no less skewed within certain segments of the motherhood movement. Take, for example, the ballyhooed "mommy wars," or heated debates over women's abandonment of the professions for homemaking and motherhood. Vehement declarations of choice are somewhat beside the point when the freedom to choose comes with a law degree in one hand and ring on the other.

And so what role can teenage mothers and organizations like Girl-Mom.com play in the larger motherhood movement? In the immediate sense, GirlMom aims to provide support and resources in the face of an overwhelming and almost universal lack of support for young mothers. Girl-Mom.com members know that marginalizing young mothers only compounds many of the challenges they already face. They also know that young mothers thrive when they are confident in their abilities, have supportive networks in place, and a community of peers with whom they can thrive.

In a broader sense of the motherhood movement, teenage mothers and organizations like GirlMom, challenge patriarchal models of fertility and motherhood. They challenge the notion that motherhood is a privilege secured through the market economy either in the form of high family wages or employment security (Orloff 112). They challenge the inherent contradictions of a model simultaneously based on the concept of the traditional family and the universal worker (Lessa).

They challenge more complex concepts of fertility, motherhood, choice, feminism, patriarchy, racism and classism. Furthermore, they challenge pro-choice feminists and pro-choice members of the motherhood movement alike, to strengthen the reproductive rights agenda for all by respecting and supporting young mothers' rights to bare and raise their children (Kelly 2000: 61).

Conclusion

If Girl-Mom.com exemplifies the accomplishments of a successful online grassroots movement, it more significantly exemplifies the accomplishments of young mothers and the challenges we are capable of meeting. Girl-Mom.com is run both for and by young mothers, and as such, places additional responsibilities on the shoulders of young women already tasked with the never-ending work that comes with raising children. Beyond the additional workload, online harassment, and periodic inactivity, Girl-Mom.com remains held together as a community by the guiding principle that teenage mothers deserve the respect and encouragement that enables all mothers to achieve self-worth and independence.

Works Cited

Assensi, Kathleen. "I Was A Teenage Transsexual Super Mom." [n.d.]. *Girl-Mom.com* <http://www.girlmom.com/node/26>. Accessed: 20 December 2010.

Crews, Allison. "And So I Chose." *Girl-Mom.com* [n.d.] Web. <http://www.girlmom.com/node/46>. Accessed 20 December 2010.

Crews, Allison. "When I Was Garbage." *Girl-Mom.com* [n.d.] Web. <http://www.girlmom.com/node/46>. Accessed 20 December 2010.

Geronimus, Arline T. and Sanders Korenman. "The Socioeconomic Consequences of Teen Childbearing Reconsidered." *The Quarterly Journal of Economics* 107.4 (1992): 1187-1214.

Kelly, Deidre. "Stigma Stories: Four Discourses About Teen Mothers, Welfare, and Poverty." *Youth and Society* 27.4 (1996): 421-449.

Kelly, Deidre. "Warning Labels: Stigma and the Popularizing of Teen Mothers' Stories." *Curriculum Inquiry* 27.2 (1997): 165-186.

Kelly, Deidre. "A Critical Feminist Perspective on Teen Pregnancy and Parenthood." *Teen Pregnancy and Parenting: Social and Ethical issues.* Eds. David Checkland and James Wong. Toronto: University of Toronto Press, 2000. 53-70.

Lavender, Bee. "Young, Gifted, and Pregnant." *The Guardian* 31 March 2007. Web. <http://www.guardian.co.uk/lifeandstyle/2007/mar/31/familyandrelationships.family>. . Accessed: 9 September 2010.

Lessa, Iara. "Discursive Struggles Within Social Welfare: Restaging Teen Motherhood." *British Journal of Social Work* 35.2 (2006): 283-298.

Hirshman, Linda. *The American Prospect.* 21 November 2005. Web. Online: <http://www.prospect.org/cs/articlesarticleId=10659>. Accessed 21 December 2010.

Orloff, Ann. "Explaining U.S. Welfare Reform: Power, Gender, Race and the U.S. Policy Legacy." *Critical Social Policy* 22.1 (2002): 96-118.

Pillow, Wanda S. *Unfit Subjects: Educational Policy and the Teen Mother.* New York: Taylor and Francis Books, Inc., 2004.

Traister, Rebecca. "Bristol Palin stammers the truth." *Salon,com* 18 February 2009. Web. <http://www.salon.com/mwt/feature/2009/02/18/bristol_palin/index.html>. Accessed: 4 July 2009.

Vinovskis, Maris. *An "Epidemic" of Adolescent Pregnancy?* New York: Oxford University Press, 1998.

18.

"When you are coming out of the gate placed way behind as a woman and a woman of color . . . it's a huge pile on top of you to work your way through"

The Latina Mami Collective, Austin, Texas

CRISTINA HERRERA

LATINA MAMI IS A COLLECTIVE for working-class Latina mothers residing in the Austin, Texas area. Founded in 2000 in Austin by Gloria Pérez-Walker, a 23-year-old first-time mother, Latina Mami strives to serve as a major resource network for Latina mothers by running projects that have included a babysitting cooperative, support groups, and bilingual newsletters on parenting written by Latina mothers. Currently, Gloria Pérez-Walker is involved in advocacy work for parents of children with disabilities, making her role in Latina Mami less active, although the group is still operating. This chapter will provide a discussion of Latina Mami, with a focus on a context for better understanding the significance of the group, its philosophy, and history.

Context

The epigraph quoted above from a blog entry on Latina Mami's website underscores one of the major reasons this mothers' collective was created: to provide support in myriad forms for a historically marginalized, underserved group: working-class Latina mothers. Created by and for working-class Latina mothers, Latina Mami demonstrates the unique, creative ways Latina mothers and other mothers of color have attempted to improve their lives as women and mothers when "the system" fails to do so.

Support services in Austin did not address cultural diversity and the experiences and needs of working-class mothers of color. By providing resources such as babysitting, cultural events, and maternity and baby clothes, Latina Mami aims to empower and educate Latina mothers despite social, economic, and language barriers they may face. Moreover, because Latina Mami is run entirely by and for whom they identify as working-class Latina mothers, the group acknowledges the multiple ways in which their motherhood is experienced: as non-white, historically working-class women living within a dominant culture. As scholars such as Evelyn Nakano Glenn, Patricia Hill Collins, and others have argued, factors including gender, sexuality, race/ethnicity, and socio-economic status will impact how women mother their children, and thus motherhood must be studied and

Latina Mami Collective members.

understood within these multiple, intersecting contexts. These scholars emphasize that motherhood is not experienced universally.

According to an interview conducted by Marrit Ingman with Latina Mami's founder, Gloria Pérez-Walker, the need to create a group for Latina mothers was a result of what Pérez-Walker witnessed around her, that is, "even 'liberal' Austin was racially bifurcated, that her fellow activists were white and privileged, that segregation was thoroughgoing" (Ingman). For Pérez-Walker, a central question that arose when she became a new mother was, "where was the support for Latina women struggling with the challenges of motherhood?" (Ingman). According to Pérez-Walker, "Instead of finding support, I found demeaning classes and support groups where I was treated as a 'client.' I was disgusted" ("Partners"). Because existing maternal support groups and organizations in Austin did not take into account the unique needs and challenges faced by non-white, poor, and working-class mothers, Pérez-Walker has sought to change this reality by creating Latina Mami. Further, this "client-centered," non-culturally-specific perspective held by support groups and maternity organizations in Austin, according to Pérez-Walker, fails to consider the varied forms of assistance needed by mothers of color:

> When I look at the stats on Latinas both native and foreign-born, we have children in our teens or early twenties and have more children on average than the rest of the population, I have to wonder why others aren't working in a more culturally sensitive fashion with our group of women.

> Parenting support and community involvement are necessary for us to succeed, and for our children to succeed. Why are we still considered clients instead of fellow community members who can and should learn skills to transfer to our families and neighborhoods? ("Partners")

As Pérez-Walker asserts, support groups for mothers have not considered "motherwork" as community-oriented, instead viewing it as a private interaction between mother and child. In addition, some support groups universalize motherhood, as if this is experienced the same way, under the same circumstances, among all women. In addition, Pérez-Walker wanted to instill her young son with Mexican cultural values that he would not find in Austin: "I was a young mother in a mostly white city and realized that my son was not going to grow up in a large Mexican family as I did" (e-mail correspondence). Pérez-Walker's statement affirms what Patricia Hill Collins says about African-American motherhood, which may also apply to many mothers of color, including Latinas: "... the assumption that mothering occurs within the confines of private, nuclear family households where the mother has almost total responsibility for child-rearing is less applicable to [mothers of color]," considering that in some African-American (and Latina/o) communities, "other mothers," that is, community members, share responsibilities of caring for children (qtd. in O'Reilly 2008: 147-148). Thus, Pérez-Walker is correct to state that mother support groups in Austin have largely been organized from an Anglo-centric, middle-class perspective that reflects cultural biases toward Latinas, who are statistically shown to have higher fertility rates and more likely to be single mothers than non-Latina women (Gonzales 2). It may also be said that the creation of a group such as Latina Mami enables disenfranchised, marginalized women to become active and visible members of their community-at-large. As such, these groups *make* women visible when the surrounding culture refuses to acknowledge their existence, much less provide for them.

This insistence on making Latina mothers visible members of their community, that is, making Latina mothers seen rather than ignored, is highly reminiscent of the well-known mothers' group, Madres de la Plaza de Mayo in Argentina, who made their motherhood public by protesting Argentina's "dirty war" and the subsequent imprisonment, death, and "disappearances" of thousands of people during the years 1976-1983 (Bejarano 132). Of course, protesting the brutalities carried out by a military government is not Latina Mami's mission, but it is important to acknowledge that present-day Chicana/Latina protest movements and mother groups such as Latina Mami, are part and parcel of an overall extensive history of Latina and Latin American mothers' protest movements, activism, and unyielding attempts to make their motherhood seen and heard. Both in the United States and Latin America, mother groups and protest movements led by mothers have been highly visible.

Considering that traditionally "Latina mothers' responsibilities and assigned roles are strictly placed within the confines of the home and workplace, and they are forbidden by gendered norms and standards of citizenship to use their status as mothers for anything other than the proper rearing of their children," the very public nature of Latina and Latin American mother groups and protest movements, is politically subversive in and of itself (Bejarano 126). Chicana sociologist Mary Pardo's statement about the Latina grassroots, mother-centered activist group, "Mothers of East L.A.," may also be applied to Latina Mami in the context of Latina and Latin American motherhood movements and activism: "The women ... have expanded the boundaries of 'motherhood' to include social and political community activism" (4). Latina Mami, then, in its efforts to make public the needs of working-class Latina mothers, challenges "traditional" Latina/o cultural standards of motherhood as home-based and private. As Pérez-Walker argues, for mother groups to better serve diverse groups of women, they should acknowledge that mothers are community members as well as mothers, and the surrounding community will, in many ways, impact how Latinas mother and care for their families. To better grasp the purpose and philosophy of groups such as Latina Mami, this social and historical context of Latina and Latin American mother protest and activism should be taken into account.

History and Philosophy

Interestingly, however, although Latina Mami's philosophy reflects a socio-political consciousness that has critiqued the city of Austin's unequal social treatment of mothers of color, the term "feminist" is not used to describe the group. Gloria Pérez-Walker founded Latina Mami in response to what she felt was an overwhelming lack of support services and resources for working-class Latina mothers and their children in the Austin area. According to the Latina Mami philosophy stated on their website, what makes this collective unlike others is its emphasis on "the need to support the unique cultural experience of the Latino population: Indigenous, African, Mestizo, Asian, yet tied together through colonial history." Latina Mami's philosophy further states, "We understand that children and families can only benefit when they have healthy, involved, and informed mothers." Thus, the group's mission aims to unite motherhood with self-empowerment.

According to Pérez-Walker, Latina Mami "provides peer support for other women and uses a collective model. Women assist other women by using their own ongoing narrative as a way of processing the daily events in their lives" (e-mail correspondence). In other words, by using a familial, more intimate mode of connection, Latina mothers in the group receive validation and cultural understanding:

> ...It's that shared experience, it's that resistance to the dominant culture, it's relating to other mothers and also getting their feedback on the most human of things: childrearing. I think that's helped most of our mamis not to feel "crazy" and to find that support at just the right time. Most of the women are well aware of the fact they need one another and Latina Mami is something that is similar to the way we all grew up. For instance,

Latina Mami Collective member and her children.

> I had a meal with several Latina mamis the other day—they are worried about one of our collective members who hasn't been seen and whose husband has a history of abuse toward her. So it was informally decided how to intervene on her behalf: one woman stopped by the house, another organized a time for the women to get together (to talk about Latina Mami but another key motive was to get the woman in question to have other women around her and open up if she could), another called in to her work, another set up a kids' playtime. That's the intervention I am talking about. Note that in all of that, there was no idea of making her leave and go to a shelter, etc etc. Latinas are very different in their support, and realize that it takes a little more time and effort with our mamis in order not to alienate them. (e-mail correspondence)

Thus, in addition to providing services such as a baby-sitting cooperative, clothes exchanges, and support groups, Latina Mami also has a record of providing individual support for Latina mothers who are thought to be in physical danger. By intervening in what could be a violent situation, as Pérez-Walker states above, she and the mamis resist the culturally-sanctioned model of suffering, victim-

Latina Mami Collective members and their children.

ized motherhood. Once again, these efforts to ensure a woman's overall health reveals the group's philosophy and beliefs, namely that well-being is fundamental for women to thrive as community members and mothers. A radio show called "Mamis of Color," which entails much of Latina Mami's mission of providing Latina mothers and other working-class women advocacy and social support, was also formed but is currently off the air. The radio talk show addressed parenting concerns from people of color, among other related topics. Latina Mami also has a Facebook page, demonstrating the collective's efforts to broaden its outreach using multiple media outlets.

Contributions to the Motherhood Movement

It is not surprising that Latina Mami does not use the term "feminist" to describe its organization, given that in the United States the second wave of the Women's Movement was heavily critiqued by Latina and other women of color activists for what they deemed was racial and class bias inherent in Anglo women's feminism (García 192). While children, family, and motherhood were often critiqued by Anglo feminists because of the argument that family structures perpetuate patriarchy and sexism, early Latina feminists, although critical of sexism, were reluctant to break away from their respective families, whom they viewed as a source of emotional support in an often harsh, racist, and classist society. Even today, self-identified Latina feminists and other feminists of color have consciously constructed a politic that reflects their multiple identities and the problematics of universalizing the label "woman." Moreover, while some Latina feminists have been critical of Roman Catholicism's and Latino culture's history of idealizing yet simultaneously punishing mothers, Latinas as a whole have not argued that motherhood is necessarily an obstacle or impediment, as some second wave Anglo feminists originally argued. Latinas may then regard the concept of feminism with suspicion, considering that for many Latina mothers, according to Pérez-Walker, "they're simply in survival mode" (Pleticha). In other words, for many working-class women of color, Anglo-centered feminist politics and practice seemingly have little relevance in their day-to-day lives.

As Latina feminists and writers such as Cherríe Moraga, Ana Castillo, and others have argued, one of the reasons feminism has perhaps not "caught on" with a great number of Chicanas and Latinas is because of what the writers have perceived as mainstream feminism's failures to reach out to women of color and make it accessible to women who comprise diverse experiences. Further, many Latina mothers, although they may express feminist beliefs, may be reluctant to identify as feminists because of the belief that this label somehow "attacks" motherhood and mothers, especially given that motherhood is valued among many Latinas and Latinos. Nevertheless, important questions should be considered when it comes to defining mother groups as feminist and political. As Andrea O'Reilly posits, "Does the mother have to identify as a feminist for her mothering to qualify as a feminist practice? Or, more pointedly, can we have a practice of feminist mothering without a politic of feminism?" (2000: 2). It would be useful, then, to begin by defining what is meant by "feminist mothering."

According to O'Reilly, "a theory of feminist mothering begins with the recognition that mothers *and children* benefit when the mother lives her life, and practices mothering, from a position of agency, authority, authenticity, and autonomy" (2000: 11). Feminist mothering aims to "empower" mothers, in direct contrast to narrow, constricting views of motherhood propagated by patriarchal, sexist ideologies (O'Reilly 2000: 4). As the late Chicana feminist writer Gloria Anzaldúa and others have explained in-depth, Latina motherhood has traditionally been defined in narrow terms that have reinforced a binary of "good" and "bad" motherhood. Not surprisingly, then, one component of Chicana/Latina feminism has been a redefinition of motherhood, a liberation of motherhood so to speak, from a dualistic view that makes all mothers suspect and vulnerable to patriarchal practices and ideologies. In Latino patriarchal standards of motherhood, mothers are subject to punishment for "failing" to live up to rigid expectations that polarize some mothers as good, others as bad. Thus, Latina scholars, activists, and writers have consciously challenged this concept of motherhood, instead constructing motherhood that makes empowerment, visibility, and activism possible.

Latina Mami's philosophy, while not identified as feminist, nevertheless echoes O'Reilly's (2000) definition of feminist mothering cited above. It may be stated, then, that although Pérez-Walker does not label her group as "feminist," Latina Mami's philosophy of uniting motherhood with community involvement and activism, is feminist in theory and practice. Yet as Pérez-Walker's statements throughout this chapter have underscored, existing theories of motherhood, mother groups, and the motherhood movement have ignored Latinas as a group and have otherwise failed to document the contributions Latina mothers and scholars have made to improve the lives of Latina mothers.

Although Latina Mami's message of mother activism and involvement makes it a valuable contribution to the existing motherhood movement, it should be noted that historically, because of gender, race/ethnicity, and socio-economic status, the mothers who comprise this group have been discouraged and in some cases prevented from claiming and voicing a socio-political consciousness. As I explained briefly as well, the unique circumstances of women of color in the United States were often ignored and misunderstood by leaders of the Second Wave Women's Movement; thus, mother movements must be careful to avoid universalizing mother experiences. Latina Mami is conscious of itself as a group that provides a voice and subjectivity for a group of women that is still marginalized in mainstream United States society, but one that has a valid, necessary place in the 21st century motherhood movement. As Latina Mami's mission and philosophy make evident, social, historical, and economic contexts of Latina motherhood must be carefully considered for agency and empowerment to be possible for this group of women. In order for motherhood movements to be more politically viable, underrepresented groups such as Latina mothers (and indeed, all mothers of color) must be viewed as central, not marginalized members of society-at-large. Latina Mami adds a much-needed component to the existing motherhood movement by addressing how factors such as race/ethnicity and social class combined with gender inform a woman's mothering practices. While the motherhood movement is vital and necessary for women, more culturally-specific goals must be addressed. For mother groups and the movement itself to more fully engage diverse groups of women, a universal model of motherhood should be challenged; sensitivity to and a more comprehensive understanding of the interrelationship between race/ethnicity, gender, sexuality, and socio-economic status is needed. In addition, by using a non "client-centered" approach, Latina Mami can provide a model to current mother groups in order to better provide services to underrepresented groups.

Works Cited

Bejarano, Cynthia L. "Las Super Madres de Latino America: Transforming Motherhood by Challenging Violence in Mexico, Argentina, and El Salvador." *Frontiers* 23.1 (2002): 126-150.

Castillo, Ana. *Massacre of the Dreamers.* New York: Plume, 1994.

García, Alma M., ed. *Chicana Feminist Thought: The Basic Historical Writings.* New York: Routledge, 1997.

Gonzales, Felisa. "Hispanic Women in the United States, 2007." Pew Hispanic

Center. 14 May 2008. Web. <http://pewhispanic.org/files/factsheets/42.pdf>. Accessed: 18 March 2010.

Ingman, Marrit. "Meet Gloria Perez-Walker." *AustinMama.com.* 17 Feb 2010. Web. <http://www.austinmama.com/gperezwalker.htm>.

LatinaMami. May 2009. Web. <http://lagloria.typepad.com/latinamami/>. Accessed: 30 Jan 2010

Moraga, Cherríe. *Loving in the War Years: lo que nunca pasó por sus labios.* [1983]. Cambridge, MA: South End Press, 2000.

O'Reilly, Andrea. "'I come from a long line of Uppity Irate Black Women': African-American Feminist Thought on Motherhood, the Motherline and the Mother-Daughter Relationship." *Mothers and Daughters: Connection, Empowerment, & Transformation.* Eds. Andrea O'Reilly and Sharon Abbey. Lanham, MD: Rowman & Littlefield, 2000. 143-159.

O'Reilly, Andrea. "Introduction." *Feminist Mothering.* Ed. Andrea O'Reilly. Albany: State University of New York Press, 2008. 1-22.

Pardo, Mary. "Mexican American Women Grassroots Community Activists: 'Mothers of East Los Angeles'." *Frontiers: A Journal of Women Studies* 11.1 (1990): 1-7.

"Partners in Policymaking." 2007. <http://www.partnersinpolicymaking.com/testimonials/tx1.html>. Accessed: 4 Mar. 2010.

Pérez-Walker, Gloria. 2010. Web. <http://gloriaperezwalker.homestead.com/>. Accessed: 11 March 2010.

Pérez-Walker, Gloria. E-mail correspondence. 31 March 2010.

Pleticha, Kim. "The Mommy Wars: The Case for a Cease Fire." *The Mothers Movement.* Web. <http://www.mothersmovement.org/features/cease_fire/cease_fire_p1.htm>. Accessed: 2 Feb. 2010.

19.
Single Mothers by Choice

No Time to Wait for a Perfect Partner

VERONIKA NOVOSELOVA

SINGLE MOTHERS BY CHOICE (SMC) is a non-profit U.S.-based organization that was established by Jane Mattes in 1981 to provide support and assistance to women who raise children as sole parents. This large international support network grew out of an informal get-together of several mothers in Matte's living room, when she decided to share her mothering experience with other women who were raising children by themselves. Today SMC provides several thousands of its members with information on various subjects related to parenting, ranging from genetic testing to financing an adoption. Local SMC branches organize networking events for single mothers on a regular basis.

The following sections of the chapter will describe aims, philosophy and activities of SMC, lay out milestones in its history and discuss the challenges that the organization faced in its early days. The chapter explains why the necessity for such an organization exists; it seeks to relate the activities and philosophies of SMC to a larger motherhood movement while acknowledging the ways in which SMC principles may appear problematic within a feminist discourse.

Philosophy and Purpose

Single Mothers by Choice is a networking organization that helps women to consider the possibility of becoming single mothers either by inception or by adoption, and provides peer support network, both off- and online, for those who have already chosen a path of single motherhood. It also aims to clarify public's confusion around single motherhood by choice. According to the SMC website, the word "choice" in the title of the organization refers to the "serious and thoughtful decision to take on the responsibility of raising a child by ourselves" ("Philosophy"). This statement from the SMC website serves as a motto of the organization:

> We are of all races, religions, ethnic groups, and lifestyles, from all over the United States and abroad. The main thing that we have in common is our belief that a woman can successfully raise a child on her own. ("F.A.Q.")

The philosophy statement of the organization declares that a single mother by choice would prefer to raise children alone, rather than in an unsatisfactory relationship. Many of SMC members have come to decision to become single mothers not because they reject marriage or do not find any benefits in a two-parent family model. Quite the opposite, at some point in their lives the majority of SMC members had imagined themselves as being a part of a traditional husband-and-wife household. As Melissa Ludtke observed from a series of interviews with unmarried older mothers, for the most of them single motherhood is a "second choice": they would rather prefer to raise a child with a partner, if there was a chance (111). Since SMC members have not met a significant other who would be willing to enter into parenthood with them, they had to let their dream of Mr. Right go and to grieve over unfulfilled expectations around family and marriage.

It seems that many SMC members have come to the realization that they could not afford to wait for marriage while their fertility is declining. A woman's desire for marriage may be pushed aside by the desire to have a baby, fuelled by the variety of biological, personal and social messages telling her not to postpone motherhood any longer (Ludtke 109, 112). "I have been dating and looking for a mate, but it did not work out. So eventually it was now or never," said Sarah,[1] a management consultant from Alberta and a member of SMC, about her decision to become a single mother at the age of 42. Initially she tried to choose a donor from a sperm bank. Browsing through candidates "was like online dating only with serious consequences," she said. Eventually, a married couple, who are good friends of Sarah, suggested donating the husband's sperm to her. It took her three attempts to get pregnant using her friend's sperm, and finally Sarah became a mother of a baby girl.

A single mother by choice, unlike a woman who becomes a primary caregiver for her children after a divorce or a partner's death, has actively chosen to conceive or adopt a child, knowing from the onset that a father will not be involved in parenting and that she would be raising a child as a sole parent, at least in the beginning. A divorced or widowed woman, who already has children from a previous relationships, could apply for the membership in SMC if she is planning to have another child as a single mother or is going to adopt a child on her own. The reasoning behind the exclusion of divorced or widowed women with children from SMC membership is that such families face problems not typical for single mothers by choice: emotional trauma caused by the loss of a parent, stress related to the divorce, drop in the family income, child support and visitation issues. A single mother by choice would probably grapple with more specific questions such as embryo donation or donor identity release.

Being a single mother by choice does not mean that a woman signs up for being single for the rest of her life. Some members do find partners and marry after having a child as single mothers by choice, and others become less interested in finding a partner than they were before entering motherhood. Even though it becomes harder to schedule time for romantic encounters, especially during the early stages of motherhood, many women find dating to be more enjoyable after the baby is born because the pressure to find a perfect daddy-to-be and to settle down is gone (Mattes 194; Ludtke 109).

In a telephone interview, Mattes emphasized that SMC is not an advocacy group. Even though single motherhood may be a suitable option for some women, the organization does not advertise lone parenthood as a choice for everyone. Mattes acknowledges that a woman should decide independently if this decision is good for her and her child. Single mothering may be more difficult than co-parenting, since there is no sharing of childcare responsibilities and a woman can rely only on herself in terms of time and money. Philosophy of SMC implies that a woman should be sure in her decision to parent alone; she should have sufficient financial resources, commitment and a sound network of relatives and friends who are willing to help. "Good support system is very important," Mattes said.

SMC can be praised for empowering women to exercise freedom in reproductive decision-making, and at the same time the organization can be criticized for elitism and classism. As Jane Bock pointed out, single mothers by choice claim the right to parent solely by emphasizing their fiscal capability and presenting themselves "as competent, ethical, and mainstream mothers" (62). Usually being in a privileged class position, they intentionally separate themselves from other single mothers, mainly poor and teenage mothers "by chance"—those who allegedly did not actively choose motherhood and who have been historically seen as problematic social actors. In this way, SMC philosophy contributes to the ideological division between "legitimate," older, educated and respected single mothers and those single mothers who parent outside of the "good" mothering discourse.

Members

SMC members are single mothers or unmarried women who are considering the option of starting a family without involvement of a partner. Members could be divided into three groups: "thinkers" who are considering pros and cons of single motherhood and are not sure about the decision to parent alone, "tryers "who are going through stressful stages of adoption or trying to conceive, often through donor sperm insemination and with the help of new reproductive technologies, and the third group that consists of women who have already become mothers. They are "single mothers who are mature and responsible and who feel empowered rather than victimized" (Mattes xxi). Not all women who join the organization finally venture to have children without a father. After weighting all the issues concerning single motherhood, some members decide that finding a loving soul mate comes first.

Single mothers by choice try to distance themselves from teenage mothers with whom they are sometimes wrongly associated. The average age of a SMC member is 35 years. Jane Mattes, the founder and the director of the organization, said that recently both younger and older mothers—in their late 20s and 40s—have started joining SMC. Despite the fact that more and more women are having children later in life, mid-40s is generally a cut off point for women who are thinking about becoming single mothers by choice. The overwhelming majority of SMC members are heterosexual, have a university or postgraduate degree and an accomplished career that serves a reliable source of income. The median income of SMC members is higher than then median income of the average American man (Mattes 10). Although SMC members are predominantly coming from middle- and upper-classes, women in a financial need can join and may receive a scholarship covering a part of a membership fee.

History

SMC was founded in 1981 by Jane Mattes, C.S.W., a psychotherapist in New York City. Soon after Mattes had her son as a single mother by choice in 1980, she decided to organize an informal meeting to share her experiences and concerns with other women who had been raising their children without involvement of a partner (Mattes xix). Initially there were seven people in the group, and its size was growing gradually. After *The New York Times* published an article about these gatherings, which involved approximately 30 women at that time, the group led by Mattes was flooded with phone calls and letters from across the United States (Mattes xxi). American women were asking for more information on single motherhood by choice and were looking for the ways to join. Already by 1982, a year after the first small gathering in Mattes' living-room, these meetings grew into a non-profit corporation that currently has its members all over the world, primary in the United States, Canada and Europe.

Mattes wrote about the history of the organization in *Single Mothers by Choice: A Guide Book for Single Women Who Are Considering or Have Chosen Motherhood*, which includes chapters on legal, social and moral aspects of becoming a single mother, addresses "daddy issues" and offers advice for mothers on dealing with child development issues specific to one-parent families. The book provides a balanced account of experiences of single upper-middle-class mothers.

Activities

Main SMC activities are information and support services. SMC members receive a quarterly newsletter with articles on various aspects pertaining to single motherhood and on more general issues concerning parenting. For the fee of $25.00, a non-member can order a subscription for the four newsletter issues. SMC also maintains a number of e-mail lists that are members-only: a list for general discussion, lists devoted to certain topics such as adoption[2] or infertility treatments, and a few lists designated to discuss questions specific to parenting a child of a certain age.

Several times a year SMC offers an all-day workshop in New York. It is designed for women who are contemplating the possibility of becoming single mothers. Its goal is to enable women to clarify their concerns and decide if single motherhood by choice is a right option for them. Members of SMC regularly update a blog, where they share their worries, hopes, ideas and thoughts on single motherhood.

The blog reflects the diversity of perspectives that SMC members have towards pregnancy, adoption, mothering and marriage; entries in the blog are available to the public.

Local chapters of SMC hold regular meetings that allow mothers to network with each others and provide a peer-group for children. Trish, a teacher and a single mother by choice from Ontario, said she has received an "amazing support" from SMC. In addition to gaining knowledge about single motherhood by choice, she made a couple of good friends, including one of her closest friends, through the local group. Trish always wanted to have kids, at least two of them, but she had never felt particularly ready to start a family. When at the age of 32 she went to a routine physical exam, the doctor noted that if Trish ever wanted to have children, it was a good time to start trying. "The doctor almost made a decision for me," Trish said. From that moment she began seriously considering the possibility of becoming a mother and joined SMC online community. It took her three years to get pregnant, and now Trish says she is happy with her two-year-old twin girls and has never regretted her decision to become a single mother by choice.

Challenges

In the North America, lone motherhood has always been a perceived as a threat to the social order:

> Throughout the last century, society has, on mass scale, done the following to single mothers: shamed them, infantilized them, forcibly removed their children, abandoned them, condemned them to poverty, deemed them mentally ill, sterilized them against their will, and blamed them for all of society's ills. Evidently, single mothers have been violated, punished, and controlled because of their position outside of a heterosexual marital union. (Ritcey 26)

In the second half of the 20th century, when as a result of social, political, economic and cultural changes many women attained a greater freedom in reproductive decision-making, the public attitude towards lone mothers started shifting, but single motherhood still carried a lot of stigma.

SMC faced the most challenging period in the early days of its development, when misinterpretation of SMC activities by mainstream media and general public was common. It was not unusual for Mattes to be asked by a news reporter why single mothers by choice hate men and disregard a traditional family. "We were seen as radical women opposing marriage," Mattes said. Some individuals assumed that a word "choice" in the title of the organization stood for the rejection of marriage rather than for choosing motherhood (Mattes 17). Public opinion on single-headed families has changed dramatically since 1980s when SMC was founded. Recent Hollywood romantic comedies such as *The Back Up Plan* and *The Switch* bring the subject of single motherhood by choice forward, and make it look as a strategy acceptable for mature professional women. Popular books on childbearing outside marriage, such as *Single by Chance, Mothers by Choice: How Women are Choosing Parenthood Without Marriage and Changing the American Family* by Rosanna Hertz and *Choosing Single Motherhood: The Thinking Woman's Guide* by Mikki Morrissette, are geared towards the growing number of unmarried women who are considering having a child without a partner. Mattes pointed out that when her guidebook was published in 1994, single motherhood by choice was not very well understood and people were unfamiliar with it. "Now almost everybody knows a woman who done this [became a single mother by choice]," Mattes said.

Current Context

The amount of lone-parent families is on the rise in Western countries: in the United States the percentage of children born to unmarried women rose from 18.4 percent in 1980 to 39.7 percent in 2007, and in Canada it rose from 12.8 percent to 27.3 percent respectively (U.S. Census Bureau 840). SMC membership is increasing steadily, and the organization is opening new chapters around the world. Currently more women have two children as single mothers by choice, which indicates their growing confidence in balancing motherhood and a career. The rise of second births to unwed college-educated women marks the difference between the starters of SMC and current members of the organization.

Jane Mattes connects the growing number of older professional women who decide to parent solely with the achievements of women's movement that made it possible for women to enter labour markets, support themselves financially and choose a lifestyle they prefer (Mattes 12). Openly stating that a woman does not necessarily need a male partner to raise a child does not sound radical anymore. Even though backlash against single mothers is still present, having a child outside the institution of marriage invokes less amount of moral panic than it used to. The stigma attached to mothers who raise children on their own is fading, especially in relation to affluent women who do not rely on state or institutional support. "Single motherhood became normalized to some extent," Mattes said. A single mother by choice, Trish is thinking about a possibility of having a third child and does not consider her choice to be something extraordinary: "I'm not going around saying I'm a single mother, but I certainly don't hide it. I am just a mother, like any other."

The Importance of SMC to Motherhood Movement

SMC importance for larger motherhood movement lies in promoting empowered mothering that allows women to dissent from the traditional two-parent family model. However, while asserting that an unmarried woman is capable of successfully raising children on her own, Mattes stresses the importance of a positive male role model in children's lives. She contends that boys need a man in their live for "masculine identification" and girls need "the experience of loving and being loved by a man" (Mattes 162).

The organization debunks the stereotype that children born to unmarried women are destined to live in poverty, drop out of school and engage in illicit activities. SMC philosophy statement also emphasizes the diversity of single mothers, who are often homogenized in public discussions. Nevertheless, SMC differs from other single mothers support groups by incorporating "a very classist element to their discourse" (Bock 83) which manifests itself in framing the decision to parent alone as legitimized by high income and college education.

Conclusion

Even though single motherhood is becoming more accepted, the traditional view holds that a child needs both a mother and father for healthy growth and development. Heterosexual two-parent family is still the dominant model against which all other families are compared (Mannis 122). Unwed mothers, along with lesbians, minority or welfare mothers, are often labeled as deviant or bad mothers (Arendell 1195). By claiming that adult single mothers are perfectly able to raise happy and healthy children, SMC supports women who do not conform to the standards of culturally normalized mothering. The organization promotes the autonomy of middle- and upper-class mothers and asserts women's ability to exercise agency in their daily lives.

[1]The names of the interviewees are changed *to protect their privacy.*

[2]About 25 percent of SMC members have adopted a child. SMC members assist each other with going through the adoption paperwork both domestically and internationally, and discuss which agencies and countries make it easier for single women to adopt a child.

Works Cited

Arendell, Terry. "Conceiving and Investigating Motherhood: The Decade's Scholarship." *Journal of Marriage and the Family* 62 (2000): 1192-1207.

Bock, Jane D. "Doing the Right Thing? Single Mothers by Choice and the Struggle for Legitimacy." *Gender and Society* (Special Issue: Emergent and Reconfigured Forms of Family Life) 14.1 (Feb., 2000): 62-86.

Hertz, Rosanna. *Single by Chance, Mothers by Choice: How Women are Choosing Parenthood Without Marriage and Changing the American Family*. New York: Oxford University Press, 2006.

Ludtke, Melissa. *On Our Own: Unmarried Motherhood in America.* Los Angeles: University of California Press, 1999.

Mannis, Valeria S. "Single Mothers by Choice." *Family Relations* 48 (1999): 121–128.

Mattes, Jane. *Single Mothers by Choice: A Guidebook for Single Women Who Are Considering or Have Chosen Motherhood.* New York: Random House, 1994.

Morrissette, Mikki. *Choosing Single Motherhood: The Thinking Woman's Guide.* New York: Be-Mondo Publishing, 2005.

Ritcey, Joanne Marie. *Hegemonic Heterosexuality, Moral Regulation and the Rhetoric of Choice: Single Motherhood in the Canadian West, 1900–Mid 1970s.* Diss. University of Alberta, 2009.

Single Mothers by Choice. Philosophy. Web. <http://www.singlemothersbychoice.com/philosophy.html>. Accessed: 21 January 2011.

Single Mothers by Choice. F.A.Q. Web. <http://www.singlemothersbychoice.com/faq.html>. Accessed: 21 January 2011.

U.S. Census Bureau. Statistical Abstract of the United States: 2011. International Statistics. Accessed 21 January 2011. Web. <http://www.census.gov/compendia/statab/2011/tables/11s1336.pdf>.

20. Incarcerated Mothers: Mothers First and Foremost

Legal Services for Prisoners with Children

KAREN SHAIN

IN 2007, DENISHA LAWSON WAS incarcerated at Family Foundations, a small mother-infant prison facility in San Diego, California. Denisha came to Family Foundations while she was pregnant and gave birth to her daughter Esperanza (which means hope in Spanish) a few weeks prematurely. Soon after she brought Espy back to the prison, the baby got sick. Denisha knew her daughter was sick but prison officials wouldn't take Espy to the doctor, even as her condition deteriorated. Finally, Denisha sat down in front of the administrative office and refused to move until her daughter received treatment. By the time Espy got to the emergency room, she was in near cardiac arrest. She suffers from breathing difficulties to this day. Denisha was totally traumatized by the situation, felt angry and afraid because she was not allowed to care for her baby adequately. But she rose above it all, fought hard and saved her daughter's life (Moore).

Denisha sued the California Department of Corrections and Rehabilitation (CDCR) on behalf of her daughter and herself. After several years of litigation, during which CDCR argued that it was not obligated to provide medical care to Esperanza, since the newborn was not technically incarcerated, the suit was settled in 2010.

Pauline Latu found out she was pregnant while being held at Contra Costa County Jail. Pauline was sent out to court at least a dozen times during the seven months she was in jail. Each time she was taken to court jail in chains—around her waist, around her ankles—attached to another prisoner. Each time, she was terrified that she would fall and not be able to protect herself or her pregnancy. When she was taken to the hospital with pre-eclampsia, she was shackled to the bed. Pauline contacted us because she didn't think this was right. She didn't think it was right for her or the other five pregnant women who were then at the jail.

Already the mother of five, at the age of 24 Pauline knew what Denisha knew as well—that being incarcerated is not the same thing as being a bad mother. Every person who is held behind bars has the right to humane conditions and every parent has the right and duty to protect, care for and maintain a relationship with their children.

Legal Services for Prisoners with Children: Mandate

Legal Services for Prisoners with Children (LSPC) seeks to transform the harm to people, families and their communities caused by mass incarceration through three overarching strategies: to restore the human and civil rights of people inside prison and following their release to the community; to release people from prison and reduce the number of people behind bars; and to reunify families and communities impacted by incarceration. Our Family Unity Project sits at the center of this vision: by protecting mothers' rights, seeking their release, and fighting for the reunification of their families, we unite the struggles for criminal and reproductive justice.

For people in prison, the concept of "reproductive justice" must be seen in the context of their overall lack of freedom and the tremendous strength and effort it takes to realize any form of social and racial justice. People in prison cannot choose where they live, when they can go outside, what they can eat or who touches them. Prisoner health care is so abysmal that there is no guarantee that a woman will be able to bear children after she is released. We believe that reproductive justice for people in prison includes basic rights of self-determination: the right to determine if and when to have children and under what circumstances, the right to a healthy outcome to pregnancy (including but not limited to the right to end an unwanted pregnancy), and the right to a continued relationship with their children (including the right to determine with whom and where their children will live and an assurance that they will be able to have regular contact with their children).

LSPC is a 33-year-old advocacy organization based in California. Started by MacArthur Award winner Ellen Barry after she graduated from law school, the organization began by providing direct services to incarcerated mothers at a federal prison outside of Oakland. By the mid-1980s, California was in the midst of a massive prison expansion explosion fueled by the so-called War on Drugs, and LSPC began receiving letters from pregnant women in county jails across the state who were experiencing miscarriages stemming from abominable pre-natal care. In 1985, LSPC represented incarcerated mothers who were trying to get access to the newly-formed mother-infant programs, named the California Prisoner-Mother Program (CPMP). These programs, which exist to this day, allow mothers of young children to live with their children during their incarceration. Once the program was initiated through statute, it took several years of state inaction until pregnant women as well as mothers and their children were allowed to transfer to these facilities, the result of one of our first class action lawsuits (*Rios et al. v. Rowland et al.*).

Context: Women in Prison in California

In the mid-1980s, California saw a major expansion of the prisoner population as the War on Drugs exploded across the state. The resulting prison construction was unprecedented. In 1990, the Central California Women's Facility (CCWF) opened in Chowchilla, California. CCWF reflected the impact of the prison expansion on women, soon to become the fastest growing sector of the California prisoner population. While far outnumbered by the men, California and Texas vie for the largest number of women in prison in the United States. Before 1990, California Institution for Women, the state's only state prison for women, held approximately 1,000 women. CCWF was built to hold 3,800 women and its twin prison, Valley State Prison for Women (VSPW), opened in 1995 across the street. Together, the two Chowchilla prisons represent the largest women's prison complex in the world (Talvi).

The impact of incarceration on families of prisoners has grown as the number of people in prison, particularly women, has risen. The number of children who have a mother in prison has increased by 131 percent between 1991 and 2007. Almost half of these mothers were single parents before they went to prison and most of these children went to live with relatives, friends or were placed into foster care (Simmons).

Incarcerated women tend not to be violent. According to California's Department of Corrections and Rehabilitation (CDCR), 49 percent of women in prison are there for non-serious, non-violent crimes *and* have no history of serious or violent crimes. Only 14 percent of those admitted in 2009 were admitted for crimes against persons. (California Department of Corrections and Rehabilitation) The rest are there for a variety of crimes, such as welfare fraud, bad checks or drug offenses. Given this situation, one has to wonder why these women are incarcerated in the first place, rather than receiving the drug treatment and other services they need. Such a concept is anathema to the growth of the prison industry in California and the national movement to be as tough on crime as possible.

Many women are incarcerated during their childbearing/childrearing years. While the fastest growing portion of the prisoner population is over the age of 55, more than two-thirds of the women admitted in 2009 were between the ages of 18 and 40 (California Department of Corrections and Rehabilitation). Because of increasingly long sentences as a result of mandatory minimums and three strikes, incarcerated women are either separated from their children for the bulk of those children's childhood or are not able to have children at all. One response to this situation was the creation of mother-infant programs, designed to allow women to do their time while raising their children.

Mother-Infant Programs

Pursuant to legislation enacted in 1978, the California Prisoner-Mother Program (CPMP) opened its doors in 1980. Generally, eligible women must have shorter, less serious prison sentences and be pregnant or have a child or children under age six. From the beginning, there were serious problems with access to the program. Originally, it was very difficult for any incarcerated woman to get into CPMP. Five years after the program started, fewer than 15 women were participating. Many

Denisha and Esperanza, October 2010

women only heard about the program through other prisoners. Some women had to wait over two years after submitting their applications before they were notified of their application status. Delays were often the result of applications being lost or incorrectly processed.

In addition to suing the state to allow women to access the CPMPs, we had to address the serious problem that pregnant women were not being allowed to apply for the program until after their babies were born. LSPC staff worked to change this policy in the legislature as well as the courts. In 1988, additional CPMP regulations were passed and prison rules were implemented establishing that (1) pregnant women could be placed directly into the program before delivery, (2) women convicted of manslaughter may be considered if they committed the crime in response to a physically abusive male partner, and (3) mitigating circumstances could be considered to approve an otherwise ineligible applicant.

The Family Foundations Program (FFP) opened in 1999 pursuant to 1994 legislation. This program differs from the CPMP in several significant ways. The most important is that the judge, with input from CDCR, sentences the woman to FFP and she is transported there directly from county jail, rather than being sent to a state prison first. Second, FFP is specifically a drug treatment program—in order to be sentenced there, women are supposed to have a drug abuse problem. Third, unlike the CPMP, the mother does not serve her full sentence in the program. Rather, she serves one year at the program and then is paroled to one year of "aftercare." In this program, she could serve more, or less, than her original sentence.

Returning to our story about Denisha and Esperanza, after Espy was taken to the emergency room, we interviewed several women whose stories were remarkably similar—children were getting sick or injured and the prison authorities would not allow them to see a doctor. The most egregious incident involved a five-year-old who came to the program in early November. Soon after arriving, she complained of headaches, nausea and dizziness. Her mother was concerned and asked to have her daughter taken to the doctor. Authorities refused and the child got sicker. Authorities stated that the child was merely manipulating the system and she wasn't really sick. After two months of vomiting and debilitating headaches, the little girl finally was taken to the emergency room in early January where she was diagnosed with a malignant brain tumor. Luckily, the child survived and is doing well. Litigation is ongoing in this case.

As a result of the scandalous conditions at Family Foundations San Diego, LSPC began an investigation of all of the mother-infant prison programs in California. Our final report, published in November 2010, is the result of interviews with women at all six facilities, some staff and family members. The report culminates in recommendations concerning the physical plant, programming, childcare, food, relationship to the outside world, retaliation, re-entry, and of course, provision of medical care. Despite all of the recommendations regarding conditions of confinement for these mothers and their children, our over-riding recommendation is that the state must "create a real alternative to incarceration for primary caregivers of children that provides services to these families outside of the jurisdiction of CDCR" (Shain, Strickman and Rederford).

Stop Shackling!

In the United States, there is a growing movement to halt the shackling of pregnant women during labor and delivery. In 2005, a bill was passed in the California legislature (Lieber) that banned the shackling of pregnant women during labor, delivery and recovery. This ban covered all women in state prisons, county jails and juvenile facilities. There is an exception for women who are deemed to be a danger to themselves, their babies or others. Since the ban went into effect in 2006, there has not been a single instance of violence or escape by women who were not shackled. While the state prisons halted the practice of shackling soon after the ban went into effect (January 2005), counties have been much slower at implementing the new law. In 2009-2010, LSPC polled the counties to determine their compliance. Sadly, less than 1/3 of the counties were able to state that their written policies are in 100 percent compliance of the anti-shackling ban (Shain, Strickman, Kjaergaard and Smith).

In 2009, Pauline Latu contacted us about her pregnancy care at Contra Costa County Jail. In an interview, she stated:

> The shackling was ridiculous. I went to court 8 to 10 times while I was in jail. Every time, they would put a chain around my stomach,

my feet and my hands. I had to shuffle. I would be attached to a male prisoner—what would have happened if he had tried to take off? I had to walk down the street like this. I told the deputies that I was pregnant. One told me, "You did the crime, you do the time."

When I was taken to the doctor I would be handcuffed in front with two deputies on each side. One time coming from court, I was in the bullpen with lots of other people. There was no space to move around or sit down. I was sick and throwing up. I felt like I would pass out. I knocked on the door, told the deputy I couldn't breathe. I was there all day from 7:00 a.m. until 4:30 p.m.

Once when I was in jail, I got sick and I was in a lot of pain. The ambulance came. The deputy wanted me to be shackled around my feet, but the ambulance driver said no. They had a big argument and I ended up being shackled by one arm to the gurney. In the hospital, they shackled both of my ankles to the bed. I had to tell someone when I had to go to the bathroom. Then I would be unshackled, then attached by one ankle to a long chain that didn't reach all the way to the bathroom and I would have to use a commode. This was when I was about seven months pregnant. When I went back to jail, they shackled my ankles and hands to the ambulance.

I was very depressed and stressed out. I would cry every night. I really missed my kids. I felt like I was being punished for killing somebody.

Our conversations with Pauline reminded us that pregnancy is much longer than its final hours, and that the human rights and dignity of an incarcerated woman must be protected throughout her entire pregnancy. A coalition of organizations—LSPC, Center for Young Women's Development, American Civil Liberties Union of Northern California, All of Us or None and American College of Obstetrics and Gynecology—co-sponsored a bill authored by State Assembly member Nancy Skinner that would have ended the practice of shackling pregnant women at any time during their pregnancy unless there was a security or medical necessity to do so. The bill passed through the legislature unanimously but was vetoed by the governor. A large grassroots effort supported the legislation. Pauline Latu testified in support of the bill at the Assembly Public Safety Committee—the first time she had ever been to California's capitol or participated in the legislative process. She told us afterwards that she would always remember that day and promised to tell her children about the experience when they were older.

Incarcerated Mothers Face Myriad Challenges

In the mid-1990s, the *Prison Litigation Reform Act* was passed. This federal legislation severely limited prisoners' ability to form class action lawsuits. In the past 15 years, LSPC has adapted by moving into the grassroots organizing and public policy arenas.

Pauline Latu a week before giving birth

Since 1983, the CDCR has increased the number of state prisons from 11 to 33, while the University of California system built one new university. But even though the numbers of prison beds kept increasing, the number of actual prisoners increased even more quickly! The result is massive overcrowding, huge costs for overtime for prison guards, and decreasing program services for those caught in the net.

There are currently over 10,000 women housed in California's state prisons. It is estimated that at least that many are in county jails and juvenile facilities. In the Chowchilla prisons, women are crammed into eight-person cells. Two-thirds women of color, disabled women, pregnant women, women with HIV, older women (some as old as 80), young women (some as young as 18), transgender men, all live together as best they can. As California's notorious financial crisis spirals and budget cuts throughout the state are rampant, any attempt at providing decent programming for prisoners has halted. Drug treatment programs, parenting classes, educational activities have all been cut.

Approximately 85 percent of incarcerated women report that they are survivors of physical, emotional or sexual abuse. The result is a powder keg of post-traumatic stress. With no therapeutic programming designed to address this problem, women experience prison as a continuation of the previous abuse. Psychiatrist Terry Kupers compellingly provides a recipe for creating madness in prisons. Below is his "recipe":

> Begin by over-crowding the prisons with unprecedented numbers of

> drug-users and petty offenders, and make sentences longer across the board. Dismantle many of the rehabilitation and education programs so prisoners are relatively idle.
>
> Add to the mix a large number of prisoners suffering from serious mental illness.
>
> Obstruct and restrict visiting, thus cutting prisoners off even more from the outside world.
>
> Respond to the enlarging violence and psychosis by segregating a growing proportion of prisoners in isolative settings such as super-maximum security units.
>
> Ignore the many traumas in the pre-incarceration histories of prisoners as well as traumas such as prison rape that take place inside the prisons.
>
> Discount many cases of mental disorder as "malingering."
>
> Label out-of-control prisoners "psychopaths."
>
> Deny the "malingerers" and "psychopaths" mental health treatment and leave them warehoused in cells within super-maximum security units.
>
> Watch the recidivism rate rise and proclaim the rise a reflection of a new breed of incorrigible criminals and "super-predators."

While Kupers' work is primarily with men incarcerated in solitary confinement, the impact of these conditions on women who have already experienced horrifying life experiences can only be imagined. In fact, the resilience and strength of these women who are able to survive prison conditions and re-enter an increasingly unfriendly and unsupportive community on the outside with their sanity intact is amazing! Add to that, their ability to reunite with their children, resurrecting a functional family unit with very little support, and we can begin to imagine the power that these families could have if there were a reasonable safety net to support them.

In addition to being incarcerated under worsening conditions, prisoners in California are increasingly unable to make even a small salary for the work they must do in order to gain "good-time credits." According to the 13th Amendment of the United States Constitution, "Neither slavery nor involuntary servitude, *except as a punishment for crime* whereof the party shall have been duly convicted, shall exist within the United States, or any place subject to their jurisdiction" [emphasis added]. Prisoners who used to make as much as $.75/hour are now doing the same jobs without any pay at all. Unable to pay for even the most basic hygiene products such as tampons and toilet paper, women are forced to ration these products and often must request tampons one at a time on an as-needed basis. We heard about an elderly woman at California Institution for Women disciplined for having too much toilet paper in her cell. (Toilet paper has joined a growing list of contraband items.)

Mothers getting out of prison are now expected to survive in California, a state that is facing a grave economic crisis, the immediate impact of which is the devastation of any semblance of a social safety net. Those whose children are in foster care or in the custody of others must prove that they have the economic ability to support their children. They must have a place to live and a job, both of which are extremely difficult to come by.

All of LSPC's work is based on the expressed needs of those most impacted by the system of incarceration in California. Over one-half of our staff are formerly incarcerated; all but one Board member has either been in prison or has a family member who was incarcerated. In our experience, the fact that an incarcerated woman is a mother has a profound impact on the way she serves her sentence. Mothers in prison face all of the issues of incarceration that everyone does—sentencing and appeal issues, harsh conditions of confinement, re-entry problems, etc. An incarcerated mother has to worry about visitation problems, reunification requirements, and the health and welfare of her children as well as her own.

Because California's two largest women's prisons are far from major urban centers, most children never get a chance to visit their mothers. Contact has to happen by telephone, which is very expensive for grandmothers whose dollars are already stretched by caring for young children. Chana's son is three years old. Chana hasn't seen him since she got to Valley State Prison for Women in Chowchilla a year ago. He is being cared for by Chana's grandmother. Chana tries to call but it's very expensive and difficult to get through. Chana expects to be released within the next 18 months, but she is very worried that she will lose her parental rights in the meantime.

> I write my son letters, trying to keep busy. I am always worried about him. I write to different workers—trying to find out who my attorney is, trying to find someone to help. When I try to call home, the phones are blocked. My grandmother doesn't understand the phone system and has the wrong kind of [long distance] service. It's been a year since I saw my child. I get upset and stressed when I don't hear from him. I get pictures of him, I want to hear his voice.

We have recently begun working with the Mother-to-Mother Alliance based in Valley State Prison for Women. The Alliance is dedicated to providing incarcerated mothers the tools necessary to fight for their parental rights and to maintain relationships with their children. We are currently working with leaders of the Alliance to create and implement a training program for women to become "family law assistants" to help other incarcerated women file the forms they need to fight for their rights. We also plan to hold workshops at the prison for pregnant women to explain their legal rights regarding their pregnancy and what they need to do to ensure that their babies are placed with the caregiver of their choice pending their release.

Together, LSPC and the Mother-to-Mother Alliance will provide incarcerated women the tools they need to fight to preserve their parental rights and maintain contact with their children. We will work with pregnant women to explore their options so they can make the best decisions possible for their babies and themselves. We provide technical and legal support while the women themselves make decisions about the direction of our work.

Conclusion

Incarcerated mothers are much like mothers everywhere. They love their children. They worry that their children will not get enough to eat, will not get a good education, will not have adequate housing, will not thrive. They lose sleep over their own ability to provide for their children and give them the love and nurturing that all children need and deserve.

LSPC's Family Unity Project is committed to working on these issues with our clients who are mothers. When Denisha called and said she needed help getting care for her daughter, and when Pauline wrote and said she was facing unspeakably difficult conditions in the midst of her pregnancy, we tried to be there. Our concentration on these and other issues are directly related to the needs of the women we visit and the women and family members who contact us. As we state in our pamphlet, "Bill of Rights for Incarcerated Parents:"

> Every day at Legal Services for Prisoners with Children we hear the voices of mothers and fathers seeking to maintain a parental relationship with their children despite their own incarceration. We hear from incarcerated parents who are desperate to reunify with their children. We are contacted by prisoners who long to establish a meaningful relationship with their children. We believe that all of these parents should be entitled to certain basic human rights of parenthood. Please join us in fighting for these rights. (Legal Services for Prisoners with Children)

By combining grassroots organizing, litigation, and legislative and administrative advocacy strategies, LSPC has successfully worked with our clients to expose the harsh reality of being a mother in prison. With the leadership of extraordinarily brave, brilliant and resilient currently and formerly-incarcerated mothers, we are proud to highlight the work of these mothers as part of the progressive motherhood movement.

Works Cited

California Department of Corrections and Rehabilitation. *Characteristics of Felons New Admissions.* 2009. Web. <http://www.cdcr.ca.gov/Reports_Research/Offender_Information_Services_Branch/Annual/ACHAR1/ACHAR1d2009.pdf>. Acessed: 16 January 2011.

Chana. Interview. Karen Shain. July 2010.

Kupers, Terry A. "How to Create Madness in Prison." Jones, David. Humane

Prisons. Ed. David Jones. Oxford: Radcliffe Publishing, 2006. Web. *<www.minutesbeforesix.com/MB6Files/.../Kupers%20Humane%20Prisons.pd>*. Acessed: 16 January 2011.

Latu, Pauline. Interview. Karen Shain. 2010.

Legal Services for Prisoners with Children. "Bill of Rights for Incarcerated Parents." 2009. Web: <www.prisonerswithchildren.org/wp-content/uploads/Incarcerated-Parent-Brochure-22.pdf>.

Lieber, Sally. "Assembly Bill 478: Female Inmates and Wards." 2005. Web. <http://www.leginfo.ca.gov/pub/05-06/bill/asm/ab_0451-0500/ab_478_bill_20051006_chaptered.pdf>. last accessed 1/16/11.

Moore, Solomon. "Caifornia Investigates a Mother and Child Prison Center." *New York Times* 6 July 2007. Web. <http://www.nytimes.com/2007/07/06/us/06women.html?_r=1&ref=solomonmoore>. Acessed: 16 January 2011.

Rios et al v. Rowland et al. No. 330211. Superior Court of California, County of Sacramento. 1985.

Shain, Karen, Carol Strickman, Mia Kjaergaard and Courtney Smith. "Stop Shackling: A Report on the Written Policies of California's Counties on the Use of Restraints on Pregnant Prisoners in Labor." 2010 Web. <http://www.prisonerswithchildren.org/pubs/stop_shackling.pdf>. Acessed: 16 January 2011.

Shain, Karen, Carol Strickman and Robin Rederford. "CDCR's Mother-Infant Prison Programs: An Investigation." 2010 Web. <http://www.prisonerswithchildren.org/pubs/cpmp_report.pdf>. Acessed: 16 January 2011.

Simmons, Charlene and Emily Danker-Feldman. "Parental Incarceration, Termination of Parental Rights and Adoption: A Case Study of the Intersection Between the Child Welfare and Criminal Justice Systems." *Justice Policy Journal* (2010). Web. <http://www.cjcj.org/files/Parental_Incarceration.pdf>. Acessed: 16 January 2011.

Skinner, Nancy. "Aseembly Bill 1900: Pregnant Inmates and Wards: Least Restrictive Restraints." 2010. Web. <http://www.leginfo.ca.gov/pub/09-10/bill/asm/ab_1851-1900/ab_1900_bill_20100901_enrolled.pdf>. Acessed: 16 January 2011.

Talvi, Silja. *Women Behind Bars: The Crisis of Women in the U.S. Prison System.* Emeryville: Seal Press, 2007.

21.
The Right to Mother – DAWN-RAFH Canada
25 Years of Activism for Reproductive Control of Our Bodies

JEWELLES SMITH

According to 2006 Statistics Canada data, 15.2 percent of women in Canada live with disabilities. Of these women, approximately 13 percent are of childrearing/bearing age, that is, 464,630 Canadian women (Statistics Canada). Although DisAbled Women's Network (DAWN) Canada was not primarily an organization formed for mothers, the network has addressed the rights of and challenges experienced by women with disabilities (WWD) who are or who hope to be mothers. During a span of nearly 25 years, initially as DAWN Canada and later, DisAbled Women's Network of Canada – Réseau d'Action de Femmes Handicapées du Canada (DAWN-RAFH Canada) has resolutely demanded the right of WWD to parent. Through several projects and reports, DAWN Canada/DAWN-RAFH Canada has candidly discussed the lived experience of women who are currently parenting, as well as the stories of women who were denied the right to parent. Highlighting these shared stories of women across Canada, DAWN's reports address the discrimination against WWD as well as the outright denial of the basic human right of all Canadians to have and raise a family.

This chapter will examine the context and mandate of the organization; a brief history of the work of DAWN Canada/DAWN-RAFH Canada as related to mothering. The Activities section will review some of the projects completed over the 25-year span of the organization. Being a national, diverse organization has many challenges—a few of these will be addressed in the next section. In the final two sections I will discuss some of the future goals that DAWN-RAFH Canada has set, and provide some conclusions on mothering, disability, and human rights.

Context: Why is a Network of Disabled Women Crucial in Canada

In 1985, several women who were activists nationally and locally in their communities recognized that the experiences of WWD were not being represented in the organizations that they were working with. I was fortunate enough to contact via email one of these founding members, Jillian Ridington. According to Ridington, Joan Meister was the driving force behind that first, 1985 network meeting of 17 women from across Canada. In a recent email interview, Ridington (2011) wrote:

> DAWN Canada was really Joan Meister's brainchild. I had met her when I was doing research for The Disabled Persons Coalition Against the Budget, a short-lived organization that was formed by disabled activists in response to severe cutbacks in services by the Social Credit government of BC in the early 1980s.

The women who gathered together knew firsthand that other organizations in their communities were not addressing the particular challenges of WWD: feminist organizations at that time were white, middle-class, able-ist and oblivious to the diversity of experience of *other* women including women living with disabilities. Many groups of women criticized the movement for the non-inclusive nature of feminism at that time. In *Sister Outsider*, Audre Lorde wrote:

> By and large in the women's movement today, white women focus upon their oppression as women and ignore differences of race, sexual preference, class, and age. There is a pretense of homogeneity of experience covered by the word *sisterhood* that does not in fact exist. (116)

Lorde addressed the failing of the women's movement in 1984 to recognize "race, sexual preference, class, and age." Even within the "outsider" movement, disability was not recognized as an axis of oppression. WWD were the "forgotten sisters" (Dowse and Parkinson) of the woman's movement. It took women living with disabilities, like the women of DAWN Canada, to draw attention to their situation.

These early women of DAWN knew that women living with disabilities experienced very particular experiences of isolation, poverty, discrimination, and violence. According to Ridington in "Who Do We Think We Are? Self Image and Women with Disabilities" one of the identified issues at the founding meeting was a "*lack of access to the women's movement*" [emphasis mine]. As DAWN Canada moved forward this exclusion was clearly addressed in position papers and reports. Currently, DAWN-RAFH Canada board and staff identify relevant national and local projects and strongly encourage them to include the experience of women with disabilities in their work.

Whether an organization was woman-centered, or disability-focused, the particular experiences of *women* with *disabilities* was often overlooked and remained invisible. DAWN Canada was formed out of the recognition of this invisibility and the necessity to recognize and change the situation of WWD.

During that initial meeting, the women in attendance identified the key struggles that they were experiencing and witnessing in their communities. These issues included, among others, recognizing the discrimination against women and girls with disabilities in relation to their reproductive rights and freedoms. The women at that meeting made the decision to include mothering and reproductive rights in the project proposals. According to Ridington (1989a):

> We realized early on that, although there was a lot of material available for parents of children with disabilities, there was little or nothing about the challenges faced by women with disabilities who were mothers. So we were adamant from the beginning that we would look at this issue, and we included it on the grant proposals and the interview questions right from the start.

This commitment to speak out about the experiences of mothers who lived with disabilities has been carried forward in the organization. DAWN-RAFH continues to address the challenges of WWD who are mothers.

Mandate: How Does DAWN-RAFH Canada Meet the Needs of Mothers with DisAbilities?

DAWN-RAFH Canada is made up of members who are women with disabilities representing women from across Canada: urban and rural, French and English speaking, as well as women of colour, older women, girls, LBTQ women, new Canadians, and women who are mothers. To ensure the success of their mission to end the poverty, isolation, discrimination and violence experienced by women with disabilities, DAWN-RAFH Canada has adopted a mandate of Leadership, Partnership and Networking. For the past 25 years, the organization has developed a network of international, national, provincial and local organizations, effectively drawing attention to the situation of WWD in Canada. Partnering with organizations across the country has many benefits for WWD who are mothers. First, DAWN-RAFH Canada strives to ensure that mothers with disabilities have the same opportunities and rights that non-disabled parents take for granted. Secondly, DAWN-RAFH Canada works towards guaranteeing that mothers with disabilities have freedom of choice in all aspects of their lives[1] by helping to make certain that women can access the services and supports that they need. Working to develop relationships with organizations will increase awareness of the issues of WWD.

DAWN Canada produced a number of groundbreaking papers in the late 1980s and early '90s. Jillian Ridington's work largely came out of a national survey that DAWN conducted at that time: the 1988 General Study of the Needs and Concerns of Women with Disabilities. Ridington's first paper, "Who Do We Think We Are? Self Image and Women with Disabilities" in part discussed the beginnings of DAWN Canada, and then addressed the many self image challenges of WWD set against the already impossible body image of society at large, including self-image at school, in relationships, within the family, as parents, and in the context of aging. In "The Only Parent in the Neighbourhood: Mothering and Women with Disabilities," Ridington candidly discussed the challenges of WWD in the context of parenting and reproduction rights. She discussed information around the right to reproduce—or not (1), the right to adopt or foster children (2-3), and the denied rights and violation of women who experienced forced sterilization. Further, Ridington addressed issues around the need for girls with disabilities to have access to sex education and health information and pregnancy (3). She wrote about making mothering accessible, including how this pertains to housing, transportation, childcare, self-care, and household tasks (3-4). Truly, this paper was groundbreaking in discussing the experiences of WWD who are or hope to become mothers. In "Beating the Odds: Violence and Women with Disabilities," once again, Ridington tackles a topic that is so often ignored by the larger community. WWD are more likely to experience violence and abuse than any other group. The few studies that have looked into violence against women with disabilities indicate that up to 60 percent of WWD experience violence (DAWN-RAFH Canada Women with Disabilities Factsheet). "The absence of attention to this issue from both disability and violence researchers has contributed to the 'invisibility' of the victimization of women with disabilities" (ibid).

Violence may come from family members, community members, care-givers, institutions, peers, or partners. Often women and girls with disabilities are not believed when they report abuse. According to Ridington, "[t]he most common reasons women gave for not reporting were fear (64 percent of women who said they did not report the abuse) and dependency (55 percent)" (5). Finally, DAWN Canada created the still relevant report, *Meeting Our Needs: Access Manual for Transition Houses* (Masuda and Riddington). This manual informed much of the follow-up project "The National Accessibility and Accommodation Survey" by DAWN-RAFH Canada.

Beginning in 2007, DAWN-RAFH Canada developed a survey for women's shelters across Canada. This survey, the National Accessibility and Accommodation Survey (NAAS), included a section of questions that directly pertained to WWD who were mothers, and who were seeking emergency shelter. This survey revealed that mothers were the least served by the present model of emergency shelter. Many shelters have a room and a bathroom that are accessible; however, they rarely create accessible spaces in other areas of the shelter. Most often this is due to funding challenges (Smith 2009b: 23). Further, shelters report that although women can have their caregiver attend them within the space, funding to support parenting is not available. "Shelters have told us that government workers have recommended returning custody of children to the able-bodied abuser, rather than provide funding to accommodate mothers with disabilities in shelters" (25).

After attending several housing focused conferences and forums in 2009 on behalf of DAWN-RAFH Canada, I was struck by the absence of affordable appropriate housing for disabled mothers. Often subsidized housing units make the assumption that either a disabled person will live alone in the apartment, or that a caregiver might live within the home. There are very few housing units that are accessible throughout the unit, and there are limited units that have more than one bedroom. Addressing this need by speaking to local MLAs, MPs, and city officials is an example of the work DAWN-RAFH Canada is currently undertaking.

History

DAWN-RAFH has had great success in drawing attention to the experience of women with disabilities. However, there have been many challenges both internal to the organization and to the larger mothering movement. Any movement is only as strong as its weakest link, and the "forgotten sisters" (Dowse and Parkinson)—women with disabilities—are a population that is almost invisible to the general public, especially those who are or who hope to become mothers. Whenever DAWN-RAFH Canada is discussed relative to other mothering movements, it is crucial to acknowledge intersectional levels of discrimination to ensure that all future actions include the voices of mothers who live with disabilities. DAWN-RAFH Canada has been able to achieve visibility of the issues through the completion of large projects that illuminate the challenges of mothers with disabilities. The future of DAWN-RAFH Canada is exciting with a number of projects planned, and as always, the experience of mothers will be included.

In the Preface of the 1992 *Meeting Our Needs: Access Manual for Transition Houses*, the authors provide a short history of DAWN's early days. According to Shirley Masuda and Jillian Ridington in June 1985:

> After three days of intense discussions, DAWN Canada was born with an elected Board of Directors. The women who were at this first meeting identified six areas of major concern to women who have disabilities: access to the women's movement and services for women, employment, parenting, self-image, sexuality, and violence against women with disabilities. (vii)

Unfortunately, many of these issues must continue to be a priority for DAWN-RAFH Canada in 2011. The organization is hopeful that with the ratification of the *United Nations Convention on the Rights of Persons with Disabilities* (*CRPD*), Canadians will become aware of the rights of WWD in the context of parenting; as well, DAWN-RAFH Canada hopes this Convention will provide tools to fight all violations of these rights.

The early commitment of the women of DAWN to include questions related to mothering in their surveys truly created a remarkable document on the experience of women with disabilities who are also mothers. Jillian Ridington's paper: "The Only Parent in the Neighbourhood: Mothering and Women with Disabilities" (1989b) continues to be a relevant document 22 years later as many of the challenges that WWD were having at that time continue today.

After the "Sowing the Seeds" conference in 2006, the office was relocated to Montreal and the decision was made to centralize the operations. Further, to reflect and entrench the bilingual values of the organization, the name was changed

Béatrice and Micalla at her former daycare.

and legally incorporated to the DisAbled Women's Network of Canada – Réseau d'Action de Femmes Handicapées du Canada (DAWN-RAFH Canada).

The six issues identified initially during the "Sowing the Seeds" conference were: mothering; self-image; employment; health; sexuality; and violence. Three of these areas came to be the focus of the subsequent "Bridging the Gaps" project, funded through Status of Women Canada. While a catalyst, this conference was not the sole reason to focus on violence against women with disabilities, as well as on employment and housing issues. These arose from necessity: two of the women were mothers with disabilities and one of the mothers actually was homeless. The project focused on two areas of concern—violence and housing—by conducting the National Accommodation and Accessibility Survey (NAAS). The NAAS addressed the emergency housing issues of all WWD. It contained an entire section of questions that focused on housing challenges for mothers with disabilities who have custody of their children and are accessing shelters. The NAAS reinforced the anecdotal evidence the organization had gathered—that WWD face many barriers to emergency shelter access, and mothers with disabilities experience even greater barriers (Smith 2009b, 2009c; *The Motherhood Movement*). In addition to the historic and persisting issues, DAWN-RAFH Canada is also committed to tackling emerging issues. Issues regarding transportation, traumatic brain injury, the provision of assistance in times of disaster or humanitarian aid, access to technology and assistive devices, as well as attendant care, have an important impact on women with disabilities, both in a positive and negative way.

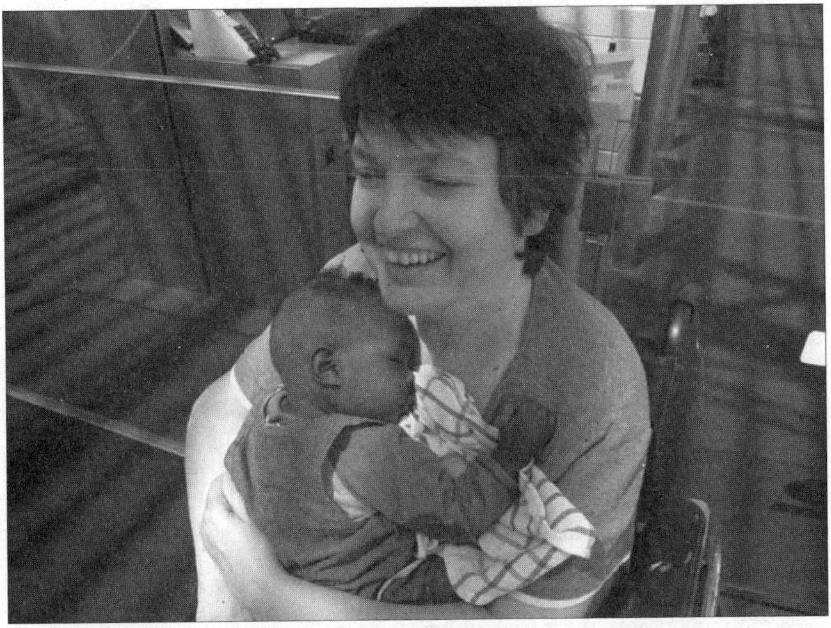

Nathalie and Oscar about to get on the plane to Montréal.

Historically, women with disabilities have experienced many violations of their right to parent, ranging from forced or coerced sterilization; sexual abuse and assault; as well as forced abortion. Too often, girls born with disabilities received little or no sexual education—based on the assumption that persons with disabilities are asexual. Further, WWD have experienced restricted access to the right to adopt or foster children and often face the loss of custody during divorce and separation—based on the false assumption that children are better off with an able bodied, possibly abusive father, rather than with a disabled mother. There is a lack of resources for disabled mothers and their children. This author currently represents DAWN-RAFH Canada on the files related to mothering with a disability and, along with other mothers with disabilities across Canada, is raising awareness about the false assumptions that enable these violations.

Early Activities of DAWN Canada

DAWN Canada came out of the gate clearing a wide path for their sisters to follow. Initially the brainchild of Joan Meister, the first women of DAWN Canada met together in Ottawa in June 1985. Here they set a mandate for the coming years. The early group consisted of Joan Meister, Shirley Masuda, Jillian Ridington, and Pat Isreal—working to represent the diverse population of the country, they contacted women from across the country to participate in the first meeting in 1985. Maria Barile assisted in organizing translations and interviews in Quebec.

After establishing their mandate, these women applied for and received funding to address the issues they had identified in their initial meeting. The majority of the funds went towards conducting a national survey of WWD and producing four DAWN Canada position papers, one of which was "The Only Parent in the Neighbourhood: Mothering and Women with Disabilities." These position papers, especially, "Beating the Odds: Violence and Women with Disabilities" identified the extent that violence and abuse was affecting WWD in Canada. After identifying that there were few, if any, resources for disabled women to turn to when experiencing violence, Shirley Masuda and Jillian Ridington wrote *Meeting Our Needs: Access Manual for Transition Houses*. This manual is still referenced today, and recent work of DAWN-RAFH Canada updated the information. DAWN received funding from the Family Violence Prevention Program of Health and Welfare Canada to create the manual.

The early work that DAWN produced regarding reproductive rights included education about sexual health, access to contraception, the right to refuse sterilization, the right to adopt and foster, consent, abuse and reporting assault, and access to and refusal of abortion was groundbreaking. The survey that had been conducted, as well as subsequent interviews, revealed the challenges, neglect, and discrimination that WWD experienced in Canada.

As with any group, there were disagreements. According to Jillian Ridington in a January 2011 email conversation I conducted, one of the most contentious topics for the women was abortion. She wrote:

> Those of us who had experience in the Women's Movement of the '70s, like Joan and myself, were supporters of abortion rights. This group was primarily also women who were disabled later in life. Women who were born with disabilities tended to be anti-abortion, on the grounds that, had their own mothers been able to abort them, they might not be here.

This is a great example of the diversity of opinion that exists within any group of women. The complexities of a demographic and the desire for each member to have her rights regarding her body respected are an assumed right by so many non-disabled women in Canada. Equal access to the same reproductive rights has been the goal of the women of DAWN from the beginning.

Recent and Current Activities of DAWN-RAFH Canada

With their new bilingual name, and refocused mandate, DAWN-Canada has been working tirelessly to address the issues that WWD are facing. The organization supports and informs other government organizations and institutions across Canada about the needs and experiences of women with disabilities. Carmela Hutchison (current President, DAWN-RAFH Canada), and Bonnie Brayton (Executive Director, DAWN-RAFH Canada) have both presented to the Standing Committee on the Status of Women numerous times since the reformation of the organization in 2007.

One of Brayton's first acts as Executive Director was to attend the May 3, 2007 Study on Economic Security—Subgroup Women with Disabilities. Hutchison has also presented to the Committee on December 2007 (speaking against the de-funding of the court challenges program), and March 12, 2009 (speaking on the impact of Employment Insurance regulations on people with newly diagnosed disabilities and people with episodic disabilities). The Office for Disability Issues (ODI) works closely with the organization to discuss prospective projects and the importance of gender issues in the context of disability issues.

Representatives, staff, and board members are also active within their own communities and attend events that address issues such as housing, violence, mothering, accessibility, employment, and education (to name a few). There are several provincial DAWN groups, and they conduct research and work specifically related to their provinces.

DAWN-RAFH is able to assist and reach out to women by: conducting outreach with all WWD across Canada; addressing issues of poverty, employment equity, violence and abuse, mothering, sexuality, health, New Reproductive Technologies (NRT), isolation, and access to services; providing and remaining a resource for and about women with disabilities and their concerns; working in coalition with others who share the same concerns for social justice and equal rights ("Our National Network"). Women can contact the organization directly through the 800 number, email, or board members. Many of the projects, reports, and activities of the organization are also available for the public on the organization's website (www.dawncanada.net). All recent reports and most articles are available in both French and English.

Although DAWN Canada had conducted a survey of women's shelters in 1989, when the follow-up project, NAAS, was initiated in 2006, the survey results showed that little progress had been made for women with disabilities entering shelters and transition houses (Smith, 2009a, 2009b, 2008b). Especially clear was how few resources there were for women living with disabilities who are also mothers. When faced with a choice to leave an abusive home, or to lose access to their children, many women choose to stay (Smith 2008a). It is imperative that resources are developed to keep women safe and to support them as parents. As an organization, following the analysis of the NAAS, DAWN-RAFH Canada has published the findings, addressed audiences at conferences and forums, and acted as a resource to shelters and transition houses across the country. In addition to research projects, DAWN-RAFH Canada also uses caucus discussions; public dialogue; presentations to policy makers and government; and, most importantly, education on how to address accessibility issues (including physical and attitudinal) to fulfill its mission. Whenever addressing accessibility issues, staff and researchers highlight the challenges for women who are also parents.

There is much work to be done in this area, starting with an entire societal shift that has to accept that individuals with disabilities are fully functioning members of society and retain the same parental rights as other members of our communities. Girls and women with disabilities have a right to access information on sex, reproduction, and health. Women with disabilities should have equal access to information about reproduction, childbearing risks, and adaptive equipment for birthing and for caring for their children as their non-disabled sisters. Access to birth control, as well as information about abortion needs to be made available and accessible. For women who cannot or choose not to birth their own children, and who still wish to parent, access to adoption and fostering should be available as an option, just as it is to other women and parents. Women with disabilities should also have equal access to new reproductive technologies.

Some headway has been made with regard to equal rights through the *CRPD*. Art. 23 of the Convention focuses solely on the rights of PWD to marry, and to raise a family without interference from the state. Canada played a key role in developing the *CRPD*, and on March 11, 2010, Canada ratified the agreement. Disability organizations and activists are keeping a keen eye on how Canada will act to enshrine this international agreement into law and practice of the country and provinces.

Further, DAWN-RAFH Canada responds to numerous inquiries from mothers with disabilities across Canada who require support. Whether escaping violence, struggling to find appropriate and affordable housing or facing myriad other challenges, DAWN-RAFH connects these mothers with suitable resources. DAWN-RAFH Canada also responds to inquiries from women who experience barriers when they try to become involved in scholastic and recreational activities with their children due to inaccessible venues or a lack of willingness of the community organizations to work with them. DAWN-RAFH Canada is accepting of all self-identified women with disabilities within a supportive and non-judgmental atmosphere.

Challenges

DAWN-RAFH Canada is thankful to the women who step forward to take on the challenges associated with the network: they not only assume the risks of any who try to make society more progressive; they often risk their health as well. In addition to the organizational challenges a Canadian non-profit organization faces, the women who comprise DAWN-RAFH Canada have to deal with daily disability issues that make ordinary challenges nearly overwhelming.

Like all non-profit organizations, access to funding for day to day operations is often hindered, and past DAWN members have written about the difficulty they had maintaining the network over the years. Unlike other non-profit organizations that do not employ WWD there is a further obstacle to fund accessibility supports in the workplace as well as at speaking events (including adaptive equipment, accessible workspaces, travel arrangements, caregivers). The additional cost of the disability issues makes funding pressures even greater. Some WWD experience fluctuations in their health and energy, and some women may only be able to work on an adapted and part time schedule. DAWN-RAFH Canada has worked hard to identify strategies and funding to employ a diverse group of women. Many government grants do not recognize the need to be flexible in grant funding arrangements.

Nathalie and Osca going to the pharmacy.

Further, as DAWN-RAFH Canada is a cross-country organization, geographic distance and the diverse needs of the women involved require very creative and technical solutions, which are difficult and not always feasible. Early members have written about the challenges of maintaining contact. However, new technologies are being built with more thought given towards accessibility. Access to the Internet, Skype, and having a toll free phone number have helped to increase communication between women. The voice of women who do not have easy access to technology must be preserved and sometimes there is no replacing the need for face to face interaction and support.

Accommodation of mothers who are also WWD has been a challenge; however, writing as a mother living with disabilities, and working with the organization, I can say that DAWN-RAFH Canada has been amazing in accommodating my own accessibility needs, even as they relate to my two sons who both have support needs. Some of the challenges from my perspective have been health, childcare, accessible technologies to complete work, access to Internet, and time. Like other mothers who are activists, I have noticed that as my sons grow and become more independent, I am able to commit myself more easily to projects.

In any organization like DAWN-RAFH Canada, success depends on getting the message into the public dialogue. Raising awareness is made more difficult because of the current social stigma surrounding disabilities and the way media approaches feminism. However, the rise of new media venues via the Internet has enabled very cost effective ways of distributing the publications of the organization. DAWN-RAFH Canada uses social media, websites, and networks of the women who work for and volunteer with the organization to reach out and distribute information. They have been working to document and provide copies of past and present projects, publications, and interviews on their website. Further, the women of DAWN-RAFH have committed to providing both French and English copies whenever possible.

The current political environment needs to be more receptive to finding solutions to the difficulties faced by mothers in general, and to a greater degree, for mothers with disabilities in particular. By structuring the organization as a series of provincial boards that are affiliated in a national sense, access to MLA's can be tailored on a provincial level while relationships with Federal representatives benefit from a centralized source. The organization continues to seek ways to reach out to political and community leaders to address the concerns of WWD in Canada. Further, the organization has partnered with international organizations on occasion.

Future Goals

The results of the NAAS project show that there is still much work to do regarding WWD and their needs. DAWN-RAFH Canada will continue its work in addressing the issues women with disabilities experience. The organization plans to take the NAAS project into its next phase. Part of this project will focus on the needs of mothers with disabilities who require the services of shelters and transition homes across the country. Additionally, the organization will develop tools that community groups can use in structuring programs. With the ratification of the *CRPD*, DAWN-RAFH Canada hopes to see stronger recognition of the experiences of WWD, especially within the context of their legal rights.

Relation to Larger Motherhood and Feminist Movement

The women who originally formed DAWN understood all too well the distance between their experience and the larger movements (whether disability or feminist focused). The roots of the organization were formed around this exclusion in an attempt to demonstrate that the issues faced by women living with disabilities are not solely the domain of feminist nor disability organizations, but are common to both. Although some change has occurred, very often feminist, motherhood and disability organizations neglect to address the particular challenges of disabled mothers. In "Beating the Odds: Violence and Women with Disabilities," Ridington states:

> For almost 20 years, the "second wave" of Canadian women's movement has been working towards true equality for women. We have worked to overcome sex role stereotyping, and abusive images of women.... We have struggled to come to terms with racism in the women's movement. But Feminists are only just beginning to recognize that no woman can

> achieve security and equality until all women—including women with disabilities—are safe and equal. We see it as the responsibility of the women's movement to join us in changing society's treatment of … women with disabilities. (9)

Although the larger feminist movement has come to recognize the diversity of women's experience, and the complexity and intersections of discrimination of women, too often there continues to be a disconnection between groups of women. The issues that mothers face directly relate to their class, race, education, marital status, sexual orientation, financial situation, and dis/ability. Understanding the intersections and subsequent challenges of women within these contexts will hopefully create dialogue between groups who are working on similar issues. DAWN-RAFH Canada is committed to networking with other organizations of women by providing leadership in the context of dis/Ability.

Although many organizations may complete a particular project that focuses on WWD, the women believe they would be better served through inclusion in all projects, policies, and campaigns. We have a saying in the disability movement: "nothing about us without us." Although WWD have some struggles that may differ from their sisters, at the core, they experience the same challenges relative to gender. The invisibility of disabled women within the feminist movement only exacerbates their isolation. And too often within the disability movement, challenges related to gender are not recognized. By ignoring the intersections of disability and gender, women who experience multiple intersections of discrimination experience further isolation and poverty. Parenting and so often single parenting becomes another place of discrimination for disabled women. As Women with Disabilities Australia (WWDA) stated in their 2009 policy paper, "Parenting Issues for Women with Disabilities in Australia: A Policy Paper by Women with Disabilities Australia":

> *The Convention on the Rights of People with Disabilities* (*CRPD*)[1] [2007, Article 6], in acknowledging the impact of multiple discriminations caused by the intersection of gender and disability, prioritises [sic] women with disabilities as a group warranting specific attention and calls on States Parties to take positive action and measures to ensure that women and girls with disabilities enjoy all human rights and fundamental freedoms (*CRPD* Article 6) [7] (23-24).

Conclusion

For all WWD, the ultimate and achievable goal is to have the same choices, and the same legal rights as women without disabilities, including choices regarding motherhood. Although the *CRPD* has solidified these rights in international law, the only way that WWD will experience the same full rights as other women and citizens in their communities is by reaching out to and working with other groups.

Connecting to the larger motherhood movement and vocalizing our needs is a crucial part of the networking and leadership role that DAWN-RAFH Canada holds. Because disability can affect a person at any age, from any background, in any community, clearly, all organizations that work with or are formed by mothers need to be aware of the special challenges that women with disabilities experience. By creating a larger awareness and support network, DAWN-RAFH Canada hopes to eliminate barriers for women with disabilities as they navigate their mothering journey.

[1] *United Nations Convention on the Rights of Persons with Disabilities (CRPD)*, ratified by Canada March 11, 2010. Article 23:
1. States Parties shall take effective and appropriate measures to eliminate discrimination against persons with disabilities in all matters relating to marriage, family, parenthood and relationships, on an equal basis with others, so as to ensure that:

> a. The right of all persons with disabilities who are of marriageable age to marry and to found a family on the basis of free and full consent of the intending spouses is recognized;
> b. The rights of persons with disabilities to decide freely and responsibly on the number and spacing of their children and to have access to age-appropriate information, reproductive and family planning education are recognized, and the means necessary to enable them to exercise these rights are provided;
> c. Persons with disabilities, including children, retain their fertility on an equal basis with others.
> [...]

4. States Parties shall ensure that a child shall not be separated from his or her parents against their will, except when competent authorities subject to judicial review determine, in accordance with applicable law and procedures, that such separation is necessary for the best interests of the child. In no case shall a child be separated from parents on the basis of a disability of either the child or one or both of the parents.

Works Cited

"Convention on the Rights of Persons with Disabilities." Article 23. United Nations. Canada ratified March 11, 2010. Web. < http://www.un.org/disabilities/convention/conventionfull.shtml>.

DAWN-RAFH Canada Website. "Our National Network." 27 August 2010 Web. <http://www.dawncanada.net/ENG/ENGnagional.htm>.

DAWN-RAFH Canada. "Women with Disabilities and Violence Factsheet." Web. <www.dawncanada.net/pdf/WomenDisabilitiesViolence.pdf>. Accessed 30 January 2011.

Canada. Parliament. House of Commons. Standing Committee on the Status of

Women. *Evidence*. 39th Parliament, 1st Session, Number 053. Ottawa, Ontario, 3 May 2007.

Canada. Parliament. House of Commons. Standing Committee on the Status of Women. *Evidence*. 39th Parliament, 2nd Session, Number 007. Ottawa, Ontario, 4 Dec. 2007.

Canada. Parliament. House of Commons. Standing Committee on the Status of Women. *Evidence*. 39th Parliament, 40th Parliament, 2nd Session, Number 009. Ottawa, Ontario, 12 Mar. 2009.

Dowse, Leanne and Annie Parkinson. "Forgotten Sisters: Recognising and Responding to Domestic Violence in the Lives of Women with Disabilities." Paper presented on behalf of Women with Disabilities Australia (WWDA) at the Domestic Violence, Disability and Cultural Safety National Forum 2007, Diverse and Inclusive Practice: Redrawing the Boundaries. Brighton-Le-Sands, NSW, Australia, November 8-9, 2007. Web. <http://www.wwda.org.au/dowsedv07.htm>.

Lorde, Audre. *Sister Outsider: Essays and Speeches.* 12th ed. Freedom, CA: The Crossing Press, United States, 1998.

Masuda, Shirley with Jillian Ridington. *Meeting Our Needs: Access Manual for Transition Houses.* DAWN Canada. 2nd ed. Toronto, Canada, 1992.

Motherhood Movement, The: You Say You Want A Revolution, The Film. Dir. Joy Rose. Prod. Museum of Motherhood, in collaboration with the Association for Research on Mothering (ARM) and The Motherhood Foundation Inc. (MFI). 2008. Web. <www.motherhoodmuseum.org/themmovementfilm.html>.

Ridington, Jillian. "Beating the Odds: Violence and Women with Disabilities." Toronto: DAWN Canada, 1989a.

Ridington, Jillian. Email correspondence. January 2011.

Ridington, Jillian. "The Only Parent in the Neighbourhood: Mothering and Women with Disabilities." 1989b. DAWN Canada, Vancouver, Canada. Web. <http://www.dawncanada.net/ENG/ENGmother.htm>.

Ridington, Jillian. "Who do We Think We Are? Self Image and Women with Disabilities." 1989a. DAWN, Vancouver, Canada. Web. <http://www.dawncanada.net/ENG/ENGwho.htm>.

Smith, Jewelles. "A New Dawn: An Update on 'Bridging the Gaps' and Access to Women's Shelters." *Abilities Magazine* 78 (Spring 2009a): 43. Web. <http://www.abilities.ca/organizations/2009/04/30/dawn_rafh_forum/>.

Smith, Jewelles. "Bridging the Gaps: Survey Examines Accessibility at Women's Shelters." *Canadian Women's Health Network* 11.2 (2009b): 23-26. Web. <http://www.cwhn.ca/en/node/41613>.

Smith, Jewelles. *Bridging the Gaps: Violence, Poverty & Women's Shelter—An Update on Non/resources for Women with Disabilities.* Project Report. Montreal: DAWN-RAFH Canada, November 2008b. Web. <www.ywcacanada.ca/data/research_docs/00000056.pdf>.

Smith, Jewelles. "DisAbled Mothering: Building a Safe and Accessible Community." Presented at the Association for Research on Mothering (ARM) Conference:

"Mothering, Violence, Militarism, War and Social Justice" with embedded Motherhood Movement Conference. York University, Toronto, October 23-26, 2008a. Web. <http://www.dawncanada.net/pdf/DisAbled%20mothering.doc>.

Smith, Jewelles. "Disabled Women and Shelter Access: Early Findings of the National Accessibility and Accommodation Survey." DAWN-RAFH Canada. June 2009c. Web. <www.dawncanada.net/.../Early_Results_of_the_NAAS_A_Summary_June_2009.doc>.

Statistics Canada. "Persons with Disabilities, by Age Group and Sex (2006)." 22 06 2009. Web. <http://www40.statcan.gc.ca/101/cst01/health71a-eng.htm>. Accessed: 7 January 2011.

Women with Disabilities Australia (WWDA). "Parenting Issues for Women with Disabilities in Australia: A Policy Paper by Women with Disabilities Australia." April 2009. Web. <http://www.wwda.org.au/parentingpolicypaper09.pdf>.

22. Mocha Moms

Lifting as We Climb

R. DIANNE BARTLOW

Let us not say we know this, or we know that, and practise nothing; but let us practise what we do know.

—Maria Stewart

MARIA MILLER STEWART, A FREE black from Hartford, Connecticut (Guy-Sheftall 25) has been widely recognized as one of the first women in the United States to speak publicly to a mixed audience of men and women, black or white in the early nineteenth-century (Conway and Waters 4). She stands "at the beginning of an unbroken chain of black women activists whose commitment to the liberation of blacks and women defines their life work," (Guy-Sheftall 25). Stewart inferred that "by prudence and economy in their domestic concerns, and their unwearied attention in forming the minds and manners of their children," African-American women "laid the foundation" and were seminal to the future outcomes of their children (Stewart 28). A central precept of the Mocha Moms Inc. philosophy is a devotion and commitment to their children, families and communities. Support of members is crucial to the implementation of the organization's mission.

At the core, Mocha Moms, Inc. is a support group for mothers of color who have chosen not to work full-time outside of the home in order to devote more time to their families and communities. While some members do work part-time, have home-based businesses, or choose alternative, less demanding career paths, what is critical to the organization's mission is to honor and support the decisions made by its members to prioritize their families without judgment. Formed in the summer of 1997 by four mothers of color in Prince George's County, Maryland, Mocha Moms, Inc. now has a roster of 2500 members including some men with over one-hundred chapters throughout the United States ("About Mocha Moms"). While the predominant constituency of Mocha Moms, Inc. is comprised of African-American mothers, the organization is inclusive of people from all religions, races, educational backgrounds and income levels, and individuals who support the organization's mission (English-Figaro).

Mocha Moms, Inc. National Board. Fom left to right: Vanessa "Max" Russell, LaShaun Phillips-Martin, Kenya Robinson, Kim Scott, Kuae Kelch Mattox, Cheli English-Figaro, Esq., Shalaun Newton, and Gabriela Sanchez.

Mandate

There are seven main pillars that are part of the Mocha Moms, Inc. national platform. These include: 1) Non-exclusivity: Any at-home mother of color or race is welcome in addition to any individual who supports the organization mission. To this end, dues are set at a relatively low rate of $40.00 per member. 2) Community activism: Beyond benefiting the community at large, members are able to cultivate skills not being used in their roles as mothers. Children are also able to witness their mothers improving and giving back to the community. 3) Support for work-at-home mothers: Creation of a database of home-based businesses owned by Mocha Moms, Inc. to enable mothers who work-at-home to connect and network. 4) Non-partisanship: Mocha Moms, Inc. welcomes members of all political and religious affiliations and does not support political candidates or parties. 5) Strong commitment to marriage, support of member partners, and mothers in setting the foundation for the family while learning to grow as a partner and parent. 6) Health and Wellness: Promotion of optimum health for members, their families and communities. 7) Education: Includes promotion of member's children and children throughout the nation ("Our National Platforms…").

History

Mocha Moms, Inc. initially began with the publishing of the *Mocha Moms* newsletter with the goal of connecting at-home mothers of color with each other, and to validate their decisions to stay at home, in addition to providing them with information that would aid them in learning how to be optimal parents in recognition of the view that parents are the most important influences in their children's lives. In the summer of 1997, four mothers in Prince George's County,

Maryland formed the support group. There are now over one-hundred chapters through the United States ("About Mocha Moms"). Co-Founder Cheli English-Figaro suggested when the organization first started, there was always the promise it would grow. "The trend toward women leaving full-time employment had already been established as families across the United States were re-discovering the benefits of having a home-based parent." However, according to English-Figaro, "African-American families were not recognized as being part of that trend in large numbers." She adds, "We knew though, that African-American home-based moms existed and that if we built this organization, they would come." English-Figaro says "But even with that knowledge, we never anticipated the explosive growth which occurred." She asserts, "We were amazed and completely awestruck by the number of women who wanted to be a part of the organization" ("Cheli English-Figaro, Esq.").

Context

Central to the mission and purpose of Mocha Moms, Inc. is the understanding that the organization is essential because historically, mothers of color, particularly African-American mothers, have not had the opportunity to devote the majority of their time to caring for their own families ("About Mocha Moms"). The absence of agency in this regard stems from longstanding stereotypes about what constitutes Black womanhood. "The vast majority of African-American women were brought to the United States to work as slaves in a situation of oppression," according to sociologist Patricia Hill Collins (4). One seminal stereotype applied to Black womanhood by dominant culture is the "welfare mother," which denotes a desire on the part of African-American women to be content in sitting around to collect welfare, while shunning work and thereby passing on bad values to their offspring. In the popular imagination, this welfare woman fails to pass on a work ethic (Collins 79). Key, is that the "…authority to define societal values is a major instrument of power, elite groups, in exercising power, manipulate ideas about Black womanhood," according to Collins. "They do so by exploiting already existing symbols, or creating new ones" (69). In contrast to this stereotypical view of African-American women, cultural critic bell hooks asserts "Historically, black women have identified work in the context of family as humanizing labor, work that affirms their identity as women, as human beings showing love and care, the very gestures of humanity white supremacist ideology claimed black people were incapable of expressing" (133). The Mocha Moms, Inc. mission illuminates this later assessment with its focus on support of mothers, family and community.

Objectives

The Mocha Moms, Inc. objective is to serve as advocates for mothers and to encourage the spirit of community activism and volunteerism within its membership ("About Mocha Moms"). Upwards of 90 percent of Mocha Moms have college and advanced degrees, and an overwhelming majority as previously indicated, are African-American (English-Figaro). One example: Mocha Moms Co-Founder and President Emerita is a graduate of Yale University and Columbia University School of Law. Prior to leaving full-time employment outside the home, she practiced law in New York and Washington. Now, she works part-time running her family business from home (English-Figaro). Meeting and achieving this alternate goal was tied to the impetus for starting Mocha Moms, Inc. English-Figaro says she and her husband had just moved 350 miles from their home state when they had their first child and, had no support systems in place to aid in their childcare needs. The decision for her to stay at home with the children was a difficult one financially and emotionally. Most people, including her own father, did not agree with or understand the decision. However, after the initial shock wore off, her parents offered to help them financially in order for her to remain at home. Mocha Moms, Inc. was born a few years afterwards (English-Figaro).

For outgoing Co-Southwest Regional Director and now National Director of Community Services Kenya Robinson, the road to Mocha Moms, Inc. came when her spouse who had previously shared in helping to pick up their daughter from daycare, needed to take a business trip out-of-town. When the sole duty of picking up her daughter fell to Robinson, she and her husband also decided she might become a full-time at home mom. Her daughter was eight months old when she made the transition to be a full-time stay-at-home-mom. She says she came across an *Essence* magazine article on the Mocha Moms, Inc. organization. Impressed with the organization, Robinson subsequently helped to charter a chapter in the Southern California area. Recently, she started her own home-based event planning business which includes cake decorations. It has been so successful according to Robinson, that she and her husband with two additional children in tow, are contemplating whether they will open a store-front to accommodate the growing needs of her business. For Robinson, she now has the best of both worlds. She adds, "Kids at day, cakes at night."

Given the talent and upward mobility of its membership, harnessing and cultivating the skills of the Mocha Moms membership is crucial to the organization's goal of not only uplifting their families, but also their communities. In her article "Black Club Women and the Creation of the National Association of Colored Women," Stephanie Shaw suggests, historically, African-American women have worked for self-improvement in a variety of settings and, particularly during the antebellum period. This involved a duty and obligation to the race (435). Shaw asserts a key goal of the National Association of Colored Women was "Supporting the less able and improving the standards of living," which "meant providing these services," which "pushes the activities of these women beyond traditional 'charity work' and, in fact, represented community development" (440). Mocha Moms, Inc. has made these mandates a cornerstone of their community involvement objectives.

Activities

The "Boys Booked on Barbershops," "National Marrow Donor Program," and the "Black Women's Health Imperative" are among the plethora of community service initiatives Mocha Moms, Inc. has been engaged in throughout the nation through the organization's 100 affiliated chapters. "Boys Booked on Barbershops" facilitates the practice of reading for boys (and girls) primarily with books written by and about African Americans in the context of their regular visits to barbershops (and beauty shops) where many spend a significant amount of time. "The National Marrow Donor Program" is focused on educating the Mocha Moms membership about the National Cord Blood Donor Program and, collaborating with select partners to increase cord blood donations particularly where pre-natal clinic education is concerned. The "Black Women's Health Imperative" which was founded in 1983, aids members in becoming educated health care consumers and advocates for the improvement of health status and well-being for themselves and their families. Mocha Moms, Inc. community service programs have been so successful that the organization has been featured in news stories including a segment on the *NBC Nightly News with Brian Williams* program.

Challenges

According to Cheli English-Figaro, one of the main challenges for Mocha Moms, Inc. is to remain relevant, retain members, and to help members stay focused on its mission and connected to the organization, particularly after children reach school age and, at a time when different parenting demands arise. Kenya Robinson adds, "When kids get older and have activities like ballet and soccer, parents don't always have time to attend meetings because their priorities shift." She says one challenge is to help to better service these parents as well.

Future Goals

Mocha Moms, Inc. hopes to provide more visibility for its National Conference, and to increase member interest and participation in the organization in addition to publishing a book on parenting and home management. Other goals are to increase partnerships with the wider community, and creating a greater on-line presence. English-Figaro says of the organization, "We are still in our infancy, we just want to grow and reach more people."

Relationship to Larger Motherhood Movement

In thinking of the organization's relationship to the larger motherhood movement, English-Figaro suggests, "I think we diversified it." That diversification can be viewed in contrast to the early body of Anglo-American feminist perspectives on motherhood that tied motherhood to oppression, and saw it defined by patriarchal culture in particular (O'Reilly x-xi). In her book, *Toni Morrison and Motherhood: A Politics of the Heart*, Andrea O'Reilly suggests we can understand Morrison's view on the dimensions of black motherhood including "motherwork, motherlove, and the motherline" as demonstrating a "political enterprise with social consequences" (x). O'Reilly argues that one distinct aspect of the tradition of African American motherhood is the recognition that mothers and motherhood "...make possible the physical and psychological well-being and empowerment of African American people and the larger African American culture." To this end, O'Reilly explains "Black women raise children in a society that is at best indifferent to the needs of black children and the concerns of black mothers." Thus, "The focus of black motherhood, in both practice and thought, is how to preserve, protect, and more generally empower black children so that they may resist racist practices that seek to harm them and grow into adulthood whole and complete" (4). The Mocha Moms, Inc. community involvement efforts certainly mirror the tenants of black motherhood illumined by O'Reilly not only by the organization's literal focus on community, but also its concern about their children in particular. Moreover, its recognition of the trend toward African-American mothers and parents who opt to stay at home to care for their children and to support its members, illuminates the work the organization is engaged in. This assessment is also evidenced by the mainstream media attention Mocha Moms, Inc. has received, honing in on the difference the organization is making in the lives of their children and communities.

Conclusion

Stephanie Shaw asserts that "self-help and racial uplift were always important objectives of black women's public activism" (441). The Mocha Moms, Inc. organization fits squarely within this historical trajectory, particularly in its role to expand the organization. Shaw explains that whereas the anti-slavery societies and associations of free blacks in the antebellum period maintained a local orientation in their activism, in the post-emancipation period, black women's organizations eventually forged national connections. She adds, the voluntary associations formed by club women around the turn of the century did not only embrace local women with shared traditions and outlooks who were from the same families, churches and neighborhoods or regions. Instead, this effort represents an aspect of diversity that did not preclude the organizing efforts of African-American women, but "encouraged the creation of a national structure to perpetuate the historical traditions of self-help, community development, and racial uplift..." (441). The Mocha Moms, Inc. organization builds on this legacy of African-American women's activism. Their innovativeness provides a direct contradiction to dominant cultural views of black motherhood, what it means, and the significance of self-definition in fulfilling its mission of empowerment. Mocha Moms, Inc. "is a novel idea.

People are surprised we exist. We're not just making coffee but we're giving back to community" (English-Figaro).

Works Cited

Collins, Patricia Hill. *Black Feminist Thought: Knowledge, Consciousness, and the Politics of Empowerment*. New York: Routledge, 2000.

Conway, Carol B. and Kristin Waters. "Introduction." *Black Women's Intellectual Traditions: Speaking Their Minds*. Eds. Kristin Waters and Carol B. Conway. Hanover: University Press of New England, 2007. 1-10.

English-Figaro, Cheli. Personal interview. 13 Dec. 2010.

Guy-Sheftall, Beverly. "Maria Miller Stewart (1803-1879)." *Words of Fire: An Anthology of African-American Feminist Thought*. Ed. Beverly Guy-Sheftall. New York: The New York Press, 1995. 25.

hooks, bell. *Feminist Theory: From Margin to Center*. Cambridge: South End Press, 2000.

Mochamoms.org. "About Mocha Moms, Inc." [n.d.] Web. <http://mochamoms.org/article.html?aid=14>. Accessed: 10 Dec. 2010.

Mochamoms.org. "Cheli English-Figaro, Esq." [n.d.] Web. <http://www.mochamoms.org/article.html?aid=431>. Accessed: 10 Dec. 2010.

Mochamoms.org. "Letter From the Co-Founder." [n.d.] Web. <http://www.mochamoms.org/article.html?aid=467>. Accessed: 10 Dec. 2010.

Mochamoms.org. "Our National Platforms…." [n.d.] Web. <http://www.mochamoms.org/article.html?aid=10>. Accessed: 13 Dec. 2010.

O'Reilly, Andrea. *Toni Morrison and Motherhood: The Politics of the Heart*. Albany: State University of New York Press, 2004.

Robinson, Kenya. Personal Interview. 17 Dec. 2010.

Shaw, F. Stephanie. "Black Club Women and the Creation of the National Association of Colored Women." *We Specialize in the Wholly Impossible: A Reader in Black Women's History*. Eds. Darlene Clark Hine, Wilma King and Linda Reed. Brooklyn: Carlson Publishing, Inc., 1995. 433-447.

Stewart, M. Maria. "Religion and the Pure Principles of Morality, the Sure Foundation on which We Must Build: Productions of Mrs. Maria W. Stewart." *Words of Fire: An Anthology of African-American Feminist Thought*. Ed. Beverly Guy-Sheftall. New York: The New York Press, 1995. 28-29.

23.
Queering the Family Tree

LGBTQ Parenting Network, Sherbourne Health Centre

RACHEL EPSTEIN

THE LGBTQ PARENTING NETWORK (PN) was founded in 2001 at Family Service Toronto, and in 2007 moved to the Sherbourne Health Centre (SHC), an innovative health centre located in downtown Toronto. The SHC houses community development projects such as the LGBTQ Parenting Network and Supporting Our Youth (SOY)—a program for queer and trans youth, as well as providing primary health care, counselling, support, outreach, health promotion and education programs to Lesbian, Gay, Bisexual, Trans, Queer (LGBTQ), homeless, and newcomer communities in Toronto and beyond. The PN is now a permanent program of the SHC, employing two full-time staff, as well as contract staff, students and volunteers.

It is difficult to speak about the work of the PN in the context of "motherhood," given that our work and our constituencies include lesbian, gay, bisexual, trans and queer parents, prospective parents and their families. However, much of our current work across the spectrum of LGBTQ identities grew from the historical insistence on the part of queer women on their right to parent free from discrimination. In 1997, Dykes Planning Tykes (DPT), a course for lesbian/bi/queer women considering parenthood, was born in Toronto. In many ways, the work of the PN grew from and was informed by the content and popularity of this course and the courses it has spawned—Daddies & Papas 2B (DP2B), Trans-Masculine People Considering Pregnancy, and, recently, Queer and Trans Family Planning(s).

Mandate

The LGBTQ Parenting Network promotes the rights and well-being of lesbian, gay, bisexual, trans and queer parents, prospective parents and their families through education, advocacy, research, social networking and community organizing.

History

The history of the PN is both a personal and an institutional story. In 1986, having been an activist in Vancouver for many years, I moved to Toronto. When I left

Vancouver, a small group of lesbians, calling themselves the Lavender Conception Conspiracy, were meeting together to share information and to support each other in their desire to become parents. In those days, lesbians trying to get pregnant had nowhere to go for information. There were no organized support groups or programs or courses. Groups such as the Lavender Conception Conspiracy were a response to this lack of information and resources and to a social climate that was markedly unhospitable to the idea of lesbians as parents. Lesbians courageous enough to fight for judicial custody of their children in the U.S., almost always lost (88 percent of the time) (Chesler). Many, understanding the legal climate of the time, chose to relinquish custody in favour of liberal access (Rayside). In Canada, the climate was not dissimilar, with courts distinguishing between "good" and "bad" lesbian mothers (and gay fathers); the good ones being those who were not visible, militant, or sexual (Arnup). In 1977, Francie Wyland wrote, "Only once in Canada, and fewer than a dozen times in the United States, has a known lesbian mother been granted unconditional custody of her children" (cited in MacKay 16).

In 1991, when I got pregnant through a fertility clinic in Toronto, the doctor who inseminated me routinely required lesbians to write a "letter to the doctor," convincing him to provide access to insemination services. There were other doctors and fertility clinics that required lesbians to undergo psychiatric assessments in order to gain access to donor sperm, others simply denied access. In Quebec, clinics refused to give unmarried or lesbian couples access to donor insemination (Nicol 188).

Non-biological lesbian parents had no legal right to their children—women were courageously committing themselves to children with no guarantees that they would be protected in their parenting roles. Gay fathers, in some instances, were choosing to stay in heterosexual marriages for fear of societal homophobia and the loss of their families. Those who were visible were struggling with disclosing their sexual orientation to children and spouses, with the consequences of a homophobic legal system, and with their own identities. Trans and bisexual parents were virtually invisible—and where trans people were visible as parents, they were subject to excruciating discrimination.

During my pregnancy, I went back to university and began to do research on lesbian parenting-related subjects. I visited lesbian moms in their kitchens and living rooms to ask them about their lives and about who did what in their homes (Epstein 2003). I interviewed non-biological lesbian parents and became acutely aware of the vulnerabilities attached to this position. As my child got older, I researched the school experiences of kids with queer parents (Epstein 2004). My long-standing admiration of butches led to interviews with butch-identified women who chose to give birth (Epstein 2002). My work as a professional mediator led to mediations and planning sessions with queer parents and prospective parents who were attempting to work out the inevitable issues that arise whenever two or more people try to do anything together, let alone something as complex as parenting.

Queering the Family Tree Poster, 2005
<http://www.lgbtqparentingconnection.ca/research/queeringthefamilytree.cfm>.

In 1997, Kathie Duncan (our midwife at my daughter's birth) asked me to plan and co-facilitate a course for lesbian/bi/queer women considering parenthood, as part of the Queer Exchange, a community-education program sponsored by the Centre for Gay and Lesbian Studies. We called it "Dykes Planning Tykes." Twenty dykes wanting to plan tykes arrived at the doors of the University of Toronto's International Student Centre—excited, eager for information, and for community.

We talked about fertility, insemination, adoption, and co-parenting; we brought in a lawyer, a midwife, and panels of lesbian parents. We role-played how you might respond to a doctor who denies you reproductive services. We laughed a lot, and we all got a little choked up when people came in with babies.

Since 1997, over 500 people have taken Dykes Planning Tykes (DPT), and it has spawned Daddies & Papas 2B (DP2B), a course for gay/bi/queer men considering parenthood, Trans-Masculine People Considering Pregnancy, and Queer and Trans Family Planning(s) for those who identify outside of the gender binaries implied by DPT and DP2B. The courses are run jointly by the LGBTQ Parenting Network at the Sherbourne Health Centre, where I work, and Queer Parenting Programs at The 519 Community Centre, both in Toronto. My colleagues, Chris Veldhoven, Nila Gupta, j wallace, and I continue to expand and modify the courses each year, based on community feedback.

These courses are integral to the work of the LGBTQ Parenting Network, a program I was hired to coordinate in 2001, possibly the first program in Canada to receive on-going funding to provide resources, information, and support to lesbian, gay, bisexual, trans and queer parents, prospective parents, and their families.

The work of the PN was originally informed by a series of ten focus groups conducted at the Network's inception in 2001. In these groups we heard from people across the spectrum of LGBTQ parenting: long-time lesbian moms, gay dads, LGBTQ parents of colour, single parents, bisexual parents, trans parents, and people considering parenthood. In summary, participants identified five key needs: information and support in order to create families; get-togethers with other LGBTQ parents to talk about common issues; a desire for their children to know other children growing up in similar families; concerns about their children's experiences in schools and daycares and strategies to best protect and equip them; and finally, a need for queer-positive professionals of all sorts.

The work of the PN, now in its tenth year of operation, continues to reflect the key concerns expressed in the initial focus groups. We offer four different family planning courses; run a community discussion series called *Up For Discussion*; organize social and recreational events for LGBTQ families (as do our colleagues at The 519 Community Centre); have initiated many school-related projects and events; develop print and on-line resources, including posters, brochures and newsletters, that reflect and advocate on behalf of LGBTQ families. A major part of our work involves the training of professionals interested in making their services more welcoming and accessible to LGBTQ families. And we are deeply involved with community-based research on LGBTQ parenting, research that directly informs our programs, resource development and practice.

Context

The last 30 years in Canada has been marked by staggering social, legal and political change in relation to LGBTQ families. The social and political climate

I ♥ my LGBTQ Family Cards, 2010. Artist: Willow Dawson. <http://www.lgbtqparentingconnection.ca/research/iheartmylgbtqfamily.cfm>.

has shifted from one that forced queer people to deny huge parts of themselves in order to keep their children, to one where we can increasingly claim our sexual and gender identities *and* our right to parent. Legal victories include the right to both "stranger" and second parent adoption, birth registration amendments that allow two women, and in some cases, single and/or coupled gay/bi/queer men, to register directly on their child's birth certificate, and, significantly, a case popularly known as AA/BB/CC (*A.A. v. B.B. and C.C.*, 2007. ONCA 2), which allowed, for the first time, legal recognition of more than two parents *and* those parenting together outside of conjugal relationships. The same-sex marriage debate served to markedly influence public opinion and support for the existence of LGBTQ families.

And yet, despite these victories, our experiences in most institutions, including daycares, schools, health care facilities, and fertility clinics continues to be informed by profound heteronormativity (the assumption of the normalcy of heterosexuality) and cisnormativity (the assumption that one's biological sex corresponds with one's gender identity). In Prince Edward Island non-biological parents are not allowed to legally adopt their own children through second parent adoption, and as recently as 2001, close to half the Canadian population believed that gays and lesbians should be denied the right to parent (Leger Poll). Despite unprecedented legal and social recognition, many LGBTQ parents still fear that their children will be taken away from them, struggle with questions about their own legitimacy as parents, and find that current family law does not adequately recognize or protect their families. These tensions underlie the lives of queer parents in Canada—the tensions between our history and current realities, between the enormous gains we have achieved and the ways our right to parent continues to be undermined. These tensions affect our daily lives, our consciousness, and the strength of our sense of entitlement to bring children into our lives.

Objectives

The programs of the LGBTQ Parenting Network aim to empower LGBTQ parents and prospective parents by providing information, resources and support. Our work aims to counter culturally persistent ideas about the negative impact of LGBTQ parenting on children, and to foster the knowledge, borne out in current research and experience, that LGBTQ people not only have the right and the ability to be parents, but that LGBTQ families provide unique and interesting opportunities for the children growing up in them. We affirm the existence and visibility of LGBTQ families through events, workshops, and the development of resources. We add to knowledge of LGBTQ parenting by conducting community-based research that informs our practice, and we advocate for LGBTQ parents and prospective parents, both individually and systemically.

Activities

Family Planning Courses

As outlined above, the LGBTQ Parenting Network, in partnership with The 519 Church Street Community Centre, offers four courses for prospective parents: Dykes Planning Tykes, Daddies & Papas 2B, Trans-Masculine People Considering Pregnancy, and Queer & Trans Family Planning(s). These courses run in 12-week or weekend intensive format, and, through presentations, small group discussions, audio-visual materials and guest speakers, explore some of the key practical, emotional, social and legal issues related to LGBTQ parenting. These family planning courses are a cornerstone of the PN's work, as they so profoundly challenge commonly-held views about the negative impact of LGBTQ parenting on children, and are a powerful vehicle for empowerment and community-building. Groups of people who have met in these courses frequently continue to meet and provide on-going support to each other as they embark on their journeys towards parenthood.

Research

Much of the PN's practice is informed by community-based research. In partnership with Dr. Lori Ross in the Health Services & Health Equity Research Section of the Centre for Addiction and Mental Health (CAMH) we have carried out research projects on the experiences of queer women during conception,

I ♥ my LGBTQ Family Cards, 2010. Artist: Suzy Malik.
<http://www.lgbtqparentingconnection.ca/research/iheartmylgbtqfamily.cfm>.

pregnancy and the first year of parenting, and a study of LGBTQ adoption in Ontario. With funding from the Canadian Institutes of Health Research, we are currently engaged in an Ontario-wide study on LGBTQ experience with fertility clinics and assisted human reproduction (AHR) services. Partners on this project are the PN, CAMH, Dr. Leah Steele, graduate student Stu Marvel, research assistants Datejie Green and Scott Anderson, and an advisory committee composed of key players in the world of AHR. Through the efforts of Jake Pyne, a placement student with the PN, we have recently conducted focus groups with trans parents, a critically under-researched group. The PN has also carried out an independent research project involving interviews with queer spawn (the children of LGBTQ parents), teachers, and LGBTQ parents, about school experiences and concerns (Epstein et al. 2009).

Advocacy and Social Justice

The PN advocates with and on behalf of LGBTQ parents and families in individual instances, and in three major areas: Assisted Human Reproduction, Adoption and Family Law Reform.

Assisted Human Reproduction

In 2008 the PN established the AHRA/LGBTQ Working Group, a group of Toronto-based service providers (physicians, nurses, fertility counselors, midwives, community development workers, lawyers), researchers (university, institutional, community-based), and consumers of reproductive technologies who, collectively, have decades of experience working with and on behalf of LGBTQ individuals and communities. Some fertility clinics estimate that as many as 15-30 percent of their clients are members of LGBTQ communities (statistic cited by Toronto-based fertility clinics at joint session of Dykes Planning Tykes/Daddies & Papas 2B, 2007). As such, the AHRA/LGBTQ Working Group has followed with keen interest the development of the *Assisted Human Reproduction Act.* We view ourselves, our clients, and the communities of which we are a part, as key stakeholders in the implementation and enforcement of the Act. In 2008, the AHRA/LGBTQ Working Group compiled some of its key concerns and recommendations in relation to the Act.[1] The PN currently sits on the Patient, Multiple Births, and Editorial Committees of the AHR Agency in Ottawa. In light of the recent ruling on the constitutionality of much of the AHRA, the Working Group anticipates an important role for itself in articulating LGBTQ concerns to provincial governments as they grapple with the implications of this decision.[2]

Adoption

Between 2006 and 2008, in partnership with CAMH, the PN conducted a research project on LGBTQ adoption in Ontario. The project involved a survey of 97 public, private and international agencies licensed to handle adoption in Ontario, and interviews with 43 LGBTQ people from across the province who had completed, or were in the process of completing, an adoption.[3] The project resulted in a brochure for LGBTQ people considering adoption, and a booklet for adoption workers that samples personal narratives on the positive/supportive and negative experiences of LGBTQ persons in the adoption process and provides practical suggestions for adoption workers seeking to support LGBTQ prospective adoptive parents. As well, we have offered and continue to offer training workshops for adoption and foster workers across Ontario, and have published research results in two academic articles and one book chapter (Ross et al. 2009a; Ross et al. 2009b; Eadie et al.).

Family Law

The PN has acted as an expert witness in several key Ontario legal cases related to LGBTQ parenting, and myself, my co-parent and daughter, were parties in the 2006 Charter challenge that changed birth registration procedures for lesbian parents in Ontario. PN research contributed to testimony presented for this case and was cited in the judge's decision. The case resulted in the ability of two women, if they use an anonymous sperm donor, to register both their names on their child's birth registration, eliminating the need for second parent adoption. This case also influenced the abilities of gay/bi/queer men to register their children's births, singly and in couples. The PN continues to advocate for family law reform that recognizes and protects the diversity of LGBTQ family structures.

Education and Training

The LGBTQ Parenting Network offers educational workshops, trainings, public speaking, and lectures on a wide range of LGBTQ parenting issues and themes.

We have provided trainings to health, legal, social work and education organizations, service providers and professionals, to university and college students in midwifery, nursing, medical, child care and social work programs, as well as in academic programs, including Women, Gender and Sexuality studies, Criminology, and Child and Youth studies. We have also presented in hospital settings, high schools, to supervised access workers, family resource programs and at Pride and other LGBTQ events.

The PN offers specific in-service training to sperm banks and fertility clinics interested in improving their practice with regards to LGBTQ clients. We have worked with many of the downtown Toronto clinics and look forward to continuing to develop these connections in Toronto and beyond.

Community Events / Discussion Forums

The PN, often in partnership with the Children's Aid Society of Toronto, coordinates a discussion forum series called *Up For Discussion*, providing space for LGBTQ parenting communities to discuss important and/or controversial issues. Recent topics have included the debate surrounding anonymous sperm donation, the current state of family law and its ability, or not, to adequately recognize and protect LGBTQ families, and the information needed by queer parents to negotiate the Toronto public school system. We frequently organize special events for Family Day, the new statutory holiday celebrated in February in Ontario, with an emphasis, again, on the need to recognize and support *all* families.

Peer Support Groups

The PN provides support to peer-led support groups as needs arise. To date, we have provided on-going support to groups for single moms, adoptive parents, parents of colour, trans men, trans women, co-parents, and parents of multiples.

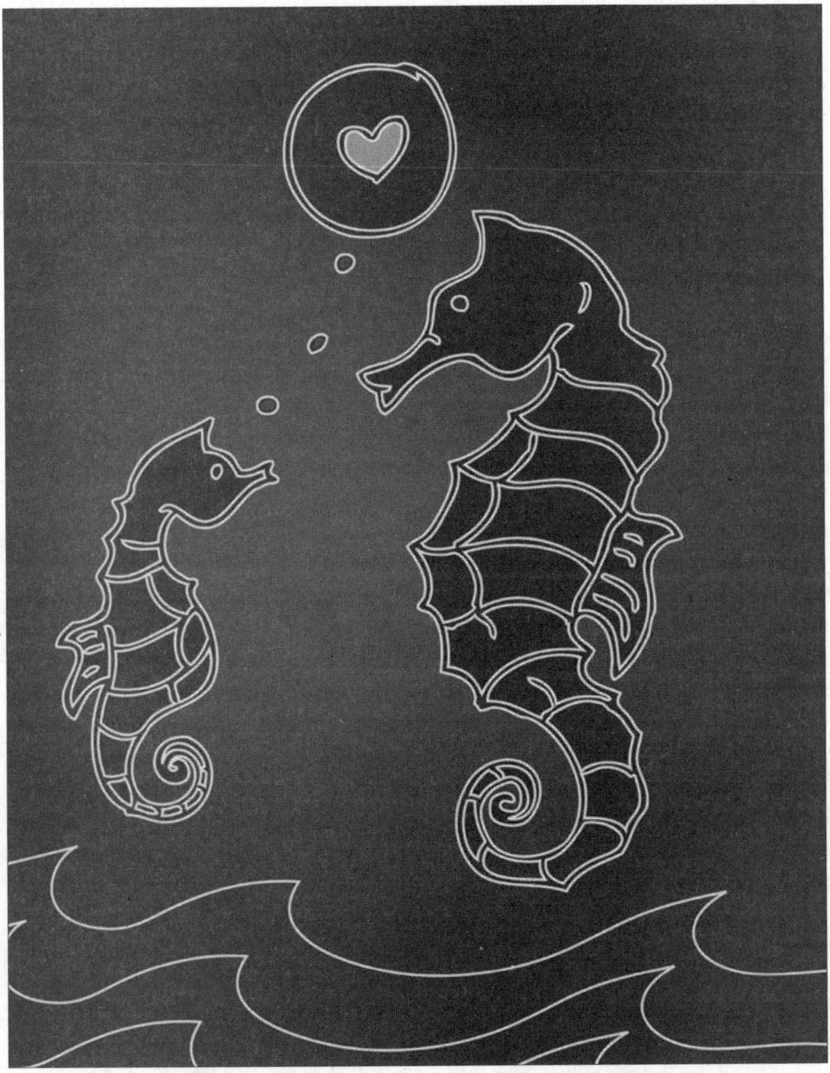

I ♥ my LGBTQ Family Cards, 2010. Artist: Suzy Malik. <http://www.lgbtqparentingconnection.ca/research/iheartmylgbtqfamily.cfm>.

Print and On-Line Resources

As part of our objective to increase visibility, provide information and advocate on behalf of LGBTQ families, the PN develops print and on-line resources. One of our most popular is the *Queering the Family Tree Poster*, conceived and designed in 2005 to celebrate the diversity of families within which children live and thrive. The poster, developed as a collaboration between the PN, Family Service Toronto, CAMH, Gay Fathers of Toronto, Chinese Family Services and TGStation, was inspired by stories from children living in LGBTQ-led families about the "Family

Tree" exercises they do in school. Typically these exercises assume that all children live in conventional nuclear families. The fill-in-the-blank format, with spaces for a "mom," "dad," "maternal grandparents," and so on, often excludes children of LGBTQ-led families, as well as others. Funded in part by a grant from the Lesbian and Gay Appeal of Toronto (now The Community One Foundation), the poster was designed to bring visibility to LGBTQ-led families and to generate discussion about homophobia, transphobia and discriminatory attitudes towards LGBTQ-led families in schools.

Bilingual (French/English), brightly-coloured and emblazoned with a range of terms to describe sexual orientation and gender identity, the poster represents and celebrates the diversity of families. The poster's border translates the word "family" into 35 languages. To date, more than 30,000 copies of the poster have been printed and are on display in schools, community centres, health centres and hospitals, daycares, libraries and homes across Canada, the United States, and as far as Australia. Recently, in collaboration with the Father Involvement Research Alliance and The 519 Community Centre, we developed another poster to celebrate GBTQ fathers.

The Queer Parenting Information Brochure Series provides parents and prospective parents with information on a range of topics, and we regularly send out an e-newsletter (available for sign-up on our website), and once a year put out a hard copy newsletter, *Pride & Joy*, featuring news related to LGBTQ parenting and, most popularly, birth and adoption announcements. Most recently, with coordination by PN program assistant Mariko Tamaki, we worked with seven Toronto-based artists to develop, as an alternative to traditional Mother's Day/Father's Day/Family Day cards, a series of cards to celebrate the parents, caregivers, and other important people in the lives of kids in LGBTQ families. The cards were launched at an "I ♥ My LGBTQ Family" event, featuring a writing workshop for teenagers with LGBTQ parents.

Challenges

Queer parenting communities in Toronto are fortunate, relative to communities in most other parts of Canada, in that we have access to programs that receive secure funding and are able to hire full-time staff to carry out their work. However, despite this privilege and stability, the PN continues to be under-funded and under-staffed. Our work would be more comprehensive and our staff less pressured and overworked, if we were able to hire more full-time staff members.

Probably the biggest challenge we face, given our financial and staff limitations, is our desire to address the needs and concerns of people across the range of identities and experiences that exists amongst queer families. Lesbian, gay, bisexual, trans and queer parents share many similar circumstances and needs; and, at the same time, experiences and needs differ according to sexual orientation and/or gender identity, racialization, ability, geographical location, age, how one became a parent, etc. We are a relatively small organization, and thus limited in what we can do. Our strength is that we are well-rooted in queer parenting communities in Toronto, which assists us in identifying and responding to needs and concerns as they arise; our limitation is that we cannot be deeply rooted in *all* queer parenting communities, and therefore there are always exclusions. As is true for most activist groups, it is a challenge to adequately recognize and address the complexities and intersectionalities of people's lives in the development of social programs.

Future Goals

The year 2011 marks the tenth anniversary of the PN. It is ten years since we held the series of focus groups that initially informed our work, and we are currently developing an on-line survey to formally check-in with our constituencies and to receive feedback and direction from the people who use our programs and, even more importantly, from some of those who do not.

We look forward to the research results of the trans parent and AHR studies, and to the knowledge transfer activities that will stem from them. We anticipate producing a video about the experiences and concerns of trans parents for use by both service providers and trans communities; and to working with AHR clinics and staff to provide in-service educational workshops based on our research findings.

We continue to develop and expand the LGBTQ Parenting Connection website as a comprehensive resource on LGBTQ parenting, and are in the process of transferring the family planning course manuals to an on-line format.

Most significantly, we are recognizing the need for more programs for older children who have grown up in LGBTQ families. While there are programs that run regularly for younger children (for eg. COLAGE–Children of Lesbians and Gays Everywhere), there is a lack of spaces for older children/young adults to gather.

Stefan Lynch, the first director of COLAGE, has coined the terms "queer spawn" and "culturally queer" to describe young people with queer parents. As our kids get older many of them seek a place in queer communities. They have grown up here, and yet do not always feel fully welcomed. One young woman, as part of an interview about her experience as a queer spawn, describes the ways that she recognizes queerness in others, but how they do not always recognize it in her:

> It's greatly influenced who I am because I feel a connection to the LGBT community in Toronto. It's weird because as a heterosexual female I am not recognized by that community. Like if I'm walking down Church St. I'm not recognized as a member of their community, however I feel like I am, it's an odd kind of place to be. When I see a lesbian couple walking down the street, I feel like "Hi!' you know. If I'm with one of my moms they kind of acknowledge each other, but when I'm alone I never get that acknowledgement from other people.... It's kind of like a little secret I have with myself sometimes, that they can't see, but you know.... (girl, 16, lesbians moms)

Our children are challenging us to create spaces in our communities that affirm and welcome them—particularly those who are, in Lynch's terms, erotically straight, but culturally queer. Abigail Garner refers to the "bicultural identity of heterosexual children who are linked to queerness through their heritage." While not all children of LGBTQ parents identify as straight or cisgendered, those that do sometimes find that it is not always clear where they fit in relation to queer or straight culture. Anti-homophobia/transphobia initiatives in schools usually focus on queer and trans youth, often excluding queer spawn, who are uniquely positioned at school. The homophobic/transphobic/heterosexist teasing or harassment of which they may be targets are not necessarily due to their own sexual orientation or gender identity but most often stem from their parent's sexual or gender identities and their family structures. They may be straight-identified themselves, but find themselves identifying with and defending queer people and cultures. (Epstein et al. 2009)

As more and more queer people have children, and as our children grow up, it is crucial that we do not, even inadvertently, exclude them from queer spaces. The PN is currently exploring ways to provide meaningful programming for the older children of LGBTQ parents.

Relationship to Larger Motherhood Movement

What has come to be known as the "lesbian baby boom," has its roots in the women's health movement of the 1970s and 80s. At a time when the medical establishment was not forthcoming in its support of other-than-heterosexual parenting, lesbians sought ways to bring children into their lives. As part of a growing lesbian and gay activism, with links to feminism, the women's health movement, and other progressive social movements of the time, the early days of lesbian conception were characterized by a feminist, self-help, empowerment model of women's health. The women's health care movement was about women taking control of their bodies and their reproduction and lesbians desiring children set out to do so. Many got pregnant at home, relying on knowledge of cervical mucous, known sperm donors or donors known to third parties, and syringes (not typically the mythical turkey baster, though it remains iconic). Small groups of women met to share information, knowledge and support. Women helped each other find men willing to be sperm donors, carried sperm for each other, shared knowledge about fertility and insemination, and supported each other through the roller coaster of conception, including the disappointments and heart break of miscarriages and infertility.

At the same time, lesbians were often rendered invisible and/or discriminated against in the early years of the women's and motherhood movements. And, although LGBTQ parenting has found its place on the map, queer women continue to face challenges in the motherhood (and fatherhood) movements, where parenting can still be narrowly viewed as primarily a heterosexual and cisgendered activity.

Feminism, and the motherhood movement, are based in an analysis of discrimination against women and the ways that motherhood, as a "woman's" activity, has been devalued. The insights and practices of feminism have unequivocally transformed the landscape of politics, and parenting, in North America. LGBTQ movements could not have made the gains they have, without the contributions of feminism. Simultaneously, LGBTQ communities have much to offer motherhood/fatherhood movements, particularly in terms of expanded understandings of gender and its relation to parenting. LGBTQ families profoundly challenge rigid and essentialist cultural assumptions about the femaleness of "motherhood" and the maleness of "fatherhood," calling into question assumptions about the need for male or female "role models," and about the gendered nature of parenthood. For example, some children of trans parents whose parents transitioned after becoming parents, simultaneously refer to their fathers as "dad" and "she," and their mothers as "mom" and "he," offering a powerful critique of the assumption that fathers are always men and mothers are always women (Canfield-Lenfest 16; Feakins 363).

[1]The complete Word document of this article is available for download at <www.lgbtqparentingconnection.ca>.
[2]Full decision can be read online at: <http://www.cfas.ca/images/stories/pdf/2010scc61judgement.pdf>.
[3]A summary of the research results is available at <www.lgbtqparentingconnection.ca>.

Works Cited

Arnup, K. *Lesbian Parenting: Living with Pride and Prejudice*. Charlottetown, PEI: Gynergy Books, 1995.

AHRA/LGBTQ Working Group. *The Assisted Human Reproduction Act* and LGBTQ Communities, 2008.

Canfield Lenfest, M. *Kids of Trans Resource Guide*. San Francisco: COLAGE, 2008.

Chesler, P. *Mothers on Trial: The Battle for Children and Custody*. New York: McGraw-Hill, 1986.

Eadie, A., L. Ross, R. Epstein and S. Anderson "To Bi or not to Bi: Bisexuality and Disclosure in the Adoption System." *Who's Your Daddy? And Other Writings on Queer Parenting*. Ed. R. Epstein. Toronto: Sumach Press, 2009. 124-132.

Epstein, R. "Our Kids in the Hall: Lesbian Families Negotiate the Public School System." *Mother Outlaws: Theories and Practices of Empowered Mothering*. Ed. Andrea O'Reilly. Toronto: Women's Press, 2004. 131-144.

Epstein, R. "Lesbian Families." *Voices: Essays on Canadian Families*. Ed. M. Lynn. Toronto: Nelson Canada, 2003. 76-102.

Epstein, R. "Butches with Babies: Reconfiguring Gender and Motherhood." *Journal of Lesbian Studies* 6.2 (2002): 41–57.

Epstein, R., B. Idems and A. Schwartz "Reading, Writing, and Resilience: Queer Spawn Speak Out About School." *Who's Your Daddy? And Other Writings on Queer Parenting*. Ed. R. Epstein. Toronto: Sumach Press, 2009. 215-232.

Feakins, J. "I Am My Father's Son." *Who's Your Daddy? And Other Writings on Queer Parenting*. Ed. R. Epstein. Toronto: Sumach Press, 2009. 363-367.

Garner, A. *Families Like Mine: Children of Gay Parents Tell It Like It Is*. New York: HarperCollins, 2004.

Leger Poll. 2001. CLGRO Newsclippings

MacKay, L. *Children and Feminism*. Vancouver: The Lesbian and Feminist Mothers Political Action Group, 1982.

Nicol, N. "Politics of the Heart: Recognition of Homoparental Families in Quebec." *Who's Your Daddy? And Other Writings on Queer Parenting*. Ed. R. Epstein. Toronto: Sumach Press, 2009. 180-196.

Rayside, D. *Queer Inclusions, Continental Divisions: Public Recognition of Sexual Diversity in Canada and the United States*. Toronto: University of Toronto Press, 2008.

Ross, L. E., R. Epstein, C. Goldfinger and C. Yager. "Policy and Practice Regarding Lesbian, Gay, Bisexual, Transgender, Transsexual and Two-Spirit Adoption in Ontario." *Canadian Public Policy* 35.4 (2009a): 451-451.

Ross, L. E., R. Epstein, S. Anderson and A. Eady. "Policy, Practice and Personal Narratives: Experiences of LGBTQ People with Adoption in Ontario, Canada." *Adoption Quarterly* 12.3,4 (2009b): 272-293.

III.
Maternal Advocacy

24. The Mother Centers International Network

MONIKA JAECKEL

THE MOTHER CENTERS INTERNATIONAL NETWORK (MINE) connects and supports the Mother Centers worldwide. Core elements of mine's networking support include naming, claiming, analysing and conceptualising the Mother Center experience, defining shared concerns of mothers and families world wide as well as strategies for action, organizing peer-learning workshops to collectively learn from the large experience of Mother Centers from around the world, harvesting their knowledge and linking it to mainstream debates, organizing international campaigns, supporting local and national negotiations and advocacy, creating partnerships with important stakeholders in society, linking the Mother Center movement to like-minded groups and movements, providing Mother Center start up knowledge, and supporting the further spreading of Mother Centers as well as supporting innovations and further development in the existing Mother Centers.

The first three Mother Centers were founded in Germany, as a model project funded by the German Federal Family Ministry. Within two decades they have spread into 20 countries. Mother Centers currently exist in Albania, Argentina, Austria, Bosnia, Bulgaria, Cameroon, Canada, Czech Republic, Germany, Hungary, Italy, Liechtenstein, Kenya, Nepal, The Netherlands, Poland, Russia, Rwanda, Slovakia, Spain, Switzerland and the U.S. It is estimated that there are over a thousand Mother Centers worldwide, linked by regional, national and international Mother Center networks.

Mother Centers seem to answer a historic need. They recreate family and neighborhood structures where they have been weakened by modernization, (Western Europe, North America), by socialist regimes (Czech Republic, Bulgaria), by war (Bosnia, Rwanda), or by poverty and aids (Cameroon, Kenya). Mother Centers represent another kind of globalization, a globalization from the ground. This has created the need for a global network: MINE, which was founded in late 2000. MINE connects and supports the Mother Centers movement. The network stands for a world that places social cohesion and community building at the base of development, re-integrates the culture of care into public life, and recognizes the central role of women in peace building and development.

MINE has been certified as Best Practice by United Nations Habitat and won the Dubai International Award for Best Practices to Improve the Living Environment in 2002. Since then, MINE has received many requests for support to start up Mother Centers in countries as diverse as Sudan, Guatemala, India, Ethiopia, Albania, Iraq and Burundi. As an organization operating on a voluntary basis, MINE has not been able to respond adequately to these requests. MINE can only function if the decision-making, programming, and planning is carried by the grassroots leaders, but if implementation is not dependent on their non-existent extra time.

Our desire is to bring out the strength of the network, "the spinning of the gold of the Mother Center movement" in a more organized and professional way, in order to be more efficient and reach further. Stretching the existing (human) resources at the present state of development of the network is not productive any more. Giving start-up support to Mother Centers in Burundi for example simply costs more than doing so in Austria, while at the same time the capacity of the women there to jointly raise the money is lower. So the challenges to fulfill our potential are about as large as our ambitions.

Background

What is remarkable about the development of the Mother Centers into a global movement is that it has been a spontaneous process. There has been no governmental or NGO program through which Mother Centers were disseminated. It happened "by itself," as the result of members' self-help and peer learning.

This chapter is based on the publication *Spreading like Wildfire: The Development of Mother Centers into a Global Movement*. The publication was the result of the study: "The Elements of Spontaneous Dissemination of Social Practice The Experience of the Mother Centers," commissioned by the Bernard van Leer Foundation. It sets out to examine the factors behind this seemingly miraculous dissemination process. How does the transfer of knowledge happen at the grassroots level? What makes Mother Centers a movement? What are the secrets of their success? What can be learned from this process?

It was a qualitative study conducted in several phases. In the first phase, 35 in-depth interviews were held with initiators of Mother Centers and Mother Center networks in Bosnia, Canada, Czech Republic, Germany, The Netherlands, and Slovakia, following a questionnaire previously sent to the country's networks. Individual and group interviews were conducted between February and June 2006. Participants were selected by the national and regional networks, as well as by local Mother Centers. A first analysis of the interviews was presented to the Mother Center Network at its international conference: "How Do We Want To Raise Our Children?" held in Bratislava at the end of November 2006. In a second phase, comments and feedback to the first analysis of the material were gathered and integrated into the final text.

The results of the study are presented in the authentic voices of the women interviewed. This follows the experience of the original Mother Center book, *Mothers in the Center – Mother Centers,* which played a major role in spreading Mother Centers and creating the movement.[1] The book was published as a storybook, told in the words of the women who participated in the establishment of the first centers. This made it easy for readers to identify with their peers and the concept of the mother centers. In *Spreading like Wildlife,* the same approach is taken to safeguard grassroots ownership of the rich harvesting of experience and knowledge generated by a movement that has spread bottom up on the basis of self help.

This chapter is a summary of the complete book in which, however, only one voice is presented: that of author Monika Jaeckel. Monika Jaeckel has committed the larger part of her life to movement-building. Since 1968, when she was at the forefront of the student movement, she has been active in organizing, researching, and inspiring the empowerment of grassroots women's groups. She was part of the team of researchers who were the midwives to the birth of the Mother Centers and she founded MINE. Sadly, in November 2009 she succumbed to uterine cancer.

In recognition of her contribution to the Mother Center movement, passages from *Spreading like Wildlife,* by Monika Jaeckel, were chosen for this chapter.[2]

The Result of a Successful Partnership Between Grassroots and Academia

Academia has played a pivotal role in the creation and dissemination of Mother Centers. The concept of Mother Centers was developed by researchers at the German Youth Institute in Munich. The fact that it developed into a grassroots self-help movement was due to the fact that methods of action research were applied and that ways of practising equitable partnerships between grassroots groups and their academic partners were explored.

The idea of Mother Centers started with a process of careful listening to and bringing out the authentic voices and ideas of parents and families. Issues were framed according to the understanding and self interpretation of families themselves, versus preconceived professional ideas about them. With this research approach, the issues became visible that families were raising themselves, as did their solutions.

An important element involved shifting from the usual "deficit orientation" (families have problems and need professional help) to a "resource orientation," that identifies the resources and capacities of the groups concerned as well as the enabling conditions under which these capacities can be activated and made productive for society. Families have skills and competencies. What they need are enabling structures to apply their capabilities.

A further element that contributed to grassroots ownership of the research process, consisted of creating reflective space for the participants of Mother Centers, to reflect on what was happening in their centers and to extract the implications and lessons learned and document their experience in a story-telling format.

Outside the Mother Center Plamen (Flame) in Zavidovici, Bosnia.

Kitchen crew at Aboriginal Mother Center Vancouver, Canada.

The research team was also a valuable partner by supporting negotiations with local authorities with academic evidence and by identifying allies for the Mother Center concept from universities, the media, ministries, foundations, international grassroots organisations and other stakeholders.

Claiming A Public Place for Families

Mother Centers are local grassroots initiatives that run self-managed public meeting spaces in the neighborhood. These are places where mothers and their children meet on a daily basis, can focus on their needs and interests, exchange knowledge and experiences with peers, receive and generate mutual support in child-rearing tasks, engage in capacity building and further education, and initiate family support services like childcare, eldercare, healthcare, hot meals for school children, laundry, janitors or other household services.

Mother Centers are based on self-help and participation, following the motto that everybody is good at least at one thing, which they can contribute to the center and to the community. The atmosphere is informal, the centers operate on a drop-in basis. Activities involve projects that help lower expenses for families and that support families in their parenting tasks and everyday chores as well as in times of crisis. Most centers run projects like a second-hand shop, a toy library, holistic health services, or skills training such as language courses, computer courses and job retraining. Advocacy groups on issues like children's environmental diseases, single parenting or family friendly urban facilities, are part of what happens in Mother Centers.

Mother Centers are local switchboards of information and exchange, a place where issues and talents can become visible. Everything that happens in the community can be discussed there on a daily basis. Anything that needs immediate attention or response can be attended to collectively. There is openness, fluidity and transparency of decision-making. Everyone is welcome in the center, and can participate and be part of it. Things do not happen behind closed doors, or by invitation alone, but "in public," in the "public living room."

Children are a welcome and regular part of Mother Centers, and Mother Centers run many programs for children. At the same time, however, the focus is on the mothers. Activities also revolve around the interests and needs of the mothers. This creates public space that is shared by adults and children and a different kind of childcare than in most programs.

You can join a Mother Center by having a cup of coffee in the coffee shop or by a visit to the Mother Center's second-hand store. Childcare is offered on a drop-in basis for all ages during the opening hours of the center. Depending on their size and how long they have been operating, Mother Centers reach between 50 and 1000 families in the neighbourhood.

In Mother Centers women are supported to join forces to improve the lives of their families and communities, connect with families from different social and cultural backgrounds, gain acknowledgment for their everyday life expertise, fight poverty and social exclusion and participate in local governance. Mother Centers generate peer support systems in conflict and crisis situations. They create employment and access to the labor market. For children the centers create an expansion of their social and physical space and experience. They experience an introduction and integration into public life in a protected environment.

Princess Máxima visits the Mother Center in Bos&Lommer, Amsterdam, The Netherlands.

Mother Centers International Network meeting, Czech Republic.

An Expression of the Desire for Community

Mother Centers are contagious, and generate a spontaneous response. The spreading of the Mother Center concept is described by many as a form of "recognition" of an idea and vision that already exists inside. The concept taps into a deeper knowing, something is touched and resonates within, and the picture immediately becomes alive. Mother Centers seem to be understood spontaneously because they relate to a deep knowing and yearning for community.

Conservative forces in society often respond to the longing for community with traditional and somewhat outdated concepts, which often gives the impression of trying to turn back the clock. Mother Centers relate to the need for community in a modern way. Putting the values of community and care into a modern context, means developing conditions for social bonding and social responsibility to develop freely, and based on choice, not based on moral rules or family obligations. The task is to create the conditions to balance today's individualistic lifestyle, against social responsibility and socially reliable networks. Family needs to be defined in a wide and culturally diverse way, socially reliable networks need to extend beyond family and clan structures, to include social units and networks based on common interests and preferences.

For a sustainable future, family and community solutions are needed that work for women, who are increasingly developing an awareness of their right to equality and in many cases are also increasingly having fewer children; as well as for children and youth, who are increasingly becoming dysfunctional in urban settings.

Opening up nuclear family structures to local support networks in the neighborhood brings a shift towards more of a collective responsibility and organization of reproductive tasks, towards "community parenting." Mother Centers are paving new ways for community, which translate easily to contemporary conditions of caregiving.

What Makes Mother Centers Unique?

Some of the major challenges of contemporary societies include an increasingly individualised and aging society as well as increasingly multicultural populations. While family, kin and neighborhood networks are thinning out, the question of social cohesion and social values needs to be re-framed under contemporary conditions. How to live together in social peace and harmony, how to generate social care and responsibility and how to rebuild the social fabric in diverse, conflict-torn, pluralistic societies are issues underlying many of the current concerns around the isolation, alienation and anonymity of communities, the increase of violence, the re-emergence of fundamentalism, the non-engagement of youth and the lack of a pro-active civil society.

Mother Centers are an answer to the weakening of social ties, family, kin and neighbourhood networks in many different social, cultural and historical settings. Mother Centers are being self-created all over the world by women who see the

Move the Pram – Move the World, International Mother Centers Action Day, Bratislava, Slovakia, 2006.

need for community support for the everyday task of raising children. They reinvent family and kinship under contemporary conditions by creating extended family structures in the context of neighbourhood and community. They create buffer zones for many of the challenges of contemporary society such as individualization, alienation, isolation and clientelization.

What makes the approach of Mother Centers unique is that they provide a unique blending of public and private, the formal and informal. They reintroduce the culture of care into public life. They create public space that feels private. Public space in the context of family and neighbourhood networks stays personal. At the same time it gives access to public recognition and visibility. This unique Mother Center blend has often been described by the term "public living rooms".

Mother Centers combine many elements that make them increasingly attractive not only to mothers with small children, but also to youth as well as seniors. Many of the Mother Centers are evolving into multi-generational centers, offering a mix of private and public care to all age groups, that maintains a family-like quality while providing support, relief and back up also to the care-givers.

Strategies of Dissemination

Mother Centers spread through peer learning and peer sharing. News about the Mother Center idea is spread through word of mouth as well as by the media. Often it only takes a little spark such as an article in a magazine or a program on television for the seed to be planted. Examples of how initiatives for Mother Centers were born include women getting into a conversation with each other in the pediatrician's waiting room, a group of friends in a housing estate hearing about the idea, or a message on the announcement board of the local supermarket.

The next step is learning more about the concept by asking for more information from existing Mother Centers and very often by visiting one in the area and seeing the concept in practice. The Mother Center book, *Mothers in the Center – Mother Centers,* which published the stories of the women who built up the first three Mother Centers in Germany, played a very important role in spreading the idea and inspiring new initiatives. For the more recent Mother Centers, the Internet is becoming an increasingly important channel of information and exchange.

The Mother Center movement developed through a process of peer networking and learning from each other. Issues that are key for centers to get started and survive, such as how to register as an official entity, look for rooms, write proposals, or get funding, are passed on from center to center.

When ten to twenty Mother Centers have been founded in a region or a country, the process develops into the creation of a regional, or national, Mother Center network that takes on the task of spreading information and giving start-up support in a more organized manner.

The Creation of Networks

The spreading of Mother Centers was supported by the creation of regional, national and international networks. Networking is an important element to enable Mother Centers to gain influence in society. The development of the Mother Center movement is marked by the creation of regional, national and international Mother Center networks.

Mother Center networks contribute to the local Mother Centers as well as to the movement at large, both internally as well as externally in many ways and through various services and activities. One of the main activities involves organizing peer learning workshops to collectively learn from each other's experience and to spread innovations developed in the network. An important part involves developing internal structures to support leadership development and conflict resolution within the centers and the movement.

Another important role the networks fulfill is in helping to analyze and conceptualize the Mother Center experience, identifying the innovative elements and the essentials that make them work and guarantee their quality. Through taking up contact and exchanging experiences between the Mother Centers worldwide, an understanding of the global dimensions of motherhood is developing within the Mother Center networks, and the situation of children and families is becoming visible internationally. Networking supports the linking of like minded groups and the defining of shared concerns as well as strategies for change.

The networks spread the news about Mother Centers in both verbal and written form. They link the experiences and perspectives on families and their environment, as they are developed in the everyday life of the centers, to mainstream debates and developments, and they broker partnerships to other stakeholders. They also take on an important role in advocacy and enhancing the influence of families, both by supporting the local centers in their negotiations with local authorities as well as by creating regional, national and international agendas and campaigns. The networks create nationwide and international opportunities for Mother Centers to portray their work and voice their concerns.

Successes

The spreading of the Mother Center movement has created many effects and benefits, both for the families involved as well as for society at large. Mother Centers have a strong impact on the participating families as well as on municipalities and communities.

The success of the Mother Centers on the ground is based on specific elements that work together to create the "Mother Center magic" and success formula:

- Mother Centers operate in self management. Mothers are "the experts" in the centers. Their everyday life experience is acknowledged as expertise. Professionals have a supportive role and engage in equal partnerships.
- The centers' approach is resource, not problem, oriented. Women are not approached by asking them to define their problems. Instead they are asked to define the skills and resources they have to contribute to community building and community solutions.
- Mother Centers claim a public "room of their own." They are not harbored in rooms of other organizations for limited periods of time. The initiatives have full time access to their rooms.
- Work in the Mother Centers is remunerated and tasks are spread among the participants. Voluntary work is additional, not a substitute for paid work. On average for every paid hour in the centers about two extra

hours of voluntary work is generated.

•Children are welcome and an integral part of the centers, but the focus is also on the interests and needs of the mothers.

•Mother Centers function more like family than like institutions. The 'corporate culture' is personal and adapted to family rhythms. It follows women's ways of learning, and women's ways of doing things.

•Mother Centers function on the basis of collective leadership and a culture of leadership support. Learning to work together is a major focus. Conflicts are not avoided but an accepted part of it and efforts are undertaken collectively to work through conflicts.

•Mother Centers are melting pots in the community for women of diverse social, cultural, religious and ethnic backgrounds. Diversity is celebrated and integration and peace building methods are an integral part of the daily programs.

•Mothers' expertise in dealing with care giving and the everyday life of communities is channeled into advocacy, local governance and policy making.

•Mother Centers also claim reflective space. Taking time out for peer learning exchanges as well as for regular seminars to reflect on the daily experiences, the lessons learned, and the way forward, are an integral part of their functioning.

The benefits to the participating women, their families and communities include: assistance in parenting and family issues; improving the quality of child rearing; active roles for women and more gender equality in families and the community; support for the reintegration of women into the labor market and for work-life balance; creation of income generating activities and services that are well attuned to the needs of families; integration of youth as well as the elderly; support for family health and well being; revitalization of local culture and local neighborhoods; diversity management and social cohesion at community level; and providing families with a voice and influence in shaping their environment.

Challenges

In the process of growing into a global movement the Mother Centers encounter many challenges, which are highlighted in this section. Challenges include internal, organizational questions and communication issues, as well as challenges related to external issues and players. The Mother Center movement is in itself in many ways challenging, both to the participants as well as to the outside world, in as much as it involves many innovative aspects that often do not fit into conventional concepts, and usual ways of thinking and doing things.

Mother Centers raise challenging issues like the question of how to create value and acknowledge non-monetary sources of capital like time, care, presence, diversity and social networks. They are involved in finding ways to recognize and validate informal skills and informal work. They deal with taboo questions like the poverty of families in affluent societies and the question of qualitative poverty, a poverty of social relations in conditions of material wealth, and how to balance economic and social development.

Mother Centers question the division between private and public, the gap between institutional and informal structures. They develop a culture of public participation beyond professionalisation and formal representative democratic structures. Mother Centers are a model of civic ownership of public space that counteracts the trend of public space being taken over by formal institutions and market forces. These are not easy processes. The issues that Mother Centers find themselves struggling with come with many challenges both internally and externally. Solutions have been found to varying degrees, but many of the difficulties described remain challenging.

Ways Forward

While the challenges and difficulties that the Mother Center movement is currently facing were being described very vividly in the interviews that were at the base of this study, solutions and ways forward also became apparent. Sometimes they were implied and sometimes very clearly and intentionally described. Responses to the challenges were also a focus of the inputs in the second phase of the study. The final section of this analysis lays out the ways forward as they are being perceived and presented by active members and leaders of the Mother Center movement. In looking forward, Mother Center protagonists place a good deal of value on the issue of sustaining and nurturing the visions for which Mother Centers stand. Many centers and networks conduct regular events to raise awareness of the common values, visions and goals. Some of the most prevalent visions are described.

A major focus both of individual Mother Centers as well as the Mother Center movement as a whole is directed towards the issue of sustainability. The Mother Center movement has consistently grown for the last 30 years and also individual Mother Centers show a considerable degree of sustainability. Very few centers have closed down again. Nevertheless the issue of sustainability was very much in the forefront during the interviews. Many women felt that there was not enough political and financial support to keep the centers and the Mother Center networks going in the long run. This arose mainly from the feeling that the successes and gains of the movement were due to an "overdose" of voluntary work, that women (and families) were over stretching themselves to keep things going, that there were not enough reserves to face current issues of cut-backs in social welfare policies and that the issue of burn-out of Mother Center leaders was becoming prevalent.

A major condition for the sustainability of Mother Centers was identified as the availability of public rent-free rooms. It was named as an indispensable condition for the emergence and survival of Mother Centers. In countries where the Mother Centers have spread spontaneously and quickly like in Germany, or the Czech Republic and Slovakia, this is greatly due to the fact that local government and other organizations provide rooms free of charge to community groups. In poorer countries like Bosnia by contrast, local governments see public space as an economical asset through which to make gains. This creates a big barrier for Mother Centers as well as civil society in general to develop. In the context of developing countries this seems to create a crucial bottleneck.

In the experience of the Mother Center movement a very clear correlation emerges between the development of Mother Centers and the policies of local government in the respective countries. Although Mother Centers have also been taken up, for instance in the slums of Nairobi or in a village in Cameroon, these initiatives have remained singular and have not resulted in the spreading of the centers throughout the whole country.

If local government does not take on the role of providing public space that is not tied to commercial interests, other stakeholders in society are needed to create this precondition for civic involvement. Public space is key to any policy that aims at increasing the involvement of women in civil society and governance. The emergence of civil society depends on public space. Personal freedoms and equalities are not enough, there needs to be opportunities for public discourse and encounters. The privatization and commercialization of public space in the context of globalization constitutes a heavy challenge for democracy.

While secure and long-term access to space and funding was seen as key to the sustainability of Mother Centers and the Mother Center movement, it was by no means perceived as the only element needed. Visions and strategies for the way forward also addressed issues of professionalization and organizational development as well as internal and external relationships.

[1]The original book, *Mothers in the Center – Mother Centers,* was published in German. The translation of this book into English has not been published, but it can be downloaded at <http://www.mine.cc/MC.pdf>.
[2]The full text of this book—as well as many other artices—can be downloaded from Monika Jaeckel's website <www.MonikaJaeckel.com>.

Works Cited

Jaeckel, Monika. *Spreading Like Wildlife: The Development of Mother Centers into a Global Movement.* Den Haag, 2007. Web. <http://www.mine.cc/files/wildfire.pdf>.

Jaeckel, Monika. Hildegard Schooss, and Hannelore Weskamp. *Mütter im Zentrum – Mütterzentrum. Bilanz einer Selbsthilfebewegung (Mothers in the Center – Mother Centers. Revised and updated edition).* München: Aktualisierte und erweiterte Neuausgabe, 1997.

25. The Birth and Evolution of the National Association of Mothers' Centers

My Radical Hope

LORRI SLEPIAN
WITH LAURIE SYLLA AND ROSANNE WESTON

THE NATIONAL ASSOCIATION OF MOTHERS' Centers (NAMC) grew out of a mothers'-centered movement begun in the early 1970s. It took root in the vision of creating ethical, growth-promoting environments for mothers where they could safely speak the truth of their maternal experience to each other. These environments became Mothers' Centers and Mothers' Center Circles. The NAMC exists to support and assist in replicating these Centers and Circles, and to advocate for women's economic empowerment throughout the U.S. The NAMC's vision is a society where the work of taking care of others is valued, supported, at the center of public discussion, and a priority in public policy.

Purpose/Philosophy/Culture

The purpose of the original Mothers' Center was to create a space where women could take a deep look at the impact of pregnancy, the birth experience, adoption, and child-rearing on themselves and to serve women at all stages of mothering. The founders wanted a space where we all could study and understand our work as mothers. We needed to listen to ourselves as well as to the "experts of the day." We had to sift what these experts taught through our own experience. We had to respect our mother-work as a source of knowledge and we had to say what was true for us, without fear of disapproval.

The philosophy of the Mothers' Center movement and of the NAMC is centered on the belief that, in an atmosphere and culture that values women, children and families; fosters deep connections among women; embraces ambiguity and diverse viewpoints rather than insisting on the one "right" way; and raises the voices of women, mothers can become the experts on the developmental and societal needs of themselves and their families. This philosophy is operationalized in the Mothers' Center settings through: consensus decision-making, where the goal is to have everyone feel her voice has been heard and respected, even when there is not universal agreement on a decision; encouragement of members to approach and receive each other with an assumption of the other's integrity and good intentions

Mothers' Center Facilitator Training Group, New York

and to respond to each other with empathy; non-hierarchical roles and participatory democracy; maintenance of a spirit of inquiry that supports peer-professional intellectual exchanges between recognized experts and expert women/mothers; a commitment to empowerment by validating women/mothers as they become aware, gain understanding, and take action to claim what they are entitled to. Each center strives for financial sustainability in numerous ways.

This Mothers' Center culture is one in which women do a radical thing. They speak and tell the truth. This culture has had a profound impact over the years, trickling down the generations from Mothers' Center members to their children, their sisters, and their families. It changes the way we relate to each other. In a Mothers' Center, you can hear the mother voice and feel the maternal power. Mothers' Center culture allows us to learn that a mother has an intrinsic right to discover what gives her life meaning, both within and alongside her role as mother. It is a culture that supports the right to mother in healthy ways and supports our children's right to grow in healthy, loving families. It is a culture that insists that the world must pay attention to the needs of woman/children/families.

History

Before the Beginning

When I was raising my four boys, I noticed how easily I was affected by the judgments of others, how readily I took on guilt or shame or pride based on how others perceived my children. If my child was too noisy or had a difficult time in

Mothers' Center National Conference Roundtable with Mothers' Groups

school or with playmates, how easy it was to see them as lesser and to slip into self-criticism with the resulting loss of self esteem. Over the years, I heard other mothers report that same experience with self blame. The critical voice was very hard to silence.

I came to realize that we mothers are deeply affected by the developmental changes, the behavior, the experiences, the successes, and the failures of our children. These changes in our children have been studied by many researchers, but our responses to the developmental struggles of our children and how we mothers cope with them had not been looked at as developmental challenges. No researcher had named them yet, much less studied them. Yet, just as our children do, we grapple with issues of separation and attachment, of intimacy and boundaries. Our own questioning about our self-worth and development, however, typically happened alone, in isolation.

If you were lucky, maybe you found places to talk about the stresses of fatigue and the battles around toilet training. But where did you talk in safety about the blows to your own self-esteem, about the ambivalence, the anger, and the guilt, as well as the learning and insights about development that we gained from our mother-work? The idealized mother was a happy, energetic, fulfilled mother and to feel different from that was to make yourself an oddball, an aberration.

I often thought and studied in silence, on my own. I turned to the works of the major psychological theorists of the time. It occurred to me that much of what they knew came out of their own lived experiences, and how much knowledge there was to be gained from the study of *our* own mothering, as well as the study of child development. I became certain that we could all contribute to human knowledge if we each paid attention to our inner world, to the inner self that is our source of knowledge. Noticing, tolerating and understanding our feelings can ultimately lead to thoughts and actions that are compassionate and creative. This paying attention is our best tool for knowing and learning, for developing our children, ourselves, and humankind.

I began to wonder what would happen if mothers everywhere worked with conscious intention to instill the concepts of ethics, empathy and kindness in our children. I imagined the power of "conscious mothering" as the attention all mothers could give their children to help them develop the emotional resources they need to reach their highest development. I later discovered in the book, *Toni Morrison and Motherhood: A Politics of the Heart,* written by Dr. Andrea O'Reilly, that Toni Morrison had used this term to describe the deliberate attention black mothers give to developing their children's emotional resources to counteract growing up in a racist society.

Sara Ruddick, in her book, *Maternal Thinking: Toward a Politics of Peace,* coined the term, "maternal thinking" for seeing everything through the "mother lens." Conscious mothering married with maternal thinking is our maternal power, what I like to think of as the "maternal force." Conscious mothering, that is, intentional, growth-promoting, ethical, character-shaping mothering, cannot assure that our children will follow our teachings, but our conscious mothering increases the likelihood that they will have the emotional resources and the commitment to humanity and to themselves that could raise up humankind.

But where and how could we study ourselves and our mothering?

The Beginning

In 1973, Patsy Turrini, a clinical social worker, designed a research study of women's experience of pregnancy, birth, and early childrearing. Participants met in research groups, and, as I was already a facilitator in Women's Liberation consciousness-raising groups, I was asked to facilitate one of these early mothers' groups. It struck me that women could be brought together around the issue of mothering, without having to address the feminist vs. non-feminist battle. I wanted to organize an army of women to change the conditions of women's lives. No one was talking about the needs of mothers back then. It was a time that we didn't even think that mothers had inherent rights. I felt we could add power to the women's liberation movement by having a side by side movement focusing on mothers.

In the mothers' research groups, women began to understand the complexities of becoming and being mothers. The women began to really understand what was needed for their own development as well as for their children's and families' development and happiness. Exchanges about the birthing experience, that most *deeply* felt and *profoundly* life-changing event, brought strong connection among the women. They began to put words and value to their Motherwork. They came together for mutual support and advocacy. Most of all, they decided on a mission—that of advocating for a Mothers' Center in every neighborhood as a necessary public good, much as you would have a library or a fire station. They became the beginning of a Mothers' Movement.

When the research project concluded, Patsy Turrini drew on the social work elements of research, service, and advocacy to create the basic structure of what would become the Mothers' Center model. I focused on how to shape a growth-promoting ethical culture that would bring women together and make more possible the building of a mothers' movement. Synergizing these elements, Patsy, 15 other women, and I birthed the first Mothers' Center. It opened in Long Island, NY in January, 1975. In that Center we created an environment built on the principles of open, non-judgmental, honest sharing, and the women streamed through our doors. Peer-facilitated groups were formed in which members talked about birthing, adoption, nursing, anxieties, their children's behavior, their own often-puzzling reactions, postpartum depression and marriage. News of the Center spread by word of mouth and magazine articles. Women contacted us from all over the country. In 1981, the Family Service Association of Nassau County created the Mothers' Center Development Project (MCDP) and gave us an 800 number. The phone rang constantly. The MCDP evolved into a national, non-profit organization—The National Association of Mothers' Centers. Since its inception, NAMC has reached tens of thousands of women.

Essence of the Model: Core Elements of a Mothers' Center

Mothers' Centers and Mothers' Circles are mother-driven. They are places where women/mothers are valued as women and as mothers and where they can come together and grow in a safe, supportive environment that affirms and expands their knowledge and allows them to try to new things and new approaches. Many communities now have Mothers' Circles rather than Mothers' Centers simply because of resource issues and the lack of societal support for establishing Mothers' Centers in every community. Mothers' Circles preserve the core element of group discussion within the same cultural framework as the Mothers' Center, without the larger structure of a center.

A core element of both Mothers' Centers and Mothers' Circles are facilitated groups, typically using a questionnaire with focused, open-ended-reflective questions. We maintain a spirit of inquiry because we know we can learn from each other. The amount of wisdom women gain through their mothering experience and in their being attuned to their developing child is astonishing. In these groups we learn how to listen, really listen, and how to respond so that the speaker feels heard. We use group facilitators who are offered ongoing training and consultation.

All group members take on group responsibilities to help the group go well. Each of the mothers speaks of their own personal experience, not a third party's. Each is asked to be aware of group time, and try to be fair about it. They are asked not to interrupt. Advice is not given unless it is asked for. They are to think about what they learned that day and to keep all that is said in the group confidential.

Many of the groups and centers offer childcare. Our childcare is based on psychological development theories that respect the child and the mother's needs. We teach and consider constructs of separation, attachment, individuation, and temperament to the members and to the child care workers. If needed, children are allowed to return to their mothers for comforting, and then encouraged to return to the children's room as they are ready.

We use a non-hierarchical system where people take on positions as they feel ready and stop when they need to. There are no elections. It is a participatory democracy where members have opportunities to use and develop their skills.

The center uses a steering committee to do the nuts and bolts work of running a center. Other committees are formed as needed. In a Mothers' Center, committees are both task and group focused, using aspects of the group process while getting the work done in a respectful way.

We are always open to the newest information in many areas of knowledge. We invite in experts in areas such as brain development, parenting, safe childbirth practices, child development, women's history, health issues, public policy issues and so on. We take in the knowledge of experts and we give them ours from our own knowledge base. In that way we have a valuable peer-professional exchange. We find that *all* of these practices change beliefs, values and perceptions. Members often acquire a more comprehensive, more inclusive view of the world.

The members internalize their Mothers' Center experience and take that out to the world. We have many times seen mothers feel more able and empowered to speak and to do. They are much better able to advocate for what they need. The power of the Mothers' Centers is that the structure and the culture of the organization support an empowerment process that unfolds in these five ways:

- *Becoming aware, paying attention and noticing:* Women notice and become aware of what happens inside them, what they are feeling, what their physical responses are, and they learn from these as they listen to others.
- *Validation:* In speaking together, women receive validation for their own thoughts feelings and experiences. Validation is *most* important because without it you can feel alone and crazy in your mothering journey. Such aloneness diminishes mental health.
- *Gaining understandings:* Understandings emerge when you reflect on what you hear in a setting of non-judgmental connection and compassion. With gained understandings, the sense of self deepens and the view of the world enlarges.
- *Entitlement:* At this point women are stronger and feel entitled to different and better responses to their needs, wants and rights as mothers.
- *Taking action:* Because they feel entitled and are informed, they are able to take action and make changes in their families, in their schools, in their communities. They make changes in the way doctors, elected officials,

Three moms at Mothers' Center, Bellmore, New York

> and public institutions respond to them. They, aware and strong and connected to each other, become part of the Mothers' Movement.

Each Mothers' Center and Mothers' Circle grew out of the desires of women/mothers to connect with other mothers, share experiences and learn from each other and from others. The NAMC helps women who wish to establish a Mothers' Center or a Mothers' Circle in their communities. A number of tools are available free on the NAMC website and additional resources, such as start-up kits, discussion guides, and facilitators' manuals are available from the NAMC website.

Activities and Accomplishments

In the past 37 years, the NAMC has been creating places where women can develop an understanding of who they are as mothers and as women and empowering them to work together toward a fair and equitable society that would benefit their children, their families and themselves. It has been providing training, technical assistance and support to existing Mothers' Centers and to women who want to start new Centers. The NAMC also discovered ways to replicate the Mothers' Centers' nurturing and empowering culture outside of the free-standing Center model, and we now embed that culture into our Mothers' Center Circles, held in living rooms and libraries across the country. Over the years, the NAMC has helped countless women establish numerous Mothers' Centers and Mothers' Circles. Many have endured, and others have been more short-lived in nature. The population of mothers of young children keep knocking on our doors as the need is still there. Unfortunately, adequate resources and community support are not always easily available.

In the 1970s, we were instrumental in stopping the use of the drug scopolamine for reducing childbirth pain, as it caused some women to have psychotic reactions. We pressed for sibling visitation in the maternity wards, and we got the dads into the delivery rooms. We disseminated essential information to parents and professionals about postpartum depression. In 2005, along with the Postpartum Resource Center of New York, we created a new project—the Circle of Caring—which was offered to women coping with postpartum depression.

Since 1980, we have put together national and regional Mothers' Center Conferences, where people from across the country meet to share and learn the most updated information affecting women, health, families, children, and Mothers' Centers. In 1996 we held the first of our annual Work/Life Conferences, gathering parents and business representatives to converse about evolving family-friendly workplace policies and what more needs to be done. In 1997 we created a cross-cultural leadership program for mothers and their eleven to thirteen-year-old daughters, reaching across economic and racial lines, and in 1998 we developed Mothers Make a Difference! aimed at teen mothers and women in emergency and transitional housing. We began a worksite support program for parents in 1999, bringing our first group to the office of the FBI in New York City, and in 2000 we issued the Mothers Declaration of Rights.

We further responded to the critical, evolving economic and work/life balance needs of mothers by creating the MOTHERS initiative, an economic rights initiative. Utilizing the power of social networking we promote our advocacy efforts through our "(Wo)man in Washington" blog, and a monthly MOTHERS e-news. The blog has gained prominence, respect and trust within the women's public policy community and our readership has grown.

Our blog writer and advocacy coordinator, Valerie Young, is our real-time voice in Washington, DC. She has often said that she is the only one at events speaking up for mothers, even when the meetings are organized by women's groups, around women's issues. The NAMC believes that it's necessary to strengthen the voices of mothers so we can have a greater impact on public policy issues addressing the needs of women.

In 2009, the NAMC became the host of the Alfred P. Sloan awards ceremony for Business Excellence in Workplace Flexibility in the Long Island region of New York. These are prestigious, coveted and competitive awards for employers on Long Island who are interested in their employees and addressing work and family life while benefiting their bottom line. And in 2010 we co-hosted with Rutgers University a "What Women Want" conference, presenting research findings on mothers' broad support for corporate and public policies addressing work/life issues.

Mothers' Centers Regional Conference, Connecticut

Today, we are still advocating for safer births and compassionate care, for every mother to have a Mothers' Center program in her community, and for mothers to gain economic and social rights. Motherwork needs to be much more valued, recognized and accommodated in our society, and the National Association of Mothers' Centers is making that happen.

Our work on growing the network and the motherhood movement continues through our cooperation with the Mothers Centers throughout the world. The U.S. Mothers' Center model grew out of a 1973 research project of Patsy Turrini, which ultimately resulted in the opening of the first Mothers' Center in 1975 in New York. In 1976, research done in Germany by Monika Jaeckel ultimately resulted in the model used there and in other countries. Both models continue to proliferate. To this day, the U.S. and German models differ but are connected through the Mothers Center International Network for Empowerment (MINE) in sisterhood and in dedication to mothers' development as parents and influential citizens of the world.

Challenges

NAMC's efforts to institutionalize a mother's right to a neighborhood Mothers' Center in our country has so far been slowed by societal constraints. The need for Mothers' Centers is not widely recognized as people often take motherhood for granted. Identifying funding sources is a difficult task, as funders are faced with bottomless requests to help meet urgent survival needs on a daily basis. Articulating our message in a way that resonates with and is inclusive of *all* women/mothers, regardless of political perspective, is challenging.

Some challenges have been organizational and others more core to our mission. How do we remain true to our principles and stay relevant in an evolving society? How do we respond to the changing roles of fathers and other caregivers? How do we prioritize our work when the need is so great and the resources inadequate? How do we maximize the impact we can have in supporting women/mothers and in creating new possibilities for humanity that allow us to reach our highest and fullest potential?

Our original dream was built on the premise that mothers had a right to have Mothers' Centers in every neighborhood as an essential service. Initially, we were enormously successful at making steady progress toward this goal. Then, the huge sea change that occurred when massive numbers of mothers began working outside of the home, either by choice or necessity, forced a shift in organizational priorities. Building and maintaining Centers became difficult because the mothers were now struggling to meet the demands of both the home and workplace, leaving them less volunteer time to devote to nurturing the Centers. We made an organizational decision that the best way to help women/mothers now would be to tend to the immediate need of addressing the policies that pertain to women's employment and economic well-being. The necessity of this became even more apparent after the release of Ann Crittenden's groundbreaking book, *The Price of Motherhood,* in 2001. We are focused on workplace and social policy change that confronts the outdated and inexcusable lack of childcare, sick time, part time job opportunities with benefits, flexible work hours, along with continued pay inequity, and other structural barriers that women/mothers face.

Future Goals

We must expand our programs, reach more mothers, establish more Centers and Circles and continue growing our work /life economic advocacy in order to strengthen the Mothers' Movement. To succeed at creating a more humane civilization we must support each other in efforts to bring the maternal into the work of constructing a different civilization. Women must take their place as leaders in our world.

We must find a different way to live: a way with more security and less violence; a way that offers women more economic opportunity; a way that supports and values the work of caregiving; a way that makes possible a more fully developed humanity.

Relation to Larger Motherhood Movement

The NAMC has helped mothers break through their isolation from each other, to learn from each other and to care about each other. We have created ethical,

Mothers Declaration of Rights

The work of mothering can have enormous benefits; the beneficiaries of this work are not only the mother and child, but families and society as well. The work of mothering also creates enormous demands. It requires inordinate physical and psychological energy, and is often performed with limited social support and access to historical wisdom and current research. It may have long term and often unanticipated negative economic repercussions for the woman and her family. We believe that mothers have the right to perform this vital and essential work in a supportive environment, one that acknowledges the value of her work and accounts for her economic, social, educational, psychological and physical needs. Every mother, every child, every family deserves nothing less.

Therefore, we believe in the following rights:

Economic

- To have unpaid caregiving conceptualized as work and valued accordingly by society (i.e., included in the census, accounted for in GDP calculations, counted in welfare rights, credited toward social security benefit calculations…)
- To pursue occupational goals as well as family ones (i.e. availability of good part time jobs, childcare subsidies, workweek reduction/flexibility…)
- To have training to upgrade or optimize her skills as well as childcare provisions to facilitate utilization of training opportunities

Social

- To have a Mothers' Center in every community—comfortable and safe community space
- To have safe, affordable childcare options available to any family who needs it
- To be entitled to parenting support services
- To lead a life free from violence and discrimination

Educational

- To have more influence/voice in the areas of maternal health, birthing practices, women's health and research
- To be entitled to information about maternal and child development
- To have information about the work of women/mothers who went before us

Psychological and Physical

- To value mother knowledge gained from the attunement to self and child
- To acknowledge the value of maternal experience to the growth and development of the mother
- To support the emotional health of pre- and post-partum women
- Access to adequate health and mental health care before, during and after pregnancy and child birth to ensure optimal outcomes for infant and maternal health

—NAMC © 2000

growth-promoting environments in which we listen to, validate, and empower women/mothers. This is the key to forging a mothers' social change force, a Mothers' Movement. Mothers in our programs widen their vision to identify what, in our society, makes mothering difficult and then work for changes that are needed. The NAMC has worked in collaboration with mothers' groups around the world committed to this work.

Conclusion

The goal of the National Association of Mothers' Centres is to unleash mother power in our society by creating the political, economic, psychological and social environment that allows women/mothers to flourish while they develop their children, their families, and themselves.

Let's imagine the world as it should be and work to make it happen. As Susan B. Anthony said when the women's movement was focused on gaining the right to vote, "FAILURE IS IMPOSSIBLE." Yet, in the United States, it took more than a century for women to gain what seems like a "no-brainer" now. Our new goals might well take longer to achieve, but with a strong mothers' movement we *can* bring about a more highly developed humanity and a less violent world. With a strong mothers' movement, "failure" *is* impossible.

Works Cited

Crittenden, Ann. *The Price of Motherhood.* New York: Metropolitan Books, 2001.

Mothers Ought to Have Equal Rights (MOTHERS). Web. <www.MothersOught-ToHaveEqualRights.org>.

O'Reilly, Andrea. Toni Morrison and Motherhood: A Politics of the Heart. New York: State University of New York Press, 2004.

National Association of Mothers' Centers (NAMC). Web. <www.MothersCenter.org>.

Ruddick, Sara. *Maternal Thinking: Toward a Politics of Peace.* Boston: Beacon Press, 1989.

"Your (Wo)man in Washington" blog. Web. <www.WomaninWashington.org>.

26.
Empowering First-Time Mothers
The Feminist *Coping with Change* Maternal Health Promotion Program

FIONA JOY GREEN

THE WOMEN'S HEALTH CLINIC (WHC), located in downtown Winnipeg, Manitoba is a feminist, community-based health centre that offers a range of services to women from teens to elders. Understanding health to mean "a state of complete physical, mental and social well-being and not merely the absence of disease or infirmity" (WHO), the WHC promotes and advocates "the health and well-being of all women by facilitating empowerment, choice and action" (WHC, 2009). Opening in 1981, and certified through the *Canadian Council on Health Services Accreditation* in 2003, the Clinic's holistic approach emphasizes prevention, education and action, and encourages women to learn all they can about what contributes to their health and well-being so they can make informed choices.

Since 2001 the WHC has offered the innovative feminist psycho-educational *Coping with Change Program* (*CWC*) to promote maternal health and well-being through building knowledge and support for mothers, community members, and service providers regarding the emotional changes that occur after introducing a baby, whether by birth or adoption, into the lives of women and their families. *CWC* is based on the feminist philosophy that mothers are at the centre of care, and that shifts in social expectations and relational pressures are as equally important to physical changes in understanding women's transition to motherhood. *CWC* addresses the social expectations placed on new mothers and the changing nature of personal and familial relationships, rather than solely focusing on the needs of the children or the physical or biological changes many new mothers experience. Through workshops it offers a prevention model of care that integrates the practices of feminist consciousness raising and feminist praxis during the "teachable moments" when postpartum women are wondering about the normalcy of their feelings. These successful approaches mean a cognitive shift and behavioural change for participants and practitioners who come to view postpartum emotional adjustments as a continuum rather than as a singular medicalized view of postpartum depression.

I begin this chapter by explaining the philosophy, purpose and history of *CWC*, follow with a discussion of the program's activities and outcomes, along with some of the challenges it has faced and strategies it has used to deal with those obstacles, and conclude by outlining the future goals of *CWC* and the relationship of the program with the motherhood movement.

Philosophy and Purpose of *Coping with Change*

In a climate of the mother/child dyad and family support programming, where most programs for mothers focus on the child or on the physiological changes mothers may be experiencing, *CWC* offers a different perspective based on the feminist philosophy that mothers are at the centre of care, and that shifts in social expectations and relational pressures are as equally important to physical changes in understanding women's transition to motherhood. The program focuses on the needs of women by addressing the social expectations placed on new mothers and the changing nature of personal and familial relationships, rather than solely focusing on the needs of the children and on the physical or biological changes many new mothers experience.

The purpose of *CWC* is to offer a prevention model of care to new mothers by successfully integrating the practice feminist praxis—unifying knowing and doing for the purpose of making social change—during the "teachable moments" when postpartum women are wondering about the normalcy of their feelings as mothers. It also seeks to engage the feminist practice of consciousness raising, of speaking collectively to share personal awareness and experience and to find authority in that knowledge, to normalise their experiences, to encourage them to recognize and acknowledge their strengths as mothers, and to identify when their experiences may require further attention.

History

Jody Thomson, the Mothers Program Coordinator at the Women's Health Clinic, developed *CWC* from her experience working one-on-one and with a group of women who self-identified with being "postpartum depressed."[1] In the process of listening and speaking with these women, she helped them normalize their experiences, identify their strengths, and recognize when their issues could become a concern requiring more attention. In the process, Thomson recognised new mothers need support in learning how to identify personal stresses and understand how a baby can create more complex problems that require a new set of coping skills (Thomson). She created *CWC* to address these overlooked areas of maternal health by demystifying the transition to mothering and caring for a child/ren by providing mothers with honest and meaningful information about the work and realities of parenting.

Since its inception in 2001, *CWC* has worked with two specific groups: 1) pregnant and postnatal mothers, and 2) government and community service providers who work with mothers in Manitoba. Data collected from an evaluation of *CWC* that I conducted in 2007 shows that between 2001 and 2007 approximately

580 pregnant and/or postpartum women participated in the Program through 83 one-on-one support sessions, individual presentations or workshop series and that approximately 140 female service providers were also educated about *CWC* through a dozen train-the-trainer sessions, of which five were full-day sessions.[2] The goal of the five session program—which can be presented individually as part of a workshop series, or through one-on-one support—is to offer a framework that helps mothers to identify the emotional and lifestyle changes that often arise after the arrival of a baby, to normalize those changes, and to recognize when they may need more support (Thomson).[3] This approach assists mothers in understanding their new role and eases some of the stresses associated with this transition, and helps them develop tools for dealing with their needs.

Activities

CWC engages new mothers in discussions that reveal the realities, myths, silences, and emotional adjustments in the transformation process of becoming a mother. Rather than focus on the child and on the physical changes new biological mothers may experience like most other self-help programs for new mothers, *CWC* engages the feminist philosophy that places women at the centre of care, acknowledging and deconstructing the larger social norms and expectations placed on mothers, and providing coping strategies for mothers dealing with these various maternal physical, mental and social changes. The five sessions are:

- *Getting to Know You: Your Birth Experience* encourages participants to understand the relationship between their birth experience and its effects on their emotions.
- *Emotional Adjustments: What Are They?* Educates and normalizes the spectrum of emotional adjustments felt by women during the postpartum period.
- *Relationships: Adding Someone New to the Mix* explores the changes that occur in relationships after a baby arrives, looks at new ways of understanding women's needs as mothers, and how to communicate those needs effectively to others.
- *Networking: How to Break the Isolation* develops the mother's support systems by practicing how to ask for help and identifying who can be asked for help.
- *Self-care: I Am Important Too!* helps women recognize stress by understanding their critical voice and learn new coping strategies.

All sessions follow a similar structure to provide consistency of expectation and to help create a space where women can risk expressing their feelings, experiences and fears associated with mothering. Each two-hour gathering begins with the facilitator introducing herself and the topic for the day, and is followed by a facilitated check in to see how the week has been for participants and an icebreaker activity to ease folks into the session and to prepare them for further discussion around the topic. Once the moms have settled in the facilitator provides information through a verbal and/or visual presentation with handouts on the topic. Participants are encouraged to engage with the information and to share their own knowledge by participating in specific exercises to help them appreciate and reinforce what they know. Each session concludes with an informal opportunity for moms to comment on anything they may have learned from the day's session or to ask any final questions while they choose a small item for themselves, such as hand cream or bath salts, from the self-care basket that is passed around at this time. The purpose of the self-help basket is to celebrate each mother as an individual, and to reinforce the importance of taking care of herself at a time when most of her energy and attention is given to her child.

As a way of encouraging mothers to participate in and foster a meaningful experience with *CWC*, the facilitator and moms address the importance of recognizing the difficulties of mothering and speaking about their experiences of parenting. This means acknowledging that while at times it is hard to accept diverse parenting practices and attitudes, people do parent differently. Being non-judgemental is central to the leadership of *CWC* and to creating a space where participants are given equal opportunity to express themselves and to participate fully. During the first meeting the group discusses the importance of confidentiality, openness, and non-judgemental attitudes and behaviour, the merit of allowing people to express themselves without interruption, and the value of respecting the need for folks to opt out of discussion when necessary (Thomson). This discussion and an informal agreement around how the group will conduct itself helps to build a positive group dynamic and to shape a safer place for participants to talk about parenting.

Facilitators use the guided process of consciousness raising to encourage women to speak collectively about their personal experiences, to see how they are connected to larger social and political structures, and how these understandings can shape their analysis and help them develop language to make sense of themselves in relation to the world around them (Fulton). In the process, moms come to draw upon the authority of their own meaning making and together develop a language that verifies their own accounts and offers trustworthy knowledge that is a reliable basis for action.

For example, in "Getting to Know You: Your Birth Experience" mothers are encouraged to capture and express their experiences of birth through drawing while they are prompted with questions like "Were you overdue, premature, or right on time? Did you have a vaginal birth or c-section? or, Was it a long labour?" to help them understand the relationship between their birth experience and its effects on their emotions. When the drawings are complete the moms regroup to share their birth experiences and often relate them to their pictures. Through sharing their memories and listening to those of others in the group, the moms come to understand how their birthing experiences, while personal, private and individual, also take place in a social and political context rather than being limited to their own making. The recognition of not being alone in their experiences of birthing, even when other women's experiences differ somewhat from their own, provides participants with a sense of normalcy and belonging. By the end of this session, mothers begin to recognize that their experiences of birth, while unique, are also part of a larger collective experience of women that is not often candidly spoken about, nor understood. They also begin to see how they often put their own needs behind those of others and that taking care of one's self is not selfish, but rather, a loving act.

The activity of drawing/telling birth stories is essential to the facilitator-training workshop Thomson does with professionals who work with pregnant and postpartum mothers. Service providers express the importance of reconnecting with their own birth experiences and to the act of telling and being empathetic while listening to birth stories—whether birth/mothers or not—as it helps them to understand their own personal feelings or other practitioners' birth experiences and the potential feelings their clients might also experience.

A core component of all sessions is acknowledging and normalising women's feelings and showing them and their families how to recognize when those feelings could become a problem (Thomson). Rather than reinforce the common belief and rhetoric of postpartum depression so prevalent in the media and popular culture, the Program presents a radical new outlook that it is normal for new mothers to experience a variety of emotional responses in the postpartum period, and that listening to women's bodies and taking time to care for one's self is healthy and okay.

The continuum of postpartum emotional adjustments is introduced and supported by information that may include the fact, among others, that postpartum emotional reactions are among the most common complication of pregnancy and often the most unrecognized. While postpartum psychosis is the least experienced type of postpartum response, it is the image that often screams from newspaper headlines and is commonly showcased in dramatic TV shows and movies. The linear graph below used in *CWC* sessions helps explain and normalise the continuum of feelings women may experience (Thomson 2006):

←--→

Baby Blues	Psychosis
Normal	Worsening of normal

Throughout the sessions, mothers continue to identify and talk about their feelings and stressors associated within and outside of mothering along with the various available treatment options. They report being empowered in being able to identify what is normal, to make time for themselves outside of their parenting duties that assist in decreasing negative feelings often experienced postpartum, and being more aware of postpartum issues. Service providers, too, speak of the importance of these exercises in the work they do with pregnant and postpartum women and in the personal shifts they have in understanding postpartum.

Within the collective and interactive discussion groups provided, participants learn to shape language and develop analysis that is drawn on their own knowledge and in ways that make sense of themselves and others; in other words, they participate in the recurrent cycle of integrating theory (ways of understanding the world) with action (ways of speaking and acting in the world) and of also incorporating action and theory with the result of creating partial change in society (Fulton). They share information, theorizing, and language addressing postpartum responses, make sense of their own knowledge and realities, and question and resist those of society. Women's experiences of postpartum emotional adjustments are validated and normalised throughout, and mothers are introduced to the more meaningful language of postpartum emotional adjustment developed by Thomson in her ongoing work with postpartum women. The realities and knowledge of postpartum mothers become the basis for creating and using a new theory that more accurately describes the complexity and continuum of the emotional transition women undergo in the first three years of mothering.

Service providers come to a similar view of maternal experiences and health with new language that assists in creating an understanding and promotion of maternal health that moves beyond merely physical and biological ailments to one that includes social and emotional adjustments that are beyond the narrow confines of maternal bodies. As one provider notes, they come to "understand that our system is quite medical and we need to consider women's experiences" and the need to be "less quick to prescribe what the 'system' might dictate to do, and spend more time exploring the mother's statements." They spoke of needing to recognize that moms are having these thoughts and need to be asked about them to empower mothers as knowledgeable agents.

Challenges, Responses and Successes

Mothering continues to be an aspect of women's lives that is foreshadowed by erroneous societal assumptions that caring for children is innate, and if not, then at least an easily socialized skill that women possess and, therefore, doesn't require much attention or support. An initial challenge *CWC* faced was integrating their knowledge within WHC. Today, continuous training with all new staff is necessary to shift the common societal belief that "mothering is easy" as there is still work to be done to dispel this hazardous myth.

Another challenge initially confronted by *CWC* was a lack of interest from government agencies to incorporate their curriculum and approach when the agencies attempted to create policies and programs around maternal health. Again, due to the perseverance and ability to raise and address the importance of mothering and the value of a preventative approach to care for mothers by Jody Thomson and Sharon Young, the feminist approach and substantive content so fundamental to *CWC* is becoming entrenched within the curriculum and delivery of the provincial Healthy Baby Community Support Program, which is a component of *Healthy Child Manitoba*, and has a series of services for children, youth, and families. Having Young share the model of care offered by the WHC larger Mothers Program with the Canada Prenatal Nutrition Program (CPNP) advisory committee—a federal government body of Public Health Agency of Canada—and also being a key informant in the Public Health Agency of Canada (PHAC) funded research project "Beyond the Baby Blues—A Needs Assessment for tools, strategies, education resources related to antenatal depression and post partum depression among at-risk and vulnerable populations served by Community Action Program for Children (CAPC) and Canadian Prenatal Nutrition Project" has also been hugely influenced by the philosophy and practice of *CWC* and are understood and adapted into other funded programs.[4] Thomson and Young note how members of a postpartum mental health working group associated with the *Winnipeg Regional Health Authority* (WRHA), including mental health practitioners, Public Health nurse specialists, psychiatrists, and consumer based groups like *Mood Disorders of Manitoba* are hearing and using the term postpartum adjustments when addressing the realities and issues associated with postpartum women and maternal health promotion and education.

Future Goals

CWC will continue to offer its program across Winnipeg and to expand their connection with smaller communities beyond its boundaries—such as in the cities of Brandon and Steinbach—where provincially funded and run programs have fully adopted *CWC*. The freestanding midwife led Birth Centre expected to open in Winnipeg in May, 2011 is going to offer a "full range of services throughout pregnancy, childbirth, postpartum and early parenting" (CBC). *CWC* anticipates training participants involved in the centre's new midwifery and birthing programs to ensure a feminist and preventative model of care is provided.

CWC also expects to continue to participate on committees and in decision-making meetings around policy development, implementation and delivery models and practices of care for mothers. Before taking a medical leave from *CWC*, Thomson developed two new *CWC* programs that address prenatal care and teen mothering and are currently offering community workshops to newcomer groups to Winnipeg. The Province of Manitoba is lacking in these areas, with the WRHA, for example, offering prenatal programs without any evaluative procedure or data collecting mechanism to measure the effectiveness of the content or delivery of their programming. At the time of this writing, Thomson is expected to soon return within weeks to her position as Team Leader of the Mothers Program and expects to launch these two much needed programs through WHC and to influence the WRHA policies and programs.

Relation to Motherhood Movement

Coping with Change is essential to the motherhood movement. The feminist and mother-centered philosophy and practice developed in and used by *CWC* is the foundation of the entire model of the larger Mothers Program at Women's Health Clinic, which offers two additional programs to assist mothers. Sherpa Mothers is "a peer support program that offers women who are pregnant and/or have children under the age of one an opportunity to be matched with a trained volunteer for guidance and support through the changes mothering brings," while Families Connecting is a Healthy Baby Community Support Program designed to assist soon-to-be and new parents to connect with health service providers and other parents with children in their communities" (WHC). Through its individual, outreach and group programs, and its role in influencing mothers, government policy, program development, and educating service providers who work daily with mothers, *CWC* provides a powerful model of empowered mothering and an alternative script and praxis for motherhood.

Understanding the complexities of maternal health and the transition to motherhood simultaneously empowers mothers and disrupts and offers an alternative theory to the erroneous, dangerous and medicalized label of postpartum depression. The feminist concept postpartum emotional adjustments coined by Jody Thomson, actively used by mothers, service providers, and government agencies validates the authority and knowledge of postpartum women, and displaces the previously used mainstream concept of postpartum depression that pathologies women with language that articulates the authority of women's postpartum experiences and knowledge. Mothers, practitioners and policy makers are empowered to actively demystify the myths around postpartum expectations, experiences and responses as they learn about and honour the continuum of feelings normally associated with childbirth and mothering children.

I want to acknowledge and thank the support and input of Jody Thomson and Sharon Young of CWC in this project.

[1]The Mothers Program includes a variety of supports for mothers, including Families Connecting Support Groups, the Sherpa Mothers Program, and the Coping with Change Program. For more information, visit <http://www.womenshealthclinic.org/counselling/>.

[2]The following information is taken from an evaluation I conducted in 2007 that consisted of separate interviews with Jody Thomson, creator of *Coping with Change*, three service providers, and a mothers' focus group of three. All participants in the interviews were self-selected from contacts provided by the Program. The evaluation also included an extensive review and analysis of written evaluations from all of the mothers who had taken *Coping with Change* program and all of the service providers who had taken train-the-trainer workshops between 2001 and 2007. Detailed demographic information about the participants was not collected and, thus, is not available. Questionnaires given to mothers asked them to evaluate what they liked, didn't like, learned and wanted more of from the sessions, while practitioners were asked to evaluate if and how the sessions helped them change

their thinking, feelings and actions, as well as what was most helpful in the session and what could be improved upon. Most participants were lower- and middle- class mothers in their first year after birth, although pregnant women and women past their first year of parenting also participated in *Coping with Change*. They may have been members of various Winnipeg 'Y' Neighbour groups, participants in Healthy Baby Programs sponsored by the Provincial Government of Manitoba, residents at a local prenatal and postnatal residence offering a wide variety of programs for mostly First Nations single, pregnant women or new mothers, or members of teen groups, family centers, and other community mothers' groups. If the session was conducted in partnership with an existing program, child minding for the children of participants was determined by the policy of that program. When offered by *Coping with Change,* only babies were welcome due to lack of funding to provide care for older children. Train-the-trainer participants included local and rural public health nurses, midwives, *Family First* home visitors, *Healthy Baby* group facilitators, *Healthy Start for Mom and Me* facilitators, mental health practitioners, social workers and psychologists.

[3]For more detailed information about *Coping with Change*, see Green, 2009.

[4]The Canada Prenatal Nutrition Program (CPNP) provides long-term funding to community groups to develop or enhance programs for vulnerable pregnant women and aims to reduce the incidence of unhealthy birth weights, improve the health of both infant and mother and encourage breastfeeding. CPNP enhances access to services and strengthens intersectional collaboration to support the needs of at-risk pregnant women offering services of food supplementation, nutritional counseling, support, education, referral and counseling on health and lifestyle issues. Announced in 1994 by the Government of Canada, CPNP was one of the programs promised in Creating Opportunity and is developed and delivered in partnership with the provinces and territories through joint management agreements and with First Nations and Inuit communities.

Works Cited

"Birthing and Mothering Support." Women's Health Clinic. Web. <http://www.womenshealthclinic.org/counselling/>. Accessed: 09/18/2010

Canada Prenatal Nutrition Program (CPNP). Public Health Agency of Canada. Web. <http://www.phac-aspc.gc.ca/dca-dea/programs-mes/cpnp_main-eng.php>. Accessed: 9/18/2010.

CBC News. "Birth Centre to be built in Winnipeg." Web. <http://www.cbc.ca/canada/manitoba/story/2010/01/21/mb-birth-centre-winnipeg.html#ixzz0zoyUDMV>. Accessed: 09/17/2010.

Fulton, K. L. 2001. "Living Strategically: the Praxis of Feminist Professing." *Feminist Strategies Féministes: An Interactive Feminist Scholarly Journal/Une revue savante féministe interactive.* Web. <http://unb.ca/PAR-L/strategies/Fulton.htm>. Accessed: 25/2/2009.

Green, F. J. "Coping with Change: Integrating Feminist Praxis with Maternal

Health Promotion and Education." *Journal of the Association for Research on Mothering* 11.1 (2009): 11-25.

Healthy Child Manitoba. Web. <http://www.gov.mb.ca/healthychild/>. Accessed: 09/18/2010.

Public Health Agency of Canada. Government of Canada. "Helping mothers Deal with Maternal Depression." Web. <http://www.phac-aspc.gc.ca/media/nr-rp/2010/2010_0126-eng.php>.

Thomson, J. *Coping with Change: A Facilitator's Guide*. Women's Health Clinic. Winnipeg, Manitoba, 2006.

Women's Health Clinic (WHC). "Our Mission Statement" on the "Who We Are." Women's Health Clinic. 2009. Web. <Clinic webpage. http://www.women-shealthclinic.org/Public/about.html>. Accessed: 25/2/2009.

Women's Health Clinic (WHC). "Birthing and Mothering Support." 2010. Web. <http://www.womenshealthclinic.org/birthingmothering>.

World Health Organization (WHO). Preamble to the Constitution of the World Health Organization as adopted by the International Health conference, New York, 19-22 June, 1946; signed on 22 July 1946 by the representatives of 61 States (Official Records of the World Health Organization, no. 2, p. 100) and entered into force on 7 April 1948. Web. <http://www.who.int/about/definition/en/print.html>. Accessed: 25/2/2009.

27.
Honouring Our Grandmothers' Spirits

Warriors Against Violence Society

DONNA LESTER-SMITH AND JOYCE FOSSELLA

> *We are faced with so many things, violence, drugs, alcohol. So we're going back to our culture, to the old ways; taking our children back into the longhouse, taking them into the sweat lodge ... It's coming back strong. The cycle of healing. We're healing a lot of people of the suffering when they went to [residential] school.... Their cycle is coming back. They're giving themselves back to the Great Spirit. It is good to sit with an elder. It is good medicine for us.*
>
> —Verna Kirkness (173)

IN 1997, CHANGE OF SEASONS, AN Aboriginal[1] men's anger counselling organization was forced to close its doors because of injurious government funding cuts. Despite this fiscal setback, two group members recognized that funding shortfalls did not negate the necessity for Aboriginal cultural practices to heal family violence. In 1998, Joe Fossella Sr. (*Sechelt* and *Hawaiian Nations*) and Daniel Parker (*Burrard, Squamish, Hawaiian* and *Chilean Nations*) founded the current community organization, Warriors against Violence Society (WAVS) (pronounced "waves"). Soon after WAVS first opened their doors to assist men wanting to change their behaviours, their partners counselled the WAVS facilitators for their mistaken exclusion: women asked, how can we heal our families when men and women are segregated from one another in our healing process? The women spoke, and WAVS listened—Co-author Joyce Fossella (*Lil'wat Nation*) and Gail Parker (*Blackfoot* and *Chippewa Nations*) became co-facilitators alongside their husbands. Currently, the counsellor-trained facilitators provide three consecutively run 28-week socio-educational sessions a year; co-ed group sessions are held on Monday evenings while men and women gather separately to support one another on Thursday evenings.

We, as authors, acknowledge that some of our readers might question this gender-inclusive decision; however, as will be woven throughout this chapter, WAVS' primarily urban Aboriginal participants require a worldview different from mainstream ways of healing. The essence of the Indigenous worldviews from which we seek meaning of our worlds is not only a commonality between diverse Indigenous peoples: it is also of timeless value. Indigenous worldviews include contemporary balanced and harmonious health and Ancestral guidance towards our well-being. Indigenous worldviews have existed since time immemorial (Archibald; Cajeté; Castellano; Cole; Graham). Health worldviews, in particular, are relevant to and effective in Aboriginal communities because they honour the diversity, concerns, and suggestions of all Aboriginal peoples, even the most silent and marginalized of voices. Gregory Cajeté (2000) reminds us that being torn between "different ways of living and looking at life is a place of great confusion, but it can also be a place of great compassion and clarity" (189). Indeed, Indigenous peoples continue to contextualize gender tensions. For instance, on the one hand, *Cowichan Indian Tribes* Elder, Sarah Modeste, describes her perceptions as a result of the violence she endured throughout her life. "If I didn't have my training that my Elders gave me I wouldn't be living.... It's really horrible to be, to be a woman. You're a nurturer of life, you're a nurturer for your family—and then someone does that to you." On the other hand, Sarah has also implored co-author, Donna to "not forget our men. They, too, have experienced violence as a result of unhealthy Western influences" (Personal communication, 2006).

We have subdivided our chapter into the following categories, as noted in italics. Our subsections are not exclusive of one another; rather, they offer a culturally-specific layering of WAVS. Further, for the purposes of this chapter, we use "WAVS" as an inclusive acronym referring to the agency, its co-founders, co-facilitators, members, and cultural wellness/intervention model. *Western Theories and Intervention Practices of Family Violence* are prolific throughout our dominant societal notions of health, healing, and well-being. This is a given. Nevertheless, we do not position *Indigenous Theories of Family Violence and Intervention Practices* as completely adversarial to Western ways; rather, Warriors Against Violence Society is indexical of a more culturally appropriate fusion of these two health paradigms. Joe Fossella has reminded us, "It is a good thing to learn Western ways too, so that when we also know Indigenous knowledge, we can be stronger in both" (personal communication, October 2, 2009). The WAVS' *Philosophy* seeks to ensure that violence and abuse are not recycled to future generations. The Indigenous methodological approach of *Healing through Aboriginal Storytelling* offers a fresh vantage point that encompasses the hearts and minds of many First Nation peoples. We intuit that *Aboriginal Motherhood and Ways of Being* include a wealth of personal perspectives about the relationships between intergenerational motherhood and the WAVS organization. Yet, despite the motherhood movement—inclusive of multiple ethnicities—present-day ideological and fiscal *Concerns* for WAVS remain embedded in misperceptions of race, class, gender, and ultimately, power. Although the *Significance of WAVS* seems universal—an outcry to end violence primarily perpetrated against all women and children based on respectful and relevant ethnicity standards—is, more than ever, vital to the richness of diverse worldviews in which we live. In *Closing*, we bring paradoxical attention to the fact that Indigenous knowledges, since time immemorial, follow cyclical patterns of nature, of healing, and of wellness, rather than Western ones of linearism.

Western Theories and Intervention Practices of Family Violence

Western views of our world, women, and Aboriginal women in particular, are often intricately embedded in racial discourses (Smith). Western philosophies of superiority over Canada's First Nation peoples can best be understood in the historical context of government mandated residential schooling for most Aboriginal children in Canada between the 1840s and the 1990s. These institutions, begun by mostly Roman Catholic and Anglican missionaries, were later institutionalized by *The Indian Act* of 1876, which sanctioned Canadian government personnel (Ministry of Indian Affairs) to remove Aboriginal children from their homes and be placed in residential schools (Battiste; Chrisjohn, Young, and Marun; Lester-Smith; Vedan). *The Indian Act* was enacted in 1876 by the Parliament of Canada under the *Constitution Act*, 1867, which provides Canada's federal government exclusive authority over First Nation peoples living on land reserves. Shawn Wilson states, the Act is "a form of dysfunction that's been institutionalized for Aboriginal people" (103). Residential schools have impacted a multitude of social determinants facing Aboriginal peoples today, such as control, power, basic safety, traditional ways of knowing and being, and dominant attitudes of racism and oppression (Farmer). Mason Durie asserts, "The results of colonization were consistently cataclysmic. A common pattern emerged: loss of culture, loss of land, loss of voice, loss of population, loss of dignity, loss of health, and wellbeing" (1138).

Present reality dictates that extreme numbers of Aboriginal peoples and their wellness paths remain marred in family violence primarily because of cultural loss. As many as eight out of ten Aboriginal women have experienced violence, both within their own communities and in the greater society. Rates for partner/spousal abuse are significantly higher among Aboriginal women than Aboriginal men, and among non-Aboriginal peoples (RCAP; Statistics Canada). Contemporary notions of violence against women can be traced back to the Roman Empire, c. 700 B.C., whereby wives were considered chattel—akin to cattle livestock—owned and governed by their husbands (Lemon). Under Roman Laws of Chastisement, women had little control over their lives; male authority was not to be challenged (Heinemann; Lemon; Martin).

Contemporarily, Correctional Services Canada (CSC) has become a somewhat negative icon for historically-based, patriarchal-driven policies. We acknowledge our pivotal unease with such standards for good reason—approximately 40 percent of men *and women* who attend WAVS have been previously incarcerated or are presently mandated to attend by federal and provincial court systems, parole officers, and the Ministry of Children and Family Development. CSC's governing mandate is to oversee and punitively house societal offenders, particularly Aboriginal men and women who are incarcerated at rates much higher than the non-Aboriginal peoples (Department of Justice Canada). For example, "In

Lil'wat Elder Flora Wallace (1925–2005), Joyce Fossella's mother

2003/04 Aboriginal people made up 19.8 percent of the BC prison population) and "in 2004/05, 38 percent of youth in custody were Aboriginal and 14 percent were female" (Gray1). It is because of these disconcerting reports that WAVS' framework of healing becomes vital for many Aboriginal peoples.

Indigenous Theories of Family Violence and Intervention Practices

The 2003 report by Michael and Judie Bopp and Phil Lane, Jr., *Family Violence in Aboriginal Communities*, confirms colonial and current social perceptions and experiences as key contributors to the rising rates of family violence. The importance of addressing historical theories and reasons for the inequality in health among Aboriginal and non-Aboriginal populations cannot be understated. Scholars like Marie Battiste, Yvonne Boyer, Marlene Castellano, and Madeleine Dion Stout continue to question—*why*—and continue to seek prioritizing answers. Yes, other agencies throughout Vancouver also assist families wrought with violence. But, at this time, only WAVS provides the traditional tools and ways of knowing specific to many urban Aboriginal peoples' primary needs for traditional teachings and culturally-relevant ways of healing (McCaleb; Vancouver Status of Women Resource Guide).

Efforts to address such disparities include explorations by Honore France and Rod McCormick, who began a counselling program. The Helping Circle model was designed as a culturally-relevant approach to Aboriginal peoples by combining a number of traditional cultural methods such as the Medicine Wheel, legends, and nature with current non-Aboriginal counselling practices. The Medicine Wheel is often used as a traditional and/or symbolic model to guide people toward harmonious well-being, symbolically indicative of a relationship with and between individuals and the four elements and seasons of nature, the four races, and the four dimensions of the individual: the physical, emotional, social, and intellectual (Castellano; Graveline; Loiselle and McKenzie; Turton; WAVS). Similarly, Loring Jones explores the complexities of family violence in many First Nation communities and its association with a number of co-morbid problems (i.e., genocide, racism, forcible expulsion from ancestral lands, and removal of children from Indian homes). Within mainstream healthcare system, policies and practices are often culturally ineffective for Aboriginal peoples; Aboriginal health-knowledges and ways of being are frequently pushed aside with disbelief and/or disdain. Bridging the chasm between Western knowledge and Indigenous ancestral/contemporary knowledge is crucial for today's Aboriginal peoples to prevent and/or to heal from family violence for generations to come.

Warriors Against Violence Society

WAVS has been providing services to urban Aboriginal peoples of Vancouver, BC, since 1998. The agency is a rarity in Canada, in that it innovatively brings together men, women, and youth with trained facilitators to emphasize and impart cultural teachings, thus helping participants to interpret the reasons they find themselves engaging in oppressive and violent behaviours. The agency's unique mandate is culturally-based, operating on the core belief that healing and wellness are best achieved by acquisition and restoration of traditional Aboriginal customs and approaches. Two recurring themes within WAVS are: 1) Understanding the legacy of shame and violence from generations of colonization, and, 2) Understanding the positive effects of wholistically bringing together culture, tradition, and ceremony as effective components of healing from family violence (Aboriginal Healing Foundation; Archibald et al.; Benoit, Carroll, and Chaudhry; Legacy of Hope Foundation).

WAVS Philosophy

WAVS demonstrates an understanding of oppressively-rooted anger, along with wholeness, completeness, and wellness within their intervention model of healing from, and ending, family violence. As Dan Parker, Co-founder of WAVS, highlights:

> *I just wanted to understand. If someone had told me why I was picked on in the school yard, what that was all about, then maybe I would not have been so angry* [throughout my life]. (Personal communication, Oct. 2nd, 2009)

WAVS introduces a number of *best practices* to address Parker's inquiry, such as personal ownership of the violence that each offender does to another person; building on personal strengths; pragmatically sharing their comprehensive familial experiences; traditional humility; cultural teachings; and, engaging members' voices by heartfelt demonstrations of trust, confidentiality, listening, understanding, and Aboriginal storytelling. Likewise, by focusing on the sharing/learning traditions of group-meeting sharing circles, participants learn ways to heal traditionally, contemporarily, and wholistically. In traditional sharing circles, a sacred eagle feather or an Aboriginal carved "talking stick" is passed around the circle. The person holding the sacred item is the only speaker at the time, while all others respectfully listen and remain silent until their turn to speak. Circle participation, when done respectfully, reflects the basic traditional and philosophical worldview of Aboriginal peoples regardless of whether it is done from a healing perspective, a learning/teaching approach to harmonious well-being.

The agency's intervention model rests on the cornerstone that traditional healing practices are paramount to a strong sense of health and wellness. Many Aboriginal peoples believe that First Nation peoples are all spiritually connected in health dis-ease and in health wellness (Archibald; Holmes; Little Bear). Culturally-relevant health practices may include belief in the symbolic "Medicine Wheel" teachings inclusive of the four health realms: physical, spiritual, intellectual, and emotional aspects of our well-being. Medicine Wheels can be important methods for "looking after ourselves in a well-balanced way and [that] the rewards can be achieved by doing this [i.e., compassion, respect, acceptance, pride, strength, kindness, firmness]" (WAVS 51). Other significant health practices include sacred ceremonies (i.e. sweat lodges, burning and smudging, and ceremonial brushings); sacred healing herbs (i.e., sweetgrass, sage, cedar, tobacco, and juniper); and Aboriginal-based counselling.

Re/learning ways of being rests on a theoretical cornerstone; traditional healing practices are paramount to a strong sense of health and wellness for many Aboriginal Peoples. Family Violence, both directly and indirectly, affects our Elders, mothers, fathers, brothers, and sisters. For many First Nation peoples, healing from violence is complex; traditional and contemporary Indigenous ways of healing include awareness and honour of life with respect for self, others, and environment by living in physical, emotional, intellectual, and spiritual balance. Bridging the gap between Ancestral wisdom fused with present-day healing practices remains vital for urban Aboriginal peoples. One such philosophical approach is Aboriginal storytelling.

Healing Through Aboriginal Storytelling

Lewis Mehl-Madrona integrates storytelling into his medical practice to enhance healing. His belief is that hearing stories of healing told by a peer is intrinsic to healing; it enables a person to imagine his/her own healing. Jo-ann Archibald believes that stories and the work they do have distinct shapes, but when combined to create meaning, they are transformed into new, (healthier) designs. She considers Aboriginal stories as multiple threads of cedar bark used to weave a basket together. Cheryl Turton suggests, "Stories from the oral tradition, also called myths or legends, provide valuable insight into the cognitive orientation, or health-world view, guiding the health beliefs of Aboriginal peoples" (2). Yet, another significant way of storytelling is through song. Joyce explains: There became a time of revitalization for the musical members in our *Lil'wat* family, strongly encouraged by our parents. Songs became a vital connection of traditional well-being for my family.

The transformative power of Aboriginal storytelling is also evident in the WAVS violence intervention model, whereby facilitators and participants alike share their past soul-wounds in order to heal their present-day health struggles toward their future well-being. Participants confirm that hearing the personal stories of the facilitators, who have healed from family violence themselves, offers inspiration and hope that members, too, can make positive changes in their lives. As underscored throughout our written composite, here, Joyce and I believe that motherhood resonates throughout Warriors Against Violence Society.

Aboriginal Motherhood: Our Ways of Being

As First Nation daughters, granddaughters, great granddaughters, aunts, mothers, grandmothers, and great-grandmothers, we understand the importance and the significance of our motherhood roles. Our matriarchal predecessors had to be strong, powerful women. Although both of us did not personally meet our great grandmothers, we did know our grandmothers. In *Stl'atl'imx*, Joyce refers to her grandmothers as *kwe'kwa7* (pronounced Kuka), while Donna's maternal grandmothers are known as *Kokum* in *Michif*, a blend of Cree and French Métis. Joyce's mom knew the language well enough to have carried it in her and with her so that she, as a mother, a grandmother, and an Elder, could bring it to her family and community.

Our *Kukas* and *Kokums* learned from their grandmothers and mothers, generational knowledge meant to be passed down to us. Joyce shares: they modeled for us, values that, past and presently, honour our traditions, respect others and Nature around us, excellent work ethics, self-sufficiency, dignity, and pride. We were expected to learn, through our grandmothers' living experiences and teachings, respect for others. It was a way of life for everyone to respect our Elders, guests in the home or in the community, and to never point fingers at others or make fun of anyone for any reason. As well, we learned to listen to the person speaking, and only then, speak when it was appropriate, and in a respectful manner. Our maternal ancestors honoured our traditions by speaking our first language, *Stl'atl'imx*, despite *The Indian Act* (1876) laws forbidding the use of any Aboriginal languages in Canada.

About our collective familial traditions, we offer this pointed exemplar: Duncan Scott, head of the Department of Indian Affairs between 1913 and 1932, makes transparent his goals of power over First Nation peoples: "Our object is to continue until there is not a single Indian in Canada that has not been absorbed into the body politic, and there is no Indian question and no Indian department" (cited in Jamieson 50). Despite such barriers to honouring our maternal Ancestral ways, our grandmothers continuously taught our tradition, our language, and in my family, our revitalization of cultural song and dance. Joyce continues: "they also passed on their knowledge of traditional medicines, foods, and their preparations. These teachings are valuable and necessary for survival of our people. Every spring and summer, it was necessary that we pick berries, roots, and medicines and also fish and hunt to prepare for the winter when food would be scarce. Our parents and Elders would dry the fish and meat by the wind or smoke them over fires. If our peoples did not prepare for the winter months, we could starve or get sick. Stored foods sustained our families until the snow and ice melted, when they would begin this cycle once again. We were taught to always do our best at any job. My family's music talents brought back memories to build upon, to be shared, and to encourage creativity. Mom taught our family to *never be stingy with your culture, your talent. Always share it, pass it on*. My Dad had strong values about his children getting an education. He believed that, because our family had talents, we had a responsibility to respectfully share them with other people. As a musician who played in the Mt. Currie Band, our dad loved to listen to us and to attend all of our performances. As a family, we always said to him, "We thank you for being the provider you are."

In the implicit and explicit seemingly *competition* between the better of two worldviews, Indigenous and Western knowledges and appreciation of our Elder family members can, indeed, be at their best when a fusion of the two becomes deeply re/rooted, understood, and practiced. Presently, however, our collective knowledges reveal that accountability for health policy-making for the benefit of urban Aboriginal peoples has yet to be found. Prevailing wisdoms still do not encapsulate culturally-reverent, traditional ones as best they could.

Concerns

Community agencies such as BC Corrections Branch, Correctional Services Canada (CSC), Ministry of Children and Family Development, Vancouver, Aboriginal Children and Family Services Society, and Vancouver Transformative Justice Services, all refer both men and women to WAVS. In other words, multiple communal, provincial, and national bodies remain fully aware of the transformative healing that WAVS offers; likewise, funding policies continue to insist on a segregation model of healing from family violence. They typically insist on colonially insolating Aboriginal family members from one another, as the far-reaching *Indian Act* of *1876* still dictates, as indirectly evidenced in this email note between Joyce and Bruce Wood, founder of Change of Seasons, the closed program from which WAVS was born.

> *Joyce:* Hi Bruce, I was wondering if you know about funding for men's programs. I haven't applied for any such funding because I have not come across that opportunity,
>
> *Bruce:* I do not know of any designated funding sources (private or public) for men's programming outside of Quebec. Some people suggest (sarcastically) that corrections money is "men's programming" which I find insulting. The paradox here is that progressive organizations [inclusive of men] across Canada have no access to funds and refuse to compete with women and children's programs for limited generic funding opportunities. But "fathers' rights" and other organizations have successfully competed for and won funding for so called *grief work* with men. Victoria and Nanaimo have examples of such programs for men. Their funding came at the expense of women's shelters and children's counselling programs. Quebec is a much better place with more progressive funding models for men and women's work. (Fossella and Wood, Personal communication, August 23, 2010)

Patriarchal attitudes continue to pervade Aboriginal health politics and healing leadership. Wood aptly confirms that government funding bodies, primarily dedicated to women and children, have yet to fully understand that traditional Indigenous healing practices are inclusive of the entire family unit, rather than exclusionary.

Other vital costs that WAVS must absorb include child-minding for attending members, and food. Food is traditionally served at the beginning of each meeting for upwards of 30 participants and 10 children, who arrive hungry and appreciative that they can have a substantial meal each group-night. Beyond these costs, funding for organizational capacity is also severely limited. For example, much of Joyce's executive director workload is on her own volunteered time. In order to keep the organization in good standing, someone has to focus on organizational management—someone has to manage behind the scenes. Programs can only continue if the organization is operating, and without the organization, we cannot continue with the programs. The agency struggles with minimal funding to meaningfully support as many participant-needs as possible.

Significance of WAVS

Participants learn to honour their spirits by loving themselves and by accepting and practicing traditional teachings in a culturally-sensitive, contemporary environment. They learn to respect others and to learn from their mistakes. Most participants gain pride about the color of their skin; knowledge about their culture and familial histories; and, self-esteem, despite past and present colonial oppression. As Knowledge Keeper Joe Fossella reiterates, "Most [WAVS clients] are stuck and say 'I am just from Vancouver,' but at the end of the 28 sessions they are able to identify who they are and where they come from, and love themselves for who they are as well" (WAVS program summary DVD, 2000). Once they learn to balance their healthy selves, they can discover how to make positive changes that foster a better quality of life for their families. In time, some participants begin contributing to their community in positive ways through volunteer work, employment, and participation in community events and gatherings. As Aboriginal, Métis, and Inuit peoples, our Ancestral teachings display women's nurturing, caring, and compassionate natures, and why our men need to be equally honoured as an integral part of the wholistic family unit. Our grandmothers' teachings were once shared with their children, who, in turn, would pass the knowledge onto future generations. Generations of First Nation peoples have learned that survival takes work—and the reward—is life.

Closing Thoughts

A written chapter such as ours, which attempts to follow standard beginning-middle-end storied templates, may wrestle with ideological tensions. Nevertheless, we accept this challenge with honour and gratefulness for the opportunity to share WAVS' cyclical natures of past, present, and future aims, such as: establishing social connections and ways of being; learning from role models (i.e. Elders, mentors, educators, and traditional teachers); anchoring oneself in tradition (i.e. Elder guidance, beliefs, arts, music, and dance); and, seeking both Indigenous and non-Indigenous support from one another.

Numerous WAVS participants believe the provided intervention model is essential to their healing, as some of their testimonies, below, reveal. When asked what they learned from the program through anonymous mid and final-session evaluations, some wrote,

> *That everyone gets angry and has deep issues that stem from childhood, that we can learn positive alternatives to deal with anger.*
>
> *Better relationships with mate, children, grandchildren, and people in general.*
>
> *This group is here to support me. We have similar stories. The energy at home has changed. My kids come with me more because they know I won't explode.*
>
> *My family used to refer to me as "'the dark cloud." The support I have received from this group has enabled me to be more supportive to my family and loving.*
>
> *It's given me the necessary tools to improve my home life and helped me to grow spiritually.*
>
> *Ask, not hit.*

As apparent in the above healing considerations, both WAVS—an Aboriginal community health agency—and we, as authors, believe the most effective way of confronting violent attitudes and behaviours is through culturally-sensitive, socio-personal group "storywork" (a term coined by Archibald). Much of the anger that participants express is directly or indirectly linked to a profound loss of culture. Urban-living Aboriginal men, women, and youth express that they do not know how to speak their native languages, are not aware of their traditions, and often feel displaced in mainstream society. Since our youth are our future societal leaders and health policy-makers, more than ever, it is crucial that we best understand and articulate the wholistic traditional practices of a community-based agency such as Warriors Against Violence Society.

> *A warrior is finding that strength to bring back our traditions.*
> —WAVS Participant, March 30, 2010

[1]The *Constitution Act* Section 35 (2), 1982 and the Royal Commission on Aboriginal Peoples (RCAP) use the term "Aboriginal" to refer inclusively to Aboriginal, Inuit, and Métis peoples. We interchangeably use the terms Aboriginal, First Nation, and Indigenous. Where appropriate, we also use the term Indigenous as inclusive of First Peoples globally, and the many similar/diverse issues they face such as colonization, language revitalization, maintenance of Indigenous Knowledge Systems, land-based and cultural rights, and, individual, family, and community health and well-being. Further, We pluralized the term people (i.e. peoples) as respect towards the diversities of Aboriginal peoples' living in Canada today, who are "culturally, historically, linguistically, and socially diverse" (National Aboriginal Health Organization: 4).

Works Cited

Aboriginal Healing Foundation. "Where are The Children? Healing the Legacy of Residential Schools." 2011.Web. <http://www.wherearethechildren.ca/en>.

Archibald, J. *Indigenous Storywork: Educating the Heart, Mind, Body, and Spirit.* Vancouver: University of British Columbia Press, 2008.

Archibald, J., E. Jovel, R. McCormick, R. Vedan and D. Thira. "Creating Transformative Aboriginal Health Research: The BC ACADRE at Three Years." *Canadian Journal of Native Education* 29.1 (2006): 4.

Battiste, M. *Reclaiming Indigenous Voice and Vision.* Washington: University of Washington Press, 2000.

Benoit, C., D. Carroll, and M. Chaudhry. "In Search of a Healing Place: Aboriginal Women in Vancouver's Downtown Eastside." *Social Science and Medicine* 56.4 (2003): 821-33.

Bopp, M., J. Bopp and P. Lane. *Aboriginal Domestic Violence in Canada.* Ottawa: The Aboriginal Healing Foundation, 2003.

Boyer, Y. "Aboriginal Health: A Constitutional Rights Analysis." *Discussion Paper Series No. 1, Aboriginal Health: Legal Issues.* Saskatoon: National Aboriginal Health Organization and the Native Law Centre of Canada, 2003.

Cajeté, G. *Look to the Mountain: An Ecology of Indigenous Education.* Dorango, CO: Kivaki Press, 1994.

Campbell, J. C. "Health Consequences of Intimate Partner Violence." *The Lancet* 359.9314 (2002): 1331-6.

Canadian Constitution. *Constitution Act.* 1982. Web. <http://www.bloorstreet.com/200block/sconst82.htm>.

Castellano, M. B. "Ethics of Aboriginal Research." 2004. Web. <http://www.indigenous.ca/docs/ethics percent20of percent20aboriginal percent20research.pdf>.

Chrisjohn, R., S. Young and M. Marun. *The Circle Game: Shadows and Substance in the Indian Residential School Experience in Canada.* Penticton, BC: Theytus Books, 2006.

Cole, P. *Coyote and Raven Go Canoeing: Coming Home to the Village.* Montreal: McGill-Queen's University Press, 2006.

Department of Justice Canada. 2011. Web. <http://www.justice.gc.ca/eng/>.

Dion Stout, M. *Knowledge Exchange: Successful Approaches for the Prevention of Aboriginal Family Violence, Final Report.* Workshop in Gatineau, Quebec: Public Health Agency of Canada's Family Violence Prevention Unit. 2009. <http://www.awotaan.org/downloads/Aboriginal_FV_Workshop_Final_Report.pdf>.

Durie, M. "Understanding Health and Illness: Research at the Interface between Science and Indigenous Knowledge." *International Journal of Epidemiology* 33.5 (2004): 1138-43.

France, M. H. and R. McCormick. "The Helping Circle: Theoretical and Practical Considerations of Using a First Nations Peer Support Network." *Guidance and Counselling* 12.2 (1997): 27-31.

Gray, L. *Inventory of Aboriginal Services: Issues and Initiatives in Vancouver Justice.* 2011. Web. <http://vancouver.ca/COMMSVCS/SOCIALPLANNING/initiatives/aboriginal/tools/directory/pdf/AboriginalDirectory-Complete.pdf>.

Graveline, F. J. *Circle Works: Transforming Eurocentric Consciousness.* Halifax, NS: Fernwood Publishing, 1998.

Health Canada. *Canada Health Act Annual Report.* 2006. Web. <http://www.hc-sc.gc.ca/hcs-sss/alt_formats/hpb-dgps/pdf/pubs/chaar-ralcs-0506/chaar-ralcs-0506-eng.pdf>.

Holmes, L. "Heart Knowledge, Blood Memory, and the Voice of the Land: Implications of Research Among Hawaiian Elders." *Indigenous Knowledges in Global Contexts: Multiple Readings of our World.* Ed. G. B. S. Dei, B. Hall, and D. Goldin Rosenberg. Toronto: University of Toronto Press, 2000. 37–53.

The Indian Act. Library of Parliament. 2009. Web. <http://dsp-psd.pwgsc.gc.ca/collection_2009/bdp-lop/prb/prb0912-e.pdf>.

Jamieson, K. *Indian Women and the Law in Canada: Citizens Minus.* Ottawa: Advisory Council on the Status of Women, 1978.

Jones, L. "The Distinctive Characteristics and Needs of Domestic Violence

Victims in a Native American Community." *Journal of Family Violence* 23.2 (2008): 113-8.

Kirkness, V. J. *First Nations and Schools: Triumphs and Struggles.* Toronto, Ontario: Canadian Education Association, 1992.

Legacy of Hope Foundation. Web. <http://www.legacyofhope.ca> 2010.

Heinemann, S. *Timelines of American Women's History.* New York: A Roundtable Press Book/Perigee Book. 1996.

Lemon, N. K. D. *Domestic Violence Law: A Comprehensive Overview of Cases and Sources.* San Francisco: Austin and Winfield Publishers, 1996.

Lester-Smith [neé Hill], D. M. *Aboriginal Women Living with HIV: An Empowerment Perspective.* Master of Arts, University of British Columbia-Okanagan, 2008.

Little Bear, L. "Jagged Worldviews Colliding." *Reclaiming Indigenous Voice and Vision.* Ed. M. Battiste. Vancouver, BC: University of British Columbia Press, 2000. 77-85.

Loiselle, M., and L. McKenzie. "The Wellness Wheel: An Aboriginal Contribution to Social Work." Paper presented at the First North-American Conference on Spirituality and Social Work, University of Waterloo, Ontario, 2006.

Marsden, D. "Creating and Sustaining Positive Paths to Health by Restoring Traditional-Based Indigenous Health-Education Practices." *Canadian Journal of Native Education* 29.1 (2006): 135-45.

Martin, D. *Battered Wives.* New York: Pocket Books. 1976.

McCaleb, J. L. "Story Medicine." *English Journal* 93.1 (2003): 66-72.

Mehl-Madrona, L. *Coyote Wisdom: The Power of Story in Healing.* Vermont: Bear and Company, 2005.

Modeste, S. "Title Unknown." *Hidden From History: The Canadian Holocaust–The Untold Story of the Genocide of Aboriginal Peoples.* 2011. Web. <www.hiddenfromhistory.org/VoicesoftheCanadianHolocaust/tabid/57/Default.aspx>.

National Aboriginal Health Organization. *An Overview of Traditional Knowledge and Medicine and Public Health in Canada.* Ottawa: Author, 2008.

Public Health Association of BC. *Responding to Health Inequalities: The Role of Public Health.* Vancouver, BC: Paetzold Health Education Centre, 2008.

Royal Commissions on Aboriginal Peoples (RCAP). Volume 1: Looking Forward, Looking Back. Ottawa, Canada: Author, 1996.

Smith, L. T. *Decolonizing Methodologies: Research and Indigenous Peoples.* London: Zed Books, 1999.

Turton, C. L. "Ways of Knowing about Health: An Aboriginal Perspective." *Advances in Nursing Science* 19.3 (1997): 28-36.

Vancouver Status of Women. *History in our Faces on Occupied Land: A Race Relations Timeline.* Coast Salish Lands: Vancouver Status of Women, 2008.

Vedan, R. W. *How Do We Forgive our Fathers: Angry/violent Aboriginal/First Nations Men's Experiences with Social Workers.* Ph.D. Simon Fraser University, 2002.

Warriors Against Violence Society (WAVS). *Facilitator Training Manual.* 1998.

Wilson, S. *Research is Ceremony: Indigenous Research Methods.* Halifax: Fernwood Publishing, 2008.

28.
Our Family Coalition

Mothering on the Curve

HEAVEN WALKER

THE STONE WALL RIOTS IN 1969 were a turning point in the struggle for Gay and Lesbian rights and had paved the way towards the LGBTQ liberation movement. Many women who were married with children finally felt empowered to claim their lesbianism and leave their marriages. However, as lesbian mothers began to make their way out of the closet, they were met with a very harsh reality. The courts were very conservative and favored traditional marriage and the nuclear family. This caused many lesbian mothers to lose custody of their children. The American court system was so riddled with homophobia that in the case of lesbian custody battles, it had adopted a policy of women and children last.

In the documentary "Mom's Apple Pie: the Heart of the Lesbian Custody Movement" many women recollect the pain of losing custody of their children to their ex-husbands when they came out of the closet as lesbians. Barbara "Boo" Price stated that "There wasn't a single case in the United States in 1972 in which a lesbian mother had won, not only won custody that hadn't happened, but even won normal visitation rights" (*Mom's Apple Pie: The Heart of the Lesbian Mothers' Custody Movement*). This fact is illustrated by one woman's painful testimony of her battle with the courts. She states "All I did was cry through the whole court, I cried because it didn't matter what I said and I didn't have an attorney, I couldn't find an attorney to legally represent me at the time. I thought I could go to court and tell the judge, look, he's dealing drugs, my kids are safer in my household and they just ignored that part. Being a lesbian is worse than living around drugs ... and that's what the message was from the judge at that time" (*Mom's Apple Pie: The Heart of the Lesbian Mothers' Custody Movement*).

Melissa Hart was deeply wounded by the injustice of the courts as a child and spoke of her experience, stating "I think divorce is devastating to young children in general, but to be taken away from an absolutely wonderful mother, I mean this was our girl scout leader ... to be taken away from her because she was sleeping with a woman and dropped into our father's extremely abusive and volatile household, it was devastating" (*Mom's Apple Pie: The Heart of the Lesbian Mothers' Custody Movement*).

The outcry of the injustices suffered by lesbian mothers and their children led to the creation of a Seattle-based organization called the Lesbian Mother's National Defense Fund (LMNDF). The LMNDF provided legal resources and funding to lesbian mothers in the midst of custody battles. Their motto was "Raising our children is a human right, not a heterosexual privilege." The LMNDF provided assistance to over 400 lesbian mothers (*Mom's Apple Pie: The Heart of the Lesbian Mothers' Custody Movement*).

The Lesbian Mother's National Defense Fund was eventually dissolved in the 1990s as it became more commonplace for lesbian mothers to win custody of their children. We are very fortunate to live in a time where being a lesbian does not automatically render you an unfit mother in the eyes of the court system. However, in the twenty-first century, lesbian mothers and LGBTQ families are presented with new challenges: lack of visibility, isolation, and social intolerance and/or unacceptance. Lesbian mother Judy Appel founded the organization "Our Family Coalition" to address these issues.

History and Mandate

Our Family Coalition was founded by the 2002 merger of two San Francisco Bay Area California organizations serving lesbian, gay, bisexual, and/or transgendered families—the Berkeley, California-based "Our Family," and the San Francisco-based "All Our Families Coalition." Our Family was founded in 1994 by a group of East Bay lesbian and gay parents with infants as a social and educational organization for lesbian, gay, bisexual, trans-gendered, and questioning families. All Our Families Coalition was founded in 1996 by and for lesbian, gay, bisexual, and transgendered families to provide LGBTQ families with services and referrals that addressed their needs, helped them to support each other, and also provided resources and structures to help LGBTQ families to advocate for themselves in their respective communities. Since the merger of the two organizations in 2002, Our Family Coalition has grown to over 700 member families, with many more that participate in their activities and utilize their services. Our mandate is to promote "...the equality and well-being of lesbian, gay, bisexual, transgender and queer families with children. We foster community leadership in advocacy efforts that promote social justice" ("Our Family Coalition, 2007-2011.").

Context

Lack of visibility is a problem that affects many mothers. We live in a society where mothers and mothering are devalued and many women feel disempowered as mothers. In her book *Daughters of the Moon,* Fiona Morgan states "In patriarchy there is perhaps no greater oppression than that experienced by mothers. We are the invisible source of the entire race, yet our gifts are exploited, even as they are denied recognition. Praises are given to the progenital male as god or husband, who is seen as the source of all. The womb is his property and the foundation of his marketplace; his vessel which gives him birth and sustenance. Mothers themselves learn to be self-effacing, and are often completely unaware that they carry the all-powerful gift of life, and that their sustaining energy nurtures all of society." Lesbian mothers and LGBTQ families as a whole suffer a severe lack of visibility, which in turn leads to social unacceptance. This invisibility can lead to feelings of disempowerment and oppression. Our Family Coalition exists to provide visibility and promote social acceptance of GLBT people and their families.

Objectives

The first objective of Our Family Coalition is to provide support to LGBTQ parents by addressing issues of isolation by providing social networking events and support groups. These social networking events and support groups enable LGBTQ parents and families to see themselves and their individual experiences collectively represented through the experiences of other families. Over the past year OFC has expanded its reach to include public advocacy and policy structure. OFC promotes advocacy and policy making by trying to make elementary schools more inclusive by increasing LGBTQ visibility and awareness through age and development appropriate education that will make children feel safe around issues of gender and sexual orientation.

Activities/Programs

Social Events: In the last year Our Family Coalition hosted over 150 events. Our Family Coalition hosts many events in both San Francisco and the East Bay where families can connect and have fun together. OFC recently hosted a multifaith holiday party where families brought food that was important to the holiday celebrations of their respective faiths, built gingerbread houses, made holiday crafts, and enjoyed a magic show. Other activities include but are not limited to the: Thanks for Families Thanksgiving Celebration, Monster Mash Halloween Potluck, African American Hair Workshop, Family Garden at Purple Moon Dance Project, San Francisco Pride Family Garden, Family Arts Bridge Camp, and the Back to School Family Potluck Picnic.

School Advocacy Program: Our Family Coalition works with parents, teachers, administrators and others to create more welcoming schools for the children of LGBTQ headed households, address gender stereotypes, and break down anti-gay bias at an early age. OFC's School Advocacy Program offers a wide variety of services that support LGBTQ families with children in elementary schools, including:

- anti-bias trainings for service providers, elementary age students, teachers and administrators;
- leadership training for parents to advocate on behalf of their children to create safe and welcoming school environments;
- school fairs and forums;

- work to create and strengthen school district policies on LGBTQ inclusion;
- staff presentation at schools; and
- developing written and web-based public information materials ("Our Family Coalition, 2007-2011").

Peer Support Groups: Our Family Coalition support groups provide a forum for LGBTQ individuals to meet, explore shared concerns, receive assistance from their peers, and learn from experts. There is a diverse offering of support groups. The following Support Groups are offered by OFC:

- *Mammas & Pappas* provides parents the opportunity to expand their circle of LGBTQ parents, swap parenting tips, and explore concerns shared by all parents as well as those of special interest to LGBTQ families. This group will also help children of LGBTQ families to build lasting friendships with other children growing up with LGBTQ families. Each month Mamas & Papas hosts a family dinner, parent-led discussion, and activity groups for LGBTQ parents with kids ages 0-12.
- *The Transgendered Parent Support Group* is an opportunity for transgendered parents to connect with peers and get mutual support. The first half hour is usually spent socializing and the remaining time is dedicated to group discussion.
- *The LGBTQ Parents of Color Support Group* is an opportunity for families of color to connect with peers and get mutual support. This group sponsors a monthly social where dinner and activities for children of all ages is provided.

The Prospective Parent Potluck provides an opportunity for LGBTQ prospective parents to meet and network with other LGBTQ prospective parents. These meetings alternate between San Francisco and the East Bay, and usually feature a guest speaker and materials provided by OFC that can help LGBTQ families to embark on the journey of parenthood.

Parent Education: Our Family Coalition holds educational workshops that raise awareness and provide support and resources on topics that are of particular interest to LGBTQ families. Past Parenthood Education workshops have included the following topics: Legal Workshops; Coming Out to Your Children; Speaking with Children About Their Biological Origins; Talking with Your Children About Adoption; Resource Panel for Prospective Parents; Wills, Power of Attorney, and Estate Planning; Domestic Partners and Second-Parent Adoption.

Social Justice: Our Family Coalition strives to increase visibility and achieve justice and full equality for LGBTQ families. Along with their families, they work with local, state and national coalitions to advocate for change on issues relevant to LGBTQ families, including marriage equality and healthcare reform. In the media and in political forums, they work to improve public perception and policy for LGBTQ families. Our Family Coalition recognizes that its families live within every

Appel-Bernstein family.

community, and are of every racial, ethnic, cultural, and socioeconomic group. As a result, they strive to work in collaboration with other social justice issues such as immigration, welfare rights and disability rights to further the rights of all families. OFC's Social Justice Campaigns are as follows:

Marriage Equality: Our Family Coalition was proud to play an active role in the fight for Marriage Equality in California. They were plaintiffs in the recent Marriage cases that won the right of same-gender couples to marry in California in 2008. OFC was also active in the unsuccessful efforts to defeat Proposition 8, which defined marriage as a union between a man and a woman, and overthrew the California Supreme Court ruling that legalized same sex marriage in 2008. OFC will continue to advocate for Marriage Equality and the families that are disenfranchised by marriage inequality.

Safe Schools: Our Family Coalition works with parents, allies, community based organizations and elected officials to make preschool and elementary schools more welcoming to the children of LGBTQ families and to integrate inclusive curriculum into the Bay Area schools. OFC's experience continues to suggest that parents are among the best agents of change in district-level policies and play an integral part

Bennett-Frankfurt family.

in OFC's work. They work with parents to facilitate policy changes that support welcoming and bias-free elementary school environments. These can include district-wide curriculum and/or staff training policies; attention to Assembly Bill 537 compliance at the elementary level, including greater accommodation of gender-nonconforming students; and other approaches. OFC is currently working on policy issues with district personnel in Berkeley, Hayward, Oakland, San Francisco, and Albany ("Our Family Coalition, 2007-2011").

Health Care: Our Family Coalition is proud to be a founding member of the newly formed LGBTQ Health and Human Services Network, housed within Equality California, a statewide coalition of LGBTQ and allied organizations working to provide non-HIV health and human services to LGBTQ Californians and their families. The Network works to prioritize the health needs of the LGBTQ community in California and connect existing organizations with statewide funding sources that have not necessarily been directed toward LGBTQ communities in the past. In addition to advocating for funding, the Network also works to improve the cultural competency of state agencies that serve or interact with LGBTQ communities in the provision of state health or human services. Our Family Coalition brings the voice of parents and their unique health concerns to the table ("Our Family Coalition, 2007-2011").

Immigration: Under federal law, legal residents are unable to petition for their same-sex partner or spouse to immigrate to the United States. The policies of the INS have a magnified impact on LGBTQ families who in addition to being separated from their partner and children may face heightened homophobia in their family of origin. Our Family Coalition recognizes that this is an issue which affects their members and their families. OFC supports Immigration Equality in its efforts to

Daniels-Merrill family.

aid LGBTQ immigrants and their families. "Immigration Equality is a national organization that works to end discrimination in U.S. immigration law, to reduce the negative impact of that law on the lives of lesbian, gay, bisexual, transgender and HIV-positive people, and to help obtain asylum for those persecuted in their home country based on their sexual orientation, transgender identity or HIV-status. Through education, outreach, advocacy, and the maintenance of a nationwide network of resources, we provide information and support to advocates, attorneys, politicians and those who are threatened by persecution or the discriminatory impact of the law" ("Our Family Coalition, 2007-2011").

Welfare Rights: Women of color and LGBTQ people both suffer under national and state welfare policies such as the federal *Personal Responsibility and Work Opportunity Reconciliation Act* (PRWORA). These policies promote restricting access to welfare services through family caps, two-parent income ineligibility, and suitable home requirements. These policies ultimately promote marriage and the so-called "nuclear family" as the answer to getting and staying off of welfare. The combination of such policies with positive reinforcement tactics like welfare benefits bonuses for welfare mothers who marry have a magnified impact on LGBTQ parents on welfare, which are not able to marry their spouse under federal law. Our Family Coalition works with welfare advocates supporting broader community efforts and bringing the voice of LGBTQ parents to the struggle for more productive and supportive welfare policies ("Our Family Coalition, 2007-2011").

The *Access Program* seeks to increase visibility and access for LGBTQ families. Our Family Coalition offers training and technical assistance for health, mental health and social service providers, so they can better serve LGBTQ families with

Dries-Sindelar family.

children. In order to achieve this goal OFC provides the following services through the Access program.

- •Conducts pre-training meetings with organizational or clinic management to identify key areas of service provision and clarify training needs.
- •Conducts two or three hour LGBTQ Family Cultural Competency trainings for all staff and management. The trainings combine anti-bias curriculum with data about LGBTQ families and practical actions that the agency can take to be more welcoming to LGBTQ families and prospective parents.
- •Provides post-training technical assistance to work with staff to implement action steps identified during the training.
- •Conducts evaluations to determine the impact of its work ("Our Family Coalition, 2007-2011").

Informaton and Referrals: Our Family Coalition seeks to better serve LGBTQ headed families and prospective parents in the San Francisco Bay Area by connecting them with applicable and welcoming resources. Our Family Coalition offers information and referrals for LGBTQ adoptive families looking for counselling, health related services, and information or support with adoption related matters. OFC also maintains a resource database that contains state and national websites and resources relating to: bisexual parenting; family building; co-parenting; coming out to our children; gender nonconformity in children; parents of color; single parenting; transgender issues; and transracial adoption.

Fiscal Projects

Our Family Coalition sponsors projects that align with their mission. Currently, Our Family Coalition is the fiscal agent for Family Arts Bridge (FAB) Camp and Somos Familia.

Somos Familia is the only organization oriented to Latino families with children who are lesbian, gay, bisexual, transgender, queer or questioning (LGBTQ). Located in the East Bay, it is a primarily volunteer-run, family-driven effort, supported by many community partners. Somos Familia seeks to build the capacity of families to support their youth and to speak out on the importance of family and community acceptance. Somos Familia strives to create safe spaces for youth, families and allies to meet together. Somos Familia works together to increase acceptance of LGBTQ people in our community to create a world where families and community allies embrace their youth of all sexual orientations, gender expressions and identities.

Family Arts Bridge Camp or FAB Camp (for short) is an arts-based non-profit family camp for all kinds of families representing diverse backgrounds, including families with lesbian, gay, bisexual, transgender members, and their friends and allies ("Our Family Coalition, 2007-2011").

Publications

Our Family Coalition produces a number of publications to better serve, as well as increase the visibility and understanding of LGBTQ-headed families. These publications are produced by OFC and other resources that serve the LGBTQ community and their families. OFC publications include a *Quarterly Newsletter*, a bi-monthly e-newsletter, Program materials from educational workshops and access programs, "Best of the Gay Bay" family resource guide, handouts and reports such as *Our Families: Attributes of Bay Area LGBTQ Families* and the "Family Values" poster featuring LGBTQ families.

Quarterly Newsletter: OFC's print newsletter is sent to hundreds of households and organizations. With many of the articles, including the cover piece, written by fellow LGBTQ parents, our quarterly print newsletter provides a forum for current and prospective parents to share, reflect and learn from each others' stories and experiences. Contributions from experts of varying fields from child development to legal to estate planning provides LGBTQ parents and individuals with resources, up-to-date developments, current news, and much more.

Best of the Gay Bay: A 2007 Membership Survey stated that over 70 percent of the members would find a resource guide of parents' recommendations of LGBTQ friendly services, organizations, and activities very valuable. Since that time, hundreds have shared their opinion and completed the "Best of the Gay Bay" Families Survey that led to the *Best of the Gay Bay Family Resource Guide.*

Program Materials: Our Family Coalition creates materials and handouts for their School Program and Access Program for Service Providers. These materials include literature such as a Quick Facts sheet on LGBTQ-headed households, and Resources for Safe & Inclusive Schools for LGBTQ Families. OFC also produces handouts and reports on LGBTQ families such as *Our Families: Attributes of Bay Area LGBTQ Families*, which is a collaborative publication about Bay Area LGBTQ families with children and their basic demographics ("Our Family Coalition, 2007-2011").

The Family Values Poster Project is a full-color 18" x 24" poster that features LGBTQ families. Family Values Posters are offered free to schools and non-profit organizations to promote diversity awareness, and acceptance. Pictures from the Family Values Poster project are included in this article.

Challenges

The task of trying to create LGBTQ visibility and acceptance and a society that is fully equal to all is no small feat. This year alone, OFC engages in challenging advocacy projects that range from tackling institutional heterosexism to providing access to all social and health services. However, the specific challenge that OFC faces is trying to serve the needs of a diverse community which includes addressing issues of immigration, welfare rights, disability rights, the concerns of families of varying cultural backgrounds and income levels so that everyone's experience is valued and all voices are heard.

Future Goals

Our Family Coalition is currently the largest local LGBTQ family organization in the country. They have truly made groundbreaking steps in the Bay Area. This year OFC focused its attention on performing Inclusive Elementary Schools forums to talk about how to make elementary schools more welcoming to LGBTQ families and gave sample lesson plans of the Welcoming Schools Curriculum. The Welcoming Schools Curriculum is an LGBTQ inclusive approach to addressing family diversity, gender stereotyping, bullying, and name calling in K-5 learning environments. OFC's work paid off when the Berkeley California unified School District became the very first district in the country to adopt the Welcoming Schools Curriculum. Unfortunately, OFC is currently primarily only serving the Bay Area. The Bay Area is an area known for its liberal politics and openness to new ideas. OFC would like to first expand statewide so that it may serve other regions of California that are not as progressive. Eventually OFC would like to expand nationally so that all may benefit from its groundbreaking work. If OFC continues to grow and expand it will benefit mothers of every background regardless of their sexual orientation. Lesbian mothers will no longer have to feel isolated, invisible, or unaccepted. Mothers of all sexual orientations will benefit from the Welcoming Schools Curriculum program that OFC is campaigning for. Mothers of all gender identities and sexual orientations will benefit from knowing that their child's school is addressing issues of bullying and name-calling.

Jadalah-Karraa family.

Society tells women that mothering is intrinsic in our DNA and that women are all meant to be mothers. We are also expected to automatically know how to be good mothers. We are not told about things like postpartum depression, possible difficulty with breast feeding, loneliness, sleep deprivation, isolation, and guilt over these feelings. Many mothers suffer in silence and their suffering may manifest into severe postpartum depression.

Mothers often feel invisible to the rest of society and many face discrimination because of the fact that they are mothers. Immigration policy is extremely gender biased and ignores the stories and the needs of immigrant mothers and their children. Working mothers are particularly susceptible to discrimination. Many women do not get hired for certain jobs, or promoted in their current job because of the fact that they are mothers. Mothers are often seen as a "conflict of interest" to the professional world. Single mothers suffer discrimination of many kinds because they are mothers that have failed to propogate the status quo of the nuclear family. Lesbian mothers are twice as susceptible to discrimination as they face the challenges of a culture that is not accepting of mothers or LGBTQ people. They suffer an extreme invisibility as it is often assumed that they are either heterosexual or that they are not mothers because they are lesbian. Immigrant Lesbian mothers face extreme hardship as their families are not recognized and are vulnerable to legal separation.

The Motherhood Movement seeks to end gender-based discrimination that mothers face as well as empower mothers as feminists in their own right. Our Family Coalition seeks to provide strong support systems and resources to LGBTQ families, and end discrimination based on sexual orientation, or homophobia. Homophobia is a form of gender-based discrimination. In essence, the Motherhood Movement and Our Family Coalition have the same goal and the contributions of each organization will aid in changing the cultural climate of discrimination, to that of tolerance and acceptance.

Conclusion

Mothers have often felt invisible, and isolated. When you become a mother it is often hard to remember who you are outside of your role as a parent. This disconnection from self can lead to extreme postpartum depression. The more depressed you become, the more you isolate yourself. It is often wise to seek the company of other mothers in order to ease some of the tension that is often felt by mothers, especially new mothers. However, if you are a lesbian mother you may feel rejected or judged by mothers in traditional heterosexual relationships. Even if the other mothers are welcoming and accepting you may still feel isolated or like an outsider. If you are a single mother, this feeling can be greatly exacerbated.

We all come from different backgrounds and we all travel different roads, but the destination is the same. As mothers we are all activists and agents of change. We birth a new world with the children that we rear. As feminists we honor ourselves as mothers and as a diverse community of women. We understand that we are all part of a sacred sisterhood, no matter what path has led us there. Our Family Coalition paves the way toward a just world for all and provides community and support for the mothers on the curve who have taken a road less travelled.

> *Do not go where the path may lead; go instead where there is no path and leave a trail."*
>
> —Ralph Waldo Emerson

Works Cited

Mom's Apple Pie: The Heart of the Lesbian Mothers' Custody Movement. Dir. Jody Laine, Shan Ottey, Shad Reinstein." Perf. Kate Clinton. Frameline: 2006, Web. <http://cart.frameline.org/productdetails.asp?productcode=t655>.

Morgan, Fiona. *Daughters of the Moon Tarot.* Novato, CA: Daughters of the Moon, 2000.

"Our Family Coalition, 2007-2011." Our Family Coalition: The Bay Area LGBTQ Family Organization. Web. <http://ourfamily.org>. Accessed: 1 Feb 2011.

29.
Family and Home Network

Listening, Learning and Leading for Over 25 Years

CATHERINE H. MYERS

THE U.S. NATIONAL NON-PROFIT organization Family and Home Network (FAHN) helps parents and children spend generous amounts of time together. FAHN focuses on children's needs for warm, nurturing relationships with their parents—and on parents' experiences and feelings as they take the time to meet their children's needs. Parents define "generous amounts of time" for themselves and their children; individuals and circumstances vary greatly and each family changes over time. FAHN advocates for inclusive policies that support parents regardless of how they choose to share and/or divide income-earning and caregiving responsibilities. Our advertisement-free publications and website offer parents opportunities to learn, to share their experiences, and to express their feelings. FAHN reaches out to policymakers, think tanks, other parent organizations and the media. Our members and leaders include both women and men, crossing the spectrum of politics, religion, ethnicity, race and socio-economics.

Family and Home Network's mandate and a history of its 25 years begin this chapter. Next, the Context and Objectives are explained, followed by the organization's Activities in two subsections: *Publications; Outreach and Advocacy.* Challenges examines major issues past and present, then the organization's current Goals are described. FAHN's involvements with other organizations are recounted in Relationship to the Motherhood Movement. Wrapping up this chapter are the Conclusion and information about our new Website, built by volunteers using open source content management tools and equipped with state-of-the-art social networking features.

Mandate

At its founding in 1984, the organization was devoted to "mothers at home: smart women who have actively chosen to devote their exceptional skills and good minds to the nurturing of their families" (Mothers at Home, "Dedication"). With time, the mandate of the organization has evolved and expanded to include families in which parents share and/or divide the income-earning and caregiving responsibilities in a great variety of ways. Family and Home Network's efforts on behalf of at-home mothers—as well as at-home fathers—continues; its mandate has become both more inclusive and more focused on the critical importance of nurturing relationships between children and parents. FAHN provides information and affirmation to parents, supporting them as they decide how to care for their children. Important aspects of the organization's efforts include speaking out to the media and to policymakers, advocating for inclusive family policies and encouraging parents to speak up for themselves.

History

Family and Home Network is a 501(c)(3) nonprofit organization, founded in the state of Virginia in 1984 by Linda Burton, Janet Dittmer and Cheri Loveless, and originally named Mothers At Home. A 1987 fact sheet listed the goals: "to help mothers at home realize they have made a great choice; to help mothers excel at a job for which no one feels fully prepared; and to correct society's many misconceptions about mothering" ("Minutes of Board of Directors Meeting, Mothers at Home"). At that time, prevailing messages were that women could (and should) "do it all" and that success and self-worth were measured by academic and workplace achievements. Media reports depicted working mothers as the epitome of modern, enlightened women; in comparison, at-home mothers were referred to with demeaning stereotypes from 1950s-era television sitcoms.

The founders initially focused on a monthly publication for at-home mothers: *Welcome Home.* They described "a new mother emerging"—not a housewife of the 1950s but instead:

> "a mother who has decided to put her family first without putting herself last. ... At a time when women have a host of attractive options, she is consciously choosing to devote her exceptional skills and good mind to nurturing her family. And she is doing it by spending as much time as possible at home" ("Mothers at Home brochure: No one...").

During the first year of publishing *Welcome Home*, the founders were stunned by the candor, passion and insight of letters from readers. In April 1984 they testified at a Congressional Hearing about what they were hearing from mothers: the call for family policies that offered *true* choices—not just more child care, but also more economic and social support for mothers who wanted to care for their children themselves (Burton, Loveless, and Dittmar).

Linda, Janet and Cheri felt compelled to write a book; they wanted to help reverse the then-prevailing stereotype of mothering at home as outdated and unimportant. *What's a Smart Woman Like You Doing at Home?* includes essays by the co-founders, excerpts from *Welcome Home* readers' letters, and a report on the widespread misuse of statistics on "working mothers." Going straight to the source—an expert at the U.S. Department of Labor (DOL), the founders discovered

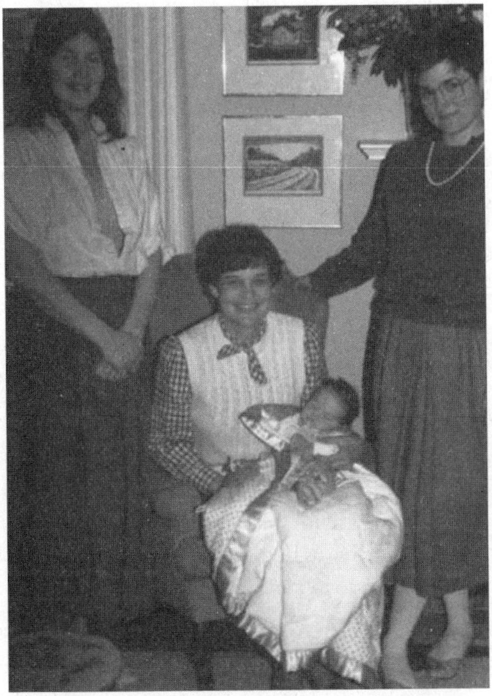

Cheri Loveless, Janet Dittmer, and Linda Burton, Co-founders, Mothers at Home

that the DOL statistics include mothers who have at least one child age 18 or younger, and they divide mothers into two categories: employed or not employed. The definition of employment includes mothers who do any work at all for pay (even as little as one hour per week), mothers who provide child care for other children while also caring for their own children, mothers who work without pay for a family operated enterprise at least fifteen hours per week, and mothers who are on maternity leave. There is nothing wrong with the statistics themselves, but they are often used in a context that leaves the impression that the DOL's "working mothers" are all mothers of young children who are employed full-time. This is simply not true. The founders started speaking up to the media and policy makers about misuse of the DOL statistics. Today, FAHN continues to object to misuse of statistics and also provides information on our website about other statistical information and about some of the research studies that examine the complexities of mothers' labor force participation (Family and Home Network, "Statistics").

By the time *Smart Woman* was published, the founders' growing families included a combined total of thirteen children, ranging in age from one to eleven years old. With great support from their husbands and children, they had achieved extraordinary success and now it was time to spread the workload further. One-by-one the founders removed themselves from day-to-day operations of the organization, after preparing others to take the reins. Cheri would be the last to leave, after a year-long effort to articulate the organization's policy perspectives in a concept paper (Mothers at Home, *Mothers Speak Out on Child Care*). I volunteered to help with the typing and production of this paper and received invaluable mentoring from Cheri and from Heidi Brennan, who, with her education and interest in government, led the organization's public policy efforts for decades. Cheri and Heidi drew me in to the project, taking time to explain as they analyzed, wrote, and edited.

Those early years laid critical groundwork for the organization's continued success. First and foremost was the task of developing the philosophy behind the organization's work. The founders listened to mothers' thoughts and feelings, helping mothers connect with each other to share their concerns and ideas. The depiction of mothers by media representatives and policymakers did not align with what the founders were hearing from mothers themselves; the organization's public relations and outreach work challenged prevailing misconceptions. The organization faced a daunting workload. Early on, the founders recruited and inspired volunteers—who were encouraged to bring their babies and children along when they came to work or to meetings. Volunteers were critical to the organization, tackling everything from serving as Chair of the Board of Directors to stuffing envelopes.

From the beginning, a volunteer Board of Directors (which originally included the founders) has governed the organization. In 1989 the Board of Directors created a Management Team to separate the Board's governing role from the day-to-day operations of the organization. Management Team departments included Administration, Publications, Marketing and Public Relations, Human Resources, Development and Public Policy. Each department had a Director; some also had staff and volunteers. Staff positions were part-time, paid jobs, ranging from four hours per week to fifteen hours per week; staff members often contributed additional volunteer hours. Procedures were designed to meet the needs of the part-time staff, priorities included flexible hours and a welcoming office space for children. When the organization moved to a new office, it had sliding glass doors installed on opposite sides of a middle room, creating a play room with access to the administrative office and the conference room so that mothers could work and keep an eye on their children at play, and children could have ready access to their mothers. At a time when many advocates of "family-friendly" practices called on businesses to provide more services to care for children (including special childcare for children who were ill) so parents wouldn't have to miss time on the job, our organization figured out how to operate with flexibility and cooperation. We also had a level of chaos and multi-tasking that sometimes stretched us thin (an especially memorable Board meeting was conducted with seven little boys going back and forth from the playroom to their moms' laps.) We learned how to work in a family-friendly environment that suited us—mothers taking time to breastfeed and rock a baby to sleep, toddlers "helping" with the mail, children in laps at meetings and diverted by a colleague during a phone call. Some work, including editing, could be done at home. With children along, we accomplished much, including the on-time publication of our journal every month for 22 years (220 issues) as well as publishing four books and representing the organization to the media and policy makers.

Through the 1990s, the organization flourished. *Welcome Home* won numerous national awards, including four prestigious Parents' Choice Awards. Hundreds of media inquiries were answered each year and the organization's leaders were quoted in major newspapers and magazines. FAHN leaders conferred with authors doing research for books on motherhood and policy issues, they attended

FAHN tenth anniversary picnic

national conferences, talked with legislators and took part in policy presentations at Washington, DC, think tanks. Infrastructure was improved; several of our tech-savvy husbands volunteered their time to set up a computerized database to replace our 3 x 5 card file of subscriber records. Two more books and other special publications were created, drawing on material that had been published in *Welcome Home.* In 1994 we celebrated the organization's tenth anniversary with a family picnic.

Over the years, the organization had been reaching out to at-home fathers and also acknowledging the interdependent partnership between at-home parents and their income-earning spouses. While maintaining its special focus on at-home mothers and fathers, the organization was expanding its outreach and emphasizing that parents themselves had to decide how to share and/or divide the income-earning and caregiving responsibilities. Parents must become informed about the critical importance of nurturing relationships and about the generous amounts of time needed to build those relationships with their children. FAHN spoke out in opposition to the media-devised "Mommy Wars," and called for recognition of the many creative ways mothers and fathers care for their children, as well as recognition that today's "working mother" or "working father" might next year be "at home" and vice versa. After much discussion and an often-frustrating search for a new name, in 2002 the Board of Directors changed the organization's name to Family and Home Network.

At the beginning of the twenty-first century, like most publishers of magazines and newspapers FAHN was struggling to respond to the challenges of the internet. The exorbitant cost of office space in the suburbs of Washington, DC, was a serious strain; when we moved to a less expensive space in a renovated basement, our office flooded repeatedly. We tightened our budget year after year, eliminating the marketing that might have increased subscription numbers. Finally in 2004 we decided to suspend publication of *Welcome Home* and close our office. Except for a very part-time bookkeeper, FAHN is all-volunteer again, supported by member donations and continuing its work through sales of its books, special publications, free e-newsletter and its new website.

Context

The primary motherhood issue that FAHN addresses is the critical importance of consistent, intimate relationships with our children. Closely related issues are cultural and political factors that make it hard for parents and children to have generous amounts of time together; these factors include: cultural messages that tie self-esteem to achievement in the workplace, materialism, isolation in our communities and the pressures of advertising. In recent decades many family policies have been crafted to support equal opportunities for women in the workforce and have a narrow focus on "working families." Such policies usually offer no support to families with an at-home mother or an at-home father, nor do they support entrepreneurial parents or tag-team parents, who take turns at work and at home.

Objectives

Family and Home Network speaks up for at-home mothers and at-home fathers, for families who use a wide variety of work/family strategies in order to spend generous amounts of time with their children—and for those who would like more time with their children. FAHN offers affirmation and encouragement to mothers and fathers who forgo or cut back on paid employment as well as information about the critical importance of nurturing and examples of the many ways in which parents meet their families' needs. FAHN advocates for inclusive public policies; such policies would embrace the wide range of strategies parents use in meeting their income-earning and caregiving responsibilities.

Activities

Publications

For 22 years, the main activity pursued by the organization in fulfilling its mission was the publication of its monthly, advertisement-free journal, *Welcome Home.* Its 32 pages were written, edited and illustrated by parents, for parents. *Welcome Home* included personal essays, poems, letters from readers, a monthly "problems and solutions" column, artwork and photographs. In addition, there were informational articles covering a range of topics in categories including Health and Safety, Time to Care (about volunteering in the community), Back in the Kitchen (healthy family recipes), book reviews, Media on Mothers (examples of positive and negative media reports), Public Policy analyses and opinion on cultural issues including consumerism and advertising.

Parents' interests and questions have inspired FAHN's editors and leaders to seek information and make it available through our publications. One topic of great interest is the importance of nurturing relationships between parents and their children. We point to expert opinion on the importance of the parent/child relationship, and to the latest research on nurturing from neuroscience and biopsychology. We also report on researchers' disagreements, such as those about the National Institute of Child Health and Development's long-term study on the effects of child care. And we didn't forget older children and their parents. When Harvard University's Center for Health Communications released a report on parenting teens, *Welcome Home's* editors sought out brief narratives from parents as examples of each of the five "basics" identified by the researchers (Simpson; (Family and Home Network, "Raising Teens"). Many readers were interested in topics of affordability, and in our media and policy work, we were often faced with comments such as: *A family with an at-home parent is fine for those with high incomes, but most parents have to work.* We knew that many families lived on moderate incomes, that many made significant sacrifices and/or did a lot of financial planning to make it possible to have a parent at home. And we knew that it was incorrect to simply divide mothers into two categories: at work or at home. In order to collect data and recruit families willing to talk with reporters and policy makers, Marian Gormley (Public Relations/Marketing Director) and Heidi Brennan designed an in-depth survey on family finances and recruited participants through a notice in *Welcome Home*. Over 100 families completed the survey, sharing details of their family finances as well as their thoughts and feelings about the choices they'd made. We reported on findings in *Welcome Home* and were able to refer reporters to families across the U.S. who, in spite of modest incomes, managed to have a parent at home (Myers).

Affirmation and information for parents who spend generous amounts of time with their children is offered in other publications from Mothers at Home/Family and Home Network, including our books: *What's a Smart Woman Like* You *Doing at Home?; Discovering Motherhood; Motherhood: Journey Into Love;* and *Blow-Drying the Frog and Other Parenting Adventures*. In addition, "Best of" collections from *Welcome Home* cover approximately 40 popular topics.

Outreach and Advocacy

FAHN offers information and advocates on behalf of families to other organizations, media representatives, government officials and elected representatives.

The 1989 effort by co-founder Cheri Loveless to produce a concept paper: *Mothers Speak Out on Child Care* (MSOOCC) lay the groundwork for many years of public policy advocacy. This paper examined some common misconceptions about mothers and work, about the media's portrayal of mothering issues, and about policy options. It included an explanation of the way statistics on mothers and employment are often misused. Most importantly, MSOOCC gave voice to mothers whose stories were not being heard by policymakers. We mailed copies of MSOOCC to leaders of other mothering organizations, to professionals and members of the media and to the Governor of each state—asking for feedback and endorsement. Our team of volunteers, mothers with children in tow, delivered MSOOCC to every Congressional office at the Capitol in Washington, DC, (Mothers at Home 1989).

Over the years, representatives of Mothers at Home/Family and Home Network (MAH/FAHN) have testified several times at Congressional Hearings, and we've attended countless policy briefings, symposiums and conferences at Washington DC think tanks. Our advocacy work is nonpartisan. In 1990, when one-fourth of Wellesley's students signed a petition in protest of Barbara Bush's appearance as their graduation speaker because she had "just" been a wife and mother, MAH/FAHN wrote a thank you letter to the first lady for her eloquent and educational speech (Butterfield; Brennan; Bush). In 1992, when there was public outcry over Hillary Clinton's "I could have stayed home and baked cookies" comment, MAH/FAHN wrote an editorial in support of her, noting that her comments were made in the context of our culture's stereotypes and misconceptions about motherhood (Koppel and Judd; Brennan and Myers 1992). FAHN initiated a project with the federal Child Care Bureau to develop *Accessing Support for All Parents,* a free guide for parents exploring their child care choices, available in print and online (NACCRRA and Child Care Aware).This project marked the first time the Child Care Bureau addressed the choice of having a parent forgo or cut back on paid employment to provide care, and the first time it offered resources to at-home parents. At the invitation of the Child Care Bureau, Heidi Brennan and I presented a handout and poster at the 2002 State Administrators Annual Meeting (Myers and Brennan).

In 2003 FAHN launched its Campaign for Inclusive Family Policies—calling on policymakers to craft policies that support families regardless of the ways in which parents share and/or divide their income-earning and caregiving responsibilities. Issues that impact families are complex—tax policies, child-care subsidies, work and family policies—and we work to ensure that policy makers and the media understand the range of choices families make in caring for their children. We reach out to other parent organizations, inviting their feedback on the Campaign for Inclusive Family Policies (Myers and Board of Directors, Family and Home Network).

Challenges

Financing our work has always been a challenge. We made modest efforts to approach foundations, without success—MAH/FAHN is nonpartisan and doesn't seem to fit the expectations of many foundations, which tend to identify with either conservative or liberal viewpoints on family issues. When we approached corporations to ask for sponsorship we were told privately that corporations could not risk offending working mothers by giving support to MAH/FAHN. The renewal rate on *Welcome Home* subscriptions was over 60 percent, an extremely high rate in the magazine industry. Most of our new subscribers came from word-of-mouth contacts and reader's gift subscriptions to friends and family. Readership surveys showed that over half our subscribers regularly shared their magazines with others (thereby reducing our subscription revenue but increasing readership numbers). The price of subscriptions was kept as low as possible in order to enable families on a budget to afford it (and we gave a free subscription to anyone who couldn't afford to pay). There was disagreement among leaders over the use of advertising as a revenue stream, with some advocating for *Welcome Home* to carry ads while others believed the advertisement-free journal provided a much-needed refuge for mothers from our culture's consumer culture; the "no-advertising" perspective prevailed. For many years, individual contributions solicited through an annual fundraising drive made up the difference between subscription revenue and costs; a small group of contributors sustains the organization today.

The organization's advocacy work has always been an entirely volunteer effort. In the policy arena, advocates for working families have access to funding and institutions that support their work; some comes from those with a financial stake in legislation. Those with a financial interest include corporations who seek "family-friendly" accolades as well as childcare corporations whose profits increase when more children are placed in their care. Fifty-five major corporations are partners of Corporate Voices for Working Families, a "national business membership organization representing the private sector voice in the dialogue on public policy issues involving working families"("Corporate Voices for Working Families"). In the family policy debate, the financial resources these corporations provide help to create a very unbalanced playing field—grassroots organizations advocating for families who do not fit the "working family" model operate with severe financial limitations. Understanding the influence of these market factors is the first step in being able to hold them at bay.

Society's misconceptions about mothers and families, and "working mother" perspectives adopted by many mainstream media representatives and academicians have made it difficult at times to engage in mutually respectful conversations at public meetings. MAH/FAHN leaders worked hard to make it clear that our organization was not working in opposition to working mothers, but our mere presence seemed to offend some people. Disapproval has been conveyed in various ways, including one professor who shook her head "no" while a FAHN leader introduced the organization's work, a representative of a working mothers' magazine who refused to acknowledge or speak to a FAHN representative at another meeting, and many individuals who accused FAHN leaders of "setting back the women's movement" or of being naïve in our statements that a life at home with children could be fulfilling. We were warned repeatedly of the financial risks of at-home motherhood (though the same concern is rarely raised on behalf of at-home fathers, and working mothers can also suffer great financial harm from divorce). It is a big challenge to discuss issues related to children, time, and employment. We continue to learn and to gather evidence to support inclusive family policies.

Goals

Family and Home Network aims to increase awareness about the critical importance of nurturing and to increase opportunities for parents to spend generous amounts of time with their children. We work to accomplish this by offering affirmation, information and advocacy through our publications and our website, as well as by speaking out to the public, to reporters and authors, to academicians, public policy analysts and legislators.

Relationship to the Motherhood Movement

FAHN communicates with and cooperates with mothers' organizations as well as with fatherhood organizations and other parenting groups. We see ourselves as colleagues with other organizations, and freely share resource lists of other organizations with our readers, encouraging them to seek out the support they need, wherever they find it. Some of our readers wanted local support groups, and FAHN knew others were doing this work well; we referred people to other organizations rather than trying to establish our own local groups. In the early 1990s we attempted to form a coalition of mothers' groups in order to work cooperatively on media outreach and policy issues, but each organization's own internal time and resource pressures were too high, there was no funding for staff or communication tools—this effort failed.

FAHN representatives participated in many national conferences, including the Harvard Women's Leadership Conference, several conferences organized by Family Support America for the purpose of forming a national parenting organization (this never came to fruition), caregivers' groups associated with United Nations meetings, and annual conferences of the National Association of Mothers' Centers. FAHN leaders wrote a public policy article for *Mothering* magazine (Brennan and Catherine H. Myers, "Beyond the Child-Care Debate") A member of our Board of Directors served on the Motherhood Council founded by Enola Aird. FAHN has long-time relationships with leaders of many other mothering organizations and publications; we reach out to discuss policy issues and are actively seeking feedback on our Campaign for Inclusive Family Policies.

We are grateful to those in the motherhood movement who have organized conferences and meetings at which FAHN has benefited by learning more about others' work and by strengthening relationships. From the motherhood movement, FAHN has gained an appreciation for others' challenges, courage and persistence. We also enjoy the feeling of camaraderie with many amazing women. We would like to see those engaged in the motherhood movement take time to listen deeply to each others' perspectives, to find common ground on issues and to build stronger alliances. FAHN brings to the motherhood community our many years of listening to mothers, our experience in fostering communication among people with diverse views, and our experience with the importance of editors' work in challenging rhetoric and clarifying viewpoints. FAHN also brings to the motherhood movement its commitment to including fathers in discussions of family issues, both personal and political.

Conclusion

Family and Home Network has been listening closely to mothers and fathers for over 25 years, facilitating parent-to-parent communication and speaking up to the media and to policymakers on behalf of families. FAHN focuses on children's needs for warm, nurturing relationships with their parents as well as on parents' experiences and feelings as they take the time to meet their children's needs. The publisher of an award-winning monthly journal for over two decades, today FAHN reaches out through its extensive website and E-News, its books and other publications. The organization's strengths include its volunteers and supporting members, its wealth of parent-written essays and articles, its knowledge of scientific research on nurturing, its experience in policy analyses and its relationships with other parenting organizations. FAHN has faced serious challenges in recent years; it succeeded in finding and learning to use new technology and it is engaged now in addressing its financial well-being. FAHN anticipates both promising opportunities and significant challenges as it continues to help families spend generous amounts of time together.

Works Cited

Brennan, Heidi. "MAH Update." *Welcome Home* Dec. 1990: 16-17.

Brennan, Heidi L. and Catherine H. Myers. "Beyond the Child-Care Debate." *Mothering* Spring 1991: 120-123.

Brennan, Heidi L. and Catherine H. Myers. "The Over-baked Cookie Cliche." *Welcome Home* July 1992: 25.

Burton, Linda, Cheri Loveless, and Janet Dittmar. *What's a Smart Woman Like You Doing at Home?* Washington, DC: Acropolis Books, 1986.

Bush, Barbara. "Remarks of Mrs. Bush at Wellesley College Commencement." 1 June 1990. Web.

Butterfield, Fox. "At Wellesley, A Furor Over Barbara Bush." *The New York Times* 4 May 1990. Web.

"Corporate Voices for Working Families." Web. 30 Nov. 2009.

Family and Home Network. "Raising Teens." Web. 13 Jan. 2011.

Family and Home Network. "Statistics." *Family and Home Network.* 2010. Web. Accessed: 19 Jan. 2011.

Koppel, Ted, and Jackie Judd. "Making Hillary Clinton an Issue." 26 Mar. 1992. Web.

"Minutes of Board of Directors Meeting, Mothers at Home." 27 Feb. 1987.

Mothers at Home. "Dedication." *Welcome Home* Jan. 1984: 1. Print.

Mothers at Home. *Mothers Speak Out on Child Care.* Merrifield, VA: Mothers at Home, 1989.

"Mothers at Home brochure: No one was speaking for today's mothers at home... so we decided to speak for ourselves."

Myers, Cathy. "MAH's Affordability Project." *Welcome Home* Jan. 1999: 24-26.

Myers, Catherine H. and Board of Directors, Family and Home Network. "Campaign for Inclusive Family Policies." 2003. Web. 12 Jan. 2011.

Myers, Catherine H., and Heidi L. Brennan. "Wholehearted Family Policies: More Choice for Parents, Cost Savings for Government." July 2004.

National Association of Child Care Resource and Referral Agencies (NACCRRA) and Child Care Aware. "ASAP: Accessing Support for All Parents." 2006. Web.

Simpson, A. Rae. *Raising Teens: A Synthesis of Research and a Foundation for Action.* Cambridge, MA: Center for Health Communication, Harvard School of Public Health, 2001. Web.

30.
Attachment Parenting International

Nurturing Generations of Mothers, Children and Families

SALLY DEAR-HEALEY

Do not kiss your children so they will kiss you back but so they will kiss their children, and their children's children. —Noah benShea

When a woman is pregnant, her growing body often becomes the unwitting object of attention—privately and publicly. Although well-meaning, advice offered by friends, family, and often complete strangers sends conflicting and confusing messages, especially to the first time mother. In response, many women seek information and advice from "experts," including health care providers, who they have been taught to believe *should* have the *right* answer(s). But what if the professional advice they get does not support—or directly contradicts—the mother's or families personal beliefs and values? What happens when the mother is expected, and often directed, to engage in behaviors and practices that contradict her instincts and intuition?

In today's culture, success is often defined in terms of material and economic wealth. Early independence is idealized and mainstream practices such as the "training up" of children to engage in socially acceptable feeding, elimination, sleep, discipline and behavior patterns is well accepted. Yet there are others whose focus is on beliefs, behaviors, and practices that emulate a more deliberate "people before things" approach to parenting which emphasizes the development of secure attachment and interdependence and both values and respects the mother's unique role in this process. While information and support for more mainstream practices is readily available, where do these "alternative" mothers and families find information and support for *their* values and *their* choices?

It is not unusual for women to seek out or gravitate towards other like minded women. In return they receive communal support along with the opportunity for open and affirming conversation. Often their children become friends and families gather together, forming significant emotional and social bonds. This same "like seeks like" inclination set the stage for a meeting between two women whose casual conversation eventually led to the creation of Attachment Parenting International, Inc., otherwise known as API, which serves as the "mother ship" for uniting women, children, and families who are committed to API Principles.

In addition to providing support for mothers who practice attachment parenting, API serves as a trusted resource for evidence based research and up-to-date information on a variety of topics related to mothering, parenting, and child development. Membership in API provides multiple benefits including access to publications such as API's quarterly magazine *The Attached Family*,[1] an annual subscription to *The Journal of API*,[2] *API Forums*,[3] *API Speaks*,[4] *API Reads*,[5] *Parenting Compass*,[6] and numerous other informational and educational materials. Members also receive discounts on API teleseminars and have access to local API parent support group meetings, the lifeblood of the organization.

In this chapter, I introduce API as an integral part of the motherhood movement, examine API's Principles, provide an overview of the organization, and acknowledge some of their past and present challenges. In closing I will offer some insight into API's future aims, goals, and direction. Attachment Parenting's ultimate goal is to create "a more compassionate world." With that laudable mission in mind, let us take a more detailed look at the history of the organization.

A Chance Meeting

In 1980, two young women—Barbara Nicholson and Lysa Parker—met in Nashville, Tennessee. Parker had just moved to the area from Texas and was interested in meeting other mothers in her new community, so she packed up her children and headed to a La Leche League (LLL) meeting. Nicholson, a leader applicant at the time, was enthusiastic about sharing what she was learning and, after a few conversations; the two quickly realized they shared many of the same ideas, beliefs, and values.

Fourteen years and many conversations later, Parker and Nicholson went from having their "own little support" group to establishing Attachment Parenting International, Inc., a not-for-profit organization dedicated to raising children to be strong citizens and creative contributors to society. Today, API serves mothers and babies worldwide by means of its sixty Support Groups, one hundred accredited active Leaders, approximately one thousand members, and more than ten thousand subscribers.

API boasts an impressive Board of Directors, Advisory Board and Resource Advisory Council (RAC) whose members represent a wide range of disciplines, professions, and organizations dedicated to the emotional and physical well-being of mothers/parents, infants/children, and families. Although not a complete list, some of the more notable members include Sir Richard Bowlby, Bt., son of attachment theorist Dr. John Bowlby; Jan Hunt, Child Psychologist and Director of The Natural Child Project; pediatrician Dr. William Sears and his wife Martha Sears; Dr. Elliott Barker, Psychiatrist and Founder of the Canadian Society for the Prevention of Cruelty to Children (CSPCC); and Peggy O'Mara, Editor of Mothering Magazine.

On the financial side, API is a 501(c) (3) nonprofit member supported organization. According to Guidestar.org, for the fiscal year ending 12/31/2009,

First API Meeting: Lysa Parker, Camille McNutt, Kathy Bishop, Barbara Nicholson, Karen Fletcher and Nancy Crow, January 1994

contributions and program services brought in revenues of $415,401 and there were $400,965 in expenses, leaving the organization with $49,301 in total assets. As with most not-for-profits, many of these assets are reinvested back into the organization.[7]

Over the years API has had partnered—locally, nationally, and globally—with a host of other mother and family centered individuals and organizations. The list, although not exhaustive, includes La Leche League, Mothering Magazine, Lamaze International, Infant Massage USA, Attachment Parenting Canada, and Search Institute. With just over 60 people on staff, the vast majority of which are volunteers, API impressively serves as both a clearinghouse and community of practice within the larger motherhood movement for attachment parenting research, education, and support.

One of the most notable and influential aspects of API is their philosophy, communicated through what they refer to as *The Eight Principles of Attachment Parenting*. These "principles" serve as a critical source of both inspiration and support.

The Eight Principles of Attachment Parenting

The Eight Principles of Attachment Parenting form the core of APIs philosophy which advocates that children's physical and emotional health and well-being are equally important, and that there is a direct connection between how we parent and how our children develop. The Eight Principles are 1) prepare for pregnancy, birth, and parenting, 2) feed with love and respect, 3) respond with sensitivity, 4) use nurturing touch, 5) ensure safe sleep—physically and emotionally, 6) provide consistent and loving care, 7) practice positive discipline, and 8) strive for balance in personal and family life. No matter where a person is on their mothering/parenting journey and regardless of what they may have done, said, or experienced in the past, API does not impose judgment, blame or ultimatums. Instead they offer the Eight Principles and trust that mothers and families will make decisions that are best suited to their individual beliefs and values. In addition, API openly recognizes the challenges that many mothers face, especially when their beliefs and values conflict with more socially pervasive beliefs and practices. The often overwhelming pressure to conform can interfere with a mother's ability to develop a responsive relationship with her baby. In response, API encourages mothers to recognize, try to understand, empathize with, and respect each individual child's unique natural inner rhythms and be patient with themselves.

While it is not practical to go into depth on each within this chapter, I will employ Principles 1, 4, and 5 to illustrate how they may be used as guides.

Principle 1: Prepare Yourself for Pregnancy, Birth, and Parenting

While API's overall focus is on parenting, Principle 1, *Prepare Yourself for Pregnancy, Birth, and Parenting,* maintains that an emotionally and physically healthy prenatal period plays a crucial role in the short- and long-term development of the child and the mother, as well as the development of mother-child and family relationships. Towards that end, mothers are invited to reflect on childhood experiences, as well as their current attitudes, beliefs, and behaviors; and work through any negative emotions they might have. The goal is for mothers to empower themselves, starting before their baby is born, by becoming more knowledgeable about their options for birth, feeding/weaning, sleep options, and discipline—four of the most talked about and highly debated topics in parenting. Good nutrition and physical activity are also encouraged.

Principle 4: Use Nurturing Touch

Principle 4 outlines the benefits of nurturing touch and provides research which shows that humans not only survive, they thrive on touch and the sense of connection it provides. For example, nurtured babies nurse better and gain weight faster, cry less, and are calmer. Other benefits include the stimulation of growth promoting hormones, improved intellectual and motor development, and the regulation of babies' temperature, heart rate, and sleep/wake patterns. Nurturing touch can come in the form of skin-to-skin contact, breastfeeding, joint baths, massage, and babywearing. In order to avoid forced or premature independence, API cautions against the overuse of devices designed to hold a baby independently, such as swings, jumpers, plastic carriers, and strollers.

Recognizing that everyone deserves to receive the gift of touch, API extends the acceptable "touch time" to children well beyond what many people consider appropriate by openly endorsing nurturing touch with children of both gen-

First API exhibitt, La Leche League conference, Indianapolis, October 1994

ders—no matter how big or old they are. Nurturing touch can come in the form of frequent hugs, snuggling, back rubs and massage, or more physical play.[8] The purpose is to encourage children of all ages to connect with their own physicality and appreciate touch for the reconnection and health benefits it provides. In addition to reducing stress, nurturing touch also stimulates brain chemicals that are crucial for healthy growth and development, including secure, rather than avoidant, attachment.

The potential for nurturing intentional touch is especially intriguing given the research which suggests that cultures high in physical affection, touch, holding or carrying have a lower rate of adult physical violence (Prescott; Heller 71). While we would like to believe that all children receive nurturing physical affection, and we receive and provide adequate amounts of it in our own families, the high rates of violence in today's society suggest differently. To increase awareness and counter that trend, API provides research that both encourages and supports nurturing touch with hopes of creating a less violent and more peaceful world.

Principle 5: Ensure Safe Sleep—Physically and Emotionally

The topic of sleep—specifically naps and bedtime—is often a contentious issue among mothers, between a woman and her husband/partner, and even between a mother and her child's doctor, inviting debates, judgments, and ultimatums. Through Principle 5, API maintains that babies and children's needs are not limited to their waking hours and suggests that the parent's role is to be responsive and help their child regulate their own emotions throughout the day. According to the API website,

> Parents are … encouraged to explore the variety of different sleeping arrangements, and to chose the approach that best allows them to be responsive at night. Individual babies" sleep patterns and needs vary a great deal. Remain flexible and understand that it is developmentally appropriate and normal for babies to wake up during the night to feed and seek contact.

In their quest to provide a safe and suitable sleeping environment for their child, and get a good night's sleep themselves, mothers may find themselves confused or misled by options and opinions promulgated by the media and healthcare providers regarding where, when, and how long a baby/child "needs" to sleep. They are often told to put their baby down in its crib, in a separate room, for scheduled naps and bedtime before he/she is fully asleep. But what if a mother wants to have her baby close by? What if, instead of putting the baby in a separate bed in a separate room, she provides a suitable sleeping space somewhere in the parent's room, a practice referred to as "co-sleeping?" What if she chooses to practice the "family bed" and brings the baby to bed with her? For many mothers, children, and families these serve as preferable alternatives.

API offers research based guidelines which help mothers/parents make safer choices about where their family sleeps while honouring their, and their child's, needs.[9] Standing strong against the national fear-based "Babies Sleep Safest Alone" campaigns, API launched its *Infant Sleep Safety Campaign,* which serves as a valuable resource to parents, partners, and the media regarding infant sleep.

No matter where a baby/child sleeps during the day or at night, they often wake because they are hungry or lonely. The child who wakes frequently or doesn't nap—or both—can be frustrating and tiring for everyone in the family, especially the mother. Mothers are frequently told to let their babies cry "because it's good for the lungs" and that they will "spoil" their baby, or they are being "manipulated," if they pick their baby up too quickly. Unsure and unsupported, many of these mothers seek guidance from their child's pediatrician or follow one of the popular "sleep training" methods, such as "Ferberizing," so popular in Western cultures.[10] Relinquishing their right and instinct to comfort their own child, many mothers cry along with their babies, only on separate sides of the door. In response, API draws upon research which suggests that the practice of letting a baby "cry it out" or "self-sooth" is inconsistent with the infant's neurological and developmental abilities. These practices result in detrimental physiological effects on the baby by increasing the stress hormone cortisol in the brain. They also set the stage for the cycle of "protest-despair-detachment" that, according to attachment theory, happens when a child who is trained not to cry learns to repress—rather than express—his feelings (Sunderland 79).

Ultimately, attachment parenting provides mothers with strategies and tools that will help to minimize daily stressors so that their relationship with their child is strengthened and the child grows up feeling more secure and connected. Mothers are additionally supported in their efforts to help their child develop an internally guided conscience based on compassion for others. These bonds of attachment and trust are formed whenever parents consistently and compassionately respond to their infants and child's needs, whether the mother remains home, returns to work, or needs childcare. Finally, API also recognizes that sometimes mother's feel out of balance and stress the importance of ensuring the mother's needs, not just the child's, are recognized, validated, and met to the greatest extent possible.

These Principles, beliefs, and practices serve as the basis for APIs major contributions to the motherhood movement.

API's Role in the Motherhood Movement

Attachment Parenting International holds a unique and vital place in the motherhood movement, especially for those women whose beliefs about and expressions of mothering and motherhood challenge mainstream beliefs and practices. While the overall goal of the women's movement has been a quest for equality, mothers, mothering, and motherhood have not always received their fair share of (positive) attention, nor have they always been given fair and equal treatment. Despite debates on the essentialization of womanhood via motherhood, or the mothering "propaganda" that touts motherhood as the "new feminist frontier," the reality remains that motherhood *is* an experience unique to women and, if we are going to support *all* women, we need to support *all* mothers—no matter their age, race/ethnicity, social class, sexual orientation, or economic standing.

API provides support for women who, although they may not be inherently nurturing, wish to learn about and practice mothering in a nurturing way. They do not attack or marginalize women who choose not to mother, or mother differently. Instead of taking a position and purporting that motherhood is the "chosen" profession, and that no other profession is as rewarding or satisfying, API simply supports women who *are* mothers.

In return, by applying a variety of theoretical and analytical lenses, as well as opening the venues by which information could be shared and discussed, the motherhood movement gave space and meaning to the terms "mother," "motherhood," and "mothering" as viable topics worthy of serious study and consideration. The movement successfully vindicated mothers in their quest for women's rights within the home at the same time it acknowledged how unproductive and damaging silence and ignorance can be. While the complexities of both definition and experience continue to be teased out, and there are still a variety of "camps," without the motherhood movement these discussions would not be taking place, mothers would have less access to information and support, and organizations like API would not exist.

Obstacles/Challenges/Issues

No great thought or worthwhile organization is without its critics, growing pains, and challenges, and API is no exception. According to Samantha Gray, API's Executive Director and Business Management Coordinator, some of the greatest challenges over time have been "overcoming myths, economic conditions, being a not-for-profit organization, and working in prevention—not crisis—mode."[11] Yet, despite the current economy and focus, API has experienced increased growth along with greater understanding and appreciation as families—facing their own challenges—look to attachment science and parenting for answers and support. In fact the lean nature of the organizations structure has worked to its advantage as they pioneer innovative approaches to management and organization and embrace new technologies that streamline operations and facilitate new alliances and enhanced networking.

Interestingly enough, one of API's biggest challenges is helping people to understand what attachment parenting is, and what it is not, and putting the focus on attachment security not practices per se. Attachment parenting is not a parenting "style" or "choice." It is merely the way that parents used to take care of their children before the advent of modern medicine and the appearance of child health/care "professionals" who—trained within a culture that values independence versus interdependence—warned parents that they were being "indulgent" and "manipulated" if they were readily available and responsive to their children, and that their children would suffer as a result. Attachment parenting is about being attentive, not indulgent or permissive. It also takes into account the age of the child. While some Principles—in whole or in part—may be viewed as optional, the science of attachment is well-researched and simply does not bear this out.

Another significant challenge has been obtaining the funding needed to maintain and expand parent education programs including the production of more books, videos, audios, and virtual webinars. Although parents are one of our world's greatest natural resources, and whatever is done to help parents directly supports and benefits their children, we live in a time where more value and emphasis, and therefore more money, is put on programs that focus on teachers; mentors, afterschool programs, and daycare. The focus seems to be on everyone but the mother/parent(s).

The current economy has also had a negative influence on generating new and sustaining memberships, as well as the number and size of philanthropic contributions used to fund API programs and outreach. Many people within the API network, some of whom are highly educated, have chosen to live off one income so that the other parent can be the primary caregiver. These families, along with others who are struggling to make do with two incomes, simply do not have discretionary funds available to pay for memberships in organizations, no matter how worthy. In response, API is in the process of expanding it philanthropist network through their partnership counsels.

None of this would be possible without the efforts of many volunteer hours, provided primarily by API parents, many of whom see their efforts as a way to maintain their educational and professional expertise. This personal touch is part of what makes API so unique. In the past volunteers have instituted innovative methods to balance family and work like cross training, job sharing, team arrangements, and technology so that they can operate in a completely virtual situation.[12] While this volunteer support is essential to the survival of the organization, and although there has been relatively little turnover in the long term, the reality is that API needs to reach more mothers/parents and gain new funding sources if the organization is going to survive.

Future Aims, Goals, and Direction of the Organization

There is much in store for the organization as it moves into the future. Upcoming projects include expanding their Parent Education Program, increasing the number of Support Groups, and initiating a program to complement API's grassroots network with a mass media awareness and social marketing campaign. Parents and professionals will have opportunities to connect at local gatherings, API conferences, the AP Community of Practice, and through the publication of *The Attached Family* magazine, while *The Journal of API* will help API expand its research and assessment efforts and be duly recognized in the professional and academic community.

Recognizing that advocacy and outreach are essential to the education of policy and law makers, especially those who work in public health and the care and custody of children, API has reached out to the judicial system by developing toolkits for attorneys and judges and providing resources to families and advocates. In their quest to serve *all* families, API is increasing their focus on the specific and unique needs of previously underserved communities. This includes making their resources available in different languages and expanding their international focus.

API is committed to providing information, support, and networking opportunities to otherwise un- and under-served mothers in a similarly engaging and supportive manner. Many of these families do not have the "luxury" of going beyond caring for their child's basic needs. By focusing on expanding the availability of information and support to low income parents/families and other marginalized populations, new communities of support will be created. Toward that end, local support groups host programs in shelters and public housing communities with plans to expand to prison communities, especially those with established parenting programs. These communities also connect mothers with other, and perhaps more experienced mothers, who can model first-hand the API Principles and talk honestly, and knowledgably, about child development and what it is like to do attachment parenting on a day-to-day basis.

Yet another project will focus on educating the media, a prime source of misinformation and misunderstanding, especially when it comes to "hot" issues like co-sleeping, babywearing, inter-dependence versus independence, feeding, and sleep. Toward that end API created a list of questions, along with supporting research, that will help reporters ensure the reliability and accuracy of their information, as well as take other sources and viewpoints into consideration.

This may prove particularly challenging in light of the vast discrepancy between the interests and budgets of major corporations and a not-for-profit humanistic organization such as API.

Conclusion

In conclusion, Attachment Parenting is not simply the name of an organization within the women's movement. As previously stated, their primary mission is to promote strong, healthy emotional bonds between children and their parents through the Eight Principles of Attachment Parenting philosophy which promotes active, intentional, conscious, and intuitive nurturing to fulfill a child's basic needs for trust, empathy, and affection.

Few other organizations encourage mothers to be totally responsive to an infant or child's emotional needs. Few others provide research that supports these practices in accordance with each individual child's personality and developmental abilities. Few others encourage mothers/parents to trust that their child's emotional and developmental needs will be met if they do. Recognizing that the ultimate responsibility of raising a child falls on the shoulders of the mother, API publicly affirms that mothers should have the right to mother their children in ways that feel mutually nurturing and rewarding. When parents live in places where practices such as co-sleeping, babywearing, extended breastfeeding, and non-violence are considered alternative, or even deviant practices, API's information and support may even be lifesaving. Among the patchwork of mothering organizations—some more mainstream than others—API is the thread which has held the fabric of many "alternative" families together.

[1] *The Attached Family* is a quarterly print magazine containing in dept articles to educate and support families on Attachment Parenting (AP) from conception through the teenage years, and even in parenting adult children. TheAttachedFamily.com, published as a weekly ezine, is the online extension of this publication.
[2] *The Journal of API* is Attachment Parenting's newest venture. While targeting professionals serving parents, the publication will also be available to all API members.
[3] *API Forums* give space for conversations about topics of general interest (healthcare/wellness, parenting, children's celebrations, relationships, etc.), which allow members to explore the day-to-day challenges and joys of raising attached children as well as Circumstance- and Principle-Specific Forums, a Professionals Forum, an API Around-the World Forum, and an API Support Group Forum.
[4] *API Speaks* was launched in April of 2008, as part of Attachment Parenting International's larger effort to offer interactive content through their web site.
[5] *API Reads* is an online book discussion group.
[6] *Parenting Compass: Guiding the Way for Parents Through Compassion,* is API's newest members" publication.

[7]http://www2.guidestar.org/organizations/62-1574168/attachment-parenting-international.aspx#
[8]Play which involves wrestling or tickling should follow the lead of the child and should not be forced.
[9]http://ocfs.ny.gov/main/babiessleepsafestalone/video_psa_eng.html
[10]The Ferber method of sleep training, based on Dr. Richard Ferber's 1985 book, *Solve Your Child's Sleep Problems*, lays out a seven-day timetable for how long to leave one's baby alone before going in to comfort him or her. By day seven, the baby is crying for as long as 45 minutes before being reassured (http://abcnews.go.com/GMA/OnCall/story?id=1317690). API reports that sleep training techniques such as these can have short- and long-term detrimental physiological and psychological effects on babies and mothers.
[11]Conversation with Samantha Gray on 2/18/2011.
[12]Because API is run by volunteers who can live on opposite sides of the country, or the world, the vast majority of their communications and work is done via virtual office space, email, and conference calls. This also presents a challenge in terms of fundraising since there isn't a "storefront" location people can go to or connect APIs efforts with. The establishment of partner councils should help them overcome this challenge.

Works Cited

Heller, Sharon. *The Vital Touch*. New York: Henry Holt and Co., 1997.

Prescott, J. W. (1990) "Affectional Bonding for the Prevention of Violent Behaviors: Neurobiological, Psychological and Religious/Spiritual Determinants." *Violent Behavior.* Ed. L. J. Hertzberg, G. F. Ostrum and J. R. Field.(pp. 95-124). Great Neck, NY: PMA Publishing, 1990. 95-124.

Sunderland, Margo. *The Science of Parenting*. New York: DK Publishing Inc., 2006.

31. Choice Moms

Building Community, Resources and Services for the Choice Mom Community Worldwide

CHRISTIN GEALL

CHOICE MOMS IS A PRIMARILY a web-based support group for women "thinking, trying, waiting or becoming single mothers by choice." The organization runs a number of communications and community-building initiatives, such as online discussion groups and workshops. Through these venues, Choice Moms offers resources and support to mothers who have chosen single-parenthood.

Mikki Morrissette, a journalist and mother based in Minneapolis, coined the term "Choice Mom"[2] when writing her book, *Choosing Single Motherhood: The Thinking Woman's Guide*, in 2005. She later launched the Choice Moms website in March of 2006. In its first year, the site garnered approximately 800 visitors per month; in 2011, the site averages 4,000 visitors a month.

Choice Moms hosts a number of discussion boards. In October of 2005, Morrissette and five other women launched the first, to great success. (It recently topped out at 1,200 members.) A number of topical boards have been added to meet demand. Choice Moms also offers podcasts called "Choice Chats." In an April 21, 2010, blog post Morrissette wrote: "Choice Chat podcasts have been downloaded more than 21,000 times; the most popular topics (in order): 1) negotiating with a known donor, 2) what donor-conceived adults want to know, 3) at-home insemination, 4) fertility basics."

Philosophy

Choice Moms' philosophy, as stated on the website, is centered on "building community, resources and services for the Choice Mom community worldwide." The three pillars of Choice Moms are communication, community and support. The banner of the home page reveals Choice Mom's reach. It reads: "Thinking; Trying; Waiting; Becoming; Being; Events." Profiles of choice moms, recent news, and feature articles offer visitors multiple points of connection. The Choice Moms network also extends through social media; links for Twitter, Facebook and You Tube also appear on the home page.

Digging deeper into the site, keywords offer areas of interest to women, such as:

"Our kids; Fertility; At-home insemination; Donor conception; Known donor; Adoption; Stories of other Choice Moms; Money matters; Telling and talking, to our children and others, about this choice; Building a support network; Stress relief, holistic and organizational; Emotions about this choice and regional resource guides."

Mandate

According to founder Morrissette, the mandate of Choice Moms is threefold:

> 1) To create a supportive, welcoming, educational environment for single women who consciously decide to become mothers without a partner.
> 2) To create print and online tools of communication, as well as to advocate for Choice Moms and their children.
> 3) To create points of connection that bring women together in special events and activities designed to help them celebrate this journey, share their struggles and concerns, and learn the best ways to dedicate themselves to the lives of their children.

Challenges

Choice Moms founder, Morrissette, first identified herself in a recent interview "as a journalist by background, not a business person." Her primary focus is on "content development and sparking conscious conversations and connections." However, in order to meet those goals, Choice Moms has had to generate revenues. Hence, the financial challenges facing the organization, as reported by Morrissette: "I pay a website designer, podcast editor, and occasionally my discussion board moderators when they've been accomplishing a lot. I try to pay myself, based purely on whether I've sold sponsorships. And I pay a 30 percent commission to any Choice Moms who recommend a new sponsor who comes on board." She goes on to note that, "it's largely a volunteer labor of love."

Morrissette's greatest challenge is a shortage of time. She listed her managerial duties as including, "maintaining a robust website, moderating blog comments, two discussion boards, an occasional podcast (lower priority right now) and occasional book sales, in tandem with six networking events per year requiring travel."

In order to keep costs low, Morrissette works from a home office. Revenues from workshops help fund the organization, in addition to sponsorships. She noted that, "the most expensive aspect of the business are the workshops I do. I have a primary sponsor for those, without whom I wouldn't be able to do them (California Cryobank), that remains hands off in terms of format. We confer about the now six host cities to visit each year, and the selection of dates. I charge a nominal fee to women who attend the workshops. That's the primary source of revenue. I do have website advertisers and other sponsors who are increasingly providing value-added resources for women—such as e-books on specialty topics (fertility, dealing with emotions), and a new Welcome Kit to new moms that just launched."

Choice Moms currently has a volunteer board. Regarding their advisory capacity, Morrissette said, "My board has met once since I incorporated in 2006. Obviously, it's pretty loosely structured. I primarily rely on advisory board input based on anything happening in discussion with community."

Activities

Choice Moms networking events connect like-minded women who are thinking, trying, waiting or becoming single mothers by choice. In 2011, Choice Moms will meet in Toronto, Boston, Raleigh, Seattle, Los Angeles, and Philadelphia. A sponsorship from California Cryobank supports these events.

Choice Moms also advocates on behalf of the community. Morrissette has served as a spokesperson for mothers who choose single-parenthood. She also ensures any media stories relevant to the community are promptly posted to keep Choice Moms informed.

Relationship to Wider Motherhood Movement

Despite the challenges of running an online community and national and international workshops, Morrissette is positive about Choice Moms' future:

> The women who tap into the resource benefit a great deal from learning from the wisdom of others, talking out loud about their fears, and sharing their insights and tips with each other. We have a worldwide community, and this year I'm starting to use local coordinators in certain places to help generate Regional Guides for the website, such as in Canada, U.K., Australia and certain high-traffic U.S. cities.

Morrissette refers to these geographic regions as "markets."[2] Based on its history of growth, Choice Moms membership should continue to grow as it expands its geographic reach.

The options for single women wishing to become mothers have also increased. In a recent Cambridge University survey, 60 percent of Choice Moms reported having used anonymous donor conception to build their family; 15 percent by a known donor; 12 percent through adoption; 12 percent by other means (some indicated open-identity donor as a distinction from anonymous; others: foster care, embryo donation).[3]

Choice Moms supports these women who may not have been represented in the wider motherhood movement. By providing access to information, hosting networking events and fostering a discussion of the challenges and joys of single parenting, Choice Moms has succeeded in building a strong support network for a growing number of twenty-first century mothers.

[1]Morrissette acknowledged in a 2008 *Globe and Mail* article that the group "Single Mothers by Choice," founded in 1981, by psychologist Jane Mattes, significantly influenced her decision to become a parent. However, she felt mothers, such as herself, might benefit from a shorter, clearer name—one that dropped the world "single."

[2]See: <http://www.choicemoms.org/blog/347/where_are_choice_moms_and_what_matters_to_us>.

[3]See: <http://www.choicemoms.org/blog/112/data_on_choice_moms>.

Works Cited

Morrissette, Mikki. *Choosing Single Motherhood: The Thinking Woman's Guide*. Self-published. 2005.

32. Bad Mother's Club

The Online Safe Haven for Australian Mums: Politically Incorrect or Reality Parenting?

AMANDA COX

THE BAD MOTHER'S CLUB HAS become the safe-haven for Australian mums to speak openly and honestly about their experiences of childbirth and parenting, the trials, tribulations and dilemmas they face every day, and the opportunity to let off steam in a supportive and non-judgemental online environment. Launching online in 2006 out of needs by the founder, the business also now offers a number of offline opportunities for mums to meet up and let their hair down and is branching into books; both fiction and non-fiction and a portal for resources for Australian mums, that focus on the reality of their daily lives as opposed to expert opinion and information.

Predominantly, it is the safe haven of white, middle-class Australian mothers, aged 30-45 years with one or more children of school age. Both married and single, due to separation, mothers make up a significant proportion of the member base, many of whom are stay at home mothers, working part time, or are running their own business from home. A good portion of these women have experienced some form of depression in their lives, particularly around the time they became mothers. Postnatal and general depressions are most common, with some having experienced anxiety disorders.

Many have joined in order to find a place where they fit in, not enjoying or having moved on from their first time Mother's Group, feeling ostracised for not conforming to the "right" way to mother or adhere to the "good mother" standards set out by mainstream media, parenting publications and the myriad parenting books available on the market. All wish to feel accepted for who they are, the parenting and other choices they make, and to find support and friendship, without being told what to do, or how to do it. Young mums, aged 25 and under with young children are prevalent on the site, however aren't as active as those with older children. First time mums, and mothers with young babies, pop in, yet are rarely active on the site.

Context

While there appears to be a strong movement towards the support and recognition of mothers in Australia, in terms of valuing their role as mother, the implementation of paid maternity (and paternity) leave and the increase in family friendly workplaces, there also appears to be a conscious decision towards divisiveness. Mainstream media, in particular, deliver stories intent on creating discussion and division within the community, whether it be who pays for women to stay at home and raise children, via increases in tax, or the "best" way to bring up baby. The use of loaded words and expert opinion are frequent, yet the acceptance of differences between women, the needs of individual families and even the belief and values of mothers, including cultural values, are regularly neglected.

Parenting publications who purport to be all-inclusive often publish parenting related stories along the lines of whatever the latest research states, whether biased or even conducted under appropriate and research-acceptable standards or not. Reporting of such research is so common, and the increase in the number of parenting information websites and "mummy bloggers" only aids in widespread dissemination of the word. Unfortunately, the research is, more often than not conflicting, with suggestion that one particular parenting style is the "right" way one week, followed up the next by another acceptable, yet contradictory style. All of which are accompanied by terms such as "long term emotional damage" and "psychological disorders in the future" in relation to the outcome of the child.

Thus, women, mothers, are left conflicted and confused, with a persistent self-doubt over whether they are doing the "right" thing, or permanently damaging their children. Ultimately, Mother Guilt is the basis of which all stories are reported, whether by mainstream media, parenting publications or the websites of experts, support organizations with a particular slant or your every day mummy blogger. This is taken a step further with not only a schism between mothers and their parenting styles and beliefs, but also between mothers and the rest of society; the pitting of one "side" against another, with no apparent middle ground or grey area.

Terms such as "mummy wars" have sprung up, and could just as easily relate to diverse parenting practices, for example, controlled crying versus co-sleeping, as to whether breastfeeding in public is acceptable or taking prams into small cafes is a safety risk and annoying to other customers. Mothers are not only feeling confused about which is the "best" or "right" way to parent, they are also doubting their intuition and their own values, and feeling guilty as well as devalued. Isolation is setting in due to, as previously mentioned, not conforming to the latest, most referred to parenting technique in their mothers group or play group, or wondering if they go out for a coffee they will be welcomed, shunned or asked to leave.

Notwithstanding is the evident need to keep some thoughts and feelings to themselves, due to fear of retribution or repercussions. Admitting you are having a bad day, you're tired or not coping is tantamount to admitting you are a "bad mother" and that perhaps you shouldn't have had children at all. To admit to

Amanda Cox

wanting to go back to work for your own benefit, whether emotional, psychological or financial, often leads to questioning as to why you had children in the first place, alongside pointed remarks about selfishness and what is best for the child.

It seems, in Australia at least, that once you have a baby, you are no longer a person with needs, thoughts, feelings or a personality of your own. You have, for all intents and purposes, the extension of your baby. You are little more than the incubator you were, also without thoughts and feelings, during your child's gestational period.

Purpose and Philosophy

The purpose of Bad Mother's Club is simply to provide a safe, welcoming, supportive and non-judgemental, if not anonymous, online space for Australian mums to openly and honestly express their thoughts, feelings and attitudes about their own experiences with parenting, seek advice, support and information from others in similar circumstances, share information and resources.

Understanding of the context in which we are currently parenting is embraced, and rather than discuss which persuasion is best for our children, and ourselves, we allow for women to accept and understand who *they* are, acknowledging and accepting their beliefs, values and parenting styles. Support can then be offered on these grounds, whilst also allowing for mums to vent; express any difficulties or bad days they are having, concerns they have or confusion they are experiencing.

Being able to get a stressful situation off your chest, and onto a web-based forum, in itself, can make people feel better. Opening a discussion, and allowing for the expression of "grey areas," for example, not everyone finds breastfeeding easy or natural for any number of reasons, goes some way to educating others, and also provide an understanding of circumstances and situations not often spoken about in the mainstream media or parenting organizations, both on and offline. Our philosophy is "you're not bad, you're just dealing with reality the best way you can, with what you have."

Taking into consideration the vastly different parenting styles, beliefs and values, accepting that everyone is unique and has their own way of doing things that suit *them* is the basis of the organization. That there are far too many "experts" out there telling us what to do, without any apparent acknowledgement that there is a life outside our kids, or that, perhaps, we as mums have our own thoughts and feelings, too, is also a strong philosophy underlying what we do.

This is important for a number of reasons. First and foremost, we believe a happy mummy makes for a happy and healthy family. Loss of self, being available only for the children and/or putting the child first at all times, has the effect of leading to unhappy, and potentially depressed mothers. This, of course, has the potential to impact on the family in a negative way; unhappy children, deteriorating relationships and high-stress households, for example.

That the expert focus is all child-based leads to mothers feeling not only undervalued and ignored, but also completely disregards the emotional and psychological changes that occur from time to time in the process of parenting. Lack of sleep, for example, leads to over-tiredness, which in turn significantly impacts on levels of tolerance and ability to perform disciplinary actions or to just get through a day without yelling.

The cycle of guilt, feelings of being a "bad mother" and the doubting of intuition is perpetual and spiralling downwards. Of course, having all talk aimed at you, but centred around the needs, wants and what is "best" for your child, can only have the impact of having mothers feeling worthless, unimportant and that their own needs and wants are of no value whatsoever. Resources and articles offered to members and visitors of the site have strong satirical and humorous perspectives on expert advice and living with children, including activities and behaviours expected of mums in the twenty-first century.

Written mostly by the founder of the site, with input via the online forums and online surveys from members, newsletter subscribers and colleagues, the articles and other resources, such as e-guides and facts sheets, are all based on and around parenting generally, or mothering specifically. Usually, the relate to the actions we are often required to perform as mothers, whether it be preparing school lunches, combing hair for nits, or looking after yourself during or post pregnancy.

The focus is always on the mother. For example, where head lice is the topic, rather than repeat the information and advice offered by any number of parenting or government health websites, and notes home from the school, the focus will be on the actions the mother is required to perform; spending hours combing hair, rushing out to spend a fortune on nit treatment at 10:00 p.m. The tone is always comical, with an extreme look at the situation at hand.

Other articles relate to the actions and behaviours of other people, from the Mother-In-Law, to husbands and partners, children's behaviours and development and members of the local community. These articles also have a humorous perspective to all too common circumstances. Recipe and household tips also feature on occasion, again with a satirical twist and include a facetious look at the information and recipes imparted by other websites. A greatly simplified version, with the "expert" tone, is then imparted to our readers.

Members have also provided their own written accounts of personal experiences in depression, stillbirth and miscarriage, and other accidents and situations that include being a mother, or involving their children. These provide an avenue with which other mothers who have experienced similar to relate and feel less isolated and alone. Social and media discourse are challenged, and obvious, common problems, circumstances and situations are highlighted in a fun way that not only cause a mother to smile, but to actually think about her own situation and behaviours; a less than subtle reality check, without the guilt.

Ultimately, however, the articles are about seeing the lighter side of parenting, pointing out the obvious, offering a different perspective and a light-hearted alternative to mainstream "should do's." They're about giving mums the opportunity to laugh, at themselves, the world, or just because, as opposed to mothers comparing themselves or feeling unsure about the "right" way to do things.

History

The Bad Mother's Club was conceived in 2005, a result of my own needs to find an online support group that fully understood the implications of postnatal depression, both for the mother herself and those around her. Although a significant number online parent support sites existed at the time, where well known and had been around for quite a while, an underlying conformist attitude was present. Members of these sites appeared to have to conform to particular parenting methods or philosophies, to restrain themselves from divulging certain information or saying particular things, and to pretend that all was good in their world.

Discussion on the online forums, for the most part centred around drug free vaginal birth, the practice of controlled crying was strictly forbidden and having your baby attached to you all day every day was the only acceptable method of mothering. This was evident in the forum posts themselves, some verging on bragging, and backed up by comments from others. Words such as "super mum" and reference to being "amazing" were common.

Quite the reverse was true of those who posted questions asking for support for controlled crying, where other members had no hesitation in advising how "bad" it was, judging and, rather than supporting and offering alternatives, would condemn the original poster. Similar was true of those who requested information relating to experiences on which drugs to use during birth, or caesarean sections.

Some websites were unashamedly promoting their particular slant. Other forums and sites that offered no particular philosophy, as a rule, still appeared inundated with self-righteous members who had no hesitation in advising others how things "should" be done, and openly condemning, through phrases such as "you are damaging your child" and "if you are not giving your child the best start, you shouldn't be allowed to have children."

Conformity also revolved around the "happy life" syndrome, where discussion around children's milestones and cutesy behaviours were acceptable, as were successful breastfeeding stories. Stories, in particular, that overcame some form of adversity, whether it was mastitis or an interfering mother-in-law, in order to conform and perform whatever the latest mothering discourse was (co-sleeping, baby wearing, flashcards for children under one to teach them to read) were most popular.

On the contrary, support for particularly bad days or depressive episodes were poorly handled, with other members of the sites condemning behaviours or spoken-out-loud thoughts, arguing over parenting practices rather than encouraging or assisting, or blatantly judging others for their beliefs. A particular example was a post-natally depressed mother, unable to cope and opening up to her online support group, advising she was not coping and just wanted to leave the house, never to return because she hated it so much. Instead of support, understanding and suggestions to seek help from a doctor or specialist support organization, she was accused of being a "terrible mother" and that good mothers do not think like that. Accusing her of all manner of bad parenting, she was also advised that she should be putting her children and their needs first. To leave them, regardless of her mental and emotional state, would be the worst thing a mother could do, according to the replies to her cry for help on this particular forum.

Unlike these other sites, and particularly because of this last example, Bad Mother's Club's forum was set up to provide not only a safe place to vent, and speak openly and honesty about parenting experiences, thoughts, feelings and requests for help. The forums are also highly moderated to ensure that judgement, pressure to conform to certain (other's) expectations, condemnation and deprecation are absent. As a result of the openness and honestly, a community that offers empathy, support, and the sharing of experiences has emerged. This is evident, particularly when discussion of children's behaviour and management of such behaviour arises. Where most other parenting sites the focus is the best way to manage the behaviour, and usually involves on what the latest and loudest research or reporting advises is "good for the child," our forums allow for others to share how they managed the behaviour. More importantly, they consider the circumstances of the mother, and what disciplinary/positive reinforcement behaviours *she* feels she can implement and cope with, and where she may need support or other ideas.

Bad days, it is understood, have been evident in parenting for generations, yet the opportunity to speak honestly of them has been ill received. Again, the site provides the opportunity to let off some steam, but also allow others to share their similar experiences, offering not only support and how others managed particular situations, but also removes those feelings of isolation and inadequacy. The lack of acceptance with frank discussions about certain parenting experiences, whether it be mode of birth, inability to breastfeed, or you've inadvertently left your glass of wine in reach of the toddler, who has either spilled it on the heirloom rug, or drunk the contents of the glass, exacerbates the feelings of guilt and "bad mothering." Sharing the experiences, and having others share theirs, enables a connection and friendship, but also knowing you are not alone and others do really understand and appreciate you and your feelings. To discuss only the feelings of the child, and how the child can best be served, as mentioned earlier, only leads to feeling devalued in oneself.

The main focus of other sites also seemed to be that of the baby; whether it was the promotion and advertising of products or information and resources. All advice was focussed around the baby and its physical and psychological wellbeing, with little or no regard for the wellbeing of the mother. These messages of "baby first" gave the impression that the mother was merely a machine and you stopped being a parent, and your kids stopped being kids, once they hit two- or three-years of age. Little information, resources and discussion occurred for and around the over-twos.

Products and information for and to support mothers were lacking. It highlighted the "put your child first" mentality, which, for me conflicted with my "but if I'm happy and do things for me, I can be a better mum." Personally, I was unsure of how to manage particular behaviours in my children in certain circumstances, like being overtired or stressed, and could find no information with which to aid me in this.

The fact that a mother had any feelings at all appeared non-existent, except for the often humorous acknowledgement about lack of sleep. Dealing with managing a baby while extremely sleep deprived, despite this acknowledgement, was in severe deficit. That any other thought, feeling or emotion was evoked in mothers was not up for discussion. Anywhere.

Having experienced postnatal depression, and now the mother of a two-year-old and four-year-old, lacking in support and opportunities to connect with likeminded others, I created this place. Although resources, articles and information relating to advise for sleep deprived and/or stressed mothers are still in their infancy, with only few available, acknowledgment that mothers are people unto themselves, with thoughts and feelings separate from the child is strongly evident on the forums. The entire site comes with the acceptance of a wicked sense of humour, and you were allowed the use of profanity; two conditions that were banned on all other online forums and chat rooms at the time.

Profanity, while seemingly a minor issue, is allowable because we acknowledge that some mothers use this sort of language. We also understand that, at times, particularly when stress levels are high, that the use of profanity can help to emphasise the seriousness of a situation, or it may just help to make the author of the post feel just that much better. Rather than see it as "offensive" as some other forums do, we understand that no offence is intended. Instead we see it as being just a part of who a particular member is, or as an aid to a stress outlet, or both.

Humour plays another, very important role, in that, first and foremost, it causes readers to smile, and hopefully laugh. During periods of feeling down, stressed and not coping a small laugh during their morning can make all the difference, pulling them out of their sad reverie. For others, it has provided the opportunity to consider their situation or circumstance from another perspective, or to enable them to see the funny side of a particular incident. It may be as simple as a member explaining of her discontent at her toddler covering the house in talcum powder before she leaves for work, and another member seeing the humour in the situation. "Laughing at the misfortune of others" and "it's funny because it wasn't me, this time" have become an unofficial catch phrases on the forums. Whilst they change the tone of the original post for one member, it enables other members to see the lighter side, and, ultimately, the original poster can see the funny side of the situation as well.

A large part of this humour is my own personal blog, which initially started as a series of articles on the website itself, and is now an entity on its own; *Diary of a Mad Cow* (http://www.diaryofamadcow.com.au). The purpose of this blog was to encourage and, at times, force me to see the humour in my own life during particularly dark days. I write, for the most part, about the day-to-day goings on of my family, seeing each potentially stressful or annoying situation from the perspective of others, enabling me to see the funny side of it.

Articles written for the site are drawn from these experiences, as well as those of the members on the forums. The humorous aspect has aided significantly in Australian mums feeling less isolated and more adequate in their parenting abilities. Partly, this is due to knowing others have dealt with very similar experiences. Another aspect is the ability to put their lives into perspective; whether it be someone having a similar, yet worse, experience and coming through the others side, knowing that others have similar feelings about being a "bad mother" or just knowing that their children's behaviour is "normal."

Another mother speaking of their children's behaviour; for example boys playing with their penises from a young age, climbing everything or an unrelenting obsession with trains can have a greater impact on feelings of normality than can an expert-written information article or parenting book. Neither of which generally touch on such behaviours in any pertinent way. Adding a touch of humour to such experiences, whether via the blog or articles, or posts on the forums, adds not only the opportunity to laugh at the exploits of others, but also a level of relatability and connection with other humans (mothers) that can't be achieved through the medium of imparting information only.

The site, originally, was realmums.com.au launched in March 2006, with "Bad Mother's Club" officially launched in 2007 as an offline venture, including magazine and events. Events centred around providing mums with a night off and away from their families, and include dinners at a nice restaurant and movie nights. The two sites—Real Mums and Bad Mother's Club—merged, with an all online focus, with the exception of a small number of the social gatherings (dinner, movies etc) throughout the year. Mums' Night Out!, a cocktail party complete with DJ, giveaways and entertainment, occurs annually and is the biggest of the events. At times, the events, particularly Mums' Night Out! supports a charitable organization which supports women, including post natal depression, domestic violence and various others, with raffles or a portion of proceeds being donated to the organization chosen.

These events provide an extension of the social and friendship connections made via the online forums, as well as an opportunity to put faces to the now extremely familiar and friendly names, get out of and away from the home, and, possibly most importantly, to provide, in person, the support, hugs and well-wishes that are often offered during discussions online. They allow for greater connection, empathy and understanding for members that go towards enhancing the online experience.

Although, initially, and possibly incredibly idealistically, the site was for *all* mothers, with the catchphrase "whatever sort of mum you are, you are a real mum" it has become the safe haven for the white, lower-middle class Australian mum, with children beyond the baby stage, who refuses to conform to what she "should" be doing, according to the mainstream media and organizations with the loudest voices. Members are approximately 30-45 years old, with at least one school aged child. They are both married and separated in equal proportions. Many are working part time or are running a home based business, with fewer stay at home mums. Those who admit to not willingly conforming to the expectations or the stereotype of the stay at home mum; the mum with the tidy house, clean clothes and participant of play groups who does puzzles and drawing with her children.

White Christian values are evident amongst members, and the theme and feel of the site itself, however, religion and political stance are not generally topics of discussion, nor are they referred to discussions. Some have openly declared their atheism and/or lack of religious skew, although a slight majority are of one Christian faith or another. A smattering of other religions, including Muslim and Buddhist are also present.

Feminist perspectives are also clearly evident, particularly in terms of choice (relating to working versus staying at home) and mothers being women in their own right, however this appears more perceptible in terms of the feel of the site, as opposed to any particularly strong argument or stance for feminism. Or against it, for that matter.

Although, both personally and from the perspective of longer term members of the site, who still refer to themselves as "real mums," the term "bad" is one that does not sit all that comfortably. There is, however, the subconscious feeling of safety and acceptance with the title "bad mother's club." The site has attracted women whom, for one reason or another have felt at some point like a "bad mother"; whether this is because they have returned to work against adversity and expectation of others, experienced depression, not been able to keep up with commonly accepted expectations or have been ostracised from their mothers group. Thus, their feelings of being a "bad mother" have resonated with the site title; they seem to be able to grasp the definition and philosophy of the term "bad mother" and to relate to it a little better, as opposed to the term "real mum," which is often misunderstood initially. They *feel* like a bad mother, and they have somewhere to go that accepts them for who they are.

Thought the title of the site is Bad Mother's Club, there is common reference to the term "real mum" throughout the forums, article titles and articles themselves. This is most evident when a member may post a discussion thread that refers to themselves as a "bad mum," along with a lengthy discussion as to why the feel this.

Members, particularly those longer term ones, are quick to point out the reality of the situation, their own personal experiences and common beliefs, concluding with reinforcing their support and that the member is not a "bad mother" but a "real mum." In other words, whilst they may be feeling bad over the incident, they reacted in the only way possible to them at that moment, given the circumstances that they were in at the time and that "this is reality."

The site started out as "real mums" because I didn't consider anyone a "bad mum" for whatever life—and reality—threw at them. This underlying value remains; the term "bad mother" is to give mums a place to start with that they can relate to and makes sense to them. All around us, in the media, parenting websites and publications and society in general, we are constantly being referred to as a "bad mother"; understanding the concept of reality in circumstances can be difficult and hard to relate to. It is, therefore, over time that members begin to change their mindset about themselves and have greater understanding and acceptance of what is happening around them that they being to refer to themselves as "real mums" as opposed to "bad." Progress!

They realise that what they are doing isn't "bad," *per se*, but is a consequence of the realities of their life. They are dealing with reality the best way they can, with what they have.

Activities

Bad Mother's Club is essentially an online forum, creating a safe and supportive community of Australian (and a few international) mums. Members must be registered to access and post on the forums, free of charge. Given the nature of the site, the forums are highly moderated to ensure no flaming or judgement of others, however the examples set by the admin, moderators, and the community created usually self-excludes those who do not wish to be accepting of others.

The need for this type of forum has arisen out of the increase in reporting of parenting practices and behaviours, whether the highlighting of a particular incident whereby the actions of a parent have resulted in some harm to the child, often with judgement based commentary, or the over-reporting of the latest research on one parenting technique of another. Over scrutinization of parenting practices, coupled with deliberately divisive coverage, has lead to websites and support groups that embrace one particular practice or another, shunning those who choose alternative methods of parenting. Sadly, factions have been created and the search for supporting and finding a community in which they fit has lead some mums to feel isolated, guilty and condemned for their beliefs. Even someone who chose to birth vaginally and drug free could be ostracised should she have trouble breastfeeding and opt for bottle feeding instead.

Australian mums needed a safe place in which they could discuss, openly and honestly, all aspects of their parenting, regardless of their particular parenting practice or belief, without fear of judgement or retribution. While an accepting, empathetic safe haven, the forums are moderated. Moderators are a small group of longer-term members, with an obvious passion for the site and what it stands for. They are unpaid for their role, however have a strong desire to see the site and forums remain as intended. They are usually selected based on their participation within the community and their ability to be empathetic and compassionate, and have a broad understanding and acceptance of various views, values and beliefs. It is important, also that they are able to refer to appropriate authorities and specialist resources when necessary. To date, it has been unnecessary for us to exclude or ban anyone based on behaviours seen as being against the supportive, accepting and non-judgemental values of the site.

Self-selection/self-exclusion usually occurs due to an aversion to profanity, or because they have strong beliefs about a particular parenting practice, such as breastfeeding, and are unable to accept that others choose not to practice this particular custom. That we offer support to all is irrelevant; some do not feel comfortable with a site that supports those who chose to parent "the other way," whatever that other way may be.

Although just about any discussion on any topic is allowed, and an airing of views and beliefs is permitted, we do not allow "telling" others how to do things, nor do we allow personal attacks, derogatory or judgemental comments. Sharing of experiences along the lines if "I did this" are encouraged, but we discourage "you should do" or other terms that are a direct instruction as opposed to supportive comment. Non-supportive comments, such as replying to request for help with bottle feeding with "I wouldn't give my precious baby poison," or that blatantly state a particular parenting practice is damaging to the child are not tolerated. Obvious judgements are removed, as are direct or personal attacks. Judgement can be a grey area and comments are taken on a case by case value. Some comments are perceived by some as a "judgement" where, for others, they are a funny response to someone. Personalities are taken into consideration as best as possible, and all members have the opportunity to contact administration (myself and two other, long term members) should they have any concerns.

We also highly encourage discussion of various parenting articles and research in the media, as well as prominent stories and goings on. Again, personal attacks, or attacks based on parenting styles, judgements etc. are not tolerated. Obviously, we also don't tolerate pornography, racist, sexist and other discriminatory discussion.

The site also includes "just for fun" activities such as a Book Club, Wine Club and fun challenges that focus on the health and wellbeing of mums. These clubs and challenges are all conducted online, with specific forums and scheduled live chat times set up for discussion, and another opportunity to connect and chat.

Book Club encourages mums to take time out for themselves, and facilitates the opportunity to do this; giving mums a "valid" reason to spend some time sitting and reading. We understand time constraints and conduct Book Club bi-monthly, with an online sign up form for those who wish to participate. Email updates with the latest Book Club book for discussion are sent out to the list, including links to sites where the book may be purchased. A specific forum is set up on the boards to discuss the latest book, and a bi-monthly, online live chat is set up specifically for book club members to connect and discuss—or not—the book.

Wine Club has a similar concept, with the ability to purchase wines online through a "partner" organization. A specific board has been set up to discuss wines, however regular discussion and live chat along the same lines as Book Club, are still to be organized.

A quarterly Challenge, organized by one of the moderators, is designed to ensure members do something for themselves. It may be as simple as purchasing themselves a Mother's Day gift, or participating in a specific, self development activity; journaling, creating something, changing a habit or creating a new habit. Pinpointing a self-destructive behaviour, such as a particular self-talk, participating in the Challenge and discussion it on the boards with other challengers (and supporters) can be empowering.

The site also offers articles and tips, all with a fun, humorous and sarcastic tone, for the enjoyment of all visitors. They relate to all aspects of parenting, and provide a fun, light-hearted look at parenting. Importantly, the site also provides a list of support organizations that focus on parenting and related activities, such as breastfeeding support, maternal and child helplines. Other resources, relating to mental and emotional health and wellbeing, including suicide helplines and specific postnatal depression organizations are also available. Contact information for organizations focussed on specific causes such as reflux support groups, kids' helplines, still birth and miscarriage, breast cancer etc. are is also readily available.

Many of our members have joined in search of support in their day to day parenting, and the site has been specifically set up to be devoid of experts and expert information, the provision of these contact details is imperative to refer members to should they need the expert and professional help. Although we have a specific, and private, board for those experiencing depression, for example, we are not equipped to be offering medical or professional advice. Therefore, we have the contact details of various depression support organizations to refer our members to, to ensure they have the help they receive. This applies, also, to those members experiencing a particularly difficult time, where we can refer them easily to suicide helplines and other organizations.

The list of contact details for various support organizations adds to the supportive aspect of the website, as well as providing us with relatively easy access to information we feel may be necessary for members in particular circumstances. These helplines and organizations are not affiliated with the site, but are pertinent organizations that support mothers in all aspects of their mothering role. They are a separate, yet important, source of support and information.

Bad Mother's Club offers a paid membership area, providing extra privacy and security on specific online forums, live chat and scheduled online chat times, and member only resources and information with a more serious slant. The initial idea of the site, in general, was to provide a free safe haven for all Australian mums. We also wanted the forums available at any time for anyone who needed them, without having to wait for administration approval. Therefore, given this and the relatively lax security in relation to who could join and when, some of our members requested additional security. Included in this was a significant amount of time and work put into the site and the recruitment of article writers, software purchased for activities most requested, such as live chat, and various other resources. Time and finances forced the decision to keep the site as a free, anonymous, anyone can join at any time situation and chase advertising, or focus on providing what I had intended the site to be; a safe haven.

The decision was made to charge a small fee per year for a membership, which ensured member only, private areas of the site, and to include various activities for those who paid. The payment of membership ensured two things; 1) that only those that really wanted to be involved would be, and 2) that we had specific details of members, including full name, address, phone numbers and other details, increasing the security and safety of members in the members only areas. The rest of the site, to join, only required a valid email address and a pseudonym (username).

All members have access to the majority of the site, with paid members having access to forums that are hidden from visitors and non-participating members. Most of those who have joined the paid membership area have been members on the forums for approximately six to twelve months. A smaller number who have particular circumstances and feel, potentially, more vulnerable to judgement and criticism, particularly those who have experienced depressive illnesses, have joined the paid membership shortly after registering on the site. These members, however, tend not to be as active or involved in community activities, on or offline, as the longer-term members. Paid members also have the opportunity to participate in other activities that support other members, or are just for fun. These include live chat, where we have both scheduled live chat nights, as well as access to organize their own chats at any time.

A Random Acts of Kindness initiative has also been set up, exclusively for paid members, whereby members are sent a list of the details (names, addresses and birthdates) of other members and invited to indulge in a random act of kindness. This may be as simple as sending a "thinking of you" card, should they notice another member going through a difficult time on the forums, a birthday card or gift, or something small for no particular reason. This has been well received, enhancing the community feel of the site and a source of enjoyment for those who receive RAKs and post about them, including pictures, on the boards.

Quarterly offline social events are being scheduled in Melbourne, Victoria for members, including an annual Mums' Night Out! semi-formal ball. Mum' Night Out! is the largest of the events, and is particularly aimed at giving mums a safe, fun and enjoyable night out. This event is a cocktail party, complete with food, drinks and a lot of dancing. It has also offered, over the years, entertainment in the form of fashion parades and female comedians, and raised funds for charitable organizations that support women, including breast cancer groups, domestic violence and post-natal depression. Other events include smaller, sit down dinners and movie nights, with the intent of providing mums with a night off from the family, the home and their day to day lives, and to just sit back, relax, have fun and chat with other mums.

Challenges

Australia is currently, and has been for some time, in a maelstrom of parenting advice and politically correctness and the emotional and physical wellbeing of our children is besieging parents. Research and the media are that forefront, deliberately creating divisive commentary in order to generate discussion, and, undoubtedly, attract more readers and viewers.

Parenting experts, too, are resorting to loaded and emotive language and phrases in a bid, it seems, to "guilt" parents into buying their latest program/book/service. It seems everyone is an expert, and certainly with the increase in online platforms, such as blogs, e-newsletters and the ease with which one can set up a website, in which to preach, it is easier to advocate for a particular parenting practice.

Our children's emotional and physical wellbeing is used as a threat to tempt us to conform one way or another. This has lead to mass confusion in the "right" way to parent, and, sadly, has lead to a position where mothers apparently feel the need to "choose a side" and create "warring" factions. It is no longer acceptable to "go with your gut" and do what suits each mother. Instead, it seems we must stick to certain invisible guidelines and keep well within their boundaries. The greatest challenge the Club has faced is the inability for many parenting groups and experts to understand and appreciate we aren't against any particular parenting philosophy or practice, merely to support mothers in relearning to trust their intuition and find the method that best suits them. The aforementioned divisiveness seems to have created a situation whereby support for a particular parenting practice automatically assumes you are against another. If you support bottle feeding, then, by default, you must be anti-breastfeeding.

All too commonly, advocates and support groups, and to a large degree, other parent support sites, are unable to see that one can support both equally and without judgement for the choices women make. As a result, many who wholeheartedly support breastfeeding, for example, see the Club as the adversary, a rebel against the cause and as having a detrimental effect on their efforts to raise breastfeeding rates. A similar viewpoint stands for all parenting practices; including sleep and settling methods, attachment parenting and various other styles. Quite the opposite, however, is true as rather than argue for one method over another, we have encouraged, through support and sharing our own experiences, mothers to find the value that sits most with them, and where she can find the appropriate, professional support she may need. At the very least, she has relaxed, removing the stress and guilt surrounding the issue at hand, and sits comfortably in her choice with the help she needs.

All of this has led to misinterpretation of the purpose of the site, and, subsequently, ill-informed discussions about the potential "damage" to Australian children as a result of the site. Some argue that we are encouraging women to stop breastfeeding, for example, thereby not giving our children the "best start in life" and all that goes in hand with this belief. Others suggest that supporting women in returning to work, because that is what they wish to do, is encouraging women to be selfish and disregard their children. Some fanaticists argue for the potentially psychologically damaging environments of childcare centres, despite the lack of evidence to suggest such extreme effects as they are suggesting occur. No consideration for the mental or emotional health of the mother and her ability to parent effectively is ever considered in these arguments.

The honesty of the site and its members has also created much controversy, with media and experts implying such openness to be detrimental to the well-being of members and/or their children. Members openly admitting that they sometimes don't like parenting and/or sometimes don't like their children, it is said, can have a "negative effect on the children." This statement, however, has never been qualified, explained or elaborated. I am at a loss as to what, exactly, it implies. Countering the comment has, thus far, been a futile exercise given the political correctness of the society in which we parent, and the obdurate views of those who make such statements. Similar to accepting the different values and practices of others, accepting that being open and honest about parenting requires the maker of such statements to consider their own behaviours, and, perhaps, also to agree to something that is not an acceptable statement to make in public. At least, it's not yet acceptable.

Experience with members, however, has been that making such statements as "not enjoying parenting," particularly in an environment where it is safe to make such declarations has resulted in feelings of acceptance and relief. Similar to venting a particular frustration, admitting to such feelings has allowed for a freedom, and a removal of certain expectations. The "you should" is no longer a part of their day to day parenting, so they no longer feel they "should" sit on the floor with the toddler and paint if they don't enjoy it. Instead, they find they can embark on activities they *do* enjoy, with their children, because they are no longer bound by these expectations. Even more simply, sometimes they just feel better and a little less stressed having got something that had been weighing them down off their chest. Parenting becomes easier, yelling and shouting at the children lessened and "good" mothering more evident.

Of course, it is also highly politically incorrect for a mother to use profanity at all, ever. Having a sense of humour, particularly in relation to parenting and/or children is also heavily frowned upon. Swearing at, around or in relation to children is never acceptable, with many arguing it is *the* reason we have such high rates of violence, disrespect and lack of appropriate behaviour in our society. On the forums, however, profanity is a means with which to convey just how frustrating an incident is, or how infuriating a circumstance. Some mums just swear, for no other reason than they just do. At times, it is also a release for some members, allowing for a much more impactful verbal vent.

Making jokes about parenting and/or children, whether it be a jovial "I'll just lock them in the cupboard to get some peace and quiet" or "free to good home" comments; the saviour of the stressed out mother, often result in judgements made about parenting abilities. "Good" mothers, apparently, don't even joke about such things. In fact, to even think such things, regardless of the circumstances, are the work of "bad" mothers; those that should never have been allowed to have children in the first place. Humour also allows for an emotional stress relief, either enabling the member to make light of a particularly demanding or nerve-racking situation and taking the edge off it, or to provide another member with a much needed laugh. It also has the effect of providing an alternative viewpoint to a particular situation and the possible perception that things aren't as bad as they seem.

Both the use of profanity and humour can go a long way to relieving and diffusing stressful circumstances, whether it's a child throwing yet another tantrum, or a mother about to throw one of her own, that could potentially result in harming a child. An example of the effect of humour on mums is this comment from a new member: "I just found my way here after reading some mad cow articles. After my whole family changed their undies, I started thinking of some funny things that have happened around here lately. Isn't it lovely to see your life as a comedy instead of a drama?"

Challenges were overcome through persistence, challenging media/news reports and research through blogging and the writing of articles, and promotion through social media networks. The blog (*Diary of a Mad Cow*) has been a considerably helpful medium through which to challenge discourse and research, or, at the very least, highlight alternative perspectives, exclusions and biases within media reports and the reporting of research. Adding an amusing tone to the blog posts, and the articles published on the site have not only been entertaining, but have had the effect of encouraging people to really think about what is actually being delivered. The humour has allowed for me to be more confronting and thought provoking, whilst at the same time causing readers to reflect on their own circumstances and/or behaviours. Rather than feeling judged, they are able to relate, and, hopefully, see the impact of their own actions. Despite being confronting at times, all articles and blog posts are at the same time respectful and understanding of various parenting practices.

Whilst adversity towards me, personally, and the site has at times been difficult to overcome, testament from members along the lines of "you saved my life today" has had a profound impact. Knowing that providing a supportive and safe haven hasn't been "just a bit of fun" but has significantly impacted and changed the lives of a number of Australian mums has been a definite encouragement and motivation to continue.

Challenging the discourse has been one mode of overcoming adversity, the rest has been the profound realisation that I can't please everyone, and that not everyone will like what I do, whether because it challenges their own beliefs and values, or challenges them personally to do something about their own lives is unclear. Thus, my focus has become to continue to provide for the members, visitors and readers that do appreciate and understand the concept of the organization, and to continue to support them and their needs.

Cultivating relationships with the media enabled the opportunity to publicise a more accurate message about the Club. Ultimately, it has been about finding just who my target market is, and providing, for them, the tools, information and resources that assist them in their lives. The mainstream media and online publication of my works, through blogging, articles and social media sites, such as Facebook and Twitter have expanded my reach, increasing not just to my target market, but also my alleged adversaries and others who aren't quite sure where they sit in relation to "good," or "bad," parenting, If nothing else, thought is provoked and hopefully this is having an impact on how society views, accepts and understands the diversity in parenting and its practices.

Ultimately, the support and community created through the online forums, and the members it has attracted, speaks volumes. Regular members turn to the forums several times a day for connection, community and friendship, or just someone to talk to that can relate and support them. Other members may appear and post when they are having a particularly difficult time, or have a question that requires a non-biased and pragmatic answer. Others still are feeling like bad mothers over a particular incident and seek reassurance, acceptance or understanding.

Comments such as "I love this website—it ALWAYS makes me feel so much better about my bumbling motherhood skills!!" are commonplace, resulting from the honesty of members responding to cries for help from other members. Community is created, and enhanced, through not only the ability to share "I'm the worst mother in the world" stories in a safe place, but also through the replies and responses of other members of this community. Other, more serious and sensitive comments are along the lines of "without this site, I would have killed myself" and the similar "you have saved my life" are usually accompanied by statements that reflect the supportiveness, non-judgement and acceptance of the community of members. This particular statement sums up the feel of the site, and its importance to Australian mums:

> Every mum on this forum has YOU personally to thank for the love, support, advice, commiserations and celebrations 'cos if you hadn't done it, this forum wouldn't exist and we wouldn't have formed the concrete, dependable friendships we have. You ARE CHANGING LIVES.

More than this, the organization has created, at least within its own community, an acceptance that everyone has their own beliefs, values and ways in which they parent, and, extreme behaviours not withstanding, all of these values and practices have a place. They are all acceptable, beneficial and personal. Mostly, we have a profound understanding that here is a place for everyone, and that place may or may not be Bad Mother's Club.

Future Goals

Although the site has a well established community and support structure in place, there are plans to expand the current paid membership structure to include more resources and access to information, as well as small gifts and opportunities for mums to consider and look after themselves, have some time out and ensure their own health and wellbeing is not overlooked. More options for members that will also go a long way to making their lives easier, whilst at the same time, ensuring the philosophies of the Club will be implemented. This will include such measures as including the Book Club component within the membership itself, sending the books to members, facilitating discussion and organizing specific live chat times to discuss the book in real time. This saves the member searching for the book, either at the library or local bookstore, or purchasing online. Similar inclusions will work also for wine club and the quarterly events, whereby the ticket price is included in a monthly membership fee, saving the member the trouble of having to book a ticket separately.

Expanding on the resources and information currently available online through the site is a major goal. More detailed and informative, researched articles, facts sheets, e-books and e-courses will be made available to members, relating to all manner of parenting and life, from childhood development to behaviour and discipline, and relationships to looking after yourself. Tools and products that assist mums in organizing daily family life, as well as life aspects such as work, business or their own social life will be made available, both as an electronic, downloadable version as well as a tangible, sent out in the mail product. Meal planning and preparation will also be a large part of this, including tools to help with the evening meal. Obviously, the reality of people's lives, such as long work hours, both parents working, and various extra-curricular and after school activities which can affect the cooking of the evening meal, will be addressed. Much of the cooking shows and tips are conducted and presented by professionals, with little consideration given to bus lives, financial constraints or lack of interest in performing this particular task. Acknowledging these issues will, again, create connection and feelings of being heard, allowing for an increased chance of making an impact in this area of parenting.

A series of facts sheets and guides, relating to all aspects of parenting and children's ages, as well as specific parenting health issues, such as post-natal depression are planned. This includes a series of books, devoid of experts and with the same humorous tone, yet important information, as the rest of the site. The humorous tone can help to remove, to a degree, the significance that many feel about particular issues, and at the same time creates a connection, understanding and relateability. Readers can see themselves in similar situations, and are more open to understanding the situation and seeing it for what it is. The lack of expert and being told what and how to do things is replaced by the sharing of stories, tips, experiences and ideas. Once again, this allows for more ability to relate to the issue at hand, thus a greater likelihood of being able to act on it.

Of course, including the thoughts, feelings and behaviours of the mother, including being over-tired, stressed and confused, factors which are neglected in other parenting books, will offer a different set of coping strategies. They will not only address that mothers *do* actually feel these things, but also how they affect decision making, tolerance and ability to act on expert suggestion, as well as how to manage these factors. Books based on the site owner's personal blog, *Diary of a Mad Cow*, are currently in the process of being published, with plans for a series of books in the near future. As the site is focused on the health and well-being of mothers, an expansion of the site to include more opportunities to share information and advice, as well as increased opportunities to attend small, affordable events throughout Australia are also in the goals for the future.

The Larger Motherhood Movement

The larger motherhood movement has, for the most part, identified the needs of the modern mother; whether it be care for the children, support, resources or whatever, and has made vast progress in terms of securing such provisions as workplace childcare centres, family friendly workplaces, and myriad services and support agencies to enable and empower mothers to fulfil their dreams.

Recently, Australia introduced a paid maternity leave scheme, a follow on from an initiative allowing for paternity leave. Websites that specialise in resume writing and training for mums to return to the workforce have appeared, a number of which also facilitate the placement of mums into workforces. Alternatively, other organizations work with workplaces to facilitate a more family friendly environment, whether this be work hours, the option to work from home or childcare facilities on site. Websites that help mums set up their own business are now commonplace and grants are made available through local council, local business and large business to assist them in getting started.

Unfortunately, it seems the movement has been almost muted with the increasingly vocal well-meaning, yet often uninformed or highly opinionated advocates of various causes; whether it is a push for children under five to be cared for in their own home, or increasing support for paid maternity leave, and more. Every aspect of parenting, parenting practices, and the health and wellbeing, safety and security of our children has a voice. A LOUD voice.

Almost daily exposure of how we are doing wrong by our children, putting them in danger or not giving them the best start in life is thrust upon us. So much so that mothers, especially working mothers, are being blamed for the increase in childhood obesity rates, unsupervised and undisciplined children, low literacy rates (although there is no evidence that literacy is declining among non-migrant children) and the like. Mother's being away from their children in the first five years of their life, according to these advocates, are a blight on society and causing more harm than good.

These statements have a profound effect on mothers, particularly those that do not enjoy spending all this time with their children, or those that are at work, whether they feel they have a choice in the matter or not, or who perhaps have other commitments or issues that require they spend time away from their children. Feelings of guilt at doing the "wrong" thing, the thing that causes obesity, or accidents or a child slow to read, are enhanced. Confusion over the decision they "should" have made, or feelings of inadequacy because they don't "love parenting" perpetuate the feelings of guilt and being a "bad" mother. All of which, inevitably, lead to an unhappy mother.

So vocal are these various organizations and groups, embarking on missions to get their message across, seemingly without regard for the views of others, albeit with the best of intentions, they have inadvertently created chaos and confusion. Breastfeeding support organizations, for example, are regularly quoted in the media as condemning the behaviours and actions of those whom they refer to as "anti-breastfeeding." They appear to have divided people, whether mothers/parents or not, into "pro-breastfeeding" and "anti-breastfeeding," either for or against it, with no discussion, mention or conversation around choice, circumstance or the fact that some people just can't. The discourse that "if you don't breastfeed then you must be anti breastfeeding" is evident amongst these group

An example of this relates to a blog post I wrote some time ago, that suggested that if mothers wanted respect when breastfeeding in public, they also had to respect those around them, and to earn respect; a reaction to a spate of online condemnation, some misguided, against those who are against breastfeeding. The "discussions" I referred to involved copious amounts of name calling and accusations, and no respect or understanding for the circumstances or beliefs of others. In suggesting "respect must be earned" and "to respect others," breastfeeding advocates, including a spokesperson for a breastfeeding organization, commented that my views were akin to the Nazi's treatment of Jews and the "segregation of blacks."

This line dividing parenting practices has extended to my, personally, being accused of being anti-breastfeeding *because* I had a caesarean section. The fact I did breastfeed was overlooked, and this concept and connection between the two issues, whilst incomprehensible, highlights just how strict guidelines for "good" versus "bad" parenting are. That you must adhere to certain practices to be considered a "good mother" is definite. These rules apply not just to breastfeeding, but also to every other parenting practice. Working versus staying at home, childcare and sleeping/settling are often the keys to discussion.

Bad Mother's Club, because mothers on either side of that line can feel "bad" or guilty due to judgements by others and prevalent media messages, allows for discussion around all these issues and more, regardless of which aspect is spoken of. Women seeking support for breastfeeding, generally or in public, will receive it, without condemnation, just as those who wish to bottle feed will receive the same level of support.

Challenging these staunch views has been on the one hand, difficult due to not just the unrelenting views of those who have them, but also their apparent inability to accept and appreciate different circumstances and views. They seem unable to recognise that we are not disputing or dismissing their beliefs, or even arguing against them, just that there are other perspectives to be considered. On the other hand, the challenge hasn't been all that difficult due to a collection of supportive and compassionate women who frequent the Club, who have the capacity to share experiences and suggestions without condemnation or judgement, and to support others. They also demonstrate the capacity to avoid replying to, or discussing, topics they feel they are unable to contribute to, supportively or positively, or that are significantly against their beliefs.

The site's guidelines also highlight the need for support and acceptance, and moderation of particularly sensitive topics is increased. In short, we don't discriminate between parenting practices, beliefs and values, and allow for open discussion of all, but not limited to, parenting related topics. We do, however, restrict or keep a close watch on discussion that is judgement based, discriminatory, condemnatory, accusatory, or telling others what they "should" be doing, rather than sharing stories and experiences from a personal perspective. Commencing replies with "I tried this…" as opposed to "you should do/try…" are preferable.

These guidelines and moderation remind newer members of the site's aim and objective to support mothers in their choices and to restrict, or remove entirely, feelings of guilt and inadequacy. Sharing stories and experiences, as opposed to telling someone to do something because it's the way you did it, helps to build connection and friendship. It also provides for a more supportive environment that mothers feel comfortable frequenting and joining discussion on, which has evidently occurred on the site, with members regularly commenting that the site has provided them with support, a safe place to be themselves and enabled them to forge strong friendships.

This motherhood movement, particularly in Australia it seems, is fighting to be heard, and struggling against the sanctimonious rhetoric of various groups, or caught up in the aforementioned "warring" between factions; commonly referred to in the media as the "mummy wars." The messages are lost in the bid to create a divisiveness that, in turn, continues to feed the media; the "mummy wars" are the source of daily "news" and the apparent reasoning for the "war" or divisiveness between mothers, or groups of mothers, is perpetuated and reinforced. Groups and advocates use social media, like Facebook and Twitter, to back up, or disagree with, media coverage of particular topics, using emotive and, often, judgemental language. Given these groups are relatively unmoderated, there is little to stop personal attacks or the distribution of misinterpreted, whether accidental or deliberate, information from spreading further. Misinformation, as well as valid research, is often used to back up a belief, and to add fuel to personal attacks and attacks on the actions of others.

Bad Mother's Club, where possible, tends to avoid participation in such discussion, however discussion on the topic itself, or that other discussion have got out of hand, may appear on the forums. Whilst all members are entitled to their opinion and encouraged to share it, non-judgement and removal of personal attacks are enforced. Our aim is that if we can pass on this message of support and non-judgement, and share emotional experiences without overly persuasive language or with the intent to change the belief of someone else, that we can, at the very least, encourage them to accept that other perspective, points of view, and, most importantly, personal experiences and circumstances do exist. These other viewpoints and experiences are just as valid, and our intent is to enable others to see this, too. Through all of this, over the last five years or so, Bad Mother's Club has drawn on the confusion caused, the motherguilt inducing information and research, and the self-serving, often sanctimonious oratory from the experts, leaving mothers wondering which way is the "right" way to parent.

The Club has, in its own way, created its own "motherhood movement," in that it is leading a "change of attitudes and beliefs associated with this thing called motherhood." It is offering reason and logic to the most vocal of experts and parenting groups and their philosophies, providing an opportunity to consider options realistically and to shun, where necessary, those messages that lead to feelings of guilt and inadequacy. This may be as simple as respectfully correcting the language or tone used on the forums, for example, when someone says "I'm the worst mother in the world, I left my baby to cry because I couldn't cope." Our response is to reassure the mother in questions, point out the reality of the situation (you're tired, its understandable you feel like this, this is normal, lots of women feel it), usually with the personal experience of someone else (I've been there, too) and aid her by suggesting activities she can do that will help her feel she can cope again. Or, let her know that leaving a baby to cry on one occasion is not going to have any long lasting or remotely damaging effect. We've, to a degree, assisted her in feeling less guilty about the situation by reassuring her she is normal, and that any ill effect on the baby is unlikely. We've assured her she is normal, and not "the worst mother" as a number of other members have done the same, and have told her so.

In terms of the overarching motherhood movement, Bad Mother's Club serves to "normalize" the variety in mothering experiences, beliefs and values, and also seeks to create an acceptance between mothers, and mothers groups, that each has their own personal needs; whether it be returning to work, or remaining home and being a full time mum.

To a degree, thus far, acceptance has led to a reduction in divisive discussions and an increase in the amount of support mothers have for each other. This is partly through encouraging empathy and understanding of the experiences of others, and the safety, openness and honesty with which members can share their experiences. It allows for others to get a better understanding of a variety of circumstances and practices, without having them forced upon them. Leadership by administration and moderators has also forged the appropriate behaviours on the forums, reinforced by feedback from users of the forums. At least, within the site community it has made a difference ("thank you for your support, I could not have done this without you all"), and is slowly impacting on other visitors, readers and, in particular, the media. Blog posts and forum discussion on popular topics, or those in the recent media, attract greater attention from non-members, and our handling of such discussion, the acceptance and acknowledgement of both sides of the coin and other, pragmatic discussion provide those with stubborn viewpoints a respectful, yet realistic perspective. For example, the aforementioned blog post on respect and breastfeeding in public highlighted the fact that someone giving a breastfeeding woman a "glare" may, in fact, be nothing to do with her and everything to do with the person in question having a bad day. Suggestions that a person is "getting her out of the public eye for fear of offending others" included the alternative that perhaps they were offering her a comfortable place to feed, with less distraction and nicer chairs.

Challenging the mass media reports, research and expert through blogging has provided the opportunity for readers to think objectively about the subject matter they are bombarded with, as does the use of humour, the exaggeration and satirising of parenting practices and experiences in articles and information. Tactfully and respectfully highlighting different perspectives, such as those referred to above, via the forums, articles and resources on the site and through the blog enable readers to accept, although not necessarily agree with, the information without aggression or defensiveness. There is not much for them to defend, given the manner in which they are challenged. Respectfully imparting information, whilst also accepting that which you are challenging, has more of an impact and is more likely to be heard and remembered, than attacking a person for their beliefs.

Conclusion

Despite the term "bad mother" being a deterrent for some, or a particularly useful scapegoat for others, it has done a considerable amount for the motherhood movement and a much-needed source of support for Australian mums. It has provided them, in its name alone, a connection and relateabilty they feel they can understand, and the lack of judgement enables them to feel safe and welcome. Its acceptance of all parenting styles has reinforced the supportive nature of the site, but also impacted on societal beliefs, albeit in a tiny amount, but effectively enabling others to understand and appreciate the views of others.

More specifically, it has provided an alternative place for a particular group of mums, those who feel they don't conform to the current, loudly touted expectations of society, a safe haven and source of support and practical information. The freedom of speech and use of humour and satire considerably lessens the significance of the messages constantly confronting mothers, and leaves them feeling less of a failure and more normal than the TV commercials and parenting books and magazines leave them believing they are.

The aim, now, is to infiltrate the rest of society with this message and reduce the divisiveness not just between mothers and mothers groups, but also between parents and business owners, the childless by choice, educational facilities and various other aspects of our community.

The aim, now, is to recreate the village that raises our children.

33. Feminism by Stealth in the Suburbs

The Feminist Mothers Discussion Group

ANDREA FOX

THE FEMINIST MOTHERS DISCUSSION GROUP (FMDG) was established in 2005 and eventually acquired over sixty feminist mothers as members. The group existed for the sole purpose of discussion and was neither a service nor a political advocacy group. The FMDG sought a mother-centred perspective rather than a child-centred one. The aim of discussions was not to talk about our children, but rather, about our experiences as mothers. The mother's perspective on mothering has been marginalised and the vast majority of material produced about motherhood is child-centred. It was this feature that made our discussion group a feminist one—it meant not only that we applied a feminist process to our discussions, by being woman-centred, but that we also chose subjects which would allow a feminist lens to be applied to topics of motherhood. This decision put the FMDG in stark contrast to all other mothers' groups we had come across.

Members were typically highly educated and the vast majority of us were also middle-class. Although some queer mothers regularly attended the discussions it would be fair to say that most of us were heterosexual. The age range of members varied from those in their early twenties to those in their late sixties, however the majority of us were somewhere in our thirties. About three-quarters of the group would have identified as working-outside-the-home mothers (including part-time, full-time, contractual, and working from home), while the others saw themselves as predominantly stay-at-home mothers (SAHMs). However, most of those SAHMs planned to return to the workforce at some point in their future. Occupations in the group included an economist, lawyers, doctors, directors of non-government organizations, academics, a journalist, teachers, nurses, a musician, a ship cook, a yoga instructor, community workers and university students. A handful of irregular participants had never worked outside the home.

Almost all of us had small families, that is, between one to three children in total and many members were first-time mothers. All the mothers who joined our group readily identified as feminist, although for some there was no previous history of activism or feminist activity in their lives and their participation in the group was part of an exploration into their feminist identity. And of course, a good number of the women in the discussion group strongly identified as feminists and had been significantly involved in political feminist activity.

The FMDG ran monthly meetings around pre-arranged topics focusing on the intersection of feminism and motherhood. Some examples of these topics included libido and parenthood; queer parenting; domestic labour negotiations in the home; "mother shock"—adjusting to new motherhood; the "mummy wars"; and, the "yummy mummy" phenomenon. The purpose of the discussions was to provide space for mothers otherwise marginalised by their feminism, and to build a community of like-minded parents for support. It was feminism by stealth; feminism in the suburbs; feminism when the children were asleep and tucked up in their beds.

This paper details the origins and progress of the FMDG and includes an examination of its mandate, history and context, its objective and activities, the challenges it faced, the future for the group, and its relationship to the larger motherhood movement.

Mandate

The FMDG provided a space for feminist mothers to explore, through a facilitated discussion, how their feminism impacted on their mothering and conversely, how their experiences of motherhood shaped their feminism. Each discussion topic was framed with these two questions in mind—how is feminism affecting your mothering and your mothering affecting your feminism? The aim of the FMDG was to bring together and support the feminist parenting community of Brisbane and to help strengthen the collective power of the feminist movement in Australia.

History and Context

The Feminist Mothers Discussion Group (FMDG) was established in Brisbane, Australia in 2005. It was initiated by myself and another feminist, Kitty Carra, following the births of our daughters. Carra and I met in our early twenties when we were both working for the same non-government organization in the women's sector. We share some common elements in our background including—childhoods spent outside of Australia (and mostly in developing countries); some family similarities; qualifications in male-dominated disciplines; an interest in artistic pursuits; and, strong long-held feminist identities. We had a decade of close friendship behind us before we started the FMDG in our thirties and that closeness has allowed us to work almost intuitively together as co-facilitators.

Carra was, by the time we put together the FMDG, the mother of two while my own baby daughter was, at that time, my only child. We found our mutual interest in feminism intensified with the prospect of potentially raising a new generation of feminists. Our interest in starting a discussion group with other feminist mothers was primarily to explore the impact of motherhood on our feminism, but we also wished to examine the practice of feminist mothering, and we very much wanted to combat the sense of isolation that was our experience of motherhood. Already out of the loop as feminists—as we were no longer at university, and had also both left jobs in the women's sector to work in the mainstream—this was also coupled with a feeling of "not fully belonging" to the motherhood club we had joined. Contemporary motherhood was surprisingly old-fashioned; it was also competitive, homogenous, sexist, conservative, materialistic, unimaginative, cautious, unquestioning, stifling and artificial. Basically, it was no place for a feminist.

I hasten to add that it was not an altruistic act on Carra's and my part in forming the FMDG—we started it because we wanted to talk about what was happening to us. We provided what we needed and in doing so also provided a very useful service for other women like us, that is, educated middle-class feminists, but we readily acknowledge that the FMDG may not have been a perfect fit for mothers who differed greatly from that demographic.

Borrowing from our experience as facilitators for the general feminist discussion group Carra and I ran under Brisbane Feminism Online (www.brisbanefeminismonline.net), and also from our work in facilitating feminist workshops at events such as *Ladyfest*, we decided to establish a feminist discussion group for mothers. We photocopied a handful of flyers to stick up around playgrounds and daycare centres, spread the word among friends and eagerly awaited our first meeting. At our first discussion group we met members of the Association for the Research of Motherhood Australia and we subsequently linked up with them to promote the group further.

The FMDG eventually acquired over sixty members who circulated in and out of attendance. On any one evening attendance at a discussion could total anywhere from four to twenty mothers. While membership included a wide variety of mothers—queer and straight; Australian-born and immigrant; new mothers and grandmothers; partnered and solo; custodial and non-custodial; English speaking and non-English speaking backgrounds; Christian cultural backgrounds and Muslim cultural backgrounds; stay-at-home and working-outside-the-home; low and high incomes—it always remained a relatively middle-class group of mothers who were highly educated, so whether we achieved much in the way of diversity is questionable. The FMDG recruited members primarily through word of mouth and this undoubtedly contributed to a narrow class representation. The topics we ended up choosing for discussion probably also reinforced our group's demographics. Examples of such middle-class concerns include—the "yummy mummy" phenomenon; slacker parents; the commerical co-opting of "mother love"; the sexualisation of little girls in advertising; and the emergence of a trend in "mothers who do cocktails."

Objective and Activities

It is tempting to write simply that mothers need to talk, a lot, and that this is the objective we fulfilled with our facilitated discussion groups. It is both more complicated than this, and not, too. The need for an emotional and cerebral outlet for mothers is great and part of what the discussion group provided was peer support through listening, reflecting, reframing, and sharing of similar experiences. However, we readily acknowledged we lacked the resources and motivation to act as a support group, with each of us as exhausted and as confused as the next, and we all maintained fairly robust and healthy boundaries in our discussions. Participants often shared deeply reflective aspects with the group and there was an informal understanding of confidentiality in discussions.

The FMDG provided space for us to reframe feminist theory as personal experience. It was not particularly a forum for the sharing of studies and the critique of theories. In forming the group Carra and I openly acknowledged that everyone's feminism was different, and although we probably identify as radical feminists ourselves, the group was reasonably third-wave in terms of its emphasis on inclusiveness and personal experience. The discussions were not particularly confrontational and nor were they all that academic in style; we did not concern ourselves much with challenging others' feminisms, instead we sought out shared experiences. This probably assisted the FMDG in coping successfully with its mix of both "novice" and "experienced" feminists. It also separated the discussion group from other feminist forums, such as those found on-line or those conducted in university tutorials, which can tend more towards open and fierce debate. We recognised that mothers already face multiple forces of division—eg. the so-called "Mummy Wars," and also, different styles of parenting. What we needed was a greater sense of unity.

During the past decade motherhood has entered the contemporary media conversation. Today there is significant exploration of mothers in the media: celebrity mothers, "yummy mummy" fashion trends, and "bad mother" news reports are all common in today's mainstream journalism. The FMDG was an important forum for us as feminists in unpacking how motherhood was being presented in the media and for better developing our own critical analysis of these messages.

The FMDG was held once a month. Carra and I decided to hold the discussion group in the evenings, this marked the event as one that was distinctly "adult" in tempo and immediately differentiated us from playgroups. Evenings allowed Carra and I to claim space for ourselves as individuals outside of motherhood and we hoped it would inspire other members similarly. The discussions were held over light suppers with wine. The venues we used included community halls, quiet bars, a room at a university, and in some instances a studio in Carra's home. Factors such as centrality, proximity to public transport, safe parking, disability access, and comfort were always factored into the selection of venues. By and large the evening time was widely supported by members as it simplified childcare arrangements. During the latter stages of the FMDG's existence the meetings were moved to Carra's house in order to accommodate the arrival of her third baby and to allow sole parents to more readily bring their children with them where childcare alternatives were not available.

Challenges

Among the challenges the FMDG faced was the identity of the group. At one point we considered a shorter, snappier name—"Thinking Mothers"—but this was subsequently abandoned following feedback from the group indicating that they saw identifying as a feminist to be an important first step in joining the discussion group.

One member was critical of our evening meeting times and felt that this clashed with her attachment parenting. This complaint surprised Carra and I, as we both leant towards attachment parenting ourselves. Meeting in the evenings was very symbolic for the group and for us, the facilitators; it represented a reclamation of ourselves as individuals outside motherhood—women with a "night life." For those of us still overwhelmed by the shock of new motherhood having an evening event to attend felt positively revolutionary. From a practical point of view an evening meeting time was generally easier to negotiate with partners and family members because the caring tasks they were taking on in our absence tended to be less onerous "after bedtime." However, we tried a weekend day-time meeting on several occasions in response to that member's complaint and found that it was unfortunately not successful. Weekend time was apparently seen as "family time" by many members.

The bulk of the obstacles the FMDG met and overcame related to the nature of discussion groups and how they are facilitated—how to make sure discussion was shared equally among "chatty" and "quiet" members, how to resolve conflict when it arose, how to steer conversation but not become intrusive, and how to gauge the energy levels of the group accurately enough to allow discussions free reign when that was needed and conclusion when that was called for.

A defining moment for Carra and I as facilitators was the introduction to the group of an interesting young mother who had both the capacity to dominate discussions and also a tendency to fall into talking at great length about her children. De-briefing as facilitators after that discussion we realised that we had both observed the discussion losing its energy as soon as conversation turned exclusively to talking about someone's child/children. We were able to identify what became a critical point for the FMDG—the driving force of the discussions and indeed, what marked them as so different to those generated by other gatherings of mothers—our discussions were to be about ourselves and not our children; about motherhood rather than mothering. From that time onwards we were more direct with members about that distinction and this problem has been overcome. We wanted space to talk about ourselves and our journey as feminists, and not about our baby's teething problems and our children's school difficulties. Where we talked about teething problems it was in terms of the effect of our baby's fussiness on our experience of post-natal depression; and where we discussed schooling difficulties it was in relation to the way in which mothers, and not fathers, seemed to provide the invisible labour that kept our schools running. The group was feminist both in its process and its content. The process was feminist in that it was woman-centred and the content was feminist in that the topics were focused on the application of a feminist analysis.

Recruitment efforts were an ongoing activity and we were continually seeking new ways to reach hidden pockets of feminist mothers. In truth, smaller discussion groups were far and away the more successful discussions. Larger discussion groups are more difficult to facilitate, and are unlikely to foster the kind of intimacy that leads to breakthrough discussions. Some of the methods we used for promotion of the FMDG included distributing flyers around playgrounds, parenting rooms and at daycare centres; conducting an interview on radio; various measures on the Internet; and as previously mentioned, through word-of-mouth. Our most successful recruitment exercise was a film event we held at a university where we presented the Canadian independent short film, "The Unmartyred Mother" followed by a discussion.

One of the most significant challenges we met in facilitating discussions, which was a problem from time to time both with the FMDG and with other feminist discussion groups Carra and I ran, was inspiring members to do the readings before the discussions. While members were generally enthusiastic participants in terms of attendance and opinion, the readings were met with some resistance. Some discussions frustrated me, and were probably limiting for other members also, because of the lack of progress we could make in analysing a particular topic where the majority of participants had not done the readings. In these instances a good part of the discussion had to be devoted to filling the other members in on the background of the topic and to also summarising the readings for them. The subsequent discussion often lacked depth as there was only time remaining to hear people's initial reactions to a topic. For this reason books, which would otherwise be good jumping off points for a discussion, held limited value in discussion groups. The lesson from this is that people, particularly mothers, are time-poor and that discussion groups need to have the flexibility to accommodate varying levels of energy among participants. The most insightful discussions occurred when the topic was something controversial enough to have had wide and recent media coverage and participants were already reasonably well-versed on the issues. An example of this was when we discussed the debate that occurred in Australia over famous artist, Bill Henson's photographic nudes of pubescent girls. Other highly successful topics were those that were relatively universal and rich in emotion, but which are rarely explored openly such as post-natal depression, "mother shock" in the first year, and intimacy with one's partner after having a baby.

We never encountered any serious conflict during the Feminist Mothers Discussion Group, although the same cannot be said for other feminist discussion groups we have facilitated. Perhaps the smooth sailing was the result of luck or maybe it was that mothers, as participants, make a particular effort for cordial discussions.

The Future

The FMDG has taken a temporary hiatus while I adjust to my second baby and another return to work, and while Carra settles into a challenging new work role. We plan to re-establish the group this year as we master our new responsibilities. Although it was a shame to pause the discussions when the FMDG had reached a peak in numbers, we have found through previous experiences facilitating discussion groups that they often benefit from the reflection and renewal that can happen during such a break. Carra and I are currently considering assembling a one-off feminist discussion group tour of some of the major cities of Australia.

Relationship to the Larger Motherhood Movement

The FMDG is not a service nor a political advocacy group. Its place in the motherhood movement, even localised to Australia, is small; however its impact on those who participated was considerable. The FMDG was cherished by its members. It is no exaggeration to say that the monthly evening meetings felt like an escape for us all. Members often reported that successfully attending a discussion evening, even just in and of itself, felt like an achievement for them—it was seen as another step towards their bid to carve out time and identities for themselves beyond motherhood. Attendance was not without its challenges—sick children, busy partners, work deadlines all stood in the path of mothers joining us each month. The discussions went for a minimum of two hours, and three hours was not unheard of. In several cases a woman's attendance at the discussion marked her first time ever away from her infant, such was the value she placed on the discussion and such was the urgency she felt for having this time in solidarity with other mothers. It was a radical act and male partners sometimes teasingly referred to the discussion group as our "witch's coven."

The FMDG was so successful that Carra and I began to wonder how discussion groups had ever fallen out of vogue—inexpensive, low-maintenance, entertaining and incredibly satisfying—why weren't they springing up all over the place? But the FMDG, to our knowledge, was the first of its kind in Brisbane.

Some of the mothers had a strong history of identifying as feminists and had participated previously in some way in the women's sector but a significant number of the mothers had no prior history of activism or feminist activity and were building their feminist identities through the discussion groups. As previously mentioned under Objective and Activities, the FMDG deliberately steered clear of the pitfalls Carra and I had seen in other spaces for feminists. We recognised that the real enemy was the patriarchy and not each other and we discouraged members from measuring feminist outcomes against one another—turning away from such ideas as who had the most feminist marriage or the most feminist parenting arrangements etc. We concentrated on "the personal as political" and on debunking common myths and stereotypes about mothers that are used to divide and conquer women. And because the FMDG was not particularly academic in tone it did not require of its members a formal education in feminism. This probably made our group accessible if not always entirely satisfying for academics from a gender studies background.

Fortunately Carra and I did not find ourselves needing to regularly defend feminism in meetings, an activity which can slow down and distract serious discussions. The "I am not a feminist, but..." problem did not present itself in the FMDG. Possibly this is because of our group's name, which had the appeal of being self-selecting—by joining the group one had to more or less declare oneself a feminist. Carra and I believed that members had engaged in a hugely transgressive act already as mothers, by merely declaring to others that they were going out that evening to attend a feminist discussion group.

The group served a number of purposes for its members, including for both Carra and I as co-facilitators. The discussion group helped women to reclaim their identities as individuals and feminists; it also allowed us to better define our parenting as feminist mothers; and finally, it empowered us to negotiate fairer outcomes in our lives, both inside and outside the home by recognising the patriarchal framework that underpinned our experiences. For instance, knowing that you are not the only mother who finds it absurd that she is doing the bulk of the night parenting with a baby, and that other couples have tackled the division of tasks and devised something fairer greatly strengthens one's own bargaining position.

The FMDG also provided authority to our feminist parenting, and an avenue for sharing knowledge and support among like-minded mothers. One loyal participant said her interest in attending the group was in large part due to the fact that she was soon to become a grandmother for the first time and that she didn't feel any connection with other grandparents she knew on account of her feminist and queer identity. We were no longer the odd parents out at the playgroup, fighting gender stereotypes with our children. We found solidarity among the mothers attending the FMDG.

Two such examples of where the discussion group supported changes to parenting practices are as follows. The first involved a mother of two little girls. After attending her first discussion group she openly wondered if she were suited to a feminist mothers' group. She explained that both her daughters were devoted to all things pink and she wondered not only if we would assume she had failed some sort of feminist parenting test but also whether there was anything all that wrong with girls liking pink. Her questions led to an interesting discussion in our group about how rejecting traditional visions of femininity could be a misogynist act in itself. Several months after this discussion this same mother came back to the group to tell us about an act of protest she had initiated. She had been looking through a children's clothing catalogue and had noticed their use of verbs like "play" and "run" to describe all the boy pictures and adjectives like "pretty" and "sparkling" to describe all the girl pictures. The mother wrote a letter of protest to the clothing label complaining about the sexism. She attributed her ability to recognise the sexism in those advertisements and her confidence to make a complaint to her participation in the FMDG.

The second example involved a meeting where we discussed feminist aspects to raising sons. This discussion was enormously popular. Many of the mothers said they came away with a sense of endorsement for their parenting. They felt they had more courage now in allowing their sons the space to cry, express feelings, show affection in public and to remain closely bonded to them—all acts which were viewed as transgressive for masculinity in the wider world and for which they had previously encountered criticism as mothers.

There were numerous life-changing moments in the course of discussions. Because the discussions were centred on us, as mothers, rather than on our children a level of intimacy quickly developed that was conducive to the truth-telling and honesty that is fundamental to feminism. Among the topics we were able to cover on account of this developing sense of trust were depression, divorce, difficulties bonding with children, parenting failures, and breastfeeding as part of our sex lives.

Additionally, the FMDG also encouraged us to be more political. The discussions motivated us as feminists to see our personal experiences in political contexts and ultimately to incorporate more activism in our broader lives. Among the events the FMDG hosted were guest speaker events on same-sex parenting, and another on the sexualization of girls; a table at a UNIFEM breakfast; and a film event on mother-guilt at a university. These types of events both ignited our thinking and also lifted our analysis to a new level.

Conclusion

I would like to inspire readers to consider establishing their own feminist mothers discussion group. Feminist discussion groups are relatively easy to run and enormously rewarding for participants—there are few more enjoyable ways to spend a free evening out. There is an enormous, untapped desire out there among women for discussion groups, particularly among mothers. In my opinion, women, particularly those isolated by domestic toil, are desperate for more philosophy, more self-analysis, and more intellectual conversation in their lives. Mothering is still very much ghettoized and women rarely get opportunities to examine their lives and work. To this day we continue to receive inquiries about joining our feminist discussion groups, including requests by men to start a mixed discussion group.

Discussion groups benefit from the presence of a facilitator and in our experience having two co-facilitators greatly lightens the load for the facilitators. Having two facilitators also means that the facilitators have someone to de-brief with afterwards, which if the discussion has been particularly "fast and furious" can be essential. We would emphasize the importance in distinguishing your mothers' discussion group from a playgroup—ground rules that discourage the presence of children unless they are "babies in arms" and which also limit the extent to which the conversation may be about your own children can greatly assist in lifting the discussion from the usual trappings. However, room should be made for children to be nearby at discussions if there are mothers attending who don't have alternative care arrangements.

We have also observed that feminist discussion groups are always enhanced by the participation of a few core members who reliably and regularly attend. Feminist discussions groups tend to go through peaks and troughs in terms of attendance across the year and various members will participate for a while and then fall away and re-join the group later. If the discussion group is continually encountering an entirely new mix of people each meeting you will find the discussion somewhat stilted until rapport is developed, and this can make facilitation demands particularly onerous. Once a core group is established the discussion group will have the necessary stability for long-term survival.

34.
Toronto Feminist Mothers

A Work In Progress

TANIA JIVRAJ

I WENT TO MY FIRST Association for Research on Mothering (ARM) conference two years ago at the recommendation of my professor at Ryerson. There began my awakening as a mother, woman and person. As a new mother, a single mother, I was desperate to find others for support. I had gone to different mothers' groups, but felt as if I would be reproducing a gender role that I was unhappy with, though I did not have the words at the time to express even the notion of "gender roles." The amazing, controversial and inspiring women speakers and attendees at the conference… Blew. My. Mind. I have not been the same since. I have begun to explore myself and the world around me in a critical way. My daughter will not grow up in the world that I did. ARM has since transformed into the Motherhood Initiative for Research and Community Involvement (MIRCI).

History

MIRCI parents other groups, one of which is Mother Outlaws. Mother Outlaws is discussed in another chapter in this book. Briefly, it derives its name from Adrienne Rich's book, *Of Woman Born: Motherhood as Experience and Institution (1986)*. Rich uses the term Mother Outlaw to describe the act of mothering against the norms imposed by a society that enforces patriarchal definitions of motherhood. These definitions create motherhood as an institution that traps mothers within a narrow binary of "good" mothers and "bad" mothers". It is from this notion of resistance to imposed norms that the Toronto Feminist Mothers (TFM) group was developed and is developing. Initially, I understood TFM members as exploring the act of parenting in a manner that is conscious and more reflective of personal and familial needs and values. This understanding is expanding into one that recognizes parenting as a cooperative effort within communities that are affected by political agendas. It is a *parenting* that is diverse and is respectful of the complexities of human relationships and does not rely on Hollywood's martyr mom or evil stepmother as its foundation. It is an active participation in challenging the institution of motherhood allowing mothers to parent "out"side "laws" that are reflected in media, policies, cultural norms and obligations. The

Toronto Feminist Mother's group was borne out of Mother Outlaws in 2009. Thankfully, this came just in time for me. I was invited by my then professor (now my friend, but always a teacher) May Friedman to a feminist mom's group. I came to my first meeting knowing I was a bad mother and pretty sure I was not as smart as everyone else. A feminist mom's group? I read a bell hooks book once … does that make me a feminist? Two years later, I don't know if labelling my parenting style is beneficial—and I feel confident that "being smart" is not the point. I have now read two bell hooks books and few others too. But I'm pretty sure that's not what makes me a feminist. I eventually was asked to coordinate the group and did so for two years in 2009 and 2010.

Toronto Feminist Mothers

The Toronto Feminist Mothers are at times an eclectic group of women from diverse socio-economic and religious backgrounds with somewhat varying skin tones and splashes of queer identities and sometimes very homogeneous in our privileges and oppressions. The membership list sits at around 150 members from across southern Ontario with attendance to meetings ranging from two to fifteen. The group meets monthly at different members' homes with women contributing light snacks and following a never discussed but somehow adhered to policy of "no alcohol." The meetings are not a social event. Nor are they a support group, though I do find simply being in the company of the TFM a rejuvenating experience. It is so nice to have so many short cuts in discussions. For example, not having to explain why I would attend the protests surrounding the G20 in Toronto in the summer of 2010. I currently see the group as one of exploration. A place where a space is created in which I feel free to jump in, raw in my interpretations and potentially exposing myself as unconsciously towing the line of privileged discourse that values dominant ideologies further marginalizing and exploiting people who do not fit within Canada's notion of the good citizen and the good mother. It is a place to challenge popular knowledge and investigate the inherited assumptions of what is deemed "natural" in our society. It is in the space where I have developed a new awareness of who I am and who I would like to be. It is a lot of work.

Mandate

Though I am presenting my impressions, I am thankful and ever grateful for the hours of discussions and mental challenges that the Toronto Feminist Mothers meetings have provided me with, and am absolutely convinced that many of "my" impressions were borne from these meetings. On that note, I would say that I feel we do not have a formal mandate. Nor does our group have an informal one. The Toronto Feminist Mothers' group is a space for people who self-identify as feminist mothers to shape and be shaped in a continuous and organic community process as people and as mothers. I feel that the group changes its focus as the membership and the political and social environment changes. The TFM group has one criteria for membership, and that is associating oneself as a feminist mother, with the terms "feminist" and "mother" being fluidly and self-defined. This lack of mandate is not static and is ripe for change, or not.

Context

Why do I need to go to a feminist mom's group? Because following my daughter's birth, I was headed down a dangerous path. One paved with the submission of mothers before me and maintained by a legacy of peoples reinforcing the notion of the naturalness of motherhood-martyrdom. I felt that anything but complete surrender to the duty of my biology would have me demonized and ostracized for non-conformity. As a person who takes her duties very seriously, I wholly embraced motherhood-martyrdom, without knowing that this was what I was doing. It was not a conscious decision, but one whose route was determined without my participation. Worse yet, it appeared that the people around me were following directions from the same map. How could it be then, with nicely paved roads and everyone using the same map, that I felt so lost? I was not content to give up my independence, my body, my coffee, my sexy high heels and strapless dresses, drinks with my friends, and late night movies with sushi and non-pasteurized cheese. It was very difficult to spend each day … and night … and the following day … and the next night … with someone I did not know who took my sleep, my body and every available space previously afforded to my being. Why is her dad a great parent because he changes diapers yet my diapering capabilities were not a consideration in rating my parental abilities? It was impressed upon me by historical roles of mothers that all this was natural for women, so it is not considered work. I'm supposed to not only be fine, but to love this change. Women have been doing since the beginning of time. It's what you do because you love your daughter. Love her? Sure. It's just that I had no idea who this person was at the time. Yet because I had internalized the "social correctness" of this unconditional love, and so have those around me, it was inconceivable for me to not be ok with it.

A definition of internalized oppression that gets straight to the point is from the Women's Rural Advocacy Programs, an organization providing services for battered women and their children, "Internalized oppression means the oppressor doesn't have to exert any more pressure, because we now do it to ourselves and each other. Divide and conquer works." I live in a country where the Conservative government's human resource minister, Diane Finley, does not believe in implementing a national subsidized child-care program because that "…would ensure that parents are forced to have other people raise their children," and that "We do not believe in that" (Hennessy). I was not contacted before the minister made this statement. Of course, even if she had tried to call me, I probably would not have answered the phone being either at work, in class, at my placement for school or possibly in the library … or sometimes I even sleep. Divide and conquer indeed! There are good moms who stay home and care for their own children and there are other moms. My voice was silenced before I even spoke. This is not just an anecdote of an out of touch Minister, but a reflection of deep and thick and heavy assumptions of gender roles that have been elevated to the status of general knowledge that has infused society so profoundly so as to marginalize us to the point where we, well I, agree with it. I am not part of the "we" the government is talking about. The reality is that I find it difficult to find the time to reflect on how such comments, decisions, limited representations of mothers in the media impact me as a mother in everyday situations. The way I choose what to think about and the way in which I think about what I have chosen to think about (read it over a few times, it eventually makes sense) is formed within a context where I have already accepted my position in relation to others. My internal map is structurally unsound and only guides me back to the place that reinforces that it is natural for women to love their children unconditionally. I am perpetually lost following a map built on a lifetime of sexist notions of what is right and correct for me as a mother. Even going home is not much solace. In Maya Angelou's book, *Letters to My Daughter*, she says, "I believe that one can never leave home. I believe that one carries the shadows, the dreams, the fears and dragons of home under one's skin, at the extreme corners of one's eyes and possibly in the gristle of the earlobe" (6). Then I was directed to the Toronto Feminists Mothers where time and space is laid out for just such reflections.

Objectives and Activities

My home was built on unjust foundations where I was not allowed to question the injustice because, "Oh, Tania, that's just how things are." Where I am wrong to not accept that our society is set up to benefit one group and marginalize those who question that life and society could be reframed towards greater equity rather than a blanket acceptance of privilege and oppression. So I go to the feminist moms' group. The group is about questions. Then questioning why we are asking those questions. Then coming up with answers, maybe, and understanding that our perspectives are limited. It is always challenging ourselves and each other and not accepting a status quo that perpetuates unequal power distributions within our own lives and how these are formed by greater societal injustices.

In becoming part of the feminist mom's group, I don't have to be a nice polite mother. It feels mostly amazing and sometimes shocking to discuss such disparate topics as what does a feminist mother look like to giving partners hormones so they could also breast feed. I love NAMING issues and looking at greater systemic inequalities that challenge my capabilities to parent with less remorse for all my supposed failures. It was so nice to say, "My child is being such a jerk right now," and no one called the Children's Aid Society (CAS). Of course, no one outside the group would have called CAS either, but how could I, a mother, call her daughter a jerk!? Let the list of my inadequacies begin. I am more comfortable with myself and as a result I feel that my relationship with my daughter is gentler, kinder and so much more forgiving. The group discusses issues of race and class and ableism in mothering as well as the biases against single parents and how the not so subtle messages of demonizing mothers who do not fulfill society's notion of the good mom are reproduced in policies that reward mothers for staying at home. For example, that Canada has no national childcare is not an accident. The Toronto Feminist Mothers discussed this issue in terms of a heteronormative and gender analysis. It only makes economic sense since women in Canada in 2010 still earned only 72 cents for every dollar men earned (Conference Board of Canada). A friend recently spoke to me of her internal conflict at hiring a caregiver, because there were no day care spots and she has a full time job. If we had national day care, she would not have to be conflicted. She could be a mother and a full time wage earner, as is her right, without having to make excuses or feel guilt. Especially telling, is that Canada has changed immigration policies to allow women from what Western discourse would call developing countries, to come to Canada and work as Live-In Caregivers in often precarious working conditions where their rights are easily abused within the invisible confines of a stranger's home. Why would our government change immigration policies rather than institute a national day care and why are these policies created in such a way to further isolate and marginalize women, often mothers themselves, to positions of increased vulnerability? It is from these connections of government policies to community interactions to personal troubles that the TFM attack discussions. It is from these connections that the TFM are now looking at redefining motherhood and activism. It has taken us two meetings to reconfigure activism into mothers as agents of change, with plans of further discussions as to how to frame this within a context of feminism, motherhood and mothering and our own personal needs and goals.

Challenges

I am uncomfortable with who is not represented each month at the TFM meetings. We are missing the vital voices of adoptive parents, queer mothers, trans-mothers, recent immigrant mothers, mothers-to-be, older mothers and young mothers. I want to call all my social work friends right now to find out what other mothers I have neglected. I won't do this, so you can see how even after two years of challenging the notions of what a "mom" looks like, I still struggle to challenge my own assumptions. Of course I am conflicted, by naming "other" mothers, of which I include myself. I am a mixed-race, single mom with more than three mental health diagnoses. I am an older (mature?) university undergraduate student living off student loans in a rental apartment who relies too heavily on macaroni and cheese for dinner, albeit not from a box. I am the other or the alternative lifestyle mother in comparison to the mother who is immediately accepted because she looks and acts the part that is expected in Canadian society. This is a look and a part that I do not fit. There is so much to unpack. We have talked about expanding awareness of the TFM to beyond the people that we know, which brings up another challenge. Everyone is very busy and further commitments can be complicated.

For example, I recently had to relinquish my role as coordinator of TFM since my work, school, and parenting responsibilities made my involvement too sporadic to keep the momentum of the group going. It is now heading in a new direction, with Rebecca Lee as our fearless coordinator. I am so far away from giving up my life for the needs of my child. I am thrilled, excited, inspired and yes, tired. It's a strange bird, this feminist moms' group. Each month I look forward to the next meeting, then a few hours before the meeting I don't want to go. I have so much to do. There are other things that take priority. Yet, I force myself. After the meeting, I am exhilarated. These moms rock my world! I can't wait for next month. All revolutions must start in a living room at some point.

Organization's Importance in the Motherhood Movement

It is this small revolution that makes the Toronto Feminist Mothers' group so pertinent to the Motherhood Movement. It is a grassroots initiative that creates a safe space for self-identified feminist mothers to reflect upon and challenge not simply how to parent, but how our decisions are informed by disparate values imposed upon us by formal and cultural institutions. The TFM group is completely organized and directed by its' members—by the moms for the moms. A space for voices using words in a unique way to help create a different understanding of what it means to be a mother. I see our fluidity and lack of formal mandate as one of the strengths of the group as it is this flexibility that will allow the members to continually question assumptions that we carry as "natural truths" within the realm of our beings. It is about being uncomfortable with others and ourselves and sitting in that uncomfortable place, yet in a safe space within the bosom of the TFM. We may not know which direction to take, but we know we are not alone and that the struggle to redefine and address the inequities of how society is currently presenting "mothers" is not one that we will accept in its homogenization of such incredible and diverse mothers—mothers that I know and mothers I do not.

Works Cited

Angelou, Maya. *Letters to My Daughter.* New York: Random House, 2009.

Hennessy, T. "Guilting Parents Out of Child Care." *Rabble.ca.* 2011. Web. <http://www.rabble.ca/blogs/bloggers/trish-hennessy/2011/02/guilting-parents-out-child-care>.

Conference Board of Canada. "Society: Gender Income Gap." 2011. Retrieved from Web. <http://www.conferenceboard.ca/hcp/details/society/gender-income-gap.aspx>.

Women's Rural Advocacy Programs, 15 Nov. 2007. "Internalized oppression." Web. <http://www.letswrap.com/nadvinfo/internal.htm>.

Rich, Adrienne. *Of Woman Born: Motherhood as Experience and Institution.* New York: Norton, 1986.

IV.
Maternal Activism

35.
Mothers Are Women

KRISTEN ABATSIS McHENRY

MOTHERS ARE WOMEN (MAW) WAS a Canadian organization founded in 1984, whose purpose was to bring mothers together in order to make social connections, provide support, and discuss issues relevant to mothers who had made the conscious decision to stay at home and care for their children.

Mandate

This organization specifically worked on the issue of women's unpaid work and advocated for society to value the contributions women's motherwork makes to society. According to MAW (1992b), "Motherwork embraces three components: reproductive labour, the bearing and nursing of children; domestic labour associated with the physical care of children; and emotional labour related to the emotional and social development and well-being of children." MAW sees motherwork as an important and valuable contribution to society. Members of MAW sought to break their isolation, find support, and advocate on behalf of at-home mother's interests in Canada. According to the MAW constitution the organization's purposes are:

> 1. Providing a forum for sharing experiences, resources and information;
> 2. Encouraging individual women to develop their abilities to create changes on both personal and societal levels;
> 3. Working to control and define the conditions of motherhood and environments in which children are raised through political analysis and action;
> 4. Working for the recognition of women's unwaged labour whether in the home, on the farm, in the community or wherever else it occurs; and
> 5. Linking our efforts with those of women around the world.

Presently, Mothers Are Women is not an active organization. However, during its period of activity, MAW was successful in garnering national attention for the issue of unpaid work. It was nationally politically active, and allied with the

Canadian women's movement, all while providing local level support for mothers who choose to stay at home and care for children. It is important to examine the history, structure, issues, and tactics used by MAW in order to best understand its relationship to the women's movement and the motherhood movement.

History

Mothers Are Women originated in 1984 and began as a type of support group for stay at home mothers who felt very isolated and undervalued by society. MAW was originally based out of Ottawa, Canada. MAW's initial purpose was to connect women who wanted to have analytical discussions about their roles as mothers while providing support, information, and advice that many new mothers feel in need of. For example, Marla Waltman Daschko who joined MAW in 1989 saw the group as a way to connect with other women who "cared about the world." Many of the members of MAW felt similarly in that their new role as mother was isolating them from their previous work colleagues.

Many of the members felt their identities were shifting but also that members of society often judged women who care for children as "doing nothing" or "not working." MAW saw this as extremely problematic and began to get involved in addressing the issue of women's unpaid work. MAW pointed out that the Canadian government had many programs available for women in the paid labor force, but few programs for women who chose to stay at home with their children. In addition political parties such as the Conservative Party, the Liberal Party, the New Democratic Party, or the Reform Party, all lacked policies directed at mothers at home. MAW saw mothers at home as a marginalized and unrepresented constituency. Therefore MAW aimed to make their voices heard and strive for better political representation and programs for mothers at home.

At a certain point the focus and nature of MAW began to change and evolve. Many incoming members identified as feminists and were interested in being more politically active as a group. In many ways MAW was a reflection of the feminist position that "the personal is political." Some of these members felt as though the women's movement in Canada did not accurately represent mothers and therefore there was a need for a group who identified as feminist and mothers. MAW was a unique organization in that it identified as feminist mothers. In fact MAW was often assumed to be affiliated with more conservative right wing organizations of mothers. This is interesting given the differences between the stated principles of MAW and ideologies found in conservative right wing motherhood organizations. In this sense, MAW was distinct from other organizations based around the identity of motherhood.

Members and Structure of Organization

Early on, MAW made a conscious decision to be cooperative rather than a hierarchical organization. The decision to be cooperative was a defining feature of MAW.

They strived for achieving group consensus and in times where that was difficult resorted to majority vote (MAW Constitution). MAW was made up of officers, committee chairs, a steering committee, regional representatives and members. MAW held over 600 members by the '90s. MAW had a very diverse membership, made up of Jewish women, white women, working and upper class women, and women of color. Jane Ellens' states MAW was "an articulate diverse group of women with wide ranging perceptions of their lives and their place in society. Through all the differences however there emerged a number of common threads which ultimately formed the core of the MAW philosophy and goals" (Ellens 1). According to Ellens, all of the members felt a shared sense of isolation and alienation as mothers at home.

MAW was built on the free time of volunteer mothers and eventually came to obtain a good deal of funding from the Secretary of State. According to Kellerman "Much of MAW's work, including the publication of *Homebase,* would not be possible without the funding which we have received from Secretary of State, Women's Program. Since its inception in 1984, MAW has received grants ranging from $8,000 to $14,000 per year. The Women's Program, funded by the federal government, provides grants to groups engaged in education, lobbying and advocacy work on status of women issues. We are grateful to the Secretary of State for their support of our projects to improve the economic and social status of women at home and to support women as at-home mothers" (Kellerman 3). This funding allowed MAW to expand their reach and implement their key programs like "Count Us In" and "Work is Work is Work."

Context

Early on MAW strove to break the isolation of mothers at home. They accomplished this through discussion groups, workshops, and the publication of *Homebase* magazine. The first issue of *Homebase* magazine was published in 1985 and was distributed quarterly. The *Homebase* magazine was instrumental in moving MAW from a local organization to one with a national membership. Lisa Menard headed this magazine for some time, but many of the members were involved in the production and distribution of *Homebase. Homebase* magazine strove to provide information relevant to women choosing to be at home with children. Therefore the magazine featured articles on child friendly businesses, restaurants with high chairs, safe places to nurse in public, how to build a babysitting co-op, and the financial difficulties of choosing to stay home with children. The main goal of *Homebase* was to ensure that mothers at home felt connected and had access to resources and information on motherwork.

Objectives

One of the early projects MAW worked on was to get involved with Canada's formal women's movement. At the time, the National Action Committee (NAC) on the

Status of Women represented Canada's women's movement. NAC has since been disbanded. However, at the time the NAC was claiming to represent the women of Canada. Therefore MAW felt it important to join NAC and become actively involved. MAW's membership was accepted in 1987, and they proceeded to put forth resolutions that represented the mothers of Canada. MAW's goal was to have NAC represent the position that "women can be feminist and mothers. Our work may be unpaid but it is still work" (Daschko).

Unfortunately, this position was not readily accepted by NAC (Luxton and Vosko 52). Therefore MAW and NAC often clashed. While NAC claimed to represent all women of Canada including women of color, working mothers, Jewish women, and transgender women, they did not represent mothers who chose to stay at home. While NAC claimed to be very inclusive, in the perspective of MAW they were very exclusive in many ways. The exclusion of stay at home mothers became apparent in NAC's constant focus on fighting for government funded daycare without a focus on valuing the work and childcare that women who stay at home do. Daschko argues NAC "would talk about childcare as if all women wanted government funded childcare." MAW felt that the NAC did not acknowledge childcare work as important or valuable.

MAW and NAC continued to clash and MAW members were often critiqued for not being true feminists. This was truly unfortunate for the political alliance between MAW and NAC and was very demoralizing for MAW as an organization. However, MAW did join other groups such as the National Council of Women and worked with organizations such as the National Advisory Committee on Women in Law. MAW adopted more of a national focus in order to expand its membership and spread their philosophy to new audiences. One of the ways MAW accomplished these goals was through the *Homebase* magazine. In addition MAW sought to make alliances and connections to scholars, policy makers and feminists who were working on the issue of unpaid work. Specifically, they wished to make conceptual connections and political alliances between the United Nations Conference held in Beijing and women living in Canada. As a result, in 1995 they launched a workshop titled the "Global Kitchen."

Activities

In the early '90s, MAW began to focus on the issue of women's unpaid work. They did a number of projects such as "Work is Work is Work" and "Count Us In." Fortunately, they were able to receive funding from the Status of Women to pursue these projects. MAW began these projects by first conceptualizing how unpaid work should be defined and measured. This led MAW to the issue of the census. The "Count Us In" project, which began in 1994, focused on creating questions that measured unpaid work and care giving for the 1996 Census. In addition "Count Us in" wished to draw national attention to the unpaid work that women do in society. Proposed census questions were distributed to MAW members through the *Kitchen Table Revolution.* This was a newsletter created in

1994, which updated members, women's organizations, and policy makers on MAW's activities and future plans. In addition, the goal of this newsletter was to provide information and facts with the goal of further educating the general public and MAW members about women's unpaid work. MAW desired to have a say in the questions used in the census and the way unpaid work is measured. Other mother based organizations such as the Canadian Alliance for Home Managers and B.C. Voice of Women, and Women to Women worked together with MAW to include questions of unpaid work in the census (Luxton and Vosko 56). There was a considerable amount of media attention given to these groups and the campaign. MAW member Evelyn Drescher also publicized the issue of women's unpaid work by speaking at a UN conference. The media attention helped make women's unpaid work a national issue and garnered more support for MAW as a national group. According to Luxton and Vosko it was MAW's affiliations with the NAC and the Federated Women's Institutes of Canada that led to the success of the "Count Us In" campaign (57). MAW played a pivotal role in getting the Canadian Government to begin to measure women's unpaid contributions to society.

Challenges

One of the possible reasons for the decline of MAW was its shift in focus from local support to national politics. MAW began as a locally based support network for mothers. However, MAW soon evolved to be a political organization that focused on connecting mothers across the nation. This shift in focus led to a decline in membership at the local home base of Ottawa. Moreover, many new members were not interested in national level political activism but were more interested in the connections and personal level support that MAW could offer women in their community.

In addition, many members' lives were changing and for personal reasons some wanted to be involved in MAW in a less prominent way. The original members of MAW looked to the new members to emerge as leaders of MAW. However, this did not end up being the case. For example, there was no one who wished to take over the responsibility of *Homebase* magazine. Grace Johnston argues that it may have been an issue of women being unable to put in more unpaid hours than they were already doing in their homes (2010). Ultimately a lack of time to devote to MAW due to other responsibilities may have played a role.

Future Goals

A change in government brought a decline in funding for MAW. This was significant because many of the key projects pursued by MAW, such as "Work is Work" and "Count Us In," relied on government funding for support. Therefore, a lack of funding is one element that factored into the decline of MAW. Despite the fact that MAW chose not to continue on as a formal organization, their contributions to the motherhood movement and the women's movement are truly important.

MAW successfully connected mothers throughout Canada and encouraged them to fight for better political representation, connect with women and mothers, and strive for society to value women's motherwork. Despite MAW's success, the members ultimately chose to disband MAW in the 2004.

MAW and the Motherhood Movement

Many members of MAW did not feel connected to a larger motherhood movement. In fact MAW felt very isolated from other motherhood organizations. While there was a sister organization in the U.S. (Mothers at Home), MAW was not connected in any formal way. According to Marla Waltman Daschko, MAW was "it's own movement in a sense with few allies. We didn't feel part of something larger" like a motherhood movement. Grace Johnston echoes this sentiment, arguing that at the time there was no notion of a larger motherhood movement, there was no sense of other voices speaking out on these issues. MAW was what linked women to other voices. Specifically *Homebase* magazine helped link women together. Occasionally, MAW would receive messages back from subscribers with sentiments like "you saved my life, and I was feeling isolated and crazy and unimportant, thank you for your magazine" (Johnston).

Conclusion

MAW was a political organization in many ways, but throughout its existence it maintained a focus on improving women's personal lives. MAW was a pioneer in the motherhood movement in Canada. Their desired goals to break up mother's isolation, provide support, educate and inform were all achieved. On a personal level, MAW was very empowering for its members. According to Marla Waltman Daschko, "it saved me." MAW offered personal support and emphasized the strength and value of women's contributions to society. Grace Johnston argues that MAW demonstrated the power and impressiveness of women working together in a non-competitive way. The many successes of MAW made members such as Daschko believe that "one person can accomplish change and do so much in the world." This sentiment demonstrates the impact MAW had on its members and on the potential role women can play in changing the world.

Works Cited

Daschko, Marla Waltman. 2010. *Personal interview.* August 17.

Ellens, Jane. *Mothers Are Women. Report.* 1986.

Johnston, Grace. 2010. *Personal interview.* August 23.

Kellerman, Mauren. *History of Mothers Are Women.* 1990.

Luxton, Meg. "The UN, Women, and Household Labour: Measuring and Valuing Unpaid Work." *Women's Studies International Forum* 20.3 (1997): 431-439.

Luxton, Meg and Leah F. Vosko. "Where Women's Efforts Count: The 1996 Census Campaign and 'Family Politics' in Canada." *Studies in Political Economy* 56 (1998): 49-78.

Mothers are Women (MAW). *Appendix One: Political Parties and the At Home Mother.* 1992a.

Mothers are Women (MAW). *Appendix Two: Definition of Terms.* 1992b.

Mothers are Women (MAW). *Short History.* 1992c.

Mothers are Women (MAW). *Draft Action Plan for MAW Annual General Meeting.* June 24, 1992d.

Mothers are Women (MAW). (Daschako, Marla Waltman). *Report: Spring.* (#35) 1994a.

Mothers are Women (MAW). *Report: Count Us In Project: Stage 1.* June 1994b.

Mothers are Women (MAW). *Final Report: Women and Unpaid Work: Count Us In! Stage 1.* 1994c.

Mothers are Women (MAW). *Interim Report: Women and Unpaid Work: Count Us In: Stage 2.* 1995.

Mothers are Women (MAW). *Project Proposal Women and Unpaid Work: Count Us In! Stage 3.* 1996a.

Mothers are Women (MAW). *Final Report on the Activities Carried Out for Step By Step: Unpaid Work and the Census.* 1996b.

Mothers are Women (MAW). *Information on NAC.* 1997.

Mothers are Women (MAW). *Constitution.* Ottawa, Canada. March 29, 2001.

Placksin, Sally. *Mothering the New Mother.* 2nd ed. New York: New Market Press, 2000.

United Nations Platform Action Committee (UNPAC). "Valuing Unpaid Work." Summary of Keynote Address given by Evelyn Dresher of Mothers are Women at UNPAC. May 1999 Women & the Economy. Web. <www.unpac.ca/economy/valuingunpaidwork.html>. Accessed: August 18, 2010.

Wagman, Shawna. "Will Mothers Are Women Survive?" *Herizons* March 2005.

36.
MOTHERS Uniting and Organizing for Change

The Next Step in Building a Mothers' Movement

LINDA LISI JUERGENS

MOTHERS OUGHT TO HAVE EQUAL Rights (MOTHERS) was founded in September 2002 by the National Association of Mothers' Centers (NAMC) to address the issue of the economic impact of being a mother or caregiver in the United States. At the time, NAMC had a 27 year history of addressing the needs of mothers and raising their consciousness to the role they could play in affecting change. The NAMC's leadership had been using the term "mothers' movement" for years to describe the end result of mobilizing women involved in Mothers' Centers. The research done by Ann Crittenden for her 2001 book *The Price of Motherhood: Why the Most Important Job in the World is Still the Least Valued* validated years of women's stories about their experiences during the transition to motherhood and beyond. Early in 2000 the NAMC created a Mother's Declaration of Rights which was a more formal statement of the issues addressed in their programs including economic as well as social, educational, psychological and physical rights. Ann's facts were a perfect match with NAMC's mission. MOTHERS was created by the NAMC in conjunction with Ann Crittenden as the advocacy arm of the national organization to inform, educate, and motivate women regarding the connection between their personal situations and the larger world of public policy, corporate culture and societal norms. MOTHERS is a grassroots effort made up of mothers from all over the U.S. who are becoming more and more active advocates for their own economic well-being and subsequently that of their families. The founding of MOTHERS was the direct result of a collaboration between Ann Crittenden and the NAMC, facilitated by the years of work the NAMC has done in helping women raise their voices on their own behalf and on behalf of their children and communities.

How MOTHERS Came To Be

MOTHERS (Mothers Ought To Have Equal Rights) was founded in 2002 as an advocacy initiative of the National Association of Mothers' Centers (NAMC) to address the economic impact of being a mother. The philosophical base which created the fertile ground that nurtured the founding of MOTHERS comes from

Roundtable Mothers Groups, NAMC National Conference 2008

the NAMC. The model of the Mothers' Center program includes many principles from the women's movement and the consciousness-raising work of the '60s and '70s. Instrumental in the adaptation and implementation of these principles was Lorri Slepian, a founder of the Mothers' Centers and an NAMC founder. Her visionary leadership always included the goal of the optimal development of humanity through the mobilization of mothers. Over the years of her involvement she repeatedly used the phrase "building a mothers' movement."

At the outset, the originator of the Mothers' Center model, Patsy Turrini, conceived of and conducted research to study the lives of mothers, their hard work, their feelings, their sufferings. She set out to explore the unmet needs of mothers and to examine self-reported changes in their self-esteem and confidence during the transition to motherhood and beyond. Ms. Turrini's research was conducted in 1973 in discussion groups which were so well-received by the participants that they wanted to replicate the experience for other mothers. Seventeen volunteers and a few social workers worked together for over a year to create a model for self-reflection, service, consciousness-raising, research, empowerment and advocacy. Among those women was Lorri Slepian, who facilitated a research group and brought the idea of a mothers' movement to the fore from the beginning.

The first Mothers' Center in the world was opened in January 1975 in Hicksville, New York, after a year of work by research participants, community volunteers, and social workers.

As a result, in addition to mother-to-mother support and an information exchange in discussion groups, the program offered insights into how the personal is political and how mobilizing individually and together is a powerful tool for change. At the heart of the program are the communication skills that are modeled and practiced in Mothers' Center programs. These skills give the women a way to connect to each other in the most therapeutic way and also provide the confidence and the tools to approach just about anyone they encounter resulting in more positive outcomes. At home, it impacts on how they communicate and connect with their children, their partner or spouse and their extended family and friends. In the public sphere, the family doctor, their child's teacher or the principal of their school, their employer, as well as "the powers that be" in their communities and in government are no longer intimidating or overpowering. The skills learned at a Mothers' Center are similar to conflict resolution and negotiating skills that, once mastered, are gifts that have a lifelong impact.

The combination of a raised consciousness, increased confidence, and usable communication tools create a perfect storm to transform mothers into effective advocates on both personal and societal levels. While the centers began to spread from Hicksville to other states, for the most part the advocacy efforts were personal and local in nature. For example, mothers banded together in the Long Island region of New York to push for sibling visitation in maternity wards after hearing scores of mothers say how frustrating it was for their two and three year olds to be kept away from them during their hospital stays. At that time women were hospitalized for anywhere from three days for a vaginal delivery to six days or more for a caesarean section. One Mothers' Center member mobilized her community to clean drug paraphernalia from the grounds at her child's school so that the children could be allowed to utilize that space. In addition, mothers were routinely prevented from bringing strollers into card stores, clothing stores, the public library and other public places. There were precious few places where mothers were welcomed with their children in tow. These are the kinds of issues tackled by women in Mothers' Centers from the beginning of the program.

The network of centers grew each year, first under the auspices of Family Service Association, a Nassau County (New York) social service agency, and later in 1994 as the NAMC outgrew the scope of a county agency and became a national non-profit organization in its own right, and with its own Board of Trustees. At this point the national continued to provide the same support, consultation and training for the local centers but became more vocal about the role the national could play in helping women get their needs met. The NAMC became more and more the voice of the women who attended our local programs. Group facilitators documented the types of issues facing women and how they were dealing with them. Increasingly, the NAMC functioned as a repository for what was happening to women all over the country. Staffers could be counted on to be on the pulse of issues facing mothers, collecting their creative solutions, and validating their frustrations. As the NAMC continued to grow and was recognized as a source for information about mothers, the more opportunities arose to highlight these issues on a national level. Local, regional and national publications became more interested in what we had to say. By the mid-'90s, the media was focusing more and more on parenting, and all of a sudden we were "in the know" about a topic of interest. We branched out into work/life issues as women were returning to the workplace more quickly after becoming a mother.

The NAMC's first foray into a political issue was the Million Mom March, held in 2000 in Washington, DC. Mothers were very committed to addressing the issue of curbing gun violence that was increasingly affecting our children even in what used to be the safety of their classrooms. The timeliness and seriousness of this effort made NAMC's involvement inevitable.

The impetus for the creation of the MOTHERS initiative was word spreading among the leadership of the NAMC about Ann Crittenden's book *The Price of Motherhood: Why the Most Important Job in the World is Still the Least Valued.* Her research documented the various ways in which caregiving work is invisible, undervalued and certainly not supported. Word of the focus of the book spread like wildfire throughout the organization. At last someone was articulating what we knew to be true, something our members had been struggling with for years, something we didn't have the words to even describe accurately. Crittenden's contribution in crystallizing the issues so clearly and pertinently sparked readers everywhere to dream of addressing the economic consequences of the caregiving work mothers do every day. At last, the action steps to make a dramatic change come about were getting clearer. The public policy options, the necessary changes in corporate culture and the kinds of economic supports that might help were coming into focus.

After an outreach from Mothers' Center founder and NAMC Board member Lorri Slepian resulted in several meetings with Ann Crittenden, NAMC Board of Trustee Co-chair Rhonda Kave and Lorri Slepian went back to their headquarters in New York with a commitment from Ann to work together to start the ball rolling to create an initiative called MOTHERS (Mothers Ought To Have Equal Rights). NAMC leadership including Board of Trustee Co-chair Rosanne Weston, Executive Director Linda Lisi Juergens, Board member Kim Foglia, social work consultant Livia Polise and staffer Lori Rappa Rodriguez worked remotely with Ann to pull together a diverse group of women representing different issues and constituencies for a Steering Committee Retreat to create next steps.

With the help of author Naomi Wolf, a meeting place was secured at the Woodhull Institute for Ethical Leadership, a retreat center in Ancramdale, New York, founded "so women would have a place of their own" and "a place to grow, to develop new goals, and infuse ideas with strength and empowerment." It was a kind of Seneca Falls moment when a diverse group of women from various organizations met at the Woodhull Institute in September 2002 to plan next steps in the formation of a new organization whose goal was to advocate for reducing the economic impact of being a mother in the United States. What a synergistic start.

MOTHERS hit the ground running after that September 2002 meeting with a website www.MothersOughtToHaveEqualRights.org—created by web developer and NAMC Board member Kim Foglia—and its first Mother's Day Action for May 2003 in place.

From the inception of MOTHERS, the core concepts of non-judgmental communication, a collaborative and transparent leadership structure, and a profound respect for differing perspectives, all stemming from the philosophy of the NAMC, laid the groundwork for its work to improve the economic situation for mothers.

What MOTHERS Does

MOTHERS informs, educates, assists and motivates women to take an active part in the political process, primarily on issues regarding the economic impact of being a caregiver. MOTHERS hosts annual Mother's Day Actions, maintains a website, disseminates an e-newsletter, collaborates with other organizations on relevant actions, and produces both a blog entitled Your (Wo)man in Washington (www.WomaninWashington.org) and a column entitled DC Dispatch which are brilliantly written by Valerie Young, one of the women who joined us at our Woodhull meeting and who now serves in Washington, DC, as our Advocacy Coordinator.

Our Mother's Day Actions to date:

- •2003 *No More Zeroes:* women faxed their Social Security statements to their legislators circling all the zeroes representing years of no income due to unpaid caregiving work;
- •2004 *Get Out the Vote: Host an Economic ABCs Workshop*—women hosted discussions in their homes and communities with MOTHERS' discussion outline about the economic hit they were experiencing as mothers and caregivers with the goal of making sure women got out to vote in the next election season;
- •2005 *MOTHERS Book Bag*: a website listing books of interest to mothers that dealt with diverse topics including public policy, public discourse, culture and parenting trends; site included reviews and interviews with authors;
- •2006 *CEASEFIRE in the "Mommy Wars":* targeted at the media to insist they stop using inflammatory language to pit mothers against each other, usually working vs stay-at-home, when their self-interest would bring them together to work for similar changes;
- •2007 *Paid Family Leave Efforts*: a campaign to inform the electorate and legislators about the profound difference having paid family leave would have on families;
- •2008 *Top 10 Gifts Mothers Really Want for Mother's Day*: a list that bypassed traditional flowers and candy—although those are appreciated—to focus on real solutions and societal changes that would support essential caregiving work;
- •2009 *Mile for Mothers*: (in conjunction with the international MC network) first attempt to mobilize MC women to walk a mile in their community to highlight the important work of their center and the need for support for mothers;
- •2010 *Mile for Mothers expanded* (in conjunction with the international MC network) first annual nationally centralized walk added to local

activities to honor the value of mothers' work and to highlight needed support for that work.

Our efforts help mothers and those who support mothers' issues to keep abreast of: current opinions and perspectives; legislative possibilities; implications of proposed legislation; media coverage pertinent to our issues; research; and current events.

MOTHERS aims to offer information to help individuals form personal opinions and take action. MOTHERS aims to enable women to raise their voices as so many issues could benefit from the perspective of mothers. Furthermore, we make getting information and becoming active as easy as possible for the novice and the person who is short on time but committed to being involved.

The Mandate of MOTHERS

MOTHERS was founded to address the economic impact of being a mother or other caregiver in the United States. Our goal is to inform women of this impact, to educate them about the current state of affairs as well as the possible solutions in all realms (in workplaces, in public policy, in their communities, in their homes) and to give them the tools and the motivation to work for change.

The Challenges for MOTHERS

Challenges inherent in the work of mobilizing mothers include:

Mobilizing women who are in the midst of their own personal transition to motherhood. This normal developmental crisis helps women grow in many ways but is also a difficult time to ask them to focus outward with the confidence they once had and will regain as they get their footing in their new role of mother.

Reaching mothers who are already time starved as they struggle in today's difficult economic and political environment. Not only are new mothers emotionally cocooned with their babies to meet their 24 hour a day needs, in many cases they are also forced into a quick return to paid employment to make ends meet. There is often little spare energy or time to devote to more global concerns.

Making complex political machinations understood as quickly and easily as possible. Discussions and wording of potential legislation are complex and include enough legalese that precious few citizens can discern how to interpret the details or assess their impact without explanation.

Finding ways to collaborate wherever possible with like-minded groups to bring the biggest collective voices possible to issues of concern. Territorial issues and power struggles can make collaborative efforts few and far between.

Bringing diverse and what may appear at first glance to be unrelated information and support to bear on the issues we espouse. It is imperative to look at our issues with a 360-degree view at how the areas of economic stability, competitiveness in the global marketplace, early care and education of children, social justice,

Mile for Mothers Walk ribbon cutting, Boardwalk at Long Beach, New York, May 1, 2010.

Start of the Mile for Mothers Walk, Long Beach, New York, May 1, 2010.

gender equity and much more are interrelated. This requires some "out of the box" thinking. Making a case from all these different vantage points strengthens our cause and can bring quite unexpected support from disparate quarters.

MOTHERS Response to Challenges

Mobilizing women in the midst of the adjustment to motherhood:

Those who attend Mothers' Center programs are involved in groups where their experiences and emotions are validated, assisting them in moving through this transition with less anxiety and loss of confidence. Even for those not involved in these programs, all MOTHERS communications validate the importance and life-changing aspects of becoming a mother, assisting with her adjustment to her new life responsibilities. All communications are done in a non-judgmental, respectful way and all programs model exemplary communication skills that women utilize in every aspect of their lives. These skills are particularly useful in giving women the confidence to engage in advocacy efforts of all kinds.

Reaching mothers who are already time-starved:

MOTHERS offers information in small bits and pieces, easy to digest in the few moments it takes to open an e-mail or click the link to a blog or website. Women are addressed respectfully, acknowledging their power to help change happen, whenever they are ready to take that on. Even the smallest steps are valued and encouraged.

Making complex legislative language accessible:

MOTHERS supporters receive the *DC Dispatch* column and alerts on new posts to the Woman In Washington blog. The *DC Dispatch* takes a look at what conversations are happening in the nation's capital, among whom, and with what potential outcomes. The Woman In Washington blog covers both timely and personal issues about women's roles as mother and caregiver in various circumstances. It connects them to the economic security of women throughout their lifespans and most compellingly as they reach old age. The Mothers e-news editions further highlight work being done by other organizations as well as research results and current print and electronic media that bring greater understanding to the issues and to possible solutions. These methods of communication generally include a brief, easily digestible synopsis followed by a link to a more in-depth analysis so that even those who don't read further have a basic grasp of the issue.

Finding ways to collaborate with others:

With the goal of promoting the growth of a broader mothers' movement to affect change, in April 2008, the National Association of Mothers' Centers of the U.S. began the process of assembling a convocation at their 24th National Mothers' Center Conference *MOTHERS '08: Thinking Beyond Ourselves and Beyond Today* in Hauppague, New York. The conference brought together 18 diverse mothers organizations to share information about their unique perspectives, to explore common issues and to strategize about future collaborations and joint actions on behalf of mothers. The keynote speaker was Ellen Bravo, a policy analyst and advocate who shared her personal story of involvement as well as bringing women to their feet in support of public policies that address the needs of mothers and families. The next gathering occurred at the October 2008 Toronto ARM international conference *You Say You Want a Revolution,* where the foundation for the International Mothers Network was laid, thanks to the leadership of Dr. Andrea O'Reilly and the interest of mothers groups from around the world. Both of these opportunities helped create a bond, a familiarity and an understanding of both the differences and commonalities among a diverse spectrum of organizations and missions. These "getting to know each other" steps are absolutely necessary in order to produce a sisterhood of open-minded, sensitized women who will bring new ideas and possibilities for collaboration from their organizations to the larger network and vice versa.

Bringing diverse support to our advocacy issues:
MOTHERS leadership and supporters come from collaborations focused on:

- early care and education of children
- the economic benefits of family support and quality care for children
- the positive impact on corporations' bottom line when flexible workplace practices are implemented
- family friendly community development
- gender equity
- social justice
- empowerment of women and girls and more.

Future Aims / Goals / Challenges

These are the goals we have already begun tackling which will continue to be relevant as we progress into the future:

Keeping alive the history of where women and mothers have been, what steps were taken to make change happen and how far we've come.
MOTHERS, although founded in 2003, is built on a long history of women facing and sharing personal stories and identifying the accompanying political implications. We must keep in mind and share with younger women the context of a long term effort by many women over 100 years to improve the lot of all women. While stories of suffragettes may feel like the distant past to young women in their 20s and 30s, there are many women who can bear witness to more recent circumstances that circumscribed the opportunities available to women.

In the U.S., as recently as the 1970s there was still a respect for the authority of the professional, causing many women to take at face value what their doctor recommended as treatment or prevention. Other women felt intimidated to interview a doctor to ensure that during pregnancy and delivery her expectations and values would be respected and hopefully matched. Countless birth stories were humiliating episodes featuring condescending medical professionals treating women like misbehaving children. Postpartum depression was swept under the rug if acknowledged at all. Scores of women were sent home with the stern message to "snap out of it" received like an abrupt slap in the face.

By the mid-'70s women were graduating from prestigious universities in greater numbers, entering male-dominated professions, and were getting their feet wet in tenure and partner track positions in universities and corporations. (As a 1970 college graduate I was still asked at each interview if I could type. There was no training, apprenticeship or internship offered for a beginning employee who happened to be female.)

On the economic front, women's earning potential was considered a short-lived luxury evidenced by the fact that as late as 1974 a lender would refuse to count the wife's salary when calculating how big a mortgage a couple could qualify for when buying a home. It was assumed the wife would become a homemaker as soon as their first child arrived. Women business owners (who tended to be the widows or single daughters of a deceased prior male owner) were denied the credit they needed to sustain or grow their firms.

While not dwelling in the past, we cannot lose sight of where we've been as we forge a new path. The stories of women who have gone before us are powerful and need to be accessible to provide a context of the journey to date. The stories of our contemporaries are equally powerful and point to what still needs to be done. Hopefully, the stories of the future will reflect that change.

Breaking down the barriers that divide mothers unnecessarily.

Mothers are most often defined by their differences in the media, in research and in public policy discourse. Are they working mothers or at home mothers? Are they opting out or breaking the glass ceiling? Are they opting out or being pushed out? Are they breastfeeding or bottle-feeding? Are they natural childbirth proponents or interested in a medicated birth? Are they rich or poor? Educated or not? Urban or rural? Straight or lesbian or bi? These distinctions are often what get the attention, create the buzz and controversy and get the media attention. While some of these distinctions directly influence how we might stand on or perceive certain issues and are important to address in their own right, the constant focus on our differences diverts our attention from the preponderance of issues we have in common. The tactic of pitting one woman's choice and/or circumstance against another's predictably provides much heat but little light. Bringing women together based on their shared experiences rather than segmenting them can bring a louder voice and a more effective action plan.

Helping mothers feel powerful as change makers and provide the skills to advocate confidently.

Mothers need to be introduced to the possibility that things do not have to be the way they are and that they have a significant part to play in making necessary and beneficial change happen.

One of the challenges here is that in the U.S., gender roles have historically played a significant role in all aspects of society. There is evidence of a noticeable shift, though progress is still slow, as fathers recognize the value of being an active participant in their children's lives and their elder parents' lives, as women's inroads into leadership positions in all areas are increasing, and as women battle daily to be the best they can be in both their public and private lives. Women are still under-represented in the halls of government and in corporate boardrooms and over-represented (and underpaid) in caregiving work.

We've faced a particular challenge in the U.S. as our national culture, history, traditions and heritage are built on the concepts of rugged individualism and taking care of one's own. Public assistance and support is most often seen as being for those who are lazy or stupid or both. There is an underlying fear that people will take advantage of "the system" and get something for free that everyone else is working hard to achieve. These are so ingrained in us that women buy into the notion that it was their decision to have a child so they must take full responsibility. There is not so much a group consciousness that we all can use support and that support will result in better outcomes for all citizens and the country as a whole.

Many issues are assessed using the logic of a manufacturing, production model where the inputs and outputs are concrete and easily measurable. The softer outcomes related to social supports don't quite fit the mold well enough to offer the clarity and certitude that other types of outcomes do, plus may take longer to come to fruition. And there's always the almighty dollar at play. The cost vs profit is often the determining factor, and when the profit of social supports may be years down the road as we track the development of our children, our families and our community, the lack of that more immediate profitability can derail and undervalue these essential efforts.

There is most often NO sense of entitlement to support from the larger society. (Two compelling examples of this are: the U.S. is one of five industrialized nations worldwide that does not mandate any paid family leave—the other four countries are Lesotho, Liberia, Papua New Guinea and Swaziland. And in 24 of 50 U.S. states it is NOT illegal to refuse to hire a mother because of her responsibility for her children.)

And to complicate things, there is virtually no financial support available to women starting Mothers' Centers in the U.S. There is an underlying assumption that mothers *give* care—they don't *need* care or support. Unless a program is specifically for a population of mothers that is seen as critically at risk (from poverty, illness, addiction, for example) there is generally no assistance available. Centers pay fair market value rents for their spaces and are often required to have substantial liability insurance to cover any accidents or injuries that may occur in that space. These programs are founded by and operated by volunteer mothers who raise the necessary funds locally through their own efforts. So even as we make the case that the work mothers do is invaluable, our society is telling them in so many ways that they don't merit attention or support.

This is why the Mothers' Center method to bring women to a greater sense of entitlement starts with the MC culture which acknowledges individual differences, includes skill building in non-judgmental communication, promotes an assumption of integrity, a willingness to address areas of conflict, and a validation of the importance, value and challenges of motherwork. Each individual participant is brought into this way of interacting, affecting not only the functioning of her center, but profoundly influencing her parenting, her relationship with her partner and her social and work life. Those skills in turn support good conflict resolution and negotiating as well as giving women the confidence and words to advocate for themselves and their families. It is at this point that the women really feel their power and can begin to move to another level of advocacy in a more public forum. It follows that the National Association of Mothers' Centers eventually created its MOTHERS initiative (www.MothersOughtToHaveEqualRights.org) to provide information and action steps to advocate for public policies to mitigate the economic impact of being a caregiver.

So first and foremost, this work must continue to bring women along this path.

Work hand-in-hand with other mothers' organizations wherever feasible to grow our voices and our influence, no matter how small these steps are, and to get publicity for these efforts.

A unified voice can only come about piece by piece as mothers' groups craft joint messages and partnerships for joint action. Starting first with other women's organizations as our partners, our voices need to merge and grow and our footsteps need to resound together wherever possible for change to occur. The common messages may be limited at first and perhaps somewhat global in nature. The joint actions likewise may be limited initially. And almost as important as the joint action is the promotion and publicizing of those actions by all involved to help build momentum and credibility.

One aspect that MOTHERS has contributed to this effort, as mentioned above, is the utilization of the Mothers' Center culture, that is, its frank acknowledgement of differences between us, non-judgmental communication, an assumption of integrity and a willingness to address areas of conflict. Our organization functions according to those principles at all levels, and brings those components to conversations with other organizations.

While we must acknowledge the limitations in terms of availability worldwide, we cannot underestimate the power of the internet and the opportunities it presents for virtual events and actions. In every way possible we need to keep the lines of communication open, inform each other, invite each other, learn about each other, build trust between us, respect each other and begin to work together, acknowledging that each of our sister organizations will bring its own unique skills and perspectives to any collaborative efforts.

The NAMC / MOTHERS has joined a very large U.S. coalition called the National Council of Women's Organizations, consisting of over 200 member organizations representing over eleven million women. When signing on, organizations do not agree to agree with everyone else's issues, but agree not to actively work against each other's issues. Joint actions and partnerships help build momentum and gain more publicity and credibility. Working together even in the smallest ways increases the impact by virtue of the additional weight of the joint voices. We can do the same internationally.

I want to acknowledge the Grassroots Women's International Academies offered by the Mother Centers International Network for Empowerment (MINE) which has brought together many diverse groups over many years to share best practices and learn from each other. The growing network of Mothers Centers internationally has had much success mobilizing their members for public actions in support of mothers and families in communities across the globe.

Engage diverse stakeholders drawing from every possible area of expertise.

We see potential support in these areas:

Researchers: The importance of the role mothers play in the development of children has gotten increased attention in the last decade. Brain development researchers have been making a compelling case for the absolute importance of good care and an empathic connection to a caregiver for babies zero to three. Brain synapses that develop during these formative years are critical for their future optimal growth and development. Some of this early growth is not possible to replicate later on so this early window of opportunity must be utilized. Emotional intelligence is another topic that draws some conclusions about the kind of care and connection babies and children feel toward adults and their ability to self-regulate and manage the ups and downs of living.

Economists and business leaders: The former head of the Federal Reserve Bank, Art Rolnick, a very respected economist, began to talk about the return on the investment in early education for children from zero to three years. This was a departure from the usual assessments about the success of education which were traditionally limited to looking at first grade through high school. Not only did Mr. Rolnick understand the huge importance of the early years of development and the need for adequate care, he saw the link to future productive citizens and most importantly, convinced the business community in the state where he worked of the vital nature of this kind of investment. He calculated that the return on investment in early care was sixteen to one, an incredibly high return as investments go. In that way he was able to transform the thinking in his sphere of influence, the business community—a sphere that a few years earlier would never have stayed awake for a discussion of the needs of newborns and toddlers.

Law enforcement officials: Researchers once again come into play here, having compared the public cost of remedial services for students who are falling behind as well as court involvement and prison for those who subsequently turn to crime. Once again, a moderate investment in early care and education reaps huge savings in comparison to the costs of retraining delinquent students and incarcerating those who cross the legal limits. The organization Fight Crime, Invest in Kids has taken the lead in this area.

Environmentalists: Concerns regarding environmental degradation and increased traffic and gas emissions dovetail well with work/life initiatives that serve workers' diverse responsibilities. Offering flexible work hours, telecommuting, staggered shifts throughout an industry or geographic area, all benefit mothers and other caregivers who need these kinds of work policies to deliver adequate care while simultaneously meeting environmental goals.

Global competitiveness: Many international comparisons and rankings have been done to highlight the vast differences between even neighboring countries. In the United States, women earn at least 45 percent of the total income brought in by families. No country can afford to ignore the importance of that income to the family and their nation. Yet women are often underpaid, not employed, discriminated against, overlooked, and under-educated. In the U.S., while the national Census data shows that women are closing the wage gap so that women now make about 78 cents compared to each dollar a man earns, when women's incomes were compared to men's over a 15-year period by the Institute for Women's Policy Research, women actually made 38 cents compared to a man's dollar. This discrepancy was due to women's caregiving responsibilities over those years. How can the U.S. compete globally when half of their workforce is at such financial risk and not able to participate fully in the workplace due to the lack of supports? Add to that the fears about adequate training of our future workforce and there is real concern and beginning action to change course.

We have to look for and capitalize on these intersecting efforts. We have to engage partners from every possible connecting pathway. Much progress has been made in this arena internationally by many grassroots organizations working on development, water, environmental and health issues, utilizing United Nations initiatives and reports. Backing up our grassroots knowledge and insights with an array of partners from every field can bring support from previously unexpected areas. We need to know and use the "business case" and the "environmental case" and the "national economic case" and the "reducing cost case," etc.

It will only be by making these first few steps, no matter how tentative, that there can be any hope for larger, more elaborate, more studied and nuanced partnerships and actions in the future. By starting where the women are to bring them along to a new awareness of their latent power, by working together organizationally whenever possible, and by working with diverse partners to bolster our case, we will succeed in creating an effective mothers movement.

What MOTHERS Brought to the Motherhood Movement

From its inception, MOTHERS was focused on creating a mothers' movement. We cannot detail the goals and philosophy of MOTHERS without acknowledging the role its mother organization, the NAMC, had in informing the way it works and its goal of nurturing a Mothers Movement. One example is that MOTHERS has contributed the utilization of the Mothers' Center culture in the creation of a mothers' movement. Its frank acknowledgement of differences between us, non-judgmental communication, an assumption of integrity and a willingness to address areas of conflict are essential ingredients for collaborations among diverse organizations to occur. Our organization functions according to those principles at all levels, operates within a transparent non-hierarchical structure, and brings those components to every aspect of its work. These practices will increase the likelihood of collaboration and cooperation among diverse organizations.

MOTHERS and NAMC hosted their 24th National NAMC Conference in April 2008 which brought U.S. mothers' organizations to the table to start identifying common concerns and building the familiarity and trust necessary for true collaboration to grow. This was followed by the Association for Research on Mothering's conference in October 2008 at which representatives from mothers' organizations around the world came together to conceptualize the International Mother's Network.

Conclusion

Despite written history's neglect of women, women and mothers have been activists and community organizers for untold years. If anything, becoming a mother helps galvanize whatever strength and resolve women may have, and helps them find the power they may never have known they had, to defend and protect their children and their children's futures. With the proper support and validation mothers can be a powerful force. What is new in the twenty-first century is the increase in groups focusing on mothers' issues and the more widespread dissemination of their messages and actions thanks to technological advances. And now, a new strategy to bring mothers groups together to talk, to strategize, to collaborate, to support each other's efforts, and where possible, to present a united front is beginning to materialize both within and across country boundaries.

A mothers' movement is afoot. The National Association of Mothers' Centers has devoted many years to working on this and bringing Mothers' Center women along. The founding of MOTHERS was the direct result of the years of that work to help women raise their voices on their own behalf and on behalf of their children and communities.

I'd like to close with two compelling pieces:

A call to action:

We all have what it takes to be advocates. We show it every time we...

Think beyond ourselves and beyond today
Share a personal experience
Listen and learn from one another
Hunt for information
Make a new friend or gain someone's trust
Set priorities
Work with others to agree on a good policy
Build alliances with others
Get angry enough to do something
Find solutions to recurring problems
Realize that we are not alone
Celebrate small victories
Advocacy is for everyone. Go do it.
—Reprinted from Parent Services Project

And a brief poem the National Association of Mothers' Centers has been using for many years:

ONE WOMAN AWAKE
awakens another,
the second awakens her next door neighbor
and three awake can rouse the town,
and turn the whole place upside down.
And many awake
can raise such a fuss
that it finally awakens the rest of us.
One woman up,
with dawn in her eyes,
multiplies.
—Author Unknown

Works Cited

Crittenden, Ann. *The Price of Motherhood: Why The Most Important Job in the World is Still the Least Valued.* New York: Metropolitan Books, 2001.
Mothers Ought To Have Equal Rights (MOTHERS). <www.MothersOughtToHaveEqualRights.org>.
National Association of Mothers' Centers (NAMC). Web. <www.MothersCenter.org>; <www.motherscenters.org/blog>
Parent Services Project. Web. <www.ParentServices.org>.
Woman in Washington blog. Web. <www.WomaninWashington.org>.

37. Mothers & More

Fighting "Invisimomibility" to Make Mothering Count

JENNA VINSON

The work I do is invisible to my family. Occasionally I don't do it (when I travel, or, last year, when I was injured), the whole place goes to hell, but it never makes them understand how much I do for them, it just makes them angry when I don't do it.

—Mothers & More member, 2005

Invisimomibility is a chronic, pervasive condition in which mother's unpaid caregiving work is undervalued, leading to an inability to successfully fulfill one's caregiving, civic and paid work responsibilities and leaving primary caregivers vulnerable to social and economic risk.

—"Mothers & More Fights to End Invisimomibility"

SINCE ADRIENNE RICH'S INFLUENTIAL TEXT, *Of Woman Born,* feminist writers have been making visible the ways in which many mothers are isolated from the public sphere, assigned the role of care worker as a natural condition of their femininity, and then bombarded with prescriptive images of what a good mother is.[1] The combination of isolation, pressure, and naturalization of caregiving makes the unpaid *work* of mothering invisible to both the community and the nation at large. This leads to serious economic and emotional costs for women. I open this chapter with the epigraphs above in order to highlight the parallel between the frustration many mothers may feel about their domestic work going unnoticed in the family and the lack of mechanisms to account for the value of this work in the broader national context. The Center for American Progress reports that women are still more likely than men to be poor, and suggests one of the key contributors to this inequity is that women do more unpaid caregiving work than men (Cawthorne). Furthermore, the U.S. Bureau of Labor Statistics reports that full-time working women still make only 80 percent of the income that salaried full-time working men do. Women remain more likely than men to be positioned in part time jobs that often offer no benefits and little job stability. Though married women with children had salaries comparable to women without children, unmarried women with children earned 14 percent less then unmarried women without children (U.S. Bureau). Add to these nationally-identified economic disparities, the under-represented challenges that Arlie Hochshild called "the second shift"—the considerable amount of time women spend on housework and caring for children after returning home from work—and it becomes clear that paid and unpaid mothers alike face severe socioeconomic challenges.

Mothers & More is a non-profit organization that connects mothers and mothering advocate organizations to address these economic disparities through the strategies of grassroots activism and virtual communities. Comprised of over 100 chapters around the nation and a vibrant online network, Mothers & More uses tactics of visibility and connectivity to demand that mothers' work count. On their website they emphasize, "By uniting mothers to act on our own behalf, we seek to eliminate policies, practices and attitudes that unfairly impact mothers as caregivers" ("Where We Stand"). Since it began, Mothers & More has served over 100,000 mothers. This chapter will give a brief overview of the history, philosophy, and activities of Mothers & More. In the end, I suggest that Mothers & More has made important contributions to mothering movements by modeling strategies for resistance and bringing attention to the social and economic impacts of mothering work.

What is Mothers & More?

Mothers & More is a non-profit, volunteer driven, member-based organization dedicated to raising awareness about the difficult and often unrecognized work that mothers do to raise children and run households. Mothers & More also nurtures members' sense of identity as they balance these often stressful and financially challenging tasks. The homepage of the Mothers & More website exclaims, "Mothers Need Playgroups Too!" and uses images and phrases that welcome women to join in their vision of a mothering community. Mothers & More members are given an opportunity to interact with other mothering women and a space to resist sacrificing their other "selves." Yet, it would be a mistake to assume that Mothers & More is simply a series of support groups for local women to socialize and vent. Mothers & More has a political agenda that, like many feminist practices, builds from personal struggle into broader, collective action. In this sense, Mothers & More tackles two large obstacles that many mothers face: the sense of isolation or loss of friendship that can accompany transitions into motherhood and the economic impact of having children.

The History of Mothers & More

Mothers & More began in 1987 in Elmhurst, Illinois, as a small support group named "Formerly Employed Mothers At Loose Ends," or FEMALE. Founder Joanne Brundage created FEMALE as a social outlet for "sequencing" mothers. Sequencing is a term coined by mass communications scholar Arlene Rossen Cardozo, who argued for the value of "having it all, but not at once" (Cardozo).

The term is most often used to refer to heterosexual, married, middle-class adult women who leave the workplace or reduce their working hours to accommodate caring for children (Mothers Movement 2005). Sequencing is made possible by having a partner who is well-paid in a full-time job. However, Brundage and other sequencing mothers found that transitioning from self-supported paid worker to full-time unpaid caregiver is not without its challenges—despite what the 1980s supermom myth told women at the time. In creating FEMALE, Brundage was looking for a safe space to vent with other "like-minded women" about her transition from full-time U.S. Postal Service employee to full-time stay-at-home-mother-of-two ("History"). In an interview with *Mothers Movement Online,* Brundage explained that forming the group "was pure personal desperation on my part, after being home full-time for a year with a very crazy, colicky infant and wondering if I'd ever find another mother who was home and not in a total state of bliss about it—someone who shared the ambivalence, the grieving, and the guilt over the grieving I felt about leaving the paid workplace to be home with my children" (2005). Brundage did find four women to meet once a week in her home, and they soon began to network to find others. Brundage quickly learned that the group's focus appealed to many women's concerns at the time. She explained, "When we put a small blurb in the women's section of the *Chicago Tribune* in late December, we got calls from 64 women in 48 hours, from all over the Chicagoland area. And when a letter to the editor describing the group was published in the March 1988 issue of *Ms. Magazine*, we grew to hundreds of members, across the country and beyond, literally overnight. Clearly, we had touched on an unfulfilled need" (2005).

From the beginning, the leaders of Mothers & More have been aware that the feminist mantra "the personal is political" means that women cannot just voice frustration about material inequalities for mothers and women in the workplace (though, clearly, this is an important part of the process). Members must also engage in political work to initiate social change. In 1991 the meaning of the acronym FEMALE tellingly changed to "Formerly Employed Mothers At the *Leading* Edge" and then finally "Mothers & More" in 2000. As the support group grew, the members decided to change the name to "reflect the organization's commitment to educating and motivating businesses and government about the value and necessity of all mothers' work to our society—paid and unpaid" ("History"). "Mothers & More" is meant to reflect a broader understanding of who Mothers & More are and what they want to accomplish as an organization; members are mothers who work part-time or full-time, mothers who stay at home, or mothers who have left the workforce temporarily but all of whom do valuable *work* to raise children.

Mothers & More Philosophy and Mandate

According to the Mothers & More mission statement, this non-profit organization is committed to "improving the lives of mothers through support, education, and advocacy. We address mothers' needs as individuals and members of society and promote the value of all the work mothers do." More specifically, Mothers & More recognizes the tension between carework and work for profit in our society, and the organization does its best to educate their members about the real material effects of these tensions. They write, "Two different but equally important types of work are fundamental to the structure of our society and the growth and stability of our economy: market work, which centers on the production of material foods and profit-making, and caregiving, which maintains the health and well-being of the population" ("The Challenge"). While there are policies and practices in place to guarantee many full-time workers income, social security, benefits, and retirement, there are few ways to literally account for the work that mothers do to raise children. Furthermore, Mothers & More emphasizes that many workplace structures are not conducive to people who parent: "mothers are the ones most hurt by this imbalance because we are the ones who do the bulk of the caregiving work and often perform both market work and caregiving work. Both are vital to society and both require time, energy, and resources" ("The Challenge"). Thus, Mothers & More mandates that there needs to be 1) a new understanding of mothering as work in order to improve mothers' material conditions and reflect that mothering practices have value and 2) a reorganization of established workplaces to change "public policies, private practices, and cultural attitudes" about mothering as work.

In order to meet the above-mentioned goals, the organization lists "Mission & Beliefs":

- A mother is more than any single role she plays at any given point in her lifetime. She is entitled to fully explore and develop her identity as she chooses: as a woman, a citizen, a parent or an employee.
- All the work mothers do—whether paid or unpaid—has social and economic value.
- Caregiving work is real work with real social and economic value.
- All women deserve recognition and support for their right to choose if and how to combine parenting and paid employment.
- All mothers, all children and all families are unique. We respect the wisdom of each mother to decide how to care for her children, her family and herself.
- Mothers have the right to fulfill their caregiving responsibilities without incurring social and economic penalties.
- The transitions women make into and through motherhood are challenging and can be difficult.
- Together, mothers are powerful.

The Challenges of Mothers & More

Mothers & More addresses the challenges many mothers face including: the loss of both friendship and sense of self that can accompany the transition into motherhood, the tough financial choices women must make to raise children, and the dearth of social and economic support for paid and un-paid mothers alike who need steady income, benefits, childcare, and future economic security. While the organization finds ways to address these large and complex challenges, they also face internal obstacles to keep Mothers & More moving. In a 2005 interview with *Mothers Movement Online*, Brundage reflected on the challenges the group faced in mobilizing mothers to act for social change. Specifically, Brundage cited the generational difference between "Boomer" moms and "Gen-Ex" moms in the organization. She explained that many members from the older generation identify with larger feminist movements to equalize conditions for women, but many members from the younger generation are skeptical of the feminist movement or think that there is no longer a need to advocate for equal conditions. Brundage suggested that since newer Mothers & More members experienced relative equal opportunity in education and career choices, they are often "blindsided" by the inequalities of the child-rearing experience.

Furthermore, Brundage mentions the well-known feminist challenge to channel personal reflection and social gatherings into political movements for change. She explains that though many Mothers & More members are comfortable discussing individual life changes in the support group context, many members feel less comfortable engaging in "work that could be considered 'political,' even if it's just political with a small 'p'" (2005). Brundage believes this unease may stem from fear of confrontation, the desire to avoid a "negative or bitchy or whiney" persona, and the persistent belief that mothers should be selfless creatures. She tells *Mothers Movement Online,* "Somehow, being a 'good' mother and taking care of our own wants and needs seem mutually exclusive. This is why, within Mothers & More, we have spent a lot of time and energy on consciousness raising (by reinforcing a positive message that you can be a loving mother and still look out for yourself) over issues identification."

Mothers & More Taking Action

Despite these challenges Mothers & More has seemingly not slowed down since it began in 1987. This non-profit continues to grow and diversify its efforts to support women and bring attention to the need for change. As mentioned above, Mothers & More includes a dual focus: supporting women individually through the challenges of adult middle class motherhood and advocating for policy changes in regards to unpaid mothering work and flexibility for parents in the workplace. Mothers & More taps into the power of building from the ground—or local communities—up by situating flexible and diverse chapters around the nation and also spearheading larger national efforts to combat "invisimomibility."

Building Community: Mothers and More Chapters

Mothers & More's membership program supports the needs of individual mothers in local communities across the nation. Women can join Mothers & More by paying an annual membership fee of $45 (special discounts and offers are advertised on the website). Membership includes access to local chapters' monthly meetings and special events, the Mothers & More online publication *Forum*, and online discussions on a variety of topics with members across the nation. A Mothers & More membership also includes the PERKs program of discounts and deals with a variety of vendors and attractions in the United States. Finally, membership with Mothers & More entitles mothers to position themselves in a variety of leadership roles in the organization or local chapter.

Though Mother & More's name, mission statement, and plan of action have shifted throughout the years, founder Joanne Brundage notes that the demographics of Mothers & More have remained relatively stable (*Mothers Movement Online*). According to their 2010 member survey, Mothers & More members are typically in their late thirties, well-educated (88 percent have college degrees and 39 percent have professional degrees), married, with two children. Around half of the members do paid work (47.5 percent) while the other half "do not work for pay" (52.5 percent). An impressive 88 percent of the members who report that they do not work for pay mention that they will return to work someday. This highlights, again, Mothers & More's appeal for sequencing women.

Fighting "Invisimomibility": Mothers & More Strategies of Visibility

Close reading of the past actions of Mothers & More reveals that this organization uses strategic visibility to intervene in negative representations of mothers and bring attention to "the fact that mothers live and work in a society that presents significant barriers to their ability to succeed as women, citizens, parents, or participants in the workforce" (Mothers & More). Indeed, Mothers & More thinks of creative ways to play with the politics of visibility to question cultural assumptions of motherhood. By tapping into the ways that mothers are already made visible, the organization seeks to change the potentially problematic ways that the nation acknowledges mothering work. For example, Mothers & More developed "The Apple Awards" to both recognize progressive representations of the realities of caregiving work and to critique social constructions that make light of the obstacles mothers encounter or divide mothers across lines of difference (think *Mommy Wars*). In July of 2005, the "Apple of our Eye" award was given to celebrity Brooke Shields for braving scrutiny to bring attention to postpartum depression and stand up for women's right to choose how to treat their depression. In contrast, Mothers & More gave their "Apple Pie in the Face" award to celebrity clinical psychologist Dr. Phil McGraw for his television episode called "Mom vs. Mom," which intentionally tried to pit working mothers against stay-at-home mothers.

One of the main venues for Mothers & More action has been Mother's Day campaigns. Since 2003, Mothers & More has approached each Mother's Day as an opportunity for raising awareness of the variety of obstacles many mothers face in being recognized for the *work* they do to raise children. These campaigns are part of the organization's POWER plan—a detailed plan of action that stems from Mothers & More's core belief that "together mothers are powerful" (see core beliefs listed above). Each Mother's Day campaign has a different theme—with creative propaganda like shirts, buttons, and canvas totes that reflect this theme—but all of the campaigns work to improve the way in which mainstream society *sees* mothers. For example, in 2003 the theme was "Making Mothers Count" and was dedicated to making unpaid caregiving work visible. Members wore buttons that stated "I'm a Mother. I Care. I Work. I Count" and distributed cards with "Mom Metrics" such as the facts below:

> •81 percent of [U.S.] women will become mothers.
> •69 percent of mothers work for pay in addition to providing 2/3 of all unpaid family care.
> •Unpaid caregiving is not counted as work in the Gross Domestic Product.
> •Women spend an average of 11.5 years out of the workforce, [caring] for children or elderly parents. For each year out of the workforce, a mother receives 0 credit toward Social Security benefits.
> •Among young women and men without children, women now make 98 percent of men's wages. Yet, mothers make 73 percent or less of the wages of all others in the workforce.
> •[Two] of the world's wealthiest nations—The U.S. and Australia—do not provide paid parental leave for full-time employees. ("Mothers Day campaign 2003")

All in all Mothers & More collectively held 55 special events in 22 states during this first campaign. Some other notable themes have included 2004's "Mothers—the Real Story: Mom's Media Reality Check" which deconstructed stereotypes of middle class moms in the media, 2005's "Mothers—The Real Story: It's About *Time*" which advocated for the American Time Use Survey (ATUS) as a tool that could make visible the amount of time women spend on unpaid caregiving work, 2006's "Mothers At Work" that used construction signs and activities to bring attention to mothering as *work*, and 2008's "Connecting Mother's Voices," which was dedicated to saving the ATUS by collecting signatures on letters to President Bush and other key political officials. Finally, Mothers & More discovered the "Power of a Purse" during their 2010 campaign when they brought attention to "the social and economic factors that put mothers at greater risk of poverty" by collecting purses for low-income mothers:

> The purse symbolizes a woman's economic power, something we wish for all women, especially mothers in need. No matter where a mother is on the social ladder, there is "power in her purse" having money of her own to control, to buy things and provide for herself and her children.

> Mothers & More also had a goal to collect 10,000 purses for mothers in need around the country during the Mother's Day season. That goal was met! ("Mothers Day Campaign 2010")

Because of this last campaign's great success, Mothers & More plans to keep this focus for the 2011 Mother's Day campaign.

Though each year's theme varies, common strategies of Mother's Day campaigns are 1) getting mothers to meet in a central location to exchange stories about the "real" struggles of mothering that are often silent in the mainstream media; 2) educating the public and promoting the Mothers & More philosophy that mothers' unpaid carework should count for more economically and socially then it currently does; 3) gathering important information about members of the organization through blogs and surveys which push against cultural assumptions of motherhood; and 4) connecting leading researchers and advocate organizations on motherhood via the PowerLoop—an online discussion forum. In this way, Mothers & More has functioned as one of the first entities *connecting* mothers, organizations, scholars, and advocates to create knowledge and action that betters the material experiences of mothers.

Partnering for Progress: Mothers & More Community Collaborations

Beyond supporting individual women in local chapter meetings and making visible the work mothers do in large national campaigns, Mothers & More also acknowledges the community outreach efforts of chapters across the nation. In 2007, Mothers & More "Features" editor Kathy Johnson posted an article to the discussion forum about chapters partnering with the Women Build sector of Habitat for Humanity. By reporting on local chapters' partnership with Habitat for Humanity, Mothers & More helped ensure a steady supply of volunteers for Women Build and brought attention to the fact that single mothers occupy 60-80 percent of Habitat for Humanity homes.

Another example listed in the organization's "Community Outreach" section is the work local chapters did to guarantee the success of the Lilly Ledbetter Fair Pay Act of 2009. Lilly Ledbetter was a Goodyear employee who discovered she made 40 percent less than her male peers. She lost her 2007 Supreme Court case against Goodyear Tire & Rubber Co. because she did not file her complaint within the 180 day period stipulated in the 1964 *Civil Rights Act*; however, Ledbetter's case inspired legislation to amend the *Civil Rights Act* that demands equal pay for equal work—no matter when employees discover the inequity. In 2008, Mothers & More chapters in Minnesota came together to develop tools to lobby the senate for the *Lilly Ledbetter Fair Pay Act*. Writing letters, calling key senate representatives, and co-hosting an event called "Mothers' Voices: Constituent Concerns about Fair Pay in Context of Motherhood," Mothers & More members used personal stories of their experiences with inequality in the workplace to advocate for the passing of this act. The *Lilly Ledbetter Fair Pay Act* was signed into law by President Obama in 2009.

Connection to Larger Mothering Movement(s)

Though this anthology makes clear that there is no cohesive twenty-first century motherhood movement, I will end by considering what Mothers & More offers in terms of advocating for better conditions for women raising children. Mothers & More contributes to mothering movements a model of how to use strategies of visibility to counter the invisibility of unpaid mothering work and the economic disparities that women who mother face. Taking advantage of the ways mothers are already made visible—in the press, mainstream television, and a national holiday—this national organization hopes to change the vision of motherhood. Beginning as a local support group dismayed by the 1980s stereotype of a supermom doing it all and the actual tensions that accompanied "sequencing" one's childbearing, Mothers & More has helped to change the economic and social value of mothering. They maintain that the work mothers do should be reflected "in reforms to retirement savings plans, Social Security and disability insurances" ("The Power Plan"). This organization recognizes that the only way to do this is to build collaborative movements with their members and with other organizations working on economic issues for women. Their mission relates to other national mother-centered organizations, such as Momsrising and NOW's Mothers & Caregivers Economic Rights Committee, which emphasize that the social value of motherhood and economic value of carework are inextricably related. This organization contributes specific attention to middle-class adult women who mother and the unique financial challenges they face in leaving or negotiating the paid workplace to raise children.

Yet, Mothers & More also centers on the second-wave feminist practice of acknowledging the personal conflicts, contradictions, and struggles of individual women's lives (Campbell 174). By keeping central the focus on locally situated chapters—initiated and run by local women—this organization models a well-recognized process of resistance: beginning with reflection on personal and collective struggle, moving into an understanding about how the personal is implicated and constructed by the socioeconomic context, and, finally, strategizing for action. Whether or not each chapter functions in this way is up for debate. Brundage's concerns about the challenges of continuing the organization's political efforts showcase the potential stagnation of small groups where "there is no persuasive campaign … only the very limited realm of therapeutic, small group interaction" remains (Campbell 178). However, small groups can be sites for developing a belief in the need to resist social structures that negatively impact women who mother. Moreover, as Mothers & More's interaction with Habitat for Humanity's Women Build sector illustrates, having an expansive ready-made social network of like-minded mothering women can be a beneficial resource for engaging collective pursuits quickly. Mothers & More chapters have the potential to collaborate with other efforts to respond to the diverse issues women who mother face.

Finally, I suggest that Mothers & More continues the work begun by Adrienne

Rich's emphasis on the *institution* of motherhood by continuing to dissociate the work that women do to raise children from "natural" or biological understandings of reproduction. The struggles that accompany mothering work are in no way a natural condition of women's ability to reproduce, and women should not be unfairly disadvantaged because of the lack of economic and social structures to support mothering women in the United States. As a final example, in 2002, Mothers & More published a press release to intervene in public conversations about research that suggested women who wait to have children face more problems conceiving. Former advocacy manager of Mothers & More Judith Stadtman argued:

> This is not a woman problem or a mother problem. It's not a symptom of the limitations of female biology—it's a symptom of the limitation of our society to create workplaces that offer equitable opportunities for all employees....The work/family conflict is not going to be resolved by women making more timely reproductive decisions and reining in their professional ambition accordingly. Our entire society must recognize the value of caregiving to the wider community and we must restructure our workplaces and institutions to fully include women with family responsibilities. ("Mothers & More Clarifies")

Stadtman's efforts to shift attention away from "women" or "mothers" as a coherent category of people to blame for social struggles (such as, the struggle of infertility) to the wider socio-economic context in which women must make reproductive decisions, is an important and critical move. Though Mothers & More focuses primarily on middle-class adult mothers' representations and issues, their core beliefs and rhetorical tactics connect in exciting ways with other mothering movements like the movements for welfare mothers' rights and the young mothers' movement(s) for respect and support.

[1]It is important to note that visions of (good) motherhood are raced and classed. For example, the works of Angela Davis, Dorothy Roberts , and Rickie Solinger illustrate how some mothers—especially immigrant, poor, and/or minoritized women—face societal assumptions that they are not natural, capable, or otherwise fit mothers.

Works Cited

Campbell, Karlyn Kohrs. "The Rhetoric of Women's Liberation: An Oxymoron." *Readings on the Rhetoric of Social Protest.* 2nd ed. Eds. Charles E. Morris III and Stephen H. Browne. State College, PA: Strata Publishing, 2001. 172-84.

Cardozo, Arlene Rossen. *Sequencing: A New Book for Women Who Want Marriage, Career, and Family.* New York: Atheneum, 1986.

Cawthorne, Andrea. "The Straight Facts on Women in Poverty." The Center for

American Progress. 8 Oct. 2008. Web. <Americanprogress.org>. Accessed: 16 February 2011.

Davis, Angela. "Surrogates and Outcast Mothers: Racism and Reproductive Politics in the Nineties." *The Angela Y. Davis Reader*. Oxford: Blackwell, 1998. 210- 21.

Hochshild, Arlie R. *The Second Shift.* New York: Viking Penguin, 1989.

Mothers & More. Web. <mothersandmore.org>. Accessed: 16 Feb 2010.

Mothers & More. "Mothers & More Fights to End Invisimomibility." Press Release. 2 May 2008. Web. 16 Feb 2010.

Mothers & More. "Mothers & More Clarifies Career/Family Issue." Press Release. 22 Apr. 2002. Web. 16 Feb 2010.

Mothers Movement Online. "Shaping the Pro-Mother Agenda: An Interview with Joanne Brundage, Founder and Executive Director of Mothers & More." March 2005.

Rich, Adrienne. *Of Woman Born: Motherhood as Experience and Institution.* 10th ed. New York: Norton, 1986.

Roberts, Dorothy. *Killing the Black Body: Race, Reproduction, and the Meaning of Liberty*. New York: Pantheon Books, 1997.

Solinger, Rickie. *Pregnancy and Power: A Short History of Reproductive Politics in America.* New York: New York University Press, 2005.

United States Bureau of Labor Statistics and United States Department of Labor. *Highlights of Women's Earnings in 2009.* Report 1025. June 2010.

38.
Welfare Warriors

Fighting for the Lives of Mothers and Children

PAT GOWENS

SINGLE MOTHERS IN MILWAUKEE, WISCONSIN came together in 1986 to create mamas media. We were moms in poverty who received child support through the welfare system—a stigmatized but essential economic resource. Angry and frustrated with the scape-goating and prejudice against us for caring for our children with government support instead of abandoning them like most of their dads had done, moms decided to create mass media to combat the stereotypes while uniting our communities of single moms.

The Warriors were inspired by a mothers' group in Cuernavaca, Mexico, who published a newspaper by, for, and about low-income mothers and children. We decided that the United States could also benefit by such a publication. Before our first issue of *Welfare Mothers Voice* hit the streets, we were pushed into the streets and the political arena by dramatic events that would lead to an ugly escalation of the war on the poor in national and state governments. Once we realized we were becoming activists, as well as journalists, we ended an extended internal debate and came up with our controversial name: Welfare Warriors.

This is the story of Welfare Warriors' growth from a Milwaukee mamas' group into a national and international network organizing and advocating for economic justice for families in poverty. It is the story of learning from, as well as inspiring, other single moms to take action and unite for economic, social and political survival during a period of increased economic onslaughts against poor women and children. And it is the story of our foremothers in whose footsteps we were following—the African American mothers' movement that swept the United States from 1965 to 1975.

Mandate

Pack the halls with angry mothers
Ma ma ma ma ma ma ma ma ma
Still families without the father
Pa pa pa pa pa pa pa pa pa

We work hard to raise up lives
Ma ma ma ma ma ma ma ma ma
While Clinton lies and terrorizes
Blah blah blah blah blah blah blah blah blah

Linda Ray, a member of the Welfare Warriors, wrote this song in 1995 when the U.S. war on the poor was being openly escalated. The Clinton administration, both Bill and Hillary, had decided to eliminate the only public child support program available to low-income single moms—Aid to Families with Dependent Children (AFDC). Welfare Warriors wrote 50 similar songs. Along with activist moms' groups around the country, we took them to the streets and legislatures in our Mamas Media campaign to educate and agitate to stop corporate attacks on government support for our families.

Our mandate was clear: we must make our own communities, and the larger population, understand that poverty was not a personal failing; it was the result of economic injustice caused by unpaid motherwork, disability, low wages, violence, and social stigma. But how would we accomplish this education and organizing, while at the same time validating and strengthening single mothers who had been so battered and belittled by ignorance and bigotry? How could we keep our vision of winning social and economic change without being bogged down in providing "services" for suffering families? We had to look to our foremothers to find the answers.

History of Single Moms' Struggles and First U.S. Mothers' Movement

Historically mothers in the patriarchy have suffered a lot. But single mothers, especially never-married and divorced moms, have always endured economic and emotional hardship—and are often treated as outcasts. In 1935 the U.S. passed the *Social Security Act.* It created a child support program for children, specifically for the children of widows. Called Social Security Survivors benefits, it provided a monthly check for 18 years for any minor children deprived of a parent (with a work history) through death or disability. Within the same program, they created Aid for Dependent Children (ADC).

Unfortunately by the end of 1935, the Congress decided to separate the ADC program from the Social Security Survivors Benefits. The Survivors benefits were for the mothers who were seen as "deserving." If you lost your man through death, it is not your fault. But the Aid for Dependent Children was for the "undeserving" moms. If you lost your man through abandonment, that's your fault, you're the bad mama.

That began a huge social and economic division. The different treatment of moms in basically the same situation was phenomenal. For moms who were receiving child support from the government under ADC, there was a massive amount of policing, social stigma, and hatred. Paper-work policing was supplemented with household raids. Social Services people would raid homes in the middle of the night searching for evidence of a man in the house. The most serious welfare fraud felony a mom could commit was to allow the children's *father* to stay in the home. Big Brother was a jealous husband.

Single mothers suffered intensely between 1935 and 1965, especially African American moms and other women of color. Social services people were already prejudiced against poor single white women. Think of what they did to the women of color in poverty. They just said, "No, we can't help you. Goodbye." (That type of "front-line deterrence" is what Temporary Assistance to Needy Families [TANF] does to everyone now.)

African American single mothers faced a deadly struggle, being denied the little bit of financial support available to white women. By 1965 moms reached a point of explosion. Single moms were tired of being humiliated, tired of being told they were worthless because they were raising their kids instead of abandoning them. And the Civil Rights movement had made it very clear to most Americans that we had the right to fight for what's right—to fight against oppression.

In 1965 a national movement began, the first mothers' movement in the U.S. There had been pockets of welfare moms organizing locally since 1963. But the National Welfare Rights Movement, led and run by mostly African American single moms on welfare, was created in 1965. This very powerful movement lasted from 1965 until 1975.

The successes won by the mothers in this movement, both black and white, was phenomenal. These women were the lowest of the low—stigmatized, poor, alone etc. They fought until they doubled the welfare roles. In both rural and urban areas millions of eligible moms had been illegally denied this economic support. The moms began to notify everyone that a welfare program existed and that moms could fight for a child support check from ADC when illegally denied. In state after state the mothers also organized increases in the cash support that a family received.

In 1971, the mothers' movement won a Supreme Court decision that outlawed home raids. Social Services could no longer invade a home searching for evidence of a man. By 1972, the moms won the creation of SSI, a poverty program for people with disabilities. (A third of the moms on welfare suffer from disabilities.) And they won Energy Assistance, a subsidy to help heat homes.

Smaller victories in some states included getting checks distributed twice a month instead of just at the beginning of the month. And moms in most states won clothing allowances for the children at the beginning of the school year.

Creative Strategies Win Impressive Victories

What strategies and tactics did this mothers' movement use to make these huge improvements in the lives of their families? First they bombarded the Civil Rights offices to address their issues. Womens' and mothers' issues had been mostly overlooked until then. This generated some recognition of the mothers' issues. The paid staff and support people of the new mothers' movement were mostly

Members of LA's Every Mother Is A Working Mother group present Congresswoman Patsy Mink (Hawaii) with a T-shirt at a Congressional briefing in June 2002.

middle-class professionals. They were successful at organizing support primarily from white churches and black and white professionals. Ironically the mothers hired two men to run the National Welfare Rights Movement and to raise funds for the movement. Eventually this resulted in a lot of class and race and sex strife and struggles.

The tactics that the moms used were similar to the Civil Rights movement. In 1968 over 5,000 mothers marched on Washington, DC. They also took over local welfare departments. In Milwaukee, the moms marched 70 miles to our state capitol. But they did not just march on the Capitol, they lived in the Capitol building. They cooked and ate and slept in the building for a couple of weeks. They bothered and harassed and harangued the legislators until they passed bills to improve the welfare system.

The activist moms also targeted big business. One tactic was research. They researched the reality of poverty pimping and the real welfare recipients, the wealthy corporations. They showed how much government money was going to big business (decades before the 750 billion-dollar bail out). They exposed the corporations as the real welfare queens and showed how poverty pimps were making money off the welfare programs. They began writing too. They wrote a book called *Welfare Mothers Speak Out* in 1972.

The mothers' movement lobbied across the U.S. for an adequate guaranteed income for all families. That was one of their key demands.

Besides going to welfare departments and legislators, the women also targeted big business for actions. 50 to 100 women would go to a Boston store, take clothes off the racks and bring them to the checkout counter. There they would announce "Oh. We have no money in our checks for clothes. Sorry I can't buy

Welfare Warrior children.

this." They would go to a big hotel, sign up for rooms and then announce. "We don't have money in our AFDC checks for rent, so we thought we could stay here." The actions created chaos. The tactic was to put pressure on big business, who control the legislators to a large degree, to pressure the legislators to pass the mom's proposed bills.

Johnny Tillman was the Executive Chairwoman of the National Welfare Rights Movement. In 1962 Tillman was one of the early local organizers with a group called "Mothers Anonymous." Because of the criminalization of mothers on welfare, they did not want to use their names. Johnny Tillman is famous for her much–quoted statement "Every woman is one man away from welfare."

Another important and successful tactic was the proliferation of mothers' groups across the U.S. Even after 1975 when the national movement folded, other moms around the country continued to organize. A truly impressive moms' group organized in Las Vegas Nevada. In *Storming Caesars Palace*, published in 2005, Annelise Orleck describes the Welfare Rights Movement in Nevada.

The African American moms in Las Vegas were mostly poor immigrants from the south who were suffering incredible degradation, living in mud towns on the west side of Las Vegas. They had no medical care, few city services, and rarely managed to get a welfare check. Social Services constantly raided their homes and regularly denied checks to eligible families. The moms heard about the national welfare rights movement. So they began to organize in Las Vegas.

They decided to target big business too. Who would you target in Las Vegas?

Welfare Warriors make war on poverty.

Welfare Warrior moms on strike.

The casinos, of course. So, despite the casinos' connection to the mafia, they organized a huge march in 1968 on Caesars Palace. They won support from movie stars and activists across the country. They actually went into Caesars Palace and sat down to eat there. One irony in this action was that black people were not allowed into the Casinos except to clean or wash dishes or perform for white audiences. Yet hundreds of African American moms and kids marched into Caesars Palace.

They accomplished their goal. The idea was to show the U.S. people that they would not have fun gambling in Las Vegas because there are crazy women there storming casinos and protesting for decent welfare support. The casino owners had to put pressure on the state legislators to listen to the moms.

Nevada was so backward that it was the only state in the nation that did not allow foodstamps in their state. So the mothers were fighting from the very bottom up, for the most basic survival. They were tremendously successful.

After a few years of organizing, the Las Vegas moms got an abandoned hotel with a swimming pool donated to them. They set up their "Operation Life" in that hotel where their children were able to swim in the pool. They created a health clinic there, the first one on Las Vegas' west side. They created a library for their community, a daycare, a senior housing program and a jobs program. They were suffering from constant midnight raids in their homes, which were eventually stopped. They literally took hostage of the director of the welfare department to demand an end to the raids.

After endless lobbying at their capitol, the Las Vegas moms finally got Las Vegas to allow foodstamps in Nevada. They continued organizing until 1990, 15 years after the end of the National Welfare Rights Movement.

Context of Current Struggle

In 1996, despite massive organizing on the part of activist mothers groups across the United States, the Clinton administration succeeded in terminating the 61-year-old child support program—AFDC. Congress replaced it with Temporary Assistance to Needy Families (TANF). The TANF program is temporary support and a forced work program. Mothers must work off the support check, even though the average monthly check is only $370 for a family of three. Moms must work for 30 hours in unpaid work activities. That means we have mothers working in the public schools for no pay, in Head Start for no pay, in parks and housing projects for no pay, and working at all types of social services and non-profits for no pay. Mothers are even working in the army base for no wages. If a mom fails to complete the required hours, the TANF agency sanctions (reduces) her tiny check. Any business that wants a mom, a slave mom, can have one. Mothers call this system the "New Millennium Slavery."

In addition to forced work, TANF also imposed a deadly five-year time limit for receipt of this child support. And states can decide to impose even shorter time limits. (Wisconsin has a two-year time limit.) So TANF is now a states-rights program. States may create whatever policies they want within the general federal guidelines. We are now back to pre-civil rights movement—if we want to sue to stop any of these injustices, we have to sue in all 50 states.

Under these harsh time-limits, no matter how destitute a mom is, or how sick or needy she or her children may be, or what challenges she faces in child rearing, she can't receive any public support for her children after she exhausts her time limits. A shocking effect of these time limits is a massive army of U.S. moms now raising children with zero income. In 2010, we have over six million people in the U.S. living with zero income, most of these are moms and their kids.[1]

The Mothers Are Crying and the Babies Are Dying

Another TANF provision allows states to require moms to leave their babies *at any age* to seek work and perform unwaged work. Under AFDC, single mothers could care for their own children until they were in school full-time at age six years. In states like Wisconsin, single breadwinners have to leave their babies at only three months. This has caused a huge increase in infant mortality, the highest in the U.S. With no mom available to protect the children (and no other back-up parent around) babies are dying needlessly. In Milwaukee's African American community we have had a 37 percent increase in infant death since TANF began. In Wisconsin, an eleven percent increase.[2] And the statistics do not include the many deaths of toddlers and older children.

Examples of these deaths are heartbreaking. The first public TANF death in Milwaukee occurred when a single mom could not find daycare for her sick nine-month-old nursing infant. She dare not miss work so she took the child to the health clinic where she worked. They did not allow her to keep the child with her so she left him in the car and checked on him every two hours. She found him dead at the end of her shift. She was prosecuted criminally and lost her three-year-old as well.

A young mom with three toddlers was working seven hours a day at a non-profit for no pay. The YWCA TANF agency sanctioned her check for missing time at her unwaged "job." Her gas was turned off when she was unable to pay her bill so she was using a space heater. A young family friend was caring for the three babies because the TANF agency had not yet provided the mother with child care. The inexperienced caregiver put the children down for a nap in their room with the space heater on. It started a fire and the adult got out, but all three children were burned to death.

A mom with a severely disabled (cerebral palsy and retardation) 13-year-old son in a wheelchair asked the Goodwill TANF agency to allow her to care for her son during the summer as had been her custom. The workers denied her the time off as well as child care for the boy. So the distraught mom went to work and her 14-year-old son cared for his brother. He put him in the tub for a bath and left him while he made lunch. When he returned, the disabled boy had burned himself to death by turning on the hot-water faucet.

TANF Endangers the Workforce

Although TANF's impact on children is our greatest nightmare, TANF has also had a devastating impact on the workforce. Now we have five million moms each year who must "choose" to do unpaid work—if they can't get hired. They will take any job for any pay to escape TANF's new millennium slavery/public servitude. All of the part-time, low-wage, no-benefit Wal-Mart, Walgreens, fast food, and Manpower temporary agency employers are dancing in the streets. They finally have all the workers they want.

Those billionaire corporations lobbied Congress and Clinton to give them the single moms. That is how the TANF program was passed. Big business said "we want the moms ... especially the mothers in college." About 25 percent of the moms on AFDC had been pursuing post-secondary education. In Milwaukee between 1995-1996 over 16,000 single moms were forced out of college to do 30 hours unwaged work for a puny TANF welfare check. Across the U.S. several million moms have been denied education under TANF. Naturally big business wanted the educated moms first for their starvation-wage jobs.

Imagine the horrible impact on single moms—no longer allowed to get any post-secondary education, yet somehow expected to single-handedly keep her family safe and economically solvent. And instead of getting education or job training, the moms must work 30 hours unwaged work! So of course moms who *could* get hired at Walgreens, McDonalds, and temp agencies took those dead-end, no-benefit jobs. Big Business now has millions of forced workers across the country to choose from which has kept minimum wage at a sub poverty level.

Not only does welfare reform destroy single-mom families and the workforce, it is also a rip off for the taxpayers. Most Americans believe that the cost of welfare has been reduced because the roles have dropped from five million to two million. But in fact the cost to the taxpayers has increased from $15 billion to over $17 billion.[3] This is a transfer of income from the poor (who used to receive benefits) and low-wage worker (who used to staff welfare agencies) to the middle and upper-income professionals who now administer all benefits. Clearly we had to develop creative and powerful strategies to combat these newest betrayals of single mothers and children, as well as the betrayal of the workforce.

Tactics and Goals of the Second Wave of the Single Mothers' Movement

When Welfare Warriors came together to validate moms struggling to survive single motherhood, social stigma, and poverty in 1986 we knew little about the earlier mothers' movement. We simply wanted to put an end to the devastating bigotry we faced as single moms. And we wanted to smash the myth of our "dependence." We knew that needing support did not make us "dependent," that all single moms need support for children—in fact economic support is legally mandated. We refused to be labeled "dependent" because the dads *depended* on us to singlehandedly raise their children and *depended* on the government to support them.

We decided to create visible public media, like a welfare mamas' TV sit-com or soap opera. But as low-income single moms we did not have the resources to accomplish such a lofty goal. Fortunately we learned about The Marias in Cuernavaca Mexico who published a moms' newspaper and organized mothers' workshops. We modeled our publication, *Welfare Mothers Voice*, after them.

The *Voice* has been instrumental in meeting our goal to give a voice to moms in poverty, some of the most silenced and maligned women in the country. It has been exciting for moms to finally hear their own words and ideas in an international publication. I recently ran into a mom who told me she has been "suffocating" because she couldn't find the truth anywhere. She was overjoyed to find our quarterly publication, *Mother Warriors Voice*. (In 2006 we changed our publication's name from *Welfare Mother Voice* to *Mother Warriors Voice* to put "mother" up front and to include a broader organizing base.) The 56-page, ad-free *Mother Warriors Voice* has been a great success. It is 24 years old with distributors, subscribers and readers across the U.S. and Canada, and some subscribers in Europe, India and Africa. It covers resistance in the war on the poor worldwide and gives a voice to mothers to network, vent, and share information.

Moms in Welfare Warriors t-shirts.

Our publication began reaching moms in other cities, first in Wisconsin, than across the country and eventually around the world. Single moms were inspired to start up their own groups and publications after reading *Welfare Mothers Voice* and realizing that a group of welfare moms had created it. We wrote an *Organizing Handbook* to share our ideas and tactics with moms who wanted to start up a group in their town. The *Voice* became the key to reaching and inspiring other moms to take on the bigoted politicians and media that promote the war on the poor. With help from the Warriors, moms from Hawaii to Maine have created dozens of organizations to educate and agitate for economic justice.

From Media to Activism and More

It is hard for a single mom not to believe the social stereotypes and slander that label single moms as "lazy, loose, liars" and "dependent" women. After all it must be true about someone! So moms always insist, "not me, maybe she is, but not me." This causes a deadly divide-and-conquer division between moms. To address this division, we decided to create as many types of mamas media as possible. We began a sort of "Single Moms Are Beautiful" campaign like the "Black is Beautiful" strategy of the civil rights movement.

Before our first issue of *Welfare Mothers Voice* hit the streets of Milwaukee, we mothers were pushed into the streets too. Our unexpected activism was the result of a new wave of cynical political preying on poor mothers and children. Tommy Thompson was running for governor of Wisconsin, promising to reduce our children's government support (AFDC). Moms were enraged and demanded we take our anger to the streets. From this moment we were no longer simply journalists; we would also use street theatre to make our voices heard.

We learned an important organizing lesson from this first public action. The moms who were most vocal about taking action, never showed up! Since then we have followed an iron-clad rule: *No member can propose an action, activity or event unless she is willing to take responsibility for organizing that action or find someone else to do so.* That policy has saved us endless hours of brilliant discussions of great ideas … that no one commits to implementing!

As soon as moms began reading *Welfare Mothers Voice*, we heard from both excited moms and desperate moms. Women were delighted to read stories by moms that told the truth, for a change, about single-mother families. They wanted to get involved. But moms also called for help surviving the welfare no-sayers, violent partners, corrupt landlords, and indifferent schools.

Moms Line Teaches Bureaucratic Self-Defense

To address these problems we quickly established a Moms Line staffed by moms to teach callers a Three-Step-Plan of Self-Defense against Bureaucratic no-sayers. To train the Moms Line staff we researched and wrote the *Moms Survival Self-Help Manual.* It covered issues from public benefits laws and policies to housing policies to surviving violent partners. In the past 24 years we have trained thousands of moms and grandmoms and some dads in this Three-Step plan.

When callers to our Moms Line cried out for help after Social Services had taken their children on false allegations of abuse and neglect, we created a support and action group to help them. We named the group MaGoD, Mothers and Grandmothers of Disappeared Children, after the mothers in Argentina who marched in their plaza weekly to demand the return of their disappeared children and grandchildren.

To supplement our journal and activism we created t-shirts and bumper stickers. Our first t-shirt "Every Mother Is A Working Mother" was followed by "Because I'm the Mom, that's why." Our most popular bumpersticker is "Stop the War on the Poor." The scariest one reads "If they take your child, demand a jury trial."

Creating Language to Challenge the Anti-Mother Propaganda

By 1995 we felt an urgency to make politicians and progressives understand that caring for children is WORK that requires *time and money.* We had observed that neither capitalists, nor socialists, nor feminists, nor labor organizers acknowledged the reality of the unwaged WORK done by all caregivers. This dangerous oversight led in part to the deadly welfare reform that was sweeping the land and ending vital safety net resources for families. So we created the word MOTHERWORK to validate and make visible the WORK that moms do. And of course we made bumperstickers and t-shirts and songs with this important slogan: Motherwork *is* Work.

An entertaining new media emerged when Linda Ray arrived at a MaGoD meeting singing new lyrics to *Jingle Bells*:

I thought I'd find a job
So I looked everyday
For every buck I earned
Welfare took one away
And when I lost my job
Back to the welfare mill
I thought it couldn't get much worse
Than Tommy called on Bill

That began our practice of using music to get our message out and to make our street theatre more fun. Even the kids in our MAY (*Mother and Youth)* Project have created a couple of songs and love singing many of the 50 songs now compiled in our songbook, *Songs from the Mamas Movement.* And the activist moms around the country take these songs to their streets and legislators.

Challenges

The second wave of the U.S. mothers' movement has not yet seen the types of success that the earlier mothers' movement won. We are still fighting the billionaire corporations and Congress who have ravaged our U.S. safety net, eliminating most public housing and much of the cash support for families, single people and the disabled. These are dangerous times and we are not going to surrender in this violent war on the poor worldwide.

About a dozen U.S. groups have survived along with Welfare Warriors. Boston Moms who also started in 1986 are still publishing their *Survival News.* In Minneapolis/St. Paul the Welfare Rights Committee won a million dollars last year for moms and children by stopping proposed state cuts on the poor. Direct Action Welfare Group (DAWG) in West Virginia and Low-Income Families Empowerment through Education (LIFETIME) in Oakland have been successfully organizing since the '90s to win the right for moms to attend college while receiving TANF. Every Mother Is A Working Mother, out of Los Angeles and Philly, are organizing with Welfare Warriors to change the lawless Child Welfare system that wrongfully takes children from impoverished moms. Parents Organizing for Welfare and Economic Rights (POWER) in Washington state and the Welfare Coalition in Ohio are winning a voice in their state's TANF reauthorization.

Outside of the U.S. some moms groups are seeing more successes. A Tokyo single moms' group beat welfare time limits in Japan in 2008. And this year a group in Israel put an end to their "Wisconsin Plan," a punitive welfare program based on TANF.

Future Goals and the International Motherhood Movement

Welfare Warriors has expanded our goal to fight for a Government Guaranteed Child Support Program for all children modeled on the European family pension or child allowance plans. In most European countries, every family with a dependent child gets a check each month—rich and poor. This combats the divide-and-conquer strategies that enable politicians and corporate media to pit poor against nearly poor and middle-class people. It frees moms from chasing after the elusive dads for their much-resented child support. And it is a means of validating the motherwork done by all who care for children.

Our membership in the International Motherhood Movement has assisted us in this goal. Mothers from across Europe have been providing us with information about amounts and types of family pensions in their countries.

Welfare Warriors brings to the new International Motherhood Movement our 25 years of experience organizing with groups across the U.S. and the experience of our foremothers in the first wave of the Welfare Mothers' Movement.

[1]*New York Times,* January 2, 2010.

[2]Start Smart Milwaukee, 1442 N. Farwell, Milwaukee, WI 53202

[3]TANF Financial Data, U.S. Dept of Health and Human Services, Administration for Children and Families.

Works Cited

Milwaukee Country Welfare Rights Organization. *Welfare Mothers Speak Out.* New York: W.W .Norton and Company, 1972.

Orleck, Annelise. *Storming Ceasar's Palace.* Boston: Beacon Press 2005.

Welfare Warriors. *Songs from the Mamas Movement.* Welfare Warriors, May 2004

West, Guida. *The National Welfare Rights Movement, The Social Protest of Poor Women.* New York: Praeger Publishers, 1981.

39.
MomsRising

A Million-Member Organization Working to Ensure Family Economic Security and to End Discrimination Against Mothers

KRISTIN ROWE-FINKBEINER AND MARY OLIVELLA

MOMSRISING IS A MULTICULTURAL GRASSROOTS organization of more than a million members (with a blogging and social media reach calculated at over three million) who are working in the United States to achieve family economic security, to end discrimination against mothers, and to ensure that all children have a healthy start in life.

MomsRising uses the power of online organizing in coordination with on-the-ground activities and dynamic media outreach to educate the public about problems facing American families and to propose common sense solutions. We provide the public with an opportunity to amplify their voices in order to take their concerns to leaders who are in a position to bring about positive change.

MomsRising uses M-O-T-H-E-R-S as an acronym to describe our overall advocacy and cultural change focus:

M = Maternity/Paternity Leave
O = Open, Flexible Workplaces
T = Toxics Free Childhoods
H = Healthcare for All Kids
E = Excellent and Affordable Childcare
R = Realistic, Fair Wages
S = Sick Days for All, Paid

We also address other issues of priority for mothers including breastfeeding rights; food insecurity and nutrition, fair housing and stopping immigration enforcement practices that promote human rights abuses for families in this country. Our MomsVote campaign is also a central piece of our work.

Established in 2006, MomsRising has gained over a million members in four years and has developed a social media network that extends our work to three million people. In 2010, Forbes named MomsRising a "Top Website for Women," along with other non-profits and for-profits like Oprah. MomsRising's members are organizing and speaking out to improve public policy and to change the national dialogue on issues that are critically important to America's families.

This chapter describes the context and history of MomsRising as well as our mission and key results areas, strategies for movement building, and a look at some future goals.

Context and History

As the stated in *The Economist* magazine in December of 2009, "If the empowerment of women was one of the great changes of the past 50 years, dealing with its social consequences will be one of the great challenges of the next 50." *The Economist* article goes on to state that the "cost of motherhood" is the biggest issue before us today. With over 80 percent of American women becoming mothers by the time they are 44 years old, awareness of that cost—and of the need for solutions—is increasing.

Indeed, families are reeling from this great societal shift. In the past three decades, the percentage of working women has skyrocketed (from 63 percent of 25 to 34 year old women in 1975, to 81 percent in 1999). However, the public and private policies that affect parenting and the workplace have remained largely unchanged. The result is that parents of all socio-economic backgrounds are struggling to integrate the needs of their children with the demands of their workplaces. It is this universality of the experience of motherhood that has created a fertile ground to build a non-partisan and multicultural grassroots movement of millions of people who share a common concern about the need for family economic security as well as for protecting the health and safety of our next generation.

The recent growth of many motherhood organizations including MomsRising certainly attests to the salience and potential of the motherhood movement to address these challenges for our generation. Our country's current motherhood movement has been born from the long line of women for whom the responsibility of civic engagement was a given—and for whom the inequalities faced by women was a wall to be broken down.

To advance women's equality today, MomsRising is helping to build the motherhood movement in recognition that before many women even get to the glass ceiling, they are impeded by the maternal wall.

Here's what that the maternal wall looks like: Women without children make 90 cents to a man's dollar, women with children make about 73 cents, and single moms make about 60 cents to a man's dollar.

It also looks like this: A recent study found that mothers are 100 percent less likely to be hired than non-mothers with equal qualifications. And this impacts a huge number of women given that over 80 percent of women have children by the time they are 44 years old.

The maternal wall begins to explain why so many women, families, and children are living in poverty, why so few women are in national leadership, and also why not enough children are getting the healthy start they need in life.

It is within this context of understanding the impact of discrimination against mothers that Joan Blades (Co-Founder and President of MomsRising) and Kristin

Rowe-Finkbeiner (Co-Founder and Executive Director) were prompted to write *The Motherhood Manifesto* and to co-found MomsRising in May of 2006, along with the founding team of Vice President Mary Olivella and Campaign Directors Katie Bethell, Ashley Boyd, Anita Jackson and Donna Norton.

MomsRising first began building its movement by connecting with many other non-profit organizations to establish "who was doing what" and to begin making policy partner relationships. In these partnerships, MomsRising focuses on grassroots engagement while policy partner organizations focus on current policy analysis. In this way, a broad, symbiotic movement has been growing that maximizes the expertise of many organizations working together. Currently, over 200 national and state organizations have elected to become publicly aligned with MomsRising. These organizations represent a wide variety of groups including faith groups, child advocacy groups, unions, healthcare organizations, parenting groups, family advocacy groups, women's organizations, and mothers' organizations.

From the very start, MomsRising worked with policy partner organizations to find the moments in which the voices of moms could make a difference on moving policy matters. For this effort, MomsRising has offered a mixture of on-the-ground and online opportunities for members to engage, including sending out emails calling for change that could be shared with and forwarded to friends and co-workers in order to grow a movement. In addition, one of the first national grassroots efforts that MomsRising took on was to organize hundreds of house parties across the nation where groups of women watched the documentary film version of *The Motherhood Manifesto* and discussed what was going on in their lives and how they wanted to make a difference.

MomsRising strives to always offer members multiple opportunities for taking action online and on-the-ground with engagement opportunities that require varied amounts of volunteer time including signing a petition, sending a letter to Congress, writing an op-ed for a local paper, making calls, attending meetings with elected leaders, being spokespeople at events, and organizing local MomsRising members. Members regularly make their presence known at state capitals or on the hill in DC to meet personally with Congressional representatives. Members also promote educational and advocacy actions via social media outlets including blogging, Facebook, and Twitter

Not only does MomsRising focus on engaging grassroots members to directly move legislation forward, it's clear that the personal stories of MomsRising members resonate with the media and policy-makers alike and can be a tremendous asset to the overall effort of moving forward family economic security policies. As such, MomsRising has made many requests to members inviting them to share their personal stories relating to healthcare, fair pay, housing discrimination, childcare access, sick days and much more—and has been flooded with stories with each request. MomsRising now has a treasure trove of thousands of member stories told by very diverse mothers and fathers that are leveraged to explain what's really going on across America to leaders, to the media, and to build public support for economic security measures that are critical for families. The stories of mothers are powerful. For example, recent research by the Herndon Alliance found that the best way to build public support for health reform in the U.S. is by women sharing personal health care stories paired with a fact or two about health reform.

By message testing and savvy use of technology, along with a fusion of old and new grassroots engagement tactics, MomsRising has been successful in growing an economic, geographic, and culturally diverse, powerful membership. We have used this power to build public will for paid family and medical leave, affordable child care, flexible work options, access to paid sick days, and an end to the wage and hiring discrimination which penalizes so many mothers, especially mothers of color. In addition, MomsRising works to increase empathy for immigrant families—particularly those who face immigration enforcement practices that separate children from their parents.

At our core, MomsRising believes that together we can build a nation where children, parents, and businesses thrive, and we can end discrimination against mothers.

Mission, Goals and Key Results Areas

MomsRising's mission is to build a more truly family-friendly nation in which women and mothers have achieved economic equality. Our top line goals are to: grow the movement; garner media coverage to change the culture; win legislative policy changes; engage with traditionally underrepresented communities; experiment and learn new online and on-the-ground tactics; and to listen to and serve our members/constituency.

The following are MomsRising's key results areas and metrics for assessing progress towards achieving these results.

1. MomsRising is building a strong multicultural movement of people who care about family economic security and well-being. *Metrics: Weekly and annual measurement of new members, member retention, unsubscribes from our membership, and full incorporation of our "Raising All Voices" diversity initiatives across the organization.*
2. MomsRising is changing our national culture so change can happen in public policies, private interactions, and workplaces. *Metrics: Number of media hits per week and year.*
3. MomsRising is exercising our power to pass family-friendly policies at the state and federal levels and to change the culture. *Metrics: Number of actions per year and per member, as well as the number of target policies moved forward or passed.*
4. MomsRising rapidly responds to emerging opportunities in partnership with aligned organizations in order maximize our collective impact and to ride the wave of change, instead of waving at the wave. *Metrics: Number of rapid response actions per year that helped with the above key results areas. Number of aligned policy partners we work with each year.*

MomsRising members march to bring visibility to family economic security issues.

5. MomsRising is working to increase organizational internal capacity. *Metrics: Funds raised from the base, large donors, and foundations. Infrastructure staff hired in order to maintain and maximize our organization.*

Across all aspects of MomsRising, we are working to build a massive multicultural movement of mothers and others where the MomsRising membership and issues areas reflect the top concerns of all mothers in America.

Objectives include:

•Ensure that all staff weaves the analysis of social/racial justice through their programs.

•Ensure that the MomsRising membership reflects the diversity of the American public.

•Maintain strong partnerships with state and national organizations that represent traditionally underrepresented communities.

•Ensure that women of color feel included when they first visit our website and when they read our outreaches by ensuring cultural competency in the content of our text and choice of visuals, as well as through the diversity of our bloggers and the visibility of our partner organizations.

•Target maintaining a diverse staff team along with offering fellowships and internships, and cultivating key volunteers.

•Ensure the MomsRising Team is well-equipped and supported in implementing the RAV initiatives, including by hosting regular in-service trainings and prioritizing fundraising for RAV initiatives to ensure adequate organizational resources.

MomsRising members walk the Halls of Congress to deliver thousands of stories from mothers across the country calling for change in family policies.

Strategies and Tactics for Movement Building

In order to effectively build the movement, MomsRising has found that it is essential that we be nimble and responsive to emerging cultural and media trends. Rapid response is key. We also constantly test our messaging. We test to see what messages resonate with our members, as well as track engagement in depth using metrics on a weekly, quarterly, and annual basis.

MomsRising has found that when designing modern citizen engagement campaigns, there are two key barriers: 1) People are busier than ever, leaving little time for activism and engagement. Three-quarters of mothers are now in the labor force, and women are juggling an unprecedented number of roles simultaneously. 2) People are now awash with messaging due to the proliferation of television and cable channels, along with the now nearly unlimited Internet options for media. Each person now gets over 3,000 media or marketing hits per day.

Given these two major hurdles, at MomsRising we focus on Four Essential Elements of Modern Campaign Mobilization and Engagement in order to help leap those barriers, educate leaders, engage people in campaigns, build a movement, and win. Here are the four essential elements:

1. Be nimble and responsive. Ride the waves of change (and news) as they go through the media, instead of waving at them as they pass you by.
2. Constantly test creative and effective strategic engagement opportunities and messaging with members, using Key Result Areas (and associated metrics) to stay on target toward your long-term organizational, educational, and movement goals.

3. Be in dialogue with membership, not broadcast. MomsRising also prioritizes listening and being in dialogue with our target audiences so they can help shape the debate, instead of just broadcasting out our own pre-set messaging.
4. Have as many avenues for citizen engagement open as possible at the same time so that busy people can choose what they have time to do in each given moment. In addition, many layers of citizen engagement actions working together at the same time are often most effective (MomsRising calls this the "Layer Cake").

We provide as many avenues as possible for citizen engagement because people are busier than ever before, particularly moms. In fact we have a term for our most highly effective method of creating change by using multiple avenues for actions at the same time. We call it the "Layer Cake." Here's a sample sketch of our Layer Cake approach which is a multilevel, systems approach for grassroots organizing where each tactic augments the other to build a powerful impact:

- Layer One—*Synergistic Collaboration Work:* MomsRising thrives on collaboration with organizations which serve as policy experts in each given issue area. We have now over 200 aligned organizations.
- Layer Two—*Citizen Engagement Supported by Technology:* Examples include one-click actions that can send an email directly to a leader or a letter to the editor of a local newspaper. Or an invite to make phone calls.
- Layer Three—*Citizen Presence Proxy:* To further leverage our online actions, MomsRising often organizes simultaneous on-the-ground engagement opportunities by creating ways for parent's voices to be heard without them having to be physically present at the place where an action is taken.
- Layer Four—*On-the-Ground Engagement and Community Leadership Development*: MomsRising cultivates and trains citizen leaders to lead community meetings with elected leaders and to become spokespeople for parents throughout their community and state.
- Layer Five—*Traditional and New Media Outreach*: Every MomsRising Multi-Layer Campaign includes proactive outreach to traditional and new media outlets like mother bloggers and others.

It is with these methods that MomsRising is:

- Growing our membership—from zero in 2006 to over 1 million now in 2010;
- Garnering media coverage—MomsRising garnered over 1,000 points of mainstream media coverage by our second year with escalating coverage subsequently;

•Helping to build public will for moving policies forward which had long been stuck.

With these tactics MomsRising has played a significant role in passing policies through Congress such as health reform, the *Lilly Ledbetter Fair Pay Act,* and increasing unemployment compensation and childcare funding. At the state level we have partnered with other groups to pass paid family leave in New Jersey and Washington State, and move paid sick days forward, as well as to get rid of toxic children's products and increase funding for early learning.

Future Goals

MomsRising strives to continue to grow the movement of moms in America. As part of that movement we hope to focus in the future more on creating a robust on-the-ground monthly discussion group program across the nation, a candidate recruitment program, a text messaging wing, along with additional increased avenues for people to make their voices heard.

Conclusion

While MomsRising stands on the shoulders of giants in the American women's movement who paved the way for modern women, currently works in collaboration with many strong policy partners, and is effectively bringing the voices of mothers forward in the national dialogue; there is still work to be done. In the U.S., having a baby is a leading cause of a "poverty spell"—a time when income dips below what's necessary to cover food and rent. Further, maternal discrimination runs rampant with both wage and hiring discrimination. For example, mothers with equal resumes as non-mothers are hired 100 percent less of the time according to a recent Cornell University study; and mothers are offered $11,000 lower starting salaries than non-moms with equal resumes. This discrimination has rippling repercussions. The USDA reported that one in four children are experiencing food scarcity in the U.S. due to family economic limitations. With most families now needing two breadwinners to make ends meet, the lack of family friendly policies combined with the hiring and wage discrimation that mothers experience creates a critical situation. The voices of mothers are needed now more than ever.

Fortunately, moms are coming forward and change is starting to happen. Below is a selection of member voices sharing what working with MomsRising has meant to them:

> *I felt like I was out riding the suffragist trains with Alice Paul and Lucy Burns! It was exhilarating to be part of the process that made paid family leave happen, and an honor, really, to help impact families. MomsRising has made advocacy timely, doable and effective—I'm ready for our next mom mission!*—Leslie

Working with MomsRising, particularly on the Power of ONEsie campaign, reinforced my faith in our democratic system. When we put those onesies up at the Washington State capital and Senators and Representatives stopped in their tracks to watch what we were doing, I was reminded that we DO have a voice, that we CAN change things and that we MUST do what we can, however wacky and outlandish, to remind our leaders that they are here for us and that families need to come first! —Colleen

When the Senators came out after the vote to give us hugs and high-fives, half of us we're in tears we were so excited! It hit me then just how ground breaking and powerful our work is. Washington is the second state in the nation to have this kind of policy—and we did it! —Katie

When the vote in the House seemed in jeopardy, we needed an impactful way to influence legislators beyond making calls and e-mails. What better way to reach legislators than through their stomachs? I recruited a group of moms to bake 50 dozen cookies in a very short time. Within days of the crucial House vote, 600+ cookies were delivered to all 98 representatives with hopes of leaving a powerful impression in their minds (and stomachs!). I was overwhelmed at the quick response from the moms willing to help out on such short notice despite their hectic schedules. We'll never know what kind of impact a little batch of cookies made, but I like to think it pushed at least one or two votes over the edge! —Marisa

When Ken and I committed to wear MomsRising shirts everyday until this bill passed, we believed we would be wearing the same shirts everyday for the next few years. Instead, our community spoke loudly that it supported this bill, our government listened intently and, when this bill is signed into law, we will be taking off our daily uniform after only 4 months. While we will be setting our Rosie & Baby t-shirts aside, what will not be set aside is that we can help to make history. We look forward to the year 2009 and the lucky babies who will have more time with their parents. —Yvonne

I'm amazed at the collective brain power and commitment of all the folks involved with keeping things rolling with MomsRising. What I appreciate most is the all-inclusive nature of this organization. If you've got an idea, then run with it! That's how the "Power of the ONEsie" campaign got its start. I'm thankful for the opportunity and means to help make a positive impact for a cause that's truly worth believing in—the family! —Maris

You can visit MomsRising online. We invite you to sign on and get engaged while you're visiting.

40. Jennifer Schumaker's 500 Mile Walk for Togetherness

NATALIE WILSON

JENNIFER SCHUMAKER WALKED ACROSS CALIFORNIA in the Spring of 2006 in order to raise awareness about LGBTQ rights and issues. A lesbian mother of four, Schumaker envisioned her walk as a way to deconstruct the entrenched "us and them" way of thinking that dominates both public and private discourse, especially in relation to sexuality. As noted on her website, she believes that "any discussions or debates that use the words 'we' and 'they' to polarize communities are erroneous and destructive." Thus, Schumaker's vision of togetherness is not aimed at merely dismantling the hetero/non-hetero binary, but at moving beyond dualistic, judgmental thinking altogether, and at making all humans visible. As the website reads, "Jennifer is not only walking for LGBT people and their families, but also for anyone who feels invisible in our society. Jennifer dedicated her walk to a 12-year-old boy named Dakota, who has cerebral palsy. When Dakota was seven, Jennifer heard him call himself 'the Invisible Man.'" Schumaker often invokes Dakota's story when writing or talking about her activism, emphasizing that nobody, regardless of race, sexuality, disability, or any other difference should be rendered invisible by society.

As Schumaker describes, "the purpose of the walk was at once social, familial, and personal. I needed to contribute to the visibility of a largely invisible, often derided community. I also needed to show my children, one of whom was already professing to be gay, that personal empowerment is a choice. Additionally, I needed to give myself a difficult chore to gain perspective so that the negative messages toward me as a lesbian would not turn to feelings of victimhood. I had already moved through throwing off victim feelings as a young Catholic feminist and Theology scholar. I needed to claim a place for myself, one step at a time, as an empowered, purposeful person."

History and Context

Schumaker's "Walk for Togetherness" draws on three key practices: first, the enactment of "just a normal mom" or an "everymom" identity in order to manipulate this status into what Andrea O'Reilly (drawing on Adrienne Rich) defines as a "mother outlaw" identity[1]; secondly, an invocation of a "personal is political" methodology that not only reconsiders and expands mothering practices but also builds on the long traditions of women's protests surrounding concepts of nationalism and "the good citizen;" and thirdly, an enactment of embodied activism, a form of activism that resolutely refuses "abstract rationalism" and instead foregrounds the ways in which national and international policies and institutions effect mothers and their families.

Schumaker has translated her own personal frustration concerning the ways that she and her children are disenfranchised by society due to heteronormative mandates into a profoundly public activist movement. While drawing on her status as an everymom (and in particular on tropes such as soccer mom and carpool mom), Schumaker expands the definition of mothering to include LGBTQ activism. Noting that when she was planning the walk in 2005 that it was still rare to hear about gay people in a "normal context" (and especially to hear about lesbians), she emphasizes the need to normalize and legitimize non-heterosexuality in everyday life. Recognizing her own privilege as a white, suburban mother figure, Schumaker felt responsible to use her privilege to help others. As she notes, "There's a certain respectability with being a mom that gives me privilege that some of my LGBT sisters and brothers don t have" (qtd. in Sherman, para. 5). However, as Schumaker notes, she realized she didn't "want to rest on that privilege" (qtd. in Conlan, para. 16). This realization is, as she puts it:

> really the crux of this walk. I am very aware that I have a lot of privilege in this society, and if I can share that with people who maybe wouldn't get received the same way I have, hopefully I can open some dialogue that will include people who do feel more invisible than I do, people who don t necessarily have the confidence or the privilege to speak up. (qtd. in Conlan, para. 16)

Explaining that she "felt called to do something" that would be an "example of moving through the fear into understanding and acceptance," she decided to embark on a walk across California to raise awareness about LGBTQ discrimination and societal disenfranchisement. As she explains,

> I needed to use the integrating forces of who I was—woman, mother, and homosexual—to try to help ease the fear triggers people had and have toward gays and people who are transgender. As a mother I could see that I might have some power to soften those fear responses by introducing my queer self to people and letting them start the process of relaxing their fears to the queer natures in my LGBTQ brothers and sisters. (qtd. in Conlan, para. 16)

Emphasizing the need to use everymom privileges to help others, Schumaker is nevertheless acutely aware that being a lesbian ejects her from the everymom club.

However, the fact that she has four children, lives in suburbia, and "does not look like a stereotypical lesbian," gives her a "normal" edge. Recounting the tendency of people to not hear the lesbian part when she introduces herself, Schumaker notes "My physical appearance seems to elicit certain recognitions and activate comfort stereotypes." As she explains, her "normal" appearance is not used to trick people into a comfort zone, rather, she uses this appearance privilege as a bridge towards open, non-discriminatory communication. According to her, "the privilege comes in being white, extroverted, feminine, mom-like (whatever that means), dressed decently, etc" and allows her to successfully enact activist mothering. Because Schumaker occupies a number of privileged social identities, she is able to, in effect, deliver their messages to a much wider audience by drawing upon these privileges. However, as Schumaker emphasizes, the way she enacts this type activist mothering is via drawing on her personal identity/appearance as a means through which to change the other (and as a result, society as a whole), or, as she puts it, "it is very important that outlaw mothering be seen in terms of the 'mother other' outlook—that just by quietly revealing simple facts about my life and personhood, there can be a revolution in the thoughts and categories *in the other.*" Here, Schumaker reveals that her quiet mode of delivery functions as a deliberate attempt to change others in non-confrontational ways. This type of delivery, as the successes on her blog attest, has the effect of making people who would otherwise be disinclined to consider the merits of a non-heterosexist society to hear the message of inclusiveness, equality, and togetherness rather than to hear "lesbian" and shut their ears.

Objectives

Schumaker is particularly committed to what feminists call everyday activism. In her explanation of these everyday activisms, Schumaker reveals that activism is not only about walking 500 miles, but also about the little daily steps of promoting awareness and togetherness:

> I would buy my groceries and I would say, "Remember, a Lesbian spent money here today." I would get my car towed, and I would say, "Hey, guys, remember you helped out a Lesbian today." I would leave a plane, and I would look at the crew and say, "Hey, remember, ten percent of your passengers are Gay, Lesbian, Bisexual or Transgender." It was never easy. Sometimes my face would get a little red. Sometimes I had to ask myself if I could really do this.... But if it isn't easy for an extremely hyper, extroverted person like me, how are other people doing it? (qtd. in Conlan, para. 12)

While this concept of everyday activism is well-known within the feminist community, Schumaker is helping to bring this conception of activism to a wider audience. Her approach to activism emphasizes that everyday acts that

Jennifer Schumaker's two sons meet her in San Francisco, with Dakota, to whom the walk was dedicated. Photo: Wendy Muglia

may happen in the line at a grocery store or while picking up the kids at school are just as important as the "big acts" of marching, picketing, or petitioning. Championing this mode of everyday activism delivery seems a crucial move in terms of expanding the parameters of what it means to be activist in a way that makes activism an activity open to all mothers rather than just to those who can travel to DC or who have the time/money privilege to be able to picket, petition, lobby, run for office, etc. By showing that activism can be delivered at the Boy Scout meeting, at the park, or during the lunch break, Schumaker brings to the fore a mode of activist delivery open to all. Or, to put it in her own words, she is a "pioneer." As she explains,

> In some ways, I feel like this big pioneer. I even looked up "pioneer" in the dictionary one day. It means someone who goes into new territory or brings a new idea to a new area. I can say that being backstage at your kid's junior theatre production and helping with the other moms and

> having a button on that says, "I'm much Gayer than I look," probably fits the pioneer definition. (qtd. in Conlan, para. 9)

Here, Schumaker redefines what it means to be a pioneer. While the word traditionally calls to mind notions of male settlers who colonized "new" sections of land in order to expand U.S. power and profit, Shumaker's use of the word emphasizes doing things not for personal or national gain, but for the betterment of all humanity. As a pioneering activist, Schumaker continually breaks new ground with her activist goals and, like other contemporary activist mothers, does not limit her purview to one group, issue, or platform. She is active in groups such as Scouting for All, San Diego Family Matters, Marriage Equality U.S., and Equality California. She regularly attends political protests and rallies and frequently lobbies Governor Schwarzenegger to pass inclusive legislation. In addition to her extensive activism surrounding LGBTQ issues, Schumaker emphasizes her solidarity with all people who are rendered invisible by society, be it due to their race, age, body-size, health, and/or immigrant status. As she explains, "I frame my need for inclusion in the wider issue of what barriers exist to full inclusion and respect for anyone."

Activities: Embodied Activism

As mothers, women are often forced into a keen awareness of the embodied nature of existence. As Adrienne Rich explores in *Of Woman Born*, the body often becomes a trap for women, and especially mothers. As Rich notes, "The body has been made so problematic for women that it has often seemed easier to shrug it off and travel as a disembodied spirit" (40). Hence, women have been encouraged to forget their bodies, to deny the bodily realities of pregnancy and birth, to hide the embodied practices of breastfeeding, to deny the profound ways in which they, and their children, are shaped by their facticity as embodied beings. However, many maternalist activists and activist mothers staunchly refuse the call for bodily forgetting. Like Rich, who refers to her "determination to heal—insofar as an individual woman can, and as much as possible with other women—the separation between mind and body," activists like Schumaker specifically highlight the embodied nature of existence (40). By carrying out what I term embodied activism, Schumaker delivers a form of feminist activism that utilizes embodiment to further particular political causes. In so doing, she takes her place in a long history of embodied activist mothers.

Schumaker enacts embodied activism via both her mode of delivery (walking) and her insistent foregrounding of the body in her writing and speeches. As she explains,

> I can say that just as a laughing, sleeping or crying baby drew my complete, absorbed attention, the need to Walk, to DO SOMETHING sustained and deliberate and intentional called to me, from just a few

Jennifer Schumaker hugs Dakota, to whom the walk was dedicated. He is saying in her ear, "You did great. Now we're not invisible anymore." Photo: Wendy Muglia

> months after I realized I was lesbian. Everything about the world looked different, just like when you're a new mother. Everything seemed to have more weight, but, due to allowing myself to be who I truly was, everything also seemed to have more possibilities. I wanted to make sure those possibilities leaned decidedly toward joy and hope and love and growth, not toward protest and sadness and despair. I guess the walk was as much mothering my inner child as it was setting an example for my children and providing hope or inspiration to others who needed it.

Schumaker thus consistently draws on the physicality of mothering and on the inherently *embodied* nature of our human condition. The normal bodily act of walking is juxtaposed with what some would see as a radical request to be treated as equally human regardless of one's social positioning, sexuality, or (dis)ability. Such enactments of embodied protest are by no means new to feminist activist traditions—from the Women of Greenham Common to the Madres de la Plaza de Mayo to Grannies for Peace, feminist activism has been a profoundly embodied practice that utilizes the body in very unique ways to protest. From the dancing and holding of hands around nuclear silos that the Women of Greenham Common practiced, or the chaining of oneself to old growth trees that Ecofeminists have enacted, or the lying nude en masse to call for peace as the women of Baring Witness do, female activists the world over use their bodies to enact protest. Such acts also draw attention to the way social injustices harm individual bodies. Perhaps the particularly embodied emphasis of female activism is in large part due to the fact that, as Rich puts it, "The woman's body is the terrain on which patriarchy is erected" (55). As Schumaker's activism emphasizes, homophobia is damaging to female, male, and transgender bodies in that it defines some types of bodies and bodily practices as abnormal.

Noting that she purposefully chose a physical form of activism via which to deliver her message, Schumaker recounts the physical terror she felt before the walk, a terror that she says caused her to wake repeatedly at 3:00 a.m. in the weeks leading up to the walk. Linking this embodied fear to the fear pregnant women often experience before delivery, Schumaker associates the feeling of pressure women feel as the baby's head presses on the cervix to the pressure she felt to be an activist. As she relates,

> The deeper I get into my activism, the more I actually remember the physical feeling of the baby's head beginning to push down in my pelvis; this is something that I could never really feel before unless it was actually happening the four times, nor could I recall the feelings in any real way between births or in the years following. Now, the feelings I have about the potential for peace and change and my place in those births are so near to the imminent signs of childbirth that I am at times simply blown away, at times on me knees in wonder.

Recounting that when people told her not to do the walk, she felt they "might as well tell me not to have the baby," Schumaker links her activism to birth, to a physical eventuality that cannot be stopped. However, she also emphasizes that, as with birth, "it's about pushing when the time is right," that the birthing of particular activist movements will not be as healthy or productive if one "pushes too soon." This notion of "pushing too soon" seems a useful way to read earlier incarnations of maternalist activism. In previous eras, women could only "push so much" and found ways to be activists via manipulating their accepted (and respected) status as mothers. However, now that many women have broken away from the chains of domesticity, mothering activists are able to push a lot harder and push in a lot of different directions and ways.

Challenges, Achievements, and Future Goals

Schumaker recounts that she was privy to many criticisms while planning and carrying out her *Walk for Togetherness*. In fact, the press coverage of her walk almost never failed to consider who was taking care of her children while she was gone, if she missed them, and how they were fairing—as if her status as a mother was more important than the activism she was carrying out. Thus, as analyst Ahmed Amr indicates, for activists such as these women to succeed "we need a sudden outbreak of journalism in America." For, although Schumaker is undoubtedly making changes and delivering activism in new ways, the waves of change would come all the faster and bigger if the press offered analytical coverage that actually took the issues they focus on—war, imperialism, homophobia, poverty, prejudice—to task. In effect, it is as if the media holds steadfastly to a staunch maternalist frame that refuses to see women as activists or give the stories of activist mothers the coverage they deserve. As Schumaker relates, "At first I was frustrated that there was no major media coverage, but as I made my way up the coast, the walk became front page news in small town papers. That turned out to be an incredibly uplifting turn. I began to see the power one person had to touch people, to really relate and to nurture their consciousnesses by being on their streets, eating in their cafes, staying with their neighbors." Sadly, the walk didn't garner national media coverage.

However, Schumaker's walk has inspired other women to become active in LGBTQ issues. She knows of some who have done their own walks and/or started websites. She shares that she hopes her walk demonstrated "that the attention to the positive things and nurturing is more powerful than the traditional understanding of power—which is that direct conflict and polarized discourse make change.... So many people believe that we have to directly confront negative behavior every time, when the truth is, if we take a few moments to think of what we want in its place, we can model and encourage that without ever mentioning the aggressive or negative behavior."

Schumaker's activism is an important example of the philosophy of hope and positivity. As she says, "change really does happen one heart and mind at a time.

You might be able to reach hundreds, thousands or millions of hearts and minds at a time, but they still each change as individuals. The safer and more relaxed the discourse, the more likely the participants might experience a shift toward more human togetherness."

Conclusion

From Mary Wollestonecraft's famous message that female children deserve equal education to Mother Mary Jones emphatic call for worker's rights, mothers around the world have long delivered activist messages. In fact, while mothers have historically been associated with home and hearth, a feminist look at history reveals that motherhood often radicalizes women, prompting them to want to change the world for their families and children.[2] As Kristin Rowe-Finkbeiner argues in her polemic, *The F Word: Feminism in Jeopardy*, for many women "motherhood brings to the fore social inequalities that must be addressed politically" (150). This "bringing to the fore" that Rowe-Finkbeiner refers to has inspired political engagement, or, in my terminology, activist mothering, on the part of Schumaker and many others.

If the work of mothering activists such as Schumaker is any indication, the twenty-first century will deliver many new conceptions of activist mothering. However, as (m)others, we cannot wait for mainstream, national media to wake up. Instead, we must take it upon ourselves to seek out independent media, to follow the blogs and websites and writing of activist mothers like Schumaker, to vocalize our support for an inclusive, peaceful world at the polls, the PTA meeting, and the school pick up. If all of us activist mothers offer vocal and visible support, we can change the tide, for, as Andrea O Reilly notes, "it will be mothers, empowered and united, who will create the just and caring society, that feminist new world, we seek for ourselves and our children" (2006: 50). Drawing inspiration from the fact that this century opened with the Million Mom March, we must embrace "the politics of the possible" and look forward to a better tomorrow (Frazer 56). Schumaker did just this with her 500-mile walk, marching across California to honor the vision of a better, more inclusive world.

[1]See, for example, O'Reilly, *Mother Outlaws: Theories and Practices of Empowered Mothering* (2004).

[2]For a discussion of motherhood as a radicalizing (and intellect inducing) experience, see Ellison, *The Mommy Brain* (2005).

Works Cited

Amr, Ahmed. "Counteroffensive: Bush launches 'Operation Cindy Sheehan'." *Palestine Chronicle* August 28, 2005. Web. <http://www.palestinechronicle.com>.

Conlan, Mark Gabrish. "Lesbian activist starts walk for togetherness." *San Diego Indymedia* April 8, 2006. Web. <http://sandiego.indymedia.org>.

Ellison, Katherine. *The Mommy Brain: How Motherhood Makes Us Smarter.* New York: Basic Books, 2005.

Frazer, Nancy. "Feminist Political Theory." *Contemporary Feminist Theories.* Eds. S. Jackson and J. Jones. New York: New York University Press, 1998. 50-61.

McReynolds, John. "Walking the Walk, Talking the Talk." *Lompoc Record.* May 9, 2006. Web. <http://www.lompocrecord>.

O'Reilly, Andrea, ed. *Mother Outlaws: Theories and Practices of Empowered Mothering.* Toronto: Women's Press, 2004.

O'Reilly, Andrea. *Rocking the Cradle: Thoughts on Feminism, Motherhood, and the Possibility of Empowered Mothering.* Toronto: Demeter Press, 2006.

Rich, Adrienne. *Of Woman Born: Motherhood as Experience and Institution.* New York: W. W. Norton, 1976.

Rowe-Finkbeiner, Kristin. *The F Word: Feminism in Jeopardy.* Emeryville, CA: Seal Press, 2004.

Schumaker, Jennifer. "Love, Loss, and Lots of Walking." *The Advocate.* May 31, 2006. Web. <http://www.advocate.com>.

Schumaker, Jennifer. Personal interview. August 14, 2006.

Schumaker, Jennifer. 2005. *Walk for Togetherness.* 2005. Web. <http://www.walkfortogetherness.org/about.htm>. Accessed: September 26, 2008.

Sherman, Pat. "A Mother's Message." *San Diego Union Tribune* June 25, 2006. Web. <http://signonsandiego.com>.

Wollestonecraft, Mary. *A Vindication of the Rights of Women.* [1872]. Boston: Astera, 2010.

41.
The LGBT Family Coalition of Quebec

NANCY NICOL, WITH SPECIAL THANKS TO MONA GREENBAUM

THE LESBIAN MOTHERS ASSOCIATION OF Quebec (LMA) was founded in October 1998, by Mona Greenbaum and Nicole Paquette in response to a series of obstacles they faced in fulfilling their desire to have children. At the time, there was no form of relationship recognition or parenting rights for same-sex couples in Quebec. When they approached a fertility clinic in Quebec, they were refused access to donor insemination as a lesbian couple. Eventually Mona and Nicole found a sympathetic doctor who agreed to provide insemination. Once Mona became pregnant, given that there was no recognition of same-sex relationships, the couple launched the first case for co-parent adoption by a lesbian couple in Quebec in the spring of 1998.

When their son Léo was just six weeks old, Mona and Nicole shocked at the lack of basic information, isolation and legal obstacles that they faced, held a meeting at their home, for lesbian mothers and lesbians who wanted to become parents. Forty women showed up and the Lesbian Mothers Association was born. By 2002, it had grown to represent 500 lesbian families throughout Quebec, becoming the largest lesbian organization in the province. In 2005, LMA played an important role in the establishment of a gay men's parenting network, the Papa-Daddy group; and in 2008, the LMA, the Papa-Daddy group, and transgender parents and future parents came together to form the Lesbian, Gay, Bisexual and Trans-identified (LGBT) Family Coalition of Quebec.

The Coalition is a bilingual group of LGBT parents and future parents that advocates for the legal and social recognition of LGBT families. They provide workshops for future parents and parents with young children, hold picnics and activities for LGBT families, organize conferences and educational workshops throughout Quebec, and work to increase the visibility of LGBT families and raise public awareness of the reality for LGBT families.

Context and Challenges

Over the course of their history, the LMA and the LGBT Family Coalition have played an important role in transforming the legal status of LGBT families in

Quebec as well as advancing broader social awareness. The challenges they faced were significant. Despite the fact that Quebec was the first province in Canada to include non-discrimination on the basis of sexual orientation in provincial human rights legislation in 1977, the government continued to discriminate against gays and lesbians for the next 25 years under 54 different statutes related to family and relationships.

By the early 1990s discrimination against gays and lesbians in terms of relationship recognition and family status was exacerbated in part by the AIDS crisis. Montreal was devastated by the AIDS epidemic, one of the hardest hit communities in North America. Gay men and lesbians living in relationships faced tremendous hardships due to the absence of recognition as "next of kin," denial of visitation rights in hospitals, the absence of bereavement leave, denial of pension benefit or health benefits for same-sex partners, and denial of the surviving partner's right to mourn as homophobic relatives of the deceased excluded same-sex partners from family funerals. At the beginning of the 1990s, La table de concertation des lesbiennes et gais du Québec / The Roundtable of Lesbians and Gays of Québec, a coalition of LGBT groups in Quebec, put pressure on the Quebec Human Rights Commission for a public enquiry into discrimination and violence against gays and lesbians. They launched an organizing drive throughout Quebec calling on organizations and individuals to testify before the Commission (Hendricks and Leboeuf; Demczuk). In June 1993, the Commission held ten days of public hearings in which 75 organizations and individuals gave testimonials.

Among those testifying was Anne Robinson, a professor of law from Laval University, who spoke on same-sex families, same-sex adoption, and the extreme obstacles that lesbians encountered in the courts during custody disputes. Robinson called for recognition of same-sex relationships and families and, for the first time in Quebec, publicly supported the right of lesbians and gay men to marry. On June 1, 1994, the Commission released its report, *De L'Illégalité à l'égalité / From Illegality to Equality,* which made forty-one recommendations dealing with a range of issues including supporting same sex relationship recognition, recognition of parenting rights for same-sex partners and same-sex marriage. Building on the report's recommendations, La coalition québécoise pour la reconnaissance des conjoints et conjointes de même sexe / the Québec Coalition for the Recognition of Same-Sex Relationships was founded in 1996, to press for legislative change to recognize same-sex relationships and families.

A well-organized lesbian community had existed in Montreal since the 1970s with deep historical links to a strong feminist movement in Quebec. Lesbians had participated in the women's movement and were involved in the establishment of women's health care services, pro-choice organizations and clinics throughout the 1970s and 1980s. During that time, lesbian mothers' organizations remained small support groups, principally made up of mothers who had divorced a man and who lived in a reconstituted family with their children. The issues for lesbian mothers of that period were invisibility, social stigma, isolation, and bitter battles over custody rights in divorce cases. Lesbians often lost custody of their children

Lesbian Mothers Association, Montreal, 1998. Left, foreground, is founder Mona Greenbaum and her partner, Nicole Paquette, with their infant son Léo.

on the grounds that merely by being a lesbian, a woman was considered as "unfit" to parent by the courts. (Caldwell; Chamberland; Demczuk).

By the time the Lesbian Mothers Association was founded in 1998, the context had shifted: the Human Rights Commission had recommended relationship recognition and parenting rights for same-sex couples and a broad-based coalition was mobilized to fight for those rights. In 1999, Bill 32 was passed, redefining the term "spouse" in 39 provincial laws and regulations to include same-sex spouses in common law relationships; but there was still no recognition of same-sex parenting or adoption by same-sex couples. Lesbians who wanted to become parents faced prejudice and ignorance as well as denial of access to services. Lesbian couples who had children faced obstacles since only the birth mother was accorded any legal status in relation to the child.

At the same time, more and more lesbians were establishing families as lesbian couples or as single women outside of heterosexual relationships. The issues for these women were reproductive rights, access without prejudice to fertility clinics, the ability to negotiate their relationships to known sperm donors or to co-parent as three-parent families, and recognition and legal rights for both mothers. The LMA reflected a higher level of confidence and sense of entitlement than lesbian mothers groups of the previous decade. Mary Lamey, a member of the Political Action Committee of the Lesbian Mothers Association, reflects this rising sense of entitlement:

> Once you decide that you're going to live as a lesbian, you've already thrown off what the world's expectations are, right! The world already says that you shouldn't be a lesbian. So once you've crossed that frontier, you've made a decision. Are you going to not have children because the world says you shouldn't have children, that this is some sort of social

> experiment? No, you know who you are, and you know what your motivations are. If the world … is not always a kind place [and] you want your kids to be safe in the world, then the world's got to change, not your kids.

Initially, the LMA acted as a support group, seeking to overcome isolation, working to build community, doing educational work and sharing information about supportive doctors. But very quickly the LMA became a political organization, engaging in social movement organizing and becoming active in the Lesbian Issues Committee of the Federation of Women of Quebec (FFQ) and the Coalition for Same-Sex Relationship Recognition to win support and recognition of their families. FFQ activist and author, Evangeline Caldwell, describes the role played by the LMA and the Lesbian Issues Committee in raising awareness within the FFQ with respect to lesbian parenting,

> We got the same question in nearly all the workshops, which was, "Well, tell us about the children. How are the children going to do in these families?"…By then there had been a sufficient critical mass of research by the American Psychological Association and other critical associations, that had said that the developmental path of children in same-sex families was absolutely normal. There was no problem. So, we were able to impart that type of information. But a few of us were also able to say, "Well, you're talking about me; my partner and I have a child." And then, out comes the picture. "And here's my little boy." And then the little boy's picture gets passed around the table, and someone pipes up and says, "Oh, I have a little boy that age." And then the conversation goes to, "Oh, well I have a little grandson that age." So, we would talk about our sons and grandsons, or daughters and granddaughters… And I think having those types of moments is really important because it not only demystifies [lesbian families], it makes it just part of what is it to be another family. It was incredibly useful in giving women who didn't necessarily have any experience with same-sex families a glimpse of a same-sex family… And when we came to the general assembly [of the FFQ] the political platform of supporting [same-sex] marriage and full parental and filiation rights was passed by an overwhelming majority. (Caldwell)

Apart from working to raise awareness about lesbian families, the LMA also supported lesbians in their desire to have children, assembling and providing educational resources as well as information on doctors who were open to providing insemination. When access to family planning and donor insemination continued to be a problem for lesbians, the LMA took matters into its own hands by establishing their own insemination services for lesbians. Mona Greenbaum explains:

Lesbian Mothers Association, Pride Day, Montreal 2002.

> We did our own insemination. My partner's a doctor, so we were able to do it. We started our own mini sperm bank. We had a big liquid nitrogen tank. Lesbians would order sperm and keep it in our tank and ring our doorbell at five in the morning, [saying:] "It's time, we're going to do it before work." And they would come and pick up their little vials. It was complicated and none of us were fertility experts, so it was kind of hit and miss. It was actually the lesbian mothers' sperm bank. (Greenbaum 2004)

Fighting for Legislative Change

On November 8, 2001, the Quebec government released a "White Paper" on preliminary legislation that would introduce a limited form of Civil Union for same-sex couples (Cloutier 1). The proposed legislation provided hospital visitation rights and some benefits for same-sex couples, but fell far short of equal rights and recognition of same-sex relationships. Moreover, it contained nothing with regard to recognition of same-sex parents and the right to adoption. The Coalition for Recognition of Same-sex Relationships, which for months had been asking for a meeting with the Minister of Justice to advise the government on any proposed legislation, reacted with outrage to the limited extent of rights contained in the White Paper. It demanded and got a meeting with the Justice Minister, Paul Bégin. At that meeting, Bégin agreed to hold a Parliamentary Commission and accept presentations on the legislation. The Coalition responded with an extensive public campaign and organizing drive to prepare papers and organizational presentations for the Parliamentary Commission, similar to what they had done in 1993 for

Lesbian Mothers Association banner and Simon, Pride Day, Montreal 2002.

the Quebec Human Rights Commission. In particular, the LMA launched a press campaign to raise awareness in Quebec about the needs of same-sex parents to have their families recognized and to be given full rights as parents. LMA members Amy Barratt and Mary Lamey describe their efforts,

> Amy: We heard about this Civil Union Bill … and we realized this is where we needed to lobby. And our focus was not on marriage or civil union. We needed to get parental rights and this is our chance. We needed to get them in this bill because if this bill passes without them it's going to be ten years before they do anything else on gay rights… Lesbian Moms had been open to doing interviews but it really became a mission when they introduced the Civil Union law.… Anyone who wants to talk to us, we're going to talk to them. We're going to get our image out there and demystified.
>
> Mary: And … the Justice Minister had said, "public opinion isn't there; we've done polling and it's like 30 percent of the population think that parental rights should be included." So we said, we've got to get public opinion up.
>
> Amy: That's right! He said bring the numbers up and we'll see what we can do.
>
> Mary: So we said, people don't know us; everyone's going to know our families by the time this bill comes before the National Assembly!… We did every interview, anyone who asked. We were like page three girls in the *Journal de Montreal* (laughs), which is like being page three girls in the *Toronto Sun!* It was not the place I thought we'd ever see our

> picture!... We talked with people who were totally obsessed with, 'how did you get your baby?' [We said] how we got her is not important. Here's what matters: we have a child and she needs to have her rights protected. (Barratt and Lamey 2004).

Mona Greenbaum describes their campaign and the impact of the widespread media attention it captured:

> People realized that we existed. I don't think people knew that we existed before that. I mean, we, back in 1998, we didn't know that we existed! So, you know, all of a sudden it came into the public domain, about lesbian parents. So there were a lot of interviews and a lot of debating back and forth whether or not we should have rights as parents. I think Quebec society had evolved enough to that point where the majority of people were very clear that couples, gay and lesbian couples, should be recognized; but when it came to kids, it was very "iffy." People didn't know. The group had gone from being just a social and support group, an information group, to being a political group. And those women were very involved and they knew that we were fighting for something very important that was going to affect all of us on a very personal level. (Greenbaum 2004)

Representing the fruition of years of organizing by the Coalition for the Recognition of Same-sex Relationships, a broad spectrum of civil society came forward to present briefs supporting same-sex relationship recognition and parenting rights to the Parliamentary Commission including a range of labour, LGBT, and community-based organizations. Mona and Nicole presented a brief on behalf of the LMA. The president of the Federation of Women of Quebec presented a paper to the Commission and appeared before the media to defend lesbian and gay parenting rights and relationship recognition (Caldwell; Demczuk). The CSN's (Confédération des syndicats nationaux) presentation called for the recognition of same-sex adoption and parenting rights. As well, it successfully persuaded the National Assembly members and Minister of Justice Bégin that Civil Union should not be established as a separate category for homosexuals as was originally proposed in the legislation, arguing that a separate Civil Union provision only for lesbians and gay men would constitute a segregated status, violating the dignity of same-sex couples by maintaining a discriminatory status. Rather, the CSN argued, Civil Union should be open to anyone regardless of their sexual orientation (Lagacé). In a key presentation to the commission, psychology professor, Danielle Julien (UQAM) submitted a comprehensive dossier of over 20 years of research which concluded that children raised by lesbian or gay parents had no differences in their development, including no differences in terms of their sexual orientation, than children raised by heteosexual parents (Cloutier).

Irene Demczuk, acting as the co-ordinator and the spokesperson for the Coalition, decided that the National Assembly should also hear from the children of lesbian and gay parents. She asked three youths who had been raised by lesbian or gay parents to present their perspectives to the Parliamentary Commission. Their testimony proved to be a turning point in the hearings. One of the youths, Annick Gariépy, told the National Assembly that her mother had always hidden her lesbianism and that even on the day of her testimony her mother did not know she would be testifying before the Commission. She went on to explain to the Assembly why they should vote to extend parenting rights and recognition to lesbians and gay men:

> My mother is a mother who is there for me, who has given the best of herself. She is encouraging, attentive, available, devoted: all the qualities that a mom should have. As I was saying earlier, it has only been four or five years since I started to reconcile myself with my mother's sexual orientation. I stopped feeling humiliation to have a parent often associated with pedophilia, abnormality—a parent seen as outside the norm. I often asked myself, and this is in my testimonial, how could a feeling as noble and as beautiful as love have inspired in me feelings as devastating as shame? As a child I was mortified by this situation. Continuing to play ostrich and denying them rights normally recognized for heterosexual parents constitutes more of a menace to the family than could ever be the inverse, contrary to what some may think. How could giving all of one's love and dedicating your life to a child be a menace to society or to the family? Why ask gays and lesbians to renounce a part of their humanity in the name of this difference? (Quebec National Assembly)

The testimony of the three youths moved the members of the Quebec Assembly to tears and profoundly influenced the proceedings. Minister of Justice, Paul Bégin, describes the impact on the legislature of hearing the experiences of lesbian mothers and the children raised by lesbian and gay parents, saying:

> [It was] a memorable moment… for 30 seconds [after they spoke] I was still trying to figure out, what I was going to say, if I would be able to speak. I looked around, and there were tears in the eyes of the deputies; everyone was choked up… I don't remember what I said… I wanted to say that I loved them; that it was extraordinary what they had just done. It opened the floodgates for everyone. An unforgettable moment.… And I'd say it was the same for about 60 percent of the groups [who presented testimonials], it was always their personal experiences [that mattered]. Mme. Paquette and Mme. Greenbaum and other people came to tell us what they experienced in their lives. And you got the sense that everybody was drinking in their words, listened and understood

their experience ... and that it was inhuman; that you couldn't say all kids were equal when theirs were treated like that.

Following the Parliamentary Commission, Paul Bégin rewrote the legislation, Bill C-84, to establish Civil Union for both heterosexual and homosexual couples in Quebec. With regard to parenting rights for same-sex couples, Bill C-84 modified fifty-four laws of the filiations provisions of the Civil Code of Quebec to establish new assisted procreation rules (donor insemination) and extended equal adoption and parenting rights and recognition to same-sex couples. For the first time in Canada, *both* mothers in a lesbian couple gained the right to sign the birth certificate upon the birth of their child, thus eliminating the necessity of having to go through a process of co-parent adoption in order to secure parenting recognition for both parents. The LMA brought their children to witness the vote on the legislation in the National Assembly of Quebec (it was the first time that children were allowed into the National Assembly during a vote). Together they stood as witnesses in the National Assembly as members rose and voted unanimously and without abstentions to support the legislation. In contrast to other jurisdictions in Canada where there had been strong dissent to the passage of such legislation, particularly over the question of same-sex parenting rights and adoption, the National Assembly of Quebec voted unanimously and without abstentions in favour of Bill C-84.

The passage of Bill C-84 and the changes to the filiations provision of the Civil Code came as a result of a highly organized campaign for same-sex relationship recognition and parenting rights for same-sex couples. Prior to the Parliamentary Commission, polls indicated that only 35 percent of Quebec society supported parenting by lesbians and gay men, but by the time the legislation was passed, the debate, the coalition's work, and the LMA media campaign had significantly influenced public awareness.

The LGBT Family Coalition of Quebec Organizational Activities

In the wake of these legal and social advances in rights in Quebec, the LGBT parenting networks have grown in confidence and organization. In May 2005, the LMA published *Respect and Self-Esteem: Talking about sexual orientation and gender identity with our kids*. In October 2006, the LMA launched the first Québécois book for young children that depicted families with same-sex parents, *Ulysse et Alice,* (Bertouille and Favreau) and worked with the Montreal School Board to develop a teacher's guide to accompany the book's introduction into schools. In the fall of 2005, the LMA helped to found the Papa-Daddy group for gay fathers. In 2008 the LMA and the Papa-Daddy group formed the LGBT Family Coalition of Quebec (Coalition des familles homoparentales) to work together for the legal and social recognition of gay, lesbian, bisexual and trans-identified families. This group has now become the largest LGBT organization in Quebec.

In July 2004, the LMA joined a working group of ministry representatives and LGBT community organizers that eventually worked under the Quebec Human Rights Commission to produce a report for the Ministry of Justice entitled *De l'Egalité juridique a légalité sociale: vers une stratégie nationale de lutte contre l'homophobie / From Legal to Social Equality: Toward a national strategy against homophobia.* The report surveyed the needs and demands of the LGBT community in Quebec and was completed in 2007. This publication became the blueprint for "*la politique québecoise de lutte contre l'homophobie*"/ *the Quebec Policy Against Homophobia*, launched by Quebec Justice Minister, Kathleen Weill, in December 2009. Fifty-four LGBT organizations, trade unions, civil society stakeholders and researchers have come together to collaborate with the Quebec government to make sure that this policy translates into real action according to the priorities of the LGBT community. The action plan will be launched in the spring/summer of 2011.

The mandate of the LGBT Family Coalition is to create resources that can be used in primary and secondary schools, daycares, doctors' offices, community organizations or social services to raise public awareness about the diversity and reality of LGBT family structures. Today, the coalition offers free training sessions to institutions that work with children or families, to combat homophobia and promote inclusion.

While a great deal of research has been done over the past two decades focusing on whether children raised by lesbian mothers differ from children raised by heterosexual parents, far less work has been done to examine experiences unique to sexual minority parents and their children, such as the impact of homophobia on LGBT families (Vyncke). As the children of members of the LMA began to grow and enter the school system, new challenges were presented for the coalition. They found that their children at the primary and high school level were very cautious about talking about the fact that their parents were gay or lesbian. Even in the most progressive schools, their kids would hear homophobic insults every day in the schoolyard. When words like "faggot," "gay" and "lesbo" are commonly used insults it was not surprising that the children of lesbian and gay parents did not feel comfortable talking about "mommy and maman" or "papa and daddy." At the same time, many educators did not have access to resources which addressed homophobia or the reality of LGBT families.

So, in November 2007, the LMA applied for funds from the Ministry of Education to develop educational resources to combat homophobia in the schools. Their goal was to educate professionals including school staff and medical and social services personnel, to the realities of same-sex parented families and to combat homophobia in the schools. In March 2008, they received funding to carry out the project and produced a ground-breaking resource kit, "*Regards sur les familles homoparentales: s'ouvrir à leurs réalités pour mieux répondre aux besoins des enfants*" in June 2009. Targeted to professionals who work with children, the training and resource kit raises awareness on the devastating effects of homophobia on all children. The English version, *Family Diversity: Strategies to Fight Homophobia and Promote Inclusion*, was completed in November 2010.

The project was carried out by the LGBT Family Coalition drawing on research and expertise contributed by Dr. Danielle Julien (UQAM), as well as researchers at McGill University, to communicate research about LGBT families to non-experts and professionals working with children. The Coalition trained teams of facilitators who carry out the training in schools, social and health services, and community organizations throughout Quebec. The project consists of a three-hour workshop and a kit of educational resources and activities to assist professionals in dealing with homophobia in their institution, to deconstruct the myths and stereotypes around LGBT families and to motivate people to act. Each institution receives lesson plans, a best practices guide, posters, and lists of books and videos to help them work against homophobia and toward inclusion. Included in the materials are video testimonies of children of LGBT parents, to help professionals understand the experiences of homophobia that children of LGBT parents encounter. To date, over 3,000 professionals have gone through the *Regards sur les familles homoparentales* training sessions and some 700 future teachers have taken the program as part of their undergraduate degrees; and the numbers keep growing.

Contribution to the Motherhood Movement

Over the years the LMA and the LGBT Family Coalition have overcome isolation, provided education, and built a strong support mechanism for LGBT families which has lead to a vibrant and engaged community. They produce a quarterly newsletter which informs the members on issues affecting LGBT rights in general and parenting issues in particular, including news on struggles at the domestic and international level. In recent years the LGBT Family Coalition has developed parenting courses which deal with a large number of questions: How do I form a family: adoption, international adoption, adoption through the mixed bank, surrogacy, co-parenting, natural childbirth, donor insemination? What are our rights and responsibilities as lesbian, gay, or trans parents in Quebec? What are the rights of known and unknown donors? Do we need to write a donor contract if we are inseminating at home? What does a contract have to say? Does getting married give our children extra legal protection? Whose name goes onto the child's birth certificate? They deal with issues in transracial adoption, dealing with homophobia at school or daycare, surrogacy, as well as issues facing new parents from sleepless nights to baby proofing your home.

Led by founder, Mona Greenbaum, they have built bridges between lesbian, gay men and transgender communities and developed a diverse, multi-faceted organization. And with all the work of building an organization, challenging injustice and societal prejudice, they come together in celebration and play as well as the more serious work of the day. They organize trips to the beach, picnics in the parks, Pride Day outings and trips to the maple sugar bush for sugaring-off when the sap runs in the springtime.

Much has changed since Annick Gariépy told the Quebec National Assembly in 2002 about the shame and prejudice which forced her mother to live in hiding, and which caused her as a child to feel humiliated because her mother's sexual orientation was "often associated with pedophilia, abnormality." The LMA has provided a social network and support to thousands of LGBT parents to have a family, to live with dignity and pride, and to celebrate the diversity of their families. They have challenged the hetero-normative presumption of parenting, and the painful internalising of those assumptions which caused many lesbians to question their ability to parent. Instead of questioning the "fitness" of lesbians, gay men, bisexuals and transgender people to parent they have worked to overcome the homophobia and prejudice that does profound damage not only to LGBT people but to society as a whole.

Conclusion

The LGBT Family Coalition's current work in the schools in Quebec is a reflection of both their successes and the challenges they face. Children of LGBT parents still encounter prejudice at school and there are insufficient resources to raise awareness and overcome marginalization. Groups like the LMA and the LGBT Family Coalition of Quebec have been at the forefront, challenging unjust laws, overcoming barriers, developing ground-breaking educational resources and seeking change. The gains they have achieved since the mid 1990s are a remarkable achievement, but the work of overcoming prejudice and building a new society where every child is treated equally and every family is accorded dignity and respect remains a work in progress.

This paper is based on research done by Nancy Nicol for her documentary, Politics of the Heart/ La politique du coeur, *funded in part by a Social Sciences and Humanities Research Council of Canada (SSHRC) Creation/Research Grant. The film is distributed by Vtape <http://www.vtape.org/contact.htm> and by Night at the Indies <http://www.nightattheindies.com/merchandise.nicol.asp>. An earlier revised version of the paper was presented at the conference "Heresy, Blasphemy, and the Freedom of Expression," University of Central Florida, Orlando, Florida, in January 18–20, 2007. Parts of this paper were also used in an paper entitled: "Politics of the Heart: Recognition of Homoparental Families in Quebec," published in* Whose Your Daddy? And Other Writings on Queer Parenting, *ed. Rachel Epstein (2009). I would like to thank Pascal Hugo Plourde for his research assistance and the interview subjects for agreeing to participate. This research was conducted in accordance with Canada's Tricouncil Statement on Research Ethics. All interviews were conducted by Nancy Nicol, except as noted.*

Works Cited

Barratt, Amy and Mary Lamey. Interview with author, Montreal, QC, 30 July 2004 and 20 August 2005.

Bégin, Paul. Interview with author and research assistant Pascal Hugo Plourde, Quebec City, 4 September 2004.

Bertouille, Ariane, with illustrations by Marie-Claude Favreau. *Ulysse et Alice.* Montréal: Les Éditions du Remue-Ménage, 2006.

Caldwell, Evangeline. Interview with author and research assistant Pascal Hugo Plourde, Montreal, QC, 7 May and 29 July 2004.

Chamberland, Line. Interview with author and research assistant Pascal Hugo Plourde, Montreal, QC, 9 May 2004.

Cloutier, Mario. "Québec reconnaîtra l'union civile homosexuelle, Paul Bégin travaille à un avant-projet de loi consacrant les droits des couples de meme sexe." *Le Devoir* 9 November 2001: 1.

Demczuk, Irene. Interview with author and research assistant Pascal Hugo Plourde, Montreal, QC, 7 May and 1 August 2004.

Greenbaum, Mona. Interview with author, Montreal, QC, 6 May and 2 August 2004, 5 September 2007.

Greenbaum, Mona, and Nicole Paquette. Interview with author, Montreal, QC, 2 August 2004.

Hendricks, Michael, and René Leboeuf. Interview with author and research assistant Pascal Hugo Plourde, Montreal, QC, 8 May and 2 August 2004.

Lagacé, Francis. Interview with author and research assistant Pascal Hugo Plourde, Montreal, QC, 7 May and 29 July 2004.

Lamey, Mary. Interview with author, Montreal, QC, 30 July 2004.

LMA Newsletter 9.3 (March 2008).

LMA Newsletter 9.4 (June 2008).

LGBT Family Coalition Newsletter 10.2 (December 2008).

LGBT Family Coalition Newsletter 10.4 (June 2009).

LGBT Family Coalition Newsletter 11.1 (September 2009).

LGBT Family Coalition Newsletter 11.2 (December 2009).

LGBT Family Coalition Newsletter 11.3 (March 2010).

LGBT Family Coalition Newsletter 11.4 (June 2010).

LGBT Family Coalition Newsletter 12.1, (September 2010).

LGBT Family Coalition Newsletter 12.2 (December 2010).

LGBT Family Coalition Newsletter 12.4 (June 2010).

LGBT Family Coalition Newsletter 13.3 (March 2011).

De L'Illégalité à l'égalité : Rapport de la consultation publique sur la violence et la discrimination envers les gais et lesbiennes. Québec Human Rights Commission (Québec Commission des droits de la personne et des droîts de la jeunesse). May 1994.

Nicol, Nancy. Director. *Politics of the Heart / La politique du coeur*. Film. Toronto: Intervention Video Inc., 2005. Distributed by http://www.vtape.org, http://www.givideo.org/ang/orgA/orgA.html and http://www.nightattheindies.com/merchandise.nicol.asp.

Quebec National Assembly. 2nd Session, 36th Legislature, June 2002 Bill C84, *Act Instituting Civil Unions and Establishing New Rules of Filiation.*

Quebec National Assembly. 2nd Session, 36th Legislature, Parliamentary Commission, 6 February 2002. *Testimony by M. Ludovic Maillé-Prévost, Mmes Julie Pétrin and Annick Gariépy.*

Robinson, Anne. Interview with author and research assistant Pascal Hugo Plourde, Quebec City, 4 September 2004.

Vyncke, Johanna, *Équipe de recherche sur la famille et son environnement,* Ph.D. Candidate Department of Psychology, Université du Québec à Montréal, 2009.

42. Changing the World One Mother at a Time

The International Mothers and Mothering Network

MELINDA VANDENBELD GILES

THE INTERNATIONAL MOTHERS AND MOTHERING Network (IMMN), formerly the International Mothers Network, is a global consortium of over 80 motherhood organizations, which provides a collective virtual space for the motherhood movement. The IMMN was officially launched on International Women's Day, March 8, 2009. The purpose of the IMMN is to link maternal activist organizations and galvanize a strong collective voice representing the rights and needs of mothers globally. It is about providing a space of empowerment, a space of information sharing, a space for community building and a space for bringing together progressive mothering groups who are all fighting for the same cause through various different means.

Mandate

Andrea O'Reilly, founder and director of MIRCI (Motherhood Initiative for Research and Community Involvement) and Associate Professor in the School of Women's Studies at York University, describes the IMMN as "a space for mothers and scholars. A safe space to share ideas, collaborate and move forward through research and activism." The IMMN web site states, "IMMN's focus, in particular, is on progressive mothers groups—mothers from the global south, mothers in poverty, mothers who are activists, mothers with disabilities, welfare mothers, grandmother caregivers and others, who are vested in feminist perspectives on maternal well-being, health; including but not limited to, safety, freedom of expression, equal rights, benefits for families and caregivers and support for organizations that encourage a platform for continued pragmatic change-work." In other words, it is a virtual collective space in which progressive researchers/activists/artists can converge in the sharing of mothering knowledge and practices.

History

MIRCI (previously identified as the Association for Research on Mothering) was pivotal in organizing and initiating the conversation that led to the creation of the IMMN.

Beginnings of the International Mothers and Mothering Network, October 26, 2008.

It was during the annual ARM conference in October 2008 ("Mothering, Violence, Militarism, War and Social Justice"), that the IMMN was first conceptualized. As O'Reilly says, "We wanted to think about social change not just in terms of social policy, but in terms of advocacy, health, creative resistance." And so, as O'Reilly phrases it, "We brought the leading organizations together and we talked." And talk they did. For three hours. "What do we need to do? What does the motherhood movement look like? Who does it serve? What are its goals? Who are we excluding?" One can only imagine the palpable energy within a room occupied by 24 members of the leading mothering organizations all converging in one space to discuss their collective desire to make mothering a pivotal issue in both public policy and societal consciousness. One can also imagine the potential site of controversy. "I think it was like what the early feminist movement would have been like," is how O'Reilly describes the moment. It was a pivotal moment in (her)story.

Context and Objectives

Beginning with 24 organizations at the inception of the International Mothers and Mothering Network, there are now over 80. Some of the participating organizations include: Literary Mama, Brain Child, Mamapalooza, Mother Centres International Network for Empowerment (MINE), Mothers Acting Up, Mother Outlaws and Moms Rising. The diversity of these organizations reveals the confluence of creativity, innovation and resourcefulness existing within such a powerful coalition of groups. All of these organizations are actively supporting mothers, dealing with anything from mothers who are incarcerated to welfare reform to poverty in the global south.

Challenges

Of course, attempting to collectively unite diverse interests inevitably presents several challenges. Everyone could agree that providing visibility for the motherhood movement was pivotal, providing a network for information sharing and community building. A web site provides a platform. It provides a space where people can share information, thoughts, and find empowerment through a collective goal. However, the specific objectives of each organization differ. In a neoliberal era of particularism, the challenge of uniting beneath a common cause can be difficult. However, the IMMN proves the possibilities inherent within the collective. As O'Reilly says, "We need to talk about a motherhood movement, not motherhood movements. We say a feminist movement with feminisms in there. We need to have a sense of belonging uniting all these different women and motherhood organizations. We have to come together because only a movement can bring about social change. We have to say: there *is* a motherhood movement."

The Motherhood Movement

Despite their differences, O'Reilly says all participants at the conference could agree that "motherhood is devalued in our culture, invisible, unpaid, and women are still responsible for this work." What is the goal of the motherhood movement? "We want to create a world where mothering work is honoured, respected, supported," says O'Reilly. Indeed, 35 years after the birth of feminism, women are still struggling. O'Reilly discusses how the oscillation of forces during the 1980s, including the impact of neoliberalism, consumerism, the rise of smaller families, the rising culture of fear, the feminist backlash, all contributed to how motherhood has been, and continues to be perceived. The 1990s identity politics opened a space for gender studies yet at the same time limited the hard-fought space of women's studies, effectively taking the already marginalized discussion of motherhood off the agenda. An interesting reversal, however, has taken place in the 2000s.

"In the early 2000s people started asking: Can we say there's a motherhood movement, groups of women and groups of organizations mobilizing around a particular cause—mothers? If you asked that in 1999, the answer would have been no. If you asked that in 2000, the answer was yes. Something happened." Indeed, as O'Reilly says, something *did* happen. All of the mothering organizations that participated in the 2008 conference, with the exception of a handful, had been created in the past twelve years. As O'Reilly explains, "Mothers' needs weren't being met in the labour movement. They weren't being met in the feminist movement. It came out of virtual necessity."

Although there are a number of mitigating factors for this increasing interest in all things mother-related, O'Reilly posits a fascinating—and often unrecognized—thesis. "I argue that it's largely demographics. The third-wave feminists are now mothers. Born 1965, they were 35 in 2000. Guess what they were do-

Association for Research on Mothering conference, 2008. Photo courtesy of Joy Rose.

ing? Having babies! These are the women that benefited from the baby boomers' feminist movement. The argument is that these young women, they grew up with the political savvy, the education, with the knowledge of political mobilization. White, able-bodied heterosexual women can, to a large extent, avoid excessive patriarchy. The wage gap is not between men and women. It's between parents and non-parents. These women hit patriarchy full-force only when they became mothers." And the shock of it forced them to speak out—and to continue speaking out.

Future Goals

Plans for the future include the MIRCI May 2011 conference on Motherhood, Activism, Advocacy, and Agency, which the International Mothers and Mothering Network will be co-sponsoring. The other event will occur in May 2012. Dr. O'Reilly has revealed some of the exciting plans. "We will bring together the top twenty motherhood scholars and motherhood organizations in North America. Bring them together for a day and a half. They will answer two questions: What do mothers need? How do we get it?" Well-known and respected authors such as Sharon Hays, Meredith Michaels and Ann Crittenden will be there. "We're going to get these people in a room and they're going to present their view, but in a very practical, useful way. What changes do families need? What changes in public policy? What changes in work-place practices? We want to document what's wrong and with evidence. And then figure out what to do about it."

Conclusion

Social change is never easy. Nor is providing a collective forum where mothering voices can be heard. But with individuals such as Andrea O'Reilly providing inspiration, we can get that much closer. We must always remember that the day we become complacent is the day we become complicit. The International Mothers and Mothering Network provides a visible recognition of the motherhood movement and its forceful impact. As O'Reilly states, the purpose of the IMMN is "to make visible the motherhood movement, disseminate information, create community amongst the diverse motherhood organizations, and push forward into the public world the needs of mothers." It's about putting the needs of mothers on the public agenda and into the public space of awareness. And to do this requires a combination of research *and* advocacy. O'Reilly talks about the need to integrate these two dimensions. "We're trying to model IMMN on MIRCI, but in a much different way and more activist-based. But I say research *is* activism." After all, "We need the research to figure out what's going on and how to fix it. We need those people doing the papers. And we need the activists to disseminate it and help produce better research. To do better research, you have to ask better questions."

The International Mothers and Mothering Network provides a virtual collective space where over 80 mothering organizations list their web sites, providing an extremely useful information source. Yet through the conferences and active sharing of knowledge and experience, it also provides a very real place of social engagement. It is a visible reminder that the motherhood movement *does* exist, and is only getting stronger. One mother at a time, we *can* collectively change the world.

Works Cited

O'Reilly, Andrea. Personal interview, MIRCI conference on "Mothers and the Economy: The Economics of Mothering," Toronto, October 22, 2010.

43. Mother Outlaws

Building Communities of Empowered Feminist Mothers in the Mother'hood

LINN BARAN

We were conspirators, outlaws from the institution of motherhood; I felt enormously in charge of my life.

—Adrienne Rich

Mother Outlaws recognize that mothers and children benefit when the mother lives her life, and practices mothering, from a position of agency, authority, authenticity and autonomy.

—Andrea O'Reilly (2004)

THE IDEA FOR MOTHER OUTLAWS was initiated in 2004 by Andrea O'Reilly, the founder and director of the Motherhood Initiative for Research and Community Involvement (MIRCI), as an opportunity for self-defined feminist mothers in the Toronto area of Ontario, Canada, to regularly meet with one another to discuss the challenges and triumphs they personally experienced in their endeavors with feminist mothering.

MIRCI is the feminist scholarly and activist organization on mothering and motherhood developed from the former Association for Research on Mothering at York University (1998-2010). Alongside Mother Outlaws, MIRCI houses the *Journal of the Motherhood Initiative* (formerly the *Journal of the Association for Research on Mothering*), the International Mothers and Mothering Network (formerly IMN), The Young Mothers Forum, and Demeter Press.[1]

An integral aspect of MIRCI's community building for researchers, academics, activists, and mothers interested in the topic of motherhood is to provide resources and opportunities for making the connections between "lived mothering" and "examined motherhood," essentially bridging divides between academe and activism. For this reason, Mother Outlaws was considered an important community outreach initiative for MIRCI. The meetings were intended as an opportunity for women to gather together and discuss the links between their own feminist mothering practices and strategies for political and social change.

This chapter will examine the relevance of the image of being a "mother outlaw" to discussions of maternal activism and the wider mother's movement, specifically in relation to current theories on feminist mothering and maternal empowerment. I will highlight the feminist theory and socio-political context for Mother Outlaws' emergence and the outreach initiatives pursued during its history. Finally, I will emphasize how both growing communities of "mother outlaws" who choose to mother from a position informed by their feminism and the increasing feminist scholarship on the theory, practices and politics of an "outlaw motherhood" serve an important role in the motherhood movement of the twenty first century.

Philosophy and Mamafesto

The philosophy and "mamafesto" of Mother Outlaws has always been best described using the two quotes listed on our website and above from Adrienne Rich and Andrea O'Reilly. Published in 1976, Adrienne Rich's classic feminist text, *Of Woman Born: Motherhood as Experience and Institution,* was the first scholarly publication to draw the groundbreaking distinction between two meanings of motherhood, one superimposed upon the other. Rich's central claim in this work was that mothering, "the potential relationship of any woman to her powers of reproduction and to children", should be distinguished from the institution of motherhood, "which aims at ensuring that potential—and all women—shall remain under male control" (13). In making this clear delineation between motherhood and mothering, Rich suggested that in order to realize the transformational possibilities of an empowered and feminist mothering, women must become "*outlaws from the institution of motherhood.*"

Undoubtedly, Rich's distinction between motherhood and mothering remains a central tenet for several feminist scholars suggesting that feminist mothering can lead to both maternal activism and personal empowerment (see Green 2005; O'Reilly 2006, 2008). However, a missing piece for some scholars to Rich's important call for an "outlaw motherhood" was exactly how women could envision, achieve and experience such empowered feminist mothering in their daily lives.

Almost 30 years later, Andrea O'Reilly in her edited collection, *Mother Outlaws: Theories and Practices of Empowered Mothering*, continued the conversation started academically by Adrienne Rich in not only further exploring how the patriarchal construction of motherhood disempowers women, but more importantly how a "mother outlaw" can move beyond "powerless responsibility" to a means of making motherhood their own source of empowerment.

In her introduction to this collection, O'Reilly discusses the need for feminists to define and imagine "empowered mothering, or what can be termed 'outlaw mothering' or 'mothering against motherhood" (2004: 4). O'Reilly acknowledges that Adrienne Rich's distinction between two modes of motherhood is what eventually "enabled feminists to recognize that motherhood is not naturally, necessarily, or inevitably oppressive; a view held by many early second-wave feminists but that if freed from motherhood, mothering could be experienced as a site of empowerment; a location of social change" (2). Furthermore, this collection of essays introduced readers to an alternative model for empowered mothering that was distinguished from patriarchal motherhood, and at the same time made a clear link between Rich's earlier work and what could be envisioned as "mothering against motherhood."

The initial Mother Outlaws mamafesto, so to speak, took into consideration both Adrienne Rich's call for a mode of mothering outside of what she named "the institution of motherhood" and Andrea O'Reilly's suggestions for an empowered feminist mothering that acknowledged a woman's agency, authenticity, authority and autonomy.

These two essential feminist theories were considered the starting points for Mother Outlaws in offering women a place and space to discuss how feminist mothers can rewrite the rules of patriarchal motherhood through a conscious re-creation of a new discourse and practice on empowered mothering. More specifically, a "mother outlaw" was defined during the group's origins as a woman who chooses to negotiate the tensions, fringes and margins of patriarchal culture and its prescriptive ideologies for motherhood by engaging in mothering practices that challenge and resist the status quo.

History

> *Come to Jean Rosenthal's house on Monday night. Talk about your real feelings. Women's group forming.*
>
> —Jane Lazarre

In Jane Lazarre's classic feminist memoir *The Mother Knot*, she discusses how she and her friend posted flyers with the above statement in their neighborhood to reach out to other mothers. In many ways, Mother Outlaws began in 2004 as a similar attempt to build a figurative "Jean Rosenthal's house"; a safe space for feminist mothers to gather as a community and discuss their real feelings about current constructions of motherhood and their personal experiences with mothering in opposition to the prescriptive ideologies that currently prevailed.

In my presentation entitled "Mother Outlaws: Community Outreach in the Margins of the Mother'hood" delivered at a MIRCI conference in 2006, I discussed the important role that community-based family resource programs and child-parent centres have always played in bringing mothers together. My analysis highlighted the grassroot origins of these community-based programs—that is, they were initially organized by mothers and for mothers and often with a feminist analysis during the second wave of feminism—to point out why I believed something essential had gone missing in current operations of predominantly government managed "early years centres." Most specifically, I was concerned that recent trends toward "intensive mothering" (Hays) were being accelerated by neo-liberal discourses that emphasized how parents (albeit mothers) should focus their parenting on "maximizing children's brain development" in order to make them more "school ready" (Wall). It was felt at this time that parenting classes for improving children's cognitive development were not only dominating neighborhood programs but superseding previous opportunities where mothers could meet together, build community, and experience a sense of empowerment by sharing their individual experiences.[2]

Mother Outlaws was conceptualized to fill this community gap and most importantly, to bring back a feminist critical examination of mothering from the margins of the mother'hood.

It has been understood by many feminist scholars of motherhood that having a community or network of supportive peers is essential for women who choose to challenge and resist dominant discourses. In her book, *Feminist Mothers*, Tuula Gordon (1990) emphasizes this point:

> ..."feminist mothers" have been able to develop critical orientations towards societal structures and cultures, stereotypical orientations and myths of motherhood. They do that in the context of exploring how the personal is political, and with the support of the networks of women which place them beyond "collective isolation." (150)

For this reason, the provision of a judgment free space for mothers to share their personal experiences in challenging dominant discourses of motherhood was not only central to the mission of Mother Outlaws, but also built on the history of earlier feminist consciousness raising groups of the women's movement. In speaking collectively about how personal mothering challenges are linked and connected to larger social and political structures, Mother Outlaws strived to operate on the level of "changing minds to change the world." The key theories of "outlaw motherhood" as envisioned and expressed by both Adrienne Rich and Andrea O'Reilly were introduced to participants.

And, in building on the work of feminist theories that call for a "transformational consciousness" to mobilize mothers into "inclusive maternity coalitions" (O'Reilly, Porter and Short), the Mother Outlaw meetings were designed to transform the way feminist women talked to one another about their mothering experiences and to develop strategies of community activism that could lead to making life better for all mothers.

The Mother Outlaws group continued to meet in this format under my leadership and coordination as the Community Outreach Liaison for MIRCI. Initially, the Mother Outlaws' meetings were very casual in format and held in participants' homes. The gatherings involved potluck dinners and allowed women the opportunity to share their personal stories of feminist mothering in a supportive group setting while elucidating connective key themes of both struggle and triumph. Over time, the group meetings organically evolved into more specific discussions on current motherhood issues from a feminist perspective, often with an invited guest speaker on a proposed topic.

In many ways, I feel this directional change of Mother Outlaws was a key evolution of the process of feminist praxis—feminism in action. As expressed by Fiona Joy Green, "feminist praxis occurs when women participate in the recurrent

Linn Baran, Andrea O'Reilly, and Mary Kay Blakely at launch of the Mother Outlaws' Speakers Series, 2007. Photo: Renée Knapp

cycle of integrating theory (ways of understanding the world) with action (ways of speaking and acting in the world) and of also incorporating action and theory with the result of creating change in society" (2009a: 21).

In celebration of Mother's Day and the International Day of Families, *Mother Outlaws* hosted a panel in 2007 that was held at a local community centre and open to the general public. This panel was entitled "Redefining Motherhood and Family for the 21st Century" and speakers at the event included Joanna Radbord, Andrea O'Reilly, Diana Gustafson, and D. Memee Lavell Harvard. The event drew wide attendance and interest for the discussions about lesbian mothering, feminist mothering, non-residential mothering and aboriginal mothering.

Due to the success of this panel, it was mutually decided by both myself and Andrea O'Reilly that Mother Outlaws could begin to operate on a wider and more public scale. The idea was that Mother Outlaws could move from "consciousness raising" to actually "raising the roof." That is, there was a growing momentum amongst participants to move discussions from reflection to action. Mother Outlaws' events were subsequently held during the annual spring and fall MIRCI conferences in Toronto, and were open to local and international conference participants. Most importantly, a continuing Mother Outlaws' Speakers Series was designed that would feature presentations and panels by invited guest speakers on various current topics related to feminist motherhood. The main intention for the Speakers' Series was to hold free forums in accessible community venues in the Toronto area that would be publicized widely and open to the general public. At the same time, it was felt that a recognizable image needed to be created for Mother Outlaws. A logo and t-shirt design were designed by myself and Toronto-based artist Vanessa Rieger. I will discuss more about this image in the community outreach section below.

The Mother Outlaws Speakers' Series (along with our t-shirts) was officially launched in October 2007 at MIRCI's annual fall conference with invited guest speaker Mary Kay Blakely delivering a presentation entitled "Raising Outlaws: Beyond the Boundaries of the 'Good' Mother."

Over the next two years, the Mother Outlaws Speakers' Series brought together both local and international scholars, activists, authors and artists to present their work at community-based panels that included the following topics:

- •Mommy Blogs: Mothers, Feminism and the Blogosphere
- •The Mommy Wars: The Rhetoric and the Reality
- •Mining, Mothering and Mending Women's Bodies in the Democratic Republic of Congo
- •The Challenges and Rewards of "Other Mothering"
- •Navigating Work and Family: Dad's Experiences
- •Care work and Caregiving
- •New Frontiers in Maternal Activism
- •Spiritual Mothering
- •Ancient Birth Goddesses and their Symbols
- •Feminist Motherlines: Connections and Dis/Connections across Generations
- •The Mothers' Movement … Moving Forward.

Additionally, with widespread curiosity continuing to grow about Mother Outlaws via social media outlets, I began receiving several inquiries about the potential establishment of Mother Outlaws groups in other cities and countries.

One particularly memorable post about our community initiative was written in 2006 by feministmoms.blogspot.com, which defines itself as "a blog of resources about the emerging mothers' movement as well as personal thoughts about being a feminist mother." The entire post is listed below:

> **Bay Area Needs a Mother Outlaws Group**
> It appears as though Toronto is the place to be for feminist moms. Not only is Toronto the host of the only research center dedicated to the study of feminist mothering, the Association for Research on Mothering, but it also has an active feminist mothers group, Mother Outlaws. I have been in awe of what the Mother Outlaws are doing. These women get together to discuss raising children according to their feminist principles and give each other advice and political inspiration. We need this in the Bay Area!! Email me if you would like to start a Mother Outlaws group.
>
> If you are lucky enough to live in the Toronto area, here are the de-

> tails about their group: "Mother Outlaws recognize that mothers and children benefit when the mother lives her life, and practices mothering, from a position of agency, authority, authenticity and autonomy." Mother Outlaws are community gatherings in the Toronto area for women interested in: Discussing current motherhood issues from a feminist perspective—Sharing the links between their own mothering practices and social change.
>
> The gatherings occur at members' homes in the Toronto area for a potluck dinner and informal discussion on a specific topic or at scheduled special events.
>
> **Real Options (Part 2): Mothering and the Politics of Choice**
> We are currently witnessing an interesting new way of speaking about "choice" for women, their families and their children. At increasing levels, stories in the mainstream media focus on mothers choosing to "opt-out" of participation in the workplace and present work/family issues in an "either/or" way. The way "choice" is often used in such debates often has the effect of reducing the number of available options. In addition, if the real constraints on women's choices are ignored, then the effect is to individualize problems and to erase or minimize social responsibilities. Of course, there are alternatives to seeing mothers outside of the media fuelled "mommy wars." This meeting will allow women to share their own "real" stories on the choices, decisions, and negotiations they have made as mothers seeking work/family balance. Stories that go unreported if unspoken. For more information and to RSVP, please contact: Linn Baran, Mother Outlaws Co-coordinator.

In 2009, Mother Outlaws and MIRCI did re-establish, alongside our other community initiatives, the original informal discussion group in Toronto to be held regularly every month in participants' homes (see "Toronto Feminist Mothers" by Tania Jivraj in this collection).

Community Outreach: Creating a Recognizable Image and Representation for Mother Outlaws

A key component of Mother Outlaws remains community outreach in both spreading the word about our events and also establishing our title as a recognizable image of "feminist mothering against the institution of motherhood." That is, our intention in 2007 was that Mother Outlaws could become a cultural signifier of mothers who are overtly feminist and proudly activist.

In several ways, the relationship between motherhood and feminism continues to be largely misrepresented in media depictions and popular culture. The growing discourse of how "cool" or "hip" it is to be a "bad mother" or "desperate housewife" clearly was not addressing the real experiences of many feminist mothers.

Mother Outlaws at the Toronto SlutWalk, April 3, 2011. Photo by Kim Breland.

The Mother Outlaws' logo was designed basically with the focus of creating an accurate visual representation of the statement "This is REALLY what a Feminist Mother Looks Like." I worked on creating a logo in collaboration with my niece and Toronto-based artist Vanessa Rieger to conceptualize feminist mothering as both a lived resistance and proud defiance to the restrictive social norms of "good" motherhood.

As previously mentioned, a "mother outlaw" is defined as a woman who chooses to engage in mothering practices that challenge and resist the status quo. For this reason, my creative idea was to deliberately "play" with the imagery of a "women's room" and more specifically signage that depicted mother/child and breastfeeding friendly spaces. I wanted to suggest that an alternative "space and place" can exist for mothers to feel empowered for themselves and not just to benefit their child. This final suggestion in our imagery was paramount to emphasize Mother Outlaws as a "mother-centered" expression of feminist motherhood. The figure depicted in our logo also was a testament to the belief that mothers can find "room" to practice agency and resistance in their daily lives that will lead to personal empowerment.

The figure in our logo is without the stereotypical "skirt" that often denotes women from men in space configurations for the reasons of disrupting gender categorizations. Secondly, "she" is holding a child but not necessarily breast feeding to suggest both that mothering is not a biological imperative nor one that can only be experienced by biological mothers. And finally, and most importantly, in emphasizing the potential for empowerment in resisting dominant discourses of motherhood, our figure is raising her "well-biceped" arm in a statement of defiant personal strength

In several ways, I feel the Mother Outlaws' image truly "rocks the cradle!" The oft repeated sentiment that "the hand that rocks the cradle rules the world," although comforting, still implies a powerless responsibility to mothers in patriarchal constructions of motherhood. In echoing the title of Andrea O'Reilly's (2006) collection of personal essays, in order to *truly rock the cradle*, connections must be made amongst motherhood, feminism, and the possibility for an empowered mothering. That is, Mother Outlaws[3] is a movement to change minds, change signs, and then change the world.

Our Mother Outlaws logo and t-shirts continues to draw wide interest. Their presence at several activist events including International Women's Day marches and rallies continue to initiate positive responses about their implied meaning.

The Importance of Mother Outlaws to the Motherhood Movement of the Twenty-First Century

In conclusion, I feel that as a cultural signifier for the empowering process of resistance to dominant discourses of motherhood, Mother Outlaws has achieved a recognizable image and reputation in the feminist mothering community. Many feminist mothers and feminist scholars of motherhood have long recognized that motherhood, as it is lived and represented in patriarchal culture, can be deeply oppressive to women. The importance of Mother Outlaws is that it offers an alternative view of motherhood, one that acknowledges the potential for maternal empowerment as well as how resistance and maternal agency can lead towards social and political change.

When mothers who are feminists come together to discuss how motherhood and feminism intersect in their personal and professional lives, they are not only moving out of collective isolation and finding validation for their maternal practices and scholarship, they are indeed challenging and changing patriarchal motherhood.

I believe the motherhood movement of the twenty-first century is very similar to the women's movement of the 1960s and the 1970s. Both are instrumental in making long lasting transformations to patriarchal belief systems. Furthermore, in moving beyond the critique of patriarchal motherhood to discuss and situate feminist mothering practices as not only sites of resistance that are empowering to women and children but transformative to the current socio-political landscape, the theory of an "outlaw motherhood" is a ground breaking initiative for the future theorizing that continues in the motherhood movement.

By engaging in a feminist praxis of thoughtful reflection and action on current motherhood issues, Mother Outlaws transforms the current constructions of motherhood and allows for an "outlaw mothering" to be realized and validated in popular discourse, political initiatives and academic scholarship.

Recent feminist literature on the importance of "mothering against motherhood" (Green 2009b; Horwitz; O'Reilly 2010) continues to open the way for future scholars, mothering activists and mothers themselves to integrate more fully the practices of being a "mother outlaw" into their scholarship, activism, and daily lives.

In closing, I would like to offer the statement made by Shawna Lewkowitz, a mother in London, Ontario who wrote the following in her blog about her own first Mother Outlaws group meeting:

> *I absolutely loved having this group of women in my living room—especially when my young daughters returned home with my partner after an evening out. Having strong, passionate women sending that energy out into our home felt right, real and radicalizing. I want my daughters to be surrounded by strong women who advocate for change and for that energy to surround and influence them. They already have this just by nature of our community, but bringing a group of women dedicated to feminism and speaking that into their space made it feel more tangible.*

[1]Although the Association for Research on Mothering (ARM) at York University was the initial site for Mother Outlaws' emergence in 2004, ARM eventually evolved in 2010 to become the Motherhood Initiative for Research and Community Involvement (MIRCI). For purposes of clarity in this chapter, the acronym MIRCI will be used consistently when explaining the origins and history of Mother Outlaws. [2]I would like to acknowledge and thank Andrea Gordon, family issues reporter with *The Toronto Star*, for her continuous support over the years for the mission of Mother Outlaws, ARM and MIRCI through several of her newspaper columns and personal blog posts.

[3]For more information about Mother Outlaws, see out new website: <www.motheroutlaws.org.>

Works Cited

Baran, Linn. "Mother Outlaws: Community Outreach in the Margins of the Mother'hood." Presentation at panel Supporting Mothers and Motherwork: Agency and Resistance., Association for Research on Mothering 10th Anniversary Conference: The Motherlode. Toronto, 2006.

Blakely, Mary Kay. "Raising Outlaws: Beyond the Boundaries of the 'Good' Mother." Special Mother Outlaws Event, Association for Research on Mothering Conference: Maternal Health and Well-Being. Toronto, 2007.

feministmoms.blogspot.com. "Bay Area Needs a Mother Outlaws Group." Blog post. 2009

Gordon, Andrea. "'Hangout' still holds magic." *The Toronto Star* December 4, 2006.

Gordon, Tuula. *Feminist Mothers.* New York: New York University Press, 1990.

Green, Fiona Joy. "Feminist Mothering: Challenging Gender Inequality by Resisting the Institution of Motherhood and Raising Children to be Critical Agents of Social Change." *Socialist Studies* 1.1 (2005): 83-99.

Green, Fiona Joy. "Coping with Change: Integrating Feminist Praxis with Maternal Health Promotion and Education." *Journal for the Association for Research on Mothering* 11.1 (2009a):11-25.

Green, Fiona Joy. *Feminist Mothering in Theory and Practice, 1985-1995: A Study in Transformative Politics.* NewYork: Edwin Mellen Press, 2009b.

Gustafson, Diana. "To Be or Not to Be: Questioning the Decision to be a Non-Resident Mother." Presentation at panel Unbecoming Mothers: Redefining Motherhood and Family for the 21st Century. Toronto, 2007.

Hays, Sharon. *The Cultural Contradictions of Motherhood.* New Haven: Yale University Press, 1998.

Horwitz, Erika. *Through the Maze of Motherhood: Empowered Mothers Speak.* Toronto: Demeter Press, forthcoming 2011.

Lazarre, Jane. *The Mother Knot.* New York: McGraw-Hill, 1976.

Lavell-Harvard, D. Memee. "The (Ab)Original Mother Outlaw: Celebrating Traditional Aboriginal Culture as a Source of Modern Feminine Power." Presentation at panel Unbecoming Mothers: Redefining Motherhood and Family for the 21st Century. Toronto, 2007.

Lewkowitz, Shawna. *doulamama.wordpress.com*. Personal blog, 2009.

O'Reilly, Andrea. *Mother Outlaws: Theories and Practices of Empowered Mothering.* Toronto: Women's Press, 2004.

O'Reilly, Andrea, Marie Porter, and Patricia Short. *Motherhood: Power and Oppression.* Toronto: Women's Press, 2005.

O'Reilly, Andrea. *Rocking the Cradle: Thoughts on Motherhood, Feminism and The Possibility of Empowered Mothering.* Toronto: Demeter Press, 2006:

O'Reilly, Andrea. "Worth It in the End: The Rewards and Risks of Feminist Mothering." Presentation at panel Unbecoming Mothers: Redefining Motherhood and Family for the 21st Century. Toronto, 2007.

O'Reilly, Andrea. *Feminist Mothering.* Albany: SUNY Press, 2008.

O'Reilly, Andrea. "Outlaw(ing) Motherhood: A Theory and Politic ofMaternal Empowerment for the Twenty-first Century." *Motherhood at the 21st Century: Experience, Identity, Policy, Agency*. Ed. Andrea O'Reilly. New York: Columbia University Press, 2010. 366-380.

Radbord, Joanna. "*Lesbian Mothers and the Law.*" Presentation at panel Unbecoming Mothers: Redefining Motherhood and Family for the 21st Century. Toronto, 2007.

Rich, Adrienne. *Of Woman Born: Motherhood as Experience and Institution.* 1976. New York: Norton, 1986.

Wall, Glenda. "Is Your Child's Brain Potential Maximized? Mothering in an Age of New Brain Research." *Atlantis* 28.2 (2004): 41-50.

44.
The Mothers Movement Online

RACHEL SUTZ PIENTA

THE MOTHERS MOVEMENT ONLINE (MMO) (2003-2008) was an independent, online-only media project featuring essays, commentary, interviews, reviews, and fact-based reporting on the politics of women, work and family in the United States (www.mothersmovement.org). While the website is still accessible, it is not currently active. It exists in an archival mode for informational purposes. Prior to 1999, there was little mainstream reporting on the work and family balancing issues faced by working mothers beyond the media-driven, somewhat sensationalistic popular culture depictions of the "mommy wars."

Judith Stadtman Tucker conceptualized the Mothers Movement Online as a forum for online grassroots organizing that would provide a venue to address such issues as global work and families, maternal employment issues, and the economic destinies of working women. Tucker had been part of a discussion group via her involvement with "Mothers and More."At one point, the discussion group involved 200 women, and Tucker kept hearing stories about workplace experiences that particularly focused on facing gender inequality after having children. She soon realized that little research and few resources were available to women facing workplace gender inequality challenges after having children, and the Mothers Movement Online evolved to fill the information void.

History and Background

The decision to launch MMO was an offshoot of Judith Stadtman Tucker's previous work with Mothers & More, a non-profit organization comprised of a nationally-coordinated network of local chapters focused on "support and advocacy" for professional class mothers transitioning in and out of the full-time paid workforce. In online forums and face-to-face discussions, Mothers & More members related their personal encounters with structural and cultural barriers to combining childrearing with a satisfying career, and expressed frustration with the disconnect between the promise of equal opportunities for women and the lack of practical support for maternal employment in the United States. As a result of such group discussions and related program planning, the Mothers & More Advocacy leaders adopted the terminology of "the motherhood penalty," "work-life conflict," and "the mothers' movement" to describe mothers' discontent and their desire to improve social conditions that limit mothers' employment opportunities and life satisfaction.

National news outlets periodically covered trends in maternal employment—typically through the lens of the so-called "Mommy Wars"—but prior to 2006, reporting on public opinion and social research supporting the need for national action on paid parental leave and other "family friendly" policies was rare. As the Senior Manager of Mothers & More's Advocacy program, Tucker suggested that the organization could take the lead by publishing an online resource directory with links to news items and public interest research reports to expand popular awareness of "mothers' issues" and the pressing need for policy reform. In the interest of building momentum for a grassroots social movement, she prepared a formal proposal and recommended that this information stream be fully accessible to the public, rather than offered as a proprietary, members-only service. Ultimately, the team concluded that devoting resources to an open-source media project was inconsistent with Mothers & More's goals and operating principles. Tucker then decided to launch the project on her own, and the first edition of the Mothers Movement Online (MMO) was published in April 2003.

Although several independent media projects featuring maternal narrative and social commentary launched around the same time, the MMO was unique for its focus on exploring motherhood as a political status and emphasizing the need for collective action to achieve social change. In the late 1990s, cultural and social messages in the United States would have suggested the mistaken idea that the problems of gender inequality for working mothers had been resolved. The efforts that began with the passage of Title VII in the 1960s and culminated with the passage of the *Family Medical Leave Act* during the Clinton years may have led many to believe that working mothers had achieved occupational parity. However, as Tucker herself discovered after the birth of her own children, the world had not entirely changed for working mothers—despite landmark legislation aimed at addressing gender inequality. More work was needed to address the structural and institutional issues that continued to perpetuate gender based economic disparities. Tucker also recognized that cultural issues and prevalent gender ideologies had to be examined to fully address the challenges faced by working mothers.

To achieve the organization's goals, Tucker applied herself to the task of translating the conceptualization into actual operational practices. The mission of MMO was reflected in the core editorial standards: MMO did not publish parenting advice or reviews of parenting advice books, and only reviewed maternal memoirs that offered a meaningful feminist analysis of the author's experience or otherwise sought to disrupt the dominant ideology of motherhood. Personal essays featured on the site had to address some political aspect of motherhood and validate the diversity of maternal experience. Commentary and articles were fact-checked for accuracy. The publication's guiding philosophy was that motherhood is a complex and important topic which is worthy of serious political analysis, and content was selected to popularize that perspective. Another important goal was to report on the findings of relevant social research and create a bridge between the academic work on women and working families and the potential movement activists.

Tucker (2011) said,

> Overall, I saw MMO as having a central role in documenting the political arguments, ideological conflicts, and activities of the emerging 21st century mothers' movement. I was concerned that the next generation of mothers would hit the same roadblocks as my own cohort of mothers, and be just as perplexed that status quo had never been challenged. I wanted to ensure there was a record of the thinking and debates happening in the maternal community. As was true for feminist analysis of motherhood in the second wave, a lot of this will vanish from view but hopefully future generations of mothers will be able to find some remnant of it and it will help them understand their own experience is part of a greater historical arc.

The Mothers Movement Online worked to provide a forum for dialogue and a venue for framing and discussing the discourse on and around the issues faced by working mothers. Furthermore, MMO also published writing that proposed improved policy solutions for American women.

Purpose of the Organization and Activities

As a media project, the MMO did not have members—only readers and contributing writers. Before the site was moved to archive mode in 2008, it attracted over 30,000 readers a month. Most were from North America, but MMO also had readers in Europe and Australia. Most of the contributing writers were college educated and were predominantly white, but the site encouraged and included a diverse range of maternal voices.

All content was (and is) free—there is no registration required for access. Also, there is no advertising on the site. There was no active marketing for the site, but as the MMO grew in popularity Tucker was asked to give media interviews and received some exposure for the site in that manner (MMO articles were also mentioned and quoted in the mainstream press, which increased visibility and traffic). Readers generally came to the site through web searches and links. In its heyday, MMO was one of the top ten non-commercial motherhood sites so it had a fairly good ranking in Google and other search applications.

The Future of Mothers Movement Online

By 2007-2008, there was more and better mainstream news coverage of women, work and family, and the original impetus for MMO was less relevant. At that time, Tucker personally also reached the conclusion that more writing and talking about the motherhood problem was unlikely to activate mothers for change. Tucker (2011) stated that,

> For the mothers' movement to make the transition from concept to collective action, we would need to develop the capacity for strategic political organizing. As I turned my focus to learning the best practices of grassroots organizing, I had less time for planning and publishing the site. In late 2008, I discontinued adding new content to the site, although all editions are still available as an online archive.

Challenges Faced by the Organization

Like many independent feminist publishing projects from the second wave, the issue of sustainability was difficult to resolve. As a self-funded project with no paid staff, the life of the MMO was entirely dependent on Tucker's ability to feed and nurture it, which was a full-time job. Tucker explained that when she decided that she needed to focus on a different path to movement building, it was impossible to keep the MMO going. It was both a philosophical and strategic decision to keep MMO free of advertising and subscriber fees, but it also limited avenues for funding the work of writing, editing, and producing the site.

The Mothers Movement Online and the Motherhood Movement of the Twenty-first Century

Amber Kinser cited Tucker's website The Mothers Movement Online as an example of "work that explores how contemporary mothers have used technology to support and grow women's power in mothering knowledge" (5). While the MMO site has been dormant but available in archive form since 2008, Tucker remains a vocal advocate on mothering and work issues. In January 2010, in an article for WomensMedia.com, Tucker commented on the barriers that working women with children still face as in the form of policy shortfalls and motherhood penalties:

> Maternity remains a significant drag factor on women's earnings and employment outcomes—a phenomenon work-life researchers call "hitting the maternal wall." Legal experts note the recent increase in litigation resulting from employer discrimination against workers with caregiving responsibilities, a pattern known as "family responsibilities discrimination," or FRD. FRD can be as blatant as a supervisor telling a worker she can either be a good employee or a good mother but not both at the same time, or as insidious as reassigning a talented achiever to a dead-end job when she returns from maternity leave.

In 2011, American women find themselves under attack from an increasingly conservative Congress. Across the nation, state governments have also experienced conservative shifts that have translated into anti-women policies such as cuts to maternal health care and reductions in childcare subsidies. The gains seen prior to 2008 have been experiencing steady erosions in the intervening years as the policy pendulum has reversed. Working women with families now find themselves battling to hold onto healthcare and pension contributions while other key support services are scheduled for the legislative and executive chopping blocks at the local, state, and federal levels across the nation.

The enduring legacy of The Mothers Movement Online is the foundation it provided for continued advocacy and organizing efforts. MMO, under the leadership of Judith Stadtman Tucker, helped to establish a voice for women on issues related to mothering, wage earning, and the world of work. Prior to the establishment of online forums and information sharing conduits such as MMO, the notions of mothers as workers was often reduced to a cartoon caricature or used as a plot device in a Hollywood film.

Susan Douglas, in *Enlightened Sexism,* broached the topic of women and work in light of the American recession in the latter half of the last decade, circa 2007 and later. In 2011, the new economic picture generated by the extended American recession has created an income structure in which unprecedented numbers of single mothers and married women have become the sole income for their families. The messages of MMO in the new economic reality have become more salient than ever, as more women find themselves navigating the world of work while balancing family concerns in precarious financial times.

While the presidential election of 2008 brought issues of motherhood and the world of work to the forefront of national discourse, the years after the election of President Obama would see women lose critical ground as a conservative pendulum shift gained momentum after the 2010 midterm elections. At the time this chapter went to press, the national discourse included a media battle on breast feeding between former vice presidential candidate Sarah Palin and First Lady Michelle Obama along with pending legislation that ranged from criminalizing miscarriages to redefining "forcible rape." The "mommy blogs" and mother-focused websites that emerged in the wake of The Mothers Movement Online face the stubborn obstacles that persist from the twentieth century as well as new challenges to surmount in the twenty-first century. The movement is far from over.

Works Cited

Douglas, S. *Enlightened Sexism: The Seductive Message that Feminism's Work is Done.* New York: Times Books. 2010.

Kinser, A. Motherhood and Feminism. Berkeley, CA: Seal Press. 2010.

Tucker, J. "Personal Interview." February 2011.

Tucker, J. "Uncle Sam: No Friend to Working Mothers." *Women's Media.* 2010.

Web. <http://www.womensmedia.com/balance/206-uncle-sam-no-friend-to-working-mothers.html>. Accessed: February 21, 2011.

V.
Violence, Militarism, War and Peace

45.
How to Mobilize One Million Mothers
The Million Mom March and the Power of the Social Network

RACHEL SUTZ PIENTA

THE MILLION MOM MARCH BEGAN as the brainchild of Donna Dees-Thomases during the summer of 1999. Influenced by the activism of Sarah Brady and galvanized by the horror of the Granada Hills, California gun massacre, Dees-Thomases conceived a mission statement for what would become a national movement to bring together mothers across the country to advocate for and with victims of gun trauma for saner gun laws (Dees-Thomases, Hendrie and Feinstein). Estimates put the crowd that gathered to protest gun violence and advocate for stricter gun control in Washington, DC, on Mother's Day, May 14, 2000 somewhere between 400,000 and 700,000 (Meagher and DiQuinzio).

In 1999, other victims of gun trauma had launched another national campaign that offered a grassroots solution to the American gun epidemic. The Bell Campaign, modeled after Mothers Against Drunk Driving (MADD), was created to prevent gun death and injury, and to support victims of gun trauma. Organizers of the Million Mom March and the Bell Campaign would join forces in 1999 under one umbrella as the Million Mom March. After the Mother's Day rally in May 2000, the Million Mom March merged with the Brady Campaign to Prevent Gun Violence (DiQuinzio).

Philosophy, Purpose, and Mission

In the U.S., gun control is a partisan issue that tends to divide along political lines. The Republican Party supports the rights of gun owners as written according to the Second Amendment of the United States Constitution. Members of the Democratic Party tend to favor stringent gun control. In 2010, political newcomers in the form of the Tea Party also became a force in the arena of gun rights discourse.

The origins of America's longstanding love-hate relationship with firearms are rooted deeply in this young nation's colonial past. The right to bear arms was codified in the Second Amendment to the United States Constitution, and the Revolutionary era patriots who would become the nation's forefathers after independence had been won with guns. An inherent part of the American national identity is based on the historical foundation of hard won independence from imperial tyranny and the perception that the firearms of patriots carried the day.

Fast forward over two centuries later to the United States of the present day. Gun control has become a polarizing political issue. Organizations such as the National Rifle Association (NRA) influence national elections and public policy with strategic financial infusions and well-organized media efforts to lobby for gun owners' Second Amendment Rights, while gun control advocacy groups such as the Brady Campaign organize and lobby for stricter regulation and stronger government oversight.

History

In 1999, victims of gun trauma launched a national campaign that offered a grassroots solution to the American gun epidemic. The Bell Campaign, modeled after Mothers Against Drunk Driving (MADD), was created to prevent gun death and injury, and to support victims of gun trauma. To support victims of gun trauma, the Campaign offered information, education, and victim advocacy to survivors of gun trauma. As chapters developed, members offered compassionate support through self-help groups and resource referral.

In recent years, political campaigns and politicians expanded the gun control versus Second Amendment rhetoric in the wake of well-publicized shootings and proposed ballot initiatives. Since 2006, a global movement to limit the trafficking of small arms has gained impetus in the form of the International Arms Trade Treaty via the United Nations. Under President Bush, the United States cast the lone dissenting vote (172-1) against a measure that would implement tracing and controls to limit the illicit trade in small arms and light weapons. In 2009, under President Obama, Secretary of State Hilary Clinton announced a reversal of United States' policy and issued a statement in support of the treaty.

The treaty is opposed by American gun rights advocacy groups such as the conservative U.S. think tank the Heritage Foundation, which said that it would not restrict the access of "dictators and terrorists" to arms but would be used to reduce the ability of democracies such as Israel to defend their people (Mohammed). The National Rifle Association, one of the most influential gun rights advocacy organizations and a powerful lobbying group in its own right, has also opposed the treaty. While the treaty addresses the illicit global trade of small arms, it does not limit the ability of sovereign nations to regulate gun ownership within its borders—as opponents seem to fear.

In Pennsylvania, gun control briefly dominated the public discourse in the 2010 governor's race after a shooting in Philadelphia made national headlines. The shooter in the September 12, 2010 murder held a Florida gun permit that had been obtained via an Internet application—an application procedure that would be identified as the "Florida Loophole" by gun control advocates.

In Florida, where gun permitting is administered by the Commission on Agriculture and Consumer Services, the gun rights issue was not addressed by either candidate for that seat—even though crimes committed with Florida gun

CA Chaper activists, Chief Dunbar, community outreach event.

permits were making headlines in Pennsylvania and other states. However, the Republican candidate and ultimate victor in the race, Congressman Adam Putnam, had been endorsed by and received a sizable campaign contribution from the NRA. Speaking as the current executive director of Unified Sportsmen of Florida and past president of the NRA, Florida resident Marion Hammer stated, "Adam's solid pro-sportsmen, pro-Second Amendment, pro-freedom record has earned him our endorsement and our gratitude. No other candidate in this race has the background of dedicated legislative service that he has demonstrated to the cause of freedom, the Second Amendment and protection of constitutional rights" (qtd. in Remington). Putnam's stated stance assured Floridians he would be a staunch advocate on behalf of gun owners, "I have always fought to protect the Second Amendment, the rights for self-defense and have sponsored anti-crime legislation throughout my career. As commissioner, one of the most important responsibilities is protecting Floridians' right to carry, and I will ensure that eligible citizens who seek a concealed weapons license receive the most efficient service possible" (Remington). Elected on the same ticket in 2010, Florida governor Rick Scott also assured gun owners he would advocate for their interests, "As a member of the NRA and a hunter, I'm a strong supporter of the Second Amendment. I will protect our fundamental right to keep and bear arms."

While Florida's governor and the Commissioner of Agriculture enjoy the support of the NRA and the hunters, a number of Florida's mayors have joined a national coalition for gun control, Mayors Against Illegal Guns, led by New York City Mayor Michael Bloomberg. The policy gap between the stance adopted by

CA Chapters speak at press conference on AB 2235 9-1-09

CA Chapters with Governor at signing ceremony for Assembly Bill 962 15-15-09

local leaders and the executive branch of the state is emblematic of the American cultural and political divide on the gun issue. The Mayors' coalition, like the Brady Campaign and the Million Mom March, advocates for responsible gun ownership via government regulation,

> As mayors, our highest responsibility is to enforce the law and to protect the people we serve. One of the most difficult challenges we face in meeting this responsibility is preventing criminals from illegally obtaining guns and using them. The issue of illegal guns is not conservative or liberal; it is an issue of law and order—and life or death. We support the Second

Amendment and the rights of citizens to own guns. We recognize that the vast majority of gun dealers and gun owners carefully follow the law. (Mayors Against Illegal Guns)

In January 2011, gun control and gun rights would dominate the public discourse and once again make headlines after the Tucson, Arizona shooting of Congresswoman Gabrielle Giffords during a public appearance at a Safeway grocery store that left six dead and injured 18 others.

The impetus for what would eventually become the Million Mom March began in 1994, on the streets of New York City, when Mary Leigh Blek's son Matthew, a 19-year-old college freshman was murdered on a street in Manhattan (Kelly 216). Mary Leigh Blek, a continent away in California, was a former nurse and stay-at-home wife prior to her son's death. Her son's death motivated her to work for sound public gun policy while she learned to adjust to life without Matthew.

She would later learn that the 15-year-old who killed her son, Matt, got the gun via a street purchase. It was determined that the gun had been first purchased in a Southern state with more lenient gun laws and then sold illegally out of a car trunk in a New York City neighborhood. She wanted people to know, she said, "If it happened to me, it could happen to you" (Blek).

What she said next, though, and what she has done in the 16 years since her son's murder, is remarkable. Blek explained her motivation to turn her personal tragedy into a national movement to advocate on behalf of victims of gun violence: "The idea—the death of your child—is so sudden, so senseless, you want to stand on rooftops and shout so somebody else's child gets to live."

Blek, supporting what she terms "common-sense gun laws," rather than a total gun ban, began to organize locally with other parents who had lost children to gun violence (Kelly 216). Her organization, modeled after Mothers Against Drunk Driving (MADD), would eventually grow into the Bell Campaign, as an organization devoted to preventing gun death and injury, and to supporting victims of gun trauma (Bell Campaign; Kelly 216). Early group activities included aiding victims after the Columbine shootings in Colorado. The group expanded its efforts nationwide in 1999 with the aid of a $4.3 million grant from the Richard and Rhoda Goldman Fund. She first organized the Bell Campaign with the intent of organizing mothers against gun violence. The organization would later join forces with Donna Dees-Thomases' Million Mom March group—Dees-Thomases' own response to the mass shooting at the North Valley Jewish Community Center in Granada Hills, California.

Later, the organizations would merge with the Brady Campaign. Today, Blek's ongoing advocacy goals and work include bringing accountability into gun ownership and having a background check for all guns.

Activities of the Organization

One of the most visible activities of the organization was the march organized

Lie-In demonstration at Chico State, 2008

in 2000 by Donna Dees-Thomases. Dees-Thomases founded the Million Mom March, and would eventually collaborate and combine efforts with Blek, to bring people to Washington, DC, as a highly visible political event with the idea that concurrent marches would be held in cities across the nation. After Blek agreed to the union, the organization began to grow into a movement (Kelly 216) that would later join forces with the Brady Campaign.

In 2004, the Million Mom March staged the "Halt the Assault Tour" to promote the renewal of the Federal Ban on Assault Weapons (DiQuinzio). While the Million Mom March lost that battle when Congress failed to renew the ban in the fall of 2004, the war against gun violence would continue with the work of grassroots chapters and the national advocacy efforts under the auspices of the Brady Campaign.

In 2010, the Million Mom March organized a national petition campaign against Starbucks in response to a corporate policy that would allow gun rights advocates to meet while exercising rights to the open-carry of firearms in the coffee houses. The petition stated the following:

> Dear Starbucks,
>
> I demand that Starbucks stand up for the safety of your customers and bar guns in your establishments. Guns don't belong in restaurants and coffee shops where children and families gather. It puts families and law enforcement at risk. Reverse your corporate decision. (Brady Campaign)

Efforts to protest Starbucks' corporate support of open-carry laws included demonstrations by Million Mom March chapter members at Starbucks' locations in their local communities.

The organization also celebrated the tenth anniversary of the first Million Mom March at the Brady's Center Gala at the National Museum for Women in the Arts in May 2010.

Following the Roadmap Created by Mothers Against Drunk Driving

The mothers who coalesced to form what became the Million Mom March used a grassroots strategy modeled after Mothers Against Drunk Driving. Mothers Against Drunk Driving is an organization considered to be one of the greatest grassroots organizing successes in the United States and was also started by a grieving mother. In May 1980, Candy Lightner's thirteen-year old-daughter, Cari, was struck and killed in a hit and run accident by a drunk driver while she was walking to a church carnival. In the aftermath of Cari's death, Candy Lightner and her friends would learn that there were no laws to address drunk driving in California and few legal avenues for victims to pursue in the court systems. MADD's first office was located in Cari Lightner's old bedroom (MADD).

As would happen 20 years later with the Bell Campaign and the Million Mom March, a movement that began on one side of the nation developed a face and a presence on the other side of the country when Cindy Lamb, the mother of Laura, a five-month-old drunk driving victim, the nation's youngest paraplegic, started a MADD chapter in Maryland (MADD). In October 1980, Candy Lightner and Cindy Lamb became the national faces for Mothers Against Drunk Driving after speaking together at a press conference on Capitol Hill.

By 1982, Mothers Against Drunk Driving had grown to 100 chapters nationwide. That same year, with Executive Order 12358, President Ronald Reagan created the Presidential Commission on Drunk Driving and charged it to undertake the following mandates: (a) heighten public awareness of the seriousness of the drunk driving problem; (b) persuade States and communities to attack the drunk driving problem in a more organized and systematic manner, including plans to eliminate bottlenecks in the arrest, trial and sentencing process that impair the effectiveness of many drunk driving laws; (c) encourage State and local officials and organizations to accept and use the latest techniques and methods to solve the problem; and (d) generate public support for increased enforcement of State and local drunk driving laws. Later that year, Congress passed a federal bill awarding highway funds to states with anti-drunk driving efforts. MADD's advocacy efforts would ultimately result in passage of the *Uniform Drinking Age Act* in 1984—legislation that would deny highway funds to states that did not raise the drinking age to 21.

Since 1984, economists, policy analysts, and the American Medical Association have expressed differing opinions on the effectiveness of the series of laws that became known as MLDA21s (see Corlin; Trapp). However, regardless of differing viewpoints about the association between the reducing teen alcohol consumption and reductions in traffic fatalities, the influence of MADD as an advocacy organization that changed how an entire nation's legal system and concomitantly, its culture, addresses the issue of drunk driving, is undeniable.

Challenges: The Growth and Evolution of the Million Mom March

Like Mothers Against Drunk Driving two decades earlier, the organization that first began as the Bell Campaign as a way to address grief and to advocate for the victims of gun violence grew state by state and chapter by chapter. After the Million Mom March in the United States' capital with concurrent marches around the country, the organizers utilized early forms of social networking via the Internet and late night conference calls that fit into the busy schedules for working and stay-at-home mothers around the nation.

Challenges

President Clinton, in the wake of the 1994 mid-term elections, may have best summed up the challenges faced by the Million Mom March when he stated, "The NRA is the reason the Republicans control the house" (Homsher). While the pendulum of public opinion swings from election to election and the rhetoric varies annually and state by state with each legislative session, the message of gun control advocates has remained constant. For the women who continue to organize and advocate under the auspices of the Million Mom March, gun control continues to be "about reinforcing a norm of responsible gun ownership and use" (Jacobs). The NRA, however, bills itself as, "as America's foremost defender of Second Amendment rights." The organization, with nearly four million members, views attempts at government regulation as an encroachment upon Second Amendment Rights and has a successful track record of effectively mobilizing members on the state and national level.

Future Goals

Between 2007 and 2010, the United State Supreme Court heard cases related to gun rights and the Second Amendment for the first time since 1939. Mary Leigh Blek believes, along with Criminologist and Professor James Alan Fox, that the Supreme Court's recent ruling on gun control is helpful and that with the Court's "recognition that various government bodies maintain the authority to regulate gun ownership and licensing" reasonable public policy related to gun control is within reach (Fox cited in Blek).

In *United States v. Miller*, the 1939 decision "suggested that the right should be understood in connection with service in a militia" (Greenhouse). In 2007, a

Million Mom March in Washinton, DC, May 2000.

case related to the Washington, DC, handgun ban appeared before the Court and the ban was struck down. Subsequently, the *McDonald v. Chicago* ruling nullified "many city and state bans on handguns, but left the door open for carefully worded legislation that restricts gun ownership" by clarifying Second Amendment rights related to self defense for non-militia members (Rice).

The organization's continuing goals closely align with Professor Fox's stance. According to Blek, the following measures represent reasonable public policy goals that the Supreme Court's majority might deem as legitimate. Most importantly, she stated, these policies would help save precious lives by preventing guns from falling into dangerous hands. In one year in the United States, 30,896 people died from gun violence and 78,622 people survived gun injuries (National Center for Injury Prevention and Control (NCIPC). Blek asked, "What are we waiting for?"

The future goals of the Million Mom March as outlined by President Emeritus Mary Leigh Blek:

- Repeal of federal restrictions on the wide-ranging use of ATF trace data for identifying patterns of illegal gun trafficking.
- Control of bulk sales of firearms.
- Require licensed firearms dealers to maintain up-to-date records and to report all stolen or lost inventory.
- Require background checks on all gun purchases and for registration of all guns and transfers of ownership.

Mary Leigh Blek with grandson addresses crowd at Chapter press event

Another current initiative of the Million Mom March, in partnership with the Brady Campaign, is advocacy for childproof guns:

> POSITION: The Brady Campaign supports making all newly manufactured or imported handguns "childproof." Childproof handguns can be designed so they can be fired only by their owner or someone authorized by the owner. (Brady Campaign "Childproof Handguns")

According to the Brady Campaign, childproof handguns would use existing technology to increase gun safety:

> Gun manufacturers can make handguns childproof by integrating a mechanical or biometric lock into the handgun's design. An internal mechanical lock works like the lock on a briefcase. The owner punches in a code and the lock releases, allowing the owner to open the briefcase. Biometric locks release when the fingerprint or hand-grip of the owner/authorized individual is read by the lock's scanner. Biometric locks are more secure than mechanical locks. (ibid)

In the wake of the 2011 shooting in Tucson, Arizona that injured Congresswoman Gabrielle Giffords and left six dead, including a nine year old girl, gun control proponents have called for tighter restrictions on access to guns, including additional screening for mental health issues that might render a person unfit for safe gun ownership.

The Motherhood Movement and The Million Mom March

The first Million Mom March was conceptualized as a campaign that would appeal to mothers and used iconic imagery associated with motherhood in American culture—linking, for example, the association between "mothers and apple pie." The Bell Campaign was first conceptualized by a grieving mother who sought to make some sense out of the senseless—in the case of Mary Leigh Blek, the shooting death of her son Matt in 1994. The model for her organization was based on another grassroots' mother-focused organization, Mothers Against Drunk Driving. The Million Mom March was launched on the national stage at a major rally on Mother's Day 2000 in Washington, DC.

Feminism and motherhood have long had a tumultuous, controversial relationship (Kinser). To be a feminist or to embrace feminism is to think in terms of women as advocates and as actors with a certain amount of agency. The concept of motherhood is emotion-laden and fraught with social expectations based on cultural frameworks (DiQuinzio). Women such as Mary Leigh Blek, Donna Dees-Thomases, and Sarah Brady all used their status as mothers as the basis for their civic participation and the foundation for their activism. The inherent idea on which the main premise of the Million Mom March is founded is that these are mothers organizing against gun violence. Patrice DiQuinzio asserts that "women's civic engagement is more likely to be accepted when it is based on motherhood, since motherhood has long been seen as women's distinctive and most appropriate role" (227). However, as noted by Amber Kinser, "feminists have also channeled a great of energy into critiquing motherhood as a source of women's oppression, isolation in the home, and exclusion from paid work and career opportunities" (1).

The role of the Million Mom March in the Motherhood Movement is multifaceted. As an organization that organized around and built upon the lessons learned from other successful foremothers in grassroots organizing, the women of Mothers Against Drunk Driving, the mothers who coalesced into the group that would celebrate its tenth anniversary in May 2010 as the Million Mom March have further cemented the power of mother-based advocacy efforts. As co-founder Mary Leigh Blek observed, the Million Mom March provided a blueprint for grassroots organizing on the working mother's schedule. Conference calls were scheduled at night to accommodate the hectic calendars of mothers with children. Local Million Mom March chapters embraced the Internet and numerous web-based social and new media tools such as Facebook to expand their grassroots' organizing efforts.

Critics of the Million Mom March have argued that the organization and others like it have helped to create notions of "essential motherhood" and that their existence has functionally served to characterize agency and activism that is motherhood-based as further legitimating the motherhood identity or status as "the basis for women's moral authority" (DiQuinzio 236). Proponents of empowered motherhood advocate for a broader conceptualization of the mothering experience that does not give extra weight to the voices those women who mother in accordance with traditional, patriarchal norms (Kinser).

Conclusion

The Million Mom March helped to ring in the new century in May 2000 with a massive demonstration orchestrated by an estimated 750,000 mothers in Washington, DC. Ten years after its inception, the Million Mom March organization continues to be a national voice advocating for sane gun control laws in the United States. The role of the Million Mom March in the twenty-first century Motherhood Movement has been to serve as a model for grassroots organizing that has stood the test of time while adapting to and embracing evolving technologies in order to facilitate more effective advocacy.

Works Cited

Bell Campaign. "New Grassroots Campaign to Support Gun Victims, Responsible Gun Policies to Be Launched May 25." *Common Dreams News Wire* May 23, 1999. Web. <www.commondreams.org/pressreleases/may99/052399a.htm>.

Blek, Mary Leigh. Personal interview, 30 June 2010.

Brady Campaign to Prevent Gun Violence. "Million Mom March Supports Common-Sense Gun Controls." 2011. Web. <http://www.bradycampaign.org/chapters/>.

Brady Campaign to Prevent Gun Violence. "Childproof Handguns." 2011. Web. <http://www.bradycampaign.org/legislation/childsafety>.

Brennan, Chris. "Onorato Again Slams Corbett On Florida Gun Permit Loophole." *Philadelphia Daily News*. 20 September 2010. Web. Philly.com.

Brown, Peter H, and Daniel G. Abel. *Outgunned: Up Against the NRA: The First Complete Insider Account of the Battle Over Gun Control*. New York: Free Press, 2003.

Corlin, Richard F. "The AMA's goal and role in preventing gun-related injury." *American Medical News* Dec. 17, 2001. Web. < http://www.ama-assn.org/amednews/2001/12/17/edca1217.htm>.

Dees-Thomases, Donna, Alison Hendrie, and Dianne Feinstein. *Looking for a Few Good Moms: How One Mother Rallied a Million Others against the Gun Lobby*. Emmaus, PA: Rodale, 2004.

DiQuinzio, Patrice. "Love and Reason in the Public Sphere: Maternalist Civic Engagement and the Dilemma of Difference." *Women and Children First: Feminism, Rhetoric, and Public Policy.* Ed. Meagher, Sharon M. and DiQuinzio, Patrice. New York: State University of New York Press, 2005.

Greenhouse, Linda. "Supreme Court Agrees to Hear Gun Control Case." *New York Times* 2007. Web. 20 November 2007.

Homsher, Deborah. *Women & Guns: Politics and the Culture of Firearms in America.*

Armonk, NY: M.E. Sharpe, 2001.

Jacobs, James B. *Can Gun Control Work? Studies in Crime and Public Policy.* Oxford: Oxford University Press, 2002.

Kelly, Caitlin. *Blown Away: American Women and Guns.* New York: Pocket Books, 2004.

Kinser, Amber. *Motherhood and Feminism.* California: Seal Press, 2010. Print.

Mothers Against Drunk Driving (MADD). "History of MADD." 2005. Web. <http://www.madd.org/about-us/history/>.

Mayors Against Illegal Guns. "About the Coalition." 2010. Web.

Meagher, Sharon M. and Patrice DiQuinzio. *Women and Children First: Feminism, Rhetoric, and Public Policy.* SUNY Series in Gender Theory. Albany, NY: State University of New York Press, 2005.

Mohammed, Arshad. "U.S. reverses stance on treaty to regulate arms trade." *Reuters* October 14, 2009. Web. <http://www.reuters.com/article/2009/10/15/us-arms-usa-treaty-idUSTRE59E0Q920091015>

National Rifle Association (NRA). *A Brief History of the NRA.* 2010. Web.

Remington, Tom. "Vote Adam Putnam, Florida Commissioner of Agriculture." *Maine Hunting Today* October 27, 2010. Web. <http://mainehuntingtoday.com/bbb/2010/10/27/vote-adam-putnam-florida-commissioner-of-agriculture>.

Rice, Mary. "Supreme Court Rules on Gun Control, Second Amendment." Personal Money Store. 2010. Web. 28 June 2010.

Scott, Rick. "Our Second Amendment Rights." Rick Scott, Republican for Governor, 2010. Web.

Spitzer, Robert J. *The Politics of Gun Control.* Chatham, NJ: Chatham House, 1995. Print.

Trapp, Doug. "Physicians, gun owners tangle over Florida 'don't ask' gun bill." *American Medical News* Jan. 31, 2011. Web. < http://www.ama-assn.org/amednews/2011/01/31/gvsa0131.htm>.

United Nations. *International Arms Trade Treaty Aim of Draft Resolution Approved By Disarmament Committee. Seven More Texts Recommended to General Assembly; Comprehensive Nuclear-Test-Ban Treaty, Small Arms Among Issues Addressed.* New York: United Nations, 26 October 2006.

46. United Mothers Opposing Violence Everywhere

Moving Up, Moving Outward

LAURA PENNINGTON

UNITED MOTHERS OPPOSING VIOLENCE EVERYWHERE (UMOVE) was founded by Audette Sheppard and 16 other mothers in August of 2001. The organization was founded by Ms. Sheppard as a reaction to her own son's death due to gun violence. The goal of the organization has been to provide a place for support for grieving and spreading the word about stopping violence. The goal of their organization is two-pronged: caring and understanding. At present, Audette Sheppard is still the leader of this group. This chapter provides a brief overview of the history and activities of this organization, the challenges and future goals, and a conclusion about how UMOVE fits into the broader motherhood movement. At present, UMOVE does not appear to be operational due to its lack of a website and contact information, which made obtaining information for this chapter particularly difficult.

History and Activities

The founding of UMOVE was an important step for the motherhood movement in recognizing a problem that all mothers, regardless of a personal connection to a violent event, could relate to. In addition, the outcry made by one mother touched not only other mothers but people in the community who supported her beliefs and were touched to get involved in the overall issue.

Sheppard's outcry and personal example of reaching out to other victims certainly inspired others to get involved: NBA player Jamaal Magloire vowed to mentor a young man orphaned after his mother was murdered. Magloire also promised to set up a trust fund for the young man. This is perhaps one of UMOVE's greatest successes, in that their attempt to reach out and raise awareness has initiated a "call to arms" for those who may be able to help or provide support to families (Doucette).

UMOVE was relatively successful initially in bringing awareness to the issue of violence in Toronto itself. The city of Toronto proclaimed October 21, 2004 as "UMOVE Day of Non-Violence." The following year, Toronto experienced what many called "The Summer of the Gun." This prompted UMOVE to foster a gun-control awareness campaign. During that summer, 52 people were violently killed. This provided a catalyst for the group to unite and advocate for tighter gun control. This is an excellent example of UMOVE connecting their movement to specific issues or legislation that impacts their mission.

One of UMOVE's most successful activities has been providing support and events for families and friends of victims of violent crime. In December of 2007, UMOVE hosted a Christmas party for 40 children who had lost parents, siblings, and relatives. At the time of the party, half of the people murdered in Toronto had been gunned to death. During an interview at this party, Sheppard noted that she planned and participated in these events because she felt that although it was too late for her own child, raising awareness might help to prevent other families from experiencing that same loss and grief ("Children scarred by violence focus of party") .

Thus far, UMOVE has been most successful as a globally recognized effort to address violence and to prevent future losses. It is easily a movement with which many women (as well as men and children) can identify, and the potential of this organization is unlimited with the proper resources and support.

Challenges and Future Goals

One of the greatest challenges for UMOVE is that it doesn't have a website or a place where the women who are part of the movement can go to find information about the organization, implement regional activities, and relate to one another. I believe that the most important challenge ahead of UMOVE is moving itself into the digital age; for example, a website with an active forum list could help connect mothers to one another and provide a list of clear resources, information about the organization, and help make the movement against violence more global. This could also connect UMOVE to other motherhood organizations that could band together to combat violence, as even those mothers who haven't experienced this issue personally are likely to support the overall mission of UMOVE.

The most crucial thing UMOVE can do to improve its mission is, therefore, to create a consistent web presence. Given that Sheppard herself has made it a focus to reach out to those impacted by violence, the membership and activities of this organization are only likely to increase upon to creation of an accessible, user-friendly website where mothers from around the world can connect and share ideas. Currently, the only web-based resource for UMOVE is a Facebook page with a few posts from over 12 months ago. If utilized, a Facebook page would serve as an excellent resource to reach out globally to those women interested in eradicating violence. In the search to discover UMOVE's Internet presence, the author contacted several people who had posted on the UMOVE Facebook page. Those members and supporters suggested contacting other people. Unfortunately, none of those leads were successful in locating an active member of the UMOVE movement.

If UMOVE aims to move "upwards and outwards" as the title of this chapter suggests, a volunteer public relations specialist should be one of the first goals after the creation of the website. An international campaign to alert women to the goals of UMOVE would create a powerful membership base. UMOVE could then clarify specific policy goals and use their voice as a group of mothers to advocate for greater protection of children. A public relations specialist would also be crucial in monitoring the news for information about other mothers and families impacted by violence, both to reach out to these families and to use their voice as a mission-motivated organization to make statements. Developing a clear and active voice in issues regarding violence will help UMOVE address national and international concerns. Cementing their role as a leader both in grief assistance and public policy support will make the organization more legitimate, respected, and well-known.

UMOVE faces an additional challenge in that violence across and within countries has not really decreased since their founding. Families continue to be impacted by violence on a daily basis—what role then, is there for UMOVE to continue moving forward? Should the organization continue to focus on grief management and support or attempt to take a more forward step in trying to actually reduce violence? Obviously trying to reduce violence will be difficult because there are many factors at play; it's difficult to even guarantee justice to the families. In order for UMOVE to have a significant impact, they must incorporate their movement into larger movements focused on violence and children. Only when societies recognize the many challenges that violence presents and how prevalent the issue is will a real focus be given to the issue as a whole. This is why it is crucial that UMOVE connect itself to the larger movements against violence and develop a clear mission statement about the focus of the group. UMOVE has great potential to create an international network of women opposing violence.

Relationship to the Larger Motherhood Movement

UMOVE has the potential to fill an important space providing both an outlet and an organization where women can come together to combat violence. UMOVE has been successful incorporating itself into the motherhood movement by choosing to focus on an issue that is international in nature: the grief and pain mothers experience upon the loss of a child. This is an issue that plagues societies worldwide; despite different cultures, languages, laws, and ways of life, women, and men, are certain to experience anger and sadness at the loss of children to violence. In fact, childless women and men are also likely to support the mission of this organization, making UMOVE relevant and important in today's world. .

Conclusion

UMOVE's creation recognized a worldwide problem of mothers experiencing pain, grief, and loss of loved ones due to violent activities. The organization provides an outlet for those women going through this process for certain public policies that could help prevent violence. At present, however, UMOVE seems unorganized and inaccessible. There is no website, email address for the founder, or use of social networking for UMOVE. The first step for this organization is to recognize that in order to reach more potential members and supporters, the group must create a home for itself on the Internet where women can find and connect with one another. The location of a public relations specialist to keep the organization up to date and connect UMOVE with relevant activities and stories is also important for cementing the organization into the larger non-violence and motherhood movement. In order to move "up and outwards," UMOVE must reevaluate its goals, leadership, and make the organization more easily located. If the organization is successful in doing this, UMOVE will fulfill a crucial role for mothers in society today.

Works Cited

"Children scarred by violence focus of party." *National Post* December 19, 2007. Web. <(http://www.canada.com/cityguides/toronto/story.html?id=85e91271-749c-4d55-9cb3-e9574599baae&k=95509)>.

Doucette, Chris. "NBA Star vows to help boy orphaned by murder." *Toronto Sun* June 5, 2010. Web. <http://www.torontosun.com/news/torontoand-gta/2010/06/05/14279191.htm>.

47.
Taking Back the Streets, Helping Victims Heal

"Mothers In Charge" in Philadelphia

ABIGAIL L. PALKO

MOTHERS IN CHARGE—THEIR VERY name attests to the proactive stance that the members of Mothers In Charge have claimed for themselves, projecting an image of power. These are not victims, but women who can make a difference, embodying in their activism Sara Ruddick's theory of "maternal thinking." In their call to action against the gun violence that afflicts the city, the group has had a marked impact on the city of Philadelphia and the surrounding suburbs through their anti-violence initiatives and has brought comfort to countless women with the resources that they provide for the surviving friends and families of victims.

History

The story's first act is not a new one—nor, sadly, is it unique. But the response, the second act, has been anything but complacent. In December 2001, 24-year-old Khaaliq Jabbar Johnson became yet another victim of gun violence in Philadelphia when he was shot eight times by "a violent repeat offender" over a triviality—a parking space (Miller). The impact on his mother, Dorothy Johnson-Speight, was life-changing in a very public way: in the midst of her pain and grief, she connected with Ruth Donnelly, among other grieving mothers (Miller), to found Mothers In Charge in 2003 "as a community advocacy and support organization for families affected by violence" (Mothers In Charge). Mothers In Charge, a nonprofit organization, is a grassroots support organization for the surviving family members and friends of victims of violence, guided by an anti-violence mission.

Under the guidance of Dorothy Johnson-Speight, who has spent her career as a licensed family therapist advocating for the rights of children and families, Mothers In Charge has undertaken numerous public-service activities. The organization explains its mission, promotes these various initiatives, and offers support to survivors through a large website. On this website, the organization describes its members:

> Mothers In Charge is comprised of impassioned mothers, grandmothers, aunts, and sisters who are committed to working towards savings lives.

> Most of the members have experienced the horror of having a son or daughter or loved one murdered. Because of the death and the life of their loved one, each mother and member is committed to saving lives and preventing another mother from having to experience this terrible tragedy. (Mothers In Charge)

These women have been empowered by the tragedies that have touched their lives.

Philosophy

The mission of Mothers In Charge is two-fold: in collaboration with school districts, youth and faith-based community organizations, they offer educational programs, as well as provide grief support to families affected by violence (Mothers In Charge). On their website, they articulate their philosophy:

> The mission of Mothers In Charge is violence prevention, education and intervention for youth, young adults, families and community organizations. In addition, Mothers In Charge works with elected officials on legislation to support safe neighborhoods and communities for children and families and collaborates with community and faith based organizations.
>
> Mothers In Charge will advocate for families affected by violence and provide counseling and grief support services for families when a loved one has been murdered. (Mothers In Charge)

This dedication to "ending the cycle of violence in Philadelphia" ("Mothers In Charge Air Documentary on Violence") has led to the spread of Mothers In Charge's influence nationwide.

Mandate

Mothers In Charge operates under the mandate that Dorothy Johnson-Speight perceived and accepted after her son's tragic murder: to provide support to Philadelphia-area families victimized by violence and to sponsor public education initiatives to prevent gun violence. Her fellow members, in turn, have accepted her mandate as their own. For the members of Mothers In Charge, the ultimate success would be sparing other mothers the pain they have endured: "Their purpose is to change things so that other mothers won't have to live with the grief that never goes away" (Miller).

Challenges

As the home page of their website proclaims in appropriately red capital letters, "blood is spilling at a record rate—not only on the streets of Philly—but in sup-

Antonio, Tiana, and Ayanna in the photo bank data entry room of the Mothers In Charge headquarters, recording information about a recent Mothers In Charge event.

posedly friendlier locales, according to police statistics" (Mothers In Charge). The hard facts and figures are the bedrock reality that informs all of the challenges they face, as well as their varied responses to these problems. In 2010 alone, there were 306 recorded homicides in the City of Philadelphia. Of these three hundred victims, twelve were age seventeen or younger, 118 were young adults (between the ages of 18 and 25)—and 242 of the victims were African American. The members of Mothers In Charge constantly live with the knowledge that they have lost a loved one to this violence and that it is ongoing. The challenges they face, therefore, arise from the personal nature of their calling, a violence that seems to increasingly target women, and the racial elements of the problem and the efforts (Johnson-Speight, interview).

The nature of the grief that the members of Mothers In Charge have endured combines with their mandate to offer several specific challenges. In Philadelphia, repeat offenders are frequent perpetrators of the crime and violence that Mothers In Charge works to eradicate (including the murderer of Johnson-Speight's son); over the past few years, both homicide rates and the number of non-fatal shootings have been rising; and an overwhelming percentage of both the victims and the perpetrators are African Americans (Miller). This is a problem that afflicts the entire community, though, not just the African Americans in Philadelphia. Efforts to reduce the gun violence that has so personally impacted the members of Mothers In Charge has led them to identify the numbers of at-risk young adults in the community—both male and female—as a challenge and an area where they can make a positive impact. The bloodshed and the violence that have devastated communities is not just a Philadelphia problem—it is a nationwide problem (Miller). The activities that Mothers In Charge sponsors are designed to meet these varied challenges.

When asked what challenges Mothers In Charge confronts, Dorothy Johnson-Speight enumerates several. The first two are related to image, and a third is funding, which is always an obstacle. In disheartening ways, the media re-victimizes those who have lost a loved one to violence through an assumption (sometimes implicit, sometimes verbalized) that an opportunity for the violence to occur was there because the victim's mother was not a good mother. She then must deal with judgments about her mothering and the attendant victim-blaming on top of the pain and grief caused by her child's murder. In a related issue of perception, there is also a reluctance to get involved in issues pertaining to violence; as Johnson-Speight (2011b) explains, "People just don't get involved. Violence is such an ugly thing; people can be blind, thinking, 'If my child isn't involved, it doesn't involve me.' [But] it will take getting everyone involved to make a difference, getting people to understand the impact and how everyone is involved even if you think you haven't been affected."

Activities

Mothers In Charge is a vibrant organization whose members "make themselves a visible presence in the community, appearing at peace rallies, anti-violence seminars, and gun legislation protests" (Miller). In December 2008, Mothers In Charge premiered the documentary *Stop the Violence: a Message to Youth*, that they created. *Stop the Violence* features two sides of violence: the stories of women who lost loved ones to violence and the stories of young men who were jailed for committing violent crimes ("Mothers In Charge Air Documentary on Violence"). Another documentary that features the group is the recently premiered *Mothers In Charge: No Greater Pain*, a documentary about the organization and the impact of violence that was screened at Villanova University in January 2011. *No Greater Pain* was produced by Villanova's Center for Justice, and was initiated by Dorothy, who saw this partnership as an opportunity to draw attention to the Mothers In Charge's commitment to bringing about change (Johnson-Speight 2011a). Of the 15 students involved in producing the documentary, not one had lost someone to violence, a detail which Johnson-Speight (2011b) offers as evidence of the power of community-wide involvement in the anti-violence project. Mothers In Charge is currently working on a teacher's guide for this documentary, to further its potential reach and pedagogical impact.

Other public outreach efforts have also focused on highlighting the ways that positive involvement in the community can contribute to the healing that Mothers In Charge champions. The organization published *Mothers In Charge — Faces of Courage*, a chronicle of the grief that mothers experience when their child is killed by violence, in Spring 2009. In Spring 2010, Mothers In Charge expanded its activities to bring a mentoring program to Philadelphia. The group began working on "1000 Women for 1000 Girls," a program designed to offer young women mentorship by pairing them with a Philadelphia-area woman. According to the press release, "the program's goal is to give a 'positive female direction' to girls in need" (May).

A crucial component of Mothers In Charge's outreach efforts is their violence prevention initiatives; they support multiple programs that work to counter violence in several very different ways. The programs that Mothers In Charge have sponsored in the past seven years include: The Billboard Campaign, The Female Rites of Passage Program, Grief and Loss Male Teens Support Group, The SMART Program (Saturday Morning Alternative Reach and Teach), Reading STARS Program, Message In The Music, and Men 4 Mentoring Program. They also sponsor grief-relief efforts through their (new) Mothers In Charge victims support center, including the grief support meetings, "Grief Support: The Process."

The Billboard Campaign is conducted in partnership with Clear Channel Outdoors, Inc. (who offers financial support through subsidizing the cost of putting up the billboards in affected neighborhoods). This campaign consists of billboards that feature the photos of victims of unsolved murders and display information, including an anonymous tip line. This campaign, designated "The Taking Back our Streets to SAVE our Children Citywide Billboard Campaign," was launched in March 2004 with a public unveiling of one of the first billboards. The campaign strategically places these billboards throughout Philadelphia and in close proximity to the crime scenes. Other pertinent information includes the reward that is offered for anonymous information related to the crime (the victim's family raises the reward money); information about the crime can be shared through an anonymous tip line or the Mothers In Charge website. The tip line on the billboard connects callers to the police, who then follow up on information. But the billboards are much more than a simple call for information. According to Johnson-Speight, they are "a way for those responsible for the crime to know the victims are not forgotten. People are concerned and caring, are working for justice for them. It can be overwhelming for a family to initially see it, because it's larger than life up there" (interview). But the billboards are a reminder that their loved one lives on in people's memories and actions. When a new billboard goes up, Mothers In Charge makes flyers of the billboards, and members canvas the community to distribute the flyers to cars passing on the street and at businesses in the neighborhood. Members take to the streets to urge people to come forward with information. The billboards have become a tangible landmark throughout the city, viscerally and forcefully spreading Mothers In Charge's message through the power of visual advertising.

Mothers In Charge has developed multiple programs to educate teenage children. The Female Rites of Passage Program is conducted in partnership with Carson Valley Children's Aid (a local non-profit, child welfare agency formed by the merger of the Carson Valley School and Children's Aid Society) and the community; Female Rites of Passage provides education and support for young women, ages

Candace and Ayanna record the names of new members and new volunteers.

13-18. Carson Valley Children's Aid, which has several Neighborhood Centers in Philadelphia and Montgomery County, as well as a Behavioral Health Center in Philadelphia, offers a comprehensive continuum of care to children who have experienced abuse and/or neglect or have medical, behavioral or emotional needs that require specialized care. (Carson Valley Children's Aid)

With the Grief and Loss Male Teens Support Group, Mothers In Charge offers support to young males victimized by the loss of a loved one to violence. Mothers In Charge also sponsors the Men 4 Mentoring Program, through which concerned men work with at-risk youth in the community and in the Philadelphia Prison System. Mothers In Charge targets teenagers' interest in music through Message In The Music, a program they describe as "designed for youth at risk to help improve writing skills, violence prevention, address conflict resolution, and develop critical thinking thru [sic] writing and positive music." In the past, they have also offered mentoring through programs like Reading STARS Program, a collaboration with the Greater Philadelphia Cares organization that offered individual reading mentoring, and The SMART Program, a collaboration with the Philadelphia School District's Saturday school program that taught life-skills such as anger management, conflict resolution, and time management; unfortunately, due to funding restrictions, these last two programs have been discontinued.

In their efforts to address the root causes of street violence, Mothers In Charge has turned their attention to keeping women out of prison, and a key component of this campaign is the Thinking for a Change program. This program is a national curriculum that teaches life skills and anger management with the goal of reducing recidivism rates, and Mothers In Charge sponsors it at Riverside Correction Facility, the women's prison with the Philadelphia Prison System. As of October 2010, approximately ninety women have completed the program. The challenges that face a newly-released woman, however, are greatly compounded if she has children to support, offering problems that the program alone cannot solve; in the fiscal year 2010, 6,061 women were released from Philadelphia jails to the streets, after their "lives and careers [were] interrupted" (Kase). Consequently, Johnson-Speight added a re-entry jobs program for graduates, and has hired several women herself to work at Mothers In Charge. Mothers In Charge's involvement with the women at Riverside was prompted by an appeal for help from an inmate who had just learned of her son's murder (Kase). Wondering if the mother could have helped her son if she had not been in jail, Johnson-Speight realized the need to explore alternatives to incarceration and reduce recidivism (Kase). And the program has been successful:

> ...The Mayor's Office says close to 400 people have gotten jobs through the program in the last 15 months. Recidivism rates for those who have completed the program hover around three percent, says Michael Resnick, chief of staff for Deputy Mayor for Public Safety Everett Gillison. That's far below national rates, where studies peg recidivism between 58 and 67 percent over two to three years, and over a 20-year period as high as 82 percent, according to a study by Correctional Counseling Inc. (Kase)

As Johnson-Speight explained to Annette John-Hall, "The idea is to heal these women so they can be better parents, so they won't end up being part of Mothers In Charge," to help the women offer the good parenting that might protect their children from becoming either victims or perpetrators of violence. In their work at Riverside, the members of Mothers In Charge have taken on "prevention advocacy on the ground level with the women who could have the most profound influence on their children but who don't because they're incarcerated," going to Riverside two nights a week to mentor the inmates (John-Hall). With this program, Johnson-Speight is, as John-Hall proclaims, a visionary: "she understands that recidivism prevention and violence prevention go hand in hand" (John-Hall). In addition to education initiatives, Mothers In Charge also sponsors grief support projects, including the Mothers In Charge Victims Support Center, which provides support to the surviving family members and friends of victims of violence through a bi-weekly grief support meeting that includes the communal emotional support of a group dinner and bereavement education and information on surviving the loss of a loved one. As the Mothers In Charge website explains, these sessions are meant to:

> offer unconditional love, support, and understanding to all who come. One thing that is frequently discussed at our meeting is the despair of thinking you are on the road to "recovery," when all of a sudden you

> seem to be back at square one. But are you really? Let's keep in mind most of us have had no previous experience in "recovering" from the loss of a child. Therefore, we have no point of reference—it's all new to us. Actually the "roller coaster" of emotions is perfectly normal. In the very beginning most of us seem to vacillate between total numbness and excruciating pain. (Mothers In Charge)

The organization is currently working on developing a workshop to be held in August 2011 on the "Victimization of Victims"; this workshop will address the challenge (mentioned above) that surviving mothers often face, a media portrayal that invites condemnation of their mothering practices as the cause of violent crime. Ultimately, the grief support initiatives are an integral part of their educational mission: in helping women through the grieving process, Mothers In Charge is teaching them that they can be empowered mothers, too.

Members of a Larger Motherhood Movement

As they explain on their website, each of the members of Mothers In Charge hopes to "turn a personal tragedy into a medium for change." Their collective understanding of this personal mandate is quite powerful: "They realize that positive change cannot happen within communities without addressing the issue of senseless and random violence. They know that in the names of their lost sons and daughters, they can and must serve as the catalyst for change." Like many other activist motherhood groups, such MADD, Mothers In Charge partners with the larger community to effect change. They have partnered with numerous organizations and companies in the Philadelphia region over the years, including:

- National Comprehensive Center for Fathers
- Council for Relationships
- Women Organized Against Rape (WOAR)
- The School District of Philadelphia
- The City of Philadelphia
- Carson Valley Children Aid
- Philadelphia Police Department
- The Department of Human Services
- Charlie Mack Party for Peace Celebrity Weekend
- Interfaith Peace Walk
- The Brotherhood of Huntingdon Street
- Men United for a Better Philadelphia

They have also moved beyond Philadelphia and chapters have been established in Norristown, PA; Atlantic County, NJ; Broward County, FL; and New York, as has a national and international conference presence.

A vibrant, vital maternal activist group, Mothers In Charge live out Sara

Ruddick's theory of maternal thinking in their daily efforts to make Philadelphia (and the larger world) a safer place, a place free of the effects of gun violence. As Ruddick argues, "All of women's work—sheltering, nursing, feeding, kin work, teaching of the very young, tending the frail elderly—is threatened by violence. When maternal thinking takes upon itself the critical perspective of a feminist standpoint, it reveals a contradiction between mothering and war" (148). Reflecting on her group's connection to a larger network of activist mothers, Johnson-Speight (2011b) offered her dream that "we would one day see mothers affected by violence to stand up and say no more," like those who recently protested in Egypt. This will take a coalition of mother groups, she notes, but there is, as she declared, "strength in numbers." Ruddick suggests that "[a]t its best, maternal nonviolence is a reality in the making" (183); the members of Mothers In Charge work with other mothers, helping women see that they are empowered as mothers to make a difference, striving toward the day when a nonviolent world will render their organization obsolete.

Works Cited

Carson Valley Children's Aid. "CVCA Overview." Web. <http://www.carsonvalley.org/about.aspx>. Accessed 7 February 2011.

John-Hall, Annette. "Mothers In Charge seeks to ease female inmates' return to freedom." *The Inquirer* 21 January 2011. Web. <www.philly.com>. Accessed 9 February 2011.

Johnson-Speight, Dorothy. Interview with Patty Jackson. [n.d.]. <http://www.youtube.com/watch?v=HD4FH92Lh1w&feature=player_embedded#>.

Johnson-Speight, Dorothy. "No Greater Pain." *NBC News* 28 January 2011a. Web. <www.youtube.com/watch?v=YvWtVniT_2o&feature=player_embedded#>.

Johnson-Speight, Dorothy. Personal Interview. 10 February 2011b.

Kase, Aaron. "Philly Works to Keep Moms Out of Jail." 26 October 2010. Web. <www.philadelphiaweekly.org>. Accessed 9 February 2011.

May, Jennifer Ellis. "Mothers In Charge begins a mentoring campaign after seven years in Philadelphia." *Examiner* 12 May 2010. Web. <Examiner.com>. Accessed 19 January 2011.

Miller, Larry. "Mothers In Charge founder sees growing need to fight violence." *The Philadelphia Tribune* 15 June 2009. Web. <http://news.newamericamedia.org>. Accessed 19 January 2011.

"Mothers In Charge Air Documentary on Violence." 5 December 2008. Web. <http://www.nbcphiladelphia.com>. Accessed 19 January 2011.

Mothers In Charge, Inc. "Stop the Violence—Get Involved." Web. <mothersincharge.org>. Accessed 19 January 2011, 7 February 2011.

Ruddick, Sara. *Maternal Thinking: Toward A Politics of Peace.* 2nd ed. Boston: Beacon Press, 2002.

48.
Parents Against Police Brutality in *Every Mother's Son*
A Profile of Mother-Warriors Seeking Justice in New York City

AMBER FATIMA RIAZ

To a mother, a child is a child, a soul is a soul.
—Kadiatou Diallo, *Every Mother's Son*

A PUERTO-RICAN CATHOLIC WOMAN. A Liberian Muslim woman. A New York Jewish woman.

What could these women possibly have in common? As the film *Every Mother's Son* documents, they are united by one of the least talked-about phenomena of the 1990's—innocent young men tortured and/or killed as a direct result of the use of excessive force at the hands of New York police. In a movement hauntingly reminiscent of the grieving mothers of the Plaza de Mayo, Argentina, these and countless other mothers unite on the streets of New York to demand justice for their sons, to hold the police and the political establishment accountable for the victimization of specific communities in the name of "protecting" the citizens of New York and of "reducing crime." This paper will begin with an account of the three stories highlighted by the 2004 film, and will then discuss the association founded by the parents of the victims of police brutality, to showcase the incredible transition from grieving motherhood to activist seeking change in the political establishment.

The film *Every Mother's Son* was produced and directed by Kelly Anderson and Tami Gold in 2004, and has been nationally broadcast through PBS. According to the Andersongoldfilms' (the production company's) website, the film has received numerous awards, including the Audience Award at the Tribecca Film Festival, and an Emmy Nomination for Outstanding Achievement in Directing. Lasting about an hour, the film documents the tireless struggle of parents seeking justice for innocent young men killed by the special Street Crime Unit set up by Mayor Rudy Giuliani in the 1990s to fight street crime in New York. Anderson and Gold assert, in their director's statement, that they had been looking for a unique way of documenting the issue of police brutality, and found it in the stories of the mothers of the victims.

The first story profiled in the film *Every Mother's Son* is that of Iris Baez, mother of Anthony Baez, a Puerto Rican who had been born and raised in Bronx, New

Doris Busch Bosky, Iris Baez, Kadiatou Diallo gathered in a church.

Iris Baez, mother of Anthony Baez, wearing a button with her son's photograph, during a protest march.

York. In December 1994, Officer Francis Livoti arrested Anthony Baez when his football hit the side of his patrol car. According to Marilynn S. Johnson, author of *Street Justice: A History of Police Violence in New York City*, "Baez resisted cuffing" due to which "Livoti used an illegal chokehold that killed the asthmatic Baez"

(Johnson 292). According to the interview in *Every Mother's Son*, Iris Baez insists that her son did not have asthma, and that Livoti used excessive force to "subdue" Baez. The killing sparked a series of protests and meetings "led by the National Congress for Puerto Rican Rights and ... Parents Against Police Brutality, founded by Iris Baez and Margarita Rosario, the mothers of two of the victims" (Johnson 292). Livoti was acquitted of all charges on October 7 1996, due to insufficient evidence. According to a statistic quoted in the film, 107 civilians were killed due to use of excessive force by police between 1994 and 1999.

The second story highlighted by the film is that of Kadiatou Diallo, mother of Amadou Diallo. In 1999, Amadou, a Muslim immigrant from Liberia, was shot by four policemen, while re-entering his own apartment building. The police officers claimed they supposed him to be a rape or robbery suspect, and approached him. Diallo reached into his pocket and pulled out his wallet, apparently assuming he was being robbed as the four men were in plainclothes. The officers mistook the wallet for a gun, and shot at him. Out of the forty one shots fired, nineteen hit Diallo. The incident sparked protests and sit-ins, and a civil disobedience movement "modeled on the antiapartheid movement" (Johnson 297) was launched. Mothers from Parents Against Police Brutality were in the forefront of the movement, gathering in front of the "police headquarters in lower Manhattan" (Johnson 297). According to Johnson, the protests gained tremendous momentum: "more than twelve hundred people were arrested during three weeks of protests" (Johnson 298). The movement helped focus national media attention on the issue of police brutality but had little impact on the outcome of the Diallo case—the four officers were acquitted of all charges by a jury in Albany.

The third story is that of Gary "Gidone" Busch's mother, Doris Busch Boskey. When police knocked on the door of Busch's basement apartment in response to neighbour complaints that he was playing his music too loudly, Busch emerged in the traditional garb of a Hasidic Jew, a small claw hammer clasped in his hands. Police asked him to put his weapon down, but Busch protested that the hammer was a religious symbol, not a weapon. The police pepper-sprayed him and when he ran up the stairs in pain, they shot him. As in the previous two cases, the officers responsible for the killing were not charged.

The common thread in these three cases is the activism of the mothers of the victims. Supported by groups like the October 22nd coalition, 100 Blacks in Law Enforcement who Care and the Lower East Side Call for Justice, the mothers of the victims hold regular rallies and meetings, speaking in schools and raising awareness about the issue of police brutality and excessive force. The film takes great pains to profile mothers who not only grieve for their sons but also continue to raise their voice against the political establishment, reaching out to other parents who have suffered similar losses. What the film fails to show is the impact these voices have managed to have on the political establishment. The film ends with Iris Baez's speech to an audience of young New Yorkers urging them to understand the root of the problem before condemning it. She insists on the re-training of police officers, contending that the "police cannot police itself" and constantly asking how brutality and the use of excessive force can be stopped. The film ends with Baez's insistence that she continues to be vocal about the issue because she does not want Anthony's death to be in vain.

The group of mothers profiled in the film has found strength in numbers. United under the umbrella of the group Parents Against Police Brutality as well as the Anthony Baez Foundation (founded by Iris Baez), the mothers have drawn upon their anger and their grief, using the system itself to hold the administration and the police department accountable for their actions. According to Marilynn S. Johnson, the continued protests and demonstrations against the Street Crimes Unit, first established by Mayor Rudy Giuliani to fight street crime and notorious for its abuse of individual civil liberties, led to Attorney General Janet Reno's undertaking to "expand the ongoing pattern or practice investigation to include a study of the NYPD's stop-and-frisk policy" (298). Johnson shows that

> The state attorney general, the city's public advocate, and other public and private organizations also launched investigations of policing and disciplinary practices in the city.... Most notably, the U.S. Civil Rights Commission announced in May 1999 that it would conduct a major investigation of police practices and their impact on civil rights in the city. (298-299)

The report of the Civil Rights Commission when released after almost a year of investigations, was ridiculed and disparaged for its shoddy reporting by the NYPD and Mayor Rudy Giuliani's office. The Commission's report critiqued "everything from recruitment and training to policing policies and discipline" (Johnson 299). The report criticized the department's stop-and-frisk policy, showing a "dramatic racial disparity among those stopped by the NYPD" (Johnson 299). In spite of the resistance put up by the NYPD as well as Mayor Giuliani, the Commission's report had some impact on the department's policies, and more misconduct cases were disciplined after the report was released. According to Johnson, "the department's disciplinary rate for CCRB-substantiated cases continued to rise, reaching 74 percent in 2000, a more than twofold increase over the 1994 rate" (301), a rate which is a direct tribute to the efforts of civilian protestors like the mothers and parents of victims of police brutality.

Since the terrorist attacks of 2001, however, the issue of police brutality seems to have dropped off the city's agenda. The policemen and firefighters have become heroes, "even to young residents of poor, nonwhite neighborhoods" (Johnson 302). The priorities of the department itself have shifted, no more evident than in the closure of the Street Crime Unit in early 2002. As Johnson shows however, the potential of other forms of repression is all the more, given the city's investment in anti-terrorist operations and the rising support for racial profiling targeting young Muslim and Arab males under the circumstances.

The changes wrought within the NYPD, and the increased accountability of police actions even before the issue itself became irrelevant in 2001, is a testament to the activism of the grieving mothers briefly outlined in this paper. As Johnson acknowledges, it is due to civilian pressure and scrutiny that a department as secretive as the police department in any city can maintain the delicate balance between ensuring safety and security of citizens and preserving individual rights and liberties. Even though the policemen responsible for the deaths of Anthony Baez, Amadou Diallo and Gary Busch were not brought to justice by the courts, the fact that the department itself was forced to change and to acknowledge the importance of individual rights and liberties allows us to assert that the deaths were not completely in vain.

Works Cited

Johnson, Marilynn S. *Street Justice: A History of Police Violence in New York City.* Boston: Beacon Press, 2003.

Every Mother's Son: A Film. Dir. Tami Gold and Kelly Anderson. Andersongold Films Inc., 2004. Videocassette. Web. <http://www.andersongoldfilms.com/beta/everymothersson/synopsis/index.html>.

49.
No Body, No Crime?
The Mothers of Acari and the Struggle for Justice and Non-Violence

TATIANA MOURA AND RITA SANTOS

THE 1990S WITNESSED THE GROWING lethality of police action in Brazil and specifically in the city of Rio de Janeiro. The *chacinas* (massacres)—a term used to describe the collective murder or summary execution of a group of people by the police or by the militia (which usually consists of police officers, ex-police men, fire-fighters and private security officers)—such as the massacres of Acari (1990), Candelária (1993), Vigário Geral (1993), and Baixada Fluminense (2001) irreversibly marked the lives of the people of Rio de Janeiro. By making visible the growing lethality of police action in Rio de Janeiro, these events resulted in a significant shift in the popular image of the so-called "*Cidade maravilhosa*" (wonderful city). As a result of this shift, Rio became known instead as the "*Cidade partida*" (broken city) (Ventura), an allusion to the geographical borders of violence, which further isolated the poor areas of the city from its wealthy neighbourhoods (Araújo 2007). While the incidents of police brutality occur more frequently in the poorest areas of the city, executions have spread geographically in the past two decades. Nevertheless, the poor communities remain the most affected by police violence, as the neighbourhoods (or slums) in which they live are the focus of the police force's crime suppression initiatives.

The public exposure of these massacres, and its repercussions, was facilitated by survivors and relatives of the victims, as well as human rights organizations, which reported the cases to the authorities and the public. The "Acari case," the focus of this article, involved the disappearance of eleven youth, mostly inhabitants of the Acari *favela* (slum), in a northern suburb of Rio de Janeiro, and was reminiscent of the terror tactics used during the dictatorship period. This incident prompted a pioneering form of post-dictatorial anti-violence militancy by mothers of the murdered and disappeared, and led to extensive media coverage as well as important international recognition and support.

The Mothers of Acari is an organization made up of survivors and relatives of victims of human rights violations resulting from urban violence in Brazil that keep alive the memory of the Acari massacre, by challenging the popular adage in Brazil to "forgive and forget." The Mothers of Acari's actions in this realm, as well as those of other civil society groups protesting against state-sanctioned violence, are examples of new social movements in Brazil that struggle for the advancement of democracy in all spheres and aspects of social and political life.

This chapter analyzes the trajectory of the Mothers of Acari, particularly the way they perceive themselves and their struggles. After a brief history of the group, we examine the ways in which they demanded justice and reparation from the State, and the strategies used by the group to articulate their demands. The group's challenges, obstacles, and alliances will also be examined, as well as the organization's relationship to the larger motherhood movement.

Context: State Violence in Rio de Janeiro in the Post-Dictatorship Period

Despite recent advances,[1] Brazil currently remains as one of the most violent countries in the world, with gun-related mortality rates similar to many war scenarios. In 2006, Brazil registered 35,969 gun-related deaths (Rede de Informação Tecnológica Latino-Americana et al. 94), 2,235 of which occurred in the city of Rio de Janeiro, the state with the highest prevalence of gun-related deaths.

The State-led massacres and summary executions, during the military dictatorship, remain still today one of the most visible expressions of State-sanctioned violence in Rio. The conception of public security in the 1980s and '90s, profoundly militarized, was influenced by the Doctrine of National Security, which, during the military dictatorship took root in Brazilian society and politics and was aimed at eradicating political opponents to the authoritarian regime (Coimbra). With the transition to democracy, the category of "internal enemy," used during the dictatorship to refer to the regime's opponents, shifted its meaning and began to target the most impoverished segments of the population: the young, poor and *favelado* (those who live in the *favelas,* or slums).[2]

According to the *Instituto de Segurança Pública* (Institute of Public Security), from 1998 to 2009, 10,216 deaths were registered as a result of State-sanctioned violence (averaging 2.4 deaths per day). Data of the period of 1993-1996 (Cano) show that the number of dead civilians, as a result of police confrontations, compared to the number of policemen killed on duty is 41 to 1; that is, for each policeman killed on duty, 41 civilians are murdered. This proportion is significantly higher than the international average and irrefutably points to the excessive use of police force and practices of summary execution (Cano). According to Human Rights Watch's 2009 Report "Lethal Force: Police Violence and Public Security in Rio de Janeiro and São Paulo," between 2004 and 2008, police forces in the states of Rio and São Paulo alone killed over 11,000 people. Cases of execution by the Rio police (2,176) were higher than the number of deaths perpetrated by the police in South Africa during the same period (1,623), a country with higher homicide rates than those registered in the state of Rio de Janeiro.

The motherhood group that is the focus of this paper is part of a new kind of maternalist movement (Humphrey and Valverde) that emerged during the post-political transition (democratization) period, or during post-war periods, in response to what Koonings and Kruijt have labelled "new violence" contexts, that is, scenarios where the democratic State is still in the early stages of its consolidation and in which coexist mechanisms of legal democratic organization and manifestations of State and criminal violence. In some of these contexts, the combination of growing social and economic disparities; low rates of development and high unemployment rates; unplanned urban growth and the increasing fragility of quality urban infra-structures; increasing availability of firearms and the centrality of violent cultures in interpersonal and community relations; and widespread impunity, has given rise to what has been called "newest wars" (Moura; Moura, Afonso and Soares): a highly concentrated incidence of armed violence in urban territories within larger scenarios of institutionalized peace.

History

On the 21 July 1990, eleven young people went to a farm in Suruí, in the Baixada Fluminense, Rio de Janeiro, to spend the weekend. The farm was owned by the grandmother of one of the youths. When the weekend was over, they decided to stay a few more days. According to some testimonies, on July 26, six men visited the farm, claiming to be policemen. After speaking to the older ones—Luiz Carlos, Moisés, and Wallace—they took the entire group to a van and drove away. That was the last time these eleven young people were ever seen.

Among the eleven youth of Acari that disappeared that day were Cristiane Leite de Souza, 17 years old, daughter of Vera Lúcia Flores Leite (deceased); Rosana de Souza Santos, 19 years old, daughter of Marilene Lima de Souza; Luiz Henrique da Silva Eusébio, 16 years old, son of Edméia da Silva Eusébio (murdered); Hudson de Oliveira Silva, 16 years old, son of Ana Maria da Silva; Edson Souza Costa, 16 years old, son of Joana Euzilar dos Santos; Antônio Carlos da Silva, 17 years old, son of Laudicena Oliveira do Nascimento (deceased); Viviane Rocha da Silva, 13 years old, daughter of Márcia da Silva; Wallace Oliveira do Nascimento, 17 years old, son of Maria das Graças do Nascimento; Hédio Oliveira do Nascimento, 30 years old, son of Denise Vasconcelos; Moisés Santos Cruz, 26 years old, son of Ednéia Santos Cruz; and Luiz Carlos Vasconcelos de Deus, 32 years old, son of Teresa Souza Costa.

There are many versions about what happened that morning. One version maintains that after being tortured, these young men and women were locked into a van, which was later set on fire. Others claim that the bodies had been fed to the lions of a nearby farm owned by a civilian policeman. A vet taken to the scene, however, argued that because of the young age of the lions it would not have been possible for them to eat eleven people.

On January 28, 1992, the newspaper *O Dia* published information obtained from the Secret Service of the Military Police that revealed that eleven civil and military policemen had taken part in the apprehension of these young men and women. The names of the policemen involved were connected to an extermination group named *Cavalos Corredores*[3] (Running Horses), which would later also be involved in the massacres of Candelária and Vigário Geral[4] in 1993. These policemen were part of the 9th Battalion of the Military Police, Rocha Miranda, a section with jurisdiction over the *favelas* (slums) of Acari and Vigário Geral (Araújo 2006).

The police investigation conducted during the inquiry was unable to collect enough evidence to back up the assumption that the young men and women had been murdered and then forcibly disappeared. As a result, some mothers of the disappeared began to associate and conduct investigations on their own after their working hours. This was the beginning of the Mothers of Acari.

Due to the activism of the Mothers of Acari, significant national and international attention to the disappearances/murders of these individuals mobilized the State apparatus to investigate the case. It is important to take into account the political context underlying the massacre. The Acari massacre took place in the last year that Moreira Franco acted as head of the State's affairs (1987-1990), unfolding during the Brizola government (1991-1994). According to Cristina Buarque de Hollanda, the Brizola government strived to create a "positive social identity of the poor," and its main challenge was to "discipline the police" (32). In this context, the massacre of Acari can be understood as an act of retaliation by some sectors of the police against the Brizola government's new policy of public security.

Drawn Together by Loss: The Genealogy of the Mothers of Acari

Similar to other current groups made up of relatives of victims of urban violence, the experience of the Mothers of Acari is marked by a three-fold condition: class, gender (women-mother), and social-geographical location (*favelado*). The Mothers of Acari manipulate and subvert the roles attributed to women by the patriarchal society, especially those of mother and wife, as a strategy to enter the public sphere. By politicizing the private domain, instead of eliminating motherhood as a reference in the construction of femininity, they bring the perspective of motherhood to the forefront in confronting the political system. During this process of collectively creating a "political role for motherhood" (Howe 47), their own self-image is altered and, as a result, also their very own meaning of motherhood and care; as well, societal stereotypes that define women as apolitical and passive are challenged. In the words of Marilene,

> We became something different. We were mothers but we were out there. It was the first time mothers from poor neighbourhoods rose and began searching for their offspring and demanding for justice. People started calling us Mothers of Acari, since most of us came from the community. It was only after that that I realized that there was a group of mothers, in Argentina, called Mothers of Plaza de Mayo.
>
> In these 20 years I/we succeeded in many ways. Personally, my personal growth and my growing concern for other people and my sense of solidarity since the tragedy are key. When I look back, I am

> so different and so distant from the Marilene in 1990, sitting at home, cooking for her husband and children. And I can't go back and I don't want to. I became aware of so many things that hinder me from going back to be the Marilene I used to be. During the course of our militancy I learned so much about the different treatment that people get in Brazil as a result of our postal code, of poverty and stigmatization. And now I fight for my daughter, Rosana, but also for other people, for other sons and daughters whose lives are being taken away by the street judges.

During this 20-year period (1990-2010), the Mothers of Acari rallied, organized public demonstrations and marches, particularly on the anniversary of the disappearance of their children, and also in the event of new massacres, such as Vigário Geral and Candelária. On these occasions, they invaded public institutions; lobbied authorities (namely regarding the lack of progress of their police inquiry, the possibility of a national reparation fund for victims of State violence, and the establishment of a national holiday in honour of victims of State-sanctioned violence); gave interviews; occupied public offices; and travelled to other countries to share with other people and other mothers their personal account of violence and mourning.

The Mothers of Acari have also maintained contacts with human rights activists, non-governmental organizations, public entities, and the media. The *Centro de Articulação das Populações Marginalizadas* (Centre for the Articulation of Marginalized Populations) (CEAP) was their first important contact, offering them initial guidance by providing basic information and knowledge about police inquiries and the legal process, assisting them in drafting press releases and preparing them for media interviews, and offering them a space to conduct their meetings and events. Amnesty International followed the case, which also got the attention of the former French first lady, Danielle Mitterrand. The Mothers of Acari met other mothers and groups of relatives of victims in the State, inspiring the formation of other groups. They also established relationships with similar groups in other countries, such as the Mothers of Plaza de Mayo in Argentina.

The murder of one of the most active mothers, Edméia da Silva Eusébio, after a visit to a prison in Rio de Janeiro in 1993, allegedly with the aim of obtaining more information about the Acari's case, constituted an important landmark in the history of the group. Edméia's death, which remains unsolved to date, resulted in a decrease in the mothers' participation, especially those who were inhabitants of the *favela*, while it reinforced the image of the mothers as a symbol of struggle for peace in the city. The newspaper article "*Mães de Acari fazem reunião mas têm medo*" ("The Mothers of Acari meet but are fearful") (*O Povo*), and the testimonies of some of the mothers, illustrated the fear and suspicion of the mothers after the death of Edméia, describing their precautions in getting around the city and in organising rallies and meetings. In many of their accounts, they mentioned the sensation of being followed and the need to be accompanied during their initiatives (Nobre; Araújo 2007). After the death of Edméia, two mothers, Vera Flores and Marilene Souza, assumed leadership of the group.

From Mourning to Struggle: Public Denunciation, Mobilization and Activism

As described by Schirmer (3), the practice of forced disappearance, popularized by repressive regimes in Latin America, particularly in the 1970s and '80s, was perceived as the perfect crime: it was hard to prove who was responsible, thus denying the status of victim to the disappeared, and it hindered the completion of the mourning process by the family of the disappeared. In fact, disappearance disrupts the lives of those who remain in many ways. After the disappearance of their children, the daily routine of the Mothers of Acari was severely altered. As Vera used to say, "someone is missing from my house." And that routine can only be re-established with the return of the disappeared, or with the clarification of what happened. Disappearance thus seems a flawless instrument of social control, frustrating the emergence of collective forms of resistance. In reality, however, the uncertainty about the whereabouts of the disappeared gave rise to protests by mothers. If, on the one hand, disappearance can hinder the completion of the grieving process by the relatives and indefinitely maintain the sense of hope that prevents family members from assuming their loved ones are dead, and thereby preventing their participation in militant movements; on the other hand, the absence of definite news can prompt protest, including the demand of the return of bodies and of judicial sanctions.

After the initial experience of the traumatic event, these mothers moved from shock and indignation to politics, positioning themselves as political actors in the public sphere, aimed at fighting impunity and obtaining reparation. The first meetings were held in the house of Edméia, in Acari. Subsequently they started visiting places near the farm where their children were last seen, searching for traces of their sons and daughters. They researched clandestine cemeteries, prison facilities, monitored diggings and police searches, as well as the judicial trajectory of the case. Their search for information became increasingly public, with growing solidarity among the inhabitants of Acari for the mothers' appeals.

The search for justice is also the search for truth. The Mothers of Acari thus publicly denounced State-sanctioned violence, committed with impunity, and demanded reparation. To confront the State's inability to justify its actions, the group resorted to primordial ties (mother-son/daughter) as a way to legitimate their demands.

As a result of the mobilization strategy used by the Mothers of Acari, as well as by similar groups, that revolved around the creation of an informal network of support and provided solidarity to people in similar circumstances, the protest gained momentum with every ceremony, mass, and demonstration. With the gradual transformation of the public denunciations—which were no longer based on the specific case of Acari, but were broadened to encompass other cases of police violence—other relatives of victims of violence, mostly mothers, joined the group. The public denunciation of these atrocities is, thus, a key element of the activity of these groups.

Strategies

Taking into consideration the Acari case, we are able to identify some strategies used for public denunciation: first-hand depositions or testimonies from the mothers at various events; public mourning rituals; denunciation through activist organizations and movements (local and international); and denunciation through the media.

Personal Testimonies

The testimonies of these mothers represent an attempt to preserve their children's memory, to refuse stigmas and stereotypes that brand the writing of that memory. In many occasions over the past 20 years, they used public appearances at human rights events, women's human rights marches, university lectures, State ceremonies, public *fora*, such as the National Public Security Forum, and award granting ceremonies to raise awareness of the life stories of their missing sons and daughters, and their search for their childrens' whereabouts and their quest for justice. These events enabled them to deconstruct many stereotypes reinforced by the media and public officials, mainly policemen,[5] concerning the Acari's case, namely the recurrent reference to the involvement of some of the missing youth in drug trafficking and armed robbery.

Public Mourning Rituals

Public mourning rituals have gathered together mothers who lost their sons or daughters at the hands of the police brutality, death squads or militias. In 1993, Mothers of Acari, joined by other mothers of missing or dead children, created Mothers of Cinêlandia. For five years, 150 to 180 mothers gathered every Monday afternoon, on the footsteps of Rio de Janeiro's *Câmara de Vereadores* (Counsellors Chamber) in silent protest to denounce the death or disappearances of their children, to demand information on the whereabouts of their sons and daughters, displaying photographs of the victims. These public rituals have led to the growth of other mother organizations who have lost sons and daughters murdered by the police or death squads.

Association with Other Activist Organizations and Movements

The local and international pubic denunciations enabled the Mothers of Acari to keep networking with other mothers, such as Mothers of Cinelândia, Mothers of Rio, and social movements like the *Rede de Comunidades e Movimentos Contra a Violência, SOS Queimados, Fórum Reage Baixada*, and several NGOs that made it possible, to some extent, to form powerful linkages to draw even more attention to the violation of their rights, and the rights of their children. The joint drafting

Mothers of Acari and Mothers of Cinelândia protest outside the Cousellors Chamber, Rio de Janeiro, 1994. Tortura Nunca Mais Image Records.

of reports and news briefs on State-sanctioned violence and the criminalization of poverty (Wacquant) in Brazil, as well as the joint organization of public events enabled them to consolidate their partnership with international human rights organizations such as Amnesty International and succeed in forging political alliances with key municipal and state deputies which culminated in the insclusion of these topics in the public agenda. For instance, since the early stages of the drafting of the PRONASCI program (the National Program of Public Security and Citizenship[6]), the Mothers of Acari, as well as other mothers' groups, were invited to Brasília to participate in the public debates of its priorities. The 2007 visit of the United Nations Representative Philipe Alston to Brazil included a meeting with the Mothers of Acari and other human rights organizations, while the 2009 Amnesty International Report on Brazil, *Picking up the Pieces: Women's Experiences of Urban Violence in Brazil* relied on the information gathered by the Mothers and the other organizations.

The Mothers of Acari's association with the Centro de Articulação das Populações Marginalizadas (CEAP) was particularly important. CEAP wrote a report on the "Acari case" and, based on that report, Amnesty International, the Brazil-France Solidarity Committee and the France-Libertés Foundation led by the former French first lady Danielle Mitterrand, were made aware of the case. From then on, the case had international attention and this gave rise to the international denunciation of the crimes against human rights committed in Brazil. An example of this can be found in the news article cited below:

> The governments of France and Sweden, along with another 50 countries will denounce Brazil for human rights violations in the World Confer-

> ence on Human Rights that will take place next June [1993] , in Vienna. The policy-makers have shown concern for the disappearance of the eleven youth, which took place in July 1990, and culminated with the murder of one of the Mothers of Acari, Edméia, last Friday [15 May 1993]. (*O Dia* 1993)

According to CEAP, the clarification of the circumstances of the massacre was key for Amnesty International and the Brazilian government. Since the murder of Edméia, the executive secretary of CEAP has been talking to national and international media about the case. He is hopeful that the French government will take a strong stand on human rights violations in Brazil in the near future (Araújo 2007).

In 1994, the Mothers of Plaza de Mayo, together with Danielle Mitterrand, organized the first Meeting of Mothers of Missing Persons in Paris with political leadership, to which the Mothers of Acari were invited. In this context, the writing of the book *Mães de Acari: uma história de luta contra a impunidade*, by the reporter Carlos Nobre, was of utmost importance. The book, written with the input of the Mothers of Acari, helped the group to denounce the human rights violations in Brazil to the international community.

This public denouncement of State-sanctioned violence in Brazil at the international and national level made the struggle of the Mothers of Acari visible on a wide scale. This was central in the process of putting State-sanctioned violence on the public agenda in Brazil, especially due to the mutually exclusive understanding of human rights and public security which continues to reign in Brazil today (Araujo 2007). It was also valuable since it demonstrated the connections between the use of violence and repression in contexts of dictatorship, war and post-war and formal peace scenarios, such as in Brazil, and allowed the sharing of stories and strategies of resistance to that violence and repression.

Significantly the Mothers of Acari did not create their agenda of political action in isolation: their participation was connected to activities developed with or by other formal organizations, such as, more recently, the *Rede de Comunidades e Movimentos contra a Violência*, established in 2004, and which brings together various relatives of, and victims of violence, from different city locations. The work of this association was particularly relevant and politically important as it was able to increase awareness of human rights violations and violence in Brazil as cross-cutting the whole society and the extension of solidarity and mobilization around a common cause, increasing their prospects of drawing attention to the impact of State-based violence in the country and the fight against State impunity as well as prevention strategies.

Relationship with the Media

If, on the one hand, the media in Brazil has contributed to consolidating social stigma especially towards the *favelas* and its inhabitants, and legitimating the criminalization of poverty (Silveira), on the other, it also publicized denunciations of the murders and made visible the demands of groups such as the Mothers of Acari. In fact, along with reports voicing authoritative sources on the case, mainly the police and judicial actors, some media accounts, particularly in more popular (non-elitist) newspapers such as *Jornal O Povo* and *Dia*, began voicing the concerns and initiatives of these women and drawing attention to violence taking place in the suburbs of the city, hitherto invisible in the media, enabling the issue to become part of the public agenda.

Apart from the press coverage, the Mothers of Acari also managed to get some important TV coverage. For example, in 1996, the soap opera "*Explode Coração,*" by TV Globo, which focused on the story of a kidnapped child, drew attention to the actions of the Mothers of Acari and the Mothers of Cinelândia. The Mothers of Acari filmed some scenes in the soap opera, which contributed to further dissemination of their struggle (Freitas). The participation of the Mothers of Acari in that soap opera made many headlines.[7] This was particularly significant since the popularity of soap operas in Brazil, as well as its potential to raise social awareness on a variety of topics, has been well documented by several media and education experts (La Ferrara, Chong and Duryea).

The media interest in the Mothers of Acari is the result of the discursive strategy adopted by the mothers to generalize their search for justice and generate empathy by resorting to emotive symbols and language associated with their personal tragedy and their identities as mothers, as well as the possibility of its recurrence, thereby affecting many other mothers as well.

As Vera often put it:

> Our eleven children went missing. Then 21 youth were killed in the [*favela* of] Vigário Geral and now 29 more died in the [poor communities of] Baixada. So, there are times when we feel down. But other people "push" us. I know that I will fight until the end, I need to know what happened to my daughter. But also, now I got to know a lot of people, a lot of tragedies and I can't let go. It's my mission now: to contribute to violence reduction in the state of Rio de Janeiro and in Brazil. If there is one thing that I have learned, is that it can happen again.

Challenges

Criminalization of Poverty and the Favela

The strong prejudice against the *favela* and the *favelado* represents one of the largest obstacles towards the greater effectiveness of Mothers of Acari denunciations. It reinforces the difficulties already faced by the *favelados* in their claim for rights (mainly socio-economic), as was with the case of Mothers of Acari, who had to break the ground by talking about dispossession in a criminalized territory. In the words of Vera,

> I couldn't understand how eleven young people disappeared and nothing happened. Until that moment I had never been inside a police precinct. I was, we were, terrified at the time. Time passes and the possibilities of pursuing the investigation become narrower. And in the Acari case the waiting was the result of bad conduction of the investigations. Acari was perceived as the most dangerous place in the city. The law enforcement agents didn't want to go there and do their investigations. For example, Laudicena, the owner of the farm, was only able to notify the police four days after the van was stolen, the van used to drive the our children away, when those of us from Acari called the press and denounced the disappearances.
>
> At that time we faced several obstacles, but, to me, the main one was that we couldn't get in contact with the authorities! And that was so shocking to me! I have always thought that they were there to help us, to assist us. But, no. And this was an obstacle we, all mothers, shared. The Acari case wasn't solved because the authorities weren't interested. (cited in Moura, Afonso and Soares 83)

Similar to Argentinean, Salvadorian and Guatemalan mothers, these mothers faced a serious situation of family disruption and financial difficulties, while dealing with emotional and social exhaustion associated with being viewed as the "mother of thugs," which carries a similar weight to the "subversive" label, common in the contexts of political violence aforementioned. This element, of legitimate victimization, is central to the new movements of relatives of victims against violence, as compared to the previous kind of maternal anti-violence activism. While in both contexts victimization is legitimated, the "thug mother" stigma seems to have more weight in the State's attempts to "de-politicize" this violence. As a result, the mothers of such victims struggle to protest the killing of their children both at the internal level (debates over the legitimacy of relatives of drug-traffickers victims) and external level (recognition by the public opinion and the political spheres).

Despite the visibility, the Acari case was never resolved and no reparative measures were taken. Today, 20 years after the Acari murders, there is the possibility of taking the case to international courts. The case of the Acari forced-disappearances expired in 2010. However, with the issuing of the certificates of "presumed death" in 2010, the case can now be brought before the Inter-American Human Rights Commission, which can examine the case and its admissibility before the Inter-American Court of Human Rights. At the end of this process, the Commission will issue recommendations to the Brazilian State. If these recommendations are not followed, the Commission will bring the case to the Court and put Brazil on the stand.

While the Acari case generated a lot of publicity, in the city of Rio de Janeiro, when a middle-class citizen dies, the population's collective indignation is powerfully exhibited. When a resident of the *favela* dies, there is much less sympathy and indignation and in the protests that occur as a result of these deaths there are fewer people. Furthermore, there is also a sort of horror competition: as massacres accumulate, it becomes harder to maintain public attention on older cases.

Politicization/institutionalization

Unlike other mother movements of missing persons and political prisoners of repressive Latin-American regimes, the majority of mothers of the groups of survivors of Rio de Janeiro were poor and marginalized. Thus, they are not only more vulnerable to violence, but find it also more difficult to mobilize against such violence due to a lack of resources. As Araújo (2007) claims, while the Mothers of Plaza de Mayo, for instance, posit social justice at the centre of their discourses and actions; identify capitalism and imperialism as enemies; and defend political leaders such as Evo Morales and Hugo Chavez as potential alternatives for Latin America, the Mothers of Acari focused their narratives on the denunciation of the criminalization of poverty in Brazil. In so doing, they failed to name a specific enemy or to present a specific transformative project for Brazilian society.

In other words, if the tragedy prompts awareness and at times militancy or victimacy, as described by Mats Utas, the justification of these public demands and denunciations stems from a previously ascribed social role—the *mater dolorosa*—which grants moral immunity to the pleas and from which it is difficult to break loose. This is further complicated by the advantages that this status brings: media attention, direct access to social and political authorities as well as celebrities (Moura, Santos and Soares 220).

Future Perspectives: "A Large Family of Relatives of Violence in the Making?"

Since 2007, and partially due to the decrease of the group's activity as a result of the death of one of its most active mothers, Vera Flores, there have been signs of greater alliances with the wider movement of the victims and relatives of victims of armed violence in Rio de Janeiro and in Brazil. The participation of two of the main activists of the group in the "Support Program for Relatives of Victims of Police-led Massacres"[8] has allowed a more direct and continued contact with other relatives of victims of urban violence, as well as with other organizations and interlocutors such as research groups and arts-based communities.

During the course of this program, and for the first time in the history of the mothers movement in Brazil, the idea of collectively writing a book and preparing a documentary honouring the memory of the loved ones and the daily struggle of these survivors began to take shape. Marilene Souza was amongst the editorial team that pulled together the book, *Auto de Resistência: Relatos de Familiares de Vítimas de Violência Armada*, which was published in 2009 (Moura, Afonso and Soares). Additionally, Vera and Marilene became involved in project of the documentary *Right to Mourn,* by Luis Carlos Nascimento, together with the other mothers of the group. The documentary was released at Rio's International Film

Festival, in September 2009, and recently won the award for Best Documentary at the International Film Festival of Bolívia, in Santa Cruz de La Sierra. Marilene Souza, in particular, has taken on an active role in meetings and conferences on public security regionally and nation-wide, bringing together a network of people (mainly women) willing to engage in activism. This is thus a key moment in that it marks the emergence of a new organizational level.

Recent events, particularly the issuing of the first certificates of "presumed" death for the Acari's case,[9] and the potential re-opening of the case of Edméia's death (Notícias Terra), as well as the involvement of the Mothers of Acari in nation-wide initiatives such as the one concerning the institution of a national day in memory of the victims of violence and impunity in Brazil,[10] can also be interpreted as opportunities to establish a survivors' organization in the State of Rio, as well as signs of mobilization around a potentially national association.

The Organization's Importance in the Motherhood Movement

The Mothers of Acari, as well as the other organizations of relatives of victims, and victims, of violence that have been emerging since the 1990s in Brazil, maintain a genealogical relationship with the older maternalist movements that surfaced during the dictatorships of the 1970s and '80s in Latin America. These movements, which emerged as a result of the mass disappearances caused by military dictatorship regimes in the region, have influenced the surfacing of new maternalist groups in the advent of post-democratic transition or post-war period in Latin America. These groups are the new faces of the struggle against prevailing insecurity and injustice, resulting particularly from multiple and transformed forms of State abuse and negligence.

Despite the fact that these new groups of relatives vary in terms of their demands, goals, organizational level, legal status, size and scope of action, they share with the older organizations their agents (women, mostly mothers); the personal and on-going experience of protesting government impunity for new forms of State-sanctioned violence; political mobilization around personal tragedies—particularly disappearances—as well as common narratives and actions characterized by informality and spontaneity, and shared grief for interrupted motherhood and loss.

One difference relates to the difficulty of obtaining public and political recognition of the State's responsibility (through action or systematic neglect) in their personal tragedies. As a result and in greater scale than observed previously, a distinct form of political management of these movements seems to be surfacing, one based on the hierarchization of victims according to their responsibility status.

Yet another important difference is related to the degree of institutionalization of the older and newer victims' groups. Despite the fact that, with time, some of these groups structure themselves politically and strategically in institutional terms, most of them remain organized around a group of activists who organize themselves through networks and movements created as a result of the traumatic memory. The organized collective participation of women, similarly to men, is the result of deliberate choices, often taken due to the personal experience of violences and of macro political circumstances (war, dictatorship, hybrid scenarios) and micro (if the relatives are politicized or not, for instance), as well as social, economic and cultural contexts.

Through their activism, the Mothers of Acari, as well as other allied mothers' groups of victims of urban violence, have contributed to fostering a new form of citizenship amidst the "new violence" scenario. Their experiences may give rise to new models of motherhood and mothering and, as a result, of new expectations around what means to be a woman, which will have positive repercussions in the family sphere, both immediate and extended family relations.[11]

The personal experience of violence and grief (*mater dolorosa*), and later the politicization of motherhood, enabled the entrance of these women into the public sphere. The reconstitution of lives and ties around grief through maternal activism, identified by them as a process which facilitated "scaring" and "closure," has enabled, to a certain extent, the construction of a new identity associated to their practices in the political realm (solidarity building, rights awareness and mobilization), transforming their meanings of motherhood. This resonates with Hebe Bonafini's, president of the Mothers of Plaza de Mayo, statement:

> I was a housewife and I barely attended school.... My life changed, my values changed. This struggle has heightened my solidarity ... a miracle happened, the dead children gave birth to their mothers. (cited in Freitas)

Their political experience changed their discourse and knowledge, enabling them to learn more about their rights and how to exercise them. Obviously, this "new" exercise of (maternal) citizenship coexists alongside maternal stereotypes such as those of "authoritarian mother," "good mother" and "victimized mother," and of "absent father" and "father-provider." This experience, in spite of allowing these mothers to re-visit and re-invent their personal and maternal identities, has some limitations, namely class and gender-based barriers that hinder full and equitable access to their basic human rights.

Conclusion

In the face of contemporary processes of the criminalization of poverty, where social policies are transformed into surveillance policies, designed to monitor, control and repress popular classes, which political meanings can this associative experience of mothers and relatives of violence have? Similarly to other groups of relatives of victims of violence in Brazil, the Mothers of Acari have become social and political actors that interact and question the State as a result of its direct and overt violence, as well as its failure in the public security realm. Their criticism targeted the State's neglect mostly in socio- and geographically-marginalized territories such as the *favelas*, which experience conflicts involving drug factions, corrupt police forces and the militia.

In fact, while suffering and grief prompted action, the justice demands made by this group, as well as the relations forged with the State's judicial and police apparatus, forced their transition from "moral communities" (based on the personal and collective sharing of grief) to "political communities" (political action and discourse based on their collective experience and solidarity in grief, around which they rebuild their lives).

Using elements of the political culture of anti-dictatorship struggles in Latin America and the sentiment of loss as a source of support and credibility, the Mothers structure their demands and activism. The formats of their protest, including resorting to the universal appeal of motherhood, family ties and death mourning rituals, visible in the public use of personal photographs and objects from the disappeared, as well as forms of demonstration which resonate grieving practices, namely silent vigils and religious ceremonies.

Among the greatest achievements of the Mothers of Acari is indeed the democratization of the human rights for the marginalized and poor. However, the Acari case also suggests the persistence of socio-spatial hierarchies, visible in the distinctive patterns of activism participation of the *favela* mothers and the mothers originated from outside the *favela*. This corroborates the fact that the criminalisation of the *favela* and of the *favelado* was indeed one of the main obstacles to public legitimation faced by the Mothers of Acari.

Finally, the personal experience of violence and grief and the use of their maternal identity for political action has enabled two significant changes: the construction of a new identity related to the public sphere, which they associate to the "birth" of their citizenship, and ultimately the re-examination and re-invention of their private spheres, particularly their personal identities and the meanings of motherhood.

[1]According to the report "Redução do Homicídio no Brasil" in 2006 the country registered 34,648 deaths caused by firearms, while the previous study, in 2003, indicated 39,325 deaths in these circumstances. That represents 4.677 of lives saved in the country, especially among men. Regarding gun-related mortality rates, there was an 18 percent decrease. The rate dropped from 22 to 18 deaths per 100 thousand inhabitants (Health Ministry and Justice Ministry, 2007), still far from the value indicated as reasonable by the WHO, which set the bar at the one digit figures per 100 thousand inhabitants.

[2]The most obvious example of this policy was the institution in 1995, during the government of Marcelo Alencar, of the so-called "Far-West Award," in place until 1997, an award granted to the Military policemen for acts of bravery in the command of the corporation. Often, the awarded policeman was distinguished

by the participation in actions that resulted in the killing of alleged criminals (see Justiça Global).

[3]The policemen were named *Cavalos Corredores* because when they entered the slums they sounded like a troop advancing into enemy territory, spreading terror, invading houses, extorting money, and battering people.

[4]The massacre of Vigário Geral took place in the *favela* of Vigário Geral, located in the northern part of the city of Rio de Janeiro. It occurred on the morning of 29 August 1993, when the *favela* was invaded by an extermination group made up of over 50 armed men, who broke into people's houses and executed 21 residents. The massacre of Candelária took place on the morning of 23 July 1993 , near the church of Candelária, in the centre of Rio de Janeiro. Six homeless minors and two young adults were murdered by the military police.

[5]An example of this sterotyping can be seen in the book *Cavalos corredores: a verdadeira história—fatos reais,* written by Colonel Larangeira, a member of the 9th police batallion, responsible for patrolling the *favela* of Acari and the surrounding area, and also one of the main suspects of the forced disappearances. In the book, Larangeira challenges the label of "Mothers of Acari" since, in his opinion, this title (an allusion to the Mothers of Plaza de Mayo) is not worthy of a group of mothers whose children were involved in drug trafficking. According to the Larangeira and other police officers, the disappearance of the youth was motivated by conflicts over the distribution of drug trafficking income and was conducted by a rival criminal group.

[6]PRONASCI is a nation-wide program developed by the Ministry of Justice of Brazil which aims to prevent and react to criminality in the country. The project articulates security policies with social initiatives. The program's key areas of work are the training and qualification of the professionals of public security; the restructuring of the penal system; the fight against police corruption; and the involvement of the community in violence prevention. Amongst the target population of the program are public security professionals; at risk youth, ages 15-24, in conflict with the law or imprisioned; and military reservists, often lured by organized crime due to their expertise in firearms use and repair.

[7]For example, the magazine *Isto É*, on the 3rd of April 1996, highlighted their participation in the soap opera, the media attention devoted to them and their role in the creation of a similar movement in São Paulo, the Mothers of the Sé Square (Freitas).

[8]The program, conducted by Cândido Mendes University, Brazil, and University of Coimbra, Portugal, has sought to contribute to amplifying the voice of the existing women's groups advocating for justice and reparation in Rio de Janeiro, through the promotion of their emotional and psychological strengthening as well as access to information and to justice. It gathered women from groups such as the Mothers of Maracanã, Mothers of Via Show, and the Mothers of Baixada. The program encompassed psychosocial support through a self-help group; free psychosocial assistance and legal advice; and a training course of Popular Legal Educators, addressing topics such as human rights, the Brazilian criminal justice

system, income generation and public speaking skills (see Moura, Santos and Soares).

[9]Marilene Souza has asked for the support of Amnesty International to pressure the General's Attorney to re-open the case of the death of Edméia da Silva Euzébio, murdered in 1993, in Praça Onze, under mysterious circumstances. A witness heard recently by the State's General Attorney appears to be able to identify who killed Edméa and to clarify the circumstances of the disappearance of the eleven young Acari men and women, whose crime expired on the 25th of July 2010.

[10]See <http://lutocomomae.blogspot.com/2010/12/aviso-de-pauta.html>.

[11]These issues dialogue with the debate of Giddens (1993) on the transformation of intimacy.

Works Cited

Alston, Philip. *Report of the Special Rapporteur on Extrajudicial, Summary Or Arbitrary Executions. Mission to Brazil.* 2008. United Nations Human Rights Council. Web. *<www.extrajudicialexecutions.org/.../media/2008%20Brazil%20report8.pd>.*

Amnesty International. *Brazil: Picking up the Pieces—Women's Experience of Urban Violence in Brazil.* 2009 http://www.amnesty.org/en/library/info/AMR19/001/2008/en

Araújo, Fábio. "Com as patas dos cavalos: a criminalização dos pobres e das lutas sociais." *Geografares: Revista do Departamento de Geografia/UFES* 5 (2006): 139-151.

Araújo, Fábio. "Do luto à luta: a experiência das Mães de Acari." Master's thesis, Universidade Federal do Rio de Janeiro, Instituto de Filosofia e Ciências Sociais, Programa de Pós-Graduação em Sociologia e Antropologia, 2007.

Cano, Ignácio. *Letalidade Policial no Rio de Janeiro: a atuação da Justiça Militar.* Rio de Janeiro: ISER, 1998.

Coimbra, Cecília. *Operação Rio: O mito das classes perigosas: um estudo sobre a violência urbana, a mídia impressa e os discursos de segurança pública.* Rio de Janeiro: Oficina do autor, 2001.

Correio do Brasil. "Depois de 20 anos, Justiça expede certidão de morte presumida." 19 de Outubro de 2010. Web. <http://correiodobrasil.com.br/depois-de-20-anos-justica-expede-certidao-de-morte-presumida/186915>.

Freitas, Rita C. S. *"Mães de Acari": preparando a tinta e revirando a praça—um estudo sobre mães que lutam.* Ph.D. thesis, Rio de Janeiro: Escola de Serviço Social, Universidade Federal do Rio de Janeiro, 2000.

Giddens, A. *A transformação da intimidade: Sexualidade, amor e erotismo nas sociedades modernas.* São Paulo: Universidade Estadual Paulista, 1993.

Health Ministry and Justice Ministry (2007), "Redução de Homicídios no Brasil." 2007. Web. <http://www.deolhonoestatuto.org.br/index.php?option=com_docman&task=doc>.

Hollanda, Cristina Buarque de. "Polícia e direitos humanos: política de segurança pública no primeiro governo Brizola (Rio de Janeiro: 1983-1986)." Master's thesis, Instituto Universitário de Pesquisa do Rio de Janeiro, 2005.

Howe, Sara. "The Madres de la Plaza de Mayo: Asserting motherhood; rejecting feminism?" *Journal of International Women's Studies* 7.3 (2006): 43-50.

Human Rights Watch. "Lethal Force: Police violence and public security in Rio de Janeiro and São Paulo." 2009. Web. <http://www.hrw.org/en/news/2009/12/08/brazil-curb-police-violence-rio-s-o-paolo.

Humphrey, Michael and Estela Valverde. "Human Rights, Victimhood and Impunity: An Anthropology of Democracy in Argentina." *Social Analysis* 51.1 (2007): 179-197.

Instituto de Segurança Pública. "Estatísticas sobre incidências criminais e admnistrativas do estado do Rio de Janeiro." 2010. Web. <http://www.isp.rj.gov.br/Conteudo.asp?ident=231>.

Justiça Global. "Relatório Rio: Violência Policial e Insegurança Pública." 2004. Web. <www.global.org.br/portuguese/arquivos/relatorio_rio1.pdf>.

Koonings, Kees and Dirk Kruijt. *Armed Actors: Organised Violence and State Failure in Latin America.* London: Zed Books, 2005.

La Ferrara, Eliana, Alberto Chong, and Suzanne Duryea. "Soap Operas and Fertility: Evidence from Brazil." Working Paper, Bureau for Research and Economic Analysis of Development, 2008.

Leite, Márcia Pereira. "As mães em movimento." Eds. Patrícia Birman and Márcia Pereira Leite. *Um mural para a dor: movimentos cívico-religiosos por justiça e paz.* Porto Alegre: UFRGS, 2004. 54-67.

Moura, Tatiana. "Novíssimas guerras, novíssimas pazes. Dasafios conceptuais e políticos." *Revista Critica de Ciências Sociais* 71 (2005): 77-96.

Moura, Tatiana, Carla Afonso and Barbara Soares, eds. *Auto de Resistência. Relatos de familiares de vítimas de violência armada.* Rio de Janeiro: 7 Letras, 2009.

Moura, Tatiana, Rita Santos and Barbara Soares. "Auto de Resistência. The Collective Action of Women Relatives of Victims of Police Violence in Rio De Janeiro." *Journal of Motherhood Initiative* 1.2 (2010): 215-225.

Nobre, Carlos. *Mães de Acari: uma história de luta contra a impunidade.* Rio de Janeiro: Relume-Dumará, 1994.

Notícias Terra. "Mães de Acari ainda tentam descobrir onde estão seus filhos." *24 July 2010,* Web. <http://noticias.terra.com.br/brasil/noticias/0,,OI4584247-EI5030,00 Maes+de+Acari+ainda+tentam+descobrir+onde+estao+seus+filhos.html>.

O Povo. "Mães de Acari fazem reunião mas têm medo." 22 January 1993.

O Dia. "Anistia Mobiliza 52 países para denunciar Brazil por violações de direitos humanos." 15 May 1993.

O Dia. "O grupo Cavalos Corredores não é fruto da imaginação da imprensa." 28 January 1993.

Rede de Informação Tecnológica Latino-Americana, Instituto Sangari, Ministério da Saúde, and Ministério da Justiça. *Mapa da violência dos municípios brasileiros* 2008. Brasília.

Right to Mourn. Documentary. September 2009. Dir/Prod: Luis Carlos Nascimento Web. <www.lutocomomae.com>.

Schirmer, J. "'Those Who Die for Life Cannot be Called Dead': Women and Human Rights Protest in Latin America." *Feminist Review* 32.3 (1989): 3-29.

Silveira, Martim. "Brazilian Favelas in the Media: A History of Stereotyping." 2009. Web. <www.transcend.org/tms/2009/10/brazilian-favelas-in-the-media/>.

Utas, Mats. "Victimcy, Girlfriending, Soldiering: Tactic Agency in a Young Woman's Social Navigation of the Liberian War Zone." *Anthropological Quarterly* 78.2 (Spring 2005): 403-430.

Ventura, Zuenir. *Cidade Partida.* Rio de Janeiro: Editora Companhia das Letras, 2000.

Wacquant, L. *Prisons of Poverty.* Minnesota: University of Minnesota Press, 2002.

Vink, Nico. *The Telenovela and Emancipation: A Study of Television and Social Change in Brazil.* Amsterdam: Royal Tropical Institute, 1988.

50. Mothers Against Trafficking Humans

GLENDENE GRANT

MY NAME IS GLENDENE GRANT and on March 29, 2006 we realized that my second oldest of four daughters was missing. Jessica (Jessie) Edith Louise Foster was born on May 27, 1984 in Calgary, Alberta and was raised in my hometown of Kamloops, BC. When she was 16 years old, Jessie moved back to Calgary to live with her dad and stepmom. She was in grade eleven and she finished her high school years there. Jessie graduated on June 1, 2002; she had just turned 18 years old.

When Jessie was 20 she had been living on her own for almost two years. She decided to put her belongings in storage and come back to Kamloops to spend some time with her family. While she was living here she got a call to go on a "trip" to Ft. Lauderdale and Key West, Florida, and even though I was not happy about it, she went for a few days. When she got home she had some wonderful pictures of parasailing on the Atlantic Ocean and out on a big beautiful boat and jumping on a water-trampoline, also on the Atlantic Ocean. You could tell by these pictures that she was having the time of her life.

I was relieved when Jessie got home from that trip, so when she got a call a few weeks later to go on another one, I was quite upset. But Jessie told me I had nothing to worry about, and she left to go to Manhattan, New York and Atlantic City, New Jersey. Like her first trip, Jessie kept in touch with us while she was gone. She called me, her sisters, and her friends several times on both trips.

Jessie then called me the night before they were to leave Manhatten. She was in the lobby of the hotel they were staying at, and she was very upset. She said that her "so-called" friend asked her to prostitute herself so they could get some money together for their flight home the next day. She told us that he said he spent all his money at a casino. Though she was mad at what he suggested when she called, she told us that she was not worried about him doing anything to her. She said he was just being a (jerk), and that he was not the type of person who would harm her. She hung up and went back upstairs to her room.

The next day Jessie called and she told me their flight plans had changed. Instead of coming home to BC from New York via Toronto, Ontario, she said they were going to go to Las Vegas, Nevada first. I did not like this at all, but she told

Jessie's grad pictures with her sisters, from the Nancy Grace Show, January 27, 2011.

me she had to go, and she would call me later. She called me two times along the way, and she called me again from Las Vegas. When Jessie got to Las Vegas I was pretty much beside myself, after all, this person she was with had already tried to "talk" her into prostituting. What else might he be capable of?

Jessie got to Las Vegas on May 13, 2005. It was exactly two weeks until her 21st birthday. She told me that she was going to stay in Vegas until her birthday and celebrate it there. I told her that I was not happy with this choice. I also told her something that is hard for me to think about now. I told her that I needed another contact number for her in Las Vegas, because if something happened to her, or to her cell phone, how would I contact her? I said, *who would I call if you went missing*? Even though I did not have a premonition that something was going to happen, I did know that *if* something did, I really needed someone else to be able to contact. So she gave me a number that I did not need until March of 2006, when Jessie went missing.

Our nightmare began then, and with it I decided that there were things I could do. And I would do them. This included educating others about this horrific crime that resulted in the disappearance of my daughter, and to try to keep anyone else from becoming a victim of human trafficking.

On March 28, 2006 Jessie spoke on the phone to her older sister, Crystal, several times. They were making plans to meet up in Kamloops, at my house, where Jessie's car was parked (and is still parked) in my backyard. Jessie has paid for a month of car insurance and that came in the mail *after* we knew something was wrong—but that little insurance card was one of the many things that proved to us that Jessie was definitely planning on coming home when she went missing.

We hired a private investigator right away and he found out some very shocking things about what had been happening to Jessie for the ten months she had been kept in Las Vegas. He found out that Jessie had been beaten and hospitalized, and that she had been forced to work at an escort agency and was even arrested two times, for solicitation of prostitution—for a total of five charges. I have often thought that either Jessie was the dumbest prostitute in Las Vegas ... or she was trying to get herself arrested. As her mother, I honestly believe that Jessie thought if she could just get arrested, she would be sent home, but all that happened was she got arrested, and then sent back with the person who was forcing her to prostitute herself in the first place.

The police did not want to file a report in the beginning. They came up with all kinds of excuses not to: *wrong police office; she may be in Mexico; she probably chose to leave and start a new life ...* anything but: *okay, let's get this report filed.*

When we turned to other officials for help, they completely disregarded us, or gave us the completely useless information. The worst thing of all was that the North Las Vegas police department, the ones in charge of the investigation, simply did not seem to care at all about Jessie, her disappearance, or us. Right from the beginning they told us that she either chose to leave and start a new life, or that the Mojave is a big desert and she will turn up one day. *They refused to consider a third option: that she was kidnapped.* That she was taken away against her will because she was going to leave, and perhaps they knew that she would not return this time. The officer in charge has been disrespectful to me for years. He does not reply to any of my emails or return any of my phone calls. He also never returns calls to people phoning in with tips, and so I also believe, they do not follow up on any one of them. I know this to be true, because I have had people call me to tell me they are waiting for the police to get back to them after they left a message, but no one has ever called them.

The FBI told us that because Jessie was arrested for prostitution, they would have to decline to help. After all, she dared come to their wonderful Sinless City to work at an illegal activity, why should they help? However, if they had been open-minded, I believe the FBI would have been involved in helping find Jessie.

We contacted our Canadian Consulate General, and the Consul/Consular Program Manager in Los Angeles, California (ironically, there is not one in Las Vegas) one time, but she never gathered any information and never got back to us. After several months of leaving messages with the Consular Program Manager not responding, Jessie's dad sent an email begging for her to help us. He said, *remember when you told me you were not just an Ambassdor, you're your were also a mother. Please ... help us.* She emailed back, with this comment:

> As a parent, we try to warn our children of the dangers of travelling alone. Referring Jessica to publications such as "Her Own Way: Advice for the Woman Traveller" and reading the travel report for the United States on the Consular Affairs website is part of our pro-active approach in helping Canadians to avoid problems when they are travelling outside of Canada. Ultimately, the traveller must weigh the risks of travelling to

Pamela Martin (CTV) and Glendene Grant at Hope in the City luncheon, November 25, 2010.

> certain locations that have reputations as unsavoury places, such as Las Vegas. Most of our distressed Canadian cases for our mission originate in Las Vegas. Many people are robbed there or get into other trouble and ask for us to bail them out after they have put themselves in risky situations. We are limited in what we can do in these situations.

I can't believe that they told us that their brochure would have protected Jessie. But when someone is not willing to get involved in a serious situation, this is the kind of answer they give you. And, where did they get the idea that Jessie "traveled" to the U.S. "alone"? She was not alone and she was not "traveling," not what we would think of as travelling, anyway.

I did get a very good response from the RCMP Victim Services. They called us for years to make sure we are okay, but unfortunately, there was not really anything they could do to help us.

Context: What Will M.A.T.H. Actually Do?

I have been thinking about how to describe what Mothers Against Trafficking Humans (M.A.T.H.) will actually do but it is not easy, as there are many things it *needs* to do. M.A.T.H. needs to be an organization that will help turn human trafficking victims into survivors and in order to do that, we need to provide:

> *Housing*: a safe house for the women to be able to start their recovery with counselling and schooling so they can begin their new lives. This will not be short term; when they are ready, they will need their own place to live, with furnishings.

Counselling: there are so many different types of counselling they will need—post traumatic stress; rape; all forms of abuse (mental, emotional, physical, sexual have been done to these women) and it will be hard to trust and live a productive life again.
Doctors: to ensure the women are able to get as physically healthy as possible; it is likely they have not had proper care for a long time. If they have any diseases, they need proper treatment to ensure they are able to become healthy again.
Dentists: the women's teeth and gums would not have been high on the list of things that a human trafficker would have thought about taking care of, and there is a good chance they may even need extensive dental care after being rescued.
Education/Training: in order for a victim to become a survivor, she must be able to get schooling to help her get a job, she will need a career and most times when a victim becomes a survivor, their career choice has something to do with helping others, like a counsellor or a nurse.

M.A.T.H. will do fund-raising to ensure we are able to provide the things needed to help a human trafficking victim become a survivor. M.A.T.H. will do human trafficking education to the police, front line workers, parents and youth.

Education is power.
•Police need to be able to recognize a human trafficking victim in order to save them—they need to be educated on what to do. *Education is power.*
•Frontline workers need to be able to recognize a human trafficking victim if they are ever able to help them to become a survivor. *Education is power.*
•Parents need to know what to be aware of with their children, teens and young adults—knowledge is power and without it, they are a potential victim. *Education is power.*
•Our youth need to know how to protect themselves from ever becoming a human trafficking victim and how to talk to their peers and hopefully prevent it from happening to one of them. *Education is power.*
M.A.T.H. will keep the public aware of other cases and potential cases. M.A.T.H. will actually do so much more.

History

Founded in April 2010, Mothers Against Trafficking Humans (M.A.T.H.) came to me because 1) I am a MOTHER and 2) my daughter is a victim of HUMAN TRAFFICKING. I thought, Do the MATH. There are over 27 million victims of human trafficking and the crime brings in over 43 billion dollars annually.

As the founder of M.A.T.H. and the mother of a trafficked victim I have taken it upon myself to bring attention to all things to do with this crime of modern-day sexual slavery.

I educate students in high schools. I talk to mothers whose daughters have been caught up in the sex-trade industry or they believe their daughters are being groomed to be a victim, which is what happened to my own child. I have been asked to be the guest speaker at fundraisers for organizations that are trying to open houses to help human trafficking victims become survivors (among many other things these organizations do). I am invited to launches of new human trafficking organizations that are opening their doors. I am on the Fredrick Douglass Family Foundation's Board of Directors for a human trafficking education program. I am opening the western chapter of Canada Fights Human Trafficking. I talk to people everywhere I go and open their eyes to modern-day human trafficking. I let them know that there are more good people than bad, and if we stick together, then one person at a time we will win over evil.

I am just one person, and I know I am making a difference.

Mandate

First and foremost, I want to see a decline in the number of human trafficking victims there are annually, and with that I would like to see the victims rescued and given the help they deserve to become survivors. I believe that if there are enough people educated and trained to spot and rescue modern-day slaves, and if there are enough places to take them so they have the chance to get well, then we will be well on the way to taking care of this huge problem.

I believe that if the criminal codes match the crimes and the crimes are punishable by sentences that will perhaps have others reconsider the crimes they will commit, then again, we will be well on the way to combating human trafficking ... and winning.

I believe that if we start educating our citizens while they are still children, teach our children when they are still very young, like we do when we caution them about pedophiles, about drugs, they will know what they are up against as they grow up. *We can do it,* and we can do it without scaring them too much, while protecting them against yet another, horrific crime.

Activities

I have been to many different events from Vancouver to Edmonton to Toronto and back again, helping raise awareness and funds for various organizations with speaking engagements and visits to a number of then including, but not limited to, the following:

•The 19th Annual Women's Memorial March (Vancouver, BC, 2010).

•I was the guest of honour at the "Glendene and Jessie Foster Award" hosted by the Walk-With-Me organization, founded by human traffickng survivor, Timea Nagy (Toronto, Ontario, 2010).

•After meeting Member of Parliament Joy Smith in at the Walk-With-Me event, she asked me if I knew about her Bill C-268, introduced at the Canadian House of Commons First Reading January 29, 2009, to get a mandatory minimum jail sentence for someone convicted of human trafficking of a minor. I told her yes, and that I fully supported it. She asked me, if they felt it would be needed, would I be willing to go to Ottawa to speak to the Senate Committee about Jessie and my point of view on this topic. I told her of course. This was not necessary, and her bill was passed by the Senate of Canada, at Third Reading on June 17 and received Royal Assent and came into force on June 29, 2010.

•The Salvation Army's Hope in the City named me the Hope Giver of the Year (Vancouver, British Columbia, 2010).

•The Maple Leaf Alberta Projects, a committee in Edmonton, Alberta working towards providing hope in the lives of teenage girls (Edmonton 2010).

•Professor Benjamin Perrin's book launch. I was one of his special guests, and when he talked about his book, he specifically talked about Jessie and told his audience that this story was as true as they come, the victim's mother is sitting right there (Vancouver 2010).

•The Alliance Against Modern Slavery as a presenter at the Freedom Benefit Concert and a guest speaker and panel guest at the Inaugural Conference (Toronto, 2011).

•Award-winning writer Andrew Kooman, author of *She Has A Name*, contacted me about speaking at his event and doing a workshop about human trafficking. The event, called "Raise Their Voice: The Trafficked and Exploited" (http://raisetheirvoice.com/raise-their-voice-the-trafficked-exploited) will include several keynote speakers, including MP Joy Smith (Red Deer, Alberta, 2011).

•The Soroptimist International of the Langleys invited me to be on their panel to discuss a National Action Plan as proposed by Joy Smith, MP Winnipeg. There was a march that proceeded down main street to the location and then the forum. It was not open to the public at that point so they could have an honest discussion about how we can be effective in our own communities (Langley, BC, 2011).

•I have been to the Lower Nicola Indian Band to give my talk to kids between the ages of six and 18. We discussed human trafficking and I gave them info about trying to stay safe.

•For two years or more now, I have gone into high schools and have given my presentation to school assemblies for Anti-Hate Week; to several grade 12 law classes; to grade 10 social studies classes; to schools in my city; schools in my province of British Columbia and also schools in Alberta—to talk about Jessie Foster's disappearance and to educate them about human trafficking, to give them dating tips and more.

•I talk to people in line-ups; at grocery stores; on the city bus; in airports; on airplanes; in hotel lobbies; to cab drivers; to every single person who lets me. I make sure that people know this crime happens HERE. No matter where HERE is, it can happen and the only way to prevent it from happening to us, it so be educated.

What I would like to see, legally, is human trafficking charges and convictions result in punishments that fit the crime. I want to know that the perpetrators are not going through a revolving door, where they are back on the streets in three months. We need mandatory minimum sentences for all human traffickers convicted of this horrific crime. Canada, as a British colony, abolished slavery in 1807 and that is over 200 years ago, yet slavery continues like the dirty little hidden secret that it is. Though it is certainly not very "little." But, the secret is slowly being let out to the world.

On September 29, 2003, the United Nations Convention Against Transnational Organized Crime came into force on 25 December 2003 with two protocols, including: the Protocol to Prevent, Suppress and Punish Trafficking in Persons, Especially Women and Children (the Trafficking Protocol). To which I say, *happy holidays.*

Our country of Canada long ago outlawed trafficking-related conduct. Key Criminal Code offences relevant to trafficking in persons include kidnapping, extortion, forcible confinement, conspiracy, the controlling or living off the avails of prostitution, as well as organized crime offences.

On November 25, 2005, the same time that Jessie was planning to come back home to Canada for a "visit" (or whatever it was; all I know is she put a lot of information and pictures in her storage locker in Calgary, which we had access to after Jessie went missing, and which was very helpful to us), all this work was strengthened with the reform of our Criminal Code to specifically prohibit trafficking in persons (in living, breathing human beings); benefiting economically from trafficking; and withholding or destroying identity, immigration, or travel documents to facilitate trafficking.

Then Canada stepped up to help the victims of human trafficking become survivors. In May 2006, just two months after Jessie went missing, a new policy was announced by the Department of Citizenship and Immigration. This policy allows Immigration officers to give temporary resident permits to trafficked persons, for a period up to 120 days.

What our government needs to do is take the stance that Sweden and other Nordic countries have taken and, as a result, have practically gotten rid of prostitution, pimping and human trafficking over there. In 1999, they adopted what is called the "Swedish model," but over the years, after driving the criminals and victims out of Sweden and into Denmark, Norway, Iceland, other countries have followed suit.

The "Nordic model" completely decriminalizes those who sell sexual acts while support services are offered to exit prostitution. As it helps the victims, it does not help "the johns"; it criminalizes the purchase of sex acts in order to stop the demand, which expands prostitution and contributes to modern-day sexual slavery. The message that is sent is very powerful. *It is simply not okay, ever, for a human being's body to be for sale.* Our flesh, blood and bones are not commodities to be bought or sold to the highest bidder, or even the only bidder.

The "Nordic model" takes all criminal liability off those who have been forced into prostitution; those being exploited are victims and they are treated like that and helped in every way possible. Then the police, the courts and judges do the rest. Those who feel it is all right to *buy* a human being are then charged, convicted and humiliated by having all their family, friends, co-workers, and boss know what they are being charged with. What the "Nordic model" is aiming for in the future is to completely eradicate prostitution—not to legalize it, as that ultimately would result in expanding it.

What we need to do as citizens who want this horrific crime to end, is exactly what Crime Stoppers says to do and I completely agree: *Remove the Blue Blindfold* (http://www.publicsafety.gc.ca/media/nr/2010/nr20100907-eng.aspx).

Another way to help put a huge dent in human trafficking is to stop it from being a hidden secret. Talk about it to everyone you know. Discuss it with your family: kids, siblings, parents, friends, schoolmates and teachers, your co-workers and your boss. Your government officials and people you see everyday. *That is how we can combat human trafficking—one person at a time.*

Challenges

There are many challenges in taking M.A.T.H. from a Facebook group (4,252 members) and cause (4,885 members) to a non-profit organization without any formal training or help from anyone. But this will not stop me, because there is a lot of need for this type of organization. There is really nothing in Western Canada set up to help human trafficking victims. The biggest challenge is to get members of Canadian parliament and local citizens involved so we can raise funds to build or open the doors to *Jessie's House* and to keep them open as we help the victims who turn to us.

Jessie's House will be another challenge, as we will need to have only educated and trained personnel working to help save the victims.

Even though I have named these things as challenges, I truly believe that my biggest challenge is something that I meet every day. I live with the horrific realization of having a missing and maybe even murdered child.

Relation to the Larger Motherhood Movement

Anytime an individual or group works towards a similar goal, we are working together. To bring forth a movement that will help women live a safer life is always the answer we are looking for. In relation to the larger motherhood movement, M.A.T.H. has the same purpose as many others: to help victims become survivors.

There will always be a need for organizations like M.A.T.H. and all the others that have been founded to bring forth the changes needed to protect and ensure women's human rights … and men's, women's, and children's right, to live a life safe from the threat of kidnapping and more.

51.
American Mothers Fighting the Vietnam War

Another Mother for Peace

MEGHAN GIBBONS

We who have given life must be devoted to preserving it.
—Another Mother for Peace

As U.S. casualties in the Vietnam War mounted, 15 women in Hollywood, California formed a group that called itself Another Mother for Peace (AMP). Disturbed by the prospect of sending their sons to fight in a distant war with uncertain goals, the mothers organized in 1967 around the nonpartisan slogan "War is Not Healthy for Children and Other Living Things." The majority of AMP members were average mothers with sons who already had been called to fight or who could eventually be drafted. Among them were mothers who had already lost sons in the conflict and wanted to save other mothers the same grief. The group's origins in Hollywood attracted several celebrity mothers who heightened media attention for AMP—Joanne Woodward, Felicia Montaleagre Bernstein, Betsy Palmer, and Barbara Avedon—among them. The AMP group grew by word of mouth and widespread media coverage of the Vietnam War and its opponents. By 1971 AMP had its own office and a staff of fourteen. A major component of its activism was education about the war and how mothers could oppose it. To this end AMP produced a regular newsletter that counted 400,000 subscribers by 1970.

One of AMP's first goals was to lobby Congress to end the draft. The women did so by contacting members of Congress—and even their wives—to influence their votes on key legislation. In the meantime they counseled young men about how to avoid the draft by claiming conscientious objector status or by going to jail instead of enlisting. While AMP recognized that this solution was a bandaid on a much larger problem, such public activities allowed the women to contribute to the wider discourse around the war.

Purpose and Strategies

From the beginning AMP members realized that their power resided in their identities as mothers. They capitalized on this power in their discourse, one that feminist theorists would likely describe as essentialist. Claiming to be solely devoted to their children, they brought their innately nurturing, emotional temperaments to the protest campaign. Although essentialism has long been critiqued by feminist scholarship, the mothers in AMP used it to their advantage, in what has been called "strategic essentialism" (Friedman). The idea that women/mothers have been biologically or divinely designed for certain ends underlies this approach. Thus, their temperament, emotional make up, and even intellectual capacities can be explained within this context. The essentialist rhetoric applied by AMP mothers relied upon larger, often unspoken narratives of women's "essence." In this narrative, certain qualities are so "irreducible, unchanging, and therefore constitutive" of the mother or woman, that they cannot be altered (Fuss 1997: 250).

AMP embraced this essentialist framing of motherhood, a move that separated it from other groups in which women worked against the Vietnam War in the same era, Women Strike for Peace and Students for a Democratic Society among others. The founders of AMP argued that their roles as mothers gave them a special authority: "We who have given life must be dedicated to preserving it" (AMP Newsletter 1970). In identifying themselves first as mothers, the members carved out a space for their discourse that fell between traditional politics—public, patriarchal, hierarchical—and traditional motherhood—private, domestic, personal. In this way they were able to escape from the rules and expectations of both of these spaces and create a new maternal politics.

AMP newsletters and publications sought to emphasize the group's belief that mothers should have a special role in the debate about the War. One of their first mass mailings was organized around Mother's Day and sought to identify this day of homage to mothers with the group's opposition to the war. One thousand cards were printed and sent by mothers to members of Congress with this message: "This Mother's Day I don't want candy or flowers. I want an end to war." The first printing of the cards drew such attention that AMP printed another 10,000 then 100,000, and finally a total of 200,000, were printed (Woodward 1967a). From their early newsletters and correspondences one can see the mounting energy as the women realize that their cause is taking on a life of its own. In one newsletter the mothers report that, "we can barely keep up with the requests for mailings" (AMP Newsletter 1969).

AMP eschewed traditional, formal politics. Its approach to winning members was personal, linking women to each other one-to-one. As one newsletter describes: "we work on a person to person basis.... we need responsible, caring people like yourself who can reach out to friends to make our association known...." Their rhetoric discouraged its members from thinking of themselves as traditional political subjects. In their first mailing on April 24, 1967 they stress that even mothers who have never been politically active could participate. One such mother, Mrs. Billie Backer, whose son, Jimmy, was killed in Vietnam at age 19, was profiled in an AMP newsletter with: "the shock radicalized Mrs. Backer, who had never before been politically active, had seldom read a newspaper and had never even voted." AMP argued that this transformation was occurring in mothers across the country. An Iowa mother, Peg Mullen, who later became a well-known Vietnam War protester, described how her son's death in the war impacted her: "I became the angriest mother in the world. That's when my protest began" (*And Another Family for Peace*).

Cultivating a non-political identity by AMP members was central to its strategy. Its mission statement explains that "AMP does not take positions on issues other than Peace....it supports no political party, but urges its members to support peace candidates of their own choice." (AMP website). Throughout its Vietnam activities AMP tread carefully around the issue of their political nature, catering to several types of women, particularly those with little experience in formal politics. One of AMP's celebrity leaders, screenwriter Barbara Avedon explained that, "We've had letters from all over the country from women who want peace but who would never demonstrate or walk a picket line" (qtd. in Lilliston 19). The high profile actress, Joanne Woodward, wife of Paul Newman and one of the founders of AMP, even described herself as more "maternally oriented than politically" (Radcliffe). AMP's mailing campaign appealed to rural women as well, those who couldn't travel to cities for rallies or direct lobbying. Regular newsletters encouraged such women to "meet informally in their own homes with their neighbors each week to write letters to their representatives in Washington" (AMP Newsletter 1969). Despite its "non-political" rhetoric, AMP urged women to take actions with political impact: write letters, send telegrams, march on Washington. Strategically they didn't call this activity "politics" to avoid backlash from those who saw women's and mothers' appropriate place in the private sphere.

In a remarkable digression from traditional patriarchal politics, AMP's early discourse does not claim to know how to solve the problem of Vietnam: "We aren't pretending to have the answer. We are just interested in women expressing themselves and possibly making the world a better place to live" (Avedon qtd. in AMP Newsletter May 1967). While their earliest publications claimed that "We have no stand. We are apolitical," their actions were directed at formal authorities who would take political action (Woodward qtd. Secrest 1967). They lobbied Congress to pass specific measures around the war and send campaign contributions to the "doves" they wanted to be re-elected. AMP'ers even wrote to the wives of Senators who had voted for renewed military appropriation in 1972: "We were disappointed ... not to see your husband's name listed along with those.... who voted against the $70 billion dollar military appropriations bill" (Letter from AMP 1972). Despite all of this political action, the mothers can claim that their group is "apolitical" because they never ally themselves with any party or platform.

Challenges

From the beginning AMP relied heavily on essentialist images of mothers. The notion that mothers—and all women—were biologically or divinely created with particular qualities fundamentally distinct from males was the basis for this approach. The group authorized itself with archetypal images of motherhood such

as, "A Mother's dream of peace is older than time." (Woodward 1967a, AMP mailing). All mothers, they claimed have a "deep yearning" for peace. (AMP newsletter 1967). Transnational conflict between mothers was impossible, they argued, because of their shared experience of motherhood: "No mother is the enemy of another mother" (Angie Brooks AMP newsletter 1970). AMP's archives are filled with mothers' writings around their spiritual and physical bonds with their children, most with some naturalist imagery of the mother as biologically connected to her child. A 1969 editorial in *Harper's Bazaar* has one mother explain that, "I believe that the reverence for life must live especially in female loins. ... Each child who dies ... in the final obscenity of war is lost by every woman who has ever borne a child—and by all those women who have not, but whose maternity is no less vibrant" (Gittleson). It is not only childbirth but the energy and devotion of childcare that makes mothers particularly connected to children: "We labor to bring children into the world...we sacrifice to raise them. And every mother all over the world rears her young with the same love and concern. And then these children are ripped from us" (AMP newsletter 1970).

AMP's rhetoric argued that the experience of motherhood, despite differences in race, nationality, and class, gave mothers a shared essence: they were sensitive, patient, and nurturing. These shared qualities gave mothers a unique perspective on politics and increased their capacity to work across difference. Privately, though, these mothers proved themselves to be much more complex: their activism was not always patient—they could be demanding and impatient in their campaigns. They were not merely weeping mothers, the *mater dolorosa.* They were at times very angry and quite willing to show it. They were not always polite; they could be rude and confrontational. They were not only emotional beings; they were quite rational and intentional in their campaigns.

While AMP recognized the power of essentialist rhetoric, it understood that such essentialism could be dangerous. Essentialism had been used to argue that only men should operate in the "public" world of business and politics, while women belonged in the "private" world—raising children, keeping home, cultivating religious and moral values. Patriarchal nationalist groups could use AMP's own rhetoric to shame them back into the domestic sphere, arguing that public protest by mothers was unnatural. AMP's rhetoric also clashed with feminist groups who claimed that one could not be liberated and act primarily from a maternal space—which had been traditionally dominated by patriarchal constructions of motherhood. Betty Friedan captured this sentiment in her critique of maternalist rhetoric with, "I don't think that the fact that milk once flowed within my breast is the reason I'm against the war" (qtd. in Echols 1989).

Negotiating these potential conflicts, AMP purposefully defined its motherhood in expansive ways. Its members could be domestic or professional, public or private, sexually "liberated" or conservative. Above all mothers who participated were most certainly patriots and democratic citizens. AMP's office in Beverly Hills was intentionally decorated with a large American flag which Barbara Avedon explained as fundamental to their identity: "The Flag is here because it's our Flag and we're Americans and we're proud of it. We are not a protest movement. We are an assent movement" (Lilliston 1967).

Individual members made the point that they, too, were loyal to the nation. As one AMP member put it: "It's not that I'm against America.... It's just that I'm against war by any government" (Mrs. Billie Backer 1970).

Trends in Women's Activism

In the struggle to define motherhood for the purposes of political action, AMP had to address several elements of maternal identity that were contested in the 1960s and 1970s. The growth of the second wave of feminism and the backlash against it, had heightened awareness of several paradigms related to female identity: essentialism, emotion as episteme, sexuality, and the division of the private/public spheres. The 1960s feminist movement began to examine gender identities as socially and culturally constructed, and questions about women's "nature" abounded: were women more "naturally" suited to childcare and domestic work or had they been constructed this way so that men could maintain economic power? Were women more "naturally" emotional or had they been stereotyped this way by patriarchal systems that privileged reason? The brilliance of AMP was that it did not try to answer any of these questions for its members or potential members. Nor did it try avoiding these topics that were so heatedly debated in so many circles of their era: mothers/women on all sides of these debates could join AMP.

The popularity of white middle class cultural feminism was another influence in AMP's era. These feminists believed that the most effective means to counteract patriarchal power was to create a women's culture that would embrace anti-patriarchal values. Oriented towards the production and valuation of a "women's" culture, this movement focused on the "mother" as a universal category, rather than on "woman," which had encountered serious problems in incorporating differences in race, class and sexuality. The category of "mother," while unable to completely transcend these differences, refocused attention on shared characteristics with a biological basis. Qualities such as nurturing, patience, and gentleness were celebrated by cultural feminists as innately female, and mothers were afforded special status: "the capacity to bear and nurture children gives women special consciousness, a spiritual advantage, rather than disadvantage" (Barbara Deming's qtd. in Echols 253). U.S. cultural feminists saw this construction as empowering mothers/women in "natural" qualities and private experiences already in their domain. But much like essentialism, constructing mothers in such terms had the potential to return them exclusively to the private, domestic sphere and keep them out of public politics. Other feminists argued that mothers/women had to develop qualities that might not be "natural" to them such as aggression, independence, and rational thought, and apply them in the public sphere. As the New York Radical Women explained, "until women go beyond justifying themselves in terms of their wombs and breasts and housekeeping abilities they will never be able to exert any political power" (qtd. in Echols 55-56).

Within this context the use of emotion in public, political discourse was a risky move. The mothers of AMP relied heavily on emotion in their public calls to end the War. The group was founded explicitly as a "group of worried mothers." (Woodward 1967b). At the same time the group tread carefully on emotions that might be considered unappealing in women—especially anger. One member confesses that, "In recent times I have not wept gently. I have wept with rage, with frustration and with horror" (Gittleson). Although this mother admits to her anger, it is tempered by her feminine side, which weeps—evoking the tender image of the *mater dolorosa*. Her grief makes her anger palatable as she explains that, "no woman can confront her own motherhood on the happy, close and carefree family holiday of May 11th [Mother's Day] without grieving for tragic, careworn parents all over the world whose children have been lost" (Gittelson). In public protests the mothers evoke the desperation and impotence that they felt in fighting for their cause. One poignant photo from a march at the White House shows a mother wearing a large placard that reads, "My Son Died in Vain in Vietnam" (Swerdlow 158). Billboards were plastered with advertisements such as "Please No, Mr. Nixon, Not Our Sons" and "Mom and Dad, Your Silence is Killing Me" (Swerdlow 97). These mothers used their emotions to powerful effect and, in the process, legitimized their right to base political action on emotions, a move that flew in the face of traditional, patriarchal, reason-based politics.

The role of politicized women as sexual beings was also a notable issue for AMP. The coverage of AMP by the popular press paid particular attention to members' attractiveness. Numerous newspapers articles and feature stories on the group tried to reconcile what were contradictory images for some: sexual, attractive women who were also intelligent political activists. A newspaper article from AMP's archives on the group's origins is topped by a large photograph of two AMP members, a writer and a TV actress, both very attractive by conventional white, middle-class standards. The headline reads "A Gentle Reminder by Two Doves," suggesting the pacifist politics of the women and the natural temperament of their gender.

The copy describes their campaign as "the gentlest protest of all" and notes that "blond, pretty Whitney Blake was drawn to the movement "by the cute little cards" that AMP produced. She may be working for AMP now but she is not one of those radical leftist women. In fact, the article focuses on how Whitney "wanted to see the fighting stopped, but I didn't really want to get involved" (Craib). The profiling of a private woman who got involved with AMP despite her clearly feminine appearance and propensities is an example of how AMP tried to market itself in compliance with mainstream gender roles.

Formal Women's Activism

AMP's activities should also be seen in the context of social change movements in the U.S. Women were at the forefront of several reform movements during the last two centuries. Sexual morality, abolition, the temperance movement and the suffrage movement were all nineteenth century movements run by women. In the twentieth century women gathered during WWI (1915) and called themselves the Women's International League for Peace and Freedom. The Women's Peace Party, also formed in 1915, similarly called upon "the ideology of nurturant motherhood" to explain its pacifism (Steinson 259). Resting on the Enlightenment notions of women's private natures, both groups affirmed that because of their maternal roles, women were different from men "temperamentally, psychologically, and intellectually.... women instinctively gave their unselfish devotion to the nature and protection of life" (Steinson 259). Several other women's peace groups formed in the 1920s, including the Women's Peace Union, the Women's Peace Society and the National Committee on the Cause and Cure of War (Swerdlow 33). Many of these groups extended their motherhood alliances across borders, arguing that women/mothers of different nations could understand each other's sufferings and losses like no other. But not all U.S. mothers shared this vision. Another group of women, "patriotic maternalists," organized themselves into the largest of several patriotic preparedness leagues, the Women's Section of the Navy League (WSNL), for example, was born in 1915 (Strange 21). WSNL's rhetoric tied women's support for the war to their "instinct of motherhood" which would show them that "women's protective functions made it their duty to demand strong military defenses" (Steinson 266). The group also linked the maternal instinct to women's traditional domestic and child rearing roles.

Conclusion

AMP redefined motherhood in its own terms, creating a political force that called a powerful patriarchal state to account for its foreign policy. On the surface they performed motherhood by rules with which their audiences would be familiar. They were patriotic mothers whose passion for their sons and the ethics of the War motivated their opposition to the Vietnam conflict. They were not gender reformers or revolutionaries. They channeled their emotions only in service to their child-centered cause. The group constructed its authority by relying on essentialist rhetoric and the history of women's moral reform movements in the U.S. It carefully negotiated both second-wave feminism and patriarchal maternalists.

In private, though, some AMP members' experiences transformed their views of the state, the family and political action. Conservative forces had tried to insist that mothers choose between their sons and the state. Although AMP tried to deconstruct this false dichotomy, social pressure was intense to ally with one or the other. As one mother noted after the death of her son in Vietnam, "I love my son more than I love my flag or my country and I would lie down and die for any of my children before I would let them give up their lives for President Nixon and the other politicians who are asking us to survive through this tragedy…" (Backer).

At the same time many AMP members came out of the movement more confident and more capable. Peg Mullen's book about her personal experience, *Unfriendly Fire: A Mother's Memoir,* was made into a TV movie starring Carol Burnett, which was reportedly viewed by 64 million Americans (Brown). The AMP mothers had proven that they could make themselves heard on their own terms. AMP's survival in the ten years beyond the Vietnam War—the group stopped its newsletters in 1986—showed that politicized motherhood was a force with powerful roots. Mothers are not easily silenced by traditional methods, either political or social. AMP's rebirth in 2003 after the U.S. invasion of Iraq is another sign of its timeless message and the willingness of a new generation of mothers to carry the torch for peace.

Works Cited

And Another Family for Peace. Dir. Donald MacDonald. Library of the American Friends Service Committee. Films Incorporated. Cambridge, MA, 1971.

"Another Mother for Peace." March 3, 2011. Web. <http:www.anothermother-forpeace.org/about>.

Another Mother for Peace (AMP). AMP archives. Swarthmore College Peace Collection: Swarthmore, Pennsylvania, June 1967.

Another Mother for Peace (AMP). *AMP Newsletter* May 1967.

Another Mother for Peace (AMP). *AMP Newsletter* April 1968.

Another Mother for Peace (AMP). *AMP Newsletter* 1969.

Another Mother for Peace (AMP). *AMP Newsletter* March 19, 1970.

Another Mother for Peace (AMP). *AMP Newsletter* May 14, 1970.

Another Mother for Peace (AMP). *AMP Newsletter* June 1970.

Avedon, Barbara. *Los Angeles Times,* May 8, 1967.

Backer, Billie. Letter to AMP. Smithtown, New York: June 6, 1970. AMP Archives.

Craib, Ralph. "Gentle Reminder by Two Doves." *San Francisco Chronicle* April 15, 1967.

Department of Defense. *Why Vietnam?* Motion picture. United States: National Audiovisual Center, 1965.

Brown, Les. "ABC's 'Friendly Fire' Drew 64 Million." *New York Times,* April 25, 1979.

Echols, A. *Daring to Be Bad: Radical Feminism in America 1967-1975.* Minneapolis: University of Minnesota Press, 1989.

Elshtain, J. B. *Private Man, Public Woman: Women in Social and Political Thought.* Princeton, NJ: Princeton University Press, 1981.

Friedman, Susan Stanford. *Mappings: Feminism and the Cultural Geographies of Encounter.* Princeton, NJ: Princeton University Press, 1998.

Friendly Fire. Arch Marbel Productions. American Broadcasting Company. Executive Prod. Martin Starger. April 22, 1979.

Fuss, Diana. *Essentially Speaking: Feminism, Nature and Difference.* New York: Routledge, 1989.

Fuss, Diana. "The Risk of Essence." *Feminisms.* Eds. Sandra Kemper and Judith Squires. Oxford University Press: Oxford, 1997. 250-258.

Gittleson, Natalie. "Needles and Pins: How to Win the Human Race." *Harper's Bazaar* May 1969.

"Happy Mother's Day, Mrs. Smith." *Catholic Free Press* May 1970.

Lilliston, Lynn. "Mothers Campaign for Peace Talks," *Los Angeles Times* May 8, 1967.

Moses, C. G. and H. Hartmann, eds. *U.S. Women Struggle: A Feminist Studies Anthology.* Chicago: Board of Trustees of the University of Illinois, 1995.

Mullen, Peg. *Unfriendly Fire: A Mother's Memoir.* Iowa City: University of Iowa Press, 1995.

Radcliffe, Donnie. "Mothers Stump for Pace." *The Evening Star* February 6, 1969.

Secrest, Meryle. "Through Anti-War Christmas Card: Mothers Wish Peace on Earth." *Washington Post* November 10, 1967.

Steinson, B. J. "The Mother Half of Humanity: American Women in the Peace and Preparedness Movement in WWI." *Women, War and Revolution.* Eds. C. R. Berkin and C. Lovett. New York: Holmes and Meier, 1980. 259-284.

Stone, L. *The Family, Sex and Marriage in England,* 1500-1800. New York: Harper Row, 1977.

Strange, Carolyn. "Mothers on the March: Maternalism in Women's Protest for Peace in North America and Western Europe, 1900-1985." *Women and Social Protest.* Eds. Guida West and Rhoda Lois Blumberg. Oxford: Oxford University Press, 1990. 209-244.

Swerdlow, A. *Women Strike for Peace: Traditional Motherhood and Radical Politics in the 1960s.* Chicago: University of Chicago Press, 1993.

Woodward, Joanne. Letter to AMP supporters. April 29, 1967a. AMP archives. Swarthmore College Peace Collection. Swarthmore, Pennsylvania.

Woodward, Joanne. Letter to "Friend." April 24,1967b. AMP Archives.

Woodward, Joanne. *Evening Star.* Washington, DC: February1969.

52.
The Mothers of the Plaza de Mayo

MARGUERITE GUZMÁN BOUVARD

THE ARGENTINE MOTHERS OF THE Plaza de Mayo appeared on the political scene in the aftermath of the military coup of 1976 that ushered in one of the most flagrant and brutal military dictatorships of our times. The military Junta suspended all government institutions and set out to capture subversives, a loosely defined label that included anyone who might oppose their rule. It carried out its aims without compromising its image abroad, inventing its deadly policy of *disappearances,* dragging thousands of young people from their homes, their places of work and their schools by plainclothesmen in unmarked cars. A group of mothers of the *disappeared* began meeting in secret in 1977 and created a formal organization in 1979 with the goal of establishing a democratic system and finding their children. Other groups opposed the Junta, but only the Mothers of the Plaza de Mayo dared to publicly protest and to demonstrate on behalf of their *disappeared* children in the Plaza de Mayo outside the Presidential palace. It was an act of extraordinary courage, and an organization that inspired women around the world. Despite the fact that their own lives were in danger, their organization was founded upon mutual respect and affection and operates as a direct democracy. The Junta's collapse was followed by a series of unstable governments and the end of opposition, except for the Mothers who wanted to keep the memory of their *disappeared* children and the Dirty War alive in a country that turned its back on this period. Today, the Mothers, who are elderly, remain politically active.

History

The Military Junta regarded leftists and reformers as a threat to Argentina's way of life and made their destruction one of its main goals. However, because the Junta did not want to incur international censure for its policies, as General Augusto Pinochet had in Chile, it resorted to the deadly practice of *disappearances.* In what is now referred to as the Dirty War, thousands of gifted and idealistic young adults vanished into the 365 hidden concentration camps scattered throughout Argentina where they were tortured and secretly executed in the most abominable

Mothers marching at night in Buenos Aires. Photo: Gerardo dell'Orto

Mothers demonstrating outside the cathedral where government authorities are attending Mass,1990. Photo: Gerardo dell'Orto

ways, such as being thrown from airplanes into the Atlantic Ocean or the river in La Plata. An estimated 30,000 Argentines were murdered, not including whole families who were *disappeared,* and thus had no one to testify on their behalf. Whole classes of medical students at the university disappeared. Many pregnant women vanished into concentration camps until they gave birth. In a horrendous twist of fate, members of the military whose wives were unable to have children adopted their babies.

Because all opposition was forbidden during the Dirty War, the most astonishing group that openly defied the government was a group of mothers of the *disappeared.* In the beginning, they fit the norm of Argentine mothers in a traditional and patriarchal society that viewed the aged and women as powerless. Those who were not stay-at-home mothers worked in areas commonly reserved for women such as primary-school education, social work and retail sales. Fueled by anger, they would develop a political organization and style that contradicted a culture whose politics historically has been based upon ideological fragmentation and military intervention.

The Mothers first met outside the Ministry of Interior, police stations, army barracks where many of them were kept waiting for hours in their futile search for their *disappeared* children. It was a brutal introduction to the world outside the home and its political system. The Mothers personal lives, the comfort and structure of their routines were turned upside down. They were propelled into a netherworld with no rules, no institutions to respond to their concern. They lived in surreal limbo, deprived of all information and recourse, stripped of social support and comprehension.

In their anguish and perplexity, the Mothers began to compare notes on their situation. They gathered secretly in each other's homes, arriving separately and at different times so as not to attract the attention of the ubiquitous security police because the Junta passed a decree forbidding any public meetings. They also met in churches where they would silently pass each other notes.

Because the Mothers' tragedies were invisible, sharing their situations helped them perceive a political pattern. Each story had a terrible poignancy, often creating disagreements within families. Elsa Fanti de Mansotti was in her forties when her only son was *disappeared.* He and his wife were dragged away by the security forces while staying at his mother-in-law's house with their little girl and their nine-day-old baby while his wife was recovering from the delivery. Beside the anguish of the *disappearance* of the young couple, there would be years of conflict between the two families over custody of the grandchildren. Susanna da Guidano's physicist son was a dragged away in front of his wife and baby. But Susanna's granddaughter and daughter-in-law would not approve of her politics. Comparing their stories and sharing their grief brought the Mothers into the political arena.

On April 30, 1977, fourteen of the Mothers decided to meet in the Plaza de Mayo right in front of the Presidential Palace, risking arrest and assassination, for the military barracks were only a mile away from the Plaza. They thus claimed the geography of dissent, for the Plaza is where Argentina proclaimed its independence from Spain in 1816 and where groups of citizens gathered since then with their political demands. Many of these women had not received a high school education, but they soon established links to Mothers in other parts of Argentina. At a time when any opposition was banned and even friends and family members

Mothers demonstrating in the Plaza de Mayo. Photo: Gerardo dell'Orto

Demonstrating Mothers being attacked by police. Photo: Eduardo Longoni, 1982

of people suspected to be opponents of the regime were being *disappeared,* the Mothers continued to demonstrate in the Plaza de Mayo outside the presidential palace every week.

The Mothers were quick to take the initiative when security forces sought to attack them. They would change the date of their marches at the last minute.

They would join religious processions and talk to people about their cause. When the police arrested one of their members during a march, 60 Mothers stampeded into the police station shouting, "*if you take one you have to take us all.*" The overwhelmed officers were only too happy to get rid of so many vociferous women. By these actions, the Mothers thus not only transformed the Argentine image of motherhood, but also began working to transform the entire political system.

In the early years of the *disappearances*, only those who were personally involved had any awareness of what was happening. Argentina had a dual reality. Everyday life proceeded as usual including soccer matches celebrated with great fanfare and national holidays observed while thousands of people were being taken away by the Junta security without a trace. The ultimate victim of the policy of *disappearance* was the family, whose stability, structure and privacy were deeply affected. The children, siblings and often parents of the *disappeared* suffered severe traumas and were plagued with psychological problems.

Although the Dirty War happened between 1977 and 1983, many of the security forces responsible for torture and *disappearances* are still at large, and after the Junta fell, the country did not want to look back at this terrible period for too many years. However, the Mothers of the Plaza de Mayo continued to march, demonstrate, and speak out to remind the country of this period.

I first visited the Mothers in 1989 because I planned to devote a chapter about them in a book on women and human rights. My response to them went deeper than that of a scholar or a human rights activist. As a mother, I could feel their anguish and soon experienced a profound love for each one of them. That led me to participate in their demonstrations. Being with the Mothers and marching with them transformed me. I saw how they used both their grief and their anger to create a powerful political force. In the midst of heightened tensions and mutual hatred among the various political groups, I witnessed a totally new way of carrying out politics. The Mothers' evolution from simple housewives to powerful political leaders is a story of the revolution of hope, a story I wanted to share with a generation who no longer believes that the individual, especially older women, can have an impact on events. Their continuing political work celebrates the values their *disappeared* children worked for and change for those who are oppressed. I see each mother as a flame moving through chaos and injustice, illuminating the possibilities of the human spirit, a vision I will always carry.

I also learned about fear and how useful anger can be in overcoming it, although women who become angry are generally thought of as "bitches." During my visits I accompanied the Mothers as they were followed by security police, some of them taking videos of their marches from their cars. Their president, Hebe de Bonafini, survived an assassination attempt in front of her home the week before I arrived. She invited me to stay with her to test me. I was terrified during our midnight bus trip to the city of La Plata. Over time I learned that fear was compromising my work with the Mothers and became enraged at the continuing presence of the police and disguised security guards. It was liberating: I found myself taking photos of police who were on the rooftops in the Plaza with their rifles pointed at

Evel Aztrabe de Petrini in the Plaza de Mayo
Photo: Marguerite Guzmán Bouvard

the crowd during a violent confrontation provoked by security forces. One of the mothers called to me, "Run Margarita, run," as two tiny women over seventy years old took me by the hand and led me away from the Plaza.

Finding Allies and International Support

The Mothers learned important survival techniques that included reading the newspapers about foreign dignitaries visiting Argentina and getting in touch with them to explain their situation and persuade them to attend their marches. They became a strong match for the Junta as they forged ties with supporters in Western Europe and the United States. Lisbeth Den Uyl, the wife of the Prime Minister of the Netherlands, created a support group for the Mothers of the Plaza de Mayo (SAAM). They became the first champions for the Mothers, bringing together women from all walks of life, writers, executives, politicians and housewives. SAAM organized demonstrations in their country, sponsored exhibits, and raised funds to help finance the Mothers' activities. Its members were also able to pressure their own governments, giving the Mothers yet another weapon against the Junta. Soon, other support groups throughout Western Europe, including France's President Mitterand's wife who headed the human rights organization, France Libertés, followed SAAM as the Mothers raised their concerns abroad.

As the years passed, the Mothers' numbers would swell into the hundreds and include a network of Mothers in the interior provinces and support groups staffed by exiles and nationals throughout Western Europe. At a time when any opposition was banned and anyone suspected to be opponents of the regime were being *disappeared,* the Mothers continued to demonstrate in the Plaza de Mayo every week. At a meeting with the President of the Junta to discuss the whereabouts of their children, they insisted "*You are not going to remove us from the Plaza until you tell us what happened to our children. Because you won't take responsibility for your*

Hebe de Bonafini serving lunch in the Mothers' House
Photo: Marguerite Guzmán Bouvard

actions, you are more cowardly than anyone."

What set the Mothers apart from other dissident groups in Argentina was their bravery, their audacity and the manner in which they outwitted the Junta at a time when many people sought refuge from their fear in the belief that if one remained quiet and focused one's attention on personal matters, nothing would happen. Because so many journalists were *disappeared*, the only people who dared to publicly protest were the Mothers. In so doing they risked their lives. Indeed their first leader, Azucena de Villaflor de Vincente and two other Mothers were *disappeared* by Alfredo Astiz, a member of the security forces. Astiz had disguised himself as Alfredo Nino, someone who had lost his parents and needed the Mothers' help. He is still at large today.

In August 1979 the Association of the Mothers of the Plaza de Mayo was registered in a formal charter, creating an organization promoting democratic values. By this time, they had developed a vast network of communications and cooperation with Mothers in the city of La Plata and in the interior. Headed by their new president, the outspoken and charismatic Hebe de Bonafini, the Association moved into a small office financed by their supporters in Western Europe. This was a first step in what would become a long act of defiance against the terrorist state. The women had sought help from a variety of human rights' organizations but they felt that they were a distinct group and that it would be better for them to work on their own.

The Mothers of the Plaza de Mayo politicized motherhood by wearing white shawls on their heads that were intended to represent baby shawls or diapers as well as opposing military power by their peaceful demonstrations.

The Junta referred to the Mothers as *Las Locas* or *the Crazy Ones*, thus equating political dissent with social deviance. In addition to threatening them physically, it deliberately ridiculed them as a tactic to isolate and weaken them and as an

Noemi de Alvarez Rojas and Eliavera Diaz de Triana
Photo: Marguerite Guxmán Bouvard

an example to any group who might oppose the regime. When the Junta blamed the *disappearances* on nihilistic subversion, the Mothers called a press conference in the Plaza de Mayo to deny the statement and to blame the abductions on the government. Given the fact that so many journalists had *disappeared,* speaking out was unusually courageous. It was the beginning of the war of words between the Mothers and the government.

The Mothers broadened their struggle during he late 1970s and early 1980s. They traveled to the United States, to Geneva where they met with Theo Van Boven, head of the United Nations' Human Rights Commission, to the Vatican, and throughout Europe to denounce the *disappearances* and seek the support of democratic leaders. They carried out a frenetic round of visits that brought the Mothers to any country willing to receive them and listen to their message, from Sweden, to Canada, to Korea, to Australia. With their white shawls they circled the globe, self-appointed ambassadors on behalf of the victims of state-sponsored terrorism. They thus gained an international reputation, and claimed space in opinion sectors throughout the world for their plight and their humanitarian values. From their intrusion into a political arena that proscribed any form of opposition, they joined the arena of international diplomacy. In 1980 they were nominated for the Nobel Peace Prize and shortly after received the Norwegian Prize of the People for having qualified for the Nobel Prize. In 1992 they were awarded the Sakharov Prize for Freedom of Thought from the European Parliament.

Speaking Truth To Power

The Mothers have always refused to align themselves with any political party although they sponsored political debates in their office. They identified themselves as a collective, claiming that they have socialized maternity, meaning the *disappeared* child of one is the child of all of the Mothers. From the early days of their organization, the Mothers have maintained that truth is revealed both by speaking and acting. They have shown that in revealing the inconsistencies and weaknesses of the system, truth can constitute a form of power against a repressive system. They have thrust themselves into the arena of national politics by shaping political dialogue and thus awakening political consciousness. By defining their own political vocabulary in a way that unites the public and private spheres, they have forged a space in political awareness, echoing the work of the Brazilian social theorist, Paulo Freire, who wrote that power begins with the formulation of our own perceptions of reality. The space the Mothers claimed for ethics illuminated the lies in the Junta's propaganda, just as the Junta's efforts to silence them revealed the Mothers' profound influence.

The military Junta collapsed in 1983 as a result of its defeat during the ill-fated Falklands War and growing popular disaffection. A transitional government was created and elections were scheduled for October 1983 to restore a constitutional government. Some top commanders of the military were tried and convicted, but after a series of abortive military uprisings, prosecutions were dropped and those convicted received amnesty. That the transitional government persisted in harassing the Mothers with tear gas and night sticks as they marched in the Plaza was proof of the importance of their voice. As usual, they fought back with pointed statements. For instance they claimed that if their voice were not as strong they would not have experienced harassment from the government.

By this time, the Mothers had not only acquired political sophistication but had formulated a vision of Argentina that would pit them against the exigencies of the new regime, a fragile democracy still embattled with a powerful military. Many human rights groups felt that it was necessary to suspend criticism of the new government's policies in order to ensure its survival. They also felt that too much pressure on the military would cause it to revolt and attempt to regain power. The Mothers' radical stance resulted in a drop in membership. A number of Mothers left because they believed that justice would be best served by supporting the new government and working with the political parties. From the Mothers' organizational perspective, insufficient pressure on the military would create the same result. Because of this stand, the Mothers were widely considered as difficult, intransigent women. When President Alfonsin was urging everyone to *"heal the wounds"* and move on, the Mothers were in the Plaza with their banners and thousands of followers, denouncing him. They proclaimed "*if the wounds were still bleeding people would remember what had happened.*" They also chanted "*while the President had the government, the military still had the power.*" They continued to demonstrate and chant their slogans, a new one every year, responding to the government's effort to ridicule them and to ignore the events that occurred during the Dirty War.

The government began to malign the Mothers by circulating rumors about them and by publicly criticizing them. In response they came up with searing slogans of their own. Besides enduring verbal harassment from the media and government officials, the Mothers also suffered many instances of violence that they traced to the President's inner circle. The Mothers always linked the continual stream of death threats they received throughout the 1980s and 1990s to the security forces and ultimately to the government. They publicly stated that both the robberies of their computers and the trashing of their large office on Yrigoyen Street called The Mother's House, happened shortly after President Carlos Saúl Menem, Raul Alfonsin's successor, had criticized them.

The political effectiveness of the Mothers resulted from their ability to forge a new public language, proclaiming their goals while revealing the hollowness of certain government policies. They also manifested their presence by publishing their own newspaper and by demonstrating throughout the country at important political events. They were taking an important space in the political arena that reflected their power.

Defying the government under Saúl Menem was risky business in Argentina where the executive has traditionally dominated the Congress. President Menem made the presidential system even stronger by replacing three-fourths of the Supreme Court justices and by passing a large number of measures by decree, completely circumventing the Congress. When a judge spoke out against the government's practice of torturing criminals, Menem dismissed him. The President tried to evade any response to the Dirty War. While the country continued its politics as if nothing had happened, many of the perpetrators of the horrible deaths of a generation of young people and whole families were never brought to justice. But the Mothers continued refusing to allow the government to dominate the political dialogue. Every year since 1981, as part of their 24-hour march on Human Rights Day, they have unveiled their new slogans intended both to defy the government and to empower their followers. For instance, after yet another failed military coup, they adopted the slogan "*to resist is to combat,*" teaching their followers that power lies with those who oppose military force rather than with those who resort to it.

The Mothers' office, the Mother's House, was a perfect example of their meshing of motherhood and politics. There is a room where the Mothers once met with their lawyers who volunteered their services and where they received journalists from abroad. On the upper floor there is another room where they produced their monthly newspaper and a large room with photos of their own *disappeared* children lining the walls and space for their private political gatherings. But at noon the desks were cleared and lunch prepared. After a heated discussion one of the Mothers often reached under a table, pulling out her sewing machine to create a banner for their weekly marches. The Mothers also prepared dinners for their young supporters who arrived after their jobs and dedicated their evenings to helping them. People who suffered from crimes committed by the still present security forces arrived at their office to ask for help and received it both from their lawyers and by the Mothers taking them to the Plaza to speak out.

Developing A Political Program to Ensure Maternal Values Around the World

The Mothers continued asserting the claims of motherhood against the state and their efforts to transform the political system, reflecting their definition of maternal values as concern for the well-being of all children through health care, education, full employment, grass-roots participation in government and the international pursuit of peace. In their claims and in their defiance of the governmental policies of Presidents Raul Alfonsin and Carlos Saúl Menem, they came to refer to themselves as revolutionary mothers.

In March 1994, the Mothers sponsored an international conference of activist mothers' groups. The meeting held in Paris was organized by Ada Allesandro, who lives there and is the coordinator of the Mothers' support groups. The purpose of this extraordinary conference was to forge an international movement of mothers and women on behalf of human rights that would strengthen each organization within its respective country and create a new presence in international politics. Hebe de Bonafini's travels around the world brought her into contact with other mothers' associations that were working on behalf of justice. The Mothers' office in Buenos Aires hosted Latin American Mothers who came to learn from their experiences. Armed with their belief in the ability of committed women to effect changes in values and political practices, the Mothers set out to transform a troubled globe.

Because of the difficulties of even contacting women's groups in war-torn countries such as Bosnia-Herzegovina, the Israeli-Occupied Territories, the Western Sahara and Sri Lanka, it took almost two years to arrange for the gathering. For three days at the end of March, 1994, representatives of fourteen organizations met in Paris, including women who had flown from Sarajevo, Zagreb, Belgrade, Brazil, Kiev, Jerusalem and other places around the world. There were women, such as the Sinhalese and Tamil members of the Mothers Front in Sri Lanka who could not leave their war-torn countries but who wanted to attend. Many of the participants had never left their countries before. A number of them risked their lives in attending because their governments regarded their presence as a traitorous act. Although they came from different cultural backgrounds, all shared the common bond of having suffered oppression and the loss of family, and were struggling against various forms of injustice. They were united by their activism, their ability to give each other affection and support, and their goal of ensuring human dignity.

Speaking to each other of the horrors they had endured and of their attempts to confront dangerous authoritarian governments, they broke the silence imposed by political persecution. Although their political circumstances and cultures were highly diverse, their stories revealed a common path from personal tragedy to courageous activism. As they listened to each other, Israeli and Palestinian women overcame national hatred, and three women's organizations from the war-torn former Yugoslav republic found mutual support in their efforts to end armed conflicts and establish peace among Muslims, Croats and Serbs (Bouvard 1996).

The Mothers also inspired the organization of the Mothers of East Los Angeles led by Juana Gutierrez in the United States. They protested against putting an incinerator, a prison and an oil pipeline in their community. They rallied against dumping toxic wastes in poor Latino Communities, gathering crowds of hundreds of women. These courageous and outspoken mothers not only achieved their goals, but also received an award from President Bill Clinton.

Meanwhile, in Argentina politics continued as if nothing had happened and many of the perpetrators of the horrible deaths of a generation of young people and whole families continued to evade justice.

Victory

It was not until President Nestor Kirchner came to power in 2003 that the death threats and harassment of the Mothers ended. They knew that that he had personally suffered during the Dirty War and they considered him as an ally.

By then, they were no longer shunned by the media and didn't need to publish the newspaper they sold in the Plaza. Every issue of that paper always featured on its last page the photo of a member of the military responsible for the *disappearances* with his face portrayed behind bars beneath the title Gallery of Oppressors. Recently, a well-known newspaper "Pagina Doce," (Page 12) published a book of the Mother's Gallery of Oppressors that went through two printings in just one year.

In 2004 President Kirchner began the process of establishing a museum in the Naval Mechanics School, the site of a former concentration camp where many of Dirty War's worst atrocities took place. As usual, the Mothers were not in agreement with the government's decision. Their outspoken leader Hebe de Bonafini said, "*Museums mark the end of a story and we haven't reached that point in Argentina yet. It is much too soon to be setting up a museum because the historical events are too recent*" (cited in Rohter 2004).

In the spring of 2006, it was discovered that the naval intelligence agency continued to spy on public officials, journalists and political leaders, including the President. As a result all naval intelligence activities were suspended and the director was fired pending a complete investigation. The Mothers marched in protest.

Later, President Kirchner directed the Supreme Court to nullify the pardons and amnesty laws that protect military violators. He also agreed to help extradite those who were hiding in other countries. In an unprecedented act of international judicial cooperation, Ricardo Cavallo, a former naval officer accused of kidnapping, torturing and murdering hundreds of people at the school of Naval Mechanics in Buenos Aries, was extradited to Spain from Mexico where he was accused of genocide and terrorism (Daly). Outside the court, a crowd of protestors marked the occasion with banners recalling the *disappeared* from the Dirty War. Kirchner also purged the military, removing the Dirty War generation from command positions. Although many people in Argentina do not remember or are not interested in what happened during the Dirty War, the Mothers continue to proclaim their crimes.

The first trial involving charges of torture at a notorious military prison began in 2006, with a former coast guard officer receiving life in prison. Héctor Febres was accused of torturing people seized by government agents and taken to the feared Navy Mechanics School, the largest clandestine torture center of the era; an estimated 4,500 prisoners had passed through its cells and were never seen again (*New York Times* 2007). When he was ready to denounce his colleagues he was found dead in his cell, poisoned with cyanide ("Argentina's dirty war"). Government prosecutors also brought a series of charges against former state security agents and their civilian allies for crimes committed during the Dirty War. Among these criminals, Rev. Christian Von Wernich, a Catholic priest, was finally convicted of participating in the torture. Until then, the Mothers had kept on marching by his church and organizing demonstrations against him.

One of the pilots responsible for throwing scores of people into the ocean, Julio Alberto Poch, was arrested in Spain in 2009 and extradited to Argentina in 2010 (*New York Times* 2010). In spite of these arrests, many of the most notorious members of the Security Forces are still at large. In fact many other former military leaders including General Jorge Videla who ruled the Junta between 1976 and 1981, have never been brought to justice. He was charged in connection with human rights abuses but still lives under house arrest like many other former military leaders.

On the 30th anniversary of the military coup the Mothers put up posters and billboards vowing, "*Nunca Mas*," (Never Again) (Rohter 2006). They carried a banner with photos of the people abducted during the coup, the photos of their children that still line the walls of their office. This time the streets were filled with protestors, not only Argentines but also with Uruguayans (many of whom were also *disappeared*) and Chileans. There were also special museum displays, photographic exhibitions, public forums and television programs joining the public outrage. But it was only that group of older women, the Mothers, who had been consistently marching and speaking out in public.

Overcoming resistance in Congress, President Kirchner succeeded in making the date a permanent holiday called the National Day of Memory for Truth and Justice. Many Argentines marched and held commemorative vigils across the country, with some gathering outside the homes of former officials of the Dirty War and hurling eggs, rocks and insults. Meanwhile, in provincial cities such as Cordoba that had been a stronghold of death squads, masked men broke into the homes of human rights' groups.

The Mothers were always the ones to move beyond fear and take to the Plaza and the streets. During the Dirty War, they even spent one night before a military parade, painting the outside walls of prison cells with images of the military behind bars, and angry criticisms on the pavements where the soldiers would march.

Given the national response, the Mothers decided to end their 24-hour Resistance March on Human Rights Day in 2006. Sara Brad, a Mother from Tucuman noted, "*This is the last Resistance March, but we are going to continue each Thursday in this Plaza and other plazas of the provincial affiliates like always. Our fight will continue in other spaces and with other projects, but with the same strength. The only fight that is lost is the one you give up*" (cited in Trigona).

In 2007, the Mothers celebrated the thirtieth anniversary of their organization. It attracted thousands of supporters and the media in Argentina and other countries. Their supporters in Europe also marked the occasion. Britain's BBC's *Women's Hour* flew down one of its reporters and a few women's groups from Western Europe attended.

The current President Cristina Fernández de Kirchner is committed to seeing trials against the oppressors by the end of her term in 2011. The Mothers support her efforts with their relentless struggle. The Mothers' numbers have dwindled but they continue to be active, to speak out and march with their children and grandchildren, many of whom are children of the *disappeared.* The Mothers continue fighting for a more just and egalitarian society. They have established a university to train people in human rights and they have also created a number of centers in slum areas to teach adolescent children at risk as well as supporting indigenous peoples in their country. With the help of a radio journalist who had been silenced during the Dirty War, they created a new radio program for their organization.

The Mothers of the Plaza de Mayo have left an important legacy by fashioning the political dialogue, taking space in the streets, reaching out to the United Nations and the Organization of American States, and fanning out throughout the country on behalf of political change. Thus they proved that no dictatorial regime is invulnerable, that mothers banding together with ties of affection and common goals can become not only a a formidable source of dissent but also an end in itself. Today, the Mothers of the Plaza de Mayo remain a rare example of powerful elderly women.

They have shown mothers around the world how to overcome fear and create political change that will honor motherhood and democracy. Most importantly they developed ways of making their goals visible in countries that use any means possible to ignore them, such as the media, death threats, circulating rumors and engaging in violence. They have demonstrated how they are able to educate a country not only about what horrendous acts are occurring even though they are hidden, but also how to react to them and create change. They have revealed that for a committed organization of mothers, anything is possible. Their history has become a beacon that will remain in our memory and serve as a model for contemporary mother activists.

Works Cited

"Argentina's dirty war: the museum of horrors." BST 17/05/2008. Web. <http://www.telegraph.co.uk/cora/content/display>.

Bouvard,Guzmán, Marguerite. *Women Reshaping Human Rights: How Extraordinary Women Are Changing the World.* Lanham, MD: Rowman & Littlefield, 1996.

Bouvard, Guzmán, *Marguerite, Revolutionizing Motherhood: The Mothers of the Plaza de Mayo.* Lanham, MD: Rowman & Littlefield, 1994.

Bouvard, Guzmán, Marguerite. "Mothers as Agents of Political Change: The Mothers of the Plaza de Mayo at 30 Years." Spring 2007. Web. <www.womensvoicesforchange.org>.

Bouvard, Guzmán, Marguerite, Interviewed on BBC Women's Hour, celebrating the Mothers' 30 Years. May 2007.

Bouvard, Guzmán, Marguerite. "Mothers Working Together for Peace, Sara Ruddick and the Mothers of the Plaza de Mayo," *Maternal Thinking; Philosophy, Politics, Practice*, Ed. By Andrea O'Reilly, Demeter Press, Toronto, Canada, 2009.

Daly, Emma. "Argentine Extradited to Spain for Genocide Trial." *International Herald Tribune* June 30, 2003.

New York Times. October 18, 2007.

New York Times. January 6, 2010.

Rohter, Larry. "Debate Rises in Argentina on Museum of Abuses." *New York Times* February 2004.

Rohter, Larry. "On Coup's Anniversary, Argentines Vow 'Never Again'." *New York Times* March 25, 2006.

Trigona, Marie. "Argentina's Mothers of the Plaza de Mayo Pass on a Legacy of Defending Human Rights." March 9, 2006. Web. <http://towardfreedom.com/home/content/view/769/54/>.

53.
The Mothers of Laleh Park

The Mourning Mothers of Iran Demand an End to Violence

SUSAN LOGSDON-CONRADSEN

IN JUNE 2009, THE MOURNING MOTHERS of Iran, a civil society group, was formed by mothers whose children were killed, imprisoned, or disappeared during the state-sanctioned violence that occurred after the disputed June 12 presidential election. They came together to demand justice and truth about what happened to their loved ones and quickly grew to include supporters. Their principle demand is government accountability for the deaths, arrests, and disappearances of their children and other Iranians. However, they also call for abolishment of the death penalty and the release of political prisoners.

The group is not affiliated with any political organization and uses non-violent ethics and measures to bring attention to the atrocities and violence within Iran. Every Saturday they dressed entirely in black and gathered silently for an hour in various parks in Tehran. For several months the Mourning Mothers continued their weekly vigils risking bodily harm, harassment, and arrest, despite the fact that their gatherings were routinely targeted by security forces. Presently they are unable to hold vigils in Tehran due to pronounced security forces but continue to be active in the blogosphere and other aspects of social media and have become global icons of humanitarian rights. The Mourning Mothers have changed their name to the Mothers of Laleh Park. However, many groups have formed around the world to show solidarity with them and use the name Mourning Mothers of Iran, and many news reports also utilize the name Mourning Mothers of Iran.

In discussing the Mothers of Laleh Park this chapter will examine the history surrounding the formation of this group, the significant challenges it has continually faced from the Iranian regimen, and discuss how this group falls into a long history of mothers risking their very lives to provide a voice for their silenced children, demand human rights, and protest violence.

Mandate

On their official website (*Iranian Park Laleh Mothers*) the Mothers of Laleh Park describe their primary purpose as fighting for justice for their lost children. Specifically, they "demand those responsible for ordering and carrying out the

Placard held up at weekly vigils featuring slain Iranians, including Neda Agha-Soltan on the far right.

individual and mass executions, ethnic and religious massacres, imprisonments, tortures, rapes, assassinations, raiding and ransacking the homes, pillaging the dormitories, etc., since the 1980s to be brought to justice." Thus a main goal of these Iranian mothers is to get answers and justice from the authorities. The group's philosophy is one of non-violence, both in its activism and in its demands of the Iranian government, and they repeatedly advocate for an end to violence, including a repeal of the death penalty. They also advocate for human rights and demand the release of political dissidents stating that they "support all non-violent and equalitarian activities". The Mothers of Laleh Park have issued various statements in support of releasing women's rights activists and other human rights activists and preventing executions.

History

The Mothers of Laleh Park is a grassroots group that spontaneously arose in response to increasing violence from the Iranian regime in June 2009. That month a huge protest rose up from the general public and university students following the disputed presidential election in which President Mahmoud Ahmadinejad was re-elected. On June 20th, referred to as Black Saturday, during the massive protest, several women and men were killed, and others were beaten, raped, tortured, and imprisoned. A woman, Neda Agha-Soltan, was shot and died within minutes on the streets; her death was videoed on a witness's cell phone and posted on YouTube and Facebook within minutes. Within hours the footage had gone viral and created international outrage. Neda's death has been described as "the defining sequence in the 10-day uprising against the regimen in Tehran, a gruesome manifestation of Ayatollah Ali Khamenei's threat to use force on the tens of thousands of people contesting the outcome of the presidential election" (Tait and Weaver). Authorities

Collage of Mothers of Laleh Park

quickly prevented Neda's family from holding an Islamic funeral out of fear of creating a martyr for the opposition and they threatened mosques against holding a service. Despite these measures Neda became a martyr with her image placed on placards held up on the streets in Iran, and she has come to symbolize government repression and a rallying cry for freedom (Drash and Nasr).

The Mothers of Laleh Park was formed initially by the mothers whose children were killed or disappeared during this protest of the presidential election. Neda's mother, Hajer Rostam Motlagh, and Parvin Fahimi, the mother of Sohrab Arabi, a 19 year old man who was killed when the basiji militia opened fire on the protestors in central Tehran, are two of the more publicly known Mothers of Laleh Park. The Mothers decided to hold a silent vigil near the place and time (7:00-8:00 p.m.) of the killing of Neda Agha-Soltan at Laleh Park. Dressed in black and holding candles, roses, and/or photos of their children they held a silent vigil on Saturday June 27 th.They were attacked by security forces and many were detained, but despite the attempts to disperse them, over 500 women continued with the sit-in and gatherings.

On July 3, 2009 the Mourning Mothers issued a statement to other Iranian mothers. They stated:

> Dear Mothers! Our mother instinct has forced us to demand justice for our children and freeing those who are unlawfully detained in prisons. We invite you to join our grassroots peaceful gatherings in the above-mentioned parks on Saturdays of each week. To our boys and brothers in the security forces! We are your mothers. We treat you with respect as mothers. Respect us and our wishes and refrain from inflicting harm onto your mothers. Our sighs will follow you if you treat us with violence. (Setrakain)

From then on, until they were prevented by security forces, the group gathered every Saturday in a peaceful and silent protest and membership in the Mourning

Collage of Mothers of Laleh Park

Mothers grew to include mothers of political prisoners and those whose children had been killed, tortured, raped, detained, or disappeared during the past 31 years.

On July 31, 2009, on the 40th day of Neda's death, there was a large protest to commemorate her death, and security forces were apparently caught off guard at the amount of mourners in five different cities. At the cemetery of Neda's grave approximately 10,000 people came to mourn. There were reports of random beatings with batons from the security forces initially with violence intensifying later in the day (Daragahi and Mostaghim).

Context

Although the Mothers of Laleh Park formed in the aftermath of the state sanctioned violence in June 2009, their focus has been on injustices and violence over the last 31 years. For the last three decades Iran has attracted global attention for its human rights violations including unlawful detainment, torture, and cruel executions. A particularly dark period of Iranian History occurred in 1988 when during a couple of months, 4,500–10,000 Iranian prisoners were declared killed or missing according to Amnesty International (Amani and Anzi). Similar to the prohibition of a memorial service for Neda, these families were not allowed to hold a service and were pressured to be silent. In fact, the families were not told of the massacre until months later and the executed prisoners were buried in unmarked and unknown mass graves; one of these mass graves at Khavaran was later accidentally discovered. The Human Rights Watch declared in 2005 that the "deliberate and systematic manner in which these extrajudicial executions took place may constitute a crime against humanity under international law" (Haeri). Since 2005, President Ahmadinejad's "administration has pursued a multi-phased campaign to neutralize dissent at universities and 'Islamicize' higher education" including imprisonment, banning education, and restricting student activities ("Iran: Escalating Repression").

Since the June election, Iran has further increased repressive measures against

Iranian civil rights activists. In June 2009 a blanket detention order was issued that empowers the police to take anyone into custody for any reason; according to the International Campaign for Human Rights in Iran over 1,000 individuals were arrested in January and February of 2010 alone (Slackman). Official reports indicate that over 5,000 activists have been arrested since the election, although this is widely considered a gross underestimate, and hundreds of activists are being locked up in an attempt to silence them ("From Protest to Prison" 5). Speaking out against the regimen carries serious consequences. For instance, Bahareh Hedayat, the first women elected to the national student organizations committee and the first secretary of the Women's Commission of the Office to Foster Unity was arrested on December 30, 2009 and charged with national security crimes including "propaganda against the system" and "participating in illegal gatherings" and sentenced to nine and a half years in prison ("Iran: Escalating Repression").

Objectives

The events of Black Saturday were a tipping point for these mothers. Many had endured hardships over the years and did not speak out, but the continuation and the increase in violence and suffering brought these women, these mothers, together. According to human rights activist Asieh Amini, a journalist and woman's rights activists who worked with the Mothers of Laleh Park, this group arose from a demand from the people for action. "I dare say that the most important motivation behind the formation of this group, which soon grew too big to be able to say who was and who was not involved in it from the beginning, was to prevent the repetition of the political asphyxia and the horrific silence that predominated the '80s and continue to this day" (Amini). Thus the Mothers protest the violence and the silencing of the mourners and demand transparency and justice for human rights violations that have occurred for decades. As one mother wrote (anonymously):

> Gentleman! What leaded us to become close to each other were neither political organizations nor individual comments, in fact that was no one except you. It was your actions that linked us together. Know and be aware that this common pain caused by you will get back to you one day. Fear and be afraid of the day that all mothers and families who during these thirty-one years went through lots of pain and sorrow but kept quiet, will stand up to demand justice together; the day that all of you have to accept responsibility for your actions. Be sure that this day will be, according to history. Be aware and don't cause anymore sorrow. Signed, "A scathing Mother." ("Set Free Mourning")

The activities and mission of the Mothers of Laleh Park received so much public support and media coverage that it grew from a small group into a transnational one, spreading to other cities and countries where there were Iranians and other

Demonstration in Hamburg February 6, 2010

activists who wanted to take part in their mission. Nobel Peace Prize Laureate Shirin Ebadi made a plea to activists worldwide at an Iran pro-democracy in July 2009 rally in Amsterdan to show their support of the Mourning Mothers by assembling in parks in their own countries wearing black between the hours of 7:00 and 8:00 p.m. Many groups around the world have spoken out in support of the Mothers of Laleh Park, and have formed Mourning Mothers of Iran support groups and hold peaceful demonstrations including in Vienna, Stockholm, Hamburg, Frankfort, Oslo, Rome, Cologne, San Francisco, and London.

Activities

Initially the Mothers of Laleh Park gathered in peaceful and silent protest at Laleh Park and other parks in Tehran to protest the state-sanctioned violence during the protests after the disputed presidential election in June, 2009. However, they also held peaceful demonstrations in various parks, cemeteries, or in front of prisons to commemorate the victims of violence during the last 31 years. The Mothers stated their primary demands were releasing all political prisoners, identifying and holding those responsible for the murders and tortures during these three decades, and ending capital punishment. For many months they met in silent and peaceful protests in parks, with security forces frequently breaking up the demonstrations.

Currently security has prevented them from massive park demonstrations, but the Mothers continue to be active using technology and social media, and some members have continued to participate in gatherings outside of prisons and cemeteries up until the time of this writing. They have an official site for the Mothers of Laleh Park/Mourning Mothers of Iran in English that they use to publish statements issued by the Mothers, related articles and updates, and links to groups that provide solidarity with the Mournful Mothers of Iran. For instance, at the time of this writing they wrote a statement on December 27, 2010 to release Hakime Shokri and Neda Mostqimi (two members arrested for attending a vigil at a cemetery) and another on December 24, 2010 to cancel the execution of Habib Allah. In a statement they state:

> we give you an ultimatum once again to pay attention to our demands, and end the arrests of the supporters of bereaved families.... Now think to yourself [to realize that] our movement of Mothers of Laleh Park not only has not been a risk to national security but also it has been a source of comfort and calm for the bereaved families in the tense and tumultuous days and months. We, the Mothers of Laleh Park, condemn all the executions, massacres, and killings of the last 32 years as well as the self-willed arrest and detention of our loved ones. ("Release Hakime")

They also have a Facebook page titled Mourning Mothers of Iran and one titled Iranian Mourning Mothers for Justice and Freedom.

Challenges

The Mothers have faced significant and repeated challenges since their formation including being harassed, beaten, arrested, and detained. As the Iranian regimen has increased repressive actions towards activists, and strove to suppress public demonstrations and silence protestors, the Mothers silent vigils were repeatedly targeted and ultimately suppressed. Holding any type of public protest became increasingly difficult, and according to Amnesty International the last massive public demonstrations (of any activists/protestors) took place in December, 2009 with subsequent attempts to hold broad public protests on the anniversary of the founding of the Islamic Republic on February 11, 2010 prevented by heavy security forces ("From Protest to Prison").

The arrests of Mothers occurred during vigils initially but more recently occurred in the women's homes in the evenings with children present. While detained they have been denied several rights including medical treatment, visitation, and the right to legal defense; some have been held for months, and at least seven mothers were put in solitary confinement in Evin Prison (Amani and "Iran: Mourning Mothers"). To illustrate the incredible challenges to their own life and liberty, and the commitment of the Mothers to continue their protest, a few details on the known arrests will be provided.

According to one of the Mothers of Laleh Park, Mrs. Khadueh Moghadam, in the first week of the Mothers vigil, 20 members were caught (Ghazi). Another massive arrest targeting the Mothers of Laleh Park occurred on December 5, 2009 when the police attacked the Mothers, who were silently walking shoulder to shoulder, and arrested 29 members. This was the government's attempt to suppress a large rally planned for the following Monday by preventing the Mothers from participating. Large numbers of police and plain-clothes agents occupied the park, preventing protestors from entering. The regime's efforts to prevent all activists from assembling included slowing the internet to prevent information from leaving the country and to prevent the opposition from using one of their main methods of mobilization (Fathi). Despite the regime's attempts, protestors came out in large numbers on December 7th, and due to the high numbers of other protesters detained, the Mourning Mothers were released.

The following month another massive arrest of 33 Mourning Mothers occurred during a silent vigil on January 9, 2010. According to Payvand Iran News, eyewitnesses said they were violently forced into police vans by over 100 police and agents, many were beaten, and 10 were taken to the hospital ("Iran: 30 members"). On January 13, 2010 the U.S. Department of State issued a statement by Secretary Hilary Clinton urging release of the Mourning Mothers in Iran as did other activist groups including Amnesty International. Iranian authorities released 31 of them by January 14, 2010 but kept one member, Farzaneh Zeinali.

In early February of 2010 five supporters were arrested in their homes and sent to Evin Prison due to their activities with the Mourning Mothers ("Iran: Free Mourning"). Those detained were Omobeyne Ebrahimi, Elham Ahsani, Jila Karam Zadeh Makvandi, Fatemah Rastegari, and Laila Seifalahi. As public support for the Mothers of Laleh Park grew, authorities ran news stories accusing them of various crimes. For instance, in October of 2010, two Mothers, Jila Tarmassi Mahdavian and Akram Zeinali Neghabi and their daughters were arrested in their homes in Tehran. Iranian papers said that the women were suspected of espionage and were collaborating with the dissident People's Mojahedin of Iran (PMOI) organization based in France. There were reports of the women being tortured and pressured to make false confessions against Zahra Rahnavard (the wife of Mousavi, the opponent of Ahmadinejad in the 2009 election) to indicate she had collaborated with the PMOI ("Iran: Four Mourning Mothers" and "State Pressures"). The Mothers of Laleh Park made a statement officially rejecting the false accusations emphasizing that "the very fact that these mothers' quests are civil and not political in nature proves that they have nothing to do with political organizations. Therefore, the current accusations against these mothers are contradictory to the reality of their peaceful and civil activities. The imprisonment and persecution of these mothers is a violation of the basic human and citizenship rights" ("Petition to Free"). The Mothers continue to assert that they are a peaceful and justice-seeking group who do not have any ties to political organizations, and stated "with all respect to Mrs. Rahanvard, we have never had any connection with her and our group is a popular and spontaneous gathering that has worked towards reducing violence in our society" ("State Pressures").

At the time of this writing in early January 2011, these two mothers who had been detained for months were recently released.

However, two supporters of Mothers of Laleh Park were still in prison, Neda Mostaghimi and Hakimeh Shekari. On December 5, 2010 they were arrested at an event to commemorate the birthday of slain human rights activist Amir Arshad Tajmir at his gravesite. In prison they have allegedly been subjected to severe intimidation and torture with the goal of forcing them to make self-incriminating confessions; they are being accused of "having ties to foreign based websites, writing protest slogans on banknotes, and organizing activities of the Mourning Mothers" ("Centre to Defend"). In fact, a year and a half after they formed, the Mothers of Laleh Park are under "growing suppression" and have "been pressured to make televised confessions" (Ghazi).

Future Goals

The Mothers of Laleh Park are a powerful voice within and outside of Iran. As Shirin Ebadi, Nobel Peace Prize winner has said, "every time that the Mourning Mothers gather they are beaten up and attacked by police. Therefore if you want to see what lies ahead, what lies in the future of Iran, you can rest assured that it is the Mourning Mothers that will bring democracy to Iran" (Kielburger and Kielburger). The influence of the Mourning Mothers, and an indication of the fear the regime has of their influence, is echoed by Mr. Hadi Ghaemi, director of the International Campaign for Human Rights in Iran, who stated "it shows how frightened they are of their own people, when they can not tolerate mothers who are holding a silent vigil and want accountability" (Slackman).

In the most recent interview with a member, Khadijeh Moghadam in January 2011, she states that The Mothers of Laleh Park (referred to in this article as Iran's Grieving Mothers) continue to work towards putting "a stop to violence" since this is "the main reason" behind the creation of the group (Ghazi). In their own words, from their website, they state:

> We, the Mourning Mothers of Laleh Park, condemn any act of violence and discrimination, and request immediate and unconditional release of the mother(s) in jail. We insist on our three main demands:
> 1. Fair and public trial of those who ordered and executed the murders and massacres of the last 31 years;
> 2. Abolishment of the death penalty;
> 3. Release of all political prisoners and prisoners of conscience;
> We, the Mothers, shall not give up until all our demands are met."
> ("Let Us Remember")

They have elaborated on their future goals to include the end of any homicide and the attainment of equality. They state: "The Mothers of Laleh Park consider execution (death penalty) a form of organized murder, and are against any type of homicide in any form and shape, and under any pretext including stoning and Qessas (an eye for an eye). The Mothers demand abolition of death penalty. The Mothers of Laleh Park, who themselves have been and continue to be victims of violence and discrimination against women, support all non-violent and equalitarian activities. The Mothers hail all the dignified women and men [who value freedom] ("About Us").

Relation to Larger Motherhood Movement

History holds several examples of mothers effectively using the symbolic and ideological power of motherhood to demand justice and push social reform on several social issues including the suffrage movement, progressive era social movements, prohibition, conservation, and peace movements. The practice of employing widely accepted social constructions of motherhood to effect change has combined understandings about the collective sentiment of "mother" as an all-loving, nurturing, selfless, caring person who puts her children above all else, with the cultural rhetoric of respect and honor granted towards mothers. These women develop their mother-activist identity embedded within their social community through their personal experiences and for some, such as the Mothers of Laleh Park, the event that pushes them into full public political activism is the loss of a child.

The Mothers of Laleh Park join the ranks of several other mother activist groups in history that use an ethics of non-violence to protest the deaths of their children and the violence in their countries. In some countries where women's rights are limited, and people's voices are suppressed, mother activists have been able to publicly challenge militant regimes by maximizing on maternalistic motivation and authority, in ways that would be less feasible for men. For example, it is not socially acceptable to open fire on a group of mourning mothers. However, historically this maternal image has not protected these groups from arrest, torture, or in some cases, disappearance or murder, and the women involved risked family alienation, public rebuke, arrest, and great personal harm in their fight against the powerful, often militant state, for social justice. The Mothers of Laleh Park join the ranks of some other powerful mother-led grassroots groups protesting state violence, including the widely known Mothers of the Plaza de Mayo in Argentina. Other similar groups include the following: *The Committee of Soldiers' Mothers in Russia,* a protest group founded in 1989 demanding their son's rights and protesting the cruel conditions in the Russian military which grew into a powerful organization with 300 chapters and official political status; China's *Tiananmen Mothers* led by Ding Zilin after her son was killed in Tiananmen Square, who have been collecting and disseminating human rights violations in China for over 15 years; *The CoMadres of El Salvador or Committee of Mothers* who mobilized in the 1970s when their children who were protestors disappeared and were awarded the Robert F. Kennedy Human Rights Award in 1984; *The Four Mothers Movement* in 1997 which contributed significantly to ending the "silent war" between Lebanon and

Israel with Israel's unilateral withdrawal from Lebanon in 2000; and *The Peace Mothers*, a women's civil rights group in Turkey with the mission of promoting peace between Turks and Kurds.

Conclusion

The Mothers of Laleh Park formed in the aftermath of the violence following the disputed presidential election in Iran in June 2009 by a group of mothers whose children had been arrested or killed. They decided to "take a 'motherly' action, something non-political for none of us were political activists of any sort" and hold peaceful vigils to call for an end to the violence (Ghazi). From the beginning, some members were arrested, harassed, and beaten but they continued to meet and hold demonstrations and voice their demands for justice and their call for an end to the violence. To this day, a year and a half after their formation, despite their continued persecution and the security forces preventing them from holding vigils and arresting them if they attend memorials, they are utilizing their influence to continue to fight for justice and an end to the violence in Iran. Around the world groups have formed to show their solidarity with the Mothers of Laleh Park, and The Mourning Mothers of Iran have become global icons for human rights (Amani).

Works Cited

"About Us." *Iranian Park Laleh Mothers*. [n.d.]. Web. 4 January 2011.

Amani, Elahe. "Women in Prison: Iran Women Rights Defenders Undeterred by Prison Detention." *Iranian.com*. 6 Mar. 2010. Web. 2 Jan. 2011.

Amani, Elahe and Lys Anzi. "'Mourning Mothers Iran' Stand with Activist Mothers Worldwide." *Women News Network*. 8 Oct. 2009. Web. 30 Dec. 2010.

Amini, Asieh. "Please Stop Joking." *Iranian Park Laleh Mothers* Oct. 2010. Web. 29 Dec. 2010.

"The Centre to Defend the Families of the Detained and the Fallen issued a statement announcing that the arrested Mothers are under pressure and duress to make false confessions." *Iranian Park Laleh Mothers* Dec. 2010. Web. 3 Jan. 2011.

Daragahi, Borzou and Ramin Mostaghim. "Iran Security Forces Retreat as Huge Numbers of Mourners Gather at Cemetery." *Los Angeles Times* 31 July 2009. Web. 27 Dec. 2010.

Drash, Wayne and Octavia Nasr. "Neda's Mother: She was Like an Angel." *CNN.com*. 5 Nov. 2009. Web. 23 Dec. 2010.

Fathi, Nazila. "Mothers Arrested Before Opposition Rally in Iran." *The New York Times* 7 Dec. 2009. Web. 19 Nov. 2010.

"From Protest to Prison: Iran One Year After the Election." *Amnesty International* 8 June 2010. Web. 3 Jan. 2011.

Ghazi, Fereshteh. "Iran's Grieving Mothers Not Deterred by Armed Suppression." *Payvand Iran News* 1 Jan. 2011. Web. 3 Jan. 2011.

Haeri, Safa. "Ministers of Murder: Iran's New Security Cabinet." *Iran Press Service* 15 Dec. 2005. Web. 2 Jan. 2011.

"Iran: Free 'Mourning Mothers' Supporters." *Human Rights Watch* 5 Mar. 2010. Web. 27 Dec. 2010.

"Iran: Four 'Mourning Mothers' Arrested for Spying." *Adnkronos International English* 14 Oct. 2010. Web. 2 Jan. 2011.

"Iran: Mourning Mothers Supporters in Solitary Confinement at Evin Prison." *Women Living Under Muslim Laws* 19 Feb. 2010. Web. 30 Dec. 2010.

"Iran: Escalating Repression of University Students." *Human Rights Watch* 7 December 2010. Web. 4 Jan. 2011.

"Iran: Rights Defender Dedicates Award to Women Activists." *Human Rights Watch* 10 Nov. 2010. Web. 30 Nov. 2010.

"Iran: 30 Members of Mourning Mothers Detained in Tehran." *Payvand Iran News* 1 Jan. 2010. Web. 18 Nov. 2010.

Iranian Park Laleh Mothers. N.p., n.d. Web. 30, Dec. 2010.

Kielburger, Craig and Marc Kielburger. "Can Iran's Mothers Achieve what Sanctions Can't?" *The Star.Com.* 22 Mar. 2010. Web. 30 Nov. 2010.

"Let Us Remember the Month of Azar." *Iranian Park Laleh Mothers.* December 2010. Web. 3 Jan. 2011.

"Petition to Free the Mothers of Laleh Park." *Iranian Park Laleh Mothers* October 2010. Web. 3 January 2011.

"Release Hakime Shokri and Neda Mostaqimi Immediately and Unconditionally." *Iranian Park Laleh Mothers* 27 Dec. 2010. Web. 3 Jan. 2011.

"Set Free Mourning Mothers Akram Neghabi and Jila Mahdavi." *Iranian Park Laleh Mothers* 1 Nov. 2010. Web. 2 Jan. 2011.

Setrakain, Lara. "Statement from Mourning Mothers of Iran." *Posterous* 3 July, 2009. Web. 30, Dec., 2010.

Slackman, Michael. "Arrests by Iran are a Bid to Quell Wide Protests." *The New York Times* 10 Feb. 2010. Web. 11 Nov. 2010.

"State Pressures Stepped Up on Iran's Mourning Mothers." *Payvand Iran News* 14 Oct. 2010. Web. 29 Nov. 2010.

Tait, Robert and Matthew Weaver. "How Neda Soltani Became the Face of Iran's Struggle." *Guardian New and Media Limited* 22 June 2009. Web. 23 Dec. 2010.

54. The Committee of Soldiers' Mothers in Russia

Anti-War and Human Rights Activists

SUSAN LOGSDON-CONRADSEN

THE UNION OF THE COMMITTEES of Soldiers' Mothers of Russia (UCSMR) is a federation of regional committees with a head office in Moscow. It is a non-governmental organization (NGO) established in 1989 that has worked for decades to protect soldiers rights, and lobby for military reform, and it played an important role in ending the two Chechen wars. The UCSMR has worked tirelessly to expose human rights violations within the Russian military including deaths and serious injuries from the practice of *dedovschchina,* a systemic practice of harassing/hazing first year conscripts by elder soldiers (Zdravomyslova). In addition, it has worked to improve conditions for soldiers, lobbied for legislative reform, secured amnesty for deserters and conscientious objectors, and actively and prominently campaigned to end conscription and radically reform the military into a volunteer, professional army (Glasser 1). Before 1998 it was known as The Committee of Soldiers Mothers (CSM; when referring to the group before 1999 CSM will be used). A conflict in the leadership in 1996 caused Valentina Melnikova to form the UCSMR (Glasser 1)

This organization of primarily volunteer, middle aged mothers, began as a small grassroots organization and grew into "one of the most prominent civil-society groups in Russia" (Caiazza). The UCSMR is considered "Russia's most respected soldiers' rights group" (Glasser 1). Currently the UCSMR has hundreds of affiliated groups all over Russia and many of the branches see more than 100 cases a week. The CSM/UCSMR has been awarded several international prizes for their protection and advocacy of the human rights of soldiers and their activism in the Chechen war. They were awarded the Sean McBride medal from Germany in 1995, the Prof. Rafto Award from Norway in 1995, the Right Livelihood Award (the Alternative Nobel Prize) in 1996, and the Friedrich Ebert Foundation Award from Germany in 2000 (Jagudina 169-170).

In discussing the UCSMR, this chapter will discuss the political climate that influenced its formation, a history of its activities including the ways in which its focus has shifted during peacetime and wartime, the challenges it has faced and the more authoritarian climate in which it currently functions, and discuss how this organization utilizes the symbolic power of motherhood to attain legitimacy.

Portrait of the original committee that was awarded the Alternative Peace Prize © Right Livelihood Award Foundation <www.rightlivelihood.org>.

Mandate

On their official website (*Union of the Committees of Soldiers' Mothers of Russia)* they state that their "main goal … is human rights protections of draftees, soldiers, and their parents." They define these human rights activities as including "dealing with the individual complaints on human rights violations in the armed forces; organizing human rights education of draftees and their parents; operative consulting of the regional soldiers mothers' NGO." Since their formation they have consistently fought to protect the rights of draftees and conscripts both during military service and the conscription process itself (Eichler 494). They work to expose human rights violations, call for an end to *dedovschina*, publish research on deaths in the military, provide legal help to families and conscripts, call for increased accountability and transparency, and lobby for military reform including a true alternative service option and transitioning to a voluntary professional army. The UCSMR demands military reform due to the physical harm endured by conscripts and thus emphasizes human rights rather than pacifism or antimilitarism as its philosophy (Glasser 2). The group functions as a "watchdog, bringing complaints of military abuse to national attention that would otherwise not receive press coverage" (Poolos).

History

The CSM formed during the reforms of perestroika when Gorbachev introduced a policy of transparency and openness within government institutions known as

Mothers Against the Chechen War, 1996.
© Right Livelihood Award Foundation <www.rightlivelihood.org>.

glasnost, leading to less censorship and greater freedom of information (Zdravomyslova). The organizers of UCSMR acknowledge the importance of this historical period and state that it was formed "because of the freedoms that accompanied the fall of communism" (Hunt). At this time various organizations were created with the goal of democratizing Soviet institutions, including organizations of soldiers' mothers that were attached to military commissions and under military supervision (Jagudina, 163-164). Other organizations developed independently including the CSM in Moscow, which began as a small grassroots organization under the leadership of Maria Kirbassova following her experience with the army. Kirbassova's son was attending university when he was drafted and she requested that he be assigned to a unit related to his education. This request was mocked by the commander. Later her son became suicidal and his commander stated "So what? Look, if he hangs himself, we'll look into what happened." This "cold-hearted answer provoked her political activism" and she organized fellow parents at the university to protest the conditions in the army and its draft policies (Caiazza). The message of this group resonated with many Russian women at a time when there was an increase in individual empowerment and women's political activism and organization at the local level, leading to the emergence of the CSM (Caiazza).

The CSM started a media and lobbying campaign, handing out leaflets to deputies in the Congress and holding a vigil outside the Kremlin. A popular daily newspaper began regularly covering their activism and as media coverage grew the movement spread with affiliates forming across Russia (Jagudina 165). Their first victory was when 170 soldiers were returned to the university from which they had been illegally taken (Albert). A mass media campaign and the growing pressure from CSM activists later led to the release of 176,000 students who were drafted illegally during 1987-1988 (Jagudina 165).

After this the CSM began to focus on exposing the widespread violence within the Soviet military and lobby for "concrete mechanisms to be put in place to protect conscripts and to prevent barracks violence" (Elkner 2-3). As soldiers or their families reported about the atrocities conscripts were experiencing, the CSM learned about severe beatings and torture that many first year conscripts were undergoing through *dedovshchina* (systemic severe hazing of younger recruits by older soldiers) (Jagudina 165). They began to collect statistics on the number of peacetime injuries and deaths in the military and, in 1990, the CSM widely publicized the frequency of peacetime deaths which they claimed was 15,000 during the previous four years (Elkner 3). There were mass rallies over these peacetime deaths and a series of hunger strikes designed to raise public awareness of these deaths (Elkner 10). The grief of mothers who lost their sons during peacetime generated a great deal of public support.

Human rights violations within the conscription process also became the focus of the CSM, including the drafting of soldiers who had medical issues which justified exemptions, the forcible removal of young men, and the accelerated conscription process (Jagudina 165). Under pressure from the CSM, the military in 1989-1990 revealed that they called up "unfit conscripts" including ex-convicts and invalids in order to fill draft quotes (Jagudina 165). In response to the violence within the military barracks, local CSM chapters offered refuge and assistance to conscripts who fled due to abuses and provided legal assistance to deserters. They also advised families and held weekly meetings on how to qualify for legal exemptions from military duty, and they provided copies of unpublished guidelines for deferments to assist in securing a deferment. The CSM began lobbying for military reform, specifically to create an army of professional volunteers rather than conscripted soliders, and they worked with deputies of several Supreme Soviet Committees to place military reform on the state's agenda in the early 1990s. In response to the CSM's demands, Gorbachev signed a non-official decree demobilizing the construction battalions in the army where younger recruits were regularly mistreated by older servicemen (Zawilski 2). In 1990 Gorbachev also created a commission of Supreme Soviet deputies and soldier's mothers with the purpose of investigating the causes of non-combat related deaths (Jagudina 166)

The activities of the CSM grew once the first Chechen war began in 1994. It began organizing and holding regular anti-war demonstrations and was the first Russian NGO to publicly issue an anti-war statement in November 1994. According to Valentina Melinkova, the spokesperson for CSM, their offices received 100 phone calls and 200 letters daily inquiring about the war after the start of the first war (Zawilski 2). The popularity of the organization increased greatly during 1994-1996 in part due to media coverage of their activities but also due to widespread disagreement with the government's war efforts (Glasser 2). Some

Committee of Soldiers' Mothers in Russa demonstration, 1996.
© Right Livelihood Award Foundation <www.rightlivelihood.org>.

of their most famous activities took place during this time when they organized groups of mothers who marched to the front lines of Chechnya, entering into dangerous conflict zones, to search for their missing sons. As one mother told the *New York Times,* "I just leaped over the fence into the military compound and grabbed [my son]" (Caiazza). The Russian media showed footage of the Mothers braving artillery fire in Chechnya to rescue their sons (Zawilski 7) and the striking images of these mothers taking their sons away from military service had a major effect on "raising awareness and turning public opinion against the war" (Caiazza). Over twenty groups were sent during the first Chechen war to reclaim their sons and many were successful; after one trip in January 1995 approximately 100 Russian servicemen were returned home (Sperling 243). It is important to note that the CSM mothers worked closely with Chechen mothers during this time, staying in their houses and coordinating exchanges of prisoners of war (Eichler 495).

One of the largest and highest profile events was the March of Maternal Compassion and Protest against the War in Chechnya which took place in 1995. The March began at the Tomb of the Unknown Soldier in Moscow and went to the Chechen capital Grozny, going "directly down the line of military engagement" (Jagudina 167). The purpose of the March was to collect accurate information, show anti-war attitudes, and ultimately bring peace (Zdravomyslova). Over 300 individuals participated and they marched until they were forced to stop by armed forces; 150 marchers were detained for five hours and forced to return to the city Narzan outside of Chechnya (Jagudina 167). These daring acts, which were

The chairman of Sochi Committee in Chechnya.
© Right Livelihood Award Foundation <www.rightlivelihood.org>.

widely publicized, led to the rapid growth of CSM and gained them wide public acceptance. The group waged a very effective "Western-style public relations war against the government through press conferences, press releases, letters to the editors of major newspapers, and calls to policy-makers" and gained international attention and support; further, it is believed that their activities played a role in ending the first Chechen war (Caiazza).

In addition to rescuing their sons, the CSM was active in trying to protect the rights of conscientious objectors and deserters. After intense lobbying on the part of the CSM, 500 soldiers who refused to fight in Chechnya as conscientious objectors were granted amnesty and immunity in 1995-1996. In addition, at the end of the first war the CSM convinced the Duma to include deserters and evaders in the general amnesty for Russian and Chechen soldiers in 1997. They also succeeded in their campaign for amnesty for 40,000 soldier-fugitives who had left the military due to suffering from human rights violations (Jagudina 168; Glasser 1).

During the inter-war time period between the two Chechen wars, from August 1996-1999, the CSM continued to work on military reform by collecting statements from Russians opposed to war, and organizing demonstrations and conferences. They also searched for missing individuals from the 1994-1996 war and worked to establish rehabilitation centers for soldiers and their families. Throughout, they continued their legal assistance for soldiers and their families and held their weekly human rights school advising families on their rights in the conscription process (Zawilski 8).

When the second war in Chechnya began in 1999 the UCSMR resumed its anti-war activism, primarily through issuing statements and open letters to authorities and holding press conferences. The context in Russia had changed since the first war however, and the mass media was now under the control of the military and the activities of the CSM did not receive the same attention and positive coverage (Eichler 498; Jagudina 168). In addition, the public was initially more supportive of this second war seeing it as necessary for anti-terrorism efforts, and the UCSMR was one of the only organizations protesting the war (Sperling 244). During this time the UCSMR actively collected statistics on the numbers of casualties in the war by visiting cathedrals, documenting testimonies from soldiers and families, and using hospital records to calculate accurate statistics that the state would not release (Sperling 243). They publicized these statistics to demonstrate that the official figures were gross underestimates of casualties and demanded that the authorities publish official lists of the dead, wounded, and missing on a regular basis. During this time they continued to network with other organizations and hold congresses and conferences (Jagudina 168). In an attempt to bring an end to the second Chechen war, members of the UCSMR initiated a process of negotiating peace talks with Chechen separatist representative Akhmed Zakayev; the Russian government and military intervened to stop the meeting (Glasser 4). In 2005 representatives of the UCSMR and those of the Chechen side met in London to discuss conditions for a peace settlement and sealed a memorandum with Akhmed Zakaev and representatives of the European Parliament ("Soldiers' Mothers Enter").

Context

The UCSMR currently operates within a country that has been restricting the activities of various NGOs. After his election in 2000, Vladimir Putin utilized his popularity and the increasing wealth from rising oil prices to "consolidate an authoritarian form of government," one in which media and watchdog groups lack the freedom to monitor the state; this weakening of critical voices within civil society has been a consequence of Putin's patriotic, anti-terrorist agenda (Eichler 498). In 2008 Putin outwardly transferred presidential power to Dmitry Medvedev after serving his two presidential terms, but Putin continues to play a prominent role in defining policy as prime minister (Orttung 2).

A major reason for the continued viability and success of the UCSMR is that it operates within accepted Soviet gender ideology which has "revered the cult of motherhood" (Glasser 2); the members explicitly accept the "prevailing notions of femininity and gender relations" (Eichler 496). The activists define themselves as mothers who are protecting their sons and thus provide legitimacy to their political activism since protecting one's child is a socially mandated mother's right (Glasser 2). At the same time as they draw upon the power of the mothering archetype they also directly challenge the long held notion of Soviet patriotic motherhood as the self-sacrificing mother who sends her son off to service willingly (Eichler 492). To the contrary, they "used motherhood as a platform from which to voice their critique of the military and the war" (Eichler 495) and are trying to "redefine patriotism in a liberal, civic way" (Sperling 237) which includes defying the state (Sperling 246).

Objectives

The primary purpose of UCSMR has stayed the same, protecting the human rights of soldiers. Within this human rights framework they work on several issues including shortening the term of service, eliminating the draft, providing exemptions for university students, and ending *dedovshchina* (Caiazza). Their ultimate goal is to "transform the nature of military service in Russia by lobbying for the legal implementation of alternative service and the transition to a professional army, which they see as key to reducing human rights violations in the armed forces" (Eichler 494).

Activities

A large part of the UCSMR's daily activities includes providing legal advice to men seeking draft exemption or evasion and to soldiers who have fled their units due to human rights violations (Eichler 494; Engleman). This need is even more pronounced as greater numbers of young men are being conscripted into the Russian military following cuts to contract personnel and retirement of officers ("Russia to draft"). They also provide assistance to families who are unable to get information on missing soldiers from the authorities. Essentially the UCSMR works to mobilize individuals to assert their personal rights in the military and counsels them on their rights and methods and assists in lodging complaints with the Ministry of Defense (Caiazza). Each year the UCSMR registers 4,000 in-person complaints and 3,000 written primary complaints, with 60 percent of them related to violations of human rights (Ignatieva 19; UCSMR website). Every Monday the UCSMR holds "Human Rights school" for draftees and their parents with 200-300 attending every week (Ignatieva 20). They also play an important role in monitoring the military (Albert) and compile statistics on estimates of peacetime deaths in the military which according to UCSMR is about 3,000–5,000 deaths annually due to "beatings, harassment leading to suicide, intolerable living conditions, denial of needed medical assistance, and excessive labor (Glasser 2-3). Other regular activities include lobbying, holding demonstrations, writing open letters and statements to public officials, working with other human rights organizations, and trying to bring public awareness to human rights violations within the Russian army (Sperling 243). They continue to demand radical military reform with an end to conscription and the formation of a professional volunteer army.

Challenges

Throughout its history the UCSMR has faced various obstacles from the military establishment. For instance, in 1991 the Defense Ministry, in an attempt to neutralize institutions that challenged its authority, called up journalists who had published stories of *dedovshchina* and draft evasion into service, as well as young deputies who had been outspoken for military reform (Jagudina 166). The mothers have been confronted by Russian military, pulled off of trains, and evicted from their offices (Hunt). The mothers are also subject to slander and negative media representations. The military press attacked mothers in the CSM (Jagudina 166) and some Russian politicians have "described the UCSMR as hysterical and irrational grieving mothers with no political competence" (Glasser 4). Others have accused soldier's mothers of being anti-patriotic and state that they are traitors that are under the influence of foreign organizations and governments (Sperling 247). Defense Minister Sergei Ivanov has also criticized the UCSMR stating that they impede military justice (Engleman).

Another challenge is that in 2006 Russia adopted a law that broadened its ability to monitor and regulate non-profit organizations, enabling the government to limit NGO activities in areas that it deems inappropriate. After this law was adopted a lawsuit was filed by the Ministry of Justice requesting the dissolution of the Russian Research Center on Human Rights, an umbrella organization which included the UCSMR. The lawsuit claimed that the Center had not completed accurately all reports of its activities for the last five years. The Center disputed this claim and submitted all documents and no further action was taken against it ("Choking on Bureaucracy" 28). For the majority of prominent human rights NGOs the state has constrained their activities and in some cases used legislation to weaken their voices, raided their offices, and engaged in other actions to impede their work. In July 2008 Putin issued a decree removing the tax-exempt status from 89 of the 101 foreign NGOs and foundations, "targeting those active in the sphere of human rights and the environment," including the International Red Cross and the World Wildlife Fund (Orttung 451).

Finally another serious challenge is that in the last decade the government in Russia has become more authoritarian and there exists "a culture of impunity… where human rights activists and opposition journalists are killed and the perpetrators are typically neither found nor prosecuted" ("Nations" 436). A recent study indicated that non-governmental organizations "can no longer be outspokenly critical of power … since NGOs and individuals who persist in voicing criticism find themselves in serious trouble" (Sieca-Kozlowski 7). Organizations that resist being co-opted by the government and continue to be critical have encountered more frequent intimidation and harassment (Eichler 500). Another significant difficulty is that in contrast to the 1990s when there were liberal parties that could voice the proposals of independent NGOs to the Duma, there are no political relays now. Essentially "the possibility for an NGO to influence the legislative process and political life is now quasi zero" (Sieca-Kozlowski 7-8). Thus the UCSMR's influence is constrained by these significant challenges.

Future Goals

The UCSMR continues to work to protect the rights of draftees and conscripts and educate the public about abuses within the military. Multiple abuses and human rights violations continue to be reported within the military, and the Human Rights Watch has issued two reports detailing what "is described as grossly abusive and humiliating treatment" (Bigg; "Conscription"; "The Wrongs"). Specifically hundreds of men are forcibly conscripted into the Russian army and are not provided any opportunity to appeal their conscription since they are deployed to their units the same day they are detained without undergoing a thorough medical examination for eligibility ("Conscription"). There are reports of men being detained while on the metro or doors broken down at their homes, some even with medical documentation that they were unfit for service (Arnold). Despite the violence within the military and the continuing problem of systemic *dedovschina,* "the state has tight control over the media" and " few cases of bullying in the army come to light" (Arnold). The UCSMR states that "80 percent of cases of violence against soldiers go unreported" (Bigg). Further, at least 1,000 conscripts die each year from noncombat related incidents including suicide and hazing, and hundreds are hospitalized (Arnold).

In their two decades of fighting for the human rights of young men the UCSMR has seen its share of successes and failures. In recent years some of the changes they lobbied for have since been rescinded. For instance, in 2004 the government announced that it was going to cancel all draft deferments ("We Have Broken") and a law on substitute service for conscientious objectors came into force which requires objectors to serve a term between 36 and 42 months compared to 24 months of conscription ("Russia: Start of"). The Secretary of the UCSMR, Valentina Melnikova, criticized this law for being a longer term and for taking place in very remote places ("Soldiers' Mothers Consider"). The UCSMR continues to call for military reform including the end to conscription and the formation of a professional volunteer army.

Relationship to Larger Motherhood Movement

Throughout its history, the UCSMR effectively utilized traditional notions of motherhood, which fit well with Russian cultural norms about gender ideology, enabling them to be very successful. The group emphasized that their members were mothers of soldiers and stressed that as mothers they personally suffered when their sons were exposed to harm. They explicitly reinforced the ideal of mothers having an innate mothering instinct to protect their children at any cost, including self-preservation. This message was particularly powerful in a country with a long history of glorifying the image of "mother" as well as the county's identity as "Mother Russia" (Caiazza). As the press secretary of UCSMR, Valentina Melnikova, said "real mothers" pull their sons out of prison and "protecting children has become parents' business." Thus the group relies "on traditional notions of motherhood in claiming its right to a political voice" (Caiazza). The UCSMR gained the support of the people who could understand the suffering and motivation of these mothers, thus legitimatizing their role in the political sphere (Caiazza).

The UCSMR join the ranks of other mother activists groups such as Las Madres de Plaza de Mayo in Argentina that have used an ethics of non-violence to protest the deaths of their children and the violence in their communities by utilizing the powerful public display of mourning. They have also shown through their cooperation with Chechen mothers that they espouse "a conception of motherhood that crosses national and ethnic boundaries" (Eichler 495). These Russian mothers have expanded on the concept of "good mothering" to include advocating for the human rights of their sons.

Conclusion

The UCSMR formed in 1989 as a grassroots group of mothers protesting the draft of their sons who were in university and grew into a large, popular, and influential Russian NGO. For over 20 years they have worked to protect the human rights of young Russian men, assisting them in the deferment process and advocating for the end of violence within the military. They played an important role in ending both Chechen wars and risked their lives to find their sons and return them to safety. Members continue to collect statistics on casualties in the military during peacetime and lobby for military reform despite residing in an increasingly authoritarian country where speaking critically against the government carries serious risks.

Works Cited

Albert, Odile. "In Russia, the Committee of Soldiers' Mothers has become a link in civil society that can no longer be muffled." Centre de Documentation Tiers Mondre de Paris, March 1997. Web. 9 Feb. 2011.

Arnold, Chloe. Russia: "Conscripts Prostitution Claims Shed Light on Hazing." *Radio Free Europe Radio Library* 21 Mar. 2007. Web. 20 Jan. 2011.

Bigg, Claire. "Russia: Brutal Hazing Incident Rocks Army." *Radio Free Europe Radio Liberty* 27 Jan. 2006. Web. 9 Feb. 2011.

Caiazza, Amy. "Russia Meets its Matriarchs." *Transitions Online*. 18 Oct. 2010. Web. 20 Jan. 2011.

"Choking on Beauracracy: State Curbs on Independent Civil Society Activism." *Human Rights Watch* 19 Feb. 2008. Web. 7 Feb. 2011.

"Conscription Through Detention in Russia's Armed Forces." *Human Rights Watch* 21 Nov. 2002. Web. 26 Feb. 2011.

Eichler, Maya. "Russia's Post-Communist Transformation: A Gendered Analysis of the Chechen Wars." *International Feminist Journal of Politics*, 8:4 (2006): 486-511. Print.

Elkner, Julie. "Dedovshchina and the Committee of Soldiers' Mothers under Gorbachev." *The Journal of Power Institutions in Post-Soviet Societies* 1 (2004). Web. 20 Jan. 2011.

Engleman, Eric. "Russian Soldiers' Mothers Work Together." *Johnson's Russia List* 14 Jan. 2003. Web. 27 Jan. 2011.

Glasser, Julie. "United People's Party of Soldiers' Mothers: An Analysis of a Grassroots Movement." *Stanford's Student Journal of Russian, East European, and Eurasian Studies* 1 (Spring 2005): 1-8.

Hunt, Swanee. "Mothers of Russian Soldiers Fight for Their Sons." *Womens E-news* 21 Mar. 2001. Web. 9 Feb. 2011.

Ignatieva, Anna. "Brutalization of Young Conscripts in the Russian Federation and the Long-term Effects." *Developing Strategies to Deal with Trauma in Children.* Eds. J. Donnelly et al. Amsterdam: IOS Press, 2005. 19-22.

Jagudina, Zaira. *Social Movements and Gender in Post-Soviet Russia: The Case of the Soldiers' Mothers NGOs.* Diss. University of Gothenburg. Web. 26 Feb. 2011.

Poolos, Alexandra. "Anti-War Mothers' Group in Russia Fears for Future." *Women's eNews.* 5 Jun. 2006. Web. 20 Jan. 2011.

"Response of the Russian Ministry of Defense to the Human Rights Watch Report 'Wrongs of Passage'." *Human Rights Watch* 21 October 2004. Web. 9 Feb. 2011.

"Nations in Transition 2010: Russia." *Freedom House.Org.* 2010. Web. 10 Feb. 2011.

Orttung, Robert. "Nations in Transit 2009—Russia." Freedom House. 2009. Web. 22 Feb. 2011.

"Russia: Start of substitute service for conscientious objectors." *War Resisters' International* 30 September 2004. Web. 9 Feb. 2011.

"Russia to Draft 320,000 Conscripts in Fall 2009." *RIA Novosti* 21 July 2009. Web. 26 Feb.2011.

Sieca-Kozlowski, Elisabeth. "NGOs and the Power Ministries in Russia: from Resistance to Cooperation?" *The Journal of Power Institutions in Post-Soviet Societies* 9 (2009): 2-9. Web. 7 Feb 2011.

"Soldiers' Mothers Enter Into Amicable Agreement with Akhmed Zakaev." *Kommersant.* 28 Feb. 2005. Web. 9 Feb. 2011.

"Soldiers' Mothers Consider the New Law Unconstitutional." *Pravada.ru* 01 Mar 2004. Web. 9 Feb. 2011.

Sperling, Valerie. "The Last Refuge of a Scoundrel: Patriotism, Militarism, and the RussianNational Idea." *Nations and Nationalism* 9.2 (2003): 235-253.

"The Wrongs of Passage." *Human Rights Watch* 19 Oct. 2004. Web. 9 Feb. 2011.

"We Have Broken the Silence on Chechnya." *Human Rights House Network* 9 Mar. 2005. Web. 26 Feb. 2011.

Zawilski, Valerie. "Women for Life Without War: Russia's Committee of Soldiers' Mothers and the Russian Chechen Wars." *The Military and Society in Post-Soviet Russia.* Eds. Stephen Webber and Jennifer Mothers. London: Manchester

University/St. Martin's Press, 2005. 1-11.
Zdravomyslova, Elena. "Peaceful Initiatives: Soldiers' Mothers Movement in Russia." *Towards a Women's Agenda for A Culture of Peace*. Eds. Ingebory Brenes, Dorota Gierycz, and Betty Reardon. Paris: UNESCO, 1999. Web. 25 Feb. 2011.

55.
Gold Star Families Speak Out

Coalitions and Anti-War Maternal Activism

JOCELYN FENTON STITT

THE U.S. ORGANIZATION GOLD STAR Families Speak Out (GSFSO) has its roots in the negative public reaction to the United State's foreign policy decisions in the wake of the September 11, 2001 terrorist attacks.[1] Several key decisions by then-president George W. Bush and his administration formed the basis for wide-spread critique, protest, and the forming of anti-war organizations. Some members of GSFSO became politicized when their children or family members were deployed overseas and/or when they were killed in the conflict. Many in the movement also decried the invasion of Iraq that was justified by the Bush administration based on intelligence of weapons of mass destruction. Anti-war protestors found that evidence either flimsy, poorly analyzed, or knowingly falsified to justify going to war. All members of Gold Star Families Speak Out have lost a loved one either in the months leading up to the 2002 invasion of Iraq, during the wars in Iraq and Afghanistan, or after returning home.

Mandate

GSFSO's first stated purpose is to "end the occupation of Iraq" and only secondly to offer support to anyone who has lost a military family member since 2001. Their website lists three main goals for the organization: to bring the troops serving overseas home immediately, to provide adequate health and mental health services for soldiers when they return home, and "Never, ever enter an illegal war again." This last section reflects the fact that GSFSO is not a traditional peace organization. Their website and other materials reflect, I believe, a coalition approach to their anti-war work. Since the members of both GSFSO and Military Families Speak Out (MFSO) are from military families, it makes sense that their members probably have a spectrum of beliefs about military engagement ranging from radical peace positions to being pro-militarization while criticizing the current wars. Their common cause is the belief that these specific wars in Iraq and Afghanistan are unjust and should end immediately.

GSFSO writes that the best way to accomplish these goals is to provide support and empowerment to those grieving a family member lost in the war and to provide outreach to these affected families. This private sphere work is complemented by their conviction that ending these wars can only happen if they "Raise awareness in the United States about the true human costs of the invasion/occupation of Iraq." Part of this human cost includes testifying to the aftermath of losing a child to war. The interlinking of the personal with the political corresponds to Natalie Wilson's idea of a maternal "embodied activism," which uses maternal experience to highlight "the ways in which national and international policies and institutions affect mothers and their families" (232). The many testimonials, articles, and interviews given by GSFSO members and documented on their website remind the public of their personal losses caused by U.S. foreign policy.

Other issues of concern for GSFSO include the lack of health care for returning soldiers, and the high rate of post-traumatic stress disorder and suicide among veterans. The issue of veteran suicide is especially important, since former service members who commit suicide are not considered officially to have died in combat. For members of GSFSO, however, they are indeed a causality of war. The high rates of veteran mental illness and self-harm and the lack of medical care for these conditions are a big concern for military family members. GSFSO challenges government classifications of those who die after their military service: "The military and government does not consider many of our loved ones to be casualties of this war; some are not counted in the official casualty list. Despite whatever political beliefs / stance people may have, we know the human cost of war; we live it every day. We are not alone." ("Living With PTSD"). Finally, the use of the U.S. National Guard in combat overseas is a new role for this branch of the military. It has traditionally be used as a civil defense branch of the armed forces involved in helping in instances of domestic crises, such as natural disasters. Around 28 percent of all forces in Iraq and Afghanistan are National Guard forces (Associated Press). Maternal peace activists harshly criticized the repeated deployment overseas of National Guard service people who never expected to serve outside the United States.

History

Many of these anti-war maternal activists first formed Gold Star Families for Peace (GSFP), a group made up of those who lost family members through military service, or its aftermath. At the outset, in late 2004 and early 2005, approximately 50 families were members of this organization, coming together through internet searches, blogging, and an affliation with MFSO (Pullin). Celeste Zappala and Karen Meredith were prominent members of GSFP, but the best-known participant was Cindy Sheehan. Major early activities included the creation of Camp Casey near then-President Bush's Texas compound in August 2005. This site was named after Sheehan's son who was killed in Iraq. Camp Casey was used as a base to protest the war, to try to arrange a meeting with the President, and to publicize their anti-war message (Sheehan; Meredith "The Crawford Papers").

GSFP splintered in October of 2005, and another group was created, Gold

Star Families Speak Out (GSFSO).[2] Gold Star Families Speak Out is a chapter of Military Families Speak Out (MFSO), an anti-war organization founded in 2002. GSFSO members consist of those who have family members who served in the military since 2002 and who were killed while serving or who have subsequently died. Karen Meredith and Celeste Zappala co-founded GSFSO have continued to lead that organization. Current membership of MFSO stands at around 4,000 families.

Context

Gold Star Families Speak Out addresses several issues relevant to mothers' political action. At the most fundamental level, GSFSO members demand accountability from their government for the deaths of their children. Their writing, websites, and public activism rely on many of the ideas of the motherhood movement: that mothers have the right to be heard and to have their voices taken seriously. Cynthia Enloe, a feminist scholar in international studies, noted in 2005 about public perceptions of peace activist Cindy Sheehan, "We want to make her the naïve mother, and if we hear that she is really politically conscious we start to doubt the authenticity of her maternal message" (Houppert 14). Women like Karen Meredith and Celeste Zappala demand to be taken seriously as mother/citizens who have a political agenda of ending a war they view as unjust. We should remember that grieving mothers protesting an ongoing war is highly unusual, as historian Michael Beschloss explains, since military families historically have not publically protested war, "We're seeing something that really is unusual because military families in history have been pretty much inclined not to do this sort of thing. It's in a way sort of part of that culture. And the fact that they are doing it now shows how deeply many of them feel about the fact that they were never convinced at the beginning of this war that it was the right thing to do" (qtd. in Hochberg). This new form of political critique has left members open to accusations ranging from treason to triviality. Members of MFSO were accused of undermining the war effort and of lending aid and comfort to the enemy (Hochberg). Mothers like Laurie Loving who spoke out publically with MFSO were belittled as being just "terrified mothers" (Rose). Popular conceptions of mothers' anti-war protests as either so dangerous as to put the country in peril or as so meaningless as to be embarrassing, tell us more about public beliefs about mothers and citizenship than they do about the actual actions taken by GSFSO. Refusing to be silenced, GSFSO members use their status as grieving mothers as the basis for a radical political platform.

Objectives and Activities

One of the main ways members of GSFSO work against cultural and media attempts to sideline mothers' political activism has been to use technology to control their own message. GSFSO's website is highly detailed, with sections for members' writings, photographs of demonstrations and vigils, links to newspaper reports and interviews with members, YouTube clips of members and actions taken, and links to other organizations. Karen Meredith maintains a website in memory of her son, blogs, and also Twitters under the name "goldstarmom." Other members make themselves available for interviews with the media and publicize their message through Op-Ed pieces.

This group fulfills their three-part mission by having multiple chapters to offer support and information to those who have lost a loved one. There are 34 state chapters. As part of their goal to provide services to soldiers who return home, they raise awareness of post-traumatic stress disorder and the high rate of suicide among veterans. They do this through their website, by speaking out about these issues in interviews and Op-Eds, and by publicizing this information during rallies and demonstrations.

MFSO's and GSFSO's more traditional forms of activism ranges from lobbying Congress to end the war, to organizing conferences and informational workshops, to giving and receiving support from other military families. The MFSO 2010 Mother's Day Action encompassed all of these anti-war approaches, by reminding members of the pacifist origins of Mother's Day, which began by honoring the deaths and casualties of the Civil War. MFSO's One Nation Working Together event in October 2010, with a coalition of anti-war groups, is a recent example of a public action. Finally, GSFSO, in concert with MFSO, have built coalitions with other motherhood movement organizations, such as CODEPINK, Women's International Peace Brigade, and the Granny Peace Brigade.

Challenges

GSFSO faces two main challenges, one ideological and the other political. On the ideological level, the activism of many of the women involved in ending the U.S. war in Iraq and Afghanistan exemplifies what Peggy Antrobus, Caribbean transnational feminist activist and co-founder of Development Alternatives with Women for a New Era (DAWN), calls the uneasy relationship within global women's movements between women who are "mobilized on the basis of motherhood and the political virtue of women's values" and those who are "concerned about the price women have always paid for this kind of 'essentializing'" (159). In other words, there is always a danger for women when they base their claims for reform on an identity, such as being a mother, which has links to essentialized notions about all women.

All female activists, from radical feminists to socially conservative women's groups, then, are caught in a binary that Carole Pateman describes as one that "continues to oscillate between 'difference' (maternal thinking should be valued and brought into the political arena) and 'equality' (citizenship not motherhood is vital for feminists)" (21). The binary between equality and difference, Pateman reminds us, is usually framed as an open question about whether gender and gender specific experiences such as mothering should be considered pertinent to politics and social change. Instead, feminists focus on a different issue: "how to subvert and change the manner in which women have already been incorporated, and so to transform the relation between 'equality' and 'difference'" (Pateman 27). The work mothers like Karen Meredith and Celeste Zappala do in the public sphere opens up the possibility that women can have equality of political participation *and* recognition of difference in mothers' experiences of public policies.

A political challenge has been keeping the wars on the public agenda. GSFSO and MFSO have maintained a consistent message of "bring the troops home now." In spite of this media attention, public interest in the issue of military family protests seemed to peak in the years 2006-2007 and has waned. In 2009 Senator Kerry lamented that the war in Iraq seemed forgotten in the wake of President Obama's election and global economic turmoil ("The 'Forgotten War'"). President Obama announced in August 2010 that the mission in Iraq was over and that the country's top priority would be the economy and creating jobs. However, as of January 2011 there were still 144,000 troops in Afghanistan and Iraq (Capaccio).

Future Goals

Future plans include coalitions with the Friends Committee on National Legislation for a weekend of action, lobbying, and training in Washington, DC, in March of 2011 to mark the ninth anniversary of the war in Iraq. A new initiative for GSFSO and MFSO is what they call "The True Costs of War Campaign": to remind the public of the human and financial costs of remaining in Iraq and Afghanistan. MFSO claims that keeping one solider for a year in Afghanistan costs taxpayers 1 million dollars ("Campaign Overview"). This campaign encourages members to send postcards to Congress and the President, to write letters to the editor, to offer to be interviewed by the media, to talk to members of their community, and to encourage people to sign a petition asking President Obama not to fund the wars overseas. MFSO provides their members with a talking-points PDF, where they remind their members: "Statistics can change minds, but only stories can change hearts. Commonly held beliefs about the war are often based on emotional reactions, not logic. The most powerful tool you have is your own personal story—the facts are here to back you up" (MFSO "The Wars"). This initiative may be responding to the U.S. public's concerns about taxes and the national debt, by reframing an anti-war position as not just moral but economic.

The Organization's Importance in the Motherhood Movement

In contrast to the marginalization women often experience as participants in social change movements, either from within the movement (Basu), or from without by the media (Ramirez), mothers have taken a leadership role within the Iraq/Afghanistan anti-war movement broadly, and are central to the GSFSO.[3] I might speculate that the media is more receptive to reporting the protests of grieving mothers when they fit into otherwise normative categories of American womanhood, such as that they are heterosexual, white, and middle-class. However, Meredith's status as a single mother and Zappala's status as an adoptive mother indicate that diverse maternal identities are embraced within the organization. In any case, the centrality of mothers as voices of the movement and as acknowledged leaders make this organization part of the Motherhood Movement, even if all of their members are not mothers.

GSFSO and MFSO activists frame their right to speak and protest in terms of their familial identity. They do this in spite of the mocking of maternal activism as too emotional, or unseemly in public. For example, Meredith argued in 2005 in a speech before the American Friends Service Committee that both mothers and fathers should speak out against the war, but that the public would be more receptive to hearing calls for peace from mothers:

> As long as the human costs are hidden, this country cannot begin to heal. The mothers' voices will end this war, they have to; and the father's can too, but it's mostly the mothers they will listen to… Imagine, for one minute, my sense of peace knowing that my speaking out might end the war one day earlier and possibly save the life of one of the pro-Bush, pro-war families. Their loved ones will come home because I raised my voice to question this war. ("Impassioned")

Meredith's writing does not necessarily invoke a essentialized idea of mothers as naturally more peaceful than fathers, but she does suggest that mothers must lead this movement because they are more credible witnesses to the destructive nature of war.

In addition to insisting on their right to be part of the public sphere debate over the war, Gold Star Families Speak Out took one of the most potent symbols of military grief and turned it into a critique of the Iraq and Afghan wars. The Gold Star is a traditional military symbol representing a family member who has died during military service. Sometimes family members wear a gold pin issued by the military, or sometimes they display a small banner bearing a gold star in their home or on their front door. Despite this long-standing tradition, many Americans are unaware of the significance of the gold star.

Some family members of soldiers killed since 2001 feel that their loss and their grief were marginalized through the Bush administration's efforts to keep a lid on media coverage of casualties. Meredith writes, "Very few people have actually met a Gold Star Mom. It is important that people know what it feels like to be in my situation" ("About"). Maternal activism insured that Gold Star mothers' perspectives were on the public agenda and put a face to the mothers who had lost children in the wars in Afghanistan and Iraq.

Many members of GSFSO advocate for a public and community-based social justice mothering practice. While not recognized as such, I argue that this reframing of public maternal subjectivity stands at the forefront of the maternal peace activists' accomplishments. GSFSO leader Celeste Zappala wages weekly anti-war protests in Philadelphia. Zappala has continued to do so even after President Obama announced the troop draw down in Iraq. Zappala argues that her political actions have a more expansive meaning than a protest over her son's death. "It's not joyfully that I can say the war is over, because it isn't," Zappala notes, "The consequences will go on forever. They've changed the name, but our people are still in danger and there are still going to be people injured or dying" (Pompilio). Thus, these activists call not just for government or foreign policy change, but for mothers themselves to change their vision of caretaking.

Conclusion

Gold Star Families Speak Out can be seen as an organization with roots in women's peace movements going back to the nineteenth-century. On the other hand, GSFSO makes a radical break with the past, by being military mothers critiquing an ongoing war, and by creating a larger base of supporters through specifying that their goal is to end the wars in Iraq and Afghanistan, rather than all wars. Claiming a voice as a citizen and a mother is difficult, since mothers have not been traditionally counted as a political constituency (Reiger 318). In nationalist discourse, mothers have been expected to embody and perpetuate the nation while not being active citizens (Stitt 2007). GSFSO and MFSO members break the binary between mother of the nation and active citizen by claiming their rights as citizens through their experiences as mothers.

[1]This chapter is adapted from a previous article, "A Gold Star for Grieving: Cindy Sheehan, Military Families Speak Out and Gold Star Families Speak Out." *Journal of the Motherhood Initiative for Research and Community Involvement* 1.2 (2010): 242-257.

[2]Private conversation with Karen Meredith, October 12, 2010. I would like to thank Ms. Meredith discussing the history of Gold Star Mothers Speak Out, her activism, and her leadership of that group. Meredith's son Lt. Ken Ballard was killed in Iraq.

[3]A 2005 *Washington Post* article noted that the majority of Gold Star Families for Peace members were mothers, which remains true for Gold Star Families Speak Out (Nieves).

Works Cited

Antrobus, Peggy. *The Global Women's Movement: Origins, Issues and Strategies.* London: Zed Books, 2004.

Associated Press. "Most Vet Suicides Among Guard, Reserve troops." *MSNCB* Feb 12 2008. Web. <http://www.msnbc.msn.com/id/23132421/>. Accessed 18 Jan 2011.

Basu, Amrita, ed. *Women's Movements in the Global Era: The Power of Local Femi-*

nisms. Boulder, CO: Westview Press, 2010.

Capaccio, Tony. "Obama Plans $42 Billion Cut in War Costs With Iraq, Afghan Troop Reduction." *Bloomberg*. Jan 20 2011. Web. <http://www.bloomberg.com/news/2011-01-20/pentagon-fiscal-2012-war-request-to-be-lowest-since-fiscal-2005.html/>. Accessed 24 Jan 2011.

"Cost of War Talking Points." Oct 27 2010. "Who We Are." Web. <http://www.mfso.org/article.php?list=type&type=61>. Accessed January 22 2011.

"Forgotten War, The." Editorial. *Washington Post*. Sep 13 2009. Web. <http://www.washingtonpost.com/wp-dyn/content/article/2009/09/13/AR2009091302444.html>. Accessed Jan 24 2011.

Gold Star Families Speak Out (GSFSO). "About Us." Web. < http://www.gsfso.org/about_us.html>.

Hochberg, Lee. "Homefront Battle." *Public Broadcasting Corporation*. Oct. 4 2004. Web. <http://www.pbs.org/newshour/bb/military/july-dec04/battle_10-04.html>. Accessed 12 October 2010.

Houppert, Karen. "Cindy Sheehan: Mother of a Movement?" *The Nation* Jun 12 2006: 11-16.

"Living With PTSD." *Gold Star Families Speak Out*. 2009. Web. <http:// www.gsfso.org/index.html>.

Meredith, Karen. "About Me." *Gold Star Mom Speaks Out*. May 22 2010. <http://gsmso.blogspot.com>. Accessed 30 May 2010.

Meredith, Karen. "The Crawford Papers." November 2005. Web. <http://www.ltkenballard.com/Crawford, percent20TX.htm>. Accessed Jan 14 2011.

Meredith, Karen. "Impassioned Plea from a Gold Star Mother. *Street Spirit*. October 27 2005. Web. <http://www.thestreetspirit.org/Nov2005/ goldstar.htm>. Accessed 12 Oct 2010.

Military Families Speak Out. "Action Center." May 2010. Web. <http://www.mfso. org/article.php?id=1380>.

Military Families Speak Out. "Campaign Overview: The True Costs of War." Web. <http://www.mfso.org/article.php?id=1416>. Accessed Jan 14 2011.

Nieves, Evelyn. "For Some, a Loss in Iraq Turns into Antiwar Activism: Gold Star Families Band Together to 'Make People Care.'" *Washington Post*. Feb 22 2005. Web. <http://www.washingtonpost.com/wp-dyn/articles/A42498-2005Feb21.html>. Accessed January 22 2011.

Pateman, Carole. "Equality, Difference, Subordination: The Politics of Motherhood and Women's Citizenship." *Beyond Equality and Difference: Citizenship, Feminist Politics, Female Subjectivity*. Eds. Gisela Bock and Susan James. New York: Routledge, 1992. 17-31.

Pompilio, Natalie. "Philadelphia Mother's Fight For Peace Continues." *Philadelphia Daily News* Aug 31 2010. Web. <http://www.philly.com/ dailynews/local/20100831_Philadelphia_mother_s_fight_for_peace_con- tinues.html>. Accessed 8 October 2010.

Pullin, Lara. "A Woman's Place is In the Struggle: Women Against War." *Green Left* 617 (March 2 2005). Web. <http://www.greenleft.org.au/node/33058>.

Accessed 14 Jan 2011.

Ramirez, Renya K. "Gender, Belonging, and Native American Women: The Activism of Cecelia. Fire Thunder and Sarah Deer." *Gendered Citizenships: Transnational Perspectives on Knowledge Production, Political Activism, and Culture.* Eds. Kia Lilly Caldwell et. al. New York: Palgrave: 2009: 157-172.

Reiger, Kerreen. "Reconceiving Citizenship: The Challenge of Mothers as Political Activists." *Feminist Theory* 1.3 (2000): 309-27.

Rose, Ryan. "Loving the Warrior, Hating the War." *Sacramento News and Review* Sep 15 2005. Web. <http://www.newsreview.com/sacramento/content?oid=43976>. Accessed 12 Oct 2010.

Sheehan, Cindy. *Peace Mom: A Mother's Journey Through Heartache to Activism.* New York: Atria, 2006.

Stitt, Jocelyn. "Gendered Legacies of Romantic Nationalism in the Works of Michelle Cliff." *Small Axe* 24 (11.3) (2007): 52-72.

Wilson, Natalie. "From Gestation to Delivery: The Embodied Activist Mothering of Cindy Sheehan and Jennifer Schumaker." *Mothers Who Deliver: Feminist Interventions in Public and Interpersonal Discourse.* Eds. Jocelyn Fenton Stitt and Pegeen Reichert Powell. Albany: SUNY Press, 2010. 231-252.

56. Raising a Ruckus with CODEPINK

Women for Peace

GAYLE BRANDEIS

PERHAPS YOU'VE SEEN US. WOMEN in hot pink holding signs of peace at Congressional hearings; women dropping 20 ft. tall lingerie-style "pink slips" with messages such as "Bush—You're Fired" from the sides of buildings; women being dragged out of political conventions for daring to speak truth to power. Women raising palms dipped in red paint to Condoleeza Rice, reminding her of the blood on her own hands. Women standing up and saying "No to War" in the most outrageous, vibrant, visible way possible.

Mandate

CODEPINK is a women-initiated grassroots peace and social justice movement working to end the wars in Iraq and Afghanistan, stop new wars, and redirect our resources into healthcare, education, green jobs and other life-affirming activities. CODEPINK rejects foreign policies based on domination and aggression, and instead calls for policies based on diplomacy, compassion and a commitment to international law. With an emphasis on joy and humor, CODEPINK women and men seek to activate, amplify and inspire a community of peacemakers through creative campaigns and a commitment to non-violence.

At a time when the media tends to ignore the peace movement, when the hundreds of thousands pouring into the streets worldwide to stop war were considered a "focus group" by Bush, when protestors were deemed "ground noise and static" by McCain, CODEPINK has aimed to give peace a voice and a face that can't be ignored. Our tactics appear to be working; former White House secretary Dana Perino once said, "It seems that increasingly Congress is being run by CODEPINK." If only this were true—but we will continue to make our presence and our message for peace known, both in Congress and beyond. As a reporter for Fox News stated, "George Bush will eventually go back to Texas, but CODEPINK is here to stay." And of course he was right—with George Bush out of office now, we are deeply committed to reminding President Obama of his campaign promises for change, and urging him to live up to the honor of his Nobel Peace Prize. One of our co-founders, Jodie Evans, recently had the opportunity to meet briefly with

CODEPINK *Mother's Day rally in front of the White House..*

Obama in person—she hand-delivered a petition signed by Afghan women and their sisters around the world, asking for no new troops in Afghanistan. She also asked Obama to bring more women to the negotiating table. "We have Hilary," he said to her, but she told him that's not what she meant. "We need Afghan women to be involved in the future of their own country," she reminded him and he looked stunned, as if he hadn't considered this before. We will continue to encourage him to heed the voices of women, of mothers, as he makes life or death decisions about war and humanitarian aid.

History

CODEPINK: Women for Peace began in 2002 as a group of women standing vigil in front of the White House, asking Bush to not invade Iraq. The protest was organized by the aforementioned Jodie Evans, a prominent social, political and community activist over the last 30 years and Medea Benjamin, longtime peace activist and co-founder of the international human rights organization, Global Exchange. Both mothers, Medea and Jodie knew great power could be generated when women band together to speak for peace. Along with Texas environmentalist Diane Wilson and the author Starhawk, they chose to call themselves CODEPINK as a direct response to the Bush administration's kindergarten color-coded security alerts of code yellow, code orange, code red. They wanted CODEPINK to counter this system of fear with a more creative, proactive system, a women-generated grassroots effort that would create and nurture peace, justice and community.

Their vigil became a daily presence on Pennsylvania Avenue over the next four chilly months, their numbers steadily growing before culminating in a week of massive action to mark International Women's Day and celebrate women as global peacemakers. Ten thousand women attended this mobilization and 25 were arrested, including Jodie and Medea, as well as authors Alice Walker, Maxine Hong Kingston and Susan Griffin. When the story of these illustrious women dressed in pink for peace hit the news, CODEPINK first entered the public consciousness as a force to be reckoned with.

Since then, CODEPINK has become a worldwide network of women and men committed to working for peace and social justice. We have become famous for confronting the warmongers, whether in the halls of Congress, the national conventions for both the Republicans and Democrats, George Bush's fundraisers, or in Donald Rumsfeld and Nancy Pelosi's houses. We have over 200,000 people on our mailing list, and over 250 local groups around the globe who work to mobilize for peace in their own communities, organizing vigils and marches and meetings with decision makers, along with other creative actions.

From 2007-2009, CODEPINK leased a row house in Washington, DC, to serve as headquarters for those who wish to hone their activist skills and be in action on Capitol Hill. The Pink House had its own House Mother—Desiree Fairooz, a mother, grandmother, and former school librarian who left the home she knew in Texas to be the heartbeat of the Pink House—rallying and cooking for the assembled activists who have come to DC to shake things up. The house was steeped in pink—pink boas and other costumes to wear to protests and street theater actions, pink banners and signs and parasols and other props. While we had to let go of the house, CODEPINK continues to be a steady, vocal presence in DC and beyond. CODEPINK has rescued the color pink from the Barbie aisle, from its stereotypical connotations of girlishness, and turned it into something fierce and alive. When we don our pink, we are reclaiming the color as a source of female power.

CODEPINK and the Motherhood Movement

The language we use during our meetings and conference calls is deeply informed by our experiences as women and mothers. When we begin a new project, we ask who wants to "mother" it along. We support and encourage one another the way all good mothers should, in a spirit of cooperation and creativity and mutual inspiration and respect. And we hope that our pink presence reminds lawmakers of the strength and influence of women, of mothers. "In the hindbrain of anyone who listens to us, we're momma," said Eileen Coles, 45, of New York, who came to DC to protest the fifth anniversary of the war. "Somewhere in their head they're hearing their mother say, 'You're doing wrong. You're being bad. Cut it out.' We are creators of life, and we have that power."

CODEPINK has reclaimed the original intention of Mother's Day, envisioned

CODEPINK's Walk in Their Shoes campaign.

by Julia Ward Howe in 1870 as a time for all the mothers who lost their sons in the Civil War to protest the senseless violence. Howe's Mother's Day Proclamation begins:

> Arise then … women of this day!
> Arise, all women who have hearts!

And later goes on to say:

> As men have often forsaken the plough and the anvil
> At the summons of war,
> Let women now leave all that may be left of home
> For a great an earnest day of counsel.
> Let them meet first, as women, to bewail and commemorate the dead.
> Let them solemnly take counsel with each other as to the means
> Whereby the great human family can live in peace…

CODEPINK resurrects this proclamation every May, bringing mothers and children together for peace picnics and parades around the country (including a mothers' and children's march at the White House and a funeral procession for mothers who lost children to war across the Golden Gate Bridge), but we also believe every day is Mother's Day; every day is an opportunity for women to rise

Aerial photograph of CODEPINK's Mother's Day action.

up and gather and take counsel as we work together toward peace—and not always solemnly. CODEPINK believes that joy and humor and play are an important part of the process. If we want to create a more hopeful future, we need to model that hope and peace within ourselves and between one another. Just as mothers learn that it's good to offer a Yes to our children after we tell them No, when we create Women Say NO to War actions, we also are sure to say Yes to peace, Yes to justice, Yes to a more sustainable future. As such, CODEPINK is an integral part of the Motherhood Movement, making the movement more visible and vocal, drawing upon the inspiration and strength of the women who have come before us, and joining in coalition with other women's and mothers' groups currently working for peace and social justice.

Making the Cost of War Visible

While we're best known for our colorful disruptions, whether we're confronting war mongers in the halls of Congress (sometimes even camping out in front of their houses), attempting to make citizens arrests of figures such as Karl Rove, showing Condoleezza Rice that she has blood on her hands, or staging "Make Out Not War" kiss-ins in front of military recruiting stations, much of CODEPINK's most powerful work is of a more quiet nature.

We have brought women's peace delegations to Iraq and Iran and Afghanistan and Gaza to gather the stories of women from those countries, voices that are not often enough heard in dialogues about war. In 2006, we brought seven Iraqi women, mostly mothers, to the U.S. and organized a speaking tour so they could share, first hand, their own stories of how the occupation in Iraq has affected their lives and devastated their families. We are currently sponsoring a couple of brave Afghan women as they tour the U.S. and Canada, speaking about their experiences in their oppressive, war torn home country and what we can do to support women there (especially through U.S. money for development rather than further war).

Our national campaign, Walk in Their Shoes, was inspired by the actions of CODEPINK New York, who set over one hundred pairs of children's shoes, each standing for a particular Iraqi child killed during the current war, in front of Hillary Clinton's Manhattan office. The powerful visual display—which of course represents only a tiny percentage of actual civilian deaths in Iraq—forced passers-by to confront the true human cost of war.

Since then, we have staged Walk in Their Shoes actions throughout the country. Passers-by are often moved to donate hundreds of pairs of shoes, to label each pair with the name and age of a woman or child killed in Iraq (and now also Afghanistan), to bear witness to the unspeakable pain this war has unleashed on the Iraqi and Afghan people.

It is easy for politicians and media outlets to portray citizen casualties as numbers on a page, as faceless, nameless "collateral damage," far removed from any real pain. But when you see a worn pair of shoes, you can't help but think of the feet that once pulsed inside. The body connected to those feet. The heart and mind and voice connected to that body. The person's whole rich and complicated life, now silenced. You wonder about the fear they must have felt when the bombs started to fall. You wonder if they tried to outrun the destruction. You wonder about the pain that ripped through them when their flesh was pierced by shrapnel, when the walls began to fall. You wonder about the unbearable grief the surviving family members grapple with still. You wonder how we ever could have started such a tragic and unnecessary war.

In our effort to stop the next war now, we have also asked CODEPINK members to download photos of Iranian children and wear them as pendants with the message "Don't Bomb Iran." We want these images to remind our friends and neighbors and lawmakers of the humanity of the Iranian people. When we see the beautiful faces of these children, how could we ever come to terms with them as potential collateral damage? How could we ever risk harming such precious young lives?

CODEPINK works hard to keep the human cost of war visible; we can't give our elected officials the luxury of looking away, of pretending that we are waging a humane and compassionate war.

Helping Mothers Around the World

We are especially proud of the work we've done with Iraqi refugees, raising tens of thousands of dollars to help women and children who had been displaced by violence in their country. Medea Benjamin traveled to Jordan and Syria in 2008 so she could witness firsthand the important and inspiring work being done by our partnering organization, the Collateral Repair Project. Not only does the CRP repair schools and feed the hungry with CODEPINK's help; they also provide very personal support. Medea saw this in the case of one Iraqi woman, Um Marianne.

A single mother whose husband had been killed, Um Marianne was unable to work legally because she was undocumented. Men preyed on her and bosses cheated her, yet she could not complain because of her precarious situation. Um Marianne wept as she spoke about leaving her daughter at home while she went off to endure sweatshop conditions. A group of Iraqi women, fellow refugees, were concerned about her and banded together to help. They approached CRP, who gave them the money to buy a sewing machine. Now Um Marianne can work from home and take care of her daughter without worrying about exploitation and other dangers. Numerous other displaced Iraqi mothers have received similar help from CRP and CODEPINK in starting small, underground businesses that can keep their families afloat.

In early 2009, CODEPINK traveled to Gaza to bear witness to the destruction wrought by the Israeli invasion that left over 1,300 dead in December, 2008. After listening to the stories of women there, we have since returned to build playgrounds and bring school supplies to children, so they can begin to imagine a more peaceful future. We are currently helping to organize a Gaza Freedom March, a non-violent action dedicated to breaching the illegal blockade, lifting the siege, and starting the process of rebuilding the occupied territory.

CODEPINK has also been working within the United States to help single mothers devastated by the current economic crisis. When CODEPINK heard the story

Cindy Sheehan and Susan Sarandon join CODEPINK Mother's Day rally.

of Jocelyne Voltaire, a single mother of four who had recently lost her eldest son, a Marine who had served in the Gulf, and was about to lose her New York home of 20 years due to a predatory lender scam, we knew we had to do something. We put out a call for donations, and within one day, raised $30,000, enough to save Jocelyne's home from auction. The outpouring of support was so generous, so heartfelt, we decided to expand our efforts to help other single mothers facing foreclosure, and toward that end, have launched HealMainStreet.org. While our government has taken billions of our dollars to bail out the wealthy, we came together to bail out a desperate mother. We modeled just what we want our government to do—bail out families facing personal disaster, not financiers. CODEPINK is committed to continuing to work for peace and justice for women both in our own communities and around the world, from New Orleans to Pakistan, often partnering with other peace and justice groups to amplify all of our voices.

Challenges

Unfortunately, CODEPINK has become the target of far-right hatred that has filled staff email boxes with profane and insulting messages suggesting that, among other things, we should be run over by trucks, forced to wear burkas, or shipped to Iraq and Afghanistan where we would get what we deserved. One site published the home addresses and phone numbers of all CODEPINK staff members, with the intent to harass us (and worse). Another site photoshopped our "Women Say No to War" banner to read "We Support the Murder of the American Troops," an image which became widely circulated, and which we often have to debunk (along with the myth that we fund terrorist organizations.) Our actions are often met with hostile counter protestors. While sometimes the hatred directed our way is frightening, and we have had to contact the police over specific threats, we can't let fear stop us. There is too much important work to be done.

Some critics, on both the right and the left, have called our tactics obnoxious, embarrassing, silly, but as all mothers know, sometimes you have to risk embarrassment to be heard. The stakes are too high for us to sit back and be polite, to stay in the background as our leaders lead us into unjust wars and economic disaster, as they strip away one right after another. CODEPINK is committed to keeping the voice of peace alive and as visible and audible as possible.

My Own Story

On a more personal note, my own involvement with CODEPINK came about because of my experience as a mother. I had been on the CODEPINK mailing list since it was founded in 2002 and had wanted to get more involved, but somehow hadn't yet found the right opening to do so. Then in the summer of 2005, I saw that their Los Angeles group was going to be staging a play about election reform and they needed local actors, including young ones. I asked my daughter Hannah—an emerging activist at the time, as well as a budding thespian—if she'd like to go to the audition, and she was excited by the prospect.

We drove down to a funky little bungalow in Venice, which turned out to be full of women of all ages, many in pink t-shirts. After demonstrating her passionate portrayal of the "child of the future" for the director, Hannah was offered a part on the spot.

As we sat in the airy front room, a woman with flaming red hair, and a pink scarf draped gracefully around her neck, burst through the door and introduced herself as Jodie Evans. While the play people talked their play talk, I followed Jodie into the cozy kitchen.

"I admire your work so much," I told her. "If there is anything I can do to help in any way, please let me know." I told her that I was a writer, that I was always looking for ways to use my voice for good.

"Thanks." She smiled and retreated to her office. About half an hour later, just before Hannah and I were about to leave, Jodie burst back into the room, teary and alive with excitement. She had just gotten off the phone with a woman named Cindy Sheehan, she told us. Cindy had just sat down in a ditch in Crawford, Texas and said she refused to leave until President Bush told her what noble cause her son had died for in Iraq. Shivers ran up and down my arms.

Jodie turned to me. "Can you write a press release about this?" she asked.

I have been writing for CODEPINK—op-eds and chants and whatever else needs to be put into words—ever since. I was eventually invited to be part of the national staff as their "Communication Goddess," and I now write the weekly action alerts that go out to our 200,000 members and ask them to sign petitions or visit their representative or write letters to the editor or find creative ways to work for peace in their own communities. I know these alerts that I write anonymously every week reach more people than my fiction ever will; not only that, they will inspire action, encourage change. I feel very grateful to be able to lend my voice to CODEPINK, and even more grateful that CODEPINK gives voice to women around the world.

Conclusion

You will keep seeing us, in our pink boas and pink slips and pink wigs, standing up for peace and justice and a more sustainable world, whether we're working to close Guantanamo, or support war resisters or remind the public that War is Not Green; whether we're holding signs that say "Bail Out Main Street, Not Wall Street" or "Stop the Next War Now."

It has been so inspiring to me to see how mothers around the world, through CODEPINK and other organizations, are working to combat war and wage peace. We are all pink under our skin. May we continue to reclaim that color, and use our voices and our visions together to create a more peaceful, joyful future for all of our children.

57.
Peace X Peace

Global Motherhood for the Twenty-first Century

MARY LISTON LIEPOLD

PEACE X PEACE (WHICH IS pronounced Peace by Peace), is an internet-based global network of mothers and others in about 110 countries. It invites and facilitates heart connections, partnerships, and diverse from-the-front-lines perspectives—all disseminated worldwide through blogs, e-mail, Facebook, Twitter, and other new media. To women at every life stage—maidens, mothers, and crones, in the classic goddess manifestations—it offers a way to extend our distinctly feminine, maternal, tend-and-befriend approach to a global arena. This chapter briefly outlines the organization's philosophy, its history, its activities since 2002, its challenges, and its vision for the future, which is also its relationship to the larger motherhood movement.

Mandate, Mission, Philosophy, and Theory of Change

To promote peace, Peace X Peace lifts women's voices, strengthens women's capacity to connect across divides, promotes women's leadership and gender equity, and nurtures the global network of peacebuilders. Through its media and its social network, it multiplies the impact of individual experience and expertise to bring exponential positive change.

Philosophically, as a women's organization and a peace organization, Peace X Peace embraces our distinctive feminine power in all of its fruitful mothering aspects. Long before written history began, mothers, sisters, grandmothers, aunts, and neighbors knew that the survival of children and the survival of the group depended on their nurturing and cooperation. These values and traits that men in traditional cultures deride as weak are the strengths the world needs now, when the greatest threats to our survival are not local but global in scope. The open structure of our inclusive network models a womanly understanding of power-with—cooperative, shared, win-win—against the still-dominant, historically masculine model of power-over—rooted in conquest, domination, and control.

In the words of our founder, Patricia Smith Melton:

> Women's ways of perceiving, organizing and interacting are rooted in

seeking security and harmony through coming together and bonding rather than dividing and building walls. Given opportunity and means, women will include, and communicate with, the stranger in order to build family. This force, ever-present, has been underrated and even unseen in a world where the feminine principles of perception, interaction, and action were not, *until now*, recognized as the key to substantive, sustainable peace.

Our theory of change is the tipping point. Malcolm Gladwell, who borrowed the term from epidemiology, defines it as that moment in an epidemic when a virus reaches critical mass. The Internet has been essential to the growth of Peace X Peace because it makes possible for the first time the global, viral transmission and multiplication of women's power for peace.

History and Activities

2001–2005: Peace Media and Global Connections

Peace X Peace began immediately after September 11, 2001, with a mother's fear and hope. Mother, poet, photographer, and playwright Patricia Smith Melton felt sure the violence would be answered with more violence, and that it was up to women to come together to right the balance. So she called on wise women like Fatima Gailani, current head of the Red Crescent in Afghanistan; Susan Collin Marks, executive vice president of Search for Common Ground; Barbara Marx Hubbard, founder of the Foundation for Conscious Evolution; novelist Isabel Allende; Koranic scholar Azizah al-Hibri; and author Jean Shinoda Bolen. Seven Muslim, Christian, and Jewish women from the North, South, East,

The 2002 Gathering

and West gathered in her home for three days in early 2002. They agreed that peace is connectedness, inclusion, wholeness, seeing the humanity in the other, and restorative justice, and that uniting women of all cultures through new and emerging technologies was the most powerful way to engage maternal energy in bringing the world to peace.

For the next nine months, as America prepared for war, Patricia and an all-woman film crew documented the peacebuilding work of ordinary extraordinary women on five continents. The result was the documentary film *Peace by Peace: Women on the Frontlines*, starring Spes Manirakiza, whose radio station counteracted hate radio during the massacres in Burundi; Colleen Kelly and other U.S. members of September 11 Families for a Peaceful Tomorrow; Argentinian presidential candidate Elsa Carrio, and the Madres of the Plaza de Mayo, who took motherhood to the public square and inspired countless other mother's movements; women entrepreneurs in Bosnia-Herzegovina; and in Afghanistan, underground schoolteacher Naheed Sharfi and Constitutional Commissioner Fatima Gailani. The film premiered at the United Nations in 2003, won film festival awards in the U.S., Canada, and South Korea, then played on PBS stations and in living rooms and church basements everywhere throughout 2004 and beyond. It was featured in a 2010 film festival in India, and continues to be watched and enjoyed around the world.

The organization Peace X Peace was incorporated in 2003 and grew rapidly, fueled by the success of the film, press coverage in media as diverse as Oprah's *O Magazine* and *Al-Jazeera*, and global personal outreach by Patricia and the staff. Its two major components were an array of media and a social network, both focused on women as builders of peace. The 2003 Peace X Peace Global Network, the earliest version of today's Peace X Peace Community, was a custom-built, pioneering web platform unlike anything else that existed at that time. It invited women everywhere, regardless of status, language, religion, race, or nationality, into a secure online space to communicate directly and personally, form lasting relationships, and take joint actions for peace.

Online social networks were still in their infancy in 2003, and those that did exist built (in Robert Putnam's term) bonding social capital, linking on the basis of affinity. The Peace X Peace Network built *bridging* social capital as it linked women across vast distances in culture and geography. Almost inevitably, conversations began with the stuff of home—children, grandchildren, food preparation—and quickly branched out. Mention of holiday preparations led to religious differences, so Baptists in Atlanta learned the daily details of Ramadan, and Muslims in Herat learned how one family celebrates Passover. Conservative Anglicans in Kenya learned about Wicca from their friends in Canada—and the connection shook, but held. When University of Baghdad professor Naba Saleem Hamid agonized over whether to stay in Iraq or leave it, her online sisters listened and helped her weigh the alternatives.

As founder Patricia likes to say: "Strangers become friends and friends become as dear as family. And you don't drop bombs on family."

Palestinian and Israeli women share a laugh on neutral ground.

2005 to the Present: High Tech and High Touch

In 2005, when it became apparent that members were enrolling at a greater rate from outside North America than from within it, staff member Linda Higdon embarked on a ten-city Celebrate Peace U.S. Tour with Peace Cereal and Spirit Rising Yoga. The partners worked with yoga studios, congregations, and peace organizations in each city to bring audiences together for Peace X Peace workshops and other events.

Over the next few years, staff members and volunteers traveled around the U.S. and to Pakistan, Afghanistan, India, Kenya, South Africa, Sudan, Sri Lanka, Uganda, Indonesia, Egypt, Israel, the UAE, and Jordan to cement friendships and promote the Global Network. In March 2006, 24 members from eight countries traveled to Washington to meet face to face in The Women's Global Initiative Forum. Sara Cobb, Director of the Institute for Conflict Analysis and Resolution at George Mason University, facilitated three days of purposeful, recorded cross-cultural conversation. The forum discussions produced an interactive online wiki for continuing the conversation and a multi-media, cross-cultural dialogue guide.

Several of the participants have since become prominent peacebuilders in their own countries and internationally. Afghanistan's Suraya Pakzad was selected as one of *Time Magazine's* 100 Most Important People in the World for 2009 because of her fearless advocacy for women. Palestinian Rula Salameh co-produced the documentary film *Budrus*, which is currently gathering awards at film festivals around the world. Michigan's Judy Satterthwaite and WISDOM (Women's Interfaith Solutions for Dialogue and Outreach in Metro Detroit) worked with David

A Peace X Peace Circle in Mali

Crumm to create the book *Friendship and Faith: The WISDOM of Women Creating Alliances for Peace*. Patricia Smith Melton was featured as an Interfaith Hero in an earlier book in the same series.

Members' caring, nurturing relationships flow naturally into face to face visits and direct joint action. Women from Iraq, Afghanistan, Mali, the Palestinian Territories, Israel, Korea, and other nations have made extended visits to the U.S. and Canada, while North American members have visited Kenya, Israel, Uganda, Egypt, and many other countries. The 2006 Washington, DC, gathering has been followed by others.

Joint projects often involve micro-enterprise and education.

Members in Uganda and other parts of Africa sent handmade jewelry to their Sister Circle in the U.S. The women sold it through their local networks and returned the profits to be reinvested in the micro-enterprise. Traveling community members recruited for hand delivery often wound up drawn into the connection.

Members in the U.S. co-invested with members of their Circle in Meru, Kenya, to found and operate a hostel for visitors. Members in Pakistan and the West Bank coordinated with local organizations and Peace X Peace to open centers where women can use computers and the internet. Members in Canada, Iraq, and the U.S. ignited the Women Stand with Iraq coalition, offering a range of concrete actions to take in solidarity with Iraqi women and families.

Members in Egypt initiated educational exchanges about women's health and hygiene, gaining information they had been denied in their home culture. Members in Israel and the Palestinian Territories co-hosted events that brought women from their communities together for friendship, education, and cultural exchange. U.S. members facilitated scholarships so Circle sisters in Afghanistan, Mali, and other countries could study in the U.S.

Peace X Peace began with the hypothesis that women could bring their distinctive capacity to tend and befriend to virtual connections that develop real trust and collaboration. That hypothesis has been borne out.

Over the years we have raised hundreds of diverse voices and developed an extensive archive of stories and statements. These include audio recordings (housed at Voice X Voice on our website) and YouTube videos, as well as blogs, newsletters, and first-person online narratives. Contributors have included Ela Gandhi, Riane Eisler, Nicholas Kristof, Louise Diamond, Lynne Twist, and other famous people. More typically, though, we offer a platform to those women (and sometimes men) whose work to strengthen the Pillars of Peace is not yet widely recognized. Often this exposure is a springboard to deeper engagement with the Peace X Peace network, the wider peace community, and the world at large.

Awards and Achievements

Interfaith Heroes (http://www.readthespirit.com/) recognized Smith Melton for creating and sustaining Peace X Peace and also for the personal diplomacy she has practiced around the world, and, particularly since 2004, in Israel and the Palestinian Territories. In late 2008 she published *Sixty Years, Sixty Voices*, a collection of interviews and portrait photos featuring 30 Palestinian women and 30 Israeli women who all believe that peace is possible for this deeply troubled

2009 Women, Power, and Peace Award Winners with Patricia Smith Melton and Executive Director Pat Morris

region. The text is in English, Arabic, and Hebrew. That year Smith Melton was chosen as a Person of the Year by OneWorld and received the Peace and Dialogue Award from The Rumi Forum. She was recognized as a Purpose Prize Fellow for 2009.

In 2008 Peace X Peace won the Technology Innovation Award from NPower and Accenture. In 2007 it was selected from a field that included Oxfam, the Humane Society, and the American Cancer Society to receive the ePhilanthropy Foundation's Best Community Building/Activism Award. Other honors have included selection as one of *Working Mother* magazine's 25 Best Companies for Women in 2006 and the Espiritu Award from the Isabel Allende Foundation in 2005. Isabel established the foundation as a tribute to her daughter, whose loss she describes in the 1995 memoir, *Paula*.

Peace X Peace gives awards as well as receiving them. Annual events have honored paired peace circles, like the St. Tereza Circle in Mubende, Uganda, and Women Building Bridges in Mount Shasta, California, and individual members like Mercy Chidi, co-founder of Ripples International in Meru, Kenya. In 2009 we honored Afghan members Fatima Gailani and Suraya Pakzad, as well as Abigail Disney, producer of the documentary *Pray the Devil Back to Hell*, and Mario Morino, founder of Venture Philanthropy Partners. Our most significant accomplishments, though, are not the awards but the relationships among women across borders and the changed awareness they have produced on all sides. One member told us, in a 2008 survey:

> Peace X Peace gives me insight into issues that are important to me both as a woman and as a supporter of peace. It also alerts me to things happening to women and their families all over the world—information that you don't necessarily get from the news media and other organizations.

Another commented: "You've given us something we can do at home, in private, without undue effort, to promote world peace."

2010 and Beyond: Collaboration and Growth

In 2010 our community includes almost 18,000 women and men in some 110 nations. Our rich web of personal and organizational connections includes both face-to-face and online relationships that span the globe. Kimberly Weichel is Chief Executive Officer, and founder Patricia Smith Melton serves on the volunteer Board of Directors. The Peace X Peace Community, the Ning social network that launched in 2010, gained 1,500 members between March and June of 2010. As of July, it was growing at a rate of 60 percent each month. This year and for the year ahead, Peace X Peace activities are focused in six areas:

E-media: Our monthly e-newsletter and weekly blog digest reach nearly 20,000 subscribers worldwide. We expect to expand that circulation through partnerships and outreach.

Other media: The book *Sixty Years, Sixty Voices: Israeli and Palestinian Women* and the documentary *Women on the Frontlines* show women's peace power in the round. The array will continue to evolve to reflect members' and partners' needs.

Peer Education and Skillbuilding: We host an online social network, the Peace X Peace Community, and an evolving online classroom to facilitate exchange of skills and resources among our community members.

Advocacy: We advocate for effective, sustained policies and programs that support and advance women.

United Nations Collaboration: We collaborate on UN initiatives for women, including the Commission on the Status of Women, Millennium Development Goals, and UN Women.

Women, Power and Peace Awards: Our annual awards event honors extraordinary women and men on the frontlines of peacebuilding.

The e-media include four blogs that are hosted on the website www.peacexpeace.org and disseminated to almost 18,000 subscribers in the Weekly Blog Digest and the monthly *PeaceTimes*. Content reflects a wide range of perspectives from the founder, staff, Board, Community members, and expert friends, centered on five Peace Principles and eight Pillars of Peace (see below). Topics broached in the blogs fuel continuing discussion in the Peace X Peace Community.

Voices from the Frontlines, our most popular blog feature, showcases women's brief first-person stories and statements. In cases when exposure could put an author at risk, as during crackdowns on political opposition in Zimbabwe and Burma, we use generic names and photos to protect her identity.

Peace Principles and Peace Pillars

The work of Peace X Peace is grounded in the following principles and Pillars of Peace:

- Sustainable peace requires women's perspectives and expertise.
- Each individual has equal standing and all have wisdom and experience to share.
- Peaceful cultures are founded on justice, equality, and cooperation.
- Open, inclusive exchanges through online communications technology lead to best solutions and actions.

Thriving communities value the social goods we call the Pillars of Peace:

- Conflict Transformation
- Cross-cultural Understanding
- Economic Empowerment
- Education
- Environmental Sustainability
- Health and Well-being
- Interfaith Dialogue
- Justice and Good Governance

A culture of peace includes all of these social goods. It was defined by the 1998 United Nations resolution on the culture of peace as "an integral approach to preventing violence and violent conflicts, and an alternative to the culture of war and violence based on education for peace, the promotion of sustainable economic and social development, respect for human rights, equality between women and men, democratic participation, tolerance, the free flow of information, and disarmament."

Challenges

A funny thing happened on the way to 2010. Online social networking—a term that had barely been coined in 2003—came to be seen as so essential that almost every major nonprofit organization added a network to its other offerings. Peace organizations and women's organizations also proliferated in this decade. The wars in Iraq and Afghanistan grew increasingly unpopular, while global financial and environmental crises gave increasing evidence that the men in charge were clueless and it was time for women to do what mothers know best: protect life in all its manifestations.

While this growing awareness is good news for the planet, the conditions that caused it brought dire financial news to many social profit organizations, including Peace X Peace. Rapidly evolving technologies and the rise of citizen journalism have also been mixed blessings. They bring new outreach opportunities to every organization and increase the potential for global connectedness. They also increase the volume and speed of the media stream, making even raised voices harder to hear. And of course, they serve repressive governments and proponents of violence as well as peace-builders.

In the face of these challenges, we have evolved continually to lead and expand. The current online Community moves us from proprietary toward relatively open source technology. Like the Creative Commons agreement that we feature on our e-publications, the open source philosophy mirrors our commitment to collaboration and our belief that trust engenders good will and good results.

Current Objectives

Objectives for 2011 are summed up in our tagline: *Raise Women's Voices, Build Cultures of Peace.* Every day women seize the opportunity to raise their voices, both publicly, through our blogs, and in the privacy of the password-protected online Community. Writers and readers both benefit immediately from a forum dedicated to women's peace-building. They learn they are not alone; that others are eager to share their passions, their challenges, and their success. They mother, mentor, and challenge each other, and are nurtured and challenged in turn.

They join us in partnering with United Nations agencies and programs that benefit women, and especially the new combined entity UN Women. Sisterly relationships with related organizations have been and remain an important part of our

Leyma Gbowee featured in Pray the Devil Back to Hell. *Photo courtesy Michael Angelo for Wonderland*

strategy. Early and ongoing partnerships include Gather the Women, the Millionth Circle, Circles of Ten, the United Nations Development Fund for Women (UNIFEM), September 11th Families for Peaceful Tomorrows, Women's Edge (now Women Thrive), Women Waging Peace (now Inclusive Security), Ripples International, George Mason University's Institute on Conflict Mediation and Resolution (ICAR), the Institute for Peace and Justice at the University of San Diego, the U.S. Institute of Peace, and the Rumi Forum.

Building cultures of peace is a long-term project. Still, we see evidence that these cultures developed and gained strength in the first decade of the twenty-first century, and that their growth is gaining speed on three levels: interpersonal, local, and global.

We see the living room circles, online forums, and cross-cultural friendships our members enjoy as micro-cultures of peace. Since our inception in 2003 we have seen relationships weather strong differences of opinion, disappointments, delays, even serious breaches of trust, and endure.

Peace X Peace e-media lift these personal gains to the next level by documenting the exchanges and sharing them. We highlight circle stories, when all members agree to waive confidentiality. Our media publicize the stories of members and others around the world who are building peace on the ground—as artists, educators, environmental activists, and entrepreneurs, as well as experts in conflict resolution, reconciliation, and rebuilding.

Our members' own networks and our sister relationships with other organizations, like One World, WorldPulse, and Positive News U.S., carry these stories beyond our circles to the level of global motherhood. We are frequently amazed to see how far a story has gone and how many people it has touched.

We know that our work builds on the achievements of many peace-building foremothers, from Jane Addams (whose mother love was universal, though she never bore a child) to peace studies pioneer Elise Boulding, Leyma Gbowee in Liberia, and many others whose names we may never know. And we are confident that our work contributes to the cascading global movement for peace and women's empowerment. Every connection between grassroots women and other builders of peace, every new idea and practical example strengthens the web.

Future Aims, Future Vision: Global Motherhood

Peace X Peace will continue to evolve, taking advantage of each new development to grow and build critical mass. Staff and members are growing increasingly sophisticated in the use of new media, like Twitter, Facebook, and cloud computing, to further increase our range and our reach. Every new member, reader, and viewer takes us closer to the tipping point where peace becomes the new cultural norm.

In the years ahead we hope to collaborate even more closely, more widely, and more effectively. Peace-building is a win-win proposition. Gains by any member of the movement for peace and human rights will benefit the rest of the movement and humanity at large.

As mothers, grandmothers, sisters, aunts, best friends, neighbors, colleagues, executives, and increasingly, world leaders, women bring a sorely needed, motherly, "Different Voice" to the resolution of our many urgent challenges. Mounting environmental, economic, and epidemiological challenges make the need for energetic global cooperation ever more clear. In the Global Peace Index, now in its fourth year, the staff of *The Economist* demonstrate by the numbers that peace is both the seed and the fruit of prosperity.

We are eager to learn about other motherhood organizations and make common cause. Planetary survival requires a global, united, motherhood movement. At Peace X Peace, we are not essentialists who believe that women are inherently peaceful, any more than men are essentially warlike. We *do* believe that mothers through the ages have cooperated and exercised boundless creativity to protect their children and the planet's future. While we welcome and celebrate men of good will as partners, we know that women have indispensable contributions to make. The nurturers, preservers, and peaceful problem solvers have been on the sidelines too long. As futurist Jeremy Rifkin asserts in *The Empathic Civilization*, humanity's choice is empathy or entropy. Women—especially mothers—are wired for empathy.

And as CEO of Peace X Peace Kimberly Weiche says:

> *Everything that isn't peace is the antithesis of mothering. If mothers don't join together for peace, who else will?*

Works Cited

Allende, Isabel. *Paula.* New York: Harper Collins, 1995.

Gladwell, Malcolm. *The Tipping Point.* [New York: Little Brown, 2000.

Institute for Economics and Peace. *The Global Peace Index.* Sydney, Australia, 2010. Web: http://www.economicsandpeace.org/WhatWeDo/GPI.

Interfaith Heroes2. Canton, MI: Read the Spirit Books, 2009. Web: <http://www.readthespirit.com>. <http://www.readthespirit.com/interfaith_heroes/2nd-annual-interfaith-heroes-month-no-29-patricia-smith-melt.html>.

JustVision. *Budrus.* Documentary film directed by Julia Bacha, produced by Bacha, Rula Salameh, and Ronit Avni, distributed by JustVision, Washington, DC, 2009. Web: <http://www.justvision.org/budrus/about>.

Peace by Peace, Women on the Frontlines. Documentary film produced by Patricia Smith Melton, directed by Lisa Hepner, distributed by Peace X Peace, Vienna, VA, 2003. Web: <http://www.peacexpeace.org/media/our-media/video>.

Pray the Devil Back to Hell. Documentary film produced by Abigail Disney, distributed by Fork Films, New York, NY, 2008. Web: <http://www.praythedevilbacktohell.com>.

Rifkin, Jeremy. *The Empathic Civilization.* New York: Tarcher Penguin, 2010.

Satterthwaite, Judy and (Women's Interfaith Solutions for Dialogue and Outreach in Metro Detroit (WISDOM). *Friendship and Faith: The WISDOM of Women Creating Alliances for Peace.* Canton, MI: Read the Spirit Books, 2010.

Smith Melton, Patricia, Editor & Photographer. *Sixty Years, Sixty Voices: Israeli and Palestinian Women.* Washington, DC, Peace X Peace, 2008.

United Nations Resolution on the Culture of Peace. November 20, 1997 (published 1998). A/RES/52/13 (UN General Assembly Resolution): Culture of Peace. Web. <http://www3.unesco.org/iycp/kits/res52-13_en.htm>.

57. Cindy Sheehan

NATALIE WILSON

CINDY SHEEHAN, A PEACE ACTIVIST spurred into action via her son Casey's death in the early days of the Iraq war, helped to reinvigorate the anti-war movement in the United States in 2005. Her success was undoubtedly informed by her role as a mother, and, moreover, by her status as the mother of a dead soldier. While drawing on traditional concepts of motherhood and the trope of the grieving mother to further her cause, Sheehan's public protests and political actions expanded the notion of what a mother can and should be.

In August of 2005, Sheehan travelled to Crawford, Texas, and started a vigil outside George W. Bush's ranch, explaining that she wanted to talk to the president, so he could explain the "noble cause" for which her son was killed (Pershing). Some 15,000 people travelled to Crawford to support Sheehan. As scholar Linda Pershing, who travelled with and researched Sheehan's activism over the course of six years, argues Sheehan's activism "captured public attention because of its intensity and raw expression of anger and outrage" (Pershing). Since her 2005 vigil at Camp Crawford, Sheehan has led numerous political actions and marches, has served as a keynote speaker at universities and peace events across the country and around the world, and ran for Congress in 2007. What started as an interrogation of the Iraq war expanded into rallies against military recruitment and retention policies, work to expose atrocities at Guantanamo Bay and calls for the president's impeachment and for action about the continuing tragedy surrounding hurricane Katrina. As an activist and public figure, Sheehan has faced much scorn and numerous threats of violence. Her activism has led to at least seven arrests.

Philosophy, Purpose, Mission and History

As Pershing documents, "Sheehan based her earliest work for peace on her experiences as a grieving mother. She soon learned that this was the most distinctive, and most powerful, characteristic of her activism, one that provides her with a special vantage point in the public discourse about the war. Consequently, she has used this as a foundation for her writing, speeches, and political actions."

In particular, Sheehan drew on her status as a mother to appeal to others to become active. Noting her story exemplifies that "One mom has shown that we can be the change in our government," Sheehan emphasizes to (m)others that they too "can be the change" (2005: 20). In fact, Sheehan (2006) goes as far as to argue that those not doing anything are accessories to the crimes of war and encourages "everyone in America to move away from the comfortable complacency that allows BushCo to kill people with impunity" (para. 10).

However, Sheehan is also careful to emphasize that it is difficult to move beyond the apathy, acknowledging that, "What kept me from speaking out in the beginning was the sense that I couldn't make a difference" (Houppert, para. 35). She further notes that "I think the people in power want you to feel helpless, because if we all find our voice, our power, we really can make a lasting difference in this country" (Houppert, para. 36). Here, using an "Everymom" stance, Sheehan notes her previous sense of powerlessness as *induced,* as one that those in power purposefully manifest in order to keep the "herds" under control. As such, Sheehan seems dedicated to motivating the "Everymom" masses and does so through a purposeful use of "Everymom language." Specifically avoiding complex jargon or vituperative rhetoric, she speaks in the voice of "the mom next door," making very clear points such as "as long as moms are having to hold bake sales to buy their sons' body armor … military service should be opposed" and asking simple questions such as the one she has repeatedly posed to George W. Bush: "If it's such a noble cause, have you asked your daughters to enlist? Have you encouraged them to go take the place of soldiers who are on their third tour of duty?" (Sheehan 2005: 31, 98)

Refusing to hide her grief or pretend it will go away after the "allotted grieving time," Sheehan draws on her status as an "Everymom" as a justified platform from which to air her grievances, while simultaneously transgressing this "Everymom" role by being too sad, too angry, too political, too public. For Sheehan, a large part of her success is no doubt related to this "Everymom" status. As Karen Houppert argues in her article "Cindy Sheehan: Mother of a Movement?":

> …part of Sheehan's power as a voice of the peace movement comes from her very lack of power as a mother. Unlike Jane Fonda, who spoke out against the Vietnam War from her privileged perch in Hollywood, Sheehan emerged as a middle-aged, middle-class Everymom who was simply raising her voice in the time-honored exception to maternal decorum: a shout to defend her kid. In fact, the rich tradition of "Don't mess with my boy!" extends across time and place from the mundane schoolyard scrap to the 1915 Women's International League to the Mothers of the Plaza de Mayo, who demonstrated for their "disappeared" sons every Thursday for years in Buenos Aires, to the contemporary Union of Soldiers' Mothers in Russia, where hordes of women are protesting their sons' conscription. (para. 22)

Like these other mother activists, Sheehan protests in her son's name, directing her condemnations of the war very specifically at George W. Bush and often roundly accusing him of murdering her son. This personalization differs from the often more generalized anti-war, peace building movements in that it takes aim at particular people in power rather than at governments in general. This too is a transgression of the "Everymom" stance, one that allies with the feminist mantra "the personal is political" in intriguing ways. In statements such as, "I often get introduced as a mother who lost her son in Iraq. I didn't lose Casey. I know right where he is. He is in a grave in Vacaville, and I know who put him there: George Bush" (Sheehan 2005: 52), Sheehan puts her personal loss in a politicized context. Refusing the often used verb "loss" in relation to her son's death, she does not allow for the erasure of the profound personal anguish caused by war and imperialism that the word "lost" enacts. Rather, she turns the passive construction surrounding "lost" into active verbs such as murder, lie, and steal.

Her plea that Bush talk with her and answer a few questions is predicated on this methodology of personalization—one that has encouraged thousands of others that opposing the war needs to be a *personal* issue undertaken by all who do not support it and that not opposing war will lead to *personal* cost. While those in power attempt to depersonalize the war with statistics and euphemistic jargon such as "collateral damage," Sheehan (2006b) repeatedly emphasizes the personal dynamics of war, emphasizing that death tolls do not account for the fact that "for those of us who have lost a son or a daughter or a brother or a sister or a father or a mother in this war, the number one is more than enough" (para. 10). Sheehan continuously personalizes grief in this way, and, more specifically, tries to make public (and political) the palpable pain and suffering war brings. For example, when she asks "How many more mothers are we going to watch sobbing over their children's flag-draped coffins before we get out in the streets and demand an end to the immoral and illegal occupation so no other mothers will have to be plunged into a pool of pain?" she publicizes the coffins the government tries to keep hidden, she politicizes the pain caused by war, and she specifically calls for action—to "get out in the streets" to demand an end to war (2006b: 21).

In addition to using an "Everymom" platform and personalizing the costs of war, Sheehan's activism also consistently draws on the physicality of mothering and on the inherently *embodied* nature of our human condition. As Adrienne Rich explores in *Of Woman Born*, the body often becomes a trap for women, and especially mothers, as they are forcibly tied to the body side of the mind/body duality. Not only do woman occupy the disparaged side of this duality *as women*, they also are quite literally tied to the body in mothering—not only to their own bodies through pregnancy, birth, and breastfeeding, but also to the body-care of their children. Thus, as Rich notes, "The body has been made so problematic for women that it has often seemed easier to shrug it off and travel as a disembodied spirit" (40). Hence, women have been encouraged to "forget" their bodies, to deny the bodily realities of pregnancy and birth, to "hide" the embodied practices of breastfeeding, to deny the profound ways in which they, and their children, are shaped by their facticity as embodied beings. However, many activist mothers staunchly refuse the call for bodily forgetting.

Like Rich, who refers to her "determination to heal—insofar as an individual woman can, and as much as possible with other women—the separation between mind and body," activists such as Sheehan specifically highlight the embodied nature of existence (40). Moreover, by carrying out what I term "embodied activism," Sheehan delivers a form of feminist activism that utilizes embodiment to further particular political causes. In Sheehan's case, the body is deployed as a visible reminder of injustice, grief, and injury both via the living, present bodies of protestors at Camp Casey, Crawford Peace House, in front of the White House, etc., and via the pictorial/oral reminders of those bodies that have been killed/injured in Iraq, Afghanistan, Guantanamo, etc.

Sheehan uses her corporeal form as a sort of screen from which to deliver pictures of her son Casey, of statistics of war atrocities, or to manifest the exhaustion brought about from protesting outside Bush's Crawford ranch in 100 degree plus weather. Mothering activists have a well-established tradition of corporeally based political engagement, or, to use a sporting phrase co-opted by Sheehan (2005), of "putting their skin in the game" (115). One of the most well established traditions of activist mothering, protesting war and grieving the loss of children as a result of war in profoundly politicized ways, markedly draws on embodied activism. In a sense, such protests have been condoned via the notion that is only natural for mothers to grieve children who have been killed in battle, wounded in service, or "disappeared" by militarized government practices in very "bodily ways" such as crying, wailing, fasting, etc. This acceptable grief fits into motherhood as an institution in which the selfless mother is to efface herself (and her body) in order to live her life through and for her children. Thus, when a child is killed or injured, the mother loses in a way her own "purpose" and well-being and by enacting grief in "acceptable ways"such as refusing food and sleep, mothers indicate that their bodies *do not matter* as much as those of their children. In fact, mothers (like widows) are often roundly chastised for not grieving enough—they are not supposed to be able to get on with their daily lives, but to succumb to tears and black veils. Thus, when "acceptable grief" moves into a more public, politicized enactment of grief and when bodily denial turns into embodied protest, the story changes profoundly.

Akin to the hunger strikes of the Suffragettes or the cross-country female activist walkers known as "Peace Pilgrim" and "Granny D," the activism of Sheehan emphasizes physicality. Sheehan, for example, often places large pictures of her son Casey around her neck which tend to hang (deliberately?) at womb height, as if to emphasize that the son she housed in her womb, gave birth to, raised, and cared for, now forms a wound on her own body—a wound of grief that will not go away.[1] Like the Mothers of the Plaza de Mayo, who carry placards with large faces of their missing children as they protest, Sheehan insists the face (and body) of her son not be forgotten by offering a pictorial replacement of his now dead body. Likewise, at Camp Casey, crosses are put in the ground as visual, material reminders of those killed. Unlike the practice of bringing dead and wounded soldiers back to the U.S. under the cover of darkness, the practice of placing tangible reminders of those killed insists viewers "see" the number of dead in the fields outside where Bush vacations. Moreover, the choice to *camp* outside Bush's ranch is in itself an embodied form of activism. While there, Sheehan and her supporters serve as embodied reminders of the lack of public support for this war, as material proof of the growing numbers of people who are calling for an end to the escalation of the military industrial complex. These activist bodies, laboring under the 100 degree plus weather of August in Texas, cannot be erased by one of Bush's smirks or smarmy platitudes—they are there, in all their materiality, sweat, sun block, and thirst, squinting into the blazing sun, reminding the world not only of the bodily cost of war, but of the bodily ways we can *protest* war and other social injustices.

In the summer of 2006, Sheehan participated in the "Troops Home FAST" hunger strike that launched on July 4. Offering a rationale for the fast, Sheehan recounts, "While others are celebrating July 4th with barbeques, we'll be showing our patriotism by putting our bodies on the line to bring troops home" ("Troops Home Fast," para. 2). Her choice of words here brings to mind the 'front lines' that put soldiers bodies at extreme risk of death and injury—the very lines that the media and the government puts under erasure by acting as if war is a 'strategy' far removed from the actual bodies that must fight and die. In addition to drawing attention to the bodily costs of war, Sheehan also continually emphasizes the ways war has damaged her own body by regularly emphasizing the ways in which her son's death manifests itself physically on her body. As she relates, she has been forced to learn "to live with a pain that is so intense that sometimes I feel like throwing up, or screaming until I pass out from sorrow" (2005: 96). Here, refusing acceptable displays of grief such as wearing black or daintily dotting away tears with a handkerchief, Sheehan emphasizes the very physical manifestations of grief—the palpable sickness, anger, and pain. Sheehan's hospitalization due to internal bleeding in late August 2006 also makes it patently clear that her activism has physical consequences. Not only is she "putting her own skin in the game" though; she emphasizes the way *all bodies* are harmed by the militaristic mentality that currently reigns supreme, that, as Sheehan writes, "chews up … flesh and blood to spit out obscene profits" (2006a: para. 14)

Importance to Wider Motherhood Movement

Camp Casey placed Sheehan, as Thom Hartmann argues in "Cindy: An Historic Perspective," in "the great tradition of the mothers of Chile and Argentina, the women who have protested against war from the times of ancient Greece through every one of America's wars, and of Julia Ward Howe" (xv). Sheehan builds on the collective activism tradition in keeping with the activist mothering groups of Chile and Argentina by attempting to forge dedicated groups of activists via the founding of Camp Casey as well as the Crawford Peace House. Simultaneously, she also enacts 'individual activism' like that of Julia Ward Howe via her willingness to serve as an iconic figurehead for the current peace movement.

Drawing on the general respect mothers are granted in society (even if this respect is mainly symbolic and does not afford real power), maternal activists such as Sheehan have long utilized acceptable mothering practices, such as a bear-like tendency to protect their children and to be devastated at their loss, to protest war, poverty, child labor, and myriad other social injustices. Sometimes this activism has (necessarily) been delivered via a maternalist framework that entrenches "motherhood" as a necessary component of womanhood on the one hand, and defines motherhood in very specific ways on the other. For example, as noted by Meghan Gibbons, the group Another Mother For Peace framed their protest within traditional notions of motherhood and protested the Vietnam War using images associated with mothers and peace, that of flowers, children, and doves. As Gibbons further notes, both the Madres de la Plaza de Mayo and Another Mother For Peace insisted on their apolitical aims and tried to frame their arguments within traditional and culturally specific tropes of motherhood and maternalism. In contrast, contemporary mothering activists are able to more radically depart from traditional ideas of motherhood, though not without coming under fire by the media and political pundits (as is discussed in more detail in the "Challenges" section below).

As Pershing notes, Sara Ruddick's theory of maternal peacemaking "provides a useful framework for understanding Sheehan's activism." As Ruddick work reveals, "mothering" can be likened to peacemaking and contrasted to militarism:

> Mothering begins in birth and promises life; military thinking justifies organized, deliberate deaths. A mother preserves the bodies, nurtures the psychic growth, and disciplines the conscience of children; although the military trains its soldiers to survive the situations it puts them in, it also deliberately endangers their bodies, minds, and consciences in the name of victory and abstract causes. Mothers protect children who are at risk; the military risks the children mothers protect. (Ruddick 148)

In addition to her importance to the wider motherhood movement, particularly in relation to maternal peacemaking, Sheehan's conception of matriotism implicitly emphasizes the need to *personalize the political*—an aim of feminism and the wider maternal activism movement generally. Referring to matriotism as a "new paradigm for true and lasting peace in the world," Sheehan (2006a) argues that "A true Matriot would never drop an atomic bomb or bombs filled with white phosphorous, carpet-bomb cities and villages, or control drones from thousands of miles away to kill innocent men, women, and children" (para. 8) Thus, matriotism emphasizes individual embodiment and interhumanity rather than the depersonalized allegiance to a nation-state that patriotism calls for. This call for matriotism places Sheehan in a long line of maternal activists who have worked to reveal, in various ways, how women have been codified as "eccentric subjects" that have "had a problematic relationship to the modern nation-state and its construction of subjectivity" (Alarcon et. al. 1). Sheehan's use of the word matriotism gestures towards this "problematic relationship," emphasizing the ways that subjectivity has been constructed along "pater" or male lines. Calling attention to the fact that women are linguistically and otherwise left out via words such as "patriotism" and concepts such as "nation," Sheehan insists, as many have before her, that we must consider the gendered implications of defining citizens, nations, and patriotism as if gender didn't matter. By foregrounding gender in her reclamation of patriotism into matriotism, Sheehan emphasizes we are not homogenous citizens, but humans shaped by gender, race, class, geopolitical location and many other axis of identity. More specifically, in her meditation on the implications of the word matriotism, Sheehan calls upon the mothers of the world to "never send her child or another mother's child to fight nonsense wars," and, in so doing, she turns the "power over" ideology of patriotism into a "solidarity with" paradigm for peace (para. 9). In so doing, Sheehan not only stresses the need to be active *at the level of language*, she also reveals a profound understanding that in order to change the world, we must change not only the words we use but also the ideologies they represent and perpetuate.

Challenges

Affiliated with other groups such as Veterans for Peace, United for Peace and Justice, CODEPINK, Military Families Speak Out, the Crawford Peace House, Sheehan's Gold Star Families for Peace (GSFP) is interestingly *not* affiliated with the American Gold Star Mothers organization. In fact, American Gold Star Mothers (AGSM), which was formed shortly after WWI, pointedly distances themselves from Sheehan. As their website reads, "Cindy Sheehan is currently in the news. She and her organization have no connection whatever with American Gold Star Mothers, Inc. We are a 501 C(3) organization and, as such, do not engage in political activities. We do support our troops. After all, they are our children." Here, not only does AGSM emphasize they are not affiliated nor do they approve of Sheehan's activities, they also deploy language that indicates Sheehan is not supporting the troops—the very insult that the mainstream press and many politicians lob at her despite the fact that Sheehan continually notes that wanting to bring the troops home and put an end to unjust war is the strongest form of support one can give. Thus, the AGSM is an organization tied to "nation building," not to protest. As Gibbons notes, AGSM "is an example of attempts by U.S. administrations to win mothers' allegiance away from the nuclear families and into the camp of the nation family." This agenda seems perfectly in keeping with the group's motto: "Perpetuating the Nobel Principles for which they fought and died"—a motto which upholds the nations state as "nobel" and refuses to question its "principles." Moreover, unlike GFSP which emphasizes the importance of family loss and grief and aims to support individual families, AGSM emphasizes duty to *nation* and supports national decisions in a way akin to a dutiful, fearful child that is reticent to question the tactics of the overbearing, dicataroral father/nation. Thus, while AGSM's deference to the nation mimics the traditional nuclear family concept wherein the family is run according to a strict heirarchy that is "ruled over" by the "head of the family," GFSP functions as a progressive family where power/roles are distributed and where questionning/protest of family/nation "rules" are not only allowed but encouraged.

The dutiful non-questionning stance adopted by AGSM colludes with their staunch criticsim of GFSP's use of the Gold Star. Acting like the "dutiful daughter/son," AGSM, along with three other groups, called for an end to what they termed the "the misuse of one of the nation's most sacred symbols—the Gold Star—to politicize efforts for ending the war in Iraq." Noting that "The American Gold Star Mothers, Inc., Gold Star Wives of America, Inc., Sons and Daughters In Touch and American WWII Orphans Network oppose the use of and reference to the 'Gold Star' in the political demonstrations being carried out in Texas and other parts of the United States," the press release went on to claim "Our loved ones gave their lives to protect the freedom to protest, and we know all too well the pain that these families are now suffering. However, the Gold Star symbol—authorized by Congress to honor a family's loss in service to our nation—must not be tarnished by partisan political demonstrations." Here, in terms that stronlgy emphasize deference to the "nation," these groups indicate that so-called "partisan political demonstrations" are akin to betraying family "service to the nation." Thus, the family is construed as part and parcel of the nation-state, as a unit that forms and owes deference to the nation first and foremost. This stance allies intriguingly to McClintock's thesis in the article "Family Feuds: Gender, Nationalism, and the Family," in which she argues that nations function as psuedo families that "punish" wayward relatives. As McClintock notes, "Nations are frequently figured through the iconography of familial and domestic space" (63). In framing Sheehan's "politics" as family betrayal, the AGSM and their affiliates position her as the naughty child who is misguidedly using the Gold Star for what they see as 'wrong' purposes. However, Sheehan uses this same tactic in order to emphasize the way the 'nation family' has betrayed her and the many other family members who it has lied to and injured. By emphasizing her role as the mother of a son killed in unjust battle, Sheehan delivers an argument that is akin to that of a daughter betrayed by an uncaring father/nation. In fact, as I will elucidate later, Sheehan draws on this sort of "father betrayal" to denounce patriotism and call instead for matriotism. Moreover, Sheehan continually frames her protest not only as that of an individual mother, but via the guise of a family protest. By including fathers, sisters, children, siblings, etc in her protest against unjust war, she emphasizes the way in which the policies of the U.S. nation hurt *all* U.S. families. And, more and more, her message has morphed into one that draws on the "global family" as she expands her activism beyond national borders and dedicates herself to needed change not only in relation to the U.S. and U.S. policy, but also in relation to other areas of injustice around the globe in Afghanistan, South Korea, Guantanamo Bay, etc. Thus, while she is the individual celebrity/matriarch activist, she nevertheless actively aligns herself and is supported by various groups, or families, if you well.

However, her involvement with a much larger peace-activsist "family" and her membership in a long-standing tradition of peace-activist mothers, has resulted in Sheehan's evolving "from the darling of the press (in the early days, when she was portrayed, Rosa Parks-style, as a grief-stricken mom who simply materialized on Bush's doorstep) to a less trustworthy spokesperson of the left's antiwar message (once her connections to a more radical peace agenda were exposed)" (Houppert, para. 25). In addition to being criticized for being "too political," the change in perception of Sheehan from a sympathetic, grieving mom to crazy, radical leftie has also come about due to her transgressing the "normal" time limits of grief and the "normal" privatized role of mother. Mothers, like widows, are supposed to grieve for a certain amount of time, then they *should* get on with their lives, which usually means attending to the children or spouse they still have living. Moreover, they are supposed to grieve and act in a privatized fashion, not on the world's stage. Expectations such as these were made patently clear regarding Sheehan through the increasingly loud outcry that she should "Go Home and Take Care of Her Kids." Cindy Sheehan (2005) has responded to this offensive message by noting that her activism is a profoundly important form of mothering, that "what I am doing is for my children, and the world's children," that "I *am* taking care of my kids, and yours, too" (118). Yet, Sheehan refused the individualized script of motherhood and insists on a more expansive concept of mothering that involves caring for the world and all its children, expanding, in effect, the idea of mothering into a global, activist one. Moreover, her comments emphasize that although she is framed as "one woman against the world" by the mass media, that she represents many women and mothers who care not only for their own children, but also for the entire world and its inhabitants. Sheehan (2005) further notes the directive to "Go Home and Take Care of Your Kids" offends her "because it is so blatantly sexist. Would anyone think of emailing George Bush when he is out and about … telling him to go and take care of his kids? Does anyone write to *any* man and tell him to go home and take care of his kids?" (118). Here, Sheehan emphasizes unequal gendered expectations—moms are supposed to "care for kids," dads are free to run the corporation, the country, or the world. Referring to "the load of misogynistic crap" that children need their mothers "constant presence in their lives so they can thrive and grow," Sheehan (2005) reveals an incisive awareness of the damaging dictates of motherhood as institution (119). This criticism of the ways in which human expectations are profoundly gendered links well with McClintock's assessment of nations as gendered:

> Women are represented as the atavistic and authentic "body" of national tradition (inert, backward-looking, and natural), embodying nationalism's conservative principle of continuity. Men, by contrast, represent

> the progressive agent of national modernity (forward-thrusting, potent and historic), embodying nationalism's progressive, or revolutionary principle of discontinuity. (66)

As McClintock argues, nations and concepts of nationalism are configured in a very gendered way. In relation to Sheehan's activist mothering, she is moving beyond being the traditional "inert" female national body into the area of (male) potency and thrust. As McClintock notes, women are "Excluded from direct action as national citizens" and thus "subsumed symbolically into the national body politics as its boundary and metaphoric limit." (62). Thus women are not meant to be *active* citizens but symbolic ones—they are supposed to symbolize patriotism through the birthing of future citizens, through revering national law, and through acquiescing to the mandates of the nation state. As symbols of nationalism, they are to function like "Lady Liberty" or "Lady Justice"—as beautiful, inert icons representing the nation's ideals. This symbolic nationalism would also seem to be enacted when, during wartime, women are so often framed not as active soldiers, policy-makers, or global ambassadors, but as weeping widows, tearful girlfriends, and bereft daughters endlessly standing by disembarking ships or mourning graveside. Given that Sheehan has refused to play the role of symbolic nationalism, it is no surprise she became a punching bag of the press as well as of political pundits. For example, as Houppert notes, "Sheehan has been lambasted for a host of infractions, ranging from charges that she has politicized her grief to rebukes for naïvely weighing in on foreign policy decisions best left in the hands of the big boys in Washington" (para. 16). Much of the criticism, as Houppert notes, is predictable: "She speaks as a mother, and her mothering comes under fire. There are the scoldings she get—typically from other women—for protesting the war instead of staying home to cook her family dinner. A tiresome charge dredged up for decades against any woman who takes to the streets for a political cause" (para. 17). Or as Sheehan puts it (2005), "the right-wing media … assiduously scrutinize the words of a grief-filled mother and ignore the words of a lying president" (74). As Pershing documents, Sheehan "has paid a hefty price for her efforts: a divorce from her husband of 28 years, rejection by friends and family members, serious illness, and character assassination by journalists, public officials, and pundits."

Conclusion

Sheehan continues her activism to this day and has broadened her anti-war scope to also focus on the environment, socio-economic inequality nationally and globally, and the plight of the Palestinian people. Bush's departure from the White House has not lessened her focus on U.S. militarism, though. In 2009, she protested at Martha's Vineyard during Barack Obama's stay. That same year, she was arrested again at a White House protest action against President Obama's continuation of wars in Iraq and Afghanistan. In 2010, Sheehan began working with the Socialist Party in hopes of forging support for a united socialist campaign for the United States presidency in 2012. She has published three books in the last few years, *Peace Mom*, *Myth America,* and *Revolution: A Love Story. Myth America II* is purportedly in the works. She also blogs, hosts podcasts and radio shows from "Cindy's Sheehan's Soap Box," a political site not sponsored by corporate dollars or owned by a radio station. As the site page describes, "Being on the air is a chance to break through with an alternative, progressive viewpoint going out to many, many listeners; people that can be affected and inspired to create change." Here's hoping this inspiring, peace activist mother stays on her soap box for years to come.

[1]See Sheehan, 2006, p. 92 for photo.

Works Cited

Ahmed, A. "Counteroffensive: Bush Launches 'Operation Cindy Sheehan.'" *Palestine Chronicle* 28 August 2005. Web. <www.palestinechronicle.com>. Accessed August 15, 2006.

Alarcon, N., C. Kaplan. and M. Moallem, eds. *Between Woman and Nation: Nationalism, Transnational Feminisms, and The State.* Durham: Duke University Press, 1999.

American Gold Star Mothers (AGSM). "National Military Family Organizations Say: Stop Using 'Gold Star' Immediately." 23 August 2005. Web. <http://www.goldstarmoms.com/>. Accessed January 28, 2007.

Frazer, E. "Feminist Political Theory." *Contemporary Feminist Theories.* Eds. S. Jackson and J. Jones. New York: New York University Press, 1998. 50-61.

Gibbons, M. "Political Motherhood in the U.S. and Argentina." *Mothers Who Deliver.* Ed. Jocelyn Fenton Stitt and Pegreen Reichart Powerll. New York: State University of New York Press, 2007. 253-277.

Hartmann, T. "Cindy: An Historic Perspective." *Not One More Mother's Child.* C. Sheehan. Kihei, Hawaii: Koa Books, 2005. xiii-xvi.

Houppert, K. "Cindy Sheehan: Mother of a Movement?" *The Nation.* Web. <http://www.thenation.com>. Accessed August 9, 2006.

McClintock, A. "Family Feuds: Gender, Nationalism and the Family." *Feminist Review* (44) (1993): 61-80.

McReynolds, J. "Walking the Walk, Talking the Talk." *Lompoc Record* 9 May 2006. Web. <http://www.lompocrecord>. Accessed August 9, 2006.

O'Reilly, A. ed. *Mother Outlaws: Theories and Practices of Empowered Mothering.* Toronto: Women's Press, 2004.

O'Reilly, A. *Rocking the Cradle: Thoughts on Feminism, Motherhood, and the Possibility of Empowered Mothering.* Toronto: Demeter Press, 2006.

Pershing, Linda. "Cindy Sheehan: A Call to Maternal Activism in the Contemporary Peace Movement." *Maternal Thinking: Philosophy, Politics, Practice.* Ed.

Andrea O'Reilly. Toronto: Demeter Press, 2009. 144-59.

Rich, A. *Of Woman Born: Motherhood as Experience and Institution.* New York: W.W. Norton, 1976.

Rowe-Finkbeiner, K. *The F word: Feminism in Jeopardy.* Emeryville, CA: Seal Press, 2004.

Ruddick, S. "Making Connections Between Parenting and Peace." *Journal of the Association for Research on Mothering* 3.2 (2001): 7-20.

Sheehan, C. *Not One More Mother's Child.* Kihei, Hawaii: Koa Books, 2005.

Sheehan, C. "Matriotism." *Truth Out.* 22 January 2006a. Web. <http://www.truthout.org>. Accessed August 20, 2006.

Sheehan, C. "2,5000 Dead: How Many More?" *The Progressive* 14 June 2006b. Web. <http://www.truthout.org>. Accessed July 29, 2006.

Sheehan, C. "Starving for Attention: Troops Home Fast, Day One." *Common Dreams News Center* 5 July 2006c. Web. <http://www.commondreams.org>. Accessed July 29, 2006.

Stolnit, Rebecca. "The Housewife Theory of History." *Alternet* 9 June 2005. Web. <http://www.alternet.org>. Accessed January 29, 2007.

"Troops Home Fast. Cindy Sheehan, Dick Gregory, Diane Wilson and hundreds more launch the 'Troops Home FAST.'" *YubaNet* 3 July 2006. Web. <http://www.yubanet.com>. Accessed July 29, 2006.

VI.
Social Change and Social Justice

59. Mothers Against Drunk Driving

How Two Mothers' Personal Pain Birthed a Social Movement

LAURA DREUTH ZEMAN

SIX CARBONDALE TEENS INJURED IN WRECK

"CARBONDALE—*Police aren't releasing the names of six Carbondale high school students injured late Monday morning in a single-vehicle wreck south of Carbondale.*

Jackson County sheriff's deputies and several other agencies responded to the crash on Chautauqua Road, near Rowden Road, about 11:45 a.m. Monday.

The 16-year-old driver and his five passengers, all 15-year-olds, were taken to Memorial Hospital of Carbondale with injuries ranging from minor to critical.

Deputies said the six boys were eastbound on Chautauqua Road, traveling at a high rate of speed. The 1998 Chevrolet Venture minivan apparently went out of control on a hillcrest and slid more than 600 feet before crashing into a tree and overturning. The van then skidded on its roof, striking a second tree.

Deputies found the minivan overturned against the tree, with three teens still trapped inside. All six boys were reported to have been wearing their seatbelts.

Emergency personnel spent close to an hour extricating the three boys. Chautauqua Road was closed nearly one-and-a-half hours Monday while crews cleared the scene.

The driver, a 16-year-old, was ticketed for reckless driving and failure to reduce speed to avoid an accident. More charges are pending the outcome of the accident reconstructionist report.

Alcohol isn't considered a factor in this crash.

Deputies were assisted by the Jackson County Ambulance Service, Southern Illinois University Carbondale police and the Carbondale Township Fire Department" (Bean).

My MADD Experience

My beautiful, athletic, academically gifted, and loving child was one of the trapped, critically injured, 15-year-old passengers who hung upside down in the back of that minivan. The 16-year-old driver was allegedly "hill hopping," an act that involves speeding up inclines so that the automobile becomes airborne at the hillcrest. The driver's blood test indicated that he was under the influence of alcohol at the time of the accident, yet below the legal adult blood alcohol content limit. For days, I sat bedside him, from emergency room to intensive care, speaking to and holding my beloved son as if we were sharing our last words, in our final moments. Months of recovery followed where we learned about the complications associated with closed head injuries like memory loss, rage, and mood shifts. My son struggled with self-medicating drug use and school failure while battling depression, physical pain, and cognitive impairments. He stopped attending school regularly, quit the wrestling team, and then signed himself out of high school. By age sixteen, he was a drug using, physically and cognitively impaired, angry, high school dropout.

No mother plans or prepares for her child to be injured or killed in a reckless driving incident involving alcohol. I was no exception. My shock was intense. I felt as if I was suspended in a state of disbelief. I could not make peace with my new reality of mothering a critically injured child who was hanging on to life. I struggled to accept the fact that my child went to school that morning healthy and alert and by lunchtime was critically injured. He naively thought he was joining a group of friends who left campus to get submarine sandwiches for lunch. For days, he babbled about being hungry because he never got his meatball sandwich. I felt helpless, shifting from shock, to guilt, to anger, and to sadness. My thoughts raced. I did not know he left school. I thought he would be okay. I never dreamed that he could be involved in an automobile accident involving alcohol before he even got his driver's permit. I was convinced I was responsible. I could not imagine my life without my beloved son. I felt isolated. At the time, I did not realize that I was not alone and that my experience was not unique. I leaned on another parent who went through a similar experience. I also sought support through the Internet.

Introduction

I discovered the organization called Mothers Against Drunk Driving (MADD) through searching the Internet for information and support. It is a resource for information from legal issues and head injuries to loss and grieving, as well as an advocacy and educational group. MADD was formed in 1980 by two mothers, Cindi Lamb and Candy Lightner, whose children were involved in auto accidents involving drivers under the influence of alcohol (Toomey). MADD's mission is threefold: to support victims of alcohol-related automobile accidents, to prevent underage drinking, and to end driving under the influence of alcohol. It seeks to meet these goals through providing victim services, educational programs, public safety campaigns, and organized legislative activities.

This grassroots social movement draws from personal pain to create social change through community building. MADD grew out of the experiences of two women in California, to a multinational organization which reportedly has chapters across the U.S., Canada, England, New Zealand, Australia, Guam, Puerto Rico, and Sweden. MADD is not without challenges and controversies. Opponents claim it outgrew its mission because public awareness has increased about the hazards of driving under the influence and because this public awareness has been coupled with a reduction in fatalities associated with alcohol (Center for Consumer Freedom). Organizational challenges for MADD include attracting and engaging victims of automobile accidents involving alcohol in order to sustain or grow its organizational missions (Weed). This chapter will examine MADD's organizational activities, challenges, social movement characteristics, and its contributions to the broader mothering movement.

Organizational Activities

MADD provides victim assistance, public awareness and educational programs, public safety campaigns, and legal advocacy through localized legislative initiatives designed to create and enforce laws that address drinking and driving. These efforts intend to address a broad spectrum of alcohol and driving-related problems from prevention to victim support following automobile accidents involving alcohol.

Victim Assistance

MADD provides a resource for parents who are experiencing feelings of shock, guilt, and loss following their children's involvement in alcohol-related automobile accidents. These services assist parents using models of care similar to those effective with individuals experiencing secondary trauma, a condition that occurs when a loved one experiences a life-threatening illness or is injured (American Trauma Society). Symptoms of secondary Post Traumatic Stress Disorder may include intense responses to the event such as shock, panic, anger, fear, and grief. Family impact can include physical and mental health problems including suicide, marital separation or divorce, job loss, and financial problems related to health care and court costs (Mercer and Evans). Researchers have found that family members have improved coping and interactions with hospital and recovery staff as well as with victims when they receive support and understand that their responses are normal (American Trauma Society).

MADD offers a multifaceted approach to assisting families through recovery from secondary trauma. The range of direct services varies based on local needs and resources and may vary from volunteers providing telephone support to informal support groups. One chapter in Windsor, Ontario, Canada, offered open support groups for grieving family members. These group therapy sessions allowed participants to explore their feelings, to give and receive support, and to increase their awareness of the trauma of their current experiences (Kroeker, Taub and Schnarr Wilhelm). Some researchers found that participants in MADD-sponsored outreach groups reported that the intervention helped them make sense of their grief experience (Mercer and Evans) and subsequently that they experienced a reduction in their secondary trauma symptoms (Kroeker, Taub and Schnarr Wilhelm).

Secondary trauma recovery is not the only aspect of support offered through

MADD. MADD's victim service and outreach includes resources, guides, and training. Many MADD chapters in the U.S. and Canada maintain websites with information and serve as links to local resources for victims and families. MADD publishes guides to understanding the criminal justice system. These resources provide information on victim rights, current laws, and information on how cases move through the system. Unfortunately, many victims die following these accidents. MADD offers volunteer training and training in compassionate care for police and health care workers, who are typically the first to interact with surviving family members; this service is called Death Notification Training. MADD also supports research and maintains archives of published statistics related to driving under the influence of alcohol fatalities, and underage drinking (Solomon, Organ and Abdoullaeva).

Public Awareness and Education

MADD sponsors public awareness campaigns and educational programs to educate about driving under the influence of alcohol and early drinking. Victim awareness is a hallmark feature of MADD educational programming. These units involve participants interacting with family members and victims who survived automobile accidents involving alcohol. The intent is to tie the act of driving under the influence with intense emotional pain experienced by survivors. Theoretically, the association of emotional victim impact with the act of driving under the influence of alcohol creates empathy toward the victims. Furthermore, the model assumes that the experience of empathy with victims serves as a deterrent to both early drinking and driving under the influence of alcohol (Theriot). MADD's youth programming also seeks to use victim awareness to deter youth from becoming passengers of drivers who are under the influence of alcohol (Bohman, Barker and Bell). For example, MADD in Hawaii uses the slogan, "tie one on for safety" on its public awareness materials.

MADD advocates abstinence from alcohol for youth as the desirable behavioral outcome. By targeting youth, it seeks to prevent alcohol-related problems before they begin. These programs have potential benefits for both the youth and the victim or family volunteers. Findings from studies that evaluated the effectiveness of these programs indicated that they tend to be most effective as deterrents for youth without prior histories of substance use or criminal charges for substance-related behavior (Bohman et al.; Theriot). Yet, these studies only examined the impact on the youth. They did not include an analysis of the impact of participating on victim panels for the volunteers. It is possible that there may be a victim benefit derived from sharing their story and believing that act of going public can prevent other families from experiencing the same pain.

Legal Advocacy

MADD's legislative initiatives have varied across nations and localities because, for the most part, localities decide these policies. A local tragedy that gains notoriety often initiates grassroots action and MADD mobilizes by using the victims' appeals to move their legislative agenda. Though varied, local chapters tend to organize around actions related to legal blood alcohol levels (Canadian Medical Association), drinking age, and general legislative efforts to reduce driving under the influence of alcohol (DeJong and Hingson). The success of these initiatives varies across local chapters and over time.

Perhaps the most successful legislative actions came in the beginning of the organization. The first-person accounts of MADD co-founders Candy Lightner and Cindi Lamb skyrocketed public awareness using victim stories. These mothers' stories were motivating factors that lead to public pressure for U.S. federal action. Under pressure by MADD, the U.S Congress later passed legislation connecting state highway funding to tighter laws regarding driving under the influence. Another significant change in U.S. policy during the early years of MADD activism included the 1984 Federal Uniform Drinking Age Act, which set the legal drinking age at 21 nationwide (Main).

Lobbying activities in Canada resulted in strengthening laws regarding driving under the influence of intoxicating substances. The Criminal Code of Canada set legal blood alcohol limits at 0.08, therefore making it illegal to drive if there was more than 8 milligrams of alcohol in 100 milliliters of blood. Blood alcohol limits are also 0.08 in the U.S., United Kingdom and New Zealand (MADD). Canadian MADD lobbied for tougher penalties for driving under the influence. This resulted in mandatory alcohol rehabilitation for repeat offenders and laws that allowed police officers to suspend the licenses of individuals caught driving under the influence of alcohol (Canadian Law). Worldwide MADD chapters continue to lobby for tougher legislation. Currently they have joined with other organizations like the Canadian Medical Association to lower the legal blood-alcohol level to levels currently adopted in Australia, 0.05, and to establish a zero tolerance policy for underage drinkers who drive (Canadian Medical Association).

The Reduced Impaired Driving Everywhere (RIDE) program is another notable indication of the success of this movement. MADD chapters across Canada lobbied for the implementation of this program, which involves systematically conducting roadside checks during periods when incidences of driving under the influence increased historically, such as New Years Eve. The MADD Chapter that encompasses the Toronto and Niagara areas of Canada reported that in December 2002 police officers conducted roadside checks of over 4,000 vehicles, which resulted in 28 arrests for impaired driving (MADD Canada). In 2009, MADD Canada sponsored #TAXI, a program where individuals can dial #TAXI on their cell phones and connect with a local cab company to assure that they have access to a ride home if they are intoxicated (MADD Canada).

Lobbing activities associated with MADD chapters evolve as proposals regarding alcohol consumption and driving emerge in legislative bodies around the world. Because the issues are diverse, MADD chapters require a growing body of knowledge and legislative strategies that can be flexible to meet the challenges as they arise. MADD maintains information links and public information resources on their websites to support local lobbying efforts.

Overall, MADD contributed to radically changing the public perceptions and behaviors related to driving under the influence. Perhaps driving under the influence was a cultural norm as recently as the 1970s, the decade preceding the inception of MADD. Take for instance the representation of driving under the influence in *Saturday Night Fever* (1977), the movie that combined disco dancing and aggressive male coming of age to became a cultural phenomenon. Drinking and driving provided a backdrop to several significant scenes. In the first driving scene, the protagonist, Tony, entered the car and asked his peers to tell him which drugs and alcohol they brought. He was told, "we have ups, downs, three ludes, two jays and half a bottle of vodka" (*Saturday Night Fever*). In the final scene that involved drinking and driving, arguably the movie climax, the group engaged in aggressive sexual acts, drove to the Verrazano-Narrows Bridge that connects the New York City boroughs of Staten Island and Brooklyn, engaged in reckless horseplay, until the driver fell to his death into the New York Harbor. Yet, the drinking was not represented in public discourse about the film, rather this was primarily represented as a film that integrated a coming of age story with music (Kupfer). The fact that audiences are unlikely to see drinking and driving casually portrayed in the top grossing films of 2010 is just one reflection of the impact that MADD had on changing the cultural perceptions and behaviors.

Challenges

Any multinational organization that wishes to make substantial changes to regional mandates needs to have strong local chapters that are capable of responding to unique initiatives and appealing to diverse constituents. Therefore, maintaining a worldwide base of active members and attracting victims of automobile accidents involving alcohol in order to sustain or grow are among the most prominent challenges MADD faces. To accommodate these challenges, MADD consists of local chapters that self-govern and create their own programming based on local needs and concerns (Weed). Frank Weed examined successful MADD chapters and found that local chapters that adapted the activism model to their own communities had the strongest likelihood of success. Adaptability requires that local chapters build networks within their communities with business and civic leaders as well as build an activist base among victims and survivors of automobile accidents involving alcohol. Therefore, while MADD maintains a central mission and identity, its success lies in the local chapters' ability to be flexible.

MADD's activism model assumes that legal change requires educating and mobilizing support. Yet, like most political movements, change draws criticism. Groups that oppose its mission have confronted MADD with multiple attacks on its activist agenda. Opposition groups have targeted their statistics, suggesting that accidents involving alcohol are actually decreasing and, therefore, there is no longer a need to tighten laws or to increase consequences. They fail to recognize that these decreases occurred largely due to the programs and laws brought about because of MADD activism, i.e., the RIDE program, stiff penalties against driving under the influence and changes in public perception of drinking and driving. Another attack suggests that its public education programs do not produce long-term change in behaviors and therefore should not be endorsed by local schools or courts (Toomey). Recent attacks include accusations that MADD forwards a prohibitionist agenda, that it is trying to end social drinking, and interfering with the free market by imposing regulations on alcohol sales and consumption (Hanson).

MADD as a Social Movement

The emphasis on the personal story is perhaps one of the foremost strategies contributing to the longevity of this organization. Social movement theorists Thompson and Davis (1997) speculate that controlling resources that are unique to the organization is critical to the success of a movement. The most important resource that MADD has is the personal story of the victims and the survivors. It uses these stories to tie members together and to mobilize collection action. With the infusion of the personal story into the organization's political efforts, public service campaigns, and educational programming, MADD has elevated the personal experience into a unifying organizational resource that it alone controls. External forces or political foes cannot change the emotionally-charged personal survivor's account. As new members join the organization, the stories also change to reflect their experiences. Stories can also differ across chapters to reflect local concerns. Therefore, personal stories are resources that change over time and locality to adjust to member interests and political conditions. This adaptability makes personal stories a highly-adaptable organizational resource controlled by the members.

Another characteristic that is associated with the success or failure of a social movement is the range of concerns embraced by the organization. Thompson and Davis suggest that organizations that have resilience are those with limited, shared interests. In that case, MADD's longevity can be associated with its focused mission of reducing automobile accidents involving alcohol. Whether its activity is public education, victim support, or legal activism, MADD consistently focuses on its central mission. For example, opposition groups have failed to engage MADD into defensive actions outside its mission. Specifically, MADD has not engaged in campaigns designed to combat opposition efforts to paint MADD as a prohibitionist group that seeks to repeal alcohol legalization (Center for Consumer Freedom). To redirect its efforts away from automobile accidents involving alcohol would reduce the power of the organization's most significant resource, personal stories, and could potentially reduce member support and ultimately, result in reduced resources.

A third factor influencing the success of social movements is the degree to which the members know each other so that they can form collective action. Thompson and Davis suggest that it is not enough that individual citizens are passionate about the same cause. They argued that if they are not familiar with each other, or if they do not know each other, then they cannot work collectively towards the same goal. For MADD, the personal story serves an additional purpose because it allows strangers to empathize with other similarly affected people along a highly emotional issue. By sharing an intensely personal and painful story, it is possible that strangers can transform into allies rather quickly. Therefore, it is possible that the survivors' intensely personal stories allow the organization to form alliances and cut through social barriers, therefore speeding the process of group cohesion.

Overall, the success of this social movement lies in its ability to focus its mission and use survivor stories as resources that communicate its message, form group cohesion, and serve as mobilizing factors in collective action. The survivor stories also serve another purpose because they attract new members. Therefore, the organization assures that growth occurs among people who share its commitment to the organizational mission of reducing automobile accidents involving alcohol. Survivors' stories, while significant, are not the only social movement characteristic that contributes to this organization's ability to recruit and mobilize new members. MADD's multifaceted programming not only serves to educate and provide support but also serves as an opportunity to attract new members. In the case of victim support, family members or victims may find they experience great relief and feel a sense of obligation or commitment to the organization. In addition, their newly formed insight into the legal system or the healing process may motivate them to share their experiences with others or to work towards changing the legal system. Public education programs and youth outreach designed to prevent alcohol-related auto accidents may attract new members from the community who were not otherwise aware of the damaging effects of these accidents. As a result, people who attend educational programs may be attracted to the mission of the organization and may join as a result. Likewise, legal action may result in building allies with members of other organizations with similar interests or among key legislators who support the organization's mission. Therefore, the activities of the organization serve not only to accomplish its mission but also to attract new members.

The Intersection of MADD and the Early Motherhood Movement

MADD emerged during a time of social movements that projected contrasting images of women and motherhood. The 1980s saw the height of the second wave of feminist social activism that considered the personal story as a political resource. At the same time, some of the most vocal opposition to the feminist movement alleged that feminists were anti-mother, thus trying to claim the motherhood agenda as one aspect of their mobilization efforts (Schlafly). The social and political environments, including the contrasting feminist and motherhood movements that existed in the United States during the early years of MADD, helped shape this organization's long-term identity.

For example, MADD's early years corresponded with feminist activism that organized in the United States to pass the Equal Rights Amendment. As MADD tried to legitimate mothers' voices as the medium for social activism, the pro-ERA movement was organizing mothers to support equal rights. Most notably, the pro-ERA movement organized events to encourage states to ratify the ERA for Mothers Day, specifically in Illinois and Florida, in 1982, just two years after the founding of MADD (Gilmore). These ERA rallies were rare events amidst a feminist movement that was widely criticized as anti-mother, to the extent that second-wave feminists often presented motherhood as a social institution that served as a barrier to women's liberation (hooks). Rather, that era of feminist activism was more likely to organize around ending rape and other forms of violence against women (Gilmore) than organizing mothers to support their own personal political agendas.

While motherhood was hardly at the forefront of the second wave of feminism during the time MADD emerged on the political scene, the concept that personal is political was a central theme in both movements. The personal as political assumes that women have common struggles and, by sharing their stories, they may understand that the solution to their problems does not lie within them but rather lies in social activism (hooks). The use of personal accounts as organizational resources reflects MADD's success using the personal story as a resource for political mobilization. Therefore, early MADD organizers were able to draw from the second wave of feminism to help shape its emerging organization.

Regardless of whether the second wave of feminism considered motherhood as a barrier to liberation, it is more certain that feminist opposition groups used motherhood as their rallying issue. Conservative activists, like Phyllis Schlafly, argued that feminists were trying to force mothers out of the home and into the work place, and tender the responsibility of child rearing to government-financed daycare centers (Schlafly). Thus, by co-opting the mother-as-protector-and-nurturer image while labeling the feminist agenda as anti-motherhood, conservative activists were able to claim motherhood activism as a feature of their social movement. To some degree, the motherhood movement in the United States that existed during the emergence of MADD had its strongest membership base among conservative anti-feminist groups. From its inception, then, MADD needed to position itself within a social context that supported feminist principles while navigating amid an emerging motherhood movement organized by conservative activists. Perhaps one of the survival strategies of this organization has been its ability to navigate the social environment that is often conflicted around motherhood.

Contributions to the Motherhood Movement

MADD certainly can contribute examples of a successful movement organized around mother's issues for persons involved in other motherhood movements. Among these examples, are the strength of personal stories as organizational resources, focused mission, adaptable local chapters that can attract members who mobilize for change, and navigating controversial political and social environments. Current motherhood activists can draw on these examples to grow support for equality for mothers in employment, childcare, and in other areas where discrimination exists.

Instances where the current motherhood movement relies on first-person accounts from volunteers as resources are numerous. One group, called MomsRising, advertised for readers to share their real stories. It stated that personal accounts demonstrate how laws and business practices influence the lives of everyday families. One mother shared her personal story to demonstrate a working relationship between an employer seeking to downsize and an employee seeking flexible work hours to accommodate her family. The site informed contributors that their personal stories were the best advocacy tool the group had to help influence legislative change (MomsRising). While MADD did not originate the use of personal stories, MADD has helped other organizations, such as MomsRising, understand the importance of these resources in attracting and engaging a volunteer base that will actualize its mission.

One strategy that contributed to MADD's sustainability as an effective organization is its commitment to a consistent and focused mission: ending alcohol-related automobile accidents. Under the tenets of this focused message, MADD provides a flexible variety of services. The Motherhood movement organizers can learn from this experience and focus their mission on ending discrimination against mothers, for instance. In order to achieve that mission they may offer a variety of services or follow legislative agendas that can change from chapter to chapter. Some local chapters may focus on childcare or flexible work. Over time, the political agenda may address living wages or parental leave. A resilient motherhood movement will be flexible to change its programming or legislative agenda as needs change, while remaining true to the organizational mission.

A final, and perhaps most significant, contribution that MADD has made to the motherhood movement is its demonstration of the importance of sustaining the movement within the social and political context of its time. MADD evolved within the context of the conservative pro-family and feminist social and political environments. Current and future motherhood movements may find that their sustainability depends on forming alliances with organizations or other movements that may not embrace the entirety of their mission in order to maximize public support. As it is true that politics makes strange bedfellows, MADD has demonstrated that the sustainability of a movement involves drawing alliances across groups that may otherwise be engaged in conflict.

The Future of MADD

MADD's plans include focusing on eliminating driving under the influence of alcohol. They also demonstrate that these plans include worldwide expansion. Efforts to expand could be supported by developing easily identifiable international chapter homepages on the Internet that would enhance MADD's mission to reach victims with information specific to their countries and local communities. Such an expansion could cater to families living in England, Australia, New Zealand, and Sweden, where the organization reports it has chapters but it does not currently have an identifiable web presence. Growth also includes attracting new members to existing chapters and mobilizing those members as volunteers. It claims that it will continue to exist until it ends alcohol-related automobile accidents, and it professes that this goal is achievable.

Conclusion

Perhaps nothing is more personal than the death of a child. This movement emerged from the pain of mothers grieving the loss or injury of their children through the acts of individuals who were driving recklessly under the influence of alcohol. MADD engages in victim support, education, and legal action to achieve its threefold mission of supporting victims of alcohol-related automobile accidents, preventing underage drinking, and eliminating driving under the influence of alcohol. This group of mothers demonstrated the strength of unity represented in the feminist activist's motto "personal is political" by using its experiences to reach out to others in similar situations, build mutual support in groups, organize for power, and create a social movement that impacted our culture for over 25 years.

Works Cited

American Trauma Society. "Second Trauma." *American Trauma Society.* 2010. <http://www.amtrauma.org/secondtrauma/secondtrauma.html>. Accessed 11 July 2010.

Bean, Sara. "Six Carbondale teens injured in wreck." *The Southern Illinoisan* 26 February 2002. Web. <http://thesouthern.com/news/local/article_bc7ce63c-9a75-53e2-890a-325bc92d50bf.html>. Accessed 11 July 2010.

Bohman, Thomas, et al. "Early Intervention for Alcohol Use Preventiona and Vehicle Safety Skills: Evaluating the Protecting You/Protecting Me Curriculum." *Journal of Child and Adolescent Substance Abuse* 14.1 (2004): 17-40.

Canadian Law. "Canadian Drunk Driving, DUI, DWI, Impaired Driving Law." 2010. *Canadian Law Information.* Web. <http://www.canadianlawsite.ca/impaired-driving.htm>. Accessed 17 July 2010.

Canadian Medical Association. "CMA Demands Lower Legal Blood-Aclohol Level." *Canadian Medical Assocation Journal* 166.1 (2002): 79.

Center for Consumer Freedom. "Mothers Against Drunk Driving." 2010. *Center for Consumer Freedom.* Web. <http://activistcash.com/organization_overview.cfm/o/17-motehrs-against-drunk-driving>. Accessed 10 July 2010.

DeJong, William and Ralph Hingson. "Strategies to Reduce Driving Under the Influence of Alcohol." *Annual Review of Public Health* 19 (1998): 359-378.

Gilmore, Stephanie. "The Dynamics of Second-Wave Feminist Activism in

Memphis, 1971-1982: Rethinking the Libtera/Radical Divide." *NWSA Journal* 15.1 (2003): 94-117.

Hanson, David. "Mothers Against Drunk Driving: A Crash Course on MADD." 2010. <http://alcoholfacts.org/CrashCourseOnMADD.html>. Accessed10 July 2010.

hooks, bell. "Revolutionary Parenting." *Maternal Theory.* Ed. Andea. O'Reilly. Toronto: Demeter Press, 2007. 145-156.

Kroeker, B, Barry Taub and R Schnarr Wilhelm. "Grief, Anger, Social Action: Experiences of the Windsor Chapter, Mothers Against Drunk Driving (MADD)." *Guidance and Counseling* 10.1 (1994): 25-30.

Kupfer, J. "'Stayin' Alive': Moral Growth and Personal NBarrative in *Saturday Night Fever.*" *Journal of Popular Film and Television* 34.4 (2007): 170-178.

Main, Carla. "Underage Drinking and the Drinking Age." *Policy Review* (June and July 2009): 33-46.

Mercer, Dorothy and John Evans. "The Impact of Multiple Losses on the Grieving Process: An Exploratory Study." *Journal of Loss and Trauma* 11.2 (2006): 219-227.

MomsRising. "Do you have paid sick days? Have you been fired or lost pay because you didn't? Tell us about it." May 2010. Web. <http://www.momsrising.org/blog/do-you-have-paid-sick-days-have-you-been-fired-or-lost-pay-because-you-didnt-tell-us-about-it/>. Accessed 19 July 2010.

Mothers Against Drunk Driving (MADD). *A Victim's Guide to the Canadian Criminal Justice System.* Oakville, Ontario Canada: Mothers Against Drunk Driving, 2009.

Mothers Against Drunk Driving (MADD). *History of MADD: Twenty-five Years of Making a Difference.* 2005. Web. <http://www.maddorangecounty.org/madd2005.htm>. Accessed 11 July 2010

Mothers Against Drunk Driving (MADD). *MADD Annual Report Fiscal year 2007-2008.* Irving, Texas: Mothers Against Drunk Driving, 2008.

Mothers Against Drunk Driving (MADD). *MADD Canada Victim Support Services.* 2010. Web. <http://www.madd.ca/english/services/index.html#5>. Accessed 11 July 2010.

Mothers Against Drunk Driving (MADD). "New MADD film drives home sobering message." 23 September 2009. *MADD Canada.* Web. <http://www.madd.ca/highlights.html>. Accessed 14 July 2010.

Mothers Against Drunk Driving (MADD) Canada. "2002 RIDE results in Toronto and GTA." *Toronto/Niagara Reports.* January 3, 2003. Web. <http://www.madd.ca/english/news/stories/n030103.htm>.

Mothers Against Drunk Driving (MADD) Canada. "Keep Irish eyes smiling this St. Patrick's Day." *MADD Canada Releases.* March 13, 2009. Web. <http://www.madd.ca/english/news/pr/p20090313.htm>.

Saturday Night Fever. Dir. John Badham. Perf. John Travolta, Karen Lyn Gorney, Barry Miller, Donna Pescow, Burce Ornstern, and Martin Shakar. Paramount, 1977.

Schlafly, Phyllis. "Feminists Consider Motherhood Oppressive." *The Moral Liberal* 11 March 2010. Web. <http://www.themoralliberal.com/2010/03/11/feminists-consider-motherhood-oppressive-phyllis-schlafly/>. Accessed 19 July 2010.

Solomon, R, et al. *Alcohol, Trauma and Impaired Driving.* 4th Ed. Oakville, ON: MADD Canada, Center for Additction and Mental Health, and the Canadian Centre on Substance Abuse, 2009.

Theriot, Matthew. "Evaluation of a Court-Ordered MADD Presentation for Juvenile Alcohol and Drug Offenders." *Journal of Offender Rehabilitation* 43.3 (2006): 49-72.

Thompson, T. and G. Davis. "The politics of Corporate Control and the Future of Shareholder Activism in the United States." *Corporate Governance* 5.3 (1997): 152-159.

Toomey, Tracy. "Amercian Beverage Licensees Attach Mothers Against Drunk Driving." *Addiction* 100 (2005): 1389-1391.

Weed, Frank. "Organizational Mortality in the Anti-Drunk-Driving Movement: Failure Among Local MADD Chapters." *Social Forces* 63.3 (1991): 851-868.

60.
Mainstreet Moms: Organize or Bust

LISA FEDERER

IN A NATION OF OVER 300 million people, some individuals find the idea that a single person can make a difference unrealistic. However, the organization Mainstreet Moms: Organize or Bust (MMOB) was founded on the notion that "bite-size actions" could indeed influence national policy. Founded in 2004 by Megan Matson, a mother of three, MMOB focuses its grassroots efforts on three main political areas: protecting children's privacy from military recruiters, promoting democracy through voting activism, and combating climate change. This chapter will discuss the history of MMOB's nationwide concerns and consider how local activism can produce results on a national level.

Philosophy

In an ever-more complex political setting of national coalitions and huge media campaigns, MMOB was formed by mothers who believed that grassroots efforts at the local level could have a positive impact on the nation as a whole. The activities of the organization are mostly simple and community-based: letter-writing campaigns and local volunteerism are mainstays of MMOB. Leveraging the power of Internet communication and the expertise of moms and "honorary moms," MMOB has demonstrated that local activism can indeed effect national change. Though MMOB has addressed a number of different local and national concerns in its six-year history, the recurring theme in all its activities is a focus on making the world that mothers would like to see for their children.

MMOB's primary philosophy is that activism should harness the skills and talents that people already have, emphasizing the impact of local and individual efforts to create broader changes on a national level. While the group encourages participation from non-mothers as well, as its name implies, its focus is on encouraging mothers to become active in politics. With their interest in ensuring a positive future for their children, MMOB argues, mothers are "hardwired for sustainability" and thus are uniquely motivated to work toward political and environmental goals.

While MMOB's philosophy emphasizes the importance of individual action, the organization partners with a number of other groups who share similar values and goals. In 2004, MMOB partnered with Working Assets to create the Leave My Child Alone coalition, which aims to educate parents about military recruitment policies and how to prevent their children's information from being shared with military recruiters. MMOB also partnered with Working Assets and VoteTrustUSA to form Pollworkers for Democracy, an organization dedicated to recruiting and training pollworkers.

History

MMOB was founded in 2004 by Megan Matson, a former advertising creative director who saw the opportunity for women, particularly mothers, to have an impact on national politics through political efforts in their own communities. Matson, who had become "tired of being a spectator to the unfolding disaster of our democracy," hoped to encourage ordinary citizens to participate in politics by providing resources that would allow them to make activism part of their already busy lifestyles. MMOB originally stood for Mainstreet Moms Oppose Bush, but after the 2004 elections, the group changed their name to Mainstreet Moms: Organize or Bust in order to reflect their broader political and environmental activism interests.

Activities

MMOB's activities center around three objectives: protecting children's privacy from military recruiters, combating climate change, and promoting democracy through voting activism. In 2004, MMOB partnered with Working Assets to form the Leave My Child Alone coalition, which aims to protect students from military recruiting. The coalition was formed in response to Section 9528 of the No Child Left Behind Act of 2002, which requires public secondary schools to release student contact information to military recruiters. In addition, the Pentagon's Joint Advertising Market Research and Studies program maintains a list of 16 to 25-year-olds that is distributed to the Armed Services for recruitment purposes. Few parents were aware of these provisions that made their children's information available to recruiters, so MMOB's coalition aimed to educate parents about how to opt their children out of these lists. In addition, the website encouraged parents to organize at the community level and work with their local school boards to protect their children's privacy.

Climate change is a significant focus of MMOB, who consider it not merely an environmental issue, but an "everything issue." MMOB calls for both awareness of and action on climate change issues. They emphasize the importance of busy mothers making time to educate themselves, suggesting that they read informational literature rather than watching television or reading fiction, and free up time by asking their children to help with household chores. MMOB also encouraged local groups to educate citizens about viable solutions to climate crisis and spark local action. In February 2007, MMOB launched their Soup and Solutions campaign, with help on the website for organizing a soup dinner in one's own community. At one time, MMOB's website offered much of this practical type of advice, with recommendations to help members organize their own local action groups, book club meetings or other events to address climate change. However, after the site was relaunched in late 2009, climate change and clean energy dominated MMOB's focus, although these efforts were limited to the Northern California area, especially San Marin.

Finally, MMOB also addresses voting issues through several approaches. First, MMOB encourages youths to vote through their Vote@18: Moms Sign Up the Senior Class campaign, in which mothers visit high school classes to speak on the importance of voting and conduct on-the-spot voter registration. In 2007, MMOB partnered with VoteTrustUSA and Working Assets to create Pollworkers for Democracy, an organization that recruits and trains individuals to work as paid pollworkers on election days. MMOB became a member of the Help America Vote ... On Paper (HAVOP) coalition, which campaigned against the use of touch-screen Direct Record Electronic (DRE) voting machines on the basis that they are costly and prone to failure. MMOB and HAVOP have organized local letter-writing campaigns, participated in litigation against DREs in California, and produced an informational video. Finally, MMOB created the Missouri Votes! campaign with author and professor Alan Gerber in 2004. Participants sent personal letters and voter registration forms to single women and unregistered mothers in an effort to educate women on the importance of voting and encourage them to learn more about the issues.

Future Goals

After the 2008 election cycle, MMOB ceased updating its website, as well as the website of the Leave My Child Alone project. Many of the resources that had been available on MMOB's site, such as guides to forming local action groups, readings lists, and pre-made banners and flyers, were removed from the site, leaving only basic information about the organization's history and philosophy. The Leave My Child Alone website continued to offer resources like letters parents could send to their local officials, but no revisions or additions were made after 2008.

Although the lack of updates to the organization's site seemed to suggest that the group had ceased its activities, an update in late 2009 indicated that MMOB's focus had "gone all-out local and fairly off-the-computer." With Matson still at the helm, MMOB had turned its attention to climate change and clean energy efforts in Northern California's Marin County. In November 2009, the site changed to a blog format, with Matson making occasional updates that primarily dealt with the June 2010 vote on California's Proposition 16, which would have made it more difficult for local governments to form Community Choice Aggregators (CCAs). CCAs allow cities and counties to aggregate energy buying power, thus giving consumers opportunities to choose cleaner energy alternatives. After

California voters defeated Proposition 16 in June 2010, the MMOB website was less frequently updated, with blog entries focusing on CCAs in California. Based on these changes to the organization's website, it appears that MMOB continues its original goals of climate change activism, with future goals more specifically focused on CCAs in Marin County.

Conclusion

Although MMOB no longer focuses on national-level activism as it once did, the organization is important for having helped many Americans re-envision their place in the world. As Matson has pointed out, the 2000 election was essentially decided by a few hundred votes in Florida; this result is proof that individual votes can and do make a difference. Whether it's through voting, promoting clean energy in one's own neighborhood, or even just opting one's own child out of military recruiting lists, "bite-sized" actions can quickly effect change when enough people gather their energy.

MMOB's special focus on mothers also has significance in the national motherhood movement. For one thing, MMOB members lead by good example—they, too, are busy moms with families to take care of, yet they still find the time for activism. Their emphasis on bite-sized action means that even the busiest mothers can find time to make a positive difference. Such a philosophy empowers women to become more active by showing them that their actions can have an effect on the issues that often concern them the most: the safety and future of their children. MMOB's letter-writing campaigns have also appealed to single and low-income mothers, encouraging women who probably would not have voted to become more politically active. Finally, MMOB mothers set an example for their own children, the mothers and voters and activists of the future.

Works Cited

Della Cava, Marco R. "Just Vote." *USA Today* August 3, 2004: 1D.

Della Cava, Marco R. "Advocacy as an Accessory." *USA Today* Aug. 3, 2004: 2D.

Krim, Jonathan, "Recruitment Tool Targeted; Privacy-Minded Coalition Seeks to Quash Pentagon Database." *The Washington Post* October 18, 2005: D05.

Lombardi, Kate Stone. "How the Army Gets What it Wants." *The New York Times* November 6, 2005: 14WC.

Marklein, Mary Beth. "War opponents target military recruiters in high schools." *USA Today* September 21, 2005: 5D.

Matson, Megan. "Mainstreet Moms: Organize or Bust." Last modified December 3, 2010. Web. <http://www.themmob.org>.

Rosenberg, Betsy. "Megan Matson and the Mainstreet Moms Organize or Bust." *EcoTalk*. Last modified December 18, 2006. Web. <http://blogsofbainbridge.typepad.com/ecotalkblog/2006/12/megan_matson_an.html>.

61. The Mother-Daughter Project

RENÉE SCHULTZ

IN 1997, WHEN TWO FRIENDS read the radical book, *Mother-Daughter Revolution: From Good Girls to Great Women* by Elizabeth Debold, Marie Wilson, and Idelisse Malavé, it fired us up. Debold, Wilson, and Malavé challenged our thinking about mothers and daughters, using the work of The Harvard Project on Women's Psychology and Girls' Development under psychologists Lyn Mikel Brown and Carol Gilligan as their foundation. Their book, *Mother-Daughter Revolution:*

> ...explores how mothers can have more power by bringing more of themselves into mothering their daughters. We present ways to transform what has been experienced as a cycle of betrayal between mothers and daughters into a powerful catalyst for social change. We see girls betrayed by a culture that diminishes women. The journey from betrayal to power traces how mothers can support girls in resisting the unnecessary losses they experience in growing into womanhood: losses of voice, of freedom, of power to do and to be in the world. This journey begins as women reclaim their powerful preadolescent voices as a prerequisite to voice lessons with their daughters. Then, mothers and daughters join to take action. (xvi)

Like the air we breathe, we'd absorbed the mistaken assumption that girls are supposed to hate their mothers during the teen years. And to make it even worse, we bought the idea that we'd be doing right by our daughters if we helped them to separate. Encouraged by their book (and the consciousness-raising model of the Women's Movement), we put out the word and gathered a group of women together to deconstruct the dominant paradigms about mothers, daughters, and the mother-daughter relationship. Our initial invitation read:

> *We thought we had plenty of time before our daughters would be approaching adolescence and making their way into the world of women, but as their bodies begin to change, we've recognized how swiftly they*

will move into themselves as young women. We want our daughters to be whole: all of their many attributes and feelings having room and given voice. We fear that in this world that diminishes women, they, too, will be diminished.

We want to join with other women in exploring how we can continue to nurture our daughters through pre-adolescence, adolescence and into adulthood. We want to explore ways that we can welcome them into the powerful community of women. We want to find ways that we can support each other as mothers and support our daughters as they are challenged by the restrictions placed on them by our culture. We recognize that they may choose to fight this oppression and we want to be prepared to fight alongside them. We each want our daughter(s) to shine in her own identity, not in the prescribed one. We want her to appreciate her many gifts and learn to use them wisely. We want her to emerge from adolescence full of her own choices and desires. We each have worked hard to reclaim lost parts. We want our daughters to rejoice in their unique selves and their "sisters."

Our goals were both simple and profound:

1. To support each other;
2. To create a new model for mother/daughter relationships;
3. To explore and grow as women and mothers;
4. To develop a model for other moms and document it;
5. To share resources.

Within a year, we mothers took it a step further and birthed several mother-daughter groups, both to pass on our knowledge as women and to have fun! And, of course, the moms kept meeting because you can't change the world by yourself.

Five years after the initial mothers group had formed, two members, Renée Schultz and SuEllen Hamkins, began meeting every other week in the couple of hours they could squeeze out of their busy lives. Over the kitchen table we began to discuss and write about what we were learning from both the mothers meetings alone and the meetings with our daughters. Inspired by our belief that these groups could be helpful to a broader community, we began reaching out to other women. From an initial professional paper in an international mental health journal to national and international talks on the mother-daughter relationship to a book, *The Mother-Daughter Project: How Mothers and Daughters Can Band Together, Beat The Odds and Thrive Through Adolecence,* the seeds for The Mother-Daughter Project were sewn.

Now mothers are using our book, *The Mother-Daughter Project,* to launch moms groups with the intention of spawning mother-daughter groups. Our book provides a framework for supporting mothers and daughters and provides a structure for age-appropriate explorations of topics to address in the correct developmental stage as our daughters mature. Our goal is to help women stay one

Celebrating ten years of mom-daughter.

step ahead of their girls when introducing the cultural deconstruction necessary to empower women.

Mandate/Philosophy

Coming of age during the Women's Liberation Movement, our lives opened up for us in ways that our mothers' lives had not. The arrival of our daughters was thrilling, in part, because we thought life was going to be different for them, an easier journey. And it is different. Girls today, especially before they hit the teenage years, take it as a given that they are as valuable as boys, that they have choices. They look around and see that their doctor, their mayor, their coach, is a woman.

At the same time, we are shocked by how the world isn't so different. In some ways it is worse for our girls, particularly during adolescence. The voices of the cult of thinness, of the sexual objectification of girls, even the social acceptability of surgical procedures such as breast implants for teenagers, are unrelenting. Likewise, as mothers we are bombarded with unrealistic expectations of mothering. The requirements of mothering go beyond what onc actually does: for example, getting up in the middle of the night to comfort and feed a crying baby, to encompassing how one should feel about it: that is, unequivocally happy. One slip and you are a bad mother. Although men are taking a greater role in active parenting than ever before, the standards are dramatically lower for fathers.

By forming the Mother-Daughter Project, we discovered that a group of mothers and daughters can do together what one woman alone cannot: form a creative subculture that provides mothers with the support they need; helps girls grow into their full power and potential; and promotes positive mother-daughter connections. Despite the social, political, and economic gains women have made over the past thirty years, sexism still harms women and girls and its dictates are often disguised as "common sense." The erroneous myths that you can never be too thin, that teen daughters must hate their mothers, and that mothers are to blame are all tales wrought by a sexist culture that prevails today. We call these stories "discourses." The Mother-Daughter Project deconstructs the dominant discourses that damage teenage girls and mothers, and breaks down mother-daughter connections. We work at creating new stories and practices that celebrate strong, self-possessed girls and women, promote healthy mother-daughter relationships, and bolster the work of mothers.

Three principles emerged that guide The Mother-Daughter Project:

1. Mothers need each other. We need to understand our relationship as daughters and we need to be able to understand our mothers and grandmothers as both mothers and daughters themselves.

2. Daughters need other mothers, *co-madres*, so they can hear the wisdom of women from many perspectives.

3. The mother-daughter relationship needs other mothers and daughters exploring power, intimacy, and voice together in community.

We're fostering an approach to mothering that includes support, vulnerability, and getting our needs met as women and mothers rather than the prevalent notion of mothers as martyrs. By interrupting the cultural message that teens are supposed to hate their moms, we provide the tools for a healthy, pro-active, mature relationship (that encourages individuation), as we work to break the cycle of separation. We are creating a community of support for mothers, daughters, and the mother-daughter relationship as we reframe women's reliance on each other as a positive model.

History/Activities

The first mothers group started in 1997 by reading *Mother Daughter Revolution* chapter by chapter with activities planned by one or two of the moms to take the group into a compassionate understanding of the material and how it related to our lives. When we heard the stories of our mothers, each coping in unique ways with the oppression of her time, we developed a new perspective on their struggles as women and a greater appreciation for the challenges they had as mothers, wives, and workers. This had been invisible to us when we were limited to seeing our mothers only through our own eyes as daughters.

We also paid attention to how our fears for our daughters (enhanced by the media) got in the way of our connection. *Allies rather than jailers* became our motto and we developed strategies that helped us hold that vision for the future when our daughters would begin venturing more independently into the world.

By the end of the first year we had formed two mother-daughter groups, which were meeting monthly and a third mom-daughter group was in the wings. Over the next ten years, the different groups progressed through developmental conversations and activities.

Mothers who are now forming mother-daughter groups find it helpful to begin by meeting in a moms' group without their daughters for the first six months. You will be inviting your daughters into this community of women. In your moms' group you'll have the opportunity to thoroughly examine your own experiences as a daughter, both in the past and present, as well as to give each other support in addressing issues that come up in parenting. It is helpful to come up with your own mission statement as a group. If your piece of The Mother-Daughter Project is wildly successful, what will it look like? Take time to write it out along with the ground rules you decide upon. It will help you if you hit a snag in the group.

Once you are ready to include your daughters, it is helpful to plan your mother-daughter group for the first year: dates, where you are going to meet, the main concept you want to address and the path you are going to take to do that, what two mothers will be co-leading a particular meeting, etc. There are helpful suggestions for each year, beginning at the age of seven, in our book. Following are a few guidelines to get you started:

- Sit in a circle, with everyone checking in about what's important in her life, both moms and daughters. It's a great way to begin each meeting and a valuable modeling of the importance of every individual in the group.
- As the girls get older, we recommend that shared leadership develop into one mom and one daughter, not her own. We encourage every possible mom-daughter combination have a turn. Strengthening the relationships of the girls with their *co-madres* is often very fruitful.
- By the time the girls are in their teens, it's often helpful to have part of the group time shared with both moms and daughters and some time

when the girls can go off by themselves and the moms can have some bonding time, too.

•Develop a simple *ritual,* like ending each group with a song. It is a powerful yet simple way of strengthening your group. One group who met for ten years went apple picking every fall to the same orchard. By the last year, the apple picking led to everyone lying on the ground on the edge of the orchard, heads together, our bodies like spokes in a wheel, as we shared from our hearts the importance of our group.

•Have moms share stories of their experiences growing up and how they handled difficult situations. It is particularly useful as our girls become more independent of us as it widens our daughters' understanding of some of the challenges they might face.

Moms continue to meet monthly separately from their daughters throughout the duration of the mom-daughter group. (Some mothers groups continue to meet after the daughters have left home and are in different parts of the country.) There is a twofold reason for continuing to meet as a mothers' group: 1) to actively support each other in the day-to-day issues that come up with your daughter, and 2) to have a small group of women who are committed to their own growth as well as their daughters. Having a safe place to share our struggles to be strong women, identify and meet our needs as individuals, and stay connected to the larger community, is invaluable. Many women, busy with the demands of mothering, work, a committed relationship, etc. find it difficult to prioritize the moms' group, but we believe supporting moms is critical to supporting our daughters. We are, after all, their role models.

Because of our book, *The Mother-Daughter Project,* there are now hundreds of mother-daughter groups throughout the United States that we know of and probably many more, as new groups start. From talking to mothers at presentations we have given on *The Mother-Daughter Project* and emails we have received, women articulate their desire to be an integral supportive part of their daughters' lives.

Challenges

When we began The Mother-Daughter Project, we envisioned mothers joining with other mothers and their daughters to change the dominant paradigm of mother-daughter separation, and that is exactly what is happening as new groups are constantly forming. As a grassroots idea and form of activism, the ball is rolling and we as an organization offer a book and website, and soon a blog. As an organization, we are building on the momentum and energy that is currently being manifested from our book, website, speaking engagements and workshops.

At the same time, we recognize that many women want more support than we are currently able to provide. We are seeking additional funding in order to train more women in this model of empowerment. Similarly, we'd like to increase the number of workshops and talks that we give to promote the wellbeing of mothers, their daughters, and the mother-daughter relationship. We would also like to provide additional trainings to social network professionals (teachers, mental health workers, clergy, etc.).

Currently, we see that many moms are desperate for support and yet scared and often unable to imagine finding enough time in their schedules to have both a moms group and a mother-daughter group (or two, if they happen to have two daughters or more). While mothers are expected to sit on the sidelines of their daughters' activities or endlessly chauffer them, taking the time for a monthly gathering to support their own needs as women and mothers can feel selfish, just as taking the time to join with other mothers and daughters to deconstruct the blatant sexism in magazine advertising, for example, can feel like "too much work." The word *feminism* is not helpful as a summary of why this matters to many women. In trying to explain that the groups are more than socializing or just for the girls, we run into moms not knowing what they need. Often women feel as though they don't deserve the time it takes to find support for themselves.

Without the moms' group component, we lose the space for moms to identify their own issues. Each of us has our vulnerabilities when it comes to living up to our own expectations of a good mother. In focusing solely on our daughters, we can forget that we moms are also daughters and women with our own particular needs and challenges.

Future Goals

We want to continue to get the word out about The Mother-Daughter Project through an increased presence on the web and additional speaking engagements and workshops in professional venues as well as directly with mothers. We are eager to foster cross-fertilization between groups. As great ideas arise, we'd love to set up a mechanism so that groups could share both their successes and their challenges. Some of this happens via email to the Project, but it currently doesn't get widely disseminated.

Our goal is to continue to be a resource for mothers and their daughters, to keep abreast of the latest research on mothers and daughters, to continue to learn directly from mothers about the challenges this new generation of mothers is experiencing, and to expand ways in which we can serve as a resource. We hope to sponsor gatherings where existing groups could send one or two representatives to meet, share ideas, and learn new skills so that they could bring back information to their groups.

Currently much of the work of The Mother-Daughter Project is voluntary and we lack the funding that will make much of this possible.

Motherhood Movement

Our first reaction was "What motherhood movement?" Though we know that the Motherhood Movement exists, it is *way too quiet!* For us, the women's movement informs our work: from circles of women talking to each other about issues of importance in their lives to deconstructing, speaking up, and supporting each other in our day-to-day reality as members of the Second and Third Waves. We come from a long line of women who want to change the world. In our moms groups, we can see how much has improved generation to generation and how far we have to go. We encourage both women and girls to explore how each of us can find our way as powerful women in the world.

Conclusion

It isn't what we do in the Mother-Daughter Project that makes it unique: it's the change of thought about what's most empowering for mothers and daughters. We know that women are valuable resources in each other's lives and we support mothers to look to other women for support beyond the early years of their children. And we know that most often a daughter's best ally throughout her teen years and beyond will be her own mother and co-madres who share the desire to change the world for mothers and their daughters. However that word gets out works for us. We offer resources but are happy to become extinct. Please.

Works Cited

Brown, Lyn Mikel and Carol Gilligan. *Meeting at the Crossroads: Women's Psychology and Girls' Development.* Cambridge, MA: Harvard University Press, 1992.

Debold, Elizabeth, Marie Wilson, and Idelisse Malavé. *Mother Daughter Revolution: From Betrayal to Power,* 2nd ed. New York: Addison-Wesley, 1993.

Hamkins, SuEllen and Renée Schultz. *The Mother-Daughter Project: How Mothers and Daughters Can Band Together, Beat the Odds, and Thrive Through Adolescence.* New York: Hudson Street Press, 2007.

62.
The Playground Revolution
Working and Stay-at-Home Parents Fight on the Same Side

SARAH COTE HAMPSON

THE PLAYGROUND REVOLUTION IS A blog by Miriam Peskowitz, author of *The Truth Behind the Mommy Wars: Who Decides What Makes a Good Mother?* In her first blog entry, Peskowitz states that her goal in creating the blog is to establish a forum for parents, both mothers and fathers, "who are dissatisfied with the alternatives for how to raise our kids and work for pay at the same time." She goes on to say that she sees the mission of the blog as essentially a *political* one. "I'm looking at the new ways that families are politicized, and the ways that mothers can think about the problems that ail us—like isolation, or overwork, or judgment, or anger, or even love—through a political lens." Over the course of the blog's two-year history, its mission was to dispel the Mommy Wars cultural myth, and to unite parents in working together to improve social and political conditions for all parents, whether working full-time, part-time, or staying at home. Though Peskowitz shut the blog down in 2006, its message is at the heart of the motherhood movement, and lives on through the action of mothers and fathers everywhere seeking to bring about social change.

The Playground Revolution is something more than a blog, though. It is a philosophy—how one woman has viewed the possibilities and the future of mother activism. This chapter will begin by discussing the cultural context of the "Mommy Wars" out of which the Playground Revolution emerged as both an idea and a blog, and discuss the history of the blog itself. It will then lay out Miriam Peskowitz's stated goals for the blog, as well as the discussions and actions that ensued during the blog's two-year history and the challenges that Peskowitz faced in meeting her vision for the blog. Finally, this chapter will lay out the future of the Playground Revolution, and how, even though the blog no longer continues, the ideas behind it still continue to be an important part of the larger motherhood movement.

Context: Challenging the "Mommy Wars"

"Do Real Women Have Mommy Wars?" asks Miriam Peskowitz in the opening chapter of her book, *The Truth Behind the Mommy Wars: Who Decides What Makes a Good Mother?* Peskowitz begins her book by describing a particular episode of *Dr. Phil.* In the episode, entitled "Mom vs. Mom" working mothers and stay-at-home mothers have been physically separated on opposite sides of the room. Over the course of the program, the mothers sling various accusations at each other. "Working moms should hide in shame for putting their kids in a filthy daycare center," is the war-cry of the stay-at-home mom, while working women lay claim to progressivism, sniping: "Stay-at-home mothers waste their education and throw us back to the 1950s" (20). But is this image really how working moms and stay-at-home mothers relate to one another? As Peskowitz recounts in an interview with *Mothers Movement Online,* the show's producers actually needed to edit the episode to make it appear more confrontational than it was. The real conversation that took place was in fact "more cooperative and supportive" than the Mommy Wars scene that played out on the air.

As E. J. Graff observes in the *Washington Post,* the Mommy Wars story is irresistible to media outlets that seek attention-grabbing headlines. "Everyone knows that a war, any war, is good for the news business. The Mommy Wars sell newspapers, magazines, TV shows and radio broadcasts, as mothers everywhere seize on the subject and agonize, in spite of themselves," says Graff. The Mommy Wars story is certainly prevalent in popular culture, and countless books, articles and television slots attest to its perseverance as a cultural talking point. But the dichotomy between working mothers and stay-at-home mothers is a false one, claims Peskowitz. In truth, working moms, moms who stay home, moms who work part-time, and stay-at-home dads all face very similar struggles with the difficulty of balancing the enormous time commitments that children and paid work both require.

Peskowitz thinks the Mommy Wars are really just about parents trying to make their way through the battlefield that is modern parenting. One of the central challenges that Peskowitz sees parents facing is the use of the language of "choice." "'Choice' is a complicated concept," Peskowitz says. "We often claim we are 'choosing' options that actually are not truly open choices" (Peskowitz 104). In recent years, "choice feminism" has become a burgeoning topic not only in media outlets such as magazines and newspapers, but has also caught fire as a popular doctrine espoused by members of the general public in such arenas as personal blogs, "mommy" message boards, and popular entertainment. "Choice feminism," which is essentially a term coined by Linda Hirshman to describe a major underlying attribute of "third-wave" feminism, is permeating American political culture. At its essence, this movement espouses a politics that defines feminist equality as the ability of women to make their own choices concerning every aspect of their lives. Whatever those choices may be, it is the ability to make that choice that constitutes a feminist act. Therefore, should a woman choose to engage in sex work, or a mother choose to leave a high-powered career to stay at home with her children, these choices can be viewed as self-determined and empowered—essentially feminist—choices (Snyder-Hall).

The Mommy Wars are palpable in online blogs and forums, as well as in media commentary, but are also present in cutting-edge feminist scholarship. A number of scholars have presented empirical evidence of a continued inequality of work distribution in the home (including housework and childcare), even when both spouses work equal amounts outside the home (Kane and Sanchez; Coltrane; Mason et al.). Choice feminists argue that feminists were the first to recognize the value of domestic work and to fight for its acceptance as "work," therefore feminists shouldn't judge women who have made a "self-empowered" decision to stay home and raise a family (Hirschmann; Snyder-Hall). However, evidence of continued inequality within the domestic sphere leads Linda Hirshman to conclude that "the real glass ceiling it at home." Feminists like Hirshman criticize choice feminism for being overly accepting of the choices women make, even if they are ultimately harmful to the women's movement. Hirshman points out, for example, that women who leave work to stay home with their children are often white and middle-class—women who are able to view work as a choice.

History: The Playground Revolution Morphs From Idea Into Blog and Back Into Idea

The Playground Revolution began as a concept, a vision of Miriam Peskowitz for what the motherhood movement should be all about. Peskowitz views the Mommy Wars culture as toxic to mothers and fathers of every stripe, since it shifts the focus from what parents really need to make their jobs easier to what ultimately becomes a mud-slinging match. Peskowitz began the blog on November 19, 2004 as a forum for parents and as a means of spreading her vision of cooperation between mothers and furthering the interests of the motherhood movement through "small change." The blog only lasted a little over two years, however, as Peskowitz found it necessary to focus her time elsewhere. "Something has to give," she says. "Internet grocery delivery, my newest time-saver delight, helps some, as do paper plates. Still, I find myself needing to limit the sheer number of different things I do. I need to clear some space so I can focus on new directions, and so I can be calmer and happier with what's in front of me right now." Thus the blog finished in November 2006, but Peskowitz's work in the motherhood movement, and the influence of the *idea* of the Playground Revolution, live on.

Mandate: A Blogger on a Mission

"The problem with the 'Women are opting out' explanation is that it treats quitting like a personal choice," argues Peskowitz. "It is, but it's a personal choice made in response to a *limited set of workplace options,* and a culture that has constricted imagination of work and family" (Peskowitz 107 [emphasis mine]). Because so many women (and men) have such diverse experiences with balancing work and family, Peskowitz believes that it is often difficult for parents from different backgrounds, or who have made different parenting decisions, to see that their struggle is the same. Peskowitz explains that her sense of the very narrow alternatives open to working mothers was heightened by her own experience early on in her parenting. In an interview with Mothers Movement Online, Peskowitz recounts:

> I know personally how hard it is to "get" how the structural issues for motherhood affect us. When my daughter was two, I had a part time job that paid decently well, and also gave me health and retirement benefits. I felt like I was on top of the world. I loved thinking of myself as the mom who could make it all work out, the mom who could win. For part of that year I thought less and less about other mothers, and less and less about the big picture. Until, that is, my schedule was changed mid year, and I found myself scrambling for a different mixture of preschool hours and babysitting, up against the gap between morning out programs on the one hand, and daycares that only provide fulltime care on the other. I was still aghast that the structures for hiring primary caretakers and caring for their young children while they worked really, truly weren't set up to help me. I started really feeling the loss of privilege and status that accompanies being a mom. (Tucker)

Peskowitz articulates the mission of her blog in her first entry. "Playground Revolution is about parents, mothers and fathers both, who are dissatisfied with the alternatives for how to raise our kids and work for pay at the same time" (September 27, 2004). She goes on to say that she sees the mission of the blog as essentially a *political* one. "I'm looking at the new ways that families are politicized, and the ways that mothers can think about the problems that ail us—like isolation, or overwork, or judgement, or anger, or even love—through a political lens." Parents need real solutions to the problems that they face in trying to balance the challenges of parenting and the challenges of working, and Peskowitz believes that the public arena is where the real Mommy Wars should be taking place. Here all types of parents may perhaps not agree on everything, but they can be working together toward the same goal—that of improving the "choices" that parents have when working out the best work-life balance for them and their families. Peskowitz envisions what this might look like in her book:

> In contrast to the largely personal attacks that filter through the Mommy Wars discussions, imagine an angry debate with real content. One side passionately argues that the federal government should provide grants or tax breaks for childcare costs and fund childcare centers with infirmaries and prepared-food counters so hungry parents can purchase healthy dinners while they pick up their kids so that everyone's night is easier. The other side argues no, and lists large and small businesses that are ready to change workplace assumptions to include the unpaid labors of

> care and nurturing in how employees are compensated, promoted, and retained, and that will give careful attention to the history of bias against mothers. Imagine that debate, one of substance. (55).

Ultimately, all parents are struggling against the structural difficulties that the American workplace presents to those with commitments outside of work. As Joan Williams argues in *Unbending Gender: Why Family and Work Conflict and What to Do About It,* both men and women who seek to balance children and paid work face the same brick wall—the pervasive norm of the "ideal worker" that is at the center of American working culture. The ideal worker is essentially childless. He or she is able to work full-time and overtime, anytime. The ideal worker does not take maternity leave or need to pick up a sick child from school. The notion of the ideal worker, in other words, presents parents who wish to work with two options: be a "bad" parent or a "bad" worker. It is the structural difficulties posed by this childless image of the ideal worker that Peskowitz hopes to address with political action.

Taking Action: "A Mom's Life is Political"

Exactly what form this political action can take varies widely, and Peskowitz enthusiastically embraces what she calls "small acts of change." In her book, Peskowitz recounts the story of Lorig Charkoudian. After being asked to take her baby into the bathroom to nurse, Lorig engaged in an active campaign to pressure Starbucks to comply with a Maryland law that allows mothers to breastfeed in public. Lorig wrote letters to educate Starbucks about the Maryland law and the benefits of breastfeeding. When that didn't work, she posted flyers and mobilized other local nursing women to participate in a nurse-in. When Starbucks sent Lorig a letter of apology just before the scheduled nurse-in, she went ahead with the protest anyway, encouraging national media outlets to cover the event, and launching a national campaign to change the policy of Starbucks. Further, the national movement gained momentum through the activists' use of the internet to organize themselves, which has propelled the effort to improve the rights and conditions of mothers who wish to breastfeed in public (208-9).

It is these small acts of change that Peskowitz set out to effect in her blog. These small acts are often just about mothers sharing information with each other. But, as was the case with the Starbucks nurse-in, mothers connecting with other mothers and sharing information can often have the effect of creating not-so-small change. Examples of Peskowitz disseminating information and calling mothers to act on it abound on the Playground Revolution blog. In October of 2004, for instance, Peskowitz blogged about the recent Paid Family Leave legislation enacted by the state of California. This law requires the state to supplement the income of mothers *and* fathers who have children *or* adopt, replacing 55 percent of wages for six weeks and allowing mothers who give birth an additional claim to disability insurance. Such a measure is a vast improvement for California residents to the federal FMLA allowance of 12 weeks of unpaid leave. Peskowitz's response was to urge her readers to spread the word about the new law, arguing that "like many things parental and child-related, affluent parents usually have the buzz before everyone else, so spread the word to everyone you know in California."

Additionally, Peskowitz encourages her readers to use Playground Revolution as a forum to communicate their solidarity with one another. She relates a story told to her by her friend about a woman whose daughter was sunburned at a beach, and was trying to help her daughter to put lotion on the burn. The daughter flew into a tantrum, screaming "you're the worst mother in the world!"

> The tantrum continued for a bit, and when there was finally a moment of silence, as she caught her breath, my friend's wife hears a woman a few stalls down say, "No. I'm the worst mother in the world." There's silence. And then, from a few stalls down the other direction, another woman raises her voice into the conversation. "No way. I'm the worst mother in the world. By far." ...One can easily imagine the mother of the sunburnt girl cringing, feeling mortified that her daughter's hurting body was her fault, and waiting for others to judge her. Instead, the women defused it all, and supported the mother.... Send me more stories like this, that's all I can say. When do we cooperate? When do we act in solidarity? (April 7, 2005).

One of the most persistent messages of the blog, however, is that parents should communicate their needs not just with each other, but with their elected officials. Peskowitz uses the blog numerous times to urge her readers to simply pick up the phone and call their representatives. "When you're frustrated about family life and/or about workplace issues, just call any of your local elected officials, from Senators on down. Tell 'em what's going on. They won't start fixing stuff until they hear more from us, and how many angry complaints from moms and dads do you think political staffers will bear before telling their boss, and before said boss jumps on the band wagon?" (June 28, 2005). Again, in January 2006, she writes, "What if everytime I felt like yelling at a child, I instead picked up the phone and called Rick Santorum's office, and Arlen Specter's too. These are the men who represent me in the U.S. Congress. Redirect that anger where it belongs." The Mommy Wars are still the prevailing cultural image of modern parenting, she laments in February 2006, "We still don't have a show that brings a Senator in to be faced by moms and dads who want affordable quality daycare." Again and again Peskowitz argues that communicating with local and national representatives is a small act that can result in big changes. "So make those phone calls. Yes, a phone call doesn't change the law. But it can help get the ball rolling. If we're going to have an impact, we have to begin moving beyond talk, and into the legislative arena" (May 5, 2006).

Challenges: The Massive and the Everyday

The Playground Revolution both as a concept and as a blog encourages mothers and fathers to tackle big issues like social and policy changes that will make a difference to the work-life balance of all parents. The challenges involved in facing these issues abound—not least because of the pervasiveness of the Mommy Wars cultural bugbear. One of the biggest challenges mothers face, Peskowitz recounts, is the lack of true "choice" when it comes to determining the best fit for them between mothering and paid work. Chiming in on a debate in the mommy blogosphere about mothers being underemployed, Peskowitz writes, "37 percent of mothers work part time. 25 percent are at home, and many, many of these mothers say they would like decent, fairly paid part time work in the professions in which they were trained. Many part time working moms are doing much less interesting work than they want. That's bad for them, and it's bad for our economy and for the productivity that the U.S. needs" (8/11/05). Tackling the image of the ideal worker, the pervasiveness of media stories that attempt to pit mothers against one another, and structural difficulties such as a lack of paid maternity leave and subsidized childcare, are all some of the enormous challenges that the *concept* of the Playground Revolution is trying to address.

Yet the Playground Revolution in its life as a *blog* also faced the comparatively mundane challenges of one woman. The challenge of a blog is that its maintenance and its mission often relies on one person to keep it afloat. Therefore, the individual's challenges become the blog's challenges. This is what happened with the Playground Revolution. Peskowitz found herself with simply too much on her plate, as a mother, an academic and a businesswoman. As she said, "something has to give." Additionally, while the heart and soul of her belief in mother activism resided in the Playground Revolution blog, sometimes the challenges of the everyday—like earning a living—need to take precedent for the individual over the movement. For instance, Peskowitz candidly explains why she chose to continue writing her other blog, Everyday Mom, while hibernating Playground Revolution.

> Why there and not here, you might ask? Simply, because Everyday Mom is sponsored by Hyland Homeopathy, and they send me a check once a month. In my calculus of time and income, that's an economic reality that matters. I resisted refashioning Playground Revolution into an advertisement-driven, income-earning site. I wanted us to enjoy ideas without who-knows-what peering over from the left-hand column. I'm glad I did, but as we all know, good blogging takes time. I can't continue to keep up both with different content on each blog.... (November 19, 2006)

Moving Forward: The Future of the Playground Revolution

The challenges that ultimately led to the blog's demise, however, do not stand in the way of the Playground Revolution's future as an idea. It is the call to political action—to "raise a fuss when a fuss needs to be raised"—that closes the blog's farewell post, in November 2006. Peskowitz herself acknowledges her certainty that the mission of the Playground Revolution will outlive her blog. In her final blog entry, she tells her readers, "To the extent that I've been part of raising political issues about mothering, parenting, and gender, I'm proud, and I look around now and see all sorts of people carrying on good work. I'm in good company, which also means I can take a well-deserved break." Peskowitz continues to be active in the motherhood movement, authoring several academic books and, more recently, the bestselling *Daring Book For Girls,* and its sequel, *The Double-Daring Book for Girls*, which encourages mother-daughter interaction and for girls to become actively involved in the world around them. Peskowitz also started a small business, MotherTalk, a place for moms to connect with other moms and discuss books and products that are of interest to women.

Though needing to allocate the time she spent working on the blog to other aspects of her busy life, Peskowitz encourages her readers to continue in the spirit of the Playground Revolution. "Change comes big, and change comes small, and all of it matters. Change enters the quiet corners of our lives and consciousness, until different sorts of decisions are made. Like that. This is the kind of revolution I've always imagined, the kind where you don't realize it's happened till you wake up one day and realize things are different, and you wonder how it all happened so quickly." Small change is the message of the Playground Revolution, and it is one that has the power to outlive a blog. The real revolution takes place every day, Peskowitz believes, and she continues with the spirit of the Playground Revolution in all of her work. In her final entry she says, "I really believe in the playgrounds, virtual and material, where we meet, talk, scheme, plan and envision. This work and play will continue for years to come. I'm so glad to be hanging out with each of you, pushing the kids on the swings while we think big and talk about the good future of the world."

The Playground Revolution In the Larger Motherhood Movement

The message of the Playground Revolution is one with the potential to resonate with many other facets of the motherhood movement. Ultimately, the new mother activists are parents who get mad—mad enough to take action to make small changes to improve the conditions in which they find themselves as parents. Mother activists, Peskowitz concludes in her book, are the new face of feminism. Because motherhood is so often relegated to the private sphere, being a mother can be isolating—a fact that does not translate easily into mobilization and mass movements. Changing public policy to recognize the work of parents, Peskowitz argues, is "the next feminist challenge, the work left to do. The story told by the new mother activists is that many of us reject classic feminism's rejection of home and family … we sought other lives: lives with children … lives that refuse the classic idea that body is split from mind, that domestic life is separate from work, that the mother cannot be public" (216).

The Playground Revolution, therefore, continues beyond the scope of the blog itself, so long as mothers find themselves dissatisfied with the conditions that interfere with their ability to make good choices about their work and parenting. So long as part-time work is inaccessible, underpaid and undervalued, there will be a place for the Playground Revolution. So long as domestic work is not recognized as *work*, there will be a place for the Playground Revolution. The motherhood movement as a whole, Peskowitz observes, is now "the startling new energy of a reviving women's movement" (216). At the heart of this revitalized movement is the call to action that is the message of the Playground Revolution—a call for mothers and fathers of all types to work together to bring about real social change.

The author would like to thank Miriam Peskowitz for her kind support and assostance in the preparation of this chapter.

Works Cited

Coltrane, Scott. "Research on Household Labor: Modeling and Measuring the Social Embeddedness of Routine Family Work." *Journal of Marriage and Family* 63.4 (2000): 1208-1233.

Graff, E. J. "The Mommy War Machine." *The Washington Post* 29th April 2007.

Hirshman, Linda. "Homeward Bound." *The American Prospect* 15th November 2005.

Hirschmann, Nancy. "Choosing Betrayal." *Perspectives on Politics* 8.1 (2010): 271-278.

Kane, Emily and Laura Sanchez. "Family Status and Criticism of Gender Inequality at Home and Work." *Social Forces* 72.4 (1993): 1079-1102.

Mason, M. A., M. Goulden and N. H. Wolfinger. "Babies Matter: Pushing the Gender Equity Revolution Forward." *The Balancing Act: Gendered Perspectives in Faculty Roles and Work Lives.* Eds. S. J. Bracken, J. K. Allen and D. R. Dean. Sterling, VA: Stylus, 2006. 9-29.

Peskowitz, Miriam. *The Truth Behind the Mommy Wars: Who Decides What Makes a Good Mother?* Emeryville: Seal Press. 2005.

Peskowitz, Miriam. "Thanks, and Look What California's Up To..." [Weblog entry.] Playground Revolution. October 6, 2004. Web. <playgroundrevolution.blogspot.com>.

Peskowitz, Miriam. "North Carolina/Bathroom Talk" [Weblog entry.] Playground Revolution. April 7, 2005. Web. <playgroundrevolution.blogspot.com>.

Peskowitz, Miriam. "Call Your Senator" [Weblog entry.] Playground Revolution. June 28, 2005. Web. <playgroundrevolution.blogspot.com>.

Peskowitz, Miriam. "The Debate Over 'We'" [Weblog entry.] Playground Revolution. August 11, 2005. Web. <playgroundrevolution.blogspot.com>.

Peskowitz, Miriam. "The Silent Yell" [Weblog entry.] Playground Revolution. January 25, 2006. Web. <playgroundrevolution.blogspot.com>.

Peskowitz, Miriam. "Mommy Wars Again" [Weblog entry.] Playground Revolution. February 22, 2006. Web. <playgroundrevolution.blogspot.com>.

Peskowitz, Miriam. "Pick Up Your Telephone" [Weblog entry.] Playground Revolution. May 5, 2006. Web. <playgroundrevolution.blogspot.com>.

Peskowitz, Miriam. "Hibernation" [Weblog entry.] Playground Revolution. November 19, 2006. Web. <playgroundrevolution.blogspot.com>.

Snyder-Hall, Claire. "Third-Wave Feminism and the Defense of 'Choice.'" *Perspectives on Politics* 8.1 (2010): 255-261.

Tucker, Judith Stadtman. "Playground Revolution: An interview with Miriam Peskowitz, author of *The Truth Behind the Mommy Wars.*" April 2005. The Mothers Movement Online. www.mothersmovement.org

Williams, Joan. *Unbending Gender: Why Family and Work Conflict and What to Do About It.* New York: Oxford University Press. 2000.

63. Mothers Acting Up

Mobilizing Mothers to Act on Behalf of the World's Children

JULIANA FORBES AND BETH OSNES

We are mothers, sisters, family;
wrapped in different cloth, standing under the same wide sky.
And we've come to the very end of our silence.

Together we've found our voice
and it is loud
and it is beautiful
and it sings a love song for our children.

IMAGINE THE POWER OF MOTHERS uniting to champion our global family. This phenomenon is so revolutionary it is difficult to even grasp its significance or what it implies for our future. To get a glimpse, imagine the radiant face of a mother re-imagining herself in new public leadership roles. Now multiply her image by a million. Sixty million. More. Around the world mothers are recognizing that our children's lives are linked; only by acting to nurture and protect *all* children, can we nurture and protect our own. Mothers Acting Up (MAU) is devoted to inspiring, educating and engaging these mothers, believing that mothers united can, and will, ensure the health, education and safety of *every* child—not just a privileged few.

Mothers Acting Up was started in 2002 by four American mothers: Juliana Forbes, Beth Osnes, Joellen Raderstorf and Erica Shafroth. While raising our children together, we became increasingly alarmed by choices our elected leaders were making, and how those choices were impacting the lives and future of every child on earth. We wanted nothing less than to inspire a political revolution—a fundamental change of values—until children's needs were no longer the bottom priority in our world's governments and corporations, but a top priority. We saw mothers[1] as the natural leaders of this magnificent revolution. Pooling our talents and experiences, we set out to create the most irresistible invitation to activism, hoping to unleash a veritable frenzy of mother leadership. Since 2002, MAU has spread to all 50 U.S. states and 24 countries through a variety of strategies, from collective actions, "how-to" recipes, public events, media stories, performances, workshops and

Three generations stand tall. Lubbock, TX, 2010.

a daily calendar. Whatever the strategy, the mission has remained the same: *to mobilize mothers to act on behalf of the world's children*. This chapter will trace our steps through sections on: Purpose, History, Principles and Programs, MAU and the Mothering Movement, Challenges, Future Goals and Conclusion.

Purpose

Though potentially the most powerful lobby for children, we mothers often don't consider ourselves "political" and traditional mothering roles have rarely included shaping policies that impact children. MAU's purpose is to encourage/incite a transformation in the hearts and minds of mothers—primarily American mothers. We don't need to *be* different. We need to *see* ourselves differently. Mothers are inherently political. We negotiate with the skill of veteran diplomats, we allocate resources so everyone eats and gets a fair share, we resolve disputes, and we judiciously spend money to ensure the wellbeing of our family. Mothers Acting Up isn't just designed to encourage mothers to include more public political activity in their lives, it is about making us aware we are *already* acting politically, and illuminating ways to leverage those actions to benefit the world's children.

Supporting this shift—mothers identifying ourselves as activists—is not as easy as you might think. Cultural attitudes play a powerful part in determining a mother's behavior and in deciding how far beyond her immediate circle she will act. From the very beginning of the suffrage movement—American women's first major step into full civic participation—the dominant power structure sought to cast suffragists unfavorably. Opponents of women's suffrage used popular iconography to represent suffrage activists as, "*unsexed, mannish, and domineering women … as spinsters who could not or would not marry or as married women who neglected their homes and children, henpecked their husbands, and generally inverted the natural order of gender politics"* (Glenn 132-133). Sound familiar? Although attitudes have certainly evolved since the last century, "female activist" still conjures up an image of a woman shouting on a street corner, neck veins angrily popping, wildly waving a placard—not an image with which many mothers identify. Part of the mission of MAU is to offer a new positive image of activism that presents acting on your beliefs as mainstream and part of the *daily* work of caring for our own children. This is critical to the movement, not just so those already engaged feel less like pariahs and still receive dinner invitations, but because *millions* of us need to feel drawn to take public action until children's lives are politically valued.

Why focus on Mothers? Because we're already passionately committed to our children's wellbeing *and*, by dint of our sheer numbers, are potentially the most powerful lobby. Given we're the ones around the world primarily raising children, mothers already see it as our job to care for them. MAU's job is to offer a compelling invitation for mothers to step into new leadership roles on behalf of *all* children. *Why*? Because our own children's future is inextricably linked to the well-being of every other child, and because children the world over are in dire need of advocates. Here are some facts about the world's children:

- •Worldwide, every day 24,000 children die due to malnutrition and mostly preventable diseases. One billion children, almost every other child in the world, live in poverty (UNICEF 2010).
- •17.5 million children worldwide have lost one or both parents to AIDS (UNICEF "Fact of the Week").
- •90 percent of war casualties are civilians—almost half of these victims are children (UNICEF "Children").
- •20 million children have been forced to flee their homes because of conflict and human rights violations (UNICEF "Children").
- •132 million children in the developing world are orphans, meaning that they have lost one or both parents. (UNICEF "Orphans").
- •Every day in the U.S., more than $1 billion is spent on the military while 2,200 babies are born without health insurance and 2,600 babies are born into poverty (MAU).

MAU's bottom line: Someone needs to step up and advocate for children—who have no political voice—and mothers are the best people in the world for the job.

History

Mothers Acting Up was launched with a Mother's Day Parade inspired by the words of Julia Ward Howe, who, after witnessing the tragedy of the Civil War, wrote in her diary, "*Why do not the mothers of mankind interfere in these matters, to prevent the waste of that human life of which they alone bear and know the cost?*"

Inaugural MAU Mother's Day Parade, Boulder, CO, 2002.

(qtd. in Richards and Elliott 1925: 159) In order to galvanize mothers, she wrote a Mother's Day Proclamation and called mothers to "*Arise!*" on a new holiday she named "Mother's Day." Howe's main goal was to organize mothers to end war, but her proclamation also urges women to focus on that which unites us, over that which divides us. In that spirit, we asked mothers on Mother's Day to include in their day of pampering, a public claiming of a new mothering role: champion for the world's children. Hundreds heeded our call. Attired in audacious costumes, many strapped on homemade stilts and paraded down Boulder Colorado's Pearl Street Mall, representing mothers as visible, celebratory, and a force to be reckoned with. There were letters to our representatives for people to sign, information on children's wellbeing, voter registration cards, and—to the delight of all—free cake. We asked people to join the movement and commit to at least one action a month, which was posted on the brand new MAU website. Many brave enough to walk on stilts, said that after being so visible in their community, they felt they could do *anything*, from getting up in front of a town council meeting to writing a letter to the editor, to visiting their Members of Congress (MOC). Their image of who they were and what they could do had been transformed; they had re-imagined themselves as powerful advocates for the world's children.

We posted a "Parade Packet" on the MAU website that included a recipe for putting on a MAU parade—from sample press releases to a recipe for building stilts. One year later, eleven cities throughout the country—including New York, Los Angeles, Cincinnati, Albuquerque and Vashon Island—hosted Mothers Acting Up Mother's Day events and celebrated mothers as outspoken advocates for

Mother speaks out in Chajul, Guatemala, 2009.

The Mother Tour Vocal Empowerment Workshop, Guatemala, 2009.

children. The courageous mothers who organized these events—several while nursing babies—overcame their own doubts and fears to make visible their commitment to protect children everywhere. There were common ingredients: mothers on stilts, a collective action on an issue facing children, a celebratory flavor, the words of Julia Ward Howe and free cake. To date there have been 90+ MAU Mother's Day events—ranging from parades to potlucks—in cities large and small across the U.S.

From the original Mother's Day launch, MAU has offered many different strategies, actions and programs—the ability to respond to changing needs and appetites being one of the great benefits of small, nimble organizations. While the Mother's Day events haven't been a current focus, they clearly established the spirit of Mothers Acting Up, which has remained strong throughout the years.

Principles and Programs

Every expression of MAU—from Op-Eds to daily actions to public events—have been guided by five MAU Principles:

1. *Be exuberant:* Since we're ACTING UP for the rest of our lives–with children at our side–our activism needs to be sustainable and joyful. Negative confrontations cause women to politically disengage. The MAU movement is organized not against individuals or policies, but towards realizing our collective vision.

2. *Follow the money:* Every dollar spent, each tax dollar collected is a vote. It's time to get educated about what we're funding with our budgets—from personal products to the government policies our tax dollars support. If anyone knows how to shop, balance a budget and make sure everyone eats, it's mothers. Make sure your dollars vote for a healthy future for all children.

3. *Connect the dots:* In our global economy, all children's wellbeing is connected. They breathe the same air, walk under the same sun, and live in countries at war or peace with each other. We need to measure the true impact of our actions—our consumption, energy & trade policies and national security strategies—not only by how they affect our children, but children everywhere.

4. *Take two-handed actions:* There are two ways to create change: direct aid and systemic change. Direct aid attends to immediate needs—donating food or providing shelter. Systemic change goes farther upstream and involves a dedicated lobby working for policy change with persistence and patience. The two handed approach is the best way to create lasting change.

5. *Know the power of collective action:* One voice calling for universal basic education is great. One hundred voices, better yet. One *million* voices and policies change and universal education is funded. Together, we can create a better world for children. The greatest challenge is to focus our energies on what unites us.

The first principle, *Be exuberant,* isn't a vague charge to be a Pollyanna and ignore the bad behavior of citizens and world leaders. It's a promise to focus on what we want to make happen, and to move towards that vision with our integrity, humor and creativity intact. Prioritizing the world's children will take more than mobilizing the very earnest. It will take more than mobilizing those already involved. It will take reaching mothers of all political parties, ages, and cultural, economic and religious backgrounds, uniting on a common concern: the health and wellbeing of children. To unite us all, we must stray from the customary way of organizing *against* something—person or policy—and organize *towards* a vision. During a MAU workshop, one mother nodded her head saying, "*I can do it if it's positive.*" It's also much easier to engage younger

Mothers Acting Up Girlcott celebrating Wild Oats, Boulder, CO, 2006.

generations—tomorrow's esteemed leaders—when the activism is creative and positive.

The second MAU Principle, *Follow the money,* is critical in bringing about political change. Nowhere are our true values more exposed than in our pocket books—whether in our personal budgets or collective tax dollars. Pay attention to what you support with your moolah: money is a tool with enormous power. Personally spend your money on products, individuals and organizations that benefit the world's children. Luckily in this day and age there are many Fair Trade products—which ensure a livable wage to whomever produced the product—from coffee to rugs to shawls. Every time you give a Fair Trade present, you've given twice, to the receiver and to the person who made the gift, who is now more likely to send their children to school because of your purchase. There are also Socially Responsible Investments, which ensure even your savings contribute to strengthening the fabric of communities. (Fair Trade resources at: Greenamerica.org, newdream.org, and Transfairusa.org.) This spirit of economic celebration continues with MAU's famous Girlcotts, our version of boycotts; still using money to create social change, but instead of *protesting* the practices of a particular business, MAU mavens support businesses whose trade and labor practices are contributing to a healthy future for all children. These events (if public) are something like street theatre and children love them (small caveat: pre-teenage.) (A full Girlcott recipe at: www.mothersactingup.org/girlcotts.)

The second aspect of *Follow the money* is central to most MAU actions: knowing what your government supports with your tax dollars. This is an eye-opening experience, in fact as eye-opening as the strongest mug of Fair Trade coffee. It's MAU's dream that every citizen know the breakdown of their federal discretionary budget—what Congress divies up—and feel some ownership in those decisions. For a teaser, here's one fact: the proposed 2010 U.S. budget request for military spending is projected to be more than 58 percent of the discretionary budget, or $663.8 billion. To put this in perspective, this number is bigger than *all other military budgets in the world combined* (U.S. Department of Defense, National Priorities Project). Creating security isn't only the domain of presidents and generals, but the domain of mothers, fathers and citizens. We all want our children to thrive—every one of us—of all political and religious stripes, of every size and color under the sun. It's the one thing we hold in common. Let's use our collective dollars to answer our common desire to ensure our children are secure.

> Governments devote billions of dollars to weaponry and nothing in comparison to bring clean water, healthcare, education, street lights—the things that really bring peace of mind and security. I'd like to see mothers ask themselves, "What does security mean to me? What does it mean for my child? My family? My community?" And then compare their answers and their needs with how governments prioritize and define security issues, and where the resources are being allocated.
>
> I'd like to see mothers, every time they hear of war, ask themselves, "Where are the women?" What are they doing? What is their solution?
>
> —Sanam Naraghi Anderlini, Co-founder of International Civil Society Action Network (I CAN) (Mothers Acting Up Calendar 2008, week of November 2)

Getting educated about where we spend our money also means finding out what we *could* be spending our federal dollars on. World leaders have committed themselves to a set of eight targets called the Millennium Development Goals (MDGs), which, if adequately funded, will cut extreme poverty worldwide in half by 2015. The world's richest governments, including the U.S., have committed to each contributing 0.7 percent of their gross national product (GNP) to Official Development Assistance. The U.S. is currently falling far short of our promised funding (U.S. Department of Defense, National Priorities Project, Convention on the Rights of the Child, Milleniumcampaign.org).

Now that we're talking about policy, we've noticed a few eyes glazing over. A quick reassurance: you don't need to be a policy wonk, have a Ph.D., or even wear panty hose to be the perfect advocate for the world's children. *You*, standing up for your beliefs, are already the perfect advocate. Not even runner up. So don't get intimidated by statistics, pie charts and policies. Use information to strengthen your leadership. And, perhaps when you bravely leap into the "policy world," you'll be hooked; policies are fascinating and are ultimately what impact the lives of children.

The third principle, *Connect the dots,* means tracing the connection between our lives and the lives of people living around the world. Warning: this principle weans us off the very familiar comfort of keeping most of the world as "other."

Recently MAU asked children if they could identify ways their lives were connected to children on the other side of the globe. Most were utterly baffled by the question. Some managed to say—slowly and loudly as though we didn't speak the same language—their lives were *completely* connected. From their perspective there was no disconnection. This is perhaps the most hopeful sign in the world today: children recognizing their intrinsic interconnection.

We can connect the dots economically, socially, politically, and in many other ways, but one of the most critical ways is environmentally. As climate change becomes recognized as a threat to life as we know it, it's clear we're all in this together. Climate change is wreaking havoc around the world, and Mother Nature is not paying attention to political maps, so the world's economically poorest—with the fewest resources—are currently paying the highest price for climate change, even though they've contributed the least to the crisis. Today, the world uses the equivalent of 1.3 planets to provide the resources we use. In other words, it takes the earth one year and four months to regenerate what we use in a year (Global Footprint Network). On the bright side, perhaps our environmental concerns will galvanize the world into greater collaboration and a historically unique recognition of our linked challenges and solutions.

The fourth principle, *Take two-handed actions*, is code for getting into the habit of always including a political, or systemic, action in your acting up. As notable nurturers, mothers, and women in general, have tended toward charity and direct aid in their activism. This is wonderful except mothers and women are conspicuously *absent* from negotiating tables where decisions are made that create the need for charity and direct aid. Such decisions include: whether to wage war, fund the Millennium Development Goals or how to structure trade policies. Given this, Jonathon Kozol's words ring especially true, "Charity for all its beauty is never a substitute for systemic justice." Mothers Acting Up urges mothers to influence elected leaders and shape public policies. The jewel in the Mothers Acting Up spirited-political-participation crown is taking Field Trips to our Members of Congress (MOC). Now, before anyone thinks, "*Oh, that is SO not me.*" Consider this: we've known mothers who initially didn't know the *name* of their Senator, but persevered to have transformational meetings with her/him. Oh wait, that was *us*. Given our humble beginnings, we've taken scrupulous notes over the years, and can offer with total confidence, the easiest step-by-step Field Trip Recipe in the world (see: www.mothersactingup.org/tools).

The last MAU Principle is: *Know the power of collective action*. We've saved the best for last, because our future, and certainly our children's future, will be determined by our ability to *unite*. We can moan and groan, wring hands, shake fists, but until we have millions of conversations about children's wellbeing, show up at each other's events, tweet and re-tweet about the world's children, use our money for change and join others working for a sane future, nothing much is going to change. Remember, bad behavior isn't new or news. It's been around for as long as humans. What *is* news is our current ability to reach across physical, economic, social, political and all other boundaries, to join forces for our collective family.

Beth Osnes performing in the Mother Tour DVD.

Together we can measure the true impact of our actions and policies by how they affect children everywhere. Together we can trace the ramifications of our personal choices and address issues that impact our entire global family. As we build our numbers, we also need to support each other, pass on hints and information, and help each other step into unfamiliar public leadership roles. We will act as each other's coaches and cheerleaders. This is the purpose behind MAU's Mother Tour.

Programs

MAU's current programmatic focus is the Mother Tour, a theatre performance and workshop that has traveled the world to create a global community of mothers moving from concern to *action* on behalf of the world's children. MAU joined in partnership with the Philanthropiece Foundation to present a program that uses theatre as a way to inspire, educate, and empower mother voices for effective advocacy. When being presented for an English-speaking audience, the program begins with a one-woman performance, *M-other*, written and performed by Beth Osnes (co-author of this chapter). The show explores what it just might take to get the people of one nation to authentically care about the children of other nations. The show's opening describes a fictional program, "Baby Swapping," created by the United Nations to generate care for the world's children. In this imagined pilot program, seven mothers from seven nations are required by their governments to swap their six-month old babies with another mother for one month. What follows is an intimate (funny, teary, provocative and hopeful) look at one of these mother's experience and her eventual realization of her interconnectedness with these other mothers, their children and their nations. The terrain of the drama offers a new global perspective through the eyes of a mother.

The performance *M-other* premièred in Boulder and has toured many cities in North America and Antigua, Guatemala. It was specifically written as a tool for inspiring mothers to act on behalf of the world's children; Beth took everything learned in the first five years of MAU and crafted it into an hour's worth of entertainment. It also allows mothers to *feel* their connection to the rest of the world, serving as an antidote to the numbing abstractions of daily news flashes. Finally, it challenges limiting attitudes about the mother role, encouraging inclusion of speaking out and acting up. We hope it becomes a reference point as mothers chart their own path towards increased participation.

> I think the hardest part about going back to my old life will be facing my old self that believed I was separate from you, separate from your families, your nations and your God … facing the part of me that believed you were "other." Everything has changed. Before I had asked, "Why me? Why now?" Now I ask, "If not me, who? If not now, when?"
>
> —Text from *M-other*

A MAU Vocal Empowerment Workshop is held in all locations visited by the Mother Tour, providing the tools, skills, practice and confidence needed for voicing our concerns regarding issues facing the world's children. Participants are led in exercises to experience the power of our embodied voices and using these voices to declare our most passionate concerns. Next, we imagine ways to use our voices to act on these concerns, and then rehearse these actions together—all working together to devise solutions to any obstacles that present themselves. Through the workshop, participants empower themselves and each other to use their voices to speak up on behalf of the needs of children. To date, the tour has traveled to communities across the U.S.—from Lubbock to Columbus—and internationally to countries as diverse as Canada, Panama, Malaysia, Vietnam, Guatemala and Ethiopia. Again, the intention is to share tools for expression that will strengthen mothers' ability to act on their most passionate concerns.

MAU and the Mothering Movement

Mothers Acting Up was honored to have participated in the historic 2008 National Association of Mothers' Centers Conference, *Thinking Beyond Ourselves and Beyond Today.* During the conference, Beth was a plenary speaker on "Empowering Mother Voices for Advocacy" and performed a stand up comedy piece, bringing the concept of mother activism to life. Both of us (the authors) subsequently presented "A Magnificent Revolution" during the embedded Mothering Movement session at the 2008 Toronto conference, *Mothering, Violence, Militarism, War and Social Justice*, hosted by Association for Research on Mothering (ARM) at York University in Toronto. Yes, there were stilts involved. To witness the birth of the International Mothers Network at the conference was enormously exciting, as from our perspective, the uniting of mothers is the most hopeful and powerful phenomenon of our age. It also can't be overstated how important it is for organizations and individuals to be able to share information and support, as we grow into movements able to transform our cultures on a large scale. In a mothering movement that primarily gains momentum from the women's movement, MAU stands somewhat apart because of its focus on children's issues. While many

Authors Beth Osnes and Juliana Forbes "acting up" for their first press coverage in 2002.

other groups collaborate with feminist and women empowerment networks, MAU tends to partner with organizations such as CARE, Global Action for Children and RESULTS—organizations that address issues such as poverty reduction, the environment, and human security. While all groups within the Mothering Movement work to empower mothers, Mothers Acting Up focuses specifically on empowered mothers to act on behalf of issues facing children around the world.

Challenges

When we first envisioned Mothers Acting Up, we imagined MAU would incite a frenzy of mother activism. That hasn't been quite the case. While the movement resonates with many, we haven't reached enough mothers to create a tipping point. Mother activism is clearly a hot topic right now, and MAU has undoubtedly played a role in that, but MAU hasn't *yet* found a broad enough audience. (Note key word "yet," as we're still passionately committed!) To truly ensure the health, education and safety of every child, we need to talk to millions of mothers. Perhaps our smallish audience is due to a love of creating new strategies without the discipline to promote them. Perhaps it is due to not directly identifying the challenges mothers face when they begin to step into new public roles. MAU has provided tools, unabashed enthusiasm and ways to take the plunge, but we've never explored some of the more challenging aspects of these new roles, such as: how much is enough when the need is so huge? Where are the new boundaries, if we see ourselves as protectors of *all* children? Will we need to sell our houses if we get too involved? How can we keep from becoming the "crazy poverty lady" in our hometown? Jane Barry wrote an article in *World Pulse* magazine exploring the struggles of women activists in maintaining a healthy balance in their lives. The last line is, "We have to change the culture of activism and heal ourselves, so that we can begin to heal others. When this cultural shift takes hold, our movement will become truly unstoppable."

Some of us may feel wary of getting involved in issues we're passionate about, because we wonder if there's any point of return. Will our commitment, grief, or perhaps anger, swamp us? Will our heart ever heal if we get too close to some of the realities we are peripherally aware of? For all of us who have felt this way—I'm thinking anyone who's seen a photo of a starving child or read an op-ed from Nicholas Kristof—addressing these questions is tremendously important. Together we must articulate a new leadership model that has the flexibility, responsiveness, and resourcefulness to address painful realities without losing ourselves. A leadership model where our *joy* sustains our ability to partner with those in need.

Future Goals

The future goal of Mothers Acting Up is to inspire millions upon millions of mothers to expand our mother identity to include acting on behalf of the world's children. *How* are we going to achieve this? Well, that's being dreamed up as we type, so stay tuned. And in the meantime, skip over to your computer and send a missive to us with your best strategy of how to reach a larger audience of mothers (and others.) We're listening.

Conclusion

The story of "us versus them" is obsolete. There is a new story. A story that begins with the health and security of our children. A story about finding solutions to challenges that benefit the entire human family. A story that recognizes our personal and collective impact on the world's children and outlines what it will take to support their common future. It is a story of enormous creativity, change and courage. It has never been told before. Mothers are integral to this new story; in fact it may not come to pass without our leadership. We must gather our formidable talents, ideas, money, dreams and desires and speak out; our children are waiting. As the MAU vision states, "Let us: *whisper* this to each other, *sing* it out in the streets, *yell* it from our rooftops, and *declare* it in our houses of government: *we will protect our children with our personal and political strength, wherever they live on earth*!

[1]Definition of "mother" used by MAU: *mothers and others who exercise protective care over someone smaller.*

Works Cited

Anderlini, Sanam Naraghi. *Mothers Acting Up Calendar.* Ed. Juliana Forbes. Boulder, CO: NSO Press, 2008,

Aird, Enola G. and Martha Farrell Erickson. *The Motherhood Study: Fresh Insights on Mother's Attitudes and Concerns.* New York: Institute for American Values, 2005.

Barry, Jane. "What's the Point of the Revolution if We Can't Dance." *World Pulse* 2010. Web. <http://www.worldpulse.com/magazine/articles/whats-the-point-of-the-revolution-if-we-cant-dance.html>.

"Children in Conflict and Emergencies." Web. <http://www.unicef.org/protection/index_armedconflict.html>.

Glenn, Susan. *Female Spectacle: The Theatrical Roots of Modern Feminism.* Cambridge, Massachusetts: Harvard University Press, 2000.

Global Footprint Network. Web. <www.informinc.org>.

Kozol, Jonathan. Web. <http://josephsoninstitute.org/quotes/fairness.html>.

Millennium Development Goals (MDG). Web. <www.endpoverty2015.org>.

Mothers Acting Up (MAU). Web. <www.mothersactingup.org/just-the-facts>.

National Priorities Project. Web. <http://nationalpriorities.org>.

Osnes, Beth. *M-other.* Web. <www.mothersactingup.org/mother-tour>.

Philanthropiece FoundationWeb. <www.philanthropiece.org>.

Richards, Laura E. and Maud Howe Elliott. *Julia Ward Howe.* Boston: Houghton Mifflin Company, 1925.

United Nations Convention on the Rights of the Child. Web. <www.unicef.org/crc>.UNICEF. "Fact of the Week." Web. <http://www.unicef.org/factoftheweek/index_53972.html?q=printm>.

UNICEF. "Orphans." Web. <http://www.unicef.org/media/media_45279.html>.

UNICEF "UNICEF welcomes Kiwanis partnership to fight deadly maternal and neonatal tetanus worldwide." Press Release. June 24, 2010. Web. <http://www.unicef.org/media/media_54057.html>.

U.S. Department of Defence. Web. <www.defense.gov>.

64.
Moms on the Move

BC Families Supporting People with Special Needs

ANDREA DOYLE HUGMEYER

The title of the 2010 National Women's Studies Association (NWSA) conference was "Difficult Dialogues II," and incorporated five major themes throughout the conference, one termed "outsider feminisms." The purpose of this theme was to highlight inquiries and epistemologies not regularly seen in traditional feminist practices, theories, and politics. Among topics such as fat studies and masculinity studies, disability studies was cited in the conference program as a prominent area of scholarship often marginalized within feminist discourse. Although historically the feminist movement created dialogue around issues and concerns of the disabled community and provided a much needed space to critique discrimination and inequalities associated with ableism, these issues are not always at the forefront of contemporary feminist thought, as the NWSA conference theme acknowledged. However, they are of paramount concern to mothers caring for differently-abled family members where experiencing adverse realities occurs on a regular basis, therefore illustrating how crucial the motherhood movement is to linking concerns of mothers, women, and differently-abled individuals. Responding to threats of severe budgetary cuts to government funded programs for special needs children in 2001, a group of moms (and some dads) marched the streets of Vancouver, British Columbia to vocalize the consequences of such cuts and cast awareness to the special needs community in BC. Following the strong response from BC community members during the 2001 protest, Moms on the Move (MOMS) was founded and has since been a consistent example of how women activists, particularly mothers, defend needs and resources for groups typically silenced, underserved, and relegated as "outsiders" in society.

History

Formerly called "Militant MOMS" after their vibrant protest in 2001, Moms on the Move currently operates as an information support network for BC special needs families. MOMS advocates recognized the insecurity of programs and funds available to the special needs population of BC under Premier Gordon Campbell's leadership (Moms on the Move). During the 2001 election, Premier Campbell campaigned for financial responsibility with an emphasis on cutting personal income taxes. Upon election, he successfully decreased income taxes by 25 percent causing BC to have the lowest base personal income tax in all of Canada (Ministry of Finance). While praised for upholding campaign commitments with the implementation of tax cuts, the new Premier and his liberal leaders found it necessary to make substantial reductions in social welfare programs (Foster). The proposed budget revisions would have cut over 20 percent of services for families throughout BC (Moms on the Move). With pressure from community advocacy groups, like MOMS, Premier Campbell made commitments to form a strong support system across BC serving children, youth, adults, and families with special needs, involved in at-risk situations, and/or with disabilities (Moms on the Move). Thus, the Ministry of Children and Family Development (MCFD) was created to manage, support, and evaluate the proposed program reductions. With the government committed to initiating this support system, MOMS shifted their platform and focused heavily on information sharing and support to the local BC parents in their network.

The Ministry reviewed existing social welfare programs across the province and proclaimed that assessing early childhood intervention programs for families with special needs children was a top priority. As a result, the MCFD mission was to "promote and develop the capacity of families and communities to care for and protect vulnerable children and youth, and support adults with developmental disabilities" (Foster 186). Despite its good intentions to balance the needs of the communities and streamline budgets, the MCFD was unable to meet the reduction goals set by the Treasury Board. Since 2001, the MCFD has undergone significant executive level changes and political conflicts, where both have acted as catalysts furthering program cuts (Foster). MOMS supporters have continued to advocate for their community needs and as a resource for families in the face of BC's political friction.

The Work of MOMS

MOMS members are entirely made up of BC volunteers working to "support vulnerable children, youth and adults, along with the families, caregivers and communities who support them" (Moms on the Move). MOMS operates under two co-administrators, Cyndi Gerlach and Dawn Steele, and an ad hoc advocacy committee that includes parents representing a wide range of disability interests. Gerlach and Steele manage the organization's website, actively posting bulletins in response to new legislation, op-ed pieces, and community events.

In addition to the relevant blogging authored by Gerlach and Steele, the organization's website has become a "hub" of support for the special needs community. The website (http://momsnetwork.ca/) offers viewers a substantial amount of information on current policy decisions impacting children and youth with disabilities. The MOMS website also provides an overview of BC's recently proposed budget cuts in 2009 and 2010, including an extensive overview of media coverage. Another significant portion of the website is dedicated to activism through tools like online petitions, YouTube videos, and templates of written statements to send to government officials. Links for numerous resource groups and organizations are featured on the MOMS website listed under the following categories: advocacy, autism spectrum disorder, down syndrome, children and youth with special needs, adults and youth in transition, early intervention, education, family support, and other disabilities.

The work of MOMS is not limited to their online presence, but rests in their devotion and face-to-face interaction with community members. In October of 2010, MOMS was part of a diverse group of stakeholders that organized a public forum in Vancouver to address government cutbacks to community living centers for adults with disabilities (National Union of Public and General Employees). Decreased accountability and screening criteria for living centers and foster homes were discussed as potential ramifications of cutting these funds. Additionally, the public forum discussed how this lack of attention to care providers could harmfully impact experiences of abuse and neglect among the individuals using these resources (Moms on the Move). The meeting generated proposals and calls to action agreed upon by the attendees as a plan for working together and moving forward. Among these actions, a letter of concerns and recommendations was crafted and sent to Jane Holland, Advocate for Service Quality asking to "intervene to stop the community living cuts, group home closures and forced relocations" (Moms on the Move). The attempt even garnered attention from the Health Sciences Association of BC, which recognized the unprecedented joint efforts of the community groups and strongly endorsed the concerns of the advocates (Health Sciences Association of BC). In an unfortunate response, Holland refused to address the problems outlined in the letter and referred the community groups to Community Living BC. Despite this setback, MOMS supporters are still working passionately to resist the $20 million cuts and closures by circulating an online petition directed to the Minister of Community Living BC. The petition is accessible on their website. The British Columbia Association for Community Living reported in early March 2011 that cases of abuse towards special needs youth living in foster care are surfacing (British Columbia Association for Community Living), an insight that MOMS, along with their community partners, had highlighted months earlier. Clearly, the MCFD, the children, and the community would have benefited from valuing and listening to the voices of special needs advocates.

MOMS and Maternal Activism

Feminist intersectional analyses of oppression acknowledge how ability operates in our culture similarly to other social markers like gender, race, sexual orientation, and class. Therefore, this paradigm is useful in understanding how ableism has impacted the lives of those involved in MOMS as a result of multiple oppressions.

This is particularly true for mothers who disproportionately act as primary caregivers compared to their male counterparts and their children. Historically, maternal activists have come together and advocated based on their shared experiences as mothers and their role as caretakers, especially as they confront inadequacies in social and political systems (Kinser). MOMS reflects these concepts in its origin as a group and how it continues to rally around issues to protect children and families.

Community building has been another significant aspect to the MOMS organization. The use of Internet technologies has made MOMS resources and communication easier and more accessible, including their participation on social networking sites like Facebook and Twitter that have acted as a catalyst for community organizing and activism. For many mothers, online communities have provided voice and agency while centering maternal expertise in the lives of their children and themselves (Kinser). MOMS initially responded to potential budgetary cuts that would heavily impact the lives of their children and the support they needed as mothers to raise their children successfully. The energy of initial protests sparked an ongoing commitment for MOMS to provide resources and build a community network for this underserved population.

Concluding Thoughts

At this current historical moment, it is critical to address the political and theoretical connections influencing and mobilizing groups largely consisting of mothers. Specifically for mothers, the motherhood and women's liberation movements have created a social landscape where women can make mothering choices on their own behalf and advocate for better social conditions in which to practice mothering. Both movements have worked together to empower women, enriching a platform for groups such as MOMS to carry out their mission. Feminism intersects with the concerns of MOMS supporters, providing insightful understandings of ableism as an oppressive social hierarchy that underscores the political conflicts associated with providing services to BC's differently-abled community. Furthermore, the convergence of feminism and disability studies exposes topics for social justice coalition building by addressing access to healthcare services, alternative forms of education, theories of identity and embodiment, and reproductive justice, to name a few. Successful activist groups like MOMS that are committed to informing, uniting, and educating families, government, and the public on the "importance of investing in children and youth with special needs and children at risk" (Moms on the Move) need more attention to disrupt their often perceived, but palpable, "outsider" status.

Works Cited

British Columbia Association for Community Living. "Foster Care System Failing

Youth with Special Needs." *British Columbia Association for Community Living Foundation.* 3 Mar. 2011. Web. 8 Mar. 2011.

Foster, Leslie T. "Back to the Future: Towards Community Governance." *People, Politics, and Child Welfare in British Columbia.* Ed. Leslie T. Foster and Brian Wharf. Vancouver, BC: University of British Columbia Press, 2007. 184-216.

Health Sciences Association for BC. "HSA Endorses Letter From Community Living Advocates." *Health Sciences Association for BC: The Union Delivering Modern Health care.* 20 Oct. 2010. Web. 6 Mar. 2011.

Kinser, Amber E. *Motherhood and Feminism.* Berkley, CA: Seal Press, 2010. Print.

Ministry of Finance. "Tax Cut Fact Sheet." *Economic Fiscal Update.* 30 July 2001. Web. 6 Mar. 2011.

Moms on the Move. *Moms on the Move: BC Families Supporting People with Special Needs.* 2011. Web. 3 Mar. 2011

National Union of Public and General Employees. "Families, Workers, Service Providers And Advocates Work Together to Address BC Community Living Crisis." *National Union of Public and General Employees.* 28 Oct. 2010. Web. 6 Mar 2011.

65.
Shifting the Paradigm

International Feminists for a Gift Economy

GENEVIEVE VAUGHAN

INTERNATIONAL FEMINISTS FOR A GIFT ECONOMY (IFGE) is a loose-knit network of activist and academic women, a virtual think-tank, begun in 2001 and based on an alternative paradigm at the heart of which is the idea of a maternal gift economy, which already exists before, beyond, and within the economy of Patriarchal Capitalism. We are devoted to thinking through this alternative paradigm, spreading the idea and using it as a basis for radical social change.

History

I have been working on the idea of a gift economy for several decades. In 1997 my first book *For-Giving, a Feminist Criticism of Exchange* was published. In 2001 I was invited to Norway to the first organizing meeting for the International Feminist University (IFUN). A number of the other women attending the meeting were interested in the gift paradigm and suggested we form a network. We invited other women and met again that fall at Stonehaven Ranch, a retreat center in Texas, which I operated according to gift economy principles. We were joined by other women who had been in contact with this paradigm over the years, many of whom had worked in or been influenced by the Texas-based all-woman activist Foundation for a Compassionate Society (1988-2005) which I had founded. A group of women from the network gave presentations at the World Social Forum in Porto Alegre, Brazil, in January 2002. Since then we have held several conferences and have travelled together (and separately) to many others. The membership of IFGE is comprised of some 100 women from about 15 different countries, many of whom communicate relatively regularly online. There are no criteria for joining or for leaving the group. There are no dues.

We do not have an explicit mandate but we are of a common mind and are dedicated to social change through maternal values and their implementation in society at large. We believe that there is a radically different paradigm based on mothering, upon which a better economy can be built. We are not assimilationists but rather we propose an alternative to patriarchal capitalism "from the inside and from the outside." That is, we believe that both the mothering values of the people inside patriarchy, and the gift-based values of Indigenous peoples have a deep common potential for social change. These also coincide with the values of people in movements everywhere who are trying to give the gift of peace and environmental healing.

In 2004 an anthology of our articles on the gift economy was published as a special issue of the Italian journal *Athanor* called *Il Dono/ the Gift: A Feminist Perspective*. In the same year we held a conference in Las Vegas, Nevada where international Indigenous and non-Indigenous women, many of whom were part of the network, spoke about the gift economy. The conference was titled "A Radically Different Worldview is Possible: the Gift Economy Inside and Outside of Patriarchal Capitalism." Among the Indigenous women speakers was Jeanette Armstrong of the Syilx people of the Okanagan area of British Colombia, who gave us a sense of a really different kind of social structure where interdependence with all life is continually acknowledged and gifting and sharing are the norm. In this extremely egalitarian society, the chief does not lead or tell people what to do but is one who has "an immense ability to listen … to put it all together and to say it back to the people." Native Hawaiian Attorney Mililani Trask discussed the gift economy as reciprocity according to the "original instructions" that humankind's role is to be "the guardians of creation." Peruvian Ana Isla showed how debt-for-nature swaps are actually new enclosures of the commons. Susan Petrilli from Italy and Australia talked about the gift in the works of Lady Victoria Welby (1837-1912), the little known "mother" of semiotics who proposed the idea of "mother sense" in the construction of the symbolic order. Yvette Abrahams discussed the Khoekhoe of South Africa saying, "if I have enough and you have enough, our gifts take on a social symbolism." Elisabet Sahtouris talked about the biology of cooperation and suggested that humans will evolve to do "business as it is done in the rainforest." Tracy Gary discussed the contemporary women's funding movement. Claudia von Werlhof from Germany did a deep analysis of Patriarchy. Peggy Antrobus, from Barbados, talked about gifting circles in the Carribean and in the diaspora. Vicki Noble discussed "The Gift of Her Body." Unfortunately I cannot mention all the amazing presentations that were given and the many thoughtful discussions that were held in the motel across the street but can refer you to the book on the conference *Women and the Gift Economy, A Radically Different Worldview is Possible* (Inanna 2007).

In 2003 I went to a conference on Modern Matriarchal Studies in Luxembourg, organized by German philosopher Heide Goettner-Abendroth. There I realized that Matriarchal Studies are a sister discipline for Gift Economy Studies. I invited Heide to hold a conference in Texas and we organized "Societies of Peace" in 2005 as the last event of the Foundation for a Compassionate Society. Since that time we have collaborated on a number of initiatives and many of the Gift Economy network members also belong to the Matriarchal Studies network and vice versa. A book of articles from the two Matriarchal Studies conferences, *Societies of Peace: Matriarchies Past, Present and Future*, was published by Inanna Publications in 2009.

Genevieve Vaughan speaking on the radio during the World Social Forum in Mali in 2006, being filmed by her daughter,Emma Rossi-Landi.

Philosophy, Purpose and Mission

This idea of the maternal gift economy requires some explanation, which I will attempt to give before talking a bit more about the network. I do not mean to say that everyone in the network would agree on everything I say here, but that many of them agree with much of it.

Our idea of mothering is not based in sentimentality or essentialism. Instead it takes the point of view that mothering is economic. Mothering is a mode of distribution of goods and services to needs. It is free—and it has to be free at least in early childhood, because young children cannot give back an equivalent in exchange for what they receive. This view makes it necessary to broaden the concept of "economy" to cover not only market exchange but free provisioning, rather than considering what is free as "aneconomic." In fact the market economy takes from and is nurtured by the free provisioning gift economy. Housework, which would add some 40 percent to the U.S. GNP (even more in some other countries) if it were calculated in monetary terms (Waring), is a huge gift that women are giving to the market economy. Profit itself is made of an extra margin of free gifts over and above expenses. There are innumerable free gifts that are flowing to the market from women, men and nature, from the poor to the rich and from the Global South to the Global North. Free gifts are taken by the few from the many and accumulate at the "top," thus creating a generalized situation of scarcity "below," which allows those at the top to gain and maintain control.

If too much abundance accumulates, it does not "trickle down" but is wasted on wars and armaments, re-enforcing the control of the many by the few. Scarcity created in this way makes provisioning-gift-giving-mothering difficult and thus both impedes gift giving and discredits it as a model.

From this point of view mothering small children is the practice of an economy that is a radical alternative to the market economy.

The idea of the gift economy has been discussed in academia for many years: from Marcel Mauss and Bronislaw Malinowsky in the 1920s to Lewis Hyde, Jacques Godbout, Alain Caille, Jacques Derrida, Pierre Bourdieu, Jean-Luc Marion and many others in the last 30 years. It has inspired a number of the contemporary movements that want to create an alternative to Capitalism. The emphasis of these thinkers on symbolic gift *exchange*, on giving back, debt and obligation, as well as the emphasis on reputation as the pay-off of gift giving, has hidden the connections of gift giving with mothering. In contrast the French feminists Julia Kristeva, Luce Irigaray, and especially Héléne Cixous (Still) have addressed the maternal gift economy, though more in terms of a libidinal economy than as a key for systemic social change.

In fact the logic and the psychology of the economy of giving directly to satisfy needs contradict the logic and psychology of the market economy. Positive human relations of mutuality and community are created by unilateral giving before and beyond the constraints of debt and obligation. The logic of exchange upon which the market is based, requires the return of goods or services of an equivalent value, and is therefore reflexive and ego oriented. Exchange concentrates on satisfying the needs of the (ex)giver. The logic of gift-giving is transitive and other oriented and it concentrates on satisfying the needs of the receiver. Unilateral giving gives value to the receiver by implication while exchange gives value to the (ex)giver by implication.

Mothers have to adapt to their young children and give to them unilaterally even when the mothers are thoroughly immersed in a society based on market exchange. This adaptation is made necessary by the biology of the children, not by the biology of the mothers. In fact, although children do "protoconversational" turntaking (Trevarthen) with their mothers and respond to them, they do not understand economic exchange until they are four or five years old. The term "exchange" is often used loosely to cover turn-taking but this obscures the distinction I am trying to make. Economic exchange is *do ut des*, which in Latin means "I give so that you may give."

Many so-called "pre"-capitalist Indigenous economies did not have markets as such. Their gift economies are elaborations of the maternal provisioning gift economy, not of the market. A number of Indigenous women who are part of our network speak to the existence of past and present gift economies. For example, Barbara Mann has written extensively on the Iroquois gift economy as lead by the women Gantowisas. Bernedette Muthien from South Africa tells us about the economy of the Khoisan, where nothing is done that would damage someone else. Rauna Kuokkanen from Samiland in Northern Europe has written about the

Heide Goettner-Abendroth and Genevieve Vaughan, Second World Congress on Matriarchal Studies, San Marcos, Texas, 2005.

Indigenous episteme that includes giving to and receiving from Nature. Shanshan Du writes about the Lahu people in China who have a society based on gender unity, and an economy of generalized reciprocity. Peggy Reeves Sanday has written extensively about the Minangkabau of Sumatra and their spiritual gift practices and Kaarina Kailo has written about the Nordic Indigenous gift imaginary.

It is possible to avoid the detour of the market and instead base all provisioning on the principles of the maternal economy. We believe that this is the direction in which our society should move to solve the terrible problems that have been created by Patriarchal Capitalism. In fact Patriarchy and Capitalism have merged because they share the values of competition and domination. While mothers can and do succeed in this system in spite of many challenges, the system itself is the problem and needs to be radically changed.

Exchange is self-reflecting and self-asserting, and so foregrounds itself while unilateral gift giving concentrates on the other and therefore the giver may remain unnoticed. This invisibility of gift giving unfortunately confirms and contributes to the over visibility of ego oriented exchange. (This is one of the reasons why motherhood movements are so important). In the mother-child processes of giving and receiving, the bodies of the members of the community are made, and their minds as well, in that their experiences are formed by these interactions. I think this free maternal transfer of need-satisfying goods and services, can also be seen as communication, a material communication, which creates bodies as well as human relations and minds and gives value as well as material goods. I have also written about language as deriving from this material gift communication

IFGE strategy meeting, Las Vegas, 2004.

(Vaughan 1997). The human species is not just *homo sapiens*, the knowing being. We are *homo donans*, the giving being, because we have to participate in giving and receiving even before we can know.

The division between the domestic sphere and the economic and political spheres can be cancelled or bridged by recognizing the maternal gift economy as an alternative economy, which already exists and which actually gives to or subsidizes the economy based on exchange. What is necessary is the liberation of the maternal economy *from* the economy based on exchange, and the gradual elimination and discrediting of the market rather than the assimilation of gift givers *into* the market. That is why many of us in the network do not believe in wages for housework or micro credit. We need to eliminate the market altogether and put in its place a generalized maternal gift economy. Even thinking about this possibility and working towards it begins to make cracks in the monolith by validating the values of gift giving over the values of exchange. This is our mission.

Activities

One of our members, Angela Dolmetsch has started an eco-village based on maternal principles in Kali, Colombia. Named Nashira, the community will house some 250 families when complete.

In Oulu, Finland, former women studies professor and now city councilor Kaarina Kailo has run for the European Parliament on a platform that includes the gift economy, opposing the neo liberal policies that have been encroaching so profoundly on the welfare state. Frieda Werden has produced at low cost a syndicated radio program of women's voices and women's news for 20 years. She speaks of the gift of community radio. Wahu Kaara of Kenya makes the connection between the gift economy as we understand it and what she calls the "life economy" of Kenyan women, which allows them to survive and thrive in spite of enormous difficulties. A project of the Foundation for a Compassionate Society, the temple of the Goddess Sekhmet in the Nevada desert near the nuclear test site functions completely on the gift economy, offering rituals in accord with the calendar of the moon and the wheel of the year as well as a space of solidarity for protestors against nuclear testing. In 1992 the land where the temple is located was given (back) as a gift to the Western Shoshone, to whom it ancestrally belonged.

Over the years the Foundation practiced the gift economy by offering free or low cost space for workshops and seminars at Stonehaven Ranch, the Grassroots Peace Organizations Building and the Austin Women's Peace House as well as many other projects informed by gift economy principles (see also the website <www.gift-economy.com>).

Our members try to integrate the idea of the gift economy in their lives, their teaching, writing and activism. We have given workshops as individuals or as a group (though not always the same people) at five of the international World Social Forums, two in Porto Alegre, Brazil, in Mumbai, India, in Bamako, Mali and in Nairobi, Kenya. We have also spoken at the Women's Worlds conferences in Norway, Uganda, South Korea and Spain and have given presentations in Finland, Italy, Ireland, Austria, Germany, Croatia, Holland and Canada, and among others in the U.S., at the Dallas Women's Peace Conference in Texas, and at the American Association for Anthropology in Washington, DC. Our most recent conference was held in 2009 in cooperation with the Modern Matriarchal Studies movement and hosted by the Association for Research on Mothering at York University in Toronto. We had the fortunate title *A (M)otherworld is Possible*, invented by Andrea O'Reilly and particularly appropriate for us, since we have spoken at so many of the World Social Forums, whose motto is "Another World is Possible." With some 30 international speakers we delved into many issues dealing with gift giving and matriarchal values. One of the benefits of holding conferences and attending them is that the women who participate get to hang out with each other, make friends and discuss all the issues that arise in the presentations. We have all stayed at the same hotels in most of these events which has made our time together even more fruitful and fun and has consolidated our networks.

Challenges

Our network activity is mostly writing and speaking about the gift economy to people who have not heard about it. Apart from our physical distance from each other, and the major efforts we must make to meet, which obviously hinder our collaboration on a daily basis, most of our challenges are theoretical. That is, they are part of the reason we exist; they depend upon a worldview that does not yet envision the gift paradigm.

Interest in the gift economy has grown exponentially in the last ten years. This is probably due to two factors, first the new context of shareable abundance, consist-

International Peace Association meeting, Calgary, 2002.

ing of information-products readily available on the Internet to a large number of people. Second, there has been a drastic change in the zeitgeist, deriving most recently from the collapse of Patriarchal Capitalism and the rescue of the banks with the money of the already heavily burdened public.

While we in the network propose a feminist maternalist approach to an alternative economy, there are many initiatives where the maternal aspect is completely unrecognized, even when there are women (and mothers) taking the initiatives. We believe that without the recognition of mothering as the basis of the gift economy these movements will not reach their potential for radical social change and will once again exclude mothers, and women along with them, thus providing new avenues for commercialization and patriarchal hegemony. It is as if each kind of initiative has a piece of the puzzle but the pieces are not being put together. The gift economy initiatives lack the consciousness of the importance of mothering. The mothering initiatives don't see that they hold a key to the gift economy, and the indigenous people as well often do not realize that the gift economy which they practice is a possible positive maternal alternative to the Patriarchal Capitalist system.

I do not think that Europeans should copy or appropriate the Indigenous ways, but that we should all start over again from the gift giving we practice as mothers and mothered children. In this way we could create a new maternal economy using Indigenous economies as models of the possible. We should realize that those economies were and are not "pre"-capitalist in the sense that Capitalism was more "advanced," but that they offer possible ways of organizing life which are more functional for human happiness. In fact the Europeans came to the Americas fresh from the Inquisition in which millions of women had been tortured and killed, ready to spread their dysfunctional Patriarchal economy and culture by brutal force. They were unable to recognize the positive alternative that Indigenous societies presented to their own developing capitalist economy so they committed genocide against them. Similar policies have been carried out in imperialism and colonialism, which have plundered societies, which were more maternal, creating flows of gifts away from local needs and towards the plunderer's markets. They have also enslaved people from these countries, taking all of their gifts, even their bodies and exploiting their free labor for the "growth" of capitalism. Any initiative for a maternal gift economy has to recognize the defects of the market system in order not to risk recreating situations of this kind. Women and mothers have been slaves and if not actual slaves have been and sometimes still are the property of their husbands. Perhaps this experience of their sisters and predecessors is one of the factors that make women now more careful and more appropriate as leaders of a movement for a maternal gift economy.

Otherwise perhaps we should learn from the Minankabau, the matriarchal people of Sumatra quoted by Peggy Reeves Sanday, who say that for a man to be a good leader "he must be like a good mother."

Recently a number of gift-giving initiatives have sprung up without any inkling that they have anything to do with mothering. Here is a list of some examples and there are many more:

- •Wikipedia
- •Free software, Copyleft (<www.gnu.org>)
- •Free cycling (<www.freecycle.org>)
- •Peer-to-Peer social networking (cooperative individualism modeled on and using the internet) (<www.p2pfoundation.net>)
- •Creative Commons license (<www.creativecommons.org>)
- •Blood banks and organ donation
- •Community gardens
- •Community pay-it-forward restaurants (<www.karmakitchen.org>)
- •Hitchhiking
- •Ride sharing
- •Bicycle sharing
- •Couch surfing (<www.couchsurfing.com>)
- •Alcoholics Anonymous
- •Burning Man Gatherings (<www.burningman.com>)
- •Rainbow Gatherings (<www.welcomehome.org/rainbow/index.html>)
- •Some alternative currencies and time banks, for example (<www.timebanks.org>)
- •Community solidarity work
- •Volunteerism and much non-profit work
- •Remittances of immigrants in the North to their home countries in the South
- •There is an interesting initiative called Charity Focus which has garnered quite a following. I subscribe to the newsletter myself (<www.

charityfocus.org>)
•Progressive philanthropy (<www.thresholdfoundation.org> and <www.womendonors.org>)
•In addition there has been a great deal of research done on altruism and generosity recently. One interesting intiative among many is Science of Generosity (<www.generosityresearch@nd.edu>)
•Another is The Center for Building a Culture of Empathy (<www.progressivespirit.com/empathy>)
•A conference on empathy at the University of Chicago in 2009 (<http://ccsn.uchicago.edu/empathy>).

I believe that problem-solving is a kind of gift-giving, the satisfaction of a need. This lets me include as gifts all the innumerable initiatives for social change that people as *homo donans* do to solve the problems created by the Patriarchal Capitalist system.

Future Goals

Our network works closely with the Matriarchal Studies network in Europe (<www.Hagia.de>) The gift economy, like matriarchy, applies maternal values in the organization of the lives of both women and men. It is the generalization of the logic of mothering to the wider social sphere that permits gifts to circulate within a community without an immediate return, satisfying needs and creating and maintaining the bonds that form the community itself. If the society does not honor women and motherhood, the gift economy becomes difficult to practice, perhaps a sort of unrealistic add-on to a supposedly more basic principle of exchange. It is our goal to disabuse activists and academics of this misinterpretation of gift giving and to help to spread matriarchal thinking and principles. We will continue to elaborate these while critiquing patriarchy and capitalism from this feminist maternalist point of view.

Recent gift economy projects which are detached from their social roots in the maternal practice claim the gift economy as men's invention, erasing its connection to mothering and denying the generalization of mothering logic and the validation of the mothering practice. All of this is an obstacle to the recognition and spread of the mothering economy as are patriarchal religious institutions, which have often claimed gift giving as their special territory, making misogynist rules and extolling sacrifice as good for the soul. Patriarchal governments transform giving into domination by giving aid with strings attached to other countries, creating economic servitude and placing the receiver countries in a "feminized" position.

In our Western society, mothering is discredited and often essentialistically identified with women-only. Fathering is distinguished from mothering and said to be its complement. In fact the idea of complementary male and female "energies" is often embraced, without recognizing the continuity of what we call "male energy" with the social construct of institutional patriarchy. I believe humanity is maternal—we are all mothered children—patriarchal dominant "male energy" is a construct that should be eliminated. "Female energy" should not try to complement or be in equilibrium with it. Being in equilibrium with the values of domination only enables them, discredits *homo donans* and distorts the integrity of the enabler.

There are also many challenges that are constituted by roadblocks in communication with our sisters. One of these is the knee jerk reaction against essentialism that is now commonplace in the feminist movement. What we are proposing is very much in line with the Motherhood Movements in general, a commonality among mothers based on their jobs of caring for small children and a commonality of humans based on the necessary experience of having been mothered. This mother-child interaction is the first and basic experience for everyone, whether the mothering is performed by women, men, siblings, or whole villages. In a process I call "masculation," males in the West are socialized in opposition to the economy of mothering as well as to the gender identity of the mother. The basic human economy is the gift economy; the market economy is an extrapolation and an aberration of the gift based on masculation. Indigenous economies, which avoided this detour, continue even now to practice gift economies in continuity with the maternal care of childhood. We need to open our minds to this possibility.

Another obstacle to the spread of the idea of the gift economy is the cynicism typical of patriarchal academics who are so caught in the ideology of exchange that they cannot believe that unilateral gift giving exists. For most of the mothers I know, the idea that they do unilateral gift giving seems quite normal. In fact one might say that Jacques Derrida's point is proved. Derrida holds that unilateral givers cannot be recognized because even recognition is a kind of counter gift. Well, we can ironically say that mothers are seldom recognized, so yes, indeed, they are doing unilateral giving. But the point is not to compete to say who is giving the purest gift. That is really irrelevant. The point is that mothers create a need-satisfying environment for their children, who as they grow up can do the same socially if they are not forced into a gift exploiting social system. Mothered children can also project the mother onto the environment and be grateful for its gifts rather than exploiting them.

To some, the gift economy appears utopian. In fact it may be hard to believe in a nurturing economy and a culture based on mothering values. Yet the society we live in is clearly dysfunctional. When boys give up their identification with their mothers they often take up hitting as a replacement for giving. Hitting is similar to giving in that it touches the other person and establishes a relationship, though one of dominance instead of mutuality and support. The false masculated gender identity embraces this substitute for giving, and even whole nations do the same, behaving according to patriarchal values of violence, competition and power over. It is necessary to stand as mothers in solidarity with men who are choosing non violent non patriarchal ways and to have the courage to teach our children of both genders the ways of *homo donans* rather than just *homo sapiens.*

Our utopia is waiting within us.

Sometimes women say, "We are already giving as much as we can. Aren't you telling us we should give even more?" We are not saying that, but we are saying that free giving should be valued. The reason giving is so difficult is that the system itself is creating the scarcity in which mothers have to live. The gift economy works best in a situation of abundance. Scarcity makes gift giving impractical and self-sacrificial. The gigantic social mechanism of the Patriarchal Capitalistic system itself creates the scarcity that is necessary to maintain control and keep the gift economy in difficulty. Thus it is not the maternal values we must criticize for making us self-sacrifice but the artificially created context of scarcity. Mothers do not choose the role of victim. It is forced on us by this context. It is only by changing the system that mothers can find the abundance necessary to do their jobs without sacrifice.

The Importance of IFGE for Motherhood Movements and Vice Versa

We are a virtual think tank that is trying to politicize and generalize values coming from mothering. Our organization can therefore be a resource for the Motherhood Movements. Similarly the Motherhood Movements, giving a voice and visibility to the great variety of mothers' concerns locally and globally, can contribute to the issues, information, and ideas that move us. We can stand in solidarity with each other. It is clear to many of us that Patriarchal Capitalism/Capitalist Patriarchy is not only unjust but a failure. What we need is therefore some kind of radically different system, one we can transition to without violence. As mothered children we have the gift economy already within us. As mothers we have to practice it with our children. Mothering gift-giving is the great undiscovered source for peace.

Conclusion

It is exciting to me to see how much the collective mindset has changed over the last decades, and how many people are now talking about and trying to practice the gift economy (even if they still do not acknowledge mothering). Our small movement is a strategic bridging among movements, an attempt to open a new direction towards change. We have learned a lot about different realities from each other, from the people we talk to and the places we have been. In Nairobi members of our audience said "we always used to do that at home when we were growing up." In Bamako we met a group of women who practiced the Dama, a traditional gift economy, though they did not know it had a name in the "West." A woman we met there, poet and activist Coumba Tourè from Senegal told us, "In the Bambara language spoken in Mali, the word for 'Hello' is the word for 'Thank you.' People address each other by thanking them for the gift of how they have lived their lives." In an interview she said "Dama is about giving, passing the gift on, moving it forward…. In all the places I have been in West Africa I have seen this gift economy at work" (Bell). We in the network are trying to pass the gift on, and the gift of the gift as well.

I will close with a comment by Kaarina Kailo. In a letter to me she writes,

> The spirit of the Gift is infectious, and should be the attitude that we bring to all political action.... Without it in politics, we risk becoming ego-oriented decision-makers that exchange services to advance our careers. With the Gift in our souls, we cannot be bought and will stand firm for the cause of building a worldview of solidarity and political practices that ensure abundance and the satisfaction of the needs of all. With the Gift, we can redistribute our responsibilities and entitlements in a more just and sustainable way.

Works Cited

Bell, Beverly. Interview with Coumba Tourè in *Gift Culture.* 2008. Web. <http://www.swaraj.org/shikshantar>.

Derrida, Jacques. *Given Time. 1. Counterfeit Money.* Trans. Peggy Kamuf. Chicago: University of Chicago Press, 1992.

Du, Shanshan. *Chopsticks Only Work in Pairs: Gender Unity and Gender Equality Among the Lahu of Southwest China.* New York: Columbia University Press, 2002.

Goettner-Abendroth, Heide, ed. *Societies of Peace, Matriarchies Past, Present and Future.* Toronto: Inanna Publications, 2009.

Kailo, Kaarina, ed. *Wo/men and Bears: The Gifts of Nature, Culture and Gender Revisited.* Toronto: Inanna Publications, 2008.

Kuokkanen, Rauna. *Reshaping the University: Responsibility, Indigenous Epistemes and the Logic of the Gift.* Vancouver: University of British Columbia Press, 2007.

Malinoswsky, Bronislaw. *Argonauts of the Western Pacific.* London: Routledge, 1922.

Mann, Barbara Alice. *Iroquois Women: The Gantowisas.* New York: Peter Lang, 2000.

Mauss, Marcel. *The Gift: The Form and Reason for Exchange in Archaic Societies.* 1923-24. London: Routledge, 1990.

Sanday, Peggy Reeves. *Women at the Center: Life in a Modern Matriarchy.* Ithaca: Cornell University Press, 2002.

Still, Judith. *Feminine Economies: Thinking Against the Market in the Enlightenment and the Late Twentieth Centuries.* Manchester: Manchester University Press, 1997.

Tourè, Coumba. 2008 (2005) Interview with Beverly Bell in *Gift Culture* http://www.swaraj.org/shikshantar/

Trevarthen, C. "Helping Synrhythmia: Infant Intersubjectivity and Companionship From Birth." *Improving the Mental Health of Parents and Their Infants: An International Perspective (Ante and Post Natal Support).* Dundee: University

of Dundee, 2005.
Vaughan, Genevieve. *For-Giving, a Feminist Criticism of Exchange*. Austin, Plain View/Anomaly Press, 1997.
Vaughan, Genevieve, ed. *Women and the Gift Economy: A Radically Different Worldview is Possible*. Toronto: Inanna Publications, 2007.
Waring, Marilyn, *If Women Counted: A New Feminist Economics*. San Francisco: Harper and Row, 1988.

66. Feminist.com

AMY RICHARDS

IN THE EARLY NINETIES A journalist best known at the time for covering celebrities and their causes, was enterprising and internet savvy enough to register the domain name feminist.com. She had little connections in the feminist world, but much interest in creating a space for feminism on what was then a burgeoning new expression and outlet for discourse, resources and thought—with a bit of consumerism. Because I had co-created an organization for young feminist activists (The Third Wave Foundation), this woman, Marianne Schnall, reached out to me for guidance on how to make connections in the feminist world and how to solidify feminist.com at the forefront of virtual feminism. I was naïve about the prospect of the internet but willing to share the names of organizations I considered to be the leaders of the feminist cause. I also shared strategies on how to position feminist issues in ways that made the site relevant to both the converted and the yet to be initiated. Before long there came a fully functioning site hosting some of the household names in feminism—Girls, Inc., Ms. Foundation for Women, National Committee on Pay Equity, VDay, Equality Now—and much traffic was being generated to the site. Initially many people came to feminist.com less because of the site's reputation and more because the site covered so many issues that it was easily searchable. Admittedly some of our earliest visitors were hostile people who, as in real time, were clearly threatened by feminism and fought back by trying to claim it as dead or irrelevant.

Mandate

From the organization's founding until now, feminist.com has been at the nucleus of contemporary feminism. A network for organizations needing a place to broadcast their messages, a place where concerned and compassionate individuals can come to learn more and to have their issues and concerns taken seriously, and a place to forge alliances across national boundaries, issues and demographics. The site is a one-stop shopping for those wanting a greater connection to feminism. Most of the connections happen simply by accessing the site and looking around. The site also offers a personal touch because the site's founder remains very person-

Amy and Webber

ally involved in overseeing the site, because there are many first person columns posted and because I run "Ask Amy"—an advice column where I field questions ranging from the absurd to the tragic. This personal touch makes all the difference in the vast internet, which otherwise seems devoid of human contact and personalized attention. Visitors to feminist.com benefit by having someone thoughtfully listen to their concerns and actually offer a response (so many people report that we were the only ones to respond); the site benefits by gleaning a better understanding of who visits the site and for what purpose. This access ensures that we can speak with more authority about who is interested in feminism and what issues should be prioritized not only on our site, but the movement at large.

The work that feminist.com does around mothering falls into three main categories: linking mothers to resources, providing a more personal interaction for mothers with questions or concerns, and essays. There are countless resources listed and linked on feminist.com. MomsRising is perhaps the most encompassing organization listed and the one feminist.com relies on to provide action alerts to our members and visitors. From MomsRising, members can learn about legislative updates and also how to take local actions in their communities, inspired by what others have done locally. MomsRising isn't just about aggregating members but creating a sense of community among mothers and those caring about motherhood issues. Feminist.com also relies on the following organizations to keep us updated:

•American Association for Marriage and Family Therapy
•American Medical Association Program on Child and Adolescent Health

- •Child Welfare League of America
- •Children's Defense Fund
- •Civil Survival: Your Rights in Divorce & Child Custody
- •Families USA
- •Family Center for Girls and Boys
- •Family.com
- •Girls Incorporated
- •Girltech
- •I Am Your Child
- •It's A Living! Career News for Girls
- •Kidshealth
- •Mining Company Guide to Daycare
- •National Center for Policy Research for Women and Families
- •National Parent Information Network
- •National Partnership for Women & Families
- •Parentsoup
- •Parentsplace
- •Parents Helping Parents
- •Parenting.com
- •Positive Parenting
- •Pregnancy and Infant Loss Center
- •Zero to Three.

There are also compassionate individuals, such as Rachel Simmons, Rosalind Wiseman, Carol Gilligan, Miriam Peskowitz and many others to provide an expert opinion on the state of girls.

The "Ask Amy" feature of feminist.com provides a unique, personal experience for mothers with questions about every topic from single motherhood and adoption (<http://www.feminist.com/askamy/girls/0707_girls07.html>) to work rights for pregnant women (<http://www.feminist.com/askamy/work/202_wk1.html>). This outlet has often been the forum for an explicit discussion of feminism and motherhood, and how the two might overlap or intersect (<http://www.feminist.com/askamy/repro/0309_rr4.html>, http://www.feminist.com/askamy/media/ 07 07_media03.html>).

Beyond "Amy's" personalized interaction with visitors, there are a variety of essays featured on the site that underscore the diversity of backgrounds and interests represented by its readership. There are essays that address the experience of mothering intertwined with other issues women face, such as maintaining professional aspirations (<http://www.feminist.com/activism/momsrising33.html> and <http://www.feminist.com/resources/artspeech/genwom/optingin.html>); politics (<http://www.feminist.com/activism/momsrising16.html>, <http://www.feminist.com/activism/momsrising16.html> and <http://www.feminist.com/activism/momsrising15.html>); and aging (<http://www.feminist.com/resources/artspeech/genwom/hotflashes.html>, <http://www.feminist.com/resources/artspeech/gen-

wom/gloriaspeech.html> and <http://www.feminist.com/resources/artspeech/genwom/onbecoming.html>).

There are also essays that highlight the experiences of mothers as a group (<http://www.feminist.com/activism/momsrising9.html>, <http://www.feminist.com/resources/artspeech/family/motherhood.html>, <http://www.feminist.com/resources/artspeech/insp/urgentmessage.html>) even though there isn't one singular way of mothering.

As exemplified by the above list, feminist.com attracts a huge audience, not exclusively mothers, thus opening up issues of motherhood beyond its natural audience. There are university students who write looking for help with a paper, high school girls who feel alone, ugly and isolated, older women who are angry that they never went public with incest charges against a family member, men wondering what their place in feminism is, among many others. Certainly there are plenty of mothers who reach out, often looking for ways to protect their children (from an abusive relative or from harassment at school), or ways to preserve themselves. The issues addressed by all visitors are both deeply personal and deeply political; while one person's rage starts with a personal injustice, such as being paid unfairly in their job, through feminist.com they often realize that there were political motivations behind the assault—a very deliberate attempt to keep some communities and demographics marginalized. What starts as one person expressing a concern, quickly translates into the realization that there are others who are like them—feminist.com provides that connection to both the shared personal stories and to the organizations coalescing them. All told, there is no way to stereotype the visitors to feminist.com. Their most shared asset is their articulation of an injustice, something that is unsettling to them and thus needs more attention. Luckily feminist.com has the resources to play the role of matchmaker. For every young woman who was raped and is tired of feeling penalized for what happened to her, there are concerned organizations that are committed to the same, thus immediately helping to remove the sense of isolation that so many people feel—and that so many people are meant to feel in a deliberate attempt to keep them marginalized.

Challenges

In the site's more than 15 years of existence, sadly there has been little evolution in the issues. In other words, women are still being discriminated against and while there might be more awareness on some women's plight, such as those young girls being raped in the Congo, there are also assumptions that because of certain gains that women have made at the top (*à la* Hillary Clinton running for president) all women are doing better, which simply isn't true. Some women being able to access positions traditionally reserved for men, is very different from all women being given a fair chance.

Though the general status of women has improved only slightly, certain issues have grown from something that only a handful of groups prioritized to being something the world has focused on, such is the case with the Taliban's restrictions on women and girls in Afghanistan. Other issues are still assumed to be too obscure for the masses to care about—such as rampant incest or divorce laws often being heavily weighted against wives. But what has remained true is that there are those who care deeply about issues even if they aren't always popular—and feminist.com has been able to amass those individuals and link them with the issues that need attention.

While some issues are well-represented, such as reproductive justice and anti-violence work, other issues remain starved for resources and legitimacy, such as better divorce laws or those helping women to win custody of their children or sexual harassment that is gross and offensive, but might not fit the narrow definition offered under the law. The organizations that do exist prioritizing these issues are often too depleted to be able to help thoroughly and especially to help in a way that is unique to a specific individual's needs. It's this grey area—where the laws are too rigid to fit a person's reality—that seem to attract the most attention on feminist.com. Because certain laws are in place, there is the faith that the injustice won't happen, but upon further inspection the law only covers a fraction of cases and this doesn't mean that injustices aren't happening, but that laws aren't malleable enough to adequately represent the number of infractions happening. There is a need to expand the laws so that individual shouldn't have to feel doubly wronged merely because their circumstances can't fit the rigid and narrow boundaries of the existing laws.

Activities

Through all of its years in existence, feminist.com has been able to make selective partnerships and through those relationships leverage even greater awareness for a cause. Feminist.com's contributions to these campaigns center mostly on our vast links, our loyal followers and our trusted brand. For instance, in the late nineties feminist.com was central to the creation of V-Day, the anti-violence awareness campaign made all the more successful because of its ties to Eve Ensler's award winning play, *The Vagina Monologues*. Through this alliance, feminist.com became a central source for resources to help eliminate all violences against women. As an outgrowth of this work, feminist.com then forged relationships with men working to end violences against women, which lead to larger conversations about men's role within feminism. More recently, feminist.com launched Our Inner Lives: Faith, Spirit and Action, a part of the site focused on spirituality, and it came to fruition as a natural outgrowth of conversations we had been having about the importance of linking spirit and action or inner and outer actions.

Context

Though feminist.com doesn't have specific branding for motherhood issues, mothers are central to both the leadership of the organization as well as issues that have been prioritized throughout the site. And many of our visitors are mothers—which they either explicitly state in their question or reveal in the details of their concerns. For instance, in all of the questions we receive about job discrimination, the majority come from women who have been discriminated against in their professions, most often because they are mothers and assumed to not be up to the task. Sadly, when we have worked closely with lawyers and advocacy groups to help with a specific case, they all admit that pregnancy or motherhood discrimination is rampant and there are too few protections. Even the most well meaning advocacy organizations have a hard time gaining traction on these issues.

Relationship to Larger Motherhood Movement

When it comes to the plethora of requests we receive to help women who are going through an unfair divorce, above all else the mothers are trying to protect their children. Of course they want fairness for themselves, but more so they don't want to see their children unnecessarily suffer. Rape and incest questions often come from an adult who experienced something in their childhood that they want to try to protect their children from. There are also numerous questions that come from parents who are trying to ensure that their daughters can play competitive sports without ridicule or that their sons treat women with respect, something they might not be witnessing at home. Many women also write personally and politically about their reproductive rights—some women have been denied a tubal ligation because they were deemed "too fit" to certainly want such a thing; other women have been seduced by the promise of IVF and other reproductive technologies and are now concerned that they have been mislead; others write about their conflicting feelings around abortion laws—while politically they don't want to stand in the way of another women's decision-making, they also consider abortion to be horrid and not in a woman's best interest. There are other women who write concerned that they won't be able to conceive and yet troubled that they so desperately want to become mothers—assuming that this desire toward uber-femininity as expressed by maternity is in conflict with their commitment to independence and a strong professional existence.

Objectives

Together these questions have helped feminist.com to expand the traditional dialogue around reproductive rights—one not exclusively focused on women's access to safe, legal abortion, but also on the range of other reproductive choices available to women throughout their lives. And while it's wonderful that many women have a range of choices, we are also painfully aware of how many women have no choice at all when it comes to their reproductive lives, and that the struggle around reproductive politics is often less about an emotional resistance to motherhood and/or terminating a pregnancy and more likely about the limitations imposed on many women's lives. For instance, many women choose abortion because they don't feel financially equipped to raise a child or because they are in unstable relationships and don't feel they want to bring a child into that scenario, nor do they feel confident enough to raise a child on their own. Their inclination toward abortion has little to do with their desire to be a mother or not and mostly to do with the internalization of what society says is required of good mothers, thus further highlighting the ways that parenthood is still an expectation primarily put upon women without any corresponding support for that role.

Conclusion

More than mothers writing to list their concerns and complaints, those who visit feminist.com are writing to correct something that seems unfair. From our observations mothers come less with an instinct to protect and more with an instinct to seek justice and fairness. It's protecting society from that unfairness. And sadly these same mothers are often confronted with far too many instances of injustices that it requires not only patience on their behalf, but bravery to go against what others have said is impossible. It's this tenacity that we have witnessed at feminist.com that confirms for us that mothers are their own ideal advocates.

67.
The Motherhood Project and Mothers for a Human Future

Motherworld Values and the Movement to Preserve Our Humanity

ENOLA G. AIRD

THE MOTHERHOOD PROJECT WAS launched in 2001, at a time when the national media seemed preoccupied with the "mommy wars"—the supposed conflicts between mothers in and out of the workforce. It was founded on the premise that mothers had more in common than not, and that the media's single-minded focus on our differences was a harmful distraction. The Project was established to bring mothers together and move the public conversation beyond the mommy wars, and to help mothers deal with the challenges posed by the increasing cultural dominance of the values of commerce and technology—which are, in many ways, the opposite of the values necessary to support mothers and the work of mothering.

Among the Project's contributions to the motherhood movement were: 1) a national symposium at Barnard College that brought together mothers from across the political spectrum to help pave the way for an end to the mommy wars; and 2) a national study that identified key items for a mothers' agenda for change. The Project was concluded in 2009, and succeeded in 2010 by Mothers for a Human Future (MHF).

MHF is an independent initiative that is building on the work of the Motherhood Project—focusing on fighting the commercialization of childhood and the commodification of children. Its work, like the work of the Motherhood Project, is premised on the view that what I call "motherworld" values are an antidote to the often-toxic values of our dominant culture. Our goal is to equip mothers to be effective leaders for motherworld values in an age that is putting us on the path to what has been called a "post-human" future.

Philosophy and Purpose

The Motherhood Project was driven by a concern that our society's priorities were being determined almost exclusively by the values of what sociologist Robert Bellah calls the "money world"—values such as self-indulgence, instant gratification, and materialism. We saw the dominance of these values as the root of our culture's devaluing of mothers, mothers' work, and children. We wanted to help build a culture with a healthier balance between money world values and the values of the motherworld: connectedness, stewardship, and other values necessary for raising and nurturing healthy, caring human beings.

From the start, the Project sought to reach across partisan and ideological divides, to unite mothers of varying political persuasions to resist the growing commercialization of American life—particularly childhood. We were alarmed by the tactics used by advertisers to reach children: working to develop brand loyalties in babies before they could even talk, using the tools of behavioral sciences to encourage children to nag their parents to buy products, and training children to be lifelong consumers. Such techniques steep children in the values of the money world—values that elevate instinct over reason and promote the idea that our worth as human beings is determined by what we buy and what we own. People steeped in money world values are less inclined to share, to be able to make and keep commitments, to care about people or ideals beyond themselves. They are more likely to treat themselves and each other carelessly, disrespectfully, and violently. They are more likely to treat each other as objects.

The same money world values that led to the commercialization of childhood have led to the objectification and commodification of children. Of particular concern is the increasingly real prospect of designer babies. A multi-billion-dollar baby business, driven by powerful economic interests, is changing how human beings are made. Sperm donors and egg donors are recruited and paid based on their looks, intelligence, height, and a range of other "desired" characteristics. With the powerful tools of genetic and other technologies, influential scientists are lifting up visions of a "post-human" future in which human beings would be custom-designed.

On the money world's terms, almost anything goes. Driven by advertisements blaring such messages as "Obey your thirst" and "Have it your way," the logic of the money world says "go, go, and keep going."

As a culture, we urgently need an alternative set of values that might help us set limits on ourselves—and preserve our humanity. At the heart of mothering are the values of *connectedness,* a sense of the interdependence of human beings; *concern for the other*, a willingness to restrain oneself for the sake of the other; and *stewardship,* a sense of responsibility to something greater than oneself. I call these motherworld values because they are embodied and cultivated in the work of caring for and nurturing children, work that, throughout human history, has been done—and is still primarily being done—by mothers. These values are essential to the health and well-being of human beings, human relationships, and human civilization. They foster the development of people capable of loving other people, building nurturing relationships, and living in community with one another. The values of the motherworld are crucial to our humanity, but they have been pushed to the margins of our society by the values of the money world.

Nearly everything in our culture—from advertising to music, to television programs, to the Internet and cell phones, to the latest scientific projects—is pushing people further and further away from essential humanizing values. I believe that the work of mothering provides a source of values that can re-connect us with our humanity—and help us set limits.

I am not arguing that all mothers live by motherworld values. Mothers are not a monolith. We have differing values and views. Most people, including those of us who mother, live by a mix of values. It is also true that many people, including adoptive mothers, fathers, and others who care for children, are deeply attuned to motherworld values. To invite mothers and others who are the primary caregivers of children to promote motherworld values in the larger culture is not to reinforce gender roles. In fact, a wider cultural acceptance of these values would mean that men would assume even more responsibility for the work of caring for children.

I am trying to mobilize advocates for motherworld values. Deciding to advocate for these values is independent of decisions about family structure, work in or out of the home, or other choices mothers should be absolutely free to make.

My point is simply that those of us who mother *have access to* a particular understanding of the human person that has, at its core, values that are crucial to the preservation of our humanity. As Sharon Hays suggests in *The Cultural Contradictions of Motherhood*, many mothers seem to see themselves as holding a "fragile but nonetheless powerful cultural position as the last best defense against what many people see as the impoverishment of social ties, communal obligations, and unremunerated commitments." Hays's point is consistent with the findings of the Motherhood Project's 2005 *Motherhood Study*, which suggests that mothers see themselves as guardians of childhood. I believe that the willingness on the part of so many mothers to make ourselves the "last best defense" is rooted in our profound, largely unspoken, understanding of the crucial role that mothers and mothering play in the human—and humanizing—story.

As a culture driven by money world values, we are speeding toward a road without guideposts, that could turn our children into objects of human design. MHF's goal is to mobilize mothers who share our perspective to be strong advocates and activists for motherworld values—to help preserve our humanity.

History

How do we help move the public debate about mothers beyond the mommy wars to focus on more important and pressing issues? How do we foster a deeper appreciation for the contributions *all* mothers make to children and society? How do we bring fresh knowledge to bear to help *all* mothers meet the challenges of raising children in an age driven by the values of commerce and technology? How do we help spark a "mothers' renaissance"—fresh, creative thinking about the potential and power of mothers?

The Motherhood Project was launched in 2001 to grapple with these questions, and we set out to bring together a diverse group of mothers to take on these issues. The Institute for American Values, which had a reputation for convening people of diverse viewpoints to address issues affecting children, families, and civil society, offered the Motherhood Project a base of operations and the assurance that it would be free to develop its own positions, independent of those taken by other Institute projects.

We established a Mothers' Council[1] to advise the Motherhood Project, to examine matters affecting mothers, motherhood, and the work of mothering, and to build coalitions with mothers' groups across the country. Our goal was to bring together mothers of diverse races, backgrounds, political affiliations, and ideologies to find common ground and foster a renewed sense of purpose, passion, and power in the work of mothering. Our objective in convening the Council was to bring together mothers of different backgrounds and views who were willing to listen to and reason with mothers with whom they might have disagreements. Our meetings were often difficult, but always respectful, and, eventually, fruitful. Among the key objectives of the Project and the Council were the preparation and dissemination of mothers' statements, appeals, and reports designed to add mothers' voices to the public debate and promote "mother-informed" public conversations.

Together, the Motherhood Project and the Mothers' Council: 1) launched a mothers' campaign against the commercialization of childhood; 2) convened a national symposium of mothers to draw lessons from the early women's movement to inform the 21st century motherhood movement; 3) conducted a national study of mothers that identified major elements of an agenda for social change; and 4) spearheaded an effort to spark mothers' conversations about the implications of new biotechnologies.

The Motherhood Project worked to build coalitions across a wide range of differences and, early on, enjoyed some success in doing so. As divisions between "left" and "right" in the political culture of the country became more pronounced, however, the Institute for American Values was drawn into the crossfire. It became increasingly difficult for the Project to build coalitions with mothers across political and ideological divides. I concluded the Motherhood Project in May 2009, and launched MHF in 2010 to try again, from an independent platform, to work with mothers across the spectrum on issues of shared concern.

Activities: Highlights of Our Work

Watch Out for Children

The Motherhood Project's first mothers' intervention into the public square was *Watch Out for Children: A Mothers' Statement to Advertisers*, issued just before Mother's Day of 2001. *Watch Out for Children* focused on the onslaught in advertising to children, a major carrier of money world values, and an issue we felt could help unite mothers. The statement showed how advertisers and marketers were using a wide range of invasive strategies to target children at younger and younger ages to turn them into lifelong consumers, and called on mothers to build a movement to protect children from the excesses of commercialism. The statement was signed by a diverse group of mothers, caregivers, and supporters, including leading scholars, advocates, and activists across the country and across the political spectrum.

The Motherhood Project followed up on *Watch Out for Children* with *A Word from the Sponsors: Industry Leaders Respond to Mothers' Questions About Self-Regulation and Advertising to Children*, a May 2004 Mother's Day report showing the limitations of industry self-regulation.

Toward Peace in the "Mommy Wars": The Barnard Symposium on Maternal Feminism

In October 2002, at Barnard College in New York City, the Motherhood Project and Mothers' Council brought together a group of mothers of diverse races, backgrounds, and political affiliations for a ground-breaking symposium called *Maternal Feminism: Lessons for a 21st-century Motherhood Movement.* Our goal was to draw lessons from the early women's movement to inform the 21st-century motherhood movement. We wanted to help minimize the risks of a maternalist/feminist divide in the 21st-century mothers' movement by reminding participants that mothers were a vital part of the early women's movement and that many "maternalists" worked closely with equal-rights feminists. Panelists included scholars Jean Bethke Elshtain and Janet Giele, authors Ann Crittenden and Sylvia Ann Hewlett, and Kim Gandy, then-president of the National Organization for Women.

At the symposium, the Motherhood Project and the Mothers' Council released a *Call to a Motherhood Movement* urging an end to the mommy wars. The *Call* envisioned a movement "in which mothers focused on gaining equal rights for mothers' work in coalition with those dedicated to the well-being of children and those focused on social and cultural reform." It called for a movement that "listens intently to the voices of mothers, recognizes that there are many paths to a successful and fulfilling life, and avoids 'one-size-fits-all' remedies." It also urged mothers to build a movement to "transform our culture so that the values that so dominate our lives, the values of the money world—radical individualism, relentless work, material success—yield ample room for the values of the motherworld—care, connectedness, interdependence, stewardship, and other values necessary for nurturing human beings and building human relationships." The symposium attracted considerable media attention and drew a positive response from mothers as far away as Australia.

The Motherhood Study: Listening to Mothers' Voices

For Mother's Day 2005, the Motherhood Project released the findings of a major motherhood study conducted in partnership with the University of Minnesota's Children, Youth, and Family Consortium and the University of Connecticut's Center for Survey Research and Analysis. The study found that mothers across the United States have a lot in common. There was no significant evidence in the study to support the mommy wars. Regardless of race or ethnicity, age, religious affiliation, geographic location, or employment status, mothers agreed to a large extent in their views on the importance of mothering, the satisfactions they derive from their lives as mothers, their concerns about negative cultural forces affecting their children, and their wishes for changes that would make the work of mothering less challenging.

The study pointed to three key elements of a mothers' agenda for social change: 1) the need for greater financial security for mothers: mothers wanted policies that address their concerns about health care, retirement, and financial vulnerability in divorce; 2) the need for flexible employment options: mothers wanted policies that give mothers—and fathers—more time for children and for personal and family relationships; and 3) the need to promote family health and well-being: mothers wanted policies to help prevent domestic violence, promote healthy marriages, improve parenting skills, and improve the quality and affordability of child care, and they expressed strong concerns about the direction of American culture and its effects on their children.

The Future for Mothers: The Motherhood and Technology Initiative

The Motherhood Project's concern about the invasion of money world values into every area of life led it to pilot a short web series in 2006, featuring conversations with experts in the field human of biotechnology, to open up a discussion on what the future holds for mothers. The goal was to help raise awareness among mothers about market-driven developments in genetics, robotics, informatics, and nanotechnology that could radically change human beings and human society.

Bioconversations

Technology is advancing at an unprecedented rate, carrying both extraordinary benefits and serious risks. Before it is too late, Mothers for a Human Future (MHF) wants to help bring mothers up to speed about the technologies that are paving the way to a "post-human" future. We want to break the monopoly on conversation and decision-making currently held by scientists and other elites, and we want to help launch a conversation among mothers about what it means to be human and what role mothers might play in preserving our humanity. As a first step toward this end, and building on the Motherhood and Technology initiative, MHF is leading *Bioconversations: Taking the Biotech Discussion Public,* a collaboration among the Public Conversations Project, Jamestown Project, and Center for Genetics and Society. Our goal is to help launch a grassroots conversation about technologies that are changing how human beings are made and the implications for mothers, children, and the human future.

Mothers for a Human Future Radio

MHF is the sponsor of Mothers for a Human Future Radio. Billed as "the place for commentary, discussion, and activism on staying human," this is a BlogTalkRadio program that features conversations about what it means to be human, the threats to our humanity, and what mothers can do to help us preserve it.

Challenges

The Motherhood Project's main challenge was that it did not fit into any particular ideological or political box. It deliberately set out to bring mothers of differing views together through its Mothers' Council. It was focused on finding solutions of broad appeal. People did not know quite what to make of us in a world that was growing increasingly polarized—a world in which people were being forced to "choose sides," politically and ideologically. The Project's focus on the notion of "motherworld" values, and its emphasis on children as well as mothers, made it an outlier in the motherhood movement. Leaders of several other mothers' organizations raised questions as to whether it should be considered a legitimate part of the movement. As the left-right culture wars intensified, the Institute for American Values became increasingly perceived as conservative. This perception, in turn, frustrated the Motherhood Project's efforts to build coalitions and made it difficult to keep the momentum going.

Like the Motherhood Project, MHF is an independent initiative that does not want to be boxed in. MHF seeks to spark a public conversation about the critical issues of the commercialization of childhood and the commodification of children in ways that help move the dialogue beyond the divisions of left and right. That is still a challenge. We nevertheless seek to build coalitions around the issues of primary concern to us and issues of concern to the broader motherhood movement.

Our Role in the Larger Motherhood Movement and Our Approach to Collaboration

The Motherhood Project's most direct contributions to the larger motherhood movement were the Barnard Symposium on Maternal Feminism and *The Motherhood Study*. The Symposium helped to give the media a different story line about mothers. Instead of writing about the mommy wars, reporters were forced to write about mothers coming together across differences. As *All Things Considered*, NPR's flagship news program, observed, what was noteworthy about this particular forum was its success at bringing together women from across the ideological spectrum and breathing new life into an old debate. The findings of *The Motherhood Study* also underlined the commonalities among mothers and suggested key items that should be part of the agenda for the motherhood movement.

Our focus at MHF is the same as it ever was with the Motherhood Project: promoting motherworld values and fighting against the commercialization of childhood and the commodification of children. We also want to support mothers' groups that are working for empowerment and equality for mothers. We believe that one of the keys to building a truly transformative motherhood movement is the inclusion of a wide range of mothers' voices. For us, allowing for mothers' authenticity, agency, autonomy, and authority means, among other things, making room for—and listening respectfully to—mothers' varied, and often divergent, views—and working hard to find common ground.

When it comes to policies to empower mothers and promote mothers' equality, we favor flexibility and oppose "one size fits all" solutions—solutions that assume all mothers think (or should think) alike or that all mothers want (or should want) the same things. We favor policies that enable mothers to choose different paths depending on what they consider best for themselves and their children. We are interested in contributing to the crafting of solutions of broad appeal.

Future Goals: Toward a Mother-informed Vision of Who We Are as Human Beings

MHF will continue to lead in the fight to end the commercialization of childhood as a member of the Steering Committee of the Campaign for a Commercial-Free Childhood. We will continue to work with the Public Conversations Project, Jamestown Project, and Center for Genetics and Society, and others to fight against the commodification of children. I am finalizing a long-gestating book entitled *Militant Mothering: Seven Things Mothers Know That Can Save Humanity*, elaborating on the themes raised in the section on "Philosophy and Purpose," above.

Our mission at Mothers for a Human Future is to critique and restructure a culture that has lost touch with what it takes to raise caring human beings, nourish the human spirit, and build healthy human relationships. In this time of crisis, mothers can help refresh our collective memory. In the face of corporate attempts to sell us on a shallow and dehumanizing consumer vision of what it means to be a human being, we believe that mothers have access to an alternative account of who we are. In the face of scientific projects that suggest that we are little more than our DNA, we believe that mothers can offer a richer, more ennobling and captivating vision of what it means to be human. We want to mobilize mothers to be advocates and activists for that richer, more ennobling, vision. We believe that the essential values of connectedness, concern for the other, and stewardship must be brought to the forefront of our national conversation and our public debates.

Time is of the essence. Once we go down the post-human road, we will not be able to turn back.

Conclusion

The economic crisis that began in 2008 opened the door for fundamental changes in American culture. We have seen what the excesses of unfettered materialism have done to the economy. It is time for us to confront what those excesses are doing to our humanity. Mothers for a Human Future seeks to help mothers reconnect with what is deepest and most at the heart of mothering—and our humanity—so that we and our children can have a human future. We call on mothers and others who share our concerns and our views to join us in the radical work of changing the dominant values of our culture—to preserve our humanity.

[1]The members of the Mothers' Council were: Enola G. Aird, founder and director of the Motherhood Project; Heidi Brennan of the Family and Home Network; Marian Wright Edelman, president and founder of the Children's Defense Fund; the actress Frances Fisher; Sylvia Ann Hewlett, founder and president of the Center for Work-Life Policy; Gia Interlandi, business consultant; Loretta Pleasant Jones, mother; author and filmmaker Jean Kilbourne; Rev. Dr. Eileen Lindner, deputy general secretary of the National Council of Churches; Michele Mason, founder and director of the Child-Friendly Initiative; Barbara Nicholson and Lysa Parker of Attachment Parenting International; Peggy O'Mara, editor of *Mothering* magazine; Andrea O'Reilly, professor, York University; psychologist and author Jacqueline Plumez; Stephanie Robinson, President and CEO, the Jamestown Project; Gloria Rodriguez, president and CEO of AVANCE, Inc.; Julianne Still Thrift, past-president, Salem College; Randi Maines Walters, a doctoral student at Howard University.

Works Cited

All Things Considered. Web. <www.npr.org/templates/story/story.php?storyId=866268>.

Bellah, Robert N. "The Invasion of the Money World." *Rebuilding the Nest: A New Commitment to the American Family.* Eds. David Blankenhorn, Steven Bayme and Jean Bethke Elshtain. Milwaukee, WI: Family Service America, 1990.

Erickson, Martha Farrell and Enola G. Aird. *The Motherhood Study: Fresh Insights on Mothers' Attitudes and Concerns.* New York: Institute for American Values, 2005.

Hays, Sharon, *The Cultural Contradictions of Motherhood.* New Haven, CT: Yale University Press, 1996.

Motherhood Project. *Watch Out for Children: A Mothers' Statement to Advertisers.* New York: Institute for American Values, 2001.

Motherhood Project. *Call to a Motherhood Movement.* New York: Institute for American Values, 2002.

68. Mothers of East Los Angeles

Trailblazers in Environmental Justice

R. DIANNE BARTLOW

You know if one of your children's safety is jeopardized, the mother turns into a lioness.

—Aurora Castillo[1]

MATEA GOLD SUGGESTS "ON THE Eastside, they are revered simply as 'the Mothers,'" and that the designation of the phrase symbolizes "the image of hundreds of women with white scarves tied over their hair,[2] marching through the streets of Boyle Heights in the 1980s to protest the construction of a state prison near their neighborhood." The journalist asserts that the Mothers of East Los Angeles (MELA) finally won a six-year battle against the state of California when a prison plan was defeated in 1992 (Gold 1).

In her article "Mexican American Women Grassroots Community Activists: 'Mothers of East Los Angeles,'" Mary Pardo explains that "Over two thousand people, carrying placards proclaiming 'No Prison in ELA,' marched from Resurrection Church in Boyle Heights to the 3rd Street bridge linking East Los Angeles with rapidly expanding downtown Los Angeles." Pardo remarks, "[t]he march marked the beginning of one of the largest grassroots coalitions to emerge from the Latino community in the last decade" (2). In this effort, MELA remains prominent among the coalitions who fought against the prison project, according to Pardo (2).

The Mothers of East Los Angeles have become "legendary" according to Gold, who points out the MELA prison protest campaign is "recounted in classes from Harvard to UCLA as an example of a powerful grass-roots movement, and routinely cited as turning point for the Eastside." Moreover, Gold suggests MELA "evokes automatic respect" in that top politicians acknowledge the members as "national role models and clamor for their endorsement" (Gold 1).

While the history of the MELA is complex, particularly in light of the historical trajectory of Latina and African American women's contribution to social change within their respective communities (Pardo 1), the activism of the MELA represents a significant juncture and moment in time in which environmental justice was served up from the bottom in profound and significant ways.

In her ethnographic study from December 1987 through October 1989, on the Mexican American women activists central to forging MELA efforts around environmental justice, Mary Pardo argues their contributions illuminate a dimension not readily apparent in the mechanisms of how grassroots politics is conceptualized. According to Pardo, MELA's activism "illustrates how these Mexican American women transformed 'traditional' networks and resources based on family and culture into political assets to defend the quality of urban life." She adds, "Far from unique, these patterns of activism are repeated in Latin America and elsewhere," and "...arises out of seemingly traditional roles, addresses wider social and political issues, and capitalizes on informal associations sanctioned by the community," including religion as a guiding precept, which while "commonly viewed as a conservative force," is nonetheless "intertwined with politics."[3] Pardo adds, the MELA women in her study often spoke of their communities and their activism "as extensions of their families and their activism as extensions of their family and household responsibility." Thus, Pardo suggests, "The central role of women in grassroots struggles around the quality of life, in the Third World and in the United States, challenges conventional assumptions about the powerlessness of women and the static definitions of culture and tradition" (Pardo 1).

MELA core activists Aurora Castillo,[4] Juana Gutiérrez,[5] Lucy Ramos, and Lucy Delgado are among key members at the forefront of the organization's founding. (Villalobos; Pardo 2-3, 5; Del Pozo 2011b). Monsignor John Moretta is also a seminal figure, credited with guiding the mothers efforts and, with creating the name, "The Mothers of East Los Angeles" (Villalobos; Mothers of East L.A.). Also significant is MELA's historical collaboration with prominent business entrepreneur Frank Villalobos who was a major force in the "Coalition Against the Prison," with fellow business leaders Steve Kasten, and Carmine Baffo (Mothers of East L.A.).

Pardo explains MELA is comprised of a loosely knit group of over 400 Mexican American women who have since mobilized to oppose several other projects detrimental to the quality of life in the central city (2). Currently, there are 100 active MELA members (Del Pozo 2011b).

Mandate

Several significant mandates have comprised MELA's activism and have centered around the Boyle Heights prison project protest, a battle fought and won; and the east Los Angeles city of Vernon toxic waste incinerator project, which has also been defeated. There was also a Santa Barbara oil pipeline that was to run through MELA's immediate community, that the organization was successful in stopping. In this latter effort, MELA was able to successfully derail plans for an above-ground pipeline that would have carried oil from offshore rigs in Santa Barbara through the mostly middle-and low-income neighborhoods of East Los

Original MELA members posing at a hazardous waste site at Whittier Boulevard and Lorena Street. At far left is Aurora Castillo, winner of the 1995 Goldman Award for environmental justice. At right rear are, from left to right, Josie Del Pozo, Lucy Delgado, Henrietta Castillo, Rosa Limon, Lucy Ramos, Lupe Lopez, Terri Griffin, Erlinda Robles, Stella Macias, and Irene Meras. Photo courtesy of Alex Villalobos and Barrio Planners.

Angeles to the port of Long Beach, bypassing affluent white coastal communities, according to the *New York Times* ("Mothers' Group Fights Back").

Additionally, MELA succeeded in stopping a hazardous waste treatment plant near a high school and had the JCI company's conditiónal-use permit revoked for storing hazardous waste improperly (Villalobos).

MELA also rejected the proposal for the installation of a second power plant in Vernon which would have been created on a larger scale than the first one. The mortality rate and the diseases stemming from such a project took precedence in the decision by MELA to reject the proposal. MELA Executive Director Diana Del Pozo (2010) asserts, "We told them, we're not for sell, there's nothing you can give us because you can't give us those lives back." She adds, "Those affected with asthma will be our young and elders, and that can't be fixed, that's permanent."

With regard to MELA's suceessful effort in forestalling the installation of the second power plant in Vernon, Del Pozo (2010) elates, "Talk about a victory. When they told us we could never win" and that "they had too much money and strong attorneys and we had nothing, I can tell you one thing, we had heart and we knew what we wanted and we went after it and we won." She adds, "We won for other communities that couldn't stop power plants from going up in their own backyards ... that's the power that is so valuable that I am so lucky to be a part of."

A related victory is MELA's efforts in supporting Assembly Speaker John Perez' bill AB56 to lift neighboring Vernon's city hood. Villalobos explains the latter victory is monumental in that "no one in the nation has done something like

MELA parade, 1986. In the vehicle are, among others: Frank Villalobos, Veronica Gutierrez, Carlos Garcia and Jose Luis Garcia.

MELA victory rally: Cesar Chavez, Robert Blake, Fr. John Moretta, Lucy Ramos, Carlos Brron, Carmine Baffo, Jose Luis Garcia, Hortensia Fuentes, Frank Villalobos, Steve Kasten, Gloria Melina.

that" in "taking city hood away from a city." With only 100 residents in Vernon and city council representatives residing outside of the area, what is key, will be the annexation of the city of Vernon to Los Angeles (Villalobos).

Villalobos suggests the issues in Vernon revolve around not only the power plants and incinerator projects, but also what he views as "lawlessness in elections, recycling plants, laxidasical waivering of permitting" and provisions for extensions for companies who have not met obligations for environment safety. Villalobos says Exide, a battery producing and recycling company, is one such example. The company, he suggests, is currently trying to expand but should be shut down (2010).

Fighting a toxic dump in the city of Kettleman, California was also a MELA environmental justice effort. In that case, many pregnant women were maimed and a number in the cattle rich agricultural community had birth defects. MELA members went to protest against the toxins found in the soil (Villalobos).

MELA was also successful in defeating the drilling of wells under the ocean in Pacific Palisades and along the California seacoasts of Catalina and Palos Verdes (Villalobos).

History

Journalist Matea Gold suggests "[t]he story of the Mothers began in the mid-1980s, when the state proposed building a $100-million prison across the Los Angeles River from Boyle Heights." She adds, [t]o Eastside residents, it was yet another undesirable project being dumped in their community. Many whose families had been forced to move by previous government projects, such as the construction of freeways and housing projects, felt that the prison was a slap in the face" (1). This was a time when "some 10,000 residents of East Los Angeles were displaced in the 1950s and early '60s when several freeways and Dodger Stadium were built." Consequently, there was an increase in noise and pollution ("Mothers' Group Fights Back").

"People living in Third World countries as well as in minority communities in the United States face an increasingly degraded environment. Recognizing the threat to the well-being of their families, residents have mobilized at the neighborhood level to fight for "quality of life" issues. Pardo argues the common notion that environmental well-being is of concern solely to white middle-class and upper-class residents ignores the specific ways working-class neighborhoods suffer from the fallout of the city "growth machine" geared for profit" (5).

Pardo adds, "Latinos, the majority of whom live close to the center of the city, must confront the distilled social consequences of development focused solely on profit. The Mexican American community in East Los Angeles, much like other minority working-class communities, has been a repository for prisons instead of new schools, hazardous industries instead of safe work sites, and one of the largest concentrations of freeway interchanges in the country, which transports much wealth past the community" (5).

"Although women played a key role in the mobilization," MELA members "emphasized the group's broad base of active supporters as well as the other organizations in the "Coalition Against the Prison," according to Pardos. "Their

The Optimist Awards Night, 1986. From left to right, Juana Gutierrez, Lucy Ramos, Frank Villalobos and Aurora Castillo.

intent was to counter any notion that MELA was composed exclusively of women or mothers and to stress the 'inclusiveness' of the group." Pardo adds, "[a]ll the women who assumed lead roles in the group had long histories of volunteer work in the Boyle Heights community; but formation of the group brought them out of the 'private' margins and into 'public' light" (Pardo 3-4).

Diana Del Pozo (2011a) adds,."At the time, it was a different generation. These women were at home raising the children," and were not mothers who worked outside of the home for wages, but MELA members "were able to utilize their time in a different format." Del Pozo suggests, "[t]hey were able to figure out that there was a need and they were able to fill that. That was the ideal part."

"The need of the community is what the calling really was, it wasn't a calling to any one person but I think it was when it was needed, the community was awakened all at once and they knew they had to come together to form something to be an active group to make something happen" (Del Pozo 2011a).

Context

Mary Pardo indicates that "[i]n general, the women of MELA are longtime residents of East Los Angeles; some are bilingual and native born, others Mexican born and Spanish dominant." Pardo adds, "All the core activists are bilingual and have lived in the community over thirty years." MELA members have been active in parish-sponsored groups and activities, and some have had experience working in community-based groups stemming from schools, labor supports groups, and neighborhood watch associations (Pardo 1).

"In 1984, the state of California commissioned a public relations firm to assess the political difficulties facing the construction of energy-producing waste incinerators" which included a report on the "personality profile" on residents most likely to organize effectively against any opposition to the projects (Pardo 1). The report concluded that only those individuals with socio-economic upper standing would oppose such a site while older people with only a high school education or less, would likely not oppose the facility (1).

MELA Executive Director Diana Del Pozo, who participated in marches and meetings with her grandmother Josephine Del Pozo, recalled the people making the presentation on behalf of the first Vernon incinerator project. She says they thought the MELA members "we're a bunch of old ladies" in thinking they were going to get a green light or support of a grassroots organization, but "they realized they weren't dealing with old ladies, but women who knew what they wanted for the community." Moreover, according to Del Pozo, "[t]here's always an effect and these ladies had been the watchdog all along to understand that" (2010). This is but one context in which MELA has emerged to fight on behalf of environmental justice.

According to Frank Villalobos who along with Monsignor John Moretta maintains a close working relationship with MELA members, there are still older MELA members who are now in their seventies that remain a part of the organization. The first president of MELA Lucy Ramos, is one such example. She was also recently re-elected as president. In addition, there are younger members who are the daughters that have assumed leadership posts in MELA. "The activism is alive and well" (Villalobos).

Diana Del Pozo states "[o]ne of the best things is the fact that it's a grassroots organization and I'm actually a third generation [member] which speaks volumes for what it [MELA] really stands for which is the strength and backbone of the community." So often she says women in the community share their bond to the MELA by virtue of their own grandmothers, aunts, mothers, and sisters involvement in the organization. According to Del Pozo (2010), "I can remember as a teenager protesting the prison, and I can remember protesting the incinerator they wanted to build." She says some of her fondest memories are watching her grandmother, now deceased, engage in activism. Moreover, though she was not college educated, Del Pozo says of her grandmother, "She was so ahead of her time."

Objectives

The key objective of MELA is to fight against environmental injustice according to Executive Director Diana Del Pozo (2010). She asserts, "That's been our number one issue all along and even to validate ourselves. We understand that when we get put in the mix when it comes to that issue, we have a long standing reputation of actually knowing how to fight the fight." She adds, "We will not play games." MELA is also interested in public safety to reduce crime in the targeted area near Resurrection Church, and they collaborate with other community groups such as the organization Community for a Better Environment (CBE), among others fighting toxins released in marginalized ethnic communities such as a predominantly black community organization in south-central Los Angeles to block the construction of a toxic waste incinerator in an adjacent city (Villalobos; "Mothers' Group Fights Back").

Activities

MELA is currently fighting against a facility for the mentally ill, a project that came in under the pretext of senior housing and without an entitlement. After five years, it has become apparent many young people are being serviced at the facility and not solely seniors. Villalobos says while there is a need for mental health to be provided, the way in which the patients are released into the community is detrimental to community members. Other MELA projects include a ten-unit affordable housing complex for families.

Recently, MELA received over one million dollars from the Reformulated Gasoline Settlement Fund to create filtered environments via hepafilters and air conditioners in seven public school classrooms at six elementary schools and one high school in east Los Angeles. Three public and parochial schools will be serviced. Currently, each school, including the high school, is located within 500 yards from a freeway, and were identified as "hotspots," according to Villalobos. "Right now, when you open the doors or the windows to let the air in you get the ambient, toxic contaminated air into the classrooms." With many of the schools near freeways, there is a high incident of asthma in the area, thus creating a need for filtered environments to be installed at the schools (Villalobos).

MELA also works with Villalobos' company Barrio Planners[6] on a Mariachi Festival that has run for twenty consecutive years (Villalobos). Since 1986, MELA members have been meeting every Monday, and for the last twelve consecutive years, MELA has been engaged in a community neighborhood watch program that meets every Monday at Resurrection Church as well (Villalobos).

Challenges

One of the biggest challenges for MELA is raising money for the organization, particularly in that MELA projects are seen by some as controversial in confronting big industries. "When you take 'em on, it's hard ball—you fear for your life sometimes. It's not easy," according to Villalobos. Del Pozo (2010) says MELA fights "the big money, the big names, and big attorneys … it's kind of neat to continue the great reputation it has." Another challenge is attempting to stay ahead of the curve when an environmental justice emergency occurs, according to Del Pozo (2010).

Future Goals

Del Pozo hopes every child will get hepafilters in their schools and that the effort can be extended nationwide and even worldwide. She would also like to see the hepafilter installation program extended in homes affected by the toxins and pollutants in the Boyle Heights community (2011b). "We know for sick kids who are ill in our community with asthma and other ailments, it's not genetic, it's due to environmental causes" (2010).

Conclusion

This is a story about the prison, the community and the role that Mothers of East L.A. played and how within that structure they were the leading organization that survived all of the others in staying with the issue," according to Villalobos. "MELA is a leader. It's not like they are just green today, they've been green for twenty-five years" (2010). Diana Del Pozo asserts, "The environmental justice wins would be our biggest accomplishments but, more time would be how we help organize our community to be able to win for themselves." She adds, "We always seem to come out victorious because we have the volume and the heart to come forward (2010). We're looking for the betterment of everyone" (2011b).

[1]As quoted in Pardo (4).

[2]The organization's founding document suggests the women wore white scarves on their head because the color denotes peace, dignity, and respect.

[3]Comparatively, and as far back as the 1800s, Black women did not see a contradiction between political action and domesticity, according to Paula Giddings (52). For many Christian Black women, a major source of religious validation came from the Bible. Thus, through Jacqueline Grant's analysis we can begin to see the intersection of family, religion and political activism in the lives of Black women (Grant 211) (see Giddings; Grant).

[4]Aurora Castillo is the 1995 recipient of the Goldman Environmental Prize for environmental justice. Castillo continued to be a force behind MELA until her death in 1998 at the age of 84 (Villalobos).

[5]Juana Gutiérrez left MELA in 1990 and has since founded the nonprofit community-based group Mothers of East Los Angeles, Santa Isabel (MELA-SI), in her parish. She has been recognized by dozens of local, state, and national entities as an outstanding leader. She also received the President's Service Award Citation (see "Juana Gutiérrez Biography").

[6]Barrio Planners is an architectural, urban planning and design company and serves in an advisory capacity to MELA. Over the years, MELA members have given many of their awards to Villalobos in gratitude for the work Barrio Planners has conducted and collaborated on with the group since its inception. Attorneys Andy

Yamomoto and Joel Reynolds have also worked closely with MELA and Barrio Planners of many their environmental justice platforms (Villalobos).

Works Cited

Del Pozo, Diana. Personal interview. 10 Dec. 2010.

Del Pozo, Diana. Personal interview. 15 Feb. 2011a.

Del Pozo, Diana. Personal interview. 21 Mar. 2011b.

Giddings, Paula. *When and Where I Enter: The Impact of Black Women on Race and Sex in America*. New York: Bantam Books, 1999.

Gold, Matea. "The Mothers' Saga: How a Movement Split in Two: Activism: A plan for a prison near Boyle Heights spurred a group of women to action. Along the way, a bitter division occurred, and it endures to this day." *Los Angeles Times* August 29, 1999: 1. Web. <http://articles.latimes.com/print/1999/aug/29/local/me-4843>. Accessed 8 Feb. 2011.

Grant, Jacqueline. *White Women's Christ and Black Women's Jesus: Feminist Christiology and Womanist Response*. Atlanta: Scholars Press, 1989.

"Juana Gutierrez Biography—Women Reshaping Human Rights: How Extraordinary Activists Are Changing the World." Web. <http://www.jrank.org/cultures/pages/3942/Juana-Gutierrez.html>. Accessed 8 Feb. 2011.

"Mothers' Group Fights Back in Los Angeles." *New York Times* December 05, 1989. Web. <http://www.nytimes.com/1989/12/05/us/mothers-group-flights-back-in-los-angeles.html?pagewanted=print&src=pm>. Accessed 8 Feb. 2011.

Mothers of East L.A. Web. <http://www.mothersofeastla.com>. Accessed 18 Aug. 2011.

Pardo, Mary. "Mexican American Women Grassroots Community Activists: 'Mothers of East Los Angeles'." *Frontiers* 11.1 (1990): 1-7.

Mothers of East Los Angeles (MELA). Founding document (Revised). May 15, 1991.

Villalobos, Frank. Personal interview. 15 Dec. 2010.

VII.
Writing, Researching, and Performing Motherhood

69. An Association, a Journal, and a Press of Our Own

The Motherhood Initiative for Research and Community Involvement, the *Journal of the Motherhood Initiative*, and Demeter Press

ANDREA O'REILLY

If there's a book that you want to read, but it hasn't been written yet, then you must write it.—Toni Morrison

Maternal voices have been drowned by professional theory, ideologies of motherhood, sexist ignorance, and childhood fantasy. Voices that have been distorted and censored can only be *developing* voices. Alternately silenced and edging toward speech, mothers' voices are not voices as they are, but as they are becoming. —Sara Ruddick

THE MOTHERHOOD INITIATIVE FOR RESEARCH and Community Involvement (MIRCI), formerly the Association for Research on Mothering (ARM), the *Journal of the Motherhood Initiative* (JMI), formerly the *Journal of the Association for Research on Mothering* (JARM), and Demeter Press, are the first and still the only feminist research organizations, publications, and publishers, devoted specifically to the topic of mothering-motherhood. The Association for Research on Mothering (ARM) was founded in 1998, the *Journal of the Association Research on Mothering* was founded in 1999, and Demeter Press in 2006. From 1998–2010 ARM and its journal and press were housed at York University in Toronto, Canada. In 2010 ARM left York University and was re-established as an independent non-profit research organization known as the Motherhood Initiative for Research and Community and Involvement (MIRCI). The Motherhood Initiative has more than 500 members worldwide including scholars, writers, activists, social workers, midwives, nurses, therapists, lawyers, teachers, politicians, parents, students and artists. They come from more than 20 countries, as well as numerous local and international agencies and governmental, social, and community groups that work for, and on behalf of mothers. The *Journal of the Motherhood Initiative* is a bi-annual, scholarly, peer-reviewed journal funded in part by the Social Science Research Council of Canada (SSHRC). Each journal is thematic in focus and includes 12 to 24 articles per issue, as well as numerous book reviews and poetry. Demeter Press, MIRCI's publishing division, publishes two to five titles per year on a variety of diverse motherhood topics. The association, journal, and press are directed by founder, Andrea O'Reilly.

Andrea O'Reilly, Director of MIRCI *at 2006 tenth anniversary conference holding the* National Post *that featured a story on the conference.*

Context

Adrienne Rich opened her now classic work *Of Woman Born: Motherhood as Experience and Institution* with a poignant observation: "We know more about the air we breathe, the seas we travel, than about the nature and meaning of motherhood" (11). In the three plus decades since *Of Woman Born* was published, the topic of motherhood, as Lauri Umansky has documented in *Motherhood Reconceived: Feminism and the Legacies of the Sixties*, has become increasingly central to feminist scholarship. However, despite the centrality and significance of the topic of motherhood in academe, as evidenced by the numerous books and articles published each year on motherhood, and the growing number of university classrooms across the disciplines and academic levels that are now teaching this topic, a scholarly association on the topic of motherhood did not exist prior to the founding of ARM. Indeed, scholars from a multitude of fields (including but not limited to Sociology, English, Family Studies, Psychology, Women's Studies, Canadian Studies, Cultural Studies, Religious Studies, Anthropology, Law, Fine Arts, Political Science, History, Communication, and Literature) name motherhood as their central research area, yet they did not have a scholarly association they could "call their own," an association that specifically focused on their research interests. At the first motherhood conference at York University in 1997, we identified the absence of a scholarly association on motherhood as a missing piece in the field of maternal scholarship; as well, numerous researchers called upon us to develop a scholarly association to meet this need. In response to these requests and in recognition of the reality that a scholarly association on motherhood was urgently needed and long overdue, we established the Association for Research on Mothering.

While the above narrative provides the academic background for the establishment of ARM/MIRCI, it only tells half the story. It must also be noted that the foremost reason for its creation was that I, as a young feminist mother and scholar new to the field of motherhood studies, urgently and desperately needed such a community. Feminists rightly say that the personal is political, and nothing could be truer for how and why ARM happened in my life. Di Brandt opened the prologue to her book *Wild Mother Dancing* by discussing how the birth of her first child in 1977 called into question all she had learned—or thought she had learned—in the Masters English Literature program she completed that same year. She writes, "It was like falling into a vacuum narratively speaking. I realized suddenly with a shock, that none of the texts I had read so carefully, none of the literary skills I had acquired so diligently as a student of literature had anything remotely to do with the experience of becoming a mother" (3). Similarly, I entered motherhood the same year I completed an Honours BA in English and Women's Studies. When I became a mother unexpectedly at the age of 23, in the final year of my degree, I reflected back on the courses I'd taken and realized I'd never had a single course in which motherhood was discussed in a thorough way—and this was in coursework leading to a degree in Women's Studies. Numerous and diverse topics were covered including health, work, education, sexuality, aging, and violence against women, but not the topic of motherhood. Moreover, the few times motherhood did become the frame of reference, it was, more often than not, presented as either "the prison of domesticity" theme of late nineteenth century literature or the "motherhood-as-patriarchal-trap" paradigm of early 1970s feminist thought. With the notable exception of a Canadian Women's Writers Course, none of my undergraduate courses included a maternal perspective on the women's issues studied, nor did the professor call attention to the absence of motherhood in the course or position it as a worthy and deserving topic for feminist scholarly inquiry.

Two years later, I began my Ph.D. in English, giving birth to my second child four months later in December 1986, and my third child three years after that. At twenty-eight years old with three children born in five years and the only mother in my Ph.D. program, I hungered for stories and theories by and about mothers and wondered, as did Di Brandt, "Where ... were the mothers, symbolic or otherwise, whom I might have turned to in that moment of aloneness and desperation?" (4). In 1990, I designed a third year Women's Studies course on motherhood to address and correct the silencing and marginalization of motherhood in academe; it was the first course on this topic in Canada. As I note in a 2006 article written on the design and teaching of this course, York University did not offer a single course on the subject of motherhood as late as 1991, despite housing two large and successful Women's Studies programs and a student population of 40,000. I have taught this course now for close to 20 years, and while it certainly has been

Demeter books and journal issues tables at 2008 and 2010 conference.

important for the development of motherhood scholarship and my own survival as a mother scholar, I needed and longed for more. I still longed for a community to sustain and support the work I was doing as a mother academic and as a scholar of motherhood, a place where I did not have to defend or justify my motherhood scholarship or my identity as a mother academic. Necessity is indeed the mother of invention, and so ARM was born.

Mandate

MIRCI and its journal, and Demeter press, were formed to promote, showcase, and make maternal scholarship visible, and to accord legitimacy to this academic field. Our mandate is to provide a forum for the discussion and dissemination of research on motherhood and to establish a community of individuals and institutions working and researching in the area of mothering and motherhood. MIRCI promotes maternal scholarship, both at the university and community level, by bringing together interested individuals and organizations to share their insights, experiences, ideas, stories, studies, and concerns about mothering and motherhood. As we all know, scholarship at the university and community level is enriched by dialogue and debate, is broadened through knowledge/resource sharing, and is sustained by a sense of belonging. As MIRCI exists to simultaneously build a community of maternal scholars, both academic and grassroots, and promote maternal scholarship, it also developed in recognition of the centrality of motherhood in most women's lives. We are all daughters and most women are mothers if we mean this to include "othermothers" as described by Patricia Hill Collins, spiritual mothers as mentors, or any woman who is deeply concerned about children. Whether paid or otherwise, many women engage in work that is culturally or politically considered as an extension of the maternal function: teaching, nursing, and in particular, elder care. This view is neither essentialist nor pro-natalist; it simply acknowledges that discourses of motherhood inform all women's lives regardless of whether they are biological mothers or not. Normative ideologies of the "good mother," public policies on maternity leave, childcare, and so forth, legal rulings concerning same-sex adoptions, governmental decisions about children's education and maternal healthcare, workplace policies on mothering and employment and so on, have an affect on us all, albeit in different ways. MIRCI exists to provide a forum for women to discuss with one another their maternal experiences, both as they are structured by these controlling discourses and as they are lived in resistance to them. We established the Motherhood Initiative to create a maternal community that, as Sara Ruddick among others has argued, is essential for the empowerment of mothers.

The work of MIRCI is guided by six principles and objectives all centered upon the promotion of scholarship on motherhood and the empowerment of mothers:

1) We assert that motherhood is deserving of serious and sustained scholarly inquiry.
2) We seek to correct the child-centeredness that defines much of the scholarship on motherhood and develop research and activism that examines mothering-motherhood as experience, institution, and identity, from the perspective of mothers.
3) We endeavour to establish Motherhood Studies as an autonomous, independent, and legitimate scholarly discipline.
4) We are an explicitly feminist organization that regards mothering

as work that is important and valuable to society. However, at MIRCI we emphasize that the essential task of mothering is not, and should not be the sole responsibility and duty of mothers. Men and the larger society must share in the responsibility and work of childrearing. To this end, we argue that the word "mother" is best understood as a verb rather than a noun: it is an activity that one undertakes rather than an identity one has.

5) We contest, challenge, and counter the patriarchal oppressive institution of motherhood and seek to imagine and implement a maternal identity and practice that is empowering to mothers. MIRCI recognizes that mothers, children, and society benefit when the mother can live her life and practice mothering from a position of agency, authority, authenticity, autonomy, and advocacy/activism.

6) We are committed to social change and social justice and regard mothering as a socially-engaged enterprise and a site of power wherein mothers can affect social change, both in the home through feminist childrearing, and outside the home through maternal activism.

In realizing these objectives MIRCI is committed, in both membership and research, to the inclusion of all mothers including First Nations mothers, immigrant and refugee mothers, working-class mothers, lesbian mothers, mothers with disabilities, mothers of colour, and mothers from other marginalized groups. Our conferences and publications present and explore the diversity of maternal experience across race, class, culture, ethnicity, sexuality, ability, age, and geographical location, and many of our conferences and publications focus on mothers from specific marginalized groups including, for example, conferences and journal issues on "Lesbian Mothers," "Young Mothers," "Mothering in the African Diaspora," "Mothering and Poverty," and "Mothering, Race, Ethnicity, Culture, and Class." As well, in choosing motherhood topics for our Demeter Press titles, we are committed to featuring perspectives and issues that have been overlooked or under-researched in current scholarship. Many Demeter Press titles are the first ever book-length works on a particular motherhood topic including *Until Our Hearts Are On the Ground: Aboriginal Mothering, Oppression, Resistance and Rebirth*; *Latina/Chicana Mothering*; *South Asian Mothering; Black Motherhoods*; *Queering Maternity & Motherhood: Narrative and Theoretical Perspectives on Queer Conception, Birth and Parenting*; *Muslim Mothering: Local and Global Histories, Theories, and Practices*; *Incarcerated Mothers: Oppression and Resistance*; *Mennonite Mothering;* and *Other Mothers, Othermothering.*

As well, MIRCI is committed to the creation of an international network of maternal researchers that includes both scholars and community workers so as to bridge the gap between academe and activism. A central aim of our conferences and publications is to provide a forum wherein knowledge can be shared and dialogue can be fostered between activists and academics. By creating a space that brings together activists and academics, students and mothers, researchers and community agencies, one that links "lived mothering" with "examined motherhood," we can learn how to best implement supports addressing the diverse experiences, insights, and concerns of mothers. All our conferences are well attended by activists and several past conferences have featured activists including Ariel Gore, Loretta Ross, Jeanette Corbiere Lavell, Dawn Memee Lavell-Havard, Sky Hawk, Sandra Steingraber, and Cindy Sheehan, among others, as keynote speakers. Activism has also been the central theme of several MIRCI conferences including the 2008 conference on the "21st Century Motherhood Movement," the 2010 conference "Motherhood, Activism, Advocacy, Agency," and the 2010 Public Forum on "Young Mothers and Empowerment." To further facilitate these initiatives, MIRCI established Mother Outlaws in 2004, community gatherings in the Toronto area for women interested in discussing current motherhood issues from a feminist perspective and sharing the links between their own mothering practices and social change, (discussed in chapter 43). Then in 2008, MIRCI established the Toronto Feminist Mothers discussion group, (discussed in chapter 34), and also in 2008 the International Mothers Network, now the International Mothers and Mothering Network, the first global consortium of motherhood organizations, which currently boasts 80 member organizations worldwide (discussed in chapter 42). Overall, MIRCI aims to examine motherhood from both a scholarly and activist standpoint across a wide range of diverse maternal perspectives, and to establish new fields in maternal scholarship. In these endeavors we are guided by the six principles listed above, and, in particular, are motivated to establish Motherhood Studies as a scholarly discipline.

History

In the summer of 1996, shortly after completing my Ph.D. in English and while teaching as contract faculty at York University, I was invited by Nancy Mandell, director of the Centre for Feminist Research at York (CFR), to host an event on motherhood for the centre. Professor Mandell had been a member of my dissertation committee (on the topic of Motherhood and Toni Morrison) and she thought that motherhood, being an under-researched subject in feminist scholarship, would be a timely topic for an event hosted by the centre. Initially, we thought of having a small afternoon event—a luncheon or a tea—to discuss a particular motherhood theme, and considered Jewish mothering as a topic since the centre was engaged in research on feminism and Judaism at that time. However, after a handful of meetings and discussions with scholars outside the university we decided on a day-long conference entitled "Mothers and Daughters: Moving into the Next Millennium" to be held in 1997, and sought funding for this through the Social Science and Humanities Council of Canada. The grant required a detailed program including a list of the presenters and keynote speakers and full abstracts of the papers presented. So with just six weeks before the grant deadline, I sent out invitations to established motherhood scholars to be keynote speakers and distributed a call for papers to recruit session presenters. As this was in the very

Renée Knapp and Andrea O'Reilly, "Mothering and the Evironment" conference, 2009.

Pat Gowens at 2010 MIRCI conference "Mothers and the Economy; Economics of Mothering."

early days of the Internet, before there were a plethora of websites and when email was often tediously slow, a great deal of correspondence was still done by fax and phone. So I phoned, faxed, and emailed all the leading motherhood scholars on my "wish list"—those that I had read for my dissertation and taught in my Women's Studies course on motherhood: Christina Looper Baker, Sara Ruddick, Paula Caplan, Maureen Reddy, Patricia Bell-Scott, Marianne Hirsch, Naomi Lowinsky, Valerie Walkerdine, and Suzanna Dunuta Walkers, to name but a few. And to my amazement and delight, most said YES! Each day that I arrived at the centre I would find the fax machine full and often jammed with a stack of abstracts, and my desk littered with those now old-fashioned pink phone message slips, most marked urgent. Most of the abstracts were sent with a personal note, often scribbled, saying how much this conference meant to them, how thrilled they were to be able to attend a conference on motherhood, and how much this was so very needed in their research and lives as motherhood scholars.

I remember one day when I was feeling particularly overwhelmed by the flood of interest and the deluge of calls and emails requesting immediate confirmation of acceptance, Nancy stuck her head in my office and said "Andrea, with this motherhood thing, I think you are on to something." Indeed, in less than six weeks I had received more than 160 abstracts from scholars around the world, all eager to be part of this very first international conference on motherhood. I received the grant, and the one-day conference, originally envisioned as an afternoon tea, become a three-day conference in September 1997 that was attended by close to two hundred researchers and activists from more than a dozen countries around the world. Over the three days of this hugely successful conference it become more than apparent that a second conference on motherhood was urgently wanted and needed, and so the CFR hosted a second international conference on motherhood on the topic "Mothers and Sons Today: Challenges and Possibilities" in September 1998. From these two conferences three books—*Redefining Motherhood: Changing Identities and Patterns* (1998); *Mothers and Daughters: Connection, Empowerment, Transformation* (2000); *Mothers and Sons: Feminism, Masculinity and the Struggle to Raise our Sons* (2001); and a journal issue ("Looking Back, Looking Forward: Mothers, Daughters, and Feminism" *Canadian Women's Studies/les cahiers de la femme* (Vol 18. Nos, 2 & 3, 1998) were published. All received many more submissions than could be published and this, along with the overwhelming response to the conferences and subsequent publications, revealed that motherhood scholars needed and wanted a "space and place of their own" where their research would be supported and respected. In response to this demand the Association for Research on Mothering was formed and officially launched at the 1998 conference.

From 1998 to May 2010 ARM was housed at York University; over these 12 years I lobbied York for financial support to cover some of our operational costs but was unsuccessful. In March 2010, after the new faculty at York made it clear that no funding would be forthcoming, I made the decision for ARM to leave the university and, in May 2010, it was established as an independent non-profit research organization, renamed as the Motherhood Initiative for Research on Community Involvement (MIRCI). MIRCI continues the work of ARM with a renewed emphasis on community engagement and community and research partnerships.

Activities

The overall and organizing objective of MIRCI is to establish a community of and for maternal scholars and activists and to disseminate and promote research on motherhood. We seek to achieve this by way of numerous initiatives including conferences, community-academic research projects, journal publications, and Demeter Press books.

Conferences

Since 1998 ARM/MIRCI has hosted more than 40 conferences on a variety of diverse motherhood topics including "Mothers and the Economy, The Economics of Mothering"; "Mothering and the Enivornment: The Social, The Natural, The Built"; "Mothering and Migration"; "Mothering, Violence, Militarism, War and

Participants at past ARM/MIRCI conferences.

Social Justice"; "Mothering and Work"; "Mothering, Literature, Popular Culture, and the Arts"; "Maternal Health and Well Being"; "Mothering, Law, Politics and Public Policy"; "Mothers without Their Children"; "Mothering, Sex and Sexuality" and "Mothering and Fathering: Visioning, Creating and Sustaining a Culture of Peace."In October MIRCI hosts its annual conference, and in May a second conference is held to celebrate Mothers Day (both in Toronto, Canada). Recently, conferences were held in February at international locations: Puerto Rico in 2010 and Lisbon, Portugal, in 2011. Most of our conferences are held in Toronto, though in 2000 our annual October conference was held in Milwaukee, Wisconsin and two of our May conferences were held in New York (2008 and 2009). In 2012, an international conference is planned on Mothers, Mothering and Science and plans are underway for a second European conference in February 2012.

In 2001, an Australian chapter of ARM was established and they have hosted six international motherhood conferences in Australia over the last ten years. Two noteworthy conferences in MIRCI's history include "The Motherlode: A Complete Celebration of Motherhood" in 2006, our tenth anniversary conference which was attended by more than 250 people, and in 2008 the first-ever international conference on the 21st Century Motherhood Movement, which featured 28 leading motherhood organizations and led to the establishment of the International Mothers Network (now named the International Mothers and Mothering Network). Each conference features keynote addresses by leading motherhood scholars or activists (on average there are between 5-15 keynote presenters at each conference) and 50-250 presenters. Past keynote speakers include (in addition to the activist keynote speakers listed above) Sara Ruddick, Marilyn Waring, Martha Albertson Fineman, Patricia Hill Collins, Meredith Micheals, Andrea Doucet, Kim Anderson, Ann Crittenden, Nancy Folbre, Joan C. Tronto, Eva Feder Kittay, Rickie Solinger, Dorothy Roberts, Patrice DiQuinzio, Chris Bobel, Andrea Buchanan, and Faulkner Fox to name but a few. Along with academic panels most MIRCI conferences also include workshops and literary events. MIRCI conferences are attended by scholars, students, activists, community agencies, mothers, and professionals from many diverse fields including law, education, nursing, midwifery, social work, and government.

Research Projects

A central aim of MIRCI, particularly in the last few years, is to establish research partnerships with Community Agencies in order to research particular motherhood themes or issues from both a scholarly and activist perspective. Supported by funding from SSHRC, MIRCI, along with various community groups such as the National Association of Mother Centres and 1900 Sheppard, has undertaken a research project entitled "Young Mothers and Empowerment Programming: Education, Health, Advocacy and Agency," which seeks to effect real change in the lives of young mothers. The project explores how best to broker, leverage, mobilize, and implement the current research and activism on maternal empowerment and related innovative research on young mothers and empowerment.

Andrea O'Reilly and Marilyn Waring, "Mothers and the Economy: Economics of Mothering" conference, October 2010. Photo: Kim Breland.

The findings from this research will be presented at the MIRCI public forum on Young Mothers and Empowerment in May 2011. The conference explores the question: What do young mothers need to achieve economic, social, familial and personal wellness and prosperity? More directly, the conference will show that programs with a mother-empowerment perspective and philosophy result in better outcomes than ones that do not employ such a perspective because by placing an emphasis on maternal agency, authority, authenticity, autonomy, and advocacy/activism, they are able to empower mothers to be stronger women and more effective mothers. As well, the conference will present various models of such empowerment in the areas of education, health, advocacy and agency which may be incorporated into programming for young mothers currently offered by social agencies. Another public forum based on a partnership between MIRCI and selected twenty-first motherhood organizations, "What Do Mothers Need? Empowering Mothers/Maternal Empowerment: The Motherhood Movement, Motherhood Studies, Perspectives and Possibilities across Activism and Scholarship" will take place May 2012.

Journal of the Motherhood Initiative for Research and Community Involvement (formerly the *Journal of the Association for Research on Mothering*)

In early 1999, after a few months of operation, the advisory board of ARM met to

Performing Feminist Motherhood: Outlaw Mothers in Music, Media, Arts and Cultural Expression, May 16, 2008 in New York City. Photo: Kim Breland.

discuss how the association could better meet the objectives of our mandate. The board agreed that one of the key ways to best serve the mandate of ARM would be to establish an international scholarly journal on the topic of mothering and motherhood. It was decided that the journal would be international in scope but would also feature articles written by Canadian scholars. The journal's mission would be to promote a scholarly investigation of mothering and motherhood in which the important differences of race, class, sexuality, ethnicity, nationality, and ability are foregrounded. Finally, the focus of the journal was to be inter-disciplinary and multi-disciplinary, inviting submissions from numerous diverse fields and encouraging research that crossed disciplinary boundaries.

From spring 1999 to fall 2009 ARM published a scholarly peer-reviewed biannual journal called the *Journal of the Association for Research on Mothering* (in spring 2010 it was renamed the *Journal of the Motherhood Initiative for Research and Community Involvement*). Each journal issue focuses on a particular motherhood theme or issue and showcases the newest and best in maternal scholarship. The topic for each issue is decided upon by the journal advisory board and is based on the themes of ARM conferences. *JARM/JMI* have published 24 issues on topics as diverse as "Mothering and the Environment: The Social, the Natural, the Built," "Mothering, Bereavement, Loss and Grief," "Mothering, Violence, Militarism, War and Social Justice," "Mothering, Sex and Sexuality," "Maternal Health," "Mothering and Work: Mothering as Work," "Carework and Caregiving," "Mothering and Literature," "Grandmothers and Grandmothering," "Mothering,

Religion and Spirituality," and "Mothers and Sons."

As the *only* scholarly journal on motherhood, the defining mission of the *Journal of the Motherhood Initiative* is to publish the best current scholarship on motherhood, and to ensure that this scholarship considers motherhood both in an international context and from a multitude of perspectives including differences of class, race, sexuality, age, ethnicity, ability, and nationality. As the journal examines motherhood in an international context and from many diverse perspectives, it also examines each motherhood topic from a diversity of disciplines and aims to ensure that both the Humanities and Social Sciences are represented in each journal issue. The top scholars in the field have been published in our journal (including Sara Ruddick, Linda Rennie Forcey, Susan B. Boyd, Molly Ladd-Taylor, Lorna Turnbull, Joanna Radbord, Margrit Eichler, Nancy Mandell, Ann Duffy, Susan Driver, Patrice DiQuinzio, Deidre Kelly, Marguerite Bouvard, Susan Driver, Emily Jeremiah, Andrea O'Reilly, Deidre Hill Butler, and Margaret Morganroth Gullette).

The journal also publishes between ten and fifteen book reviews in each volume in addition to a selection of poetry from new and established poets. Each issue of *JARM/JMI* has featured a Folio on an established poet's work since 2004. The Folio includes an introduction by the Literary Editor, currently Jane Satterfield (formerly, Rishma Dunlop) and approximately 15 poems of that poet's work; photography is also included in the Folio. Featured Folio poets include Clarinda Harris, Meena Alexander, Ann Fisher-Wirth, Priscila Uppal, Katherine Smith, Kathryn Rhett, and Judith Arcana among others. The Young Mothers issue included the section "Young Mothers Speak Out," which included poetry, photography, cartoons, artwork and essays by 20 young mothers.

Our journal is well read and loved as evidenced by the following comments received from motherhood scholars. Lynn O'Brien Hallstein from Boston University describes JMI as, "The premier journal for both scholars and activists interested in learning how motherhood and mothering are being understood intellectually and politically." Joanne Detore-Nakamura from Embry-Riddle Aeronautical University writes, "The journal provides a forum for serious academic study and for high calibre creative writing concerning what is one of the most important functions of society—mothering." Likewise, Louise Ripley from York praises JMI as "One of the best academic journals available. Highly interdisciplinary with a variety of different kinds of writing, well edited, newsworthy, challenging, it is one journal that I always read cover-to-cover as soon as it arrives. I also find it useful in my teaching, in all three areas." JMI is widely cited in current motherhood scholarship, subscribed to by many university libraries, and is internationally known and recognized as the leading journal in the field; it is read by scholars, researchers, students, academics, and practitioners worldwide.

Demeter Press

Launched in 2006, Demeter Press is the first scholarly and feminist press to

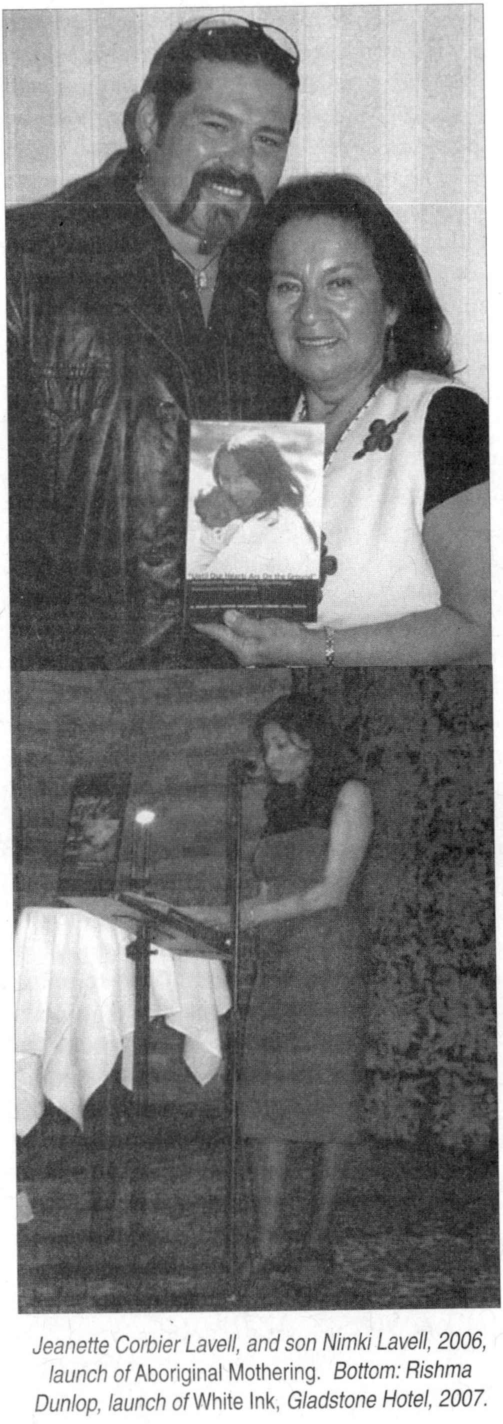

Jeanette Corbier Lavell, and son Nimki Lavell, 2006, launch of Aboriginal Mothering. *Bottom: Rishma Dunlop, launch of* White Ink, *Gladstone Hotel, 2007.*

specifically focus on the topic of mothering and motherhood. Demeter Press, a peer-reviewed press, publishes two to five titles a year on various diverse motherhood topics, with a commitment to publishing work on under-researched motherhood topics as discussed above. Past and forthcoming titles include (in addition to those cited above) *Mothering and Adoption* (2011); *Maternal Pedogogies Inside and Outside the Classroom* (2011); *Mothering: Anthropological Perspectives* (2011); *The M Word: Real Mothers in Contemporary Art* (2011); *Giving Breastmilk* (2010); *Mothering Canada* (2010); *Mothering and Blogging* (2009); *Mother Knows Best: Talking Back to the Experts* (2009); *Mothering in the Third Wave* (2008); *Maternal Theory: Essential Readings* (2007); and *White Ink: Poems on Mothers and Motherhood* (2006).

The press is named in honour of herstory's most celebrated, empowered, and outraged mother: the Goddess Demeter. Demeter was the Greek Goddess of agriculture and fertility who unleashed her power when her beloved daughter Persephone was abducted and taken to the underworld by the God Hades. Overcome with rage and grief, Demeter withheld the coming of spring after which the chief god Zeus, now faced with the plight of the earth's bareness, had no choice but to demand that Hades return Persephone to her mother. In *Of Woman Born* Rich interprets the Demeter-Persephone story as a compelling representation of every daughters' "longing for a mother whose love for her and whose power were so great as to undo rage and bring her back from death," and signifying "every mothers' longing for the power of Demeter and the efficacy of her anger" (240). In patriarchal culture, where there are so few examples of empowered mothering and mothers in literature and life, Demeter's triumphant resistance serves as a model for the possibility—and power—of feminist mothering. Overall, as a division of the Motherhood Initiative for Research and Community Involvement, Demeter Press supports MIRCI's mandate to promote motherhood scholarship and to build a sustaining community of maternal researchers by publishing a wide array of writing on mothering-motherhood by poets, community activist and scholars.

Challenges

As with most motherhood organizations, our biggest challenge is funding. While I have been very successful in securing SSHRC grants, these grants, as anyone who has submitted one knows, require an enormous amount of time and energy to prepare and are highly competitive. Such grants are also only available for specific, time-limited initiatives, such as conferences, a journal publication or a research project, and do not provide base funding for the day to day operational costs of an organization. The operational costs for MIRCI and Demeter Press are particularly high as we maintain an active membership, undertake two to three conferences a year, publish a journal issue bi-annually, and two to five Demeter Press titles each year; this magnitude of work requires a part-time director, a full-time staff person, and several part-time staff. As well, MIRCI and Demeter Press, engaged as they are in the publishing of books and journals, have the ever-increasing cost of book production, printing, and mailing to finance. A single journal issue or Demeter Press title costs between $9,000 and $20,000 to publish, with more money required for distribution and promotion. These costs are covered solely by membership dues, subscriptions to our journal, and sales of Demeter Press books. We are fortunate and deeply appreciative to have so many loyal motherhood scholars who renew their memberships and subscriptions each year and purchase our Demeter Press titles for themselves and others. MIRCI and Demeter Press would not exist without this support. Demeter Press will become eligible for publishing grants as it is further established over the next few years; it is our hope that this division of MIRCI will obtain some base funding, though the overall costs of MIRCI and its journal will continue to be financed by memberships and subscriptions

Future Goals

As with most motherhood organizations our goal over the next few years is to increase our membership and subscription base in addition to Demeter Press sales. In so doing, we aim to ensure our financial viability so that we may continue the important and necessary work of promoting the advancement of maternal scholarship and the empowerment of mothers. As well, we aim to strengthen and broaden community involvement in MIRCI and to develop a more international network of maternal scholars to ensure that the study of motherhood-mothering is situated in a fully global context. To achieve these two aims MIRCI is establishing a presence on Twitter and Facebook.

Relationship to Larger Motherhood Movement

Thirteen years ago I published my first book on motherhood with Sharon Abby, the edited collection *Redefining Motherhood: Changing Identities and Patterns* which opened with Adrienne Rich's oft-cited quote, "We know more about the air we breathe, the seas we travel, than about the nature and meaning of motherhood" (11). By 1998, 20 years after the publication of Rich's landmark *Of Woman Born*, most academic disciplines, from anthropology to women's studies, were engaged in some form of motherhood research. Although scholarship on motherhood still struggled for legitimacy and centrality in some disciplines, it was acknowledged that Motherhood Studies was emerging as a distinct field within the larger disciplines of Feminist Scholarship or Women's Studies. In the last decade the topic of motherhood has emerged as a distinct and established field of scholarly inquiry. Indeed, today it would be unthinkable to cite Rich's quote on the dearth of maternal scholarship as the above collection did a mere 13 years ago. A cursory review of motherhood research reveals that hundreds of scholarly articles have been published on almost every motherhood theme imaginable. The *Journal of the Association for Research on Mothering/Journal of the Motherhood Initiative* alone has examined motherhood topics as diverse as sexuality, peace, religion, public policy, literature, work, popular culture, health, carework, young mothers, motherhood and feminism, feminist mothering, mothers and sons, mothers and daughters, lesbian mothering, adoption, mothering, race and ethnicity, and the motherhood movement, to name a few.

In 2006, I coined the term Motherhood Studies to acknowledge and demarcate this new scholarship on motherhood as a legitimate and distinctive discipline, one grounded in the theoretical tradition of maternal theory developed by scholars such as Patricia Hill Collins, Adrienne Rich, Sharon Hays, Paula Caplan, Susan Maushart, Andrea O'Reilly, Fiona Green, Miriam Johnson, bell hooks, Patrice DiQuinzio, Susan Douglas and Meredith W. Micheals, Alice Walker, Marianne Hirsh, and Sara Ruddick. Indeed, similar to the development of Women's Studies as an academic field in the 1970s, Motherhood Studies, while explicitly interdisciplinary, cross-disciplinary and multi-disciplinary, has emerged as an autonomous and independent scholarly discipline in the last decade. The recent publication of the first encyclopedia of motherhood (O'Reilly 2010: 3 volumes, 700 plus entries) confirms the coming of age of mothering research, demonstrating that motherhood scholarship has indeed been recognized and legitimized as a scholarly discipline.

I believe that MIRCI has played a pivotal role in the advancement of maternal

MIRCI, Mother Outlaws, and GrrrlVirus at Toronto SlutWalk, April 3, 2011. Photo: Kim Breland.

scholarship and the establishment of Motherhood Studies as a scholarly discipline. The following comments from motherhood scholars and activists seem to confirm this. Sara Ruddick, author of the landmark motherhood text *Maternal Thinking* writes, "There is no question in my mind, no doubt at all, that MIRCI provides a distinctive kind of support, inspiration, opportunity, and discipline that makes the world better for mothers." Meredith W. Michaels, author of the popular book *The Mommy Myth: The Idealization of Motherhood and How It Undermines Women* voices a complimentary remark: "MIRCI has transformed research on the family and so provided policy makers at all levels with access to a reservoir of knowledge and understanding of motherhood." Likewise, Jen Lawrence, founder of BlissNotes.com, praises MIRCI as "one of the few organizations that takes the practice of mothering and what it means to be a mother seriously." Lawrence drives home her point poignantly: "In a world that either ignores mothers (save for one Sunday a year) or views us only as a consumer group, MIRCI gives mothers from all walks of life a real voice." "MIRCI's contributions to the fields of motherhood and feminist studies are incalculable. Its work is academically sound, cutting-edge, and extremely useful to people outside the academy. It has also played a crucial role in helping to build the international motherhood movement," writes Enola G. Aird, founder of Mothers for a Human Future. Dawn Lavell-Harvard, President of the Ontario Native Women's Association, states that, "MIRCI plays a powerful role in the lives of mothers around the world and has served as a focal point for research in mothering. But most importantly, MIRCI has provided a voice for women when they are at a time in their lives they have felt voiceless and that their experiences were not accurately represented by the mainstream culture."

Further, I would argue that the motherhood research that has been developed and disseminated in and through the work of MIRCI is essential for effective maternal activism. Feminists have long recognized the important affiliation and interface between research and activism, and regard both research and activism as necessary to making social change possible. Maternal scholarship provides the knowledge for understanding and responding to the discrimination, devaluation, and dissatisfaction that mothers often experience, making possible an organized movement to challenge and change such. MIRCI, as the first and still only scholarly association on motherhood, provides this necessary research for maternal activism. As explained above, the overarching objective of MIRCI is to discuss, develop, and disseminate research and community involvement that has social use and relevance in order to effect real change in the lives of mothers. In both theory and practice MIRCI is informed by a view of academic research that defines good scholarship as—to borrow from the noted scholar and activist Angela Davis—that which has social relevance and use, and the worth of which is measured by its impact on society and the achievement of a just and equitable world. Thus, MIRCI is vital to contemporary maternal activism and the success of the larger 21st century motherhood movement not only because of its credibility as the first, and still only, research association on motherhood, but also because of the socially relevant nature of its research and the impact of such.

Conclusion

I sit writing this chapter on the first spring-like weekend after what seems like a particularly long winter. If truth be told, I would rather be outside in the sunshine working in my garden than here in front of a laptop on the living room couch. Nonetheless, I am here for the same reason I agreed to organize that first conference on motherhood 15 years ago as a new Ph.D. and as an overworked and exhausted contract faculty: this work needs to be done and someone has to do it. Such reasoning is far less altruistic than it sounds: 15 years ago I needed a community of motherhood scholars to sustain and support me in my life as a feminist mother and in my work as motherhood scholar and I still need it now. Recently, some have said to me that such hard work and vigilance are no longer needed since motherhood studies now appears to be firmly established as an academic discipline, one that has secured the legitimacy and respect that I had hoped for. Yet, as a recent email correspondence confirmed, I know that the foothold that motherhood studies and mother academics have secured in universities and in scholarship is precarious at best. Last fall, I had the misfortune of engaging in an email exchange with a male graduate student who seemed to have nothing better to do with his time than attack me, MIRCI, and motherhood scholarship. Common sense would have dictated that I ignore his tirade and press the delete button but I could not help myself. Included in his increasing hostile emails were comments like: "no doubt that this organization and its publications are devoid of real intellectual merit"; "we know there is next to zero mothering going on in academia, which is a fine choice, but let's not pretend otherwise"; "Demeter Press is just one more publishing house with clear intention; promotion of books with little intellectual content" and finally "'mothering' is one of those pseudo scholarly topics which bring lots of research money from the numerous pseudo scholars who make up the committees at SSHRC, simply because it meets the PC feminist criteria of 'activism.' The posture of academic feminists, most of whom are childless, acting as mothers cannot be taken too seriously." And just yesterday he sent me another email that described maternal scholarship as "anti-intellectual hogwash." His words, while likely (and hopefully) not representative of how motherhood studies and motherhood scholars are viewed in the academe today, nonetheless serve as a reminder that the place we have worked so hard to secure for ourselves as mother scholars must be sustained and needs to be safeguarded. So this unnerving and compelling reminder is what keeps me on the couch rather than in the garden on this promise of a spring day—that and I know that more days of spring are sure to follow.

Works Cited

Brandt, Di. *Wild Mother Dancing: Maternal Narrative in Canadian Literature.* Winnipeg: University of Manitoba Press, 1993.

Chernick, Myrel and Jennie Klein, eds. *The M Word: Real Mothers in Contemporary Art.* Toronto: Demeter Press, 2011.

Craddock , Karen T., Nicole Banton and Saundra Murray Nettles, eds. *Black Motherhoods.* Dunlop, Rishma, ed. *White Ink: Poems on Mothers and Motherhood.* Toronto: Demeter Press, 2007.

Eljdupovic, Gordana and Rebecca Jaremko Bromwich, eds. *Incarcerated Mothers: Oppression and Resistance.* Toronto: Demeter Press, 2012 (Under Contract).

Fast, Kerry and Rachel Epp Buller, eds. *Mennonite Mothering.* Toronto: Demeter Press, 2013 (Under Contract).

Friedman, May and Shana L. Calixte, eds. *Mothering and Blogging: The Radical Act of the MommyBlog.* Toronto: Demeter Press, 2009.

Geissler, Shawna, Lynn Loutzenhiser, Jocelyne Praud and Leesa Streifler, eds. *Mothering Canada: Interdisciplinary Voices / La maternité au Canada: Voix interdisciplinaires.* Toronto: Demeter Press, 2010.

Green, Fiona J., and Deborah Byrd, eds. *Maternal Pedagogies: In and Outside the Classroom.* Toronto: Demeter Press, 2011 (Under Contract).

Kinser, Amber E., ed. *Mothering in the Third Wave.* Toronto: Demeter Press, 2008.

Latchford, Frances, ed. *Adoption and Mothering.* Toronto: Demeter Press, 2011 (Under Contract).

Lavell-Harvard, Dawn Memee and Jeanette Corbiere Lavell, eds. *Until Our Hearts Are On the Ground: Aboriginal Mothering, Oppression, Resistance and Rebirth.* Toronto: Demeter Press, 2006.

"Looking Back, Looking Forward: Mothers, Daughters, and Feminism." *Canadian Women's Studies/les cahiers de la femme*. Vol. 18, No. 2&3 (Spring/Fall 1998).

Morrison, Toni. "Women's History." About.com. Web. http://womenshistory.about.com/od/quotes/a/toni_morrison.htm>.

Mortenson, Joani, ed. *Queering Maternity & Motherhood: Narrative and Theoretical Perspectives on Queer Conception, Birth and Parenting*. Toronto: Demeter Press, 2012 (Under Contract).

Nathanson, Jessica and Laura Camille Tuley, eds. *Mother Knows Best: Talking Back to the "Experts."* Toronto: Demeter Press, 2009.

Olwan, Dana, ed. *Muslim Mothering: Local and Global Histories, Theories, and Practices*. Toronto: Demeter Press, 2012 (Under Contract).

O'Reilly, Andrea, ed. *Maternal Theory: Essential Readings*. Toronto: Demeter Press, 2007.

O'Reilly, Andrea. *Mothers and Sons: Feminism, Masculinity and the Struggle to Raise Our Sons*. New York: Routledge Press, 2001.

O'Reilly, Andrea and Sharon Abbey. *Mothers and Daughters: Connection, Empowerment and Transformation*. Lanham, MD: Rowman & Littlefield, 2000.

O'Reilly, Andrea and Sharon Abbey. *Redefining Motherhood: Changing Identities and Patterns*. Toronto: Second Story Press, 1998.

Reyes, Angelita. *Other Mothers, Other Mothering*. Toronto: Demeter Press, 2013 (Under Contract).

Rich, Adrienne. *Of Woman Born: Motherhood as Experience and Institution*. 1976. New York: W.W. Norton, 1986.

Ruddick, Sara. *Maternal Thinking: Toward a Politics of Peace*. New York: Beacon Press, 1989.

Sangha, Jasjit Kaur, ed. *South Asian Mothering*. Toronto: Demeter Press, 2012 (Under Contract).

Shaw, Rhonda and Alison Bartlett, eds. *Giving Breastmilk: Body Ethics and Contemporary Breastfeeding Practice*. Toronto: Demeter Press, 2010.

Smith Silva, Dorsia and Janine Santiago, eds. *Latina/Chicana Mothering*. Toronto: Demeter Press, 2011 (Under Contract).

Umansky, Lauri. *Motherhood Reconceived: Feminism and the Legacies of the Sixties*. New York: New York University Press, 1996.

Walks, Michelle and Naomi McPherson, eds. *Mothering: Anthropological Perspectives*. Toronto: Demeter Press, 2011 (Under Contract).

70. Birthing and Re-Birthing Down Under

From ARM-A to AMIRCI

MARIE PORTER AND JULIE KELSO

IN AUSTRALIA, WE HAVE A mythical creature called the bunyip. The bunyip belongs to Aboriginal culture, but this figure is known all over Australia. Marie Porter has been fascinated with the story of the bunyip since she was about three years old. In 1982, she saw a copy of another book about the bunyip—*The Bunyip of Berkeley's Creek* by Jenny Wagner. She bought it to read to her young grandson. He loved it and the book has had countless readings over 18 years to five grandchildren. In this book the bunyip emerges from Berkeley's Creek with no idea of who he is or what he looks like. He seeks the answers to these questions in the Australian bush. After vainly questioning several Australian animals, he finds a man busy writing in a notebook. When the bunyip asks the man his questions, the man does not look up, but replies that bunyips look like nothing because "bunyips simply don't exist." The poor disheartened bunyip walks back into the bush and that evening he sits by a billabong (a waterhole). His sadness turns to joy when another creature emerges from the billabong asking the same questions that he had asked himself. He could reassure this creature that she was a bunyip just like him and that she looked beautiful.

This story reminds Marie of her journey into mothering research. When she began her research, she frequently could not even find the word "mother" in an index of a book focusing on culture or society. She found few researchers in this field, and could not find an appropriate academic association to join until the establishment of the Association for Research on Mothering (ARM), founded by Associate Professor Andrea O'Reilly at York University in Toronto, Canada, in 1997. Marie attended ARM's first official conference and was overjoyed at being surrounded by about 120 scholars all researching in the area of motherhood. Like the bunyip, she no longer felt alone.[1] The support of ARM members legitimated her work in her mind.

In Australia an organization that focused on the academic study of mothering did not exist. In 2000 several mothers, including Julie Kelso and Marie, who were both Ph.D. researchers at the University of Queensland, formed a committee to plan a day devoted to presentations focusing on the study of mothering. This informal structure became a formal association in 2005, taking the name

Andrea O'Reilly, Lorelei Carpenter, elke emerald, and Marie Porter

"The Association for Research on Mothering-Australia" (ARM-A). ARM-A is a non-profit incorporated feminist organization that exists to promote research into mothering/motherhood/mothers. In August, 2010, at our Annual General Meeting, we voted to change the name of our Association to the Australian Motherhood Initiative for Research and Community Involvement (AMIRCI) to maintain our connection with the Canadian ARM now changed to MIRCI. In this chapter, we outline the history of the Australian Association, the reasons we established it, the background to our choice of name, our philosophy and our goals. We have had our successes and our failures, and will outline these aspects of our experiences.

History

For many years Julie and Marie shared an office. We are both mothers. Marie is the mother of three sons, all of whom were adults in 2000, but because of the severe disabilities and health problems of her youngest son she was still engaged in hands on, day-to-day mothering.[2] Julie was a young, single mother with a very young daughter. We were both working on our doctoral theses when we decided to organize a day-long seminar on mothering. Several other mothers were happy to support this idea. We formed a committee and advertised the event. To our stunned amazement, we had abstracts come in from nine different countries and from 35 different tertiary institutions. Our day-long seminar, "Motherhood: Power/Oppression" turned into a three-day conference, with three concurrent sessions running. It was a stimulating, interesting, and enjoyable event that revealed to all of us present that there were many academics both in Australia and overseas interested in studying mothering. We realized that there was a hunger and a need for this area of study to be acknowledged. Since then we have held five international conferences in Australia on mothering and the sixth will be held in April, 2011. These conferences have become a meeting place for scholars, and others, interested in research in this area.

In 2005, Andrea O'Reilly was the keynote speaker at our third International Mothering Conference, "Theorizing and Representing Maternal Subjectivities." A group of scholars in attendance decided that an Association for Research on Mothering should be formally established. It was proposed that the Association be national and be used as a vehicle for future growth of the study of mothering by obtaining funding to establish a maternal scholarship research centre; conducting seminars; organizing conferences; and seeking to obtain recognition for "our" field as a legitimate area of academic study. This valuable field of research would seek to raise critical awareness of the particularities and complexities of mothering as embedded in Australian society.

Aims and Objectives of the Association

The aims and objectives of the Association are to promote maternal scholarship as a distinct field within feminist studies and related areas of research; to offer peer support for researchers within this field of scholarship through social activities, conferences and reading and commenting on others' work; and to promote awareness of the importance of mothering and mothers in academia and the wider community.

Membership

Our membership is predominantly composed of scholars but we welcome anyone interested in promoting maternal scholarship and empowering mothers. We are committed to the inclusion of all mothers, those people who do motherwork, and those people interested in mothers/mothering. We recognize that the experience of being a mother varies through dislocation, discrimination, culture, and context and that diversity is part of our commonality (Collins). Our patron is colleague and friend, Dr Jackie Huggins, a prominent Indigenous scholar at the University of Queensland. She has supported the Association since the first conference at which she gave the keynote address.

The Name and Core Philosophy

We chose the name "Association for Research on Mothering-Australia" (ARM-A) because it clearly stated that our organization was aligned with Association for Research on Mothering (ARM) at York University in Toronto, Canada, but shifted the focus to Australia and the Pacific region.[3] As a group, when we were setting up the Association, we understood that the academic study of mothering was not highly regarded or recognised either in Australia or internationally. We sought the strength of unity. We still seek that strength which is the reason that we have

Andrea O'Reilly, Tamara Ditrich and Marie Porter at the end of the 2005 conference.

changed the name of our Association as we outline later in the Chapter.

We had other reasons for choosing the name ARM-A. As a play on the word "armour," our title recognized the battle we often face trying to get maternality, motherhood and motherwork recognized and valued. This punning on a masculine metaphor of war is strategically utilized to foreground the fight that women have faced, and still face, in instituting a feminist symbolic value for the figure of the "mother" in our societies, beyond "her" patriarchally-defined, oppressive conceptualization. Rejecting the biologically determinist positioning that reduces women to the equivalent position of mother, we accept Sara Ruddick's definition of mothering and motherwork as the work required to grow, preserve and train a newborn into a responsible adult. We therefore see mothering/motherwork as a gender-neutral endeavour. That is, motherwork is understood as a particular form of work that needs to be valued and recompensed, whether performed by a man or a woman. Moreover, the name, ARM-A also speaks to the need to (re)evaluate, (re)present and indeed (re)create, with valour, symbolic representations of women and maternity that serve as progressive possibilities for women. We insist that our female bodies and their productive capacities, along with the work those bodies provide, have never been truly valued in the West, and further that such a de-valuing functions as a major component of women's oppression. Thus, our intellectual endeavour concerns the fight against this dominant anti-feminist ideology by persistently and insistently re-inscribing women's "labour" (in all senses of the term) into the realms of culture and society.

Finally, there is another possibility that arises through the enunciation of our name: ARM-A is somewhat homologous with the French word amour (love). As a feminist body of scholars, we are dedicated to the revaluing of women's roles in society, particularly their status as women and mothers, for the purpose of promoting a valuable love and friendship between women: a strong and genuine sisterhood. As a feminist association researching motherhood, motherwork and historical and cultural conceptualizations of "mother," we are, in other words, intellectually committed to the development of a symbolic female genealogy.

Despite choosing our name for such good reasons, we decided to change the name of the Association at our Annual General Meeting held on the 26 August, 2006. We still believe in the concepts outlined above. These ideas still guide our Association, but we feel strongly that it is important that our relationship with the Canadian Association is highlighted because we strongly believe that there is strength in unity. We want to make our wish to promote 'a valuable love and friendship between women: a strong and genuine sisterhood', highly visible. Andrea O'Reilly and members of ARM have always been available to support us. Hence when ARM became the Motherhood Initiative for Research and Community Involvement (MIRCI), we decided to change our name to the Australian Motherhood Initiative for Research and Community Involvement (AMIRCI), thus maintaining our obvious connection with MIRCI in Canada.

Events and Activities

In conjunction with MIRCI and the School of History, Philosophy, Religion and Classics, and the Centre for Research on Women, Gender, Culture and Social Change, in the School of English, Media Studies and Art History, The University of Queensland, we have organised four of the five Australian conferences. The first conference, held in 2001, was followed by "Performing Motherhood: Ideology, Agency and Experience," held at La Trobe University, Melbourne in 2002. Our third conference, "Representing and Theorizing Maternal Subjectivities," was held in Brisbane in 2005 as was our fourth conference, "The Mother: Images, Issues and Practices," held in 2007. "The Mother and History: Past and Present," was held in 2009. Our sixth Australian International conference, "Mothers at the Margins," will be held at the University of Queensland from the 27th to 30th April, 2011.

Our conferences have been successful, well-attended with a good range of papers presented by scholars from all levels of the academic world, from various tertiary institutions and from various countries. Since that first conference, all conferences have run for two and a half days with two days of three concurrent sessions. We have been pleased at the growing diversity of the papers as more participants now come from Asia and a few from Africa.

Some events within our conferences have added another dimension to the academic focus. Our patron, Jackie Huggins, always organizes an Indigenous Elder to welcome people to the Australian land. When we were lacking Indigenous participation in our first conference, we again turned to Jackie for ideas. She suggested that we organise a Conversation Circle with three Indigenous Elders and give them a 90-minute time slot. These mothers related how they had mothered and answered questions from the participants in the circle. This was so popular we repeated it three times. At our fourth conference the leading Indigenous group of dancers performed for us. The several presentations by artists have been similarly popular.

Many of the conference presentations have been published. A selection of papers from the first conference can be found in *Motherhood: Power and Oppression*, edited by Marie Porter, Patricia Short and Andrea O'Reilly, and published by Women's Press, in Toronto. A selection of papers from the third conference form the book *Representing and Theorizing Maternal Subjectivities* (2008), edited by Julie Kelso and Marie Porter, and published by Cambridge Scholars Publishing in Newcastle, United Kingdom. In 2010, Cambridge Scholars Publishing published *Mother Texts: Narratives and Counter Narratives*, which is based on presentations from the fourth conference, and is also edited by Julie Kelso and Marie Porter. Papers from the fifth biennial conference, are published in the latest issue of *Hecate*.

Over the years, we have arranged a few seminars, and Association members living in, or close to, Brisbane have met eight to ten times per year for discussion over lunch. With the help of Brisbane-based members, Marie prepared a course for undergraduate students in their second year of study at the University of Queensland. We were (reluctantly) allowed to run the course, "The Mother: Images, Issues and Practices," in second semester in 2007. While Marie co-ordinated the course and did many of the lectures, the local Association members were all guest lecturers in their fields of expertise. The students ranged from 17 to 50 and were all women. They rated the course well, finding it interesting and stimulating. Due to various problems, both personal and institutional, the course has not been offered again.

The Association provides support for many new researchers. We are contacted by email frequently for advice and support, for our thoughts on a certain area of research, for availability of books and for their suitability. We always reply to the best of our knowledge.

Challenges and Issues

We have had many challenges and continue to face them. We have been successful in obtaining support for conferences, but other funding has eluded us. The conferences have had the effect of establishing that there is a legitimate field of academic research which centres on mothering. This recognition is particularly evident amongst women, but, unfortunately, it does not seem to be seen as important by many of the hierarchy (almost all men) in tertiary institutions. There seems to be little institutional support for (and sometimes open hostility to) the development of this area of study.

Our experience of support from other feminist scholars can be summed up as enthusiastic when we are together at a conference, but this enthusiasm drowns afterwards in the busy lives and heavy workloads we all seem to have now. Hence, our membership is relatively high in the years we have conferences, but drops

Julie Kelso and Carole Ferrier, 2009.

off dramatically in the alternate years. The result is that the same few members end up doing the work and have become tired over the years. Our hopes that each state would form a group of interested members and have regular meetings as we have done in Queensland failed to materialise. Part of the problem is the vast distances we have in Australia and, comparatively, the low population. This problem could be overcome to a large degree by the use of telephone hook-ups and the Internet—a solution we used recently.

In Brisbane our small group of active members have supported each other academically, personally and socially. Here we want to acknowledge the incredible support given over many years by Tamara Ditrich, Jenny Jones and Lisa Raith who all research different aspects of mothering/motherhood. Without these dedicated people ARM-A would have failed. The major problem for the Brisbane group has been time. We are all working on a Ph.D., lecturing, researching or publishing. We are all mothers with families. To work and maintain family connections and support family members, including adult family members when a crisis occurs, is time consuming. We have had many crises—illnesses, accidents, marriage breakups and deaths. It is women who are already busy with motherwork and voluntary work (both unpaid and undervalued) and other work (paid), who have added more unpaid work to their load.

A Common Challenge in a Patriarchal Culture?

Here we divert from direct focus on our Association to acknowledge issues in our culture which we believe make it more difficult not only for mothers, but also for their organizations. A major challenge to the development of maternal research in Australia is the general attitude towards mothers and the work they do in bearing and rearing their children. This attitude may be a common challenge to mothers in Western (and other patriarchal) societies. Mothering is not

Jenny Jones and Lisa Raith, stalwarts of AMIRCI.

recognized as work in any way that counts in the Western social system (Oakley; Cowan; Gieve; DeVault; Pocock; Home; Porter). Feminists have written about mothering as work, highlighting, in vain, how mothering requires and develops skills just as paid work does (Maher; Ruddick; Porter). In their motherwork with their children, mothers are continually working, observing, thinking, discussing with peers, trialling, adapting, and repeating these processes. These practices, formally recognised as routine for skilled or professional workers, attest to the skills mothers gain and hone in their work (Maher). Nonetheless, mothers at home who are not in paid employment, are seen as not working by many people because the word "work" is reserved for those people who are in paid employment. To many mothers, paid work is easy in comparison with motherwork (Horin).

Moreover, motherwork never seems to end. Even when children have reached adulthood, mothers usually have family calls on their time. Motherwork becomes grandmother work, caring work with elderly parents and work to support adult children through the various traumas that may afflict them. For example, it is usually the mother who looks after the adult disabled son/daughter when no support, or not enough support, is available. It is frequently the grandmother who will care for children when nurturing care is required, but is either not available or not affordable. The result is that mothers are usually very busy and find it difficult to find time to take on any more voluntary work. It is obvious that despite the achievements of feminism mothering is still problematic for women and can lead to social and economic disadvantages.

Linked to this challenge is the issue of money. Mothers' disadvantages in the paid work sphere result in few women achieving entry to the upper echelons of society. Thus few mothers have the type of influence and the money that many men have. Many men with influence and money will support particular associations. Few men are interested in supporting mothers' organisations. It is not helpful that motherhood is generally not valued in the wider society. The mothers who were interviewed for the research published in *The Transformative Power in Motherwork* (Porter), spoke about the high value that they placed on mothering whether it was their own mothering or mothering in general. They saw mothering as enrichment to their lives, and understood its value to society, despite the low social value put on mothers and their work. A belief in self-worth and in the value of the work undertaken is difficult to maintain when that work is not validated by the society, yet most mothers value their motherwork.

Changes Down Under

Julie and Marie had been heavily involved with the Association since its informal beginnings in 2000, with Marie being President of the Association once we were officially incorporated in 2005. In 2009, Marie was feeling quite exhausted from trying to keep everything going in the midst of four years of illnesses her husband had endured. She believed that the Association would benefit from new ideas and from some younger members who are more in touch with grassroots mothering organisations. She resigned the presidency. Julie stayed on the committee for some weeks, then resigned due to the pressures of her employment. The committee voted in a new president, secretary and treasurer. Unfortunately, we lost both the treasurer and the secretary. These positions were taken up again by former office bearers to ensure the survival of the Association. Jenny Jones, who is finishing her doctoral thesis, has taken on the position of treasurer again and Vivienne Muller is the secretary. The new President, Dr Joan Garvan, has just finished her doctoral thesis and, consequently, has not had the time she needs yet to devote to the Association. Despite this situation, she has made a good start by organizing a symposium. In 2010 the Australian National University hosted an International Women in Asia Conference. Joan, as President, organized a one day symposium to be held on the day after the conference.

Conclusion

We hope that AMIRCI will flourish because there are many scholars in Australia studying various aspects of mothering and we are the only academic organisation. We consider it important that mothering is made visible in all areas of society, and that mothers have a voice that is heeded. When women discover that we are studying mothering, without fail they remark that such study is needed. Men who are interested will ask (sincerely) what that means and will listen respectfully. Many men dismiss such research as women's stuff, certainly not one of the serious areas of life—not like economics, or politics, or paid work. It is, nevertheless, the most important and valuable work done in any society as it involves raising the next generation—without mothers, society and the human species would not survive.

We acknowledge that because ARM-A was established by a committee, several people-especially Jenny Jones, Lisa Raith and Joan Garvan—have had input into the ideas in the official ARM-A pamphlet, the basis for this Chapter.

[1]Marie has since attended many ARM conferences.
[2]Marie's son, Anthony, died on the 5 December 2000, aged 31.
[3]In 2009 the Association for Research on Mothering (ARM) in Canada broke its link with York University and changed its name to The Motherhood Initiative for Research and Community Involvement (MIRCI).

Works Cited

Collins, Patricia Hill. "Shifting the Center: Race, Class, and Feminist Theorizing about Motherhood." *Mothering: Ideology, Experience, Agency.* Eds Evelyn N. Glenn, Grace Chang, and Linda R. Forcey, London: Routledge, 1994. 45-65.

Cowan, R. S. *More Work for Mother: The Ironies of Household Technology from the Open Hearth to the Microwave.* New York: Basic Books, 1983.

DeVault, M. L. *Feeding the Family.* Chicago: University of Chicago Press, 1991.

"Focus on Mothering." *Hecate* 36.1,2 (2010).

Gieve, K. "Rethinking Feminist Attitudes Towards Motherhood." *Feminist Review* 25 (March 1987): 38-45.

Home, A. The Work that Never Ends: Employed Mothers of Children With Disabilities." *Journal of the Association for Research on Mothering* 6.2 (2004): 37-47.

Horin, A. "The Secret Circle." *Mother Love.* Ed. D. Adelaide. Sydney: Random House, 1996. 167-177.

Maher, J. "Skills, Not Attributes: Rethinking Mothering as Work." *Journal of the Association for Research on Mothering* 6.2 (2004): 7-26.

Oakley, A. *Woman's Work: the Housewife, Past and Present.* New York: Random, 1976.

Pocock, B. *The Work/Life Collison.* Sydney: The Federation Press, 2003.

Porter, M. *The Transformative Power in Motherwork.* Newcastle: Cambridge Scholars Press, 2008.

Porter, M. and J. Kelso, eds. *Mother-Texts: Narratives and Counter-Narratives.* Cambridge: Cambridge Scholars Press, 2010.

Porter, M. and J. Kelso, eds. *Theorising and Representing Maternal Realities.* Cambridge: Cambridge Scholars Press, 2008

Porter, M., P. Short, and A. O'Reilly, eds. *Motherhood: Power and Oppression.* Toronto, Women's Press, 2005.

Ruddick, S. *Maternal Thinking: Toward a Politics of Peace.* Boston: Beacon Press, 1989.

Wagner, Jenny. *The Bunyip of Berkeley's Creek.* Harmondsworth, UK: Puffin Books, 1975.

71. Mapping Maternal Subjectivities, Identities and Ethics

SIGAL SPIGEL AND LISA BARAITSER

MAPPING MATERNAL SUBJECTIVITIES, IDENTITIES AND Ethics (MaMSIE) is an international interdisciplinary research network based in the Department of Psychosocial Studies, Birkbeck, University of London. Founded in 2007 by Lisa Baraitser and Sigal Spigel, it aims to focus attention on the maternal in cultural, political, aesthetic, psychosocial and theoretical configurations. MaMSIE creates spaces for interdisciplinary conversations about the maternal across different knowledge and practice communities including psychoanalysis, feminism, philosophy, visual and performance art, literature and creative writing and the empirical social sciences. It aims to open up and sustain critical debates about the maternal, and explore its unique site at the potent intersection between scientific possibilities, psychosocial practices and cultural representations. Interdisciplinarity and the transversal relations between theory and practice are at the heart of MaMSIE's concerns. It has an open and growing membership of over 350 scholars, practitioners, artists and activists worldwide, who attend events, contribute online to the wiki, and submit academic and artistic work to the peer-reviewed journal, *Studies in the Maternal.*

History and Aims

MaMSIE was founded as a response to what many feminists have pointed out as a fundamental fault line in Western culture—while the maternal appears to be celebrated as the generative source of life, Western culture itself is simultaneously founded on the symbolic "murder" of the mother, and her silencing in order that the masculine, auto-affective, bounded, singular speaking subject can emerge into sociality. 'She' has been variously identified as the leaky affective body, the troubling "one" who splits in two, the necessary but undifferentiated 'environment', the container or receptacle who eludes shape or form, the placeholder for "dumb" reality, the name for the border between thought and biology, or the limit of thought itself. This makes the maternal a peculiarly troubling element of both our psychic and social imaginaries, and in cultural and political life more widely. MaMSIE therefore emerged as an attempt to provide an interdisciplinary space

for those involved in academic, artistic, clinical and activist practices, in which explorations and conversations about the maternal in all of its elusive, multiple, troubling and generative aspects could take place, therefore continuing the work of an earlier generation of feminists in countering these matricidal tendencies. One of our initial aims was to create a forum in which we could begin to draw together and map many broad and differing contributions made by those working in diverse disciplinary spaces, creating a cartography of contemporary understandings of the maternal, and conversely, exploring how this complex and nuanced notion of the maternal could help us think more effectively about subjectivities, identities and ethical relations more generally.

By "maternal" we mean to indicate an open and continually evolving series of significations that may include motherhood (and indeed fatherhood) as diverse lived and embodied experience, but also indicates a structural principle in psychic and social life, a constitutive and regulative fantasy, a unique form of care labour, a relational web, a cyborg techno-body, and many more as yet uncharted meanings.

During the last decades we have witnessed a growing interest in the maternal in academic literatures as well as a burgeoning of maternal creative writing, blogging, online magazines and journals, maternal digital media and visual and performing arts practices. At the same time we have seen a rapid and dramatic "publicization" of the pregnant body, birth, lactation and parent-craft in the media and popular culture more widely. And yet, the work of linking up these contributions into something we may term "Maternal Studies" has been less forthcoming. The reasons for this are likely to be multiple, and may have something to do with the ongoing devaluation and denigration of the maternal that runs alongside the emergence of these new maternal publics. Arguably, one of the principle aims of second-wave feminism was to increase representation, visibility and opportunity for women in public life. What seems necessary at this juncture is an ongoing and careful critique of the ways that certain aspects of maternal experience, and certain mothers' experiences emerge forcefully into the public sphere, whileothers remain occluded, marginalized and despised. Therefore, one of the urgent tasks of what we are calling Maternal Studies is to identify and respond to the blind-spots in our current research and theoretical understandings, and trace the discourses at work in the uneven distribution of what is deemed intelligible as maternal practice, experience, agency, subjectivity, identity or ethics. This work is currently being undertaken by a range of scholars, psychoanalysts, writers and artists who are members of the MaMSIE network and whose work has appeared in *Studies in the Maternal*, including: Kim Allen, Caroline Bainbridge, Elisabetta Bertolino, Rosemary Betterton, Olga Cox Cameron, Adriana Cerne, Polona Curk, Sudeep Dasgupta, Bracha L. Ettinger, Noreen Giffney, Gillian Howie, Maggie Humm, Wendy Hollway, Tracey Jensen, Amber Jacobs, Katerina Kitsi-Mitakou, Gail Lewis, Paula McCloskey, Gavin Miller, Tina Miller, Jenny Mitchell, Patricia Moran, Anne Mulhall, Laura Mulvey, Chrysanthi Nigianni, Jayne Osgood, Michael O'Rourke, Rozsika Parker, Griselda Pollock, Kate Pullinger, Joan Raphael-Leff, Tracey Reynolds, Alison Rowley, Renata Salecl, Lynne Segal, Margrit Shildrick, Lena Simic, Alison Stone, Fanny Söderbäck, Rachel Thomson, Imogen Tyler, Sofie Van Loo, Anne Verougstraete, Angie Voela, Fintan Walsh, Estela Welldon and Christine Wilks, amongst many others.

As well as the constant work of mapping and widening such conditions of intelligibility, there is also a need to keep going back to what we term "maternal subjectivities"—the affective, and at times mute and inarticulate aspects of maternal experience. As daughters, mothers and maternal scholars, we wish to facilitate the emergence of a cultural space within which the maternal can re-emerge, re-remembered in all sorts of ways, in a bid to hold onto the intergenerational and temporal dimensions of this elusive subject position, and without attempting to pin it down, explore its contemporary contours. We also wonder how the almost incomprehensible relational constellation that constitutes a mother as a mother by dint of her relation to an other who is her child, this particular ethical matrix, might have contributed to the gap between the centrality of motherhood and mothering in so many aspects of life and its evasive or polarized representations in imaginary and public arenas. In keeping with feminist strategies that have sought to open our thinking about personal and individual identity by taking the female subject as the "norm" (Battersby), the MaMSIE Network extends this project by suggesting that we ask what would happen to our notions of identity, subjectivity and ethics if we took the maternal subject as if it were the norm. Exercising a deliberate imaginative engagement with what it is like to live in an ongoing relation to that peculiar species know as a child, it would ask the question "what is it like to live alongside this other life form, *as if it were normal*?" (Baraitser).

Troubled by maternal subjectivities, identities, and ethics, we want to stress that our explorations constitute a nascent but distinct field. This is especially important given the absence of the maternal as a visible part of the teaching syllabuses of most academic courses across the disciplines, certainly in the UK context, even those whose purported remit is gender, sexuality or women's studies. As we know, The Association for Research on Mothering (now the Motherhood Initiative for Research and Community Involvement) is one of just a handful of research centres dedicated to the study of motherhood and mothering worldwide. This is now shifting significantly in both the European context, and worldwide. Interestingly, some of the new networks and projects in the UK work at the interface between maternal embodied experience, politics and cultural representations, such as *birth rites*, that explores the politics and practices of child birth through contemporary art work, whilst others continue the sociological tradition of studying motherhood within the context of families and parenting, such as the Cambridge Interdisciplinary Reproduction Forum at the University of Cambridge, and the informal network Parenting Culture Studies, based at the University of Kent. The variety of contexts in which we find maternal scholarship taking place calls into question the nature of this new emergent field. What do we mean when we talk about the maternal? Is it a useful analytic category? As more and more children grow up in blended families, how do we now understand the meanings of birth, surrogate, foster, step, adoptive and transnational mothers, let alone the intricate and diverse practices of mothering across varied geopolitical terrains? What might we mean by "queer mothering," and "queer maternal bodies," and how are lesbian, gay, transgendered and disabled maternal practices shaping and changing the ways we understand reproduction, birth, and parenthood? Should the study of the maternal incorporate discussions of parenting and fatherhood; should it take place within the wider context of studies of the 'family'? The opening up of these questions, questions that emerge out of the interdisciplinary nature of our work, is one of the major aims of MaMSIE.

Activities

MaMSIE is open to those interested in the maternal, and particularly in maternal subjectivities, identities and ethics. It includes practitioners of all kinds: mothers, activists, health professionals, policy makers, writers, academics, artists, performers, psychoanalysts, educators, trainers, birth specialists, and is always keen to welcome new voices and perspectives. MaMSIE organizes events such as conferences, symposia, workshops and other forums for discussion, which are open to members and non-members alike. It collects and collates scholarly and aesthetic work on the maternal through an online library and facilitates discussion among its members through an interactive wiki. In addition, MaMSIE has established a new online, interdisciplinary, peer-reviewed, scholarly journal, *Studies in the Maternal* that is published twice a year, and accepts submissions from a range of scholars, practitioners and artists. It also provides graduate training for emergent academics through an internship programme. A steering committee meets regularly to offer advice and support on the development of MaMSIE and *Studies in the Maternal.* Current committee members include Rebecca Baillie (Artist and Art Historian, University of Essex), Gail Lewis (Reader in Identities, Open University), Kate Pullinger (Author and Reader in Creative Writing and New Media, De Montfort University), Rachel Thomson (Professor of Social Research, Open University) and Imogen Tyler (Senior Lecturer in Sociology, University of Lancaster).

While MaMSIE's founding event aimed at simply mapping the variety of work taking place on the maternal across a range of disciplinary and practice boundaries, subsequent events have focused on different themes using the maternal both as an analytic category and as a site for exploration in its own right. Thus, the second event, "Interrupting Maternal Voices: Between the Theoretical and Empirical" (held in Birkbeck in 2007), aimed at exploring ways in which the maternal acts as a particularly sensitive site for understanding the supposed juncture between theoretical and empirical practices and domains. We looked at the ways "the personal" surfaces in theoretical thinking through engagement with the maternal, and the kinds of tensions that then arise between these supposedly divided realms. "Maternal Representations and Maternal Aesthetics" (Cambridge, 2008) focused on manifestations of the maternal in visual and creative work, whilst "Mum's the Word" (De Montfort University, 2009) explored configurations of maternal in contemporary literature. "M(o)ther Trouble" (Birkbeck, 2009) revisited the long-standing and productive intersection between psychoanalysis, feminism and the maternal and was accompanied by an exhibition by the artist and psychoanalyst Bracha L. Ettinger at the Freud Museum in London. "Motherhood, Servitude and the Delegation of Care" (Birkbeck, 2011) aimed at generating a dialogue between two rich and substantial bodies of feminist scholarship: work on the history of domestic labour, service and servitude and current debates about globalism, migration and the care industries, recasting existing scholarship through the lens of maternal studies. As part of the conference we organized a digital media competition, in which we invited digital artists to respond to the title "Maternal Subjectivities: Care and Labour." Some of this digital artwork will be published as part of a forthcoming special issue of *Studies in the Maternal*, as well as being included in an online exhibition on the MaMSIE wiki.

The issues raised and debated at MaMSIE events are therefore rich and varied. These debates are often marked by a sense of urgency around growing inequalities for women who mother, and the ongoing complexities of the politics of reproduction. Overall, these events have highlighted the need for a variety of dedicated forums to draw together the many different genealogies of the maternal, and what we may call "maternal futures." This prompted the formation of the journal *Studies in the Maternal.* Co-edited by Lisa Baraitser and Sigal Spigel provides a scholarly forum for critical research on motherhood, mothering and the maternal. Published twice yearly, the October issue is a Special Issue organized around a specific theme, and the May issue is an open issue, which may include contributions pertaining to any topic related to the maternal. In addition each issue includes an intergenerational conversation between what are usually termed "second-wave" feminists and what could be referred to as the "daughters" of this generation. Arguably, one of the main objectives of feminist thought throughout the generations has been to highlight the significance of the practice of genealogy, the investigation, that is, into the history of a subject position or a given system of thought, especially thought that appears to have no history. If, as we have argued here, one of the manifestations of the maternal in Western culture is as the very limit of thought, this makes the need for this mode of feminist genealogy especially important. We hope that these conversations, as well as the ongoing exchange of ideas that occurs through MaMSIE's activities, will contribute to such a genealogical enterprise, enabling the emergence of heterogeneous maternal subjectivities that can coexist alongside one another.

Challenges and Future Goals

There is no doubt that motherhood has remained a problematic issue for feminism and feminists. Whether viewed as embodied practice, theoretical construct or social relation, the maternal challenges hard-won feminist notions of autonomy whilst at the same time serving as the nodal point through which "the central concepts of feminist theory are elaborated, and a site at which these concepts are challenged and reworked" (DiQuinzio xi). MaMSIE aims to take part in the ongoing work of challenging and reworking central concepts of feminist theory (concepts such gender, sex and sexuality, love, care, power, embodiment, affect, inequality, and ethics), through posing the question of the maternal for feminist theory itself. It is our view, however, that the maternal subject, perhaps more than any subject position, is downright slippery, and because of the tendency to disappear from various discourses that specifically try to account for maternal subjectivity, it requires a deliberate and strenuous effort to hold the maternal in mind. Critical discourses that use the maternal as their departure point—such as research into new reproductive technologies for instance—are expanding, and rightly so, as explorations of these issues open out onto broader themes, such as the relationship between reproduction and capitalism. While these discussions are integral to MaMSIE, we attempt to focus on the concomitant difficulties and potentialities of holding onto the maternal through these debates. Further more, as Sara Ruddick has argued, maternal and paternal practices continue to remain distinct. Although she understands parenting as the "complex ongoing work of responding to children's needs in particular economic and social circumstances," work that is not *prima facie* associated with either sex, the younger the children and the more physical their demands, the more likely this work will be assigned to women (206). To talk only of parenting denies the history and current practice of female mothering—including women's disproportionate responsibility for childcare, despite the feminization of the work-place (Ruddick). Other feminists have pointed out that it is not just an issue of maternal practice. Paternal bodies are not mediated by the same cultural expectations and norms as maternal bodies (Park), and yet other feminists have worked with this difference to render a theory of "sexuate" difference that refuses to devalue one component in the binary masculine/feminine, and instead offers the maternal-feminine as the principle of two positively valued subjects in an economy of excess (Irigaray).

These heterogeneous positions remain at the heart of MaMSIE's explorations. We hope to continue offering a hub for discussions regarding what constitutes maternal work, mothering and the maternal, and how these contribute to a feminist sensibility that constantly challenges fixed, unitary, static and unsituated notions of subjectivity, identity and ethics. In addition, Terry Arendell stated a decade ago that we need to pay more attention to the lives of particular mothers—to mothers' own voices—and to the lives and voices of diverse groups of mothers. "We need work that connects mothers' personal beliefs and choices with their social situations" (Arendell 1201). It is our hope that MaMSIE's various activities will provide spaces for such work, and for the theoretical analyses that allows coherent accounts of those connections to be made.

Works Cited

Arendell, T. "Conceiving and Investigating Motherhood: The Decade's Scholarship." *Journal of Marriage and the Family* 62 (2000): 1192-1207.

Baraitser, L. *Maternal Encounters: The Ethics of Interruption*. London: Routledge, 2009.

Baraitser, L. and S. Spigel. "Mapping Maternal Subjectivities, Identities and Ethics." *Studies in the Maternal* 1.1 (2009): 1-13.

Battersby, C. *The Phenomenal Woman: Feminist Metaphysics and the Pattern of Identity*. London: Polity Press. New York: Routledge, 1998.

DiQuinzio, P. *The Impossibility of Motherhood: Feminism, Individualism and the Problem of Mothering*. New York: Routledge, 1999.

Irigaray, L. *An Ethics of Sexual Difference*. Trans. C. Burke and C. G. Gill. Ithaca: Cornell University Press, 1993.

Park, S. M. "Adoptive Maternal Bodies: A Queer Paradigm for Rethinking Mothering?" *Hypatia* 21.1 (2006): 201-226.

Ruddick, S. "The Idea of Fatherhood." *Feminism and Families*. Ed. H. L. Nelson. New York: Routledge, 1997. 205-220.

72.
Supporting Feminist Scholarship and Activism

National Women's Studies Association Feminist Mothering Caucus

ARLENE SGOUTAS

In memory of Jessica.

THE FEMINIST MOTHERING CAUCUS (THE Caucus) is a Constituency Group of the National Women's Studies Association (NWSA). Established in 1977, NWSA is a professional organization dedicated to leading the field of women's studies and gender studies, as well as its teaching, learning, research, and service wherever they be found. NWSA leads the field of women's studies in educational and social transformation ("About NWSA"). Within the association there are caucuses, taskforces and interest groups. Caucuses are designated groups that are under-represented within society or NWSA as an organization ("Communities"). As a constituent group of the NWSA, the Caucus is organized to not only support the scholarship work on feminist mothering but also to address the needs of mothers and parents through its conference program and accommodations. This chapter will include the history, philosophy, purpose and mandate of the Caucus in addition to its challenges and future goals. This history is only a brief and incomplete account of its activities.

History

The Feminist Mothering Caucus began in 1998 as the Feminist Mothers and Their Allies task force within NWSA. NWSA task forces are oriented toward an issue or problem relevant to the policies and principles of NWSA and women's studies that can be solved through action. Task Forces, however, do not require representation within the governance structure, and can accomplish their projects without its intervention. Among those academic mothers who belong to NWSA and were involved in the creation of the task force were Kathe Davis, Batya Weinbaum, Rivka Polatnik, and Andrea O'Reilly. According to one of its founding members:

> The mission of the task force originally was to establish accessible, centrally located 24 hour childcare for women who seemed to want to bring their kids to the conference; to get sessions and programming that was both experiential and scholarly; to have a plenary session on mothering leading towards an embedded conference on the theme;

> and to have the programming that we organized be operating as a track throughout the conference that all could attend rather than be conflictual. (Weinbaum)

In 2005 the Feminist Mothers and Their Allies task force became a Caucus. Then, in June 2007, the task force submitted a proposal to change the name to the Feminist Mothering Caucus. The proposal was adopted and read as follows:

> We, the members of the Feminist Mothers and Allies Caucus, wish to change the Caucus name to the Feminist Mothering Caucus. An additional statement is included in our by-laws to qualify our use of the phrase, "feminist mothering," as "a practice not bound by gender or biology. Anyone who practices or is interested in feminist mothering is welcome." Our intent in changing this name is to communicate to all NWSA members that the Caucus is inclusive and welcoming. Further, contemporary feminist theoretical language around motherhood and mothering suggests that we should adopt the term mothering, which is about practice as well as identity, rather than mother, which is more limited to identity.[1]

Since becoming the Feminist Mothering Caucus, the Caucus has worked to build and sustain a community dedicated to its philosophy, purpose and mandate.

Philosophy, Purpose and Mandate

As a constituent group of the NWSA, the Caucus is organized and operated exclusively for charitable and educational purposes which include:

- To employ a broad but pointed anti-oppression agenda and perspective in pursuit of these goals;
- Working to ensure that the NWSA recognizes and addresses the needs of mothers and parents through its conference program and accommodations;
- Supporting scholarship on feminist mothering;
- Promoting activism in NWSA and the larger community that support all those who mother to make and enact informed choices about parenting, and that works to promote real options for all those who mother.

To achieve these goals the Caucus engages in several activities:

- Ensure the existence of regular panels, workshops, roundtables and plenaries on feminist mothering at NWSA;
- Establish networking opportunities for feminist mothers and parents as well as scholars of motherhood/mothering;

2006 plenary session, "Mothering as Resistance/Activism/Social Change.

- •Ensure the existence of quality, affordable childcare at NWSA;
- •Develop recommendations for the profession in re. to mothers and parents in the academy;
- •Work in coalition with organizations that support our goals and/or promote feminist mothering (Feminist Mothering Caucus Operating Documents).

These activities are carried out by the elected officers and the membership of the Caucus. As of November 2010 the caucus has 99 members listed. Any person who is a member of NWSA and who supports the Caucus' goals is eligible for membership in the Caucus. The term of membership is one year renewable at the end of the term provided the member continues to qualify for membership and has paid annual dues to NWSA and to the Caucus, or has been granted an NWSA dues waiver. Meetings of the Caucus members take place annually at the NWSA Conference. The meeting is convened by the chair and by one of the co-chairs. The following is a list of past and present leadership of the Caucus:

- •2004–2005 Aimee Berger
- •2005–2006 Aimee Berger and Jessica Nathanson
- •2006–2007 Jessica Nathanson and Evette Hornsby-Minor
- •2007–2008 Evette Hornsby-Minor and Arlene Sgoutas
- •2008–2009 Arlene Sgoutas
- •2009–2011 Arlene Sgoutas and Heather Hewett

The purpose of the annual meeting is for the Caucus constituency to meet, to vote upon matters of Caucus governance, to recognize the activities of the last year, and to plan the activities for the coming year. Annually there is a Caucus-sponsored panel at the NWSA national conference. One success that the original task force had worked toward was a plenary session on the current research on mothering that took place in 2006. The session was entitled "Mothering as Resistance/Activism/Social Change" with speakers Andrea O'Reilly, author of *Rocking the Cradle: Thoughts on Motherhood, Feminism and the Possibility of Empowered Mothering*, and Gwendolyn Mink.

Challenges and Obstacles

A constant challenge for the task force is meeting the childcare needs of its membership in order for them to participate in the NWSA annual conference. Historically this challenge has led to the perception among some members that as a feminist institution, NWSA was not inclusive to the perspectives and needs of mothers. There are two main factors that contributed to this perception. One is that there was a lack of institutional memory, so that every year, the Feminist Mothers and Allies Task Force felt that it had to advocate to get childcare information far in advance (not just cost, but information about the childcare provider). The goal for the Task Force was for members to receive information on the availability of childcare during the call for papers. Thus, mothers would have adequate information in time to make arrangements for travel.

Another factor that contributed to the perception that NWSA was not inclusive of mothers is that centrally located, affordable childcare for the entire conference was not available. Indeed, due to the ongoing complaints around the lack of accessible, reliable childcare the task force initiated three petitions over a five-year period "calling on the organization to provide convenient, safe, and affordable child care—and to make clear in advance of conference registration what kind of care is available" (Wilson A16). Since NWSA had difficulty in providing the type of childcare described above, Task force members would coordinate an alternative, informal childcare arrangement for those who were interested (Nathanson). This period of struggle, many within the original task force felt, led to the creation of ongoing childcare at NWSA conferences.

Ultimately NWSA routinely began to provide on-site childcare at their annual meetings in 2005. According to officials at NWSA, however, the task force did not play a direct role in its creation (Provance). The concerns around childcare have, and continue to be, an issue at the national conference. The difficulty to ensure that academic and activists with small children can attend and participate in the annual meeting of NWSA is an ongoing topic of discussion for the Caucus.

Future Aims and Goals of the Caucus

At this time, the main focus of the Caucus leadership is to create various subcommittees to offer its members more opportunities to get involved in the work of the Caucus. Among the subcommittees to be created is a communications group to work on using various technologies to keep the group connected in between conferences. This subcommittee would also work on the development of the newly launched Feminist Mothering Caucus website (www.feministmothering.com/) that was created after the 2009 NWSA conference with the help of one of its members, Dr. Amber Kimber. Another subcommittee would work on building a better relationship with NWSA to analyze the childcare needs of its membership and assist in providing alternative means for parents to attend the annual meeting. Further, this subcommittee would provide suggestions to help send a message to conference attendees that it is inclusive of families. Related to this work would be a third subcommittee that would offer family-inclusive social events at the NWSA annual conference in addition to the creation of a message board for families during the conference. A fourth and final subcommittee would work on the annual official panel for the Caucus at the annual conference as well as seeking out co-sponsorship of panels with other Caucuses and Task Forces. The goal is to get the membership more involved and invested in the goals of the Caucus.

Conclusion

The important function of the Caucus to the motherhood movement in general is to provide a forum and to build a community for feminist scholarship on motherhood and mothering. While feminist research on motherhood has focused on many topics, these studies have been informed and shaped by larger inquiries: namely, how do we challenge patriarchal motherhood? How do we create feminist mothering? How may we challenge and change patriarchal motherhood by way of a theory and practice of empowered maternity? In order to answer these types of questions, the Caucus promotes the link between the theory and the practice to explore the oppressive and the empowering dimensions of maternity, first identified by Adrienne Rich.

[1]The text for the resolution, which was proposed and adopted in June 2007, was provided by NWSA through on online correspondence with Patti Provance.

Works Cited

Feminist Mothering Caucus. National Women's Studies Association. "Feminist Mothering Operating Documents." 2006.

Nathanson, Jessica. "Feminist Mothering Caucus." Message to the author. Email. 10 June 2010.

National Women's Studies Association, n.d. Web. 10 June 2010.

Provance, Patti. "Feminist Mothering Caucus information." Message to the author. 08 June 2010.

Weinbaum, Batya. Letter to Amber Kinser. 3 February 2010. TS.

Wilson, Robin. "Parents Say Women's Studies Association Provides Inadequate Child Care." *The Chronicle of Higher Education* 16 February 2001: A16.

73. Matriarchies as Mother-Centered Societies

HEIDE GOETTNER-ABENDROTH

MATRIARCHIES ARE NOT JUST A reversal of patriarchy, with women ruling over men—as the usual misinterpretation would have it. Matriarchies are mother-centered societies.[1] They are based on maternal values (care-taking, nurturing, motherliness) that hold for everyone: for mothers and those who are not mothers, for women and men alike.

The matriarchal concept of *motherliness* is not the romantic image so often portrayed in patriarchy, a fiction that devalues the notion of motherliness and makes it appear merely sentimental. The sentimental perception of motherliness reflects a systematic effort to obscure the fact that motherhood is the most important function in any society.

Matriarchal societies are consciously built upon maternal values and motherly work, and this is why they are much more realistic than patriarchies. They are, on principle, need-oriented. Their precepts aim to meet everyone's needs with the greatest benefit. So, in matriarchies, mothering—which originates as a biological fact—is transformed into a cultural model. This model is much more appropriate to the human condition than the way patriarchies conceptualize motherhood and use it to make women, and especially mothers, into slaves.

Modern Matriarchal Studies investigates and presents matriarchal societies from all over the world. These investigations focus not only on the past, but also pay attention to still-existing societies with matriarchal patterns in Asia, Africa, the Americas, and the Pacific area. Contrary to common belief, none of these is a mere reversal of patriarchy. Rather, they are all gender-egalitarian societies, and many of them are fully egalitarian. This means they have no hierarchies, classes nor domination of one gender by the other.

With matriarchal cultures, equality means more than just a levelling of differences. Natural differences between the genders and the generations are respected and honoured, but they never serve to create hierarchies, as is common in patriarchy. The different genders and generations have their own dignity, and through complementary areas of activity, they function in concert with one other.

This can be observed on all levels of society: the economic level, the social level, the political level and the areas of their worldviews and faiths. More precisely, matriarchies are societies with complementary equality, where great care is taken to provide a balance. This applies to the balance between genders, among generations, and between humans and nature. And maternal values as ethical principles pervade all areas of a matriarchal society: care-taking, nurturing, and peacemaking.

The Deep Structure of Matriarchal Society

I would like to explain this in more detail, with respect to different levels of matriarchal societies.[2] *At the social level,* matriarchal societies are based on the clan, and on the the "symbolic order of the mother." This also means maternal values as spiritual principles, one that humans take from nature. Mother Nature cares for all beings, however different they may be. The same applies to motherliness: a good mother cares for all her children, embracing their diversity.

This holds true for men as well. If a man in a matriarchal society desires to acquire status among his peers, or even become a representative of the clan to the outside word, then "He must be like a good mother" (as the matriarchal Minangkabau of Sumatra say).

But in matriarchies, you don't have to be a biological mother in order to be respected as a woman, because matriarchies practice the common motherhood of a group of sisters. Each individual sister does not necessarily have to have children, but together they are all "mothers" of any children that any of them have. This motherhood is founded on the freedom of women to decide on their own about whether or not to have biological children.

This is possible because matriarchal people live together in large kinship groups, formed according to the principle of *matrilineality*. The clan's name, and all social status and political titles, are passed on through the mother's line.

Such a matri-clan consists of at least three generations of women, along with their brothers, nephews and maternal uncles. In classic cases, the matri-clan, or a lineage of a clan, lives in one big clan-house. This is called *matrilocality.* Their spouses or lovers stay only over-night, in a pattern called "visiting-marriage." These principles of matrilineality and matrilocality put mothers at the center; in this way women guide their clans without ruling.

In order to achieve social cohesion among the clans of a village or town, complex marriage conventions have been developed that link them in mutually beneficial ways. The intended effect is that all inhabitants of a village or town are related to each other by birth or by marriage. This shapes a society that sees itself as a big clan, where everybody is "mother" or "sister" or "brother" to everybody else. Thus matriarchies are *non-hierarchical, horizontal societies of matrilineal kinship.*

This social order based on motherhood includes far reaching consequences for the *economic level:* Matriarchal economy is a subsistence economy. There is no such thing as private property, and there are no territorial claims. The people simply have usage rights on the soil they till, or the pastures their animals graze, for Mother Earth can not be owned or cut up in pieces. She gives the fruits of the fields and the young animals to all people. Parcels of land and a certain number of animals are given to each matri-clan, and are worked on communally.

Most importantly, women have the power of disposition over goods and clan houses, and especially over the sources of nourishment: fields, flocks and food. This is the important distinction which makes a society a "matriarchal" one, and differentiate it from merely "matrilineal" ones. All the goods are put in the hands of the clan mother, the matriarch, and she distributes them equally among her children and grandchildren. She is responsible for the sustenance and protection of all clan members.

In a matriarchal community, the clans enjoy perfect mutuality: every relative advantage, or disadvantage, in terms of acquiring goods is mediated by social guidelines. For example, at the seasonal festivals of the agricultural year, clans that are comparatively better off will invite all the inhabitants to be their guests. The members of such a clan organize the banquet, the rituals, and the music and dances of one of the annual festivals—and then give away their goods as a gift to all their neighbours. By doing this, they gain nothing except honor. At the next festival in the cycle, another lucky clan will step up, outdoing itself by inviting everybody in the village or neighbourhood, entertaining them all, and dispensing presents.

Since this is the general attitude, matriarchal economy can be called a "gift economy." It is the economic manifestation of maternal values, which prevents development of an exchange economy and instead fully achieves a "gift economy," as Genevieve Vaughan has formulated it.

Due to these features, matriarchies can be called *societies of economic reciprocity, based on the circulation of gifts.*

The patterns of *the political level* follow the principle of consensus, which means *unanimity* regarding each decision. To manifest a principle like this in practice, a society must be specifically organized to do so, and matrilinear kinship lines are, once again, the starting point.

The basis of each decision-making is the individual clan house. Matters that concern the clan house are decided upon by the women and men in a consensus process, of which the matriarch is the facilitator. Each person has only one vote—even the matriarch—and no member of the household is excluded.

The same applies to decisions concerning the whole village or town. The clan delegates meet together in the village council, but do not make decisions themselves; they simply communicate the decisions that have been made in their clan houses, and move back and forth, until a consensus decision is reached by the whole village. The same applies at the regional level. The delegates move between the local council and the regional council back and forth, until consensus of all the villages and towns in this area is reached.

The origin of all politics is in the clan houses, where the people live, and in this way, a true "grass roots democracy" is put into practice. The result of these practices is that matriarchies are *egalitarian societies of consensus.* This clearly shows how maternal values also permeate political practice.

But such a societal system as matriarchy could not function as a whole without a deep, supporting and all-permeating spiritual attitude. *At the spiritual and cultural level,* matriarchal societies do not have hierarchic religions based on an omnipotent male God. In matriarchies, divinity is immanent, for the whole world is regarded as divine: as feminine divine. This is evident in the widely held concept of the universe as the Great Goddess who brought forth everything by birth, and of the earth as the Great Mother who created everything living. And everyone, and everything, is endowed with divinity by virtue of being a child of the Great Mother Nature.

In such a culture, everything is spiritual. In their festivals, which follow the cycle of the seasons and the cycle of life, everything is celebrated. There is no separation between sacred and secular, so the everyday tasks also have ritual significance. In this sense matriarchal societies are sacred ones.

So, we can see here that the entire societies are constructed in the image of the creative Mother Nature. "Mother Nature is our teacher," as the Minangkabau of Sumatra say. This divine mother is reflected in every woman's being, and in her abilities to create. Every social, economic and political action is informed by the principle of the world's all-encompassing maternal attitude.

Therefore, on the spiritual level, matriarchies are *sacred societies and cultures of the Divine Feminine or Goddess.*

Matriarchal Politics

In 1986, I founded the "International Academy HAGIA, Academy for Matriarchal Studies and Matriarchal Spirituality" in Germany. It is dedicated to the exploration of matriarchal societies past and present and their worldwide existence. In that way modern Matriarchal Studies developed as a new socio-cultural field of knowledge. Many women participated in the teachings, and the knowledge about matriarchal societies spread.

Later, I guided two World Congresses on Matriarchal Studies, and here, the research on matriarchal societies was presented to a wider public by international scholars. In 2003, the first congress, titled "Societies in Balance," took place in Luxembourg/Europe, and the second one, titled "Societies of Peace," was held 2005 in San Marcos, Texas. Both congresses, but especially the second one, brought together indigenous researchers, mostly women and some men, from many of the world's still existing matriarchal societies.[3]

Through all these activities, it is becoming increasingly clear that this radically different model of matriarchal cultures will have great significance for our future as women and mothers. Therefore, I would like to suggest new mother-centered, egalitarian, and peaceful societies to explain what we mean by "Matriarchal Politics." Of course, we cannot imitate traditional matriarchal societies, but we can gain much stimulation and insights from them, which have been lived over millennia.

From this outline of modern Matriarchal Studies, it has become clear, that it deals with knowledge about non-patriarchal, egalitarian social, political and cultural patterns that are basically peace-oriented. This knowledge is urgently needed in this late phase of globally destructive patriarchy, with its institutions based on hegemonic masculine models, practices, and values.

Today, it is becoming increasingly clear that matriarchal patterns have great significance for both present and future societies. For matriarchies are not abstract utopias, constructed according to philosophical concepts that can never be implemented. On the contrary, they have existed throughout long historical periods until today. They embody an enormous amount of intellectual creativity and practical experience, and belong indispensably to humankind's cultural store of knowledge. Their values show how life can be organized in such a way that it is based on needs, is non-violent and peaceful, is simply *humane.*

The path towards a new egalitarian and peaceful society is called "Matriarchal Politics" (Goettner-Abendroth 2007). Of course, modern western people cannot imitate traditional matriarchal societies, but they can gain much stimulation and insights from them which—unlike theoretical utopias—have been lived over millennia.

Economically, the lesson of matriarchies is—in my opinion—to find a new subsistence economy, based on local and regional units. The communities of this economy work self-sufficiently and create circles of gift giving. The resulting quality of life is more important to them than producing a great quantity of goods. Women are the mainstays of these economic structures, they know it very well. Thus, regionalization and gift giving circles created by the initiative of women is a tool for a matriarchal economy.

On the social level, I think it is necessary to create and support groups and communities, based on affinity. They may be traditional existing communities, or alternative new ones. These affinity communities are formed on the basis of a spiritual-philosophical rapport between the members, who feel as siblings by choice, and they can be named "symbolic clans." The symbolic clans have the tendency to become matriarchal, if they are initiated and lead by women. The decisive factors are the needs of women, and especially of children, who are the future of humanity.

On the political level, the matriarchal consensus principle is of utmost importance for a truly egalitarian society. The consensus principle is the foundation for building new matriarchal communities. Following this principle, the small units of these new symbolic matri-clans are the true decision-makers, but this can only be practised up to the regional level. According to the subsistence perspective, flourishing and self-sufficient regions are the political aim—not the big nation states, state unions and super powers.

On the cultural level, the lesson of matriarchies is to leave all hierarchical religions with a claim to the total truth or unitary "master narratives." Instead, it is necessary to regard the world as holy, to love and to protect it, because according to matriarchal culture, everything in the world is divine.

Like that, matriarchal spirituality can once again infuse everything and thus become an inherent part of everyday life. At the same time, what again becomes apparent is matriarchal tolerance, for nobody has to "believe" anything. There is no dogma and no teaching, but the continuous, manifold celebration of life and the visible world.

The path to a new egalitarian society can only be holistic, without being vague. It has to be concrete, without getting lost in disconnected details. I call it a "matriarchal model." It is a clear vision that could become a practical guideline for integrating the actions of different peacemakers that would make their efforts more effective. In my opinion, much of the economical, social, political and spiritual work that is being done by alternative movements today implicitly embraces the matriarchal model described in this paper. In this sense, we are all together on this path toward a more just and peaceful world-society.

(Translation by Karen Smith)

[1]For more detailed discussion, see Goettner-Abendroth (1988-1995, 1991,1998, 1999, 2000, 2004) and Sanday (1998, 2002).
[2]See, for example, the traditional society of the Iroquois peoples in Mann; the Minangkabau society (Sumatra) in Sanday (2002); and diverse examples from America, Africa and Asia in Goettner-Abendroth (1999, 2000).
[3]Papers from the 2003 and 2005 World Congresses on Matriarchal Studies were published in Goettner-Abendroth (2009).

Works Cited

Autorinnengemeinschaft, eds. *Die Diskriminierung der Matriarchatsforschung—Eine moderne Hexenjagd* (Collective Authorship, eds. *Discriminating against Matriarchal Studies—A Modern Witch Hunt*). Bern: Edition Amalia, 2003.

Goettner-Abendroth, Heide: *Das Matriarchat I. Geschichte seiner Erforschung (Matriarchy I. History of Research),* Stuttgart: Verlag Kohlhammer 1988-1995.

Goettner-Abendroth, Heide: *Das Matriarchat II.1. Stammesgesellschaften in Ostasien, Indonesien, Ozeanien (Matriarchy II.1. Matriarchal Societies in Eastern Asia, Indonesia and Pacific Area).* Stuttgart: Verlag Kohlhammer, 1991, 1999.

Goettner-Abendroth, Heide: *Das Matriarchat II.2. Stammesgesellschaften in Amerika, Indien, Afrika (Matriarchy II.2. Matriarchal Societies in America, India, Africa).* Stuttgart: Kohlhammer-Verlag, 2000.

Goettner-Abendroth, Heide. "Matriarchal Society: Definition and Theory." Ed. Heide Goettner-Abendroth. *Societies of Peace: Matriarchies Past, Present and Future.* Toronto: Inanna Publications, 2009.

Goettner-Abendroth, Heide. "Matriarchal Society: Definition and Theory." *The Gift.* Ed. Genevieve Vaughan. Rome: Meltemi (Athanor Books), 2004.

Goettner-Abendroth, Heide. *Matriarchat in Südchina. Eine Forschungsreise zu den Mosuo (Matriarchy in Southern China: A Research Trip to the Mosuo People).*

Stuttgart: Kohlhammer-Verlag, 1998.

Goettner-Abendroth, Heide. *The Way to an Egalitarian Society. Principles and Practice of a Matriarchal Politics.* Winzer: Edition Hagia/Germany, 2007.

Mann, Barbara Alice: *Iroquoian Women. The Gantowisas.* New York: Peter Lang, 2000.

Sanday, Peggy R. "Matriarchy as a Sociocultural Form: An Old Debate in a New Light." Paper presented at the 16th Congress of the Indo-Pacific Prehistory Association, Melaka, Malaysia, July 1-7, 1998.

Sanday, Peggy R. *Women at the Center. Life in a Modern Matriarchy,* Ithaca, NY: Cornell University Press, 2002.

Vaughan, Genevieve. *For-Giving: A Feminist Criticism of Exchange,* Austin, 1997, PlainView and Anomaly Press, 1997.

74. Moms Rock! with MAMAPALOOZA

LYNN KUECHLE AND JOY ROSE

MAMAPALOOZA IS A MULTI-MEDIA and events company connecting women, mothers and families through music, art, activism and education for cultural, economic and social awareness. MAMAPALOOZA is comprised of live festivals across the United States and in three countries, with an online presence reaching over 100,000 families annually. As a trademarked branding vehicle (circa 2002, branding a genre of mom-made art and business), which empowers women to express themselves in all forms, MAMAPALOOZA has given context to the concept that "mothers have something to say." Founded by Joy Rose in 2002, MAMAPALOOZA has pioneered a new culture of mother-created performance, business and activism. MAMAPALOOZA's mantra is MOMS ROCK!

In this chapter we will explore the history of the company, the philosophy and social change movement, as well as some of the challenges faced by the organization and how it relates to the overall Motherhood Movement. Finally, the future of the organization will be briefly explained.

History

In 1997, while performing with her band "Housewives on Prozac," (the first Mom Rock Band, aptly named to comment on the progress of the women's movement in the "momasphere"), singing songs like "Fuzzy Slippers" with lyrics; "I wipe my baby's chin with my college diploma, and wonder how I ever got here," Joy Rose, founder of MAMAPALOOZA coined the phrase "MOMS ROCK" and sought to highlight mother-work by putting the ironies of her own life experience into performance. She created buttons, stickers, magnets, tee shirts and media buzz with the key phrases "MOMS ROCK," "Housewives On Prozac," "Baby Slave," "Domestically Challenged" and "Not Your Typical Housewife" to name a few. At this time in history, being a mom who was an entertainer was not "cool"—children were considered a liability in the professional and performing arts world. Many performers would not bring the fact they had children to the attention of the public, hiding it on their resume and album credits. Joy recognized the inspiration and foundation for many of her creative and commercial endeavors were her four young children. It was the transformation of her solo-self to mother-self that churned the creative wheels and poetic musing. Additionally, Joy was diagnosed with SLE (LUPUS) immediately following the birth of her last child in 1994. The contemplative years following the long illness set the stage and contributed to the courage she found to live life with new standards and expectations. Music and creativity played a large part in healing. The inspiration she found by 1997 propelled her towards pledging to effect change around her. She attributed some of the root causes of her illness to the stress she experienced as a young wife "caught in a conspiracy of perfection." During the years following her professional music career, art and retail experience in New York City, she noted she had "fallen into the trap of the perfect fifties wife. I was a stay at home mom, who had lost myself on the journey to family." Joy committed to shifting the psycho-spiritual legacy portrayed in films like *A Woman Under the Influence* (1974), and books like *Women and Madness* (Chesler); she wrote her own story into music for an equity production of what became a hit show "Shut Up And Drive" (1998 Schoolhouse Theater, New York), and which sold out every performance for six weeks in 1999. In these performances, songs like, "Eat Your Damn Spaghetti," and "I Don't Think Like My Mom Anymore," were sprinkled with covers like; "I Am Woman" and "Harper Valley PTA." She set out to influence her community with the kind of personal passion and self-expression she perceived as vital to elevating the human condition, especially with regard to women, mothers and family structure. Although much of this early work was intuitive, the great liberation process included changing outmoded "made for TV" perceptions of mothers being "perfect," "well coiffed," yet distinctly "un-cool" all over the world.

Over the next seven years Joy poked fun at out-dated ideas of backroom 1950s kitchen divas and suburban soccer moms, leading her band and recording team into a broader arena, catching the attention of major national and local media outlets, such as: *Good Morning America*, Fox News, BBC, *USA Today, People Magazine*, NPR Radio, and Sirius/XM Satellite Radio and newspapers as far away as Scandanavia. In 2004, Jill Brooke wrote, "Mommy rebellion: tracking the course of mutiny against the tyranny of parental expectations" for *The Chicago Tribune.* In the article, Brooks quotes Rose: "We've become slaves to our kids. I tried to be the perfect mom but then I buckled. It's time for a little liberation and I want to give moms permission to nourish a piece of themselves." It seemed that a movement was looming.

The first international editorial piece linking "Housewives On Prozac" and subsequently MAMAPALOOZA to a greater cause was an article by Molly Gitny on May 7, 2004, called "Mother's Day Rocks for Break-the-Mold-Moms."

> Fed up with definitions of motherhood that they find oppressive and restrictive, a growing number of U.S. moms are kick-boxing and slam-dancing their way toward a new interpretation. They're wearing fishnet stockings and platform heels to the playground. They're taking up scuba

> diving and bringing their kids in tow. But it's not just about the latest fashion or exercise trend. These moms are organized, forming coalitions and spreading the message that women can raise happy, healthy children and still be true to themselves.

Roberta Hershenson, in the *New York Times,* circa 1997, noted the early mama-movement trend in "Band Sings About What It's Like To Raise A Family in the '90s." "When such women have fierce creative energy and a tendency to break the mold—consider themselves foot soldiers for meaningful lives within the family." This was followed by CBS Sunday Morning, Channel 7 *Eyewitness News,* and local papers. The origins of this new consciousness was manifesting in music in church basements, coffee houses and clubs in the New York Metro area and suburbs spearheaded by Rose, a full five years before it ended up on a MAMAPALOOZA stage. The Molly Gitny piece led to a multi-page spread in *Ladies Home Journal* on HOP Band, "Women Who Rock 'N Roll" (Muchnick) and *The London Times,* "'We are global, college-educated women who came out of the feminist movement,' says Rose. 'We have briefcases and business suits, but when we get into the arena of the home, it has not changed that much through the years'" (qtd. in Dixey).

The first MAMAPALOOZA event took place on a single stage in Manhattan in 2002. Declaring May as "Mother's Month," citing the idea that one day of the year was not enough to honor all moms, the festival idea included plans to highlight some of the amazing mothers Joy Rose had met along the way. The first festival included Corliss Whitney, a 70-something high-stepping ex-Rockette, Tina de Varon ("If Mama Ain't Happy"), a committed professional mother-recording artist, Alyson Palmer ("BETTY"), whose pregnant image was the template for much of the original MAMAPALOOZA art and print, and several activist poets including Monique Avakian and Jen Ed. Since then Joy has used her notoriety and public persona and sought to define Mom Rock ("we wouldn't be mom-rockers without kids, we'd just be rockers") to change the landscape for women artists, musicians, artists, dancers, filmmakers, writers, business owners, educators and moms of all kinds, and to provide a different type of venue and stage to celebrate and examine the role of motherhood. MAMAPALOOZA festivals have been created in coffee houses, clubs, zoos, parks, college campuses, YWCAs and family expos.

In 2004, the wave of publicity was in full swing and so were a library of new books including *Bitch In The House* (2004) and CDs from burgeoning mom bands like The Mydols (USA), The Mothers (England), MotherLode Trio (USA), Placenta (USA), Veen Malner "Anakey" (Australia), Sue Fabisch, "Mommy Music" (USA), Merry & The MoodSwings (USA), Tiffany Petrossi "Rockin' Moms" (USA) and MomSense, as well as comedians like Nancy Lombardo's comedy show called Momedy™. Nancy Keates, in 2004 in *The Wall Street Journal,* wrote,

> For some moms, joining a band has solved the problem of whether they'll go back to work when their kids get old enough for school. Psychologists

> say that at a certain point, full-time mothers need more stimulation. While middle-aged men have long incorporated bands into their midlife-crisis repertoire, women were more often bogged down with PTA meetings and chauffeuring kids to after-school recitals. It's the musical version of the irreverent "momoirs" that are showing up in bookstores, and web sites that chronicle suburban-mom angst with names like Skateboard Mom, Mamaphonic and Hip Mama.

The year 2004 saw the founding of the "Mom Egg" Poetry and Prose publication by MAMAPALOOZA artists and additional theatrical and literary events were added to comedy, music and social events around New York City, with author Jamie Cat Callen, Alana Ruben Free and Marjorie Tesser blazing the way. By 2005 MAMAPALOOZA had moved to six cities: Detroit, Washington DC, Dallas, Nashville, San Francisco and New York City. In 2006 it doubled again, producing twelve festivals during May as well as compilation CDs and accompanying festival magazines. Festivals, Expos and specially created stages now reach approximately 100,000 bodies a year, in person. The gatherings range in size from 20,000 (Mayfair in Collingswood, New Jersey) to 75 people (Columbus, Ohio annual MAMAPALOOZA Festival); the average is between 4,000 to 10,000. In San Francisco, California, Buffalo and New York, mayors presented certificates declaring "MAMAPALOOZA DAY" to event coordinators Tiffany Petrossi and Annette Daniels Taylor. A small mother-centric music publishing company opened in association with MAMAPALOOZA as well, dubbed MamaPUBlooza by founders Pilley Bianchi, Carol Lester and Joy Rose. In 2009 Joy Rose was given the Susan B. Anthony award by NOW-NYC for her work on behalf of girls and mothers, while the MAMAPALOOZA Festival was named "The Best In Girl Power'" event by *Westchester Magazine* in New York. In 2010, Joy brought MAMAPALOOZA to New York Talk Radio and WBAI Radio—"The Women's Desk, Feminist Perspectives"

Candy Band at MAMAPALOOZA, Detroit, 2005.

—while branded stages were featured at Earth Day L.A., two "Go Green Expos," five baby expos, duly dubbed "BeBe Paluzza'(s)," Detroit Mamapalooza, Collingswood New Jersey Mamapalooza, Kensico Dam Mamapalooza, Buffalo, New York, Columbus Ohio, San Francisco, California, Orange County "Taste Of Ladera," California, and Manhattan flagship Mamapalooza Festival with complimentary comedy, burlesque, poetry and a "Mother Studies" conference with performances at multiple venues around New York City.

As of 2011, MAMAPALOOZA Inc. continues its mission of creating programming and media with the dedication of artists, local event coordinators, community partners, universities, a dynamic advisory board and volunteers who have successfully pioneered this new culture of mom-branded everything. Today, this mama-media empire is comprised of events, workshops, radio, online TV, festivals, publications, *MAMZINA* Magazine, blogs, "Mom of the Year," "Band of The Year" and "Mom Rock" awards, conferences, MamaZip licensing programs, CDs and an online MamaMember community that connects, entertains and empowers mothers internationally and has moved beyond the month of May into yearlong productions and paid hourly positions through its MOMbassadors.com program.

Philosophy

The philosophy of MAMAPALOOZA is to create a virtual and public space where mother artists, activists, business owners, community service agencies and the community at large can gather to celebrate the shared experience of womanhood with a special emphasis on mothers. MAMAPALOOZA provides a platform that alerts mothers to the support services in their community and inspires them to investigate their own creative and entrepreneurial spirits.

Herstorically, women in the arts would not include their age or the fact that they were mothers on their bios at all. Being a mother made you somehow irrelevant and unappealing. The first step was to convince women to articulate the ways mothering had informed and influenced their perspectives of creativity. A subculture emerged and "Mom Rock" was born. By creating specific MAMAPALOOZA events each spring for an entire month and labeling it as "May is Mother's Month," people began to pay attention as the events were held across the United States, in Australia, England and Canada. Media outlets began covering events happening in their areas and the public began to embrace Mom-art. The movement gained attention with a specific focus on women and the arts being a financial and activist enterprise.

In a culture that worships youth and raw sexuality, women over a certain age and certainly women who admit to motherhood, are back-shelved as no longer relevant. As late as the 1990s, American culture simply did not view mothers as sexy or sharp. That has changed. Since MAMAPALOOZA's emergence, organizations and slogans like "Hot Moms Club," MILF Club, "Entrepreneurial Mom," and "Moms In Business Unite" have emerged. *Rolling Stone* magazine regularly touts celebrity rocks stars with pregnant bellies as does *People* magazine. While

Moey's Music Party performs, MAMAPALOOZA *Festival, New York City, 2009.*

MAMAPALOOZA is not concerned with celebrity baby bumps, it does acknowledge the women inside the role of mother and is a proud player on the landscape that somehow expanded over the last ten years to make way for these mothers of reinvention. Hollywood has recently taken notice. The movie *Motherhood* (2009), with Uma Thurman playing a New York City mom of two, chronicles the tribulations of the modern mother's chaotic work/life balance while she tries to maintain a piece of her former self by submitting a writing sample to win a MAMAPALOOZA contest.

MAMAPALOOZA is a movement, a community and a resource, which supports women by encouraging them to get creative and give something back to themselves. The underlying mission is to have mothers understand and truly believe that by choosing motherhood they have unlimited new material with which to express themselves and to validate their experiences as mothers. The MAMAPALOOZA mission is to:

- Establish a new art form that speaks to the unique and collective perspectives of women who are mothers, giving them the opportunity to share this with the world.
- Create sustainable programming and opportunities through ongoing events, merchandising, and media outreach.
- Act as a resource and lifestyle guide for mothers seeking support in mainstream and alternative settings.
- Support the choices mothers have made, while educating and empowering them in order to support these choices.

MAMAPALOOZA recognizes and honors the growing awareness of moms; their personal stories, their power as both consumers and constituents, and their continuing need and desire to creatively express themselves while building Mom-based businesses that sustain them. MAMAPALOOZA recognizes that art is a tool for social change and encourages women to use their medium to build self esteem, break down stereotypes, create unity, encourage diversity, inspire individuality and empower future generations.

Creating a Movement Through the Arts

Creating a new art genre is an overwhelming challenge. However, strides have been made. When MAMAPALOOZA began, mom-branding—of anything—did not exist; let alone Mom-branded entertainment or business. Part of the early challenge was to establish a critical mass of women who were invested in defining their "mama" music, art, literature, comedy, poetry, theater, business, etc.

Relying on typical big-budget marketing strategies to change ideas and challenge social norms was not an option for this grassroots group. Rather, using the arts as an instrument for shattering stereotypes and informing social activism was a perfect choice.

In 2004, the RAND Corporation was commissioned by the Wallace Foundation to study the impact of the arts. The research resulted in a published report called *Gifts of the Muse: Reframing the Debate about the Benefits of the Arts* (McCarthy et al.). The purpose of the report was to inform policy makers on how spending money on the arts can benefit the community. Their findings also show that an organization like MAMAPALOOZA can benefit individual mothers, communities, and the movement at large. The RAND report cited the intrinsic benefits to individuals as well as communities, which include:

1) *Captivation*—"The initial response of rapt absorption, or captivation, to a work of art can briefly but powerfully move the individual away from habitual, everyday reality and into a state of focused attention"(xv). Mothers are often inundated with the day to day activities of mothering responsibilities, and having an outlet that will bring them to another place is very beneficial to the emotional and mental wellbeing of mothers.

2) *Pleasure*—"An imaginative experience that is often a more intense, revealing, and meaningful version of actual experience"(xvi). Thinking about motherhood through a variety of artistic genres can allow mothers and others to see motherhood as the varied and complex experience that it is.

3) *Expanded capacity for empathy*—"The arts expand individuals' capacities for empathy by drawing them into the experiences of people vastly different from them and cultures vastly different from their own"(xvi). One of the biggest challenges mothers experience is judgment from other mothers and society at large. Having a more empathetic view of motherhood and for mothers would allow mothers to exhale a collective sigh of relief.

4) *Cognitive growth*—"The intrinsic benefits described above all have cognitive dimensions. When individuals focus their attention on a work of art, they are 'invited' to make sense of what is before them"(xvi). In recent years, motherhood has become more and more reliant on the "experts"; causing mothers to think about their own mothering experience from a cognitive perspective can help them feel like they have some authority over their own experience.

5) *Creation of social bonds*—"When people share the experience of works of art, either by discussing them or by communally experiencing them, one of the intrinsic benefits is the social bonds that are created"(xvi). Motherhood can be very isolating. In recent times mothers have become increasingly independent in their experience. An opportunity to have social bonds for mothers can be a lifeline for many.

6) *Expression of communal meanings*—"Intrinsic benefits accrue to the public sphere when works of art convey what whole communities of people yearn to express"(xvi). There is a cultural element to motherhood that often goes unrecognized by mothers and by larger society.

Challenges

While the media continues to love the idea of mothers and their life outside of motherhood, the financial well-being of MAMAPALOOZA presents ongoing challenges. While MAMAPALOOZA has received major national sponsorships, the reality remains that the demographics of "artists" and "mothers" are among the most financially challenged populations. This was the fact when the organization started and continues to be relevant today. Films like *Who Does She Think She Is?* (2008) document the issue of the lack of professional women artists and specifi-

Annual Singer/Songwriter night, MAMPALOOZA Festival, New York City, with artists from around the world.

cally mother artists, and substantiate the claim that there is glaring inequality of women and mother artists. Corporations have caught on, the "mom" moniker has been used to sell merchandise, create television shows and spawn debate, but this has not financially empowered mothers in a significant way, but rather co-opted marketing images of mothers that continue to keep mothers in the same stereotypical constraints of the past. In 2005 The Women's Media Center in New York, along with MAMAPALOOZA founder Joy Rose, hosted an event called, Feminism, Finances and How Art Can Change the World. Presenters offered ongoing examples of their real life successes in combining art, work and mothering, so the stories of how it can be done are emerging, but significant obstacles remain.

MAMAPALOOZA and the Motherhood Movement

MAMAPALOOZA's initial focus was creating a language in the arts that reflected the maternal landscape, emotionally as well as culturally by amplifying the voices of mothers. In 2005, *USA Today* wrote, "the rules of motherhood are being racially rewritten—with a snarl, cymbal crash and power E-chord that would make the lads in AC/DC stand and salute" (Della Cava). "You strap on a baby, and suddenly the only archetype you have is the '50s housewife, and that stereotype is too small to hold the modern American woman," says Joy Rose, leader of the six-mom New York group Housewives on Prozac, whose to-the-point tunes include "Eat

Nancy Lombardo, MOMEDY™ and guest at MAMAPALOOZA, New York City, 2007.

Your Damn Spaghetti." "As always," she says, "rock 'n' roll is a huge medium for change, so we're using it."

Out of those founding values, an entire decade of conversations, businesses, art, music, festivals, conferences, literature, and language has emerged. The saying "Moms Rock" is readily found on bumper stickers, tee-shirts, and on novelty items around the world. Hundreds of mothers perform on stages, in theaters and performing art spaces. Mothers have brought their creativity to every art genre and their voices to a much larger public arena.

A recent study released by the online community CafeMom indicated that mothers benefit from having a source of connection and inspiration. In the web-based survey that mothers completed online, they overwhelmingly agreed that motherhood can be isolating. It has long been accepted that with the territory of motherhood comes self-sacrifice and self-depletion. If left unchecked, however, this can lead women into a state of depression and a lower value of self and self-esteem. The lost potential from low self-esteem is a terrible waste. Mothers are drawn to MAMAPALOOZA to replenish themselves. Women find support when they can get out of the house or away from the office and get up on stage. Sometimes it is for the very first time and sometimes it is picking up a profession from pre-baby days. MAMAPALOOZA believes that, while affecting the self-esteem of moms throughout the world, we will also positively affect the lives of our daughters. Founder Joy Rose asserts, "if the world view of moms changes to incorporate concepts of artistic, gorgeous, vivacious, intelligent, sexual beings living out their passion collectively, then we've done a good job."

MAMAPALOOZA events have been a vehicle for self-actualization challenging stereotypes about women who are mothers, and creating space outside the status quo. Present at outdoor festival events have been multiple social change organizations like NOW, Mothers Acting Up (MAU), Metropolitan Moms, multiple "Family Magazines," Planned Parenthood, and so many more. Using the festival as a large-scale hub, organizations as well as communities of mothers have cause to celebrate and communicate. Wikipedia states, "Festivals, of many types, serve to meet specific needs, as well as to provide entertainment. These times of celebration offer a sense of belonging. Modern festivals that focus on cultural or ethnic topics seek to inform."

Art (more specifically, music) has been a long-standing tool for political and social activism since its roots in American blues and rock, and the freedom songs of early slavery. Whether music has been used to make difficult circumstances more endurable, or used to challenge the powers that be, it elevates the spirit and turns the banal into the extraordinary. By calling attention to inter-personal issues, domestic drudgery, the banishment of self (within the context of family), economic woes, physical exhaustion during pregnancy and the early years of motherhood, and the issues women face aging and care-giving for others, individuals have been able to use the MAMAPALOOZA platform to amplify their voices and face common experiences that under normal circumstances may not be articulated. By putting lyrics, music, performance and ultimately all art forms into the context of "mother," the women of MAMAPALOOZA have been able to create a new oral history of the issues they face, while shaking free from the bonds that might keep them tied to outmoded traditions that might enslave them at worst, and mentally, emotionally, spiritually restrict them at best. This grassroots movement has resulted in the creation of hundreds of mom bands, musicals, books, readings, concerts, gatherings, CDs and publications, as well as giving women the courage to do everything from dye their hair pink, to create viable businesses. While not exactly becoming the new norm, this social-change vehicle has opened the way for a vast cooperative of woman- and mom-inspired entertainment, education, and business that continues to pave the way for individuals seeking support and community. Additionally these events make a point of making information about social services, state-run programs and health, and legal aid available to families while using free, outdoor public spaces to gather, including local and national parks, and the great lawn in front of the White House. MAMAPALOOZA, and specifically Joy Rose have certainly secured a place as one of the Motherhood Movement founders.

The Future

The ongoing vision for MAMAPALOOZA includes highlighting the challenges faced by caregivers in an ever-evolving personal, social, cultural, sexual and political landscape, by continuing to create an environment that encourages discourse, experimentation, conversation, evaluation, study, and the creation of art in all its forms of expression. MAMAPALOOZA licenses out the MAMAPALOOZA trademark to individual event coordinators, businesswomen and musicians each year so they may create events that are congruous with MAMAPALOOZA's mission.

MAMAPALOOZA continues to expand its platform to incorporate print, radio, online TV, blogging, conferencing, and news media. Its performance genre and "Mom-branded" entertainment are still a focal point that makes MAMAPALOOZA unique. The future of MAMAPALOOZA also includes raising awareness and distributing information in alliance with the non-profit Motherhood Foundation for the purpose of building the Museum of Motherhood (see chapter 75). This will dictate a new direction for MAMAPALOOZA.

MAMAPALOOZA has morphed into a multimedia organization that is wholly mom-owned and operated. Weekly online TV programming, hosted by Joy Rose, focusing on the "Not Ready For Prime Time Feminists" and Lynn Kuechle representing topical discussion and blogs for the Museum of Motherhood, along with local correspondents, broadly disseminate information about the artistic, educational and merchandising world of everything mom. Trademarks including Modern Ambassador for Maternal Advancement (M.A.M.A.™), Museum of Motherhood™, MediaMom™ and the Women's Family Network Inc. (WFNI™). have been added to the MAMAPALOOZA Inc. family.

Its grassroots festival beginnings have materialized into a solvent, year round business that is owned and operated by women and mothers, supporting a staff and reaching far into the mom-movement collective consciousness. Activist and Feminist perspectives including "green" initiatives influence the day to day and ongoing operations of MAMAPALOOZA. There is some consideration and discussion about future licensing, franchising and expansion under the MAMAPALOOZA brand. Many mothers are given more opportunities to live full lives that include caring for their children while expressing their creative, entrepreneurial and activist spirits, MAMAPALOOZA's mission is to make that a reality for all mothers. MOMS ROCK!

Conclusion

In *The Mommy Myth* (Douglas and Michaels) the authors report that mothers are rebuking the idea of devoting all of their creative energies to their children. Joy Rose, in the *Journal News,* said, "Music is rebellion. MAMAPALOOZA is really about moms breaking out of a sterotypical box and saying, "We're redefining what it means to be a modern American mother."

Because motherhood is essentially a leap into "otherhood," the paradox of motherhood is that often one takes a personal loss for the group's gain. The gains are obvious in the new life of a child who has entered the world. The *loss* on a basic level is nine (or so) months of gestation with physical, financial and emotional implications that usually extend beyond the time of birth, well into the rest of one's life and largely go socially unacknowledged. The saying "Moms Rock" is an opportunity to acknowledge mother-contributions and mother-work both literally and figuratively within the general social context and within a brand that began as a musical movement. "Moms Rock" therefore, becomes a literal and figurative expression and one that has resonated across the Western Hemisphere.

In Erica Jong's 2010 article for the *Wall Street Journal,* called "The Madness of Modern Motherhood" she questions whether modern parenting philosophies are becoming ultimatums for mothers to give themselves over to their children that have started to encourage female victimization. She believes that for some women with the idea and feeling that they need to spend every waking moment attending to their children, motherhood can become very confining, even prison-like. In the 2008 compilation CD and publication by MAMAPALOOZA called *Moms Gone Mad,* these issues were explored as well. Joy Rose said that "music is rebellion." MAMAPALOOZA is about moms breaking out of a stereotypical box. We're redefining what it means to be a modern American mother. The journey continues.

Works Cited

A Woman Under the Influence. S. Shaw (Producer) and J. Cassavates (Director). [Motion picture]. USA: Faces International Films, 1974.

Chesler, Phyllis. *Women and Madness.* New York: Four Walls Eight Windows, 1972.

Brooke, Jill. "Mommy rebellion: Tracking the course of mutiny against the tyranny of parental expectations" *Chicago Tribune* 21 December 2004: http://articles.chicagotribune.com/2004-12-21/features/0412210035_1_perfect-mom-mommy-myth-desperate-housewives.

Café Mom. *The Mom Quality of Life Index.* Café Mom, 2009.

della Cava, Marco R. "The Bands that Rock the Cradle." *USA Today* 31 January 2005. Web <http://www.usatoday.com/life/music/news/2005-01-31-rock-moms_x.htm>.

Dixey, Anne. "Socks 'N Cakes 'N Rock 'N Roll." *London Times* 11 December, 2004.

Douglas, Susan and Meredith Michaels. *The Mommy Myth: The Idealization of Motherhood and How It Has Undermined Women.*ßFree Press, 2004.

Ginty, Molly, M. "Mother's Day Rocks for Break-the-Mold Moms." *WomensENews* 7 May 2004: Web. <http://womensenews.org/story/arts/040507/mothers-day-rocks-break-the-mold-moms>.

Hershenson, Roberta. "Band Sings About What It's Like To Raise A Family in the '90s." *New York Times* 9 November 1997. Web. <http://www.nytimes.com/1997/11/09/nyregion/band-sings-about-what-it-s-like-to-raise-a-family-in-the-90-s.html>.

Jong, Erica. "The Madness of Modern Motherhood." *Wall Street Journal* 2 November 2010. Web. <http://online.wsj.com/article/SB10001424052748704462704575590603553674296.html>.

Keates, Nancy, "Mommy Loudest" *Wall Street Journal* 25 June 2004. Web. <http://mydols.com/wsj.html>.

Lombroso, Linda. "Singing". The Journal News 15 July, 2001.

McCarthy, Kevin F. et al. *Gifts Of The Muse: Reframing The Debate About the Benefits of the Arts.* Santa Monica, CA: RAND Corp., 2004.

Motherhood. J. Edelbaum (Producer) and K. Dieckmann. [Motion picture]. USA: iDeal Patners Film Fund, 2009.

Muchnick, Jeanne. "Women Who Rock 'N Roll." *Ladies Home Journal* May 2004.

Rose, Joy. "Not just a Mama..." The Hot Mommas Project." Web < http://www.hotmommasproject.org/caseview.aspx?id=642 >

Who Does She Think She Is? T. P. Boll and N. Kennedy (Directors). USA: Mystic Artists Films Productions, 2008.

Young, Erica "Mother Madness." *Wall Street Journal* 6 November 2010. Web. <http://online.wsj.com/article/SB1000142405274870446270457559060355 3674296.html>.

75.
Museum of Motherhood

The Cultural Family: Honoring Mothers in Perpetuity

LYNN KUECHLE AND JOY ROSE

THE MUSEUM OF MOTHERHOOD (M.o.M.) is the first and only facility of its kind serving as a unique resource for those who wish to study the history of mothers, mother-art and the culture of family. The Museum's purpose is to provide a space and platform that raises awareness of mother-work and amplifies the voices of women and families. Its purpose is to encourage individuals to evaluate their own experiences as mothers in authentic and mindful ways. The Museum of Motherhood serves as a unique resource and archive for everyone who wants to study mothers, from lay-people to schoolchildren to serious scholars. A physical structure for the museum is forthcoming, but there have been exhibits through an online portal and traveling exhibits that have been featured in cultural institutions, libraries, banks and city centers throughout the United States. This chapter will introduce the Museum, provide an overview of how the museum came about, describe its place within the Motherhood Movement, and give insight to iyd future goals.

Mandate

The mission of M.o.M. is to present and archive the history, evolution and cultural significance of mothers, mother-art and mother-work. The Museum will inspect motherhood and mother-work around the world, while documenting the herstory of (m)others in perpetuity. In its exhibits and programming, the Museum is dedicated to opening a public exchange and dialogue about what it means to be a mother and providing a home for existing scholarship and future research to be viewed by the public and create awareness of academia and art with mothers and motherhood as its theme.

History

After working in the entertainment industry for nearly a decade and acting as an informal activist, Joy Rose met moms from around the country and created MAMA-PALOOZA™, Inc. a multi-media and event company, which promoted mothers and

Moms of Rock, Street Exhibit, Seneca Falls, New York. Curated by Lynn Barbuto, 2009.

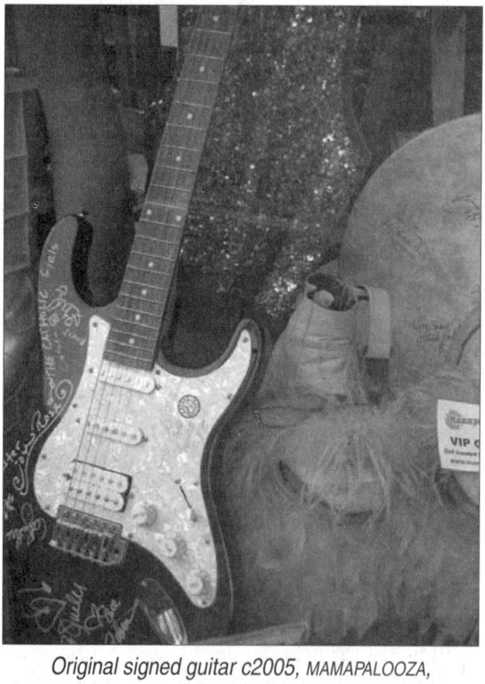

Original signed guitar c2005, MAMAPALOOZA, New York City, and performance gear from Joy Rose, Housewives on Pozac band.

mother artx (see chapter 74). Through this work, Joy helped to pioneer a larger social movement that encouraged women to experiment with breaking the mold of "traditional" mothering stereotypes. During a conversation with her good friend Gillian Crane, the concept for a Museum of Motherhood originated. Joy trademarked "Museum of Motherhood" and established the first-ever exhibit of "Mom" oribilia at 42 Main St. in Dobbs Ferry, New York in 2003, with Gillian's friendship and approval.

This first exhibit for the Museum featured books, ephemera (defined as items that are not intended to be preserved or archived), paper goods, fine art, marketing materials depicting mothers in the home and in other common roles, mom-made objects and general information about the cultural standing of mothers in North America. The exhibit remained in place through 2005. This storefront exhibit hoisted a "Museum of Motherhood" placard and hosted small gatherings of community artists, friends and mothers in an informal setting, where dialogue took place about shared experiences, frustrations, joys and cultural taboos. Mother art and literature was at the forefront. Humorous books like *Sippy Cups Are Not For Chardonnay* and *I Threw Out My Sanity With the Diapers* as well as historical and psychological texts like *Faith Of Our Mothers: The Stories of Presidential Mothers* and Pyllis Chesler's books, including *Women and Madness,* were shared and discussed. All of the literature, either written by mothers or about motherhood, provided the content that informed these dialogues. Pieces of mother-made folk art, dolls, tee-shirts and clothing from Joy Rose's band collection with quotations like "Motherhood Is The Necessity Of Invention," "Mom Is Not My Real Name," "Women Do Not Have An Expiration Date" and "Moms Rock" were featured for sale as well as Isabella Bannerman's art and mother comic strips, magnets, and buttons with funny and sassy sayings were displayed with the intention to inspire and inform. In addition, workshops about creativity and crafts-womanship were held to encourage women to get more involved with accessing their (M)other voice. Girl's birthday parties, jewelry making sessions and small gatherings focused attention on mother/daughter interactions and encouraged local youth to interact within the "MommyGirlGo-Go" store, which hosted the storefront and museum exhibit gathering space.

In 2006, Joy Rose asked MAMAPALOOZA event coordinator Terry Platz and her neighbor Bob Bickford Esq. to facilitate filing for corporate and legal 501c3 status for a non-profit body "Motherhood Foundation Inc." (MFI). Jennifer Edwards, also a MAMAPALOOZA participant, volunteered her expertise and acted as first board president for the ongoing work of the Museum. Since receiving its government approval, M.o.M. established a board of directors, research, academic and programming committees and has begun documenting the evolving role(s) of mothers as they pertain to circumstances, environment, responsibilities, health issues, influence, political position and creativity. Several grants have since been awarded, and a fundraising team has been put in place.

Initial applications, fundraising and awareness raising through sister organizations like MAMAPALOOZA, Inc., the Village of Seneca Falls, New York, Westchester Office for Women, have resulted in the current website and growing movement of mothers who wish to see a physical Museum in North America. At every MAMAPALOOZA event since 2004, a "MFI" banner has flanked the MAMAPALOOZA stage, with specific information disseminating booths cropping up at events in 2010. In 2010 the Museum Of Motherhood had a presence at over a dozen large-scale events, festivals and expos.

Context

Motherhood is an extremely complex and personal journey and is often poised as simply a "choice" made by women. In reality it is a sub-culture within society with its own set of social norms and practices, which are socially constructed. When people think of motherhood they often think of the struggles as time management, guilt, and self-sacrifice, and the only success as raising good kids and bountiful love. Motherhood and care giving in North America is unpaid and often unappreciated work, resulting in women often occupying a lower economic status. There is much more to the fabric of motherhood and family as a cultural element to our society. Health.com cited ten out of twenty-one job categories in which full time workers are most likely to report an episode of major depression in a given year. Six of the professions on the list fall under "care-giving" and "associated" professions; nursing home/child care workers, social workers, health care workers teachers and artists, entertainers and writers—all of these fall under areas of examination within the Museum of Motherhood.

As an archive devoted to educating the world about the contributions of mothers both historically and in contemporary culture, we intend to fill a longstanding void in the academic and real world with a physical and virtual library, exhibit facility, traveling productions, and resource and educational center. We honor the unsung heroes of (M)otherhood while aligning ourselves with other great existing organizations that share in the empowerment of women, love of family—in all its shapes and sizes, and other related topics.

Objectives

The Museum's purpose is to provide a place and platform that educates the general public about the history of mothers in America and around the world. It offers participants the chance to consider the different ways that mothers have birthed and raised children throughout the ages, as well as documenting the journey of mother's evolving role while promoting women and gender studies and the evolution of family.

The Museum will work to encourage individuals to evaluate their own experience as mothers in authentic and mindful ways while giving expression to the internal psyche, physical, emotional and spiritual journey of motherhood, and exposing people to the rich traditions of how family life has evolved. Additionally, the museum will share the vibrant artistic productions and achievements of mothers who are writers, painters, musicians, actors, filmmakers and individuals who have made a difference in education, literature, environment, sciences, architecture, activism, business, politics, the home and more by preserving, collecting, interpreting and producing dynamic programming that is inspirational, collaborative and informative.

We are committed to serving as a valuable resource to the community, by creating jobs, encouraging tourism, offering resources to families, generating compelling individual and community experiences. M.o.M.'s goals include a permanent library; art and history exhibit halls, family activity room, outreach center, museum store and teaching facility. We strive to amplify the voices of women and the culture of (M)others everywhere.

Examples of Museum Exhibits and Outreach

Moms Who Rock Traveling Exhibit

This exhibit was a touring visual display of "Moms Who Rock" items in upstate New York, Seneca Falls, the home of the "American Suffragette Movement,"

Moms of Rock, Street Exhibit, Seneca Falls, New York, featuring "Mom"orabilia. Curated by Lynn Barbuto, 2009.

to generate excitement and raise public support and funds with regard to the Museum of Motherhood. Items displayed included a signed spatula from Bette Midler; Barbara Streisand signed album cover; an autographed "Sweet Honey & The Rock" drum; Shirley Austin Reeves "The Shirelles" signed Poster; platform boots worn at Giant's Stadium Concerts; Joy Rose's NOW-NYC award and key to the city of Seneca Falls; Joy Rose's laminated cereal box dress from performances with "Housewives On Prozac"; a MAMAPALOOZA signed daisy rock guitar; Judy David's book, *Rock Star Mommy,* among all kinds of other "mom"orabilia. The exhibit captured the attention of tourists visiting the National Women's Hall of Fame as each windowfront lining the main thoroughfare in town was decked out with information about the Museum of Motherhood. The exhibit remained in place from the summer of 2009 through fall 2010.

Historical Installations of Mothers throughout the Ages

Pregnancy and childbirth have been documented throughout the ages. The museum will pay tribute to these mothers with excerpts of writings, such as the blog, "Down The Rabbit Hole," the author describes birth in Medieval times as:

> *"The gist of it"*
> Childbirth was considered so deadly back then, the church told women to confess their sins, and prepare their will because god forbid if you were a good Christian in this life, you'll probably burn for all eternity in the

afterlife. Get ready to die from one of the worst pains you'll feel in this one. Midwives back then were so highly regarded, not only did they work for the church, but they were trained to fight spells from witches or any other black magic your new baby might contract in this new promising age.

Why It Was So Deadly

Not only did women have to give birth the good old fashion way, but in many cases, the pain was so intense the women would die half way giving birth. Abnormal births were quite common too; the midwives with a few tricks up their sleeves, shaking the bed to reposition the baby in the womb, or turned the infant in utero.

Not only was there a physical risk in pregnancy, there is also documentation of the concerns for how women's life would change as they had more children. Shared descriptions of women's lives in the eighteenth century, which usually centered on their families; there was little likelihood of a career outside the home. Women went into childbirth uncertain not only of their own survival but of their child's, as well. It was not uncommon for a woman to give birth seven or eight times during her life, with only five or six children surviving to adulthood. Despite high mortality rates, women expected to have large families. Esther Edwards Burr, mother of Aaron Burr, was daunted by her future prospects after the birth of her second child. She wrote in 1756, "When I had but one child my hands were tied, but now I am tied hand and foot. (How I shall get along when I have got ½ dzn. or 10 Children I can't devise.)" (history.com).

Fashion was and still is relevant during pregnancy. On history.com there are descriptions such as pregnancy fashion of early American mothers: "Women had to cope with the difficulty of dressing for pregnancy in a time when the fashionable figure and undergarments called for tight lacing that shaped a woman's body into a smooth cone from the waist up to the breasts. In 1735, Sarah, Duchess of Marlborough, wrote her granddaughter reminiscing about her pregnancies and the clothing she resorted to in an attempt at comfort: "I remember when I was within three months of my reckoning, I could never endure any bodice [corset] at all; but wore a warm waistcoat wrapped about me like a man's and tied my petticoats on top of it. And from that time never went abroad but with a long black scarf to hide me I was so prodigeous big." (It is instructive to note that the duchess did not avoid going out, but covered herself with a scarf when she did.) The "warm waistcoat" described by the duchess was probably an unboned sleeveless garment that fastened at the front. In spite of the availability of looser waistcoats, some women continued to wear heavy stays or corsets during their pregnancies (history.com).

Mother Art

For the "Momma Love" project, Ali Smith photographed women performing their daily tasks of motherhood. From cuddling to feeding, she says, "the details and rituals of motherhood often go unnoticed and get taken for granted." She continues, "I found myself wanting to understand more fully." Her goal for the project is "to nurture healthier mothers and a healthier society, honest conversations about the realities of motherhood and how mothers are treated as necessary" (<www.alismith.com>).

"Sacred Feminine" by Polly Wood: Polly is a multidisciplinary artist, creating song, visual art, dance and writing, which embodies and explores the role of the Sacred Feminine in our global culture. As a mother, and as part of our community of contributing mother artists, M.O.M. organized a special online exhibit, which Polly researched and made weekly presentations of art, film, and text as it related to the "Sacred Mother." Each week, from February 17 through April 28, 2010, Polly added a new installment to the online exhibit, which was widely promoted throughout the website, blogs, and other media outlets (www.radwoman.com).

Other artists, such as Elle Dreyfus, "Pregnancy Series" (Australia); Toni Wilkinson, "m/others" (Australia); "The Prime Book," highlighting mostly mothers in transition and mothers of a certain age (USA); Jasmine Symons, "Carrying the Weight of the World" (Australia); Adrian Baker, "The Midwife" (Canada); Vee Malnar, "At Home"; and Laura Endacott, "ribs," have also been featured.

The Written Word

The Mom Egg: a collection of poems and short stories from mothers which has been published and will be sold in the Museum bookstore.

Mamazina Magazine: a quarterly "zine" that is published online and in hard copy featuring a variety of stories about mothers and showcasing mothers from various sectors of society.

The Mother Registry: is an online archive of tributes to mothers and others that are submitted by visitors to the website to honor a mother or mother figure in their life. This will continue to be a feature of the web presence of the museum and will also become a feature of the museum with quotations displayed in the physical space.

MamaBlogger365: a blog initiative starting January 1, 2011, and running through December 31, 2011, asks the question, "How does motherhood need to be reframed?" A new entry is posted each day from mothers with a wide range of experiences and perspectives. Contributors include academics, mom bloggers, artists, and laypeople write about their research, opinions and lived-experience. The purpose of the project is to raise awareness and drive attention to the fundraising initiatives of a physical space for the museum while encouraging discourse amongst individuals who are members of a variety of social stations and institutions.

Live Performance and Video Projects

The Motherhood Movement—You Say You Want A Revolution, The Film

The film, *The Motherhood Movement—You Say You Want a Revolution* captures the first ever, international summit on the Motherhood Movement, featuring

Motherhood organizations. Directed by Joy Rose, the film was produced by the Museum of Motherhood, in collaboration with the Association for Research on Mothering (ARM) and The Motherhood Foundation Inc (MFI). The film seeks to promote, showcase, and make visible maternal discussion and to disseminate information on the subject of feminist/activist mothers and the missions of International Maternal agencies. Over 23 organizations were represented at the first ever global summit at the Association For Research and Mothering Conference, York University on October 25-26, 2008, Toronto, Canada, .

We have documented and preserved presentations, interviews, and perspectives about the burgeoning "Mom Movement." Subjects include, but are not limited to: the Motherhood Movement as an important part of women's studies, activism, the three feminist waves: where are we now? Feminist mothering; women and mothers in the arts; non-traditional parenting; women and families; poor and immigrant issues, the 1950s until now; mothers and politics; mothers and the economy; motherhood unpaid; mother-work; the gift economy; matriarchal and Indigenous societies; the role of men and feminist values; future museum of motherhood; formation of an international movement.

Additional film and performance projects cover a wide variety of topics. It is the breadth of what is captured in film and performance that can begin to define our similarities rather than expose our differences. Contemporary art exhibits by Cat Del Buono, "Feeding Video" (USA) and Jess Dobkin, "Lactation Station" (Canada). Theater, TV and popular culture including: *Momz Hot Rock,* a movie by Kate Perotti (USA); *2 Angry Moms* (USA); *Mothers & Daughters* (USA); *The Motherhood Movement: You Say You Want A Revolution* (USA/Canada); *Maverick Mother,* by Janet Merewether (Australia); Christen Clifford, *BabyLove* (USA); Joy Rose, *The Housewives Lament and Shut Up & Drive* (USA); Amy Simon *Cheerios In My Underwear*, and *She's History* (USA); Sue Fabisch, *Motherhood: The Musical* (USA); Lynn Kuechle, *The Mother Monologues* (USA). Recordings and live mother-centric music and dance acts include The Mydols (USA); Tina de Varon, "If Mama Ain't Happy" (USA); Tiffany Petrossi, "Rockin" Moms (USA); Momz In Da Hood (USA), to name just a few.

Academic Scholarship

Annual Mom Conference in New York City

Each year since 2005, MAMAPALOOZA has produced a "Lifestyles and Education" conference in collaboration with the Motherhood Foundation. The first event, in cooperation with the Women's Media Center in New York City, grew to encompass academics, artists and laypeople in an expansive, multi-disciplinary landscape with multiple cooperative partners including the Association for Research on Mothering in 2008. The conference has since morphed into a "Mother Studies" conference, in conjunction with MAMAPALOOZA and its artists, but with additional focus on including academics and reaching the general public, therefore bridging a gap between inter disciplines. In 2011, professors from Minnesota

State University Mankato, Franklin Peirce University and Marymount Manhattan College formed the planning committee for M.o.M. Conference, which will move from Nola Studios (and assorted club and reading room facilities) in New York City to Marymount Manhattan College. The M.o.M. Conference accepts year round submissions through its web portal MotherStudies.org and seeks to encourage ongoing dialogue in every area of mothering and motherhood, and all related topics that affect women, mothers, feminist moms, caregivers, communities and institutions interested in sharing information, conducting research and learning about the evolution of mother.

Interdisciplinary Certificate Program

Scholars in a variety of disciplines study motherhood and mothers. Many of these scholars have gathered at the M.o.M. conferences, which has been the beginning of a variety of projects. M.o.M. has initiated curriculum for an accredited academic certificate program in "Mother Studies." M.o.M. conference committee members for "MotherStudies" are facilitating this process: a "Motherhood" course curriculum being taught at Manhattan Marymount College, New York City and at Minnesota State University. Franklin Pierce College in New Hampshire does work on establishing clarity for individuals and programs in defining goals, missions and establishing identity. Plans are underway to conduct a workshop in this area at the conference in 2011. Minnesota State University in Mankato, Minnesota has been working on plans for a certificate program. This graduate level program will introduce students to the socially constructed role of mother. The program will be multi-disciplinary in nature and examine motherhood grounded in feminist theory. Students will examine representations about mothers, in North America as well as from a cross-cultural perspective. And finally the program will offer students insight into historical representations of mother and how the role of mother has evolved over time. The program will also be in an online format which will allow students and instructors from a variety of geographical locations to be involved.

Relationship to Larger Motherhood Movement

Motherhood, no matter who is filling the role, is charged with building social capital. When children are raised well, society functions more efficiently and effectively. It has been said that "it takes a village" to raise a child. This museum will serve as the town square of that village. The Museum of Motherhood is the place for women, families, activists, academic, faith and community-based organizations to share stories, conduct research, and learn about the evolution of family. It is the receptacle and archive for the current research, libraries, works of art, and general content by and about mothers, motherhood, mothering, and caregiving from feminist, alternative and "mainstream" perspectives, and from diverse other mothers. It will offer a place to examine how mothers have been dealt with historically and the physical, emotional, psychological effects of birth, parenting and self in relation to other. Ongoing focus will be to promote organizations and individuals who are concerned with everything-mother as well as the cultural family. The cultural family is exactly that: the culture of family, its relationships and individual's perceptions within these constructs. By creating a place of valuable cultural and social information gathering, individuals, corporations, and institutions interested in studying (M)other, will have a central portal to do this. The "Motherhood Movement" per se is relatively new. Riding a wave of efforts by Joy Rose and MAMAPALOOZA, the Museum is the next logical place for archiving and then broadly disseminating the information that has been cultivated and collected in the past fifteen years. To date, Joy has passionately and personally overseen the development of M.O.M. from its initial vision; band, to movement to museum—drawn out in careful script and illustrations as far back as 2003. Her unwavering devotion and focus to see the museum become a reality has dominated her personal landscape and the bulk of her time and energies unrelentingly since it's inception. Bringing other Mother organizations on board, trusting the MFI Board; Lynn Kuechle, Cara Lee Bataglia and Gillian Crane while building relationships with funders is the ongoing story of a socially relevant, sustainable, interactive museum.

The recent and intense culture of mother art has been nurtured along and hundreds if not thousands of individuals have risen to the occasion. There is no standing-structure (yet) that will serve to harbor, nurture, celebrate and feature these endeavors. This is the home that will house all their stories. The Museum of Motherhood will honor the legacy of mothers past, present and future. It is the pivotal and crucial focal point of a larger expanded movement that encompasses all of mother history, which to date, has not been forthcoming.

In Sister Prudence Allen's book, *The Concept of Woman,* she introduces one of Socrates dialogues. "It is easy to see the virtue of man consists in managing the city's affairs capably and so that he will help his friends and injure his foes while taking care to do no harm to himself. Or, if you want a woman's virtue, that is easily described. She must be a good housewife, careful of her stores and obedient to her husband." (41) Most feminists today would take issue with a statement like this. When women cite: "I often feel like a 1950s housewife, except that my husband hasn't provided me with a wardrobe full of big flouncy dresses and I still can't bring myself to iron his shirts" (Edwards), it shows that we still have work to do.

Challenges

There are marble museums, mustard museums, train museums and money museums, but there is no museum that studies mothers, families and the history of motherhood. The biggest challenge faced by this project has been finding sources of sustainable funding. While this is a frequent concern for many organizations, this has been an internal as well as an external challenge. With so many obstacles facing mothers and families, such as poverty, homelessness, abuse, healthcare, flexible work schedules, and the simple fact that mother-work often goes largely taken for granted, MFI acknowledges it must not only work to create ongoing funding sources, but it must also challenge perceptions that we hold about mothers. Recognizing value of childbirth, care giving, mother-work and so much more, the museum is committed to facing these obstacles through vibrant identity forums and ongoing action.

Moving towards a solutions to this dilemma, identity forums led by faculty from Franklin Pierce University will be core to the content of the 2011 M.o.M. Conference in New York City. The conference being held at Marymount Manhattan College, deals with mothers' vulnerability with regard to institutions. Within that structure, we'll be directing participants to engage in ongoing questions regarding "What IS Mother?" and how we can tailor financial appeals to institutions, endowments, corporations and individuals to be focused, compelling and successful. Clarifying our mission of collecting, archiving and promoting mother work, mother art and mother/family history will enable us to begin a series of well-planned research projects quantifying the statistics, reactions, sentiment, psychology and facts of motherhood and family life experiences. Even though there's currently a proliferation of mom blogger voices and books, the movement is still lacking in cohesive studies that quantify the issues that face mothers. Much of the blog-o-sphere is devoted to marketing and coupon campaigns as well as discussion forums that, while validating mothers' experiences, does nothing to change them or create policy that can result in significant progress regarding the status of mothers. We believe understanding how policy decisions, personal choices and ideological standpoints have affected the experience of mothers in the past and present will help light the path to the future.

Funding

Many other public outreach programs are in place for raising funds for the physical museum. An on-going effort of funding was started in 2008, which encouraged contributors to the website registry to also make a donation in the name of the woman they were honoring. Letters were sent to all honorees. Recent press in *Working Mother Magazine*, Nov. 2010, the "Summer Soiree," "Legacy Tea," Working Mother Media "Silent Auction" and ongoing weekly Internet TV & radio, online "Registry for Mothers," sale of the film *The Motherhood Movement—You Say You Want A Revolution* to libraries, as well as the MamaBlogger365 initiative form the basic foundation for grassroots outreach. Partnerships with women and men of influence and means, coupled with political, academic and the steady addition of valuable M.o.M. board members will focus attention on a second tier of fundraising. The following timeline shows the steady progress being made since the inception of the museum began.

2003–2007

•Establishing Trademarks 501c3 certification and formation of the organization.

•Formation of credible board of directors and formation of the research committee.
•First visual display featuring local "Mom-orabilia," Main St. Dobbs Ferry, New York.
•Early beginnings for documentation of the Mother's evolving role, as it pertains to women's circumstances, environment, responsibilities, health, significance, influence, position and creativity.

2008–2009
•The MAMAPALOOZA/ARM Conference, New York City. Sponsored by Motherhood Foundation and the Association for Research on Mothering.
•Launched Motherhood in Motion exhibits; preparations for film development—*The Motherhood Movement,* Window treatments, Seneca Falls, New York. New Jersey Library System Arts and Culture presentations by Mothers.
•Development of Fun, Fabulous Female Facts monthly series online at M.o.M.

2010 and Beyond
•Launch MamaBlogger365.
•Completion, Promotion and Distribution of Film—*The Motherhood Movement.*
•Development of Motherhood Memorobilia and preparation for nationwide exhibit displays.
•Website Portal Development: Online Resources, Calendar, Fact sheet, educational programming, continuation of Fun, Fabulous Female Facts.
•Establishment of a world-class Museum of Motherhood in 2011 and the display online of herstory of North American Mothers, promotes women's studies and the evolution of family, while honoring the achievements of women who are mothers in perpetuity.

The Future

The future of M.o.M. is to continue along the path we have started. We plan to continue to create and promote creative and smart installations to the museum and continue to expose every sector of society to what we know, that birthing and care-giving is work that needs to be studied, celebrated, and honored. Our goal is to have a physical space in 2011. Original focus was on Seneca Falls because of its historical significance, but current interest has shifted to New York City where a viable, working budget has a chance of succeeding due to foot traffic, visibility and a wealth of community involvement.

Sustainability is a foremost objective of the museum board of directors. We know that there needs to be a reason for people to visit the museum on a regular basis. For this reason and in order for the museum to reach its full potential as a vehicle for social change, we will establish a pre-school program. The basic philosophy of the school is described in Heide Goettner-Abendroth's website: "Modern Matriarchal Studies Definitions, Scope and Topicality":

> With matriarchal cultures, equality means more than just a leveling of differences. Natural differences between the genders and the generations are respected and honored, but they never serve to create hierarchies, as is common in patriarchy. The different genders and generations have their own dignity, and through complementary areas of activity, they function in concert one other. More precisely, matriarchies are societies with complementary equality, where great care is taken to provide a balance. This applies to the balance between genders, among generations, and between humans and nature. Maternal values as ethical principles pervade all areas of a matriarchal society. It creates an attitude of caretaking, nurturing, and peacemaking.

There will be an accompanying library which will contain books by women, mothers and others discoursing on the history of motherhood as well as fulfilling the mission to preserve, collect and interpret materials and information specific to mothers who have made a difference in education, literature, environment, sciences, the arts, music, architecture, culture, activism, business, the home, and politics, as well as to document the herstory of (M)otherwork and (M)othering. Allowing mothers the time and space to explore the museum while their children are also learning and having fun will set the ground work for future proponents of the museum and future scholars.

In addition to the pre-school, the museum will offer a store that will offer with items not found in current big box stores or boutiques. Completing the plans for a fall/winter 2011 museum opening in New York City will be a presentation of "Mother The Job" as the initial founding exhibit, as well as art and photography gifts, which have already been obtained by the museum (Ella Dreyfus Photography, and more).

Conclusion

The Museum of Motherhood is for all of the unsung heroes—the women, caregivers, daughters, grandmothers, aunts, and fathers who have devoted their lives to caring for, and raising future generations. We honor, study and celebrate them in perpetuity at M.o.M. Motherwork continues to be one of the least celebrated accomplishments and yet has the most profound impact on subsequent generations. Glorified celebrity baby bumps not withstanding, the day-to-day feeding, raising, caring for, and educating of children, as well as the nurturing and the "mothering," is of the upmost importance, and moving into the twenty-first century, is occasionally perpetrated by men as well as women. By lifting people up, and witnessing their stories, we heal and empower them, and we honor them as contributing members of society. Even today, mothers struggle with a host of issues particular to their life and work choices. Issues of depression, over-work, mother-blame, lack of financial remuneration, and often-chronic pregnancy-related health issues, continue in the mother population. Workplace pay issues, healthcare obstacles and feminist and equality issues aside, issues of domestic violence and a host of other maladies that reflect mother-specific life/work, are still very much present in society. The torch must be passed to history, to begin the archival and restoration process of not only (m)other's collective memories and psyches, but also their cultural voice. This will result in the mother power, information, and a magnified point of view, that cannot be ignored, or undermined.

Works Cited

Allen, P. *The Concept of Woman: The Aristotelian Revolution 750 BC-AD 1250.* Montreal: Eden Press, 1985.

Barumgarten, L. "Fashions of Motherhood." *History.org* Web. <http://www.history.org/history/clothing/women/motherhood.cfm>.

Down the Rabbit Hole . "5 Excruciating Medical Treatments from the Middle Ages." Web. <http://downtherabbithole.posterous.com/5-excruciating-medical-treatments-from-the-mi>.

Edwards, Kasey. *MamaBlogger365—The Clock Is Ticking.* January 9, 2011,

Goettner-Abendroth, H. "Societies of Peace: Matriarchies in Past Present and Future to Modern Matriarchal Studies Definitions, Scope and Topicality." Web. <http://www.second-congress-matriarchal-studies.com/goettnerabendroth.html>.

Wood, P. "Sacred Feminine." Web. <http://www.motherhoodmuseum.org/PollyWood.html>.

Worth, T. "10 Careers With High Rates of Depression." Health.com. Web. <http://www..health.com/health/gallery/0,,20428990_1,00.html>.

76. Hip Mama

ARIEL GORE

IN THE MIDST OF THE family values campaign—that unfair fight of the early 1990s wherein a bunch of white Republicans and philandering Democrats took up rhetorical arms against *us*, a bunch of young moms raising our kids on diminishing welfare checks and large-hearted poetry—I decided that we needed a media outlet of our own.

They had the whole "liberal" media in the palm of their hands. They had those newscasters reporting on "skyrocketing teenage pregnancy" (wasn't true, rates had actually reached a plateau), "skyrocketing out-of-wedlock births" (again, wasn't true—there was no question on birth certificates about marriage, so some genius in the statistics department had started counting as "out-of-wedlock" any mama who didn't have the same last name as her baby-daddy), and "crack babies" (a label that ended up stigmatizing a whole class of children based on totally shoddy medical misinformation).

We had . . . well, we had pretty much nothing. The feminist press was reluctant to cover parenting issues because of all the work they'd done to get out from under the notion that a woman's worth is in her uterus. The radical political press was mostly a bunch of radicals without children—kids were seen as a hindrance to the revolution in a lot of circles. Folks often meant well, but they had trouble concentrating on their anarchist history text with babies babbling in the background.

There was *Mothers Underground* and *The Next Generation* and *Welfare Mothers Voice* and *Mom's Apple Pie* and likely a few other hard-to-find zines and newsletters that never made it to my Oakland, California apartment.

I wanted to make a little homemade something of my own. I had grand dreams, of course. *A media empire!* But I had very little money and third-world aesthetics and I believed something small and from the heart could make a difference. With my welfare checks and my student loan money (sorry about the electricity getting turned off every other month, Maia), I decided to make a zine.

History and Mandate

In 1993, *Hip Mama* was born as my senior project at Mills College. The mission

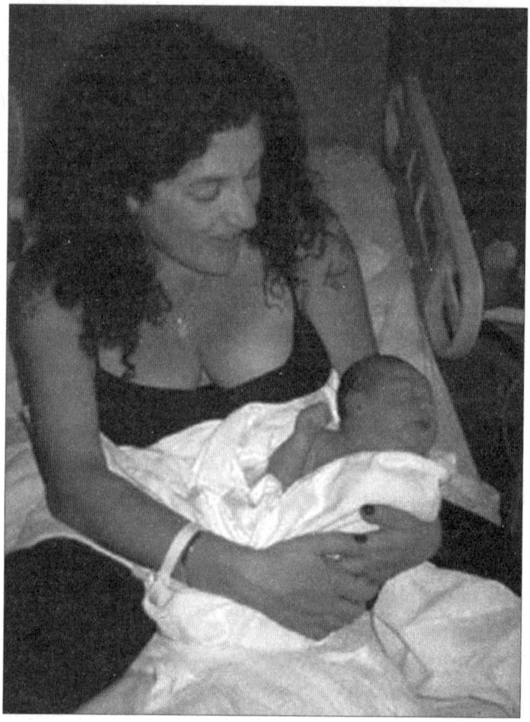

Ariel Gore with son Maximilian Gore Perez.

was simple: To provide a forum for progressive parents to tell their own stories. Most parenting magazines hire "experts" to tell mothers what to do—their goal is to round up an audience for their advertisers. *Hip Mama* would allow minimal grassroots advertising. *Hip Mama* would publish personal essays, political news and commentary, literary fiction and even poetry by parents themselves.

My best friend and radical mama, Julie Bowles, came on board and we were a two-mama-media revolution. We published feminist voices and sought to turn our readers into writers. Our idea was simple: Mothers were the experts, and the hard and real truth about motherhood needed to be told. We organized local mothers to take part in political actions. When California Governor Pete Wilson called welfare mothers "promiscuous and idle" we went right up to Sacramento with our picket signs: "We may be promiscuous, but we ain't idle."

Soon the zine's circulation was international, and we started a show on Free Radio Berkeley, the Bay Area's pirate station.

In the middle of the night, we stenciled graffiti on family courtroom walls—"Misogyny: Look it Up, Stamp it out."

Soon the mamas were coming out of the woodwork, saying, "Yes! I am here to testify that it wasn't us who poisoned the seas and raped the earth and brought down the economy. We are here, simply, keeping people alive. We are here, simply, making art and love. We are here, and we will not be silenced any longer."

Vanessa Stefanelli and Wendy De Jong and Inga Aaron and many other women whose names appeared or did not appear in the zine each joined the group for a different length of time and then moved on. Each made *Hip Mama* strong. And stronger.

There was Annie Downey's "I am Your Welfare Reform" and Allison Crews' "When I Was Garbage" and Anne Marie Keen's "Girl Mom" and Fern Capella's "This is Your Life" and Katherine Arnoldi's "How I Became a Cartoonist" and Susan Ito's "Choice" and Sarah Ongiri's "I Had a WHITE Baby" and all the stories

An early postcard promotion hipmama.com, 1997.

that changed the world in subtle and grand ways.

We gave faces to the statistics, and honored mothers—poor, young, old, single, progressive, feminist, queer—as not only breeders but as journalists, storytellers, artists, leaders, and experts.

The cover went full-color, causing many in the zine community to declare it a magazine raher than a zine, but *Hip Mama* will always be a zine: not-for-profit, mama-produced.

Soon CNN would show up at the door to my little Oakland apartment, NPR would show up, and ABC and CBS and NBC and I would by flown to Washington, DC, to debate Newt Gingrich—that architect of the "Family Values Campaign"—on MTV News. I lost the battle, as they say, in my dumb Peter-Pan collar, but I like to think we're winning the war.

Today there are thousands of blogs where working-class and middle-class and upper-class women can tell the truth about motherhood, but back then Child Protective Services would have showed up on your doorstep if you let slip half of what is commonplace in the public dialogue these days.

Sometimes, when I have the misfortune of watching TV, I think, *Great, all that work and what did we accomplish? Blue-jean diapers and The Potty Dance*? The hipification of parenting? I never cared about that. To me, "hip" always meant "aware and informed."

Activities and Expansion

In 1997, *Hip Mama* was ready to expand to the Internet. With the help of a now-defunct Internet start-up company in the Bay Area, we designed a Web community.

I wrote *The Hip Mama Survival Guide*, which was published by Hyperion.

A few years later, Bee Lavender took over the site. As she puts it in our recent email correspondence:

> The vision was simple: I would create a safe place for welfare mothers, teen parents, queer parents, the disenfranchised and lonely. We were feminist, pro-choice, sex positive, anti-capitalist, anti-authoritarian, open source, reader-written, and operated by volunteers. We were young, and passionate, and we believed in Utopia.
>
> This vision was shared by a crew of volunteer technical staff, designers, and moderators scattered across the world. And it happened—from the very start there were remarkable examples of women helping each other with tangible resources, from sharing advice, clothing, money, and food, to literally rescuing each other from chaos.

Soon, the Website was getting many millions of hits and developed a global audience. We launched a sister site, Girlmom.com, a safe haven for teen moms. Choice activist and young mom Allison Crews became the editor of Girlmom.com and that community flourished as well.

I wrote a second book, *The Mother Trip*, a collection of essays on the politics of parenting and staying sane in the chaos. Seal Press published the book in 2000 and a year later, Bee Lavender and I collected a diverse group of young mama-voices in *Breeder: Real-Life Stories from the New Generation of Mothers*.

As Bee Lavender says, "Hipmama.com started with a purpose and it has retained that directive. We are feminist, pro-choice, sex positive, anti-capitalist, anti-authoritarian, open source, reader-written, operated by and for volunteers. We are an activist tool for social change."

Each new medium—zines, websites, books, and now Facebook group, allowed for different kinds of information-sharing, networking and empowerment. While the zine has always been more literary, the Websites provide a more effective platform for community building and support. The books reached larger audiences, but *Hip Mama* zine remained the heart of the project.

Hip Mama, *2010 issue*

Challenges

In 2009, after editing and publishing *Hip Mama* for 16 years, seeing my daughter off to college, and giving birth to a second child, I was tired and broke. Volunteers would have helped me, but I felt introverted—more interested for the time being in the solitary life of the writer than the public life of the editor/activist.

I hadn't gotten over the sudden and mysterious death of Girl Mom editor Allison Crews two years earlier. Through my post-partum haze I thought: Maybe it's time to pass the zine along.

Kerlin Richter volunteered to take the reins. She was a painter, she was working on a master's degree in theology, she had a three-year-old. *Why not take on a zine as well?* In a recent email, Kerlin tells the story,

> The enormity of what I'd done took awhile to hit me....
>
> *Hip Mama* has been in this weird middle ground between magazine and zine.
>
> Yes, it's in grocery stores and, yes, it's 8 1/2 x 11, but it was just me at my kitchen table sweatin' it out in the middle of the night.
>
> The summer I took over the magazine, I went to the Portland zine symposium, and in the "Zines 101" workshop someone asked about the difference between zines and magazines. In his answer, the presenter said that some mags had started as zines but then sold out and went all professional with big staffs. His two examples were Bitch and Hip Mama. I timidly raised my hand and tried to set the record straight, but I don't think anyone believed me. I did my work on a laptop and not with a sharpie, therefore *Hip Mama* was not a zine.

There were lonely days as Kerlin tried to learn to put the zine together and run the business. She became a grad school drop out, and didn't paint much anymore. She was stressed out all the time and still getting angry letters in the mail.

But then she met Brandie who volunteered to take on the business end to let Kerlin focus on the editorial. And things got better. At the zine's annual Mother's Day party that year they met Chelsea, and through Chelsea, Amanda. And then they were four. In January, 2010, *Hip Mama* became a worker-owned collective.

The Future

"We love *Hip Mama*," Kerlin and her team say. We think it's one of the most important magazines that has ever been. *Hip Mama* is a place where divergent and rarely heard voices get to spin out into the world. Copies of the zine head out all across the globe. We've heard from countless mamas that we are the one voice reassuring them that they are not alone. That there are many ways to be a mama, only a few of which make the national scene.

Kerlin adds:

> Turns out, it's not a Slings v. Strollers world—it's a beautifully complex landscape where mothers and others struggle to define themselves and parent with every ounce of integrity we can in a world that just wants to sell us stuff and tell us what to do.

We don't need 25 ways to make our kids eat green things, we don't need to be told why everybody else is a better mama than us. Those folks will probably survive because their mags are 3/4 advertising. There are plenty of places now where we can go to find the advice we need when we need it. Go online and you can find thousands of people who agree with you, on almost any topic. There are gonna be blogs and sites aplenty. So where does that leave *Hip Mama*, as the print media world gasps for breath and falls to its knees?

We are gonna carry on, like mamas do.

Mamas can come and go and the zine will live on. *Hip Mama* will keep on providing, hopefully forever, a forum for the feminist, radical, diverse, humble, and creative voices of motherhood that might not otherwise be heard.

Works Cited

Gore, Ariel. *The Hip Mama Survival Guide.* New York: Hyperion Press, 1998.

Gore, Ariel. *The Mother Trip.* Seattle: Seal Press, 2000.

Bee Lavender and Ariel Gore. *Breeder: Real-Life Stories from the New Generation of Mothers.* Seattle: Seal Press, 2001.

Lavender, Bee. Email correspondence. July 8, 2010.

Richter, Kerlin. Email correspondence. July 20, 2010.

77. Things No One Will Tell You

Literary Mama Writes About Motherhood Outside the Mainstream Media

CAROLINE M. GRANT

LITERARY MAMA BEGAN PUBLISHING ONLINE in 2003, having evolved quickly from a local mothers' writing group into a literary journal featuring fiction, creative nonfiction, and poetry, plus book reviews and profiles of artists and writers. One of *Writer's Digests'* 101 Best Web Sites for Writers and a Forbes Best of the Web pick, today *Literary Mama's* diverse editors work from four countries and reach over 40,000 monthly readers.

Philosophy

Literary Mama was founded to give mother writers an outlet for their writing and to connect these writers, around the world, in community and conversation.

The site began as a small group of writers, led by Amy Hudock, who met in a bimonthly Berkeley group called Writing About Motherhood. As the women began to produce their own original work, they found their writing caught in a limbo outside the conventional views of motherhood commonly found in the mainstream media: either sweetly sentimental or depressingly negative. Unable to find outlets for the complex, deeply-felt, literary work about motherhood that they were producing, the group decided to found their own online magazine, a home both for their own writing and the kind of writing they wanted to read. As the group proclaimed in the *Literary Mama* mission statement, "We are a home for beautiful poetry, fiction, and creative nonfiction that may be too long, too complex, too ambiguous, too deep, too raw, too irreverent, too ironic, and too body conscious for other publications."

History

Literary Mama began in 2002 as a journal-writing class for mothers taught by Amy Hudock. After teaching a few sessions, however, Amy realized she wanted to be a participant in the class herself. She invited students from the class to form a writing group and they pooled funds to hire a childcare provider to watch over their toddlers as they wrote and discussed their work. The group met once every two weeks, for two hours, pausing for a snack break midway through the meeting to give the older kids (the ones who didn't spend the session nursing in their mother's arms!) a chance to refuel and reconnect with their moms. The women had nothing in common, at first, but their children and a desire to write. One member was a former banker, another was a neurobiologist; others had worked or were still working in education, nonprofit administration, journalism, and other fields.

The tone of the eventual website, and its reputation for offering thoughtful and constructive feedback, was set by the group, which developed a productive routine: writers emailed their work to each other, via a private Yahoo group list, several days before each meeting, and then took turns discussing the writing in person. Each member took a three-month turn as facilitator to keep the discussion on track and the feedback constructive. At first, group members offered critique in the form of answers to the following questions:

> To me, this piece is about: ______________.
> When I read this, I felt: ________________.
> Some things that are really strong about this piece are (specific examples of dialogue, sensory detail, scene-setting, clincher details): __________________.
> Some ways to make it stronger are: (specific examples of dialogue, sensory detail, scene-setting, clincher details)________________.

While group members soon moved beyond these questions in offering their feedback, the formalized response established by the writing group helped create the website's tradition of offering substantive comments to writers submitting their work.

While today we receive too many submissions for our editors to offer detailed critique to every writer, we still respond personally to every submission and we are rare, among literary magazines, in the extent to which we work closely with writers to tighten and refine their essays, stories, and poems before publication.

Soon, the Berkeley writers were producing work that they wanted to publish. Additionally, they were connecting with other mother writers whose work was both too complex to fit in the glossy parenting magazines and also too mother-centric to find a home in traditional literary journals. In the spring of 2003, the group published several issues of an online monthly magazine called *Books and Babies: Writing about Motherhood Literary Web Zine*, and then, the following fall, launched *LiteraryMama.com*. The Berkeley writers reached out to mother writers they had met via blogs, such as Andrea Buchanan's Phillymama and Lizbeth Finn-Arnold's The Philosophical Mama, plus listservs like writermamas, where they met Dawn Friedman and Katie Allison Granju.

The site was built on free blog software, Moveable Type, which worked well for a group of women in different cities and on different schedules; each editor could log in on her own time and edit and publish work. But the group worried

Literary Mama *Editors (past and present), Chicago 2009. Left to right, back: Amy Hudock, Shannon L.C. Cate, Caroline Grant, Susan Ito, Shari MacDonald Strong. Front: Sonya Huber, Nicole Stellon O'Donnell, Rebecca Kaminsky, Kristina Riggle.*

that "blog" connoted casual, off-the-cuff and unpolished writing, and so originally they took care to hide most of the blog features from the website. The site didn't accept comments, didn't date-stamp each entry, and didn't include "blog" as one of its sections, all to give the website a look as polished as the writing it published. At first, editorial decisions were made by each editor for her own section, but as the site grew beyond the original core of Berkeley writers, a masthead was created with Amy Hudock as Editor-in-Chief and Andrea Buchanan, in Philadelphia, as Managing Editor, making all final publication decisions, and the following editorial staff reading and editing pieces for their respective sections: Dawn Friedman (Commentary); Libby Gruner (Literary Criticism); Joanne Catz Hartman (Profiles); Rachel Iverson (Poetry); Rebecca Kaminsky (Reviews); Amy Kessel (Copyeditor); Sybil Lockhart (Reviews); Ericka Lutz (Fiction); Eve Daniel Pearlman (Ezine); Sophia Raday (Creative Nonfiction); Heidi Raykeil (Columns); and Rachel Sarah (Columns).

By 2004, when I joined both the writing group and *Literary Mama* (as an editorial assistant in Literary Reflections, formerly the Literary Criticism section), Amy Hudock had moved to South Carolina, leaving the group in Berkeley to run itself and formalizing the remote editorial oversight of *Literary Mama* which continues to this day. The editorial board and each individual section communicate via private Yahoo group lists to discuss submissions, plan special theme issues, solicit recommendations for reading lists, announce readings and publications, plus offer feedback and advice on managing agents, editors, and every other aspect of the publishing business. While the original group of editors consisted of neophyte writers, today our editors are all experienced writers who have published dozens of books, from poetry collections to memoirs to novels, and we are all well versed in the intricacies of the publishing business. *Literary Mama* gives us both a broad public platform to promote our work and a community of writers with whom to share our frustrations and successes.

Today, the original writing group has coalesced into a group of seven writers, all mothers, all with some association—either as editor (past or present) or contributor—to *Literary Mama.* Meanwhile, the website's editorial board has expanded over the years to include its present composition of 34 writers—all mothers, some of whom work also as teachers, editors, freelance writers, nonprofit administrators, grant writers and the like—in cities around the world. While originally the members of the editorial board happened to be primarily mothers of preschool-age children, we have broadened over the years to include the full range of mothers: single, adoptive, foster, and lesbian mothers and grandmothers, of different races, cultures, and socioeconomic backgrounds, mothering children ranging in age from babies to college students.

Activities

Motherhood has historically been overlooked as a subject for serious literary work, and mothers who write are often dismissed, considered incapable of producing significant literature. *Literary Mama* works to change that misconception. We aim to challenge readers and other media outlets to rethink the traditionally narrow focus of what mothers think and do. After all, there is no more emotionally complicated experience than motherhood, and everyone in the world can claim some relationship—good, bad or indifferent—to it. We consider motherhood an essential subject for literary exploration.

Literary Mama achieves its mission primarily by publishing the website which has, over the last four years, maintained a regular schedule of offering new content every Sunday. We publish fresh installments of our various columns every week, while the other departments—fiction, creative nonfiction, poetry, profiles, reviews, and literary reflections—publish new work once a month.

In 2005, the editors published an anthology, *Literary Mama: Reading for the Maternally Inclined.* The book project compiled a range of the best work published on the site in its first years of publication, and sold well. Readings in support of the book allowed some of the far-flung editors to meet for the first time, as well as to gather our readers for discussion; a reading at Diesel Books in Oakland attracted over seventy people. Many other book projects have developed out of work first published on the site. *Literary Mama* columns by Vicki Forman, Gail Baker, Sybil Lockhart, Sophia Raday, Heidi Raykeil, and Rachel Sarah all grew into successful memoirs. Another *Literary Mama*-inspired project is the anthology, *Mama, Ph.D.: Women Write About Motherhood and Academic Life*, which came about when reading one of Amy Hudock's *Literary Mama* columns motivated Elrena Evans to submit an essay to the site. Our subsequent editorial

Books & Babies writing group, from left to right, Amy Hudock, Heidi Raykeil, Rebecca Kaminsky and Sybil Lockhart, circa 2002.

correspondence grew into the book, which used several essays by Literary Mama contributors, including one by Amy Hudock.

Groups of *Literary Mama* editors, columnists and contributors frequently give readings, both in support of their own new publications and to promote writing about motherhood on Mother's Day. In 2009, a group of editors presented at the Association of Writers and Writing Programs conference in Chicago, speaking about the site's mission on a panel titled "*Literary Mama*: A Model of Grassroots Literary Community Building."

Building a literary community has been part of the site's mission since its founding. In the early years, it was important simply to expose readers to the variety of writing about motherhood and to expand their knowledge of the field. We maintained a comprehensive bibliography of writing by mothers and published literary criticism on the relationship between motherhood and writing. Today, our efforts focus more on building and supporting the broad network of mother writers, and we offer a variety of ways for our readers to become writers. Many of our editors and columnists teach writing, and our listings of both in-person and online writing classes and workshops have expanded from those taught by our own editorial staff to other relevant classes taught by contributors and others. Our Literary Reflections editors publish a writing prompt connected to the monthly essay, offer editorial comments on the responses, and publish one reader's response each month. Some of those writing prompt responses have developed into longer Literary Reflections essays themselves. One column, Cassie Premo Steele's "Birthing the Mother Writer," invites readers to submit their response for editorial critique and publication on the site; the editorial correspondence is narrated in a follow-up column, giving readers experience in working with an editor and making the editorial process more transparent. Finally, the blog edi-

Literary Mama *editors and contributors at Book Passage, 2008. Left to right: Sophia Raday, Rebecca Kaminsky, Sarah Kilts, Ursula Ferreira, Susan Ito, Jennifer Eyre White, Caroline Grant, Rachel Sarah, Suzanne Kamata.*

tor offers journal writing prompts which are keyed to current events and social topics relevant to parents; she provides feedback on each response, and publishes one every quarter.

Challenges

The challenge with any volunteer organization is to maintain professional standards without making any one person feel overworked or imposed upon. While we can't offer the financial benefits of working for a prestigious literary journal, we provide a writing community that supports each editor creatively. We try to maintain workloads that allow everyone to contribute at her own pace. However because out staff is unpaid, we can be agile and responsive to shifting needs: we can always add more editors and divide the work into smaller parcels. We work hard to maintain a balance between hiring enough people to handle the workload while still remaining small enough that the editors all know, trust, and feel comfortable working with each other.

As a volunteer organization made up entirely of mothers, we understand the various and demanding claims on our time: we are all on call to our children, their schools, the other organizations for which we work (whether as paid employees or volunteers); we struggle sometimes to preserve the quiet time and space to work for Literary Mama. For some editors, the school year is a busy time and summer offers an opportunity to catch up; others find the opposite is true. We know that some people may disappear, editorially-speaking, for a few weeks or months after the arrival of new child in the family, while some will be able to get online late at night—after the kids' bedtime or while nursing a baby—and will contribute via email to editorial conversations as they unfold. We accommodate our different schedules, picking up the slack for each other, facing challenges only when—because we work at great distances from each other and rely primarily on email to stay in touch—editors fall out of communication for a period.

Our main editorial challenge is simply keeping up with the volume of submissions and providing, when possible, thoughtful feedback to the writers who send us their work. Differences of opinion among the editors are rare; we want only to publish work we all love.

We face the same technological challenges that any website faces: keeping the software up to date and its content safe from hackers. The founding editors showed terrific foresight in choosing blog software to publish the site—it has allowed us the flexibility to let editors in different time zones work and edit the content—and despite having over thirty editors publishing thousands of contributions, we have always been able to publish more work.

However, the site has never had someone on staff dedicated to software maintenance or security, a weakness that was exposed in the winter of 2008, when the site was hacked and content temporarily affected. Nothing was lost, but it was as if graffiti was sprayed over some of the older archived pages. The archives were fully restored and new security measures put in place. It's critical to us, given the tradition of women's literature being lost or forgotten, and given, too, the often-transient nature of many websites, that we maintain a complete and secure archive of all our publications. In late 2009, the software was updated and the site fully redesigned, a fully volunteer effort that consumed hundreds of hours.

We are writers. We are not software developers or marketing professionals. It has been difficult over the years to attract and keep people who are interested in participating in the site's work in non-editorial ways. Making site-wide improvements is a slow process, as the priority is always on publishing fresh new writing each week.

We face financial challenges as the expenses of our software license and server maintenance increase without any real source of income. We decided in 2010 to accept limited advertising, which brings in pennies toward our monthly bills. We have considered affiliating with a university, but decided that the disadvantages of sacrificing editorial control outweighed the advantages of institutional stability—advantages that seem tenuous now, anyway, in these days of university cutbacks.

Future Goals

Engrossed with the day-to-day work of maintaining the site, it's sometimes hard to envision future projects. As *Literary Mama* moves into its eighth year of publication, we want most of all to maintain the quality and variety of writing we publish each week. We'd like to publish more diverse voices—more writing by teen moms, grandmothers, and women mothering in untraditional ways—and we'd like to offer more direct engagement with today's issues for mothers, to be a real platform for women's ideas, by publishing more op-ed columns and other kinds of timely writing. We also contemplate publishing a second *Literary Mama* anthology, perhaps with a special-issue focus.

Many of our editors and columnists offer writing and editing services independently, and we may start offering those under the *Literary Mama* banner. Most of us support ourselves as teachers, editors, and freelance writers, and we publish our poetry, memoirs, novels and anthologies in the time remaining after our other, paid work; we dream of a day when *Literary Mama* can help support us, not the other way around. To that end, we hope to find ways to nurture our editors in their creative lives, by sponsoring writing retreats for our editorial staff and by collaborating on projects with other motherhood groups.

We are always striving to reach more readers, and we'd like to connect with our audience in person by sponsoring more *Literary Mama* readings around the country.

Literary Mama's Relationship to the Larger Motherhood Movement

Literary Mama has been linked to the larger motherhood movement from its founding. We've been inspired by the long tradition of literary writing by mothers such as Emma Southworth. Southworth was a mother of two when, in the mid-nineteenth century, she was abandoned by her husband. She taught and wrote to support her family and quickly became the most well paid American writer of her time, one of a large number of mother writers in her era. In the later part of the century, however, her work was dismissed as sentimental literature and the denigration of writing by mothers began.

All of *Literary Mama's* editors and contributors, whether or not we rely on our writing to support our families, can relate to and find motivation in Southworth's life story. Despite the tremendous gains for women in our culture since Southworth's time—from suffrage to Title IX to the Lilly Ledbetter law—we all struggle in various ways with the desire to raise our children and to express ourselves in writing, while still finding a way to support our families financially. We know that claiming the time to do all of these things ourselves can be a political act, and we work to support women in their attempts to maintain a creative life while raising their children. Our efforts range from modeling (something mothers excel at), that is simply normalizing the idea of mother writers among our children, their teachers, and our communities; to more explicit political efforts in conjunction with other motherhood organizations, both activist groups like Mothers Acting Up and MomsRising, and creative arts organizations like Mamazina and Mamapalooza. We know that without political and cultural gains for women, the time and space for our writing will disappear.

We take women's voices and women's writing seriously. Other outlets can offer financial compensation to their contributors, but we take pride in nurturing our writers by offering thoughtful editorial response and a respectful, intelligent audience. As debates swirl today over the differing literary value of "chick lit," "momoirs," and literary fiction by men, *Literary Mama* continues to steadfastly support writing by mothers, about motherhood, as a significant, vital, and growing literary tradition.

Works Cited

Buchanan, Andrea J. and Amy Hudock, eds. *Literary Mama: Reading for the Maternally Inclined.* Emeryville, CA: Seal Press, 2005.

Evans, Elrena and Caroline Grant, eds. *Mama, Ph.D.: Women Write About Motherhood and Academic Life.* New Brunswick, NJ: Rutgers University Press, 2008.

78.
Yo'Mama/Literature for Life

JO ALTILIA

To tell a woman everything she may not do is to tell her what she can do.
—Spanish Proverb

LITERATURE FOR LIFE IS COMMITTED to assisting marginalized young mothers develop their "voice" as a tool for personal agency, self-actualization and building capacity. We operate an inclusive community engaging our clients to take control of their own identities as women, as mothers and as community members through participation in programs, evaluations, implementation, advisory work and employment opportunities.

Context

Literature for Life's participants are pregnant or lone parenting mothers between the ages of 13-25. They reflect the racial and ethnic diversity of the under-resourced geographic areas of the Greater Toronto Area. Most experience social isolation in one form or another, and are disadvantaged with respect to income, education, family or family support and employment. Many have been wards of the Children's Aid, living in foster or group homes. Some have participated in criminal behaviours or lived on the streets at some time before the birth of their first child. They are subjected to stereotypical myths of young motherhood. These prejudices and systemic barriers manifest in numerous ways including public abuse on transit vehicles, at banks, in malls, and by police and social assistant workers.

Most of our participants live in poverty and isolation, one-third report histories of physical and/or sexual abuse. Often they have less than a grade ten education. Generally they lack critical literacy skills. Research informs us that their children are likely to continue this cycle; they are more likely to do poorly at school, become teen parents themselves, or end up in trouble with the law—often becoming dependent on the welfare system. We have learned over the last ten years that assisting teen mothers to develop strong literacy skills increases their ability and confidence to invest in education opportunities for themselves and for their children. Literacy is a powerful tool and a first step in breaking the cycle of women and child poverty.

Statistics and studies identify young, single motherhood as a social issue or problem because they and their children are at greater risk for poverty, limited employment potential, and a host of other health, personal, educational, social and economic problems. The Status of Women Canada's publication "Social Policy, Gender and Inequality" states,

> Socio-economic disadvantage is even more pronounced among teen mothers. The consequences of precipitate pregnancy to the educational and economic futures of young mothers are well documented. As a group very young mothers are less likely to finish high school, attend college or do graduate studies than their classmates, even after controls for socio-economic background, academic ability and motivational factors have been considered.

Young mothers also tend to be seriously disadvantaged with respect to employment, perhaps, in part, as a result of educational deficits. They are much less likely than women who did not become mothers before age 18 to find the stable employment that would allow them to support themselves and their children adequately. Not surprisingly, these young women are disproportionately poor and likely to rely on public assistance for their economic support.

However, new research demonstrates that with early and meaningful intervention young mothers can take steps to improve their own outcomes and identities, and build better lives for themselves and their children. There is clearly a need among this population for such intervention programs, and that need is best addressed by programs such as Literature for Life's Women with Words Reading Circles and *Yo'Mama Magazine.*

In her Master's thesis "Reflexivity and Resistance in the Identity Construction of Young Single Mothers," Tanya Darisi presents research obtained from interviews and observations of Literature for Life's programs. Her research demonstrates how participants use reading and writing to overcome negative stereotypes and negative outcomes in their day to day lives. Darisi writes of *Yo'Mama*, "Writing articles for the magazine can also been seen as a way of accomplishing empowerment as contributors construct an alternative discourse of single young mothers and engage their audience in the resistance of stereotypes."

Programs

Literature for Life's core programs Women with Words Reading Circles and *Yo'Mama Magazine* are unique in that they specifically address the needs and interests of marginalized teen and young mothers. The programs provide safe and nurturing environments where young mothers learn to use "voice" as a tool for personal agency, self-actualization and building capacity.

Women with Words Reading Circles

Since the organization's founding in 2000 Literature for Life has distributed over 20,000 new books to more than 1,800 young mothers who have participated in our flagship direct service program Women with Words Reading Circles. Women with Words Reading Circles are held at various shelters and youth centres serving young mothers. Each week pregnant and parenting teenage women join the circles to read and discuss novels with trained facilitators. They read books that are relevant to their lives, allowing them the opportunity to reflect on issues and problems they often feel they cannot control. Through peer-to-peer discussions and writing exercises they begin to see language as a tool to express themselves and to get what they need and want effectively. They learn their voices and stories have value and meaning, leading to increased self-confidence and a renewed interest in literacy and learning. They pass these values on to their children who are then better prepared to attend and do well in school. Increased literacy skills are determinants of good mental health, as a major contributor in effective decision-making and critical thinking with a positive impact on independence, employment, and personal income capacity.

Yo'Mama Magazine

Literature for Life launched *Yo'Mama Magazine* in 2002. This quarterly health and lifestyle magazine is written by young mothers for young mothers. It is the only magazine of its kind in Canada. In contrast to the deficit-model approach to young parenting, *Yo'Mama* takes a youth-positive approach. Specifically, the goals of the magazine are organized around fostering the capacities and abilities of young mothers. Furthermore, 'written for young mothers by young mothers' is more than a tag line, it reflects the participatory and empowerment-oriented approach of the organization, which greatly improves upon the more traditional "top-down" service-delivery model that frequently alienates the population it attempts to serve.

Yo'Mama engages young mothers as contributors and as readers. It is driven by and responds to the particular interests and needs of its target audience, and as such is effective in delivering a magazine that is "client-relevant, informative and inspiring." The editorial staff decides on themes which they know are important to the audience to help them understand and to deal with issues of relevance including, parenting, health, violence, mental health, self-esteem, sexuality and more. At present, Yo'Mama is distributed to the various centres and agencies that interact with the client group.

Yo'Mama has employed over 120 young women in positions as freelance writers, photographers, editorial staff and project managers. Five thousand copies are distributed across the Greater Toronto area to shelters, hospitals, high schools, universities and government offices.

While there are various literacy organizations for adults and other programs that promote reading to children, our experience and outcome evaluations inform us that as a mother develops strong literacy skills, there is an increased capacity to create a family culture of literacy and learning, impacting the potential of two generations. One participant who is completing her third year of university reported, "For me personally, Literature for Life has been a refuge from the pain I've endured during my childhood and into adulthood. The organization's commitment to personal growth has enhanced my self-confidence and my capacity to be a better parent and role model in my community."

History

Working from a home office, I started the first reading circle at Jessie's Centre for Teenagers in November 2000. Over the years, I have often been told that "these girls" are not interested in reading or writing programs. However, of 1800 young mothers who have been members of our Women with Words Reading Circles, 120 have contributed to *Yo'Mama Magazine.* Six participants have worked for Literature for Life, returned to school and are now leaders in their communities, working full time in professions that not only pay a living wage but give them job satisfaction.

The second reading circle started at Massey Centre. At the request of a young mother in the first group, I spoke to Massey Centre and started a second circle there in 2001. We are now running eight circles across the city in shelters and social service centres. Two years ago we developed an engaging English Language Arts group designed specially to address the needs of a range of diverse learning styles and education experiences.

Yo'Mama Magazine was first conceived by the Reading Circle at Massey Centre. The women said they could not relate to the popular 'parenting' magazines available in shelters and clinics. Six dedicated women produced the first copy of *Yo'Mama* in July 2002. It was eight pages and included basic information about accessing a food bank, recipes, protecting your child against sun damage and a list of various Canada Day activities. The original editorial committee worked many long hours as volunteers to get the first three issues out the door. Eventually, Literature for Life was able to secure funding to hire a member of the client group as a full time editor as well as pay freelance fees to writers and photographers. The magazine is now a 40-page, full-colour publication.

Core Program Activities

Women with Words Reading Circles

Each week, young mothers—pregnant and parenting teenagers—gather at shelters and centres across the City of Toronto with trained facilitators to read and discuss novels together. For many participants, these books may be the first they've ever read, but over the course of the reading circles, an amazing transformation takes place. The novels become more challenging, discussions more engaging, the women involved come to understand the power implicit in language, and how to harness that power for themselves in order to effect social change and take on community leadership roles.

A major role for the facilitator is to ensure that the reading circle is a welcoming and safe environment. Failure to do so will frustrate our purposes, since achieving a level of comfort that allows each participant to be candid and share is one of our methods for success. When this happens it is part of the magic that takes place in our reading circles. Often it is the first time a mother will experience her own voice and have that voice heard in a meaningful way.

Similar to what we see in society at large, our participants are not always comfortable with the "otherness of the other" and are sometimes resistant to those of different ethnicities, religions, sexual orientation, etc. It is the facilitator's role to be aware of and effectively handle these attitudes within the group. It is important that the facilitator seize any learning opportunity that may arise through making connections and transferences for participants. For example, if participants are exhibiting judgments arising from stereotypes, it offers a teachable moment through examining the similarities between what they are feeling and expressing, to those expressed about them as a teenage mothers. This is done most effectively through inquiry that allows the participant to make the links for herself.

Fundamental to the success of the program is the ability to establish an environment of respect. To do so and to allow for the richness of each session we work from the following principals adapted from the Canadian Institute for Cultural Affairs: 1) everyone has wisdom; 2) we need everyone's wisdom for the wisest result; 3) everyone has a voice; 4) there are no wrong answers/ideas; 5) the whole is always better than the sum of its parts; 6) respect confidentiality.

The Curriculum

Whether full or half-year, the reading circles follow a pattern of four broad-themed units. They are:

a) "Me, My Place and My Community." This introductory unit features books that are palatable to participants who are often uneasy readers. These include such books as *The Coldest Winter Ever* by Sister Souljah or *White Lines* by Tracy Brown. It is important that with each new book circle, participants begin with a book where the experiences of the characters mirror their own. The group discussion provides a safe environment for participants to explore sensitive topics through the characters in the narrative without disclosing personal situations. Poetry prompts focus on understanding similes and metaphors (e.g. "I am" poems and "If I were an animal/fruit/food I'd be…"). The goal of this unit is to build confidence with reading and writing.

b)"My Place in My Family." This unit uses more advanced texts such as *The Bite of the Mango,* by Maritu Kamara and Susan McClelland, or Alice Walker's *The Colour Purple*. Journal writing is encouraged, and the poetry prompts are somewhat more sophisticated ("If I were in charge…" or "where I'm from"). The idea behind this unit is that reflection on the self and the role in the family will lead to self-awareness and confidence. It also allows participants to develop empathy through exploring possible realities of the "other."

c) "Stereotyping." The third unit addresses a key issue for participants—both in relation to their being stereotyped by others and their own stereotyping of others. By addressing the role of stereotypes, participants are encouraged to explore the impact of prejudice and bias on themselves and on others. Books in this unit often include *Lesley's Journal* by Alan Stanton or *In Search of April Raintree* by Beatrice Culleton. The writing exercises here may use several covers of other popular magazines to provoke conversations around the images presented and the way we feel about their authenticity.

d) "My Place in the Community of Women and the World." This final unit uses more difficult books such as *The Book of Negros* by Lawrence Hill, *The Birth House* by Amy McKay or *The Handmaid's Tale* by Margaret Atwood. It is intended to leave the participants with an understanding of how books can lead to larger, societal issues and concepts. Writing exercises and poetry prompts include *Goddess Knowing*, by Tricia Hersey, and *I Heard the Caged Bird Sing*, by Maya Angelou.

In addition, other books and poetry may be used. Certain poems and writing exercises are keyed to individual unit themes. Other books of popular stories, such as *Chicken Soup for the Woman's Soul* are used depending on the literacy background and learning style of participants in particular reading circles.

Publishing Voice

We believe that "publishing" the writing produced within the Reading Circles is important to building confidence in personal literacy. As indicated above, the writing produced by the poetry prompts is collected, word-processed at Literature for Life, and returned to the authors the next week. At the end of each group term, the poetry produced by participants is published and each participant receives four copies to give as gifts to friends and family. Participants are also encouraged to submit their writing (stories, fiction, poetry) to the Literature for Life's magazine *Yo'Mama* and our blog, *Womenz Wordz*. Having her submission published for distribution is an important aspect of building confidence as a woman and as a mother.

Yo'Mama Magazine

Since its inception, Literature for Life has identified numerous human rights issues faced by the target population including fair access to education, resources and supports, physical and emotional isolation, poverty, sexuality and gender, and the many mistaken beliefs about what it means to be a young mother. *Yo'Mama* was the brain child of a group of young mothers who had attended our diversity workshop held during a Reading Circle. They stated they wanted to start a newsletter or magazine to address the needs and issues of marginalized young mothers. With the assistance and support of Literature for Life, the women formed their first editorial committee and *Yo'Mama* was born.

Literature for Life has worked with hundreds of young mothers to improve

their access to education, and create greater equity in areas of literacy and self-expression. *Yo'Mama* is an extension of this work, as an outreach project that brings the same messages of education and self-esteem to a much larger audience. Many young mothers struggle and face extreme difficulty in the traditional school system, and therefore are often far behind their peers in the development of literacy skills and appreciation. *Yo'Mama* is written so that young mothers with varying degrees of literacy can access and enjoy the magazine.

The editorial process is designed to support writers of varying skill levels, and to help them build experience, skills and confidence while earning money for their work and their ideas, giving them an explicit as well as implicit value. The writers work with a professional editor who guides them through the process of pitching article ideas, doing interviews and research, and provides one-on-one assistance with style, clarity, grammar, editing, and any other issues which may arise during the writing process. Writers are given any necessary support, but are also held to high standards so that they come to understand the realities of working as a writer, and the importance of professionalism. With an emphasis on delivering quality work according to deadlines, these young women are given the opportunity to develop skills and confidence, and earn some money in a flexible, supportive environment. This kind of training and employment is not easily accessible to young people, particularly young women who are dealing with the many barriers posed to those who are young, single and pregnant or parenting. Because of Literature for Life's experience in addressing the literacy and information needs of young mothers, *Yo'Mama* has been able to tailor its content and training process to young women who otherwise would not have an adequate opportunity to express themselves, earn money, and learn about the craft and the business of writing. This experience, practice and training instill the writers with the belief in themselves and the desire to pursue further education opportunities, thus immeasurably improving their own lives, and those of their children.

Literature for Life and *Yo'Mama* also have experience creating a positive human rights and race relations environment, and a sense of community among young mothers from many ethnically diverse backgrounds. This is enhanced by delivery of workshops designed and presented by Noelle Richardson, Chief Diversity Officer of the Ontario Public Service and advisor to Literature for Life. *Yo'Mama* provides a sense of community and common ground for all young mothers, regardless of their perceived differences. *Yo'Mama* acts as a venue for young woman from different cultural perspectives to explore their own ideas and experiences, as well as those of other young women. The magazine provides information that encourages active participation in the Greater Toronto Community. As writers, these young women are encouraged to express their individual view points, while respecting and working with other young mothers, whose ideas and experiences may be vastly different from their own. With the addition of writers' workshops and quarterly editorial meetings, *Yo'Mama* fosters positive community and cultural relations by bringing a larger, more diverse field of writers together to share experiences and ideas, while building skills and relationships. The staff of *Yo'Mama* and Literature for Life is skilled in the creation of an inclusive environment that both celebrates Toronto's remarkable diversity, and emphasizes the rights of all young mothers to be treated with dignity and respect.

Yo'Mama magazine is unique in that it connects a community of young mothers who are living or returning to marginalized neighbourhoods by building a sense of shared experience and support. It challenges stereotypes, by profiling successful young mothers and by giving young mothers a voice. *Yo'Mama* creates a positive identity for marginalized young mothers and their children. It helps to make it possible in the minds of its audience, marginalized young mothers, social service workers and policy makers that young mothers can be active in the community, can continue with their education, and can indeed be "good" mothers. As well, *Yo'Mama* provides a forum in which to communicate the network of resources available to young families by highlighting various support resources and local programs available for young mothers that assist with mental health issues, education and employment.

> Once again, the idea of finding one's voice or having a voice assumes a primacy in talk, discourse, writing, and action. As metaphor for self-transformation, it has been especially relevant for groups of women who have previously never had a public voice, women who are speaking and writing for the first time, including many women of color. Feminist focus on finding a voice may seem clichéd at times, especially when the insistence is that women share a common speech or that all women have something meaningful to say at all times. However, for women within oppressed groups who have contained so many feelings—despair, rage, anguish—who do not speak, as poet Audre Lorde writes, "for fear our words will not be heard nor welcomed," coming to voice is an act of resistance. Speaking becomes both a way to engage in active self-transformation and a rite of passage where one moves from being object to being subject. (hooks)

Social Service professionals seek out ways to relate to and communicate with their clients, and according to Decision Partners' research, *Yo'Mama* addresses this need by providing illumination on various issues by the very people that are affected by those issues. In this research, it was established that *Yo'Mama* is often used by Social Service professionals to gain insight in to their clients' lives, and to open the channels of communication on a number of issues. The interviewees also had a very positive perception of *Yo'Mama,* and felt that it was empowering and inspiring to young mothers because it fosters knowledge, self-esteem and literacy skills, and, perhaps most importantly, it is relevant to their lives. The research and feedback which we have received clearly indicate that *Yo'Mama* addresses many needs in the community because it is a positive, educational voice that speaks to an audience that is too often excluded and isolated.

A collective of *Yo'Mama* contributors are now working on a project to put the magazine on line. Their intention is to include the voices of single mothers across the province and beyond.

Conclusion

Single young mothers are often victimized by stereotyping and, sometimes, discrimination, because they fall outside social norms expected of mothers. In her 2005 study of the Literature for Life reading circles, Tanya Darisi wrote,

> ...for there to be this ideal of motherhood there must also be boundaries to differentiate those who fall within normative expectations from those who do not.... One of these boundaries is between married and single mothers. Another is age. Culturally, mothering is viewed to be most properly done when within the realm of adulthood and marriage, as motherhood before the age of 20 and outside marriage is viewed as problematic. (1)

Participants' discussion within and continued outside the Reading Circle and *Yo'Mama* can be seen as a way of accomplishing empowerment in that they overcome the voices of others to establish an alternative discourse in which young mothers are repositioned as good mothers and promoted as intelligent, competent, and caring. This study shows that book circles allow participants to develop their voice and change the dominant discourses about young mothers. While the book groups discussions are one contribution to the development of voice, another is Literature for Life's publication of *Yo'Mama!*, a magazine written "by young mothers for young mothers." Writing articles for the magazine can also been seen as a way of accomplishing empowerment as contributors construct an alternative discourse of single young mothers and engage their audience in the resistance of stereotypes.

For members of a counter-normative or problematic category, resis-

> tance may be foundational to the establishment of identity. From the wrong side of a normative ideal, (stereo)typical category associations may serve as a place from which to make the move from "other" to "I" so that discursive resistance can serve as a strategy to move ideological boundaries. (Darisi 3)

Marginalized young mothers are often excluded from the larger Motherhood movement. Yet this group of mothers demonstrates through their involvement in Literature for Life's programs the power to challenge society's negative stereotypes of young mothers. How do they do this? They are rewriting an identity assigned to them by society. Through Women with Words Reading Circles and supportive peer groups, they see possibilities and hope. They begin to engage in discussions about life, through reading books and telling their stories through poetry. *Yo'Mama* provides a forum for politicization by engaging participants in solution-based discussions about mental health, relationships, violence, abuse, positive parenting and self care. Through voice and expanding experiences outside of what is familiar, they see possibilities for themselves as women and mothers. They are empowered to develop their voices, express themselves creatively and intellectually.

Promoting the benefits of literacy and the wonders of the story, Literature for Life empowers young women to expand their destinies beyond the tired clichés of teenage motherhood.

Works Cited

Coley, Rebekah Levine and P. Lindsay Chase-Lansdale. *Adolescent Pregnancy and Parenthood: Recent Evidence and Future Directions.* Chicago: The Iriving B. Harrist Graduate School of Public Policy Studies, University of Chicago, 1997.

Darisi, Tanya. "Reflexivity and Resistance in the Identity Construction of Single Young Mothers." Unpublished Masters Thesis, University of Guelph, Ontario, Canada, 2005.

Decision Partners. "Determining the Value of Yo'Mama to User Organizations, A Report to the Literature for Life Board of Directors." August 2005.

hooks, bell. "When I Was A Soldier For The Revolution." Web. <http://faculty.unlv.edu/pkane/ART230/soldier/UntitledFrame-3.html>.

Literature For Life Reading Circles. *Facilitator's Guide.* ©2008.

O'Connor, Beth. "You Have to Take It and Own It: *Yo'Mama* Magazine and Teenage Mothers' Cultural Activism in Writing from the Margins." Chicago, January 7, 2008.

Status of Women Canada. "Social Policy, Gender and Inequality." Web. <http://www.swccfc.gc.ca/pubs/pubspr/0662653327/200102_0662653327_10_e.html>.

WomezWords. Blog. Web <http://womenzwordz.wordpress.com>.

79. Literary Brainchild

Brain, Child: The Magazine for Thinking Mothers

ANN DOUGLAS

BRAIN, CHILD MAGAZINE WAS FOUNDED in 1999 by Jennifer Niesslein and Stephanie Wilkinson: two mothers with shared passions for motherhood and literary writing. Their goal was to create a publication that would allow mothers to carry on "grown up" conversations about the issues that mattered most to mothers. Forty-four issues later, their literary offspring is an award-winning publication that has become a source of information, inspiration, and support to 36,000 mothers per issue. And, despite the founders' intentions to avoid becoming too political, *Brain, Child* has also become a key ally to the twenty-first century mother's movement.

Mandate

Brain, Child: The Magazine for Thinking Mothers and its founders are very clear about what the magazine does—and doesn't—set out to do on behalf of mothers. The magazine's mandate is spelled out in the mission statement which appears on the *Brain, Child* website.

> *Brain, Child* treats motherhood as a subject worthy of literature. And in the best tradition of literature, it celebrates the diversity of mothers and their styles.... Our writers bring a down-to-earth perspective to traditional and not-so-traditional parenting subjects. And they're willing to address the big questions—our evolving identities as mothers, for instance, or what we're teaching the next generation.... You know that friend you call when you're upset and just the sound of her voice calms you? You know those friends you go out to dinner with and stay long after dessert, talking and laughing, until the waiter kicks you out? It's that kind of community.... We aim to be down-to-earth, literary, commonsensical, neither too establishment nor too crunchy, funny, poignant, honest, respectful, irreverent, relevant, intelligent.

This is fairly revolutionary stuff for a publication for mothers, even in 2011.

As the mission statement indicates, *Brain, Child*:

- takes motherhood seriously;
- treats mothers as the true experts on motherhood;
- recognizes that each mother belongs to a larger community of mothers; and
- attempts to encourage conversations between mothers within that community (conversations that are meaningful to mothers, that reflect the diversity of motherhood, and that take into account what is happening in the broader culture).

Brain, Child also has an additional mandate, one which Niesslein highlighted in a presentation to the Association for Research on Mothering (ARM) conference held in October 2008:

> The subtext … in a lot of these [personal] essays is that you aren't alone. … Exploring the emotional territory that *Brain, Child* has claimed as its niche isn't as easy as it might first appear to a casual observer, notes *Brain, Child* contributor Joanna Rossi. It requires courage and good timing: "This motherhood desperation is hard to capture because when mothers are going through it, they're too exhausted to write about it, but once out of it, it's too hard to remember. (cited in Niesslein 2008: 3)

It's that rawness and authenticity—that I'm-right-beside-you-mama immediacy—that has earned *Brain, Child* the loyalty of its readers.

History and Context

Brain, Child: The Magazine for Thinking Mothers was founded in 1999 by Jennifer

Niesslein and Stephanie Wilkinson, who shared a passion for writing and who each had babies under a year of age. As the *Brain, Child* website notes, "The pair, both with backgrounds in journalism, were itching for writing about motherhood that spoke to them. There were plenty of outlets for child-rearing tips and expert advice, but not a source of smart writing that delved into the meatier issues of that life-altering experience: motherhood" ("About Us").

The first issue of *Brain, Child* appeared in March 2000, following a year of planning. It included "essays by Barbara Kingsolver and Susan Cheever, a feature on the new academic field of ethnopediatrics, a debate on the merits of family bed, fiction, and essays by mothers addressing the stuff of real-life parenting" ("About Us"). Eleven years after its launch, *Brain, Child* remains the only print literary magazine dedicated to motherhood. Contributors have included Pulitzer Prize-winning novelists Jane Smiley and Anne Tyler, best-selling author Barbara Ehrenreich, and critically acclaimed writers Antonya Nelson, Alice Hoffman, and Susan Maushart ("About Us").

The magazine has also distinguished itself for "top-notch writing and intellectual curiosity about issues that are often culturally dismissed as unimportant," notes Niesslein (2011). For writing about motherhood and issues that matter to mothers, in other words. Personal essays that focus on the experience of motherhood are "the signature pieces of the magazine," according to the *Brain, Child* Writers' Guidelines. Writers are encouraged to "employ illustrative anecdotes, a personal voice, and a down-to-earth tone" in crafting such pieces.

Brain, Child also publishes feature articles that are based on high-quality research and reporting; shorter news items ("both stories you won't find in the mainstream media and unique perspectives on hot topics"), a debate column ("where two writers square off on a topic of controversy"), fiction, reviews, and parody. ("The parodies we like most are ones that target people, institutions, or media who don't take mothers seriously," the editors indicate.) Not surprisingly, *Brain, Child* has been embraced by mothers and the publishing community alike.

Readership

The magazine has acquired a fiercely loyal readership. According to statistics available on the magazine's website, "*Brain, Child*'s 36,000 readers are … deeply devoted to *Brain, Child*—68 percent say they read all of the magazine, including the ads—and 64 percent say they don't read any other parenting publications" ("Advertise").

"I'm extraordinarily proud of what we publish and the relationship we have with our readers," says Niesslein (2011). "I think the time really was ripe for a publication like *Brain, Child.*"

Recognitions

The magazine has also received numerous literary and publishing accolades. "In 2000, the magazine was named by *Utne Reader* as one of the five best new

Jennifer Niesslein (left) and Stephanie Wilkinson (right) at the 2010 UTNE Independent Press Awards.

magazines in the country. *Brain, Child* also won in 2003 for Best Personal Life Coverage. In 2010, *Brain, Child* received the *Utne* Independent Press Award for Social/Cultural Coverage. Since *Brain, Child*'s inception, the editors of *Utne* have nominated the magazine in the categories of General Excellence, Best Writing, and Best New Title. It is the youngest magazine to have been nominated for General Excellence. Work from *Brain, Child* won a Pushcart Prize in 2003 and was listed under "Notable Essays" in Best American Essays 2002 ("Media Kit").

Objective and Activism

Brain, Child has attempted to stake out turf for itself on the sidelines of the mothers' movement, as opposed to joining the main parade. The magazine's mission statement states: "We don't have any particular agenda, except to support thought and debate on topics of interest to mothers" ("Mission Statement").

And, during a recent email exchange, Niesslein (2011) rejected the suggestion that *Brain, Child* might be part of the mothers' movement: "Any collaboration happens on the publishing side, in marketing and advertising, when we're trying to reach the same readers. On the editorial side, we most definitely do not collaborate. We report on the mothers' movement, but we don't have a political agenda. We're not activists."

The magazine also avoids staking out political turf when it comes to its advertising policies, adds Wilkinson: "We are generally agnostic about ads—meaning, we don't have a policy that precludes us from accepting advertising from, say, baby formula companies. We try to respect the intelligence and varied experience and lifestyles and viewpoints of our readers. The only advertising we have declined to date are from companies that strike us as work-from-home pyramid schemes."

All that said, during a presentation to the October 2008 Association for Research on Mothering conference, Niesslein commented on the ways that becoming a mother can be a politicizing experience in and of itself: "You start to see connections between your experience as a mother and the stuff that either is, or should be, news" (2008: 4).

> Motherhood in general and *Brain, Child* in particular brought the world's issues home for me, but I think many mothers go through the same transformation, where they go from wondering how they will do it all by themselves to acknowledging that there are issues that they can't tackle all by themselves. (Niesslein 2008: 5)

Then she zeroed in more specifically:

> Every time a mother's voice is heard—this is what my life is like, this is what I struggle with, this is what makes life worth living—it is a political statement because we've been invisible, dismissed, for so long. But we also recognize that what we do is limited. We provide a stage and hope that players—the ones who can take it to the next level, the lobbyists and activists and policymakers and voters—will jump on it (5-6).

Challenges

The biggest challenge *Brain, Child* has faced is the very same challenge any small publication faces circa 2011—economics. "Like any independently run publication, there's always the small budget to contend with," says Niesslein (2011/. "It's just a fact of life."

"In the beginning, Stephanie [Wilkinson] and I were the only staff—everyone else was working on a freelance basis," Niesslein recalls. "We've always been largely subscriber supported; advertisers have helped us grow."

The magazine makes a point of paying its writers—not always a given for literary magazines or small publications aimed at mothers. "We believe writers are the lifeblood of this publication; we pay as much as we can, although our fees are still modest for now" ("Writers' Guidelines").

Brain, Child publishes on a quarterly basis, as it has since its inception. The magazine is distributed in independent bookstores, Barnes & Noble superstores,

Borders, and select grocery stores within the U.S. and Canada. Circulation stands at 36,000, with subscribers from every state and as far away as Sweden, Egypt, and Hong Kong.

The Future

As it looks to the future, *Brain, Child*'s editorial focus will remain largely the same, although the specific topics it covers from year to year will continue to evolve to meet the needs of its readers. "The subjects we cover have evolved over the years as the world and the issues mothers face have evolved," Niesslein (2011) explains.

The magazine will continue to nurture its relationship with its readers—a relationship that deliberately sidesteps the "we know best," expert-driven vantage point chosen by many mainstream parenting publications. "I'd say we take a conversation-among-equals approach," says Niesslein. "We don't ever condescend to readers. Personally, I think of the *Brain, Child* community as my tribe.... I think I fall in love with every issue. I have the urge when proofreading—every single time—to write the contributors and get all gushy. Part of what I love is that, eleven years in, there is still something surprising to say about life as a mother, something that makes you pause and think and, at least in my case, widens my empathy a little more."

The key challenge it anticipates will be on the financial side—a challenge all print publications are facing right now, Niesslein (2011) notes: "These aren't easy times for print publications. As I write this, just last week, *Mothering* magazine announced that they were transforming to a web-only business. All of us will have to keep figuring out new ways to thrive in a world where paper is sharing the market with the internet, ereaders, all technology that hasn't even been invented yet."

Relationship to the Larger Mothers' Movement

Brain, Child has had a more politicizing effect on the lives of modern mothers than its founders intended. By helping mothers to move out of isolation and to connect to the larger community of mothers; providing a forum where issues (both personal and small-*p* political) that matter most to mothers could be discussed on an ongoing basis; making its audience available to other more activist groups that wished to connect with its audience via advertising; and providing support and encouragement from the sidelines to working for a better world for mothers and children, *Brain, Child* made a considerable contribution to the twenty-first century mothers' movement.

Conclusion

Despite its efforts to avoid entering the activist fray or aligning themselves with identifiably political causes, *Brain, Child* has managed to politicize mothers and contribute to the twenty-first century mothers' movement in myriad ways.

And, by encouraging mothers to join in community with other mothers and to connect the dots between the personal and the small p-political events in their lives, it will no doubt continue to do so.

Works Cited

"About Us," *Brain, Child: The Magazine for Thinking Mothers.* Web. <http://www.brainchildmag.com/about/>. Accessed February 27, 2011.

"Advertise," *Brain, Child: The Magazine for Thinking Mothers.* Web. <http://www.brainchildmag.com/advertise/>. Accessed February 27, 2011.

"Brain Child Media Kit 2011," *Brain, Child: The Magazine for Thinking Mothers.* Web. <http://www.brainchildmag.com/advertise/BrainChildMediaKit2011.pdf>. Accessed February 27, 2011.

Niesslein, Jennifer. E-mail message to author, February 21, 2011.

Niesslein, Jennifer. "Welcome to the Club." Paper presented at the October 2008 conference of the Association for Research on Mothering, Toronto, Ontario.

Niesslein, Jennifer and Stephanie Wilkinson. "Mission Statemen." *Brain, Child: The Magazine for Thinking Mothers.* Web. <http://www.brainchildmag.com/about/mission.asp>. Accessed February 27, 2011.

Wilkinson, Stephanie, email message to author, February 27, 2011.

"Writers Guidelines." *Brain, Child: The Magazine for Thinking Mothers.* Web. <http://www.brainchildmag.com/contact/guidelines.asp>. Accessed February 27, 2011.

80.
Mothering

A Magazine, a Website, a Cultural Shift

PEGGY O'MARA

MOTHERING MAGAZINE WAS A CONSUMER magazine published quarterly from 1976 through 1997 and bi-monthly from1998 through 2010. Its subtitle was "the magazine of natural family living," and it had a broad readership that included granola moms, conservative moms, queer moms, professional moms, moms of color, work-at-home moms and health practitioners. At its height *Mothering* Magazine had a circulation of 100,000. *Mothering.com* was founded in 1995 and discussion boards were added in 1998. By 2011, the website had far eclipsed the print magazine as the destination for new parents. As of this writing, *Mothering.com's* discussion forums have 165,000 members and over one million threads. The site is host to 1.7 million unique visitors a month. The founder of *Mothering* could never have imagined this turn of events in the early '70s.

The Founding of *Mothering*

Addie Vorys Eavenson (now Cranson) had her first baby in 1974 and was inspired by her experience to start *Mothering*. She recognized that there were scant resources for new, natural mothers. Eavenson specifically chose the title to celebrate the act of mothering at a time when this experience was much maligned by U.S. feminists. The first issue of *Mothering* was put together in the summer of 1976 by members of the Montrose Natural Childbirth Class and other volunteers at the old Fort Smith Saloon in Ridgway, Colorado. The new parents who founded *Mothering* in the mountains of southern Colorado were natural living pioneers; they chose self-sufficiency in response to the societal instability caused by the Vietnam War. Many of us grew our own food, canned fruits and vegetables, kept chickens and goats, and heated the house with wood. This was a time when one could only find children's cotton clothing in second-hand stores; there were no natural personal care products, no packaged herbal teas or organic produce in grocery stores.

Early Cultural Influence

The 1970s was the decade of "Be Here Now" and "Do Your Own Thing" and many new social forms were born during this era, including the alternative press. *East West Journal* (1971), *New Age* (1974), *Co-Evolution Quarterly* (1974), *Yoga Journal* (1975), *Mothering* (1976) and *Mother Jones* (1976) all started within a few years of one another. These publications also spawned an alternative press distribution network that competed with and eventually supplanted the traditional magazine distribution network.

Unique among the alternative press, *Mothering* covered issues important to women with children. Early readers distrusted authority and wanted to live a principled life. They rediscovered a kind of earth feminism that embraced traditional women's roles, such as childbirth, breastfeeding and motherhood in the context of personal empowerment and enlightenment. They appreciated the home as the seminal arena for social change.

Mothering was also instrumental in the birth of the natural products industry. The early readers of the magazine were natural living pioneers who experimented with growing their own food, canning, and making their own personal care products. Many started home businesses that advertised in *Mothering* and some went on to become major companies. Ideas and practices that were reinvented by the generation that went back to the land—things like healing with herbs, growing organic vegetables, free-range chicken and solar energy—are commonplace today.

Breastfeeding was also rediscovered by this generation. In 1974 when I had my first child, only 32 percent of U.S. mothers were breastfeeding. The rate nearly doubled to 61 percent by 1982. *Mothering* has been unique among parenting magazines because every issue included a breastfeeding feature. We also advocate for breastfeeding legislation and we support the International Code of Marketing of Breast-milk Substitutes, developed jointly by the World Health Organization and UNICEF, by refusing formula advertising. Breastfeeding

Top: First issue of Mothering. *Middle: Spring 1980 issue. Bottom: Final issue, in digital form.*

is a human rights issue because four thousand babies worldwide die every day for lack of breastfeeding. Research shows that formula advertising undermines breastfeeding (Howard et al.).

Starting in the 1940s when Charlotte Aiken published the *Child-Family Digest,* modern women began to identify the potential human rights violations associated with childbirth, breastfeeding, and mothering. Breastfeeding became the feminist issue of the early twenty-first century when the U.S. media debated an infant's right to eat in public as if the breastfeeding mother and child were not part of that public. Breastfeeding mothers staged nurse-ins in response to disparaging remarks about breastfeeding made by media personality, Barbara Walters (Harmon), and others and to Delta and other airline companies that were accused of discriminating against breastfeeding mothers (Associated Press).

Worldwide health officials encourage breastfeeding for all women, but U.S. working women, especially women working in blue-collar jobs, can expect to find few if any accommodations for breastfeeding in the workplace. *Mothering* has always had a special responsibility because we publish in a country with no real social supports for parents; in fact, the U.S. is the only developed country with no paid maternity leave or family leave of any kind. It's because of the inequities faced by families in the U.S. that *Mothering* has been dedicated to being an independent media voice for families. We often forget how rare is a free press.

Freedom of the Press

In 2009, Freedom House conducted their annual survey of 195 countries and territories and found that just 36 percent had a free press. In terms of population, only 17 percent of the world's inhabitants live in countries that enjoy a free press. The 2009 report shows the seventh straight year of decline in global media freedom. Western Europe boasts the world's highest level of press freedom.

What is a free press? In the reign of Henry VIII (1509-1547), the political significance of the art of printing began to be appreciated. The King not only limited the privilege of keeping a press, he also required presses to be inspected and licensed. This was, as you know, one of the tyrannies that led eventually to the American Revolution.

Freedom of press in the U.S. constitution is not really a right unto itself, however, but an exemption from impediment. Article I of the constitution states, "Congress shall make no law respecting an establishment of religion, or prohibiting the free exercise thereof; or abridging the freedom of speech, or of the press." Freedom of the press does not mean that we can say anything at all that we like. That is license, not freedom. Freedom is mediated by the freedoms of others. We cannot speak or write a false statement of fact about another person, for example, or we could be guilty of slander or libel.

The *U.S. Telecommunications Act* of 1996 eroded freedom of press by relaxing media ownership restrictions so that one company could own up to eight media stations in a single market. According to *Advertising Age*, by September 1997 in each of the 50 largest U.S. markets, three companies controlled over 50 percent of the radio ad revenues (McChesney). Today, the media is dominated by just ten companies: General Electric, AT&T, Sony, Liberty Media, Vivendi Universal, AOL/ Time Warner/ Walt Disney, Viacom, Bertelsmann, and News Corporation.

According to Robert McChesney, "democracy requires that there be an effective system of political communication, broadly construed, that informs and engages the citizenry, drawing people meaningfully into the polity." The domination of the U.S. media by only a few points of view clearly undermines effective political conversation.

History

I wasn't thinking about media conglomerates when I discovered the second issue of *Mothering* in a natural food store in Albuquerque in 1977. I was thinking about how happy—and surprised—I was that the magazine so well articulated my point of view.

I sent my article, "In Defense of Motherhood" (Volume VII, 1978), to *Mothering* as soon as I got back home. Both *New Age* (now *Whole Living*) and *Redbook* had rejected the article, but Addie accepted it immediately as well as my poem, "There will be Time" (Volume VIII, 1978).

In early 1978, Addie called and asked me to be an editor. I was ecstatic. Fortunately, our family was already planning to move to Albuquerque where Addie had recently relocated the magazine from Colorado. I worked on two or three issues, but soon quit because I had my hands full with three kids under five.

In the summer of 1979, at my son's first birthday party, Addie told me that she wanted to sell the magazine. Of course, I told her that I wanted to buy it, but I had no idea how I would do so. I asked my dad and my cousin to loan me the $5,000 down payment, but they both said no, as did the Small Business Administration and the local bank.

Addie sold *Mothering* to Canadians Rolf and Wendy Priesnitz of *Natural Life* magazine instead. As it turned out, however, Rolf and Wendy didn't have the down payment either and Addie once again offered to sell the magazine to me, this time for no down payment. At that time *Mothering* had a circulation of 3,000, a non-existent billing system, and lots of potential. Issue 15 was our first issue. There was a lot to learn, but I was clear about the mission.

I wrote *Mothering*'s statement of purpose to reflect an egalitarian model of family that seems to me to be the most just:

> *Mothering* celebrates the experience of family life as worthy of one's best efforts and fosters awareness of the immense importance of parenthood and family life in the development of the full human potential of parents and children. As a readers' magazine, we recognize parents as the experts and wish to provide truly helpful information on which parents can base informed choices. *Mothering* is both a fierce advocate of the needs

> and rights of the children and a gentle supporter of the parents, and we encourage decision-making that considers the needs of all members of the family. We explore the realities of human relationships in the family setting recognizing that raising the heirs of our civilization well is the prerequisite of a healthy society.

Mothering has won many journalism awards over the years from *Utne Reader, Folio* magazine, and the Western Publications Association for our public service journalism, specifically our coverage of domestic violence, vaccines and autism and my editorials on the politics of breastfeeding. In 2009, I was given the National Vaccine Information Center's Courage in Journalism award. We have also been recognized in our town as a family-friendly business both by the Santa Fe Woman's Business Network and the City of Santa Fe. In 2005, the city of Santa Fe recognized us as one of the five best small businesses in Santa Fe.

Over the last five years, we have seen our community moving increasingly to the web. The very nature of information on the web is democratic so it coincides well with our intention as a publication to put the information in the hands of the parent. At the very root of feminism is the freedom to choose, the right to access enough information to make a good choice and the comfort to make that choice without coercion. The Internet allows many people to communicate with one another in a way that cannot be easily controlled or corrupted.

End of an Era

As an independent media voice, *Mothering* has been a rarity in publishing. Our work has been a labor of love as the business had never been properly capitalized and we have often been challenged by cash flow. We were already vulnerable when, in 2009, the economy slowed down and we experienced a steep decline in subscription and advertising revenue and as a result built up debt with our vendors and contributors.

While we recovered somewhat in 2010, it was not sufficient to address the 2009 debt, and in early 2011 we were further challenged by a new decline in print advertising revenue and a delay in web revenue. As a result, there was not enough money to print the January/February 2011 issue and I was forced to stop publishing *Mothering* magazine. In a final irony, the subscriptions to *Mothering* were transferred to *Natural Life* magazine where they are being fulfilled by Rolf and Wendy Priesnitz!

I hoped that by moving to Mothering.com alone, I might be able to cut expenses and continue in business, but the cash flow challenges and the debt from printing the magazine overwhelmed the business. In early 2011 I had no choice but to sell the assets of the company to pay off the debt. I will continue to be the voice and spirit of *Mothering*, but not its owner.

While the ending of the print magazine and the sale of the company is a tremendous loss to the *Mothering* community, it is also true that *Mothering* has successfully seeded the ideas of natural family living and egalitarian parenting in the larger culture. Mothering.com now has an opportunity to root and nourish these ideas as they become the values of the dominant culture.

The articles on personal empowerment, social action, and conscious mothering published by *Mothering* are unique in our culture and have personally inspired many of the leaders of the current Motherhood Movement today. *Mothering* uncovered a lost archetype of the feminine, an archetype neither passive nor subservient, but rather creative, dynamic, and original. This new breed of mother rebels against the prescribed role of motherhood and uses her mothering as a path to personal liberation.

Works Cited

Associated Press. "Mothers State Nurse-In Protests." November 12, 2006. Web. <http://www.msnbc.msn.com/id/15833953/ns/travel-news/>.

Freedom House. "Freedom of the Press 2009." May 1, 2009. Web. <http://www.freedomhouse.org/template.cfm?page=470>.

Harmon, Amy. "'Lactivists' Taking Their Cause, and Their Babies, to the Streets." *The New York Times* June 7, 2005. Web. <http://www.nytimes.com/2005/06/07/nyregion/07nurse.html?_r=1>.

Howard, Cynthia R. et al. "Office Prenatal Formula Advertising and Its Effects on Breastfeeding Patterns." *Obstetric Gynecology* 95.2 (February 2000): 296-303.

McChesney, Robert W. Corporate Media and the Threat to Democracy. New York, Seven Stories Press, 1997.

World Health Organization (WHO) and UNICEF. "International Code of Marketing of Breast-milk Substitues." Geneva: WHO, 1981. Web. <http://www.who.int/nutrition/publications/code_english.pdf>.

81. *You Say You Want a Revolution—The Film*

LYNN KUECHLE AND JOY ROSE

On the weekend of October 25, 2008 a monumental gathering of global feminist organizations with a focus on mothers gathered at York University in Toronto, Canada. The summit was arranged by the Association for Research on Mothering and was attended by hundreds of maternal activists and scholars from around the world. Filmmaker Joy Rose was in attendance and documented the event by filming conference presentations and conducting interviews with participants. The finalized product was a film entitled *The Motherhood Movement—You Say You Want a Revolution.*

Purpose

The purpose of the film was to disseminate the educational content presented at the conference and showcase the feminist/activist mothers in attendance. The film was also intended to make visible the maternal discussion that was and continues to be prevalent within many different maternal organizations. Many of these organizations work independently on specific issues facing mothers and affecting motherhood, but much of the work is interdependent with an audience that has much crossover. Putting all of the content together in one film allows the viewer to see the scope and depth of social issues that have been and continue to be of concern to these organizations. The film is also global in nature, conveying the idea that mothers are mothers no matter where in the world they reside.

Topics and Themes

We have documented and preserved presentations, interviews and perspectives on the burgeoning "Mom Movement." Subjects include, but are not limited to: the motherhood movement and its importance in the women's studies curriculum; activism; the three feminist "waves"—where have we been, where are we now and where are we going?; feminist mothering; women and mothers in the arts; non-traditional parenting; women and families of color; the poor; the 1950s to the present in terms of the role of women in the home and in the world; unpaid labor; matriarchal and indigenous societies; the role of men and feminist sons; the future of the Museum of Motherhood and the formation of an international motherhood movement.

Goals

Goals for the film include sale and distribution to academic institutions for inclusion in women's studies and other courses, in order to facilitate discussion of "Motherhood" as a course of academic studies and to disseminate information on a broad range of activist/feminist maternal topics. The tone of the film would be appropriate for College and Universitics libraries and Women's Centers, community organizations such as Mother Centers, YWCAs and domestic shelters as well as individual researchers with an area of study in Mother Studies. This historically significant film demonstrates the collective voices and power of mothers who are advocating on behalf of women and families around the world.

Relationship to the Larger Motherhood Movement

The relationship to the larger motherhood movement is two-fold. First, the film has the capacity to reach a large audience with a small amount of individual time commitment. Many of the organizations showcased in the film are run by a handful of dedicated, but very busy individuals. Disseminating their messages to the masses poses a difficult, if not in some cases impossible, challenge. Also the global representation allows people who see the film to learn about organizations and issues that they would not otherwise have easy access to. The second way that this film is related to the larger motherhood movement is the prospect of selling the film to raise money for The Museum of Motherhood (see related chapter). This is the first of many achievements that we will look back on as foundational moments within the motherhood movement.

Participants

Over 23 organizations are represented in the film and include:

•Andrea O'Reilly (Founder, Association for Research on Mothering)
•Joy Rose (Founder & President, MAMAPALOOZA and Executive Director, Motherhood Foundation)
•Alexia Nye Jackson (Mother, The Job)
•Anita Shawhanks (author, *Adolescent Pregnancy*)
•Amy Hudock (literarymama.com)
•Jewelles Smith (DisAbled Womens Network of Canada)
•Mary Olivella (momsrising.org)
Amy Richards (Third Wave Foundation)

•Tiloma Jayasinghe (Staff Attorney, National Advocates For Pregnant Women)
•Heide Goettner-Abendroth (International Academy For Modern Matriarchal Studies)
•Oleru Huda (Parliament, Uganda)
•Rebekah Spicuglia (Non Custodial Parent Community)
•Gayle Brandeis (CODEPINK)
•Audette Shephard (Chair, United Mothers Opposing Violence Everywhere (UMOVE)
•Amy Anderson (*Mamazine*)
•Jennifer Niesslein (Co-founder, *Brain, Child*)
•Laura Jiminez (Sister Song Women Of Color Reproductive Health Collective)
•Amber Kinser (Author, *Mothering in the Third Wave*)
•Genevieve Vaughan (International Feminists for a Gift Economy)
•Lynn Kuechle (Board, Museum of Motherhood)
•Enola Aird (The Motherhood Proect)
•Lorri Slepian and Linda Lisi Juergens (National Association Of Mother Centers)
•Pat Gowens and The Welfare Warriors
•Melanie Dernak (National Organization For Women (NOW))
•Rebecca Ruhlen (Breastfeeding Advocacy)
•Jill Evans Petzall (Filmmaker, *When the Bow Breaks* and *Veronica's Story*)
•Beth Osnes and Julianna Forbes (Mothers Acting Up)

Conclusion

The film *You Say You Want a Revolution* provides an easy way for individuals to learn about the Motherhood Movement and about the organizations that are blazing the trail for solving many of the issues that face mothers around the world. The film has been viewed at Universities and Academic Conferences, in college classrooms and in social service organizations. It is our hope that individuals who view the film further understand the issues surrounding modern day motherhood and also have their interest piqued to find out more about the organizations that are highlighted in the film.

Film Credits

Joy Rose, Director

Joy is making her directorial debut. As President and Founder of Mamapalooza Festivals and Mamapalooza Media, publisher of *Mamazina* Magazine and voice behind MediaMom.com, Joy can be heard on 'Don't Tell Me To Shut Up' radio, blog tv and as a featured guest speaker at places like The Women's Media Center and The What Women Want Expo, in addition to being the NOW– NYC Susan B. Anthony Award winner for her work on behalf of women and girls, and creating the 'Best In Girl Power' (*Westchester Magazine*) event at Mamapalooza, Kenisco Dam, NY. As acting Executive Director of The Motherhood Foundation, she is personally invested in seeing women's stories told, raising awareness about women's status in the world, and preserving documentation of the Maternal Feminist movement in perpetuity for The Museum Of Motherhood, academia and the general public.

Stephanie Schleicher, Editor

Stephanie is a New York-based freelance editor. She also serves as Media Coordinator for Mamapalooza, Inc, where she manages an extensive catalog of woman-produced entertainment. As a practicing artist, feminist and mother of two, she fights on the front lines of the motherhood movement all day, every day. Remember, "If you want something done, give it to a busy person."

Rebekah Spicuglia, Assistant Camera

Rebekah is a Media, Training, Web and Advocacy Manager for The Women's Media Center, where she combines her dedication to feminist, progressive values with her film production background to create and advocate for representative media. She is also founder of the Non-Custodial Parent Community blog. MSN highlighted Spicuglia as one of eight "Moms Inspired to Change History." Originally from Virginia, Spicuglia grew up in California, where she worked on several film and television projects before attending the University of California at Berkeley, earning a Bachelor's degree in Mass Communications.

Marcarthur Baralla, Cinematography and Sound

Marcarthur works as a director and cinematographer on music videos, short and feature films, commercials, documentaries and more. He established Defendshee Productions under which he produces, and currently lives in Brooklyn, NY.

Special thanks for additional editing by Jennifer Rawlings, Andrea O'Reilly, and Renée Knapp, and for musical contributions by Carol Lester, Polly Wood and Deb Chamberlin.

Organizations

Organizations

Another Mother for Peace (AMP) was founded in 1967 in California by a small group of American women concerned about the continuing escalation of the Vietnam War. The group spread across the U.S., appealing to mothers and women who feared their sons might be drafted, or already had been. AMP's non-partisan slogan "War is Not Healthy for Children and Other Living Things," and its trademark crayon-drawn sunflower, evoked maternal imagery that allowed the women a unique voice in public debate about the war. Comprised primarily of mothers, the group won widespread media coverage for their claims to be uniquely qualified to participate in dialogue about the war since their own sons' lives were at stake. The group was inactive from 1986 to 2003, but it was reborn with the U.S. invasion of Iraq when a new generation of mothers gathered around AMP's original mission to oppose war. Website: <www.anothermother.org> (see Chapter 51 by Meghan Gibbons.)

Attachment Parenting International's (API) primary mission is to educate and support mothers/parents in raising secure, joyful, and empathic children, strengthen families, and create a more compassionate world. Recognizing that every family has unique circumstances with distinct needs and resources; API also acknowledges other people in a child's life who actively foster a strong attachment relationship with the children in their care. In addition to forming Attachment Parenting support groups, API provides educational materials, evidence-based research, as well as consultative, referral, and speaker services by networking with parents, professionals, and like-minded organizations around the world. Website: <www.attachmentparenting.org> (See Chapter 30 by Sally Dear-Healey.)

The Australian Breastfeeding Association (ABA), (formerly the Nursing Mothers Association of Australia), was founded in Melbourne in 1964 by five mothers and within a few years had spread to other states. It is believed to be the second largest women's organization in Australia. The ABA's focus is on supporting mothers to breastfeed, within the context of mothering. Mother-to-mother counselling is provided by women who have undergone rigorous training; under the Code of Ethics they do not give medical advice. The training system for breastfeeding counsellors and community educators has been upgraded to Certificate IV level and continuing education is provided. The ABA has been credited with influencing the breastfeeding rate, antidiscrimination legislation, and awareness and monitoring of marketing practices within the scope of the International Code of Marketing of Breastmilk Substitutes ("WHO Code"). Website: <www.breastfeeding.asn.au> (See Chapter 16 by Virginia Thorley.)

The Australian Motherhood Initiative for Research and Community Involvement (A-MIRCI) was formally founded in 2005 after a third international conference on mothering was held in Australia. Prior to its formal establishment, a group of maternal scholars at the University of Queensland had been meeting every six weeks, holding discussions and seminars on "the maternal" and, in 2001, they organized the first international conference in Australia. A-MIRCI has grown slowly, but its successes have been in providing identity and a national meeting space for maternal scholars; in the organizing of conferences which have attracted both international and national scholars; in providing a forum for discussion and the dissemination of maternal research via conference papers and the publication of selected papers from these conferences in edited books and journals; in bringing international maternal scholars to Australia both as keynote speakers and presenters of papers; in its encouragement and support of the many scholars who are beginning their research in maternal studies; in the organization and presenting of the first course on "the mother" to be offered at the University of Queensland. Website: <www.uq.edu.au/mothering> (See Chapter 70 by Marie Porter and Julie Kelso.)

The **Association for Improvements in the Maternity Services** (AIMS) **Ireland** was formed in 2007 by mothers dissatisfied with the maternity services in Ireland. AIMS Ireland was set up with the support of AIMS UK, an organisation that has been at the forefront of improving maternity services over the past 40 years. AIMS Ireland is a consumer-led voluntary organisation whose mission is to highlight normal birth and campaign for mother- and baby-friendly birth practices that are supported by evidence-based research and international best practice. In addition to its campaign work for changes and improvements in maternity services, and carrying out research, the organisation provides independent, confidential support and information to women and their families and holds local public support and informational meetings and birth healing workshops. The organisation strives to raise awareness of birth-related issues among women, service providers, policymakers and the general public while supporting and advocating for women-centred maternity care. Website: <www.aimsireland.com> (See Chapter 10 by Christina Bermingham.)

Bad Mother's Club is an online forum and safe haven for Australian mothers to speak openly and honestly about their realities of parenting in a supportive and welcoming environment, without fear of recrimination or judgement. The Club also offers a paid membership area, including private forums, live chat and group formation, where members can discuss more sensitive issues and/or to create fun support groups, share ideas and suggestions, and have a relative level of safety, security and privacy online. Events are organised quarterly to provide members and others with an opportunity to have some time out for themselves in a safe, fun and supportive environment. Resources in the form of articles are accessible on the website, and will soon be expanding to webinars, e-courses, guides and books, videos and a plethora of information and other resources for parents, taking into account the various realities of families, and all with a dose of humour and satire. Website: <www.badmothersclub.com.au> (See Chapter 32 by Amanda Cox)

Birth Trauma Canada is an independent, volunteer run organization working collaboratively with similar organizations around the world to champion better maternity care that reflects the values and choices of all childbearing women. Founded in 1998, it has had an online presence since April, 2007. The organization offers an anonymous and non-judgemental platform for women to talk openly about their obstetrical treatment, believing that violence to childbearing women and inhumanity in obstetrics will not end until women band together and force change. Website: <www.birthtraumacanada.org> (See Chapter 5 by Penny Christensen.)

BOLD is a global movement to make maternity care mother-friendly. BOLD inspires communities around the world to organize productions of Karen Brody's critically-acclaimed play about childbirth, "Birth," and BOLD Red Tent birth storytelling circles to raise money and awareness to make maternity care the best it can be for all mothers. Since 2006 hundreds of BOLD events have taken place around the world, produced by volunteer activists in the U.S. and around the world, educating thousands of people about childbirth options and the birthing climate in local communities. Website: <www.boldaction.org> (See Chapter 12 by Kryn Freehling-Burton)

Brain, Child magazine was founded in 1999 by Jennifer Niesslein and Stephanie Wilkinson: two mothers with shared passions for motherhood and literary writing. Their goal was to create a publication that would allow mothers to carry on "grown up" conversations about the issues that mattered most to mothers. Forty-four issues later, their literary offspring is an award-winning publication that has become a source of information, inspiration, and support to 36,000 mothers per issue. And, despite the founders' intentions to avoid becoming too political, *Brain, Child* has also become a key ally to the twenty-first century mothers' movement. Eleven years after its launch, *Brain, Child* remains the only print literary magazine dedicated to motherhood. In 2010, *Brain, Child* received its most recent award, the *Utne* Independent Press Award for Social/Cultural Coverage. Website: <www.brainchildmag.com> (See Chapter 79 by Ann Douglas.)

Caritas is one of the largest non-statutory welfare associations in Germany and is guided by its Catholic belief in brotherly and sisterly love. It speaks out against social and political developments contributing to marginalization and exclusion of vulnerable members of society. Since its formative years in the late nineteenth century, its intent has been to offer an extensive spectrum of services and to reach as many people as possible. Caritas focused initially on national endeavours, but expanded its efforts internationally during the 1950s. The organization provides counselling and support in all matters related to conception, birth control, pregnancy, prenatal diagnostics, birth, postpartum, and mourning the loss of a child. Caritas also specializes in services for mothers (and children) recovering from physical and mental illnesses and provides a support system for parents of mentally and/or physically disabled children. Website: <www.caritas.de> (See Chapter 7 by Sonja M. Allen.)

Choice Moms is a primarily a web-based support group for women thinking, trying, waiting or becoming a single mother by choice. Founded by journalist and author Mikki Morrissette in 2005, the organization runs a number of communications and community-building initiatives, such as online discussion groups and regional events. Through such venues, Choice Moms offers resources, information, conversation and support to mothers who have either chosen single-parenthood or are considering it. Morrissette advocates on behalf of this community and its children, fosters a discussion of the challenges and joys of single parenting, and works tirelessly to expand the network of Choice Moms. She has seen tremendous growth in the Choice Moms brand and succeeded in building a strong support network for a growing number of twenty-first century mothers. Website: <www.choicemoms.org> (See Chapter 31 by Christin Geall.)

Cindy Sheehan is an American peace activist who was spurred into action via her son Casey's death in the early days of the Iraq war. In 2005, she helped to reinvigorate the anti-war movement in the United States through her Camp Crawford vigils held near George W. Bush's Texas ranch. At least 15,000 people travelled to Crawford to support Sheehan. What started as an interrogation of the Iraq war expanded into rallies against military recruitment and retention policies, work to expose atrocities at Guantanamo Bay, and calls for Bush's impeachment and for action about the continuing tragedy surrounding Hurricane Katrina. Sheehan continues her activism to this day and has broadened her anti-war scope to also focus on the environment, socio-economic inequality nationally and globally, and the plight of the Palestinian people. She has published three books, *Peace Mom, Myth of America,* and *Revolution: A Love Story. Myth of America II* is purportedly in the works. She also blogs, hosts podcasts and radio shows from "Cindy's Sheehan's Soap Box," a political site not sponsored by corporate dollars or owned by a radio station. Website: <www.cindysheehanssoapbox.com> (See Chapter 58 by Natalie Wilson.)

CODEPINK: **Women for Peace** is a women-initiated grassroots peace and social justice movement working to end the wars in Iraq and Afghanistan, stop new wars, and redirect our resources into healthcare, education, green jobs, and other life-affirming activities. CODEPINK rejects foreign policies based on domination and aggression, and instead calls for policies based on diplomacy, compassion, and a commitment to international law. With an emphasis on joy and humour, CODEPINK women and men seek to inspire a community of peacemakers through creative campaigns and a commitment to non-violence. While the Bush Administration's color-coded homeland security alerts were based on fear and are used to justify violence, the CODEPINK alert is a feisty call for women and men to "wage peace." While the organization is not exclusively an all-women group—men are also welcome to join—CODEPINK is particularly eager to see mothers, grandmothers, sisters, and daughters, female workers, students, teachers, healers, artists, writers, singers, poets and all outraged woman rise up and oppose the war in Iraq and Afghanistan. Website: <www.codepink4peace.org> (See Chapter 56 by Gayle Brandeis.)

Coping with Change (CWC) is an innovative feminist psycho-educational program run out of the Women's Health Clinic (WHC) in Winnipeg, Manitoba, Canada, that promotes maternal health and well-being through building knowledge and support for mothers, community members, and service providers regarding the emotional changes that occur after introducing a baby, whether by birth or adoption, into the lives of women and their families. CWC is based on the feminist philosophy that mothers are at the centre of care, and that shifts in social expectations and relational pressures are as equally important to physical changes in understanding women's transition to motherhood. The program addresses the social expectations placed on new mothers and the changing nature of personal and familial relationships, rather than only the needs of the children or the physical or biological changes new mothers may experience, and offers a prevention model of care by successfully integrating the practices of feminist consciousness raising and feminist praxis during the "teachable moments" when postpartum women are wondering about the normalcy of their feelings. Essential to the motherhood movement, CWC is the foundation of the entire model of the Mothers Program at WHC, which also offers two additional programs to assist mothers, and also strongly informs various provincial and federal policies and programs addressing the needs of mothers. Website: <www.womenshealthclinic.org> (See Chapter 26 by Fiona Joy Green.)

The **DisAbled Women's Network-Réseau d'action de femmes handicapées Canada** (DAWN-RAFH **Canada**) is a national organization. Its mission is to end the poverty, isolation, discrimination and violence experienced by women with disabilities. DAWN-RAFH Canada is working to ensure that all women with disabilities receive the services and supports they need; have access to opportunities that non-disabled people take for granted; and have freedom of choice in all aspects of their lives. Website: <www.dawncanada.net> (See Chapter 21 by Jewelles Smith.)

donum vitae is a Catholic-inspired counselling service for pregnant women of all nationalities and denominations founded in 1999. This organization is state-recognized and able to fulfill the requirements for legal abortion in Germany. Its members see it as their duty as Christians to advocate for the life of the unborn child and to help men and women during a time of personal crisis by informing them about all of their choices (including alternatives to abortion), so that pregnant women can make an informed decision. Counselling is available on topics about birth control, pregnancy, prenatal diagnostics, delivery, postpartum, abortion, and mourning the loss of a child. Specialized programs focus on the option of an anonymous birth while receiving proper medical care and supporting expecting parents on a path that includes or excludes prenatal diagnostics. Since donum vitae considers a fetus "the gift of life," as its Latin name suggests, this organization puts much of its efforts into pregnancy prevention. Website: <www.donumvitae.org> (See Chapter 7 by Sonja M. Allen.)

electivecesarean.com offers support and information to women whose birth plan is a cesarean. Its aims are to encourage clarity in the reporting of cesarean risks and benefits, which can only be achieved by separating data on different types of cesareans (for example, planned versus emergency, primary versus repeat, and maternal request with no indication versus one with medical or obstetrical indications), and to campaign for recognition that a planned cesarean at 39+ gestational weeks is a legitimate birth plan, even in a healthy pregnancy, provided the woman has an individualized consultation and is planning a small family. Importantly, electivecesarean.com does not advocate this birth choice for all women, but aims to ensure that women who do make an informed decision are not disrespected, disparaged or refused a priori. Website: <www.electivecesarean.com> (See Chapter 14 by Pauline McDonagh Hull.)

Family and Home Network (FAHN), founded in 1984 and originally named Mothers at Home, is a non-profit organization helping families spend generous amounts of time together. FAHN focuses on children's needs for warm, nurturing relationships with their parents, and on parents' experiences and feelings as they take the time to meet their children's needs. Based in the Washington, DC, area, FAHN published the award-winning monthly journal, *Welcome Home*, for 22 years. FAHN speaks out to the media and policy makers about families and works to stop the misuse of statistics on employed mothers. Today, FAHN continues to reach parents throughout the world with its publications and website, offering affirmation, information, and advocacy. Its Campaign for Inclusive Family Policies calls on policymakers to craft family policies that support parents regardless of how they choose to meet their income-earning and caregiving responsibilities. Website: <www.familyandhome.org> (See Chapter 29 by Catherine H. Myers.)

Feminist.com is a thriving online community fostering awareness, education, and activism for women all across the world. It is the Internet's definitive hub for resources and information dedicated to women's equality, justice, wellness and safety. Like a "feminist Google," Feminist.com facilitates connections between women and the many, varied organizations serving their needs and interests worldwide. Feminist.com advances women-friendly organizations, increases civic involvement, and promotes self-sufficiency, spiritual health and general wellness. For the past decade, Feminist.com has assisted its visitors in finding the causes, issues and organizations that resonate with them, leveraging the massive potential of the Internet to connect, educate, and empower. Women all over the world are actively connecting to information, organizations and each other, through the useful and varied links, activism alerts, event listings, and women-owned business listings offered at Feminist.com. Website: <www.feminist.com>. (See Chapter 66 by Amy Richards.)

The Feminist Mothering Caucus is a Constituency Group of the National Women's Studies Association (NWSA). Established in 1977, NWSA is a professional organization that leads the field of women's studies in educational and social transformation. Within the association there are caucuses, taskforces and interest groups. Caucuses are designated groups that are under-represented within society or NWSA as an organization. The purpose of the Caucus includes, among other things, working to ensure that the NWSA recognizes and addresses the needs of mothers and parents through its conference program and accommodations and supporting scholarship on feminist mothering. Website: <www.feministmothering.com> (See Chapter 72 by Arlene Sgoutas.)

The **Feminist Mothers Discussion Group** (FMDG) was founded in Brisbane, Australia, in 2005 by feminists, Andrea Fox and Kitty Carra. It established space for feminist mothers to explore, through a facilitated discussion, how their feminism impacts on their mothering and conversely, how their experiences of motherhood are shaping their feminism. Each discussion topic was framed with these two questions in mind. The purpose of the FMDG was to bring together and support the feminist parenting community of Brisbane and to help strengthen the collective power of the feminist movement in Australia. The FMDG took a hiatus across 2009-10 during the birth of Fox's second child and the emergence of Carra's new work and family arrangements, but it is currently in the process of resuming. Website: <www.bluemilk.wordpress.com> (See Chapter 33 by Andrea Fox.)

Girl Mom.com was founded in 1999 by Bee Lavender. It is a feminist pro-choice advocacy website dedicated to empowering, educating, and supporting young mothers. Rooted in her own experience of teenage pregnancy and mothering, Lavender envisaged a safe and supportive space where young mothers could gain encouragement, advice, and community from one another and their own writing; a positive space which reflected the lives and experiences of young mothers and their children rather than the dominant cultural messages of shame and blame. The structure, content and direction of Girl Mom.com is dictated by the needs and interests of the young women who design, maintain and avail of the site's resources. Girl Mom's guiding philosophy remains the steadfast belief that teenage mothers deserve the respect, encouragement, and community of peers that enable all mothers to achieve self-worth and independence. Website: <www.girl-mom.com> (See Chapter 17 by Sandy M. May.)

Gold Star Families Speak Out (GSFSO) is an anti-war protest organization founded in the fall of 2005 by Celeste Zappala and Karen Meredith. Members of GSFSO have lost a loved one in the Iraq or Afghan wars. They are a chapter of Military Families Speak Out (MFSO), which serves people with a family member, partner, or spouse in the Military. MFSO and GSFSO are united by a common belief that the U.S. wars in Iraq and Afghanistan are illegal, immoral, and unjust and must end now. GSFSO sees its mission as actively working to end the war, supporting other families who are grieving a military family member's death, and advocating for medical and mental health services for veterans who do return home. While GSFSO's membership is made up of both men and women, mothers founded the organization and have been its spokespeople and leaders from the beginning. Website: <www.gsfso.org> (See Chapter 55 by Jocelyn Fenton Stitt.)

Hip Mama has been in print since 1993. It is a worker-owned, collective-published thematic quarterly of personal stories of radically diverse experiences of parenting to promote solidarity and compassion across all boundaries, resisting the powers of silence. Its mission is to give a voice and platform for mothers to express their parenting styles that are otherwise not covered by mothering magazines. *Hip Mama* does this through being completely reader driven. *Hip Mama* is pro-choice, queer friendly, has single parent supporters, and promotes tolerance of all lifestyles. *Hip Mama* is an American Alternative Press Award-winning periodical covering the culture and politics of parenting. The magazine is widely credited with launching the contemporary mothers' movement. In spring 2010, *Hip Mama* was nominated for an *Utne* award for Best Writing. Website: <www.hipmama.com> (See Chapter 76 by Ariel Gore.)

HAGIA International Academy for Modern Matriarchal Studies and Matriarchal Spirituality was founded and continues to be directed by Heide Goettner-Abendroth since 1986. The HAGIA Academy is unique in its methods for scientific research and teaching on the subject of matriarchal cultures and societies. The program includes lectures, seminars, and intensive courses of study, exhibitions of matriarchal art, and celebrations of matriarchal spirituality following the cycles of the seasons and of life: the new Matriarchal Mystery Festivals. Every year, new informative and exploring travels are made to different countries of Europe, of Asia, Africa, and the Americas. These travels are either archaeological study travels of the historical remnants of matriarchal culture, or they are anthropological trips to visit people in existing matriarchal societies of today. As a result of the Academy's decades-long teaching activities, and the recent presentation of two large international congresses, a new movement based on matriarchal values has emerged. Website: <www.hagia.de> (See Chapter 73 by Heide Goettner-Abendroth.)

International Feminists for a Gift Economy (IFGE) is a virtual think tank of academics and activists who are working towards a shift in paradigm based on the idea of a maternal gift economy. The group has no bureaucracy, very little structure and no dues. It is comprised of some 100 Indigenous and non Indigenous women from 15 different countries who communicate on an e-list and who travel to speak at international conferences. IFGE began in Norway in 2001 when some of the women attending the founding meeting of the International Feminist University (IFUN) embraced the gift economy idea and decided to form a network to promote it and to think about it further. As a member of the twenty-first century motherhood movement, IFGE attempts to bridge among movements for social change using the idea of a common mothering gift economy. Website: <www.gift-economy.com> (See Chapter 65 by Genevieve Vaughan.)

The International MotherBaby Childbirth Organization (IMBCO) is a non-profit, non-governmental organization created to develop, regularly update, and promulgate the International MotherBaby Childbirth Initiative (IMBCI): 10 Steps to Optimal Maternity Services worldwide. The purpose of the IMBCI 10 Steps is to improve care throughout the childbearing continuum, in order to save lives, prevent illness and harm from the overuse of obstetric technologies, and promote health for mothers and babies around the world. The IMBCI's educational aims are to call global attention to the importance of the quality of the mother's birth experience and its impact on the outcome, the risks to mother and baby from inappropriate medical interventions, and the scientific evidence showing the benefits of motherbaby-centered care based on the normal physiology of pregnancy, birth, and breastfeeding and on attention to women's individual needs. Website: <www.imbci.org> (See Chapter 13 by Robbie Davis-Floyd, Debra Pascali-Bonaro, Mayri Sagady Leslie, Rae Davies, Hélène Vadeboncoeur, and Rodolfo Gómez Ponce de León.)

International Mothers and Mothering Network (IMMN), formerly the International Mothers Network (IMN), is a global consortium of over 130 motherhood organizations that provides a collective virtual space for the motherhood movement. The IMMN was officially launched on International Women's Day, March 8, 2009. Its purpose is to link maternal activist organizations and galvanize a strong collective voice representing the rights and needs of mothers globally. It is about providing a space of empowerment, a space of information sharing, a space for community building and a space for bringing together progressive mothering groups who are all fighting for the same cause through various different means. Website: <www.internationalmothersandmotheringnetwork.org> (See Chapter 42 by Melinda Vandenbeld Giles.)

Jennifer Schumaker's 500 Mile Walk for Togetherness took place in the spring of 2006. It aimed to create dialogue about LGBTQ rights and issues specifically, and to emphasize human togetherness and interconnection more generally. According to the Walk for Togetherness website, Schumaker envisioned the walk as a way to deconstruct the entrenched "us and them" way of thinking that dominates both public and private discourse, especially in relation to sexuality. As the website reads, "Jennifer is not only walking for LGBTQ people and their families, but also for anyone who feels invisible in our society. Jennifer has dedicated her walk to a 12-year old boy named Dakota, who has cerebral palsy." When Dakota was seven, Jennifer heard him call himself "the Invisible Man." Schumaker often invokes Dakota's story when writing or talking about her activism, emphasizing that nobody, regardless of race, sexuality, disability, or any other difference should be rendered invisible by society. Website: <www.walkfortogetherness.org> (See Chapter 40 by Natalie Wilson.)

Keeping Mum is a Community Art Project and activist group that includes women from Clare Birth Choice, a community group lobbying for maternity services in Co. Clare, Ireland, and for a woman's right to choose where she gives birth. Keeping Mum supports other consumer groups, politicians, policy makers and midwives in their campaign to support women in their choice of where to give birth. It provides a supportive and creative environment where women can reflect on their individual journey to motherhood and their subsequent experiences of giving birth. It also provides women with the opportunity to create artworks from their memories of giving birth. Website: <www.martinahynan.com> (See Chapter 11 by Martina Hynan.)

La Leche League International is an organization, operating in 68 countries, which primarily trains and supports experienced breastfeeding mothers to help other mothers who want to breastfeed. Founded more than 50 years ago at a time when breastfeeding rates were at an all-time low, the organization has been a source of reliable, evidence-based and practical information on breastfeeding for mothers and health care professionals. Accredited La Leche League volunteers, known as Leaders, help mothers in a variety of ways: through gro up meetings (usually held monthly), over the phone, by email, during visits to the mother's home or hospital room, at drop-in gatherings, through forums provided on the organization's website, and through various publications, including newsletters, information sheets, books and DVDs. Website: <www.llli.org> (See Chapter 15 by Cindy Cowan.)

Latina Mami is a motherhood collective in Austin, Texas. Founded in 2000 by Gloria Pérez-Walker. Latina Mami provides support for working-class, Latina mothers in myriad forms, including babysitting cooperatives, clothing exchanges, support groups, newsletters, and friendship. The group is run entirely by working-class, Latina mother volunteers and uses a culturally-specific, non client-centered model to address the unique needs and circumstances faced by a historically marginalized group. Currently, the group is in the midst of a re-organization by its founder, who also works as an advocate for parents of children with disabilities. Website: <www.latinamami.homestead.com> (See Chapter 18 by Cristina Herrera.)

Legal Services for Prisoners with Children (LSPC) seeks to transform the harm to people, families and their communities caused by mass incarceration through three overarching strategies: to restore the human and civil rights of people inside prison and following their release to the community, to release people from prison and reduce the number of people behind bars, and to reunify families and communities impacted by incarceration. The Family Unity Project sits at the center of this vision: by protecting mothers' rights, seeking their release and fighting for the reunification of their families, we unite the struggles for criminal and reproductive justice. LSPC engages in grassroots organizing, public policy, legal advocacy and coalition-building. Website: <www.prisonerswithchildren.org> (See Chapter 20 by Karen Shain)

LGBT **Family Coalition** (formerly the Lesbian Mothers Association of Quebec) was founded in 1998. In 2008, the group became the LGBT Family Coalition (Coalition des familles homoparentales du Québec) and enlarged their mandate to officially include lesbian, bisexual, transsexual, and gay parents and future parents. Since inception, the organization has advocated for the legal and social recognition of LGBT families. The group has received three "Arc-en-ciel" prizes from the gay and lesbian community. In 2002, the group was honoured for the social activism that successfully lead to the adoption of lesbian and gay parenting rights in Quebec; and, in 2008 and 2010 it was recognized for innovative projects in advancing awareness and rights for LGBT families. The LGBT Family Coalition works for the legal and social recognition of LGBT families in collaboration with government bodies and the media. Website: <www.familleshomoparentales.org> (See Chapter 41 by Nancy Nicol.)

The LGBTQ **Parenting Network** (PN) is a program of the Sherbourne Health Centre, an innovative health centre located in downtown Toronto. The PN promotes the rights and well-being of lesbian, gay, bisexual, trans and queer parents, prospective parents and their families through education, advocacy, research, social networking and community organizing. The work of the PN aims to counter historically entrenched, and often internalized, negative ideas about LGBTQ-led families, and to foster the attitude, both individually and institutionally, that LGBTQ people not only have the right and the ability to be parents, but that LGBTQ families provide children with unique and interesting opportunities. We affirm the existence and visibility of LGBTQ families through events, workshops, and the development of resources. We add to knowledge of LGBTQ parenting by conducting community-based research that informs our practice, and we advocate for LGBTQ parents and prospective parents, individually and systemically, in areas such as assisted human reproduction, adoption, family recognition and schools. To contact the Parenting Network: parentingnetwork@sherbourne.on.ca. Website: <www.lgbtqparentingconnection.ca>. To order resources listed in this chapter, go to the Rainbow Health Ontario website: <http://www.rainbowhealthontario.ca/rhostore/welcome.cfm>. (See Chapter 23 by Rachel Epstein.)

Literary Mama, an online literary magazine founded in 2003, features writing by mother writers about the complexities and many faces of motherhood. The site aims to give mother writers an outlet for their writing and to connect these writers, around the world, in community and conversation. *Literary Mama* publishes book reviews, columns, creative nonfiction, fiction, poetry, and profiles of mother writers. One of *Writers' Digest*'s 101 Best Web Sites for Writers and a *Forbes* Best of the Web pick, today *Literary Mama*'s diverse staff of volunteer editors works from four countries and reaches over 40,000 monthly readers. Website: <www.literarymama.com> (See Chapter 77 by Caroline Grant.)

Literature for Life and ***Yo'Mama Magazine*** is committed to supporting marginalized young mothers in their role as their child's first teacher, by facilitating a one-of-a-kind reading circle program throughout Toronto's underserved neighbourhoods. Through reading and sharing stories, young mothers develop literacy, empathy and decision making skills which they pass on to their children, impacting two generations. Since the organization's founding in 2000 more than 1,800 young mothers have participated in Literature for Life's reading circles, inspiring them to finish high school, pursue post-secondary educations, find meaningful employment and build stronger futures for themselves and their families. *Yo'Mama* magazine is Literature for Life's outreach program. One of a kind in Canada, this health and lifestyle magazine is written for young mothers by young mothers, most of whom are living in or returning to underserved neighbourhoods. *Yo'Mama* features tips on parenting, pregnancy, returning to school, budgeting, learning exercises, book reviews, resources and much more. The magazine gives young marginalized mothers a sense of community, connecting them with their peers who are experiencing similar triumphs and challenges. Website: <www.literatureforlife.org> (See Chapter 78 by Jo Altilia.)

Mainstreet Moms: Organize or Bust, founded by Megan Matson in 2004, is a grassroots organization dedicated to creating social and political change through "bite-sized actions." The group urges mothers to use the talents and skills they have to support grass-roots political efforts that will help create the world they would like for their children. The organization's early activities included registering single mothers and high school seniors to vote, educating parents about how to opt children out of military recruitment lists, and promoting awareness of climate change. After the 2009 Presidential election, Mainstreet Moms ceased most activities and removed sections of their website. In mid-2010, the group re-emerged, but with a more specific and local focus: climate change and energy politics in

Northern California's San Mateo County. Website: <www.mainstreetmom.com> (See Chapter 60 by Lisa Federer.)

MAMAPALOOZA is an event and multi-media company that brings mothers, who are musicians, authors, comics, dancers, filmmakers, designers, craftswomen, educators, and merchants together with community leaders and members of the community in a collaborative effort to highlight the challenges of motherhood in an ever-evolving personal, social, cultural, sexual, and political landscape. Mamapalooza recognizes and honors the growing public persona of moms; their personal stories, their power as both consumers and constituents, and their continuing need and desire to creatively express themselves and at the same time ought to have financial compensation for their artwork, performances and business endeavors. Mamapalooza is a vehicle for social change which encourages women to explore their creativity and art forms in order to build self esteem, break down stereotypes, create unity, encourage diversity, inspire individuality, and empower future generations. Mamapalooza connects women, mothers and families through music, art, activism and education for cultural, economic and social awareness. MOMS ROCK! Website: <www.mamapalooza.com> (See Chapter 74 by Lynn Kuechle and Joy Rose.)

Mapping Maternal Subjectivities, Identities and Ethics (MaMSIE) is a research network based in the School of Psychosocial Studies, Birkbeck, University of London. MaMSIE aims to focus attention on the maternal in current cultural, political, aesthetic, psychosocial and theoretical configurations. The network was founded in 2007 by Lisa Baraitser and Sigal Spigel. Website: <www.mamsie.bbk.ac.uk> (See Chapter 71 by Sigal Spigel and Lisa Baraitser.)

Maternity Coalition (MC) is Australia's national maternity consumer advocacy organization. It is a non-profit organisation committed to advancing best-practice maternity care for all Australian women and their families. MC is non-political and non-sectarian, and acts as an umbrella, bringing together support groups and individuals for effective lobbying, information sharing, networking and support. MC believes in the importance of women uniting their efforts and sharing skills and resources to achieve beneficial change in the health care system by advocating for improvements to health policy planning, decision-making and maternity services delivery which will benefit women; these include expanding models of maternity care available and supporting those models which most focus on woman-centred care. MC originated in the late 1980s to lobby state government inquiries for improved maternity services in the Australian states of New South Wales (NSW) and Victoria. By the mid-2000s the organization had grown to be established nationally and was recognized as a key stakeholder in federal and state government reviews and consultations related to maternity services improvements and reviews, as well as being invited to provide consumer representatives to a range of local and national committees covering hospitals, health departments, and midwifery education. Website: <www.maternitycoalition.org.au> (See Chapter 6 by Lareen Newman, Kerreen Reiger, and Monica Campo.)

Midwifery Collectives in Ontario, 1990-2010: The **College of Midwives of Ontario** (CMO) was established with the proclamation of the *Regulated Health Professions Act and the Midwifery Act* on December 31, 1993 to govern midwifery in the interest of public safety by: regulating the practice of the profession and governing members according to legislation, regulations, and by-laws; setting standards of qualification for persons to be issued certificates of registration; developing, establishing, and maintaining standards of professional ethics for the members; and responding to complaints from the public regarding midwifery practice. The **Association of Ontario Midwives** is the professional organization representing midwives and the practice of midwifery in the province of Ontario. It advocates for the professional interests of midwives and for the Ontario Model of Midwifery Care; provides public education and promotes midwifery as an integral part of the Ontario health care system; represents midwives to the Ministry of Health to maintain appropriate funding for midwifery services; provides ongoing peer support to all members, including educational and professional development; develops clinical and other practice guidelines and promotes midwifery research; administers a benefits package; negotiates and provides access to professional liability insurance for midwife members; and is an active member in the Canadian Association of Midwives Websites: <www.cmo.on.ca> and <www.aom.on.ca>.(See Chapter 1 by Judith Mintz.)

The Midwives Alliance of North America is a membership organization that promotes excellence in midwifery, endorses diversity in educational backgrounds and practice styles, and is dedicated to unifying and strengthening the profession, with the intent of improving the quality of health care for women and their families. As an organization dedicated to empowering women through the midwifery model of care, the Midwives Alliance envisions a maternity care system that offers high quality, affordable, and culturally competent care for all. The Midwives Alliance values the right of each woman to make informed choices regarding provider type, location of delivery, and model of care, honoring a woman's ascendency in decision-making that affects her body, pregnancy, labor, birth, and parenting style. In order to advance its strategic goals, the Midwives Alliance has launched a social justice agenda aimed at ensuring that all women have access to optimal care throughout their reproductive lives. By engaging in political advocacy, we are working to ensure access to highly skilled midwives who are able to interface with the maternity care system and are adequately compensated for their services. Website: <www.mana.org> (See Chapter 2 by Melissa Cheyney, Elizabeth Moore, and Geradine Simkins.)

The **Million Mom March** began as the brainchild of Donna Dees-Thomases during the summer of 1999. Influenced by the activism of Sarah Brady and galvanized by the horror of the Granada Hills, California gun massacre, Dees-Thomases conceived a mission statement for what would become a national movement to bring together mothers across the country to advocate for and with victims of gun trauma for saner gun laws. Estimates put the crowd that gathered to protest gun violence and advocate for stricter gun control in Washington, DC, on Mother's Day, May 14, 2000, somewhere between 400,000 and 700,000. In 1999, other victims of gun trauma had launched another grassroots national campaign that offered a grassroots solution to the American gun epidemic. The Bell Campaign was created to prevent gun death and injury, and to support victims of gun trauma. Organizers of the Million Mom March and the Bell Campaign would join forces in 1999 under one umbrella as the Million Mom March. After the Mother's Day rally in May 2000, the Million Mom March merged with the Brady Campaign to Prevent Gun Violence. Website: <www.millionmommarch.org> (See Chapter 45 by Rachel Sutz Pienta.)

Mocha Moms, Inc. initially began with the publishing of the *Mocha Moms* newsletter with the goal of connecting at-home mothers of color with each other, and to validate their decisions to stay at home, in addition to providing them with information that would aid them in learning how to be optimal parents in recognition of the view that parents are the most important influences in their children's lives. In the summer of 1997, four mothers in Prince George's County, Maryland, formed the support group. There are now over one hundred chapters through the United States. Website: <www.mochamoms.org> (See Chapter 22 by R. Dianne Bartlow.)

Moms on the Move (MOMS) was formed in 2001 as a group of special needs advocates protesting government budget cuts to social programs that would drastically impact services provided to community members throughout British Columbia. Consisting mainly of activist mothers and led by co-administrators Cyndi Gerlach and Dawn Steele, MOMS is currently the largest provincial group representing families of children and youth with special needs. The organization acts as an information sharing network for more than 1,000 BC parents and community allies. Additionally, MOMS organizes public forums to address current political concerns of the special needs community, encourages activism through letter writing campaigns and online petitions, and directs families to various resources in the province. Its mission is to educate the government and public on the "importance of investing in children and youth with special needs and children at risk." Website: <www.momsnetwork.ca> (See Chapter 64 by Andrea Doyle Hugmeyer.)

MomsRising is a multicultural grassroots organization of more than a million members (with a social media reach calculated at over three million) who are working in the United States to achieve family economic security, to end discrimination against mothers, and to ensure that all children have a healthy start in life. MomsRising uses the power of online organizing in coordination with on-the-ground activities and dynamic media outreach to educate the public about problems facing American families and to propose common sense solutions. We provide mothers and others with an opportunity to amplify their voices in order to take their concerns to leaders who are in a position to bring about positive change. MomsRising's members are organizing and speaking out to improve public policy and to change the national dialogue on issues that are critically important to America's mothers and families. Website: <www.momsrising.org> (See Chapter 39 by Kristin Rowe-Finkbeiner and Mary Olivella.)

The **Mother Centers International Network for Empowerment** (MINE), has been providing connection and communication between networks of Mother Centers throughout the world for ten years. Founded in Germany in late 2000, MINE stands for a world that places social cohesion and community building at the base of development, re-integrates the culture of care into public life and recognizes the central role of women in peace building and development. MINE strives for economic empowerment and self-sufficiency of mothers, Mother Centers, and Mother Center Networks. MINE takes female involvement in care work as a starting point for organising, and creating a location, a "public living room,"where mobilizing around the different aspects of the lives of women, children and the community can happen "under one roof." MINE has been accredited by the United Nations as best practice and has won the Dubai International Award for Best Practices to improve the Living Environment for "strengthening the capacity of civil society to revitalise local neighbourhoods and revive community life." Website: <www.mine.cc> (See Chapter 24 by Monika Jaeckel.)

The **Mother-Daughter Project** is a grassroots organization of women who support empowering mothers, daughters, and the mother-daughter relationship. We are a resource for mothers and professionals and continue to keep abreast of current research on mothers and daughters. Our book, *The Mother-Daughter Project: How Mothers and Daughters Can Band Together, Beat the Odds, and Thrive Through Adolescence*, by SuEllen Hamkins and Renée Schultz, provides a framework for supporting moms and guidelines for starting mother-daughter groups with age-appropriate explorations of topics to be addressed. Staff members are available for speaking engagements and workshops. Our goal is to offer more networking between mom-daughter groups. Website: <www.TheMotherDaughterProject.com> (See Chapter 61 by Renée Schultz.)

Mother Outlaws is as a community outreach initiative of the Motherhood Initiative for Research and Community Involvement (MIRCI) based in Toronto, Canada. Since 2004, Mother Outlaws has organized several events to establish itself as a recognizable image and cultural signifier of how feminist mothering against the patriarchal institution of motherhood can be envisioned and experienced as empowering for women. The outreach initiatives of Mother

Outlaws have included a Toronto based feminist mothers' discussion group, a continuing speakers series, special events, media coverage, T-shirt images, and assisting with the start-ups of Mother Outlaws chapters elsewhere. In building communities of "mother outlaws" who are challenging normative discourses on motherhood and expressing an empowered feminist mothering in their personal lives, activist activities, professional scholarship and work lives, Mother Outlaws is a unique initiative that connects "lived mothering" to "examined motherhood," bridging academe and activism. Website: <www.motherhoodinitiative.org/motheroutlaws.html> (See Chapter 43 by Linn Baran.)

The **Motherhood Initiative for Research and Community Involvement** (MIRCI), (formerly the Association for Research on Mothering or ARM), the ***Journal of the Motherhood Initiative*** (JMI), (formerly the *Journal of the Association for Research on Mothering*), and **Demeter Press** are the first and still the only feminist research organizations and publications devoted specifically to the topic of mothering-motherhood. The Association for Research on Mothering was founded in 1998, the *Journal of the Association for Research on Mothering* in 1999, and Demeter Press in 2006. From 1998-2010 ARM and its journal and press were housed at York University in Toronto, Canada. In 2010, ARM left York University and was re-established as an independent non-profit research organization known as The Motherhood Initiative for Research and Community Involvement (MIRCI). MIRCI has more than 500 members worldwide, including scholars, writers, activists, social workers, midwives, nurses, therapists, lawyers, teachers, politicians, parents, students and artists. They come from more than 20 countries, as well as numerous local and international agencies and governmental, social, and community groups that work for, and on behalf of, mothers. Demeter Press, MIRCI's publishing division, publishes two to five titles per year on a variety of diverse motherhood topics. The association, journal, and press are directed by founder Andrea O'Reilly. Websites: <www.motherhoodinitiative.org> and <www.demeterpress.org> (See Chapter 69 by Andrea O'Reilly).

"The Motherhood Movement" —You Say You Want a Revolution is a film that captures the first ever, international summit on the Motherhood Movement, featuring motherhood organizations. Directed by Joy Rose, produced by the Museum of Motherhood, in collaboration with the Association for Research on Mothering (ARM) and the Motherhood Foundation Inc. (MFI). The film seeks to promote, showcase, and make visible maternal discussion and to disseminate information on the subject of feminist/activist mothers and the missions of international maternal agencies. Website: <www.motherhoodmuseum.org/themmovementfilm.html> (See Chapter 81 by Lynn Kuechle and Joy Rose.)

Motherhood Project/Mothers for a Human Future (MHF): The Motherhood Project was one of the leading organizations in the mothers' movement in the United States from May 2001 until May 2009, when it was concluded and succeeded by Mothers for a Human Future (MHF). The Project was established to help move the public conversation beyond the "mommy wars," and to help mothers meet the unprecedented challenges of mothering in an age driven by the values of commerce and technology. Its work was premised on the view that "motherworld" values are an antidote to the often-toxic values of our dominant culture. Building on the work of the Motherhood Project, MHF places a special emphasis on fighting the commercialization of childhood and the commodification of children. MHF seeks to equip mothers to be effective leaders for motherworld values in an age that is putting us on the path to what has been called a "post-human" future. Website: <www.mothersforahumanfuture.org> (See Chapter 67 by Enola G. Aird.)

Mothering.com and *Mothering* Magazine: Mothering.com hosts the largest community online for natural parents. With over 165,000 members and 1.7 million unique visitors, Mothering.com is the hub of the natural parenting universe online. Mothering.com also has articles, blogs and podcasts on parenting, pregnancy, birth, breastfeeding, education, green living, health and food. Published from 1976 through 2010, *Mothering* magazine was the premier publication of the natural family living community. Its award winning coverage included childbirth reform, breastfeeding rights, and vaccinations and informed consent. Website: <www.mothering.com> (See Chapter 80 by Peggy O'Mara.)

Mothers Acting Up (MAU), is a movement of mothers (and others who exercise protective care over someone smaller) stretching traditional mothering roles to include advocating for the world's children. Why mothers? Because we're already committed and potentially the most powerful lobby for children on earth. Why the world's children? Because our own children's future is inextricably linked to the wellbeing of every other child. Collectively, you, she, we, can create a world where every child—and the planet itself—thrives. MAU's mission is to mobilize mothers to act on behalf of the world's children. MAU provides inspiration, education and tools to take action; you provide the passion. Website: <www.mothersactingup.org> (See Chapter 63 by Juliana Forbes and Beth Osnes.)

Mothers Against Drunk Driving (MADD) is a grassroots social movement that draws from personal pain to create social change through community building. MADD grew out of the experiences of two women in California, into a multinational organization with chapters in the U.S., Canada, England, New Zealand, Australia, Guam, Puerto Rico, and Sweden. MADD has a threefold mission of supporting victims of alcohol-related automobile accidents, preventing underage drinking, and eliminating driving under the influence of alcohol. Local chapters provide victim assistance, public awareness and educational programs, public safety campaigns, and legal advocacy through localized legislative initiatives designed to create and enforce laws designed to address drinking and driving. These efforts intend to address a broad spectrum of alcohol and driving-related problems from prevention to victim support following automobile accidents involving alcohol. Website: <www.madd.org> (See Chapter 59 by Laura Dreuth Zeman.)

Mothers Against Trafficking Humans (M.A.T.H.) is an organization founded by Glendene Grant in 2009, after realizing her daughter Jessie Foster, an international endangered missing woman, was actually a human trafficking victim. Though they are not yet where they want to be, as a much needed organization, M.A.T.H. will provide things that are needed for human trafficking victims to become survivors including counselling, doctors, dentists, housing, education, training, etc. M.A.T.H. has teamed up with Crime Stoppers and they are going into high schools and organizations to educate Canadians about human trafficking. M.A.T.H. also goes to different events across Canada doing human trafficking education presentations and helping to launch other human trafficking organizations. Glendene Grant has also recently been appointed the Director of the Western Canadian branch of Canada Fights Human Trafficking, so working directly through M.A.T.H. and with Crime Stoppers, she will continue to educate Canadian citizens across our nation. Website: via <www.causes.com/causes/474402> (See Chapter 50 by Glendene Grant.)

Mothers & More is a non-profit organization that connects mothers and mothering advocate organizations through the strategies of grassroots activism and virtual communities. Comprised of over 100 local chapters around the United States and a vibrant online network, Mothers & More provides mothering women with a space to socialize, focus on their individuality, and renew a sense of self-worth as women. Since Joanne Brundage began this group in the 1987, Mothers & More has used tactics of visibility—such as Mother's Day campaigns and press releases—to raising awareness about the difficult, unpaid, and often unrecognized work that mothers do to raise children and run households. In short, Mothers & More hopes to change work and federal policies that unfairly constrain women's economic security. Website: <www.mothersandmore.org> (See Chapter 37 by Jenna Vinson.)

Mothers are Women (MAW) was an organization founded in 1984, whose purpose was to bring mothers together in order to make social connections, provide support, and discuss issues relevant to mothers who had made the conscious decision to stay at home and care for their children. This organization specifically worked on the issue of women's unpaid work and advocated for society to value the contributions women make and their choice to stay at home. Early on MAW strove to break the isolation of mothers at home. They accomplished this through discussion groups, workshops, and the publication of *Homebase* magazine. The first issue of *Homebase* magazine was published in 1985 and was distributed quarterly. The magazine was instrumental in moving MAW from a local organization to one with a national membership. Presently, MAW is not an active organization. However, during its activity MAW was successful in garnering national attention for the issue of unpaid work. (See Chapter 35 by Kristen Abatsis McHenry.)

Mothers In Charge, a non-profit organization, is a grassroots support organization for the surviving family members and friends of victims of violence, guided by an anti-violence mission. Founded in 2003 in Philadelphia by Dorothy Johnson-Speight after she lost her son to gun violence, Mothers In Charge is dedicated to breaking the city's cycle of violence. They approach the problem from a multitude of angles, focusing on both the survivors of victims of gun violence and on the root causes of this violence. The organization works in collaboration with local school districts and youth and faith-based community organizations to offer educational programs. They also provide grief support to families affected by violence, and they have implemented outreach programs at the local women's jail in Philadelphia. Through their work to support survivors, especially mothers, Mothers In Charge has developed an international presence, with members appearing at international conferences and local chapters opening across the United States. Website: <www.mothersincharge.org> (See Chapter 47 by Abigail L. Palko.)

The ***Mothers Movement Online*** (2003-2008) was an independent, online-only media project featuring essays, commentary, interviews, reviews, and fact-based reporting on the politics of women, work and family in the United States. Judith Stadtman Tucker conceptualized the Mothers Movement Online as a forum for online grassroots organizing that would provide a venue to address such issues as global work and families, maternal employment issues, and the economic destinies of working women. While the website is still accessible, it is not currently active. It exists in an archival mode for informational purposes. Prior to 1999, there was little mainstream reporting on the work and family balancing issues faced by working mothers beyond the media-drive, somewhat sensationalistic popular culture depictions of the "mommy wars." Website: <www.mothersmovement.org> (See Chapter 44 by Rachel Sutz Pienta.)

The **Mothers of Acari** is a maternalist-based group created in 1990 by mothers of victims of police violence originated from the Acari *favela* (slums) and surrounding areas, after the disappearance of their children in Suruí, in the state of Rio de Janeiro (Brazil). Since the 1990s, they have been conducting research, monitoring police investigations, following the Acari judicial inquiries closely, and advocating for laws aimed at the rights of relatives of state-based violence, together with other human rights organisations. Recently, they have strengthened their ties with the wider human rights movements in Rio de Janeiro and in Brazil, particularly with the movement of relatives of victims of state violence. In August 2010, and after two decades of protest against the State's policy of "No body, no crime," one of the mothers of the group has finally received a "certificate of presumed death." (See Chapter 49 by Tatiana Moura and Rita Santos.)

While the history of **Mothers of East Los Angeles** (MELA) is complex, particularly in light of the historical trajectory of Latina and African American women's contribution to social change within their respective communities, the activism of the MELA represents a significant juncture and moment in time in which environmental justice was served up from the bottom in profound and significant ways. In her ethnographic study from December 1987 through October 1989, on the Mexican American women activists central to forging MELA efforts around environmental justice, Mary Pardo argues their contributions illuminate a dimension not readily apparent into the mechanisms of how grassroots politics is conceptualized. According to Pardo, MELA's activism illustrates how these Mexican American women transformed "traditional" networks and resources based on family and culture into political assets to defend the quality of urban life. Pardo suggests, "The central role of women in grassroots struggles around the quality of life, in the Third World and in the United States, challenges conventional assumptions about the powerlessness of women and the static definitions of culture and tradition." Website: <www.mothersofeastla.com> (See Chapter 68 by R. Dianne Bartlow.)

The **Mothers of Laleh Park**, also known as the Mourning Mothers of Iran, is an apolitical grassroots organization that formed in June 2009 following the state-sanctioned violence after the disputed presidential election. The group was created by mothers whose children were killed, imprisoned, or disappeared during the aftermath of the election. They came together to demand justice and truth about what happened to their loved ones and decided to hold peaceful vigils at the park near where one young woman, Neda Agha-Soltan, was murdered during a protest. For many months they gathered together every Saturday dressed in black and held a silent vigil for an hour. A year and a half after their formation they are still actively demanding government accountability for the deaths, arrests, and disappearances of their children and other Iranians and an end to the violence, and their persecution has only intensified. Groups around the world have formed to show solidarity with the Mothers of Laleh Park, and they are considered global icons for human rights. Website: <www.madaraneparklale.org> (See Chapter 53 by Susan Logsdon-Conradsen.)

The Argentine **Mothers of the Plaza de Mayo** appeared on the political scene in the aftermath of the military coup of 1976 that ushered in one of the most brutal military dictatorships of our times. The military Junta suspended all government institutions and set out to capture subversives, a loosely defined label that included anyone who might oppose their rule. It carried out its aims without compromising its image abroad, inventing its deadly policy of disappearances, dragging thousands of young people from their homes, their places of work and their schools by plainclothesmen in unmarked cars. A group of mothers of the disappeared began meeting in secret in 1977 and created a formal organization in 1979 with the goal of establishing a democratic system and finding their children. Despite the fact that their own lives were in danger, their organization was founded upon mutual respect and affection and operates as a direct democracy. The Junta's collapse was followed by a series of unstable governments and the end of opposition except the Mothers who wanted to keep the memory of their disappeared children and the Dirty War alive in a country that turned its back on this period. Today, the Mothers who are elderly remain politically active. Website: <www.madres.org> (See Chapter 52 by Marguerite Guzmán Bouvard.)

Mothers Ought To Have Equal Rights (MOTHERS): A groundswell of attention and efforts toward change are bubbling up from communities all over the U.S. and the world. More and more mothers groups are springing up with varied missions but with much in common regarding the worldview that caregiving work and the perspective of caregivers is given short shrift in many ways. In the U.S., the formation of Mothers Ought To Have Equal Rights is the culmination of the National Association of Mothers' Centres three decades of work with and by mothers to raise consciousness about common issues, to foster the confidence and skills to advocate effectively and to recognize that personal "choices" and circumstances are often limited or defined by outside forces like public policy or corporate culture. MOTHERS is a grassroots effort to address the economic inequities faced by mothers and other caregivers due to the constraints of public policy, corporate culture and policies, and societal norms. Website: <www.mothersoughttohaveequalrights.org> (See Chapter 36 by Linda Lisi Juergens.)

Museum of Motherhood (M.o.M.) is a world-class, international museum, family center and teaching facility with a specific, accessible physical location with both social and educational significance. The Museum documents the journey of the mother's evolving role while promoting women's studies and the evolution of family. The museum honors in perpetuity the achievements of women who are mothers while studying motherhood throughout history. The Museum is the place for women, family, activist, faith- and community-based organizations to share stories, conduct research, and learn about the evolution of family. Initial phases of M.o.M. include online exhibits that are building momentum while generating a wave of interest and expanding the financial framework necessary to purchase a home for the museum. Website: <www.motherhoodmuseum.org> (See Chapter 75 by Lynn Kuechle and Joy Rose.)

National Advocates for Pregnant Women (NAPW) is a non-profit organization dedicated to advocating on behalf of women on issues primarily related to pregnancy and parenting. NAPW is different from other women's advocacy organizations in that it combines litigation support, public education efforts, and grassroots organizing support. In other words, NAPW operates at the intersection of pregnancy, drug policy, and reproductive rights, representing a broad and diverse population of women and their families. NAPW also makes visible pregnancy-related issues that are often obscured or ignored by the abortion debate. As a result, both feminists and non-feminists alike can benefit by NAPW's consciousness-raising about the lack of agency afforded to pregnant women under the law. While their offices are located in New York, New York, their litigation and advocacy support is provided nationwide. Website: <www.advocatesforpregnantwomen.org> (See Chapter 3 by Michelle Trim.)

The National Association of Mothers' Centers (NAMC) began with the opening of the first Mothers' Center program in Hicksville, New York, in January 1975. The vision of the NAMC is a society where the work of taking care of others is valued, supported, at the center of public discussion and a priority in public policy. NAMC is a network of grassroots community programs, offered by mothers and for mothers (and fathers). Members gather for mutual support, validation, sharing of experiences, and the dissemination of information on child development, parenting and women's issues including perinatal mood disorders. Mothers' Centers help mothers tap into necessary resources and learn how to advocate for themselves, their children and their families at the local level at a doctor's office, at their child's school or in their workplace, and also in terms of public policy issues. NAMC has organized 23 National Mothers' Center Conferences to serve its membership. NAMC's advocacy arm is MOTHERS, which focuses on the economic impact of being a caregiver. The national organization also addresses work/life issues, offering an Annual Work/Life Conference since 1996 and serving as a host for the Alfred P. Sloan Awards in Workplace Flexibility in the Long Island, New York region. Website: <www.motherscenter.org> (See Chapter 25 by Lorri Slepian with Laurie Sylla and Rosanne Weston.)

Our Family Coalition: Lack of visibility is a problem that affects many mothers. We live in a society where mothers are often not venerated and feel disempowered. Lesbian mothers and LGBT families as a whole suffer a severe lack of visibility, which in turn leads to social unacceptance. This invisibility can lead to feelings of disempowerment and oppression. Our Family Coalition exists to provide visibility and promote social acceptance of LGBT people and their families. The first objective of Our Family Coalition is to provide support to LGBT parents by addressing issues of isolation by providing social networking events and support groups. Over the past year Our Family Coalition has expanded its reach to include public advocacy and policy structure. Our Family Coalition's advocacy and policy work focuses on making schools more inclusive by increasing LGBT visibility and awareness through age and development appropriate education on issues of gender and sexual orientation. Website: <www.ourfamily.org> (See Chapter 28 by Heaven Walker.)

Parents Against Police Brutality was first founded in 1995 by Margarita Rosario and Iris Baez, both of whom were mothers of young men killed by police officers in the Street Crimes Unit, established under Mayor Rudy Giuliani's government to fight street crime in New York. Iris Baez also established the **Anthony Baez Foundation: Community and Parents Against Police Brutality** in 1999. Both groups organized rallies, protest marches, sit-ins, talks, and other forms of protest against the use of excessive force and racial profiling by police in New York.

Membership is composed primarily of parents of victims of police brutality, and the organization is supported by other groups in New York, like the October 22nd Coalition, 100 Blacks in Law Enforcement Who Care, and Lower East Side Call for Justice. Along with protests, the group sponsored speeches at local high schools, and helped families conduct independent investigations into the deaths of the young men in order to hold the policemen accountable for their actions. Website: <www.andersongoldfilms.com/everymothersson> (See Chapter 48 by Amber Fatima Riaz.)

Peace X Peace (pronounced Peace by Peace), founded by Patricia Smith Melton in 2002, is a global network of women with women-focused e-media, fresh analysis, and from-the-frontlines perspectives. It engages, connects, and amplifies women's voices as the most direct and powerful ways to build cultures of peace around the world. The website features peacebuilding women (and a few good men who support women's peacebuilding) in more than 100 countries and an array of other timely blogs. In the online Peace X Peace Community, members engage with topics from the e-media and add their voices to the global conversation that strengthens the Pillars of Peace: interfaith dialogue, health and well-being, education, conflict transformation, cross-cultural understanding, environmental sustainability, justice and good governance, and economic empowerment. Turning conversation into action, Peace X Peace refers members to a wide range of partner organizations that work to root and strengthen the Pillars of Peace. Founder Patricia Smith Melton travels the world capturing women's stories and stunning portraits. Anyone can meet the real women of Peace X Peace in her award-winning documentary film, *Peace by Peace: Women on the Frontlines*, and the book, *Sixty Years, Sixty Voices: Israeli and Palestinian Women*. Women have been silent on the sidelines long enough. Shared globally, women's resources and solutions can tip an out-of-balance world towards cultures of peace. Website: <www.peacexpeace.org> (See Chapter 57 by Mary Liston Liepold.)

The **Playground Revolution** is a blog by Miriam Peskowitz, author of *The Truth Behind the Mommy Wars: Who Decides What Makes a Good Mother?* In her first blog entry, Peskowitz states that her goal in creating the blog was to establish a forum for parents, both mothers and fathers, "who are dissatisfied with the alternatives for how to raise our kids and work for pay at the same time." She goes on to say that she sees the mission of the blog as essentially a political one. "I'm looking at the new ways that families are politicized, and the ways that mothers can think about the problems that ail us—like isolation, or overwork, or judgment, or anger, or even love--through a political lens." Over the course of the blog's two year history, its mission was to dispel the Mommy Wars cultural myth, and to unite parents in working together to improve social and political conditions for all parents, whether working full-time, part-time, or staying at home. Though Peskowitz shut the blog down in 2006, its message is at the heart of the motherhood movement, and lives on through the action of mothers and fathers everywhere seeking to bring about social change. Website: <www.miriampeskowitz.com> (See Chapter 62 by Sarah Cote Hampson.)

pro familia is regarded as one of the leading non-governmental organizations in Germany and Europe. It advocates for the right of the individual to regulate conception and live a sexually fulfilled life. Since pro familia was founded in 1952, it has been educating the public, in particular the youth of Germany, about methods of controlling reproduction. The organization offers counselling services for pregnancy, prenatal genetic testing, birth, postpartum, and abortion with a focus on pregnancy prevention. It views the termination of a pregnancy as a form of birth control, operates several state-recognized clinics where the procedure can be performed, and campaigns to simplify the process. Some of its programs offer support to girls and young women, who decide to carry their child to full-term. pro familia is pro-choice for pre-implantation diagnostics and supportive of people living alternative lifestyles. Its services are offered in a variety of languages. Website: <www.profamilia.de> (See Chapter 7 by Sonja M. Allen.)

The FIGO **Save the Mothers and Infants Initiative** runs from 2006–2011. The backbone of this project, created by Dr. Mahmoud Fathalla, of Assuit University, Egypt, consists of the midwifery societies and obstetrical/gynecological professional societies of the involved countries. In the main pilot program, ten developing countries—Haiti, Kenya, Kosovo, Moldova, Nigeria, Pakistan, Peru, Uganda, Ukraine, and Uruguay—have been paired with a developed country, creating a partnership which has led to improved services and then to better health outcomes in the developing countries. Related projects operate in Ethiopia, Nicaragua, El Salvador, Guatemala, and Honduras. Each country has a separate project with a unique name and emphasis. The projects emphasize different health issues, such as abortion-related health concerns, or the top five childbirth health issues, and propose different mechanisms for change, such as process auditing, increased data analysis, or strengthening professional organizations. These projects have produced measurable improvements in population health, and have also led to synergies in surgical and emergency care. Website: <www.figo.org/projects/newborns> (See Chapter 9 by Jacqueline Ciccio Parsons.)

Single Mothers by Choice (SMC) is a non-profit New York based organization that serves women who are sole parents or who are considering this particular type of motherhood as a viable option. Jane Mattes, a psychotherapist and a single mother by choice herself, founded SMC in 1981 in order to create a support network for women who knowingly decided to raise their children without presence of a father or a partner. The majority of SMC members are women in their thirties and forties, well-educated and financially stable. Some of the members get pregnant accidentally, and others turn to adoption and donor insemination. SMC offers workshops for women who are thinking about becoming single mothers by choice, issues a quarterly newsletter and maintains a blog where members share their thoughts on single motherhood, marriage, pregnancy and adoption. Website: <www.singlemothersbychoice.org> (See Chapter 19 by Veronika Novoselova.)

Sistersong is a feminist collective that groups together Indigenous women and women of colour organizations under the umbrella of reproductive justice. Sistersong aims to support a woman's desire to avoid pregnancy and motherhood, become a parent if she so wishes and/or keep her family together in the face of child removal. Sistersong began as a collaboration between 16 member organizations reflecting four categories of racialization and ethnicity (black/African-American, Hispanic/Latina, Asian/Pacific Islander and Indigenous/Native American). By 2010, the organization had grown to 40 member organizations and 56 affiliate organizations that include women from multiple categories of racialization and ethnicity, including white allied women and men of colour. Website: <www.sistersong.net> (See Chapter 4 by Jennifer Musial.)

Sozialdienst katholischer Frauen (SkF)(Social Service of Catholic Women) specializes in programs for disadvantaged young women and mothers. Since its foundation in 1900, it is SkF's goal to empower and strengthen women and their families, so that they can enjoy a lifestyle that allows them to be equally active as an individual, in their family, as employees/employers, and as a part of society. SkF advocates for the interests of women at all political levels and its members strive to be strong, confident, and hopeful in an effort to have a positive impact on other women, including mothers. The organization promotes the prevention of unwanted pregnancies and offers counseling services for pregnancy, prenatal diagnostics, delivery, postpartum, mourning the loss of a child, and abortion, but no longer has the authority to issue the necessary papers for this procedure. SkF focuses on supporting (expecting) mothers in crisis, so that they can adjust to a life with children and become good mothers. Website: <www.skf-zentrale.de> (See Chapter 7 by Sonja M. Allen.)

Toronto Feminist Mothers (TFM) is made up of a fluid membership of self-identified mother-feminists or feminist-mothers. Discussions range from definitions of feminism, how to enact positive and sustainable change, imagining how a world structured in a radically different way would affect parenting and more. Of particular concern is the impact of messages from the media and institutions that construct people in opposition to each other rather than celebrating differences and the beauty of diversities. The group stays connected via email where books, art and news that promote exclusion of non-accepted forms of behaving as parents are posted for group involvement. Toronto Feminist Mothers meet once a month. (See Chapter 34 by Tania Jivraj.)

The Union of the Committees of Soldiers' Mothers of Russia (UCSMR) is a human rights NGO established in 1989 that works to protect the rights of soldiers and men being drafted into the Russian military. It consists of regional committees throughout Russia with a head office in Moscow. For decades it has worked to reveal human rights abuses within the army including death and injury resulting from *dedovschchina,* a systemic practice of severe hazing of new recruits, and it compiles and publishes peacetime deaths to raise public awareness. In addition, they provide legal counsel about deferment and services for deserters who leave due to violence and abuse within the barracks. The UCSMR also lobbies for radical military reform, calling for an end to conscription and the formation of a volunteer professional army. They are most well known for their activism during the first Chechen war when they organized marches into the war zone and rescued their sons. The Committee of Soldiers' Mothers, as it was known prior to 1999, won several international awards for their advocacy of human rights and anti-war activism including the Alternative Nobel Prize in 1996. Website: <www.ucsmr.ru/english> (See Chapter 54 by Susan Logsdon-Conradsen.)

United Mothers Opposing Violence Everywhere (UMOVE) was founded by Audette Sheppard and 16 other mothers in August of 2001. The organization was founded by Sheppard as a reaction to her own son's death due to gun violence. The goal of the organization has been to provide a place for support for grieving and spreading the word about stopping violence. The organization has served as a place to gather women who stand against violence globally, and has been successful in organizing grief-related events. At present, UMOVE does not appear to be entirely operational due to its lack of a main contact person and website. (See Chapter 46 by Laura Pennington.)

Warriors Against Violence Society (WAVS) has been providing services to Vancouver, British Columbia since 1998, and is a rarity in Canada, in that it innovatively brings together mainly Aboriginal men and women with trained facilitators to impart and to emphasize cultural teachings, thus to help clients (community members who attend WAVS) to interpret the reasons they find themselves engaging in oppressive and violent practices. The agency's unique mandate is culturally-based, operating on the core belief that healing and wellness are best achieved by acquisition and restoration of traditional Aboriginal customs and approaches. Two recurring themes within WAVS are to understand the: 1) Legacy of shame and violence from generations of colonization, and, 2) Positive effects of wholistically bringing together culture, tradition, and ceremony as effective components of healing from family violence. Website: <www.wavbc.com> (See Chapter 27 by Donna Lester-Smith and Joyce Fossella.)

Welfare Warriors has been fighting for the lives of mothers and children since 1986. They organize to expose and stop the war on the poor who face economic injustice resulting from unpaid motherwork, disability, low wages, violence, and social stigma. The Warriors create a visible culture to show the truth about families in poverty and to reach other mothers to organize for justice and counteract the soul numbing bigotry endured by moms who receive public child support (welfare) for children. Welfare Warriors' creations include a quarterly, international, 56-page mothers publication, *Mother Warriors Voice*; a book of *50 Songs from the Mamas Movement* with original lyrics to traditional tunes; the invention of the word Motherwork which is now used internationally; a MOMS line to train mothers and others in survival skills; a Mothers and Youth project to train children in organizing skills; a Mothers and Grandmothers of the Disappeared Children Project to reunite families wrongfully separated by Social Services; bumperstickers, pins, posters,T-shirts, and several videos; a *Moms Survival Guidebook*; and a Mothers Organizing Center in downtown Milwaukee, Wisconsin. The Warriors has inspired thousands of moms in poverty to become involved in organizing for economic justice across the U.S. Website: <www.welfarewarriors.org> (See Chapter 38 by Pat Gowens.)

White Ribbon Alliance for Safe Motherhood (WRA) is an international coalition advocating for safe motherhood as a basic human right and is a leader among those holding governments and institutions accountable for the tragedy of maternal mortality. The organization confronts the health scandal of our time: maternal mortality. WRA is dedicated solely to saving the lives of the world's poorest women who die because they do not have access to basic healthcare. More than 90 percent of maternal deaths occur in developing countries and approximately 80 percent of maternal deaths can be avoided by effective intervention. Easily treatable problems such as high blood pressure, infection, obstructed labor, or heavy bleeding needlessly kill mothers every day in developing nations. Women die while giving birth because there are no clamps to stop a mother's bleeding or no health worker to hold them. Women die because there is no one to dispense the three cents worth of magnesium sulphate required to stop death due to high blood pressure associated with pre-eclempsia. The WRA understands that maternal mortality is no longer an issue of knowledge; it is an issue of advocacy and political will. Website: <www.whiteribbonalliance.org> (See Chapter 8 by Lynn Comerford.)

Contributor Notes

Enola G. Aird, an activist mother, is the founder and director of Mothers for a Human Future (MHF), successor to the Motherhood Project. MHF is an initiative focused on fighting for the assertion of mother world values in American culture. Aird is a Phi Beta Kappa graduate of Barnard College and holds a J.D. from Yale Law School. She is completing a book on the indispensability of motherworld values.

Sonja Martina Allen holds a MA in German from Memorial University of Newfoundland. She is writing her doctoral dissertation at Queen's University on maternity images in the works of three German women writer/artists. She has published and presented on a variety of topics including children's fiction, motherhood in Germany, and cloning.

Jo Altilia: Drawing upon her experience as a teacher and community advocate, Jo Altilia established Literature for Life in 2000. Working closely with various parenting resource centres Jo has established off site reading circles and launched the innovative *Yo'Mama* and *SOLACE*, two magazines written by young mothers for young mothers.

Lisa Baraitser, Ph.D., is a senior lecturer in Psychosocial Studies at Birkbeck, University of London, a feminist theorist and writer, and a psychotherapist with a particular interest in working with mothers. Her research is concerned with articulations of the maternal in the fields of psychoanalysis, social theory, feminism and philosophy. She is author of *Maternal Encounters: The Ethics of Interruption* (2009).

Linn Baran assists the Motherhood Initiative for Research and Community Involvement (MIRCI) with community outreach initiatives to link "lived mothering" to "examined motherhood"; bridging academe and activism. In this capacity, Linn has been the Coordinator of the Mother Outlaws group and speaker's series. A graduate of York University with degrees in English Literature and Women's

Studies, Linn has worked with community-university research projects, family resource programs, and parent action groups to increase community capacity and social inclusion of all mothers with young children in service provisions and family supports. Linn's main research interest is non-traditional forms of social networks that mothers engage in to both empower themselves and resist dominant narratives of "good motherhood." She lives with her son and partner in the Beaches community of Toronto.

R. Dianne Bartlow is an Associate Professor in the Department of Gender and Women's Studies at California State University, Northridge. Her research interests include nineteenth-century Black feminism and representations of African-American women in popular music, culture, and film, and violence against women. Bartlow is also a multiple Emmy Award winning director/writer/producer.

Christina Bermingham is a Ph.D. Candidate at Dublin City University (DCU) in Ireland. Her research explores the politics of birth and maternity care and development of birth activism in Ireland. She has been a member of AIMS Ireland since 2007 joining shortly after the birth of her first son in Galway, Ireland. In 2008 she was awarded a Ph.D. Studentship from the School of Nursing at DCU and spent several years in Ireland living, researching and campaigning for changes in maternity services. She currently lives in the Boston, MA, area with her partner and son where she is finishing her Ph.D. dissertation and teaching Sociology at Massasoit Community College as an adjunct faculty member.

Marguerite Guzmán Bouvard is the author of eleven nonfiction books and six books of poetry, her latest, *The Unpredictability of Light*, won the Massbook prize for poetry. She is the editor of the *Healing Ministry Magazine* and a Resident Scholar at the Women's Studies Research Center at Brandeis University.

Gayle Brandeis is the author of *Fruitflesh: Seeds of Inspiration for Women Who Write; Dictionary Poems;* the novels *The Book of Dead Birds,* which won the Bellwether Prize for Fiction of Social Change, *Self Storage* and *Delta Girls*; and the novel for young readers, *My Life with the Lincolns.* She is on the national staff of CODEPINK: Women for Peace and is mom to one college student, one high school student, and one baby boy.

Monica Campo has been involved in Maternity Coalition and other consumer birth groups since 2004. She is currently completing her doctoral thesis at La Trobe University which examines obstetric hegemony and contemporary childbirth discourses.

Melissa Cheyney, Ph.D., CPM, LDM, is an Assistant Professor of Medical Anthropology at Oregon State University. She received her doctorate from the University of Oregon in 2005, where her research examined the U.S. Homebirth

Movement. Dr. Cheyney is a Certified Professional Midwife, Chair of the Board of Direct-entry Midwifery for the State of Oregon, and the author of the recently published ethnography, *Born at Home*.

Penny Christensen is the Executive Director of Birth Trauma Canada. As a human rights activist she works to emphasize the value of mothers, to garner respect for the human rights of mothers around the world and to reduce maternal mortality and morbidity. Penny is also active in the struggle for human rights for the women of Afghanistan. She lives in Calgary, Alberta and is the proud mother of two daughters.

Lynn Comerford is Associate Professor in the Department of Human Development and Women's Studies at California State University, East Bay, where she also directs the Women's Studies Program. She is currently completing a book on the sexual politics of child custody policy.

Cindy Cowan is a mother of four children who has been an active volunteer at La Leche League Leader for more than ten years. She writes about parenting and breastfeeding on her blog and for other publications.

Amanda Cox, also known as Mad Cow, is a mum to three boys, a wife, author, speaker, and founder of reality parenting website Bad Mother's Club/Real Mums. She also dabbled with postnatal depression, completed a degree in Health Promotion, blogs, presents on community TV, has written a book and has much more planned.

Rae Davies is Administrative Director of the International MotherBaby Childbirth Organization, health educator, doula, doula trainer, lactation consultant and long-time birth and breastfeeding advocate nationally and internationally. Rae also serves as the co-coordinator for the World Alliance of Breastfeeding Action (WABA) Health Care Practices Task Force.

Robbie Davis-Floyd Ph.D., Senior Research Fellow, Dept. of Anthropology, University of Texas Austin, is a medical anthropologist specializing in the anthropology of reproduction. An international speaker and researcher, she is author of over 80 articles and author, co-author, or co-editor of ten books, including *Birth as an American Rite of Passage* (2004) and *Birth Models That Work* (2009). A board member of IMBCO, she is Editorial Chair for the IMBCI.

Sally Dear-Healey, Ph.D. Candidate in Sociology at Binghamton University, has taught in Human Development, Sociology, and Women's Studies, and is a Childbirth Educator/Trainer and Doula/Trainer with Birth Works®. Her current research investigates ways in which beliefs and behaviours related to pregnancy, birth, and mothering are passed from mothers and daughters.

Ann Douglas is the author of 28 books, including *The Mother of All Pregnancy Books* (a mother-focused pregnancy guide). She writes "The Mother of All Baby Columns" for *The Toronto Star*. Her essays have appeared in Shari MacDonald Strong's *The Maternal is Political*, Andrea Buchanan's *It's a Girl*, May Friedman and Shana Calixte's *Mothering and Blogging*, and Kyra Anderson and Vicki Forman's *Gravity Pulls You In*. Her website is <www.anndouglas.ca>.

Andrea Doyle Hugmeyer is completing her Master's in Interdisciplinary Studies with an emphasis in Women's Studies at Oregon State University and acts as a graduate instructor in the Women's Studies program where she recently developed a course on body politics, reproductive justice, and motherhood inspired by her experiences mothering her two daughters, Hannah and Kiera.

Laura Dreuth Zeman is a Professor of Social Work and Women Studies at Southern Illinois University, Carbondale. She integrates practice and research at the point where they intersect with consumer education and mental health services. Her current research involves examining parenting children who live with disabilities.

Rachel Epstein coordinates the LGBTQ Parenting Network at the Sherbourne Health Centre in Toronto. She is editor of *Who's Your Daddy? And Other Writings on Queer Parenting* (2009), and the 2008 winner of Community One Foundation's *Steinert & Ferreiro Award*, recognizing her leadership and pivotal contributions towards the support, recognition and inclusion of queer families in Canada.

Lisa Federer is a Dean's Scholar at the University of Los Angeles, California, where she studies in the Department of Library and Information Studies. Her research interests include lesbian motherhood and medical librarianship.

Juliana Forbes is a co-founder, Interim Director and Creative Director of Mothers Acting Up. She is also an abstract painter, and mother of two.

Joyce Fossella (BA, M.ED in Counselling), is a member of the *Lil'wat Nation* in British Columbia, Canada. She has worked extensively in the First Nations community in education, employment, and health and wellness fields, and is currently the Executive Director of Warriors Against Violence Society where she has worked since 1998. Joyce co-facilitates group sessions, working with men and women addressing family violence. She has presented at various conferences, nationally and internationally, including the World Indigenous Women & Wellness Conference in Vancouver, British Columbia, and in Calgary, Alberta; the "Guns, Gangs and Drugs" youth conference in Prince George, British Columbia; and the International Critical and Feminist Perspectives in Health and Social Justice in Auckland, New Zealand.

Andrea Fox in an economist who writes about motherhood from a feminist perspective, she is the author of the popular blog, blue milk (<www.bluemilk.wordpress.com>). She is co-facilitator of the Feminist Mothers' Discussion Group and has presented at conferences on motherhood, work and family, feminism, and social media; written for magazines and newspapers; and has had her work quoted on television. Fox is the mother of two children.

Kryn Freehling-Burton is an instructor and advisor in the Women Studies program at Oregon State University. She is the mother of four and with her partner, acts, directs and writes for the theatre.

Heide Goettner-Abendroth is a philosopher and researcher on culture and society, focused on matriarchal studies. She was born in Thuringia (Germany) in 1941 and is mother of two daughters and one son. In 1973 she obtained her Ph.D. in philosophy and theory of science at the University of Munich where she taught philosophy for ten years. She has published various books on matriarchal society and culture, and has become the founding mother of Modern Matriarchal Studies. In 1986 she founded "HAGIA: International Academy for Matriarchal Studies and Matriarchal Spirituality" in Germany, and from the beginning she has been its director. In 1980 she was visiting professor at the University of Montreal/Canada and, in 1992, at the University of Innsbruck/Austria. She is one of the women, across the globe, nominated as one of the"1000 Women for the Nobel Peace Prize 2005." <www.hagia.de> <www.goettner-abendroth.de>.

Christin Geall worked as a newspaper columnist, magazine editor and communications director before completing the Stonecoast MFA. She teaches creative nonfiction at the University of Victoria. <http://christingeall.wordpress.com>.

Meghan Gibbons has a Ph.D. in Comparative Literature. She has written extensively on the activism of mothers against their nation-states in times of national crisis in the Americas, and is currently working on a book on politicized mothers in the U.S., El Salvador and Argentina. She works as a speech writer.

Ariel Gore is the author of seven books including *Atlas of the Human Heart, The Traveling Death and Resurrection Show*, and *Bluebird: Women and the New Psychology of Happiness*. She founded *Hip Mama* in 1993 and served as editor for 15 years. She is currently a visiting professor of creative writing at the University of New Mexico.

Pat Gowens is founder of Welfare Warriors and editor of its international journal *Mother Warriors Voice*. She works to provide a voice to mothers living on the edge, reports on resistance in the war on the poor, and advocates for a U.S. Child Allowance. Since 1986 Gowens and Welfare Warriors have created mamas' media, actions for economic justice, and many new moms groups. Gowens' writings include *Mothers Survival Self-Help Manual (National)* (1990) and *Moms Survival Guide (Wisconsin)* (1997). She has also produced three videos by and about low-income mothers. Gowens has been published in *MS Magazine, Off Our Backs, Belfast's Women's News, Mothering Magazine, Tokyo's Femin*, local Milwaukee publications, *Political Affairs, Dollars and Sense*, and the former *Sojourner* and *Kinesis.*

Fiona Joy Green, Ph.D., author of *Feminist Mothering in Theory and Practice, 1985-1995: A Study in Transformative Politics*, Mellen Press 2009, and co-editor of the forthcoming *Maternal Pedagogies: In and Outside the Classroom*, Demeter Press, is a feminist mother, Chair of the Department of Women's and Gender Studies and a Co-Director of the Institute for Women's and Gender Studies at the University of Winnipeg. Her research on feminist mothering can be found in various editions of the *Journal of the Association for Research on Mothering*, and in the inaugural edition of *Socialist Studies: the Journal of the Society for Socialist Studies*, and in the books *Feminist Mothering, Mother Outlaws* and *Motherhood to Mothering.* Her analysis of depictions of mothers in reality TV can be found in *Storytelling: A Critical Journal of Popular Narrative* and the forthcoming *Mediating Moms: Mothering in Popular Culture*, McGill-Queen's press.

Caroline M. Grant is the Editor-in-Chief of *Literary Mama*, where she also writes the column *Mama at the Movies.* She is co-editor of the anthology *Mama, Ph.D.: Women Write About Motherhood and Academic Life* (Rutgers University Press, 2008). She holds a Ph.D. in Comparative Literature from the University of California at Berkeley, and has published in a number of journals and anthologies.

Glendene Grant is a 53-year-old mother of four and the grandmother of three. She has four daughters, two granddaughters and one grandson. Her second oldest daughter is the victim of human trafficking and because of that she has been given the job of educating others on human trafficking.

Mona Greenbaum and her partner, Nicole, are the mothers of two sons aged thirteen and eleven. Mona founded the Lesbian Mothers Association in 1998, which is now called the LGBT Family Coalition. Recipient of numerous awards, Mona was chosen by the popular magazine *Coup de Pouce* as amongst the 20 most influential women in Quebec. In 2010, Mona was also awarded the medal of Quebec's National Assembly for her advocacy work in the LGBT community.

Cristina Herrera holds a Ph.D. in English from Claremont Graduate University. She is an assistant professor in the Department of Chicano and Latin American Studies at California State University, Fresno. Her research interests include contemporary Chicana and Latina literature, Chicana motherhood, and mother-daughter relationships. She is at work on a book manuscript that discusses mother-daughter relationships in contemporary fiction by Chicana writers.

Rodolfo Gómez Ponce de León MD, MSPH, Ph.D., is an ob/gyn from Tucuman, Argentina, where he served as Professor of Obstetrics at the National University of Tucuman and as Coordinator of OB at Hospital Avellaneda, where his influence helped keep the cesarean rate below 15 percent for ten years. He went on to graduate study at the University of North Carolina, served as Senior Health Systems Advisor at IPAS for seven years, and as Executive Director for IMBCO for two years. He currently serves as International Women's Health Advisor for Pan American Health Organization in Brazil, Adjunct Professor in MCH at University of North Carolina, and as a Board Member of IMBCO .

Sarah Cote Hampson is currently working toward her Ph.D. in Political Science at the University of Connecticut, and also serves as the Managing Editor for *Polity*, the Journal of the Northeastern Political Science Association. Her research interests include the politics of motherhood, women and politics, feminist theory, law and society, public policy, and race, gender and ethnicity.

Martina Hynan is a Ph.D. Student at University College Dublin, feminist visual artist and co-ordinator with Keeping Mum Community Art and Activist Group and member of Clare Birth Choice. She is researching the cultural politics of maternal identities from within Ireland's visual cultural landscape. She is actively involved in lobbying for improved maternity services in Ireland.

Tania Jivraj is a social work student at Ryerson University. She identifies as a mixed race, single mother of a snarky and super spunky five-year-old girl. Political, philosophical and sexual identifications are in a state of perpetual motion, thus difficult to pin down at this moment.

Linda Lisi Juergens is the Executive Director of the National Association of Mothers' Centers (NAMC) and a founder of its advocacy initiative, MOTHERS. She has spoken at national and international events and been quoted in print media on mothers' needs, parent support, work/life integration, and the economic impact of caregiving. Linda holds a Bachelor of Arts in Foreign Language and MS in Education.

Julie Kelso is Assistant Professor in Philosophy and Literature at Bond University and Honorary Research Adviser in the School of English, Media Studies and Art History at the University of Queensland, Australia. Her monograph, *O Mother Where Art Thou? An Irigagarayan Reading of the Book of Chronicles* was published recently. Julie Kelso is the editor (with Marie Porter) of *Theorising and Representing Maternal Realities* and *Mother-Texts: Narratives and Counter-Narratives.*

Lynn Kuechle is a local Mamapalooza event coordinator and Mother Studies scholar. She is also active in organizing programming and events for the Museum of Motherhood. She is also the author of *The Mother Monologues*, which recently aired on public television in the United States.

Mayri Sagady Leslie, CNM, MSN, EDDC, is a midwife on clinical faculty at Yale University. An author, educator and consultant, Mayri is the former chair of the Coalition for Improving Maternity Services (CIMS), a former member of the IMBCO Board, and a current member of IMBCO's Advisory Board. She has presented numerous times in national and international venues and is the author of *Promoting and Preserving Physiologic Birth: A Textbook for Midwives, Physicians and Nurses* (2011).

Donna Lester-Smith, of *Métis/Algonquin*, English, Irish, and Scottish heritage, is a Ph.D. Candidate at the University of British Columbia, Canada. Her work interests focus on Indigenous knowledges and methodologies, and collaborative community health research with Aboriginal peoples, including many years of practical, academic, and community experience in developing, implementing, and facilitating well-being activities. Donna's personal interests include Aboriginal community support, mentoring younger Aboriginal students, and sharing her writing skills with others.

Susan Logsdon-Conradsen is a clinical psychologist, Associate Professor, and Director of the Women's Studies program at Berry College in Rome, Georgia. Her current research focuses on mother-activism (specifically environmental and anti-violence) and gendering of parenting in the media. She is also a feminist mother who lives near Atlanta, Georgia with her husband.

Mary Liston Liepold, Ph.D., is Editor in Chief of *Peace X Peace*. Mary spent 15 years as a family daycare provider, then 25 years with national and international nonprofits. At the Child Welfare League of America from 1990 to 2005 she founded the magazine *Children's Voice* and wrote speeches, proposals, and education and advocacy materials. She has four children and five grandchildren.

Sandy M. May is a Master of Women's Studies candidate at Memorial University of Newfoundland. She is currently completing a Masters thesis entitled "A Crisis of the Spirit? Discursive Constructions of Teenage Mothers, Social Exclusion, and Social Welfare Policy." Her scholarly works include presentations on Western concepts of normative and deviant mothering, and a guest-editor position with the *Journal of the Association for Research on Mothering* (11.2 December 2009). A young mother herself at age 14, May considers her teenage daughter, Allison, to be her greatest accomplishment.

Pauline McDonagh Hull is a journalist, writer and campaigner. In 2004, she decided to address the negative portrayal of cesarean births, and in February 2006, her website *electivecesarean.com* went live. Previously, Pauline worked for five years as a broadcast journalist with *BBC News* in London. She has now co-written a book on cesarean birth, published by Prometheus Books.

Kristen Abatsis McHenry is a Ph.D. candidate at University of Massachusetts, Amherst in Political Science. McHenry also holds a MA in Women's Studies from the Women's Studies Institute at Georgia State University. Her current research interests include: breast cancer activism, the U.S. women's movement, and women's health politics.

Judith Rebecca Mintz holds a BFA Visual Arts from York University (1994) and is currently a second-year MA student at Trent University's Frost Centre for Canadian and Indigenous Studies, where her research focuses on women's narratives of the perinatal experience through literature and historiography. In addition to mothering two girls, Judith is a yoga instructor, shiatsu therapist and musician.

Elizabeth Moore, CPM, RM, is a practicing midwife, activist and woman's health advocate. For six years she has served as a Court Appointed Special Advocate for Abused & Neglected Children (CASA). Elizabeth served six years as Regional Representative for the Midwives Alliance and is currently the Public Education Project Manager for Mothers Naturally.

Tatiana Moura is the coordinator of the Observatory on Gender and Armed Violence (OGAV) and the co-coordinator of the Peace Studies Group (Centre for Social Studies, University of Coimbra, Portugal). Since 2004, together with the OGAV's team, has conducted research-action oriented projects on women and armed violence in Latin America (mainly in Brazil, Colombia and El Salvador).

Jennifer Musial completed her Ph.D. in Women's Studies at York University in 2010. Currently, she teaches as an adjunct professor at Trent University and Queen's University. Her new research projects involve an examination of the backlash against "Octomom" Nadya Suleman and a look at the passage of the Unborn Victims of Violence Act and the "Partial Birth" Abortion Ban Act in the United States. Jennifer's research and teaching interests include feminist critical race theory, popular culture studies, body studies, motherhood/pregnancy studies and feminist pedagogy. In addition to her academic life, Jennifer is a Hatha yoga teacher in Kingston Ontario.

Catherine H. Myers first volunteered for Family and Home Network in 1986, when she was the mother of two young children (she is now a grandmother of two). Catherine serves as Executive Director and is completing a Bachelor of Individualized Studies degree in Human Development, Parenting and Policy.

Lareen Newman, Ph.D., has been involved in maternity consumer groups and birth choices education since 1996. She was State President of Maternity Coalition in South Australia from 2005 to 2010 and has been consumer representative to various hospital and midwifery education committees. She is a senior social health researcher at Flinders University, South Australia.

Nancy Nicol, an award-winning documentary film director, is a professor in Visual Arts at York University. Her film, *Politics of the Heart* on the Lesbian Mother's Association is part of a series entitled: *From Criminality to Equality*, on lesbian and gay history in Canada, available through Vtape, www.vtape.org and www.nightattheindies.com/merchandise.nicol.

Veronika Novoselova received her undergraduate degree in Journalism at Ural State University in Russia. After becoming interested in understanding and researching gender, she pursued an MA degree in Women's Studies at York University, and now she is a Ph.D. student in the same program.

Mary Olivella is Vice President for MomsRising. She writes on topics related to women, families, health, and social policy. Olivella has consulted for the World Health Organization and previously directed the award-winning health promotion department at the University of California's health services and taught in the School of Public Health.

Peggy O'Mara is the editor-in-chief of *Mothering.com.* She was the editor and publisher of *Mothering* magazine for 31 years. O'Mara is the author of *Natural Family Living, Having a Baby Naturally* and *A Quiet Place.* She is the mother of four adult children, and lives in Santa Fe, New Mexico.

Andrea O'Reilly, Ph.D., is Associate Professor in the School of Women's Studies at York University. O'Reilly is founder and director of *The Motherhood Initiative for Research and Community Involvement* (formerly *The Association for Research on Mothering*), founder and editor-in-chief of the *Journal of the Motherhood Initiative* (formerly *Journal of the Association for Research on Mothering)*, and founder and editor of Demeter Press, the first feminist press on motherhood. She is co-editor/editor of 16 books including *Maternal Theory: Essential* Readings (2007), *Feminist* Mothering, (2008), 21st *Century Motherhood: Experience, Identity, Policy, Agency* (2010) and *Textual Mothers, Maternal Texts: Motherhood in Contemporary Women's Literatures,* with Elizabeth Podnieks, (2010). O'Reilly is author of *Toni Morrison and Motherhood: A Politics of the Heart,* (2004) and *Rocking the Cradle: Thoughts on Motherhood, Feminism, and the Possibility of Empowered Mothering,* (2006). She is editor of the first encyclopedia (three volumes, 705 entries) on Motherhood (2010). She has been the recipient of 20 Social Science Humanities Research Council of Canada grants. In 1998 and again in 2009 she received the University wide "Professor of the Year" award for Teaching Excellence at York University. In 2010 she was the recipient of the Canadian University and College Teachers Sarah Shorten Award for outstanding achievements in the promotion of the advancement of women in Canadian universities and colleges. Andrea and her common-law spouse are the parents of a 26 year old son and two daughters, ages 21 and 24.

Beth Osnes, Ph.D is an assistant professor of theatre at the University of Colorado, co-founder of Mothers Acting Up, creator of M-other and the MAU Vocal Empowerment Workshop, and mother of three. She has authored/co-authored numerous books, the most recent being, *Essays and Scripts on How Mothers Are Portrayed in the Theatre*, published by Mellen Press.

Abigail L. Palko holds a Ph.D. in Literature with a minor in Gender Studies. Her research focuses on twentieth-century Irish and Caribbean women novelists, with particular attention to their exploration of oppression in connection with postcolonial motherhood. The Director of Undergraduate Studies for the Gender Studies Program at the University of Notre Dame, her courses explore the role of gender in literature.; her daughter is her favorite example.

Jacqueline Ciccio Parsons, Ph.D. is a Licensed Professional Counselor (Texas). Dr. Parsons has written on numerous topics including mothers and special needs families. She teaches at the University of Texas at San Antonio, Walden University and St. Mary's University. Dr. Parsons is also the proud mother of seven children.

Debra Pascali Bonaro, Chair of IMBCO, doula and doula advocate, is producer of the documentary film *Orgasmic Birth* and co-author of *Orgasmic Birth: Your Guide to a Safe and Satisfying Childbirth Experience*. She is an internationally renowned doula trainer and childbirth speaker. Her multiple accomplishments include speaking about doulas at the White House and to various Ministries of Health in many countries.

Laura Pennington earned a bachelor's degree from Randolph Macon Woman's College, a masters degree in political science from Virginia Tech, and is currently pursuing her P.hD. in Public Administration and Policy with Virginia Tech. She is also a social studies teacher in Baltimore City Public schools.

Marie Porter is an Honorary Research Advisor in the Centre for Research on Women, Gender, Culture and Social Change at the University of Queensland. Her monograph *Transformative Power in Motherwork* examines Australian mothering in the 1950s and 1960s. She is co-editor of three books on motherhood. Marie was a founding member, and President, of ARM-A which is now the Australian Motherhood Initiative for Research and Community Involvement (AMIRCI).

Kerreen Reiger was instrumental in founding Maternity Coalition in the late 1980s and has written widely on maternity service provision and mothers' organisations, and on family change and gender issues. She teaches Sociology at La Trobe University and continues to research relationships between mothers and health professionals.

Amber Fatima Riaz is currently enrolled in the Ph.D. program in English at the University of Western Ontario. She has presented a paper on the representation of mothers in Indian film at the 2010 MIRCI conference in Toronto, and has an article forthcoming in a Demeter Press publication on South Asian Mothering. She is currently working on her dissertation on the representation of the Muslim Veil in Pakistani Literature. Her interests include Postcolonial studies, Feminist literary theory and South Asian Studies.

Amy Richards is the author of *Opting In: Having a Child Without Losing Yourself* and the co-author of *Manifesta: Young Women, Feminism and the Future* and *Grassroots: A Field Guide to Feminist Activism*. Amy is also the co-founder of the Third Wave Foundation and on the boards of Sadie Nash Leadership Project, and feminist.com (<http://feminist.com>) among other organizations.

Joy Rose is the Founder of Mamapalooza and the Founding Director of the Museum of Motherhood. She has been involved in activism for mothers for over 20 years through her band and multi-media event company, Mamapalooza Inc. She created the first "mom band" called Housewives of Prozac. She is a musician, filmmaker and entrepreneur. She lives in New York City and is the mother of four.

Kristin Rowe-Finkbeiner is Executive Director and Co-Founder of MomsRising. She authored the award winning book *The F-Word: Feminism In Jeopardy* and co-authored *The Motherhood Manifesto*. Rowe-Finkbeiner writes about public policy, motherhood, economic security, equality, health, and new feminism. Her articles are frequently discussed in women's studies classes across the United States.

Rita Santos is a researcher at the Peace Studies Group (Centre for Social Studies, University of Coimbra, Portugal) and the Observatory on Gender and Armed Violence (OGAV). She is a Ph.D. candidate in "International Politics and Conflict Resolution," University of Coimbra. Her current research interests include violence and small arms and micro-disarmament movements, demilitarisation and global society.

Renée Schultz, co-author of *The Mother-Daughter Project,* felt woefully inadequate in deconstructing the sexist discourse that permeates the mother-daughter relationship but found the support of other women invaluable in doing just that. Renée, mother of adult children, hopes that the wisdom she has gained can be passed onto the next generation of mothers before her perspective is deemed obsolete.

Karen Shain is policy director of Legal Services for Prisoners with Children in San Francisco (LSPC). She is co-author of "Stop Shackling: A Report on the Written Policies of California's Counties on the Use of Restraints on Pregnant Prisoners in Labor" (2010), and "California's Mother-Infant Prison Program: An Investigation" (2010).

Arlene Sgoutas, Ph.D., is an assistant professor at the Institute for Women's Studies and Services at Metropolitan State College of Denver. She has severed as the co-chair of the Feminist Mothering Caucus since 2007.

Geradine Simkins, CNM, MSN, DEM, is an activist, midwife, author and visionary with over three decades of experience working in maternal and child healthcare, women's health, and community-based programs. Currently, she is the President of the Midwives Alliance of North America and its first Interim Executive Director.

Lorri Slepian, LCSW, a clinical psychotherapist, was a founding mother of the first Mothers' Center in the world, past Co-Director, leadership advisor and Board member of the National Association of Mothers' Centers (NAMC). She has worked to build a Mothers' Movement since 1973 and was the motivator behind the NAMC's Mothers Declaration of Rights and a founder of its MOTHERS Initiative.

Jewelles Smith completed her Master of Arts in Women's Studies at Simon Fraser University in 2007. She is an active member on several boards. Passionate and outspoken about women and disability rights, Jewelles currently works as a research, writer and consultant. She currently lives in Revelstoke, British Columbia, with her two sons.

Sigal Spigel is a senior associate member of University of Cambridge Centre for Gender Studies. Her research is on motherhood, feminism and psychoanalysis. She is a psychologist and a psychotherapist and currently works in an inpatient unit for adolescents with eating disorders.

Jocelyn Fenton Stitt is an associate professor of gender and women's studies at Minnesota State University where she teaches courses on global feminism, postcolonial culture and theory, and feminist mothering. She is the editor, along with Pegeen Reichert Powell, of *Mothers Who Deliver: Feminist Interventions in Public and Interpersonal Discourse* (2010). She is a member of MIRCI and published and essay on maternal peace activists and grief in *JMI*'s Fall/Winter 2010 issue.

Laurie Sylla, BSW, MHSA, has been an outspoken activist on women's issues for many decades. Her work has included education, advocacy, service, and research related to rape, domestic violence, reproductive rights, and HIV. She is an active member of a movement working to make microbicides, a product that could prevent sexual transmission of HIV, a reality for women and men throughout the world.

Rachel Sutz Pienta, Ph.D., is an Education professor at Valdosta State University in Georgia. She also teaches Women's Studies part-time at Florida State University in Tallahassee, Florida. Her teaching and research interests include gender and public policy, multicultural education and diversity, and education policy and politics.

Virginia Thorley, PhD, an International Board Certified Lactation Consultant since 1985, and historian, served as a voluntary counselor with the Australian Breastfeeding Association (formerly the Nursing Mothers' Association of Australia) from 1966 to early-2008. She founded the association's Queensland Branch with the first group in Queensland in 1969. Currently she holds an honorary position in the School of History, Philosophy, Religion and Classics at the University of Queensland.

Michelle Trim, Ph.D., is a lecturer at Elon University in Elon, North Carolina. Her research interests include feminist theory and theories of technology (as they relate to agency studies), composition pedagogy, feminist rhetoric, and democratic education. She has taught classes in Women's Studies, advocacy writing, technology studies, and composition.

Hélène Vadeboncoeur holds a Ph.D. in Applied Social Sciences (Université de Montréal, Canada). Her doctoral thesis was on humanization of childbirth. In Canada, she worked for the legalization of midwifery. A board member of IMBCO, she is in charge of the Demonstration Sites Committee. She wrote *Birthing Normally After a Caesarean or Two* (2010), a guide for pregnant women.

Monika Jaeckel committed the larger part of her life to movement building. She was one of the midwifes to the birth of the Mother Centers and founded MINE. In 2009, she succumbed to uterine cancer. Much about her work, her person, and the Mother Centers, can be found on www.MonikaJaeckel.com.

Melinda Vandenbeld Giles is a Ph.D. social/cultural anthropology student at the University of Toronto. Her research interests include maternal theory, social change, urban anthropology, neoliberalism and social activism. She is currently doing fieldwork in Toronto with mothers experiencing homelessness and facing the loss of child custody.

Genevieve Vaughan has written many articles and books on the gift economy. She created an international all-women activist foundation (1987-2005). A film on her life *Giving for Giving* (2007), her songs, books, children's books and articles can be downloaded free from her website: <www.gift-economy.com>.

Jenna Vinson is a doctoral candidate in Rhetoric, Composition, and the Teaching of English at the University of Arizona. She teaches writing and rhetoric to beginning and advanced college students. Her research interests include the rhetorical construction of teenage motherhood, rhetorics of resistance, feminist theories, and visual rhetoric.

Heaven Walker received a BA in Communications and Theatre and minored in Women's Studies. She then earned an MA in Philosophy and Religion, and Women's Spirituality. She is currently full time faculty at Heald College and an interfaith minister. However, her most fulfilling work is mothering her beautiful baby boy.

Rosanne Weston is a retired psychotherapist and past NAMC Board Co-Chair. She was an early member of the Mothers' Center, becoming a group facilitator, member of the Steering Committee and, ultimately, a social work consultant to several Centers. She was a founding members of the NAMC initiative MOTHERS (Mothers Ought to Have Equal Rights) and has been devoted to the Mothers' Movement ever since she started having her own children, 39 years ago.

Natalie Wilson, Ph.D., is a lecturer at Cal State San Marcos in the Women's Studies Program where she teaches courses in feminist theory, feminist activism, and popular culture. Her book, *Seduced by Twilight*, which examines representations of motherhood in the saga from a feminist lens, was released in April 2011. She has also published essays in the areas of feminist theory, women's literature, cultural analysis, and social justice activism. She is the mother to two budding feminist activists, a son, age 14, and a daughter, age 12.

RECYCLED
Paper made from recycled material
FSC® C103567

Marquis Book Printing Inc.

Québec, Canada
2011

Printed on Silva Enviro 100% post-consumer EcoLogo certified paper,
processed chlorine free and manufactured using biogas energy.